For Photo-Paint

Note: Though some of these shortcuts work in other Corel programs, the stuff listed on this side of the Cheat Sheet pertains specifically to Photo-Paint. The image window must be active for shortcuts to work.

Menu Command Shortcuts

Command	Shortcut
Clear	Delete
Close	Ctrl+F4
Copy	Ctrl+C (or Ctrl+Ins)
Create Mask from Object	Ctrl+M
Create Object from Mask	Ctrl+up arrow
Cut	Ctrl+X (or Shift+Del)
Duplicate Object	Ctrl+Shift+D
Exit	Alt+F4
Feather	Ctrl+Shift+F
Full-Screen Preview	F9
Help Topics	F1
Mask Marquee Visible	Ctrl+H
Object Marquee Visible	Ctrl+Shift+H
Invert Selection	Ctrl+I
Level Equalization	Ctrl+E
Mask All	Ctrl+A or double-click on mask tool icon

Command	Shortcut
Mask Remove	Ctrl+D
New Document	Ctrl+N
Open	Ctrl+O
Options	Ctrl+J
Paste as New Object	Ctrl+V (or Shift+Ins)
Preserve Image	Ctrl+Q
Print	Ctrl+P
Repeat (last action)	Ctrl+L
Repeat (Effects command)	Ctrl+F
Rulers	Ctrl+R
Save	Ctrl+S
Snap Objects to Grid	Ctrl+Y
Undo	Ctrl+Z (orAlt+ Backspace)
Zoom 100%	Ctrl+1
Zoom to Fit	F4

Roll-Up Shortcuts

Roll-Up	Shortcut
Color	Ctrl+F2
Objects	Ctrl+F7
Scrapbook	Ctrl+F12
Tool Settings	Ctrl+F8

Toolbox Shortcuts

Tool	Icon	Shortcut
Arrow tool		Spacebar
Zoom In or Out		F2 or F3
Paint tool		F5
Rectangle tool		F6
Oval tool		F7
Text tool		F8

...For Dummies: #1 Computer Book Series for Beginners

For CorelDraw

Note: Though some of these shortcuts work in other Corel programs, the stuff on this side of the Cheat Sheet pertains specifically to CorelDraw.

Toolbox and Toolbar Shortcuts

Tool	Icon	Shortcut
Arrow tool		Spacebar (or Ctrl+spacebar)
Shape tool		F10
Zoom Tool		F2
Zoom Out		F3
Zoom to Selected		Shift+F2
Zoom to All Objects		F4
Zoom to Page		Shift+F4
Pencil tool		F5
Rectangle tool		F6
Oval tool		F7
Text tool		F8

Dialog Box Shortcuts

Dialog Box	Shortcut
Align & Distribute	Ctrl+A
Edit Text	Ctrl+Shift+T
Fountain Fill	F11
Grid & Ruler Setup	Double-click on ruler
Guidelines Setup	Double-click on guide with arrow or shape tool
Insert Page	PgUp at beginning of document or PgDn at end
Object Properties	Select object and press Alt+Enter
Options	Ctrl+J
Outline Pen	F12
Outline Color	Shift+F12
Page Setup	Double-click on page boundary
Spell Checking	Ctrl+F12
Uniform Fill	Shift+F11

Roll-Up Shortcuts

Roll-Up	Shortcut
Blend	Ctrl+B
Envelope	Ctrl+F7
Extrude	Ctrl+E
Layers	Ctrl+F3
Node Edit	Ctrl+F10
Pen	Shift+F7
Position	Alt+F7
Rotate	Alt+F8
Scale & Mirror	Alt+F9
Skew	Alt+F11
Special Fill	Ctrl+F
Symbols	Ctrl+F11

Menu Command Shortcuts

Command	Shortcut
Close	Ctrl+F4
Copy	Ctrl+C (or Ctrl+Ins)
Cut	Ctrl+X (or Shift+Del)
Delete	Delete
Duplicate	Ctrl+D
Exit	Alt+F4
Group	Ctrl+G
Import	Ctrl+I
New Document	Ctrl+N
Open	Ctrl+O
Paste	Ctrl+V (or Shift+Ins)
Print	Ctrl+P
Redo	Ctrl+Shift+Z
Repeat	Ctrl+R
Save	Ctrl+S
Select All	Double-click on arrow tool icon
Snap to Grid	Ctrl+Y
To Back	Shift+PgDn
To Front	Shift+PgUp
Back one	Ctrl+PgDn
Forward one	Ctrl+PgUp
Undo	Ctrl+Z
Ungroup	Ctrl+U

by Deke McClelland
Revised by Julie King

IDG
BOOKS
WORLDWIDE

IDG Books Worldwide, Inc.
An International Data Group Company

Foster City, CA ♦ Chicago, IL ♦ Indianapolis, IN ♦ Southlake, TX

CorelDRAW™ 7 For Dummies®

Published by
IDG Books Worldwide, Inc.
An International Data Group Company
919 E. Hillsdale Blvd.
Suite 400
Foster City, CA 94404
http://www.idgbooks.com (IDG Books Worldwide Web site)
http://www.dummies.com (Dummies Press Web site)

Library of Congress Catalog Card No.: 97-70369

ISBN: 0-7645-0124-0

Printed in the United States of America

10 9 8 7 6 5 4 3 2 1

1O/RY/QT/ZX/IN

Distributed in the United States by IDG Books Worldwide, Inc.

Distributed by Macmillan Canada for Canada; by Transworld Publishers Limited in the United Kingdom and Europe; by WoodsLane Pty. Ltd. for Australia; by WoodsLane Enterprises Ltd. for New Zealand; by Longman Singapore Publishers Ltd. for Singapore, Malaysia, Thailand, and Indonesia; by Simron Pty. Ltd. for South Africa; by Toppan Company Ltd. for Japan; by Distribuidora Cuspide for Argentina; by Livraria Cultura for Brazil; by Ediciencia S.A. for Ecuador; by Addison-Wesley Publishing Company for Korea; by Ediciones ZETA S.C.R. Ltda. for Peru; by WS Computer Publishing Company, Inc., for the Philippines; by Unalis Corporation for Taiwan; by Contemporanea de Ediciones for Venezuela. Authorized Sales Agent: Anthony Rudkin Associates for the Middle East and North Africa.

For general information on IDG Books Worldwide's books in the U.S., please call our Consumer Customer Service department at 800-762-2974. For reseller information, including discounts and premium sales, please call our Reseller Customer Service department at 800-434-3422.

For information on where to purchase IDG Books Worldwide's books outside the U.S., please contact our International Sales department at 415-655-3023 or fax 415-655-3299.

For information on foreign language translations, please contact our Foreign & Subsidiary Rights department at 415-655-3021 or fax 415-655-3281.

For sales inquiries and special prices for bulk quantities, please contact our Sales department at 415-655-3200 or write to the address above.

For information on using IDG Books Worldwide's books in the classroom or for ordering examination copies, please contact our Educational Sales department at 800-434-2086 or fax 817-251-8174.

For press review copies, author interviews, or other publicity information, please contact our Public Relations department at 415-655-3000 or fax 415-655-3299.

For authorization to photocopy items for corporate, personal, or educational use, please contact Copyright Clearance Center, 222 Rosewood Drive, Danvers, MA 01923, or fax 508-750-4470.

About the Author

Deke McClelland is the author of more than 30 books about desktop publishing and graphics programs for the Mac and for Windows including IDG's bestselling *Macworld Photoshop 3 Bible, CorelDRAW 6 For Dummies, Photoshop 4 For Macs For Dummies,* 2nd Edition, *Macworld FreeHand 4 Bible;* and he is the coauthor of *PageMaker 6 For Windows For Dummies,* 2nd Edition, and *Photoshop 3 For Windows 95 Bible.*

He is also contributing editor to *Macworld* magazine and frequently pops up in *Publish* and *PC World.* He received the Ben Franklin award for the Best Computer Book in 1989 and won prestigious Computer Press Awards in 1990, 1992, and 1994. When he isn't writing, he hosts the television series *Digital Gurus* for the Jones Computer Network. In his few minutes of spare time, Deke lives with his wife and aging cat in Boulder, Colorado.

ABOUT IDG BOOKS WORLDWIDE

Welcome to the world of IDG Books Worldwide.

IDG Books Worldwide, Inc., is a subsidiary of International Data Group, the world's largest publisher of computer-related information and the leading global provider of information services on information technology. IDG was founded more than 25 years ago and now employs more than 8,500 people worldwide. IDG publishes more than 275 computer publications in over 75 countries (see listing below). More than 60 million people read one or more IDG publications each month.

Launched in 1990, IDG Books Worldwide is today the #1 publisher of best-selling computer books in the United States. We are proud to have received eight awards from the Computer Press Association in recognition of editorial excellence and three from *Computer Currents'* First Annual Readers' Choice Awards. Our best-selling ...*For Dummies®* series has more than 30 million copies in print with translations in 30 languages. IDG Books Worldwide, through a joint venture with IDG's Hi-Tech Beijing, became the first U.S. publisher to publish a computer book in the People's Republic of China. In record time, IDG Books Worldwide has become the first choice for millions of readers around the world who want to learn how to better manage their businesses.

Our mission is simple: Every one of our books is designed to bring extra value and skill-building instructions to the reader. Our books are written by experts who understand and care about our readers. The knowledge base of our editorial staff comes from years of experience in publishing, education, and journalism — experience we use to produce books for the '90s. In short, we care about books, so we attract the best people. We devote special attention to details such as audience, interior design, use of icons, and illustrations. And because we use an efficient process of authoring, editing, and desktop publishing our books electronically, we can spend more time ensuring superior content and spend less time on the technicalities of making books.

You can count on our commitment to deliver high-quality books at competitive prices on topics you want to read about. At IDG Books Worldwide, we continue in the IDG tradition of delivering quality for more than 25 years. You'll find no better book on a subject than one from IDG Books Worldwide.

IDG BOOKS
WORLDWIDE

John Kilcullen

John Kilcullen
CEO
IDG Books Worldwide, Inc.

*Eighth Annual
Computer Press
Awards ≥1992*

*Ninth Annual
Computer Press
Awards ≥1993*

*Tenth Annual
Computer Press
Awards ≥1994*

*Eleventh Annual
Computer Press
Awards ≥1995*

IDG Books Worldwide, Inc., is a subsidiary of International Data Group, the world's largest publisher of computer-related information and the leading global provider of information services on information technology. International Data Group publishes over 275 computer publications in over 75 countries. Sixty million people read one or more International Data Group's publications each month. International Data Group's publications include: **ARGENTINA:** Buyer's Guide, Computerworld Argentina, PC World Argentina; **AUSTRALIA:** Australian Macworld, Australian PC World, Australian Reseller News, Computerworld, IT Casebook, Network World, Publish, Webmaster; **AUSTRIA:** Computerwelt Osterreich, Networks Austria, PC Tip Austria; **BANGLADESH:** PC World Bangladesh; **BELARUS:** PC World Belarus; **BELGIUM:** Data News; **BRAZIL:** Annuário de Informática, Computerworld, Connections, Macworld, PC Player, PC World, Publish, Reseller News, Supergamepower; **BULGARIA:** Computerworld Bulgaria, Network World Bulgaria, PC & MacWorld Bulgaria; **CANADA:** CIO Canada, Client/Server World, ComputerWorld Canada, InfoWorld Canada, NetworkWorld Canada, WebWorld; **CHILE:** Computerworld Chile, PC World Chile; **COLOMBIA:** Computerworld Colombia, PC World Colombia; **COSTA RICA:** PC World Centro America; **THE CZECH AND SLOVAK REPUBLICS:** Computerworld Czechoslovakia, Macworld Czech Republic, PC World Czechoslovakia; **DENMARK:** Communications World Danmark, Computerworld Danmark, Macworld Danmark, PC World Danmark, Techworld Danmark; **DOMINICAN REPUBLIC:** PC World Republica Dominicana; **ECUADOR:** PC World Ecuador; **EGYPT:** Computerworld Middle East, PC World Middle East; **EL SALVADOR:** PC World Centro America; **FINLAND:** MikroPC, Tietoverkko, Tietoviikko; **FRANCE:** Distributique, Hebdo, Info PC, Le Monde Informatique, Macworld, Reseaux & Telecoms, WebMaster France; **GERMANY:** Computer Partner, Computerwoche, Computerwoche Extra, Computerwoche FOCUS, Global Online, Macwelt, PC Welt; **GREECE:** Amiga Computing, GamePro Greece, Multimedia World; **GUATEMALA:** PC World Centro America; **HONDURAS:** PC World Centro America; **HONG KONG:** Computerworld Hong Kong, PC World Hong Kong, Publish in Asia; **HUNGARY:** ABCD CD-ROM, Computerworld Szamitastechnika, Internetto online Magazine, PC World Hungary, PC-X Magazin Hungary; **ICELAND:** Tolvuheimur PC World Island; **INDIA:** Information Communications World, Information Systems Computerworld, PC World India, Publish in Asia; **INDONESIA:** InfoKomputer PC World, Komputek Computerworld, Publish in Asia; **IRELAND:** ComputerScope, PC Live!; **ISRAEL:** Macworld Israel, People & Computers/Computerworld; **ITALY:** Computerworld Italia, Macworld Italia, Networking Italia, PC World Italia; **JAPAN:** DTP World, Macworld Japan, Nikkei Personal Computing, OS/2 World Japan, SunWorld Japan, Windows NT World, Windows World Japan; **KENYA:** PC World East African; **KOREA:** Hi-Tech Information, Macworld Korea, PC World Korea; **MACEDONIA:** PC World Macedonia; **MALAYSIA:** Computerworld Malaysia, PC World Malaysia, Publish in Asia; **MALTA:** PC World Malta; **MEXICO:** Computerworld Mexico, PC World Mexico; **MYANMAR:** PC World Myanmar; **NETHERLANDS:** Computer! Totaal, LAN Internetworking Magazine, LAN World Buyers Guide, Macworld Netherlands, Net, WebWereld; **NEW ZEALAND:** Absolute Beginners Guide and Plain & Simple Series, Computer Buyer, Computer Industry Directory, Computerworld New Zealand, MTB, Network World, PC World New Zealand; **NICARAGUA:** PC World Centro America; **NORWAY:** Computerworld Norge, CW Rapport, Datamagasinet, Financial Rapport, Kursguide Norge, Macworld Norge, Multimediaworld Norge, PC World Ekspress Norge, PC World Nettverk, PC World Norge, PC World ProduktGuide Norge; **PAKISTAN:** Computerworld Pakistan; **PANAMA:** PC World Panama; **PEOPLE'S REPUBLIC OF CHINA:** China Computer Users, China Computerworld, China InfoWorld, China Telecom World Weekly, Computer & Communication, Electronic Design China, Electronics Today, Electronics Weekly, Game Software, PC World China, Popular Computer Week, Software Weekly, Software World, Telecom World; **PERU:** Computerworld Peru, PC World Profesional Peru, PC World SoHo Peru; **PHILIPPINES:** Click!, Computerworld Philippines, PC World Philippines, Publish in Asia; **POLAND:** Computerworld Poland, Computerworld Special Report Poland, Cyber, Macworld Poland, Networld Poland, PC World Komputer; **PORTUGAL:** Cerebro/PC World, Computerworld/Correio Informático, Dealer World Portugal, Mac*In/PC*In Portugal, Multimedia World; **PUERTO RICO:** PC World Puerto Rico; **ROMANIA:** Computerworld Romania, PC World Romania, Telecom Romania; **RUSSIA:** Computerworld Russia, Mir PK, Publish, Seti; **SINGAPORE:** Computerworld Singapore, PC World Singapore, Publish in Asia; **SLOVENIA:** Monitor; **SOUTH AFRICA:** Computing SA, Network World SA, Software World SA; **SPAIN:** Communicaciones World España, Computerworld España, Dealer World España, Macworld España, PC World España, PC World Centro Corporate Computing Sweden, Internetworld Sweden, it.branschen, Macworld Sweden, MaxiData Sweden, MikroDatorn, Nätverk & Kommunikation, PC World Sweden, PCaktiv, Windows World Sweden; **SWITZERLAND:** Computerworld Schweiz, Macworld Schweiz, PCtip; **TAIWAN:** Computerworld Taiwan, Macworld Taiwan, NEW ViSiON/Publish, PC World Taiwan, Windows World Taiwan; **THAILAND:** Publish in Asia, Thai Computerworld; **TURKEY:** Computerworld Turkiye, Macworld Turkiye, Network World Turkiye, PC World Turkiye; **UKRAINE:** Computerworld Kiev, Multimedia World Ukraine, PC World Ukraine; **UNITED KINGDOM:** Acorn User UK, Amiga Action UK, Amiga Computing UK, Apple Talk UK, Computing, Macworld, Parents and Computers UK, PC Advisor, PC Home, PSX Pro, The WEB; **UNITED STATES:** Cable in the Classroom, CIO Magazine, Computerworld, DOS World, Federal Computer Week, GamePro Magazine, InfoWorld, I-Way, Macworld, Network World, PC Games, PC World, Publish, Video Event, THE WEB Magazine, and WebMaster; online webzines: JavaWorld, NetscapeWorld, and SunWorld Online; **URUGUAY:** InfoWorld Uruguay; **VENEZUELA:** Computerworld Venezuela, PC World Venezuela; and **VIETNAM:** PC World Vietnam.   2/14/97

Author's Acknowledgments

The author wishes to extend his grateful thank-you-very-kindly's to all the groovy folks who helped him with the book that you now hold in your hands. Julie King performed her usual miracles in revising this edition to keep everything up to date. Lee Musick turned out to be one of the best technical editors I've ever had the pleasure of working with. And Jennifer Ehrlich did her usual exemplary job of ensuring that the text is unambiguous, humorous, and grammaticologically correct.

No page of thank-yees would be complete without one directed at my charming and beautiful wife of ten years, Elizabeth. She's the cat's meow (which has confused our cat on more than one occasion).

Publisher's Acknowledgments

We're proud of this book; please send us your comments about it by using the Reader Response Card at the back of the book or by e-mailing us at feedback/dummies@idgbooks.com. Some of the people who helped bring this book to market include the following:

Acquisitions, Development, and Editorial

Project Editor: Jennifer Ehrlich

Acquisitions Editor: Michael Kelly, Quality Control Manager

Copy Editors: Susan Christopherson, Susan Diane Smith

Technical Editor: Lee Musick

Editorial Manager: Kristin A. Cocks

Editorial Assistant: Michael D. Sullivan

Production

Project Coordinator: Regina Snyder

Layout and Graphics: Cameron Booker, Elizabeth Cárdenas-Nelson, J. Tyler Connor, Dominique DeFelice, Todd Klemme, Drew R. Moore, Anna Rohrer, Kate Snell

Proofreaders: Jon Weidlich, Robert Springer, Karen York

Indexer: Sharon Hilgenberg

Special Help: Bill Barton, Copy Editor; Patricia Yuu Pan, Copy Editor

General and Administrative

IDG Books Worldwide, Inc.: John Kilcullen, CEO; Steven Berkowitz, President and Publisher

IDG Books Technology Publishing: Brenda McLaughlin, Senior Vice President and Group Publisher

Dummies Technology Press and Dummies Editorial: Diane Graves Steele, Vice President and Associate Publisher; Judith A. Taylor, Brand Manager; Kristin A. Cocks, Editorial Director

Dummies Trade Press: Kathleen A. Welton, Vice President and Publisher; Stacy S. Collins, Brand Manager

IDG Books Production for Dummies Press: Beth Jenkins, Production Director; Cindy L. Phipps, Supervisor of Project Coordination, Production Proofreading, and Indexing; Kathie S. Schutte, Supervisor of Page Layout; Shelley Lea, Supervisor of Graphics and Design; Debbie J. Gates, Production Systems Specialist; Tony Augsburger, Supervisor of Reprints and Bluelines; Leslie Popplewell, Media Archive Coordinator

Dummies Packaging and Book Design: Patti Sandez, Packaging Specialist; Lance Kayser, Packaging Assistant, Kavish+Kavish, Cover Design

♦

The publisher would like to give special thanks to Patrick J. McGovern, without whom this book would not have been possible.

♦

Contents at a Glance

Introduction 1

Part I: The Stuff Everyone Pretends They Already Know ... 7

Chapter 1: What's with All These Programs? 9
Chapter 2: See CorelDraw Run 17
Chapter 3: Ladies and Gentlemen, Insert Your Pocket Protectors! 37

Part II: Let the Graphics Begin 57

Chapter 4: The Secret Society of Simple Shapes 59
Chapter 5: Drawn It, Shaped It, Ready to Go Free-Form 79
Chapter 6: Celebrating Your Inner Draftsman 101
Chapter 7: Making Your Shapes Look Like Something 123
Chapter 8: The Fine Art of Cloning 147
Chapter 9: The Twisty, Stretchy, Bulgy World of Transformations 159

Part III: Getting the Message
Out There (Wherever "There" Is) 189

Chapter 10: The Care and Planting of Text 191
Chapter 11: Mr. Typographer's Wild Ride 219
Chapter 12: The Corner of Page and Publish 239
Chapter 13: Those Poor, Helpless Trees 249

Part IV: Corel's Other Amazing Programs 261

Chapter 14: Programs in the Night, Exchanging Data 263
Chapter 15: Everyone Say Hello to Corel Photo-Paint 273
Chapter 16: Spare the Tool, Spoil the Pixel 289
Chapter 17: Twisting Reality around Your Little Finger 311
Chapter 18: Do Dogs Dream in Three Dimensions? 341

Part V: The Part of Tens 355

Chapter 19: Ten Way-Cool Special Effects 357
Chapter 20: Ten Time-Saving Shortcuts 377
Chapter 21: Ten Little-Known, Less-Used Features 383
Chapter 22: Ten File Formats and Their Functions 389
Appendix: Installing CorelDraw 7 393

Index 399

Reader Response Card .... Back of Book

Table of Contents

Introduction *1*

Why a Book . . . For Dummies? 1
How to Use This Book.. 2
How This Book Is Organized 3
    Part I: The Stuff Everyone Pretends They Already Know 3
    Part II: Let the Graphics Begin 3
    Part III: Getting the Message Out There (Wherever "There" Is) 4
    Part IV: Corel's Other Amazing Programs 4
    Part V: The Part of Tens 4
Icons Used in This Book 4
Where to Go from Here 5
How to Bug Me 6

Part I: The Stuff Everyone Pretends They Already Know ... 7

Chapter 1: What's with All These Programs? 9

CorelDraw 9
Corel Photo-Paint 10
    Finding photos to edit 10
    Painting from scratch 11
CorelDraw and Photo-Paint Duke It Out 12
Corel OCR-Trace 13
Corel Capture 14
CorelDream 3D 14
CorelDepth and CorelTexture 15
Multimedia Manager 15
And the Rest 16
But Wait, There's More 16
Feeling Overwhelmed? 16

Chapter 2: See CorelDraw Run 17

Draw on the March 17
Interface in Your Face 18
    Title bar 20
    Menu bar 21
    Toolbar 21
    Property Bar 22
    Tools 23
    Drawing area 23

Rulers 24
Scroll stuff 24
Page controls 24
Color stuff 24
Status bar 25
The Mouse Is Your Willing Slave (And Other Children's Stories) 25
How to Deal with Complete Tools 26
A quick experiment 27
How to find buried tools 28
More tool tricks 30
Les Menus sans Soup du Jour 31
Les equivalents du keyboard 32
Alt, ma chère amie, oui? 32
The Incessant Chatter of Dialog Boxes 33
Roll-Ups, Now in Dozens of Fruity Flavors 34
Roll 'em up and tack 'em down 35
Breakaway roll-ups 36

Chapter 3: Ladies and Gentlemen, Insert Your Pocket Protectors! 37

Spank the Baby 37
How do I start a new document? 38
The enlightening Chihuahua scenario 39
How do I open a piece of clip art? 39
Adding a drawing to an existing drawing 41
Opening and importing from the Scrapbook 42
Tools for Getting Around the Drawing Area 43
Miracles of magnification 43
Zoom up to the Property Bar 46
Your very own zoombox 47
The secret magnification menu 48
Pull Your Image into View 48
The Screen Is What You Make It 50
Show me a rough draft 50
String art revival 50
Die, you gravy-sucking interface 52
Preview bits and pieces 52
Save or Die Trying! 53
Saving for the very first time 54
Updating the drawing 55
Creating a backup copy 56
Put Your Drawing to Bed 56

Part II: Let the Graphics Begin **57**

Chapter 4: The Secret Society of Simple Shapes 59

Shapes from Your Childhood 60
Rectangles and squares 60

Ovals and circles 61
Shapes with many sides 63
Ways to Change Shapes 66
Sanding off the corners 67
Turning an oval into a tempting dessert 68
Giving the pie a wedgie 70
Making a wacky shape wackier 72
Arrow Tool Techniques (Or Tricks of the Pick) 74
Kiss It Good-bye 77
Aaaugh, It's Gone! 77

Chapter 5: Drawn It, Shaped It, Ready to Go Free-Form **79**

Do Some Doodling with the Pencil 80
Understanding paths, lines, and shapes 81
Coming to grips with nodes and segments 82
Mastering the pencil 82
Experimenting with the natural pen tool 84
Nodes as You Never Knew Them 85
Bringing nodes into view 86
Using nodes to reshape your drawing 87
Meet the Node Edit Thingies 90
Your first tentative node edits 93
How to open, split, close, and join paths 95
More ways to make a break 96
Options you need once in a blue moon 98
Bouncy paths made of rubber 99
How to Upgrade Simple Shapes 100

Chapter 6: Celebrating Your Inner Draftsman **101**

You Need to Be Disciplined 102
Rulers with no power 102
Go downtown 105
Let the lines be your guide 107
The status bar tells all 110
Tell Your Objects Where They Can Go 112
Nudging with the arrow keys 112
Moving by the numbers 112
Aligning and distributing objects 115
Gang Behavior 118
Your Drawing Is a Plate of Flapjacks 120

Chapter 7: Making Your Shapes Look Like Something **123**

Fills, Spills, and Chills 124
Fill 'er up with color 124
Hasta la fillsta 125
Make the color palette your own 126

Make New Colors in Your Spare Time 127
    Choosing a color model 127
    Mixing up a batch of color 128
The Thick and Thin of Outlines 130
    Outlining a path 130
    Removing the outline 132
    Avoiding embarrassing line widths 132
    Setting better line widths 133
    Lifting an outline from an existing shape 135
    Creating custom line widths 135
    Changing line corners and caps 136
I Don't Like the Default Setting! 138
Fill and Outline Join Forces 138
The World of Wacky Fills 139
    Using the Special Fill roll-up 140
    Dragging special fills from the Scrapbook 142
    Filling on the fly 143
Save Time with Find and Replace 145

Chapter 8: The Fine Art of Cloning **147**

Clipboard Mania: Cut, Copy, and Paste 147
    Snap, crackle, paste 148
    A few little Clipboard facts 150
    Why I hate the Clipboard 151
The Gleaming Clipboard Bypass 151
    Group before you duplicate 151
    Duplication distance 153
    Duplicate in place 154
They Look Alike, They Act Alike, You Could Lose Your Mind 154
    Links on the brink 155
    The care and feeding of your clones 156
Do the Drag and Drop 157

Chapter 9: The Twisty, Stretchy, Bulgy World of Transformations .. 159

Scaling, Flipping, Rotating, and Skewing 160
    Grouping comes before transforming 161
    Scaling and flipping 161
    Using the provocative S&M roll-up 163
    Rotating and skewing 164
    Transforming by degrees 166
    Using the not-so-provocative R&S roll-ups 167
Distortions on Parade 169
A Lesson in Perspective 169
    Viewing your 2-D drawing in 3-D space (sorta) 170
    Putting perspective in perspective 172
Envelope of Wonders 173
    The ultimate distortion 173
    The envelope editing modes 175
    Push the envelope 177

Well, Extru-u-ude Me! 179

    Extruding in the real world 179

    Extruding in the workplace 180

    Extruding by the buttons 186

    Ripping apart your new 3-D object 187

Part III: Getting the Message Out There (Wherever "There" Is) 189

Chapter 10: The Care and Planting of Text 191

    A Furst Luk at Tekst 192

    Pick Up Your Text Tool 192

        Creating artistic text 193

        Creating paragraph text 195

        Navigating among the letters 198

    How to Flow Text between Blocks 199

    Before You Can Format, You Must Select 202

        Selecting with the text tool 202

        Converting from artistic to paragraph and vice versa 203

    Okay, Now You Can Format 204

        Selecting a typeface 206

        Changing the type style 207

        Enlarging or reducing the type size 207

        Mucking about with the justification 209

            Formatting options for rare occasions 210

        Dropping your caps 212

    Please Check Your Spelling 213

    Shortcut to Typographic Happiness 214

    A Different Kind of Alphabet 216

Chapter 11: Mr. Typographer's Wild Ride 219

    Learning the Rules of the Park 219

    Playing Bumper Cars 220

        Selecting and dragging text nodes 221

        Kern, kern, the baffling term 222

        Changing overall spacing 223

    Riding the Roller Coaster 226

        Orienting text on a path 229

        Changing the vertical alignment 230

        Changing the horizontal alignment 231

        Shifting text around a geometric object 231

        Shifting text in specific increments 231

        Creating text on a circle 231

        Editing text on a path 236

        Editing the path 236

        Breaking it up 237

    Meddling with Type 237

Chapter 12: The Corner of Page and Publish **239**

Pages upon Pages 240
   Adding new pages 240
   Adding pages bit by bit 240
   Thumbing through your pages 241
   Removing the excess 242
   Flowing text between pages 243
Your Logo on Every Page 243
   Establishing a master layer 244
   Hiding master layer objects on page 1 246
I Need a Bigger Page! 247

Chapter 13: Those Poor, Helpless Trees **249**

Reviewing the Basic Steps 250
Making Sure That Everything's Ready to Go 251
   Selecting a printer 251
   Changing paper size and orientation 251
   Printing the entire document 253
Printing Those Pages 253
   Printing multiple copies 254
   Printing a few pages here and there 254
Still More Printing Options 255
   Using the page preview area 257
   Printing full-color artwork 259

Part IV: Corel's Other Amazing Programs *261*

Chapter 14: Programs in the Night, Exchanging Data **263**

OLE Must Be Pretty Bad to Deserve That Windup 264
Take OLE by the Horns 264
More Ways for CorelDraw to Receive Gifts 270
   Linking, the semi-smart technique 270
   Importing, the last ditch effort 272

Chapter 15: Everyone Say Hello to Corel Photo-Paint **273**

Blasting Off with Photo-Paint 274
   Here's paint in yer eye! 274
   Turn off the toolbar! 276
Opening Existing Images 277
Viewing Your Image 279
   Using the Navigator 281
Dividing Up Your Screen 282
Creating a Brand Spanking New Image 282
   Dots per inch 283
   Select your crayons 284

Changing the Resolution and Color of Photographs 286
Saving, Printing, and Closing 287

Chapter 16: Spare the Tool, Spoil the Pixel 289

Pawing Through Your Toolbox 289
Loading Your Tools with Color 290
Lifting Colors Right Off the Canvas 292
Erasing and Undoing Your Way Back to the Good Old Days 293
Scrubbing away those stubborn stains 293
Reviewing the history of your image 295
Going back to square one 296
Drawing Lines 296
Drawing Geometric Shapes 297
Filling Your Entire Image 299
Plunking Down the Paint 300
Creating Custom Gradients 301
Painting with a Tackle Box Full of Brushes 303
Smudging, Lightening, Colorizing, and Blurring 305
Painting One Portion of an Image onto Another 307
Spray Painting with Images 308

Chapter 17: Twisting Reality around Your Little Finger 311

Specifying Which Part of the Image You Want to Edit 312
Carving out a little bit of imagery with the
wondrous mask tools 313
Fine-tuning your selection outline 317
Making manual adjustments 321
Things to Do with a Selected Image 322
Combining Images 324
Correcting Focus and Contrast 325
Bringing an image into sharper focus 326
Reapplying an Effects command 327
Making an image less dark and murky 329
Setting Your Selections Free 332
Making an object 332
Manipulating an object 333
Moving, cloning, and deleting objects 334
Scaling, rotating, and other effects 334
Stamping Some Text into Your Image 337
Adding and modifying text 338
Painting inside text 339

Chapter 18: Do Dogs Dream in Three Dimensions? 341

The Dream That Starts Like a Nightmare 342
A Beginner's Guide to 3-D Objects 345
Importing and magnifying an object 345
Changing how the object looks on-screen 346

Moving an object in 3-D space 347
Scaling and spinning the object 348
Every Object Needs a Look 350
Adding a Prefab Backdrop 351
The End of the 3-D Highway 353

Part V: The Part of Tens *355*

Chapter 19: Ten Way-Cool Special Effects 357

Chapter 20: Ten Time-Saving Shortcuts 377

Chapter 21: Ten Little-Known, Less-Used Features 383

Chapter 22: Ten File Formats and Their Functions 389

Appendix: Installing CorelDraw 7 393
If You Build the Computer, CorelDraw Will Come 393
Checking your memory 394
Inspecting the hard drive 394
Insert the CD and Watch the Sparks Fly 394

Index *399*

Reader Response Card .... *Back of Book*

Introduction

● ●

*T*he *Guinness Book of World Records* doesn't seem to offer a category for the most immense software package. If it did, the prize would clearly have to go to CorelDraw 7. This ample, expansive, sprawling, capacious, comprehensive program is so large that it consumes three CD-ROMs.

Simply put, CorelDraw 7 is an all-in-one artist's studio. It enables you to create precise illustrations, draw free-form artwork, paint electronic master-pieces, edit digital photographs, and even design three-dimensional environ-ments that look every bit as realistic — or surrealistic — as real life. The CorelDraw package also includes thousands upon thousands of pieces of clip art, fonts, digital photographs, 3-D models, and other valuable stuff.

All this combined with the program's reasonable price may explain the phenomenal popularity of CorelDraw. By some accounts, it's the most popular piece of graphics software for the personal computer.

Why a Book . . . For Dummies?

But all this power comes at a price. The CorelDraw 7 package comprises 12 programs. The central program is CorelDraw, which enables you to design professional-quality pages and artwork, but you also get Photo-Paint, Dream 3D, Depth, Scan, Texture, Trace, Capture, Multimedia Manager, and a bunch of others. If Corel could come up with a way to market its KitchenSink and Swiss PocketKnife programs, they would be in the package as well.

Needless to say, there's no way to sit down cold with this many programs and figure them out overnight — in fact, there's really no reason why you should even bother to learn all of them. How can you tell which of these programs are worth your time and which you should ignore? I can tell you from years of personal experience that a few Corel programs are very interesting, some are somewhat interesting, and the rest are pretty darn forgettable — so forgettable that I have to consult the Corel press information to remember them.

So instead of packing your brain full of a bunch of utter nonsense about a bunch of programs you'll never touch, I cover just those aspects of those programs that I think you'll find exciting, entertaining, and ultimately useful. Being a generous guy by nature, I leave the boring stuff for another book.

By the way, I should mention that this book is specifically about CorelDraw 7. I suppose that you could use it to learn about one of the other versions of the program, but quite a few commands would be different, some tools wouldn't be available, and your screen would look different than the ones pictured throughout this book. I can't say that I recommend this approach.

If you're using an older version of the program, your better bet is to look for an earlier edition of this book. Ask your bookseller for the edition that covers your version of the program. It'll make you smile again.

How to Use This Book

I tried to write this book so that you can approach it from several perspectives, depending on how you learn.

- ✔ If you're a reader — it's been my experience that only hard-core readers put up with book introductions — I hope that you'll find my writing lively enough to keep you from falling asleep or collapsing into an information-age coma.

- ✔ If you just want to find out how a command works and then toss the book back into a dusty corner, look up the topic in the index and then turn to the appropriate page. The publisher of this book creates an ample, expansive, immense, sprawling, capacious, and comprehensive index, on par with CorelDraw itself.

- ✔ If you already know your way around CorelDraw, flip through the book, check out a few of the tips here and there, and pay special attention to the information marked with the CorelDraw 7 icon.

- ✔ If you hate to read anything without pictures, just read Rich Tennant's comics. I fall into this learning group. (Good news, huh?) Folks like you and me won't learn anything about CorelDraw, but by golly, we'll get in a few yucks.

- ✔ If you want to get a quick idea of what this book is like, read the four chapters in Part V. Each chapter contains a series of short sections that not only give you an indication of the high-falutin' caliber of information in this book but also mesmerize you with my enchanting style and wit. Well, perhaps *mesmerize* is the wrong word. How about *clomp you over the head?*

- ✔ If you don't much like the idea of reading a computer book but you're so confused that you don't even know what questions to ask, start at Chapter 1 and see where it takes you. I promise that I won't leave you wallowing in the dust.

This book has been read and reread by folks who don't know the first thing about CorelDraw, and to this day, they are only marginally confused. Considering that they all led happy and productive lives before they read *CorelDRAW 7 For Dummies* and that only three of them had to seek therapy afterwards, I think that this is one heck of a book.

How This Book Is Organized

I've divided *CorelDRAW 7 For Dummies* into five digestible parts, each of which contains three to six chapters, which are themselves divided into gobs of discrete sections, which contain these funny little letter-units called *words*. I thought about including a synopsis of every sentence in the book in this introduction, but then I thought, no, it'd be better if you had a chance to read the book before the next Ice Age set in. So here are brief descriptions of the parts instead.

Part I: The Stuff Everyone Pretends They Already Know

We're all dumb about some things and smart about others. But however smart we may be about our key interests in life, we're afraid that our dumb topics will be the death of us. At any moment, someone may expose us for what we truly are — congenital half-wits. You know what I'm saying here? (Sob.) Pass me that tissue, would you? (Sniff.) Thank you. (Honk.)

So this part of the book is about answering all those questions that you had and didn't know you had, and even if you did know, you wouldn't have asked anyone because all your friends would have laughed at you and branded you an Industrial Age cretin. These chapters are like a CorelDraw information pill. Swallow them and be smart. Or at least, better informed.

Part II: Let the Graphics Begin

In this part, you get to start expressing yourself and creating some bona fide computer art. Not an artist? Not to worry. Neither are thousands of other folks who use this program. In fact, CorelDraw is specifically designed to accommodate artists and nonartists alike, enabling you to express the uniquely individual creative impulses that surge through, well, all those places that things tend to surge through. That is to say, you'll be able to get the job done. You can even throw in a few special effects for good measure.

Part III: Getting the Message Out There (Wherever "There" Is)

Many of us feel the special need to share things with other people. Reports, newsletters, and internal memos allow us to show off our personalities and mix in a bit of our literary expertise. Bold headlines like "Joe Bob Receives Employee of the Month Award" or "Sales Up in March" tell a little something about who we are and how we live.

CorelDraw knows that it's not enough to draw pretty pictures; you have to be able to back up those pictures with hard-hitting text. In these chapters, you'll discover that CorelDraw is half drawing program and half document-creation software. You can enter and edit text, design logos and special text effects, create multipage documents, and print the whole thing out on 20-pound bond paper.

Part IV: Corel's Other Amazing Programs

As I mentioned earlier, I try to steer you away from the boring and mostly useless Corel programs and concentrate on the good ones. This part of the book covers two good programs that you're sure to want to check out, Photo-Paint and Dream 3D. In fact, it devotes three full chapters to Photo-Paint, a program that is growing in popularity and is second only to CorelDraw in usefulness and artistic prowess. You even find out how to share graphics between Photo-Paint and CorelDraw.

Part V: The Part of Tens

This part of the book is a savory blend of real information and the sort of chatty top-ten lists that prevent us all from understanding too awfully much about anything. These chapters offer lists of special effects, time-saving shortcuts, obscure features, file formats, and advice for everyday living. Prepare to be entertained as you learn. Prepare to laugh and be studious. Prepare to chortle until factoids come out your nose.

Icons Used in This Book

To alert you to special passages of text that you may or may not want to read, the National Bureau of Wacky Graphics has designed the following universal margin icons and thoughtfully interspersed them throughout the book.

Here's an example of something you may want to avoid. This icon highlights a close encounter of the nerd kind, the variety of information that could land you in the intensive care ward if you were to utter it at the Annual Gathering of Hell's Angels. In other words, read if you must, but don't repeat.

Here's something you didn't know, or if you did know it, you're smarter than you thought. Don't be surprised if a single tip makes you fractions of a percentage point more efficient than you were before. It's been known to happen to people just like you.

This may be some bit of information that I've already mentioned. But you may have forgotten it, and I want to drill it into your head. Metaphorically, of course. Or it may be something that I just thought you might like to know — a friendly gesture on my part.

This icon spells danger. Or, at least, something to be watchful for. Try to steer clear of the stuff I describe here.

If you're at all familiar with CorelDraw 3, 4, 5, or 6, you may be keenly interested in how CorelDraw 7 differs from its predecessors. This icon lets you in on the newest features so that you can make the transition to Version 7 in record time. I also point out a few old features that have been changed so dramatically that you may not recognize them without a little help.

This icon calls attention to information that, while mildly interesting, is not in the least bit important to your understanding of CorelDraw. I just throw it in to keep the scandal-mongers happy.

Where to Go from Here

Different people read in different ways. You may want to check out the index or table of contents and look up some bit of information that has been perplexing you for the past few days. Or you might just close the book and use it as a reference the next time you face an impasse or some horrible, confusing problem. Then again, you could just keep on reading, perish the thought. Personally, I couldn't put the book down, but you may have more willpower.

How to Bug Me

If you want to ask me a question, tell me about a mistake, or just share your opinions about this book, feel free to write me at one of these handy e-mail addresses:

America Online: DekeMc

Internet: DekeMc@InternetMCI.com

Don't be discouraged if I don't respond for a couple of weeks. It just means that I'm in over my head with projects and deadlines (as usual). I eventually respond to every e-mail I get. If you write me by regular mail, please include a phone number or e-mail address so that I can respond.

Good luck with the book, and may CorelDraw treat you with the dignity that you — a superior, carbon-based life-form — deserve.

Part I
The Stuff Everyone Pretends They Already Know

GUS & LILY'S
DOG GROOMING

NOW USING CorelDRAW

In this part . . .

*I*magine this: You're enrolled in an introductory computing course. The professor asks you to write a simple computer program. Let's say that you're to create a program that types out a series of *A*s in a column or something equally pointless. Who cares? It's not important. Anyway, the professor takes time to carefully explain the language and logic behind the exercise. Because you secretly harbor an unusually immense brain — granted, you only use it on special occasions — you understand thoroughly. No sweat.

But when you sit down in front of a terminal at the computer lab, you realize that you lack a key bit of information. How are you supposed to get to the point where you start entering your programming instructions? The computer is on, but it just sits there blinking at you. Anything you enter results in an error message. You're so utterly clueless and overwhelmingly frustrated that you don't even know how to ask one of the pompous lab assistants what the heck is going on.

I've been there. I empathize. It stinks. The fact of the matter is, any amount of knowledge is worthless if you don't know the basics. The difficulty, of course, is that lots of folks act as if they already know the basics because they don't want to look like, well, a dummy. But let's face it, when it comes to computers, remarkably few people know what's going on. And those who do tend to be insufferable.

So here are the basics. The following chapters explain all the easy stuff that you've been pretending to know, little realizing that 90 percent of the people around you don't know it either. Soon, you'll be welcomed into the the ranks of the Insufferable Computer Dweebs, a group we're all dying to join.

Chapter 1

What's with All These Programs?

In This Chapter

▶ The uses for CorelDraw

▶ Where Corel Photo-Paint fits in

▶ The differences between CorelDraw and Photo-Paint

▶ The lowdown on Corel OCR-Trace

▶ Should you worry about Corel Capture?

▶ How CorelDream 3D can boggle your mind

▶ The utter wackiness of CorelDepth

▶ Why Corel Multimedia Manager wants to be your electronic librarian

*O*nce upon a time, back when dinosaurs roamed the earth, CorelDraw used to be a single program — weird, huh? Nowadays, the CorelDraw box includes 12 separate programs, each of which you can use independently or in tandem with its little electronic friends. This chapter introduces many of the programs and explains their relative benefits and degrees of usefulness, which range from truly stupendous to barely worth yawning over. I also tell you which chapters in this book, if any, contain more information about each program.

CorelDraw

This program started it all. Not only is CorelDraw the program after which the package is named, it's the most powerful and the most useful program of the bunch. Not surprisingly, therefore, it's the one I talk about in the most detail.

What can you draw with CorelDraw? Why, anything. Free-form graphics of butterflies or unicorns engaged in some ridiculous activity, architectural plans for a bathroom off the linen closet (I wish I had one of those), anatomical illustrations that show food going down the trachea (and the ensuing coughing fit that follows) . . . the list is endless, or at least close enough to endless that I'd run the risk of boring you into a coma if I were to continue.

Thar's math in them thar objets d'art

Math is the driving force behind CorelDraw. I know, it's sick, but it's true. When you draw a wiggly line, for example, CorelDraw notes the coordinates of the first and last points and calculates a mathematical description of the curve between the two points. CorelDraw thinks of each line, shape, or character of text as a mathematical object, which is why the program and others like it are sometimes called *object-oriented software.* When you print your drawings, the program explains all this math to the printer, which in turn draws the objects as smoothly as it can so that they all look like you drew them by hand and not with a computer.

If your printed drawings look jagged, you're using a cheap printer. You can improve the appearance of your drawings by buying a better printer or by paying to have your drawings printed at a service bureau. Both options involve the outlay of some additional cash, of course. For the whole story on printing, read Chapter 13.

Wait, there's more. You can open and edit clip art — you know, those drawings that other people create specifically so that you can mess them up. You can create wild text effects, such as a logo or two for Stuckey's. You can even design documents such as advertisements for Stuckey's, fliers for Stuckey's, and posters for Long John Silver's. (What does Stuckey's need with posters, anyway? We're all familiar with their pecan logs.)

Corel Photo-Paint

The primary purpose of Corel Photo-Paint, discussed in Chapters 15 through 17, is to enable you to make changes to photographic images. You can change the color scheme of a photo so that everyone in your family looks like they had the sense not to wear bright orange and avocado green in the '70s. You can apply special effects so that Grandma Edna's face appears molded in lead. You can retouch subtle or bothersome details such as Junior's unusually immense chin wart. You can even combine the contents of two different photos so that Uncle Mike and Aunt Rosie are standing shoulder to shoulder, even though the two of them would rather take a flying leap into the Grand Canyon than hang out in the same room together. And if that sounds like an accurate description of your family, you need all the help you can get.

Finding photos to edit

The following list explains a few ways to get photos on a floppy disk or Photo CD so that you can edit them in Photo-Paint:

✔ You can take a photograph to a service bureau and have it *scanned* onto a floppy disk, which means to read the photo and convert it to a digital image, sort of like recording music onto a CD. Some folks call scanning *digitizing.* Scanning is generally a pretty expensive proposition, around $2 to $10 per photo, depending on whether you scan the photo in black and white or in color.

✔ To locate a service bureau, look in the Yellow Pages under "Desktop Publishing." Some cities have many service bureaus. San Francisco, Los Angeles, Seattle, Chicago, New York, and all those other coastal towns have as many service bureaus as they have adult book stores. But in rural areas, service bureaus are a little harder to come by. You may have to search around a little bit. If you have friends in the computer graphics biz, ask them for recommendations.

✔ If you intend to do a great deal of scanning, you may want to purchase your own scanner. Top-of-the-line scanners run $1,000 and up, but you can get a decent scanner for under $500.

✔ The Kodak Photo CD technology provides a better alternative to scanning your images to disk, both in terms of quality and economy. For around $100, you can transfer up to 100 photos from slides, negatives, or undeveloped rolls of film to a compact disc that's identical in appearance to CDs that play music. Of course, to take advantage of Photo CD, you need a CD-ROM drive.

✔ For service bureaus that can put your images on Photo CD, look in the Yellow Pages under "Photo Finishing-Retail."

✔ You can also buy CDs filled with photographs shot by professional photographers. Called *stock photos,* these images run the gamut from famous landmarks to animals, from textures to people engaged in people-like pursuits. Corel sells its own line of stock-photo CDs, which you can buy for less than $20 a pop. You can also purchase individual images from Corel by visiting the Corel World Wide Web site, at `www.corel.com`.

✔ If you have Internet access or subscribe to an on-line service such as CompuServe or America Online, you can download photos using your modem. Watch out, though. Because of their large file size, photos take several minutes — sometimes hours — to download. You can waste some major bucks in access charges if you're not careful.

Painting from scratch

You don't have to edit photos in Photo-Paint. You can also paint images from scratch. The difference between drawing in CorelDraw and painting in Photo-Paint is that the painting process is much more intuitive. In fact, you don't need my help to paint an image. You just sketch a little here, erase a little there, fill in some details, and keep working on your image until you get it right. Kids love painting on a computer. You'll love it, too. Painting is the easiest thing you can do with any computer program, I swear.

TECHNICAL STUFF

Picture yourself done up in pixels

Ah, even in the Simple-Simon world of computer painting, Technical Stuff rears its nerdy head. Remember that I said that CorelDraw defines lines, shapes, and text using complex mathematical equations? (If not, and assuming that you care, check out the sidebar "There's math in them thar' objects d'art," in this chapter.) Well, Photo-Paint defines the entire image — whether it's a photograph or something you painted from scratch — using thousands or even millions of tiny, colored squares called *pixels.*

A Photo-Paint image is similar to a mosaic. When you get close to a mosaic, you can see the individual colored tiles. When you get far away, the tiles blur into a recognizable picture. Pixels work just like those tiles. When you magnify an image in Photo-Paint, you can see the individual pixels. When you restore the image to its regular size, the pixels blur together.

CorelDraw and Photo-Paint Duke It Out

Although drawings and images both are forms of computer artwork, the two are very distinct. Drawings created in CorelDraw feature sharp edges, as demonstrated in Figure 1-1. The second half of the figure shows an enlarged detail so that you can see what a difference math makes. Even when printed at a really large size, a drawing retains its detail.

Figure 1-1: No matter how large or small you print a drawing, you get smooth lines and high contrast.

Images created with Photo-Paint feature softer edges. One shade flows continuously into the next. *C'est magnifique, très* artsie fartsie, *n'est-ce pas?* But like Achilles — you know, that Greek guy with the bad heel — images have a fatal flaw. They look better when printed at small sizes. When images are printed large, you can see the jagged transitions between colors, as illustrated in Figure 1-2.

Figure 1-2:
When printed small, paintings look fine (left), but when printed large, they look like a stinky pile of goo (right).

You can place scanned photos into a CorelDraw program and even do some minimal editing to the photo, such as enlarging or reducing the image and applying some photographic effects. Likewise, you can open a drawing in Photo-Paint. Photo-Paint automatically converts the drawing into a pixel-based image, which means that you can then use Photo-Paint tools to edit the drawing-turned-image. But for best results, don't edit a drawing in Photo-Paint or edit an image in CorelDraw. Instead, edit in the appropriate program: CorelDraw for drawings and Photo-Paint for scanned images.

Corel OCR-Trace

Corel OCR-Trace is a conversion program. It converts Photo-Paint images to CorelDraw drawings by tracing the outlines of lines and shapes in the image. Suppose that you put pen to paper and sketched out that plan of the bathroom off the linen closet discussed earlier. Now you want to convert the plan to a CorelDraw drawing. How can you get your hand-drawn sketch into CorelDraw? Scan it, open and modify it in Photo-Paint, and then convert it using Corel OCR-Trace, that's how.

Unfortunately, converting an image to a drawing is an iffy proposition. This process relies on something called artificial intelligence, which is about as reliable as you'd expect. You have to be prepared to edit the drawing in CorelDraw.

In a time when magazine articles, TV commercials, and CNN news blips remind you on a daily basis how much new stuff is out there that you're totally unaware of, isn't it nice to know that you can get away with not knowing something? The fact is, most folks don't need to learn to use Corel OCR-Trace.

Oh, yes, that's the word *ojoucd* — no wait, it's *qohoot*

Corel OCR-Trace can also read. If you scan in a page of text, the program can convert the page to a computer text document that you can open and edit in a word processor such as Corel WordPerfect or Microsoft Word. This capability is called *optical character recognition,* or simply by its initials, OCR.

Unfortunately, OCR involves even more artificial intelligence than converting images to drawings. Depending on the quality of the page you want OCR-Trace to read, the program can easily confuse one letter for another. For example, the word *optical* may be read as *optkal, ogucd, ojoucd,* or *qohoot.* Don't get me wrong; Corel OCR-Trace is as good as most other OCR programs on the market. But it's highly unlikely that the program will read any page 100 percent correctly. In some cases, entering the text from scratch is easier.

Corel Capture

Corel Capture takes pictures — called *screen shots* — of your screen. This book is chock-full of such pictures. Unless you're documenting a program like I am in this book, Corel Capture is of no use to you.

Just in case you find yourself loving this program in direct violation of my specific instructions, here's a little something you should know: You can use Photo-Paint to edit the pictures you shoot with Corel Capture. In fact, that's exactly what I did to refine many of the figures in this book.

CorelDream 3D

When most folks think of computer graphics, they conjure up vivid three-dimensional images, the sort of stuff you can't create without computers. You know, like the animation in the movie *Toy Story,* which was created using nothing but computers.

With CorelDream 3D, you can create your own hyper-realistic, Bizarro-World, 3-D graphics. The problem is that CorelDream 3D is pretty darn complicated — like any 3-D drawing program. First you have to build a model of an object, which is roughly equivalent to constructing a geodesic dome out of Tinker Toys. Then you have to wrap a surface around the shape, which is kind of like stretching a balloon or some other elastic plastic around your Tinker Toys. Next, you have to amass all your models together and set up lights and camera angles. And when you're finished, you don't print the drawing. That would take too long. Instead, you render it to an image file, which may take a few minutes or a few hours, depending on the complexity of the graphic. After that little process is completed, you can open the image in Photo-Paint and print it.

Sound hard? Well, it is hard. The truth is that 3-D drawing is one of the most complicated pursuits humans and computers can tackle. But what the heck, CorelDream 3D is worth a look-see anyway, which is what Chapter 18 is all about. There I tell you how to get to first base with this powerful but difficult program. The rest of the bases are up to you.

CorelDepth and CorelTexture

Just in case CorelDream 3D doesn't fit all your 3-D needs, CorelDraw 7 includes CorelDepth, which you can use to create three-dimensional text effects. Version 7 also includes CorelTexture, which you can use to create custom digitized textures that resemble marble, wood, liquids, and metals.

CorelDepth can be fun. But it takes a lot of time and effort to produce decent effects. You need not only talent but extraordinary patience and determination as well. And though these are great qualities — I've often yearned for a little bit of talent, patience, and determination myself — they are well outside the scope of this ignoble little book.

As for CorelTexture, well . . . what are you really going to do with a custom texture, anyway? I suppose that if you were enterprising and had a lot of time on your hands, you could create a texture and then use it as a background for your Windows desktop, a Photo-Paint image, or a Dream 3D scene. But really, you have better things to do with both your time and your enterprising urges — don't you?

Multimedia Manager

With all the stuff you'll be creating with CorelDraw and its friends, Corel thought you may need a librarian to keep track of it all. That's where Corel Multimedia Manager comes in.

You can use Multimedia Manager to organize just about any kind of files on the planet. Suppose that you set up your computer's hard disk so that one directory contains drawings of African animals and another contains a few North American varieties. But you also want to keep track of the horse-like animals — the zebras, the mustangs, the Triggers — regardless of their home turf. Multimedia Manager is your tool. You can easily create that catalog of horse-ish critters, complete with previews and everything.

As theoretically groovy as Multimedia Manager may be, it differs from the other Corel programs in that it doesn't let you create anything (except image and drawing catalogs, of course). Multimedia Manager is just a muck-about-and-organize-things tool. That's why I don't discuss it in this book.

This program used to be called CorelMosaic, but given the popularity of a completely unrelated program also called Mosaic — which lets you browse the Internet — the folks at Corel thought it a wise idea to pick a new name.

And the Rest . . .

Remember the intro to the early episodes of *Gilligan's Island,* in which the Gleeful Castaway Singers sang "and the rest" instead of "the Professor and Mary Anne"? Well, that's how I feel about the other programs bundled with Corel-Draw 7, including Corel Script, CorelScan, and the others — they're not really worth special mention. These programs are about as effective as the Professor was at fixing the *Minnow* — and that's why I don't cover them in this book.

But Wait, There's More

That's right, if you act now, you also receive thousands of clip-art drawings, hundreds of typefaces, lots and lots of photos, and more animation, sound, and movie files than you can shake a Douglas Fir at. No other program comes close to providing this variety of ready-to-use stuff. These goodies are truly amazing and well worth the price of admission on their own. I'll be featuring much of this artwork throughout this book in the hope that doing so helps you to follow along. I'm just that kind of guy.

Feeling Overwhelmed?

If you're feeling a little bewildered, I don't blame you. Corel went a little nuts in the value department. But the fact is, CorelDraw and Photo-Paint are far and away the most useful programs of the bunch. Frankly, few users would even buy a program like OCR-Trace or Multimedia Manager if it weren't bundled with CorelDraw.

To wit, most of this book is devoted to CorelDraw, with the secondary emphasis going to Photo-Paint. But I'll bet you ten comes a runnin' to five (actually, I don't gamble, so I'm a little rusty on the vocabulary) that after you find out how to use these two wonderful programs, you can pick up on the others with remarkable ease. No doubt, then, you'll want to take a gander at my next book, *CorelDRAW For Bionic-Brained Ultra-Dweebs.* I'll probably devote the whole thing to CorelTexture.

Chapter 2
See CorelDraw Run

In This Chapter

▶ Starting Windows 95 and CorelDraw 7

▶ Exploring the CorelDraw interface

▶ Using the mouse

▶ Getting acquainted with the drawing tools

▶ Choosing menu commands from the keyboard

▶ Working with dialog boxes and roll-ups

CorelDraw is one son-of-a-gun program. But you don't have a prayer of mastering it until you and the program get a little better acquainted. You have to discover its nuances, understand some of its clockwork and gizmos, study its fruity yet palatable bouquet, and make yourself familiar with its inner psyche. In short, you need to read this chapter. Herein lies the answer to that time-honored question, "What makes Draw draw?"

Draw on the March

Entering the world of CorelDraw is a mysterious but surprisingly straight-forward process. It goes a little something like this:

1. **Turn on your computer.**

   Imagine how embarrassed you'd be if you skipped this step.

2. **Wait for your computer to start up.**

   Be patient, it'll finish soon.

3. **Enjoy a close encounter with Windows 95.**

   Yes, CorelDraw 7 requires Windows 95. If you're looking at some older version of Windows (or DOS, heaven help you), you can't use CorelDraw 7. That's just the way it goes, I'm afraid.

4. Start up CorelDraw.

The easiest way to start the program is to use the Windows 95 Start menu. Click on the Start button in the lower-left corner of the screen. A menu of items appears. Click on the <u>P</u>rograms item in the menu to display a list of folders and programs that you can run. Next, click on the CorelDraw 7 item to display yet another submenu, and click on the CorelDraw 7 item in that submenu. CorelDraw should pop-up on your computer screen momentarily.

Don't panic if you have problems with menus and mouse clicks. I cover this stuff in more detail later in this chapter.

Interface in Your Face

When you first start CorelDraw, the program produces a welcome screen that contains a bunch of buttons. You have the option to start a new drawing, open a drawing saved to disk, peruse the on-screen tutorial, or check out a description of features new to Version 7. Feel free to check out the tutorial or Version 7 preview, if you so desire, by clicking on the CorelTutor button or the What's New button. (The first CorelDraw 7 CD-ROM must be in your CD-ROM drive for the tutorial to work.) Otherwise, click on the New Graphic button to start a new drawing, the Open Graphic button to edit an existing drawing, or the Open Last Edited button to edit the last drawing you worked on in CorelDraw. For now, click on the New Graphic button.

To make the Welcome screen disappear forever — really, you don't need to be bothered with this screen every time you start the program — click on the Show This Welcome Screen at Startup check box in the welcome screen. Or, if you want CorelDraw to automatically perform one of the Welcome Screen options each time you start the program, do this: Click on the Tools menu and then click on the Options command to display the Options dialog box. Click on the General tab inside the dialog box. At the bottom of the dialog box, make a selection from the On CorelDraw Start-Up pop-up menu, which controls what happens when you start the program. (Selecting stuff from menus, dialog boxes, and so forth is covered in other sections in this chapter if you need help.)

What you see next and what I show you in Figure 2-1 is the CorelDraw 7 *interface* (pronounced *in-yur-face*). The interface is your means for working in and communicating with CorelDraw 7. All the bits and pieces that you see labeled in Figure 2-1 are bravely covered at great length and personal risk in the following sections.

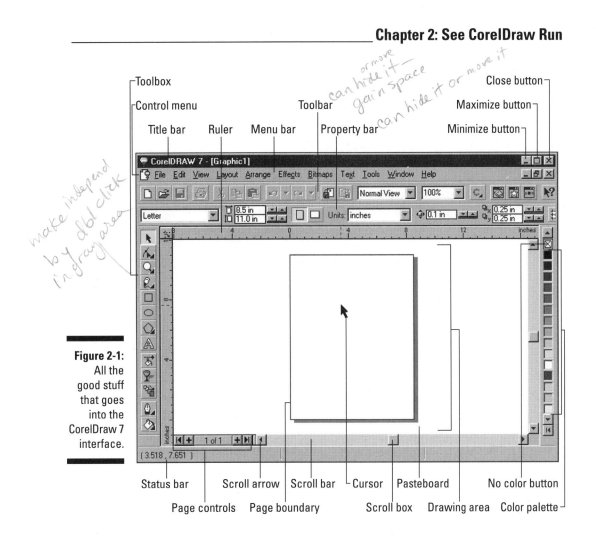

Figure 2-1:
All the
good stuff
that goes
into the
CorelDraw 7
interface.

Handwritten annotations on figure:
- Toolbox — *make independ. by dbl click in gray area*
- can hide it or move it — *gain space*
- can hide it or move it

Figure labels (top): Toolbox, Control menu, Title bar, Ruler, Menu bar, Toolbar, Property bar, Minimize button, Maximize button, Close button

Figure labels (bottom): Status bar, Page controls, Scroll arrow, Page boundary, Scroll bar, Cursor, Scroll box, Pasteboard, Drawing area, No color button, Color palette

REMEMBER

If you set your monitor's screen display to 640 x 480 pixels, some buttons on the right edge of the toolbar and Property Bar appear cut off, as in Figure 2-1. Don't worry about it; you can still access all the program's commands; you just can't do so using the toolbar and Property Bar buttons. The CorelDraw interface appears in its entirety only if you use a screen display setting of 800 x 600 pixels or higher.

To change the screen display, right-click on the Windows 95 Desktop, click on the Properties command, and then click on the Settings tab of the Display Properties dialog box that appears. Drag the Desktop Area slider to the right to raise the resolution of your monitor. But remember that the higher the monitor resolution, the greater the strain on your computer's resources. Also, on-screen things appear smaller than when you use the 640 x 480 pixels setting.

Just for the record, all the screen shots you see in this book were created using the 640 x 480 pixels setting to make the important components of the interface easier to see. Most folks who work with CorelDraw on a regular basis use a higher setting, but if I were to shoot the figures at a higher resolution, the various buttons, bells, and whistles in the interface would be too tiny to be of much help to you.

See the "Property Bar" section later in this chapter for instructions on how to move, reorganize, and resize your Property Bar and toolbar so that all the buttons are visible even at the lowest screen display setting.

If you're familiar with previous versions of CorelDraw, the Version 7 interface may come as something of a shocker. Corel is always monkeying around with the buttons and menus, and Version 7 is no exception. But though the new interface may look different, it's remarkably similar to its predecessors. Just take a few deep breaths and walk this way.

Title bar

The title bar tells you the title of the program — CorelDraw 7 — followed by the name of the document you're working on. Until you assign a specific name to your document, CorelDraw gives it the name Graphic 1.

On the left side of the title bar is the Control menu. On the right side of the title bar is the Minimize button, which has a little bar at the bottom of it. To the right of the Minimize button is either the Maximize button (a box with a bar at its top) or the Restore button (two little boxes). And to the right of that button is a Close button with an X in it. These items are common to all Windows 95 programs, but the following list tells you how they work just in case you're new to all this.

✔ When you first start CorelDraw 7, the interface appears inside a window that hovers in front of the Windows 95 Desktop and any other programs you may be using. How distracting! To cover up all that background stuff, click on the Maximize button. Now the interface fills the screen in floor-to-ceiling cinematic splendor.

✔ To restore the CorelDraw interface to its cramped quarters in a floating window, click on the Restore button, the button displaying two little boxes. The background stuff becomes accessible again.

✔ You can move the floating CorelDraw window around by dragging the title bar — that is, pressing and holding the left mouse button on the title bar while moving the mouse.

✔ To change the size of the floating window, position your cursor over one of the window's four corners or one of its four sides. Your cursor changes to a line with arrowheads at either end. Drag the corner or side as desired.

✔ If you want to get CorelDraw out of your face for a moment, click on the Minimize button to hide the CorelDraw window entirely. A CorelDraw button appears in the Windows 95 taskbar at the bottom of the screen to show you that CorelDraw is still running but is hiding. Click on the button to bring the interface back into view.

✔ To quit CorelDraw 7, click on the Close button. More on this topic in the "Put Your Drawing to Bed" section of Chapter 3.

✔ All the aforementioned options are available as commands from the Control menu, but you'd have to be a nut to use them when the title bar and buttons are so much more convenient.

Menu bar

A single menu bar appears just below the title bar. The menu bar is another one of those traits CorelDraw shares with all other Windows 95 programs. Each word in the menu bar — File, Edit, View, Quagmire — represents a menu. A menu contains a list of commands that you can use to manipulate the various lines and shapes you've drawn, change the way text looks, and initiate other mind-bogglingly sophisticated procedures.

On either side of the menu bar are the familiar Control menu and buttons that you find on the title bar and are discussed in the preceding section. They work the same way as the title bar Control menu and buttons, with one exception. Instead of controlling the entire program interface, these controls affect a single open drawing only. If you click on the Minimize button, for example, the drawing shrinks to a little title bar in the lower-left corner of the CorelDraw window. To see the drawing again, click on the Maximize button in the little title bar or double-click anywhere on the little title bar.

Menus are a pretty big topic, so I talk more about them later in this chapter.

Toolbar

The toolbar is a bunch of buttons that you can click on to access certain commands or functions, such as New, Open, Print, and so on. If you want to find out what one of these buttons does, just pause your cursor over it. A little label appears, saying something helpful, such as "Copy."

Quite frankly, I hate the toolbar. It's a stupid Microsoft idea that serves no real purpose and just clutters up the interface. Why do I harbor such hostile feelings? I'll tell you why:

✔ You can't do stuff with the toolbar that you can't do with the menu bar. Instead of clicking on the Open button, for example, you can choose File➪Open. Better yet, you can press the keyboard shortcut, Ctrl+O.

> ✔ The little button icons are so dinky that you can hardly tell one from another, and when you can, you can't tell what they do. Call me an anarchist, but I reckon that such buttons make the program harder to use, not easier.
>
> ✔ The toolbar reduces the size of the drawing area, which is really a problem when you're working on a 13- or 15-inch monitor.
>
> ✔ Corel implemented the toolbar out of peer pressure. All the other Windows programs were doing it, so Corel hopped on board. Just imagine what would happen if all the other Windows programs jumped off a cliff.

The only redeeming quality of the toolbar, in my opinion, is that you can change the zoom magnification and view mode using toolbar pop-up menus, as explained in Chapter 3. But I don't think these options warrant full-time display of the toolbar, which is why the toolbar doesn't appear in any figures after Chapter 3.

If you share my feelings about the toolbar and want to get rid of it, right-click on the toolbar between a couple of icons. A pop-up menu appears. Click on the Standard option to hide the toolbar.

Alternatively, you can choose the View⇨ToolBars command. Inside the Toolbars dialog box, click on the Standard option to turn it off and then press Enter. Either way, the toolbar vanishes and frees up valuable screen space. If you want to bring the toolbar back, choose the View⇨ToolBars command again.

Property Bar

Beneath the toolbar (or beneath the menu bar, if you followed my advice and hid the toolbar as I just suggested) lies the Property Bar, a new device added to Version 7. The Property Bar holds controls that you can use to quickly make all kinds of adjustments to your drawing, from changing the page size to rotating an object.

The controls on the Property Bar change depending upon which tool you're using. For example, when you use the text tool, the Property Bar offers controls that let you select a font and type style.

In many cases, changes you make by using the Property Bar controls are automatically applied. For example, if you click on the little up- or down-pointing arrows next to an option box, drag a slider bar, or click on an icon, CorelDraw immediately alters your selected object in response. But if you enter a new option box value from the keyboard — that is, if you click inside the option box and then type in a new value — you must press Enter to apply the value.

Like the toolbar, the Property Bar duplicates commands and options you can also access by choosing commands from the menu bar. So if you're working on a tiny screen and want to conserve space, you may want to turn off the Property Bar. To do so, right-click on an empty spot on the Property Bar to display a pop-up menu. Then click on the Property Bar item. To bring the Property Bar back into view, choose the View⇨Property Bar command.

You can move the Property Bar and toolbar to different on-screen locations if you want. Just press and hold the left mouse button on a blank spot on the bar in question and then drag the bar to its new home. Or double-click on a blank spot. Either way, the bar becomes a miniature floating window, complete with a title bar and Close button. You can resize and reshape the bar — a good fix for the screen display problem discussed at the very beginning of the "Interface in Your Face" section. To resize or reshape a floating bar, place your cursor on a corner until you see a two-headed arrow. ↔ Then drag the edge of the bar. To move the bar, drag its title bar. If you want to return the bar to its default position — anchored across the top of the window — double-click on the title bar.

You can also easily rearrange or remove buttons from the Property Bar or toolbar. Just hold down the Alt key while you drag the button. You can even drag toolbar buttons onto the Property Bar and vice versa. If you drag a button off the toolbar or Property Bar, the remaining buttons scoot over to fill the empty space.

If you prefer using the 640 x 480 monitor resolution, you can remove buttons you don't use very often to make room for buttons previously hidden from view. To return to the default toolbar or Property Bar layout, choose View⇨ToolBars. Select the check box for the bar you want to change and click on the Reset button.

Tools

The CorelDraw 7 toolbox — that strip of tools running down the left side of the drawing window — offers an abundance of tools for your drawing pleasure. To select a tool, click on its icon. Then use the tool by clicking or dragging inside the drawing area. To find out more about tools and even give one or two a test run, skip to the "How to Deal with Complete Tools" section. Or better yet, just keep reading. You'll get there soon enough.

Drawing area

Smack dab in the middle of the drawing area is the page boundary, which represents the physical size of the printed page. If you position a shape inside the page boundary, it prints. If you position a shape outside the page boundary, it doesn't print.

The area outside the page boundary is called the *pasteboard*. It's the surface on which the page sits. Think of the pasteboard as a kind of drawing repository, because you can temporarily store shapes there while you try to figure out what to do with them.

Rulers

By default, CorelDraw displays horizontal and vertical rulers along the top and left edge of the drawing area. The rulers can be helpful when you need to position objects precisely. For more about rulers, including how to turn them on and off, see Chapter 6.

Scroll stuff

The scroll bars let you navigate around and display hidden portions of your drawing inside the drawing area. CorelDraw offers two scroll bars: one vertical bar along the right side of the drawing area and one horizontal bar along the bottom. If you click on a scroll arrow, you nudge your view of the drawing slightly in that direction. For example, if you click on the right-pointing scroll arrow, an item that was hidden on the right side of the drawing slides into view. Click in the gray area of a scroll bar to scroll the window more dramatically. Drag a scroll box to manually specify the distance scrolled.

But for an even easier way to view different portions of your drawing, check out the hand tool, discussed along with other screen navigation options in Chapter 3.

Page controls

To the left of the horizontal scroll bar is a clump of page controls, which let you advance from one page to another inside a multipage drawing. I explain the nuances of these controls in Chapter 12. In the meantime, just ignore them.

Color stuff

You can change the colors of the outlines and interiors of shapes in the drawing area using the color controls on the right side of the CorelDraw interface. Click with the left mouse button on a color in the color palette to change the color assigned to the interior of a selected shape, known as the fill color. Click with the right mouse button to change the color of a shape's outline. Use the No Color button to make the fill or outline transparent.

This topic is another biggie. I cover it in my usual rough-and-tumble style throughout the rolling sagebrush and hilly terrain of Chapter 7.

You can move the color palette to a different on-screen location and display additional color swatches by using the techniques described in the section "Make the color palette your own" in Chapter 7.

Status bar

The status bar keeps you apprised of what's going on. For example, any time your cursor is in the drawing area — the place where you create your drawing, naturally — the status line tells you the exact coordinate location of your cursor. Cool, huh? The status bar also tells you a load of information about selected shapes or anything else you may want to create.

For more information about this splendid feature, check out "The status bar tells all" section of Chapter 6.

The Mouse Is Your Willing Slave (And Other Children's Stories)

So far, I've casually mentioned several ways to use your mouse. Well, it's high time I explained what I'm talking about.

Very likely, you've already noticed that when you move the mouse, the cursor moves on-screen — way to use those deductive reasoning skills. But that's not all the mouse does. In fact, the mouse is your primary means of communicating with CorelDraw. Oh sure, the keyboard is great for entering text and performing the occasional shortcut, but the mouse is the primo drawing and editing tool. In other words, you need to become familiar with the thing.

The typical mouse features two buttons on top, which register clicks, and a trackball underneath, which registers movement. If your mouse offers three buttons, the center button doesn't work in CorelDraw.

Here's a quick look at some common mouse terminology (not how mice talk, mind you, but how we talk about them, sometimes behind their furry little backs):

- To *move* your mouse is to move it without pressing any button.
- To *click* is to press the left button and immediately release it without moving the mouse. For example, you click on a tool icon to select a tool.

✔ To *right-click* is to press and release the right mouse button. In the old days, you rarely right-clicked — just to apply color to an outline and that sort of thing. But under Windows 95 and CorelDraw 7, the right mouse button takes on new meaning. In fact, I recommend that you take a moment and right-click on everything you can see. Every time you right-click, a pop-up menu appears, offering a list of specialized options. When in doubt, right-clicking may very well solve your problem.

✔ Some mice let you switch the mouse buttons so that the right button serves the purpose of the left mouse button and vice versa. In this book, I assume that you haven't switched your mouse buttons. If you have, remember that whenever I tell you to click the left mouse button, you need to click the right mouse button instead. And if I tell you to right-click, you need to left-click.

✔ To *double-click* is to press and release the left button twice in rapid succession without moving the mouse. Some programs even accept triple- and quadruple-clicks. CorelDraw does not go to such extremes.

✔ To *press and hold* is to press the button and hold it down for a moment. I refer to this operation very rarely — an example is when some item takes a moment or two to display.

✔ To *drag* is to press the left button and hold it down as you move the mouse. You then release the button to complete the operation. In CorelDraw, for example, you drag with the freehand tool (known in many camps, including this one, as the pencil tool) to draw a free-form line.

You can also use the keyboard and mouse in tandem. For example, you can draw a perfect square by pressing the Ctrl key while dragging with the rectangle tool. You can press Shift and click on shapes with the arrow tool to select multiple shapes. Such actions are so common that you often see key and mouse combinations joined into compound verbs, such as Ctrl+dragging or Shift+clicking. Don't you love the way computer marketing and journalism abuses the language? i THinX IT/z Grait.

How to Deal with Complete Tools

You can liken the CorelDraw tools to the pencils, compasses, and French curves that technical artists used back in the bad old days. The difference is that in CorelDraw, a tool never wears out, stains, runs dry, gets lost, or gets stepped on. The tools are always ready to use on a moment's notice.

A quick experiment

To familiarize yourself with the basic purpose of tools as a group, try this brief exercise:

1. Click on the freehand tool icon.

The freehand tool is the fourth one from the top of the toolbox. The freehand tool icon looks like a pencil drawing a wiggly line. In fact, I'm going to call this tool the pencil tool from now on because if I call it the freehand tool, you'll never remember which icon you need to click to get to the tool. The pencil tool works like a pencil, its icon is a picture of a pencil, and it ought to be called a pencil — so in this book, it shall.

Anyway (and thank you for allowing me to spew forth from my tiny soapbox), after you click on the tool in the toolbox, the tool is ready to use.

2. Express yourself.

I don't want to give away too much stuff about the pencil tool — I'd spoil the many surprises awaiting you in Chapter 5 — but you drag with the tool to create free-form lines. So draw something. Figure 2-2 shows a line I drew, if that's any help.

3. Roam freely. Recognize no boundaries.

Even though I stayed inside the page boundaries in Figure 2-2, you don't have to. You can draw anywhere you want inside the drawing area, either in the page boundary or on the pasteboard. Just remember, if the object you draw is outside the page, it won't print.

4. Keep on drawing.

Don't stop. After you finish drawing one line, start another one. Draw something really complicated or something really messy. Drawing with a mouse can be a real chore if you're not experienced with it. So I suggest that you spend some quality time moving your mouse around. I want you two to get acquainted.

5. Okay, that's enough already.

I mean, don't get obsessed with it or anything.

6. Grab the arrow tool.

Click on the arrow tool — at the top of the toolbox — to select it. (Corel calls this tool the pick tool. But once again, I think that this name is confusing, and therefore I refuse to fall in line. If the tool looks like an arrow, I say, call it an arrow. Besides, I don't like to talk about "picking" in mixed company.) The arrow tool lets you manipulate the stuff you draw.

Pencil tool

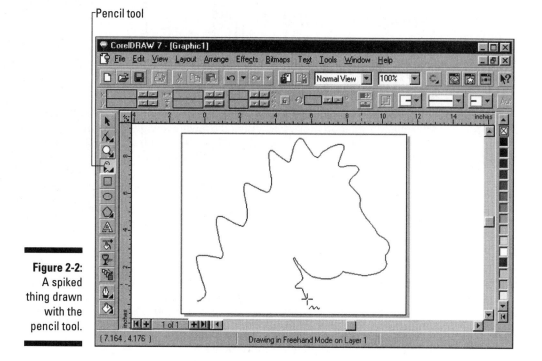

Figure 2-2:
A spiked
thing drawn
with the
pencil tool.

7. Select one of the lines.

Click on some line that you added to the drawing area. Make sure to align the tip of the arrow with the line before you click. The tip of the arrow is the hot point. I selected my wacky animal's wacky eye, as shown in wacky Figure 2-3.

8. This is the end of the line, folks.

See those enormous squares that surround the line you just clicked on? They show that the line is selected. Try pressing Delete. Oops, the line's gone. You just killed it. Way to go.

See, that was pretty easy, huh? With some time, effort, patience, and a few other rare commodities, you'll have the whole drawing-with-a-mouse thing down cold.

How to find buried tools

If you click on the bottom two icons in the toolbox — the icons for the outline and fill tools — CorelDraw displays a *flyout menu,* which is simply a row of icons for options related to the tool. Click on an icon inside the menu to select the option you want to use. For example, the options on the outline tool flyout menu, shown in Figure 2-4, affect the color and thickness of the outline around a selected shape.

Arrow tool

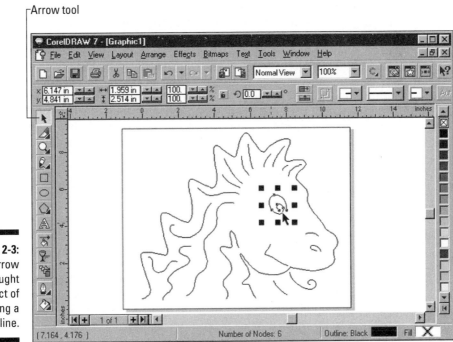

Figure 2-3:
The arrow
tool caught
in the act of
selecting a
line.

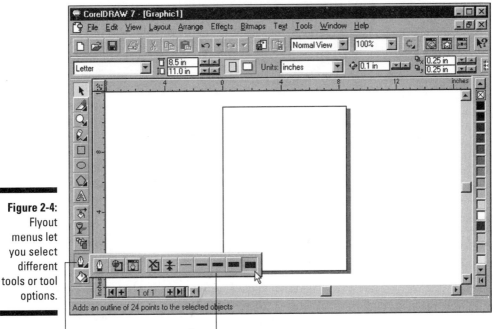

Figure 2-4:
Flyout
menus let
you select
different
tools or tool
options.

Outline tool   Flyout menu

Four other tools — the ones that have little triangles in their lower-right corners — also offer flyout menus. But rather than simply clicking to display the flyout menus for these tools, you have to press and hold on the tool icon. Then click on an icon in the flyout menu to make that tool the active tool in the toolbox.

For example, the polygon tool is one of the tools that offers a flyout menu. Press and hold on the tool to display a flyout menu filled with three icons — a polygon, spiral, and graph paper. If you click on the spiral or graph paper icon, it becomes the new occupant of the polygon tool slot.

More tool tricks

Normally, the toolbox adheres to the left side of the CorelDraw interface as if it were stuck there with denture adhesive. But you can easily move the toolbox: Simply drag it by its left or right edge, as illustrated in Figure 2-5. (Or drag any empty area around the tool icons.) After you release the mouse button, you get a new, independent toolbox complete with a title bar. You can drag the title bar to move the toolbox around on-screen.

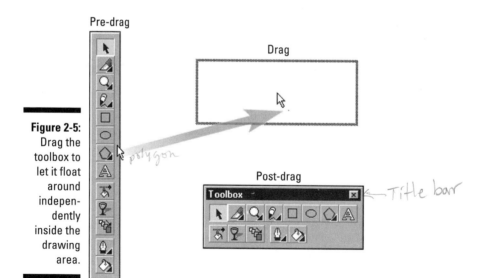

Figure 2-5: Drag the toolbox to let it float around independently inside the drawing area.

Just for laughs, here are some things you can do with the toolbox:

✔ Another way to make the toolbox float independently is to double-click in the gray area around the tools.

✔ You can resize the toolbox by dragging any side or corner.

✔ To restore the tools to their original moorings, double-click on the toolbox title bar or in the empty area around the buttons.

✔ If you want to make the tool icons larger or smaller, right-click on the gray area around the tools and select the Toolbars option. (Alternatively, you can choose View⇨ToolBars.) The Toolbars dialog box appears, as shown in Figure 2-6, offering a Button slider bar that affects the size of icons in the toolbox and toolbar. (If you don't see the slider bar in your dialog box, click on the Options button.) Drag the little tab on the slider bar to change the icon size.

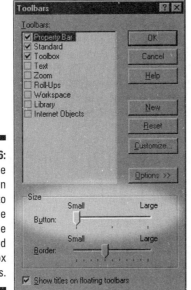

Figure 2-6: Drag the Button slider tab to change the size of the toolbar and toolbox icons.

Les Menus sans Soup du Jour

Instead of listing hors d'oeuvres and other tasty morsels, CorelDraw menus enable you to do stuff, such as open a drawing, abuse the drawing so that it's no longer recognizable, and save it to disk under the name Mud.

To choose a command from a menu, click on the menu name and then click on the command name. For example, if I ask you to choose File⇨Open, click on the File menu name to display the File menu and then click on the Open command.

Les equivalents du keyboard

In the case of File⇨Open (and many other commands), there's no reason to go to all the effort of using menus. You can simply press Ctrl+O — that is, press and hold the Ctrl key, press the O key, and then release both keys. This technique is called using a *keyboard equivalent*.

Most keyboard equivalents are listed along the right side of a menu. Some keyboard equivalents select tools and perform other functions instead of accessing menu commands. Either way, I keep you apprised of the keyboard equivalents throughout this book. If you take the time to memorize a few shortcuts here and there, you can save yourself a heck of a lot of time and effort.

Alt, ma chère amie, oui?

You can also use the Alt key in combination with other keys to access menu commands. The following steps (with French translations) demonstrate one scenario for exploiting Alt:

1. **Press the Alt key plus the underlined letter in a menu name to display the menu.**

   For example, press Alt+F to display the File menu.

2. **Use the arrow keys to navigate the menus.**

   Press the down- and up-arrow keys to highlight commands in a menu. Use the left- and right-arrow keys to display neighboring menus.

3. **If the command has a submenu, press the right-arrow key to display that menu.**

   A submenu is simply an additional list of commands designed to further refine your choice of operations. Press the left-arrow key to hide the menu.

4. **Press Enter to choose the highlighted command.**

5. **To abandon the whole menu bit, press Alt again.**

   Or press the Esc (Escape) key. Each time you press Esc, CorelDraw hides a level of menus.

Alternatively, after pressing Alt and the key for the underlined letter in the menu name, you can press the key for the underlined letter in the command name. For example, to choose File⇨Open, press Alt, followed by F and then O. (Those underlined letters are known as *hotkeys,* by the way.)

The Incessant Chatter of Dialog Boxes

Some menu commands react immediately. Others require you to fill out a few forms before they can be processed. In fact, any command that's followed by an ellipsis (three dots, like so: ...) displays either a dialog box or a roll-up. A dialog box asks you to answer some questions before CorelDraw implements the command; a roll-up stays on-screen so that you can perform an operation repeatedly without having to choose the command over and over again.

Figure 2-7 shows a sample dialog box.

The dialog box options work as follows:

✔ Many dialog boxes contain multiple panels of options. To get to a different panel, click on one of the tabs at the top of the dialog box.

✔ An option in which you can enter numbers or text is called an option box. (Propeller heads also like to call these options *fields,* strictly because it sounds more technical.) Double-click on an option box to highlight its contents and then replace the contents by entering new stuff with the keyboard. Or, if you prefer, use the arrow icons to the right of an option box or press the arrow keys on the keyboard to incrementally raise or lower the value in the option box — all without hydraulics, mind you.

✔ To conserve space, some multiple-choice options appear as pop-up menus (also known in some circles as drop-down lists). Click on the down-pointing arrow to display a menu of options. Then click on the desired option in the menu to select it, just as if you were choosing a command from a standard menu. (Note that the menus that appear when you right-click on a screen element are also referred to as pop-up menus.)

✔ You can select only one circular radio button from any gang of radio buttons. To select a radio button, click on the button or on the option name that follows it. The selected radio button gets a black dot; all deselected radio buttons are hollow.

✔ You can select as many check boxes as you want. Really, go nuts. To select a check box, click on the box or on the option name that follows it. A check mark in the box shows that the option is turned on. Clicking on a selected check box turns off the option.

✔ Not to be confused with the radio button, the normal, everyday variety of button allows you to close the current dialog box or display others. For example, click on the Cancel button to close the dialog box and cancel the current command. Click on the OK button to close the dialog box and execute the command according to the current settings. If a button name includes an ellipsis, clicking on it brings up another dialog box.

Check box   Option box

Tab   Title bar

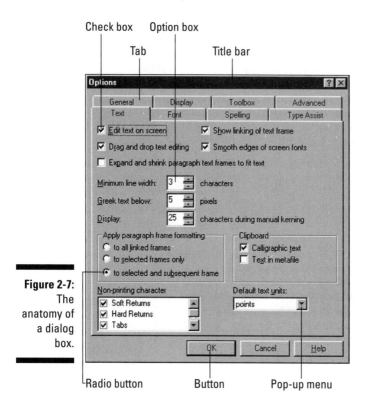

Figure 2-7:
The
anatomy of
a dialog
box.

Radio button   Button   Pop-up menu

As you can with menus, you can select options and perform other feats of magic inside dialog boxes from the keyboard. To advance from one option to the next, press the Tab key. To back up, press Shift+Tab. To select any option, press Alt along with the hotkey (the underlined letter). Or, if no option box is highlighted, just press the hotkey by itself. Press Enter to activate the button that's surrounded by a heavy outline, such as OK. Press Esc or Alt+F4 to choose the Cancel button.

Roll-Ups, Now in Dozens of Fruity Flavors

Roll-ups, like the one shown in Figure 2-8, are basically dialog boxes that can remain on-screen while you work with other functions in CorelDraw. They float above the surface of the drawing area, just like the toolbox. CorelDraw 7 offers more than two dozen roll-ups that you can display on-screen all at once, just a few at a time, or whatever. (The more roll-ups you display, the more you eat up your computer's memory, however.) Each roll-up provides so many individual options that there's no point in running through them all here. Suffice it to say that roll-ups let you do some pretty amazing stuff.

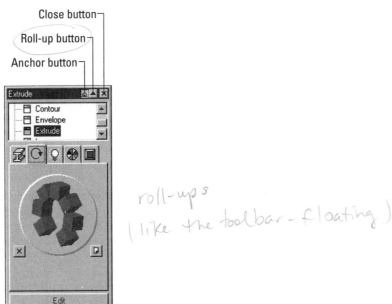

Close button
Roll-up button
Anchor button

roll-ups
(like the toolbar - floating)

Figure 2-8:
Roll-ups
float above
the drawing
area
like flat,
rectangular,
non-
rainbearing
clouds.

The roll-up in Figure 2-8, for example, lets you add depth to an otherwise two-dimensional shape. You can stretch the shape off the page, much like you'd . . . well, frankly, no real-life equivalent exists. The process is way cool, which is why I describe it in Chapter 9.

To display a roll-up, choose it from the View⇨Roll-Ups submenu or press its keyboard shortcut, conveniently located to the right of the roll-up's name. If you have more than one roll-up displayed on-screen, switch to the one you want to use by clicking on its roll-up button. The roll-up magically pops to the front of any other roll-ups that may be obscuring it from view.

Roll 'em up and tack 'em down

Roll-ups are called roll-ups because you can roll them up — strange but true. Click on the up-pointing arrow in the upper-right corner of the roll-up window to hide everything but the title bar. This way, you can have several roll-ups on-screen at once without cluttering up the interface. Click on a roll-up's arrow again — it's a down-pointing arrow now — to restore the full window.

By default, a roll-up is anchored so that it remains on-screen regardless of other activities you perform. However, if you want the roll-up to disappear after it's used once, click on the thumbtack icon just to the left of the arrow icon in the title bar. The thumbtack appears to raise up, showing that the roll-up is no longer anchored. The next time you apply an option or command from the roll-up, the roll-up disappears. If you're having problems with screen clutter, this approach is another way to eliminate it.

But if you want my opinion, you should leave the thumbtack down. Having the roll-up disappear every time you use it can be terribly disconcerting and is rarely useful.

Breakaway roll-ups

Because CorelDraw 7 offers so many roll-ups, some roll-ups are combined into related groups. For example, the Blend, Contour, Envelope, Extrude, and Lens roll-ups are all included in a single roll-up, as shown in Figure 2-9. Here are a few tidbits to keep in mind about working with these multiple roll-up roll-ups:

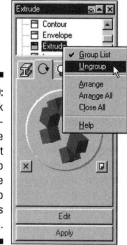

Figure 2-9:
Right-click
on a roll-
up's name
and select
Ungroup to
separate
the roll-up
from its
group.

✔ You can switch to a different roll-up in the group by clicking on its name in the scrolling list at the top of the roll-up window.

✔ To separate an item in the group into an independent roll-up, right-click on the item's name in the scrolling list. Then select Ungroup, as in Figure 2-9. Give me your roll-ups, yearning to be free.

✔ You can also combine roll-ups into your own groups, whether the roll-ups are related or not. Alt+drag the title bar of one roll-up and drop it onto another roll-up. Or, to move a roll-up from one group to another, drag the roll-up's name from the scrolling list onto the other roll-up.

Chapter 3

Ladies and Gentlemen, Insert Your Pocket Protectors!

● ●

In This Chapter

▶ Creating a new document

▶ Importing and opening clip art

▶ Magnifying your drawing for a closer look

▶ Using other zooming options

▶ Exploring the past and present virtues of scrolling

▶ Modifying the screen display

▶ Looking at a rat in startling ways

▶ Saving a drawing to disk

▶ Updating files and making backups

▶ Shutting down CorelDraw

● ●

*W*ith CorelDraw, you're the master of your creation. You can add whatever flair or flourish you deem appropriate, using whatever tool strikes your fancy. You have total artistic freedom (as much as your client or boss allows, that is). But you can't experience the heady joys that come with this absolute power until you master three basic tasks: creation, navigation, and storage. Creation is giving birth to the drawing; navigation is tooling around the on-screen landscape, moving from one part of your drawing to the next; and storage is the small but essential ceremony that ensures that all your hard work doesn't go in the tank when you quit the program. This chapter gets you up to speed on all three subjects, plus a few others for good measure.

Spank the Baby

You probably don't remember this, but when the doctor whisked you out of your mom, he or she smacked your rump to make you take in that first lungful of air and bellow like a stricken — well . . . baby. Now here you are, several thousand days later, wondering why I'm bringing up such a painful subject. The truth is, you have to perform a similar maneuver before you can begin drawing in CorelDraw.

Here's your chance to see whether you've managed to absorb anything about computers so far. Which of the following actions do you suspect results in a new document in CorelDraw?

> A. Gently but firmly slap the disk drive. There's no time like the present to teach your computer who's boss.

> B. Taunt the computer mercilessly until it cries.

> C. Choose File⇨New or File⇨Open.

Four out of five computer scientists agree that B is the best way to humble your computer into producing a new document. But recently, dissenting scientists have come out in support of answer C. In the interest of fair and unbiased journalism, I test this strange theory in the following pages.

How do I start a new document?

If you turn off the welcome screen as I instruct in the "Interface in Your Face" section of Chapter 2, CorelDraw automatically produces an empty drawing area after you start the program. (If CorelDraw does something else after you start it, choose Tools⇨Options or press Ctrl+J. After the Options dialog box appears, click on the General tab of the dialog box, select Start a New Document from the On CorelDraw Startup pop-up menu in the lower-left corner of the dialog box, and press Enter. From now on, an empty drawing area greets you every time you start CorelDraw.)

The empty drawing area represents a brand new document. This area has no preconceived notions of what a drawing is or what it should be. You can mold it into anything you want.

The problem is, an empty drawing area can be terrifying. Being confronted with a blank page is like looking inside the deepest recesses of your soul and seeing nothing — except that the experience isn't nearly so profound. Thankfully, you have other options available to you, as covered in the next section.

If for some reason — like, you're a masochist or something — you want to start a document from scratch after you've been working in the program for a while, all you need to do is select File⇨New or press Ctrl+N.

The enlightening Chihuahua scenario

Starting a brand new drawing isn't the only route to success in CorelDraw. You can approach your drawing from a different angle by opening or importing an existing drawing that can serve as a starting point for whatever you want to create.

Suppose that you want to draw a Chihuahua. Now there's a puzzle for you. You're stuck in a tiny cubicle on the third floor of an air-conditioned building in an office park — not the sort of place where a yippy little dog is likely to stroll by anytime soon. And even if you had a Chihuahua willing to serve as an artist's model, you wouldn't have a hope of drawing the animal, because the degree of difficulty for creating a realistic Chihuahua from scratch in CorelDraw is somewhere in the neighborhood of 13 on a 10-point scale.

So what's the solution? Well, in the vast CorelDraw library of clip art, you can find a drawing of a small animal that is generally accepted to be the direct ancestor to the Chihuahua. I am referring, of course, to the rat. All you have to do is shorten the tail, snip the claws, enlarge the ears, remove some whiskers, bulge out the eyes, reduce the size of the brain cavity, and add a little balloon above the creature's head that says "Yip yip," and the evolutionary transformation is complete.

But before you can do any editing, you have to open the rat drawing using the File⇨Open command, discussed next. You can find the rat on the third CD-ROM included in your CorelDraw 7 package.

How do I open a piece of clip art?

Corel now ships its clip art in the CDR format, which means that you can use the everyday, ordinary File⇨Open command to open a piece of clip art (despite what the product manual tells you). In Version 6, the clip art came in the CMX format, which required that you use the Import command to place a piece of clip art into your drawing.

The following steps tell you how to open one of the clip art drawings in the CorelDraw package. You can use the same process to open any existing drawing, whether it's stored on a CD, a floppy disk, or your hard drive.

1. **Choose File⇨Open or press Ctrl+O.**

   The Open Drawing dialog box, shown in Figure 3-1, appears.

2. **Select a disk drive from the Look In pop-up menu.**

   Click anywhere on the option box at the top of the dialog box to display a pop-up menu. Then click on the drive in which your file is stored. To find the rat, select your CD-ROM drive, which is probably the D drive.

Up One Level ⌐   List ⌐Details

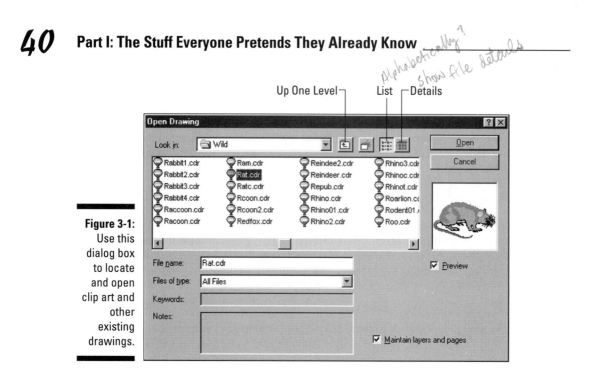

Figure 3-1:
Use this
dialog box
to locate
and open
clip art and
other
existing
drawings.

3. Open the desired folders in the central scrolling list.

Double-click on a folder name to open it. The list then displays all files
and folders inside that folder. Double-click on another folder to open it,
and so on. For example, to open the folder that holds the rat drawing,
first double-click on the Clipart folder, then on the Animals folder, and
finally on the Wild folder.

4. Select the drawing that you want to open.

To open the rat, first click on any filename in the scrolling list. Next,
press R to scroll to the drawings that begin with that letter, including
such hits as Rabbit, Raccoon, and Ram. Then click on the right scroll
arrow a couple of times to advance to the Rat.CDR file. Click on the file
to select it. Assuming that the Preview check box is selected, a preview
of the drawing appears on the right side of the dialog box so that you
can see what the drawing looks like.

5. Click on the Open button or press Enter.

You can also double-click on a filename to open the file. Whichever
method you choose, CorelDraw opens the rat inside a new drawing
area. Black squares called *handles* surround the rat, showing that it is
selected and ready to edit. You can now manipulate the rat at will.

I wish that I could tell you how to change a rat into a Chihuahua in five easy
steps, but I can't. Instead, I devote Chapters 4 through 9 to the topic of
drawing and editing in CorelDraw. I don't specifically address Chihuahua

illustrations, but you can tell that they're constantly in the back of my mind. In the meantime, here are a few additional notes on opening drawings to carry you through your working day:

✔ To close a folder and look at the contents of the folder that contains it, click on the Up One Level button (labeled in Figure 3-1).

✔ To find out more information about a file — such as its size on disk and the last time it was modified — click on the Details button (also labeled in Figure 3-1). You can then change the order in which the files are displayed by clicking on the buttons that appear along the top of the list. For example, to list the files alphabetically, click on the Name button.

✔ To hide that technical stuff and just see the filenames again, click on the List button.

You can also open a file using the new Scrapbook, as discussed in the upcoming section "Opening and importing from the Scrapbook."

Adding a drawing to an existing drawing

The File⇨Open command opens a piece of clip art as a new drawing. But if you want to add a clip art drawing to an existing drawing — say, to place the rat into a pretty field of wildflowers that you created earlier — you need the Import command.

You can add as many pieces of clip art to a drawing as you like. To place the rat or any other existing drawing into an open drawing, just perform the following easy-as-pie steps:

1. Choose File⇨Import or press Ctrl+I.

The Import dialog box, which is nearly identical to the Open Drawing dialog box just discussed, appears.

2. Locate and select the drawing.

Use the method described in the preceding section to hunt down the drawing and then click on it in the scrolling list.

3. Click on Import or press Enter.

Alternatively, you can double-click on the drawing name in the scrolling list. CorelDraw plops the drawing inside the drawing area. Your drawing is surrounded by black boxes called *handles,* which indicate that the drawing is selected and ready to edit.

CorelDraw always imports all the little bits and pieces of stuff that go into a clip art graphic as something called a *group.* If you want to select and edit individual elements in a group, you must use some special techniques, which are covered in the "Gang Behavior" section of Chapter 6.

If CorelDraw can't import a file, the file may be damaged and no longer usable. More likely, though, the file was stored in some file format that CorelDraw doesn't want to accept. Ask around and see whether anyone knows anything about the file, including where it came from. You may need to install an import filter for the file format using the installation instructions provided in the appendix to this book.

Check out the next section for an alternative way to import clip art.

Opening and importing from the Scrapbook

Version 7 provides an alternative method for opening and importing clip art: using the new Scrapbook roll-up, as shown in Figure 3-2. To display the roll-up, choose Tools➪Clipart. Or, if you like doing things the long way, choose View➪Roll-Ups➪Tools➪Scrapbook and click on the second tab in the roll-up (the one with the Corel balloon on it).

Use the Folder pop-up menu and Up One Level button to locate the Clipart folder on the third CorelDraw CD-ROM. Double-click on the Clipart folder to display all the different clip art folders; double-click on a folder to display thumbnail views of the drawings in that folder.

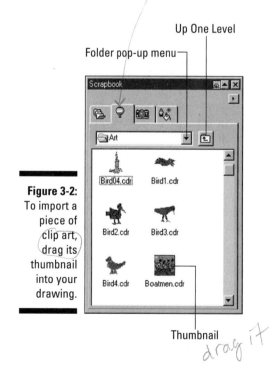

Up One Level

Folder pop-up menu

Figure 3-2:
To import a
piece of
clip art,
drag its
thumbnail
into your
drawing.

Thumbnail

drag it

When you find a piece of clip art you like, double-click on its thumbnail to open the clip art as a new drawing. To import the clip art into an open drawing, drag the thumbnail onto the drawing page. Alternatively, you can right-click on the thumbnail and choose Open or Import from the pop-up menu that appears.

If the file you want to use isn't on the CorelDraw CD, switch to the first tab of the roll-up (the one with the open folders on the tab). After locating the file, use the same methods just discussed to open or import the file. You can open regular drawing files from this tab of the Scrapbook as well as clip art files.

You can also use the Scrapbook to apply special fills and outlines to your shapes (as discussed in Chapter 7) and open photos (as discussed in Chapter 15).

CorelDraw has to generate thumbnails for each folder you open in the Scrapbook, a process that can take a bit of time if you're using a slow computer. For that reason, you may find it quicker to rely on the catalog provided with the CorelDraw 7 package to hunt down an appropriate piece of clip art rather than browsing thumbnails in the Scrapbook.

Tools for Getting Around the Drawing Area

Ah, getting around, a favorite pursuit of the Beach Boys. Of course, we all know that in reality, the Beach Boys were about as likely to get around as a parade of go-carting Shriners. I mean, it's not like you're going to confuse a squad of sandy-haired Neil Bush look-alikes with the Hell's Angels. John Denver and Richie Cunningham could play kazoos on *The MacNeil/Lehrer Report* and come off as more streetwise than the Beach Boys.

Now that I've offended everyone who's ever surfed or enjoyed falsetto harmonies, I will say two things in the Beach Boys' defense. First, "Help Me, Rhonda" and "Good Vibrations" are crankin' tunes. And second, even a bunch of squares like the Beach Boys can get around in CorelDraw. (Nice tie-in, huh?)

Miracles of magnification

When you first open a drawing, you see the full page, as in Figure 3-3. To fit the page entirely inside the drawing area, CorelDraw has to reduce the page so that it appears considerably smaller than it will print. It's as if you're standing far away from an image, taking in the big picture.

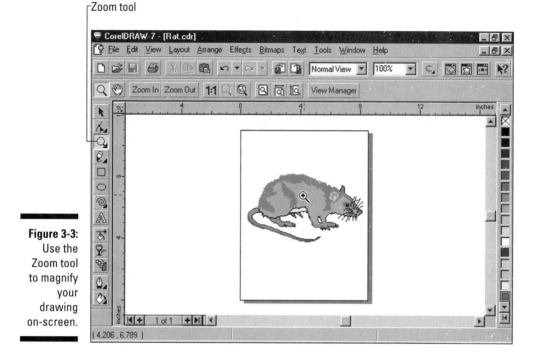

Zoom tool

Figure 3-3:
Use the
Zoom tool
to magnify
your
drawing
on-screen.

Although the big picture is great, it lacks detail. Imagine trying to edit the claws, the eyes, or some other minute feature of the rat from this vantage point. That's why CorelDraw lets you zoom in to magnify the drawing and zoom out to make it smaller.

Version 7 offers a multitude of ways to zoom in and out on a drawing, with the primary tool being the zoom tool, which you use as follows:

1. Click on the zoom tool.

The zoom tool is the one that looks like a magnifying glass. Just click on the tool icon in the toolbox to select the tool. The cursor changes to a little magnifying glass.

2. Click in the drawing area.

CorelDraw magnifies the drawing to twice its previous size. The program centers the magnified view at the point where you click. In Figure 3-4, for example, I clicked on the eyeball to center the magnified view on the eyeball.

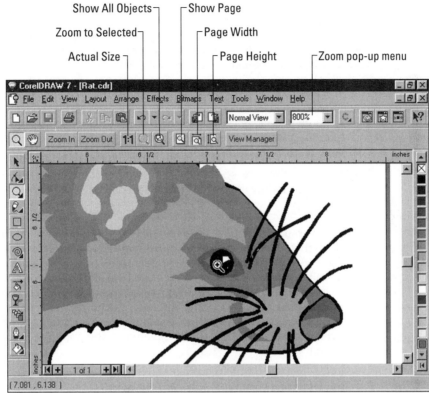

Figure 3-4:
The closer
you inspect
the rat, the
more it
looks like a
Chihuahua.

Alternatively, you can drag with the zoom tool to surround the area that you want to magnify with a dotted outline. CorelDraw fills the drawing area with the area you dragged around. Using this technique, you can zoom in to more than twice the previous level of magnification.

3. Repeat Steps 1 and 2 until your wrist gets tired.

If you selected the zoom tool by clicking on its icon in the toolbox, you can use it as many times as you like. If you selected it by pressing F2, CorelDraw reverts back to the previously selected tool after you finish zooming. You have to press F2 each time that you want to zoom.

To temporarily access the zoom tool when another tool is selected, press F2. The zoom cursor appears, and you can then click once to zoom in on your drawing. After you click, the tool that was previously selected becomes active again.

Zooming doesn't change the size at which your drawing prints. It just affects the size at which you see the drawing on-screen.

CorelDraw also offers several automatic zoom controls that zoom in and out to predefined intervals. Here's the scoop:

- ✔ To zoom out, Shift+click with the zoom tool. CorelDraw reduces the drawing to 50 percent of its former glory.

- ✔ You can also zoom out by pressing F3. The screen zooms at the touch of the key. No clicking, soaking, or whittling is required.

- ✔ To zoom in on a selected portion of your drawing, press Shift+F2. For example, select the rat's nose by clicking on it with the arrow tool. Then press Shift+F2 to get a close-up view of the critter's nostrils.

- ✔ To reduce the view so that every line, shape, and character of text is visible, including objects on the pasteboard, press F4.

- ✔ To return the view so that you can see the entire page, press Shift+F4.

- ✔ As covered in Chapter 2, I prefer to keep the CorelDraw toolbar turned off so that I have more screen space available for my drawing. But as I also mention in Chapter 2, the toolbar does offer a valuable control for zooming. You can select a preset zoom ratio from the Zoom Level pop-up menu, labeled in Figure 3-4. More importantly, you can double-click on the Zoom Level box, enter a zoom value from the keyboard, and then press Enter. This method enables you to zoom to a specific zoom level — say, 73 percent — not available on the pop-up menu or via the zoom tool.

If you want to be able to access the Zoom Level pop-up menu but you don't want to display the toolbar, do this: First, select the zoom tool. Now Alt+drag the pop-up menu off the toolbar and onto the end of the Property Bar. You now can access the menu from the Property Bar whenever the zoom tool is selected.

You'd think that this cornucopia of zooming options would be enough. But evidently CorelDraw didn't, because the program offers still more ways to zoom in and out, as covered in the next three sections.

Zoom up to the Property Bar

If trying to remember all the keyboard shortcuts for zooming makes your brain hurt, you can use the zoom tools on the Property Bar, labeled in Figure 3-4. The tools become available when you select the zoom tool. From left to right, the Property Bar controls work as follows:

- ✔ Clicking on the Zoom In and Zoom Out buttons does the same thing as clicking and Shift+clicking with the zoom tool. Click on Zoom In to magnify your view to twice the previous size. Click on Zoom Out to reduce the view by 50 percent.

✔ Click on the Actual Size button — the one labeled 1:1 — to view your drawing at close to the size it will actually print.

✔ The Zoom to Selected button zooms to the currently selected area in your drawing.

✔ Click on the Show All Objects button to see the entire drawing on-screen.

✔ Click on the Show Page button to view the entire drawing page.

✔ The Page Width button zooms your drawing so that you can see the entire width of the page. The Page Height button zooms your drawing so that the entire length of the drawing is visible.

✔ Don't worry about the View Manager button. The View Manager gives you another way to zoom in and out on your drawing. But because the View Manager eats up more of your already precious screen real estate, you're better off using the other zoom controls.

Your very own zoombox

If you're trying to save screen space and you want to turn off the Property Bar (as explained in Chapter 2), you can still access the zoom icons discussed in the preceding section. Right-click in the gray area surrounding the toolbox to display a pop-up menu and select the Zoom option. The result is a free-floating palette of zoom tools, as shown in Figure 3-5.

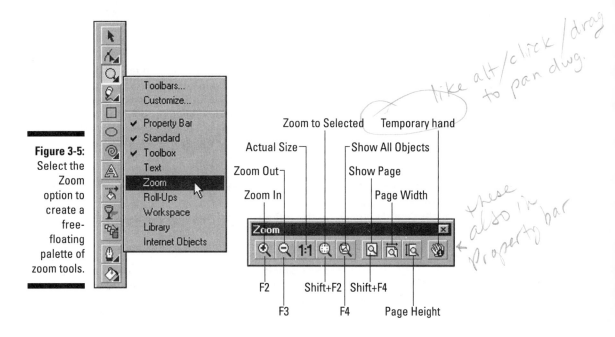

Figure 3-5:
Select the Zoom option to create a free-floating palette of zoom tools.

like alt/click/drag to pan dwg.

Zoom to Selected   Temporary hand

Actual Size ─┐   ┌─ Show All Objects
Zoom Out ─┐   Show Page
Zoom In   Page Width

these also in property bar

Zoom

⊕ ⊖ 1:1 ⊕ ⊕ ⊞ ⊞ ⊞ ✋

F2   Shift+F2 Shift+F4
F3   F4   Page Height

The tools are twins of the tools found on the Property Bar, discussed in the preceding section. (Figure 3-5 provides a handy reference to the tools and their keyboard equivalents.) You also get one additional tool, which Corel calls the pan one-shot tool and ordinary folks are sure to refer to as the temporary hand tool. Clicking on the tool icon temporarily accesses the hand tool, discussed later in this chapter. After you use the tool, the previously selected tool becomes active again.

To fix the Zoom palette in place along the right edge of the window, double-click on some gray area inside the palette. Double-click again to make the palette float independently. Click on the Close button to put the palette away.

The secret magnification menu

If you don't like any of the kazillion zoom options already discussed, select the zoom tool and right-click anywhere in the drawing area. Up pops a menu that offers you a series of zoom options. You can even select from a submenu of specific zoom ratios from 10 to 400 percent.

Pull Your Image into View

As you doubtless have already noticed, you can see only bits and pieces of your drawing when it's magnified. The scroll bars and the hand tool allow you to control which bits and pieces are visible.

Corel refers to the hand tool as the pan tool, presumably in reference to the term *panning,* which is a word used in the television and movie business. To pan the camera is to move the camera to capture a different view of the action. However, no cameras are involved in CorelDraw, and I'm guessing that you work in an office, not on a movie or television set. Therefore, I refer to the pan tool as the hand tool because the tool's icon and cursor look like a hand and just about every other program on the planet with a similar navigation tool calls the thing the hand tool.

Anyway, suppose that you can only see the nose of the rat, as shown in Figure 3-6. You want to view the animal's face and neck, an inch or so to the left. To do so, you can do the following:

✔ Drag the scroll box on the horizontal scroll bar to the left. The drawing moves in the opposite direction.

✔ Select the hand tool from the zoom tool flyout or from the Property Bar, as shown in Figure 3-6. Then drag to the right with the hand tool, as in Figure 3-7. After you release the mouse button, the drawing moves to the right.

Hand tool

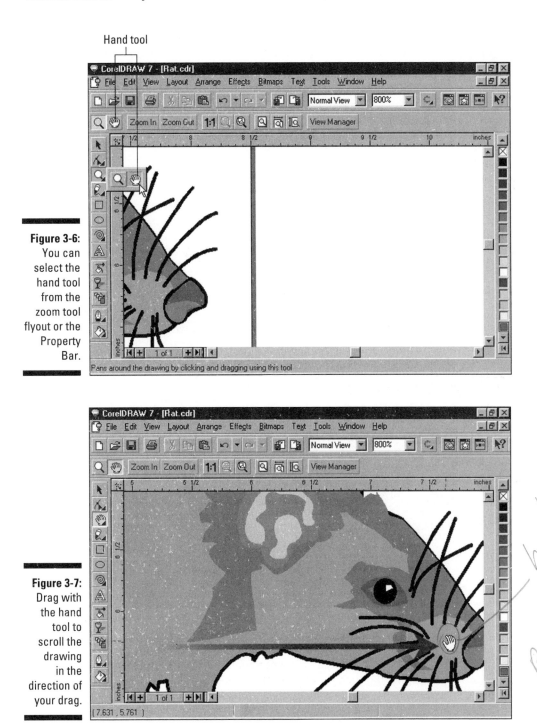

Figure 3-6:
You can
select the
hand tool
from the
zoom tool
flyout or the
Property
Bar.

Figure 3-7:
Drag with
the hand
tool to
scroll the
drawing
in the
direction of
your drag.

✔ You can temporarily select the hand tool from the Zoom palette, shown back in Figure 3-5. After you use the tool once, the previously selected tool becomes active again.

✔ Version 7 also offers a nifty keyboard shortcut for moving around your drawing. Press Alt plus an arrow key to scroll in the direction of the arrow key. Keep pressing Alt and the arrow key until you reach the area you want to view. The neat thing about this trick, called auto-panning, is that you can use it when any tool is selected, not just the hand tool.

If you get lost when scrolling your drawing and can't figure out where your drawing went, just press Shift+F4 to zoom all the way out so that the page fits inside the window. Then zoom and scroll as desired.

The Screen Is What You Make It

Another way to change how CorelDraw shows you a drawing on-screen is to switch display modes. Normally, you see the drawing in full, glorious color, with all fills and outlines intact. This view is called the normal mode. This mode is excellent in that it shows the drawing as it will print. The only problem with this mode is that it can be slow, especially when you're viewing a complex drawing. As a remedy, CorelDraw provides a few other display modes for your viewing pleasure.

Show me a rough draft

One way to speed up screen display is to switch to draft mode, which you can do by choosing View⇨Draft or selecting the Draft View option from the toolbar mode menu. In this mode, CorelDraw displays any complex special effects — such as bitmap fills — as a simple, two-color pattern instead of displaying the actual fill. If your drawing doesn't incorporate any of these effects, you don't see any difference between normal mode and draft mode.

String art revival

Another option for faster screen display is to choose View⇨Wireframe. Or if your toolbar is displayed, select the Wireframe option from the View Mode pop-up menu on the toolbar, labeled in Figure 3-8. In wireframe mode, CorelDraw displays each shape in your drawing as if it were transparent and endowed with only a thin black outline, as shown in Figure 3-8.

View Mode

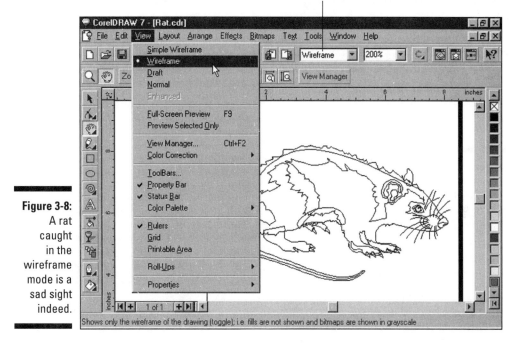

Figure 3-8: A rat caught in the wireframe mode is a sad sight indeed.

Version 7 also offers a simple wireframe mode, which displays even less of your drawing's skeletal system than wireframe mode. (Depending on how complicated your drawing is, you may not see much difference between wireframe and simple wireframe mode.) To switch to simple wireframe mode, choose View➪Simple Wireframe or select the Simple Wireframe option from the toolbar mode menu.

Wireframe and simple wireframe modes speed things up considerably because CorelDraw can display a bunch of black outlines way faster than colors, gradations, arrowheads, and other attributes that you find out about in Chapter 7. But both modes can also make it more difficult to edit the drawing. Using either of the wireframe modes is like trying to imagine how a house will look when still in the framing stage.

You only need to use the wireframe mode if CorelDraw is running exasperatingly slowly. And even then, you need to regularly switch back and forth between wireframe mode and normal mode to keep track of what's going on.

Pressing Shift+F9 switches you from the current view mode to the mode you used last. (A single command that switches you back and forth like this is known as a *toggle*.) So if you switched directly from normal mode to wireframe or simple wireframe, you can press Shift+F9 to return to normal mode. Otherwise, you need to choose View➪Normal.

Die, you gravy-sucking interface

Although the interface is absolutely essential to communicating with CorelDraw, it can occasionally prove distracting. To temporarily hide everything but the drawing itself, as in Figure 3-9, press F9 or choose View⇨Full-Screen Preview. No matter what view mode you were previously using, CorelDraw shows the drawing in full color.

Figure 3-9:
Unencum-
bered
by the
CorelDraw
interface,
the rat
appears
perceptibly
more at
ease
with its
surround-
ings.

I like to call this mode the hands-off preview mode because you can't do anything in it besides look at the drawing. The second you click the right mouse button or press a key on the keyboard, CorelDraw exits the hands-off preview mode and restores the interface. Clicking the left mouse button forces CorelDraw to refresh the screen, but that's the extent of it.

Occasionally, novices get all panicky when the interface disappears, and they assume that the only way to return to CorelDraw is to turn off the computer, pawn it, and buy a new one. I don't want this to happen to you. So at the risk of sounding repetitive, I'll repeat myself: Just press any key on the keyboard, and the interface returns.

Preview bits and pieces

CorelDraw provides one additional method for previewing a drawing. When you're working with a complex drawing, some shapes can get in the way of other shapes. You may be tempted to delete shapes just to get them out of your way. But don't, because CorelDraw offers a better way.

1. **Select the lines, shapes, and text that you want to preview.**

   I don't explain how to select stuff until Chapter 4. But to get you started, you can select a single object by clicking on it with the arrow tool. You select multiple objects by clicking on one and then Shift+clicking on the others.

2. **Choose <u>V</u>iew⇨Preview Selected <u>O</u>nly.**

   After you choose this command, it remains in effect until you choose the command again. Notice that a check mark appears next to the command name to show that the command is active.

3. **Press F9.**

   Only the selected objects appear on-screen.

Figure 3-10 shows the result of selectively previewing a few shapes that make up the rat. The poor animal looks like a gang of field mice stripped it down to its underwear.

Figure 3-10: Transforming a rat into a mole through selective previewing.

Save or Die Trying!

Saving your drawing is like locking your car. After you get in the habit of doing it, you're protected. Until then, life can be traumatic. A stereo stolen here, a crucial drawing lost there. During my formative desktop publishing years, I managed to lose so many drawings that I finally taped the motto "Save or die trying" to the wall above my computer. If you're new to computers, I suggest that you do something similar. You look up, you save your drawing, and you live happily ever after.

After all, there's nothing like spending an hour or so on a complex drawing that you've neglected to save only to be greeted by a system error, power outage, or some other electronic tragedy. Losing a drawing makes you want to beat the old fists on the top of the monitor, strangle the computer with its own power cord, or engage in other unseemly acts of computer terrorism. To avoid the trauma, save your document to disk early and update it often.

Saving for the very first time

The very first time you save a new drawing, you have to name it and specify its location on disk. Here's how:

1. Choose File⇨Save or press Ctrl+S.

The Save Drawing dialog box appears, as shown in Figure 3-11.

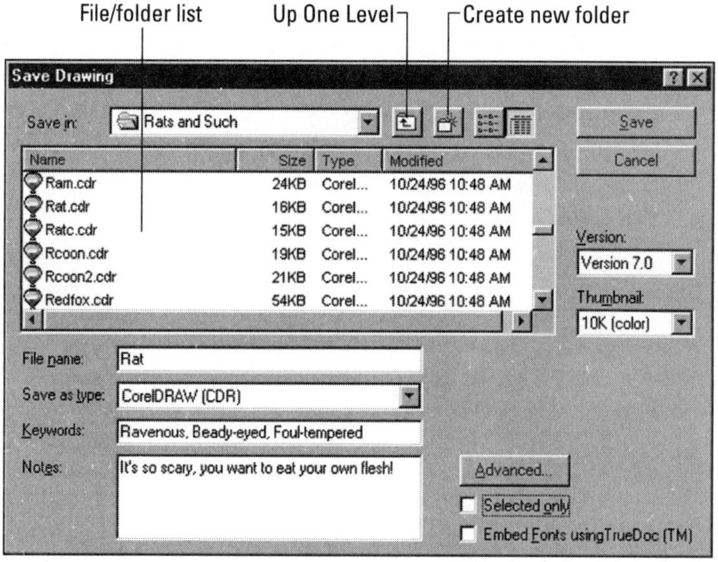

File/folder list   Up One Level   Create new folder

Save Drawing					? X
Save in:	Rats and Such				Save
Name		Size	Type	Modified	Cancel
Ram.cdr		24KB	Corel...	10/24/96 10:48 AM	
Rat.cdr		16KB	Corel...	10/24/96 10:48 AM	Version:
Ratc.cdr		15KB	Corel...	10/24/96 10:48 AM	Version 7.0
Rcoon.cdr		19KB	Corel...	10/24/96 10:48 AM	
Rcoon2.cdr		21KB	Corel...	10/24/96 10:48 AM	Thumbnail:
Redfox.cdr		54KB	Corel...	10/24/96 10:48 AM	10K (color)

File name:	Rat
Save as type:	CorelDRAW (CDR)
Keywords:	Ravenous, Beady-eyed, Foul-tempered
Notes:	It's so scary, you want to eat your own flesh!

Advanced...

☐ Selected only
☐ Embed Fonts usingTrueDoc (TM)

Figure 3-11:
Use this dialog box to name your drawing and specify its location on disk.

2. Enter a name into the File Name option box.

Gone are the days when filenames could only be eight characters long. Now you can go as high as you like. Heck, you can name the file Scurvy, Flea-Bitten, No-Good Chihuahua Wannabe if you like. As long as the name is shorter than 256 characters, you're okay.

It's also worth noting that you don't have to enter .CDR (known as the *file extension*) at the end of the filename. CorelDraw does that for you without you ever knowing. Isn't progress wonderful? (If you want to save the file in some other format than the CDR format, select the format from the Save As Type pop-up menu. The proper file extension is automatically added for you in that case, too.)

3. **Select a disk drive from the Save In pop-up menu.**

Use the pop-up menu to select the drive where you want to store your drawing. Incidentally, you can't save a drawing to CD-ROM (unless, of course, you're one of those well-financed folks who own one of the new writable CD drives). If you opened a piece of CorelDraw clip art, you need to save it to your hard drive or some other disk.

4. **Select a folder inside the scrolling list of files and folders.**

Double-click on folder names to open the folders, just as you did when opening a drawing (explained earlier in this chapter). If necessary, you can use the Up One Level button to navigate to a different folder, just as in the Open dialog box. If you want to create an entirely new folder, click on the Create New Folder button, labeled in Figure 3-11.

5. **Click on the Save button or press Enter.**

Your drawing is now saved! Come heck or high water, you're protected.

Updating the drawing

After you name your drawing and save it to disk for the first time, press Ctrl+S every time you think of it. Pressing Ctrl+S automatically updates your drawing on disk without requiring you to work your way through dialog boxes, options, or any other interface artifacts. If you remember to update your drawing regularly, you won't lose hours of work when something goes wrong — notice that I said when, not if. You'll lose a few minutes, maybe, but that comes with the territory.

If you don't trust yourself to save your drawing every five to ten minutes, you can tell CorelDraw to do it for you. Choose Tools⇨Options (or press Ctrl+J) and then click on the Advanced tab in the dialog box that appears. If you see a check mark in the Auto-backup check box, the automatic saving function is turned on. If you don't see a check mark, click on the check box to turn on the option. To specify how often CorelDraw automatically saves your drawing, enter the number of minutes between saves into the option box just to the right of the check box. Then press Enter. Now your saving worries are gone.

Creating a backup copy

If you spend longer than a single day creating a drawing, you should create backup copies. That's not a hard and fast rule, mind you, but it is a sound principle of drawing management. The reasoning is, if a drawing takes longer than a day to create, you're that much worse off if you lose it. By creating one backup copy for each day that you work on the project — for example, Rodent 01, Rodent 02, Rodent 03, and so on — you're much less likely to lose your work. If some disk error occurs or you accidentally delete one or two of the files, one of the backups will probably survive the disaster, further protecting you from developing an ulcer or having to seek therapy.

At the end of the day, choose File⇨Save As. The Save Drawing dialog box opens, as when you first saved the drawing. Change the filename slightly and then click on the Save button — way to be doubly protected!

Put Your Drawing to Bed

To leave CorelDraw, choose File⇨Exit or press Alt+F4. I know that Alt+F4 doesn't make anywhere near as much sense as Ctrl+O to open and Ctrl+S to save, but Corel isn't to blame. Microsoft demands the Alt+F4 thing from all its Windows programs. Where Microsoft came up with Alt+F4 is anyone's guess. I think that they made this shortcut confusing on purpose. This is the same company that brought you DOS, so what do you expect?

Microsoft decided to make a little more sense with Windows 95, however. In addition to using Exit and Alt+F4, you can now click on the Close button in the upper-right corner of the CorelDraw interface. This method wins my vote as the easiest way to quit the program.

Anyway, when you press Alt+F4 or click on the Close button, CorelDraw may warn you with a message that asks whether you want to save the changes you made to the current drawing. Unless you have some reason for doing otherwise, press Y or click on the Yes button. The program saves the drawing and then shuts itself down.

Part II
Let the Graphics Begin

The 5th Wave   By Rich Tennant

NATIONAL ENQUIRER PHOTO IMAGING WORKSHOP

"Remember, Charles and Di can be pasted next to anyone but each other, and your Elvis should appear bald and slightly hunched- nice Big Foot, Brad - keep your two-headed animals in the shadows and your alien spacecrafts crisp and defined."

In this part . . .

Traditional art tools are messy. Real-life ink, for example, bleeds into the fibers of the paper, goops and glumps onto the page, and stains if you accidentally spill some on your clothes. Real-life pens clog; real-life paintbrushes need washing; and real-life paintings flop over accidentally and get dust and hairs stuck all over them. Real life, in other words, is for the birds (which is only fitting because birds are wholly unequipped to use CorelDraw, what with their puny little brains and their sad lack of opposable thumbs).

CorelDraw, being a figment of your computer's imagination, is very tidy and orderly. There's nothing real to deal with. The pencil draws a line that remains the same thickness throughout its entire length. Whoever heard of such a thing? You can edit lines and shapes after you draw them. Unbelievable. And if you make a mistake, you can choose the Undo command. The real world has no equivalent. CorelDraw provides a flexible, forgiving interface that mimics real life while at the same time improving on it.

In the next six chapters, I show you how to draw, how to edit what you've drawn, how to apply colors, how to duplicate portions of your artwork, and how to create special effects. By the time you finish with Chapter 9, those Number 2 pencils you've been storing all these years will be history.

Chapter 4

The Secret Society of Simple Shapes

In This Chapter

▶ Drawing rectangles, squares, ovals, and circles

▶ Introducing nodes

▶ Rounding off the corners of rectangles

▶ Converting ovals into pies and wedges

▶ Moving shapes with the arrow tool

▶ Scaling and flipping shapes

▶ Deleting shapes and subsequently freaking out

▶ Using the Undo command

*E*ver try to draw a perfect square the old-fashioned way? Regardless of how many metal rulers, drafting arms, and absolutely 100 percent square stencils you have at your disposal, you're liable to miss the mark to some extent, however minuscule. And that's if you kill yourself over every corner and use the highest-grade engineering pens and acetate.

If you want to keep the Euclideans happy — and God knows, none of us wants to attract the wrath of an angry Euclidean — there's nothing like a drawing program for accuracy, simplicity, and downright efficiency. Suddenly, squares and circles are as easy to draw as, well, those smiley faces that little girls frequently use in their letters as punctuation at the end of jokes. You know, a semicircle mouth and two dots for eyes. Not even a circle to identify the boundaries of the head. Just a face in space, like some minimalist version of the Cheshire cat.

Well, anyway, the point is, smiley faces are ridiculously easy to draw, and so is the stuff in this chapter.

Shapes from Your Childhood

Wow, is this going to be easy! In about five minutes, you're going to laugh out loud at the idea that you once viewed computers as cold-blooded machines intent on the overthrow of humanity. It's not that computers aren't cold-blooded machines intent on the overthrow of humanity, mind you, but at least they won't seem quite so menacing.

Rectangles and squares

Click on the rectangle tool (labeled in Figure 4-1) to select it. Or if you prefer, press F6. Now drag in the drawing area. A rectangle grows from the movement of your cursor, as demonstrated in Figure 4-1. One corner of the rectangle appears at the point at which you begin dragging. The opposite corner appears at the point at which you release. What could be simpler?

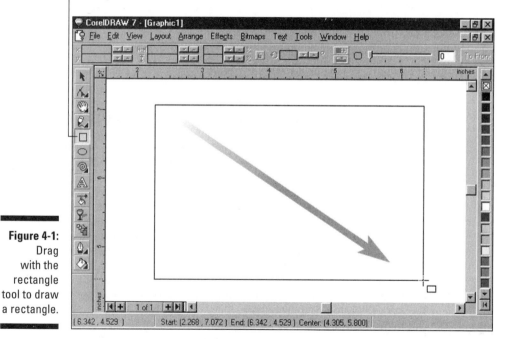

Rectangle tool

Figure 4-1: Drag with the rectangle tool to draw a rectangle.

Here's some more stuff you can do with this tool:

- ✔ Press and hold the Ctrl key while dragging with the rectangle tool to draw a perfect square. The Ctrl key constrains the rectangle so that all four sides are the same length. Be sure to hold the Ctrl key down until you release your mouse button.

- ✔ Shift+drag with the rectangle tool — that is, press and hold the Shift key while dragging — to draw the rectangle outward from its center. CorelDraw centers the rectangle about the point at which you begin dragging. A corner appears at the point at which you release.

- ✔ Ctrl+Shift+drag to draw a square outward from the center.

- ✔ Double-click the rectangle tool icon in the toolbox to draw a rectangle the size of the drawing page.

Ovals and circles

Labeled in Figure 4-2, the ellipse tool works the same way as the rectangle tool. The ellipse tool even has a keyboard equivalent, which is F7. You drag inside the drawing area to define the size of an oval, as shown in Figure 4-2. You can draw a perfect circle by Ctrl+dragging with the ellipse tool. Shift+drag to draw an oval from the center outward.

Ellipse tool

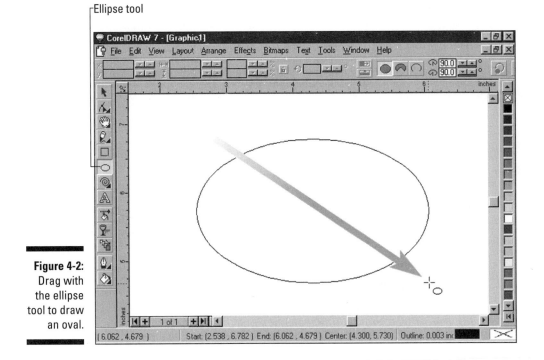

Figure 4-2:
Drag with the ellipse tool to draw an oval.

Within every oval there lurks an ellipse

Euclideans call the oval an *ellipse,* which is a shape whose outline travels at a fixed distance from two central points. You can draw an ellipse by hammering two nails into a board, tying a string between the two nails so that it has a great deal of slack, and tracing the path of the string as shown in the following figure. The slack in the string determines the size of the ellipse.

Who cares? Well, technically, an oval is less structured than an ellipse. An oval can be anything from oblong to egg-shaped to lumpy-bumpy, whereas an ellipse is always perfectly formed and exactly symmetrical vertically and horizontally, just like shapes drawn with the ellipse tool. And besides, I wanted to make sure that you appreciate the little things in CorelDraw. I mean, you wouldn't want to have to go back to board, string, and pencil, now would you?

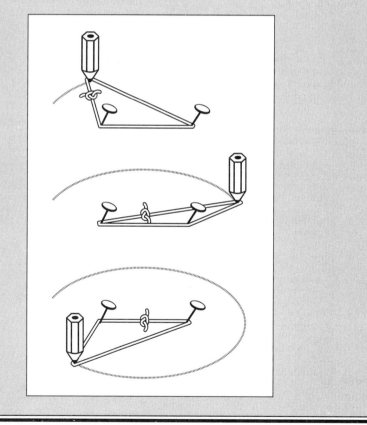

Shapes with many sides

With the polygon tool, labeled in Figure 4-3, you can draw shapes with multiple sides, such as triangles, pentagons, octagons, and all those other 'gons. You can even draw stars — boy howdy.

To draw a polygon — the generic name for any shape with three or more straight sides — select the polygon tool by clicking on it. Then drag away, as shown in Figure 4-3. Ctrl+drag with the tool to draw a shape in which all sides are the same length (called an *equilateral polygon,* for those of you interested in tossing about the technical lingo). Shift+drag to draw the shape from the center out.

By default, CorelDraw creates a pentagon, which is a polygon with five sides. But you can draw as many sides as you want. To change the number of sides, do either of the following:

✔ To change the setting for any new shapes you draw — in other words, the default setting — double-click on the polygon tool icon in the toolbox. CorelDraw displays the Options dialog box with the settings for the polygon tool at the forefront.

Polygon tool

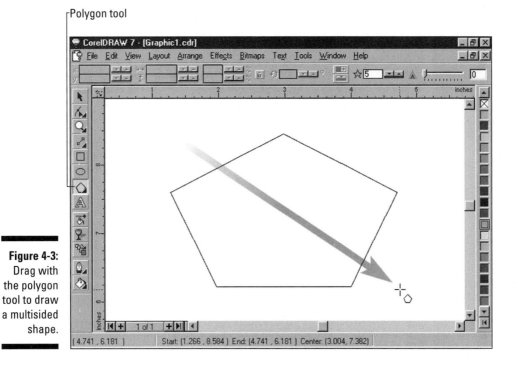

Figure 4-3:
Drag with the polygon tool to draw a multisided shape.

✔ To change the number of sides assigned to an existing shape, first click on the shape with the arrow tool to select the shape. Then press Alt+Enter to open the Object Properties dialog box, shown in Figure 4-4. (You can also open the dialog box by right-clicking the shape and selecting the Properties option from the bottom of the pop-up menu that appears.)

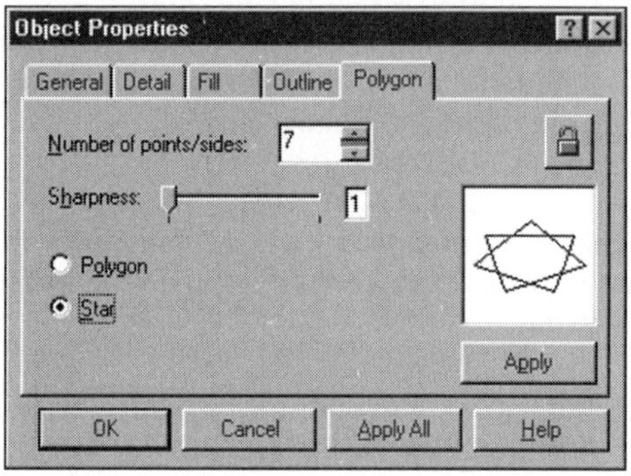

Figure 4-4:
You can decide whether to draw polygons or stars by using this dialog box.

Although the Options dialog box and the Object Properties dialog box look different, both offer the same polygon tool options, with one exception. Here's a look at your choices:

✔ Select a radio button to determine the shape of the polygon. The Options dialog box has three radio buttons: Polygon, Star, or Polygon as Star. If you select the Polygon as Star option, you create a star in which the lines of the star don't cross. But more important, the option gives you absolute control over the sharpness of the star's points. Suffice it to say, if you can't get the shape you want by selecting the Star option, try Polygon as Star instead.

The Object Properties dialog box doesn't offer the Polygon as Star option. If you want to convert an existing polygon to a Polygon as Star, you have to do it manually with the shape tool, as explained in "Making a wacky shape wackier," later in this chapter. Nor can you change an existing Polygon as Star shape into a regular Polygon shape; again, you must use the shape tool to edit the shape.

✔ The Number of Points/Sides option box establishes the number of sides for your shape. You can go as low as 3 for a triangle or as high as 500, which is, of course, an insanely large value.

✔ The Star option is unavailable in both the Object Properties and Options dialog boxes if the Number of Points/Sides value is lower than 5; by definition, a star has at least five sides.

Remember, when an option box is active, you can raise or lower the value in the box by pressing the up- or down-arrow key.

✔ If you select Star and the Number of Points/Sides value 7 or larger, the Sharpness option becomes available. The Sharpness value is also available if you select Polygon as Star. A higher Sharpness value increases the sharpness of the star's points.

✔ If you're changing the settings for an existing polygon via the Object Properties dialog box, click on the Apply button to see how the settings affect your shape. If you like what you see, press Enter to accept the changes and close the dialog box. If not, change the setting and click on the Apply button again.

When you select the polygon tool, the Property Bar offers controls for the same options as the Object Properties dialog box. If you're using a 640 x 480 screen resolution, one of the vital controls is cut off the right side of the screen, a problem I mention back in Chapter 2. If you want to use the Property Bar controls, just drag the Property Bar into the drawing window to convert the Property Bar to a floating window, shown in Figure 4-5, where you also see each of the controls labeled.

Figure 4-5:
The Property Bar controls for polygons.

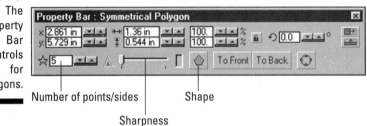

Number of points/sides   Shape

Sharpness

If no shape is selected when you change the Property Bar controls, the settings affect the next shape you draw — using the Property Bar in this way is the same as changing the options in the Options dialog box. If a shape is selected, your settings affect only the selected shape. Just as in the Object Properties and Options dialog boxes, the Star option is unavailable until you raise the number of sides for the shape to 5 or higher.

I should mention that you can similarly change the properties of rectangles and ovals. In other words, you can display the Toolbox panel of the Options dialog box by double-clicking on the rectangle or ellipse tool, or you can display the Object Properties dialog box by right-clicking on a rectangle or oval in the drawing area and selecting the Properties option. But frankly, the changes you can make inside these dialog boxes are easier to apply using a special tool called the shape tool, which I describe in the next section.

Ways to Change Shapes

After you finish drawing a rectangle, oval, polygon, or star, take a look at it. You can see one or more tiny, square *nodes* on the outline of the shape. At least that's what Corel calls them. My dictionary says that a node is a "knotty, localized swelling." If I were you, I'd try not to think about that.

As illustrated in Figure 4-6, different shapes include different numbers of nodes (the nodes are highlighted in the figure).

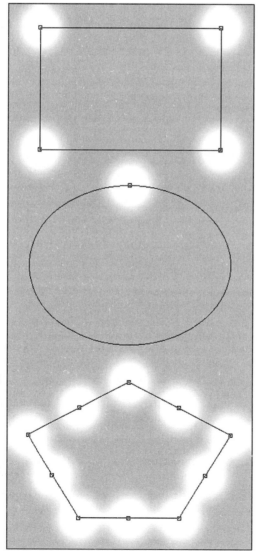

Figure 4-6:
Rectangles, ovals, and polygons include nodes that you can drag with the shape tool.

✔ A rectangle sports a node on each of its four corners.

✔ An oval features just one node. If you draw the shape by dragging the cursor downward on-screen (as shown back in Figure 4-2), the node appears along the top of the shape, as in Figure 4-6. However, if you drag upward to draw the oval — which almost no one does — the node appears along the bottom. Either way is okay.

✔ A polygon or star has one node in each corner and one in the middle of each side. So a triangle has six nodes, and a pentagon, or five-pointed star, has ten.

Although nodes are certainly decorative and particularly festive during the holidays, they also provide a bona fide function. You can change a shape by dragging a node with the shape tool, the mysterious tool of a thousand faces. Were he alive today, Lon Chaney would undoubtedly sue.

If you want to reshape an object whose nodes aren't visible, just click on the object with the shape tool. The nodes pop into view.

Sanding off the corners

When applied to one of the nodes of a rectangle, the shape tool (labeled in Figure 4-7) rounds off the corners of the shape. Here's how to perform this trick:

1. Draw a rectangle.

You can't edit a rectangle until you draw it.

2. Click on the shape tool to select it.

Or press F10 to select the tool from the keyboard.

Some particularly nerdy folks refer to the shape tool as the node edit tool, by the way.

3. Drag one of the rectangle's nodes toward the middle of the shape.

Regardless of which node you drag, CorelDraw rounds off all four corners in the shape to the same extent. Notice that you now have eight nodes, which mark the transitions between the straight and curved edges of the shape. Release the mouse button when you have sufficiently rounded off the corners.

To restore the rectangle's sharp corners, drag any of the nodes back to the corner position. Your corners should now be considered dangerous. Don't play too close to the rectangle or run around it with scissors in your hands.

F10 to get window shape tool

Shape tool   Roundness slider

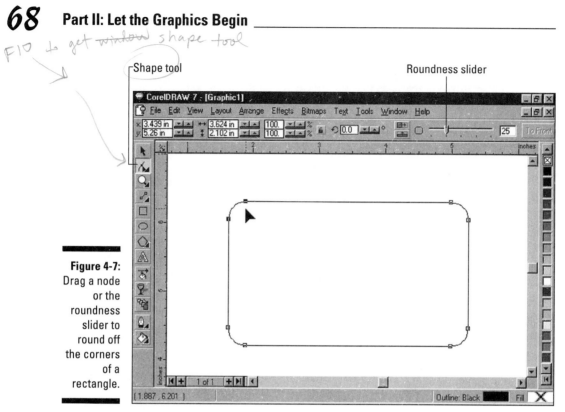

Figure 4-7:
Drag a node
or the
roundness
slider to
round off
the corners
of a
rectangle.

When you select the shape tool in Version 7, the Property Bar offers controls that give you another way to round off the corners of your rectangle. Drag the Roundess slider, labeled in Figure 4-7, to the right to make the corners more round; drag to the left to square up the corners again. You can also enter a value in the option box to the right of the slider bar, if you're feeling the need for precision. A value of zero gives you perfectly square corners.

Turning an oval into a tempting dessert

I speak, of course, of a pie. When you drag the node of an oval with the shape tool, you change the oval to a piping hot pie with a node on each side of the wedge. Truth be told, you can actually create either a pie or an arc, depending on how you drag the node, as illustrated in Figure 4-8.

✔ Move the shape tool cursor inside the oval during your drag to create a pie shape (top two objects in Figure 4-8). Like any shape, the pie has an interior that you can fill with a solid color, gradation, or what have you. (Chapter 7 talks about fills.)

✔ Move the cursor outside the oval during the drag to create an arc (bottom two objects in Figure 4-8). Notice that with an arc, the slice segments that form a V between the two pie nodes disappear. An arc is therefore a curved line with no scrumptious filling.

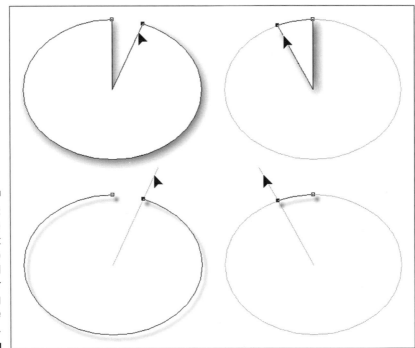

Figure 4-8:
The different ways to turn an oval into a pie or arc using the shape tool.

✔ Drag the node to the right to draw a pie with a wedge cut out of it or a long arc, as with the left two objects in Figure 4-8. (This instruction assumes that you created the oval by dragging downward from left to right, which most folks do without thinking. If you create your ovals by dragging from right to left, you nonconformist you, drag the node to the left to cut out a wedge.)

✔ Drag the node to the left to throw away most of the pie and retain a slim wedge or a short arc, as with the right-hand objects in Figure 4-8. (If you created the shape by dragging right to left, drag the node to the right instead.)

✔ Press Ctrl while dragging to constrain the wedge angle to the nearest 15-degree increment. Because a circle is 360 degrees — I don't know where Euclid got that number, maybe he had 36 toes or something — Ctrl+dragging ensures 24 equal increments around the perimeter of the oval. (360 ÷ 15 = 24, in case you're interested.)

✔ After you change the oval to a pie or arc, you can continue to apply the shape tool to either node, creating all sorts of wedges and curves. To restore the pie or arc to a circle, drag one node exactly onto the other while keeping the cursor outside the shape. Don't worry about positioning the cursor directly over either node during the drag; the two nodes automatically snap together when they get close together.

✔ If you have trouble dragging nodes to get the shape you want, try using the Property Bar controls, shown in Figure 4-9. These controls are available when the ellipse tool is selected or when the shape tool and an oval are selected. Click on the Pie or Arc icon to convert the oval into a pie or arc shape. Then click on the up- and down-pointing arrows next to the Starting and Ending Angle option boxes to create the exact pie, arc, or wedge shape you want. Click the Clockwise/counterclockwise button to reverse the Starting and Ending Angle values. (This button is grayed out in Figure 4-9 because it's available only if you selected the Pie or Arc icon.) Click the Ellipse icon to return to your original ellipse.

Figure 4-9:
The
Property
Bar when
the ellipse
tool is
active.

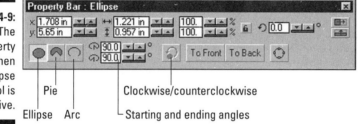

Pie

Ellipse Arc

Clockwise/counterclockwise

Starting and ending angles

Giving the pie a wedgie

Creating a pie is pretty straightforward. But because of the right/left thing discussed in the preceding section, creating the pie-and-floating-wedge effect shown in Figure 4-10 is kind of difficult. I mean, you drag one way for the pie and the other way for the wedge, so how are you supposed to get the pie and wedge to match? Well, I can tell you how, but the job involves a couple of tricks that I haven't discussed yet. Assuming that you're willing to jump boldly into the unknown, here's how the procedure works:

1. **Select the ellipse tool.**

   Remember, you can select the ellipse tool by pressing F7.

2. **Draw an oval.**

   Make sure to drag from the upper-left portion of the drawing area to lower-right or things get screwed up in steps to come.

3. **Click on the shape tool or press F10.**

   Either process selects the shape tool.

4. **Ctrl+drag the oval's node to the right. Be sure to keep your cursor on the inside of the shape.**

   This step creates a slice in the pie. Because the Ctrl key constrains your drag in increments, matching the wedge to the slice is easier later on.

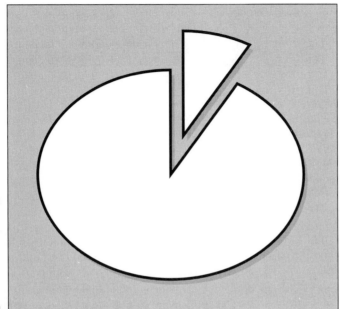

Figure 4-10:
The very
popular pie
shape with
a floating
wedge.

Otherwise, it's all up to you. How far you drag doesn't matter. You can create a thin slice or a big chunky one depending on what you want to represent — or how hungry you are.

You can also use the Property Bar controls, discussed in the preceding section, to create your pie slice.

5. **Press Ctrl+D or choose Edit⇨Duplicate.**

The Duplicate command makes a copy of the shape. I discuss this command in Chapter 8, but for now, just accept it.

6. **Reselect the shape tool (F10) and Ctrl+drag the right-hand node of the new shape to the left.**

Ctrl+drag past the upper node and toward the inside of the shape to create a wedge that matches the slice out of the original pie, as shown in Figure 4-11. Alternatively, use the Property Bar controls to create your wedge.

7. **Click on the arrow tool to select it.**

Or press the spacebar. I explain how to use the arrow tool with rectangles, ovals, pies, and all the rest in the next section. But for now, notice that the wedge becomes selected, with big corner handles around it.

8. **Press Alt+F9.**

Or choose Arrange⇨Transform⇨Scale & Mirror. Either way, the Scale & Mirror roll-up appears on-screen, as in Figure 4-12.

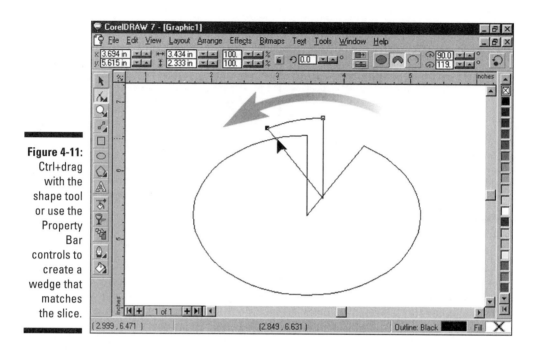

Figure 4-11:
Ctrl+drag
with the
shape tool
or use the
Property
Bar
controls to
create a
wedge that
matches
the slice.

9. Click on the Mirror Horizontal button, labeled in Figure 4-12.

Then press Enter or click on the Apply button. The wedge flips itself over, as the figure shows.

Alternatively, you can simply click on the Mirror Horizontal button on the Property Bar to flip the slice without displaying the Scale & Mirror roll-up at all.

10. Press the arrow keys to move the slice into place.

The arrow keys nudge the shape incrementally. The wedge is now moved into place.

You can also use the Object Position option boxes, labeled in Figure 4-12, to shift the slice into place. The X value moves the slice left to right; the Y value moves it up and down. (You're moving the slice along an imaginary X and Y axis, you see.)

Making a wacky shape wackier

Reshaping rectangles and ovals is a great way to while away the occasional rainy day, but you can have the most fun reshaping polygons and stars. Here's how it works:

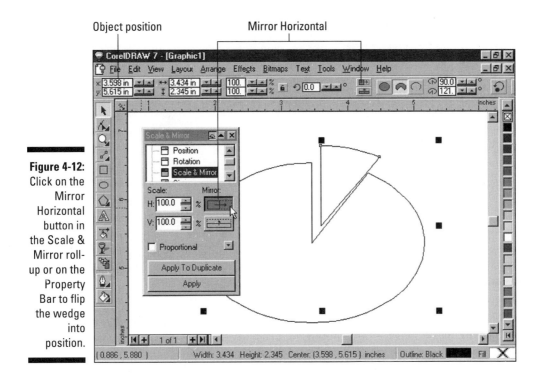

Object position   Mirror Horizontal

Figure 4-12:
Click on the
Mirror
Horizontal
button in
the Scale &
Mirror roll-
up or on the
Property
Bar to flip
the wedge
into
position.

✔ Regardless of which node you drag in a polygon, the related nodes move in kind. All side nodes move together (as you can see in shapes 2, 3, and 4 in Figure 4-13), and all point nodes move together (shapes 5 and 6). This feature ensures that the polygon or star is forever symmetrical.

✔ Just so that you can impress your friends, this kind of symmetry is known as *radial symmetry.*

✔ Try dragging a side node past a point node or vice versa to create cool geometric effects, including double stars. The effects look really great on shapes with ten or more sides.

✔ You can add or subtract sides by pressing Alt+Enter or right-clicking on the polygon and choosing the Properties option, as discussed earlier, in the section "Shapes with many sides." The polygon retains its new, weird shape however you change the Number of Points/Sides value.

✔ Click on a side node and then Shift+click on a point node. Both nodes become selected. Now when you drag one of the two nodes, both side and point nodes move together.

✔ Ctrl+drag a node to move side or point nodes in and out along a constrained axis. Ctrl+dragging is great if you want to keep things from getting too out of hand.

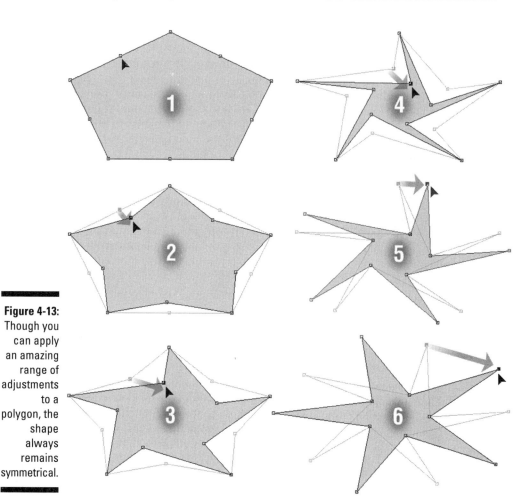

More than any other option I've discussed so far, reshaping polygons is something you should experiment with a great deal. There's simply no limit to the number of wild effects you can achieve.

Arrow Tool Techniques (Or Tricks of the Pick)

Every drawing and desktop publishing program on the planet offers a tool that looks like an arrow. Some companies call their arrows selection tools. Others call them edit tools. But wouldn't you know it, Corel — roughly the 500th company to implement such a tool — went and renamed the thing the pick tool. So when you select something, you're actually "picking" it. Just imagine if I had employed official Corel vernacular when instructing you to select the rat's nose in Chapter 3.

Everyone I know calls the tool that looks like an arrow the arrow tool. First tool among tools, the arrow tool is an editing tool, much like the shape tool. However, instead of enabling you to change details in an object like the shape tool does, the arrow tool enables you to make changes to the object as a whole.

Select the arrow tool and then click on a shape to select the shape. Be sure to click on the outline of the shape (up to this point in the book, all the shapes you've drawn are transparent, unless you've been experimenting without me). After you select a shape, it becomes surrounded by eight big black handles (called *selection handles*), as shown in Figure 4-14. The handles enable you to change the dimensions of the shape. (If you just drew the shape or you were editing it with the shape tool, you don't need to click on it with the arrow tool. The shape remains selected automatically.)

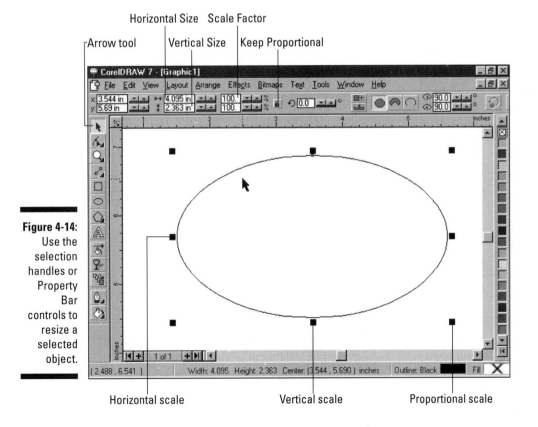

Figure 4-14: Use the selection handles or Property Bar controls to resize a selected object.

Horizontal Size   Scale Factor

Vertical Size   Keep Proportional

Arrow tool

Horizontal scale   Vertical scale   Proportional scale

You can also select shapes by selecting the arrow tool and then pressing Tab. CorelDraw selects one of the objects in your drawing. Press Tab to select the next object in the drawing. Keep pressing Tab until the object you want to select is surrounded by the black handles. To select the shape that was previously selected, press Shift+Tab.

To switch between the selected tool and the arrow tool, just press the spacebar. Press the spacebar again to return to the previously selected tool. If text is active, press Ctrl+spacebar to switch between the selected tool and the arrow tool.

To select two or more shapes so that you can manipulate them at the same time, click on the first shape and then Shift+click on the others. Or drag around the shapes with the arrow tool. To select all objects, double-click on the arrow tool icon or choose Edit⇨Select All.

The following list explains some basic ways to change a selected shape with the arrow tool.

- ✔ To scale the shape horizontally, drag the handle on the left or right side of the shape. Drag toward the center of the shape to make the shape skinnier; drag away from the shape to make it fatter.

- ✔ To scale the shape vertically, drag the handle on the top or bottom side of the shape. Drag in to make the shape shorter; drag away to make it taller.

- ✔ You can also use the Horizontal and Vertical Size controls on the Property Bar, labeled in Figure 4-14, to resize an object with precision. Use the little arrows to the right of the controls to change the values in preset increments. Or double-click on one of the option boxes, enter a value from the keyboard, and press Enter.

- ✔ To scale the shape proportionally, so that the horizontal and vertical proportions remain equal, drag one of the four corner handles. Drag in to reduce; drag away to enlarge.

- ✔ If you're a Property Bar fan, click on the little lock icon to maintain the object's original proportions when you use the Horizontal and Vertical Size controls. Note that clicking on the lock icon *doesn't* keep the object proportional when you drag the selection handles; the lock icon affects the Property Bar controls only.

- ✔ If you press Shift while dragging a handle, you scale the shape about its center. In other words, the center of the shape remains stationary throughout your drag. Normally, the opposite side is stationary.

- ✔ Ctrl+drag a handle to scale in 100 percent increments. You can scale a shape to twice, three times, or four times its previous size and even larger. You generally need a lot of extra room on-screen to pull this off. Try zooming out a few times (by pressing F3) before embarking on a Ctrl+drag.

✔ You may find it easier to use the Property Bar's Horizontal and Vertical Scale controls to scale the object. Either click on the arrows to the right of the option boxes or double-click on the option boxes, enter scale values from the keyboard, and press Enter. A value of less than 100 percent reduces the object's size; a value of more than 100 percent increases the size. Also, remember that the setting of the lock icon discussed earlier affects the scale options. If the lock icon is selected, the horizontal scale factor changes when you change the vertical scale factor and vice versa.

✔ Ctrl+drag a side handle past the opposite side to flip the shape. For example, if you Ctrl+drag the left handle rightward past the right handle, you flip the shape horizontally. Drag the top handle down past the bottom handle to flip the shape vertically. Be sure to press Ctrl when you drag, or you can distort your object. Pressing Ctrl ensures that your object remains the same size when you flip it.

✔ Notice that Ctrl+dragging has different results than using the mirror buttons on the Property Bar or in the Scale & Mirror roll-up, discussed earlier. Compare the two techniques to see the difference in how your object flips.

✔ To move a shape, drag its outline (not on the handles).

✔ Or use the X and Y coordinate controls on the Property Bar to reposition the shape. The X value moves the shape left and right; the Y value moves the shape up and down. Remember that the X and Y values reflect the position of the center of the object.

✔ If you click on the outline of a selected shape, the handles change to double-headed arrows. These arrows enable you to rotate and slant the shape as discussed in Chapter 9. To return to the big black handles, click on the shape again.

Kiss It Good-bye

To delete a shape, press Delete. It doesn't matter whether you selected the shape with the shape tool or the arrow tool or whether you just finished creating it with the rectangle or ellipse tool. Don't press the Backspace key, by the way. Backspacing doesn't do anything except cause your computer to beep at you.

Aaaugh, It's Gone!

Relax. Everything I discuss in this chapter — as well as in most other chapters — can be undone. You can undraw a rectangle or oval, restore a shape that you changed with the shape tool, return a shape to its original size, and even bring back a shape you've deleted. To undo something, choose Edit➪Undo or press Ctrl+Z or Alt+Backspace. The name of the Undo command changes to reflect the operation you're about to undo; if you choose the command after filling an object, for example, the command name is Undo Fill.

Ctrl + Z = undo

Ctrl + Shft + Z = restore the undo

Not only can you undo the last operation, you can undo the one before that and the one before that. In CorelDraw, you can undo multiple operations in a row. For example, if you draw a rectangle, round off the corners with the shape tool, and then scale it, you can press Ctrl+Z three times, first to return the rectangle to its original size, then to restore its sharp corners, and finally to delete it.

If you then change your mind, you can restore operations that you undid by choosing Edit➪Redo or pressing Ctrl+Shift+Z.

WARNING!

After you save a drawing, you lose the opportunity to undo any changes you made before you chose the Save command. Also, it is possible to run out of undos; for more information, see the sidebar "Raising the Undo ceiling until the rubble falls on your head."

TIP

Raising the Undo ceiling until the rubble falls on your head

You can find out for sure how many operations you can undo in a row by pressing Ctrl+J (or choosing Tools➪Options) and looking at the Regular value in the Undo Levels option box. You can raise or lower the value to suit your own tolerance for risk. But be aware that CorelDraw may not function as well if you use a high value. Your system may crash more often, or you may not be able to use other Windows 95 programs at the same time you're running CorelDraw.

I recommend that you set the Undo Levels value no higher than 10 unless someone who is familiar with the inner workings of your computer tells you to do otherwise. And even then, ask for credentials. Those computer know-it-alls always tell you to do something and then go on vacation when the entire system breaks down.

Chapter 5
Drawn It, Shaped It, Ready to Go Free-Form

In This Chapter

▶ Meet Shenbop, crazed adventure seeker

▶ Draw with the pencil tool

▶ Take the natural pen tool for a spin

▶ Find out all about paths, segments, and control points

▶ Go on a rampage with the shape tool

▶ Wake the neighbors with your endless curve bending

▶ Face the Node Edit roll-up without fear

▶ Hack away extraneous nodes

▶ Convert simple shapes to free-form paths

*R*emember those Mountain Dew commercials from a few years back? A bunch of guys poke their faces into the camera and express with virile bravado that they've "Jumped it," "Scaled it," yada yada yada, while images of stunt men flinging themselves into and off of everything imaginable reel across the screen. Restless daredevils overcome nature. Fledgling Odysseuses on dangerous doses.

I'm not a parent, but if I were, I think I'd have been unnerved. These young men, juiced up on too much caffeine, overconfident beyond their levels of skill and endurance, were quite obviously destined to crack their skulls open during miscalculated bungie jumps, pound their kayaks into unyielding underwater boulders, smash their ultralights into low-flying crop dusters, and invite blood blisters when constructing spice racks without adult supervision. I mean, are we really comfortable handing over the leadership responsibilities of this great nation to a bunch of super-charged yahoos? Haven't we learned anything from the super-charged yahoos currently at the helm?

I'm not sure what all this is leading up to, but I think it's a cautionary note. Some of you, Mountain Dews in hand, are naturally pumped about the skills you acquired in the first four chapters of this book. You're drawing pies with flying wedges and polygons with sharp corners while bandying about terms such as *ellipse* and *node* like a veteran CorelDraw hack. With the maddening rush of adrenaline surging through your temples combined with the dizzying sensation of newfound knowledge, you're practically psycho to throw off the chains of geometric shapes. You're itching to go free-form!

Okay, I see nothing wrong with that. Just don't overdo it the first time out. I think that Edgar Allan Poe said it best: "Quoth the raven, 'Chill, homey.'"

Do Some Doodling with the Pencil

Figure 5-1 shows an amphibian of dubious heritage whose name happens to be Shenbop. The major factor in Shenbop's favor is that he's ridiculously easy to draw. After selecting the pencil tool — which you can do by clicking on the tool's icon or by pressing F5 — you can draw Shenbop in six steps, as demonstrated in Figure 5-2. Just drag with the tool as if you were doodling with a real pencil. Your lines may look a little shakier than mine — not that mine are all that smooth — but you can do it. (For tips on drawing with the pencil, see the upcoming section "Mastering the pencil.")

In response to your drags, CorelDraw creates a series of lines and shapes, known in CorelDraw lingo as *closed* and *open paths,* as explained next.

Pencil tool

Figure 5-1:
If you can draw this cute critter with the pencil tool, you may have hidden artistic talents.

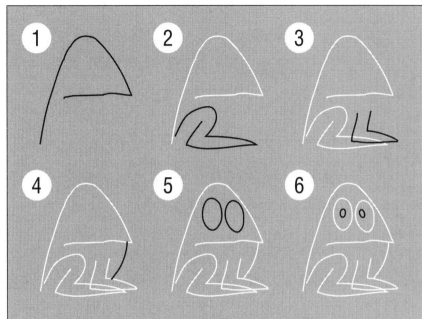

Figure 5-2:
The
six-step
Shenbop
creation
program.

Understanding paths, lines, and shapes

Anything you draw — whether it's with the rectangle tool, the ellipse tool, the pencil tool, or some other tool, is called a *path*. The origin of the term has to do with the way some printers draw mathematical objects, but just think of it this way: If you blew up a rectangle or some other line or shape onto a sheet of paper the size of a city block, the shape's outline would become as wide as a sidewalk. You could follow this sidewalk outline around the block, hence, it's a *path*. The only difference is that paths in CorelDraw are for extremely small people.

In each of Steps 1 through 4 of Figure 5-2, you draw an *open path*, in which the beginning and end of the path don't touch. An open path is, therefore, the same as a *line*. Steps 5 and 6 show *closed paths*, which are paths that loop around continuously with no obvious beginning or end. In laymen's terms, a closed path is a *shape*. For me to define common words such as *line* and *shape* may seem silly, but these terms lie at the core of CorelDraw. In fact, everything you draw falls into one of these two camps.

In Chapter 1, I introduce the term *object,* which can also mean either a line or shape. But unlike a path, an object can also be a block of text. For an object to qualify as a path, you must be able to edit its outline. So paths are a subset of objects that include lines and shapes only. Figure 5-3 shows the family tree of CorelDraw objects.

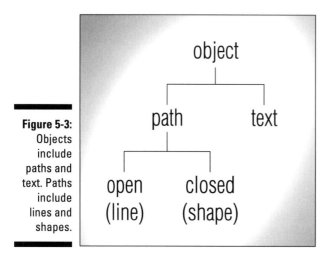

Coming to grips with nodes and segments

Immediately after you draw a line or shape, CorelDraw performs some intense calculations and assigns nodes to the path automatically, as I discuss in Chapter 4. The length of the path from one node to the next is called a *segment* (see Figure 5-4). And you thought you were finished with the vocabulary.

- If the path is fairly simple — say, requiring ten nodes or fewer — CorelDraw displays all the nodes. If the path is more complex, the program shows only the first and last nodes. It's just a display thing; all the nodes are present, they're just hiding. (If you were a node, wouldn't you be shy?)

- After you select the shape tool, the total number of nodes for a path appears in the middle of the status bar at the bottom of the screen.

- CorelDraw has a habit of depositing nodes based on the speed at which you draw. When you draw fast, CorelDraw lays down a node here, another there. When you draw slowly, the program riddles the path with nodes because it thinks that you're slowing down for emphasis. Unfortunately, densely concentrated nodes result in abrupt transitions and zigzags that make the path look jagged and irregular, as demonstrated in Figure 5-4. So try to maintain a quick and consistent drawing speed.

Mastering the pencil

If you're inexperienced at drawing with a mouse, nearly all your first hundred or so paths will be jagged and irregular. What can I tell you? Becoming a competent computer artist takes time and practice. But don't let little

Segment   Node

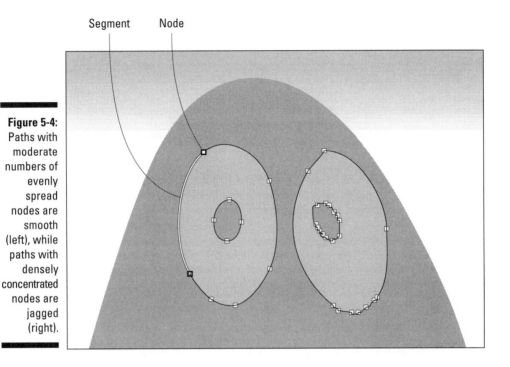

Figure 5-4:
Paths with
moderate
numbers of
evenly
spread
nodes are
smooth
(left), while
paths with
densely
concentrated
nodes are
jagged
(right).

flaws in your drawing bother you. As long as you draw approximately what you want, you can shape and mold it as discussed later in this chapter.

Here are some additional tips for creating successful pencil paths:

- ✔ To draw a straight line, click with the pencil tool to establish the first node, and then click at a new location to establish the second node. CorelDraw automatically draws a straight line between the two nodes.

- ✔ To constrain your line to a 15-degree angle, Ctrl+click at the point where you want to end the line.

- ✔ To draw an irregular polygon — such as a triangle in which every side is a different length — click to create the first node, double-click at a new location to create the second node, and continue double-clicking to establish additional nodes in the path. The program draws a straight segment between each pair of nodes. To end the polygon, click once.

- ✔ You can erase part of your path as you draw by pressing the Shift key and dragging backwards along the path. But you have to Shift+drag before you release the mouse button to end the path. Keep the mouse button pressed to resume drawing the path again.

- ✔ To complete a closed path, you have to connect with the point at which you began dragging or clicking. If you miss, the path won't close properly. You can't fill an open path. (See Figure 5-5.)

Closed path   Open path

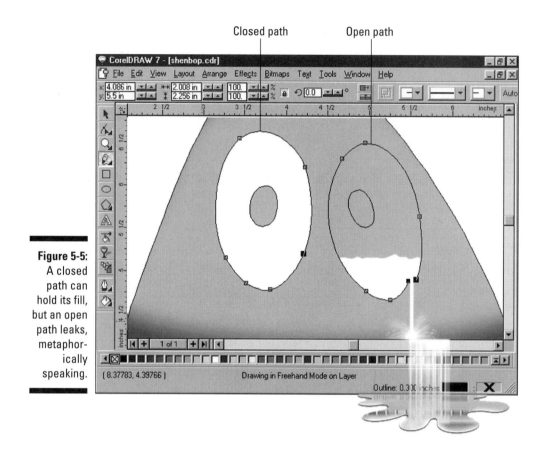

Figure 5-5:
A closed
path can
hold its fill,
but an open
path leaks,
metaphor-
ically
speaking.

> ✔ If a path does not close as you had hoped, you can press Delete and redraw the path. But you can also close the path with the pencil. Immediately after drawing an open path, drag from the first node to the last node to add a few more segments and close the path to form a shape. To close the path with a straight segment, click on the first node and then click on the last.

> ✔ You can extend any open path with the pencil. After drawing the path, drag from either the first or last node. Or click on either node to add straight segments.

Experimenting with the natural pen tool

The natural pen tool, which resides on the pencil tool flyout menu, is designed to create closed paths that look like curves. (The natural pen tool is the Version 7 twist on the former PowerLine command, found in the

Effects menu in Version 6.) You can set the tool to work in several different ways; to establish settings for the tool, double-click on the tool icon to display the Options dialog box. Here are your choices:

✔ Select Fixed Width to draw curves that are one width along their entire length. Set the width by changing the Maximum Width value.

✔ The Pressure option enables you to vary the width of the curve as you draw. If you use a pressure-sensitive pen and drawing tablet, the curve width varies depending on the pressure you apply to your pen. If you draw using the mouse, you can change the width of the curve by pressing the up- and down-arrow keys. With this option, the Maximum Width value determines how thick the curve can become.

✔ Select Calligraphy to create curves that resemble those you can create with a calligraphy pen. The width of the curve changes based on the direction of the curve. The Angle value controls the angle of the pen "nib" — changing the value is like changing the angle at which you hold a regular calligraphy pen against the paper's surface.

✔ The Presets option enables you to choose from a variety of preset line types. Select the line type you want from the pop-up menu that appears after you turn on the Presets radio button. As you draw the curve, CorelDraw displays what appears to be a standard line, but after you release the mouse button, the program creates the curve according to the line type option you selected.

Figure 5-6 shows samples of curves created using the four different tool options and then filled with black.

As you drag with the natural pen tool, CorelDraw displays what appears to be a simple line. But after you release the mouse button to complete your drag, the curve turns into a closed path. You can't draw an open path with the natural pen tool.

The controls in the Options dialog box are also available on the Property Bar when you select the natural pen tool, as labeled in Figure 5-6.

Nodes as You Never Knew Them

As discussed earlier in this chapter, it's no big deal if you don't draw your paths correctly right off the bat. Even the best and most knowledgeable CorelDraw artists spend a significant portion of their time editing and generally rehashing paths with that tool of tools, the shape tool. You can move nodes, change the curvature of segments, add and delete nodes, close open paths, open closed ones, and otherwise change a haphazard scrawl into a gracefully sinuous line or shape.

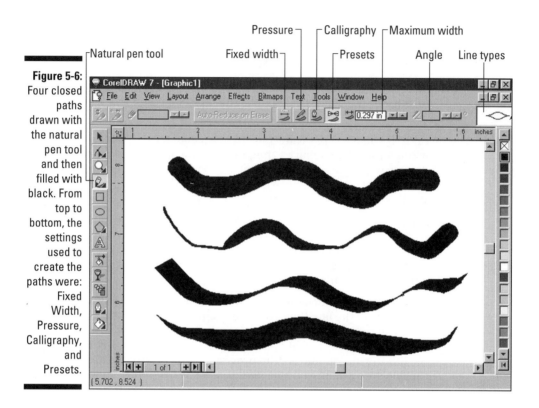

Figure 5-6: Four closed paths drawn with the natural pen tool and then filled with black. From top to bottom, the settings used to create the paths were: Fixed Width, Pressure, Calligraphy, and Presets.

Bringing nodes into view

To view and edit the nodes in a pencil or natural pen path, click on the shape tool in the toolbox — or press the shortcut key, F10 — and click on the path. The nodes in the path light up like candles on a Christma . . . er, tree of ambiguous religious origin. (We must always be PC when discussing PCs.)

Click on an individual node in the path to select the node. The node changes from hollow to black. You may also see one or two *control points* extending from the node, as shown in Figure 5-7. A purely decorative dotted line — called a *lever* — connects each control point to its node.

Control points determine the curvature of segments. And yet, unlike nodes, control points don't actually reside on the path; they float above the path like little satellites. In fact, a control point tugs on a segment in much the same way that the moon tugs at the ocean to create tides. Control points are like a detached ethereal force with special gravitational powers. But unlike the moon, a control point doesn't inspire people to howl or turn into werewolves when it's full.

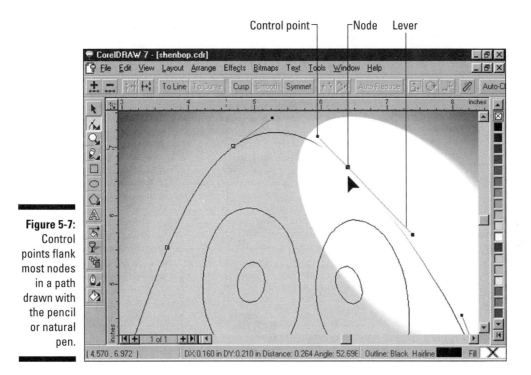

Control point — — Node   Lever

Figure 5-7:
Control
points flank
most nodes
in a path
drawn with
the pencil
or natural
pen.

Using nodes to reshape your drawing

The following items explain how to use the shape tool to select nodes and
control points as well as how to change the appearance of a path. I also
tossed in a few general notes and bits of wisdom to help you along your way.

- ✔ Click on a node to select it and display any control points associated
  with the node. A node can have no control points, or it can have as
  many as two, one for each segment.

- ✔ Segments need control points to bend them. If a segment is not bordered
  on either side by a control point, the segment is absolutely straight.

- ✔ Drag a node to move it and its control points. The segments that border
  the node stretch to keep up, as demonstrated in Figure 5-8. You can
  drag the node as far as you want; segments are infinitely stretchy.

- ✔ Drag a control point to bend and tug at the corresponding segment, as
  shown in Figure 5-9. Notice that the node remains stationary, anchoring
  the segment.

- ✔ If the node is a *smooth node,* the opposite control point also moves,
  bending its segment as in Figure 5-9. In a smooth node, the control
  points are locked into alignment to ensure a seamless arc. If the node is

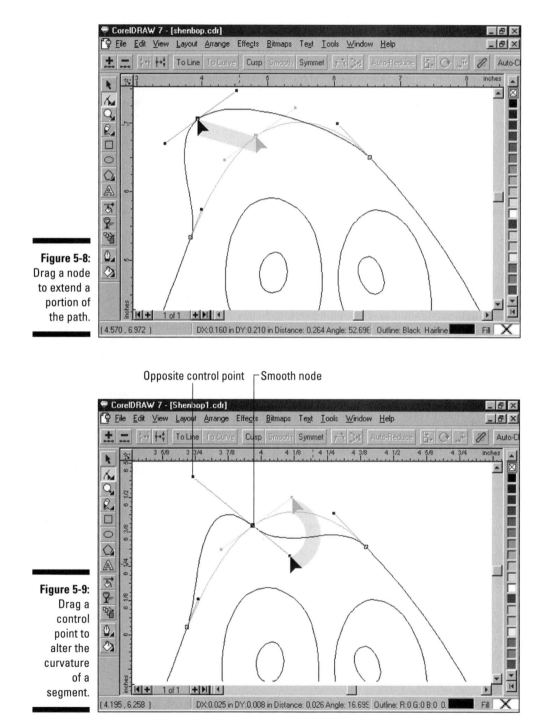

Figure 5-8:
Drag a node
to extend a
portion of
the path.

Figure 5-9:
Drag a
control
point to
alter the
curvature
of a
segment.

a *cusp node,* you can move one control point independently of its neighbor. The cusp node permits you to create corners in a path. (More on cusp and smooth nodes later in this chapter.)

✔ Are you still vague on the whole control point thing? Try envisioning a typical pencil path as a rubber band wrapped around a pattern of nails, as dramatized in Figure 5-10. The nails represent nodes in the path; the rubber band represents its segments. A sample control point appears as a round knob. The rubber band is stretched to give it tension and prevent it from crimping. A path in CorelDraw likewise bends evenly in the direction of its handle.

✔ If you don't want to deal with control points — believe me, everybody hates them — you can drag directly on a curved segment. The segment bends and stretches as shown in Figure 5-11.

✔ When you drag a segment bordered by a smooth node, the segment on the other side of that node bends and stretches with your drag. In Figure 5-11, both bordering nodes are smooth nodes, so three segments are affected.

✔ You can't drag a straight segment.

✔ To drag a node, control point, or segment in a strictly horizontal or vertical direction, press the Ctrl key while dragging.

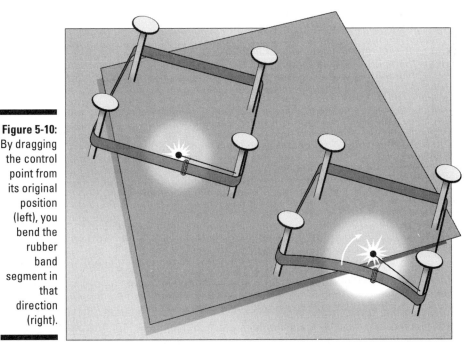

Figure 5-10: By dragging the control point from its original position (left), you bend the rubber band segment in that direction (right).

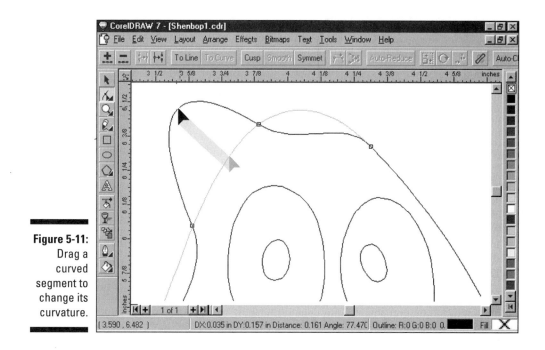

Figure 5-11:
Drag a
curved
segment to
change its
curvature.

- To select more than one node, click on the first node and Shift+click on each additional node. Then drag any one of them to move all the selected nodes at the same time.

- If the nodes that you want to select border each other, you can select them by dragging around them. As you drag, CorelDraw displays a dotted rectangle called a *marquee,* shown in Figure 5-12. Any nodes surrounded by the marquee become selected.

- Don't forget to press Ctrl+Z or choose Edit⇨Undo if you make a mistake. Or, if you prefer, you can press Alt+Backspace. No change is irreparable if you catch it in time.

Meet the Node Edit Thingies

To perform any other node-editing function, such as adding and deleting nodes, joining and splitting paths, and all the rest of that stuff, you use the trusty Node Edit roll-up or the Property Bar. To display the roll-up, featured in Figure 5-13, double-click on a node with the shape tool or press Ctrl+F10.

In earlier versions of CorelDraw, most buttons in the Node Edit roll-up were labeled with words. The meanings of the buttons weren't always crystal clear — To Line and Symmet took some figuring out — but at least you had

Marquee

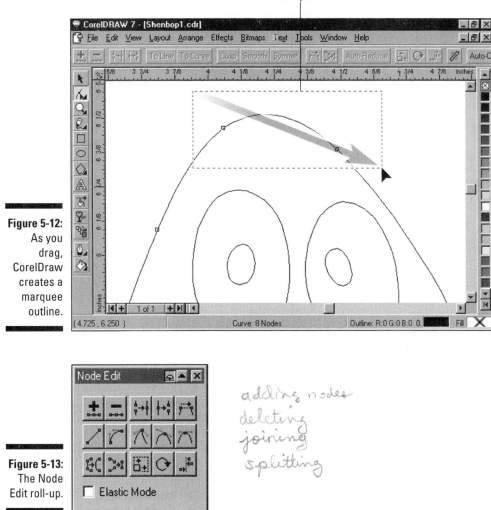

Figure 5-12:
As you
drag,
CorelDraw
creates a
marquee
outline.

Figure 5-13:
The Node
Edit roll-up.

adding nodes
deleting
joining
splitting

a clue. In CorelDraw 6 and 7, the labels are replaced by icons, few of which are the least bit recognizable.

Fortunately, Figure 5-14 includes helpful labels for each button. I also describe all the buttons in detail in the following three sections and show each button in the margin when discussing it. And in case that's still not enough, I refer to each button in the text by its order in the Node Edit roll-up. The fourth button in the first row, for example, is the one labeled *Break one node in two* in Figure 5-14. Hopefully, the result is a crystal-clear discussion of this wacky roll-up.

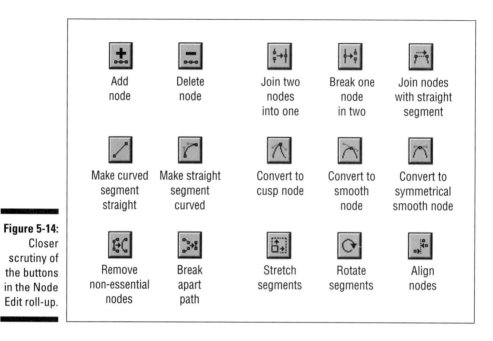

Figure 5-14:
Closer
scrutiny of
the buttons
in the Node
Edit roll-up.

Version 7 offers an additional avenue for working with nodes. When the shape tool is selected, the Property Bar offers the same controls as the Node Edit roll-up. Unfortunately, if you use the 640 x 480 pixel display setting for your monitor, some of the controls are hidden from view. To gain access to all the Property Bar controls, drag the Property Bar into the drawing area to create a free-floating palette of shape tool controls, as shown in Figure 5-15.

To further complicate things, some of the controls on the Property Bar use the old text labels discussed earlier instead of using the same icons as found in the Node Edit roll-up. Figure 5-15 sorts things out by labeling the Property Bar buttons that look different than those in the roll-up.

You may notice when looking at the Node Edit roll-up or Property Bar that many of the controls seem always to be dimmed. In many cases, the option is already in effect. For example, if you select a cusp node, the convert to cusp node button is dimmed because the cusp can't be any cuspier than it already is. Other times, the control isn't applicable. The align nodes button is dimmed if fewer than two nodes are selected, because you can't align a single node to itself. Well, I guess you could, but what's the point?

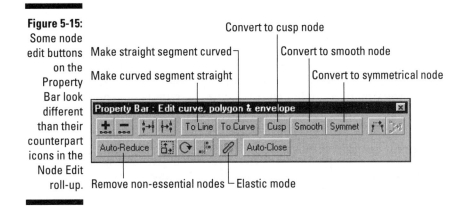

Figure 5-15: Some node edit buttons on the Property Bar look different than their counterpart icons in the Node Edit roll-up.

Your first tentative node edits

The following list explains how to use the most essential buttons in the Node Edit roll-up to add nodes, delete nodes, and otherwise wreak havoc on the whole node-oriented world. (You can also use the corresponding buttons on the Property Bar, labeled in Figure 5-15.) Get psyched, because this list is about the most exciting one you'll ever read — short of the phone book, of course.

✔ To add a node to a path, click on the spot in the segment where you want to add the node. A round sort of blob appears. It's not a node yet; it's sort of a fetal node. Then click on the add node button to bring the node into the world of the living.

✔ You can also add nodes to a shape drawn with the polygon tool. Try this: Draw a polygon, select the shape tool, and drag one of the side nodes to make the shape look like a star. Now click on any segment to create a fetal node and click on the add node button. Not only does a new node appear at the spot when you clicked, but additional nodes also spring up at symmetrical points around the shape. Drag any of these new nodes, and all the new nodes move in kind. It's very cool.

✔ To delete one or more nodes, select all the nodes you want to delete and then press Delete. Why bother with that delete node button when the Delete key is so much more convenient?

✔ If you can add nodes to a polygon, it stands to reason that you can select a polygon node and delete it as well.

✔ You can also press the + or – key on the numeric keypad to respectively add or delete a node. These keys work even when the Node Edit roll-up and Property Bar are hidden.

Excuse me for interrupting, but I feel it is my duty to come out in hearty support of the flagrant clear-cutting of nodes. The fact is, CorelDraw invariably assigns too many nodes to paths drawn with the pencil or natural pen. It's not unusual to see nodes stuck one right on top of the other, like procreating cockroaches, or wet Skittles, or some equally disgusting fluke of nature. As a rule, you need a cusp node for every corner in a path. You need a smooth node for every quarter-circle's worth of curve. Anything beyond that is garbage. Figure 5-16 shows a path before and after deleting extraneous nodes.

A little something you really don't need to know

When you draw with a real pencil, you smudge graphite directly onto the page. It's a cause and effect thing, a simple law of nature. When you draw with the pencil tool, CorelDraw tries to imitate nature using math. But because math isn't the natural state of anything except computer programs and high school calculus teachers, the line must undergo a conversion. You can tweak this conversion — thereby affecting how the pencil tool draws — using the good old Options dialog box.

Double-click on the pencil tool icon in the toolbox to display the Options dialog box. Three options have a bearing on pencil paths, as spotlighted in the figure. The first, Freehand Tracking, controls how accurately the path follows your drag. The second, Corner Threshold, helps prevent CorelDraw from following its natural tendency, which is to insert jagged corners in a path. And the third, Straight Line Threshold, determines the likelihood of straight segments in a path.

In all three cases, the values in the option boxes can vary between 1 and 10. If you develop uncanny dexterity with the mouse, you may want to test out lower values, which — taken to their extremes — encourage the path to follow every nuance and jiggle in

your drag. If your drags exhibit the kinds of tremors normally associated with small earthquakes, or if folks have a tendency to ask you why you write your letters in moving vehicles, and you actually write at a desk during the stillest of evenings while listening to endless loops of Pachelbel's *Canon in D minor,* you may want to avail yourself of higher values, which result in smoother and less jagged paths, however less accurate.

Figure 5-16:
Bad
Shenbop's
nodes are
many and
crowded.
Good
Shenbop's
nodes are
few and far
between.

Bad Shenbop   Good Shenbop

How to open, split, close, and join paths

In preceding sections of this chapter, I explain how to add and delete nodes, which amounts to super common stuff. If only for the sake of strip-mining paths, you may be engaging in these operations frequently. The next functions I describe are slightly less common, but rank right up there nonetheless. The following items describe how to open closed paths, close open ones, slice and dice paths without the aid of a Vegematic, and join them back together as effortlessly as a supercollider bonds kernels of creamed corn back onto the cob.

✔ To open a closed path, select a node that you want to split into two nodes and click on the break one node in two button. What was once one node is now two nodes. You can drag each node wherever you want.

✔ If the closed path was filled with a color before you opened it, the color disappears.

✔ To split an open path into two independent paths, select the node at which you want the split to occur and then click on the break one node in two button. The path is now split, but CorelDraw continues to think of the path as a single unit. To finalize the divorce, click on the break apart path button. Or you can choose Arrange⇨Break Apart or press Ctrl+K. The two paths can now go their separate ways.

✔ To close an open path, select both the first and last nodes in the line and then click on the join-two-nodes-into-one button. The two nodes are fused into one, and the line is transformed into a shape.

✔ The problem with the join two nodes into one button is that it moves the nodes when joining them. If you want the nodes to remain in place and connect them with a straight line, click on the join nodes with straight segment button.

Joining two completely independent open paths into a single longer path is a little tricky. Here's the step-by-step process:

1. **Select the arrow tool.**

   See, this operation is tricky already.

2. **Click on the first open path that you want to join.**

   Don't try this technique on a closed path. If you want to extend a shape, make sure that you first open the path by selecting a node with the shape tool and clicking on the break‑one‑node‑in‑two button.

3. **Shift+click on the second open path that you want to join.**

   Now both paths are selected.

4. **Press Ctrl+L.**

   Or choose Arrange➪Combine. CorelDraw now recognizes the paths as a single unit.

5. **Press F10 to select the shape tool.**

   Getting trickier.

6. **Click on the first or last node in one path and then Shift+click on the first or last node in the other path.**

   In other words, select the two nodes you want to fuse together.

7. **Click on the join two nodes into one button.**

   The two short lines are now one long line.

More ways to make a break

You can also use the knife tool or the eraser tool to break segments and paths apart. Both tools are available from the shape tool flyout menu, shown in Figure 5-17. Click and hold on the shape tool icon in the toolbox to display the flyout and then click on the tool you want to use.

✔ After selecting the knife tool, click on a path to cut it apart at that point. (If you miss the path, CorelDraw beeps at you in a highly irritating manner.) You can click on a node or on a segment. Either way, a precise incision is made.

Knife tool ⌐ Eraser tool

Figure 5-17:
Shenbop
sheds some
sweat in
anticipation
of being put
under the
knife.

✔ By default, the knife tool closes any path it touches, whether the path was originally open or closed. If you click on a line drawn with the pencil tool, for example, CorelDraw automatically adds new segments to the severed paths and creates two closed shapes. Makes about as much sense as cutting a piece of string and getting two pieces of dinnerware.

To instruct CorelDraw to stop this nonsensical closing of knifed paths, double-click on the knife tool icon in the toolbox. The Options dialog box comes to the rescue. Turn off the Automatically Close Object check box and press Enter.

✔ The eraser is another cutting tool, but rather than using it to cut at a point, you use it to slice a wide gash through the path. First, use the arrow or shape tool to select the path that you want to cut. Then select the eraser and drag across the path. The eraser tears through the path and splits it in pieces.

✔ The eraser tool leaves closed paths closed and leaves open paths open. What a sensible tool.

✔ To specify the width of the opening cut with the eraser tool, double-click on the eraser tool icon in the toolbox. You see the Options dialog box. Enter a new value into the Thickness option box — the default is $1/4$ inch — and press Enter. (Changing the value in the first option box on the left side of the Property Bar accomplishes the same thing.)

When you slice paths with the knife tool, CorelDraw breaks them into two separate objects. But when you use the eraser tool, the bits and pieces of the path remain combined into one path, which means that you can't drag the pieces separately with the arrow tool. To break the pieces apart, press Ctrl+K or click on the break apart path button (labeled back in Figure 5-14) as described in the preceding section.

Options you need once in a blue moon

I'm tempted to end my discussion of the node edit buttons right here. The buttons I didn't discuss earlier aren't entirely useless — not all of them, anyway — but they're more specialized. Most beginners and intermediates barely touch these buttons. But the buttons do serve a purpose, so you may as well know about them. The upcoming list explains the remaining options (in order from most useful to least useful) in the Node Edit roll-up and on the Property Bar.

You can apply the node edit buttons to nodes and segments drawn with the polygon tool as well as to paths drawn with the pencil and natural pen tools. Throughout, CorelDraw maintains the symmetry of the polygon, which can make for some pretty entertaining effects.

✔ The first button in the second row of the Node Edit roll-up straightens out a curved segment. (This button is labeled To Line on the Property Bar.) To use the option, click on a too-curly segment with the shape tool. A round node-wannabe appears to show that the segment is selected. Click on the button, and the segment becomes straight.

✔ The next button in the second row of the roll-up fulfills the opposite function. (The button is labeled To Curve on the Property Bar.) Click on a straight segment to get the round fetal node and then click on the button to make the segment a curve. Though the segment still looks straight, you can drag the segment with the shape tool to stretch it.

✔ To change a smooth node so that it represents a corner in the path, select the node and click on the convert to cusp node button (third button, second row of the Node Edit roll-up, labeled Cusp on the Property Bar). You can then move the control points of the cusp independently of each other.

✔ To change a corner to a smooth arc, select the node and click on the convert to smooth node button (fourth button, second row in the Node Edit roll-up, labeled Smooth on the Property Bar). CorelDraw locks the control points into alignment so that the transition between neighboring segments is seamless.

✔ The fifth button in the second row of the Node Edit roll-up (labeled Symmet on the Property Bar) locks the control points of a node into symmetrical alignment, so that the two levers are always the exact same length. The result is a variation on the smooth node that has almost no relevance in today's world. I think Peking Man used it in some sort of greet-the-dawn ritual, but nowadays, forget it.

✔ The first button in the last row of the Node Edit roll-up (labeled Auto-Reduce on the Property Bar) wins my vote as the least useful of the node edit options. This option is supposed to remove nonessential nodes automatically. But think about it for a moment. If CorelDraw were smart enough to eliminate extraneous nodes, it wouldn't have put them in there in the first place. You can rearrange some settings in the Options dialog box (as explained in the "A little something you really don't need to know" sidebar a few pages back) and get some remarkably disappointing results. But for the most part, this option doesn't do squat.

✔ The stretch and rotate segments buttons are marginally useful. You can scale, rotate, flip, and slant individual segments in a path by selecting two or more nodes, clicking on one of these buttons, and dragging a handle. To find out about the standard transformation functions, read Chapter 9. Then come back to these options and try them out.

✔ The align nodes button aligns multiple nodes in horizontal or vertical formation. You can find out more about alignment in Chapter 6.

Bouncy paths made of rubber

At the bottom of the Node Edit roll-up, you see an Elastic Mode check box (refer to Figure 5-13). The option also appears on the Property Bar, in the form of a button that looks like a rubber band (labeled back in Figure 5-15). In the past, I've been a tad unfair to this option, making libelous suggestions such as "People who know how to use Elastic Mode are dumber for it." That's true, of course, or I never would have said it. But still, being dumb can be fun, so I may as well tell you how the doggone thing works.

When Elastic Mode is on, CorelDraw moves, stretches, and rotates all selected nodes with respect to the node that is farthest away from the node you drag. Even if the far-away node is selected, it remains stationary, while the other nodes stretch away or toward it to varying degrees depending on their proximity. This option produces a spongy effect, as if the far-away node is snagged on a nail or something and the rest of the path is made of rubber.

If you turn off Elastic Mode, the selected nodes move, stretch, and rotate a consistent amount, without any rubbery stuff happening. This mode is less amusing, but it may be more useful if you're trying to achieve a specific effect. In other words, if you don't like the way a path is behaving, switch the Elastic Mode setting and see whether you like things any better.

How to Upgrade Simple Shapes

Much of this chapter is devoted to stuff that you can't do to rectangles, ovals, or symmetrical polygons. You can't move the nodes in a rectangle independently of each other, you can't adjust the curvature of a segment in an oval, and you can't drag a single node in a star independently of its symmetrical buddies.

"simple" shapes rectangle, oval, star

Not, that is, until you convert the simple shapes to free-form paths. To make the conversion, select the shape with the arrow tool and press Ctrl+Q. That's all there is to it. By pressing Ctrl+Q or choosing Arrange⇒Convert To Curves, you convert the selected shape to nodes, segments, and control points, just like a path drawn with the pencil tool. You can then edit the shape to any extent imaginable.

However, by converting a simple shape to a path, you ruin all semblance of the shape's original identity. You can no longer use the shape tool to add rounded corners to a rectangle, change an oval into a pie, or move all the points in a star together, as described in Chapter 4. The Convert To Curves command submits the shape to a state of complete anarchy.

Chapter 6
Celebrating Your Inner Draftsman

· ·

In This Chapter

▶ Disciplining yourself (and other sick ideas)

▶ Using the rulers

▶ Setting up the grid

▶ Positioning guidelines

▶ Creating guides at an angle

▶ Observing and modifying the status bar

▶ Moving objects incrementally and numerically

▶ Aligning and distributing objects

▶ Amassing objects into groups

▶ Changing the stacking order (whatever that is)

· ·

Do you have problems expressing your feelings? Are you critical of other people's driving? Do you insist on alphabetizing your guests at the dinner table? Do you distrust government, yet at the same time harbor suspicions that Ross Perot is a certifiable loony? If you said yes to any of these — except the bit about Perot — you may be a closet control freak. And you know what? That's okay. Because, doggone it, people like you. A couple of them, anyway. Well, maybe *like* is too strong of a word. Know, then. They scurry out of the room when you appear because, doggone it, people know you. Isn't that comforting?

This chapter is a call to arms for control freaks, a reawakening of the kindred spirit of the fussbudget. Together, we'll muck around with rulers, guidelines, and other tightly structured features in an attempt to precisely arrange minuscule details that no one notices but that fill you with a secret pride. I speak of the satisfaction that only a job well worried over can deliver.

I don't want to cure your perfectionism. I want you to rejoice in it! By the way, is that a grease stain on your shirt? Ha, made you look.

You Need to Be Disciplined

At least, that's what Madonna would tell you. But I'm talking about a different kind of discipline — namely, the kind provided by the big four CorelDraw control functions:

- ✔ *Rulers,* which appear along the top and left sides of the drawing area, serve as visual aids.

- ✔ The *grid* is a network of regularly spaced points that attract your cursor and prevent you from drawing slightly crooked lines and other haphazard stuff.

- ✔ You can set up custom *guidelines* between grid increments to align objects and generally ensure an orderly environment.

- ✔ The *status bar* shows you where your cursor is, the dimensions of shapes, the distance and angle of movements, and a bunch of other stuff I can't tell you right now or else I won't have anything to talk about in the status bar section.

Rulers with no power

Unlike grids and guidelines, rulers don't constrain your mouse movements or make you draw any better. In fact, they don't do much of anything. They just sit there. But rulers can be nice to have around because they show you how big objects are and how much distance is between them.

If you don't see any rulers on your screen, choose <u>V</u>iew⇨<u>R</u>ulers to display them. As shown in Figure 6-1, one horizontal ruler and one vertical ruler appear along the outskirts of the drawing area. With a little luck and a whole lot of divine intervention, the rulers may even inspire you to create something as fantastic as the Roman Colosseum (Collos.CDR), found on the third of the CorelDraw 7 CD-ROMs. (Open the Clipart folder, then the Travel folder, and then the Landmark folder to find the Collos.CDR file.)

Here's how to exploit the rulers to their fullest:

- ✔ The rulers monitor the location of the cursor using two *tracking lines.* Meanwhile, the status bar displays the numerical coordinates of the cursor, which correspond directly to the tracking lines. In Figure 6-1, for example, the horizontal tracking line appears just to the right of the $4^1/_4$ inch mark, whereas the status bar displays the coordinate 4.291.

- ✔ All measurements are made from the *zero point,* which is the point at which both rulers display the value 0. You can change the location of the zero point by dragging the ruler origin box, which appears at the

Rulers   Horizontal tracking line

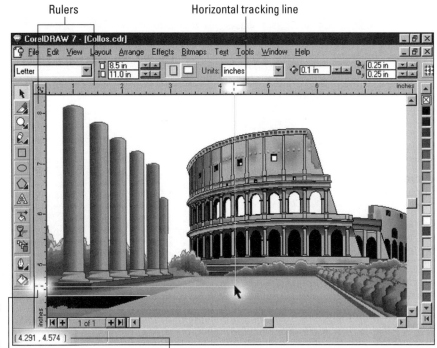

Figure 6-1:
Along with
the status
bar, the
rulers
monitor the
location of
the cursor.

Vertical tracking line Cursor coordinates

meeting of the two rulers, as shown in Figure 6-2. The point at which you release the mouse button becomes the new zero point (see Figure 6-3). To return the zero point to its original position, double-click on the ruler origin box.

✔ Rulers generally display units in inches. But if you prefer to work in a different measurement system, you can change one or both of the rulers. To quickly change the unit of measurement for both rulers, select an option from the Units pop-up menu on the Property Bar, labeled in Figure 6-3.

✔ You can also change the unit of measurement for each ruler by double-clicking on a ruler or choosing Layout⇨Grid and Ruler Setup to display the Grid & Ruler Setup dialog box shown in Figure 6-4. If the Same Units for Horizontal and Vertical Rulers check box is selected, changing the Horizontal value changes the unit of measurement for both rulers. If the check box is turned off, you can establish a different unit of measurement for each ruler.

✔ You can also display the Grid & Ruler Setup dialog box by right-clicking on the horizontal or vertical ruler and then selecting Grid and Ruler Setup from the resulting pop-up menu.

Ruler origin box

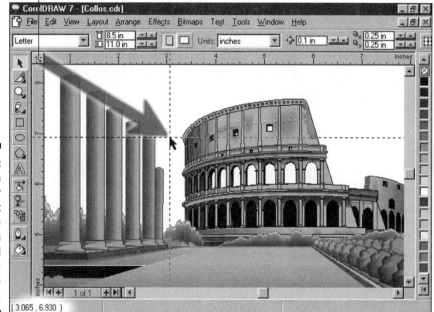

Figure 6-2:
Drag from
the ruler
origin box
to move the
point from
which all
measure-
ments are
made.

New zero points   Units pop-up menu

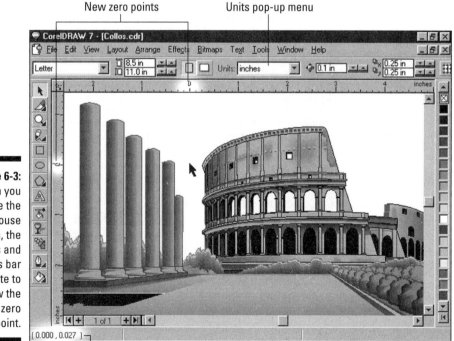

Figure 6-3:
When you
release the
mouse
button, the
rulers and
status bar
update to
show the
new zero
point.

New cursor coordinates

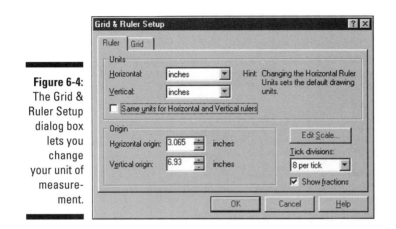

Figure 6-4:
The Grid &
Ruler Setup
dialog box
lets you
change
your unit of
measure-
ment.

✔ Use the Tick Divisions option in the Grid & Ruler Setup dialog box to specify how many division marks appear between each major ruler increment.

✔ If the Show Fractions check box is selected, CorelDraw displays ruler measurements in fractions rather than decimals (1$\frac{1}{2}$ rather than 1.5, for example).

✔ The status bar coordinates always correspond to the units on the horizontal ruler (displayed on the ruler's far right side).

✔ To get rid of the rulers, choose View➪Rulers.

Go downtown

Imagine a plan for the perfect city center, something like Washington D.C. Every block measures $\frac{1}{10}$ mile by $\frac{1}{10}$ mile. No block has an alley. Exactly 11 east-west streets and 11 north-south avenues subdivide every square mile into 100 square blocks.

Oh, sure, this layout is a little formal. It lacks spontaneity and joie de vivre, but you're supposed to be getting work done, not sitting around enjoying the scenery. Besides, your city plan is a grid, just like the one in CorelDraw.

In CorelDraw, the grid affects the placement of nodes, control points, handles, and so on. So although a free-form path can snake along wherever it pleases, its nodes are constrained to precise grid increments. The same goes for nodes in rectangles, ovals, and blocks of text. Here's how to set up a grid:

1. Right-click on one of the rulers and select Grid and Ruler Setup from the pop-up menu.

Or double-click on a ruler or choose Layout➪Grid and Ruler Setup. Any way you do it, you display the Grid & Ruler Setup dialog box.

2. **Click on the Grid tab to switch to the panel of options shown in Figure 6-5.**

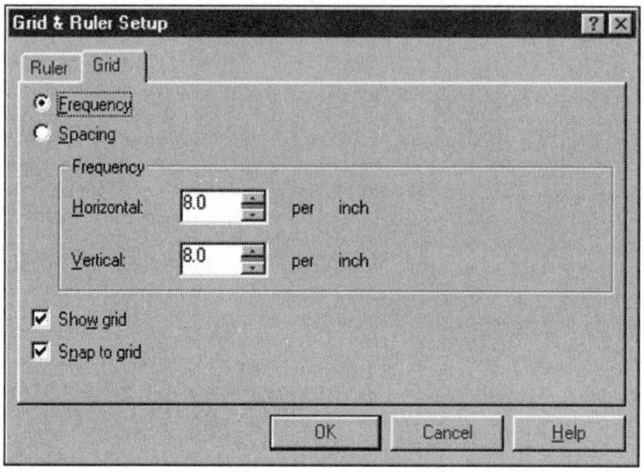

Figure 6-5:
Switch to
the Grid
panel to set
up the
wondrous
CorelDraw
grid.

Grid & Ruler Setup

Ruler | Grid

○ Frequency
○ Spacing

Frequency

Horizontal: 8.0   per   inch

Vertical: 8.0   per   inch

☑ Show grid
☑ Snap to grid

OK   Cancel   Help

3. **Define the distance between grid points by entering values into the Horizontal and Vertical option boxes.**

The option boxes work differently depending on whether you select the Frequency or the Spacing radio button. If you select Frequency, the Horizontal and Vertical values specify how many grid points you want per unit of measure. For example, if you enter a valuc of 8 and you're using inches as your unit of measure, you get 8 grid dots per inch.

If you choose the Spacing radio button, you can place grid dots at specific increments across the drawing area. If you enter Horizontal and Vertical values of .25, CorelDraw places the grid dots one-quarter inch apart. This setting would be the same as choosing the Frequency option and choosing a Horizontal value of 4; the Spacing and Frequency options just give you two different ways of looking at things.

The number of grid points per unit of measure is called the *grid frequency,* just in case you're even remotely interested.

4. **Select the Show Grid check box.**

This way, you can see the grid points on-screen.

5. **Select the Snap To Grid check box.**

When this option is active, nodes, control points, and handles gravitate — *snap* — to grid points. If you don't select this option, you can see the grid, but the grid has no effect on how you draw and edit paths. This step is the most important one. Don't skip it.

6. **Press Enter.**

Or click on OK. The grid points appear in the drawing area, as shown in Figure 6-6.

Grid point

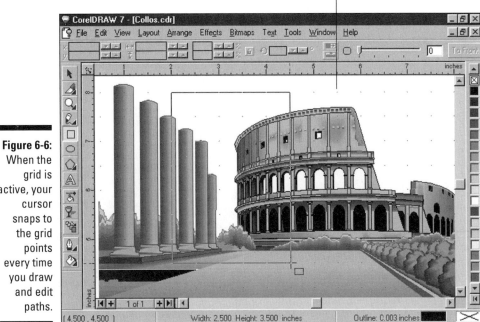

Figure 6-6:
When the grid is active, your cursor snaps to the grid points every time you draw and edit paths.

To try out the grid, draw a rectangle with the rectangle tool. Your cursor snaps from one grid point to the next, as in Figure 6-6. Incidentally, CorelDraw doesn't always display all grid points. Depending on the grid frequency and zoom ratio, the program may hide some grid points to cut down on-screen clutter (as is the case in the figure). But whether or not you can see a grid point, the snapping effect is still in force.

After you establish your grid, you can hide and display it by choosing View⇨Grid. You can turn its snapping powers on and off from the keyboard by pressing Ctrl+Y (or by choosing Layout⇨Snap To Grid).

You can also turn grid snapping on and off by selecting the arrow tool and then clicking on the Snap to Grid button on the Property Bar. (You can see the button at the far right end of the upcoming Figure 6-7.)

Let the lines be your guide

The CorelDraw grid is great for novices but loses some of its attraction after you become moderately familiar with the program. It's not that you outgrow the need for structure; that's always helpful. What you need is increased flexibility.

Guide handles Vertical guidelines Horizontal guidelines Snap to grid

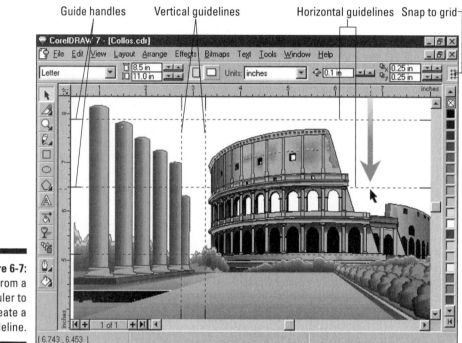

Figure 6-7:
Drag from a
ruler to
create a
guideline.

That's where *guidelines* come in. Like the rulers, guidelines are available in horizontal and vertical varieties. Like the grid, they exude gravitational force. But guidelines differ from rulers and the grid in that you can create as many guidelines as you like and place them wherever you want. You can even draw a guide at an angle.

✔ To create a guideline, drag from a ruler into the drawing area, as demonstrated in Figure 6-7.

✔ Don't see a guideline when you drag? Choose Layout⇨Guidelines Setup to display the Guidelines Setup dialog box, turn on the Show Guidelines check box, and press Enter.

✔ Dragging down from the horizontal ruler produces a horizontal guideline; dragging right from the vertical ruler produces — everybody sing! — a bright red lobster in a green varsity sweater.

Actually, that last action produces a vertical guideline. I just made up the bit about the lobster. No lobsters were made to wear sweaters in the making of this book. One was encouraged to wear a high-school letter jacket, but only briefly. The lobster is now in a recovery program (see Figure 6-8). In fact, he and I are in the same ward.

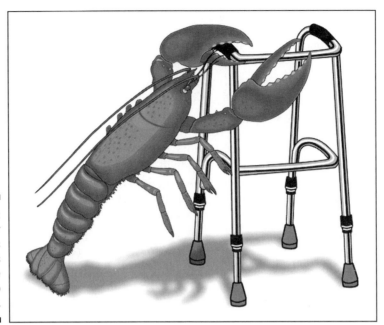

Figure 6-8:
The lobster demonstrates his indomitable will to survive.

✔ To move a guideline, place your cursor over the guideline until the cursor changes to a two-headed arrow. Then drag. Be careful, though. It's easy to accidentally drag an object when you're trying to drag a guideline (and vice versa).

✔ CorelDraw displays solid lines, called handles, at either end of every guide visible on-screen, as you can see in Figure 6-7. To change the angle of a guide, place your cursor over the handle until a curved, double-headed arrow appears. Then drag the handle to reset the angle of the guide. Notice that CorelDraw doesn't display the curved angle cursor until after you move the guide horizontally or vertically for the first time. Again, be careful to drag the guide handle and not some object in your drawing.

✔ To delete a horizontal or vertical guide, just drag it back to the ruler it came from. You can also delete an angled guide by dragging it off into a ruler, as long as you drag the guide itself and not a handle.

If you have trouble deleting an angled guide, use this method instead: Double-click the guide to display the Slanted tab of the Guidelines Setup dialog box. A list of angled guides appears on the left side of the dialog box, complete with techy coordinate data stating the location of some point on the guide and its angle. The guide on which you double-clicked should be selected. But you can also use the angle data to figure out which guide is which. Guides with positive angle values slant upward; guides with negative angles slant down. The larger the value, the more the guide slants. Select the guide that you want to delete and then click on the Delete button. If you got the right one, you can see it disappear in the background. Press Enter to make your change official. If you deleted the wrong guide, press Esc and try again.

✔ You can undo the movement of a guide — just as you can undo any other edit — by pressing Ctrl+Z (or Alt+Backspace).

✔ When the grid is active, the creation and movement of guidelines is constrained by the grid. There's no point to having a guideline that duplicates a line of grid points, so be sure to turn off the grid (Ctrl+Y) so that you can position guidelines freely.

✔ If guidelines and the grid are both active, a guideline takes precedence over either of its grid-point neighbors. The guideline has a stronger gravitational force, in other words.

✔ However, in order for guidelines to attract anything, they must be turned on. Choose Layout⇨Snap To Guidelines to turn the guideline attraction on and off.

✔ You can also turn guideline snapping on and off by clicking on the Snap to Guidelines button on the Property Bar, which is just to the right of the Snap to Grid button (labeled in Figure 6-7). The button is cut off the right side of the screen if you're using the 640-x-480 monitor display setting. For more information on this topic, see Chapter 2.

The status bar tells all

Like the rulers, the status bar doesn't affect the movement of your cursor. Instead, it provides information on everything you do in CorelDraw. By default, this information is organized into three report regions, as illustrated in Figure 6-9 and explained in the following list:

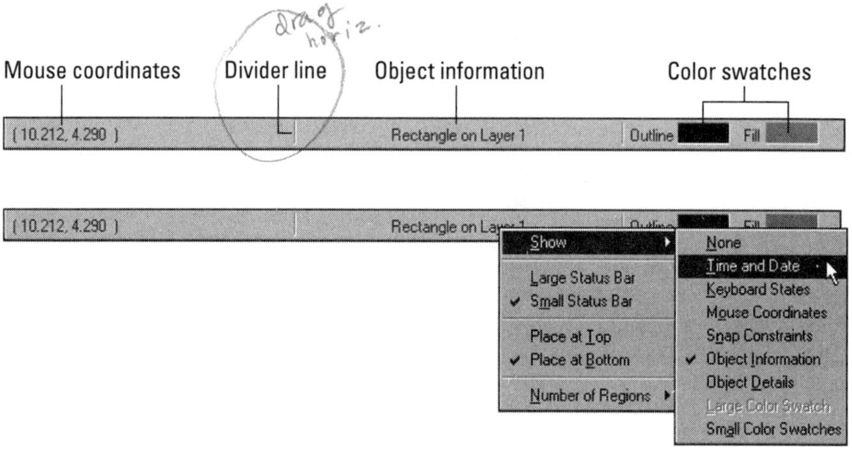

Mouse coordinates   Divider line   Object information   Color swatches

(10.212, 4.290)   Rectangle on Layer 1   Outline ▮▮ Fill ▮▮

(10.212, 4.290)   Rectangle on Layer 1   Outline   Fill

| Show ▶ |
| Large Status Bar |
| ✔ Small Status Bar |
| Place at Top |
| ✔ Place at Bottom |
| Number of Regions ▶ |

| None |
| Time and Date |
| Keyboard States |
| Mouse Coordinates |
| Snap Constraints |
| ✔ Object Information |
| Object Details |
| Large Color Swatch |
| Small Color Swatches |

Figure 6-9:
You can customize the status bar to suit your tastes.

- ✔ When your cursor is inside the drawing area, the left corner of the status bar lists the horizontal and vertical coordinates of the cursor.

- ✔ The middle report region varies depending on the operation. If an object is selected, the status bar lists what kind of object it is. When you perform certain operations to the object, the status bar reports on the operation. When you drag a node in a path, for example, the status bar tells you the distance and angle of the movement.

- ✔ The right corner of the status bar contains color swatches that indicate the outline and fill applied to the selected object. If the object is not filled or if an open path is selected, a big X appears in the fill swatch.

- ✔ The middle and right report regions appear only when an object is selected.

As shown in the lower example in Figure 6-9, you can customize the status bar by right-clicking on one of the report regions and selecting an option from the resulting pop-up menu. You can alter the status bar so that it shows different information or additional report regions. You can also allocate more room to one report region or another by dragging a divider line between two regions to the left or right.

- ✔ Change the kind of report that appears in a certain spot by right-clicking on that spot and selecting a different item from the Show submenu. For example, to display the time and date in the left corner of the status bar, right-click on the mouse coordinates and select Time and Date from the Show submenu. Experiment to see what other changes you can make.

- ✔ If you want to display additional status bar regions, right-click any-where on the status bar and choose an option from the Number of Regions submenu.

- ✔ If you have screen space to spare, you can right-click on the status bar and select the Large Status Bar option. With this option, the status bar is twice as tall as the one in Figure 6-9, enabling you to view more reports on the status bar.

- ✔ You can move the status bar to the top of the interface by choosing the Place at Top option. And naturally, Place at Bottom puts the status bar back at the bottom of the screen. (I know, I didn't have to tell you that, but my lawyer said I'd better.)

- ✔ You can also move the status bar to the top or bottom of the screen by simply dragging it with the regular old left mouse button.

Even something as useful as the status bar can get in your way. If you just want to get the thing out of your face, choose View⇨Status Bar. Choose the command again to redisplay the status bar.

Tell Your Objects Where They Can Go

In Chapters 4 and 5, I explain how to move whole objects and individual nodes by dragging them. But dragging isn't the only means for movement in CorelDraw. You can move objects in prescribed increments, by numerical distances, or in relation to each other.

Nudging with the arrow keys

The arrow keys put selected items in motion. Whether you want to move a few nodes selected with the shape tool or one or more objects selected with the arrow tool, pressing the arrow keys nudges the items incrementally in the direction of the arrow. If you press and hold the arrow key, the selected node or object scoots across the drawing area until you let up on the key.

By default, each arrow key moves a selected item $^1/_{10}$ inch. However, you can change this to any increment that you want. Just do either of the following:

- ✔ Press Ctrl+J or choose <u>T</u>ools⇨<u>O</u>ptions to display the Options dialog box and then click on the General tab. Enter a value in the Nudge option box, spotlighted in Figure 6-10. If necessary, select a different unit of measure from the Units pop-up menu.
- ✔ With the arrow tool selected but with no objects selected, change the Nudge value on the Property Bar, spotlighted and labeled in Figure 6-10.

If you press Ctrl plus an arrow key, you perform a Super Nudge, which simply means that you move the object a certain multiple of the regular Nudge value. For example, if the Nudge value is .10, and the Super Nudge value is 10, a Super Nudge moves your object .10 times 10, or a full inch. You can change the Super Nudge value in the Options dialog box.

If you press the plus key on the numeric keypad, along with an arrow key, you both clone and nudge the selected object. In other words, you make a copy of the object and nudge the copy.

Pressing Alt plus an arrow key scrolls your view of the drawing on-screen, as explained in Chapter 3.

Moving by the numbers

To move an object a specific numerical distance, you can use either the Property Bar or the Position roll-up, which you display by pressing Alt+F7 or choosing <u>A</u>rrange⇨<u>T</u>ransform⇨<u>P</u>osition.

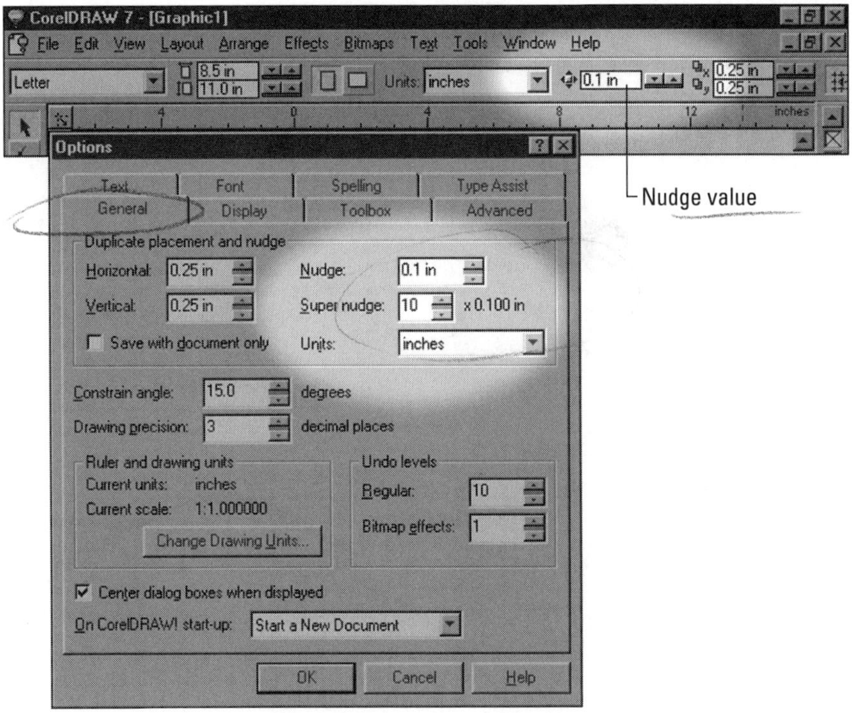

Nudge value

Figure 6-10:
The Nudge
value
determines
the
increment
by which an
arrow key
moves a
selected
object.

Moving an object using the Property Bar controls, labeled in Figure 6-11, is a cinch. Just select the object with the arrow tool and then adjust the X and Y values. You can either click on the up- and down-pointing arrows next to the X and Y option boxes, or double-click on an option box, enter a new value from the keyboard, and press Enter. The X value affects the object's horizontal position; the Y value affects its vertical position. Both values reflect the position of the center of the object.

The Position roll-up, also shown in Figure 6-11, is slightly more complicated but offers you more options than the Property Bar. You can approach moves made with this roll-up in two ways. You can either move the object relative to its current position or move it to an exact coordinate location.

To move the object a relative distance, enter values into the H and V option boxes. A negative value moves the object leftward or down. A positive value moves the object the other way.

Moving an object to a specific coordinate location is a little trickier:

1. Select the object you want to move by clicking it with the arrow tool.

2. Click on the Expand button (labeled in Figure 6-11).

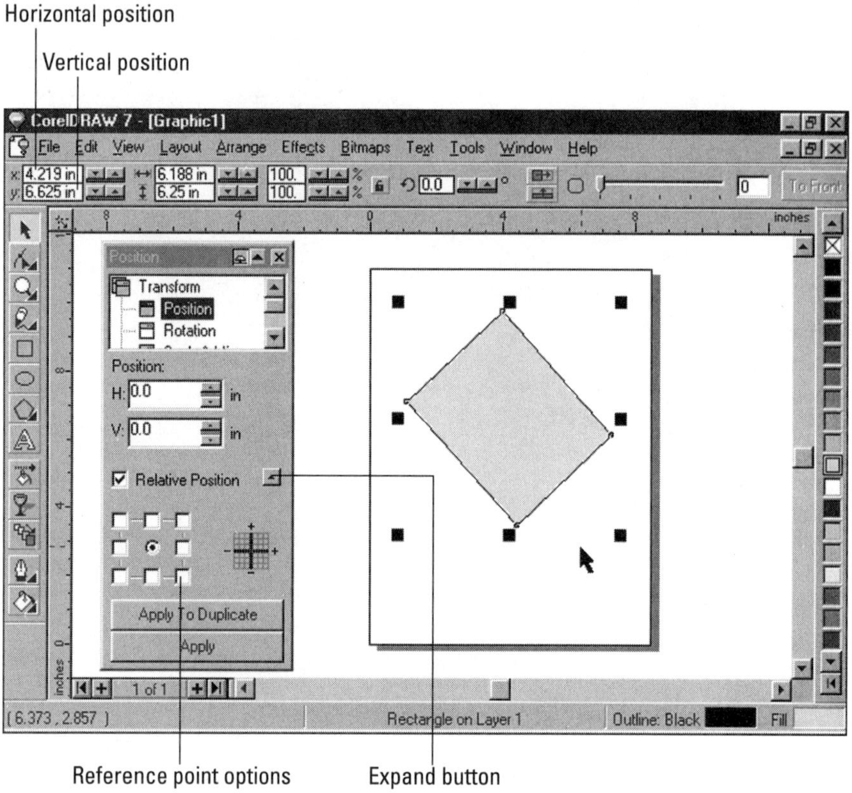

Horizontal position

Vertical position

Figure 6-11:
Use the
Position
roll-up
or the
Property
Bar
controls to
move an
object a
specific
distance or
to an exact
coordinate
location.

Reference point options   Expand button

The roll-up grows to reveal eight check boxes surrounding a single radio button. These boxes are the reference point options.

3. **Turn off the Relative Position check box.**

4. **Select a check box or radio button from the reference point options.**

The check boxes represent the eight handles around the selected object; the radio button represents the object's exact center. So, for example, if you want to position the upper-right corner of an object at a specific location, you would select the upper-right check box. You can select only one of these check boxes at a time.

5. **Enter the coordinates in the H and V option boxes.**

The coordinates are measured relative to the rulers' zero point. So, if you position the zero point smack dab in the middle of the page, all coordinates are measured from this center. By default, however, the zero point is at the lower-left corner of the page.

If you're not sure what coordinates you want to use — gee whiz, who would know such a thing? — deselect the object, move your cursor to the desired destination, and note the mouse coordinate values in the status bar. Then select the object again and enter those very values into the H and V option boxes.

6. Click on the Apply button.

Oh, by the way, the Apply To Duplicate button creates a copy of the object at the new location. Duplication is one of the subjects of Chapter 8.

The X and Y controls on the Property Bar always move the object a relative distance, regardless of whether the Relative Position option box in the Position roll-up is turned on or off.

Aligning and distributing objects

The last way to move objects is to shift them in relation to each other. Suppose that you drew a series of silhouetted soldiers marching down the road. But you were naturally so busy concentrating on making the shapes look like soldiers against an eerie twilight sky that you entirely neglected to line them up properly. So, instead of marching on a flat road, the soldiers bob up and down. To align their feet along a perfectly horizontal surface, you need to select all the soldier shapes and press Ctrl+A or choose Arrange⇨Align & Distribute.

In CorelDraw 6, choosing the Align & Distribute command displayed the Align & Distribute roll-up. In Version 7, the roll-up has been changed back to a dialog box, as in CorelDraw 5. Like the roll-up, the dialog box, as shown in Figure 6-12, enables you to evenly space objects using various alignment and distribution options.

You can also open the Align and Distribute dialog box by clicking on the Property Bar button labeled Align, which appears when you have multiple objects selected. Unfortunately, if you're using the 640-x-480 display setting for your monitor, you can't get to this button unless you drag the Property Bar into the drawing window as discussed in Chapter 2.

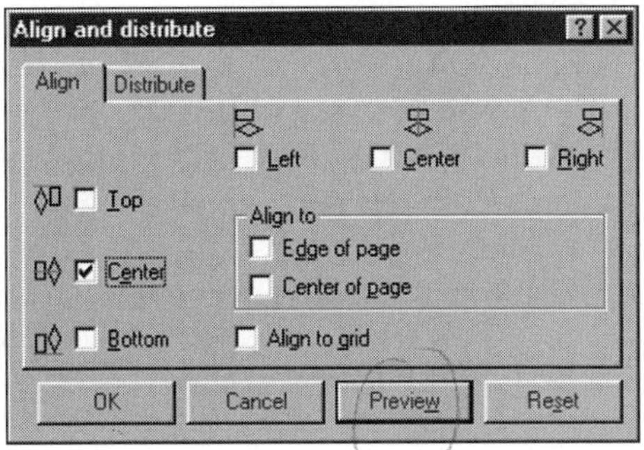

Figure 6-12:
Use these options to align selected objects.

To align two or more selected objects vertically, choose either the Top, Center, or Bottom check box from the Align tab of the dialog box. (The icon next to each check box gives you an idea of how the objects will be aligned.) To align objects horizontally, choose the Left, Center, or Right check box. You can select only one check box at a time from the vertical alignment options and one from the horizontal alignment options. To preview the effects of your choices, click on the Preview button.

CorelDraw aligns objects by their selection boxes, not by their actual edges. For example, if you choose left alignment, CorelDraw aligns the objects by the left selection boxes rather than their left borders.

Figure 6-13 shows each of the vertical alignment options applied in tandem with each of their horizontal counterparts. (The arrows surrounding the Center labels show whether the centering was horizontal or vertical.)

You don't have to select an option from both the vertical and horizontal groups. To align the soldiers along the road, for example, you would select the Bottom check box without selecting any horizontal option. In fact, you more often than not will select only one alignment option. Otherwise, the shapes bunch up onto each other, as in Figure 6-13.

If you like what you see when you click on the Preview button, press Enter or click on OK to make the alignment official. If you select one of the vertical or horizontal options but then change your mind, you can deselect it by clicking on it again. Click on the Reset button to move your shapes back to the positions they held before you opened the dialog box.

The following information falls into the gee-whiz-that-certainly-is-interesting camp of Align & Distribute dialog box knowledge.

- Select the Align to Grid check box to align objects to the nearest grid point according to the vertical and horizontal settings. For example, if you select the Top and Left alignment check boxes, CorelDraw aligns the top-left corner of each selected object to the nearest grid point.

- Select the Center of Page check box to align selected objects with respect to the center of the page. Select Edge of Page to align — that's right — to the edge of the page.

- If you don't select either check box, CorelDraw aligns the objects to the so-called *target object*. If you selected your objects by dragging around them with the arrow tool, the bottom object is the target object. If you Shift+clicked on the objects to select them, the last object you clicked is the target object.

- Use the options on the Distribute tab of the dialog box, shown in Figure 6-14, to evenly space three or more selected objects. You can choose one check box from the vertical distribution options (Top, Center, Spacing, and Bottom) and one check box from the horizontal distribution options (Left, Center, Spacing, Right).

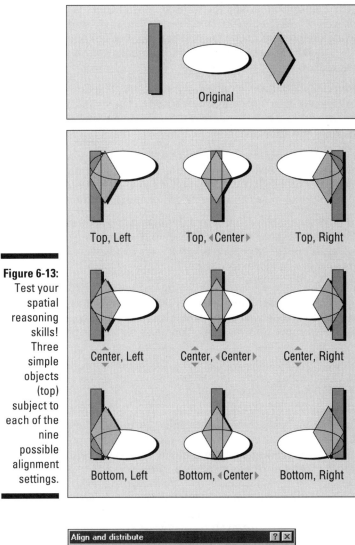

Figure 6-13:
Test your spatial reasoning skills! Three simple objects (top) subject to each of the nine possible alignment settings.

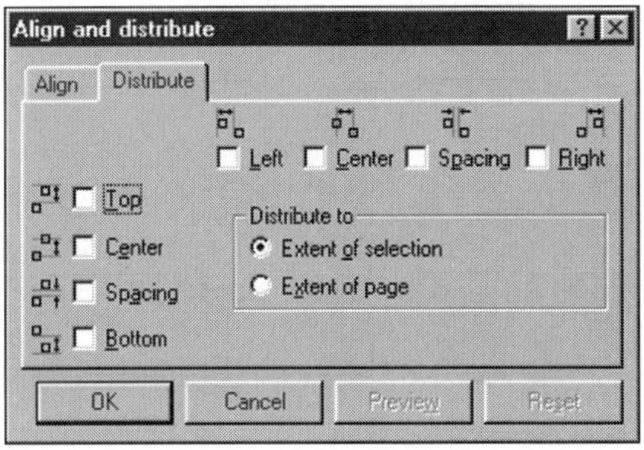

Figure 6-14:
The Version 7 distribution options.

✔ Choosing the Left option moves the objects so that there is equal spacing between the left edges of the objects. The Right and Center options space the objects according to their right edges and centers, respectively. And the Spacing option puts an equal amount of space between each object.

✔ The horizontal distribution options work similarly: The Top, Bottom, and Center options distribute objects relative to their top edges, bottom edges, and centers, respectively. The Spacing option places the objects an equal distance apart.

✔ Select the Extent of Selection option to keep the most extreme objects — leftmost and rightmost or topmost and bottommost — stationary and distribute the others between them. Or select Extent of Page to distribute the objects over the entire width or height of the page.

✔ As with the options on the Align tab of the dialog box, you can click on the Preview button to see how your chosen options move your objects. Click on Reset to put the objects back to the way they were before you started mucking around with things.

✔ The options in the Align & Distribute dialog box work only on whole objects. To align nodes selected with the shape tool, double-click on a node to display the Node Edit roll-up, and then click on the align button (see Chapter 5 for more information). You can't distribute nodes.

Gang Behavior

In the preceding section, I asked you to imagine drawing silhouetted soldiers. You probably thought that I was just trying to stimulate your interest by setting a mood. But there was a tiny modicum of method behind my madness, something that's normally entirely absent.

See, you can create a silhouette using a single shape. If, however, each of your soldiers comprise multiple shapes, the Align & Distribute options can present a problem. Figure 6-15, for example, shows a soldier made up of 18 shapes. When I aligned the shapes along the bottom, the soldier fell apart, as in the second example. This happened because CorelDraw aligns the bottom of each and every shape.

To prevent the problem, you need to make CorelDraw think of all 18 shapes as a single object. Select the shapes and press Ctrl+G or choose Arrange➪ Group. All shapes in the group now behave as a single, collective object.

✔ You can also group objects by clicking on the Property Bar button labeled Group.

Figure 6-15:
A soldier
crumbling
under
pressure is
a sad sight
indeed.

✔ To align many soldiers that are each composed of many shapes, group the shapes in each soldier — each soldier is its own group, in other words — and then apply options from the Align and Distribute dialog box, discussed in the preceding section.

✔ To bust the group up into its individual shapes, press Ctrl+U (Arrange⇨ Ungroup) or click on the Property Bar's Ungroup button.

✔ You can include groups in other groups. For example, after grouping the shapes in each soldier, you can group all the soldiers together. To restore the original shapes, press Ctrl+U to ungroup the first group. Then select each group within the previous group and ungroup it separately. Or, to ungroup all grouped objects, choose Arrange⇨ Ungroup All or click on the Ungroup All button on the Property Bar.

✔ Just because an object is part of a group doesn't mean that you can't edit it. To select a single object inside a group, Ctrl+click on it with the arrow tool. To adjust the location of nodes and the curvature of segments inside a grouped path, Ctrl+click on the path with the shape tool.

Your Drawing Is a Plate of Flapjacks

Once again, I speak metaphorically. Don't pour maple syrup on the screen or anything. Most condiments will damage your computer. My reference to flapjacks has to do with their typical arrangement in stacks. One flapjack is at the bottom of the stack, one flapjack is on top, and each additional flapjack is nestled between two others.

Now pretend that you're looking down at the flapjacks from an aerial view, like a hungry magpie. You can see the butter on the top, several flapjacks beneath that, and a plate at the bottom, as shown in Figure 6-16. Each flapjack obscures but does not completely hide the flapjack beneath it.

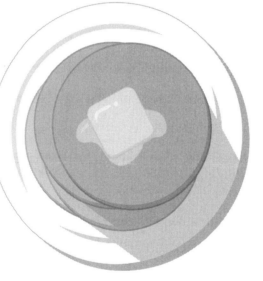

Figure 6-16:
Viewing objects in CorelDraw is like looking down on a stack of flapjacks, except not so appetizing.

CorelDraw stacks objects in the drawing area in a similar fashion. Every object in your drawing is in front of or behind some other object. When displaying your artwork on-screen or when printing it, CorelDraw starts at the back of the drawing and works its way to the front, one object at a time. If two objects overlap, the frontmost of the two partially obscures the other. This hierarchy of objects is called the *stacking order*.

If you left objects to their own devices, the first object you drew would appear at the back of the drawing, and the most recent object would appear at the front. But you can change the order of any object by selecting it and choosing one of the five commands in the Arrange➪Order submenu.

✔ Press Shift+Page Up (or choose the To Front command) to bring one or more selected objects to the front of the drawing. Figure 6-17 shows the result of selecting the face and hands of the soldier and pressing Shift+Page Up. Having moved to the front of the drawing, the face and hands conceal portions of the shapes that make up the cap and jacket. In the last example of the figure, I selected the jacket and pressed Shift+Page Up again, which covered up the buttons and medal.

Figure 6-17:
The results of moving the face and hands (middle) and the jacket (right) to the front of the drawing.

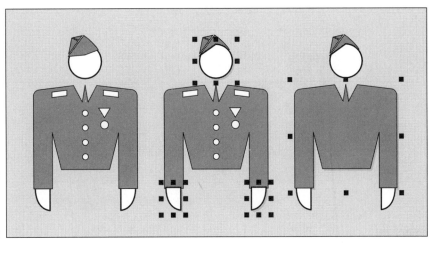

✔ Press Shift+Page Down (or choose the To Back command) to send one or more selected objects to the back of the drawing.

✔ You can also use the Property Bar buttons labeled To Front and To Back to send an object to the front or back of the stack. Sadly, these buttons are obscured when you use the 640-x-480 monitor display setting; if you want to access them, drag your Property Bar into the drawing window.

✔ Press Ctrl+Page Up to nudge selected objects one step forward. Or, if you prefer, choose the Forward One command.

✔ Press Ctrl+Page Down to nudge selected objects one step backward. If you like choosing things, choose the Back One command.

✔ As your drawing becomes more complicated, you'll want to spend less of your time choosing the commands I've discussed so far, and more time using the In Front Of and Behind commands. These commands enable you to stack objects relative to other objects. If you want to place a rat in front of some cheese, for example, select the rat, choose Arrange➪Order➪In Front Of, and then click on the cheese. To place the cheese and rat behind a cat, select rodent and supper, choose Arrange➪Order➪Behind, and click on the cat.

✔ Last but not least is the Arrange➪Order➪Reverse Order command, which reverses the stacking order of selected objects, as demonstrated in Figure 6-18. You must have at least two objects selected to use this command.

TIP

✔ You can access the entire Order submenu of commands — as well as Group and Ungroup for that matter — by right-clicking on a selected object. Right-clicking is an especially convenient way to choose the In Front Of and Behind commands.

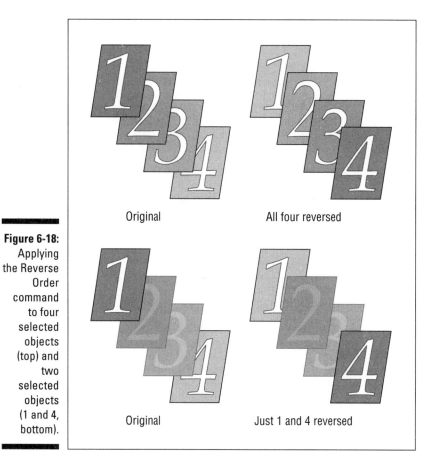

Figure 6-18:
Applying
the Reverse
Order
command
to four
selected
objects
(top) and
two
selected
objects
(1 and 4,
bottom).

Original   All four reversed

Original   Just 1 and 4 reversed

Chapter 7

Making Your Shapes
Look Like Something

•••

In This Chapter

▶ Filling closed paths with solid colors

▶ Selecting and creating colors

▶ Applying outlines to open and closed paths

▶ Using the Pen roll-up

▶ Assigning corners and caps

▶ Exploring advanced fill options

▶ Applying patterns and fills from the Scrapbook

▶ Searching and replacing fills and outlines

•••

It was an ashen morning on the blanched desert. The dusty earth was pallid, the cacti were bleached, even the lone coyote was a bit pasty. But worst of all, I myself was entirely without pigmentation.

Suddenly, I spied a flash of color on the horizon. Big, billowy clouds of green, yellow, and a sort of grapey purple were accompanied by the thunder of hoof-beats. It could mean only one thing — the Chromastazi tribe was on the warpath.

Moments later, the swiftest rider emerged from a poofy pink cloud and stopped dead in front of me. Fixing me with his terrible emerald gaze, he drew from his ceremonial paint bucket the biggest, most menacing brush I had ever seen. Before I had time to run, the warrior threw his weapon straight and true. The brush hit me full in the chest, releasing a fountain of colors. As I hit the ground, I couldn't help but notice the sky itself explode with fragments of deepest azure highlighted with streamers of pale blue and crystal white.

"Pale Shape is no more!" went up the savage cry.

Looking down at myself, I hardly believed my eyes. I was no longer transparent. Finally, I knew what it meant to be filled!

— excerpted from Memoirs of a Pioneerin' Path, 1875

Fills, Spills, and Chills

Wasn't that introduction thrilling? I remember when I first read that passage in art history class. The student body was so inspired, we spray-painted the professor.

Nowadays, what with these huge wads of computer experience under my belt, I can see the truth of the story. Regardless of how paths look or act, deep down inside, they want to be filled. It's in their nature. Take Figure 7-1, for example. On the left, you see an enhanced version of Shenbop, *primus inter amphibius*. Because all the lines and shapes are transparent, focusing on the picture is nearly impossible. The Shenbop on the right contains the exact same paths as its transparent neighbor, but the paths are filled, giving the frog form, substance, and a mighty big sense of self-worth.

Figure 7-1:
Several paths shown as they appear when transparent (left) and filled (right).

Fill 'er up with color

To fill the interior of a path with a solid color, do the following:

1. If a path that you want to fill is open, close it.

You can fill closed paths only. Open paths are inherently transparent. You can close a path by dragging from one node to the other with the pencil tool, as discussed in Chapter 5. Or select the two last nodes in the path and click on either of the join buttons in the Node Edit roll-up or Property Bar, as described in the "How to open, split, close, and join paths" section of Chapter 5.

2. **Select one or more shapes that you want to fill.**

   Using the arrow tool, draw a marquee around the shapes or click on one shape and then Shift+click on the others. To select all shapes in your drawing, double-click on the arrow tool icon in the toolbox.

3. **Click on a color in the color palette.**

   The *color palette* is the strip of color swatches on the right side of the CorelDraw window, shown in Figure 7-2. The palette contains too many colors to display all at once in a single strip, so you can click on the up and down scroll arrows on either side of the palette to display additional colors. Or, click on the left-pointing arrow at the bottom of the palette to display a pop-up menu that shows all the colors at once. (The next section explains more options for viewing the color palette.) Notice that as you move your cursor over a swatch in the color palette, the color name appears in the left corner of the status bar.

The first 11 options in the color palette are shades of gray, which are organized from black to white in 10 percent increments. For example, 50 percent black is midway between black and white. All 11 shades are ideal for creating black-and-white artwork.

You can also fill a closed path by selecting the arrow tool and then dragging a color swatch from the color palette onto the object you want to fill. The advantage of this method is that you don't have to select the object first. As you move your mouse, a little color swatch moves with your cursor. If you move the cursor over a shape that can be filled, the swatch appears as a solid square. Release the mouse button to fill the shape. If you see a hollow square, you're about to apply the color to the outline of the shape rather than to the interior.

If you see a little page icon next to the color swatch, your cursor isn't over any path. If you release the mouse button, you see a dialog box enabling you to set up default settings for your drawing tools. For more on this subject, see "I Don't Like the Default Setting!" later in this chapter.

In Version 6, you could also apply a white or black fill by selecting an icon in the fill tool flyout menu, shown in Figure 7-2. But as you can see from the figure, those icons have been stripped from the flyout in Version 7. Don't fret — you can simply apply a white or black fill using the Color palette.

Hasta la fillsta

If a shape has no fill, you can see through its interior to the objects behind it. To return a filled shape to absolute transparency, select the shape and click on the X icon at the end of the Color palette (labeled in Figure 7-2.) Or, if you like doing things the hard way, click on the fill tool icon to display the fill tool flyout menu, also shown in Figure 7-2, and click on the X button in the flyout.

No fill   Color palette

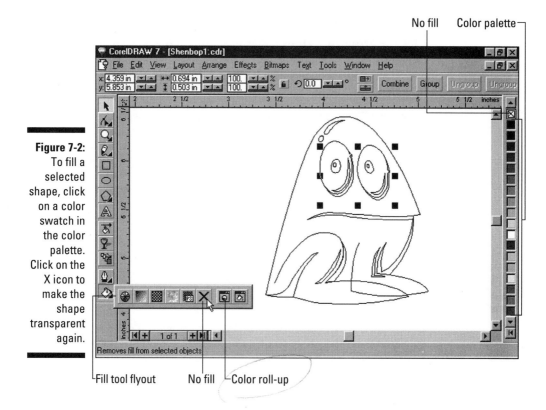

Figure 7-2:
To fill a
selected
shape, click
on a color
swatch in
the color
palette.
Click on the
X icon to
make the
shape
transparent
again.

Fill tool flyout   No fill   Color roll-up

Make the color palette your own

In this modern world, you don't have to accept the color palette that
CorelDraw gives you. You can change the colors, move the palette, and
change the way the color swatches look in a variety of terrific ways:

✔ To scroll to the beginning or end of the colors in the palette, right-click
in the gray area around the swatches — do not right-click on a color
itself — to display a pop-up menu of options. Then choose Move to
Start or Move to End.

✔ To change the colors in the palette to one of CorelDraw's other predefined collections of colors, choose View➪Color Palette. This command displays a submenu of possible palettes, many of which come
from professional color-production companies (if you can believe that
such crazy things exists).

✔ Do not select the Pantone Matching System Colors or Pantone
Hexachrome Colors option from the submenu unless you know exactly
what you're doing and you have a good reason for using spot colors. (If
you don't know what I'm talking about, steer clear of this option.)

✔ To hide the color palette and free up still more screen space, choose View⇨Color Palette⇨None.

✔ Drag a gray area around the color swatches to make the palette float independently of the interface. When the palette is floating, resize it by dragging any edge. In Figure 7-3, for example, I dragged the bottom of the palette to stretch it vertically, which reveals more color swatches.

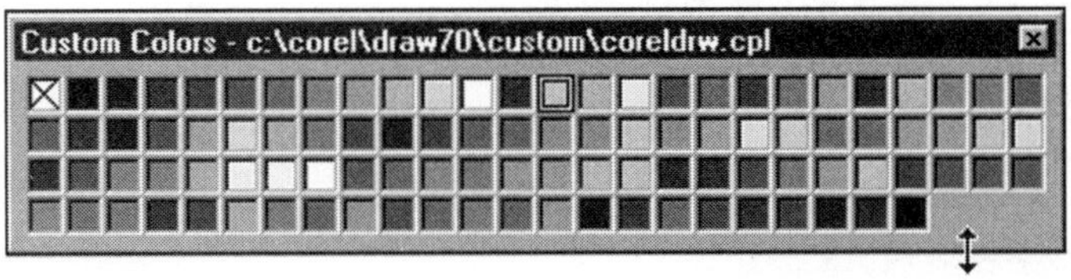

Figure 7-3:
Stretch the floating palette to see more colors at a time.

✔ To re-adhere the floating palette to the interface, double-click on the palette's title bar or in the gray area around the colors.

✔ Just because the palette isn't floating doesn't mean that you can't display more than one row of swatches at a time. To see two or more rows, right-click inside the gray area of the palette and select the Customize option from the resulting pop-up menu. Then enter the number of rows that you want to see into the Maximum Number of Rows While Docked option box, and press Enter.

Make New Colors in Your Spare Time

If you can't find the color that you want in the color palette, you can create a color of your own. But I warn you, the process is kind of messy. After selecting one or more shapes in your drawing, click on the fill tool and then click on the Color roll-up button (the second button from the right in the flyout menu, labeled back in Figure 7-2). Or, choose View⇨Roll-ups⇨Color. In response, the Color roll-up, shown in Figure 7-4, graces your screen. The following two sections tell you what you need to know about this roll-up.

Choosing a color model

Before you can understand how the Color roll-up works, you need to know a little bit about how colors work. In elementary school, you learned how to mix colors using the three primary colors — blue, red, and yellow. Commercial printers also make colors by mixing primaries, but the primaries are different.

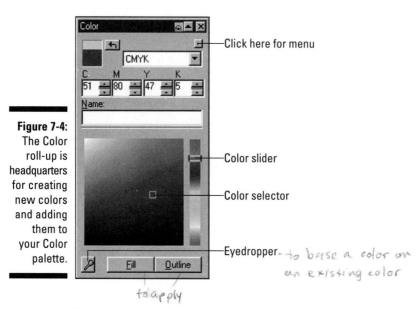

Figure 7-4:
The Color roll-up is headquarters for creating new colors and adding them to your Color palette.

Click here for menu

Color slider

Color selector

Eyedropper — to base a color on an existing color

to apply

✔ Instead of blue, printers use a light green-blue color called *cyan.*

✔ In place of red, they use *magenta,* a pinkish, purplish color.

✔ Instead of yellow . . . well, actually, they decided to hang on to yellow.

✔ And because the science of color printing is about as reliable as reading tea leaves, printers throw in black to ensure uniform dark colors.

So, there you have it — cyan, magenta, yellow, and black, better known as the CMYK (pronounced C-M-Y-K, not *simyk* or *kamick* or *ceemwac*) color model. (Incidentally, printers call black the *key* color, which is why its initial is K.) If you're printing your drawing, CMYK is the color model of choice.

If, on the other hand, you're creating a drawing for distribution on the World Wide Web or for a multimedia presentation — in other words, if your drawing will be viewed on a monitor or other television-like thing — you should use another color model, RGB. RGB stands for Red, Green, Blue, in case you were wondering. The RGB color model mixes red, green, and blue light to display colors on-screen.

Mixing up a batch of color

Because too much color theory has been known to drive people stark raving mad, the following items seek to disseminate the abstractions of CMYK and RGB into the real world of the Color roll-up.

The Color roll-up has changed significantly in Version 7, so if you're used to the old Color roll-up, pay attention:

✔ Before you do anything, select either the CMYK or RGB color model from the pop-up menu in the upper-right corner of the roll-up. Remember, use CMYK if you plan to print your drawing, and RGB if your drawing will be viewed on-screen.

✔ To create a color, you can enter values into the C, M, Y, and K option boxes (or R, G, and B option boxes, if you're using that color model). With CMYK, the higher the values, the darker the color gets. For example, 100 percent cyan plus 100 percent magenta makes deep blue. If you add either yellow or black, you darken the color. Try entering a few random values of your own to get a feel for things.

✔ When you use the RGB color model, things work a little differently. The higher the R, G, and B option box values, the lighter the colors. Entering 255 in all option boxes creates white; entering 0 in all the option boxes creates black.

✔ If you're working in the CMYK color model, you can create a custom shade of gray by entering 0 into the C, M, and Y option boxes and then entering the shade of gray in the K option box. For example, 0 percent is white, 25 percent is light gray, 50 percent is medium gray, 75 percent is dark gray, and 100 percent is black. In the RGB color model, enter the same number in all three option boxes to create gray. The higher the number, the lighter the shade of gray.

✔ Instead of entering values into the option boxes, you can also use the color slider and color selector box, labeled in Figure 7-4, to create a color. Drag the color slider to choose the approximate color you want. CorelDraw displays variations on that color in the preview box next to the slider. To refine your color selection, drag the color selector square. Notice that any changes made with the color selector or color slider are reflected by the values in the option boxes.

✔ If you want to base your new color on a color that already exists in your drawing, click on the eyedropper icon at the bottom of the roll-up. Then click on the color in your drawing. *eyedropper*

✔ To add the color to the color palette, enter a name into the Name option box. Then click on the little menu button above the pop-up menu (labeled *Click here for menu* in Figure 7-4) and select the Add Color to Palette option.

✔ To apply the color to the fill of one or more selected shapes, click on the Fill button. To apply the color to the outline of your selected shapes, click on the Outline button.

The Thick and Thin of Outlines

Although you can apply a fill to closed paths only, you can assign an outline to any path, open or closed. Furthermore, whereas a fill has one property — color — an outline has two properties: color and thickness. Known as the *line width,* or, in more gentrified circles, as the *line weight,* the thickness of an outline is traditionally measured in *points,* which are very tiny increments equal to $1/72$ inch. To put it in perspective, a penny is 4 points thick, a typical pencil is 20 points in diameter, a business card is 254 points wide, a football field measures 259,000 points from one end zone to the other, Mount Everest is 25 million points above sea level, light travels at 850 trillion points per second, presidential elections occur every leap year, and a dozen eggs contain 12 yolks.

Points are a useful system of measurement because most outlines tend to be pretty thin. Nearly all the figures in this book, for example, feature outlines with line widths of 1 point or thinner. Type is also typically measured in points.

Outlining a path

To assign an outline to a path — which is also referred to as *stroking the path* — follow these sweet and simple steps:

1. **Select the path or paths you want to outline.**

2. **Select a line width option.**

   Click on the pen tool — the one that looks like a pen nib — to display a flyout menu of six preset outline options. The last six options in the flyout, labeled in Figure 7-5, control the thickness of the outline.

   Note that when you pause your cursor over the pen tool icon, the little pop-up label says that the tool is called the outline tool. CorelDraw refers to the tool sometimes as the outline tool and sometimes as the pen tool (oops). Because the icon looks like a pen and, more important, because the roll-up for controlling the tool is called the Pen roll-up, I refer to this tool as the pen tool. And unlike Corel, I call the tool the same thing all the time. I'm just fussy about things like that, I guess.

   If a path drawn with the pencil or natural pen tool is selected, a pop-up menu offering preset line widths appears on the far right end of the Property Bar. The menu also appears for shapes that were converted to curves, as discussed in Chapter 5. If you use the 640-x-480 display setting for your monitor, though, you have to drag the Property Bar into the drawing area to access the pop-up menu.

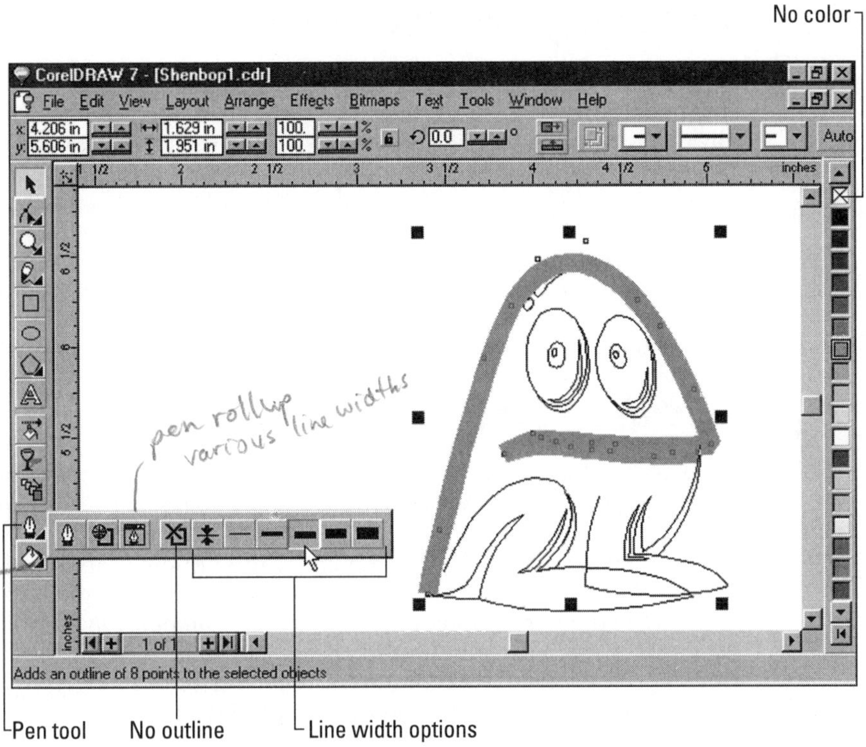

Figure 7-5: Click on the pen tool, and a flyout menu of outline options appears.

3. **Select a color for the outline.**

   Just right-click on a color in the color palette.

   You can no longer select a black or white outline from the pen tool flyout menu.

You can also change the outline color by dragging a swatch from the color palette. A little color swatch appears next to your cursor as you drag. When you see the swatch change to a hollow square, you know that you're over the area of the path that can accept the outline color. Release the mouse button to apply the color.

For a more sure-fire way to change the outline color, Alt+drag the color swatch from the palette. Now you can drop the color swatch anywhere on the shape to change the outline.

To define a custom color for your outline, use the Color roll-up as described earlier in this chapter. To display the roll-up, choose View⇨Roll-ups⇨Color or click on the Color roll-up icon in the fill tool flyout. You can no longer access the Color roll-up from the pen tool flyout as you previously could.

Removing the outline

To remove the outline of a path, select the path and right-click on the No Color button — which looks like an X — at the end of the Color palette. Or, click on the No Outline button in the pen tool flyout, labeled in Figure 7-5.

Generally speaking, you want to delete the outline of only a filled shape. If you delete the outline from a transparent shape or open path, you make it entirely invisible and run the risk of losing the path. (By the way, you can usually find a lost path by choosing View➪Wireframe to switch to wireframe view.)

Avoiding embarrassing line widths

Shown in Figure 7-6, the pen tool flyout menu offers access to several predefined line widths and also to the more functional Pen roll-up.

Each time you draw a line, the first line width option — appropriately labeled *Ridiculously thin* in Figure 7-6 — is in force. This option generally assigns the thinnest outline that your printer can possibly print. On drawings printed on laser printers and cheaper models, the outline looks okay. But on professional-level typesetters, it can result in a nearly invisible outline that doesn't stand a chance of reproducing.

Figure 7-6:
The pen tool flyout menu provides predefined line widths and the Pen roll-up.

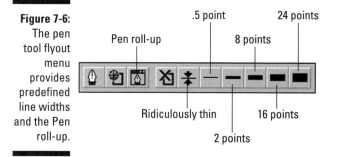

Now, I know that some of you can't imagine that you'll ever in a billion years typeset your artwork. But you may as well prepare your drawings for any event, no matter how remote you think it is. After all, you might go and win one of those Corel $1 million art contests, only to have your drawing professionally printed with ridiculously thin lines. Imagine having to describe the artwork to your grandma with her failing eyesight. "Lordy Lu," she'll cry softly, "if only you had used nice, hefty lines instead of these meager things!" Way to break an old woman's heart.

Figure 7-7 demonstrates three line weight options from the pen tool flyout menu applied to Shenbop, resulting in a story much like the one about the three bears. The first example, which shows the CorelDraw default outline, is too thin. The last example is too fat. Only the middle example qualifies as acceptable.

Figure 7-7:
Shenbop hates the predefined line weights in the Pen tool flyout and is highly embarrassed to appear in this figure.

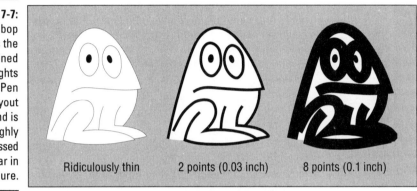

Ridiculously thin   2 points (0.03 inch)   8 points (0.1 inch)

Setting better line widths

To access other line widths, select the Pen roll-up icon (labeled in Figure 7-6) to display the Pen roll-up shown in Figure 7-8. Alternatively, you can press Shift+F7 to display the roll-up. The Pen roll-up offers several options for changing the outline of a selected path:

Figure 7-8:
Use the Pen roll-up to change outline attributes.

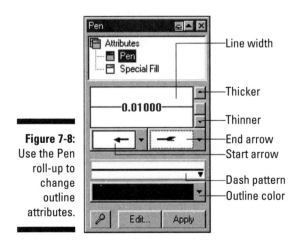

✔ Click on the scroll arrows on the right side of the roll-up (labeled Thicker and Thinner in Figure 7-8) to increase or decrease the line width in $1/100$-inch increments. The area to the left of the scroll arrows displays the line width in inches.

 ✔ If the line width is 0.003 inch (0.2 point) or thinner, a cross fills the line width area, as in Figure 7-9. The cross is an indication that your outline is too thin and may not reproduce well.

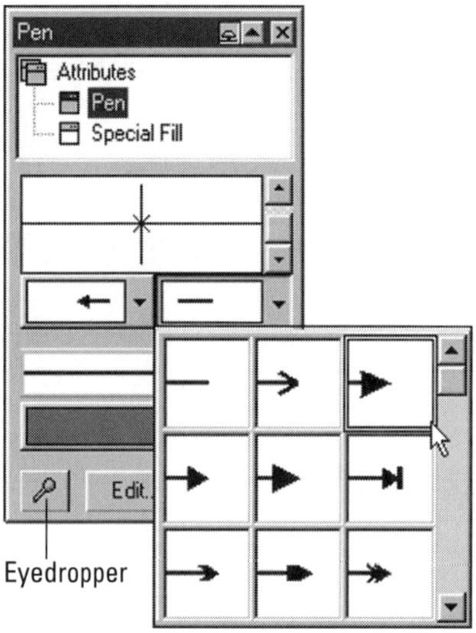

Figure 7-9:
You can select from a whole slew of arrowhead shapes.

Eyedropper

also in Property bar

 ✔ To change the line width display from inches to points, click on the Edit button. The Outline Pen dialog box appears. Select the Points option from the Width pop-up menu. Then press Enter. From now on, clicking on a scroll arrow changes the line width in 0.7-point increments.

 ✔ Click on the Start Arrow or End Arrow button (both labeled in Figure 7-8) to display a pop-up menu of arrowhead options, shown in Figure 7-9. Use the scroll bar on the right side of the menu to access different arrowheads that can appear at the beginning or end of an open path. (Arrowheads have no effect on closed paths.)

 The left pop-up menu of arrowhead options establishes the arrowhead setting for the beginning of the path. The right pop-up menu controls the setting for the end of the path.

 ✔ Click on the Dash Pattern button (just below the arrows) to display a pop-up menu of dotted line patterns that you can assign to an open or closed path.

 ✔ Click on the Outline Color button to select a color for the outline.

✔ Click on the Apply button to apply the settings in the Pen roll-up to the selected paths in the drawing area.

✔ If a path drawn with the pencil or natural pen tool (or a simple shape that's been converted to curves) is selected, you can also access the Start Arrow, End Arrow, and Dash Pattern pop-up menus from the Property Bar.

Lifting an outline from an existing shape

You can copy the outline from one path and assign it to another. Say that you have two paths, Path A and Path B, known to their friends as Fred and Wilma. To make the outline of Fred look just like the one assigned to Wilma, do the following:

1. **Select Fred and click on the eyedropper icon in the bottom of the Pen roll-up.**

   The icon is labeled in Figure 7-9 in case you need help. When you click on the icon, your cursor changes to a big, fat arrow.

2. **Click on Wilma.**

   The Pen roll-up now displays the outline settings assigned to Wilma.

3. **Click on the Apply button.**

   Now Fred and Wilma look the same, like so many other married couples.

Alternatively, you can select Fred and then choose the Edit⇨Copy Properties From command. This command displays a dialog box from which you can choose which of Wilma's attributes you want to copy onto Fred. After you click on OK, click on Wilma.

Creating custom line widths

As mentioned earlier in this chapter, the Pen tool flyout menu offers six mostly useless line widths. The Pen roll-up offers an unlimited number of line widths, but only in 0.7-point increments. If you want to access an even wider array of line widths without any weird or artificial constraints, click on the Edit button in the Pen roll-up or press F12, which brings up the Outline Pen dialog box, shown in Figure 7-10.

✔ To set the line width, enter a value into the Width option box. The value is accurate to $1/1000$ point. That's mighty accurate.

✔ Don't go any thinner than 0.3 point or 0.004 inch. Line widths between 0.3 and 0.5 point are called *hairlines,* because they're about as thick as hairs, depending on how thick your hair is, of course.

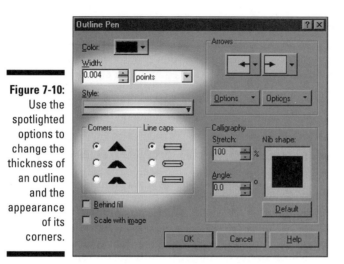

Figure 7-10:
Use the
spotlighted
options to
change the
thickness of
an outline
and the
appearance
of its
corners.

Personally, my hair rivals cotton candy for fortitude and manageability. Hairlines look like Corinthian columns compared with my hair. I suspect that my hair wouldn't reproduce well. If I were to photocopy my face, I'd doubtless look like a cue ball.

✔ To change the system of measurement, select an option from the pop-up menu to the right of the Width option box. In addition to inches and points, the pop-up menu offers millimeters and ciceros for you worldly, metric types and picas for you newspaper and magazine types.

Changing line corners and caps

In addition to the Width option, the Outline Pen dialog box offers a couple of other interesting items, which also have the spotlight trained on them in Figure 7-10. These options fall into two categories: corners and caps.

Corners determine the appearance of the outline at corner nodes in the path:

✔ First among the Corners radio buttons, the miter corner option ensures sharp corners in a path.

✔ When curved segments slope into each other to form a very acute angle, miter corners can produce weird spikes that make your path look like it's covered with occasional bits of barbed wire. You may go your entire life without encountering this phenomenon, but if you do, select one of the other two Corners radio buttons.

✔ The second radio button is the round corner option, which rounds off the corners in a path. I use this option a lot. It takes the edge off things. A real ice-breaker at parties.

✔ The last option is called the bevel corner because it lops off the end of the corner as if, well, as if the corner were beveled.

Figure 7-11 shows the three corners applied to mere fragments of Shenbop. The outlines appear black. I've represented the paths with thin white outlines so that you can see how path and outline relate. Pretty insightful, huh?

The Line Caps options determine how the outline looks at the beginning and end of an open path, as illustrated in Figure 7-11. Caps have no effect on closed paths.

✔ The first Line Caps option is the butt cap. Honest, that's what it's called. I'm not trying to be offensive to inspire controversy and sell books. Which is funny, because that's exactly what I was trying to do when I wanted to use the word *butt* in my last book and the editors wouldn't let me. Now they have to. After all, I didn't come up with the term *butt cap*. Huge corporate forces beyond my control decided on it. I'm sure that they giggled while they were at it. They must have been feeling very immature that day.

✔ Just in case you want to know what the butt (snigger) cap option does, it ends the outline exactly at the end of the path. The outline butts up (hee hee) against the node, as it were. (Guffaw!)

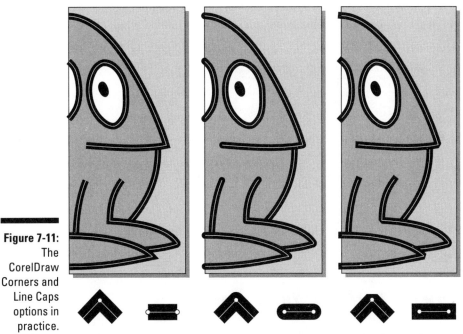

Figure 7-11: The CorelDraw Corners and Line Caps options in practice.

Miter / Butt   Round / Round   Bevel / Square

✔ The round cap does just that. It extends the outline slightly beyond the end of the path and rounds it off. Like the round corner, the round cap option gives a path a friendlier appearance.

✔ Like the round cap, the square cap extends the outline past the end of a path. But instead of rounding off the outline, it caps it off with a square. This option is useful when you want to prevent a gap between an open path and an adjacent object or when you're simply too embarrassed to use a butt cap, as when drawing for mixed company.

I Don't Like the Default Setting!

If you select an option from the fill or pen tool flyout menu or click on the Apply button in the Pen roll-up when no object is selected, CorelDraw assumes that you want to change the default attributes that will affect each and every future path you create. To confirm this assumption, the program displays the rather verbose message shown in Figure 7-12. You also see the message if you drag a color from the Color palette and drop it into an empty area of your drawing window, as discussed earlier, in the section "Fills, Spills, and Chills." If you don't want to change the defaults, click on the Cancel button. If you want to change the default settings for all future paths, select the Graphic check box and press Enter.

The Artistic Text and Paragraph Text options affect varieties of CorelDraw text discussed in Chapter 10.

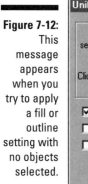

Figure 7-12:
This message appears when you try to apply a fill or outline setting with no objects selected.

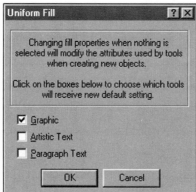

Fill and Outline Join Forces

If you gave much attention to the fully filled and outlined version of Shenbop shown back in Figure 7-1, you may have noticed something unusual about it. Namely, a few open paths, such as the main body and the legs, appear to be filled. The interior of the body covers up the background behind it; the interior of the front leg covers part of the body; and the interior of the hind leg covers part of the front leg. There's no question about it; these paths are filled.

Well, how can that be? After all, I specifically said that you can't fill an open path. I wouldn't lie — my mom won't let me — so there must be something else going on.

The answer is that the body and the legs are actually made up of two paths apiece: one closed path with a fill and no outline, and one open path with an outline and no fill. Figure 7-13 demonstrates how this works. The filled version of the path is stacked behind the outlined version of the path, creating what appears to the uninitiated viewer to be a single shape.

Just for laughs, Figure 7-14 shows the order of the paths used to create Shenbop from back to front. The paths that make up the body and legs are either strictly filled or strictly outlined, providing optimum flexibility. In fact, only the whites of the eyes are both filled and outlined. All outlines are 1 point thick. If you're really in the mood for trivia, you'll be interested to know that the border around the figure is 0.5 point thick.

Figure 7-13: A filled, closed path (first column) behind an outlined open path (second column) creates the appearance of a filled, open path (last column).

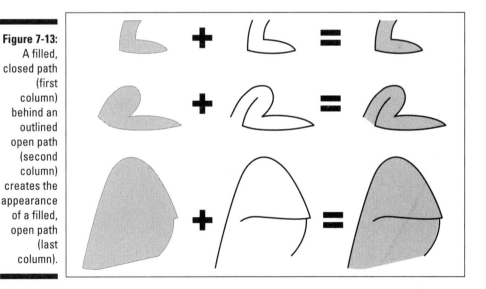

The World of Wacky Fills

In CorelDraw, you can fill your shapes with more than simple, solid colors. You can apply a variety of special fill effects, including gradations, geometrics, and textures to a shape. You access these special fill effects through three avenues: the Special Fill roll-up, the Scrapbook, and the interactive fill tool.

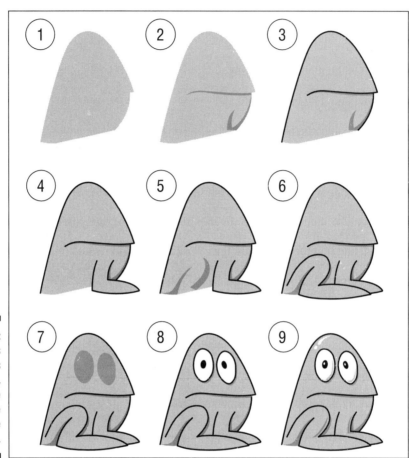

Figure 7-14:
The bits and pieces of Shenbop, from the back of the heap to the front.

Using the Special Fill roll-up

Taken to their extremes, the fill effects available through the Special Fill roll-up can prove extremely complicated. So rather than delve into tiresome lists of options and obscure settings, I introduce each effect in the most basic terms possible.

To display the Special Fill roll-up, click on the fill tool icon to display the flyout menu, and then click on the Special Fill roll-up button, labeled in Figure 7-15. As indicated in Figure 7-15, each of the buttons along the top of the Special Fill roll-up duplicates a function in the fill tool flyout menu. The only exception is the last button, PostScript fill, which is available in the fill tool flyout menu but is missing from the Special Fill roll-up. The difference between the flyout icons and the roll-out icons is that the options in the roll-up are easier to use.

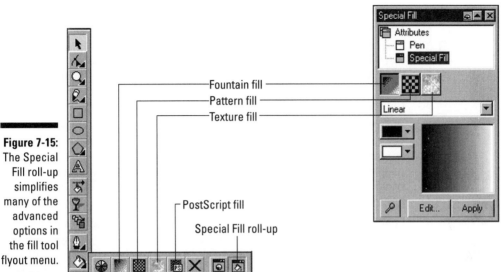

Fountain fill ——————
Pattern fill —————
Texture fill ————

PostScript fill
Special Fill roll-up

Figure 7-15:
The Special
Fill roll-up
simplifies
many of the
advanced
options in
the fill tool
flyout menu.

The following list explains how to use the options in the Special Fill roll-up, which has been slightly revised in Version 7. As with any fill effect, all the options are applicable exclusively to closed paths.

✔ Click on the Fountain fill button to fill a selected path with a gradual blend from one color to another, called a gradation or, in some circles, a gradient. Select a beginning color and an end color from the pop-up menus to the left of the gradient preview in the roll-up. Or, to lift a color from your drawing, click on the eyedropper icon and then click on the color in your drawing.

Specify the type of gradation by choosing an option from the pop-up menu directly above the gradient preview. You can create a linear, radial, square, or conical gradation. Finally, drag inside the gradient preview in the top portion of the roll-up to determine the direction or center of the gradation. To apply the gradation to the selected shape, click on the Apply button.

✔ The Pattern fill button allows you to fill a shape with a pattern of pixels. You can apply a two-color pattern, a full-color pattern, or a bitmap pattern. Select the type of pattern you want to apply from the pop-up menu above the preview box. If you select the 2-color pattern option, select the two colors from the pop-up menus next to the preview box. To change the pattern, click on the down-pointing arrow on the right side of the preview box to display a pop-up menu of options.

Similarly, the Full Color and Bitmap pattern options let you fill a shape with predefined full-color and bitmap patterns. Click on the down-pointing arrow on the right side of the preview box to display a pop-up menu of pattern choices. After you choose a pattern, click on Apply to fill your shape with the pattern.

✔ Textures are naturalistic patterns such as clouds and raindrops. To change the texture, first select a category of textures from the pop-up menu just above the texture preview. Then click on the down-pointing arrow on the right side of the preview, select the desired texture from the resulting pop-up menu, and click on Apply or press Enter.

✔ The PostScript fill button appears only in the fill tool flyout menu. It lets you apply special object-oriented patterns that are described in complex PostScript code. When you click on the PostScript fill button, a dialog box filled with a list of patterns appears. Select a pattern and click on the Preview Fill check box to see what it looks like. Press Enter after you find a fill you like.

PostScript fills have a couple of strikes against them, however. First, PostScript fill patterns don't look right on-screen. After you apply them, you don't see the pattern itself inside your shape; instead, CorelDraw just displays the repeating letters *PS*. Second, you can print PostScript fills only with high-end laser printers and typesetters that understand PostScript.

Dragging special fills from the Scrapbook

You can also apply fills to your shapes by using the Scrapbook roll-up, new to Version 7. To display the Scrapbook, choose View➪Roll-Ups➪Tools➪ Scrapbook. Or, if you have your toolbar displayed, click on the Scrapbook roll-up icon, labeled in Figure 7-16.

To browse through the available fills and outlines, click on the Fills and Outlines tab of the Scrapbook, labeled in Figure 7-16. The special fills and outlines are stored in the Favorite Fills and Outlines folder, which should appear in the folder pop-up menu automatically. Double-click on the folders that appear in the scrolling list to display thumbnail views of the available fills and outlines. To close a folder and display the contents of the folder that contains it, click on the Up One Level button, just as in the Open dialog box discussed in Chapter 3.

When you find a fill or outline you like, just drag it from the Scrapbook to your shape, as shown in the top rectangle in Figure 7-16. CorelDraw fills your shape with the effect, as shown in the lower rectangle in the figure. You don't have to select the shape before you drag. To apply the fill or outline to two or more shapes, select the shapes and then drag from the Scrapbook.

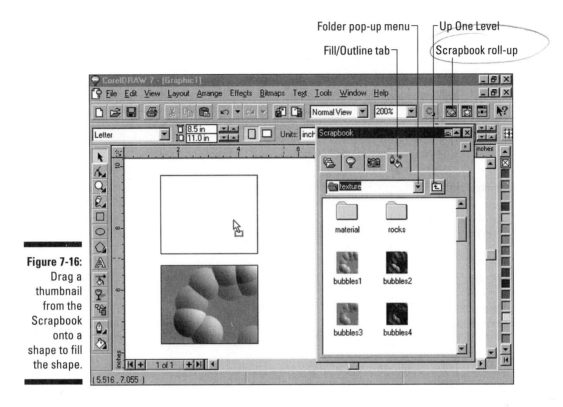

Figure 7-16:
Drag a
thumbnail
from the
Scrapbook
onto a
shape to fill
the shape.

Filling on the fly

The new interactive fill tool, labeled in Figure 7-17, gives you yet another way to fill shapes. When this tool is selected, the Property Bar displays controls that let you choose a fill type (pattern, fountain, texture, and so on) as well as many of the same controls found in the Special Fill roll-up, discussed earlier, in the section "Using the Special Fill roll-up."

By far, the biggest advantage of the interactive fill tool is that it lets you gain precise control over the position, direction, and colors of a fountain (gradient) fill. If one of CorelDraw's preset gradients doesn't suit your needs, you can create a custom gradient using the interactive fill tool. You can also edit existing gradients using the tool.

To create a custom gradient using the interactive fill tool, first select a shape. Then select the interactive fill tool, choose Fountain Fill from the Fill Type menu on the Property Bar (labeled in Figure 7-17), and drag across your shape. The point at which you begin dragging sets the beginning of the gradient; the point at which you release your mouse button sets the end of the gradient. A fill arrow appears to show you the direction of the gradient, as shown in Figure 7-17.

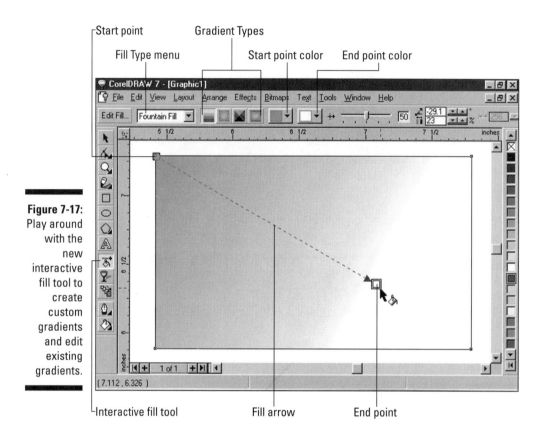

Figure 7-17:
Play around with the new interactive fill tool to create custom gradients and edit existing gradients.

After you create a gradient, you can manipulate it as follows:

- To change the gradient type, click on one of the Gradient Type icons on the Property Bar. As in the Special Fill roll-up, you can choose from a linear, radial, conical, or square gradient.

- To change the color used for the beginning of the gradient, choose a color from the start point color pop-up menu on the Property Bar. Or, drag a swatch from the Color palette onto the small box at the beginning of the gradient (labeled *start point* in Figure 7-17). To change the other color in the gradient, drag a color to the end point box or choose a color from the end point color pop-up menu. If you drag a color from the color palette, make sure that the cursor arrow, and not the color swatch, is on the start or end point box as you release the mouse button — don't try to put the swatch itself onto the start or end box.

- For even more fun, you can add additional colors to your gradient. Just drag a color from the Color palette to any spot along the dotted Fill arrow line. When you see a small plus sign next to your cursor, release the mouse button to set the color in place. A hollow square appears at the point where you added the color. If you decide you don't like your addition, right-click inside that hollow square. You can add as many colors to your gradient as you want.

✔ To change the position of colors in the gradient, drag the boxes along the Fill arrow line. For example, drag the end point box to move the end of the gradient.

✔ You can also change the angle of the gradient by dragging the end point box. To constrain the angle to 15-degree intervals, press Ctrl as you drag.

✔ If you click outside your gradient or switch to another tool, the Fill arrow disappears. But you can redisplay it and edit your gradient at any time by clicking on the shape with the interactive fill tool.

✔ You can also edit a preset gradient that you applied by using the Special Fill roll-up or the Scrapbook. Just click on the gradient with the interactive fill tool.

✔ If you want to save a custom gradient so that you can use it again, select the shape and then click on the Fountain fill button in the fill tool flyout. When the Fountain Fill dialog box appears, enter a name for your gradient in the Presets box at the bottom of the dialog box, click on the plus sign next to the Presets box, and press Enter. When you want to apply the gradient to a new shape, select the shape, open the Fountain Fill dialog box, select the gradient from the Presets box, and press Enter.

✔ You can also store your gradient in the Scrapbook. Open the Scrapbook and open the folder where you want to store the gradient. (If the gradient gradient is a radial gradient, for example, open the Radial folder.) Then select the shape that has the gradient applied and drag it to the Fills and Outlines panel of the Scrapbook. To name the gradient, right-click on it in the Scrapbook and choose Rename. You can apply the gradient to a new shape by dragging the gradient from the Scrapbook, as discussed earlier in this chapter.

Save Time with Find and Replace

Version 7 adds one additional tool that you may find helpful for filling and outlining shapes. Using the Find and Replace command, Edit⇨Find and Replace⇨Replace Objects, you can automatically replace all occurrences of a fill or outline color with another color. You can also replace one outline width with another. This command can come in handy if you want to make wholesale design changes to a drawing — for example, to replace all your thin, black lines with fat, red ones.

When you choose the Replace Objects command, CorelDraw displays the Replace Wizard dialog box. If you want to replace a color, select the Replace a Color radio button and click on the Next button. You then see the second screen of the Replace Wizard dialog box, shown in Figure 7-18. Choose the color that you want to replace from the Find pop-up menu; choose the color

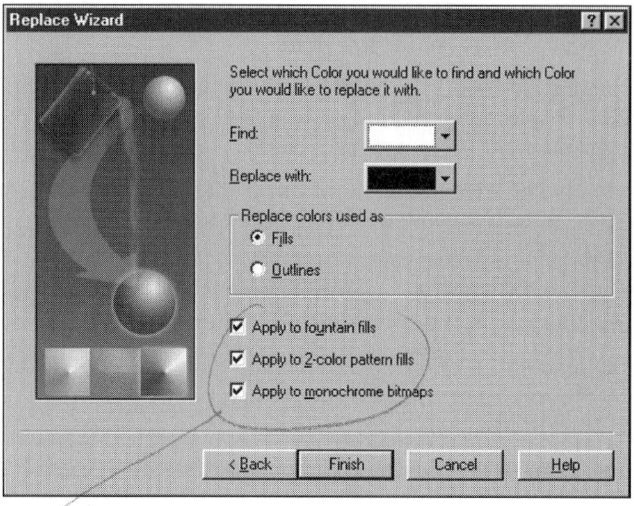

Figure 7-18:
The new
Replace
Wizard
makes it
easy to
replace all
occurrences
of a color or
line width
in your
drawing.

that you want to use instead from the Replace With pop-up menu. Select the Fills radio button to find and replace fills that match the color in the Find pop-up menu. Select the Outlines button to replace outlines that match the Find color.

The three check boxes at the bottom of the dialog box determine whether colors in fountain fills, two-color pattern fills, and monochrome (black and white) bitmap fills are replaced. If you don't want to replace colors in those fills, turn off the check boxes.

To replace an outline width, select the Replace Outline Pen Properties button in the first screen of the Replace Wizard dialog box and click on Next. (If you're currently looking at the color replacement screen of the wizard, you can return to the first screen by clicking on the Back button.) In the Find section of the resulting dialog box, enter the line width that you want to replace. Enter the new line width in the Replace section of the dialog box.

After you specify what you want to find and replace, click on Finish. CorelDraw displays a miniature Find and Replace toolbar and selects the first object that matches the criteria that you specified in the Replace Wizard dialog box. If you want to replace the color or outline for that object, click on Replace. To leave the object as is and skip to the next object, click on Find Next. Click on Find Previous to go back to the object that was previously selected. To select all objects and replace the color or line width for the entire batch, click on Replace All.

When CorelDraw makes its way through all the objects that match your find and replace request, it displays a dialog box telling you that the search mission is complete. Click on OK to get rid of the dialog box and then click on the Close button in the Find and Replace toolbar to remove the toolbar from your screen.

Chapter 8
The Fine Art of Cloning

In This Chapter

▶ The inside scoop on dinosaur maintenance

▶ How to use the Cut, Copy, and Paste commands

▶ Why I hate the Clipboard

▶ The Duplicate command and its relationship to grouping

▶ A look inside the mind of a true clone

▶ The newest rage in reproduction: drag and drop

*W*hat was the big deal with the movie *Jurassic Park?* Oh sure, lawyer-eating dinosaurs — obviously, I'm all for that. And if I were a poison-spitting Dilophosaurus, I can't imagine a tastier treat than a well-fed computer programmer. But the cloning bit, how hard can it be? CorelDraw has been able to clone things for years. You don't need any mosquito trapped in amber to clone in CorelDraw. You give me a Velociraptor, and I'll make as many duplicates as you like.

This chapter shares all my inside secrets on cloning so that you, too, can churn out as many duplicates of an object as you like. I also show you how to transfer your dinosaurs, er, objects, from one drawing to another.

Clipboard Mania: Cut, Copy, and Paste

One way to copy and transfer objects is to use the Windows 95 Clipboard. The Clipboard is a temporary storage tank for objects that you want to copy or move from one spot to another. Three Edit menu commands — Cut, Copy, and Paste — provide access to the Clipboard:

✔ The Cut command (Ctrl+X) removes all selected objects from your drawing and places them on the Clipboard. In doing so, the command replaces the Clipboard's previous contents. So if you cut Object A and then cut Object B, Object B knocks Object A off the Clipboard into electronic oblivion.

✔ The Copy command (Ctrl+C) makes a copy of all selected objects in your drawing and places the copy on the Clipboard. Like Cut, the Copy command replaces the Clipboard's previous contents.

✔ The Paste command (Ctrl+V) makes a copy of the contents of the Clipboard and places them in your drawing. Unlike Cut and Copy, the Paste command leaves the contents of the Clipboard unaltered. You can choose the Paste command as many times as you want to make copy after copy after copy.

Novices generally have problems remembering the keyboard equivalents for the Clipboard commands. Granted, Ctrl+C makes sense for Copy. Ctrl+X is a stretch, but it sort of brings to mind Cut. But where did Ctrl+V for Paste come from? The answer resides at the bottom-left corner of your keyboard. The keys are Z, X, C, and V. That's Undo (the first command in the Edit menu), Cut, Copy, and Paste. Then again, if you think of the Paste command as regurgitating the contents of the Clipboard, Ctrl+V takes on new meaning. Just trying to help.

Snap, crackle, paste

Here's an example of how you can use the Clipboard to duplicate an object:

1. Select one or more objects that you want to duplicate.

If you have a dinosaur handy, please select it now. (Incidentally, the drawing in Figure 8-1 comes from the file Tyranno2.CDR, found in the Prehist/Dinosaur folder on the third Corel CD-ROM.)

2. Choose Edit➪Copy or press Ctrl+C.

Figure 8-1 shows this step in progress. CorelDraw makes a copy of every selected object and places it on the Clipboard. This process sometimes takes a long time.

3. Toodle around.

Perform scads of operations. Work for hours and hours. Wait several weeks if you like. Time has no effect on the Clipboard. Just don't touch the Cut or Copy commands, don't exit CorelDraw or Windows 95, and don't turn off your computer.

4. Choose Edit➪Paste or press Ctrl+V.

Bazoing! (That's a sound effect, in case you didn't recognize it.) Corel-Draw makes a copy of the objects on the Clipboard and places them in the drawing area at the exact location where they appeared when you chose the Copy command. (If the Paste command is grayed out, by the way, the Clipboard is empty — go back to Step 2 and try again.)

If you don't change the location of the original objects before you choose Edit➪Paste, you won't notice any difference in your drawing,

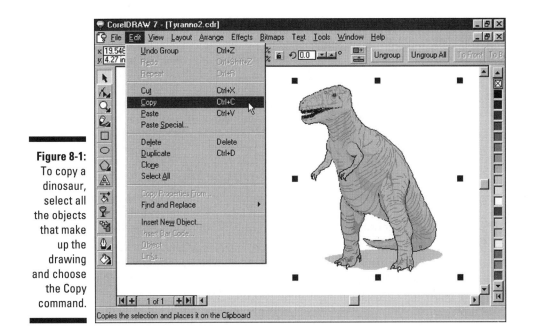

Figure 8-1:
To copy a
dinosaur,
select all
the objects
that make
up the
drawing
and choose
the Copy
command.

because the copied objects sit directly in front of the originals. Drag the
copied objects slightly off to the side to see that you do indeed have
two identical versions of your objects, as shown in Figure 8-2.

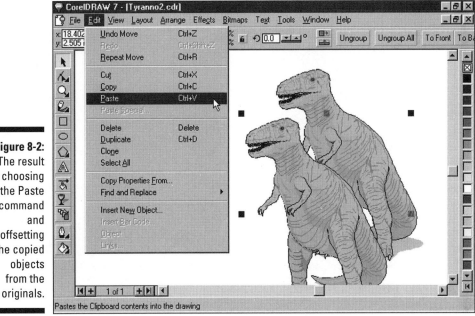

Figure 8-2:
The result
of choosing
the Paste
command
and
offsetting
the copied
objects
from the
originals.

A few little Clipboard facts

Here are a few random bits of information about the Clipboard to sock away for future use:

- The most common purpose for using the Clipboard is to cut or copy objects from one drawing and paste them into another. For example, to create Figure 8-3, I copied the tyrannosaur objects, opened the stegosaur drawing, and pasted the tyrannosaur. The two beasts should be great friends; they have so much in common. One is a tasty, crunchy dinosaur, and the other likes to snack on tasty, crunchy dinosaurs.

- The Clipboard isn't the only way to move objects from one drawing to another, though. You can drag and drop selected objects, as described in the section "Do the Drag and Drop," later in this chapter.

- If the current document contains more than one page — as discussed in Chapter 12 — you can use the Clipboard commands to transfer objects from one page to the next. If you plan on using the same object several times throughout your drawing, you may want to place a copy of the object on the pasteboard (that blank space that surrounds your drawing page). Objects on the pasteboard are available to you from all pages of your drawing.

- You can also cut, copy, and paste objects within a single-page drawing. But generally, duplicating the objects using the Duplicate or Clone command, as described later in this chapter, is easier.

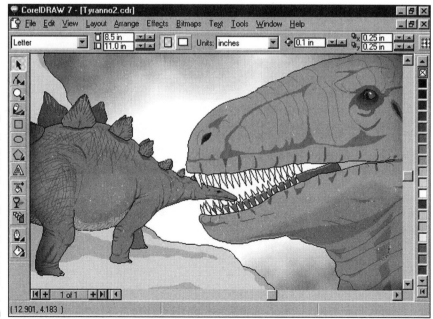

Figure 8-3:
The Clipboard enables you to combine objects from different drawings in cruel and unusual ways.

Why I hate the Clipboard

Well, I don't really hate it. It's a useful feature every once in a while. But the Cut, Copy, and Paste commands have three problems:

- ✔ Clipboard functions can be very slow, depending on the complexity of your drawing. Copying the tyrannosaur takes . . . well, let's just say that you probably have more than enough time to grab a cup of coffee — maybe even brew a new pot — while you wait. What a waste of time.

- ✔ You have to choose two commands to pull off Clipboard actions: first Cut or Copy and then Paste. What a waste of effort.

- ✔ Every time you choose the Cut or Copy command, the previous contents of the Clipboard go up in smoke. If you want to use the objects on the Clipboard over and over again, you can't go around upsetting them every time you want to duplicate something. What a waste of status quo.

The moral is, you should avoid Clipboard commands whenever possible, which is almost always. The following sections explain how.

The Gleaming Clipboard Bypass

The easiest way to bypass the Clipboard is to choose Edit⇨Duplicate or just press Ctrl+D. CorelDraw creates an exact copy of all selected objects and offsets them a quarter inch up and to the right, as demonstrated in Figure 8-4.

Group before you duplicate

When you duplicate several paths at a time, CorelDraw places each duplicated object directly in front of the respective original object. This placement means that the paths weave in and out of each other, as demonstrated in Figure 8-5, creating an indecipherable mess. Oh sure, it's great if you're buzzing on caviar and aperitifs at a tony gallery and are willing to call anything you see the highest of all possible art — "Don't you just love it, Madge? It's like Dino Descending a Staircase!" — but hardly the thing for the strictly nine-to-five crowd.

To remedy this situation, press either of the following key sequences:

- ✔ Shift+PgUp
- ✔ Ctrl+Z, Ctrl+G, Ctrl+D

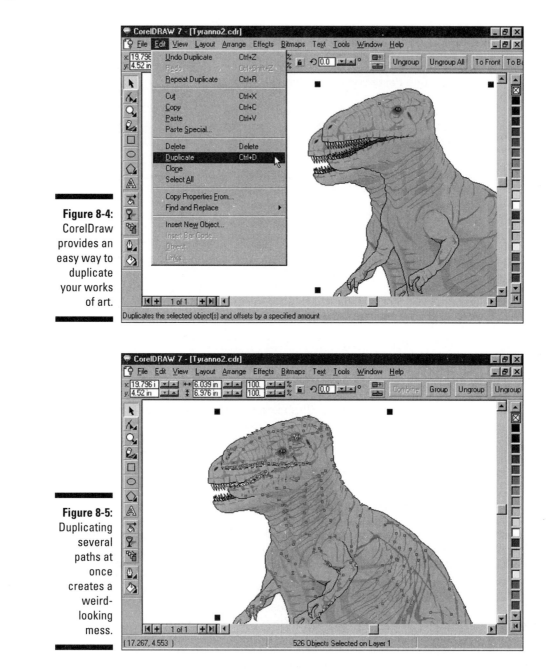

Figure 8-4:
CorelDraw
provides an
easy way to
duplicate
your works
of art.

Figure 8-5:
Duplicating
several
paths at
once
creates a
weird-
looking
mess.

The first option brings the duplicated objects to the front, creating an effect like that shown in Figure 8-4 — assuming that in your panic, you haven't clicked randomly in the drawing area and deselected the paths before pressing Shift+PgUp. If you have, you're still okay. The second sequence of keyboard shortcuts steps undoes the damage, groups the original selected objects, and reapplies the Duplicate command.

The Group (Ctrl+G) command is an ideal prerequisite to the Duplicate command. By choosing the Group command, you ensure that all your objects stay together after they are duplicated. Generally speaking, I recommend that anytime you want to duplicate five objects or more, you group them first. If you want to edit the objects, you can always ungroup them afterwards. For more on grouping and ungrouping objects, see Chapter 6.

Duplication distance

By default, the Duplicate command offsets the copied objects ¼ inch from the originals. You can change the offset by pressing Ctrl+J (or by choosing Tools⇨Options) and editing the values in the first two option boxes in the Options dialog box, spotlighted in Figure 8-6. Positive values offset the duplicate to the right or up; negative values move it to the left or down.

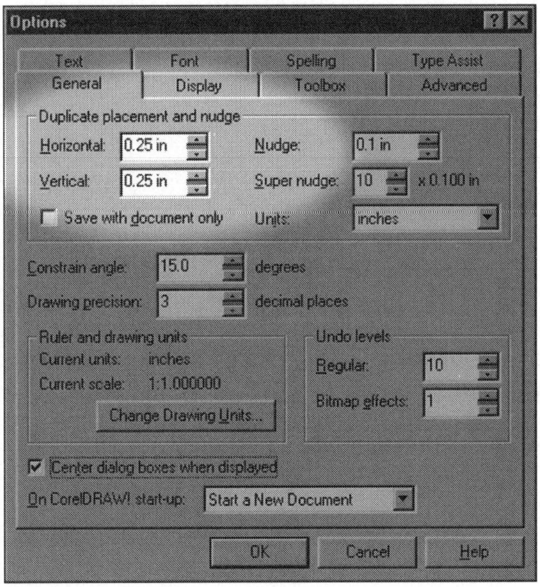

Figure 8-6:
The Horizontal and Vertical values determine the increment by which the Duplicate command offsets a copied object from its original.

Corel
Ctrl + J = settings

Options	

Text | Font | Spelling | Type Assist
General | Display | Toolbox | Advanced

Duplicate placement and nudge
Horizontal: 0.25 in   Nudge: 0.1 in
Vertical: 0.25 in   Super nudge: 10 x 0.100 in
☐ Save with document only   Units: inches

Constrain angle: 15.0 degrees
Drawing precision: 3 decimal places

Ruler and drawing units
Current units: inches
Current scale: 1:1.000000
Change Drawing Units...

Undo levels
Regular: 10
Bitmap effects: 1

☑ Center dialog boxes when displayed
On CorelDRAW! start-up: Start a New Document

OK | Cancel | Help

When the arrow tool is selected but no objects are selected, you can also use the X and Y option boxes near the right end of the Property Bar to change the duplicate offset values. The X option box controls the horizontal offset; the Y option box controls the vertical offset.

I recommend that you make these values an even multiple of the Nudge value. Better yet, make them the same. This way, if you want to line up the duplicated objects with the originals, all you have to do is press the down- and left-arrow keys.

Duplicate in place

directly over it

In addition to Ctrl+D, CorelDraw has another keyboard equivalent for the Duplicate command: the + key on the numeric keypad. That's right, just select your object and press the + key. Unlike Ctrl+D, however, the + key duplicates an object without offsetting it. You can drag the duplicate to a new location as desired. Pretty hot stuff, huh?

They Look Alike, They Act Alike, You Could Lose Your Mind

Imagine what would happen if every time Patty Duke changed her clothes, that identical cousin of hers changed her clothes, too. Or if every time Patty missed a question on a test, her cousin entered the same wrong answer. Or if every time Patty locked braces with her boyfriend . . . well, you get the idea. That's cloning.

If you're too young to remember *The Patty Duke Show,* substitute those identical twins from the newer show *Sister, Sister* for Patty and her identical cousin in the preceding analogy.

Allow me to elucidate. The Clone command creates a true twin of an object. Like the Duplicate command, Edit➪Clone creates an immediate copy, it bypasses the Clipboard, and it offsets the copy by the amount specified in the Options dialog box or Property Bar. But unlike the Duplicate command, the Clone command creates a link between copy and original. Most changes made to the original also affect the clone.

Suppose that I clone the group of objects that make up the T. Rex and move the cloned group over a little so that I can see what the heck I'm doing. Then, I select the original T. Rex and drag one of its corner handles. Instead of scaling just the one tyrannosaur, CorelDraw scales them both. Let's see those hotshots in *Jurassic Park* do that!

You can't clone multiple objects of different types unless you group them first (press Ctrl+G, click on the Group button on the Property Bar, or choose Arrange➪Group). You can, however, clone multiple selected objects that are all the same type of objects. For example, you can clone two rectangles without grouping them, but you can't clone a rectangle and a path drawn with the pencil tool.

Links on the brink

The link between a clone and its original object works in one direction only. For example, if you select a clone and apply a new fill, CorelDraw fills the clone only, as demonstrated in Figure 8-7. But if you select the original and fill it, both original and clone change, as in Figure 8-8.

Furthermore, altering a clone damages the link between cloned and original objects. You can think of the Clone command as providing three links: one that governs the fill of the objects, another that controls the outline, and a third that covers transformations (scaling, rotating, and so on). Each of the links is independent of the other two. So even if you apply a different fill to the clone, Draw retains the link between outline and transformations.

Original   Selected clone

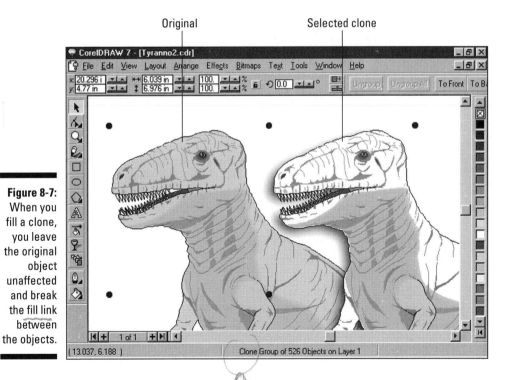

Figure 8-7:
When you fill a clone, you leave the original object unaffected and break the fill link between the objects.

Selected original   Clone

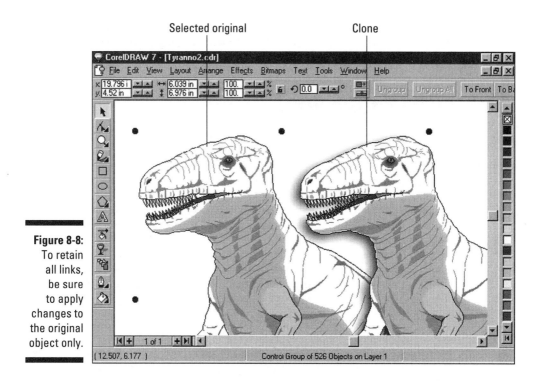

Figure 8-8:
To retain
all links,
be sure
to apply
changes to
the original
object only.

The care and feeding of your clones

Here's some more stuff to know about clones:

- You can tell whether you've selected the clone or the original by keeping an eye on the status bar. When you select a cloned path, for example, the status bar includes the word *Clone* (as in Figure 8-7). If you select the original path, the status bar says *Control* (as in Figure 8-8). In other words, *Control = original*.

- Any transformation applied to a clone severs the transformation link completely. If you scale the clone, for example, you prohibit rotating, skewing, and all the other transformations described in Chapter 9.

- If you cut the original object, you cut the clone as well. But if you then choose the Paste command, you paste only the original — the clone is lost forever.

- Deleting an object is like cutting it. So if you delete the original, you delete the clone as well. If you delete the clone, the clone and all links go away but the original object stays.

- The Copy command doesn't affect the clone. In other words, copying the original doesn't copy the clone. Nor does copying the clone copy the original.

✔ You can't ungroup a cloned group of objects unless you sever all links between clone and original. Similarly, you can't ungroup the original object until after you sever all links between clone and original. To edit an individual object in a cloned or original group, Ctrl+click with the arrow tool on the object that you want to change. (This approach is exactly what I did in Figures 8-7 and 8-8 to select the bottom object in the original T-Rex.)

✔ To sever all links between clone and original, select both objects and choose Arrange⇨Separate.

Some operations do not affect clones. For example, you don't select the clone when you select the original. If you move the original object, the clone remains stationary. And if you change the stacking order of an original object, the clone does nothing much in particular. The Extrude and Blend commands don't affect clones, either.

Unfortunately, I was unable to discover the answer to one nagging question: "If you scratch the original object's tummy, does the clone purr? Or does it bite your head off?" Experiment at your own risk.

Do the Drag and Drop

Although the Duplicate and Clone commands outclass the Clipboard in small ways, drag and drop really puts it to shame. If you have two drawings open at a time, you can move or copy selected objects by simply dragging them from one drawing and dropping them into the other. Here's how it works:

1. **Open two drawings.**

   Make sure that you can see portions of both drawings. You don't want one drawing entirely covering up the other, for example. You can choose Window⇨Tile Horizontally or Window⇨Tile Vertically to split the interface evenly between the two drawings.

2. **Select the objects that you want to move or copy.**

   If you want to copy Object A in Drawing 1, for example, select the arrow tool, click anywhere in Drawing 1 to make it active, and then click on Object A.

3. **Drag the selected objects into the other drawing.**

   In other words, drag Object A out of Drawing 1 and into Drawing 2. Your cursor changes to an arrow with a dotted page outline.

4. Release the mouse button.

When you release the mouse button, you drop the object into its new environment. Corel deletes the selected objects from the original drawing and moves them to the new drawing. It's just as if you had cut and pasted the objects, except that the Clipboard remains unaffected.

To copy the objects instead of moving them, press and hold the Ctrl key after you start dragging but before releasing the mouse button. A little plus sign appears next to the cursor, as shown in Figure 8-9. Release the mouse button to drop the objects and then release the Ctrl key.

Figure 8-9:
By dragging and Ctrl+dropping the tyrannosaur into the brontosaur paddock (top), I copy the carnivore (bottom) without upsetting the contents of the Clipboard.

Chapter 9

The Twisty, Stretchy, Bulgy World of Transformations

- -

In This Chapter

▶ Watching a mild-mannered improvisational comic flip out

▶ Getting acquainted with scaling, flipping, rotating, and skewing

▶ Transforming objects via roll-ups and the Property Bar

▶ Using rotation and skew handles

▶ Understanding how degrees work

▶ Distorting objects to create perspective effects

▶ Working in the four envelope editing modes

▶ Extruding objects to create 3-D effects

▶ Lighting 3-D objects

- -

In the movie *The Blues Brothers,* original *Saturday Night Live* cast member John Belushi does a series of back flips in a church. You think, "Wow, that's amazing! This guy is so gonzo that despite the fact that he's verging on obesity, high on nonprescription inhalants, and obviously completely out of shape (he spends half the movie breaking out in sweat), he's capable of performing complex floor exercises when sufficiently inspired."

Well, at least that's what I thought when I saw the movie in high school. Later, I learned the sad truth that it wasn't really John Belushi, but instead a padded stunt man. That fateful day, I promised myself that I would somehow make John's dream of gymnastic excellence come true. (I didn't really do anything of the kind, of course, but stay with me on this one. The whole introduction to this chapter hinges on your temporary suspension of disbelief.)

Today, I make good on that promise. In this chapter, you don't just see John do flips, though he performs quite a nice one in Figure 9-1. You see him undergo a series of elaborate transformations that would cause rational Olympic athletes at the peak of their careers to shrink in terror. By the end of the chapter, you'll swear that the guy is some kind of inhuman shape-shifter who can assume any form at will. Either that, or he's a drawing that I've subjected to CorelDraw's vast array of transformation functions.

The Belushi caricature comes from a company called Image Club, which offers a huge variety of celebrity and historical caricatures, almost all of which are splendid.

Figure 9-1:
Belushi finally does his own stunts.

Scaling, Flipping, Rotating, and Skewing

Scaling, flipping, rotating, and skewing are the big four transformations, the ones that have been available to CorelDraw users since our ancestors crafted the first version of the program out of twigs and iron-ore filings in the early 5th century. Just so that you know what I'm talking about — in approximate terms, anyway — here are a few quick definitions:

- ✔ To *scale* (or stretch) an object is to make it bigger or smaller. You can scale an object vertically, horizontally, or both.

- ✔ To *flip* an object is to make a mirror image of it, which is why CorelDraw calls this process *mirroring* and other programs call it *reflecting*. In the second example of Figure 9-1, I flipped Mr. Belushi both vertically and horizontally, making the top the bottom, the left side the right side, and vice versa.

✔ To *rotate* an object is to spin it around a central point like a top. Rotations are measured in degrees. A 180-degree rotation turns the object upside-down. A 360-degree rotation returns it right back to where it started.

✔ To *skew* (or slant) an object is to incline it to a certain degree. Like rotations, skews are measured in degrees. Just to give you some perspective, a 45-degree skew applied to a rectangle slants the shape so that its sides are perfectly diagonal.

Grouping comes before transforming

I recommend that you group all objects before you transform them. To transform the Belushi cartoon, for example, I selected all the shapes that made up the drawing by choosing Edit➪Select All and then pressing Ctrl+G. (You can also choose Arrange➪Group or click on the Group button in the Property Bar.) After grouping, you can scale, flip, rotate, and skew with a clear conscience. Grouping prevents you from accidentally missing an object — such as an eye or an ear — while transforming its neighbors.

Scaling and flipping

If you read the "Arrow Tool Techniques" section of Chapter 4, you're already familiar with how to scale and flip an object using the arrow tool. But just in case you missed that chapter, here's a quick review:

1. **Select one or more objects that you want to scale or flip.**

   Eight square handles surround the selected objects.

2. **Drag one of the handles to scale the objects.**

   Drag a corner handle to scale the objects proportionately, so that the ratio between the horizontal and vertical dimensions of each object remains unchanged. Drag the left or right handle to scale the objects horizontally only, as in Figure 9-2. Drag the top or bottom handle to scale the objects in a vertical direction only.

   Shift+drag to scale the object with respect to its center. Ctrl+drag to scale the object by an amount that's an even multiple of 100 percent, such as 200 percent, 300 percent, and so on.

   Alternatively, you can use the Property Bar object size controls or scale factor controls (labeled in Figure 9-2) to scale your objects. To change one of the Property Bar values, either click on the up- or down-arrows next to the option box, or double-click on the option box, enter a new

Vertical size ‑ Horizontal scale

Horizontal size ‑   Vertical scale   Proportional sizing   Stretch cursor

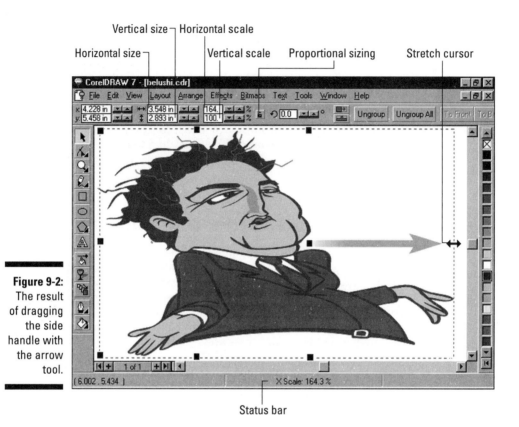

Figure 9-2:
The result
of dragging
the side
handle with
the arrow
tool.

Status bar

value from the keyboard, and press Enter. To retain the object's original proportions, click on the proportional sizing icon so that it appears to be depressed. (Depressed as in pushed in rather than as in sitting around crying all day.)

3. Drag one handle past the opposite handle to flip the objects.

In Figure 9-3, for example, I dragged the right handle leftward past the left handle to flip John B. horizontally, exactly as if he were rehearsing an episode of "Samurai Pastry Chef" in front of a mirror . . . except, of course, that he's facing the wrong direction.

To create an exact mirrored version of the object that is the same size as the original, Ctrl+drag a handle.

You can also create exact mirrored versions of objects by clicking on the Property Bar's mirror buttons, labeled in Figure 9-3. Unlike dragging the selection handles, clicking on the mirror buttons creates the mirrored image in the same location as the original image.

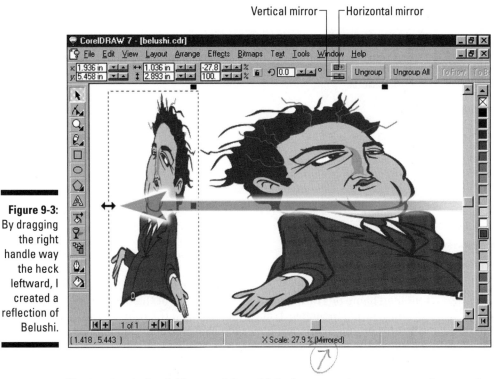

Vertical mirror — ┌─Horizontal mirror

Figure 9-3:
By dragging the right handle way the heck leftward, I created a reflection of Belushi.

Notice that in both Figures 9-2 and 9-3, the status bar measures the transformation in percentage points. A value below 100 percent indicates a reduction; a value above 100 percent indicates an enlargement. If the value is followed by the word *Mirrored* in parentheses, as in Figure 9-3, you flipped the graphic.

Using the provocative S&M roll-up

You can also scale or flip selected objects by entering numerical values into the Scale & Mirror roll-up. To do so, choose Arrange⇨Transform⇨Scale and Mirror or press Alt+F9. In response, the Scale & Mirror roll-up appears, as shown in Figure 9-4.

Most of the controls found in the Scale & Mirror roll-up are now found on the Property Bar, making the roll-up largely redundant if you display your Property Bar. But the roll-up does offer one key option that the Property Bar doesn't: the Apply to Duplicate button, which creates a duplicate of your selected object and applies the scaling or flipping to the duplicate. This option comes in handy if you want to play around to see what sort of effects you can create while still keeping your original object intact.

The Scale & Mirror roll-up is part of a group of roll-ups that go by the combined name of Transform. Scroll to the top of the list just below the title bar, and you see the name Transform above all the others. You can switch to a different roll-up in the group — such as Rotation or Skew — by clicking on its name in the list.

The options in the Scale & Mirror roll-up stretch your objects just as surely as if they were prisoners on a medieval rack, but without either the mess or the incessant groans of pain.

- Enter percentage values into one or both of the option boxes to scale the selection.
- To scale the selection by the same amount both horizontally and vertically, select the Proportional check box.
- Click on one of the Mirror buttons or enter a negative value into an option box to flip the objects horizontally or vertically.
- Click on the Apply button (or press Enter) to scale or flip the selection.
- Click on the Apply To Duplicate button to simultaneously duplicate the selected objects and scale or flip the duplicates. The original objects remain unchanged.

Rotating and skewing

To rotate or skew one or more objects, do this:

1. Select one or more objects that you want to rotate or skew.

As always, you see eight square handles.

2. Click on one of the selected objects a second time.

When you do, CorelDraw changes the square handles to a series of double-headed arrows, as shown in Figure 9-5. These arrows are the rotate and skew handles, or R&S handles for short. (The curved handles are the rotation handles, and the straight handles are the skew handles.) To return to the square stretch and mirror handles, click a third time on a selected object. Each time you click, you toggle between S&M and R&S.

3. Move the center of rotation marker as desired.

The circle in the middle of the selection is the center of rotation marker, which indicates the point about which the rotation takes place. Make sense? No? Well, think of the marker as a nail in a piece of cardboard. If you spin the cardboard, it whirls around the nail, right? In the same way, a selection rotates around the center of rotation marker. You can move the marker by dragging it.

4. Drag a rotation handle to rotate the selected objects.

Drag any of the four corner handles to rotate the selection around the center of rotation marker, as shown in Figure 9-6.

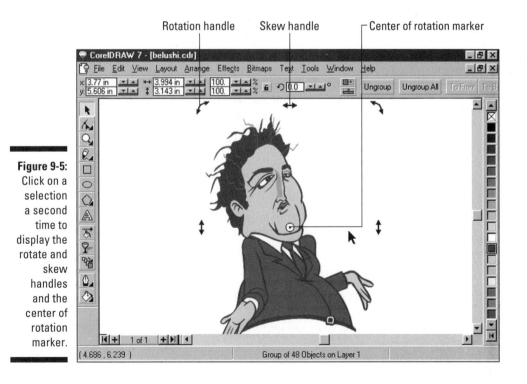

Figure 9-5:
Click on a selection a second time to display the rotate and skew handles and the center of rotation marker.

Rotate cursor   Rotation angle

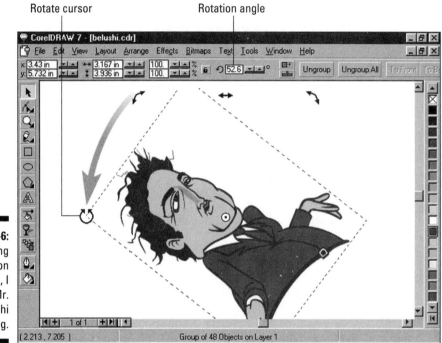

Figure 9-6:
By dragging
a rotation
handle, I
send Mr.
Belushi
spinning.

Notice that as you rotate your object, the angle of rotation is reflected in the rotation angle option box on the Property Bar, labeled in Figure 9-6. If you prefer, you can rotate a selected object by using the Property Bar rotation angle option box to rotate your object instead of dragging the rotation handles. Just click on the up- or down-pointing arrow next to the option box, or enter a new value from the keyboard and press Enter. A positive value indicates a counterclockwise rotation, as in Figure 9-6; a negative value means that the rotation is clockwise.

5. Drag a skew handle to slant the selected objects.

Drag the top or bottom handle to slant the selected objects horizontally, as in Figure 9-7. To slant the objects vertically, drag one of the two side handles.

Transforming by degrees

Keep the following things in mind when you're rotating and skewing objects:

 ✔ I don't know how much you remember from geometry class, but here's a quick refresher. Think of degrees as being measured on a clock. A clock measures 60 seconds, and a geometric circle comprises 360

Skew handle

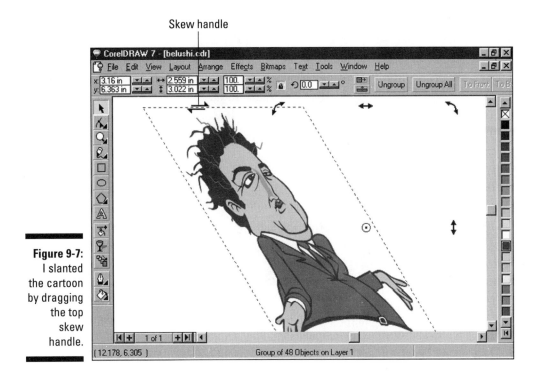

Figure 9-7:
Figure 9-7:
I slanted
the cartoon
by dragging
the top
skew
handle.

degrees. Each clock second is equal to 6 degrees, which means that the hour markers on a clock are each 30 degrees apart. So a ¹/₄ turn — the distance from 12 o'clock to 3 o'clock — is 90 degrees in CorelDraw.

✔ Ctrl+drag a handle to rotate or skew in 15-degree increments. For example, you can rotate a selection by 30 degrees, 45 degrees, and so on. All major turns — ¹/₄ turns, ¹/₈ turns, all the way down to ¹/₂₄ turns — are multiples of 15 degrees.

✔ If you don't like 15 degrees, you can change the angle by pressing Ctrl+J (or choosing Tools⇨Options). When the Options dialog box appears, click on the General tab and enter a new value into the Constrain Angle option box. After you press the Enter key, Ctrl+drag a rotation handle to see the effect of your change.

✔ Ctrl+drag the center of rotation marker to align the center point with one of the eight handles. You can also Ctrl+drag to return the marker to the exact center of the selection.

Using the not-so-provocative R&S roll-ups

You can also rotate or skew a selection by entering values into the Rotation and Skew roll-ups, respectively. To rotate a selection, choose Arrange⇨

Transform⇨Rotate or press Alt+F8. To slant a selection by the numbers, choose Arrange⇨Transform⇨Skew or press Alt+F11. Figure 9-8 shows the Rotation and Skew roll-ups, which are both part of the Transform group.

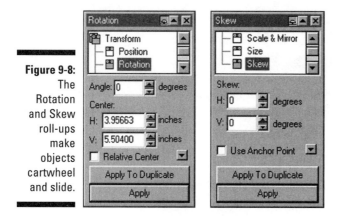

Figure 9-8:
The Rotation and Skew roll-ups make objects cartwheel and slide.

Here's how to use the options in the Rotation roll-up:

✔ Enter a degree value into the Angle option box to rotate the selection. Enter a positive value to rotate the objects in a counterclockwise direction; enter a negative value to rotate clockwise. Or, if you prefer, positive is left, negative is right.

✔ Enter values into the Center option boxes to position the center of the rotation. Select the Relative Center check box to position the center marker relative to the center of the selection; turn off the check box to position the marker with respect to the lower-left corner of the page.

✔ When in doubt, just select the Relative Center check box and enter 0 into both Center option boxes. That way, you rotate the selection about exact center. You can't go wrong that way.

And here's what to do with the options in the Skew roll-up:

✔ Enter values into the H and V option boxes to slant the selected objects. CorelDraw permits values between positive and negative 75.

✔ A positive value in the H option box slants the object backward; a negative value slants it forward.

✔ In the V option box, positive is up, and negative is down.

✔ Ignore the Use Anchor Point check box. It enables you to position the center of the skew using some hidden options — you have to click on that little down-pointing arrow to the right of the check box to get to them. Really, it's not worth the hassle.

Click on the Apply To Duplicate button to duplicate the selected objects and rotate or skew the duplicates at the same time. To rotate or skew the originals, press Enter or click on Apply.

Distortions on Parade

If scale, flip, rotate, and skew were the extent of CorelDraw's transformation capabilities, the program would be a real snoozer. It would be flexible, certainly, but hardly capable of inspiring the fanatic loyalty that accompanies this vast program. The remainder of this chapter covers three amazing transformations that you can perform with CorelDraw 7:

✔ Imagine a drawing printed on a sheet of flexible plastic in a rectangular frame. If you were to grab a corner of that plastic and stretch it, the drawing would stretch in that direction. That's what it's like to distort objects in CorelDraw using the *Perspective* function. Corel calls the function Perspective because it simulates the effect of viewing a flat drawing in three-dimensional space.

✔ *Enveloping* is like viewing a drawing's reflection in a fun-house mirror. You can bow the edges of objects inward, outward, or even along the edges of complex paths.

✔ *Extruding* an object gives it real depth by attaching sides to the shape. A square turns into a cube; a circle turns into a cylinder. CorelDraw accentuates the appearance of depth by automatically lighting the extruded shape and rotating it in 3-D space.

A Lesson in Perspective

I want to caution you against thinking of CorelDraw as a three-dimensional drawing program just because it provides a few wacky effects that simulate 3-D. In a true 3-D program — such as CorelDream 3D — you build a 3-D structure called a *model* that you can walk around and view from any angle imaginable. Then you wrap surface maps around the model, specify the reflectivity of the surfaces, light the model, apply ray tracing, and perform a bunch of other operations that very likely sound Greek to you.

The point is, CorelDraw is solidly rooted in two dimensions. Its tiny supply of 3-D-like effects are pure mockery and flimflam. All in the name of good fun. Something to do on a rainy night. If you want to get a taste for real 3-D, check out Chapter 18.

Special effects you can ignore

If you take a look at your Effects menu, you'll notice that I ignore one or two commands in this chapter, including Blend, Contour, Lens, and PowerClip. I wouldn't blame you if this fact casts a smidgen of doubt on my flawless wisdom. But the truth is, none of these commands are transformations. Here's my take on these features:

✔ The Blend command creates intermediate shapes between two selected paths. If you blend between a white square and a black circle, for example, CorelDraw creates a series of shapes that become increasingly circular as they progress from light gray to dark gray. The number-one use for the Blend function is to create custom gradations. It's a useful but hardly an eye-popping special effect. To learn how to create a blend of your own, follow the steps in the "Morph between Two Shapes" section of Chapter 19.

✔ The Contour feature is easily the least useful of CorelDraw's special effects. It fills a path with concentric versions of itself. Theoretically, you can use the Contour function to create gradations that follow the contour of a path, but you generally end up with patterns that look for all the world like shooting targets.

✔ CorelDraw's Lens function blends the colors of a selected shape with the colors in the shapes below it. You can make an object appear translucent; you can make one shape invert the colors in another; and you can create magnifying-lens effects. These are cool effects, no doubt, but they come at a price. Lens effects almost always increase the time it takes to print a drawing, and they may make a drawing so complicated that you can't get it to print at all.

✔ PowerClip lets you create stencils. In other words, you can take a bunch of objects and stick them inside another object. The CorelDraw balloon, for example, is a bunch of stripes stuck inside a balloon shape. To use the feature, you just select the objects that you want to stick inside another shape, choose Effects⇨PowerClip⇨Place Inside Container, and then click on the stencil shape. Bingo, in go your objects. But like the Lens function, PowerClip dramatically increases the complexity of a drawing. If you encounter printing errors after using this feature, don't come crying to me.

Viewing your 2-D drawing in 3-D space (sorta)

Now that I've diplomatically sorted out that tender issue, allow me to show you how to distort one or more objects using the Add Perspective command.

1. Select some random objects.

2. Press Ctrl+G or choose Arrange⇨Group.

If you don't group the objects, CorelDraw assumes that you want to distort each object individually, which can prove more than a little messy.

3. Choose Effects⇨Add Perspective.

CorelDraw converts the group to a perspective object and automatically selects the shape tool, as shown in Figure 9-9. Perspective objects are a unique kind of object in CorelDraw and require a special editing approach.

4. Drag on any of the four corner handles.

CorelDraw stretches the selection to keep up with your moves.

You can drag handles for as long as you want. Perspective objects are hard to predict at first, so be prepared to spend some time editing. If dragging a handle produces an unwanted effect, just drag the handle back or press Ctrl+Z.

When you finish editing the selection, click on the arrow tool icon. Corel-Draw exits the perspective mode and allows you to perform other operations.

Shape tool   Perspective object

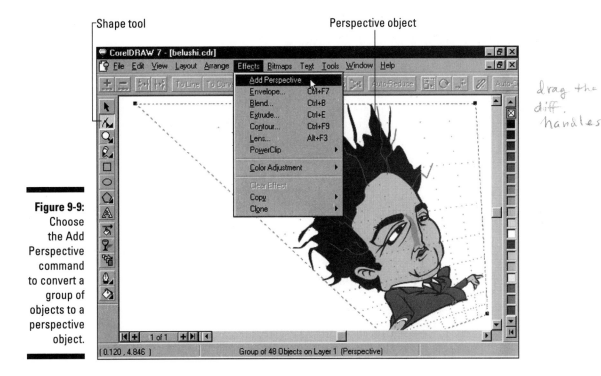

drag the diff. handles

Figure 9-9: Choose the Add Perspective command to convert a group of objects to a perspective object.

Putting perspective in perspective

Editing a perspective object is pretty straightforward stuff. But just in case, the following list contains a few items to bear in mind along with a few suggested avenues for experimentation.

✔ Ctrl+drag a handle to drag it in a horizontal or vertical direction.

✔ Ctrl+Shift+drag a handle to move two handles at once. The handle that you drag moves either horizontally or vertically; a neighboring handle moves the same distance in the opposite direction. If you Ctrl+Shift+ drag horizontally, the handle to the left or right of the handle that you drag also moves. If you Ctrl+Shift+drag vertically, the handle above or below the current handle moves.

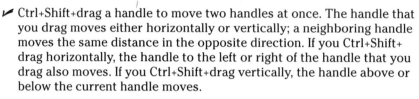

✔ Imagine that the dotted outline that surrounds the perspective object extends forever in all directions. So instead of four straight sides, you had four straight lines extending across your screen. CorelDraw marks the two locations at which each pair of opposite imaginary lines meet — that is, the point at which the left side would meet the right side and the point at which the top side would meet the bottom — with Xs called vanishing points. Unless you're far away from your object, you probably can't see the vanishing points because they're off-screen. But if you zoom out (by pressing F3) or move two opposite sides at an extreme angle to one another (see Figure 9-10), one or both of the vanishing points will come into view.

✔ The reason I even brought up this complicated topic is that you can also drag a vanishing point to further distort the perspective object. Try it to get a feel for how it works.

✔ You can no longer choose the Add Perspective command to restore the dotted outline to a rectangle and take a new stab at a perspective object, as you could in Version 6.

✔ To remove the most recent round of perspective edits from a selected object, choose Effects⇨Clear Perspective.

✔ To edit an existing perspective object, just select the shape tool and click on the object. There's no need to choose the Add Perspective command.

✔ To edit the individual nodes and segments in a perspective object, you have to convert the object back to paths. First, press Ctrl+U (Arrange⇨ Ungroup) to ungroup the object if necessary. Then, select the object that you want to edit and choose Arrange⇨Convert to Curves (Ctrl+Q).

Vanishing point

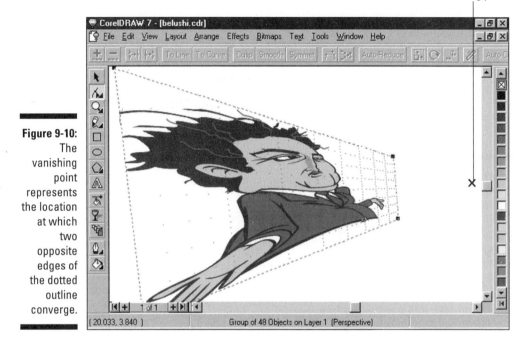

Figure 9-10:
The vanishing point represents the location at which two opposite edges of the dotted outline converge.

Envelope of Wonders

With the CorelDraw Envelope feature, you can bend and twist objects as if they were imprinted on a piece of Silly Putty. The effect is sort of like when you used to smush a piece of Silly Putty on the comics page of the newspaper and then wrap it around your little brother's face. As for why Corel calls this process enveloping, I can only guess that someone in engineering or development received a pretty gnarly package from UPS.

If you've ever taken a look at the CorelDraw Envelope feature, you probably said something like, "What the . . . ?" or perhaps more appropriately, "Duh." At least, that's what I did. But have faith. If I — king of the short attention span — could figure it out, you can too. And believe me, it's worth the effort.

The ultimate distortion

To apply envelope effects, do this:

1. **Select those objects.**

   Click and Shift+click with the arrow tool until your mouse hand goes to sleep.

2. **Group the objects.**

   The Envelope function works on only one object at a time. So if you want to distort several objects, you need to group them by choosing Arrange⇨Group, pressing Ctrl+G, or clicking on the Group button on the Property Bar.

3. **Press Ctrl+F7 or choose Effects⇨Envelope.**

   CorelDraw displays the Envelope roll-up, as shown in Figure 9-11.

Figure 9-11:
Use the
Envelope
roll-up to
distort
objects as
freely as a
rolling pin
distorts
cookie
dough.

4. **Click on the Add New button.**

   CorelDraw automatically selects the shape tool and surrounds the selection with a dotted rectangle that has eight handles — four in the corners and four on the sides.

5. **Select an editing mode.**

   The four icons in the middle of the roll-up represent envelope editing modes. For now, it's not important which one you select. I explain how each one works in the next two sections.

6. **Drag the handles to distort the object.**

   The object bends and stretches to keep up with your movements.

7. **Click on the Apply button.**

   Wherever there's a roll-up, there's an Apply button dying to be clicked.

To exit the envelope editing mode, click on the arrow tool icon. To redisplay the envelope editing handles, click on the shape with the shape tool. Or, to begin an entirely new transformation, select the object with the arrow tool and click on the Add New button in the Envelope roll-up.

The envelope editing modes

The envelope editing mode icons work like tools. Each one distorts the selected object in a unique and progressively more dramatic way:

- In the straight-line mode, CorelDraw maintains a straight side between each of the eight handles, as demonstrated in Figure 9-12. This mode is rather like the perspective distortion, except for two things: 1) you have some additional handles to play with, and 2) you can move the handles horizontally or vertically only. The left and right side handles move horizontally only; the top and bottom handles move vertically only. The corner handles move both ways.

- In the single-arc mode, CorelDraw permits a single arc to form between each pair of handles, as shown in Figure 9-13. Again, you can drag handles horizontally and vertically only. The single-arc mode works best for distorting objects into hourglass and balloon shapes.

- The double-arc mode allows a wave to form between each handle. As demonstrated in Figure 9-14, you can create rippling distortions, as if you were viewing your object under water. Just as in the straight-line and single-arc modes, you can drag handles horizontally and vertically only.

Straight-line mode

Figure 9-12: Dragging a handle in the straight-line mode.

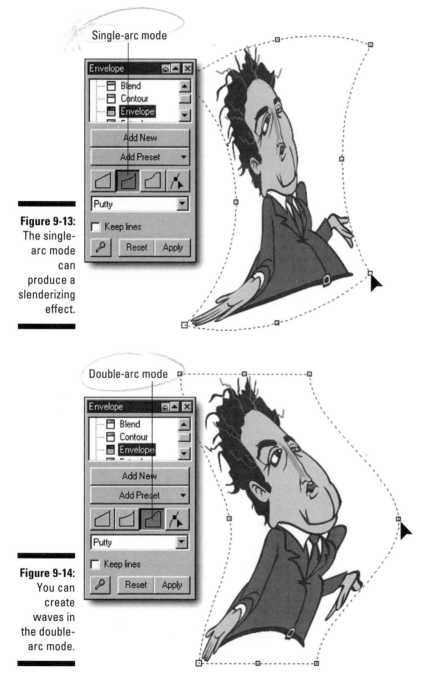

Figure 9-13:
The single-arc mode can produce a slenderizing effect.

Figure 9-14:
You can create waves in the double-arc mode.

✔ In the unconstrained mode, the sky's the limit. You can edit the outline exactly as if it were a free-form path drawn with the pencil tool. You can drag the handles — they're really nodes in this case — any which way you please. To determine the curvature of the segments between handles, CorelDraw provides you with control points, as shown in Figure 9-15.

✔ You can add or subtract nodes using the Node Edit roll-up or the Property Bar node editing buttons. (Double-click on one of the handles to make the roll-up appear.) You can even select multiple nodes at the same time. In short, if you can do it to a pencil path, you can do it to a shape in the unconstrained mode.

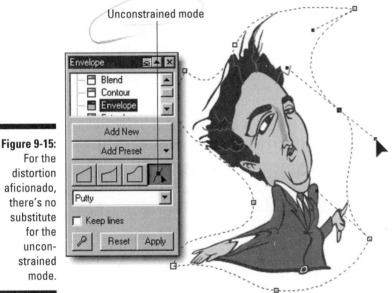

Figure 9-15: For the distortion aficionado, there's no substitute for the unconstrained mode.

Push the envelope

Just in case you're hungry for more about enveloping, here are a few tricks you may find helpful:

✔ You can use envelope editing modes in tandem with each other. For example, you can select the straight-line icon and drag one handle, and then select the double-arc icon and drag another handle.

✔ In the unconstrained mode, the Shift and Ctrl keys behave just as they do when you're editing a pencil path. Shift+click on a node to select it without deselecting other nodes. Ctrl+drag on a node to constrain the node to horizontal or vertical movements.

- In the other modes, Ctrl+drag a handle to move the opposite handle the same distance and direction as the handle you're dragging.

- Shift+drag to move the opposite handle the same distance but in the opposite direction as the handle you're dragging.

- Ctrl+Shift+drag a side handle to move all side handles the same distance but in the opposite directions. Ctrl+Shift+drag a corner handle to move all corner handles.

- If you don't feel up to editing the outline on your own, CorelDraw can help you out. Click on the Add Preset button in the Envelope roll-up to display a pop-up menu of outline shapes, as shown in Figure 9-16. Select the outline that you want to apply, and then click on the Apply button.

- You can cancel an envelope distortion anytime before you click on the Apply button. Just click on the Reset button or select the arrow tool.

- After you apply a few distortions, the dotted outline may become prohibitively wiggly. To restore the dotted outline to a rectangle and take a new stab at enveloping an object, click again on the Add New button in the Envelope roll-up.

- To remove the most recent round of envelope edits from a selected object, choose Effects⇨Clear Envelope.

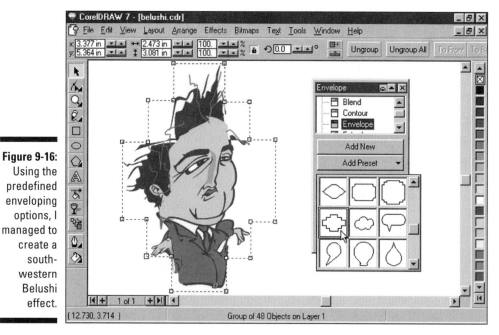

Figure 9-16:
Using the predefined enveloping options, I managed to create a south-western Belushi effect.

Well, Extru-u-ude Me!

In future years, brilliant minds no doubt will argue the merit of discussing extruding — one of the most complex functions in CorelDraw — in a ...*For Dummies* book. (Yeah, right.) But I figure, what the heck, it's a fun feature, and with enough effort, you may even figure out how to do something useful with it. In the meantime, it's a great way to waste several hours being antisocial and playing with your computer.

Extruding in the real world

First, what is extruding? Simply put, extrusion is the act of assigning depth to a 2-D shape by extending its sides into the third dimension. Naturally, that explanation doesn't make any sense, so perhaps an example is in order. Did you ever play with one of those thingies that lets you crank Play-Doh through a stencil to create snaky geometric forms, as illustrated in Figure 9-17? You cut off the snaky bit with a plastic knife, and voilà — you have a 3-D star, polygon, or other useless piece of gook. If this is your idea of a fond childhood memory, you are an extruder. Pasta machines extrude noodles. Sausage makers extrude columns of beef and pork by-products. Warts extrude out of your skin all by themselves. Life is filled with examples of extruding.

Figure 9-17: Play-Doh oozing through a stencil is an example of an extrusion.

Extruding in the workplace

For time immemorial, the Extrude roll-up has served as the central head-quarters for CorelDraw's extruding functions. Ever since the Big Bang (or thereabouts), you've been able to access this roll-up by choosing Effects➪Extrude or pressing Ctrl+E.

As with enveloping, CorelDraw can't extrude more than one object at a time. However, unlike enveloping, extruding is not applicable to groups. You can extrude a single path — open or closed — or a block of text. Sadly, I'm afraid that rules out any more transformations for John.

To extrude an object, do these things:

1. **Press Ctrl+E to bring up the Extrude roll-up.**

   The roll-up appears in Figure 9-18. Your roll-up is probably part of the Effects roll-up group, which means that you see a bunch of stuff at the top of your roll-up that doesn't appear in mine. (I pulled my Extrude roll-up out of the Effects roll-up as explained in Chapter 2.)

2. **Select a path.**

   For now, keep it simple. Select some basic shape like a circle or a star.

3. **Click on the Edit button in the Extrude roll-up.**

   A dotted extrusion outline representing the form of the extruded object appears, as shown in Figure 9-18.

   If the Edit button is dimmed, press Ctrl+Q (Arrange➪Convert To Curves) to convert the object to a free-form path. Now the Edit button is ready to go. Also, if you select an object before pressing Ctrl+E — that is, you perform Step 2 before Step 1 — the Extrude roll-up automatically goes into the edit mode. This means that you don't have to click on the Edit button. Just skip to Step 4.

   Note that after you click on the Edit button, the Property Bar displays controls related to extruding. But the buttons are all dimmed until after you create the extrusion by clicking on the Apply button in the Extrude roll-up (which you do at the end of these steps). For now, you can just lick your lips at the thought of editing your extrusion using the Property Bar.

4. **Drag on the vanishing point to change the direction of the extrusion.**

   Labeled in Figure 9-18, the vanishing point represents the point from which the extrusion emanates. If the star were a bullet rushing toward you, the vanishing point would be the gun. Kind of an ugly analogy, I admit, but accurate.

   If you don't see a vanishing point, zoom out to reveal it.

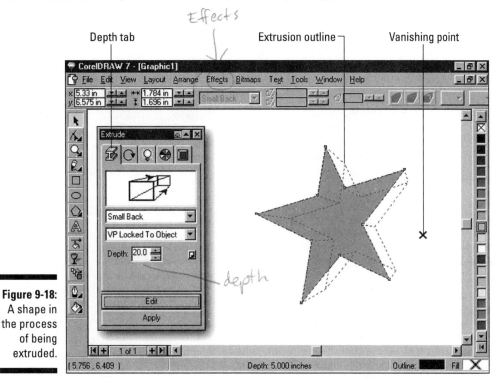

Depth tab · Effects · Extrusion outline · Vanishing point

Figure 9-18:
A shape in
the process
of being
extruded.

5. **Enter a value in the Depth option box.**

   You find the option box on the Depth tab of the roll-up, as shown in
   Figure 9-18. If the Depth tab isn't showing, click on the tab.

   The Depth value determines the length of the sides that stretch away
   from the object toward the vanishing point. If you enter the maximum
   value, 99, the extrusion outline touches the vanishing point. The
   minimum value, 1, creates a very shallow extrusion. Figure 9-19 shows
   some examples. Click on Apply to see the effects of your change.

6. **Click on the 3-D rotation tab.**

   It's the second tab at the top of the Extrude roll-up, and it's labeled in
   Figure 9-20.

7. **Drag the Corel C to spin the selected object in 3-D space.**

   Just drag around inside the roll-up, as demonstrated in Figure 9-20. Give
   it a try and see how easy it is. The front of the C is red and the back is
   blue, so you can see right away when you rotate the letter all the way
   around. Click on Apply to see what your rotation does to your object.

   Ctrl+drag to rotate in 45-degree increments. If you want to unrotate the
   object, click on the X icon.

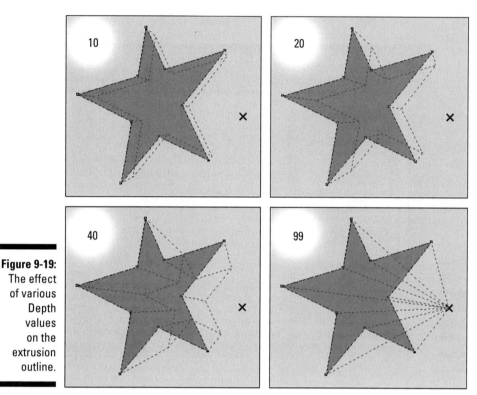

Figure 9-19:
The effect
of various
Depth
values
on the
extrusion
outline.

8. **Click on the Lighting tab.**

   This tab is labeled in Figure 9-21.

9. **Click on the first light bulb to shine a light on the 3-D object.**

   You can shine up to three lights by selecting all three light bulbs.

10. **Drag the light source markers in the cube.**

    A number in a circle indicates the location of the light source with respect to the object. Drag one of these markers to any spot in the cube where two gridlines intersect.

11. **Drag the Intensity slider to increase or decrease the amount of light.**

    Alternatively, you can enter a value between 0 and 100 into the option box. The lower the number, the dimmer the light. As before, click on Apply to see how your lights are affecting your object.

12. **Click on the Bevel tab.**

    The Version 7 Extrude roll-up contains a Bevel tab, shown in Figure 9-22. Using the options on this tab, you can create an extruded object whose edges appear beveled, as in the bottom-left object in Figure 9-22. To bevel your object's edges, select the Use Bevel check box. You can

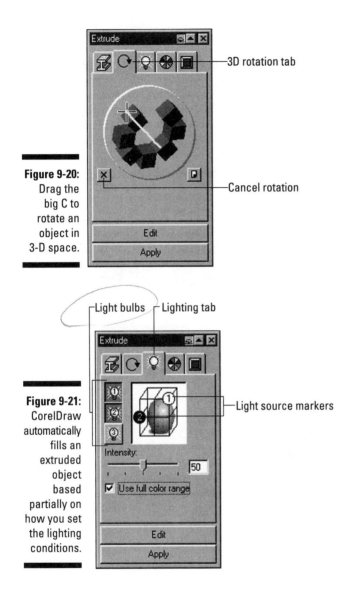

Figure 9-20: Drag the big C to rotate an object in 3-D space.

—3D rotation tab

—Cancel rotation

┌Light bulbs ┌Lighting tab

—Light source markers

Figure 9-21: CorelDraw automatically fills an extruded object based partially on how you set the lighting conditions.

then set the angle and depth of the bevel using the check boxes in the roll-up or by dragging the bevel control box in the preview area above the check boxes. Drag up or down to change the bevel depth; drag right or left to change the bevel angle.

If you select the Show Bevel Only check box, you wind up with only the beveled portion of your object, as shown in the bottom-right example in Figure 9-22. It's as if you took a knife and lopped off the rest of your object.

To preview how your object looks with the selected bevel settings, click on Apply.

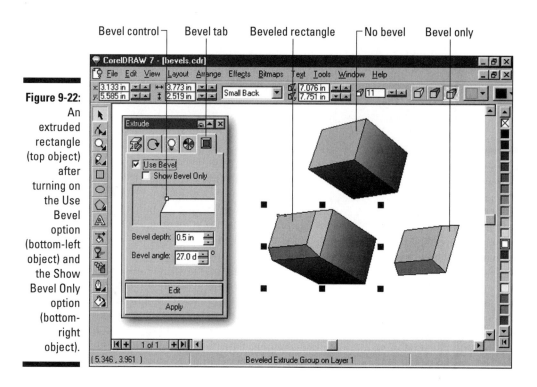

Bevel control Bevel tab Beveled rectangle No bevel Bevel only

Figure 9-22:
An extruded rectangle (top object) after turning on the Use Bevel option (bottom-left object) and the Show Bevel Only option (bottom-right object).

13. Click on the Object Color tab.

Welcome to the options shown in Figure 9-23.

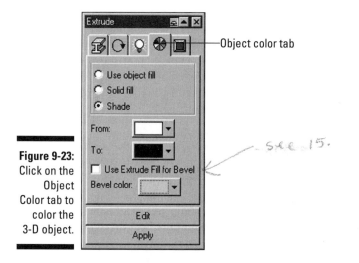

Object color tab

see 15.

Figure 9-23:
Click on the Object Color tab to color the 3-D object.

14. Select the Shade radio button to fill the partially lighted portions of the object with continuous gradations.

No reason exists not to select this option. The other two radio buttons produce boring results.

15. Select the desired colors from the pop-up menus.

The first two pop-up menus set the colors for the main object fill. For best results, select a light and dark shade of the same color. Click on Apply to check out your colors on the extruded object.

If you want your beveled edges to use a different color from your object fill, turn off the Use Extrude Fill for Bevel check box. (The option is unavailable unless you selected the Use Beveled Edges check box in Step 12.) You can then choose a color from the Bevel Color pop-up menu.

16. Click with the arrow tool.

CorelDraw automatically draws and fills the object to your specifications. Figure 9-24 shows the star from Figure 9-18 after I rotated it and lit it from the bottom-left corner. Note that this star does not use beveled edges. Call me old-fashioned, but I like my stars sharp and pointy-like.

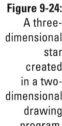

Remember that, in Version 7, clicking the Apply button simply displays a preview of your extrusion effects. To apply the extrusion for good and exit the edit mode, you must click with the arrow tool, as explained in Step 16.

Figure 9-24:
A three-dimensional star created in a two-dimensional drawing program.

Extruding is a long process, but not a particularly complicated one. Spend a little time playing around with the different controls to discover their effects, and you should become comfortable with extruding in no time. If you want to edit your extrusion, select the object with the arrow tool and then click on the Edit button in the Extrude roll-up. Or use the Property Bar controls, as explained in the next section.

Keep in mind that you can set the options on the various tabs of the Extrude roll-up in any order you like; you don't have to follow the preceding steps in the exact order I presented. If creating your beveled edges before you rotate the object is easier for you, for example, go ahead and do so.

Unfortunately for the wimps in the crowd, CorelDraw no longer offers a selection of preset extrusion effects that you can apply to objects. (The Presets tab, which provided access to the preset effects in Version 6, is replaced by the Bevel tab in Version 7.) If you want something extruded, you have to extrude it yourself, as the saying goes.

If you're technically astute and you still have a copy of CorelDraw 6, however, you can copy the CorelDraw 6 presets into Version 7 and run them by using the Script and Preset Manager. The process is detailed in the online Help system for CorelDraw 7. Personally, I wouldn't bother, though; simply creating your own extrusions is easier.

Extruding by the buttons

As mentioned in the preceding steps, the Property Bar displays controls that you can use to edit an existing extruded object. These controls become available only after you click on the Apply button in the Extrude roll-up; they're for editing the extrusion, not creating it. However, you don't have to have the roll-up displayed to use the Property Bar buttons. The buttons are displayed automatically when you select an extruded object with the arrow tool.

Also, as with other Property Bar controls, some of the buttons are hidden from view if you use the 640-x-480 display setting for your monitor. To access all the buttons, drag the Property Bar into the drawing window to create a free-floating palette of buttons, as in Figure 9-25.

The pertinent controls are labeled in Figure 9-25 and work as follows:

> ✔ You can use the vanishing point controls to move the vanishing point to a specific numerical coordinate. Unless you're really persnickety about your work or you're trying to duplicate an earlier extrusion, though, dragging the vanishing point cursor as explained in the preceding steps is probably easier.

Figure 9-25:
You can
edit some
aspects of
an extruded
object by
using the
Property
Bar
controls.

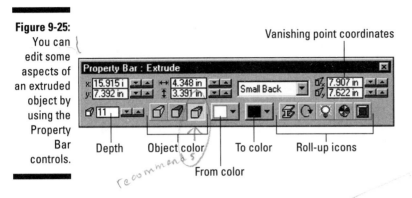

Vanishing point coordinates

Depth   Object color   To color   Roll-up icons

recommends

From color

✔ The Depth option box sets the depth of the extrusion, just like the Depth option box in the Extrude roll-up. No mystery here.

✔ The three Object Color icons duplicate the three radio buttons on the Object Color tab. The rightmost icon in the group, the Shade button, is the option I recommend.

✔ The From Color and To Color pop-up menus set the colors of the extrusion for the main object. You can't set the color for beveled edges from the Property Bar.

✔ Click on one of the five roll-up icons to display the corresponding tab of the Extrude roll-up. Come to think of it, you can probably suffer through without these buttons, which are the only ones hidden from view at the 640 x 480 monitor display setting. After all, you can always just press Ctrl+E to display the roll-up.

Ripping apart your new 3-D object

After you finish creating and lighting your object, you can break the 3-D object apart and fill it as you please. Just do the following:

1. **Choose Arrange⇨Separate.**

   This step separates the original object from its extruded sides.

2. **Shift+click on the original object with the arrow tool.**

   This step deselects the object, leaving only the sides selected.

3. **Press Ctrl+U or choose Arrange⇨Ungroup.**

   CorelDraw automatically creates the sides as a group, so you need to ungroup them before you can edit their fills.

After you separate the individual paths that make up the extruded object, you can fill each path independently to create a better-looking 3-D drawing.

Part III
Getting the Message Out There (Wherever "There" Is)

"WE SHOULD HAVE THIS FIXED IN VERSION 2."

In this part . . .

1f all you could do with CorelDraw was draw, this book would be over by now. But as luck would have it, CorelDraw is equally adept at creating documents such as fliers, newsletters, and those little wrappers that cover your hangers when they come back from the dry cleaners.

Like most desktop publishing programs, CorelDraw lets you enter and edit text, apply special formatting attributes, specify the size and orientation of a page, and print your document to paper. Unlike most publishing programs, however, it also enables you to drag letters independently of each other, create text on a circle, and actually edit the shape of characters of type. Few other pieces of software provide such a wide gamut of publishing capabilities.

At the risk of sounding like the crowned king of hyperbole, there hasn't been a tool like CorelDraw for slapping words on a bit of sliced timber since Johann Gensfleisch — who mostly went about using his mom's maiden name, Gutenberg — decided to smack some letters on a particularly abbreviated version of the Bible.

Chapter 10

The Care and Planting of Text

• •

In This Chapter

▶ Creating artistic and paragraph text

▶ Editing text

▶ Moving, scaling, and rotating text

▶ Pouring characters from one text block to another

▶ Selecting characters with one of the text tools

▶ Converting artistic text to paragraph text and vice versa

▶ Assigning formatting attributes

▶ Creating drop caps

▶ Correcting the spelling of your text

▶ Inserting symbols

• •

C reating text involves more than whacking your fingers in a hysterical frenzy against the keyboard. Remember all that stuff you learned in typing class? Forget it. Yesterday's news. I, for example, can't type — not a word — yet I write professionally, I format like a champ, and I don't have any wrist problems. Knock on wood . . . aaugh, I knocked too hard! I think I'm going numb!

Ha! Not really! See? My hand's just fine. Seemed so real, though, didn't it? And do you know why? It's not because the text is lucid and gripping. Surely you've figured that out by now. It's because the text looks good. The pages in this book appear professional — granted, in a sort of goofy way — so you naturally assume that a professional is behind them, not some crackpot like me. That, my friend, is an example of the miracle of modern computer-book writing.

In the world of corporate communications, text is judged as much by its appearance as its content. Not to put too fine a point on it, but text is art. Simply typing in thoughtful and convincing text with a hint of Hippocrene genius is not enough. You also need to know what to do with text after you enter it. And that's what this chapter is all about. (You were beginning to wonder, huh?)

A Furst Luk at Tekst

Unless you already know a thing or two about word processing and desktop publishing, this chapter is going to seem like a trip through the dictionary. You're going to learn so many terms that your brain will very likely swell up and pop. To prepare, you may want to tie a bandanna around your head and set a squeegee near your monitor.

For starters, text is made up of letters, numbers, and various symbols, such as &, %, $, and, my favorite, §, which is meaningless to most of Earth's inhabitants. If § crops up in your documents, it's a sure sign that either a lawyer or an extraterrestrial has been using your machine.

Together, these little text elements are called *characters*. CorelDraw refers to a collection of characters as a *text block* or, in deference to its path cousins, a *text object*. A text block may contain a single word, a sentence, a paragraph, or an odd collection of §s arranged in the shape of a crop circle.

In CorelDraw, you work with two kinds of text blocks:

- Use *artistic text* for logos, headlines, labels, and other short passages of text that require special graphic treatment, such as blends, extrusions, and other effects.

- *Paragraph text* is suited to longer passages, such as full sentences, paragraphs, pithy quotes, encyclopedia entries, epic poems, works of modern fiction, and letters to Grandma. You can apply certain text formatting options, such tabs and indents, to paragraph text that you can't apply to artistic text.

CorelDraw also offers access to specialized symbols, which — although they're technically not text — you can use as independent objects to highlight text objects or adorn your drawing. Symbols are organized thematically into categories such as animals, furniture, medicine, and semaphore. No smoke signals yet, but I've heard that's in the works.

Pick Up Your Text Tool

In Version 7, you create both artistic and paragraph text using the same tool, the text tool. The text tool is the third from the bottom in the toolbox — the one that looks like a big letter A. The manner in which you use the tool determines whether you plop down a chunk of artistic or paragraph text into your drawing.

Creating artistic text

To create artistic text, do this:

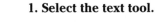

1. **Select the text tool.**

   Just click on the A icon in the toolbox. Better yet, just press F8.

2. **Click in the drawing area where you want the text to begin.**

   After you click, a vertical line called the *insertion marker* appears. The insertion marker indicates the location where new text will appear.

3. **Type away.**

   As you type, the corresponding characters appear on-screen. The insertion marker moves rightward with the addition of each character (see Figure 10-1), indicating the location at which the next character will appear.

4. **When you finish, select the arrow tool.**

   Eight square handles surround the text, as in the second example of Figure 10-1, to show that the text is selected.

   After you select the text tool, you can switch to the arrow tool quickly by pressing Ctrl+Spacebar.

Figure 10-1:
Artistic text as it appears when you're entering text (top) and after you select the arrow tool (bottom).

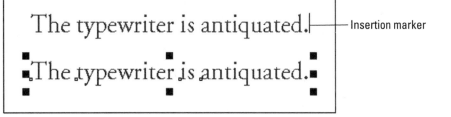

Nearly every computer program in existence lets you change text after you create it, and CorelDraw is no exception. To add more characters, select the text tool and click inside the text block at the location where you want the new characters to appear. In Figure 10-2, for example, I first clicked in front of the *a* in *antiquated* and entered the word *an*. Next, I clicked between the *d* and the *period*, pressed Enter, and entered *piece of garbage*.

> The typewriter is an|antiquated.
>
> The typewriter is an antiquated
> piece of garbage|.

Figure 10-2: Adding text to an existing text block.

Here are a few more things to know about entering and editing artistic text:

- Unlike text in a word processor, artistic text does not automatically wrap to the next line. In other words, when your text reaches the right edge of the text block, CorelDraw doesn't move the insertion point to the beginning of a new line. You have to manually insert line breaks by pressing the Enter key, just as you have to press the carriage-return key when using a typewriter.

- To move the text block to a new location in the drawing area, drag it with the arrow tool.

- The X and Y option boxes on the left end of the Property Bar give you another way to move the text block. The X value controls the text block's horizontal position, and the Y value controls its vertical position, just as with any other object. To display the controls, select the text block with the arrow tool. Remember that, as with regular objects, the X and Y values indicate the center of the text block. Also, if you enter an X or Y value from the keyboard instead of using the up and down arrows next to the option boxes, you must press Enter before your changes take effect.

- You can also use the arrow keys to move a text block. Select the text block with the arrow tool and then press an arrow key to nudge the block to a new location.

- When you drag the handles of an artistic text block with the arrow tool, you change the size of the characters. Drag a corner handle to scale the characters proportionally.

- Drag the top or bottom handle to make the text tall and skinny, as in Figure 10-3. This kind of text is called *condensed*.

- Drag the left or right handle to make the text short and fat (called *expanded text*).

✔ Click a second time on a text block to access the rotation and skew handles. These handles work just like those described in Chapter 9, enabling you to create rotated and slanted text.

✔ Alternatively, you can resize and rotate an artistic text block using the Property Bar controls, just as you can any other object. For details, see Chapter 9.

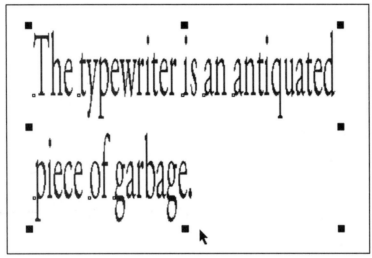

Figure 10-3:
I dragged the bottom handle with the arrow tool to create condensed text.

Creating paragraph text

To create a block of paragraph text, follow these ingenious steps:

1. Press F8 or click on the text tool icon.

2. Drag in the drawing area to create a text block.

You create a rectangular marquee, as shown in Figure 10-4.

3. Bang those keys.

As you work out your aggressions, text fills up the text block. Unlike artistic text, paragraph text automatically wraps to the next line when it exceeds the right-hand boundary of the text block, as demonstrated in the second example of Figure 10-4.

4. When you finish, select the arrow tool.

• You can switch from the text tool to the arrow tool quickly by pressing Ctrl+Spacebar.

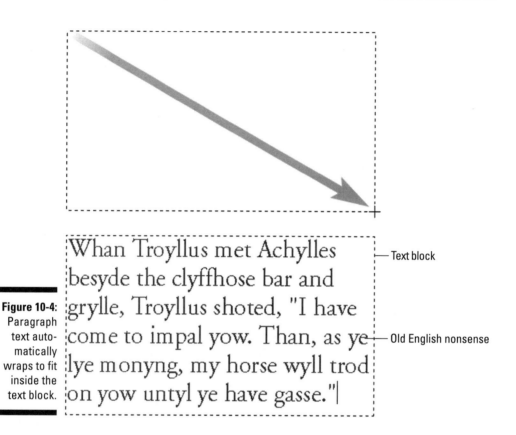

Figure 10-4:
Paragraph text automatically wraps to fit inside the text block.

Whan Troyllus met Achylles besyde the clyffhose bar and grylle, Troyllus shoted, "I have come to impal yow. Than, as ye lye monyng, my horse wyll trod on yow untyl ye have gasse."

— Text block

— Old English nonsense

- Eight square handles surround the text block, just as they do when you create artistic text. You also see little tabs on the top and bottom of the text block. The tabs are used to flow text between multiple text blocks, as discussed later in this chapter.

Some of the stuff that I said about artistic text applies to paragraph text as well. For example, you can add more characters to a block of paragraph text by clicking inside the text block with the text tool and then typing away. You can move a selected block of paragraph text to a new location by dragging it with the arrow tool, by pressing one or two arrow keys, or by using the Property Bar controls.

But a couple of operations work very differently:

✔ Dragging a corner handle scales the text block but not the text inside it. CorelDraw reflows the text to fit inside the new text block borders, as demonstrated in Figure 10-5. You can also use the Property Bar's size and scale controls to resize the text block.

✔ To resize the text block and also the text inside, Alt+drag a corner handle of the text block.

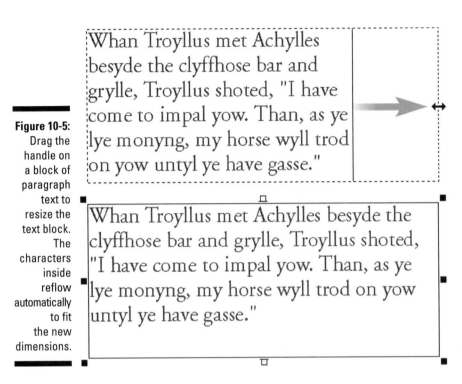

Figure 10-5:
Drag the
handle on
a block of
paragraph
text to
resize the
text block.
The
characters
inside
reflow
automatically
to fit
the new
dimensions.

✔ Normally, the text block remains the same size regardless of how much text you type. If you type more characters than the text block can hold, CorelDraw hides the extra text from view. To display it, just enlarge the text block by dragging one of the handles with the arrow tool.

✔ If you want the text block to automatically grow or shrink to accommodate your text as you type, press Ctrl+J or choose Tools⇨Options to display the Options dialog box. Click on the Text tab and turn on the Expand and Shrink Paragraph Text Frames to Fit Text check box. Note that if you turn on the option, CorelDraw doesn't let you reduce the overall capacity of the text box. For example, if you drag a side handle to make the text box narrower, CorelDraw automatically increases the height of the text box so that all the characters still fit inside the box.

✔ Click on the text block twice with the arrow tool to display the rotate and skew handles, which work the same way as for any object. You can also use the Property Bar's rotation angle control to rotate the text block.

✔ Rotating a paragraph text block rotates the characters inside, just as when you're rotating a block of artistic text. But skewing a paragraph text block slants the text block only, as shown in Figure 10-6. The characters remain upright and flow to fill the borders of the text block.

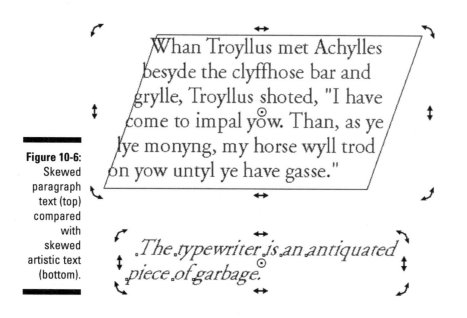

Figure 10-6:
Skewed
paragraph
text (top)
compared
with
skewed
artistic text
(bottom).

A single paragraph can contain no more than 4,000 characters, which is roughly the equivalent of two pages in this book with no figures. Okay, so maybe George Bernard Shaw would have had problems with this limitation. He and William Faulkner could have moaned about it endlessly in 10,000-character postcards to each other. But I don't think that you'll have any problems.

Press Ctrl+Shift+T or choose Text➪Edit Text to edit your text in a separate text editing window. You may find this option helpful if you're working on a particularly long section of text, like that 4,000-character postcard you're sending to George and William. After you make your edits, click on OK to close the text editing window. Your changes are automatically reflected in the drawing window.

Navigating among the letters

Whether you're working with artistic or paragraph text, you can specify the location of the insertion marker inside the text by clicking in the text block with the text tool. After you position the insertion marker, you can move it around using any of the following techniques:

- ✔ Press the left- or right-arrow key to move the insertion marker in one-character increments. Press the up- or down-arrow key to move from one line of type to the next.

- ✔ To move in whole-word increments, press Ctrl plus the left- or right-arrow key.

VERSION 7

What's that red squiggly line?

When the text tool is selected, red, squiggly lines appear underneath words that CorelDraw believes to be misspelled. The line is the CorelDraw way of saying, "Hey, bonehead, better think again!" You can either look up the word in the dictionary and fix it on your own, or right-click on the word to display a list of alternative spellings. Click on the alternate spelling you want to use or click on Ignore All to make CorelDraw leave you alone. The squiggly line changes from red to blue to show that you've inspected the word.

If you don't want CorelDraw to invade your text with its squiggly lines, press Ctrl+J or choose Tools⇨Options to open the Options dialog box. Click on the Spelling tab and turn off the Perform Automatic Spell Checking option. Or, if you want CorelDraw to perform automatic spell checking but you don't want to see blue squiggly lines for words that you asked CorelDraw to ignore, leave the Perform Automatic Spell Checking option turned on but deselect the Show Errors Which Have Been Ignored option box.

checks
↳
Spelling

- ✔ Press Ctrl and the up-arrow key to move to the beginning of the current paragraph. Press Ctrl and the down-arrow key to move to the end of the paragraph.

- ✔ Press the Home key to move the insertion marker to the beginning of the current line. Press End to move to the end of it.

- ✔ Ctrl+Home moves the insertion marker to the beginning of the current text block. Ctrl+End moves you to the end of the text block.

How to Flow Text between Blocks

As discussed previously, when you enter long passages of paragraph text, the text may exceed the boundaries of the text block. Every character that you enter still exists; you just can't see it. To view the hidden text, you can reduce the size of the characters so that they fit better, as described later in this chapter; enlarge the text block, as described earlier; or pour the text into a new text block.

That's right, you can pour excess text from one text block into another as if it were liquid. Here's how it works:

1. **Drag to create a paragraph text block with the text tool.**

2. **Enter far too much text.**

   Type in every page of *Beowulf.* This is your chance to bone up on classical literature.

Make sure that the Expand and Shrink Paragraph Text Frames to Fit Text check box is turned off on the Text panel of the Options dialog box (Ctrl+J). Otherwise, your text block grows as you add text, which prevents you from entering more text than your text block can hold.

3. Select the arrow tool.

Much of the text that you entered should not be visible on-screen.

4. Click on the top or bottom handle of the text block.

These handles are called *tabs*. The top tab is empty, to show that the text starts here. The bottom text has a little arrowhead in it to show that there's a bunch of overflow text that doesn't fit inside the text block. You can click on the top tab to pour lines from the beginning of the text block into a new text block. (Lines from the end of the text block shift up to fill the space left behind.) Or you can click on the bottom tab to pour the hidden lines of text into the new text block. In either case, after you click on a tab, your cursor changes to a page icon, as in Figure 10-7.

5. Drag to create a second text block.

Figure 10-7 demonstrates this process. CorelDraw then automatically pours lines of text originally entered into the first text block into this new text block, as shown in Figure 10-8.

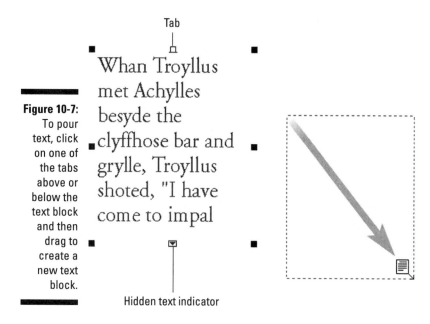

Figure 10-7: To pour text, click on one of the tabs above or below the text block and then drag to create a new text block.

Tab

Whan Troyllus met Achylles besyde the clyffhose bar and grylle, Troyllus shoted, "I have come to impal

Hidden text indicator

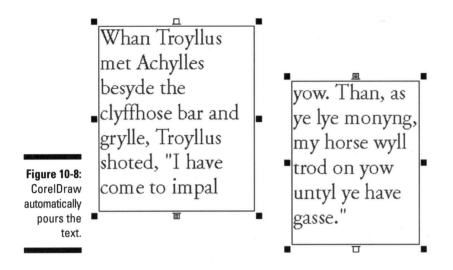

Notice that three tiny lines appear inside the bottom tab on the first text block and the top tab on the second. The lines indicate a link between the two text blocks.

To experiment with the link, keep stepping:

6. Drag up on the bottom tab on the first text block.

This step leaves less room in the first text block for the text. The overflow text automatically pours into the second text block.

7. Press Delete.

CorelDraw deletes the first text block (assuming that the first text block is still selected) but it does not delete the text inside the text block. Instead, the text pours into the second text block.

Pretty keen, huh? As long as at least one text block in the link remains in your drawing, the text remains intact. Now, if you were to delete the second text block, CorelDraw would indeed delete the text because there is no longer any place for the text to go.

When you click on a linked text block with the text tool, CorelDraw displays a dotted marquee around all the text blocks in the link and connects them with a skinny arrow. If you click on a linked text block with the arrow tool, you see the selection handles and tab only around the text block that you click on.

You can pour text between as many text blocks as you like. Okay, I bet there's some maximum, like 32 or 256 or something, but who cares? You'd be a nut to want to pour between that many text blocks! You can even pour your text across multiple pages. (I discuss multiple-page documents in Chapter 12.)

Before You Can Format, You Must Select

To change the appearance of characters in a text block, you assign formatting attributes such as typeface, style, size, and a few others that I'll get to later. But before you can do so, you have to select the text.

You can select text in two ways in CorelDraw. You can click on the text block with the Arrow tool, in which case any formatting changes will affect all characters inside the text block. Or you can highlight individual characters and words with the text tool. Your changes then affect only the selected characters.

Selecting with the text tool

Using the text tools is the preferred method for selecting text because it enables you to make selective changes. For example, you can make a single word bold or a passage of text italic. By contrast, if you select text with the arrow tool, any formatting changes that you make apply to the entire text block. The following items explain how to use a text tool to select type in any kind of text block:

   ✔ Drag over the characters that you want to select. To show that the characters are selected, CorelDraw highlights the characters by setting them against a gray background. Generally, you use this technique to select type within a single text block. However, you can drag across type in linked text blocks, as demonstrated in Figure 10-9.

   ✔ Double-click on a word to select the word.

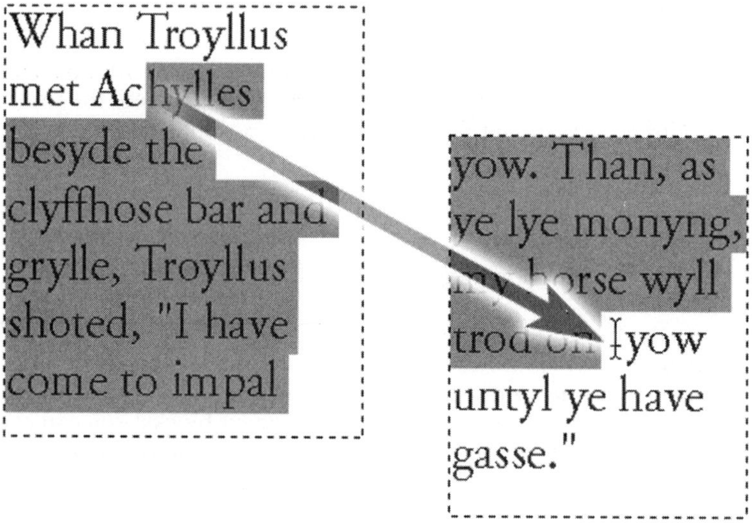

Figure 10-9:
Drag with
the text tool
to select
type in
linked text
blocks.

Whan Troyllus met Achylles besyde the clyffhose bar and grylle, Troyllus shoted, "I have come to impal

yow. Than, as ye lye monyng, my horse wyll trod on yow untyl ye have gasse."

✔ Ctrl+click on a word to select the entire sentence.

✔ Click to set the insertion marker at one end of the text that you want to select. Then Shift+click at the other end of the desired selection. CorelDraw selects all text between the click and Shift+click. For example, to select the highlighted text in Figure 10-9, I could have clicked between the *c* and *h* in *Achilles* and then Shift+clicked between the words *on* and *yow* in the second text block.

✔ Press the Shift key in tandem with the left- or right-arrow key to select one character at a time. Press Shift plus the up- or down-arrow key to select whole lines.

✔ Press Shift and Ctrl along with the left- or right-arrow key to select whole words at a time.

Converting from artistic to paragraph and vice versa

You create a block of artistic or paragraph text, but then it occurs to you that you made the wrong choice. No problem. You can easily convert one variety of text to the other.

In Version 7, the easiest way to change from one text type to the other is to select the text block with the arrow tool and then click on the Convert Text button on the Property Bar, labeled in Figure 10-7. As with other controls on the right end of the Property Bar, the Convert Text button is hidden if you use the 640 x 480 display setting for your monitor. To reveal the button, drag the Property Bar into the drawing window, as in Figure 10-10.

The Convert Text button is unavailable when a paragraph text block is too small for all your text to be displayed. To access the button, enlarge the text block to fit the text. Also, you can't use the Convert Text button to convert paragraph text that you poured into more than one text block. Nor can you convert multiple text blocks, artistic or paragraph, at a time.

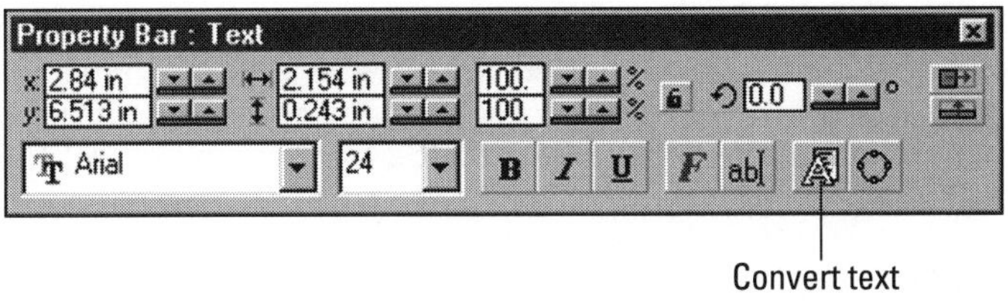

Figure 10-10:
Click on the Convert Text button to toggle between artistic and paragraph text.

Property Bar : Text
x: 2.84 in ↔ 2.154 in 100. %
y: 6.513 in ↕ 0.243 in 100. % ↻ 0.0 °
Arial 24 **B** *I* U F abl ▣ ◇

Convert text

If you prefer, you can convert your text by choosing Text⇨Convert to Artistic Text or Text⇨Convert to Paragraph Text. (The command name changes depending on the type of text block that's selected.) As with the Convert Text button, the command is unavailable if text isn't completely visible in the text block or is contained in multiple text blocks.

If you want to convert paragraph text contained in multiple text blocks to artistic text, you can also convert text by using the Clipboard. To convert paragraph text to artistic text, follow these steps:

1. **With the text tool, select the text that you want to convert.**

2. **Press Ctrl+C (or choose Edit⇨Copy).**

   CorelDraw copies the text to the Clipboard.

3. **Click somewhere inside the drawing.**

   Just don't click inside a paragraph text block. Draw creates a new artistic text block.

4. **Press Ctrl+V (or choose Edit⇨Paste).**

   CorelDraw pastes the text into the artistic text block. Now you can perform all those amazing special effects that are only applicable to artistic text, as explained in Chapter 11.

   Notice that any line breaks that existed in your paragraph text remain in the new artistic text block. But you can remove them by clicking at the spot where the line break occurs and pressing Delete.

You say you don't want artistic text? You want to be able to create long passages that flow between multiple linked text blocks? Well then, to convert artistic text to paragraph text, take the same steps, but drag to create a paragraph text block in Step 3 or click inside an existing paragraph text block.

Not sure which type of text you're looking at? Select the text and then check the status bar, which indicates whether the text is artistic or paragraph text.

Okay, Now You Can Format

After you select some text, whether it be paragraph or artistic, you can assign formatting attributes. Now, a lot of folks change the typeface and other stuff by using the Format Text dialog box, which you get to by pressing Ctrl+T or choosing Text⇨Format Text. But for simple formatting chores, using the Property Bar or the Object Properties dialog box, both shown in Figure 10-11, is quicker. (Note that in Figure 10-11, I dragged the Property Bar into the drawing window to convert it to a floating window so that all the buttons are visible at the lowest monitor display resolution, 640 x 480.)

To display the Object Properties dialog box, select the text that you want to format and press Alt+Enter. Or right-click on the text and select <u>P</u>roperties from the pop-up menu that appears. The Text panel of the dialog box, shown in Figure 10-11, appears automatically.

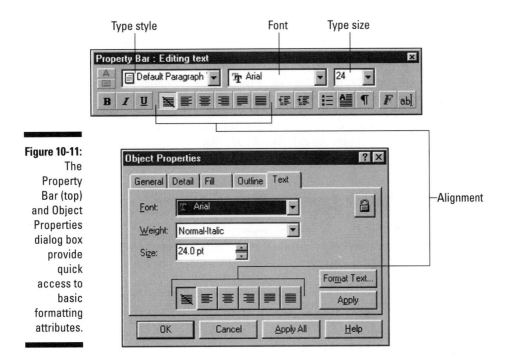

Figure 10-11: The Property Bar (top) and Object Properties dialog box provide quick access to basic formatting attributes.

If you select paragraph text, the Object Properties dialog box contains one additional option not shown in Figure 10-11: the Range pop-up menu. This option controls how formatting is applied to text in linked paragraph text blocks. You can specify whether you want the formatting applied to all of the linked blocks, the selected block only, or the selected block and the subsequent linked block. This option works only if you select your text with the arrow tool rather than the text tool.

You can also format using the Text toolbar, which you display by right-clicking in the gray area in the toolbox to display a pop-up menu and then selecting the Text option. But the Property Bar offers the same controls as the Text toolbar — and then some — making the Text toolbar redundant, in my opinion.

Using either the Property Bar or the Object Properties dialog box, you can change the typeface, type style, type size, and justification. I describe each of these formatting attributes in the following sections.

To display the Property Bar controls, shown in Figure 10-11, click inside the text block with the text tool. If you select the text block with the arrow tool, the Property Bar changes, but the type style, font, and size buttons are still available.

Remember that when you select the text block with the arrow tool, your changes affect all text in the text block. If you use the text tool, your changes affect the selected text in the text block only. The same holds true for changes that you make via the Object Properties dialog box.

To change the default settings used by the text tool, make sure that no objects are selected and then press Ctrl+T or choose Text⇨Format Text. CorelDraw asks you to specify whether you want the new settings to apply to paragraph or artistic text. After you make your selections, click on OK. You then see the Format Text dialog box, where you can change the settings for everything from font to character spacing.

Selecting a typeface

Changing the typeface is your number-one method for controlling the appearance of your text. Just in case you're wondering what I'm talking about, a *typeface* is a uniquely stylized alphabet. The idea is that the *a* in one typeface looks different from the *a* in another typeface.

Some folks refer to typefaces as *fonts*. Back in the old days — up until as recently as 20 years ago — each letter was printed using a separate chunk of metal, and all the pieces of metal for one typeface were stored in a container called a *font*. (This use of the word, incidentally, is based on the French word *fonte*, which means a *casting*, as in type casting. It has nothing to do with the baptismal font — you know, one of those basins that holds holy water — which is based on the Latin word *fontis*, which means *spring*. Dang, this is interesting stuff!)

CorelDraw includes on CD-ROM about 50 quintillion fonts that you can install into Windows (see the appendix for instructions). You can also use any PostScript or TrueType font that you've installed into Windows. If you don't know what PostScript and TrueType are, read the upcoming Technical Stuff sidebar or, better yet, don't worry about it.

To change the font of the selected text, select a typeface from the Font pop-up menu on the Property Bar or in the Object Properties dialog box. If you want to see what a typeface looks like before you apply it, do this:

1. Click on the name of the typeface in either the Property Bar or dialog box.

Or click on the down pointing arrowhead to the right of the typeface name. The pop-up menu appears. CorelDraw also displays a preview box to the side of the pop-up menu, as shown in Figure 10-12.

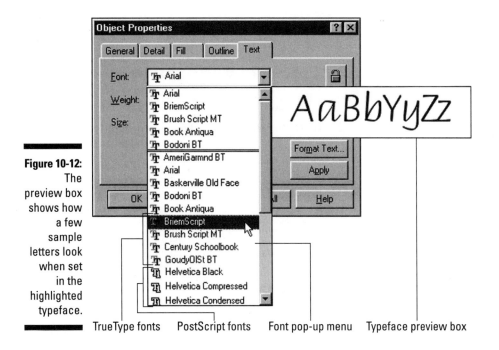

Figure 10-12:
The
preview box
shows how
a few
sample
letters look
when set
in the
highlighted
typeface.

TrueType fonts   PostScript fonts   Font pop-up menu   Typeface preview box

2. **Move the cursor or press the down- and up-arrow keys to scroll through the list.**

CorelDraw updates the preview box to show the selected typeface. If text is selected in your drawing, the actual text appears in the preview box.

Changing the type style

Most typefaces offer four type styles: plain, italic, bold, and bold italic. You can assign one of these styles by selecting the B or I button on the Property Bar. (You can also click on the U button to underline the text.) Or, select an option from the Weight pop-up menu in the Object Properties dialog box and click on the Apply button.

Enlarging or reducing the type size

As discussed in Chapter 7, line widths are measured in *points,* with one point equal to $^1/_{72}$ of an inch. Type is also measured in points. After all, type is generally pretty dinky. Even monster-big headlines in supermarket tabloids — you know, like "England Frets as Princess Di Dons Unbecoming

The typeface rivalry that isn't worth knowing about

You may not associate something as fundamental as font technology with a brand name, but the truth is, everything has a brand name. *Billy Joel* is a registered trademark, for crying out loud. So if your last name is Joel, don't even *think* about naming your kid Billy.

Anyway, the two big brands in the world of digital typography are PostScript and TrueType. Developed by Adobe Systems — the folks who created the well-known image-editing program Photoshop — the PostScript font format is the professional printing standard. Hewlett-Packard and several other printer manufacturers offer support for PostScript, as do all major brands of typesetters and other mega-expensive gadgets. Adobe also sells a Windows font manager called ATM (Adobe Type Manager) that lets you print PostScript fonts on non-PostScript printers.

Microsoft and Apple were sick of Adobe's having this monopoly in the font market. So they got together and co-developed the TrueType font format, which at the time seemed about as likely as the United States and Russia joining forces right after the Bay of Pigs to organize a worldwide polo tournament.

But they pulled it off, and Microsoft has amassed its 17th fortune selling TrueType fonts to eager consumers. Windows 95 offers built-in support for TrueType and can print TrueType fonts to nearly any model of printer. TrueType has been such a success, in fact, that Corel converted its entire 50-quintillion font library to the TrueType format.

Windows 95 even shows you which kind of font you're about to apply. Two Ts before a typeface name in one of the font pop-up menus identify a TrueType font. An outlined T1 identifies a PostScript font. (T1 is short for Type 1, which is a PostScript font variation.) Take a look at Figure 10-12 to see these identifying marks.

Swimsuit" or "Aliens Ate My Sweetheart, Then Complained about Taste" — don't get much bigger than an inch tall. For this reason, points are an ideal and time-honored unit of measure among typographers, layout artists, and others who do their best to try to attract your attention to the written word.

Type is measured from the bottommost point on a lowercase *g* to the tippy-topmost peak of a lowercase *b*. (Lowercase letters such as *b, d, k,* and others are generally taller than capital letters.) If you're familiar with typewriter terminology, elite type is 10 points tall — roughly the size of the type that you're currently reading — whereas pica type is 12 points tall.

- ✔ To change the type size, select an option from the size pop-up menu on the Property Bar (labeled in Figure 10-11). Or, double-click on the pop-up menu, enter any value between 0 (far too small) and 3,000 points (42 inches!) from the keyboard, and then press Enter.

- ✔ You can also enter a value into the Size option box in the Object Properties dialog box. Click Apply to see how the text looks in its new size.

✔ If you prefer to use inches or some other nontraditional unit of measure for your type, you can choose a different unit from the Default Text Units pop-up menu on the Text tab of the Options dialog box (press Ctrl+J to open the dialog box).

Mucking about with the justification

The row of buttons at the bottom of the Text panel of the Object Properties dialog box and the matching buttons on the Property Bar control the alignment of the lines of type in a text block. Text alignment is sometimes called *justification* — as in, "We need no justification to call this attribute what we please." Starting with the leftmost button in the dialog box and on the Property Bar and moving to the right, the alignment buttons (labeled in Figure 10-11) work as follows:

✔ The No Alignment button doesn't do much of anything. I know, that's a terrible thing to say, but it's true. Usually, this option produces the same effect as the Left Alignment button, discussed next. But when you get into the more complicated techniques described in the next chapter, the No Alignment option can wreak havoc on your text. The technical support guy I talked to claimed that he's never gotten a call about this option in his career. So not only does it not work, nobody cares about it. Good feature.

✔ The Left Alignment button aligns the left sides of all lines of text in a text block. The text in this book, for example, is left justified.

✔ The Center Alignment button centers all lines of type within the text block.

✔ The Right Alignment button aligns the right sides of all lines of text.

✔ The Full Alignment button aligns both the left and right sides of the text. As you can see in the last example of Figure 10-13, CorelDraw has to increase the horizontal space between characters and words to make this happen.

✔ Click on the Forced Full Alignment button to align the left and right edges of all lines of type, including the last line. This option is useful for stretching out a single line of text across the full width of a text block.

Figure 10-13 shows the results of applying the left, center, right, and full justification options. The gray areas in back of the text represent the text blocks.

When applied to artistic text, the justification options actually change the location of the text block on the page. If you select the Right Alignment button, for example, the right side of the text block scoots over to where the left side of the text block used to be.

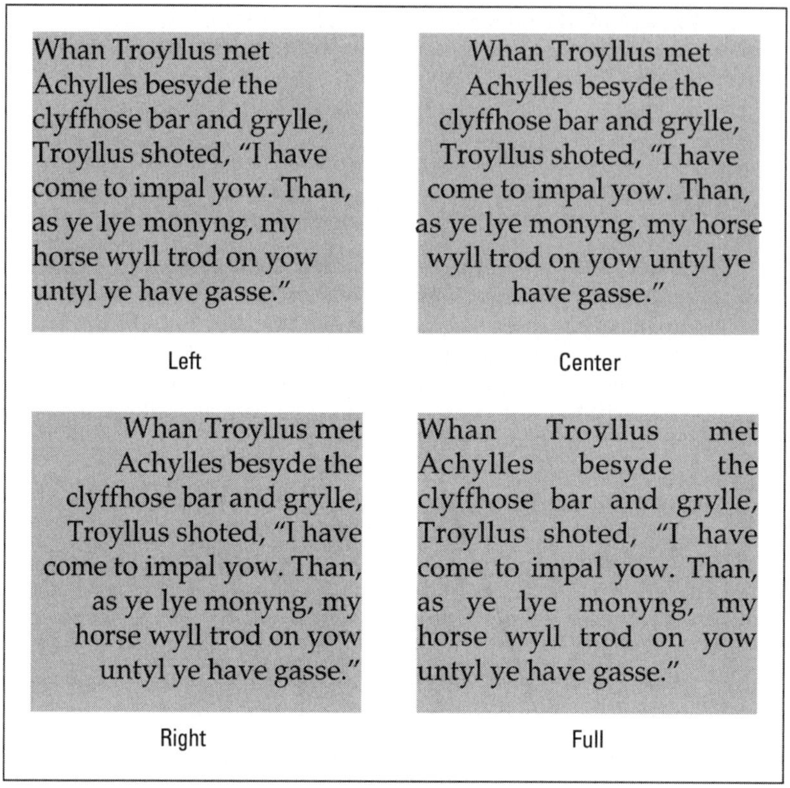

Whan Troyllus met Achylles besyde the clyffhose bar and grylle, Troyllus shoted, "I have come to impal yow. Than, as ye lye monyng, my horse wyll trod on yow untyl ye have gasse."

Left

Whan Troyllus met Achylles besyde the clyffhose bar and grylle, Troyllus shoted, "I have come to impal yow. Than, as ye lye monyng, my horse wyll trod on yow untyl ye have gasse."

Center

Whan Troyllus met Achylles besyde the clyffhose bar and grylle, Troyllus shoted, "I have come to impal yow. Than, as ye lye monyng, my horse wyll trod on yow untyl ye have gasse."

Right

Whan Troyllus met Achylles besyde the clyffhose bar and grylle, Troyllus shoted, "I have come to impal yow. Than, as ye lye monyng, my horse wyll trod on yow untyl ye have gasse."

Full

Figure 10-13: The primary justification buttons offered by CorelDraw.

Formatting options for rare occasions

In addition to those formatting attributes discussed earlier in this chapter, CorelDraw offers a mess of other formatting options that you may find interesting depending on, well, your level of interest. You can access these options by clicking on the Format Text button on the Property Bar (the button is a big letter *F*), selecting the Format Text button in the Object Properties dialog box, or just pressing Ctrl+T. CorelDraw displays the Format Text dialog box, shown in Figure 10-14, which is new to Version 7.

The dialog box changes depending on whether you select paragraph or artistic text. For artistic text, you see only the Font and Spacing tabs, and some Spacing options available for paragraph text run away and hide, too.

Here are some of the options that you may want to explore:

✔ Via the Font tab of the dialog box, you can apply underlines and other kinds of lines to selected characters of text, create superscript or subscript type, or convert characters to all capital letters or small caps (reduced-size capital letters).

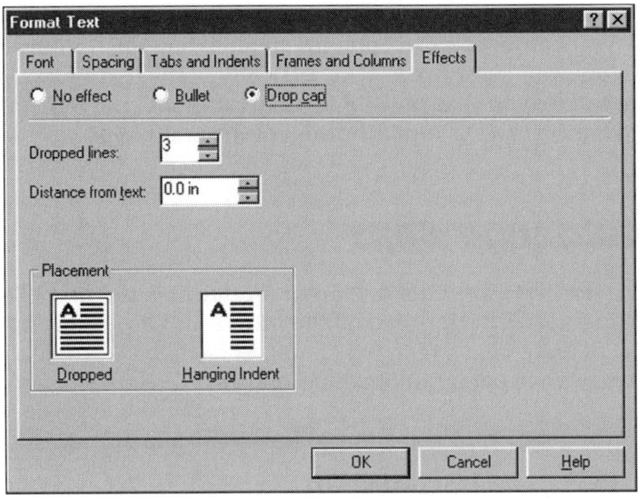

Figure 10-14:
Formatting a
drop
cap in
paragraph
text is
among the
formatting
tasks that
you can
accomplish
in the
Format Text
dialog box.

✔ The Spacing tab contains options that enable you to change the amount of horizontal space between neighboring letters and words. You can also change the amount of vertical space between lines of type. Luckily, you can more conveniently change spacing using the shape tool, as discussed in the next chapter. As mentioned before, you have more spacing options for paragraph text than artistic text.

The only unique option in the Spacing tab is the Use Automatic Hyphenation check box. Select this option, and CorelDraw automatically hyphenates long words so that they better fill the width of a text block.

✔ Switch to the Tabs and Indents panel to display an overwhelming assortment of options for positioning tabs and indents. You need to use these options only if you want to create a table of information — for example, a price list.

✔ Switch to the Effects panel to add a symbol to the beginning of a paragraph, which is useful for adding fancy bullets to the beginning of paragraphs in lists (like this one). You can also format a character as a drop cap, as explained in the next section.

✔ Click on the Frames and Columns tab to uncover options to divide the text in the active text block into multiple columns. Better yet, don't. Believe me, these options are more work than they're worth. Creating your own columns by drawing blocks of text is easier, as explained in the section "How to Flow Text between Multiple Blocks," earlier in this chapter. (By the way, the term *frames* in this instance refers to good old paragraph text blocks, not the kind of page-dividing frames that some designers use in their World Wide Web pages.)

> ✔ One option on the Frames and Columns panel that may come in handy is the Vertical Justification pop-up menu. Using the options on the menu, you can center your text vertically in the text block, spread out all lines of text so that they fill up the text block (the Full option), or align your text to the top or bottom of the text block.

Dropping your caps

Flip back to the first page of this chapter. Notice how the first character in the first paragraph is bigger than all the others and drops down into the second line of text? That oversized character is called a drop cap, and you can add one to your paragraph text in CorelDraw 7. Here's how:

1. **Select the letter that you want to format as a drop cap.**

2. **Open the Format Text dialog box.**

   You can accomplish this feat of engineering in a snap by clicking on the blue italic *F* button on the Property Bar or pressing Ctrl+T.

3. **Click on the Effects tab and select the Drop <u>C</u>ap radio button.**

   The drop cap options reveal themselves, as shown in Figure 12-14. In the first option box, specify how many lines of text you want the drop cap to sink into. In the second option box, specify how far you want to shift the drop cap from the neighboring characters. (You'll probably need to play with this setting a bit to figure out the value that works best for the font and type size you're using.)

   The two placement options determine whether your drop cap appears within the normal paragraph margins or hangs out over the left margin all by itself, as shown in the two placement icons. Click on the icon for the design that you want to use.

4. **Click on OK.**

   CorelDraw automatically resizes your selected character and formats the character according to the drop cap options that you selected.

Think that drop cap looks silly? Your first instinct may be to simply select and delete the character to get rid of it. But when you do, CorelDraw just shoves the next character in the line of text over and formats that character as a drop cap. To temporarily turn off the drop cap formatting, click on the Show/Hide Drop Cap button on the Property Bar, which looks just like the first drop cap placement icon in the Format Text dialog box. Click on the button again to bring the drop cap back.

To remove the drop cap formatting from the text block entirely, select the character and then select the No Effect button on the Effects tab of the Format Text dialog box.

Please Check Your Spelling

CorelDraw isn't a word processor. But that doesn't mean that you want to look stupid because you can't spell *leptodactylous* (which, by the way, means that you have slender toes). For this reason, CorelDraw can check and help you correct your spelling. Okay, so it doesn't know how to spell leptodactylous any better than you do. But it does know several thousand common words, and you can teach it to spell leptodactylous if you so desire.

Here's how to check the spelling of your document:

1. **Choose Text⇨Writing Tools⇨Spell Check.**

   Or right-click on a text block with the text tool and select Spell Check from the pop-up menu. Or better still, just press Ctrl+F12.

   Whichever method you use, CorelDraw begins checking the words in your document. When it comes to the first bad word, it displays the Spell Checker dialog box, shown in Figure 10-15. The misspelled word appears selected inside the Not Found option box. The Replace With option box shows the best guess CorelDraw can make at the proper spelling. The Replacements scrolling list contains other alternatives. In Figure 10-15, Draw suggested such humorless replacements for *Whan* as *What* and *When,* along with such curious options as *Han, Chan,* and *Khan.*

Figure 10-15: CorelDraw doesn't appreciate my Old English spelling.

2. **Select an alternative spelling or enter a new one.**

   If the word in the Replace With option box doesn't strike your fancy, you can click on an alternative in the scrolling list. Or, enter an entirely new spelling in the Replace With option box.

3. **Click on Replace.**

   CorelDraw replaces the misspelled word with the correct version and sets about searching for the next misspelling.

4. **Repeat Steps 2 and 3.**

   Keep checking words until CorelDraw announces that the spell check is complete. Click on the Yes button to close the Spell Checker dialog box.

If you're an alert reader, you may have noticed that the Spell Checker dialog box contains some buttons that I didn't address in the preceding steps. Not to worry — those options are described in the following list:

- What if CorelDraw flags a word as misspelled, but you want the word to appear just as it is? Take my Old English text, for example. It's 100 percent historically authentic, guaranteed by Lloyd's of London. Yet CorelDraw questions nearly every word. Just goes to show you how much things have changed since the 15th century, or whenever it was that I wrote the text. Sometimes, you have to teach Draw how to spell. If your word is spelled correctly, you can add it to the dictionary by clicking on the Add button.

- If you don't want to correct a word and you don't want to add it to the dictionary — you just want CorelDraw to skip the word and continue checking the rest of the text — click on the Skip Once button.

- To make Draw ignore all occurrences of a word throughout the current spelling session, click on the Skip All button.

- The Auto Replace button is a dangerous one. Click on this button, and you tell CorelDraw to replace the misspelled word automatically in this and all future documents you spell check — without notifying you. If you want to use this option, be sure to select the Prompt Before Auto Replace option from the Options pop-up menu in the Spell Checker dialog box so that you can see all the changes that CorelDraw is making.

- Select the portion of your document that you want to spell check from the Check pop-up menu. Your choices vary depending on what type of text is selected, but in general, you can check a specific portion of your text — a paragraph, sentence, word, or selected text — or check the entire document.

Shortcut to Typographic Happiness

You can train CorelDraw to fix your most egregious errors as you make them — without ever once bringing up the Spell Checker dialog box. To use this feature, choose Text➪Writing Tools➪Type Assist, which displays the Type Assist tab of the Options dialog box, as shown in Figure 10-16. (Or press Ctrl+J and click on the Type Assist tab.) The five significant options in this dialog box work as follows:

- Select the first check box to automatically capitalize any word that follows a period, even if you enter the letter without pressing Shift. I heartily recommend this option.

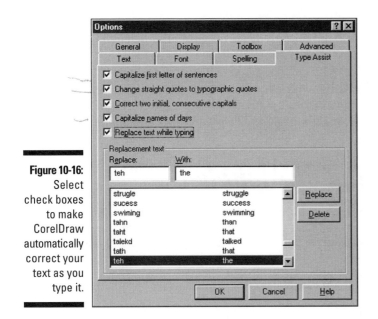

Figure 10-16:
Select
check boxes
to make
CorelDraw
automatically
correct your
text as you
type it.

- ✔ In the world of professional typography, quotation marks curl around the text. But when you enter a quotation mark from your keyboard, you get two boring, straight lines. Those lines aren't quotation marks, they're ditto marks. To turn your dreadful dittos into beautiful quotation marks, select the second check box.

- ✔ Select the third check box to correct any two capital letters in a row. For example, THe would become The. I don't like this option because it messes with words that are supposed to be formatted in all capital letters. But select it according to your own taste.

- ✔ If you forget to capitalize the names of days, select the fourth option. Too bad it doesn't correct the names of months and other proper nouns as well.

- ✔ The last check box — Replace Text While Typing — replaces abbreviations with spelled-out words. If you type **cont.**, for example, CorelDraw replaces it with *continue*. If you type **3/4** Draw replaces it with the proper fraction symbol ³/₄.

  If you don't like the way CorelDraw replaces abbreviations — you might prefer that it swap *cont.* with the *past tense, continued,* for example — select an abbreviation from the scrolling list, modify the word in the With option box, and click on the Replace button.

- ✔ You can remove entries from the scrolling list to make CorelDraw stop replacing certain words or characters you type. For example, if you find it annoying that CorelDraw changes *div.* to *division,* click on the *div.* entry in the scrolling list and click on Delete.

TIP

✔ You can also make Type Assist correct your spelling. Suppose that you constantly misspell the word *the* as *teh*. Just enter *teh* into the Replace option box, enter *the* into the With option box, and click on the Add button. From then on, CorelDraw corrects your spelling of *teh* on the fly.

If you frequently type the same long string of text, use Type Assist to speed up text entry. For example, you can tell CorelDraw to replace the characters CD7 with CorelDraw 7 For Dummies.

A Different Kind of Alphabet

The only kind of text that I haven't yet described is symbols. Choose Tools➪Symbols or press Ctrl+F11 to display the Symbols roll-up shown in Figure 10-17. This roll-up offers access to a variety of simple pictures that you can use to accent or enhance a drawing. You can even combine symbols to create drawings in and of themselves.

┌Scrolling list of symbols

Symbol font name

Figure 10-17:
Symbols
are like
alphabets
of modern
hieroglyphs.

"Little pictures?" you're probably thinking. "Wait a minute. Pictures don't constitute text. What's going on here?" Hey, take it easy. Your problem is that you're used to a Western-style alphabet, in which abstract letters stand for sounds — the same way that a dollar bill stands for a piece of gold approximately the size of a single-celled microorganism. Letters are merely metaphors for real communication.

But try thinking Eastern. Think hieroglyphics. Think kanji. These are bazillion-character alphabets in which each character represents a word or phrase. Similarly, the CorelDraw symbol library is a big alphabet. If you want to say "chair," for example, show a chair.

To add a symbol from the Symbols roll-up to your drawing, do the following:

1. **Select a symbol category from the pop-up menu at the top of the roll-up.**

   The categories are actually fonts that CorelDraw recognizes as containing something other than standard letters, numbers, and punctuation.

2. **Select a symbol from the scrolling list.**

   CorelDraw shows you every single wacky character in the font.

3. **Enter the size of the symbol into the <u>S</u>ize option box.**

   Or just use the default Size value. You can always resize the symbol later by dragging its selection handles, as you can any other object.

   Keep in mind that just as with letters in the alphabet, not all symbols in a font are the same height. The Size value is gauged by the tallest symbol in the category.

4. **Drag the symbol into the drawing area.**

   No need to mess around with the Tile option. It just repeats the symbol over and over inside a portion of your drawing, like some dreadful electronic wallpaper.

To view more symbols at a time, drag one of the corners of the roll-up.

You can edit symbols in the same way that you edit free-form paths, as described in Chapter 5. You can also fill and outline symbols as described in Chapter 7, duplicate symbols as described in Chapter 8, and transform symbols as discussed in Chapter 9. Come to think of it, symbols may be drawings after all.

Chapter 11
Mr. Typographer's Wild Ride

• •

In This Chapter

▶ Why CorelDraw is better than Disneyland

▶ Dragging characters to new locations

▶ Kerning special character combinations

▶ Changing the amount of space between characters and lines

▶ Fitting text to a path

▶ Changing character orientation and vertical and horizontal alignment

▶ Wrapping text around a circle

▶ Converting character outlines to editable paths

• •

*I*magine that you're a character of text. An H, for example. Or a P. It's not important. So far, your CorelDraw existence has been about as exciting as a traffic jam. Sometimes you wrap to the next line of type, and other times you get poured into a different text block. There are characters above and below you; you even have a few riding your rear end. It's no fun being a character in a standard text block.

But one day, you rub shoulders with a street-wise character, like an E or an S — you know, some character that really gets around — and it tells you about a world of possibilities that you haven't yet explored. You can play bumper cars, ride loop-de-loop roller coasters, even stretch yourself into completely different shapes. It's one big amusement park for text!

This chapter is your golden admission ticket. Have a blast.

Learning the Rules of the Park

Before I stamp your hand and let you into the park, a word of caution is in order. Just as too many rides on the Tilt-A-Whirl can make you hurl, too many wild effects can leave a block of text looking a little bent out of shape. The trick is to apply text effects conservatively and creatively.

If you're not sure how an effect will go over, show it to a few friends. Ask them to read your text. If they read it easily and hand the page back to you, you know that you hit the mark. If they say, "How did you make this?" the effect may be a little overly dramatic, but it's probably still acceptable. If they have trouble reading the text, or if they say "How did you *make* this?" — in the same way that they might say "What did I just *step* in?" — your effect very likely overwhelms the page and is therefore unacceptable.

Then again, I don't want to dampen your spirit of enthusiasm and exploration. Use moderation in all things, including moderation, right? So you make yourself sick on the Tilt-A-Whirl. It's part of growing up. So your first few pages look like run-amuck advertisements for furniture warehouses. It's part of learning the craft.

And if some blue-blood designer looks at your work and exclaims, "Gad, this page! Oh, how it frightens me!" you can retort, "Well, at least my text has more fun than yours." That's one way to get fired, anyway.

Playing Bumper Cars

As explained in earlier chapters, you can drag an object's nodes and handles with the shape tool. Well, this basic functionality of the shape tool permeates all facets of CorelDraw, including text. If you select the shape tool (press F10) and click on a text block, you see three new varieties of nodes and handles, as shown in Figure 11-1. These nodes and handles appear whether you click on a block of artistic text or paragraph text. They enable you to change the location of individual characters and increase or decrease the amount of space between characters and lines of text.

Text nodes

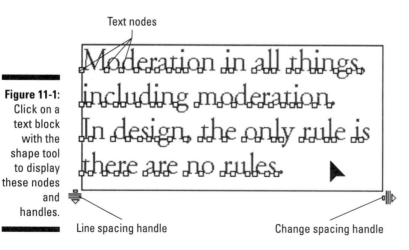

Figure 11-1:
Click on a
text block
with the
shape tool
to display
these nodes
and
handles.

Line spacing handle   Change spacing handle

Selecting and dragging text nodes

Text nodes enable you to change the locations of individual characters in a text block. You can slightly nudge the characters to adjust the amount of horizontal spacing, or you can drag a character several inches away from its text block just to show it who's boss. Here's how text nodes work:

- Each text node is associated with the character directly on its right. Click on a node to select it and its character. Black nodes are selected; white nodes are not.

- To select multiple nodes at a time, drag with the Shape tool to draw a marquee (dotted outline) around the nodes. You can also Shift+click on a text node to add it to the selection.

- If you select a few too many nodes in the process of marqueeing, Shift+click on the ones you want to deselect.

- Drag a selected text node to reposition all selected characters. In Figure 11-2, for example, I selected every other letter in the word *Moderation* and dragged the selected node associated with the *n*.

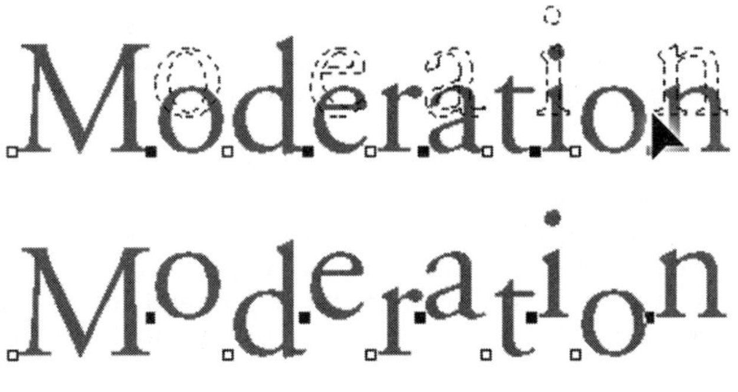

Figure 11-2: Dragging several selected characters with the shape tool (top) and the outcome of the drag (bottom).

Moderation

Moderation

- You can also change the values in the X and Y option boxes on the Property Bar to move the selected text nodes and their corresponding characters. The X value shifts the characters horizontally; the Y value moves them vertically.

- Ctrl+drag nodes to move the letters along the current line of type.

✔ Use the arrow keys to nudge selected characters without fussing with your mouse. By default, each keystroke moves the selected characters $^1/_{10}$ inch. You can change this distance by pressing Ctrl+J (<u>T</u>ools⇨ <u>O</u>ptions) and changing the Nudge value (as explained in the "Nudging with the arrow keys" section of Chapter 6).

✔ Press Ctrl+arrow key to "super nudge" the characters — that is, to move them 10 times farther than a regular nudge.

✔ To return a single character to its original position, select its node and choose Te<u>x</u>t⇨<u>S</u>traighten Text. To undo all changes to an entire text block, select the text with the arrow tool and choose the Straighten Text command.

Kern, kern, the baffling term

You can drag entire lines to offset lines of type, drag whole words, or just create crazy text blocks by dragging individual characters six ways to Sunday, whatever that means. But the most practical reason for dragging nodes is to adjust the amount of horizontal space between individual characters, a process known as *kerning*.

In *Webster's Second Edition* — the sacred volume that editors swear by (or should it be "by which editors swear"?) — *kern* is defined as the portion of a letter such as *f* that sticks out from the stem. Those nutty lexicographers say that the term is based on the French word *carne,* which means a projecting angle.

Now, I don't know about you, but where I come from: A) we don't go around assigning words to projecting angles, and B) kern means to smush two letters closer together so that they look as snug as kernels of corn on the cob. Of course, I don't have any Ivy League degree and I don't wear any fancy hat with a tassel hanging off it, but I'm pretty sure them Webster fellers are full of beans.

Not like you care. You're still trying to figure out what I'm talking about. So here goes: Consider the character combination *AV.* The right side of the letter *A* and the left side of the character *V* both slope in the same direction. So, when the two letters appear next to each other, a perceptible gap may form, as shown in Figure 11-3. Though the *A* and the *V* in *AVERY* aren't any farther away from each other than the *V* and the *E,* the *E* and the *R,* and so on, they appear more spread out because of their similar slopes.

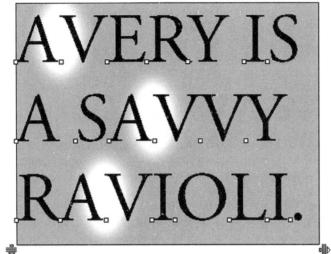

Figure 11-3:
I wish I had
a dime for
every time
we taunted
Avery with
this one.

To tighten the spacing, I first chose Tools⇨Options and reduced the Nudge value to 0.01 inch — a value that's significantly better to the art of fine-tuning text than the default .10 inch. After pressing Enter to return to the drawing area, I used the shape tool to select the *V*s as well as all the letters to the right of the *V*s. Then I pressed the left-arrow key a couple of times. (Selecting the letters to the right of the *V*s ensured that I didn't widen the spacing between any *V* and the letter that follows it.) Figure 11-4 shows the result of kerning the *A*s and *V*s. I also kerned a few other letters for good measure. (The nodes of these letters are selected in the figure.)

As it turns out, CorelDraw is pretty darn good at kerning certain letter combinations automatically. It handles the classic *AV* combination with as little thought as you and I typically devote to blinking. Even so, I find myself kerning letters just about every time I create them, particularly in headlines and other prominent text blocks. You can trust CorelDraw to do a good job, but only you can make text picture perfect.

Changing overall spacing

Dragging text nodes changes the space between selected characters only. If you want to evenly adjust the spacing between all characters in a text block, you need to drag one of the two spacing handles, labeled back in Figure 11-1.

✔ Drag the character spacing handle (located on the right side of the text block) to change the amount of horizontal space between all characters in the text block, as in the first example of Figure 11-5.

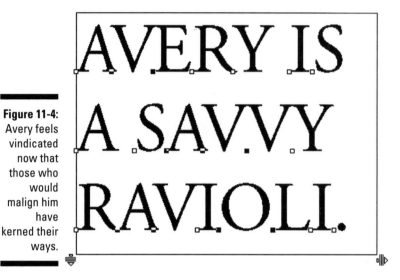

Turn off the Snap to Grid function before dragging the spacing handles. (Choose Layout⇨Snap to Grid, and if you see a check mark next to the command, click on the command to turn off the function.) With the grid off, you can drag the spacing handles anywhere you like.

 ✔ Ctrl+drag the character spacing handle to change the size of the spaces between all words in the text block, as in the second example of Figure 11-5.

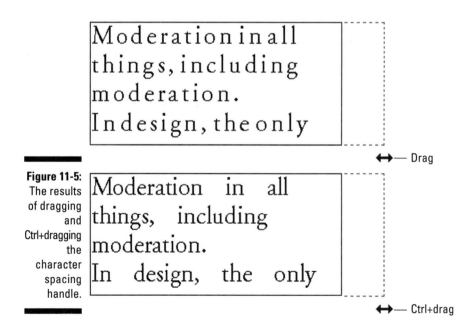

Moderation in all
things, including
moderation.
In design, the only

↔— Drag

Figure 11-5:
The results
of dragging
and
Ctrl+dragging
the
character
spacing
handle.

Moderation   in   all
things,   including
moderation.
In   design,   the   only

↔— Ctrl+drag

TIP

✔ Drag the line spacing handle (located on the left side of the text block) to adjust the amount of vertical space between all lines of type, except those that are separated by a paragraph break (created when you press Enter while typing your text). In other words, lines in the same paragraph are affected, but neighboring lines in different paragraphs are not, as the first example in Figure 11-6 shows.

✔ Ctrl+drag the line spacing handle to change the amount of vertical space between different paragraphs, as in the second example of Figure 11-6. This tip doesn't work with artistic text because artistic text has no paragraphs.

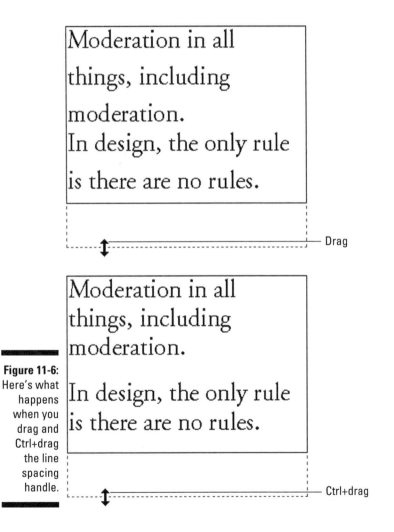

Figure 11-6: Here's what happens when you drag and Ctrl+drag the line spacing handle.

Notice that dragging a spacing handle has no effect on the size of a block of paragraph text. The block itself remains the same size, and the newly spaced characters reflow to fit inside it.

Also, changes that you make to a text block affect the characters in that text block only. If the text block is linked to another text block, some reformatted characters may flow into the linked text block, but the characters that originally occupied the linked text block remain unchanged.

Riding the Roller Coaster

CorelDraw calls the feature I'm about to discuss *fitting text to a path*. But I call it giving your text a ride on the roller coaster. After all, when your text is fit to a path, it has the time of its life, as Figure 11-7 clearly illustrates.

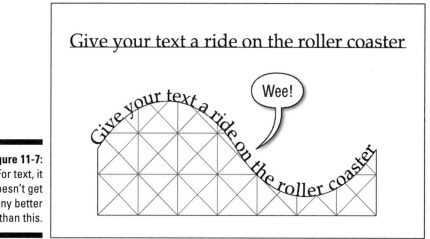

Figure 11-7:
For text, it doesn't get any better than this.

As shown in the top example of Figure 11-7, text normally sits on an imaginary flat line. This line is called the *baseline.* You can substitute an oval or free-form path for the baseline in two ways in Version 7. Both methods apply to artistic text only; paragraph text is not mature enough to ride the roller coaster.

In Version 7, you can fit text to a path quickly, like so:

1. Select the text tool.

2. Move the text tool cursor near the path.

Circles, ovals, and gradually curving paths work best, by the way, but any path is acceptable.

3. When the cursor changes to an insertion marker, click.

You should see a little A with a wavy line next to the insertion marker.

4. Type your text.

CorelDraw automatically fits your text to the path, placing the text on top of the object. (You can change the position of the text after you create it, as explained later in this chapter.) Select the arrow tool, and your text becomes selected. Click again to set the text firmly in place.

If you want to want to fit existing text to a path, follow these steps instead:

1. Select the text with the arrow tool.

2. Shift+click on the path.

CorelDraw adds the path to the selection.

3. Choose Text⇨Fit Text to Path.

The Fit Text To Path roll-up appears. If the selected path is a free-form path, the roll-up looks like the left example in Figure 11-8. If the selected path is a rectangle, oval, or polygon, the roll-up appears as shown on the right side of the figure.

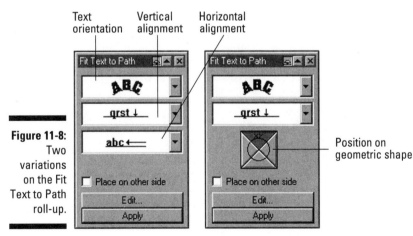

Text orientation   Vertical alignment   Horizontal alignment

Position on geometric shape

Figure 11-8: Two variations on the Fit Text to Path roll-up.

Note that the old shortcut for displaying the roll-up, Ctrl+F, now displays the Special Fill roll-up.

4. Select the desired options.

I describe them all momentarily. For now, you don't need to select anything. You can just accept the default settings and go on.

5. Click on the Apply button.

Watch the baseline adhere to that path. Those little characters are probably losing their lunches (in a good way, of course).

6. If the text doesn't attach to the path the way you had anticipated, select the Place On Other Side check box and click on the Apply button.

The text switches to the opposite side of the path and flows in the opposite direction.

The Fit Text To Path roll-up offers either three pop-up menus or two pop-up menus and a group of buttons, depending on the kind of path you're using. The options determine the orientation of characters on a path, the vertical alignment of the text, and the horizontal alignment. (The following sections explain how these options work.)

You can also use the roll-up to change the orientation and alignment of existing text fit to a path. Just click on the text with the arrow tool. Or, if you have more than one text block fit to the same path, Ctrl+click on the text block that you want to change. The text and path become selected. You can then use the options in the Fit Text to Path roll-up to manipulate the text.

When you select text that's fit to a path, the Property Bar displays many of the same controls found in the Fit Text to Path roll-up, including the orientation and alignment pop-up menus and the Place Text on Other Side option. Happily, all the controls are accessible no matter what monitor display setting you use, as shown in Figure 11-9. (Okay, so the Place Text on Other Side button is partially cut off, but you can still click on it without any trouble.)

Figure 11-9:
The
Property
Bar
controls for
adjusting
text to fit to
a path.

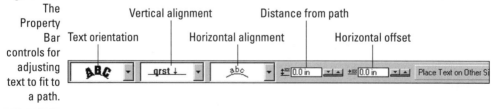

Orienting text on a path

The top pop-up menu in the Fit Text to Path roll-up offers you the choice of rotating characters along the path, skewing them horizontally or vertically, or none of the above. Figure 11-10 shows the effects of each of the options on the text from Figure 11-7, in the same order that the options appear in the pop-up menu in both the roll-up and the Property Bar.

Want my real opinion? All right, here goes:

- ✔ The rotate characters option is the most useful of the four, which is probably why it's the default setting. When in doubt, stick with this option.

- ✔ The vertical skew option is also very useful, as long as your path doesn't have any super-steep vertical inclines. Along the left and right sides of a circle, for example, characters skew into nothingness.

Figure 11-10:
The effects of the four orientation options, shown in the same order that they appear in the first pop-up menu in the Fit Text to Path roll-up and Property Bar.

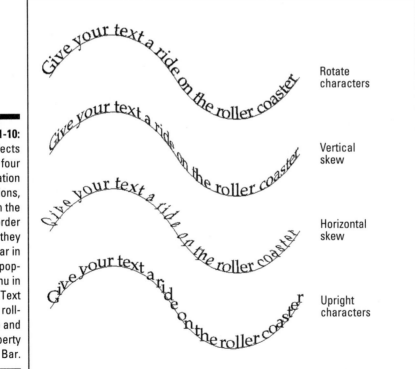

Rotate characters

Vertical skew

Horizontal skew

Upright characters

✔ The horizontal skew option is set up backward so that letters skew against the path instead of with it. The *G* at the beginning of the text in Figure 11-10, for example, should skew to the right, into the path — not to the left, away from it. Use this option only if you want to elicit comments such as "Gee, this is weird" or "Maybe we should go back to typewriters."

✔ The upright characters option is so ugly, it makes the horizontal skew option look like a good idea.

To change the orientation of text using the roll-up, select the option and then click on Apply. If you select the option from the Property Bar pop-up menu, CorelDraw automatically reorients the text.

Changing the vertical alignment

The vertical alignment pop-up menu lets you change the vertical positioning of characters with respect to the path. The options work as described in the following list. (I listed them in the order that they appear in the menu):

✔ The first option adheres the baseline of the text to the path.

✔ The second option aligns the tops of the tallest characters, called ascenders *(b, d, k)* to the path. The text hangs from the path like a monkey hangs from a tree limb, except that the text doesn't swing back and forth and scratch for ticks.

✔ The third option aligns the bottom of the hangy-down characters, called descenders *(g, j, p)* to the path, so that the letters balance like little tightrope walkers.

✔ The fourth option causes the path to run smack dab through the middle of the text like a gold chain threaded through beaded pearls.

✔ Don't you just love these clever little analogies?

✔ The last option enables you to drag text anywhere you want with respect to the path. To use this option as you're fitting text to the path for the first time, select the option from the Fit Text to Path roll-up and click on Apply. After CorelDraw fits your text to the path, drag from the text to display a positioning line. The line indicates the distance between the path and the text. When you release the mouse button, CorelDraw redraws the text at its new location. To apply this option to existing text on a path, Ctrl+click on the text, select the option from the roll-up, click on Apply, and then drag the text. (If you want to use the Property Bar, click on the text, select the option from the pop-up menu, Ctrl+click on the text, and then drag the text.)

Generally, you should stick with the default setting, which adheres text by its baseline. The one time to change this option is when you're creating text on a circle, as I describe in the section after next.

Changing the horizontal alignment

When you're attaching text to a free-form path, you can use the third pop-up menu in the Fit Text To Path roll-up or the Property Bar to change the horizontal alignment of text.

- ✔ The first option aligns the first character of text with the first point in the path. This option works like the left-justification option in a normal text block.

- ✔ The second option centers the text on the path, just as the center-justification option centers text in a normal text block.

- ✔ Starting to get the idea?

- ✔ The last option aligns the last character of text with the last point in the path. It works like — you guessed it — the right justification option in a normal text block.

Shifting text around a geometric object

When you attach text to a geometric object — rectangle, oval, or polygon — CorelDraw replaces the third pop-up menu in the roll-up with a square that contains four inset triangular buttons (see Figure 11-8). The buttons work like radio buttons; that is, you can select only one button at a time. You can either center the text along the top of the object, along the left or right side, or along the bottom. The third pop-up menu in the Property Bar offers you the same options.

Shifting text in specific increments

The Version 7 Property Bar offers two controls that give you an easy way to fine-tune the placement of text on a path. Using the first option box on the Property Bar (labeled Distance from path back in Figure 11-9), you can shift the text closer to or farther away from the path. Using the horizontal offset control (also labeled back in Figure 11-9), you can move the text horizontally along the path a specific distance.

To use the controls, just click on the up- or down-pointing arrows next to the option boxes. Or, double-click on an option box, enter a new value from the keyboard, and press Enter.

Creating text on a circle

Want to see the vertical and horizontal alignment options put into use? Well, too bad, because I'm going to show you anyway.

I don't know why, but when folks want to fit text to a path, the path they usually have in mind is a circle. Ironically, however, text on a circle is the least intuitive kind of roller-coaster text that you can create. If you simply attach a single text block around the entire circle, half of the text will be upside down. So, you have to attach two text blocks to a single circle, one along the top of the circle and another along the bottom, as explained in the following steps.

Note that the steps instruct you to create your text first and then use the Fit Text to Path roll-up to fit the text to the path. Here's how it works:

1. **Draw a circle.**

   If you need help, see Chapter 4.

2. **Create two separate blocks of artistic text.**

   Click with the text tool and enter text for the top of the circle. Then click at another spot and enter some more text for the bottom. Oh, and keep your text short.

3. **Select the circle and the first block of text.**

   Using the arrow tool, click on the circle and Shift+click on the text that you want to appear along the top of the circle. Or drag around both text and circle to enclose them in a selection marquee. (From here on, everything is done with the arrow tool.)

4. **Choose Text⇨Fit Text to Path to bring up the Fit Text To Path roll-up.**

   If the roll-up is already displayed, skip this step.

5. **Click on the Apply button.**

   The default settings are fine for now. The text adheres to the top of the circle, as in Figure 11-11. (If the text doesn't appear on the top of the circle, click the top triangle in the position square in the Fit Text to Path roll-up and click Apply.)

6. **Click in an empty portion of the drawing area with the arrow tool.**

   This step deselects everything. You have to do this so that you can select the circle independently in the next step.

7. **Select the circle and the second block of text.**

   Click somewhere along the bottom of the circle to make sure that you select the circle only. (If you click along the top of the circle, you might select the text as well.) Then Shift+click on the second block of text.

8. **Click on the bottom triangular button in the Fit Text To Path roll-up.**

   See the location of the arrow cursor in Figure 11-12.

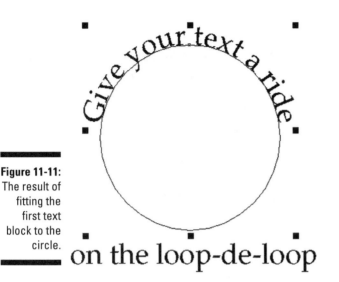

Figure 11-11:
The result of fitting the first text block to the circle.

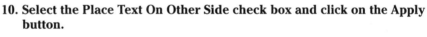

9. **Click on the Apply button.**

   The second block of text wraps around the bottom of the circle, as shown in Figure 11-12. Unfortunately, the text is upside down. To remedy this . . .

10. **Select the Place Text On Other Side check box and click on the Apply button.**

    Or just click on the Place Text On Other Side button on the Property Bar.

    The text now appears as shown in Figure 11-13 — right-side up, but scrunched. To loosen the text up a bit, do Step 11.

11. **Select the second option from the vertical alignment pop-up menu and click on Apply.**

    Figure 11-14 shows me in the process of selecting this option, which, as you may remember, aligns the ascenders of the characters to the circle so that the text hangs down.

    You can also choose this option from the Property Bar. Either way, the resulting text looks something along the lines of Figure 11-14.

12. **Click in an empty portion of the drawing area with the arrow tool.**

    Notice that the top row of type doesn't look like it's quite aligned with the bottom row. To fix this, you need to select the top text block independently of the other text. But first, you must deselect everything.

13. **Don't do this step.**

    It's unlucky. If today is Friday, shut the book and don't open it again until you've had it inspected by a psychic.

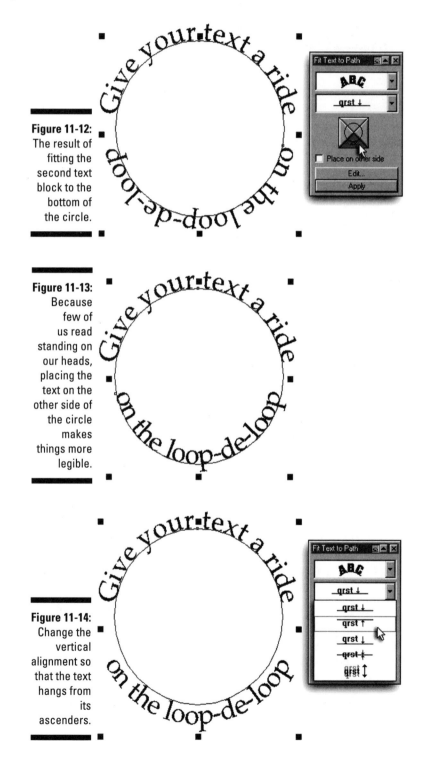

Figure 11-12: The result of fitting the second text block to the bottom of the circle.

Figure 11-13: Because few of us read standing on our heads, placing the text on the other side of the circle makes things more legible.

Figure 11-14: Change the vertical alignment so that the text hangs from its ascenders.

14. **Ctrl+click on a character in the top text block.**

    By Ctrl+clicking, you select the top text block along with the circle but independently of the bottom text block.

15. **Select the third option from the vertical alignment pop-up menu and click on Apply.**

    In Figure 11-15, you can see me selecting this option, which aligns the descenders of the characters to the circle, causing the text to walk the tightrope.

    As with other alignment options, this one is available from the Property Bar menu as well as in the roll-up.

    The top text block now aligns correctly with the bottom text block. Figure 11-15 shows text on a circle as it was meant to be.

If you want to create text on a circle on the fly — that is, by typing directly on the path instead of creating the text, selecting text and circle, and then clicking the Apply button in the roll-up — you need to approach these steps in a different order. Create the text for the bottom of the circle *first.* Place the text on the bottom of the circle using the Property Bar or roll-up, and then create the text for the top of the circle.

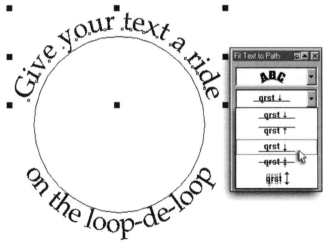

Figure 11-15:
Upper and lower text blocks align perfectly after I apply the descender option.

Remember that to change the position of a text block when you have more than one text block fit to the same path, you need to Ctrl+click on the text block to select it.

Editing text on a path

After you fit a block of artistic text to a path, you may find it difficult to edit the text with the text tools. You can do it by moving the text tool cursor around the letters until the cursor changes to an I-beam and then dragging across the text. But this technique requires dexterity and patience. The easier method is to select the text independently of the path. I touched on this technique in Step 15 of the previous section, but it bears probing in a little more depth.

- Ctrl+click *on the text* — not on the path — with the arrow tool to select the text independently of the path. If you fit two text blocks to a path, as in the previous example, Ctrl+click on the text twice in a row. (That's twice in a row on the same text.) Ctrl+clicking once on the text selects text and path together and enables you to change the orientation and alignment of the text using the roll-up or Property Bar.

- To edit the content of the text, Ctrl+click on the text to select it and then choose Text⇨Edit Text or press Ctrl+Shift+T. CorelDraw displays a separate text-editing window in which you can edit characters or words and even change the typeface, style, and size. Click on the OK button when you're done. (Don't press Enter; that just inserts a carriage return.)

- To apply new formatting, use the Property Bar controls or right-click on a letter of text and choose the Properties command to display the Object Properties dialog box, just as you do when formatting normal text. (I discuss both Property Bar and dialog box in Chapter 10.)

- Click inside the color palette to apply color to the text. Right-click on a color swatch to apply a color outline around each letter of text. Click or right-click on the X swatch to delete the fill or outline, respectively.

- Kern the text by selecting text nodes with the shape tool and then dragging them or using the arrow keys to nudge them. CorelDraw automatically constrains the movement of the text to the contour of the path.

Editing the path

You can change the fill and outline of the path to which the text is attached by selecting the object and using the Fill and Pen options described back in Chapter 7. It's very straightforward — no special tricks involved. In many cases, you'll want to hide the path by selecting the object and right-clicking on the X icon at the top of the Color Palette.

If you prefer, you can delete the path entirely, leaving just your text behind. To do so, click the path with the arrow tool and press Delete. Be careful not to select the text instead — if you delete the text, both path and text disappear.

You can also edit the shape of the path using the shape tool. Again, just be sure that you click on the path and not the text. For laughs, try dragging the top node of the circle back in Figure 11-15 to cut out a pie wedge. Without missing a beat, CorelDraw fits the text along the contours of the wedge.

Breaking it up

To detach text from a path and return it to the straight and narrow, do the following:

1. **Select the path and the text.**

   Just click on the text or marquee around text and path with the arrow tool.

2. **Choose Arrange⇨Separate.**

   This step separates the text from the path. However, the text remains all twisty-curly.

3. **Choose Text⇨Straighten Text.**

   The text returns to its plain old self.

Meddling with Type

If you're interested in creating logos or other very special text, you should know about one more command that's applicable to artistic text. After selecting a block of artistic text with the arrow tool, the shape tool, or one of the text tools, choose Arrange⇨Convert To Curves or press Ctrl+Q. CorelDraw converts the outlines of every single character in the text block to free-form paths. An A, for example, ceases to be a letter of text and becomes a triangular path with a bar across it.

After you convert the characters to paths, you can edit the paths using the arrow and shape tools (described in Chapter 5) exactly as if you drew the characters with the pencil tool. The top example in Figure 11-16 shows a block of everyday, mild-mannered text. The second example is the same block of text after I converted it to paths and edited the heck out of it.

Try this technique out a few times and you'll soon find that converted characters are as easy to integrate and edit as symbols and other pieces of clip art. Converted text serves as a great jumping-off point for creating custom logos and other exciting effects.

WARNING!

Back up your text before you make it a mess

Before converting a block of text to editable paths, you may want to first make a duplicate of the text by pressing Ctrl+D (Edit⇨Duplicate). Doing so will:

✔ Save the original version of the text block in case you really mess up the nodes.

✔ Keep the original handy for quick and easy comparisons.

✔ Provide you with an extra copy of the text in case your boss wants you to change a word or two. (I can hear your boss now. "You just have to press a key, right?")

✔ Make you so happy that you'll spend the rest of your days in a state of ecstatic delirium.

Figure 11-16:
A line of artistic text as it appears before (top) and after (bottom) converting it to paths and editing the paths with the shape tool.

Chapter 12

The Corner of Page and Publish

In This Chapter

▶ The biting sarcasm of trees

▶ Creating a multipage document

▶ Turning pages

▶ Deleting excess pages

▶ Pouring overflow text from one page onto another

▶ Repeating logos and other objects using the master layer

▶ Hiding master layer objects selectively

▶ Changing the page size

*D*esktop publishing has revolutionized the way folks churn up and spit out bits of Oregon forestry, thereby remedying the grossly inefficient way we were churning up the forests back in the 1970s. Happily, we now have more open space in which to park our cars and receive computer-created fliers that we never wanted stuck under our windshield wipers. And now you can be a part of this ever-expanding field.

Okay, that's an overstated bit of sarcasm. With the proliferation of CD-ROMs and World Wide Web pages, computers will very likely lessen our reliance on paper over time. But for now, the printed page is the medium of choice. Furthermore, although I'd love to warn you about the evils of printing, I'm in no position to lecture, having myself wasted more pieces of paper than you will probably use in a lifetime. Don't get me wrong — I'm a dedicated recycler. Ecocycle loves me. I use only the cheapest bond paper available, and I print only when I absolutely have to. Hey, you want to get off my case?

Now that I've insulted folks on both sides of the spotted owl debate, let's get down to business. This chapter and the next are devoted to output. This chapter explains how to set up your pages; Chapter 13 explains how to print them. After you finish these chapters, you'll be fully prepared to create fliers and stick them under windshield wipers with the best of them.

And remember, always use bright pink or yellow paper. That way, folks can spot your fliers nine miles from their cars and mentally prepare themselves to snatch the fliers up and wad them into balls at their earliest convenience.

Pages upon Pages

Unless you've read some outside sources or scoped out the Layout menu, you may assume that CorelDraw is good for creating single-page documents only.

Not so. Though primarily a drawing program, CorelDraw lets you add as many pages to a document as you like. (As usual, I'm sure that there's a maximum number of pages, but I'll be darned if I care what it is. I mean, if you're trying to lay out an issue of *National Geographic,* you need a different piece of software. If you have in mind a newsletter, a report, or maybe a short catalog, CorelDraw will suffice.)

Adding new pages

When you create a new drawing (choose File⇨New or press Ctrl+N), CorelDraw gives you a one-page document. To make the document a multipager, you have to add pages manually, like so:

1. **Choose Layout⇨Insert Page.**

   Or simply press either the PgUp or PgDn key. The dialog box shown in Figure 12-1 appears.

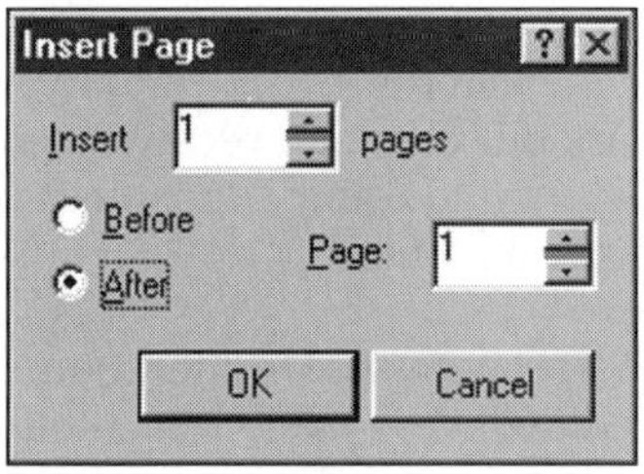

Figure 12-1:
Add pages
via this
dialog box.

> **Insert Page** [?][X]
>
> Insert [1] pages
> ○ Before   Page: [1]
> ● After
>
> [OK] [Cancel]

2. **Enter the number of pages that you want to add into the Insert option box.**

3. **Press Enter.**

   CorelDraw adds the specified number of pages to your document.

Adding pages bit by bit

The rest of the options in the Insert Page dialog box enable you to add pages sporadically rather than in one fell swoop. Suppose that you set up a four-page document and then discover that you need six pages to hold all your wonderful drawings and ideas. Using the Before and After radio buttons together with the Page option, you can tell CorelDraw exactly where to insert the pages. If you want to insert pages between pages 3 and 4, for example, you could do either of the following:

✔ Enter 3 into the Page option and select the After radio button.

✔ Enter 4 into the Page option and select the Before radio button.

Rocket science it ain't. If the pages that you want to enter aren't sequential, you have to use the Layout⇨Insert Page command more than once. For example, to insert one page between pages 2 and 3 and two others between pages 3 and 4, you have to choose the Insert Page command twice, once for each sequence.

Thumbing through your pages

After you add pages to your previously single-page drawing, CorelDraw displays a series of page controls near the lower-left corner of the screen, as shown in Figure 12-2. Here's how they work:

✔ Click on the first icon — the left-pointing arrow with a line next to it — to go to the first page in your document.

✔ Click on the left-pointing Page Back button to back up one page — from page 3 to page 2, for example.

✔ Click on the right-pointing Page Forward button to advance one page (for example, from page 2 to page 3).

✔ You can also change pages by pressing the PgUp and PgDn keys. The PgUp key backs up a page, and the PgDn key advances one page. "But wait a minute," you think. "Didn't you say earlier that the PgUp and PgDn buttons bring up the Insert Page dialog box?" The answer is yes — you're not losing your mind. If you're on page 1 and you press the PgUp key, or if you're on the last page in your document and press the PgDn key, the dialog box appears.

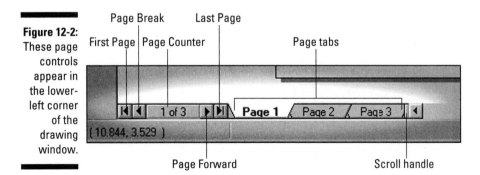

Figure 12-2: These page controls appear in the lower-left corner of the drawing window.

Page Break   Last Page

First Page | Page Counter   Page tabs

Page Forward   Scroll handle

✔ Click on the Last Page button — the right-pointing arrow with a line next to it — to advance to the last page in the document.

✔ When you're working on the first page in your document, the Page Back button changes to a + sign. The same thing happens to the Page Forward button when you're on the last page. Click on the + sign to display the Insert Page dialog box, which is set up to add pages automatically before the first page or after the last page in your document.

✔ Click in the Page Counter button to display the Go To Page dialog box, which enables you to turn to any page you like. Just enter the page number, press Enter, and off you go. (You can also access this dialog box by choosing Layout⇨Go To Page.)

✔ A series of page tabs appears to the right of the Last Page button. You can click on the tab for any page to go to that page.

✔ To increase or decrease the amount of space allotted to the page tabs, drag the scroll handle between the tabs and the scroll bar (the handle's labeled in Figure 12-2).

Removing the excess

If you add too many pages, you can delete a few of them by choosing Layout⇨ Delete Page. A dialog box, shown in Figure 12-3, asks which pages you want to delete. You can delete the single page you're viewing by pressing Enter. Or you can delete another page by entering the page number in the Delete Page option box. To delete a sequential range of pages, select the Through to Page check box and enter a page number in the option box to the right.

You cannot delete all pages in the document. That would leave you with no pages at all, and CorelDraw will have none of that.

If you delete a page that you didn't mean to delete, choose Edit⇨Undo Delete Page or press Ctrl+Z (or Alt+Backspace).

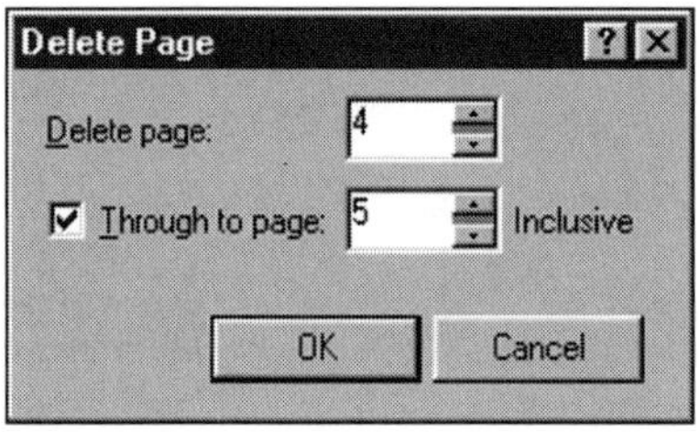

Figure 12-3:
Use this
dialog box
to kiss
pages
good-bye.

Delete Page	? X
Delete page:	4
☑ Through to page:	5 Inclusive
OK	Cancel

Flowing text between pages

As mentioned in Chapter 10, you can pour text across multiple pages. The following steps reveal the secret to accomplishing this little trick:

1. **Drag with the text tool to create a block of paragraph text.**

2. **Enter too much text for the text block.**

Be sure that the Expand and Shrink Paragraph Frames to Fit Text option on the Text panel of the Options dialog box (Ctrl+J) is turned off. Otherwise, your text block keeps growing as you type, and that defeats the purpose of this merry exercise.

3. **Select the arrow tool and click on the bottom tab in the text block.**

You get the page cursor.

4. **Go to the page where you want to flow the text.**

Use the page tabs or page arrows to navigate to the right page.

5. **Drag with the page cursor on your new page.**

Your overflow text appears in the new text block.

Isn't that a trip? Despite the fact that the two text blocks are on separate pages, they're linked.

When the text tool is selected, a dotted blue line extends from the text blocks to indicate that they're linked. A little box next to the line indicates the page number where the next linked block is located.

If you drag up on the tab in the text block on page 1, excess text flows into the text block on the page 2. Incidentally, linked text blocks don't have to be on sequential pages; they can be several pages apart. You can start a story on page 5 and continue it on page 44. You can even make a separate text block that tells readers, "Continued on page 44." These here are professional page-layout capabilities!

Your Logo on Every Page

If you're serious about creating multipage docs, I have another prescription for you. It's called the *master layer*. This function enables you to put special text and graphic objects on every page of your document without having to place them all individually. For example, if you're creating a company newsletter, you may want to show the name of the newsletter at the bottom of each page and the company logo in the upper-right corner. CorelDraw can handle the chore of inserting the name and logo on every page for you automatically.

Establishing a master layer

If you want CorelDraw to automatically place certain elements on every page of your document, you have to create a master layer and then place the elements on it. The following steps explain how:

1. Choose Layout⇨Layers Manager or press Ctrl+F3.

The Layers roll-up, shown in Figure 12-4, appears.

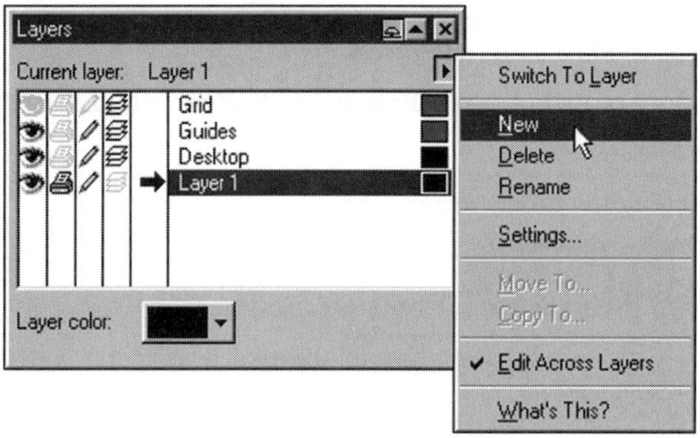

Figure 12-4:
Use the
Layers
roll-up to
create a
master
page.

2. Choose the New command from the roll-up menu.

You do this by clicking on the right-pointing arrowhead to display the menu and then clicking on the New command, as shown in Figure 12-4. CorelDraw adds a new layer — presumably named Layer 2 — to the list in the Layers roll-up.

3. Enter a name for the master page layer.

Immediately after you create a layer, its name is active, so you can just enter a name from the keyboard. Press Enter when you're done.

4. Click on the dimmed master page icon to the left of the layer name.

In Figure 12-5, I zoomed in on this special little icon, spotlighted it, and labeled it so that you won't miss it.

5. Add text and graphics to taste.

Create those logos, add those newsletter names, draw those boxes. Add everything that you want to repeat throughout your document. (Incidentally, it doesn't matter what page you're on. A master layer is a master layer throughout every page of the document.)

6. Click in front of Layer 1 in the Layers roll-up.

Or you can double-click on the Layer 1 name. Either way, that little right-pointing arrow jumps from in front of Master Page to in front of Layer 1. This step makes the original layer active again.

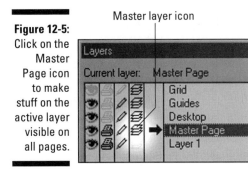

Master layer icon

Figure 12-5:
Click on the
Master
Page icon
to make
stuff on the
active layer
visible on
all pages.

7. **Drag Layer 1 up a level so that it appears above the Master Page layer.**

   In all likelihood, you want the text and graphics on the master page to appear in back of the text and graphics that you add to a page. By dragging the Layer 1 name up one notch in the list — or, alternatively, dragging Master Page to the bottom — you change the order of the layers so that the master page rests in back of the active layer.

8. **Choose <u>E</u>dit Across Layers from the Layers roll-up menu.**

   Click again on the right-pointing arrowhead to display the menu — or right-click anywhere inside the right half of the roll-up — and then click on <u>E</u>dit Across Layers to remove the check mark next to the option name. This step turns the option off so that you can manipulate objects on the current layer only, thus protecting the master layer objects.

To see how the master page that you just created works, try this: First, draw an oval or something simple on one page of your document. Then, go to another page in your document. When you turn to the other page, you see all the objects that you added to the master layer. But you don't see the oval you drew on the standard layer.

In most cases, you need only two layers in a document: one for the master page and one for your main document pages. The only reason for having more than two layers is to segregate objects in extremely complex drawings. People who go around drawing human anatomies and blow-outs of car engines — we're talking about folks with the patience of saints — use layers. However, typical novice and intermediate users have little reason to explore layers — except for creating a master page, of course — and they're all the merrier for it. I almost never use layers, and I'm an expert. At least, that's what my wife tells me every time I take the trash out to the curb. And she's not just saying it, either; you can sense that she really means it.

In any case, to find out a little more about layers — not much, mind you, but a little — read the first section of Chapter 21.

Hiding master layer objects on page 1

As a general rule of thumb, you don't display master layer objects on the first page of a multipage document. For example, what's the point of listing the name of the newsletter at the bottom of the first page? The name is already listed at the top of that page in big bold type. Very likely, the company logo is a part of the newsletter title, so there's no reason to repeat it, either.

To hide master layer objects on one page only, do this:

1. **Turn to the first page.**

   Or, if you don't want to see the master layer objects on some other page, turn to that page.

2. **Right-click on the name of your master layer in the Layers roll-up and then select the Settings command.**

   You can also select the name of your master layer and choose Settings from the roll-up menu, but right-clicking is easier. The Master Page Settings dialog box appears, as in Figure 12-6.

3. **Deselect the Visible check box.**

   This step hides the master layer objects.

4. **Select the Apply Layer Changes to the Current Page Only check box.**

   This step allows you to change the settings for the current page only.

5. **Press Enter.**

   CorelDraw closes the dialog box and returns you to the drawing area. All master layer objects have now disappeared from view. However, the objects remain visible on all other pages.

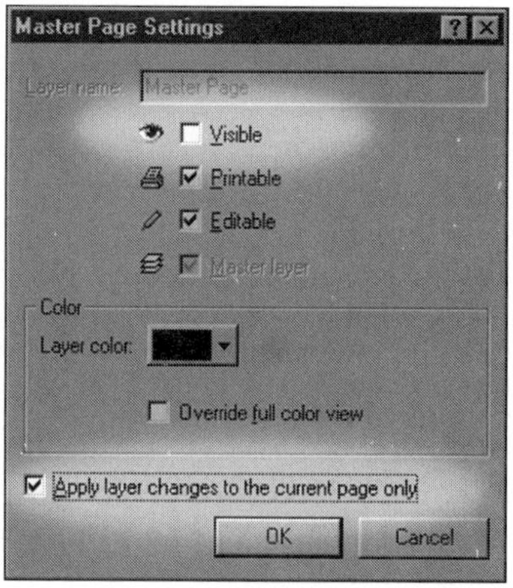

Figure 12-6: Click on each of the spotlighted check boxes to hide the Master Page objects for a single page of your document.

To get rid of a master layer entirely, click in front of the Master Layer name in the Layers roll-up and choose Delete from the roll-up menu. Or right-click on the Master Layer name and choose Delete from the resulting pop-up menu. A dialog box alerts you that you're about to delete the layer; click on OK to thank CorelDraw for the warning and move forward with the process.

If you want to hide the master layer for printing purposes, click on the little printer icon next to the master layer name in the Layers roll-up or deselect the Printable check box in the Master Page Settings dialog box.

I Need a Bigger Page!

In the United States, most folks use letter-sized paper (8 $\frac{1}{2}$ inches wide by 11 inches tall). In other countries, page sizes vary. But no matter what — at least, I don't know of any exceptions — CorelDraw is set up for the most likely scenario. If you're using the most common page size in your neck of the woods and you like your pages upright, you don't have to worry about the command I'm about to describe.

But what if you're doing something slightly different? Maybe you're creating a document that will be printed on legal-sized paper. Or maybe you're planning to print on letter-sized paper but you want to flip the page on its side. No problem. Changing the page size and orientation is simple.

You can now make most changes to your page setup by simply using the Property Bar controls labeled in Figure 12-7. A few more advanced controls reside in the Page Setup dialog box, which you display by choosing Layout⇨Page Setup. The dialog box also appears in Figure 12-7.

You can display the Page Setup dialog box quickly by double-clicking on the page border or on the gray shaded area around the right and bottom edges of the page. Or right-click on the border or shaded area and choose Page Setup from the resulting pop-up menu.

Use the Property Bar and dialog box options as follows:

  ✔ To change the size of the pages in the document, select a predefined page size option from the Paper pop-up menu in the dialog box or on the Property Bar.

  ✔ If you're unsure how large one of the predefined page sizes is, just select it. CorelDraw automatically displays the dimensions of the selected page size in the Width and Height option boxes, both in the dialog box and on the Property Bar.

  ✔ If you just want to set the page size to match the size of the paper loaded into your printer, click on the Set From Printer button in the dialog box.

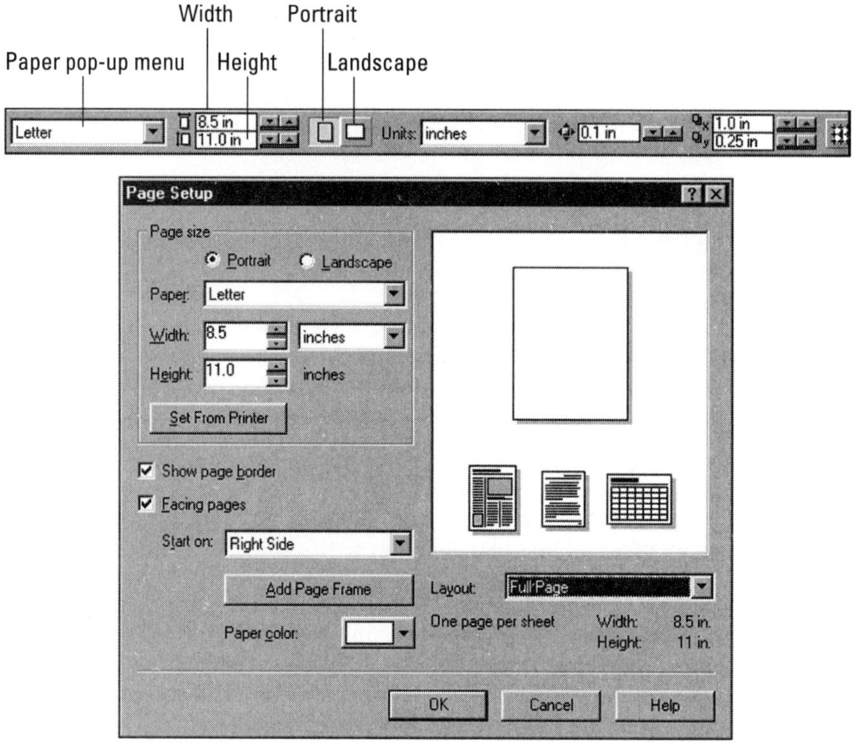

Width   Portrait

Paper pop-up menu | Height | Landscape

Figure 12-7:
To change
your paper
size and
orientation,
you can
use the
Property
Bar
controls or
Page Setup
dialog box.

✔ If none of these page sizes strikes your fancy, enter your own dimensions into either set of Width and Height option boxes. You can change the unit of measurement by making a selection from the Units pop-up menu on the Property Bar or from the pop-up menu to the right of the Width option box in the dialog box.

✔ Select the Landscape button to lay the page on its side. Select the Portrait button to stand it up again. You can access this option via the dialog box or the Property Bar.

✔ Select the Facing Pages check box in the dialog box to display two facing pages in the drawing area at once. For example, when you open up a four-page newsletter, page 2 and page 3 face each other. The even-numbered page (page 2) is on the left, and the odd-numbered page (page 3) is on the right. If you want to see these pages as your reader will see them, select the Facing Pages option.

✔ Don't even bother with the rest of the options. Unless you're creating three-fold fliers on bright pink paper, with ugly borders around each page, they're a complete waste of time.

Chapter 13

Those Poor, Helpless Trees

In This Chapter

▶ Preparing your drawing to be printed

▶ Orienting your drawing on the printed page

▶ Selecting a paper size

▶ Printing every page of a document

▶ Printing multiple copies

▶ Printing a specific range of pages

▶ Scaling the drawing on the printed page

▶ Tiling poster-sized artwork onto several pages

▶ Using the page preview options

▶ Creating color separations

*A*dvising a perfect stranger like you how to use your printer is like trying to diagnose a car problem without ever seeing the car, without knowing the make and model, without having driven more than, say, ten models in my entire life, and without even knowing what sort of symptoms your car is exhibiting. Printers come in so many different types and present so many potential printing hazards that I can't possibly give information designed specifically for your machine.

In other words, I'm completely in the dark. I'm the blind leading the blind. Sure, I can tell you how to print from CorelDraw — in fact, that's exactly what I'm going to do in this chapter — but every word that I write assumes that:

  ✔ Your printer is plugged in.

  ✔ Your printer is turned on and in working order.

  ✔ The printer is properly connected to your computer.

  ✔ Windows 95 is aware of your printer's existence.

  ✔ Your printer is stocked with ribbon, ink, toner, paper, film, or whatever else is required in the way of raw materials.

If you barely know the location of the printer, let alone anything else about the God-forsaken thing, assume for now that everything is A-OK and follow along with the text in this chapter. If you run into a snag, something is probably awry with your printer or its connection to your computer. As a friend of mine likes to tell me, "When in danger or in doubt, run in circles, scream and shout." If you shout loudly enough, someone may come to your rescue and fix your problem.

A helpful reader has advised me that the "scream and shout" quote originates "from none other than the greatest science fiction writer of all time, Robert Anson Heinlein." I'll take his word for it.

Reviewing the Basic Steps

The overall printing process includes these steps:

1. **Turn on your printer.**

2. **Press Ctrl+S or choose File⇨Save.**

   Although this step is only a precaution, it's always a good idea to save your document immediately before you print it, because the print process is one of those ideal opportunities for your computer to crash.

3. **Press Ctrl+P or choose File⇨Print.**

   A dialog box appears, enabling you to specify the pages that you want to print, request multiple copies, scale the size of the printed drawing, and mess around with a horde of other options. (I explain the various options throughout the rest of this chapter.)

4. **Click on the Properties button.**

   Up comes another dialog box that lets you make sure that you're printing to the correct printer and that the page doesn't print on its side. (Again, the options are explained later in this chapter.)

5. **Press Enter twice.**

   And they're off! The page or pages start spewing out of your printer faster than you can recite the first 17 pages of *Beowulf.*

It's magic, really. Through the modern miracle of computing, you've taken what is for all practical purposes a completely imaginary drawing — a dream known only to you and your machine — and converted it into a tangible sheet of hard copy.

Making Sure That Everything's Ready to Go

Before you tell CorelDraw to print your drawing, you should check to see whether all applicable print settings are in order. This process is like checking to see that you have your keys as you exit your house. Just as you probably have your keys, your print settings are probably fine. But double-checking things may help you avoid some grief later on.

Selecting a printer

When you press Ctrl+P (or choose File⇨Print), CorelDraw displays the Print dialog box. The dialog box offers lots of options, but for now, the only ones that you need to care about are the Name pop-up menu and the Properties button, which I zoom in on in Figure 13-1. (The entire Print dialog box appears in Figure 13-3.)

Figure 13-1:
Select a
printer and
then click
on the
Properties
button.

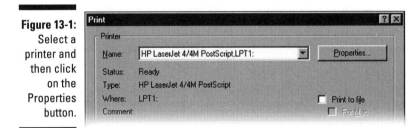

Select the type of printer that's connected to your PC from the Name pop-up menu. If you generally print all your documents from the same printer, the proper printer should already be displayed.

Changing paper size and orientation

After you choose a printer, click on the Properties button in the Print dialog box to display a printer properties dialog box like the one shown in Figure 13-2. Though your dialog box may look different from the one pictured in the figure, it should provide three or four areas of interest:

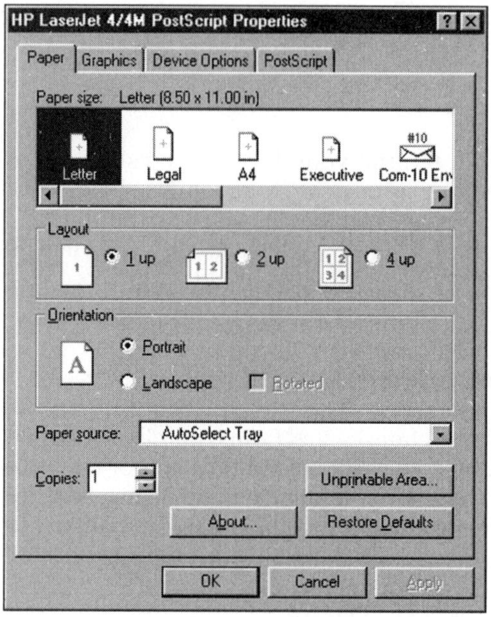

Figure 13-2:
Check this
dialog box
to make
sure that
everything's
in order.

✔ Select the correct paper size from the Paper Size list at the top of the dialog box. Ideally, the paper size should match the page size you selected for your drawing via the Page Setup dialog box or Property Bar (described just pages ago, in Chapter 12). Unless you have some special kind of paper loaded in the paper tray, you probably want to select letter-size paper.

✔ Not available for some printers, the Layout options let you group multiple pages from your drawing onto a single printed page. For example, you could select the 4 Up radio button to print four pages from your drawing on a single page, each reduced $1/4$ its normal size. This option is useful for getting a sense of what your pages look like without wasting a lot of paper and printing time.

✔ Select a radio button from the Orientation area to make sure that your drawing lines up correctly on the printed page. If your drawing is taller than it is wide, select Portrait. If not, select Landscape.

✔ Specify where the paper is coming from by selecting an option from the Paper Source pop-up menu. Some office printers have more than one paper tray. If you want to print on letterhead or some other kind of special paper, select the Manual Feed option. Then shout to the printer guy, "Shove a piece of letterhead into the manual feed slot, would you?"

You may also find a Copies option box, which lets you print more than one copy of each page in your drawing. Ignore this option for now. An identical, more convenient version of the option resides in the standard Print dialog box, as explained in the upcoming "Printing multiple copies" section.

After making your selections, press Enter to return to the Print dialog box, discussed further in the next section.

Printing Those Pages

The Print dialog box is displayed in its entirety in Figure 13-3. Naturally, I could tell you how every single one of these options work. But for the moment, I'll assume that you're more interested in getting the job done than learning about printing on an option-by-option basis. To this end, the following sections outline some common printing scenarios. Later on, I describe a few of the most important printing options on their own.

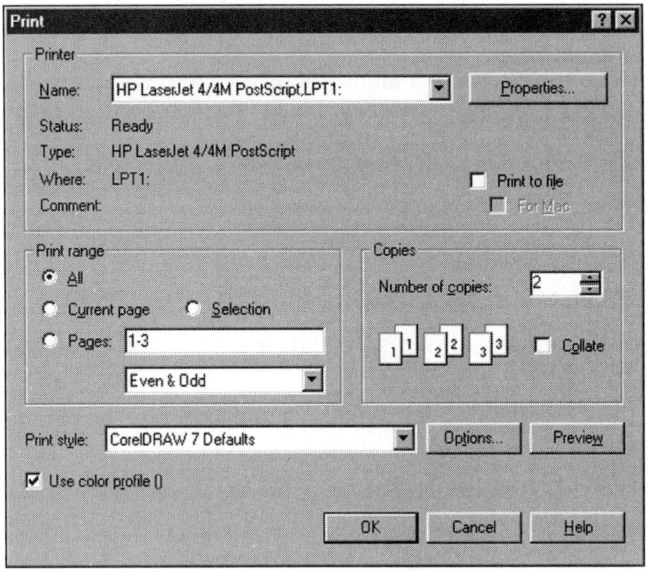

Figure 13-3:
The Print
dialog box
lets you
specify
which
pages you
want to
print and
how many
copies of
each page
you want.

Printing the entire document

To print your entire document — whether it's a single-page drawing or a multipage document — do the following:

1. **Press Ctrl+P or choose File⇨Print.**

   The Print dialog box appears.

2. **Press Enter or click on OK.**

   CorelDraw initiates the printing process.

As CorelDraw works on printing your drawing, the progress bar in the right corner of the status bar shows how close the printer is to printing your artwork. If you think of something you missed — for example, "Aagh, I forgot to draw in the toenails!" — and you're interested in saving a bit of tree, press Esc to halt the print job and return to your drawing.

Printing multiple copies

Generally, the tried-and-true method for producing multiple copies of a drawing, newsletter, or other document is to print a single copy and then photocopy it or trundle it off to a commercial printer. The latter option offers the benefit of a wide variety of paper stocks and the satisfaction of truly solid inks, compared with the malaise of toner and spotty ink cartridges supplied by computer printers. Even a fly-by-night, cut-rate commercial printer delivers better results than a photocopier.

If you don't have time for a commercial printer, and the office photocopier is out of whack, you can print multiple copies directly from CorelDraw:

1. **Make sure the printer is turned on and stocked with enough paper.**

   A full paper tray is a happy paper tray.

2. **Press Ctrl+P or choose File⇨Print.**

   There's that Print dialog box again.

3. **Enter the number of pages that you want to print in the Number of Copies option box.**

   You can go as high as 999 copies, a sufficient number of copies to send most printers to the repair shop.

4. **Select the Collate check box to group all pages in a document.**

   When Collate is turned off, CorelDraw prints all copies of page 1, followed by all copies of page 2, and so on. When the option is checked, Draw prints the first copy of each page in the document, then the second copy, then the third, and so on. The helpful little graphic to the left of the check box even changes to demonstrate what you can expect.

5. **Press Enter.**

Printing a few pages here and there

When working on a multipage document, you won't always want to print every single page. One time, you may just want to see what page 2 looks like. The next, you'll want to reprint page 6 after fixing a typo. Still another time, you'll have to print a new copy of page 3 after the first one jams in the printer. To print certain pages only, follow these steps:

1. **Press Ctrl+P.**

   You've been through this enough times to use the keyboard equivalent and quit relying on the Print command.

2. **Click on the Current Page radio button to print the single page displayed on-screen.**

   If you want to print a range of pages, double-click on the value in the Pages option box (or press Tab until the box is highlighted). Then, type in the pages separated by a dash. For example, to print pages 1, 2, and 3, enter 1–3 into the Pages option box.

   You can also print nonsequential pages separated by commas. To print pages 1, 2, 3, 5, 7, 8, and 9, for example, you enter 1–3,5,7–9.

3. **Press Enter.**

Still More Printing Options

If you want to store up some extra printing knowledge for a rainy day, you may like to know what the following options do:

- ✔ Click on the Selection radio button to print only those objects in the drawing that are selected. (If no object was selected when you chose the Print command, this option is dimmed.)

- ✔ Click on the Options button in the lower-right portion of the Print dialog box to display the Print Options dialog box, as shown in Figure 13-4. The dialog box contains options that you can use to change the size of the drawing with respect to the printed page. (These options don't affect the actual size of the objects in the drawing area, mind you; they affect output only.)

- ✔ The page preview area that was formerly part of the Print Options dialog box is now contained in the Print Preview dialog box, discussed in the next section.

- ✔ Enter values in the Top and Left option boxes on the Layout tab of the Print Options dialog box to specify the location of the drawing as measured from the top-left corner of the printed page.

- ✔ Enter a value into the Width option box to change the width of the drawing. By default, CorelDraw resizes the drawing proportionally, automatically adjusting the Height value according to your changes to the Width value. This is why the Height value is dimmed.

- ✔ To resize the drawing disproportionately, turn off the Maintain Aspect Ratio check box. The Height value becomes available so that you can edit it independently of the Width value.

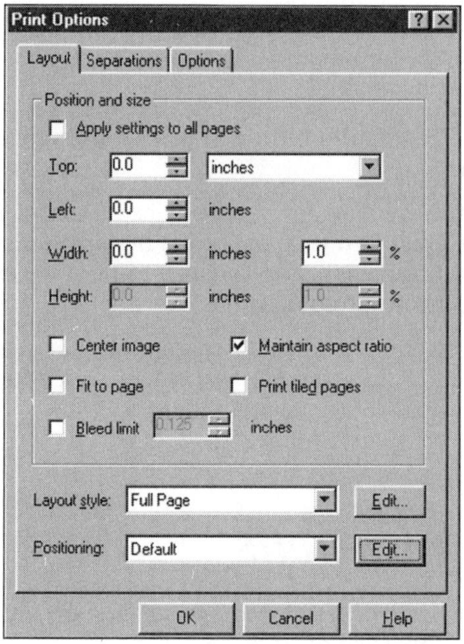

Figure 13-4:
Use the
options in
this dialog
box to
change the
size at
which your
drawing
prints.

✔ Enter values into the % option boxes to the right of Width and Height options to enlarge or reduce the printed size of the drawing by a percentage value.

✔ To center the drawing on the printed page, select the Center Image check box.

✔ Select the Fit to Page check box to reduce the size of the drawing so that it just fits onto a sheet of printed paper. This option is especially useful when you're printing poster-sized drawings on printers that handle only letter-sized paper.

✔ If you want to print a large drawing on small paper without reducing the drawing, you can cut it up into paper-sized chunks by selecting the Print Tiled Pages check box. For example, when printing an 11-x-17-inch drawing on a standard laser printer, the Print Tiled Pages option divides the drawing up into four pieces and prints each piece on a separate page.

✔ Man, is this stuff dry or what? Reading about printing options is like having sand in your mouth. Makes you want to spit. Ptwu, ptwu.

✔ Luckily, changing the printed size of a drawing using the page preview window is much easier than messing around with many of the options mentioned so far. Read on to find out how.

Using the page preview area

CorelDraw's page preview options, formerly found inside the Print Options dialog box, are now located inside the page preview window, as shown in Figure 13-5. To display your drawing in the preview window, you can either choose File⇨Print Preview or click on the Preview button in the Print dialog box. The various parts of the preview window work as follows:

✔ To increase or decrease the size of the drawing, click on the arrow tool icon and then click on your drawing. The entire drawing becomes selected. You can then drag one of the corner selection handles to proportionally increase or decrease the printed size of the drawing. As you drag, the status bar shows you the current width and height of the drawing.

✔ If the Maintain Aspect Ratio check box in the Print Options dialog box is turned off, you can drag a side or top or bottom handle to stretch the drawing without regard for the original proportions.

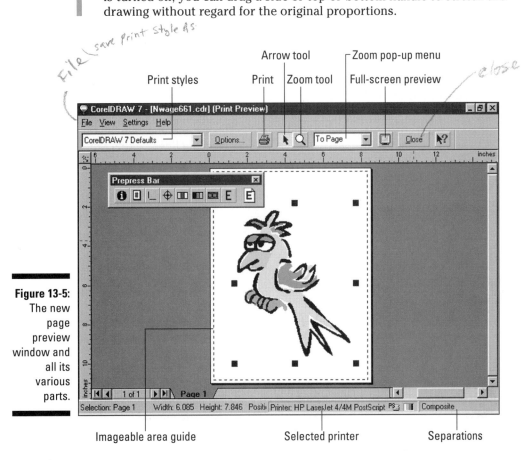

Figure 13-5:
The new page preview window and all its various parts.

- The Undo function doesn't work inside the print preview window. If you stretch your drawing beyond recognition and want to return to the original dimensions, just click on Close to close the preview window. Then, reopen the window to display your drawing at its original size.

- Click on the Options button to return to the Print Options dialog box and change any settings therein.

- Drag inside the area enclosed by the selection handles to change the placement of the drawing on the printed page.

- To zoom in on an area of your drawing, click on the zoom tool icon and click on the area that you want to inspect. To zoom out, Shift+click or right-click with the zoom tool. Alternatively, choose a zoom ratio from the Zoom pop-up menu or enter a custom zoom ratio into the pop-up menu.

- The *imageable area guide* outlines the area in which your printer can print objects. Except for typesetters and other fabulously expensive high-end printers, all printers have a dead zone around the outside of the page on which they cannot print. (Fax machines and old-style dot-matrix printers can print all the way from the top of the page to the bottom, but have dead zones along the sides.)

- If you select the Print Tiled Pages check box in the Print Options dialog box, you can enlarge the drawing to take up multiple pages. As you drag to make the drawing larger, CorelDraw adds more pages. If you make the drawing smaller, the program automatically deletes pages.

- The rulers provide additional points of reference when you're scaling your drawing. They even display tracking lines so that you can monitor the location of your cursor.

- Use the page navigation buttons and page tabs to view different pages, just as in the regular drawing window.

- Click on the full-screen preview icon to the right of the Zoom pop-up menu to fill the entire screen. Press Esc to return to the normal page preview window.

- Click on the status bar area labeled "Selected printer" in Figure 13-5 to display the Print Setup dialog box, where you can choose a different printer for this print job.

- Click on the separations area of the status bar to display the Separations tab of the Print Options dialog box, where you can specify whether you want to print color separations.

- The Prepress toolbar contains icons that enable you to add certain elements that may be required if you're sending your drawing to a service bureau for professional printing. Check with your service bureau to see which, if any, of these elements you should include. If you're not sending your drawing out for high-end printing, you can turn off the Prepress toolbar by simply clicking on the toolbar's Close button.

✔ Click on the Print icon to send your drawing on its merry way to the printer. Or, click on Close to return to the drawing window and play with your drawing some more.

If you repeatedly find yourself using the same print settings, you can save the settings as a *print style* by choosing File➪Save Print Style As in the print preview window. CorelDraw displays a dialog box in which you can give the print style a name and select which print options you want to save. After you press Enter, your print style appears on the print styles pop-up menu in the page preview window as well as in the Print dialog box. To apply the same print settings to another drawing, just select the style from the pop-up menu.

Printing full-color artwork

So far, I've covered and ignored roughly equal halves of CorelDraw's printing options. For reasons already discussed, I intend to leave it that way. But you should know about one other option, especially if you intend to print color drawings: the Print Separations check box.

Before I go any further, some background information is in order. You can print a color drawing in two ways: You can either print your drawing on a color printer, or you can separate the colors in a drawing onto individual pages. Each method has its benefits and its drawbacks:

✔ Printing on a color printer is easy, and you get what you expect. The colors on the printed page more or less match the colors on-screen. Unfortunately, a commercial printer can't reproduce from a color printout. Oh sure, you can make color photocopies, but professional printing presses can print only one color at a time.

✔ If you want to commercially reproduce your artwork, you have to tell CorelDraw to print color separations, one for each of the primaries cyan, magenta, yellow, and black (introduced in the section "Choosing a color model" in Chapter 7).

To print color separations in CorelDraw 7, do the following:

1. **Press Ctrl+P.**

2. **Click on the Options button inside the Print dialog box.**

   Up comes the Print Options dialog box shown in Figure 13-4.

3. **Click on the Separations tab.**

   This step switches you to the Separations panel. If the tab is already at the forefront, of course, you can skip this step.

4. **Select the Print Separations check box.**

5. **Click on OK to close the Print Options dialog box.**

6. Click on OK in the Print dialog box to initiate the print process.

CorelDraw automatically prints a separate page for each of the four primary colors.

You can also access the Separations tab by clicking on the separations area of the status bar in the print preview window.

Each page looks like a standard black-and-white printout, but don't let that worry you. When you take the pages to your commercial printer, a technician will photographically transfer your printouts to sheets of metal called *plates.* Each plate is inked with cyan, magenta, yellow, or black ink.

The technician prints all the pages with the cyan plate first, then runs the pages by the magenta plate, then the yellow plate, and finally the black plate. The inks mix together to form a rainbow of greens, violets, oranges, and other colors. For example, the four separations shown in Figure 13-6 combine to create a green Shenbop sitting on a royal purple lily pad. (Use your imagination — this is, after all, a black-and-white book.)

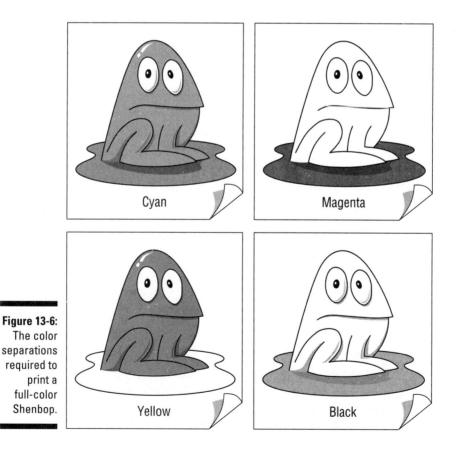

Figure 13-6:
The color separations required to print a full-color Shenbop.

Cyan   Magenta

Yellow   Black

Part IV
Corel's Other Amazing Programs

The 5th Wave   By Rich Tennant

"Of course graphics are important to your project, Eddy, but I think it would've been better to scan a <u>picture</u> of your worm collection."

In this part . . .

As mentioned in the introduction to this book, the CorelDraw 7 package contains more programs than you can shake a stick at, whatever that means. And as discussed in Chapter 1, I consider several of those programs of marginal value at best.

But the two programs discussed in this part — Photo-Paint and Dream 3D — are a different matter entirely. Photo-Paint is a highly capable program for editing photographs on a computer, which is why I devote three chapters to the subject. After introducing the Photo-Paint interface, I move on to such topics as opening images; painting inside images using traditional tools, such as pencils and airbrushes; erasing mistakes; applying effects; and cloning portions of the image to cover up blemishes and add in stuff that wasn't there in the first place. I also cover the Photo-Paint selection tools in alarming detail and explain the best way to sharpen the focus of an image and correct contrast and brightness.

Dream 3D takes you to the next frontier in computer graphics — three-dimensional drawing. Unfortunately, the frontier is pretty intimidating: Dream 3D is undoubtedly one of Corel's most complex programs. Chapter 18 eases you into the third dimension by providing a brief and gentle tour of Dream 3D. You find out how to import 3-D objects, how to move and rotate them in 3-D space, how to apply surface textures, and how to save the finished drawing as a photographic image. With remarkably little effort, you'll be rendering 3-D artwork, a practice so rarefied that fewer than 10 percent of all computer artists have ever attempted it.

In addition to covering Photo-Paint and Dream 3D, this part also contains valuable information on how to swap artwork between CorelDraw and Photo-Paint. You can use these same techniques to transfer data between other programs, too. For more on this intriguing topic, just move your eyes several inches to the right.

Chapter 14

Programs in the Night, Exchanging Data

● ●

In This Chapter

▶ How to put something you created in Program A into Program B

▶ A variety of OLE that has nothing to do with matadors

▶ South-of-the-border birthday celebrations

▶ A step-by-step discussion of embedding objects

▶ What to do if dragging and dropping doesn't work

▶ How to link objects to disk files

▶ When all else fails, import

● ●

*P*rogress and technology bring with them an element of terror. Machines help us work more productively and with less effort, but lurking in the background is an unmistakable promise: You're barely keeping up as it is. The next bit of technology is going to leave you in the dust.

At least that's the way it seems sometimes. And believe me, I'm every bit as susceptible to this phenomenon as you are. Every time I turn around, some new piece of software or hardware appears that's bound and determined to make me feel like I've been covering the computer industry for five minutes.

So when I tell you that the stuff in this chapter is a piece of cake, you can trust me — despite the fact that it discusses such nightmarish-sounding terms as *embedding* and *OLE*. Unlike those other wacko technological breakthroughs, the ones in this chapter aren't going to give you any problems. I promise. In fact, this chapter is going to solve a problem that's probably been plaguing you ever since you opened up that massive CorelDraw 7 package: How do you take something that you created in one program and put it into a document that you created in another program?

OLE Must Be Pretty Bad to Deserve That Windup

Object linking and embedding — OLE (pronounced *olé*) for short — does have a certain eerie sound to it. But that's just to amuse the computer zealots who aren't happy unless they know at least a dozen 15-syllable phrases that are guaranteed to shock their like-minded friends into frenzied states of information-age envy.

For the rest of us, OLE should be called *birthday party.* Program A gives Program B a gift of text, graphics, or other digital stuff. Program B remembers who gave it what so that if any changes or alterations need to be done, Program B can call on Program A to make the changes. Okay, it's an idealized birthday party — if your Uncle Elmer gave you a jacket that didn't fit, he'd give you the receipt instead of returning it himself — but let's just say that computer programs have better manners than that. When a program gives a gift, it guarantees the gift for life.

The reason I'm telling you about OLE is because it links all of Corel's diverse and independent programs and enables them to work together like . . . well, I think you've had enough analogies for one day. If Corel Photo-Paint gives an object to CorelDraw, you can revisit Photo-Paint and edit the object by just double-clicking on the object in CorelDraw. It's like one big, happy family. Oops, that's an analogy, isn't it?

Take OLE by the Horns

OLE isn't a command, an option, or a file. It's an invisible function built into Windows 95 that paves the way for a variety of commands and options, like natural selection paves the way for fish to walk on their fins and protozoa to attain higher educations. (Man, these analogies are going downhill.)

Now, you and I could explore every nook and cranny of OLE — and eventually this chapter explores a few of them — but the best way to really understand how OLE works is to try it out. The following steps explain how to open something in Photo-Paint and transfer it into a CorelDraw drawing by way of the age-old custom of drag and drop. You can then make changes to the image using Photo-Paint tools and commands while remaining inside CorelDraw. Will wonders never cease?

 Placing an object or image from one program into another in this fashion is known as *embedding.* (And you thought embedding was what your kids did when they smushed chocolate chips into the sofa.) The process is called embedding because Windows 95 implants — embeds — additional information about the object, such as which program created the object and how to call up the program when you want to edit the object.

1. Make sure that CorelDraw is running.

If it isn't, start the program as described in Chapter 2.

2. Start Corel Photo-Paint.

Use the Windows 95 Start menu in the lower-left corner of the screen. You know, choose Start⇨Programs⇨CorelDraw 7⇨Corel Photo-Paint 7. In a few moments, the Photo-Paint interface springs to life, filled with a bewildering array of menus and tools.

3. Inside Photo-Paint, open an image.

As in CorelDraw, you open a file by choosing File⇨Open or by pressing Ctrl+O and selecting a file inside the ensuing dialog box. In Figure 14-1, I opened the Teddy image included in the Home folder, which is inside the Objects folder on the second CorelDraw 7 CD-ROM.

If you likewise open the Teddy image or one of the others in the Objects folder, you can skip to Step 7. Corel has already done the intermediate steps for you by converting the images in the Objects folder into independent objects. If you open some other image, you have to convert the image into an object for yourself, as the next steps explain.

If you open an image from a CD, Photo-Paint may respond with a stupid message about how you can't use the Save command. (After all, you can't save to a CD, so you have to use the Save As command instead.) Press Enter to tell Photo-Paint to quit its belly-aching.

4. Select the lasso tool.

Press and hold on the rectangular mask tool's icon in the toolbox, labeled in Figure 14-1. After the flyout menu appears, select the lasso mask tool, also labeled in the figure.

5. Drag around the image to select it.

Encircle the portion of the image that you want to add to your drawing. After you draw the selection boundary, double-click with the tool. Photo-Paint surrounds the image with a dotted selection outline to show that it's selected.

6. Choose Object⇨Create From Mask.

This is a weird but necessary step. To transfer an image from Photo-Paint into CorelDraw, you must convert it into an independent object. The Create From Mask command does just that. It also automatically selects the arrow tool, which is precisely the tool you want. Now skip to Step 8.

7. Click with the arrow tool on the image.

You folks who performed Step 6 don't need to do this, which is why I told you to skip to Step 8. But you folks who skipped here from Step 3 need to specify the object that you want to select. Photo-Paint displays eight square handles around the object, just as if the object were selected in CorelDraw.

Rectangle mask   Lasso mask

Figure 14-1:
The Teddy
image as it
appears
when
opened
inside
Photo-
Paint.

8. Scale the Photo-Paint screen so that you can see the CorelDraw screen in the background.

The easiest way to embed a Photo-Paint object into CorelDraw is to drag the image from one program and drop it into the other. You have to be able to see at least a little of the drawing area inside CorelDraw to make the drop.

9. Drag the selected image out of the Photo-Paint window and Ctrl+drop it into CorelDraw.

Figure 14-2 shows the act in progress. This is essentially the same technique explained in the "Do the Drag and Drop" section of Chapter 8 — only now you're dragging and dropping between different programs. By pressing the Ctrl key midway into the drag and holding it until after you release the mouse button, you create a duplicate of the image. If you don't press Ctrl, you delete the original image from Photo-Paint and move it into CorelDraw.

10. Click on the CorelDraw title bar.

This step brings the Draw program to the front of the screen. As Figure 14-3 demonstrates, object-oriented drawings — such as Shenbop — can exist side-by-side with their image counterparts — such as Teddy — even though the two were created in separate programs.

Photo-Paint   CorelDraw

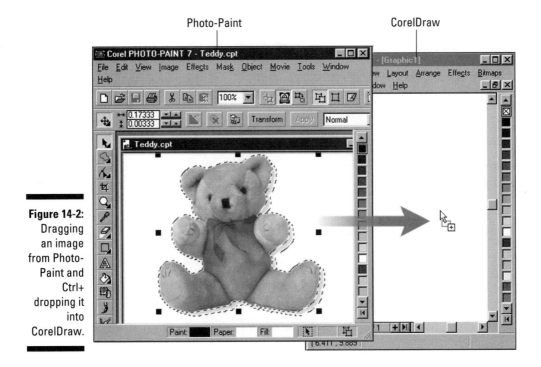

Figure 14-2:
Dragging
an image
from Photo-
Paint and
Ctrl+
dropping it
into
CorelDraw.

You may want to magnify the embedded image by clicking on it once or twice with the zoom tool. Thanks to a little thing called *resolution* — explained in Chapter 15 — an image may appear much smaller in CorelDraw than it did in Photo-Paint. So don't hesitate to zoom in.

11. Switch back to Photo-Paint.

The easiest way is to click on the Photo-Paint title bar.

12. Press Alt+F4.

You don't need Photo-Paint any more, so press Alt+F4 or choose File⇨Exit to quit the program. When a message appears asking whether you want to save the image, click on the No button. Windows 95 automatically returns you to CorelDraw.

13. Save your drawing.

Then close it. You can even exit CorelDraw, exit Windows 95, turn off your computer, and wait several weeks before performing the next step. It doesn't matter. When you're ready to go on, restart CorelDraw and open the drawing that contains the embedded image.

14. Suppose that you want to edit the image.

I don't know if *supposing* actually qualifies as an active step, but it's essential to this exercise. In my case, I wanted to make the teddy bear stick out its tongue to show its fear and loathing of cartoon frogs.

Photo-Paint   CorelDraw

Figure 14-3:
Your
drawing
may not
react as
enthu-
siastically
to
embedding
as mine
does.

15. Double-click on the image inside CorelDraw.

Or choose that wackiest of commands, Edit⇨CorelPaint.Image.7
Object⇨Edit. My, that's user friendly. CorelDraw sends a message to
Windows 95 requesting that it locate and run Photo-Paint. Windows 95
obliges. But instead of starting Photo-Paint as a separate program, as in
the old days, the Photo-Paint tools and menus take over the CorelDraw
interface. This way, you can edit the image while still viewing the rest of
the drawing in the background. As illustrated in Figure 14-4, I was able
to edit the teddy bear while keeping an eye on Shenbop. This process is
called *in-place editing.*

16. Edit the image as desired.

In case you're interested, I describe how to use the Photo-Paint painting
tools in Chapters 15 through 17. For now, just select the paint tool
(labeled in Figure 14-4) and doodle away. I added big eyes and a sticky-
outy tongue to make my bear express displeasure with his predicament.

After you double-click on your image, it may appear surrounded by a
special set of scroll bars, which let you view hidden portions of the
image. You can also scale the size of the image window by dragging the
little sizing handles — not the big handles, but the tiny ones labeled in
Figure 14-4. (The big handles don't appear unless you click on the
image with the arrow tool, but I included both sets of handles in the
figure so that you can see the difference.)

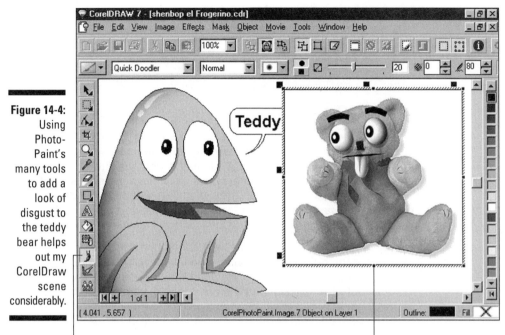

Figure 14-4:
Using
Photo-
Paint's
many tools
to add a
look of
disgust to
the teddy
bear helps
out my
CorelDraw
scene
considerably.

└─Paint tool   Window sizing handle

17. When you finish editing, click outside the image.

> Windows 95 quits Photo-Paint, hides its tools and menus, and returns you to the standard CorelDraw interface.

As an alternative to dragging and dropping, you can embed an image by copying it in Photo-Paint and pasting it into CorelDraw. In the preceding steps, press Ctrl+C in place of Step 8, switch to CorelDraw in Step 9, and press Ctrl+V in Step 10. Otherwise, the process works the same.

You now know how to take an object created in one Corel program and embed it into another. You also know how to edit an embedded object. As long as you got the preceding exercise to work, you don't have to read another page in this chapter. Just repeat the exercise every time you want to trade information between Photo-Paint and CorelDraw. But if you encountered an out-of-memory error when trying to run Photo-Paint and CorelDraw at the same time, however, or you don't have enough screen space to make Step 9 work, read on for alternative solutions.

More Ways for CorelDraw to Receive Gifts

Altogether, you can introduce objects into CorelDraw in three ways:

- ✔ You can embed the objects, as demonstrated in the preceding section.

- ✔ As I mentioned at the beginning of this chapter, OLE stands for *object linking and embedding*. I've discussed embedding, but not the other half, *linking*. You link an object by loading it from disk into CorelDraw, much as if you were opening a drawing. CorelDraw maintains a link between the object and the disk file. If you later change the disk file, the object updates automatically. (Incidentally, this kind of linking has nothing to do with the linked text blocks that I discuss in Chapter 10.)

- ✔ *Importing* an object is like giving a gift anonymously. CorelDraw has no idea where the object came from, nor can it call on another program to edit the image. As with linking, you load the file from disk into CorelDraw. But that's it. No automatic updates, no quick editing techniques. If you later change the object using a different program, you have to import it from scratch to update the object in CorelDraw.

- ✔ The beauty of importing is that it has nothing to do with OLE, so it works even when embedding and linking give your computer fits.

Linking, the semi-smart technique

You can link objects for use in CorelDraw in two ways:

- ✔ You can copy an object in Photo-Paint or some other program and then choose Edit➪Paste Special inside CorelDraw to establish a link. Unfortunately, this approach provides less functionality than simply choosing the standard Paste command — which embeds the object, remember? At the same time, this approach requires you to run two programs simultaneously, which invites the same old memory errors mentioned earlier. To sum it up in laymen's terms, this approach is dopey.

- ✔ The second and smarter way to link an object is to load it directly from disk using Edit➪Insert New Object, as described in the following steps.

The following is a typical linking scenario:

1. Create an image in Photo-Paint.

When you're finished, save it to disk. Then quit Photo-Paint by pressing Alt+F4 or choosing File➪Exit.

2. **Start CorelDraw.**

3. **Choose** **Edit**⇨**Insert** **New Object to display the dialog box shown in Figure 14-5.**

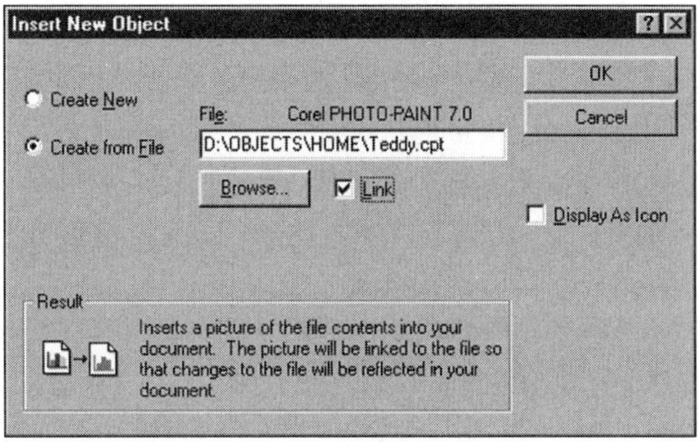

Figure 14-5:
These options create a link between your drawing and an image on disk.

4. **Select the Create from** **File** **radio button.**

5. **Click on the** **Browse** **button and locate your Photo-Paint image.**

   The Browse button brings up a dialog box like the Open dialog box described in Chapter 3. When you locate the Photo-Paint file, double-click on it to return to the Insert New Object dialog box.

6. **Select the** **Link** **check box.**

   If you don't select the check box, CorelDraw embeds the file, which can give you the same old problems you had when editing an embedded image earlier in this chapter.

7. **Click on OK.**

   Or press Tab, Enter. CorelDraw works away for a few moments and then displays the image in the drawing area.

8. **Save the drawing.**

   Then quit CorelDraw by pressing Alt+F4.

9. **Start Photo-Paint, open your image, and edit it.**

   Go nuts. Then save the image.

10. **Press Alt+F4 to exit Photo-Paint.**

11. **Start CorelDraw and open the drawing you saved in Step 8.**

12. **Save the drawing.**

Importing, the last ditch effort

If nothing else works, you can import an image created in Photo-Paint into CorelDraw. With importing, you don't retain any link to the originating program; if you want to update the object, you have to open it in Photo-Paint, edit it, and then re-import it into Draw. Here's how to import:

1. **Create and save an image in Photo-Paint or some other program.**

2. **Press Alt+F4 to quit the program.**

3. **Start CorelDraw and press Ctrl+I.**

   Or choose File⇨Import. Draw responds by displaying the Import dialog box, which I discuss in Chapter 3.

4. **Locate the image file that you want to import and then click on it.**

5. **Press Enter or click on the Import button.**

   Or, double-click on the file that you want to import. CorelDraw displays the imported image in the drawing area.

There you have it: three ways to introduce objects created in Photo-Paint into CorelDraw. Now, don't think that you have to import Photo-Paint images into CorelDraw. You can open an image in Photo-Paint, edit it in Photo-Paint, print it from Photo-Paint, and never deal with CorelDraw throughout the entire process. Like the other 50 gazillion CorelDraw functions, OLE and the Import command are merely at your disposal if you need them.

Chapter 15

Everyone Say Hello to Corel Photo-Paint

In This Chapter

▶ Fooling gullible consumers like you

▶ Starting Corel Photo-Paint

▶ Introducing the Photo-Paint interface

▶ Getting rid of nonessential interface garbage

▶ Opening images from CD-ROM

▶ Zooming and scrolling

▶ Using rulers, the grid, and guidelines

▶ Creating a new image

▶ Understanding resolution and color

▶ Saving, printing, and closing images

*I*n the world of print advertising, nearly everything you see is a distortion of reality. Food products are lacquered with hair spray, the performance of major appliances is simulated, prefab clothing is custom tailored to fit the actors. As your mom warned you, you can believe only half of what you see, none of what you hear, and the exact opposite of what you see and hear in ads.

But what goes on in front of the camera is nothing compared with what happens after the film enters the mind of the computer. Rumor has it, for example, that every major movie poster is a veritable collage of body parts and other elements. The body that you see almost never belongs to the actor whose head is pasted on top of it. In most cases, there's nothing wrong with the actor's body; it's simply more convenient to have an extra strike some poster pose and later slap one of the hundred or so head shots of the actor onto the body.

Corel Photo-Paint is the sort of program that you might use to slap well-known heads on obscure bodies. Although it's not necessarily as capable as the mega-expensive image-editing systems used by professionals, Photo-Paint performs more than adequately for the price. You can open an image stored on disk and edit it in your computer. Draw a mustache on Aunt Patty, put Grandma Ida's eyebrows on Grandpa Neil's face, or distort little baby Melvin until he looks like Mighty Joe Young. The possibilities are absolutely limitless.

Blasting Off with Photo-Paint

You start Photo-Paint by choosing Start⇨Programs⇨CorelDraw 7⇨Corel Photo-Paint 7. The first thing you see is a welcome screen similar to the one you see when you start CorelDraw. You can click on an icon to start a new image, open an existing image, scan an image using the CorelScan wizard (if you installed that option and you have a scanner), view the Photo-Paint tutorial, or view an introduction to the new features in Version 7. And if you never want to be bothered with the welcome screen again, deselect the Show This Welcome Screen at Startup check box.

After you open an image (as explained later in this chapter), the Photo-Paint interface looks something like the one shown in Figure 15-1. Don't worry if your interface doesn't look exactly like mine. For one thing, Photo-Paint doesn't automatically open an image of a slimy, crawly thing or display the Tool Settings roll-up. And if you're using a monitor resolution of greater than 640 x 480, you should see a few more Property Bar and toolbar buttons on your screen than you see in Figure 15-1. But the interface shown in the figure is more or less what you can expect to see.

Here's paint in yer eye!

With luck, you recognize a few old friends from CorelDraw when you look at Figure 15-1. Photo-Paint offers a title bar, a menu bar, Property Bar, a whole bunch of tools, a color palette, and a status bar, all of which perform like their counterparts in CorelDraw.

But just to make sure that you don't lose anything in the translation — or, perhaps more appropriate, to ensure that the translation doesn't lose you — the following list should help jog your memory:

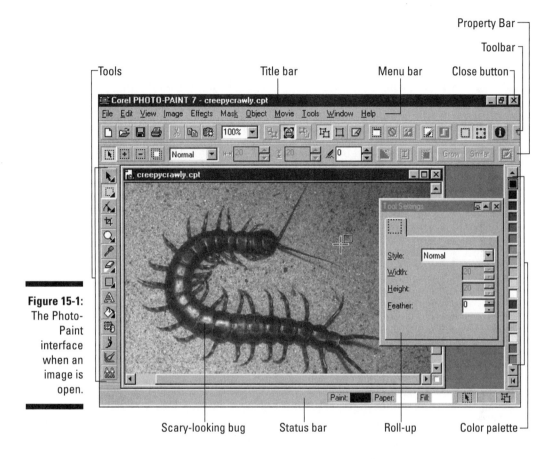

Property Bar
Toolbar
Close button

Tools — Title bar — Menu bar

Figure 15-1:
The Photo-
Paint
interface
when an
image is
open.

Scary-looking bug — Status bar — Roll-up — Color palette

✔ You choose commands from menus by clicking on a name in the menu bar and then clicking on a command name in the ensuing menu. You can alternatively press the Alt key followed by the underlined letters in both the menu and command names.

✔ Or feel free to try out the keyboard shortcuts listed to the right of the command names in the menus. Common commands — such as File➪Open and Edit➪Copy — have the same shortcuts as they do in CorelDraw — in this case, Ctrl+O and Ctrl+C.

✔ The buttons on the Property Bar and toolbar duplicate functions found in the menus. To find out what a button does, pause your cursor over the button. Photo-Paint responds by displaying a little yellow label and providing a description of the tool in the status bar. The Property Bar buttons change depending on the tool that's currently selected in the toolbox.

✔ Any tool icon that has a small triangle in its lower-right corner offers a flyout menu of alternative tools. Press and hold the mouse button on the tool icon to display the flyout menu. Then click on an icon in the flyout to switch to a related tool.

✔ You can move the toolbox to a different location by dragging the gray area around the tools. You can move the Property Bar and toolbar in the same way. To return toolbox, toolbar, or Property Bar to its original position, double-click on its title bar or in a gray area around the tools.

✔ As mentioned in Chapter 2, some of the toolbar and Property Bar buttons are hidden if you use a monitor resolution of 640 x 480. To bring the buttons into view, drag the bar into the image editing area, as just discussed. Another alternative is to remove buttons that you don't use; just Alt+drag the buttons off the bar. The remaining buttons scoot over to fill the empty space.

✔ The Tool Settings roll-up, which enables you to change the performance of the selected tool, used to appear on-screen by default. In Version 7, Photo-Paint no longer assumes that you want the roll-up displayed. To display the roll-up, press Ctrl+F8 or choose View⇨Roll-Ups⇨Tool Settings. However, many of the options in the roll-up are now also available from the Property Bar, so you may not have as much use for the roll-up as in previous versions.

The roll-ups in Photo-Paint work just like those in CorelDraw; for a refresher of all the ways to manipulate a roll-up, see Chapter 2.

✔ When in doubt, right-click on something to display a pop-up menu. You can uncover all kinds of useful Photo-Paint functions by right-clicking on tools, roll-ups, or the image itself. Generally, the functions in the pop-up menus duplicate commands found in the standard menus, but they can still come in handy.

Turn off the toolbar!

As I mention in Chapter 2, I'm not a big fan of toolbars. They take up space, their icons are scrunched and unrecognizable, and they duplicate commands that are already readily available in the menus. If you disagree — you prefer clicking on the little suckers to choosing commands or pressing keyboard shortcuts — then by all means, leave the toolbar on-screen. But if you want to free up screen space, you can hide the toolbar by simply right-clicking on the gray space around the tools and clicking on the Standard option in the pop-up menu that appears.

To bring the toolbar back, choose View⇨Toolbars, select Standard in the Toolbars dialog box, and press Enter.

The toolbars are hidden in figures from here on. That way, I can show you more of the important stuff that you need to see.

Opening Existing Images

Although you can create an image from scratch in Photo-Paint, you'll more likely be using the program to edit existing images, such as a photograph on disk or on CD-ROM. To open an image file, choose File⇨Open or press Ctrl+O. Photo-Paint displays the Open an Image dialog box, as shown in Figure 15-2. The dialog box works just like the CorelDraw Open Drawing dialog box, discussed in Chapter 3. After you select an image and press Enter or click on Open, the image opens up inside its own independent window, as shown back in Figure 15-1. Now you can edit that image till you're blue in the face.

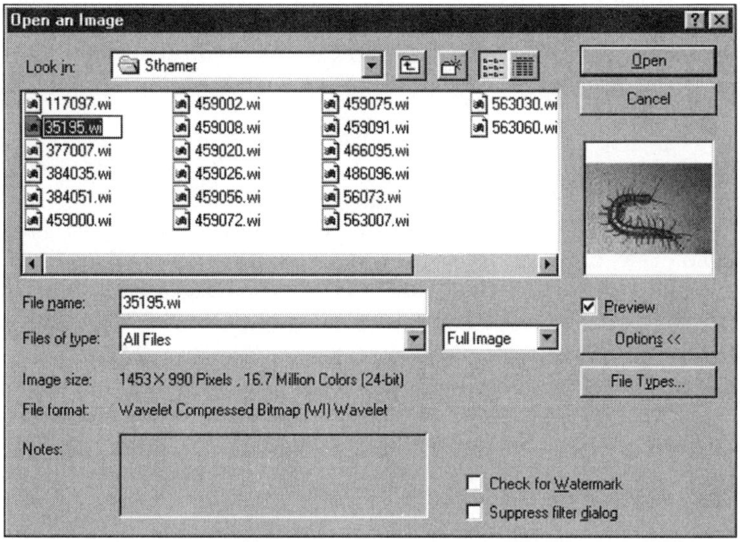

Figure 15-2:
Though Corel's image files have nonsense numerical names, you can take a peek at them by turning on the Preview check box.

Open an Image	? X

Look in: Sthamer

117097.wi	459002.wi	459075.wi	563030.wi
35195.wi	459008.wi	459091.wi	563060.wi
377007.wi	459020.wi	466095.wi	
384035.wi	459026.wi	486096.wi	
384051.wi	459056.wi	56073.wi	
459000.wi	459072.wi	563007.wi	

Open
Cancel

File name: 35195.wi
Files of type: All Files   Full Image
Image size: 1453 X 990 Pixels , 16.7 Million Colors (24-bit)
File format: Wavelet Compressed Bitmap (WI) Wavelet
Notes:

☑ Preview
Options <<
File Types...

☐ Check for Watermark
☐ Suppress filter dialog

Here are a few additional tidbits about opening images:

✔ The second CD-ROM included with your CorelDraw 7 package contains a sampling of photographic images. The images are stored inside the Photos folder on the CD.

✔ Unfortunately, the image files on the CD have unintelligible names such as 56201. (These images were originally scanned as special Kodak Photo CD files, which accounts for the random naming system.) If you turn on the Preview check box in the Open an Image dialog box, though, Photo-Paint shows you a tiny preview of what the photograph looks like when you click on the image file. If you want to play around with the many-legged creature pictured in Figure 15-1, open the STHAMER folder and select file 35195.WI, as in Figure 15-2.

✔ The images provided in the CorelDraw 7 package are *huge*. If you're using a slower computer, Photo-Paint may take a long time — several minutes, actually — to open these images. So, if the little hourglass cursor (you know, the one that your computer displays to tell you to hurry up and wait) seems to be permanently affixed to your screen, don't panic and think that your system has crashed. Just go get a cup of coffee, walk the dog, or change the oil in your car. When you return, the image should be open.

✔ Photo-Paint can open images saved in any of the most popular image formats, including TIFF, PCX, JPEG, and Photo CD. For the lowdown on file formats, read Chapter 22, "Ten File Formats and Their Functions."

✔ When you open an image off a CD-ROM, Photo-Paint displays a message telling you that the Save command is disabled. Because you can't save to a CD, Photo-Paint doesn't let you use the Save command at all. Instead, you have to use <u>F</u>ile⇨Save <u>A</u>s. Just press Enter to hide the message and get on with your life.

You can also open images by dragging them from the Scrapbook, shown in Figure 15-3. To display the Scrapbook, choose <u>V</u>iew⇨Roll-<u>U</u>ps⇨Scrap<u>b</u>ook, or press Ctrl+F12. Click on the tab that is marked with the little camera icon to display the images on the Corel CD (assuming that the CD is in your CD-ROM drive, of course). Use the Folder pop-up menu and Up One Level button to locate the folder that contains the image you want to open. Then, just drag the image thumbnail out of the Scrapbook and into the Photo-Paint editing window.

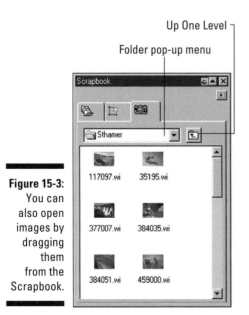

Figure 15-3: You can also open images by dragging them from the Scrapbook.

Viewing Your Image

When you first open an image, Photo-Paint displays the image as large as it can while still showing the entire image on-screen. But that doesn't necessarily mean that you can see every single pixel in the image. If you want to see one image pixel for every on-screen pixel, choose View⇨Zoom 100%. Or just press Ctrl+1. (Too bad CorelDraw doesn't offer this convenient shortcut.)

Alternatively, you can select the zoom tool, labeled in Figure 15-4, and choose the Zoom 100% icon on the Property Bar or select 100% from the Zoom Level pop-up menu, also found on the Property Bar.

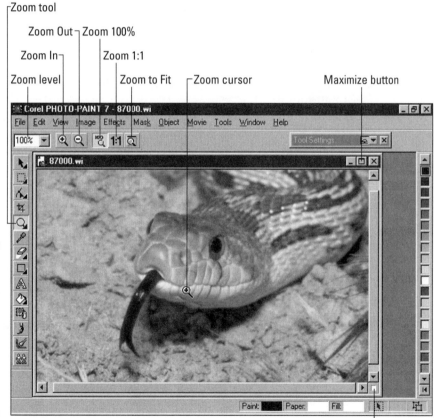

Figure 15-4: The Property Bar icons give you more ways than ever to zoom in and out on your image.

The most accurate way to see an image is pixel for pixel. Otherwise, Photo-Paint has to redraw the image slightly to make the image pixels match the screen pixels. This redrawing is only temporary — Photo-Paint doesn't change any pixel in the actual file unless you tell it to — but the screen image may give you a slightly wrong impression of how the image will print. Of course, you have to view the image at smaller sizes sometimes, but it's good to return to the 100 percent view whenever possible.

To make the image fill the screen, click on the Maximize button, labeled in Figure 15-4. Photo-Paint hides all other open images so that you can concentrate on the one you're editing. You can still view another open image by choosing its name from the bottom of the Window menu. To return an image to an independent floating window, click on the Restore button, which takes the place of the Maximize button when the window is maximized.

Here are a few other ways to zoom and scroll around inside an image:

✔ Select the zoom tool, labeled in Figure 15-4, and click in the image to magnify the image. Or, click on the Zoom In button on the Property Bar. Each click magnifies the image to the next preset zoom factor in the Zoom Level pop-up menu, found both on the Property Bar and the toolbar.

✔ Right-click or Shift+click with the zoom tool to reduce the image to next lowest preset zoom level. (In order for right-clicking to work, the Use Right Mouse Button for Zoom Out option in the Tool Settings roll-up must be selected. Press Ctrl+F8 to display the roll-up.) Alternatively, you can click on the Zoom Out button on the Property Bar.

✔ Or use the same shortcut keys you use in CorelDraw: Press F2 to magnify the image; press F3 to reduce it.

✔ To fit the image on-screen so that you can see the entire photograph at once, press F4 or click on the Zoom to Fit button on the Property Bar.

✔ You can also choose specific view sizes — anything from 25 to 1,600 percent — from the View⇨Zoom submenu and from the Zoom Level pop-up menu on the Property Bar.

✔ If you want to zoom to a custom view size — that is, a size that's not found on a menu — double-click on the Zoom Level pop-up menu, enter the view size from the keyboard, and press Enter. (Be sure to double-click the pop-up menu's option box, not the arrow.)

✔ To view the image at the same resolution that it prints, choose View⇨Zoom 1:1, or choose the Zoom 1:1 button on the Property Bar. This view gives you an approximation of the printed size of your image. (Keep in mind that this setting is different than View⇨Zoom 100%, which shows one image pixel for every screen pixel, generally making the image appear larger than it will print.)

✔ To get a close-up look at a specific area of your image, drag with the zoom tool to create a marquee. Photo-Paint then magnifies the area inside the marquee to fill the entire window.

✔ By default, Photo-Paint does not change the size of the window when you zoom in or out of the image. You have to manually resize the window.

In its past incarnation, Photo-Paint offered a size box in the lower-right corner of the image window. You dragged the size box to resize the window. In Version 7, the size box has been replaced by a button that you use to temporarily display the Navigator, as discussed in the next section. To resize the window in Version 7, just drag any corner of the image window.

✔ To make Photo-Paint automatically resize the window as you magnify or reduce the image, do this: Press Ctrl+J (or choose Tools⇨Options) to display the Options dialog box. Then select the Automatic View Resize check box on the General tab and press Enter. Now press F3 a couple of times. Photo-Paint reduces the window as it reduces your photograph. Notice that this feature doesn't work if the image window is maximized.

✔ If the image is bigger than the window, you can drag the scroll boxes in the scroll bars to reveal hidden portions of the photograph. Or you can click on the scroll arrows.

✔ But better yet, select the hand tool from the zoom tool flyout menu and then drag in the image to reveal the area you want to view.

✔ If you select the hand tool, you can also scroll the image by pressing the arrow keys.

If you don't care for the commands and tools I've mentioned so far, check out the next section, which explains the Navigator, another handy option for moving around your image.

Using the Navigator

In addition to using the scroll arrows and hand tool to display different portions of your image, you can take advantage of the new pop-up Navigator window, which takes the place of the old Navigator roll-up. Try this: Zoom in on your image until you see both the horizontal and vertical scroll bars appear. Now press and hold your mouse button on the little white box in the bottom-right corner of the image window, labeled "Navigator pop-up button" in Figure 15-4. The Navigator window appears, as shown in Figure 15-5. Without releasing the mouse button, drag the mouse to reposition the rectangle in the Navigator window. Photo-Paint scrolls your image to show the area surrounded by the rectangle. When you release the mouse button, the Navigator window disappears.

The Navigator pop-up button doesn't appear unless both the horizontal and vertical scroll bars are visible. In other words, if the entire width of your image or the entire length of the image is visible, you can't access the Navigator.

Figure 15-5:
Drag the rectangle in the Navigator window to reveal a different portion of your image.

Dividing Up Your Screen

Photo-Paint now offers a grid, guides, and rulers, just like CorelDraw. You may not have much use for these tools, but they can come in handy on occasion. For the most part, the grid, guides, and rulers work just like the ones in CorelDraw, explained in Chapter 6. The major difference is that the commands for customizing the appearance of the grid and guidelines, which appear under the Layout menu in CorelDraw, appear under the Tools menu in Photo-Paint. Also, you can't create angled guidelines in Photo-Paint as you can in CorelDraw.

Creating a Brand Spanking New Image

If you'd rather not work from an existing image — as you do every time you press Ctrl+O — you can create an empty canvas and paint a new image from scratch. If the thought of doing so appeals to you, I can only assume that you're the type who's willing to forge ahead into the barren wasteland of the blank page. You're a pioneer — perhaps a little short on common sense, but full of confidence and bravery.

To create a new image, press Ctrl+N or choose File⇨New. Photo-Paint displays the dialog box shown in Figure 15-6. I darkened the two lowest check boxes in the dialog box to show how completely irrelevant they are to creating a new image. The remaining options require you to make three decisions:

   ✔ How large an image do you want to create?

   ✔ What is the image resolution?

   ✔ How many colors do you want to play with?

You don't need any help with image size; just enter the desired width and height of the image into the Width and Height option boxes.

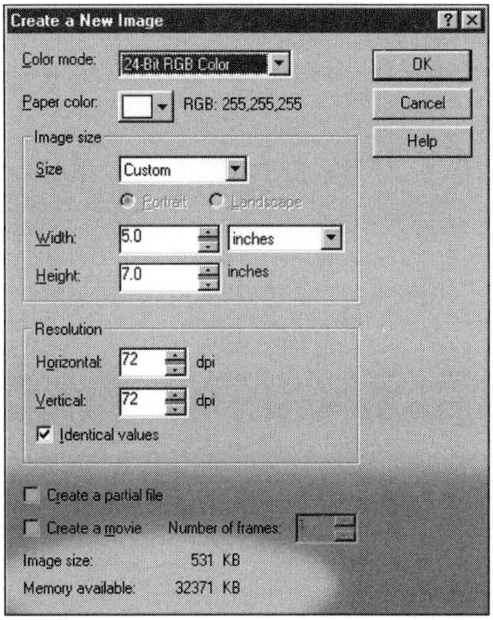

Figure 15-6:
In this dialog box, you can specify the size, resolution, and number of colors in a new image.

Resolution and color open up whole new cans of worms, however, which is why I take a little extra time to explain them in the following sections.

Dots per inch

Remember Chapter 1? I know that it was a long time ago, but you may want to take a moment and reread the "Corel Photo-Paint" section. It tells about acquiring images and covers a few other items you may have found yourself wondering about — not the least of which is how images work.

To quickly recap: Unlike CorelDraw drawings, in which objects are defined using complex mathematical equations, Photo-Paint images are made up of tiny colored dots called *pixels*. The number of pixels in an inch is called the *resolution*. So, if you create an image that measures 4 inches by 5 inches with a resolution of 72 dots per inch — or dpi (pronounced *d-p-i*) for short — Photo-Paint creates an image that's 288 pixels wide ($4 \times 72 = 288$) by 360 pixels tall ($5 \times 72 = 360$).

You specify a resolution by entering a new value in the Horizontal option box. As long as the Identical Values option is checked, you don't need to change the Vertical value; Photo-Paint automatically makes sure that both values are the same.

Do not turn the Identical Values check box off. Many printers cannot handle different horizontal and vertical resolutions. And besides, turning off the option can make for some pretty ugly results. This is one of those options that Corel throws in just to trip you up.

Select your crayons

The first option in the Create a New Image dialog box, Color Mode, requires you to specify the number of colors that you want to be able to display on-screen simultaneously. It's as if your mom required you to select a box of crayons before you sat down to color. The Photo-Paint Color Mode pop-up menu lets you select one of six boxes of crayons.

✔ The first option, Black and White, provides only two crayons, a black one and a white one. That's all you get.

✔ The second option is Grayscale, which offers 256 shades of gray, ranging from white to black.

✔ The next option, Paletted Color, contains 256 crayons (Paletted Color is the new name for the 256 Color option found in Version 6). But the interesting thing about this box is that you can swap crayons in the box for other colors. When you choose the option, Photo-Paint displays the Color Table dialog box, which shows you all the default crayons. If you don't like the default shade of a color, double-click on the color swatch and adjust the color as desired. Click on OK to close the dialog box and open the new image window. You can also swap colors after you begin working on your image: Choose Image⇨Color Table to display the dialog box and change a color swatch. Photo-Paint automatically updates any pixels using the old color to the new color.

✔ The RGB 24-Bit Color option gives you access to 16 million colors. This option provides the most versatility, but it comes at a price. A 16 million-color image takes up three times as much room on disk as the same image in 256 colors. (All the photographs on the third CorelDraw CD-ROM are 24-Bit Color images.)

✔ The 16 Color mode found in Version 6 is gone in Version 7. Instead, you get the Lab color mode, which is used by some high-end photo-editing folks. Trust me, you don't need to worry about this color mode.

✔ Neither do you need to worry about the 32-Bit CMYK option. It's specifically designed for painting CMYK images that you want to print to color separations (as described in the "Printing full-color artwork" section of Chapter 13). But you can print any color image to color separations, so the 32-Bit CMYK option makes your image more complicated without any real benefit.

For the best results, select the Grayscale option to create images that you want to print on a black-and-white printer, or select 24-Bit Color to create full-color artwork. And if you're creating images for distribution on the World Wide Web, you may want to use Paletted Color mode; limiting your image to 256 colors results in smaller image files, and smaller image files require less time to send over the Internet, particularly when saved in the industry-standard GIF file format. The other color mode options aren't particularly useful.

Oh, and by the way, you can also change the color of the new canvas by selecting a color from the Paper Color pop-up menu. In general, however, I recommend that you leave the canvas white. After all, a white background ensures bright and vivid colors; any other background will mix with and therefore dim colors that you apply with some of the painting tools. Call me crazy, but I usually prefer to apply color with the painting tools as I go along instead of imposing a color on my artwork right from the start.

Taxing your memory

In the lower-left corner of the Create a New Image dialog box, spotlighted in Figure 15-6, Photo-Paint shows you how much memory is available to Photo-Paint. If the number is low, you may have trouble opening large images.

If Photo-Paint complains that it doesn't have enough available memory to create the image size that you specify, try lowering the Resolution values. If that doesn't work, change the Color Mode option from 24-Bit Color to Grayscale or Paletted Color. And if the problem persists, lower the Width and Height values. (Note that the Image Size value in the Create a New Image dialog box refers to the amount of space that the image will consume on disk, not in memory.)

What resolution do I use?

I wish that I could just tell you the perfect resolution to use and send you on your way. But even professionals who create images day in and day out can't agree on a perfect setting. Although I can't tell you exactly what resolution to use, I can give you some guidelines.

First, a little background: Higher resolutions result in better-looking images because they have more pixels to fool your eyes into thinking that they're seeing a regular photograph. Lower resolutions result in less focused images with occasionally jagged outlines.

High-resolution images also take up more space on disk, however, and make Photo-Paint work harder and print slower. Low-resolution images are speedy to edit and print.

Therefore, use the lowest resolution value that you can get away with:

✔ If you're creating images for distribution on the World Wide Web or for display in a multimedia presentation, use 72 dpi, which is the resolution used by most computer monitors.

✔ If you just want to print the image on a laser or ink jet printer and tack it up to your wall, a value between 90 and 120 should suffice.

✔ If you're creating an image to include in a company newsletter, bump the resolution up to somewhere between 120 and 180. All the images printed in this book fall into this range. All the full-screen images — such as Figure 15-1 — were printed at 140 dpi.

✔ If you plan on printing a full-color image for the cover of a catalog or some other spiffy publication, try a value between 180 and 300.

Try printing some test images between the aforementioned extremes and see how they look. You may even want to consult with a commercial printer whose opinion you trust. There's a lot of confusion in this area — and you'll very likely get different answers depending on who you ask — so let me close with the only hard-and-fast rule: There is no wrong resolution value. What works for you is what counts.

Changing the Resolution and Color of Photographs

Resolution and color don't merely affect new images; they also affect photographs that you open from CD-ROM or disk. For example, if you open an image from the second CorelDraw CD, its resolution is 96 dpi and it contains millions of colors. To change the resolution of an open image, do the following:

1. Choose Image⇨Resample.

Up comes the Resample dialog box, which lists the width and height of the image, along with two resolution values, much the same as the Create a New Image dialog box.

2. Select the Maintain Original Size check box.

This step is extremely important! If you do not turn this option on, you run the risk of adding or deleting pixels, which you most certainly do not want to do.

3. Make sure that Maintain Aspect Ratio is checked.

This option is probably already selected, but it's worth a quick check.

4. Change the Horizontal value.

Thanks to Step 3, you don't have to worry about the Vertical value. Photo-Paint changes that automatically. (Similarly, if you change the Vertical value, Photo-Paint changes the Horizontal value automatically.)

5. Press Enter or click on OK.

To change the number of colors in an image, choose a command from the Image⇨Convert To submenu. For example, if you wanted to prepare one of the Corel photographs for inclusion in a black-and-white publication, you would remove the colors from the photograph by choosing Image⇨Convert To⇨Grayscale (8-Bit). In fact, that is exactly what I did to the photographs contained in this chapter.

Saving, Printing, and Closing

Generally speaking, saving, printing, and closing an image work very much like saving, printing, and closing a CorelDraw drawing, but you will find a few differences. Just for the record, here's how to perform these basic operations:

✔ To save an image, press Ctrl+S or choose File⇨Save. Remember, if you save early and save often, the brain you save could be your own.

✔ To save an image opened from a CD-ROM, you have to choose File⇨Save As. Photo-Paint displays the Save an Image to Disk dialog box. Here you can decide where to save the image on disk and what name you'd like to use. Because you're using Windows 95, your filenames can be virtually as long as you want (up to 256 characters).

✔ You may also want to change the file format by choosing an option from the Save as Type pop-up menu. By far the best option is TIFF Bitmap. TIFF is a standard among standards, supported by more programs than just about any other image format.

If you want to work repeatedly with an image from the second CD-ROM in the CorelDraw 7 package and your computer takes a long time to open the image, save the image as a TIFF file after you open it the first time in Photo-Paint. Then work with the TIFF version rather than the version on CD-ROM. Photo-Paint can open the TIFF version much more quickly than the CD-ROM version.

The second best format is JPEG Bitmaps, which alters the pixels in the image in order to save disk space. After you press Enter, a second dialog box appears, proffering some technical-looking options. Ignore all the options except the Quality Factor slider bar. Make sure that the value to the right of the slider is 10 or smaller. I'll say that again — 10 or *smaller*. (Higher values do major damage to the image — much more than I consider acceptable.) If the value is larger than 10, enter 10 into the option box and press Enter. Otherwise, just press Enter.

For more info on file formats, read Chapter 22.

✔ Just to be extra protected, turn on Version 7's new auto-save feature. Press Ctrl+J or choose Tools➪Options to display the Options dialog box, and then click on the Advanced tab. Check the Auto-Save Every option box, and then specify how frequently you want Photo-Paint to save your image. If you want Photo-Paint to alert you before it saves the image, turn on the Warn Me Before Saving check box.

✔ Press Ctrl+P or choose File➪Print to display the Print dialog box. For the most part, the options in the Print dialog box work similarly to those described in Chapter 13, which covers all the printing news that's fit to print. If you have more than one image open, the Documents to Print section of the Print dialog box offers check boxes for each image; select the check box(es) for the image(s) you want to print.

✔ Just as in CorelDraw, you can now preview your image before you print it by choosing File➪Print Preview. The Print Preview window works just like the CorelDraw preview window, also discussed in Chapter 13.

✔ To close the image in the foreground window, press Ctrl+F4, choose File➪Close, or click on the Close button in the upper-right corner of the image window (the one with an X on it). If you haven't saved your most recent round of changes, Photo-Paint asks whether you'd like to save the changes or chalk them up as a waste of time.

✔ Press Alt+F4, choose File➪Exit, or click on the Close button above the menu bar to get out of Dodge. If you've modified any open image since it was last saved, Photo-Paint asks you whether you might like to save the image to disk. After you answer this question for each and every altered image, you exit the Photo-Paint program and return to the Windows 95 desktop (or some other program you may be running).

Chapter 16

Spare the Tool, Spoil the Pixel

· ·

In This Chapter

▶ The Photo-Paint 7 toolbox

▶ Specifying the foreground, background, and fill colors

▶ Erasing and undoing mistakes

▶ Creating rectangles and other basic shapes

▶ Filling areas with colors, gradients, textures, and patterns

▶ Using Photo-Paint's amazing paint tool brushes

▶ Applying special effects

▶ Cloning little bits and pieces of your photograph

▶ Erasing back to the saved version of an image

▶ Using the new image sprayer tool

· ·

Chapter 15 kicks off your Photo-Paint adventure by explaining how to open and view images. But as exciting afternoons go, simply viewing an image is right up there with watching the grass grow. The real fun doesn't begin until you pick up the painting and effect tools, which I explain in this chapter.

Pawing Through Your Toolbox

Figure 16-1 offers a field guide to the Version 7 painting and effect tools. If you're upgrading from Version 6, you'll notice a few changes to the toolbox:

   ✔ The line tool is now part of the rectangle tool flyout instead of having its own slot in the toolbox.

   ✔ The pen and curve tools are gone. In my opinion, this is no great loss because these tools were never conducive to professional-looking image editing.

   ✔ A new tool, called the image sprayer tool, makes its appearance in the toolbox. I discuss this entertaining tool later in this chapter.

As mentioned in Chapter 15, the key to controlling your tools is the Tool Settings roll-up, which you display by pressing Ctrl+F8, choosing View⇨Roll-Ups⇨Tool Settings, or right-clicking in the image area and choosing Tool Settings Roll-Up from the pop-up menu that appears. The roll-up options enable you to customize a tool's performance with an astounding and sometimes excessive amount of precision, as illustrated by Figure 16-1, which shows how the roll-up appears when the paint tool is selected.

In Version 7, many of the options in the Tool Settings roll-up are also available on the Property Bar. The important options are discussed along with their respective tools in the sections that follow.

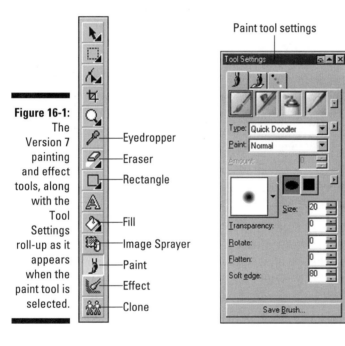

Figure 16-1: The Version 7 painting and effect tools, along with the Tool Settings roll-up as it appears when the paint tool is selected.

Paint tool settings

Eyedropper
Eraser
Rectangle
Fill
Image Sprayer
Paint
Effect
Clone

Loading Your Tools with Color

Before you can apply any color to your image, you have to specify which color you want to use. As you do in CorelDraw, you select colors from the color palette on the right side of the screen. Photo-Paint keeps track of three colors at a time — the foreground color, the background color, and the fill color. All three are displayed in the right portion of the status bar, as labeled in Figure 16-2.

✔ The line and paint tools draw in the foreground color (which Corel calls the paint color). Photo-Paint also applies the foreground color to the outlines of simple shapes — such as those drawn with the rectangle tool — and to characters created with the text tool.

Figure 16-2:
The three color swatches in the status bar represent the foreground, background, and fill colors.

Eyedropper   Color roll-up button   Eyedropper cursor   Color palette

Foreground (paint) color   Background (paper) color   Fill color

You can select a new foreground color by clicking on one of the swatches in the color palette.

✔ The background color (which Corel calls the paper color) is used by the eraser tool. Also, if you select an area and press Delete, Photo-Paint fills the selection with the background color.

To switch to a different background color, Ctrl+click on a swatch in the color palette.

✔ The fill tool uses the fill color. Photo-Paint also uses this color to fill simple shapes created with the rectangle, ellipse, and polygon tools.

Change the fill color by right-clicking or Shift+clicking on a swatch in the color palette.

To return the background, foreground, and fill colors to their default colors — white, black, and black, respectively — choose Edit⇨Reset Colors.

Lifting Colors Right Off the Canvas

When editing photographic images, you may find it helpful to match the foreground, background, or fill color to an exact color in the image. Doing so helps to hide your edits by maintaining color consistency with the original image. Sometimes, you want your effects to scream, "Look at me, I'm an electronic manipulation created in Photo-Paint!" But other times, you'd just as soon they didn't. When you're looking for subtlety, look to the eyedropper tool.

The eyedropper tool enables you to select colors from the image itself, and then turn around and apply these colors using other tools. It's as if you're siphoning color out of your photograph using a turkey baster or some other extracting device. Well, it's kind of like that anyway. The only difference is that you don't delete any color from the photograph. Oh, and unlike a turkey baster, the top of the eyedropper won't fall off in the dishwasher and melt on the heating unit.

- ✔ After arming yourself with the eyedropper, labeled in Figure 16-2, click on a color in the image to select a new foreground color.

- ✔ Ctrl+click on a color in the photograph to replace the background color.

- ✔ Right-click or Shift+click on a color to replace the fill color.

Double-click on the eyedropper icon in the toolbox, press Ctrl+F2, or click on the Color roll-up button on the Property Bar (labeled in Figure 16-2) to display the Color roll-up, shown in Figure 16-3, which lets you define a custom foreground or background color. This roll-up works essentially like its counterpart in CorelDraw, which I describe in the "Make New Colors in Your Spare Time" section of Chapter 7. But a few items work differently:

- ✔ The two colored icons in the upper-left corner of the roll-up represent the foreground and background colors. Click on the icon for the color you want to change. It becomes surrounded by a black outline to show that it's selected. Then use the color slider and color selector box to define your custom color.

- ✔ Click on the swap colors icon to make the foreground color the background color and vice versa.

- ✔ Click on the default colors icon to return to the default foreground (black) and background (white) colors.

- ✔ To add your custom color to the color palette, choose <u>A</u>dd Color from the palette's pop-up menu.

- ✔ To create a custom fill color, use the Color roll-up to establish your color, and then add the color to the color palette as just described. You can then assign your custom color as the fill color by right-clicking on the custom color's swatch in the color palette.

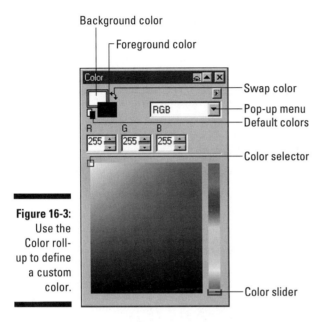

Background color

Foreground color

Swap color

Pop-up menu

Default colors

Color selector

Color slider

Figure 16-3:
Use the
Color roll-
up to define
a custom
color.

Erasing and Undoing Your Way Back to the Good Old Days

In real life, an eraser gives you the opportunity to retract a pencil stroke. But it doesn't do a very comprehensive job — you can still see some pencil remnants — and you can't use the eraser to undo other kinds of strokes, such as pen strokes, paint strokes, and big globs of black tar.

Photo-Paint 7 handily addresses this problem by offering not one but three erasers that erase everything under the sun plus a new Undo command that enables you to undo multiple operations. If necessary, you can even restore your image to the way it appeared when you last saved it to disk.

Scrubbing away those stubborn stains

Photo-Paint provides three different erasers — one that's very useful, another that's moderately so, and another that you can probably do without. The eraser flyout menu and its assortment of erasers are shown in Figure 16-4.

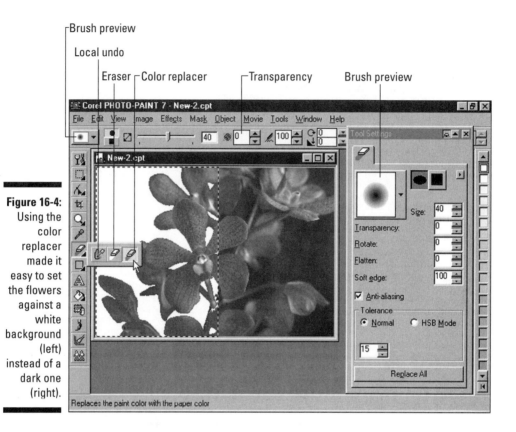

Figure 16-4: Using the color replacer made it easy to set the flowers against a white background (left) instead of a dark one (right).

Here's the lowdown on the three erasers:

✔ Drag with the Local Undo tool to selectively undo the effects of the most recent operation. Unlike Edit⇔Undo, which undoes the entire operation, the Local Undo tool restores only the portion of the image you drag over. This tool is especially useful for erasing small portions of a line you just finished drawing. I rate this tool as very useful.

Be sure to set the Transparency value (either in the roll-up or on the Property Bar) to zero to completely erase to the saved image.

✔ If you double-click on any of the eraser icons, you apply that tool's effect to the selected portion of the image. (I explain how to select stuff in the next chapter.) If nothing is selected, Photo-Paint applies the effect to the entire image.

The tool icon must be visible in the toolbox for you to double-click it. You can't double-click on a flyout icon.

✔ The standard eraser tool paints a line in the background color. But if you want to paint in white (the default background color), you're better off simply changing the foreground color to white and using the paint tool, which is infinitely more versatile. If you do decide to use the eraser tool, be sure to turn on anti-aliasing, which softens the eraser's edges. To turn on anti-aliasing, select the option in the Tool Settings roll-up or click on the anti-aliasing button on the Property Bar (if the option is turned on, the button appears depressed).

Double-click the eraser tool to fill your image or selection with the background color. (Selections are explained in Chapter 17.)

✔ As you drag with the color replacer tool, Photo-Paint replaces all occurrences of the foreground color (and colors similar to it) with the background color. This tool can be moderately useful.

For example, in Figure 16-4, the flowers in the left half of the image window were originally set against a black background, just like the flowers in the right half of the window. To change the background from black to white, I simply selected the left half of the window (as explained in the next chapter), set the foreground color to black and the background color to white, and double-clicked on the color eraser icon. If I had tried instead to use the paint tool or regular eraser, changing the background would have been a tedious chore, but the color replacer makes quick work of the job.

✔ Options in the Tool Settings roll-up and on the Property Bar let you change the size and shape of the eraser. Click on the brush preview (labeled in Figure 16-4) to display a pop-up menu of preset eraser shapes. You can also edit the Size, Rotate, and Flatten values to create a custom brush, but Photo-Paint provides you with so many presets that you probably won't need to bother.

✔ Raise the Transparency value to mix the background color with the existing colors in the image. Higher values — up to 99 — make the background color more translucent.

✔ When using the color replacer tool, you can control how many colors in the image get changed to the background color. The value in the Tolerance option box determines how close a color has to be to the foreground color to be replaced. Higher values cause more colors to be replaced; lower values replace fewer colors. (The Tolerance option box is at the bottom of the roll-up and just to the right of the HSB button on the Property Bar.)

Strangely enough, the best eraser tool isn't an eraser tool at all. It's a special function of the clone tool called the Eraser brush. Read the "Painting One Portion of an Image onto Another" section to find out all about it.

Reviewing the history of your image

As long as we're on the subject of undoing things, I should mention that the Undo command in Photo-Paint 7 now works just like the one in CorelDraw.

In the past, you could undo only the most recent operation. But now you can undo a whole series of operations. Just keep choosing Edit⇨Undo or pressing Ctrl+Z.

To do so, however, you need to change a setting in the Options dialog box (choose Tools⇨Options or press Ctrl+J). Click on the Memory tab and look for the Undo Levels option box. The default setting is 1, which limits you to undoing only one operation. Raising the value enables you to undo more operations. But keep in mind that the higher you set the value, the more you tax your computer's brain. I recommend that you set the Photo-Paint Undo Levels value no higher than 3 or 4 unless your computer has tons of memory.

If you change your mind after choosing Edit⇨Undo, choose Edit⇨Redo. Photo-Paint redoes all those operations that you just undid. (Is that a word?)

Going back to square one

Suppose that you create and save an image. Then, in a creative fit, you paint all over your image, apply a half dozen special effects, and otherwise completely muck things up. After further reflection, you decide that you absolutely hate everything you've done. No problem. Just choose File⇨Revert. Photo-Paint restores your image to the way it appeared the last time you saved it. All evidence of your embarrassing artistic flailings magically disappears.

Drawing Lines

If you simply want to draw straight lines, you have two options:

- ✔ Ctrl+drag with the paint tool. Using this method, you can create horizontal and vertical lines only.

- ✔ Pick up the line tool, which appears on the rectangle tool flyout. (The line tool icon looks like a pencil drawing a line, and it's labeled in Figure 16-5.) With this tool, you can create straight lines in any direction.

Two former companions of the line tool, the curve tool and the pen tool — both of which I found to be totally useless — have mercifully disappeared from Version 7.

My biggest complaint with the line tool is that you can't assign arrowheads to the ends of the lines as you can in CorelDraw. Still, I guess you may occasionally find a use for this tool, so here's how to use it:

✔ Drag with the line tool to draw a straight line between two points. Click with the tool and then keep clicking at different locations to draw a free-form outline with straight sides. Each time you click, you set a corner in the shape. Double-click to end the line.

✔ Be sure to turn on the anti-aliasing option (found both on the Property Bar and in the Tool Settings roll-up). Hard-edged lines have no business populating your photographs. After all, hard edges interrupt the seamless blend between pixels that is the hallmark of computer images.

✔ Using the controls on the Property Bar or Tool Settings roll-up, you can also adjust the transparency, width, and type of joint used to join two lines. In addition, you can tell Photo-Paint to automatically turn your line into an object after you finish drawing it (use the Render to Object option). For more on turning stuff into objects, see the next chapter.

✔ The options in the Paint Mode pop-up menu determine how the line color mixes with the colors in the image. For more on paint modes, see the upcoming section "Painting with a Tackle Box Full of Brushes."

Drawing Geometric Shapes

Photo-Paint provides three simple shape tools: the rectangle, polygon, and ellipse tools, which you access by clicking and holding on the rectangle tool icon, as illustrated in Figure 16-5.

✔ The rectangle tool lets you draw rectangles. Ctrl+drag to draw squares; Shift+drag to draw the shape outward from the center. You can select the rectangle tool by pressing F6.

✔ The ellipse tool draws. . . . I think you can guess the ending to that sentence. Ctrl+drag to draw circles; Shift+drag to draw from the center out. Press F7 to select the ellipse tool. (Yet another waste of a keyboard shortcut.)

✔ The polygon tool draws orange hamsters dressed in festive German drinking costumes.

No, sorry, my mistake. After reviewing my notes, I find that the polygon tool actually draws free-form shapes with straight sides. This role means that it's less like the polygon tool in CorelDraw and more like the line tool in Photo-Paint. You click to add corners and double-click when you're finished.

By default, Photo-Paint fills the shapes with the fill color. But you can also request no fill or some special fill by using the options in the Tool Settings roll-up. Click on the Fountain Fill icon in the roll-up, for example, to fill the shape with a gradation. Click on the Edit button to choose a pattern or texture for your fill. Click on the No Fill icon to make the fill transparent.

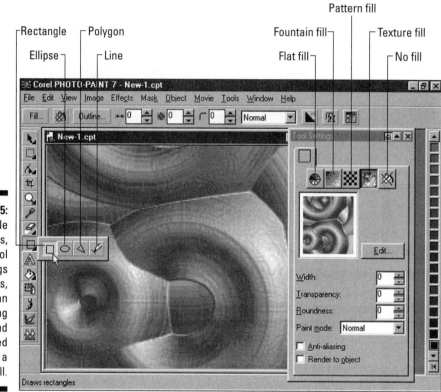

Figure 16-5:
The simple
shape tools,
the Tool
Settings
options,
and an
interesting
background
created
with a
texture fill.

Each one of these icons, labeled in Figure 16-5, directly corresponds to a special fill function in CorelDraw, as described in the last section of Chapter 7. To return a solid fill, click the Flat Fill icon.

The Tool Settings roll-up in Version 7 contains a Render to Object option that enables you to convert a shape to an object immediately after you draw it. For more about converting images to objects, see the next chapter.

You can also access the various fill alternatives by clicking on the Fill button on the Property Bar. Photo-Paint displays a dialog box that contains some of the same options found in the Tool Settings roll-up (the other options are presented as individual buttons on the Property Bar).

Although the special fill options are certainly attractive, they can't gloss over the simple fact that geometric shapes lend themselves to image editing about as well as vampire bats lend themselves to deep-sea diving. Their harsh corners and high-contrast curves interrupt the naturalistic appearance of just about any image.

So if you don't want people to be able to see from several miles off that you've been mucking about in an image, don't use the simple shape tools.

The only exception is the rectangle tool, which has one beneficial application: You can use it to draw an outline around your image. Select the No Fill icon, enter a Width value to set the outline to the desired thickness, and then draw a rectangle around the entire image.

In previous versions of Photo-Paint, the rectangle tool also came in handy for creating custom backgrounds like the one in Figure 16-5. You can still use the rectangle for this purpose: Set the Width value to 0 to turn off the outline, choose your fill, and then drag across the image. But an easier option is to use the new Fill command, described next.

Filling Your Entire Image

The new Fill command enables you to quickly fill your entire image or a selected area with a color, gradient, texture, or pattern. This command can come in handy if you want to create a custom background like the one shown in Figure 16-5, or cover your image with a partially transparent fill.

To use the command, choose Edit⇨Fill to display the Edit Fill & Transparency dialog box, shown in Figure 16-6. The various options work as follows:

- ✔ The Fill Color tab contains options that enable you to choose whether you want to fill the image with the foreground color, background color, fill color, gradient, texture, or pattern.

- ✔ Click on the Edit button to select a different texture, pattern, or gradient or to define a custom color.

- ✔ To change the fill color to a color in your image, click on the eyedropper icon and then click on the color in your image.

- ✔ The Transparency panel enables you to fade the fill so that some of your underlying image shows through. To cover your entire image with a transparent fill, choose Flat from the Type menu. Then adjust the transparency level using the Start Transparency value. Higher values make the fill more transparent.

- ✔ To create a gradient fill that fades from one level of transparency to another across your image, choose any other Type option except None. Photo-Paint displays transparency control arrows as in Figure 16-6. Drag the arrows to reposition the start and end points of the gradient. To adjust the amount of transparency at the beginning and end of the gradient, use the Start Transparency and End Transparency options.

  To create the snake-peeking-out-of-the-fog look shown in Figure 16-6, for example, I lifted a fill color from my image using the eyedropper tool and selected the Current Fill option on the Fill Color tab. Then, on the Transparency panel, I selected the Elliptical option, set the Start Transparency value to 100, and set the End Transparency value to 0. Ooh, scary.

Transparency control arrows

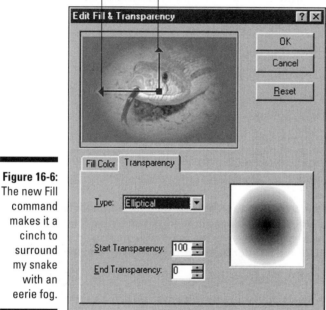

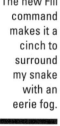

Figure 16-6:
The new Fill
command
makes it a
cinch to
surround
my snake
with an
eerie fog.

✔ If you want to fill only a portion of your image, select the area before choosing the Fill command. Selecting stuff is the subject of the next chapter.

✔ As mentioned earlier, double-clicking the eraser icon in the toolbox fills the selected area or image with the background color.

Plunking Down the Paint

The next tool on our hit parade is the fill tool, which looks like a tipped bucket with paint dribbling out of it. While the Fill command covers your entire image with a fill, the fill tool replaces an area of continuous color with the fill color.

In Figure 16-7, I set the fill color to white and clicked with the fill tool inside the archway. Photo-Paint replaced the previously black pixels with white, making the archway look like it goes right through the page. If you use your imagination, that is.

To control the range of colors affected by the fill tool, enter a value into the Tolerance option box, found in the bottom-left corner of the Tool Settings roll-up and just to the right of the HSB button on the Property Bar. Lower

Fill tool cursor

Figure 16-7:
An area of black before (left) and after (right) clicking on it with the fill tool.

values affect fewer colors. You can also select the Anti-aliasing check box or Property Bar button to soften the edges of the filled area. (In Figure 16-7, the Tolerance value was 10, and Anti-aliasing was turned on.)

You can change the fill color from a flat fill to a gradation or texture by clicking on the icons along the top of the Tool Settings roll-up. These are the same icons labeled back in Figure 16-5. The No Fill icon is absent; after all, replacing an area with a transparent fill doesn't make any sense. I mean, what is there to see behind the image? The Windows 95 desktop? The motherboard and other yucky computer innards? The center of the Earth? Without the No Fill icon, we'll never know.

Creating Custom Gradients

Just like CorelDraw 7, Photo-Paint 7 now offers an interactive gradient fill tool, labeled in Figure 16-8, which you can use to create custom gradients. The Photo-Paint version of the tool isn't quite as adept as the CorelDraw version — for example, you can create two-color gradients only.

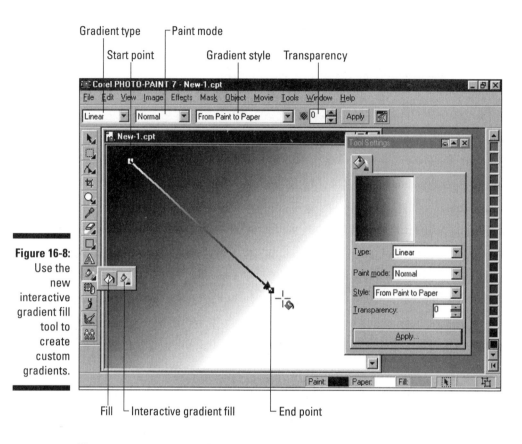

To create a custom gradient, select the tool and select a gradient type from the Type pop-up menu in the roll-up or from the Property Bar. (Don't choose Flat or None; these options don't create a gradient; rather, they enable you to replace a gradient-in-progress with a flat fill or no fill, as explained a little later.) Photo-Paint automatically fills the image or the selected area with a gradient and displays the gradient start and end point controls shown in the figure.

Drag the start or end point controls to reposition the start and end colors in the gradient, or change the angle of the gradient. Use the controls on the Property Bar or in the Tool Settings roll-up to change the gradient type, style, and transparency. If you want to return to having no fill or a solid fill, choose None or Flat, respectively, from the Type pop-up menu. For some really fun effects, play around with the different options in the Paint Mode pop-up menu, which control how the pixels in your gradient blend with the underlying image pixels.

When you're satisfied with your gradient, click on the Apply button on the Property Bar or in the roll-up. Your gradient is now set in stone; you can't edit it further as you can in CorelDraw. (Note that if you choose None from the Type pop-up menu, the Apply button is dimmed because Photo-Paint has nothing to apply.)

Painting with a Tackle Box Full of Brushes

Using the paint tool — the one that looks like a little paint brush — is simplicity itself. You merely click or drag around inside the image to lay down strokes of foreground color.

Adjusting the properties of the paint tool in the Tool Settings roll-up can be a nightmare, however. Quite simply, the roll-up offers far more options than you will ever exploit — assuming, of course, that you have a life.

So, rather than explain every available option, I'll limit my discussions to the handful of options that matter most:

✔ Shown in Figure 16-9, three tab icons appear along the top of the Tool Settings roll-up. You can click on one of these tabs to switch between the three panels of paint tool options. But don't. The second and third panels are filled with goofy options that you'll never use in a billion years. The one exception is the Anti-aliasing option found on the second panel. This option is turned on by default, which is how you should leave it.

✔ Beneath the tab icons is a row of four slightly larger icons. These icons represent the predefined brushes. Though you can see only four brushes at a time, Photo-Paint 7 offers a total of 15 brushes. To display all the brushes, click on the down-pointing arrow to the right of the icons.

Instead of explaining how each of the 15 brushes works, I show lines painted with the brushes in Figure 16-9. Each brush is pictured and labeled next to its line. The paint tool always paints in the foreground color, except when you use the Watercolor brush (second from the bottom). This brush smears existing colors in the image as if the colors were wet. (When painting on a brand new image, the brush lays down watercolor-like strokes in the foreground color.)

✔ Below the brush icons is a Type pop-up menu. If you're looking for a slightly different effect than what is offered by the 15 brushes, you can select a different effect from this menu.

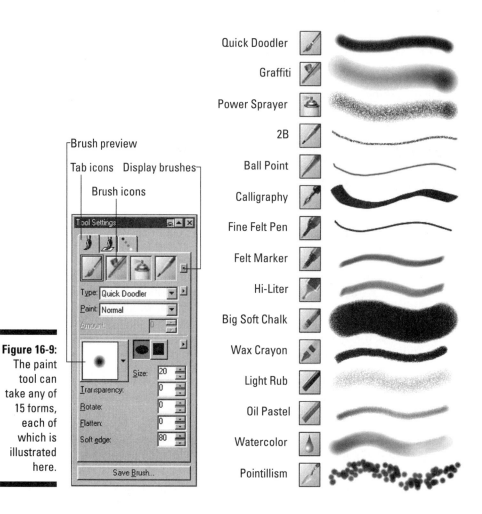

Quick Doodler
Graffiti
Power Sprayer
2B
Ball Point
Calligraphy
Fine Felt Pen
Felt Marker
Hi-Liter
Big Soft Chalk
Wax Crayon
Light Rub
Oil Pastel
Watercolor
Pointillism

Brush preview

Tab icons   Display brushes

Brush icons

Figure 16-9:
The paint
tool can
take any of
15 forms,
each of
which is
illustrated
here.

✔ To mix the foreground color with the existing colors in an image in wacky and unusual ways, select an option from the Paint pop-up menu. To explain how all these options work would take five more books. But I do want to call your attention to three fun options: Add, Subtract, and Color.

Select the Add option to lighten the colors in an image as you paint over them. This option works especially well with the Hi-Liter brush and a dark foreground color. Select Subtract to darken colors — great for use with the Felt Marker and a light foreground color. And select Color — much farther down the menu — to colorize an image with any brush. (By colorize, I mean to add color to a black-and-white image or replace the color without affecting the detail in a color image.)

✔ To change the size and shape of the brush, click on the brush preview (labeled in Figure 16-9) to display a pop-up menu of alternatives.

You can also adjust the values in the five option boxes below and to the right of the preview, but you can generally rest assured that the pop-up menu offers every brush size and shape you'd ever want.

✔ Folks who are serious about painting generally prefer to work with a cursor that represents the brush size and shape. To swap the silly paintbrush cursor for a size and shape cursor, press Ctrl+J (or choose <u>T</u>ools⇨<u>O</u>ptions), click on the General tab, select the Shape Cursor for <u>B</u>rush Tools check box, and press Enter. This option affects the cursors used by the tools that have adjustable brushes — namely, the paint, effect, clone, and eraser tools.

If you prefer a simple crosshair cursor, choose Crosshair from the pop-up menu and turn off the Shape Cursor for Brush Tools check box. With this option, all tools except the arrow tool and path node edit tools use the crosshair cursor. If you choose Shape from the pop-up menu, you get a size and shape cursor for the paint, effect, clone, and eraser tools, a crosshair for some other tools, and a cursor that resembles the tool icon for the remaining tools. Whew, that was a lot of work!

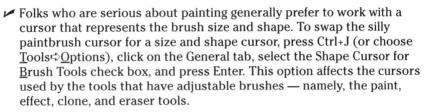

Almost all the options found on the first panel of the Tool Settings roll-up are also available on the Property Bar. If you're not sure what a Property Bar control does, pause your cursor over the control to display an identifying label.

Smudging, Lightening, Colorizing, and Blurring

The second-to-the bottom tool in the toolbox is the effect tool. As you do with the paint tool, you use the effect tool by dragging across your image. And as with the paint tool, you can adjust the way the effect tool works by selecting different brushes from the Tool Settings roll-up or Property Bar.

Altogether, the Version 7 effect tool supplies 11 brushes, displayed and labeled in Figure 16-10. Because many of the brushes work only in color, I can't show you how they work as I did for the paint tool brushes back in Figure 16-9. So, you'll have to experiment and rely on the following descriptions:

✔ The first thing I should mention is that you can change how each brush behaves by selecting an option from the Type pop-up menu. I can't tell you how every single option works — we'd be here till next Saturday (whenever that is) — but I can tell you how the brushes function in general, regardless of which Type option is active.

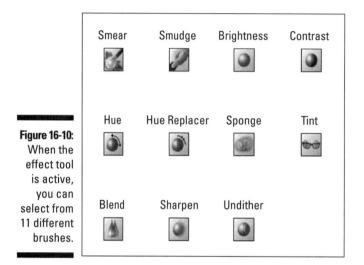

Figure 16-10:
When the effect tool is active, you can select from 11 different brushes.

✔ The Smear brush smears colors in the image. Sometimes, it smears colors as if they were wet; other times, it takes the pixels at the beginning of your drag and repeats them over and over throughout the drag.

✔ The Smudge brush mixes pixels from one area into another. It does this rather randomly, creating a rough, gritty effect. Try dragging two or three times in the same direction for the best results.

✔ Use the Brightness brush to brighten the area you drag over. Change the Amount value under the Paint pop-up menu to increase or decrease the lightening effect. You can also darken pixels by selecting Darken from the Type pop-up menu or entering a negative value into the Amount option box.

✔ Select the Contrast brush and the Increase Contrast option in the Type pop-up menu, or enter a positive Amount value to increase the contrast between light and dark pixels. Choose the Decrease Contrast option or enter a negative amount value to, well, decrease the contrast. Again, raise or lower the Amount value to increase or decrease the effect. In fact, that goes for all the other effect tool brushes.

✔ The Hue brush is really dumb. It changes every color you drag over to a different color. Red changes to green, green to blue, blue to red, and everything else to other colors in between. Now, that'll come in handy.

✔ The Hue Replacer brush replaces every color in the image with the foreground color. This brush may sound even dumber than the Hue brush, but it's actually pretty useful. It's just the thing for colorizing a color image. For example, you could change a blue dress to orange without otherwise changing the way the dress looks.

✔ If the colors in your image are too vivid or too faded and drab, you can downplay or bolster them by dragging over them with the Sponge brush. Choose Sponge Add from the Type pop-up menu or enter a positive value in the Amount option to put color into the image; choose Sponge Remove or enter a negative Amount value to suck color out.

✔ The Tint brush is the perfect tool for colorizing a grayscale photograph. After converting the image to color — by choosing Image⇨Convert To⇨RGB Color (24-bit) — you can select a foreground color and paint with the Tint brush. But be sure to decrease the Amount value to 50 or lower to allow the highlights and shadows to show through.

✔ Paint with the Blend brush to blur the pixels in an image, giving the photograph a softer quality. It's just the thing for getting that Vaseline-on-the-lens effect that was so popular in the Sixties.

✔ You could use the Sharpen brush to sharpen the focus of an image. But it doesn't work worth a hill of beans. The much better way to enhance the focus of a photograph is to choose Effects⇨Sharpen⇨Adaptive Unsharp, as described in the "Bringing an image into sharper focus" section of Chapter 17. (I know that the process sounds hard, but it's not.)

✔ New to Version 7 is one additional effects brush, Undither. This brush smoothes the transition between differently colored pixels, especially in bad scans and GIF graphics from the Web. I don't think you'll find this tool terribly effective, but it may come in handy for removing dust and scratches in a scanned photograph or for smoothing jagged edges.

Painting One Portion of an Image onto Another

The tool whose icon looks like a couple of paper dolls is the clone tool, which lets you copy one portion of an image onto another just by dragging. You can use the tool to duplicate portions of the image — take one cow and turn it into a herd, for example. Or you can cover up scratches and bits of dust that sometimes get scanned along with an image.

To use the tool, click to specify the portion of the image that you want to clone. A blinking cross appears in this spot. Then, move your cursor to a different spot and drag to clone the image. The cross moves with your cursor to show what is being cloned. You can change the clone spot any time by again Shift+clicking, or right clicking.

When you select the clone tool, the Tool Settings roll-up and Property Bar offer four brushes, shown in Figure 16-11. They work as follows:

✔ The Normal clone brush clones the image normally. This is the brush that you'll want to use most often.

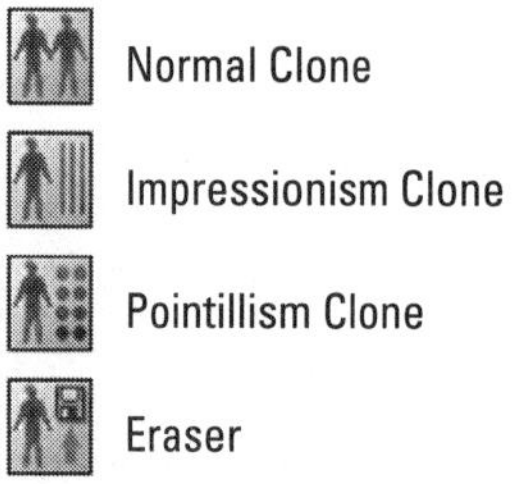

Normal Clone

Impressionism Clone

Figure 16-11:
The four
clone tool
brushes.

Pointillism Clone

Eraser

✔ The Impressionism Clone brush paints multiple lines at a time in different colors. The lines weave back and forth, so I guess you're supposed to think that Van Gogh may have used this brush. But come on, just because the guy cut off his ear doesn't mean that he was totally insane. This brush is too goofy.

✔ If the Impressionism Clone brush captures the spirit of Van Gogh, the Pointillism Clone brush embodies Georges Seurat. The brush lays down a bunch of differently colored dots. If you're painting a Hawaiian lei or a DNA molecule, it'll come in quite handy. Otherwise, it won't.

✔ In fact, the only clone tool brush that you're likely to use is the Eraser brush, which erases pixels back to the way they looked when you last saved the image to disk. This is an exceedingly useful brush. Set the Transparency value to 0 to completely erase the pixels.

Spray Painting with Images

For a fun afternoon of creative play, check out the new image sprayer tool, which "sprays" existing objects onto your image. Try this:

1. **Open a new image and select the image sprayer tool, labeled in Figure 16-12.**

2. **Click on the Load Image List button on the Property Bar (or choose the command from the Tool Settings roll-up pop-up menu).**

   After the Load Image List dialog box appears, double-click on the file SUNFLOWR.CPT. (If the filename already appears on the Property Bar next to the Load Image List button, you can skip this step.)

   An image list, by the way, is simply a file that contains the objects that you want the image sprayer tool to apply.

┌Load image list

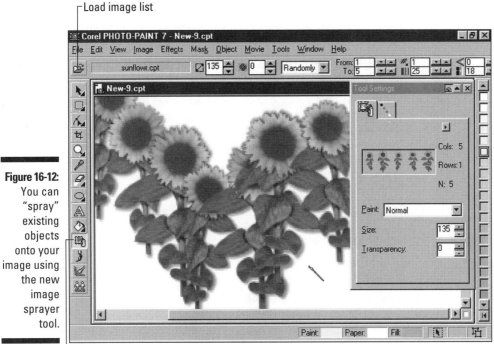

Figure 16-12:
You can
"spray"
existing
objects
onto your
image using
the new
image
sprayer
tool.

└Image sprayer

3. Drag across your image.

You should get a line of sunflowers. Keep dragging to spray more sunflowers. Using the settings in the Property Bar or Tool Settings roll-up, you can adjust the transparency and size of the sunflowers, as well as how many flowers appear each time you drag (change the Number of Dabs value).

Cool, right? Except how often are you going to need to create a bed of sunflowers? Fortunately, you have other options. In addition to the sunflowers image list, Photo-Paint provides other sample image lists in the Load Image List dialog box. You can also create your own image list:

1. Convert the images that you want to spray to objects, as described in the next chapter.

You can also spray entire images, as described later, but objects work best with this tool.

2. **Select the objects and then select the image sprayer tool.**

   Just click on the first object with the arrow tool and then Shift+click on the others.

3. **Choose Save Objects as Image List from the roll-up pop-up menu or the Property Bar.**

   If you're turning a single object into an image list, Photo-Paint asks whether you want to create a directional image list. With a directional image list, each time you drag with the image sprayer tool, you lay down a series of slightly rotated variations of your original object. If you click Yes when asked whether you want a directional image list, you're then asked to specify how many different variations you want Photo-Paint to create.

   If you don't want a directional image list, click on No. In this case, dragging with the image sprayer tool simply lays down identical copies of your original object.

   If you're saving multiple objects as an image list, you don't need to worry about this issue.

4. **Give your image list a name.**

   Photo-Paint displays the standard Save an Image to Disk dialog box, with the IMGLISTS folder open. Name your image list and press Enter.

You can also create an image list from a whole image rather than an object, although the results usually aren't as interesting. To save an image as an image list, choose Save Document as Image List from the Tool Settings pop-up menu. You then get the option of dividing your image into horizontal and vertical tiles. If you use only one horizontal and one vertical tile, each click or drag of the image sprayer tool lays down your image in its entirety. If you enter a value higher than one, Photo-Paint divides your image up into tiles. Each click or drag of the image sprayer tool lays down a different tile.

 If your image list contains more than one object, you can control how many objects the image sprayer applies by using the From and To values on the Property Bar or on the second tab of the Tool Settings roll-up. For example, if your image list contains 5 objects and you want to spray out only objects 1 through 3, enter 1 in the From box and 3 in the To box.

Chapter 17

Twisting Reality around Your Little Finger

· ·

In This Chapter

▶ Using the Photo-Paint mask tools

▶ Softening the edges of a selection

▶ Changing the sensitivity of the lasso, magic wand, and magic scissors mask tools

▶ Adjusting the outline of a selection

▶ Moving and cloning selections

▶ Cropping an image

▶ Combining images in creative and entertaining ways

▶ Sharpening focus

▶ Making the colors bright and perky

▶ Converting selections to objects

▶ Transforming an object

▶ Creating and editing text in Photo-Paint

· ·

*W*hen you were young, authority figures no doubt told you that the more effort you put into something, the more you get out of it. (You didn't believe them at the time, of course, having figured out that you could just as easily get an A by peeking at your neighbor's paper as you could by spending hours studying.)

But with Photo-Paint, the time-honored motto holds true: expend a little more effort and you enjoy greater results. Take the tools discussed in this chapter, for example. They're a little harder to use than those discussed in Chapters 15 and 16, but they can deliver amazing results. You can isolate portions of the image that you want to edit, change the focus, balance the colors, and even slap colors onto different backgrounds. Pretty soon, you'll be performing the kind of image-editing feats that make those folks at the supermarket tabloids drool with envy.

Just in case anybody's lawyer decides to take offense at that last statement, I want to state emphatically that I'm only joking. Of course supermarket tabloids don't print altered photographs. If you see a picture of a two-headed alien baby on the pages of one of these fine publications, that's a real, honest-to-goodness alien baby.

Specifying Which Part of the Image You Want to Edit

The first three slots in the Photo-Paint toolbox contain tools that enable you to select and manipulate portions of your image. Altogether, these tools — labeled in Figure 17-1 — represent the most important collection of tools that Photo-Paint has to offer.

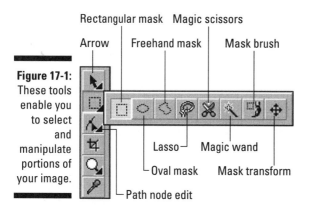

Figure 17-1: These tools enable you to select and manipulate portions of your image.

These tools fall into three categories:

- ✔ With the arrow tool — which Corel calls the pick tool — you can manipulate selections that you've converted into objects. Very likely, you have no idea what I'm talking about, which is why I examine this tool in the "Setting Your Selections Free" section toward the end of this chapter.

  To switch from any selected tool to the arrow tool, press the spacebar. To switch back to the previous tool, press the spacebar again.

- ✔ Use the eight mask tools — all available from the flyout menu shown in Figure 17-1 — to select portions of the image. (A *mask* is Corel's fancy word for a selection outline.) I discuss these indispensable tools in the very next section.

✔ The path node edit tool is twice as complicated as its name makes it sound. You draw a CorelDraw-like path one node at a time. Then you fuss around with the nodes and control points using a collection of buttons straight out of CorelDraw's Node Edit roll-up. And finally, you convert the path to a selection outline that you could have more easily drawn with one of the mask tools. If you don't mind a little advice, I suggest that you run fast, run far, and avoid this tool like the plague.

Sharing a flyout menu with the path node edit tool is the new repeat brush stroke tool. This tool lets you save a brush stroke and then repeat that same brush stroke over and over again. The brush stroke is saved as a path file, which is why the tool is found with the path node edit tool rather than with the paint tools.

Carving out a little bit of imagery with the wondrous mask tools

As in CorelDraw, you have to select a portion of an image in Photo-Paint if you want to manipulate it. But instead of selecting discrete objects — such as rectangles, polygons, and letters of text — you select free-form areas of the image, much as if you were cutting patterns out of a bolt of fabric.

Photo-Paint provides you with seven different types of scissors to cut with; they come in the form of the first seven mask tools labeled in Figure 17-1. (The eighth mask tool — mask transform — lets you modify selection outlines. I cover it separately in the next section.) Here's how these seven slick scissors stack up:

✔ Drag with the rectangular mask tool to select a rectangular portion of the image. (Corel calls this the rectangle mask tool, but rectangular mask is more accurate. Small point, but I just didn't want you to get confused by my nit-picking.) Ctrl+drag with the tool to create a square selection. Shift+drag to draw the selection outward from the center.

✔ Drag with the oval mask tool to select an oval area. (Corel calls this tool the circle mask tool, but it draws circles only if you press the Ctrl key as you drag.) Shift+drag to draw the selection from the center out (Ctrl+Shift+drag to draw a circular selection from the center out).

✔ Use the freehand mask tool to create a free-form selection outline with straight or curved sides. To draw straight sides, click to set the first point and then continue clicking to add corners to the polygon. To draw curved sides, just drag with the tool. When you finish drawing your outline, double-click to convert it to a selection.

Before you double-click to convert the outline to a selection, you can delete the last corner or node in the outline by pressing Delete. You can even press Delete several times in a row to delete the last few corners or nodes. This is a good way to fix portions of the selection outline that you don't like. Try it out with curved or straight-sided outlines.

✔ The lasso mask tool works similarly to the freehand mask tool: You click to add corners or drag to create a curved outline, and then you double-click to convert the outline to a selection. The difference is that when you double-click, the lasso mask tool tightens the selection around a specified background color. In other words, it adjusts your selection to home in on a specific portion of the image.

Perhaps an example will help to clarify: Suppose that you want to rope a calf set against an alfalfa-green background. (Ya see how I'm gittin' into the lassoin' spirit, here? Yeehaw!) If you begin dragging on the alfalfa, Photo-Paint sets green as the background color and tightens around the calf. If you begin dragging on the calf, Photo-Paint sets calf brown as the background and tightens on the alfalfa.

✔ The new magic scissors mask tool is a souped-up freehand mask tool. This tool helps you create intricate selections by finding *edges* — areas of high contrast — and automatically placing the selection marquee along those edges. This tool takes some getting used to, but you may find it handy if you can master it.

To get a feel for how the tool works, open the lizard (at least I think it's a lizard) image shown in Figure 17-2. (It's image 87068 in the Reptiles folder inside the Photos folder on the second CorelDraw 7 CD-ROM.) Then zoom in on the little guy's snout. Click near the outer edge of the lizard's back, making sure to click on the lizard and not the dark background. Now move your mouse along the edge of the lizard. Photo-Paint automatically creates a selection outline along the edge between the lizard and the background. The pixel that you clicked serves as Photo-Paint's reference point — that is, the program detects an edge when it finds pixels that contrast with the pixel you clicked.

When you get a section of the selection outline the way you want it, click to set it in place. Then keep moving your mouse along the edge of the lizard, clicking to set down new sections of the selection outline. Each time you click, Photo-Paint sets a new reference point, so be careful where you click. For best results, don't try to create too large a portion of your outline all at once (the tool's reach extends only a limited distance from the point at which you click anyway, as explained in the next section). Double-click to close the selection outline.

At any point while you're creating your selection, you can simply drag to draw a selection outline as you would with the freehand mask tool.

⌐Magic scissors mask tool

Figure 17-2:
The new
magic
scissors
mask tool
helps you
create
selections
by
automatically
finding the
edges in
your image.

Note that the magic scissors mask tool is most useful when you want to separate a complex subject from a busy, multicolored background. For an image like the one in the figure, where the background is more or less a solid color, you'd probably find it easier to use the magic wand, described next, to create your selection. But I wanted to give you a simple example so that you can clearly see how the magic scissors mask tool works.

✔ Click with the magic wand mask tool to select an area of continuous color. In the first example in Figure 17-3, I clicked in the center of the kid's forehead, at the location shown by the cursor in the second example in the figure. Photo-Paint selected a range of colors in the kid's face, extending all the way from the top of his cranium down to the base of his chin. Just to make the selected area more obvious, I pressed Delete to fill it with white.

The magic wand can take a few moments to work because it involves complex mathematical operations that tax Photo-Paint's tiny brain. Try to be patient.

✔ To create a selection outline with the mask brush tool, just drag as if you were painting with the paint tool. In the first example in Figure 17-4, I dragged around the perimeter of the kid's head. Photo-Paint traced the selection around the brushstroke. To more clearly demonstrate the selection, I pressed Delete to get the second example in the figure.

Figure 17-3:
After
opening an
image (top),
I selected
an area of
continuous
color with
the magic
wand and
pressed
Delete
(bottom).

Magic wand
mask cursor

Regardless of which tool you use to select your image, Photo-Paint displays
an animated conga line of dots around the selected area. These hyperactive
dots are known far and wide as *marching ants*. Honest, that's what they're
called. Everyone thinks that computer jargon has to be obscure and intimidating, but sometimes it's just plain silly.

If the marching ants annoy you or prevent you from seeing some part of the
image that you want to scrutinize, choose Mask⇨Marquee Visible or press
Ctrl+H to turn the command off and hide the ants. The selection is there —
you just can't see it anymore. To bring the ants back so you know where the
selection is, choose the Marquee Visible command or press Ctrl+H again.

Marching ants

Mask Brush cursor

Figure 17-4: Here I drew a selection outline using the mask brush (top) and then pressed Delete to fill the selection with white (bottom).

You can change the color of the mask marquee by choosing a different color from the Mask Marquee pop-up menu on the Marquee tab of the Options dialog box (press Ctrl+J to open the dialog box).

Fine-tuning your selection outline

If the methods just described were your only means of creating selection outlines, Photo-Paint would be a pretty poor excuse for an image-editing program. After all, it's not as if you can expect to draw a selection outline and get it just right on the first try. Suppose that you wanted to select that kid's head in Figure 17-4 and then plop it onto a baby fur seal, as I did in Figure 17-5. (By the way, that seal is image 485028 in the Animals folder.) Creating a selection this perfect requires a little effort. You have to spend a lot of time refining the selection until you get every hair, ear, and whisker just the way you want it.

That's where the Photo-Paint Tool Settings roll-up, Property Bar, mask transform tool, and Mask menu come in. These items enable you to modify selection outlines in ways too numerous to mention. I wanted to take a stab at mentioning a few of them anyway:

✓ When you use any mask tool except the rectangular mask tool, the Tool Settings roll-up includes a check box named Anti-aliasing. (This control is also found on the Property Bar; the icon looks like a big black triangle.) *Anti-aliasing* is one of the most cherished terms in all of computer-dweebdom because it sounds really technical and it means something very simple: soft edges. Unless you want jagged edges around your selection, turn anti-aliasing on for each and every tool.

Anti-aliasing is now available even for black-and-white and 256 color images, which was not the case in versions past.

✓ If you draw a selection with anti-aliasing turned off, you can't go back and apply anti-aliasing after the fact. You can, however, blur the selection outline after creating it. (Figure 17-6 demonstrates the difference between softening and blurring.) Choose Mask⇨Feather or click on the Feather Mask button on the Property Bar to display the Feather dialog box. (The Feather Mask button is just to the left of the Grow button.) Then enter a value between 1 and 200 into the Width option box. Larger values produce blurrier selections. To get the right-hand effect in Figure 17-6, I entered a value of 12.

✓ The Direction pop-up menu determines whether Photo-Paint blurs outward away from the selection outline or inward toward the center. When in doubt, select the Middle option. And always select Curved from the Edges pop-up menu. The Linear option creates harsh edges inside the blur, a singularly unattractive effect.

✓ You can also turn on feathering before you create a selection by entering a value in the Feather option box in the roll-up or on the Property Bar.

✓ When you select the lasso, magic wand, or magic scissors mask tool, the Tool Settings roll-up and Property Bar also include a Tolerance setting. (On the Property Bar, the control is just to the right of the HSB button. The pop-up label for the control reads "Color Similarity or Hue Levels" just to confuse you.) A high Tolerance value for the lasso causes the selection outline to shrink farther and avoid

Original
baby seal

After
expert
cosmetic
surgery

Figure 17-5:
Before I
could
plaster the
kid's face
onto this
innocent
arctic
critter, I had
to spend
lots of time
perfecting
the
selection
outline.

Figure 17-6:
A softened
and blurred
selection
placed
against a
white
background.

Softened (Anti-Aliasing)   Blurred (Mask⇨Feather)

more background colors. In the case of the magic wand, a higher Tolerance value causes Photo-Paint to select a wider range of related colors. And for the magic scissors, the higher the Tolerance value, the more contrast is required for Photo-Paint to find an edge. Try raising and lowering the value while using each tool to get a sense of how this option works.

✔ While we're on the subject of the magic scissors: Each time you click with the magic scissors, Photo-Paint draws an invisible square boundary around the spot you click. If you move your cursor outside that boundary, the tool loses its automatic edge detection powers. The Radius value, found both in the Tool Settings roll-up and on the Property Bar, sets the size of the invisible boundary. The higher the Radius value, the greater the reach of the magic scissors. If you're not happy with how the tool is functioning, try adjusting this value.

✔ When you use the mask brush tool, the Tool Settings roll-up and Property Bar controls enable you to change the size and shape of the brush. Fatter brushes result in fatter selection outlines. Though Photo-Paint provides quite a few options for creating a customized brush, I recommend that you just click on the brush preview on the Property Bar or in the roll-up and select an alternative brush from the pop-up menu. Unless you get seriously interested in this tool — which is unlikely — the predefined brushes should prove more than adequate.

✔ After you create a selection outline, you can move, scale, rotate, skew, or distort it independently of the image using the mask transform tool. Drag the selection with the tool to move it. Drag one of the handles around the selection to scale it.

Click on the selection with the mask transform tool to switch to the rotate and skew mode. Then you can drag a corner handle to rotate the selection outline or drag a top, bottom, or side handle to slant it.

Click again to display the distort arrows; drag an arrow to distort the marquee. Click yet again to display hollow circular handles, which you can drag to create perspective effects. When you finish manipulating the selection outline, double-click inside the outline. Or, to cancel all changes, click outside the outline.

You can use the options in the Tool Settings roll-up to move, scale, rotate, and skew the outline numerically. These options work just like their counterparts in CorelDraw, which I explain in the early pages of Chapter 9. The Property Bar also contains controls that enable you to manipulate your selection outline when the mask transform tool is selected. To switch between the various modes — scale, rotate, skew, and so on — click on the first button on the left end of the Property Bar.

✔ To select all colors throughout the image that are similar to the selected colors, choose Mask➪Similar or click on the Similar button on the Property Bar. This command is a great way to expand the colors selected with the magic wand. Suppose that you're working on a map in which all the water is blue and the land is green. If you click with the magic wand inside a lake, you select just the lake. But if you then choose the Similar command, you select all the water on the map, whether it's surrounded by land or not.

✔ The Grow command (Mask➪Grow, or click on the Grow button on the Property Bar) is a cousin of the Similar command. Grow expands the selection to include adjacent pixels that are similar in color to those along the edges of the selection outline. Photo-Paint selects pixels according to the Tolerance value set for the magic wand tool. Raise the value to select more pixels.

✔ You can increase the size of a selection by choosing Mask➪Shape➪ Expand and entering a value in the ensuing dialog box. Larger values increase the selection by larger amounts. To similarly decrease the size of the selection, choose Mask➪Shape➪Reduce.

✔ To select everything that's not selected and deselect everything that is — in other words, to invert the selection — choose Mask➪Invert.

✔ To deselect everything, choose Mask➪Remove, press Ctrl+D, or just click outside the selection with any of the mask tools except the magic wand or magic scissors. You can use the last method — clicking outside the selection — only when working in the the Normal selection mode (explained in the next section), however.

✔ To select every last pixel in the image, choose Mask➪Select All, press Ctrl+A, or double-click on a mask tool icon in the toolbox.

Making manual adjustments

All the selection modifications that I've mentioned so far are automatic. You tell Photo-Paint what to do, and it does it. But what if you want to make more precise adjustments manually? Suppose that you select a kid's head but you miss his ears. Sadly, Photo-Paint does not offer Mask➪Add Ears. So how do you add the ears to the selection?

The answer lies in the Mask➪Mode submenu. Choosing one of these four commands turns the others off. Also, each command remains in effect until you choose a different one.

✔ By default, the Normal mode is active. In this mode, every time you create a new selection outline, you deselect the rest of the image.

✔ If you want to increase the size of the selection, choose the Additive mode. To select the kid's ears without deselecting the head, for example, choose this mode, drag around one ear, and then drag around the other.

✔ To decrease the size of the selection, choose the Subtractive mode. Now you can carve areas out of the selection outline using a mask tool.

✔ The last command — XOR Mask — is kind of weird. It lets you find the intersection of two selection outlines. In other words, any pixels inside both selection outlines become selected; any other pixels do not. For example, if you draw an oval selection, choose XOR Mask, and then draw an oval selection inside the first oval, you get a donut-shaped selection (the donut is selected but the donut hole isn't).

You can also choose a mask mode via the first four buttons on the left end of the Property Bar. From left to right, the buttons are: Normal, Additive, Subtractive, and XOR Mask.

Or, if you prefer, you can access the mode commands by pressing shortcuts on the keypad (the right-hand portion of the keyboard with the numbers on it). Press Ctrl+plus (+) to choose the Additive command; Ctrl+minus (–) for Subtractive; Ctrl+asterisk (*) for XOR Mask; and Ctrl+period (.) to return to the Normal mode.

Things to Do with a Selected Image

After you select a handful of pixels, you can manipulate them with absolute impunity. Not only can you do things to Photo-Paint pixels that would make CorelDraw objects stare with wonder, you can perform these edits with relatively little effort. For starters, the following list describes a few of the minor modifications you can make to images:

✔ Drag the selection with any mask tool other than the mask brush or mask transform tool to move it to a new location. Photo-Paint leaves a background-colored hole in the wake of the moved selection, as demonstrated in Figure 17-7. (In the figure, white is the background color.) You must be working in the Normal mask mode for this technique to work. (For more on mask modes, see the preceding section.)

✔ You can also nudge a selected area when one of the mask tools is selected by pressing an arrow key. Remember, you must have a mask tool selected if you want to nudge.

✔ As in CorelDraw, pressing Shift+arrow performs a "super nudge" — that is, nudges the selection ten times as far as a regular nudge. You can set the nudge and super nudge distances on the General tab of the Options dialog box (Tools⇨Options or Ctrl+J).

✔ To clone the selected area and leave the image unchanged in the background, Alt+drag the selection using a mask tool. The bottom image in Figure 17-7 illustrates what I mean.

✔ When you clone a selected area as just described, you create a *floating selection*. The floating selection hovers above the rest of the image on its own plane, which means that you can manipulate the selection

White hole   Moved selection   Cloned selection

Figure 17-7:
Drag with a
mask tool to
move a
selection
(top);
Alt+drag to
clone the
selection
(bottom).

without harming the underlying image. In Version 7, you can float a
selection in place — that is, without dragging it from its original position — by choosing Mask⇨Float.

If you click outside the selection outline, choose the mask transform or
mask brush tool, or use any other mask tool outside the selection, you
defloat the selection. Defloating glues the selection back onto the
underlying image. You can also defloat a selection by choosing
Mask⇨Defloat.

✔ You can paint inside a selection with one of the painting or effect tools
described in Chapter 16. The selection acts as a stencil, preventing you
from painting outside the lines. (Artists also call such stencils *masks,*
which is why Corel calls the selection tools mask tools.) Try painting
inside a selection, and you'll quickly see how it works.

✔ To trace the masked selection outline with the paint, eraser, color replacer, effect, or image sprayer tool, choose Mask⇨Stroke Mask or click on the Stroke Mask button on the Property Bar. Photo-Paint asks you to specify whether you want to place the stroke along the outside, inside, or center of the selection outline. After you choose an option and click on OK, you see another dialog box in which you can select which tool you want to use to apply the stroke. Click on the Edit button to choose from a variety of tool options.

✔ To get rid of all the stuff outside the selection outline, choose Image⇨Crop⇨To Mask. This technique allows you to focus on a detail in the image. All the images in this chapter, for example, have been cropped to some extent.

You can also crop an image using the crop tool — located between the path node edit and zoom tools. Drag with the tool to surround the portion of the photograph that you want to retain. You can adjust the size of the cropping boundary after drawing it by dragging the square handles around the boundary. You can drag inside the boundary to move it. When you're finished, double-click inside the boundary to crop away excess pixels.

Combining Images

As soon as you saw the half-boy, half-seal image in Figure 17-5, you no doubt began imagining all sorts of fun things you could do with your own images, including putting your head on some buff athlete's body. By selecting something in one image and then plopping the selection into another image, you can wreak all sorts of havoc on reality.

The easiest way to clone a selection and place the clone into another image is to use the mouse to drag the selection from one image window to the other. Here's how:

1. **Open both images.**

2. **Choose Window⇨Tile Vertically to place the image windows side by side.**

3. **Select the area that you want to clone.**

4. **Choose Mask⇨Float.**

   This step creates a clone of your selection. The clone floats above your image, so you can move it without harming the underlying image.

5. **Drag the floating clone to the other image window.**

   First, make sure that the Normal mask mode is active. Then use any mask tool except the mask transform or mask brush tool to drag the selection. As you drag, your cursor changes to the mask transform cursor when you drag inside the original image window. When you cross over into the other image window, you see a regular arrow cursor with a little box attached to it.

When you release the mouse button at the end of your drag, Photo-Paint places the clone into the image window as a floating selection. You can then drag it to reposition it if need be. (You first need to click on the title bar of the image window to make that window the active window.)

6. **To defloat the clone, click outside the selection outline or choose Mask⇨Defloat.**

The clone is now permanently settled in its new home.

If you want to clone and move an object rather than a selection, select the object with the arrow tool, choose Object⇨Duplicate (Ctrl+Shift+D), and then drag the object to the other image window using the arrow tool. (Objects are explained later in this chapter.)

An alternative method of transferring selections between images is to use the Windows Clipboard. By using the Clipboard, you can cut or copy a selection and paste it into another image. Here's what you need to know:

- ✔ To remove a selection from one image and paste it into another image, choose Edit⇨Cut or press Ctrl+X. Then, inside the destination image (the one into which you want to place the selection), choose Edit⇨Paste⇨As New Selection. Photo-Paint pastes the selection as a floating selection.

- ✔ To copy a selection and paste the copy into another image, choose Edit⇨Copy or press Ctrl+C instead of using the Cut command.

- ✔ Ctrl+V, the universal shortcut for the Paste command, pastes the selection as a new object rather than as a floating selection. For more on this subject, see the upcoming section "Making an object."

Correcting Focus and Contrast

Not all images are born perfect. In fact, most images can benefit from an application of the Level Equalization and Adaptive Unsharp commands, which you can use to adjust the contrast and focus of an image.

Level Equalization, formerly known as the Equalize command, has moved from the Effects menu to the Image menu. Adaptive Unsharp continues to reside on the Effects menu, along with nearly 70 other commands that apply special effects to an image. Most of the other Effects commands create the kinds of effects that you can have a lot of fun playing around with but that serve little practical purpose. (For examples of a few of the more interesting effects, read Chapter 19.) Not so with Adaptive Unsharp; this effect can actually make your image look better instead of weirder.

Bringing an image into sharper focus

The Effects⇨Sharpen⇨Adaptive Unsharp command sharpens the focus of an image. That's right, you can actually sharpen the focus after the photo comes back from the developer. You can't bring out details where none exist — if the camera was way out of focus when you shot the picture, there's not much you can do — but you can sharpen photos that are slightly soft. In fact, you'll probably want to sharpen every single photograph that you open in Photo-Paint. Though Photo-Paint provides many sharpening commands, Adaptive Unsharp does the best job of combining ease of use and good results.

When you choose the Adaptive Unsharp command, Photo-Paint displays the dialog box shown in Figure 17-8. Here you find two previews — before and after — plus a Percentage slider bar as well as hand and zoom tools for navigating inside the previews.

Figure 17-8:
Adaptive
Unsharp
is the most
straight-
forward
and
capable
sharpening
command.

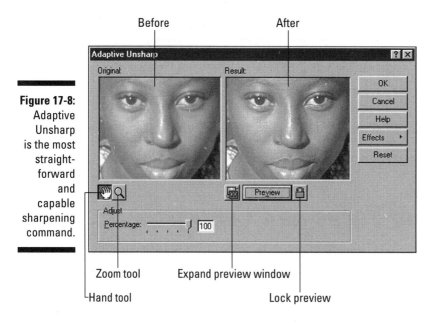

The dialog box options work like so:

✔ Drag the Percentage slider handle to decide how much you want to sharpen the image. Or enter a value between 1 and 100 into the option box to the right of the slider bar. The higher the value, the sharper your image gets.

For reference, Figure 17-9 features an image at several different Percentage values. The top picture shows the original image, which is surprisingly soft. The left examples show the results of applying Percentage values of 50 percent and 100 percent.

Because 100 percent is the highest value permitted, you may have to apply the command more than once. The right examples in the figure show the results of applying the command two and three times in a row. If you start seeing jagged pixels, as in the last example, you know that you've gone too far.

✔ To preview the effect, click on the Preview button. The right preview shows the sharpened image; the left preview shows the soft one.

✔ If you want Photo-Paint to automatically update the preview every time you change the Percentage value, click on that little lock icon to the right of the Preview button. This locks the preview function on so that you never need click on the Preview button again.

✔ Only so much of the image fits into the preview windows. To preview a different portion of the photograph, select the hand tool and drag inside the left preview window.

✔ To see more of the image at a time, select the zoom tool and right-click in the left preview to zoom out. To magnify the preview, just click with the tool.

✔ Though you use the hand and zoom tools in the left preview, Photo-Paint automatically updates the right preview as well.

✔ If you click on the expand preview window button, labeled in Figure 17-8, the left original view disappears and the right preview is enlarged, enabling you to see an even greater portion of your image. To return to the two-preview setup, click again on the expand preview button (the button scoots to the right side of the dialog box when you enlarge the preview).

✔ To close the dialog box and apply the sharpening effect, press Enter or click on OK.

Reapplying an Effects command

At this point, I feel obliged to share one tidbit about the Effects menu: After you apply any one of the menu commands, Photo-Paint displays that effect as the first command in the Effects menu. This way, you can easily reapply the effect by choosing the first command or simply pressing Ctrl+F.

Original

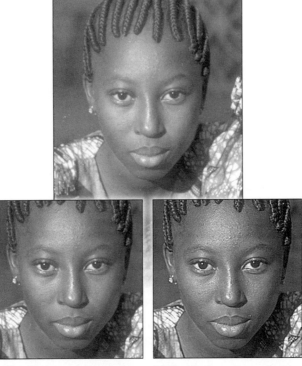

50% once

100% twice

Figure 17-9:
This image,
like many,
benefits
from
sharpening.
But be
careful that
you don't
oversharpen,
as in the
bottom-
right image.

100% once

100% three times

Just about every Effects command brings up a dialog box so that you can mess around with a few settings. If you simply choose the command at the top of the Effects menu, or press Ctrl+F, Photo-Paint reapplies the effect using the last settings that were in force.

Making an image less dark and murky

Most photographs look bright and perky on-screen. But when you print them, they typically darken up and fill in, which can lead to muddy colors and murky detail. That's where the Level Equalization command comes in handy.

Photo-Paint offers other commands under the Adjust submenu, but they are either monumentally complicated or grossly inept. Level Equalization is the exception.

Choose Image⇨Adjust⇨Level Equalization or press Ctrl+E to display the dialog box shown in Figure 17-10. (This command was formerly found under the Effects⇨Color Adjust submenu.) Naturally, when you see a dialog box as complicated as this one, your first inclination is to sweat, wring your hands, and wail pitifully. This dialog box was big and scary looking in Version 6, and it's even more so in Version 7. In fact, the dialog box is so big that the whole thing doesn't fit on-screen if you use a monitor resolution lower than 800 x 600. And if you learned how to use the dialog box in Version 6, you need to relearn everything for Version 7, because things work a little differently.

Low-point slider   High-point slider

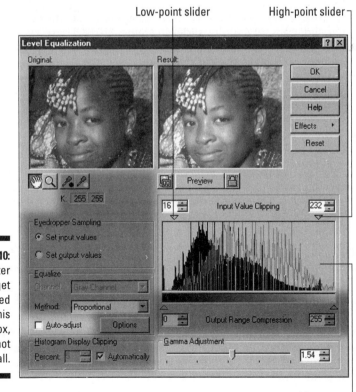

Figure 17-10: After you get acquainted with this dialog box, it's not scary at all.

Histogram

Thankfully, you can accomplish what you need to accomplish without worrying about a good majority of the controls in the dialog box. I took the liberty of shading all the parts of the dialog box that you can safely ignore. The following list tells you what you need to know to correct your image:

✔ First, that big mountain of spiky lines in the lower-right corner of the dialog box is called a *histogram*. A histogram is a graph of the colors in the image, with the darkest blacks on the left side of the graph and the lightest whites on the right. In Version 7, you actually get two histograms: a black one representing your original image, and a red one representing your image with the adjustments that you select in the dialog box.

✔ Before you do anything else in the Level Equalization dialog box, turn off the Auto-adjust option. When this option is turned on, Photo-Paint tries to even out all the colors in the image from light to dark, which results in some pretty drastic color modifications and unrealistic effects. When the option is turned off, Photo-Paint just goes ahead and does what you tell it to do without making any bad guesses of its own.

Likewise, don't try to avoid the Level Equalization dialog box by choosing the Auto Equalize command on the Image⇨Adjust submenu. This command does the same thing as the Auto-adjust option.

✔ See those two triangles above the histogram — the ones labeled low-point slider and high-point slider in Figure 17-10? These two controls enable you to darken the dark colors and lighten the light colors in your image. To make the darkest colors in the image black — not some wishy-washy gray — drag the low-point slider to the right so that it lines up with the left edge of the big histogram mountain. Then, drag the high-point slider to the left until it meets with the right end of the histogram. This step makes the lightest colors in the image white. It's just the thing for whitening eyes and teeth to make it appear as though the folks in the photograph brush regularly.

✔ To alter the lightness or darkness of the medium color — the color smack dab between black and white — drag the Gamma Adjustment slider at the bottom of the dialog box. Drag to the right to lighten the image and drag to the left to darken the image. In all likelihood, you'll want to lighten the image a little, so drag the triangle to the right.

The Gamma Adjustment slider takes the place of the Version 6 mid-point control. And just to really confuse you, the Gamma Adjustment slider works exactly opposite from the old mid-point control, which you dragged to the left to lighten the image and to the right to darken the image.

Keep in mind that the image looks brighter on-screen than it will print. Monitors project light, but the printed page reflects it. So generally, an image that looks a little too light on-screen prints just right. Make a few test prints to be sure.

✔ Use the Preview button, lock icon, expand preview window button, and hand and zoom tools as explained in the preceding section. These options just help you get an idea of how your correction will look before you apply the command.

The top example in Figure 17-11 shows an image as it appeared when I first opened it and converted it to a grayscale image by choosing Image⇨Convert To⇨Grayscale (8-Bit). The image is dark, it has bad contrast, and it's soft. The second image shows the results of applying the Level Equalization and Adaptive Unsharp commands. Needless to say, I wouldn't dream of printing an image without these helpful commands.

— Dark and soft

— Light and sharp

Figure 17-11: If you do nothing else to your photograph, make sure that you correct the colors and sharpen the focus.

Setting Your Selections Free

There comes a time in every selection's life when it yearns for independence. You can grant this independence by turning the selection into a free-floating object. You can then select and manipulate the Photo-Paint object by simply clicking on it with the arrow tool, just as you can with an object in CorelDraw.

For example, after putting all that time into selecting the kid's head back in Figure 17-5, I don't want to have to go through all that effort again if I decide to plop the head on the body of some other unwitting creature. By converting the head to an object, I make sure that I don't have to. As an object, the head remains intact and independent forever.

Making an object

To convert a selected area into an object, do any one of the following:

- Choose Object⇨Create From Mask. Photo-Paint surrounds the selection with eight handles, just like an object in CorelDraw. It even automatically selects the arrow tool, which is the primary tool for editing objects.

- An even quicker way to choose the Create From Mask command is to press Ctrl+up arrow.

- If the Preserve Image command in the Image menu is turned on (a check mark next to the command means that the command is turned on), choosing the Create from Mask command clones your selection and leaves the original image intact. If the command is turned off, converting a selection to an object leaves a background-colored hole underneath, just as when you drag a selection.

  You can toggle the Preserve Image command on and off by pressing Ctrl+Q.

- If all that stuff is too complicated, just copy the selection by pressing Ctrl+C, and then paste it by pressing Ctrl+V. (Or choose Edit⇨Copy and then choose Edit⇨Paste⇨As New Object.) Photo-Paint pastes the new object right in place and automatically selects the arrow tool so that you can play with the object.

- Photo-Paint can now automatically turn a shape you draw with the rectangle, polygon, or oval tool into an object after you draw the shape. Just turn on the Render to Object option in the Tool Settings roll-up or click on the Render to Object button on the Property Bar. You can do the same thing for lines drawn with the line tool.

✔ To turn an object back into a selection mask, select the object by clicking on it with the arrow tool. Then choose Mask➪Create from Object or press Ctrl+M.

✔ By default, text created with the text tool is also created as an object, as explained in the upcoming section "Adding and modifying text."

Manipulating an object

After you create an object, you can scale, rotate, skew it, distort it, and add perspective effects. These transformations are different from those that you perform with the mask transform tool (described in the earlier section, "Fine-tuning your selection outline"). Instead of affecting the selection outline without changing the image inside the selection — as is the case with the mask transform tool — these transformations affect the object itself.

In fact, before you can scale or rotate part of an image in Photo-Paint, you must first convert it to an object.

Of course, before you transform an object, you have to select it. If you just created the object, it's already selected. If you have multiple objects floating around inside your image and you want to select a different object, just click on the object with the arrow tool.

As in CorelDraw, you can select multiple objects by clicking on one and Shift+clicking on the others. Or you can drag around the objects with the arrow tool to surround them with a marquee.

To hide those distracting marching ants around the boundaries of your objects, choose Object➪Marquee Visible or press Ctrl+Shift+H to turn the command off. (If marching ants remain on-screen, they surround areas selected with the mask tools.) To bring the marching ants back, choose the command again.

You can change the object marquee color by selecting a new color from the Object Marquee pop-up menu on the Marquee tab of the Options dialog box (Ctrl+J).

After you select the objects that you want to modify, you can change them as outlined in the following sections.

Moving, cloning, and deleting objects

You can move and clone a selected object in several different ways:

✔ Move the object by dragging it with the arrow tool. Ctrl+drag to constrain the movement to a horizontal or vertical drag. (Remember, you can select the arrow tool by pressing the spacebar.) Because the object floats above the background image, the background remains unaffected.

✔ When the arrow tool is selected, press the arrow keys to nudge the selected object in one-pixel increments. Press Shift plus an arrow key to super nudge in 10-pixel increments. To change the nudge or super nudge distance, go to the General tab of the Options dialog box (press Ctrl+J to open the dialog box).

✔ You can also use the Object Position option boxes on the Property Bar and in the Tool Settings roll-up to precisely place the object. After you enter horizontal and vertical coordinates for the object, click on the Transform button.

✔ Alt+drag the object to clone it and move the clone. Or enter new horizontal and vertical coordinates in the roll-up or Property Bar option boxes and click on the Apply to Duplicate button. (On the Property Bar, the button is just to the left of the Transform button.)

✔ To clone the object in place, choose Object➪Duplicate or press Ctrl+Shift+D.

✔ You can make objects snap to guidelines and grid points, just as in CorelDraw. Turn on the Snap to Grid and Snap to Guidelines commands in the Tools menu. For more on snapping, the grid, and guidelines, see Chapter 6.

✔ To delete a selected object, just press Delete.

If you want to see a copy of the object as you drag instead of just the object's outline, press and hold on the object a few seconds before you begin your drag.

Scaling, rotating, and other effects

You can also apply a bunch of transformations to objects, just as in CorelDraw. Note that the way you transform objects in Version 7 is different than in Version 6:

✔ To scale an object, select it with the arrow tool. Drag a corner handle to scale the object proportionally. Drag a side handle to scale horizontally; drag the top or bottom handle to scale vertically.

✔ Click again on the selected object to display the rotate and skew handles. Drag a corner handle to rotate the object; drag a top, bottom, or side handle to slant the object.

Keep in mind that pixels are always square and upright. So when you rotate or skew an object, you don't actually rotate or skew the individual pixels. Rather, you force Photo-Paint to recolor the pixels to best represent the rotated or skewed image.

The practical upshot of this is that each and every rotation or skew causes a tiny bit of damage to the image. The recolored pixels don't look quite as good as the original ones did. If you rotate or skew the object many times in a row, it starts to look blurry and jagged. Figure 17-12 compares an image rotated three times to an image rotated the same amount once.

✔ Click a third time on the object to display the distortion handles. Drag one of these handles to stretch the image any which way. Figure 17-13 shows the results of stretching the image from Figure 17-12.

✔ Click yet a fourth time to display little round handles on each corner of the image. Drag these handles to create perspective effects.

✔ Click a fifth time to return to the scale handles.

✔ When the arrow tool is selected, the Tool Settings roll-up includes five panels of options that let you move, scale, rotate, and slant the object numerically. (Sorry, no numerical distortions or perspective effects.) These options work similarly to those in CorelDraw, as explained in Chapters 6 (in "Moving by the numbers") and 9 (in "The provocative S&M roll-up" and "Using the not-so-provocative R&S roll-ups").

You can also access the various transformation modes and options via the Property Bar. To switch from one transformation mode to the next, press and hold on the first button on the left end of the Property Bar, which displays a flyout menu of transformation icons. Click on the icon for the transformation that you want to apply.

✔ If you transform an object by dragging its handles, Photo-Paint immediately displays the results of the transformation. But if you transform the object using the Property Bar or roll-up, you need to click on the Transform button to see the results of your changes. The Transform button temporarily applies the transformation. You can cancel the transformation by double-clicking outside the object or right-clicking on the object and choosing Reset from the pop-up menu that appears.

✔ To permanently apply a transformation, click on the Apply button, double-click inside the object, or choose another tool.

✔ You can clone the object and apply the transformation to the clone by clicking on the Apply to Duplicate button on the Property Bar or in the roll-up rather than the Apply button.

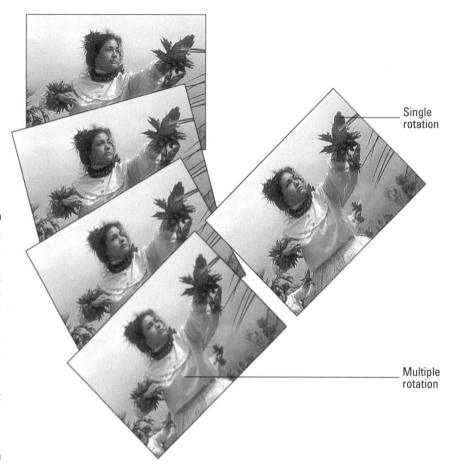

Single
rotation

Multiple
rotation

Figure 17-12:
An image
rotated
three times
(left)
becomes
blurry and
jagged,
whereas
the same
image
rotated just
once (right)
looks more
focused.

✔ To undo a transformation after you click on Apply, choose Edit⇨Undo
or press Ctrl+Z.

✔ You can flip an object horizontally or vertically by dragging a side
handle past the opposite side handle, just as in CorelDraw. Ctrl+drag to
keep the original object size as you flip. Alternatively, you can click on
the Flip buttons on the Object Scale tab of the roll-up or on the Property Bar (select the object scale icon from the flyout menu on the left
end of the Property Bar to display the Flip buttons). All these methods
both flip and move the object, though. To flip an object in place, choose
one of the commands from the Object⇨Flip submenu. (You have to
cancel or apply any transformations in progress to access these
commands.)

✔ As if all those options aren't enough, you can also rotate an object in
90-degree increments by choosing a command from the Object⇨Rotate
submenu. (Object⇨Rotate⇨Free just displays the rotate and skew
handles, as if you had clicked twice on the object.) When the rotate

Figure 17-13:
I dragged the distortion handles to create this effect.

transformation mode is active, the Property Bar also offers buttons that rotate your object 90 degrees. As with the Flip commands, you have to cancel or apply any current transformations to access these Property Bar buttons and Rotate commands.

🖊 Using the Opacity and merge mode controls in the Objects roll-up or the Property Bar, along with the new object transparency brush tool and object transparency tool, you can adjust the transparency of a selected object. For an example of how to use these features, see the section "Turn an Object into a Ghost of Its Former Self" in Chapter 19.

Stamping Some Text into Your Image

The text tool — the one that looks like an A in the toolbox — lets you add text to your image. Because type in Photo-Paint is made up of pixels, you should use the text tool only to create large letters that you want to embellish in ways that CorelDraw doesn't permit. (In Photo-Paint, small text comes out jagged and illegible because there aren't enough pixels to adequately represent the letters.) For example, after creating text in Photo-Paint, you can paint inside the letters to add stripes. You can also apply special effects from the Effects menu.

If you want to label an image, create a caption, or add other commonplace text, do it in CorelDraw. For best results, drag and drop the image as an object into CorelDraw, as described in Chapter 14.

Adding and modifying text

If you decide, after thoughtful consideration, to go ahead and create your text in Photo-Paint, you can select the text tool by pressing F8 (the same shortcut used in CorelDraw to select the text tool). Then click with the tool in the image and enter text from the keyboard. Photo-Paint colors the text in the current foreground color.

As shown in Figure 17-14, both the Tool Settings roll-up and the Property Bar contain formatting options when the text tool is selected, so you can change the typeface, size, justification, and spacing of type after you enter it from the keyboard. Be sure to turn on anti-aliasing, also available both from the Property Bar and roll-up, to soften the edges of the letters.

At this point, you may be wondering why I'm discussing text in a chapter about selections and objects. Well, I'm doing it because text in Photo-Paint is created as an object by default, and if you choose, you can create text as a selection mask. When you select the arrow tool, Photo-Paint automatically surrounds each letter of text with marching ants (assuming that Object⇨ Marquee Visible is turned on). Click on the text with the arrow tool to select it and display the standard object handles. You can then move the text, scale it, rotate it, and so on.

Figure 17-14:
You can create some cool text effects in Photo-Paint.

If you ever want to edit the characters, or change the formatting or color of the text, click on the text object with the text tool. (You know that you've properly activated the text when the marching ants disappear and a big rectangle surrounds the letters.) You can't drag across letters to highlight them as you can in CorelDraw, but you can move the insertion marker around using the left- and right-arrow keys, as well as add and delete characters from the keyboard. Click on a swatch in the color palette to change the color of the text, and adjust the formatting options in the Tool Settings roll-up or on the Property Bar to change the font and size.

 If you turn on the Render to Mask option in the roll-up or on the Property Bar, Photo-Paint creates your text as a selection mask rather than an object. You can then manipulate and edit the selection as you would any other selection. However, you can't edit or format the text with the text tool as you can a text object. To turn a text object into a selection mask after you create the text, choose Mask⇨Create from Object or press Ctrl+M.

Painting inside text

The following is a little exercise that demonstrates something you can do with text in Photo-Paint that you can't do in CorelDraw. The steps explain how to paint inside text and then apply a drop shadow to the text.

1. **Create a few characters of text.**

   Format and color it as desired. Be sure to make the text really big by entering a Size value of 200 or more. That may sound excessive, but 200 is the size of the type in Figure 17-14. You may also want to click on the B icon to make the text bold. And for a nice effect, select red from the color palette.

   Be sure that the Render to Mask option in the Tool Settings roll-up is turned off. For this effect, you need to create your text first as an object.

2. **Select the arrow tool.**

   Photo-Paint selects the text object.

3. **Convert the text to a mask selection.**

   As mentioned earlier, you can convert an object to a selection by choosing Mask⇨Create From Object(s) or pressing Ctrl+M.

4. **Change the foreground color.**

   Click on a swatch in the color palette. Make sure that the new foreground color contrasts well with the text color. May I suggest yellow?

5. **Select the paint tool.**

6. **Paint stripes inside the text.**

The yellow stays entirely inside the selection boundaries. If you followed my color recommendations, you now have red text with yellow stripes, similar to the second example in Figure 17-14.

7. **Click on the text with the arrow tool.**

Photo-Paint selects your original text object, which exists behind the stripes that you just painted.

8. **Choose Object⇨Drop Shadow.**

Photo-Paint displays the new Drop Shadow dialog box, shown in Figure 17-15, which gives you an easy way to create a drop shadow.

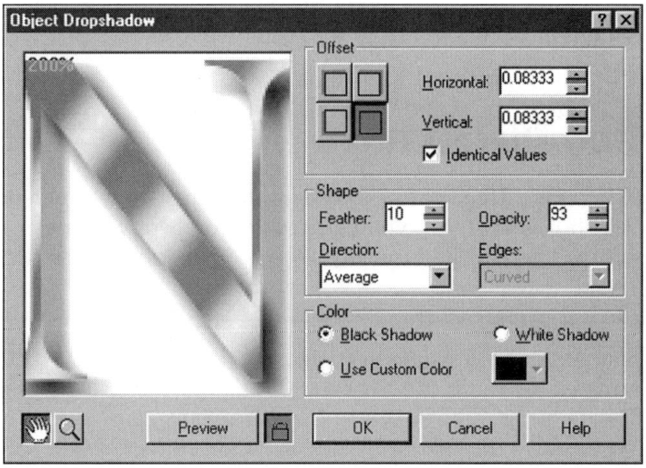

Figure 17-15: The new drop shadow command provides an easy way to place shadows behind objects.

Use the options in the dialog box to specify the position (offset), color, opacity, and softness (feathering) of the shadow. The Direction option controls the direction of the feathering. The hand, zoom, and preview buttons work just like those discussed earlier in this chapter.

9. **Click on OK.**

Photo-Paint places the drop shadow behind your text, as in the bottom example in Figure 17-14. Note that what you wind up with is a text selection mask on top of a text object. If you click on the text with the arrow tool, you select the text object. You can then adjust the drop shadow. If you choose a painting or editing tool, the text mask becomes selected, and you can then apply the tool inside the bounds of the mask. And if you delete the text object, the text selection mask remains.

If you want to gain more control over your shadow, you can paint a shadow in by hand. In that case, follow Steps 1 through 6, but choose Mask⇨Invert in Step 7. This selects the area outside the letters. Then use the paintbrush, with black as the paint color, to trace around the edges of the letters.

Chapter 18

Do Dogs Dream in Three Dimensions?

In This Chapter

▶ Starting CorelDream 3D

▶ Exploring the Dream 3D interface

▶ Importing 3-D objects

▶ Selecting a preview mode

▶ Moving, scaling, and rotating 3-D objects

▶ Applying surface textures (shaders)

▶ Adding a prefab backdrop with the Scene Wizard

▶ Rendering the finished drawing as an image

As mentioned a few hundred pages ago in Chapter 1, CorelDream 3D is a three-dimensional drawing program that enables you to create astoundingly realistic graphics. You draw and arrange shapes in 3-D space, assign textures to the shapes, and capture the final scene as an image file that you can then turn around and edit in Photo-Paint.

Sound exciting? You bet. Sound complicated? And how. It takes much longer to get to first base with Dream 3D than either Draw or Photo-Paint, and it takes weeks or even months to master the program. Three-dimensional drawing programs are among the hardest pieces of software in the universe to use. Occasionally, they have the distressing habit of baffling long-time computer artists like me.

In this chapter, I concentrate on getting you midway to first base by walking you through the process of assembling a 3-D scene. Don't get discouraged if you have to experiment to figure out how a feature works. And don't expect to understand it all overnight. By the time you finish this brief introduction, you should have a pretty sound idea of how the program works and whether or not you want to integrate it into your artistic regimen.

The Dream That Starts Like a Nightmare

Now that I've nearly frightened you into swearing off Dream 3D forever, I'd like to scare you a little further by having you start the program. Just choose Programs➪CorelDraw 7➪CorelDream 3D from the Windows 95 Start menu. After a few moments, the Dream 3D interface takes over your screen. As in CorelDraw and Photo-Paint, Dream 3D begins your encounter by asking whether you want to start an empty scene, open an existing scene, or use the Scene Wizard, which offers an assortment of ready-made backgrounds for your scene. (For more about the Scene Wizard, see "Adding a Prefab Backdrop" later in this chapter.)

After you open a scene, your screen appears something like the one shown in Figure 18-1. The layout of your screen may be a little different, depending on your monitor resolution and the option you select from the Windows➪ Workspace submenu, which enables you to choose from several different layouts. (The different layouts are designed to work with different monitor resolutions.) Some portions of the screen are familiar. Dream 3D offers a bunch of menus, a toolbar, a toolbox, and a status bar, just like Corel's other programs. But the four windows in the middle of the screen herald a decidedly different artistic approach. Sure, they're weird, but you have to get used to them:

- The *work area* is where you create your drawing. It's like the drawing area in CorelDraw, except this one shows your objects in perspective.

- To demonstrate the perspective scene, Dream 3D throws in something that it calls a *working box,* which looks like a chicken-wire cage that's missing a top and two sides. The remaining three sides represent the three planes of 3-D space. The edges where the planes meet are known as *axes.*

- The window to the right of the work area shows the hierarchy of the objects in the work area. (Now let's try that sentence again, but in English.) See, it's easy to lose items in a complex 3-D drawing. The Hierarchy window lists the names of objects and other items so that you can easily locate and select them without having to waste time searching for them in the work area.

- The Objects Browser window, below the work area, contains an assortment of predrawn 3-D objects, called *models.* Each tab in the Object Browser window represents a different folder of objects. To display the objects in that folder, just click on the folder tab. You can add additional folders and objects, as explained in the next section. To use one of the 3-D objects, just drag the object out of the window and drop it into the work area.

- The Shaders Browser window includes colors, patterns, and textures. Click on a shader and then click on the Apply button in the bottom-left corner of the Shaders Browser window to apply the shader to the selected shape in the work area. Or drag the shader and drop it right onto the object.

Work area   Working box   Hierarchy window

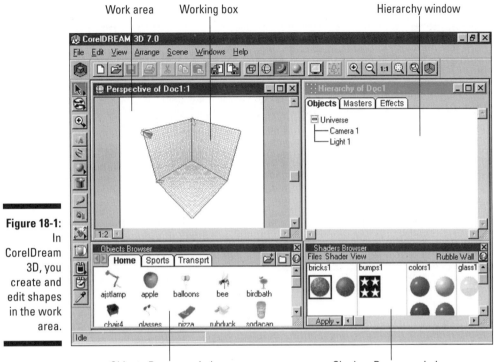

Figure 18-1:
In
CorelDream
3D, you
create and
edit shapes
in the work
area.

Objects Browser window   Shaders Browser window

✔ As in CorelDraw and Photo-Paint, you can reposition your toolbar and toolbox by dragging the gray area around the buttons. And you can hide or display the various toolbars and the status bar by right-clicking the gray area surrounding the toolbar or toolbox and clicking the name of the element you want to turn on or off.

✔ You may want to resize both Browser windows and move them into the upper-right corner of the screen to get them out of the way of the scroll bar. (Check out the Figure 18-2, which appears later in this chapter, if you want to see how I did it.)

In all likelihood, you have no immediate need for the Hierarchy window. You can cut down on the screen clutter by clicking on the Maximize button in the top-right corner of the work area window. The work area expands to fill the entire screen. The Hierarchy window is covered up, but the Objects Browser and Shaders Browser windows remain visible. If you ever need to get to the Hierarchy window later on, just choose the Hierarchy command from the Windows menu.

Three planes of pure drawing pleasure

Dream 3D's working box is really an average, everyday dimensional grid. You know how a bar graph has a horizontal X axis and a vertical Y axis? Well, the only difference between that bar graph and the working box — besides a complete absence of bars — is the addition of a third axis, called the Z axis. The X axis points to the right, the Y axis goes straight up and down, and the Z axis shoots off to the left.

Each of the planes is connected to two of the axes. The right plane borders the X and Y axes, for example. As a result, it's called the X,Y

plane. (Uninspired, but accurate.) Similarly, the left plane is called the Y,Z plane, and the bottom one is called the X,Z plane.

In CorelDraw, you have two dimensions: width (X) and height (Y). Therefore, you have just one plane, the X,Y plane. By adding a third dimension — depth (Z) — you add two additional planes — X,Z and Y,Z — to your drawing area. This third dimension is why Dream 3D presents you with the 3-D working box rather than the flat drawing area that you see in CorelDraw.

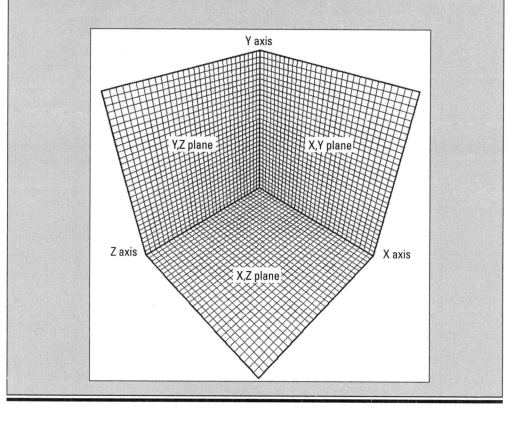

A Beginner's Guide to 3-D Objects

Dream 3D provides two ways to add objects to a drawing. You can either draw the objects from scratch or select from the hundreds of predrawn objects that Corel includes on CD-ROM.

To import a predrawn object, you can drag it from the Objects Browser and drop it into the work area. But the Objects Browser contains only a limited selection of models. More models are included on the second CD-ROM in your CorelDraw 7 box. You can add as many folders of models to the Objects Browser as you want.

To add a folder from the CD-ROM to the Objects Browser window, click on the Add Folder button in the upper-right corner of the window, labeled in Figure 18-2. A tiny Directory Selection dialog box appears. Open up the 3dmodels folder on the CD-ROM. Then double-click on a folder name that looks interesting — such as Aircraft or Fashion — and press Enter or click on the Select button. Dream 3D displays the folder and its objects in the Objects Browser window. (This process may take a few minutes, so be patient.)

If all the folder tabs aren't visible in the Objects Browser, you can scroll through the various tabs by using the folder scroll arrows in the upper-left corner of the window, labeled in Figure 18-2. To remove a folder from the Objects Browser window, click on the folder tab and then click on the Remove Folder button, also labeled in the figure.

Importing and magnifying an object

For an example of how to use Dream 3D, drag the Vicchair item from the Home tab in the Objects Browser window and drop it into the work area. A 3-D chair appears in the work area, surrounded by a box shape with handles in each corner. The box and handles show that the chair is selected.

To get a closer look, press Shift+F2 to magnify the selected portion of the drawing. This keyboard shortcut is the same one used in CorelDraw. You can also press F2 to zoom in and F3 to zoom out.

If you don't like shortcuts, click on the Zoom to Selected icon on the toolbar, labeled in Figure 18-2. (To display the zoom icons on the toolbar, right-click on an empty area of the toolbar and click on the Zoom item.) You can also click with the zoom tool or drag around the object that you want to magnify. To zoom out, Alt+click with the zoom tool.

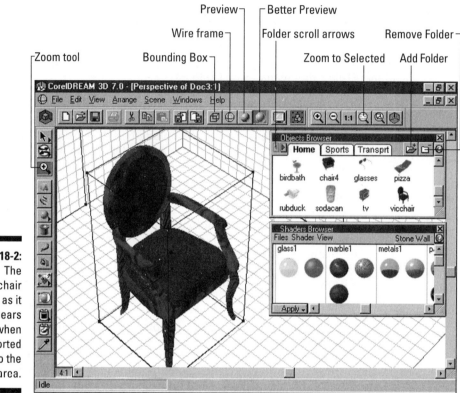

Preview

Better Preview

Wire frame

Folder scroll arrows

Remove Folder

Zoom tool

Bounding Box

Zoom to Selected

Add Folder

Figure 18-2:
The
Vicchair
object as it
appears
when
imported
into the
work area.

The little black arrow at the bottom of the zoom tool icon indicates a flyout menu containing additional tools, just as in CorelDraw and Photo-Paint. Press and hold on the zoom tool flyout to access the zoom out tool and a hand tool (drag with the hand tool to display a different portion of your work area). Click on the tool that you want to use. Or, just keep clicking on the tool icon to cycle through the different tools.

Changing how the object looks on-screen

You can also change the way Dream 3D displays the model on-screen:

✔ The default view mode is the preview mode, which shows the object in color but does not accurately show textures and other realistic stuff. You can return to this mode at any time by clicking on the preview icon in the toolbar (labeled in Figure 18-2). You can also choose View➪Default Quality➪Preview or press Ctrl+Alt+Shift+Y.

✔ If things seem to be happening too slowly, you can speed them up by switching to the wireframe mode. This mode displays coarse, chicken-wire versions of the objects without any color. Although it's not terribly accurate, this mode is much faster. To make the switch, click on the wireframe icon on the toolbar, choose View⇨Default Quality⇨ Wireframe, or press Ctrl+Shift+Y.

✔ Bounding box quality shows you just the object's selection box. You may find this mode helpful for quickly positioning objects in a complex drawing. Turn on bounding box mode by pressing Ctrl+Y or choosing View⇨Default Quality⇨Bounding Box.

✔ If you own a really powerful computer or you simply want to see more detailed versions of your objects, click on the better preview icon on the toolbar. When you work in this mode, you can see surface textures and shadows, as demonstrated in Figure 18-2. You can also turn on this mode by choosing View⇨Default Quality⇨Better Preview or pressing Ctrl+Alt+Y.

Moving an object in 3-D space

To move an object, click on it with the arrow tool — the one at the top of the toolbox — to select it. Then drag it just as in CorelDraw or Photo-Paint. You can also nudge the object by pressing the arrow keys. The nudge distance is determined by the Spacing setting in the Grid dialog box, which you display by choosing View⇨Grid or pressing Ctrl+J.

The only trick to moving an object is figuring out where the heck you're dragging it. I mean, how do you move an object side to side, forward and backward, and up and down when the only directions you can move your mouse are side to side and forward and backward? Sadly, you can't lift your mouse and expect the object to levitate in 3-D space.

Based on the way other programs work, you may think that up and down motions would be a breeze; but if you do, you're not thinking in 3-D. Granted, when you move your mouse forward and backward on the mouse pad, your cursor moves up and down on-screen. So, over time, you've come to associate forward and backward mouse movement with up and down object movement.

Not so in Dream 3D. In this program, you have to imagine that the mouse pad is sitting on the bottom plane (X,Z). When you drag the object, it doesn't move up and down; it moves back and forth. The object never moves off the ground when you drag it.

In Figure 18-3, for example, I dragged the object down. But the object moved toward me, just as my mouse moved toward me. How can I tell? By watching the tracking boxes on the two other planes (as labeled in the figure). The tracking boxes move along with the object to show how it aligns with the planes, much as the tracking lines in CorelDraw's rulers move with an object. Because the tracking boxes remain firmly fastened to the X and Z axes, I know that the chair does not move upward.

Arrow tool   Tracking boxes

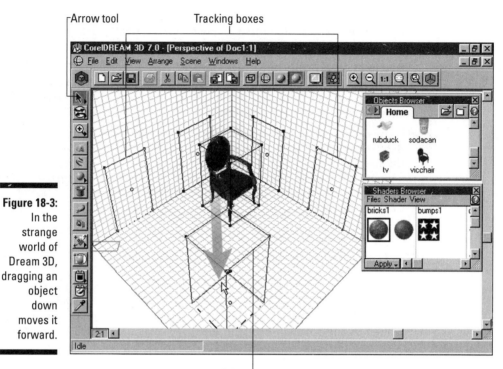

Figure 18-3:
In the strange world of Dream 3D, dragging an object down moves it forward.

Selection box

So, how do you move an object up and down? Well, it turns out that you can drag a tracking box directly. When you drag a tracking box, the corresponding object follows along with your move — on the same plane as the tracking box. In Figure 18-4, for example, when I dragged the right tracking box up, the chair moved upward into 3-D space. Because a tracking box always adheres to its plane, you can move it only two directions: up and down or left and right.

Moving an object by dragging a tracking box is frequently easier than dragging the object directly, because you don't have to translate your 2-D mouse movements into 3-D space. So when in doubt, drag a tracking box.

Scaling and spinning the object

You can also scale and rotate objects inside Dream 3D. To scale an object, drag the corner handles around the selection box. You can also drag the corner handles of one of the tracking boxes.

To rotate an object, use the virtual trackball tool, the one below the arrow tool. Though the tool has a ridiculous name, it can be very useful. Drag the selected object to spin it around in 3-D space, as shown in Figure 18-5.

Tracking box

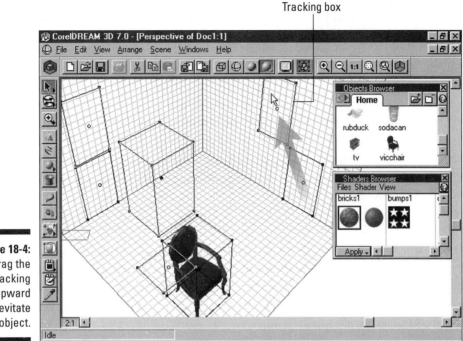

Figure 18-4:
Drag the tracking box upward to levitate the object.

Virtual trackball

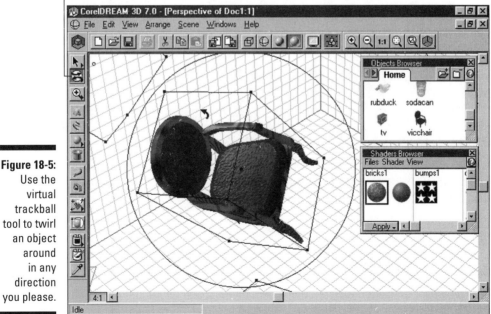

Figure 18-5:
Use the virtual trackball tool to twirl an object around in any direction you please.

Every Object Needs a Look

As I mentioned earlier, you assign colors and textures to objects using the options in the Shaders Browser window. Dream 3D calls these items *shaders* because they affect not only the color and texture of an object, but also the translucency, reflectivity, and all kinds of other properties. (Okay, so *shader* doesn't necessarily conjure up colors, textures, and all that other stuff in your mind, but it did to some daffy program manager at Corel. Unfortunately, the industry-standard term, *texture maps,* doesn't make all that much more sense.) Using shaders, you can make an object appear as if it were made out of glass, wrapped in burlap, or covered with mud.

Corel's predrawn objects comprise many separate objects, each of which you can color separately. The chair, for example, has plush blue fabric applied to the cushions and wood grain applied to the legs and trim.

In Figure 18-6, I changed the bottom cushion to stone by dragging the first shader from the Tutorial column in the Shaders Browser and dropping it onto the cushion. This step colored only the bottom cushion; I had to drag the stone shader and drop it onto the back cushion separately. To change the wood grain trim and legs to the striped pattern, I had to drag and drop the same shader onto ten different sections of the chair.

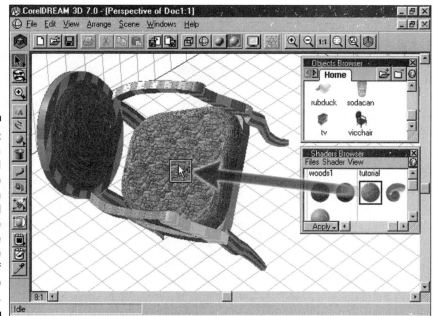

Figure 18-6:
Drag a shader and drop it onto a shape in the model to change that shape from one type of material to another.

Adding a Prefab Backdrop

Creating and spinning a single object in 3-D space is a little complicated, but nothing compared with the difficulties of putting together an entire 3-D scene. That's why Version 7 provides a Scene Wizard that you can use to add a ready-made backdrop, complete with lighting and other effects, to your scene, as I did in Figure 18-7. In many cases, you can move, shade, and otherwise edit the background elements.

If you want to add one of the backgrounds to an existing scene, choose File➪Apply Scene Wizard. To create a new scene based on a Wizard backdrop, choose File➪New and then select the Use Scene Wizard radio button.

Either way, the Scene Wizard dialog box, shown in Figure 18-8, appears. Click on the icon for the type of backdrop that you want to use, and then click on the Next button. You can then choose from an entire ready-made backdrop or put together a custom backdrop using a selection of prefab backgrounds and lighting designs. After selecting the options you want to use, click on the Done button to see the results.

You don't see the entire scene in your workspace; only objects that can be manipulated appear. The remaining elements in the scene appear when you render the object, as described next. For example, compare the scene in Figure 18-7 with the final, rendered scene in Figure 18-9 at the end of this chapter. The sky behind the open windows and the shadows on the wall appear only in the rendered version.

Figure 18-7:
The new Scene Wizard makes adding a backdrop and lighting effects relatively easy.

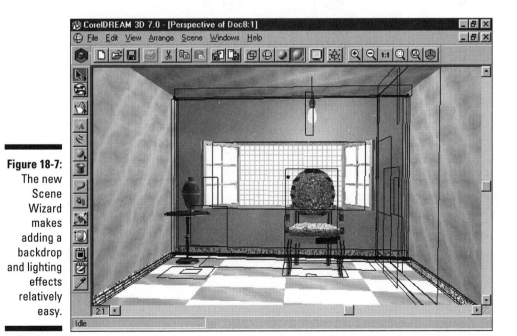

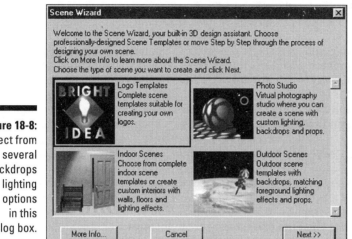

Figure 18-8:
Select from
several
backdrops
and lighting
options
in this
dialog box.

Figure 18-9:
My final
scene,
rendered at
160 dpi and
adjusted in
Photo-
Paint.

TIP

If you apply a complicated backdrop to your scene and your existing objects are at the back of the workspace, backdrop objects may obscure the existing objects. To save yourself the headache of having to relocate your objects — not an easy prospect in a crowded scene — move your objects to the front of the workspace before adding a backdrop from the Scene Wizard. You can then more easily select and reposition the existing objects.

The End of the 3-D Highway

When you finish a drawing in CorelDraw, you print it. When you finish editing a photograph in Photo-Paint, you print it. You can also print your 3D creations, but the process is a little more involved.

A 3-D drawing is so vast and complex that printing it would take far too long. So, you must perform an intermediate step called *rendering,* in which Dream 3D converts the drawing to pixels and saves it as a separate image file.

Before rendering, it's a good idea to save your drawing to disk. Though Dream 3D saves the rendered image to a separate file, you don't want to lose your work if something goes wrong. Here's how to render a 3-D drawing:

1. **Choose <u>S</u>cene⇨Render <u>S</u>ettings.**

   Up comes the Rendering Settings dialog box, which enables you to specify the resolution of the final image.

2. **Set the scene dimensions.**

   Enter the final size of the drawing into the <u>W</u>idth and <u>H</u>eight option box. You can change the unit of measure by using the pop-up menus next to the option boxes. Select the <u>K</u>eep Proportions check box if you want to maintain the original proportions of the drawing.

3. **If you have a specific resolution in mind, enter it into the Re<u>s</u>olution option box.**

   Or, if you want Dream 3D to suggest a resolution for you, enter the resolution of your final output device into the Re<u>s</u>olution option box, select the Best <u>R</u>esolution radio button, and click on the <u>E</u>stimate button. For example, if you're going to print your image on a 600-dpi laser printer, enter **600** into the Resolution option box.

4. **Select the Render <u>T</u>ime radio button and click on the <u>E</u>stimate button.**

   Dream 3D estimates the amount of time required to create the image. In all likelihood, you're looking at several minutes. Complex scenes with lots of objects can take more than an hour. Images with higher resolutions take longer as well.

5. **Press Enter.**

6. **Choose <u>S</u>cene⇨<u>R</u>ender⇨Low Res Preview.**

   Dream 3D begins generating a preview of the drawing in a new window. If you don't like how things look, close the image by clicking on the Close button, or choose <u>F</u>ile⇨<u>C</u>lose and make the necessary changes. If you do like the image, close it and proceed to the next step. Either way, you don't need to save the preview, so click on the <u>N</u>o button when the save message comes up.

7. **Choose the Perspective option from the bottom of the Windows menu.**

   Dream 3D has the irritating habit of returning you to the wrong window after rendering. Choose Perspective (followed by the name of your drawing) to get back to the work area.

8. **Choose Ctrl+R.**

   This command tells Dream 3D to begin rendering your drawing according to the settings in the Rendering Settings dialog box. The process takes a long time, so be patient. If you decide to skip it for now, press Esc to cancel the rendering or right-click the rendering area and select Abort from the pop-up menu that appears.

   You don't have to sit on your hands while you wait for Dream 3D to complete the image. Thanks to Windows 95, you can keep working in the program or switch to a different program and work in it. Unfortunately, Dream 3D renders more slowly if you make your computer do other stuff, and it may even cause the other program to pause intermittently and, in the worst cases, crash. Despite Windows 95's swell new multitasking capabilities, it's better to let Dream 3D do its stuff unhampered.

   As Dream 3D works, it shows you the parts of the image it has finished.

9. **When the image is complete, save it to disk.**

   Choose File⇨Save or press Ctrl+S. The Save dialog box appears. Enter a name for the image and select a format from the Save as Type pop-up menu. I heartily recommend that you select the Tiff (Cor) (*.TIF) option, but you can select any format you like. Then press Enter or click on the Save button.

If you don't want to go through all this rigmarole and you don't care about a precise size or resolution for your rendered drawing, you can simply choose one of the commands from the bottom portion of the Scene⇨Render submenu. The submenu contains several options for rendering your scene to various resolutions. Medium resolution should work fine for everyday uses.

After you render a drawing, you can print it by choosing File⇨Print. You can also choose File⇨Print Preview to open the same print preview window offered in CorelDraw and Photo-Paint. (For more information on printing, including how to use the various preview window elements, see Chapter 13.)

Figure 18-9 shows the final chair image after I rendered it at a resolution of 160 dpi and adjusted the brightness and contrast in Photo-Paint as explained in Chapter 17. This scene looks like a combination of a New Age retreat and a prisoner interrogation room.

Part V
The Part of Tens

In this part . . .

Sure, sure, we're all addicted to statistics and sound bites — so much so that no one knows the full story about anything. But I figure what's good enough for Moses is good enough for me. I mean, the guy kept it simple — two tablets, ten factoids — and everybody ate it up. "Thou shalt not kill" kind of sticks in your mind. It has a certain undeniable directness that's downright impossible to argue with. You can toss it out at a party or share it with a friend in a time of need.

Jill:	I swear, Jack's driving me nuts. I'm about ready to strangle the chump in his sleep.
Humpty Dumpty (a friend from a neighboring story line):	Now now, Jill. (Wagging finger.) "Thou shalt not kill."
Jill:	Oh, right, I forgot about that one. (Considers.) But I can wallop him with my pail, right? It doesn't say anything about walloping folks with a pail, does it?
Humpty Dumpty:	No, I believe that's acceptable.

Of course, the following lists don't quite measure up to the Ten Commandments (or Mother Goose, for that matter). In fact, they're more the *Guinness Book of World Records* variety of list. But they're still lots of fun and, wow, talk about memorable! You can even toss them out at a party, assuming that you want to look like a total geek.

Chapter 19
Ten Way-Cool Special Effects

● ●

In This Chapter

▶ Draw a planet with a ring around it

▶ Morph between two shapes

▶ Create a fancy shadow for your text

▶ Make type bulge like a balloon

▶ Wrap paragraph text around a graphic

▶ Put your message in the sky

▶ Turn an object into a ghost of its former self

▶ Shuffle the colors in a photograph

▶ Make the pixels beg for mercy

▶ Design your own repeating pattern

● ●

Some folks characterize CorelDraw as a functional and powerful tool for creating business graphics. They say that CorelDraw lets you assemble drawings and edit images in an efficient and timely manner. They add that CorelDraw enables you to store and catalog your graphics quickly and conveniently.

Well, I say bugger. Sure, I guess all that stuff is true, but who gives a rat's fanny? Especially when you consider the real potential of CorelDraw: It enables you to take cheesy little shapes, text, and stock photos and turn them into bizarre artistic monstrosities that overflow with an excess of special effects.

Enticed? That's where this chapter comes in. I hereby invite you to abandon all pretense of good taste and go on a computer graphics binge. Some of the techniques presented in the next few pages are based on ideas I covered in previous chapters, but don't expect any warmed-over repeats. This is your chance to indulge in some purely frivolous and largely irrelevant special effects.

Draw a Planet with a Ring Around It

I'd like to start things off with a razzle-dazzle project. But instead, the following steps tell you how to create something that looks vaguely like the planet Saturn, as in Figure 19-1. Isn't it a beauty? Can't you imagine spying that baby through the viewport of your rocket ship? Or perhaps losing communications with an unmanned probe in the vicinity of this gorgeous orb?

Figure 19-1:
Scientists aren't sure whether this is Saturn or just a sphere playing hula-hoop.

1. **Inside CorelDraw, draw a circle.**

   You do this by Ctrl+dragging with the ellipse tool. Saturn is very big, so make your circle nice and big.

2. **Press F11 or select the Fountain Fill icon from the Fill tool flyout menu.**

   The Fountain Fill dialog box appears.

3. **Select Radial from the Type pop-up menu.**

   This setting creates a radial gradation that progresses outward in concentric circles, as in Figure 19-1.

   The way things stand now, the white spot is dead in the center of the gradation, as the preview in the upper-right corner of the dialog box shows. That doesn't look right. It needs to be up and to the left a little, maybe. You can move the white spot using the Horizontal and Vertical options in the Center Offset area.

4. **Enter a value of –20 in the Horizontal option box and 20 in the Vertical option box.**

Or just drag inside the preview in the upper-right corner of the dialog box to move the white spot up and to the left.

5. Press Enter.

CorelDraw exits the dialog box and returns you to the sphere, which should look like the one in Figure 19-1, but without the ring.

6. Draw a short, wide oval centered on the sphere.

Using the ellipse tool, Shift+drag outward from the center of the sphere. This new oval represents the planet's rings. Or at least one ring, anyway.

7. Select the second-to-fattest line width from the pen tool flyout menu.

It's the one that's 16 points thick.

8. Select black as your outline color.

Just right-click on the black swatch in the color palette.

9. Select the shape tool.

You can do this by pressing F10.

10. Turn the oval into an arc.

The quickest way is to click on the arc icon on the Property Bar and then enter new values in the Starting and Ending Angle option boxes. Try a starting angle value in the 140 range and an ending angle of about 40. (See Figure 4-9 for a look at these controls.) If necessary, use the X and Y controls to reposition the arc horizontally or vertically on the sphere.

If you prefer, you can create your arc by dragging the node at the top of the oval. First, drag the node down and to the right to create a rift in the outline of the oval. Make sure to keep the cursor outside the oval so that you get an arc instead of a pie. Drag until the outline of the ring no longer overlaps the top portion of the sphere.

By the way, my instruction to drag the node down and to the right assumes that you drew the oval from left to right. If you drew it from right to left, drag down and to the left with the shape tool.

Next, drag the other node down and to the left. Again, keep the cursor outside the oval and drag until the ring no longer overlaps the sphere. You should now have an arc that looks more or less like it circles around the front of the sphere.

11. Press F12 or select the pen icon from the pen tool flyout menu.

The Outline Pen dialog box appears.

12. Select the second Line Caps radio button.

This option is the round cap.

13. Press Enter to exit the dialog box.

14. Press Ctrl+C and then press Ctrl+V.

This step copies the arc and then pastes it right in front of the original.

15. Right-click on the white swatch in the color palette.

This step makes the pasted arc white.

16. Select the 8-point line width from the pen tool flyout menu.

You could, of course, create a true 3-D sphere in Dream 3D, draw a bunch of really sophisticated rings around it, and make it look just like the real Saturn. But that would take a lot longer. And besides, you'd ruin that special Ed Wood feel of your current planet.

Morph between Two Shapes

CorelDraw enables you to blend a shape filled with one color into a different shape filled with a different color. In essence, the result is a custom gradation, as shown in Figure 19-2. The following steps explain how.

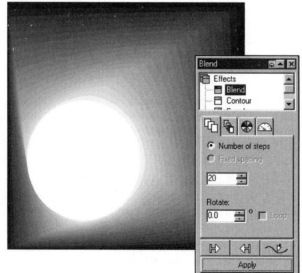

Figure 19-2:
Use the
Blend roll-
up to create
gradations
between
two shapes.

For a different way to create custom gradients, see the section "Filling on the fly" in Chapter 7, which discusses the new interactive fill tool.

1. Draw two shapes.

For this example, draw a large rectangle with the rectangle tool. Then, using the ellipse tool, draw an oval that fits inside the rectangle.

2. **Select white from the color palette.**

   Because you just finished drawing the oval, it should be selected. So clicking on the white swatch fills the oval with white.

3. **Right-click on the X icon at the top of the color palette.**

   This step deletes the outline from the oval, which is a very important step when creating custom gradations. If you don't delete the outline, borders appear between the colors in the gradation. Your oval disappears, but don't freak out; the oval is still there — it's just in temporary hiding.

4. **Select the rectangle with the arrow tool, select black from the color palette, and right-click on the X icon.**

   The rectangle is now black with no outline.

5. **Select both the rectangle and the oval with the arrow tool.**

   Assuming that the rectangle is still selected, you just have to Shift+click on the oval. Or drag around both shapes to surround them with a selection marquee.

6. **Press Ctrl+B.**

   Or choose Effects⇨Blend to display the Blend roll-up.

7. **Click on the Apply button in the Blend roll-up.**

   CorelDraw automatically creates a gradation between the two shapes, as illustrated in Figure 19-2.

By default, CorelDraw creates this gradation by generating 20 transitional shapes between the rectangle and oval, each shaped and filled slightly differently. If you want to increase the number of shapes to create a smoother gradation, increase the value in the Steps option box in the roll-up and then click on the Apply button again. Or use the Steps control on the Property Bar to make your change.

After you create a blend, CorelDraw displays a series of small squares running from the first object in the blend to the second object. These squares represent the steps in your blend.

Another way to create a blend in Version 7 is to use the interactive blend tool, which is the third tool from the bottom of the toolbox, just above the pen tool. Just select the tool and drag from one object to the other.

Create a Shadow for Your Text

Folks invariably ooh and ah when they see the effect shown in Figure 19-3, but it's really easy to create. Here's how:

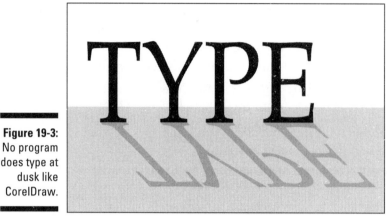

Figure 19-3:
No program
does type at
dusk like
CorelDraw.

1. Press the Caps Lock key.

This effect works best when you use capital letters only. Lowercase letters sometimes descend below the baseline, ruining the shadow effect.

2. Create some artistic text.

To create artistic text in Version 7, simply select the text tool (press F8 to do it quickly). Then click in the drawing area and type in one short line of text.

3. Enlarge the type size to 100 points or so.

To enlarge the type, first select the text by dragging over it with the text tool or by using one of the other selection techniques discussed in Chapter 10. Then choose a new type size from the pop-up menu on the Property Bar.

4. Select the arrow tool.

Pressing Ctrl+spacebar is the fastest way to select the tool. The text becomes selected.

5. Press Alt+F9 or choose <u>A</u>rrange⇨<u>T</u>ransform⇨<u>S</u>cale and Mirror.

This command displays the Scale & Mirror roll-up.

6. Click on the vertical mirror icon.

This is the icon to the right of the V option box.

You can't use the mirror button on the Property Bar for this effect. As explained in the next step, you need to apply the mirroring to a duplicate of your text, and the Property Bar doesn't have an Apply to Duplicate button.

7. Click on the Apply To Duplicate button.

This step creates a duplicate of the text block as it flips the block.

8. **Press the down-arrow key until the baselines of the two text blocks align.**

   In other words, the bottom of the letters in the different text blocks should touch.

9. **Click on a light gray color in the color palette.**

   The flipped text changes to gray.

10. **Click on the flipped text block.**

    The rotate and skew handles appear.

11. **Drag the bottom handle to skew the text.**

    This step makes the shadow appear at an angle. To complete the effect shown in Figure 19-3, I added a rectangle, filled it with light gray, and pressed Shift+PgDn (Arrange⇨Order⇨To Back) to send it to the back of the drawing.

Make Type Bulge Like a Balloon

CorelDraw is one of the few programs that lets you create type that bulges off the page, as shown in Figure 19-4. This interesting text effect is remarkably easy to create using the Envelope feature.

Figure 19-4:
This text
looks like
it's about
ready
to pop.

1. **Repeat the first four steps from the preceding section.**

   Press the Caps lock key, click with the text tool, enter a word or short line of text, increase the type size to 100 points or so, and select the arrow tool.

2. **Drag up on the top handle of the text block until it's roughly as tall as it is wide.**

   The text stretches vertically.

3. **Press Ctrl+F7 to display the Envelope roll-up.**

   Or choose Effects⇨Envelope.

4. **Click on the Add New button.**

   This step displays a dotted outline and special handles around the text.

5. **Click on the single-arc icon.**

   It's the second icon below the Add Preset button.

6. **Drag the top handle upward; drag the bottom handle downward; drag the left handle farther to the left; and drag the right handle to the right.**

   Don't drag any of the corner handles. Ultimately, you're trying to turn the square confines of the text block into a circle.

7. **Click on the Apply button in the Envelope roll-up.**

   The text now puffs out like you're viewing it through a fish-eye lens.

Wrap Paragraph Text around a Graphic

You've seen it in national magazines, newspapers, and slick fliers. Now you can join in on the fun. CorelDraw lets you wrap paragraph text around a graphic, which is just the thing for designing nifty documents that'll make your friends and coworkers drool with envy.

1. **Create a few lines of paragraph text.**

   To create paragraph text, press F8 to select the text tool. Then drag in the drawing area to create a paragraph text block and enter some text from the keyboard. Any old text will do.

2. **Draw the graphic around which you want to wrap the text.**

   Or import a piece of clip art. If you want to wrap the text around several objects, you may want to group them first by choosing Arrange⇨Group or pressing Ctrl+G. You can alternatively wrap the text around each object individually, which gives you a little more flexibility in layout but is a bit more work.

3. Right-click on the graphic.

CorelDraw displays a pop-up menu of options.

4. Select the <u>P</u>roperties option.

It's the one at the bottom of the pop-up menu. The Object Properties dialog box leaps onto the screen.

Alternatively, you can select the graphic and press Alt+Enter to display the Object Properties dialog box.

5. Click on the General tab and then select the <u>W</u>rap Paragraph Text check box.

Look for the check box in the bottom-left corner of the panel.

6. Set the text offset.

The *offset* is a fancy name for the distance that you want to place between the object and the text.

7. Click on Apply.

CorelDraw wraps the text around the graphic (assuming that the graphic is near the text, of course). If necessary, adjust the text offset and click Apply again to see the text wrap with the new offset.

8. After you're satisfied with how your text wraps around the graphic, click on OK to close the dialog box.

From now on, you can move the graphic anywhere on the page, and all paragraph text — including other text blocks on the page — automatically wrap out of the graphic's way. It's as if the graphic has some kind of force field around it. Too bad you can't apply this feature to yourself and have people wrap out of your way on the subway.

If you don't want to change the offset value, you can turn text wrap on and off for an object by simply right-clicking on the object and choosing Wrap Paragraph Text from the pop-up menu.

Put Your Message in the Sky

You can use the CorelDraw Add Perspective command and Extrude roll-up to create text that appears to zoom across the screen. Figure 19-5 shows an example in which a consumer-oriented message demands the reader's immediate compliance.

1. Create some artistic text.

You know the drill: Click with the text tool and begin typing. This time around, you can use lowercase letters if you want to. Furthermore, the type size doesn't really matter because you'll end up stretching the type all over the place anyway.

Figure 19-5:
An
important
3-D
message
solicits the
attention of
an eager
audience.

2. Choose Effects⇨Add Perspective.

Four handles appear in the corners of the text block.

3. Drag the handles until you get the desired effect.

Experiment to your heart's content.

4. Click on red or some other garish hue in the color palette.

This step colors the text so that no one will accidentally overlook it.

5. Press Ctrl+E or choose Effects⇨Extrude.

CorelDraw displays the Extrude roll-up so that you can add depth to the text.

6. Drag the vanishing point to set the direction of the extrusion.

The vanishing point is that X you see in the drawing area. To create the effect in Figure 19-5, I set the vanishing point on the left side of the text.

7. Set the extrusion colors.

Click on the Color tab of the roll-up and specify how you want the extruded text to be colored. To create the effect in Figure 19-5, I selected the solid fill radio button and black from the color pop-up menu. Click on Apply to see how your choice looks.

8. **Adjust the Depth value as needed.**

   This value, found on the first tab of the Extrude roll-up, determines how much your text is extruded. Click on the Apply button to see the results of your changes.

9. **Click on the light bulb tab at the top of the Extrude roll-up.**

   You now see the lighting options.

10. **Click on the first light bulb icon on the left side of the roll-up.**

    It's the one with a 1 in it. This step turns on the first light. Drag the little 1 in a black circle down to the lower-right corner of the box on the right side of the roll-up.

11. **Click on the Apply button.**

    Your text now appears in 3-D. If you want, you can rotate your text in 3-D space by dragging the big red C on the rotate tab of the roll-up and then clicking on Apply.

12. **To exit the extrude edit mode, click outside the text with the arrow tool.**

If you accidentally click off the text when you're creating the effect, just click on the Edit button in the Extrude roll-up to continue editing the extrusion.

After you click once on the Apply button in the Extrude roll-up, controls for making further changes to your extrusion appear on the Property Bar. For more on extruding, see Chapter 9.

Turn Your Object into a Ghost of Its Former Self

In Photo-Paint 7, you can adjust the opacity of an object in a variety of ways, all of which are illustrated in the spooky "Ghosts of the African Veldt" image in Figure 19-6. In the figure, I adjusted the transparency of the toucan, elephant, and cougar. The two giraffes, part of the original background image, are fully opaque.

Before the zoologists in the crowd start howling and pointing fingers, I want to state that I'm fully aware that cougars are not readily found on the African veldt. But I didn't have an image of a zebra, lion, or other more appropriate creature lying around. Besides, this is a ghost cougar, and when animals pass out of this world, they get to go wherever they please. This particular cougar always dreamed of going to Africa.

Figure 19-6:
I created this haunting scene by adjusting the transparency of the toucan, cougar, and elephant.

By the way, all the images in Figure 19-6 are found on the second CD-ROM in the CorelDraw 7 package. The background image is Image 480006 in the Africa folder of the Photos folder. The cougar, elephant, and toucan are ready-made objects found in the Animals folder of the Objects folder. After opening the background image, open each of the animal files. Then select the arrow tool and drag each animal into the background image window. (After you open the animal files, you see the animals already selected and ready to drag.)

✔ To adjust the transparency of an entire object, as I did for the elephant in Figure 19-6, select the object with the arrow tool. Then adjust the Opacity slider in either the Objects roll-up (press Ctrl+F7 to display the roll-up) or on the Property Bar. The elephant in Figure 19-6 has an opacity value of 49.

✔ The new object transparency tool, which appears on the arrow tool flyout menu, applies transparency to your object according to the transparency fill type that you choose from the pop-up menu on the Property Bar or in the Tool Settings roll-up. The Flat option applies uniform transparency to your object, just as if you simply selected the object and changed the Opacity slider as just discussed.

✔ The next six options fade your object into the background by applying a gradient transparency to the object. In the figure, I used the Linear option to fade the toucan into view. When you choose one of these options, Photo-Paint displays transparency controls on your object similar to those you see when using the interactive gradient fill tool or the Edit Fill & Transparency dialog box, both discussed in Chapter 16.

Drag these controls to reposition the start and end points of the transparency and to adjust the angle of the transparency blend. Use the Transparency sliders on the Property Bar or option boxes in the roll-up to adjust the level of transparency at the start and end points.

✔ The Bitmap and Texture options fill your object with a bitmap pattern or texture, respectively. Again, you can use the controls in the roll-up and on the Property Bar to select a different texture or pattern and adjust the transparency of the fill.

✔ To remove a transparency fill from your object, select the None option from the Type menu in the roll-up or from its counterpart on the Property Bar.

✔ Turn on the Use Original Transparency option to apply an additional transparency blend to an object that already has a transparency blend applied. Otherwise, the new transparency blend replaces the existing blend.

✔ Using the new object transparency brush, also found on the arrow tool flyout menu, you can "paint" transparency onto portions of your object. After selecting the cougar in the bottom-left corner of Figure 19-6, I selected the object transparency brush and painted around the outside edges of the animal. The edges of the body are partially transparent and the face is fully opaque. This cougar is trapped between reality and the ghost realm.

✔ When you use the object transparency tool, you can adjust the brush size and shape, as well as control the level of opacity, by using the controls on the Property Bar or in the Tool Settings roll-up.

The Transparency value controls the amount of transparency that you apply with each brush stroke. The Opacity value sets the maximum opacity for the object. No matter how many times you stroke the object, it can't become more or less translucent than the specified Opacity value. If you set the Opacity value to its maximum, 255, areas you touch with the tool become fully opaque. Set both the Opacity and Transparency values to 0, and you make areas you stroke completely transparent. But even though the object appears to have disappeared completely, it's still hanging around, as you can see if you click on it with the arrow tool. You can restore the object's opacity by using the tool with different Opacity and Transparency values.

Also, if you turn on the Use Original Transparency option, Photo-Paint adds the transparency value of the object transparency brush to the existing transparency of the pixels you stroke. If you turn the option off, Photo-Paint replaces the existing transparency of the pixels you touch with the transparency value set for the tool.

CorelDraw also offers an interactive transparency tool that works similarly to the one in Photo-Paint. Using this tool, you can adjust the transparency of a selected object or block of artistic text. Just select the object and select the interactive transparency tool (it's the fourth one from the bottom of the toolbox). Then choose any option except None from the Type drop-down menu on the Property Bar.

The Uniform option makes your entire object uniformly translucent; drag the Transparency slider bar on the Property Bar to change the level of transparency. The Fountain option fills the object with a transparency gradient. Drag the white and black boxes that appear on the object to reposition the angle along with the start and end points of the gradient; use the transparency sliders on the Property Bar to change the transparency level at the beginning and end of the gradient. If you choose the Pattern or Texture option, you can fill your object with a pattern or texture (big surprise there) and then adjust the transparency of the fill by dragging the transparency sliders on the Property Bar.

Shuffle the Colors in a Photograph

In Photo-Paint, you can apply some serious special effects by using commands that automatically shuffle the colors in an image. Figure 19-7 shows a few examples of these commands, found on the Image⇨Transform and Effects⇨Color Transform submenus. The labels indicate the commands used, which work as follows:

✔ Image⇨Transform⇨Invert — formerly found on the Effects⇨Color Transform submenu — changes all light colors to dark and all dark colors to light, as in a photographic negative.

✔ Image⇨Transform⇨Posterize, also a former resident of the Color Transform submenu, decreases the number of colors in a selected area to any value between 2 and 32. It's great for creating high-contrast effects.

✔ Effects⇨Color Transform⇨Psychedelic thoroughly jumbles the colors, thus fooling the viewer into seeking medical attention. You can apply this command to color images only.

Original

Invert

Figure 19-7:
An image
subjected
to the
Invert,
Posterize,
and
Psychedelic
commands.

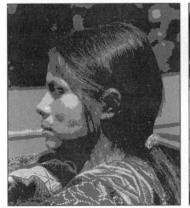

Posterize

Psychedelic

Make the Pixels Beg for Mercy

Photo-Paint stores its most amazing special effects in the 2D Effects and 3D Effects submenus in the Effects menu. Figure 19-8 demonstrates four effects from the 2D Effects submenu; Figure 19-9 demonstrates one additional effect from that same submenu plus three from the 3D Effects submenu. Though most effects in these submenus are incredibly difficult to apply — sometimes involving specialized selection outlines or other prerequisites — the eight commands demonstrated in the figures are straightforward and produce intriguing, unusual, and occasionally even attractive results.

Edge Detect

Swirl

Figure 19-8:
A few
fascinating
effects
created by
using
commands
from the 2D
Effects
submenu.

Wet Paint

Wind

TIP

- ✔ The Edge Detect command traces around high-contrast areas in your image, which is ideal for changing photographs into line art. You can trace with white, black, or the foreground color.

  For a really cool effect, set the foreground color to some bright color, such as orange or blue. Then choose Effects➪2D Effects➪Edge Detect and select the Paint Color radio button in the Edge Detect dialog box.

- ✔ Choosing Effects➪2D Effects➪Swirl curls the image toward its center, as if the image were twisting down a drain. Specify the amount of curl by using the two Amount sliders in the Swirl dialog box, and choose whether you want the image to curl in a counterclockwise or clockwise direction by selecting a Direction radio button.

✔ The Wet Paint command melts your image as surely as water melts Wicked Witches of the West. Raise the Percent value to make the drips stand out more. A positive Wetness value makes the light colors run; a negative value makes the dark colors bleed.

✔ Choose the Wind command to blast the image with a hurricane-force gale. A high Strength value smudges the pixels farther. Adjust the Opacity value to mix the blasted pixels in with the original colors in the image. Use the Direction option to control the angle of the wind.

✔ The Whirlpool command, moved from the 3D Effects submenu to the 2D Effects submenu in Version 7, brings up one of the most complicated Photo-Paint dialog boxes. Still, you can have fun messing around with the options, and nothing you do can cause any harmful effects until you click on the OK button. Even then, you can press Ctrl+Z to undo the damage. So relax and experiment. The top-left example in Figure 19-9 shows an image created with this effect.

Whirlpool

Emboss

Figure 19-9: An application of the 2D Effects➪ Whirlpool command, plus three effects from the 3D Effects submenu.

Page curl

Pinch/Punch

✔ Choose Effects➪3D Effects➪Emboss to make a photograph appear carved out of stone. You can adjust the color of the Emboss effect or select the Original Color radio button to retain the original colors in the image. You can also adjust how deeply the image is carved by changing the Depth value; change the amount of light that shines on the image by using the Levels slider; and specify the direction of the light using the Direction control.

✔ Effects➪3D Effects➪Page Curl turns up the corner of your photograph as if it were a curled page.

In Version 7, you choose the corner that you want to curl by clicking on one of the Adjust icons in the Page Curl dialog box. You can also adjust the size and orientation of the curl; make the curl more or less opaque; and choose a color for the curl and for the background area that is revealed after you apply the curl.

✔ Pinch/Punch distorts your image inward or outward. A positive Punch/Pinch value (in the Pinch/Punch dialog box) sucks the pixels toward the center. A negative value bows the image outward, as if it were projected on a balloon.

Inside most of the effect dialog boxes, you can switch to a different command on the Effects menu, the Image➪Adjust submenu, or the Image➪Transform submenu by clicking on the Effects button and choosing a command from the resulting pop-up menu. Only the commands on the Effects➪Fancy submenu and the special effects plug-ins that come with Photo-Paint are unavailable from the pop-up menu.

Also, you can click on the Reset button to return the various dialog box options to the settings that were in force when you opened the dialog box. The other dialog box controls, including the hand, zoom, and preview options, work like those discussed in Chapter 17, in the section "Bringing an image into sharper focus."

Design Your Own Repeating Pattern

My favorite special-effects command in Photo-Paint wasn't created by Corel. It comes from a company called Xaos (pronounced like *chaos*) Tools. The command, Effects➪Fancy➪Terrazzo (formerly found under the Artistic Effects submenu), enables you to design totally wild patterns by repeating small portions of your image. Here's how to put this wonderful effect to work:

1. Choose Effects➪Fancy➪Terrazzo.

Photo-Paint displays the busy dialog box pictured in Figure 19-10.

Tile boundary   Sizing handle

Symmetry button

Pattern preview

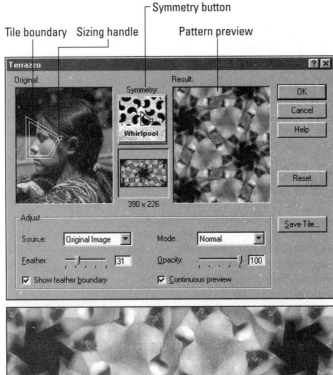

Figure 19-10:
By fooling around with the options in the Terrazzo dialog box (top), I was able to create a kaleidoscopic effect (bottom).

2. Click on the Symmetry button in the middle of the dialog box.

Another dialog box appears, offering several different ways to repeat your image as a pattern. Select the option that looks interesting — you can always come back and select a different Symmetry option if you change your mind — and press Enter. In Figure 19-10, I selected the Whirlpool option.

3. Edit the pattern tile boundary in the preview to select the area that you want to repeat.

Drag the tile boundary to move it. Drag the sizing handle (labeled in Figure 19-10) to stretch or shrink the tile.

4. Adjust the Feather value to soften the transition between tiles.

A low Feather value creates abrupt transitions between one repeating tile and the next; a high value results in soft transitions. Keep an eye on the right-hand preview to see how your changes affect the pattern.

5. Lower the <u>O</u>pacity value if you want to blend the pattern in with the original image.

I just wanted to see the pattern, so I left the value set to 100 percent.

6. Press Enter to apply the pattern.

My completed pattern appears at the bottom of Figure 19-10. Who needs a kaleidoscope when you have CorelPhoto-Paint?

If you're working on a speedy computer, you can get immediate feedback in the right-hand pattern preview by selecting the Continuous Preview check box in the Terrazzo dialog box. On a less powerful computer, the option may slow things down considerably; if you have problems, turn the option off.

Chapter 20
Ten Time-Saving Shortcuts

In This Chapter

▶ Choosing commands in the File menu

▶ Working with dialog boxes

▶ Using Alt+key shortcuts

▶ Selecting drawing and editing tools

▶ Undoing, redoing, and repeating

▶ Selecting and manipulating objects

▶ Bringing to front and sending to back

*A*nd now, from the ridiculous to the sublime. In between having fun with CorelDraw and creating every wacky special effect you can think of, you may as well work in a little productivity so that you don't go completely broke and have to put the kids up for adoption or rent them out for scientific research. To that end, this chapter presents ten time-saving mouse and keyboard equivalents (and then some). Absolutely every CorelDraw user should memorize these shortcuts — and get in the habit of using them on a regular basis.

File Menu Stuff

Ctrl+O, Ctrl+N

To open a document in any Corel program, press Ctrl+O. Press Ctrl+N to create a new document.

Ctrl+S

To save a document in any program, press Ctrl+S. Do this early and often.

Ctrl+P

You can print a document from just about any Corel program by pressing Ctrl+P. (Dream 3D is the only program that generally refuses to print, requiring you to render your drawing before you can print it.)

Ctrl+F4, Alt+F4

To close a document in Draw, Photo-Paint, and Dream 3D, press Ctrl+F4 or click on the Close button in the upper-right corner of the document window. If you haven't saved your most recent changes, press Y or Enter when prompted to do so. To quit a program and return to the Windows 95 desktop, press Alt+F4. Again, press Y or Enter to save your most recent changes when asked to do so.

Ctrl+Esc, Alt+Esc, Alt+Tab

Ctrl+Esc displays the Windows 95 Start menu so that you can start another program if you like, or shut down your machine. Alt+Esc cycles through the buttons in the taskbar at the bottom of the screen. It's a handy way to switch from one program that's running under Windows 95 to another.

But my favorite program-switching shortcut is Alt+Tab, which lets you switch to a specific program or directory window. Hold down the Alt key and then press Tab. A small window appears, listing the program or window you can switch to. If you don't want to go to that program, press Tab to go to the next one. When Windows 95 lists the desired program, release the Alt key.

Navigating Inside Dialog Boxes

You can move around a dialog box without ever using the mouse. To activate the next option in a dialog box, press Tab. To return to the previous option, press Shift+Tab.

To display the pop-up menu for an active option, press Alt+down arrow. Then use the up- and down-arrow keys to highlight the desired option, and press Enter to select it. You can also use the up- and down-arrow keys in scrolling lists.

To select a specific option, press the Alt key in combination with the underlined letter in the option name.

Displaying Menus

To display any menu, press Alt, and then type the underlined letter in the menu name. After the menu is displayed, press the underlined letter in a command name — no Alt key required — to select the command.

The Control menu is a special case. Press Alt+spacebar to display this menu.

After a menu is active, you can also press the left- and right-arrow keys to highlight different menus. Press the up- or down-arrow keys to display a menu and highlight different commands. If a highlighted command brings up a submenu, press the right-arrow key to display it. Press the left-arrow key to hide the submenu. Press Esc or press Alt again to hide the menus and deactivate the menu bar.

Simply pressing Alt no longer activates the menu bar. In Photo-Paint 7, however, you can highlight the File menu by pressing Alt and then use the arrow keys to switch to a different menu.

Zooming from the Keyboard

F2, Shift+F2, F3

In CorelDraw, press F2 and click to magnify the drawing area to twice its previous size. In Photo-Paint and Dream 3D, just press F2; you don't have to click.

To zoom in on a selected object in either CorelDraw or Dream 3D, press Shift+F2. In Photo-Paint, drag around the area that you want to magnify with the zoom tool.

To reduce the view size to half the current level of magnification in CorelDraw or Dream 3D, press F3. No clicking is required. In Photo-Paint, pressing F3 decreases the view size to the next lowest preset zoom setting.

Ctrl+1

To see one pixel in a Photo-Paint image for every screen pixel, press Ctrl+1.

F4, Shift+F4

In CorelDraw, press F4 to zoom to the maximum view size at which you can see all objects in the drawing area. In Photo-Paint, press F4 to fit the image on-screen. To zoom out so that you can see the entire page in CorelDraw or the entire work area in Dream 3D, press Shift+F4. In Photo-Paint, Shift+F4 resizes the window to fill the screen but does not zoom the image.

F9

In Photo-Paint and CorelDraw, press F9 to hide everything but your drawing or image. Press Esc to display the program interface again.

Selecting Tools

Spacebar, Ctrl+spacebar

To switch between the selected tool and the arrow tool in any Corel program, press the spacebar. The first press of the spacebar selects the arrow tool, and the second press returns you to the previously selected tool.

If text is active in CorelDraw, you can press Ctrl+spacebar instead. Unfortunately, neither Ctrl+spacebar nor the spacebar alone works to select the arrow tool when the text tool is selected in Photo-Paint.

F10

In CorelDraw, press F10 to select the shape tool and edit a path.

F5, F6, F7, F8

You can also select a few tools common to CorelDraw and Photo-Paint by using the following function keys:

- ✔ Press F5 to select whatever tool is visible in the pencil tool flyout menu in CorelDraw. F5 selects the paint tool in Photo-Paint.
- ✔ Press F6 to select the rectangle tool. Press F7 to select the oval tool.
- ✔ Press F8 to select the text tool in CorelDraw and Photo-Paint.

Undoing a Mistake

Ctrl+Z, Alt+Backspace

To undo a mistake in any Corel program, press Ctrl+Z or Alt+Backspace. If the Undo command changes to Redo after you choose it, as in Dream 3D, you can restore an operation that you undid by pressing Ctrl+Z or Alt+Backspace again.

Ctrl+Shift+Z

In CorelDraw and Photo-Paint, you can redo most undone operations by pressing Ctrl+Shift+Z.

Manipulating Objects with the Arrow and Shape Tools

Shift+click, Shift+drag

To select an object in CorelDraw, Photo-Paint, or Dream 3D, click on it with the arrow tool. To select multiple objects, click on the first object that you want to select and Shift+click on the others.

In CorelDraw and Photo-Paint, you can also begin dragging on an empty area of the document and drag around multiple objects to surround them in a marquee. To select an object, you must completely surround it with the marquee.

To deselect specific objects that are currently selected, Shift+click on them.

Alt+drag

In CorelDraw, you can Alt+drag to select all objects that even partially fall inside the marquee. This is a great way to select objects when you're zoomed in very close to them and can't marquee all the way around them.

Ctrl+drag, arrow keys, Shift+arrow keys

In Photo-Paint and CorelDraw, simply drag an object to move it. Drag and then press and hold Ctrl to move the object strictly horizontally or vertically. To nudge an object a few fractions of an inch (as specified in the Options dialog box), press one of the arrow keys.

To nudge an object in larger increments, press Shift plus an arrow key. By default, this "super nudge" moves the object ten times as far as a regular nudge. But you can change the distance of both the nudge and the super nudge in the Options dialog box (press Ctrl+J to display it).

You can also drag objects with the arrow tool and nudge them with the arrow keys in Dream 3D. The nudge increment is controlled by the Spacing value in the Grid dialog box (choose View⇨Grid, or choose Ctrl+J). But as explained in Chapter 18, moving objects in 3D space requires a different mindset than moving objects in CorelDraw and Photo-Paint.

Ctrl+click

In CorelDraw, you can select an object inside a group by Ctrl+clicking on it. This is also a useful way to select text on a curve independently of its path.

All of these techniques also work when you're editing nodes with the shape tool in CorelDraw. Furthermore, you can double-click on a node or on the shape tool icon to display the Node Edit roll-up.

Making Copies of Objects

Ctrl+C, Ctrl+X, Ctrl+V

In all Corel programs, you can copy one or more selected objects to the Clipboard by pressing Ctrl+C. To cut an object from the document and transfer it to the Clipboard, press Ctrl+X. To paste the contents of the Clipboard into the document, press Ctrl+V. (In Photo-Paint, the contents are pasted as an object rather than a selection.)

Ctrl+D, Alt+drag, Ctrl+Shift+D

In CorelDraw and Dream 3D, you can bypass the Clipboard and make an immediate duplicate of a selected object by pressing Ctrl+D.

In Photo-Paint, Alt+drag the object to a new location to duplicate it. Or press Ctrl+Shift+D.

Changing the Stacking Order of Objects

Shift+PgUp, Shift+PgDn

To bring a selected object to the front of the stacking order in CorelDraw or Photo-Paint, press Shift+PgUp. To send it to the back of the document, press Shift+PgDn.

Ctrl+PgUp, Ctrl+PgDn

You can also scoot a selected object one object forward or backward by pressing Ctrl+PgUp or Ctrl+PgDn, respectively.

Neither of these shortcuts works in Dream 3D because front and back are true spatial concepts that you adjust by dragging objects around. It's a whole different ball game.

Activating Buttons

Enter

Remember, pressing the Enter key always activates the button that's surrounded by a heavy outline.

Esc

To activate the Cancel button or cancel just about any activity, press Esc. In fact, rely on Esc to get you out of just about any weird situation when you don't know what to do.

Chapter 21

Ten Little-Known, Less-Used Features

- -

In This Chapter

▶ Understanding layers

▶ Fathoming the Blend feature

▶ Making small sense of combining objects

▶ Gaping in wonderment at CorelMemo

▶ Catching on to object databases

▶ Grasping at color trapping

▶ Assimilating the mysteries of color channels

▶ Getting the drift of scanning

▶ Wrapping your brain around lights and cameras

▶ Giving up on OCR

- -

*I*n case you haven't figured it out yet, CorelDraw 7 is a grab-bag of graphics functions. But like any grab-bag, CorelDraw is split between essential capabilities and extravagant, super-complicated excess. This chapter is about the latter. I introduce ten features that you'll probably never use. But, by gum, you paid for them, so you may as well know about them.

Turning CorelDraw into a Parking Garage

You find layers in just about every drawing program with high-end pretensions, but only a handful of experienced artists use layers on a regular basis. Except for creating master layers (as explained in Chapter 12), I would never recommend layers to anyone who isn't drawing blowouts of manifold exhaust systems, or cancer cell networks, or something equally complicated.

Here's how layers work: Imagine that all the objects in a CorelDraw document are cars. One day you realize that you have way too many cars, and you think "How can I sort out these cars to make things more efficient?" The answer is to build a multilevel parking garage.

Well, that's layers. By choosing Layout⇨Layer Manager (Ctrl+F3) in CorelDraw, you display the Layers roll-up, which lets you divide your document into a transparent, multilevel parking garage. Each layer contains a bunch of objects that are fully segregated from objects on other layers.

Unless you specify otherwise, objects on different layers don't look different, and they don't print differently. They're merely organized into separate banks to help eliminate confusion and provide greater control and flexibility. For example, you can hide different layers to get them out of your face; you can print only certain layers to isolate others; you can lock the objects on a layer to prevent accidental alterations; and you can make objects on layers appear in different colors. The icons in the Layers roll-up assist you in determining what's locked, visible, printable, and so on.

Blending between Objects

I mentioned blending as a way to create custom gradations in Chapter 19. Luckily, there's more to blending than just creating gradations. In fact, blending is one of the most complicated functions in CorelDraw. You display the Blend roll-up by choosing Effects⇨Blend. Then you select two objects, click on the Apply button, and watch CorelDraw create a bunch of intermediate objects (called *steps*) between the two. The steps gradually change in form and color as they progress from the first object to the last. You can specify how may steps Draw creates, you can rotate the steps, you can make the steps follow a path, and you can even control the amount of space between steps.

In Version 7, you can accomplish the same feats by using the new interactive blend tool and the Property Bar.

Blending is sort of like morphing — the effect you see when all those faces change into each other at the end of that Michael Jackson video. But instead of each step occurring in a different frame of videotape — creating the effect of a gradual transition — all the steps in CorelDraw appear in the drawing area at the same time. As a result, no one uses blending for any other purpose than creating custom gradations like the one featured in Chapter 19.

Taking the Old Blowtorch to Your Objects

In Chapter 17, I explain that you can manually adjust selection outlines in Photo-Paint. You can add one selection outline to another, delete a chunk from a selected area, or find the intersection of two selection outlines. Well, you can do the same thing in CorelDraw, except with objects.

Let's say that you want to create a snowman. You can take one circle and weld it to another by choosing Arrange⇨Weld. If you want to subtract a small circle from a large circle to create a doughnut, you choose Arrange⇨ Trim. And to make a circle with a flat bottom you can take a circle and a rectangle and choose Arrange⇨Intersection.

Though these are inherently useful commands, CorelDraw handles them in a really weird way. First you select just one of the objects that you want to add, subtract, or intersect. Then you choose the command to bring up a roll-up. You click on a button in the roll-up — Weld To, Trim, or Intersect With — and then click on the other object. The process would be much easier if you just selected two objects and chose a command to merge them, but simplicity is rarely the Corel style.

Slapping Sticky Notes on Your Drawing

Ever wish you could explain how something in your drawing is put together so that the next person to work on it would know what's going on? Didn't think so, but that's exactly what you can do with CorelMemo.

Inside CorelDraw, choose Edit⇨Insert New Object. When the Insert New Object dialog box appears, choose the CorelMemo 7 item from the Object Type list box and click on OK. This command starts the CorelMemo program, which displays a small window containing a digital sticky note. Enter a title at the top of the note and enter some information-rich text in the lower portion. When you're done, choose File⇨Update Graphic and then File⇨Exit & Return to leave the Memo program and place the sticky note into CorelDraw.

The problems with this ridiculous function are numerous. First, CorelDraw places the memo right in the middle of your page, which is not necessarily what you're looking at on-screen. Second, the memo takes up a ton of room in your drawing. You can rarely read the memo and view the portion of the drawing that the memo concerns at the same time.

Backing Your Objects with Data

CorelDraw lets you link data to any object. Select an object and choose Tools⇨Object Data. After the Object Data dialog box appears, click on the little data icon just below the title bar. The Object Data Manager dialog box appears, sporting a miniature spreadsheet.

Here you can enter any data you want about the selected object. Why on earth would you want to do this? Well, the Corel example is catalogs. If you had a drawing of a rotary combine engine, for example, you might want to write down the name and price of the product. Later you could print this information or export it for use in a different program. Yeah, I'm always wishing I could do that.

Trapping Colors

You may remember Chapter 13, in which I discuss how to print color separations. Cyan, magenta, yellow, and black primaries are printed on separate pages and reproduced in separate passes. That this is the same process used to print the Sunday comics in your local newspaper. Actually, nearly all color newspaper and magazine art is created this way, but the comics are the best example because they invariably have registration problems. Maybe the red in Hagar's beard is printed on Helga's face, or perhaps Robotman's outfit is leaking yellow onto a neighboring panel. These errors are caused by the fact that the cyan, magenta, yellow, and black inks aren't aligned properly.

CorelDraw enables you to compensate for bad registration by overlapping the colors a little. For example, imagine a circle with a cyan fill and a black outline. If the colors don't register exactly right, a gap occurs between the fill and outline colors. CorelDraw can fill in this gap by spreading the colors. The black outline becomes slightly thicker, and the cyan fill becomes slightly larger. This process is known as color trapping. To activate the CorelDraw trapping function, do the following:

1. **Press Ctrl+P or choose File⇨Print.**

2. **Click on the Options button in the Print dialog box.**

3. **Click on the Separations tab and select the Print Separations check box.**

4. **Select both the Always Overprint Black and Auto-Spreading check boxes in the Auto Trapping area.**

5. **Press Enter twice to start printing.**

Phew, what a lot of work. On top of that, the trapping options aren't even available for some lower-end printers.

Separating Color Channels in Photo-Paint

In Photo-Paint, you can take a color image and view it as several separate images called channels, each of which represents a primary color. For example, a CMYK image has four channels — one each for cyan, magenta, yellow, and black — just as you have four plates when printing color separations. You can view any of three channels in an RGB image — one each for red, green, and blue, the primary colors of light.

To view the different color channels in an image, press Ctrl+F9 or choose View⇨Roll-Ups⇨Channels. Then click in the column just to the left of a channel name in the image channels list in the Channels roll-up. A little pencil icon appears in the column, and Photo-Paint displays the channel as an ordinary grayscale image. To return to full color view, click just to the left of the Channels item that has the full-color thumbnail (if you're viewing an RGB item, for example, click next to the RGB Channels item).

What's the point of all this channel segregation? Well, you can apply a special effect to a single color channel to get a doubly weird effect. In addition, if a color image looks a little fuzzy, it may turn out that only one of the color channels needs sharpening. You may also want to create a psychedelic effect by selecting part of one channel and rotating it independently of the other channels.

Scanning into Photo-Paint or CorelDraw

If you sunk a few hundred bucks into a scanner, you can scan images directly into Photo-Paint. And if you also install the CorelScan utility included in Version 7, you can scan directly into CorelDraw as well.

To take a bit of real life and make it appear magically on your computer screen inside Photo-Paint, choose File⇨Acquire Image⇨Acquire. Then click on the Scan button inside the Corel TWAIN dialog box. When the scanner is done working, your photograph appears on-screen.

Alternatively, you can choose the File⇨Acquire Image⇨Acquire from CorelScan inside Photo-Paint or choose File⇨Acquire from CorelScan inside CorelDraw. This command starts the CorelScan wizard, which guides you through the process of scanning your image and then opens the image for you. In CorelScan, you can crop your image, make color corrections, and otherwise improve the quality of the image if you like.

If you don't have a scanner, however, nothing happens. You can try smushing the photograph against the screen, but I don't think that Corel has figured out how to make Photo-Paint or CorelDraw read images that way.

Assembling Your Own 3-D Movie Stage

Dream 3D lets you clutter your drawing not only with three-dimensional objects, but also with lights and cameras. Lights shine on the objects so that you can see what's going on. Without lights, you couldn't see anything. The camera controls what Dream 3D renders. Just as the audience at a movie sees what the camera films, your audience sees what Dream 3D's camera shoots.

Dream 3D offers two tools for adding your own lights and cameras. These are the Create Light and Create Camera tools, found roughly in the middle of the toolbox. Lights show up as red cone-shaped objects; cameras appear as blue rectangles. Figuring out which direction the lights or cameras are pointing is virtually impossible unless you're working in the preview or better preview mode, which can be slow on some machines. Moving the lights and cameras around and turning them toward objects is just as difficult.

If, despite these hazards, you want to edit a light, double-click on it. You can then select from different kinds of lights, control the range and brightness, add gels, and generally perform half a dozen modifications that are every bit as bewildering as they sound, if not more so. To switch to a different camera, press Ctrl+E (or choose Scene⇨Camera Settings) and select the desired camera from the Camera pop-up menu. You can even change the lens on the camera from Normal to Telephoto.

Then again, you can accept the Dream 3D default lighting and camera settings, and consider yourself lucky that you can draw some halfway decent-looking objects (if you indeed can).

Attempting Optical Character Recognition

CorelTrace can recognize the characters in the a scanned page and generate a text document that you can open in a word processor. This is absolutely the last function that I expected to see worked into a drawing package. It'll be a cold day in Port-au-Prince before you use this function.

Chapter 22

Ten File Formats and Their Functions

In This Chapter

▶ Native CorelDraw: CDR and CMX

▶ Encapsulated PostScript: EPS and AI

▶ Metafile formats: CGM and WMF

▶ CorelPhoto-Paint: CPT and WI

▶ Windows Paintbrush: PCX

▶ Tagged Image File Format: TIFF

▶ Windows Bitmap: BMP

▶ CompuServe Bitmap: GIF

▶ Joint Photographic Experts Group: JPEG

▶ Kodak Photo CD: PCD

CorelDraw supports more file formats than any other graphics program for the PC. This fact means that you can create a graphic in just about any program on an IBM-compatible or Macintosh computer and open it or import it into CorelDraw. Likewise, you can export an image from CorelDraw so that it can be opened in just about any program.

The Many Languages of CorelDraw

If CorelDraw were a person, it would be able to speak every language but . . . well, any language I may mention would be politically incorrect, so I'd better keep my mouth shut. Anyway, I've listed several file formats for your reading pleasure.

Native CorelDraw: CDR and CMX

CDR is the native file format, which means that if you just choose File⇨ Save As, enter a name, CorelDraw uses the CDR format. This format retains every bit of information about your drawing, including nodes, segments, fills, layers, and anything else you can imagine. Unless you plan to share your drawing with others or open it in another program, stick with this format.

A variation on CDR is CMX, the Corel Presentation Exchange format. Like CDR, CMX saves all information about a drawing. Corel used to store the clip art that came with CorelDraw in CMX, but now the clip art is stored in CDR.

Encapsulated PostScript: EPS and AI

PostScript is the printer language mentioned in Chapter 13. Encapsulated PostScript (EPS) is a file format that contains a complete PostScript definition of the graphic right in the file. It's as if the artwork contains a little PostScript capsule. When you print an EPS file, the program sends the PostScript capsule to the printer and lets the printer figure it out. The printer must support PostScript in order to print EPS graphics, however.

The Adobe Illustrator (AI) format is an editable variation on the EPS format. You see, when you import an EPS graphic into a program, you can't edit it. You can just place the graphic on the page and print it. But when you import an AI file into CorelDraw, you can edit every little bit of it. This format is ideal if you want to share artwork with someone who works on a Macintosh. It's also widely supported by Windows programs.

Metafile Formats: CGM and WMF

CGM (Computer Graphics Metafile) is a dinosaur-like file format that's certified by the American National Standards Institute. Predating the EPS format, I prefer CGM to EPS when I print to non-PostScript printers.

The Windows Metafile Format (WMF) is the rough equivalent of CGM in the Windows environment, though no institutions have come out to certify it. WMF is the format used by the Windows Clipboard. If you plan on transferring a drawing to another Windows program and you'll be printing to a non-PostScript printer, you may want to give WMF a try.

Corel Photo-Paint: CPT and WI

CPT is the Photo-Paint native format. Like other formats covered from here on out — PCX, TIFF, BMP, GIF, JPEG, and PCD — CPT is an image file format.

Image formats save artwork as pixels, not as objects. Though CorelDraw is perfectly capable of importing these formats, you should not save drawings in these formats unless you want to convert your graphic to pixels.

Saving your images in the CPT format is fine if you're going to be working on your images only inside Photo-Paint 7 or placing them only into a Corel-Draw drawing. If you're sharing an image file with someone who uses Photo-Paint 6, save in the Version 6 CPT format.

 Keep in mind, however, that if you save your image in any format other than CPT, any objects in the image merge with the background, preventing you from further manipulating them. So you may want to save a backup copy of your image in the CPT format before saving it in another image format.

Images in the Photos folder of the second CorelDraw 7 CD-ROM are stored in the WI format. This format takes a huge image file and smushes it down to a size that takes up less space on disk. When you open the image, Photo-Paint decompresses it, fluffing all those smushed pixels back up. Anyway, don't save your images in this format unless someone specifically requests it. Instead, use a more widely supported format, such as TIFF or PCX.

PC Paintbrush: PCX

Originally designed for PC Paintbrush, PCX is one of the most widely supported graphics formats on the PC. Recently, this format's popularity has faded. PCX is a great way to swap files with folks who use older programs.

Tagged Image File Format: TIFF

TIFF (Tagged Image File Format) was developed to be the standard image file format, even more of a standard than PCX. Although it still plays second fiddle to PCX in terms of raw support on the PC, TIFF is more likely to be supported by programs running on other kinds of computers, namely the Mac. Furthermore, if you're exporting an image for use in a mainstream desktop publishing program such as PageMaker, QuarkXPress, or CorelVentura, TIFF is the way to go. Generally a more reliable format than PCX, it offers compression options to reduce the size of the image on disk.

Windows Bitmap: BMP

BMP is the native format of the little Paint program that comes with Windows. The only reason that Corel supports BMP is for importing purposes. I don't recommend exporting to the BMP format unless you're creating graphics that will become part of your computer's system resources — for example, you can use a BMP file as the wallpaper for your Windows desktop.

CompuServe Bitmap: GIF

The GIF format was created especially for trading images over CompuServe. GIF offers compression capabilities, but it supports only 256 colors. Before you can save an image in this format, you must convert the image to an 8-bit image using one of the commands in the Image⇨Convert To submenu.

These days, lots of folks use GIF for artwork that they want to post on the Web. One advantage of this format is that you can create what's known as a transparent GIF, which simply means that you can make part of your image transparent so that a portion of your Web page shows through the image.

If transparency isn't an issue, the format discussed next, JPEG, may be a better choice because it lets you save 16 million colors and yet creates smaller files on disk. Use GIF only for high-contrast images, screen shots, and text or for creating transparent GIFs.

Joint Photographic Experts Group: JPEG

JPEG (or JPG) stands for the Joint Photographic Experts Group, the group of folks who came up with the format. JPEG is designed to compress huge images so that they take up much less space on disk. Compression-wise, JPEG wipes the floor with TIFF and GIF. However, you actually lose data when you save to the JPEG format. Usually, the loss is nominal — most users can't see the difference — but it's something to think about.

Generally speaking, you don't need to worry about the JPEG format unless you start creating very large images — say, larger than 400K — with Photo-Paint or Dream 3D. JPEG is also a common format for posting images on the World Wide Web, as discussed in the preceding section.

Kodak Photo CD: PCD

CorelDraw and Photo-Paint can import Kodak Photo CD files. Neither program can save to the format because Kodak won't let them. Photo CD is what is known as a *proprietary format.*

In case you haven't heard of it, Photo CD is the latest thing from Kodak, and it's designed for storing photographs on compact discs. You take a roll of undeveloped film to a service bureau, give the technician $30 or so, and the technician scans your photos onto a CD. As long as you own a Photo CD-compatible CD-ROM drive — which includes just about every CD-ROM drive manufactured in the last two years — you can then open and edit the images in Photo-Paint. What will they think of next?

Appendix

Installing CorelDraw 7

● ●

*O*ne thing you can say about Windows 95 is that it makes installing software a heck of a lot easier than it used to be. And when a behemoth program like CorelDraw becomes easy to install, you know that the computer gods are smiling.

If You Build the Computer, CorelDraw Will Come

Let's start off by reviewing what you need in order to install CorelDraw 7:

 ✔ **CorelDraw 7:** You need the CorelDraw 7 package with all the CD-ROMs and other goodies inside. Osmosis simply won't work.

 ✔ **A 486 or Pentium computer:** The Corel documents say that you need at least a Pentium computer to run CorelDraw 7. But the truth is that you can get by with a 486. Some operations, such as opening large images in Photo-Paint, may run too slowly for your liking, however.

 ✔ **Windows 95 or Windows NT 4.0:** None of this Windows 3.1 stuff for CorelDraw 7. You have to join the Windows 95 bandwagon if you want to run Version 7.

 ✔ **A large hard drive:** You need a lot of space for CorelDraw 7. A 1GB hard drive is best, but if you don't want to install all of CorelDraw's bells and whistles (which you probably don't), you can get by with a smaller hard drive. (I tell you how to figure out the size of your hard drive in the next section.)

 ✔ **Lots of memory:** You need at least 16MB of RAM; 32MB is recommended. (I explain how to check your computer's RAM later in this chapter.)

 ✔ **A CD-ROM drive:** CorelDraw 7 is available only on CD. If you don't own a CD-ROM drive, rest assured that it's a great purchase — one you'll come to love, and not just for CorelDraw 7.

Checking your memory

To find out whether you have enough memory to run CorelDraw 7, choose Settings⇔Control Panel from the Windows 95 Start menu. Then double-click on the System icon in the Control Panel window. When the System Properties dialog box appears, click on the Performance tab. The first item on the Performance panel is Memory. If the value is 16MB or more, you're okay. Press Esc to close the System Properties dialog box. If you don't have enough RAM, talk to your local computer wizard to find out how to get more of it into your machine.

In case you're not up on the latest terminology regarding digital storage space, here's how it works. A *byte* is a unit of space that's big enough to hold one letter of text. A *kilobyte,* or *K,* is about a thousand bytes. (It's actually 1,024 bytes, but who cares?) A *megabyte,* abbreviated *MB,* is equal to 1,000K, or a million bytes. And a *gigabyte,* or *GB,* is 1,000MB, which is a billion bytes.

Inspecting the hard drive

To check your hard drive space, double-click on the My Computer icon on your Windows 95 desktop. Click on the icon that represents your hard drive (usually drive C). In the lower-right corner of the My Computer window, you should see two numbers: a Free Space value and a Capacity value.

The Capacity value should be 200MB or more. The Free Space value is even more important because it tells you how much room on the hard drive is available for use by CorelDraw. If the value is less than 120MB, you probably need to delete some files before you can install CorelDraw 7. Or you can perform a Custom install (as explained next) and limit the programs and program components you install.

If you don't know what to delete or how to delete it, get that computer wizard on the phone and beg for help. Or just hunt and peck around your files to see what you can throw away.

Insert the CD and Watch the Sparks Fly

Assuming that your computer is prepared to install CorelDraw 7, the following steps tell you what to do:

1. **Shut down any other programs that are running.**

   At the end of the installation process, you have to restart your system. If you have any open documents that you haven't saved, you lose them during the restart. So just to be safe, close down all your open programs (except Windows 95, of course).

2. Put the first of the CorelDraw 7 CDs in your CD-ROM drive.

A few seconds after you stick the CD in the drive, a CorelDraw 7 window appears. If the window doesn't pop up automatically on the screen, double-click on the My Computer icon in the upper-left corner of your screen. Then double-click on the icon for the CD-ROM drive, which is most likely drive D. The CorelDraw windows should then appear.

If you still can't get the setup program to run, choose Start⇨Run, enter D:\Setup.exe into the Open option box, and press Enter. If you go this route, you can skip Step 3.

3. Click on the Setup button.

A setup message wastes your time for a few moments and then the Corel Setup Wizard screen appears.

4. Click on the Next button or press Alt+N.

You see a message detailing your rights under the software licensing agreement.

5. Click on Accept or press Alt+A to accept the agreement and move on.

6. Enter your name or company name and press Alt+N or click on Next.

A lot of folks get paranoid about programs asking for personal data, but you have to do it to install the program. Besides, unless you register the program, your personal data doesn't leave the confines of your computer.

After you click on Next, you see a screen asking you to confirm that you spelled your name or company correctly. If you goofed, click on the Back button to fix things. If everything looks okay, move on to Step 7.

7. Click on Next or press Alt+N.

8. Enter your serial number and click on Next or press Alt+N.

The serial number is printed on your product registration card. If you don't enter a serial number, you can still install the program, though. When you press Alt+N, Corel advises you that you need the serial number to get technical support and asks whether you want to proceed anyway. Click on Yes to do so.

9. Select an installation option and click on Next or press Alt+N.

You can choose from four options:

Full
- Typical: This option installs CorelDraw, Photo-Paint, Dream 3D, OCR-Trace, and the help, samples, and default filters and fonts files for those four programs. It requires 221MB of hard drive

space. Unless this option represents your needs exactly — are you *really* going to use all this stuff? — choose the Custom or Compact option (explained next) instead.

- Compact: Here's the option to choose if you want to install CorelDraw, its help files and its default filters only — no Photo-Paint, no Dream 3D, and no other accessories in the CorelDraw 7 package. This option requires just 44MB of hard drive space.

- Custom: Select this option to specify exactly which parts of the CorelDraw 7 package you want to install. If, like me, you're not a big fan of letting automated installation programs put whatever they like on your hard drive, this option is the best one. I heartily recommend this option.

- CD-ROM Based Setup: This option copies just enough files to your hard drive to run CorelDraw off the CDs. It eats up a bare minimum of disk space, but it causes your programs to run very slowly — far too slowly to be acceptable. Don't select this option.

10. Turn off the specific programs that you don't want to install, and then click on Next or press Alt+N.

If you selected the Custom radio button in the preceding step — good job! — a list of programs appears on-screen. If you selected Typical or Compact, skip to Step 13.

To turn off a program so that it doesn't install, click on its check box. A check mark in the box means that the program will install. If you see a plus sign next to an item, click on the plus sign to display a list of individual components associated with that item. Again, click on the check box next to the component to turn the option on or off. A gray check box means that some components associated with the item are selected for installation.

I recommend that you make the following choices (keep in mind that you can always come back and install something later).

As you select options to install and turn off other options, the installation window shows you how much disk space you need to install the selected components.

- Start by clicking on the plus sign next to the Graphics Utilities item. If you won't be tracing any scanned image to convert them to drawings (very few people do), turn off the Corel OCR-Trace check box.

- Do you have a scanner hooked up to your computer? If not, turn off the CorelScan check box. If you do have a scanner and you want to be able to scan directly into CorelDraw, leave this option turned on. However, you can scan directly into Photo-Paint without CorelScan. (For more on this topic, see Chapter 21.)

- Do you plan to catalog all your graphics, images, and multimedia files? No? Then turn off the Corel Multimedia Manager option.

- Review Chapter 1 to see whether you have use for any of the other programs in the Graphics Utilities list. If not, turn off all the options except Plug-In Filters.

- Click on the plus sign next to the Productivity Tools item and turn off all options except Writing Tools. Then click on the plus sign next to Writing Tools and turn off all the options for that item except Spell Checker.

- If you trust me to explain CorelDraw and Photo-Paint adequately in this book, you can get rid of Corel's online help files. Click on the CorelDraw plus sign and turn off Help Files and Tutors. Do the same for Photo-Paint.

11. Select the filters that you want to install and click on Next or press Alt+N.

The installation program asks you to select which filters you want to install. These filters let you open and edit drawings and images, which is very important. But some of the options are unnecessary. Turn off Animation Filters and Text Filters. The check boxes for these options turn gray instead of hollow because a couple of filters stay on regardless of your choices.

12. Select fonts to install and then click on Next or press Alt+N.

Now you can choose which of the bazillion fonts that ship with the CorelDraw 7 package you want to install. Fonts take up a lot of disk space, so be selective.

13. Choose a scanner driver — or not. Then click on Next or press Alt+N.

Next, you see a message about scanner drivers. If you don't have a scanner, just press Alt+N to move forward. If you do have a scanner and want to install a particular scanner driver, select the Please Allow Me to Select a Scanner Driver check box, and then select the driver that you want to install. Deselect the check box to install only the default Corel TWAIN driver.

14. Decide where to put CorelDraw 7.

The installer asks you to specify a directory for CorelDraw and the fonts that you selected in Step 11. Most likely, the program's default suggestions are fine, so just press Alt+N again.

15. Select the Temp check box.

CorelDraw likes to create temporary files on disk. Select the check box for your drive C and press Alt+N to continue.

16. Name the Corel program folder.

The installer wants to put all your program icons in a central place called CorelDraw 7. Press Alt+N to make it so.

17. Click on the Install button.

This step tells the installer to complete the installation. Assuming that you have enough space on disk and nothing is wrong with your CD, you can go to lunch. Installing the software takes a long time — anywhere from five minutes to an hour, depending on the number of files you're installing and the speed of your computer.

18. Register your program — or not.

When the installation is complete, you see a message asking whether you want to register your copy of the program via modem. If you have a modem and you want to register the program, click on Yes and follow the on-screen instructions. Otherwise, click on the No button and then click on the OK button.

19. Click on Yes to restart your system.

The installer asks whether it's okay to restart your system; click on the Yes button to give the installer the go-ahead. When your system restarts, you see the CorelDraw programs inside a CorelDraw 7 window on your desktop. You can also access the programs from the Windows 95 Start menu.

If you ever want to install additional programs or files, just perform the steps in this appendix again, selecting the Custom installation option.

To remove programs from your system, choose Programs⇨CorelDraw 7⇨ Corel Uninstall from the Windows 95 Start menu and follow the on-screen prompts. Alternatively, if you performed a custom install and the Uninstaller program doesn't appear on the CorelDraw 7 submenu, you can run the Uninstall program from the CorelDraw 7 installer CD (that's CD #1) by choosing Start⇨Run, entering **D:\Uninstal.exe** in the Open option box, and pressing Enter.

Index

Numbers and Symbols

2-D drawings, viewing in 3-D space, 170–171

2-D shapes, assigning depth, 179

2D Effects submenu special effects, 371–373

3-D graphics, 14–15

3-D objects, separating, 187

3-D programs and models, 169

3D drawings, printing and rendering, 353–354

3D Effects submenu special effects, 371, 374

• A •

actions
  redoing, 78
  undoing, 77–78, 295–296

Adaptive Unsharp dialog box, 326–327

Add Node (+) keyboard shortcut, 93

Additive mode (Ctrl+plus (+)) keyboard shortcut, 322

AI file format, 390

Align & Distribute (Ctrl+A) keyboard shortcut, 115

Align and Distribute dialog box, 115–116, 118

Alt-key combinations, 32, 275
  arrow keys and, 32, 50

angled guidelines, 109–110

animation files included with program, 16

arcs, 68–69

Arrange⇨Align & Distribute command, 115

Arrange⇨Break Apart command, 95

Arrange⇨Combine command, 96

Arrange⇨Convert to Curves command, 100, 172, 180, 237

Arrange⇨Group command, 118, 154, 161, 171, 364

Arrange⇨Intersection command, 385

Arrange⇨Order submenu, 120

Arrange⇨Order⇨Behind command, 121

Arrange⇨Order⇨In Front Of command, 121

Arrange⇨Order⇨Reverse Order command, 122

Arrange⇨Order⇨To Back command, 363

Arrange⇨Separate command, 157, 187, 237

Arrange⇨Transform⇨Position command, 112

Arrange⇨Transform⇨Rotate command, 167–168

Arrange⇨Transform⇨Scale & Mirror command, 71, 163, 362

Arrange⇨Transform⇨Skew command, 168

Arrange⇨Trim command, 385

Arrange⇨Ungroup All command, 119

Arrange⇨Ungroup command, 119, 172, 187

Arrange⇨Weld command, 385

arrow keys, 32, 112, 194, 198–199, 222

arrow tool, 27–28, 71, 74–77, 193, 203, 312, 334, 380–381

artistic text blocks, 192–194
  converting to free-form paths, 237
  converting to paragraph text, 203–204
  creation of, 192–194
  editing, 193–194
  Format Text dialog box, 210–212
  formatting attributes, 204–205
  insertion marker, 193
  justification, 209
  manually inserting line breaks, 194
  resizing characters within, 194

rotation and skew handles, 195

ATM (Adobe Type Manager), 208

auto-panning, 50

• B •

Back One (Ctrl+Page Down) keyboard shortcut, 121, 382

Back One command, 121

backing up text before attaching to paths, 238

backup copies of drawing, 56

baseline, 226

better preview mode, (Ctrl+Alt+Y) keyboard shortcut, 347

black, 128

Blend roll-up, 361, 384

BMP file format, 391

bounding box mode, (Ctrl+Y) keyboard shortcut, 347

Break Apart (Ctrl+K) keyboard shortcut, 95, 98

buttons, 33, 382

• C •

Camera Settings (Ctrl+E) keyboard shortcut, 388

Cancel (Alt+F4) Alt-key combination, 34

caps, 136–138

CD-ROM, saving images from, 287

CDR file format, 55, 390

CGM file format, 390

Channels roll-up (Ctrl+F9) keyboard shortcut, 387

characters, 192, 223–224

check boxes, 33

circle mask tool, 313

circles, 61–62, 231–235, 297

clicking, 25

clip art, 16, 39–43

Clipart folder, 42

Clipboard, 147–151, 204, 325

clone tool, 307–308

cloning, 147–158, 322, 324–325, 334

Close (Alt+F4) Alt-key
    combination, 288, 378
Close button, 20–21
closed paths, 80–82
    curves, 84–85
    fills, 124–125
    opening, 95
CMX file format, 39, 390
CMYK (cyan, magenta, yellow,
    black) color model,
    128–129
collating printing, 254
Collos.CDR file, 102
color
    adding/subtracting, 307
    automatically replacing,
        145–146
    blending shape's with shapes
        below, 170
    changing to different, 306
    color models, 127–128
    CorelDream 3D, 342
    custom, 299
    darkening, 304
    extruding, 184–185, 187
    fills, 24, 124–125
    gradients, 144–145
    images, 290–291
    lightening, 304
    matching Photo-Paint, 292
    number for images,
        284–285
    objects, 350
    outlines, 24, 131, 134
    photo's, 286–287
    replacing with foreground
        color, 306
    smearing, 306
    user-created, 127–129
color controls, 24–25
color models, 127–129
color palette, 24–25, 125–127,
    129, 131–132
color printers, 259
color replacer tool, 295
Color roll-up, 127–129, 131, 292
color separations, printing,
    258–260
Color Table dialog box, 284
colorizing images, 304
Combine (Ctrl+L) keyboard
    shortcut, 96
combining images, 324–325
commands
    Alt-key combinations for, 32,
        275

followed by ellipses
    (...), 33
keyboard equivalents, 32
keyboard shortcuts, 32
selecting, 31, 275
toggle, 51
condensed text, 194
Contour function, 170
Control menu, 20
control points, 87, 89, 99,
    106–107
Convert to Curves (Ctrl+Q)
    keyboard shortcut, 100,
    172, 180, 237
Copy (Ctrl+C) keyboard
    shortcut, 148, 204, 269,
    275, 325, 332, 360, 381
Corel Capture, 14
Corel OCR-Trace, 13–14
Corel Photo-Paint. See
    Photo-Paint
Corel World Wide
    Web site, 11
CorelDepth, 15
CorelDraw, 9–10
    embedding objects, 270
    exiting, 56
    interface, 18–25
    introducing objects into, 270
    linking object from
        Photo-Paint, 270–271
    math, 10
    scanned photos, 13, 387
    starting, 17–18
    versus Photo-Paint, 12–13
    Welcome screen, 18
    Windows 95 and, 17
CorelDraw 7, 2
    installing, 393–398
    photos provided with, 277–278
    programs that come in, 1
    quitting, 21
CorelDream 3D, 14–15, 169,
    341–342
    3D movie state, 388
    adding objects to drawing,
        345–346
    colors, patterns, textures, 342
    importing and magnifying
        objects, 345–346
    models, 342, 346–347
    moving objects in 3D space,
        347–348
    moving toolbar and toolbox,
        343
    printing drawings, 353–354

ready-made backdrop,
    351–352
scaling and spinning objects,
    348–349
scenes, 342
shaders, 350
starting, 342
work area, 342
working box, 342–344
CorelMemo, 385
CorelMosaic. See Multimedia
    Manager
CorelScan utility, 387
CorelTexture, 15
CorelTrace, 388
corners, 136–138
CPT file format, 390–391
Create a New Image dialog
    box, 284–285
Create From Mask (Ctrl+up
    arrow) keyboard
    shortcut, 332
Create Mask (Ctrl+M) keyboard
    shortcut, 333, 339
crop tool, 324
Crop⇨To Mask command, 324
Ctrl key, 61
cursor, 102, 305
curved segments, 84–85, 89, 98
cusp node, 89, 94, 98
customizing
    Color palette, 126–127
    digitized textures, 15
    gradients, 143–145, 301–303
    line widths, 135–136
    status bar, 111
Cut (Ctrl+X) keyboard shortcut,
    147, 325, 381
cyan, 128

• D •

Dash Pattern pop-up menu, 135
Delete key, 77, 93, 334
Delete Node (-) keyboard
    shortcut, 93
Delete Page dialog box, 242
dialog boxes, 33
    navigating, 378
    roll-ups, 34–36
digitizing, 11
display modes, 50–51
Display Properties dialog box,
    19
distorting objects, 335
distributing objects, 115–118

documents
adding pages, 240–241
deleting pages, 242
flowing text between pages, 243
master layer, 244–247
moving between pages, 241–242
naming, 20
new, 38
printing, 253–255
resizing pages, 247–248
spell checking, 213–214
double-clicking, 26
downloading photos, 11
draft mode, 50
drag and drop
duplicating or moving objects, 157–158
transferring object from Photo-Paint to CorelDraw, 264–265
dragging, 26
drawing area, 23–24
grid, 105–107
moving around, 43–50
rulers, 24
stacking order of objects, 120–122
drawing lines, 296–297
drawings
adding another drawing to, 41–43
adding objects, 345–346
adjusting, 22
backup copies, 56
clip art, 39, 41
converting paintings to, 13
draft mode, 50
free-form, 80–82
handles, 40–41
hiding interface, 52
importing, 39
magnifying, 43–48
moving on-screen, 48–50
naming, 54
normal mode, 50
opening, 39–40
orientation on paper, 252
Perspective function, 169–172
Photo-Paint and, 13
previewing bits and pieces of, 52–53
printers, 10
reducing to fit printed page, 256
reshaping, 87–90

saving, 53–55
shrinking, 21
simple wireframe mode, 51
thumbnail views, 42–43
updating, 55
vanishing points, 172
viewing 2-D in 3D space, 170–171
versus paintings, 12
wireframe mode, 50–51
zooming, 44–48
drop caps, 212
Drop Shadow dialog box, 340
drop-down lists, 33
Duplicate
Ctrl+D keyboard shortcut, 71, 151, 238, 381
Ctrl+Shift+D keyboard shortcut, 325, 334, 381–382
Duplicate without Offset (+) keyboard shortcut, 154
duplicating objects, 115
cloning, 154–157
copying and transferring, 147–151
deleting clones, 156
drag and drop, 157–158
grouping before, 151–153
linking copy and original, 154–155
objects of different types, 154–155
offset, 153–154
placing copy on pasteboard, 150
scaling or flipping, 163
several paths, 151–153
shapes, 71
transformations and controls, 156

• **E** •

Edit Fill & Transparency dialog box, 299
Edit Node roll-up, 177
Edit Text (Ctrl+Shift+T) keyboard shortcut, 198, 236
Edit⇔Clone command, 154
Edit⇔Copy command, 148, 204, 275, 325, 332
Edit⇔CorelPaint.Image.7 Object⇔Edit command, 268
Edit⇔Cut command, 147, 325
Edit⇔Duplicate command, 71, 151, 238

Edit⇔Fill command, 299–300
Edit⇔Find and Replace⇔ Replace Objects command, 145
Edit⇔Insert New Object command, 270–271, 385
Edit⇔Paste command, 148, 204
Edit⇔Paste As New Object command, 332
Edit⇔Paste Special command, 270
Edit⇔Redo command, 78, 296
Edit⇔Reset Color command, 291
Edit⇔Select All command, 76, 161
Edit⇔Undo command, 78, 296, 336
effect tool, 305–307
Effects menu, 327–328
Effects⇔2D Effects⇔Edge Detect command, 372
Effects⇔2D Effects⇔Swirl command, 372
Effects⇔2D Effects⇔Wet Paint command, 373
Effects⇔2D Effects⇔Whirlpool command, 373
Effects⇔2D Effects⇔Wind command, 373
Effects⇔3D Effects⇔Emboss command, 374
Effects⇔3D Effects⇔Page Curl command, 374
Effects⇔Add Perspective command, 171, 366
Effects⇔Blend command, 384
Effects⇔Blends command, 170, 361
Effects⇔Clear Envelope command, 178
Effects⇔Clear Perspective command, 172
Effects⇔Color Transform⇔Psychedelic command, 370
Effects⇔Envelope command, 174, 364
Effects⇔Extrude command, 180, 366
Effects⇔Fancy⇔Terrazzo command, 374
Effects⇔PowerClip⇔Place Inside Container command, 170
Effects⇔Sharpen⇔Adaptive Unsharp command, 307, 325–326

ellipse tool, 61, 70, 291, 297
F7 keyboard shortcut, 61, 70,
297, 380
ellipses, 68–70, 297
embedding, 264
End Arrow pop-up menu, 135
Envelope (Ctrl+F7) keyboard
shortcut, 174, 364
Envelope feature, 169, 174–178,
364
Envelope roll-up, 174–175,
177–178, 364
EPS file format, 390
equilateral polygons, 63
eraser tools, 96–98, 291,
293–295
exchanging data
embedding objects, 270
importing, 270, 272
in-place editing, 268–269
linking objects, 270
OLE (object linking and
embedding), 264–271
transferring objects between
Photo-Paint and
CorelDraw, 265–269
Exit (Alt+F4) keyboard shortcut,
56, 267, 270–271, 288, 378
expanded text, 194
Extrude (Ctrl+E) keyboard
shortcut, 180
Extrude roll-up, 180–186,
366–367
extruding, 169
beveling edges, 182–183
color, 184–187
depth, 187
fills, 187
light sources, 182
rotating, 181
separating 3-D objects, 187
vanishing point, 180–181, 186
eyedropper tool, 292

• F •

Favorite Fills and Outlines
folder, 142
Feather dialog box, 319
fields, 33
file formats, 389–392
File menu (Alt+F) key
combination, 32
File Open (Alt+F,O) key
combination, 32
File⇨Acquire Image⇨Acquire
command, 387

File⇨Acquire Image⇨Acquire
from CorelScan command,
387
File⇨Apply Scene Wizard
command, 351
File⇨Close command, 288
File⇨Exit & Return command,
385
File⇨Exit command, 56, 267,
270, 288
File⇨Import command, 41, 272
File⇨New command, 38, 240,
283, 351
File⇨Open command, 21, 31–32,
38–39, 41, 265, 275, 277
File⇨Print command,
250–251, 253–254, 288, 354,
386
File⇨Print Preview command,
257, 288, 354
File⇨Revert command, 296
File⇨Save As command, 56, 278,
287
File⇨Save command, 54, 250,
287
File⇨Save Print Style As
command, 259
File⇨Update Graphic command,
385
files
importing, 41–43
information about, 41
opening, 31
organizing, 15–16
Scrapbook and importing or
opening, 42–43
fill tool, 125, 291, 300
fills, 124–125
color, 24, 145–146, 300
concentric, 170
entire image, 299
extruding, 187
geometric shapes, 297–298
gradients, 141, 143–145, 301
images, 299–301
on the fly, 143–145
open paths, 83
outlines and, 138–139
patterns, 141–142
Photo-Paint images, 291
PostScript, 142
solid-color, 124–125
special effects, 139–142
textures, 142, 301
transparent, 24
Find and Replace toolbar, 146

Fit Text To Path roll-up, 228–233
floating selection, 322–323
flyout menu, 28–30
folders, closing, 41
fonts. See also typefaces, 206,
208
Format Text (Ctrl+T) keyboard
shortcut, 204, 206, 210, 212
Format Text dialog box, 204,
206, 210–212
formatting text, 202, 204–212
Forward One command,
(Ctrl+Page Up) keyboard
shortcut, 121, 382
Fountain Fill (F11) keyboard
shortcut, 358
Fountain Fill dialog box, 145, 358
frames, 211
free-floating objects, 332–337
free-floating zoom tool palette,
47–48
free-form
drawing, 80–84
ines, 27
paths, 100, 237
shapes with straight sides, 297
freehand mask tool, 313–314
freehand tool. See pencil tool
Full Screen Preview (F9)
keyboard shortcut,
52–53, 379
full-color artwork, printing,
259–260

• G •

geometric shapes, 297–298
GIF file format, 392
Go To Page dialog box, 242
Gossip icon, 5
gradations, 141
gradients, 141, 143–145, 299,
301–303
grid, 102, 105–107
aligning objects, 116
guidelines and, 110
Photo-Paint, 282
Grid & Ruler Setup dialog box,
103, 105–106
Grid and Ruler command, 103
Grid and Ruler Setup command,
105
Grid dialog box, 347
grid frequency, 106
Group (Ctrl+G) keyboard
shortcut, 118, 151,
153–154, 161, 171, 364

grouping objects, 41, 118–119
  before duplicating, 151–153
  Envelope feature, 174
  Perspective function objects, 171
  selecting single object, 119
  before transforming, 161
guidelines, 102, 108–110
Guidelines Setup dialog box, 108–109

• **H** •

hairlines, 135
hand tool, 48–50, 281
handles, 40, 41, 165
  guidelines, 109
  snapping to grid, 106–107
  text blocks, 220
hard disk, 394
hardware requirements, 393
hidden tools, 28–30
Hierarchy window, 343
histogram, 330
hotkeys in dialog boxes, 34
hyphenation, 211

• **I** •

Image Club, 160
image list, 308, 310
image sprayer tool, 289, 308–310
Image⇒Adjust⇒Level Equalization command, 325, 329
Image⇒Color Table command, 284
Image⇒Convert To submenu, 287
Image⇒Convert To⇒Grayscale (8-bit) command, 331
Image⇒Preserve Image command, 332
Image⇒Resample command, 286
Image⇒Transform⇒Invert command, 370
Image⇒Transform⇒Posterize command, 370
imageable area guide, 258
images
  background color, 291, 295
  blurring pixels, 307
  brightening areas, 306
  canvas color, 285
  cloning selection, 322, 324–325
  closing, 287–288
  color, 284–285, 290–292, 299, 307, 321
  colorizing, 304, 306

combining, 324–325
contrast, 306, 329–331
copying portions of, 307–308
correcting focus and contrast, 325–331
defloating selection, 323
deleting everything outside selection outline, 324
dpi (dots per inch), 283–284
drawing lines, 296–297
erasing, 293–295
fills, 291, 295, 299–301
floating selection, 322–323
foreground color, 290–291, 295
ghosted special effect, 367–370
gradients, 299–301
manipulating portions, 312–322
masks, 313–318
mixing pixels randomly, 306
modifying, 322–324
moving selection, 322
new, 282–283
nudging, 322
opening, 277–278
painting, 303–305, 323
patterns, 299
pixels, 284
printing, 287–288
replacing color with fill, 300
resolution, 283–284, 286
reverting to saved, 296
saving, 287–288
selecting all pixels in, 321
selection outlines, 313–322
selections as free-floating objects, 332–337
sharpening focus, 307, 326–327
shuffling colors special effect, 370
smearing color, 306
special effects, 305–307
spraying objects onto, 308–310
text and, 337–340
textures, 299–301
transparent fill, 299
undoing actions to, 295–296
viewing, 279–282
World Wide Web resolution, 286
zooming and scrolling, 280
Import (Ctrl+I) keyboard shortcut, 41, 272
Import dialog box, 41, 272

importing, 39, 41–43, 270, 272, 345–346
in-place editing, 268–269
indenting text, 211
Insert New Object dialog box, 271
Insert Page dialog box, 240–241
insertion marker, 193, 198–199
installing CorelDraw 7, 393–398
interactive fill tool, 139, 143–145
interactive gradient fill tool, 301–303
interface, 20–25, 52, 56
  Photo-Paint, 274–275
inverting selection outlines, 321
irregular polygons, 83

• **J** •

joining two independent open paths, 96
JPEG file format, 392
justification, 209

• **K** •

kerning, 222–223
keyboard, 26, 34
keyboard shortcuts, 32
knife tool, 96–98
Kodak Photo CD technology, 11

• **L** •

lasso mask tool, 265, 314, 319
lasso tool, 265
Last Back button, 242
Last Page button, 241–242
layers, 244–245, 383–384
Layers Manager (Ctrl+F3) keyboard shortcut, 244, 384
Layers roll-up, 244–247
Layout⇒Delete Page command, 242
Layout⇒Go To Page command, 242
Layout⇒Grid and Ruler command, 105
Layout⇒Grid and Ruler Setup command, 103
Layout⇒Guidelines Setup command, 108

Layout⇨Insert Page command, 240–241
Layout⇨Layer Manager command, 244, 384
Layout⇨Page Setup command, 247
Layout⇨Snap To Grid command, 107, 224
Layout⇨Snap To Guidelines command, 110
less-known features, 384–388
Level Equalization (Ctrl+E) keyboard shortcut, 329
Level Equalization dialog box, 329–331
lever, 86
line breaks, 194
line tool, 289–290, 296–297
line weight, 130
line widths, 130, 132–136, 145–146
lines, 27–28, 81–82
linked text blocks, 201–203, 205
linking objects, 270–271
Load Image List dialog box, 308–309
Local Undo tool, 294–295

• M •

magenta, 128
magic scissors mask tool, 314–315
magic scissors tool, 321
magic wand mask tool, 315
magic wand tool, 321
magnifying drawings, 43–48
manipulating objects, 27–28
marquee, 90
Marquee Hidden (Ctrl+Shift+H) keyboard shortcut, 333
Marquee Visible (Ctrl+H) keyboard shortcut, 316
mask brush tool, 315–317, 321
mask tools, 312–318, 322
mask transform tool, 321
Mask⇨Create command, 333, 339
Mask⇨Defloat command, 323, 325
Mask⇨Feather command, 319
Mask⇨Float command, 323–324
Mask⇨Grow command, 321
Mask⇨Invert command, 321, 340

Mask⇨Marquee Visible command, 316, 333
Mask⇨Mode submenu, 321–322
Mask⇨Remove command, 321
Mask⇨Select All command, 321
Mask⇨Shape⇨Expand command, 321
Mask⇨Shape⇨Reduce command, 321
Mask⇨Similar command, 321
Mask⇨Stroke Mask command, 324
masks, 313–317, 323
master layer, 243–247
Master Page Settings dialog box, 246–247
math, 10
maximizing windows, 20
memory, 394
    available to Photo-Paint, 285
    roll-ups, 34
menu bar, 21
menus, 21, 31–32
    Alt-key combinations for, 32, 275
    displaying, 378–379
minimizing windows, 20, 21
mirroring, 160–161, 165
models, 169, 342, 346–347
modifying images, 322–324
morphing between two shapes special effect, 360–361
mouse, 25–26
Move Direction of Arrow (Alt+arrow key) key combination, 50
Move to End command, 126
Move to Start command, 126
movie files included with program, 16
moving around drawing area, 43–50
Multimedia Manager, 15–16

• N •

natural pen tool, 84, 85, 130
navigating dialog boxes, 378
Navigator window, 281, 282
New (Ctrl+N) keyboard shortcut, 38, 240, 283, 377
new document, 38
Next Option (Tab) keyboard shortcut, 34, 378
Next Shape (Tab) keyboard shortcut, 76

Node Edit roll-up, 90–93, 95–96, 98–99, 118
node edit tool, 67
nodes, 66, 67, 82
    adding, 93
    aligning, 99, 118
    constraining dragging, 89
    constraining to grid, 105
    control points, 86–87, 89, 99
    cusp, 89, 94
    deleting, 93
    editing, 85–99
    Envelope feature adding and subtracting, 177
    lever, 86
    moving, 87
    Perspective function, 172
    problems dragging, 70
    removing nonessential, 99
    reshaping drawing, 87–90
    selecting, 86, 90
    smooth, 87, 94
    snapping to grid, 106–107
    splitting, 95
    stretching other nodes to, 99
    text blocks, 220
    too many, 94
    viewing, 86
normal mode, 50
Normal mode (Ctrl+period (.)) keyboard shortcut, 322
nudging objects, 112
Number of Regions submenu, 111

• O •

Object Position dialog box, 72
Object Properties dialog box, 205, 236, 365
    Alt+Enter keyboard shortcut, 64, 205
    Apply button, 65
    Center Alignment button, 209
    Font pop-up menu, 206
    Forced Full Alignment button, 209
    Format Text button, 210
    formatting text, 204
    Full Alignment button, 209
    Left Alignment button, 209
    No Alignment button, 209
    Number of Points/Sides option, 64
    Polygon option, 64
    Range pop-up menu, 205

Right Alignment button, 209
Sharpness option, 65
Star option, 64
Text panel, 205, 209
object-oriented software, 10
Object⇨Create From Mask
    command, 265, 332
Object⇨Drop Shadow
    command, 340
Object⇨Duplicate command,
    325, 334
Object⇨Flip submenu, 336
Object⇨Rotate submenu, 336
objects, 81–82
    aligning, 115–117
    bending and twisting, 173–178
    blending between, 384
    changing entire, 75
    cloning, 325, 334
    color, 350
    converting shapes to, 298
    copying, 381–382
    copying and transferring,
        147–151
    deleting, 334
    distorting, 335
    distributing, 115–118
    duplicating, 115, 147–158
    extruding, 179–187
    flipping, 160–164, 336
    grouping, 118–119, 174
    importing, 345–346
    linking, 270–271, 386
    magnifying, 345–346
    manipulating, 27–28, 333,
        380–381
    mirror images of, 160–161
    moving, 112–115, 334
    moving in 3D space, 347–348
    nudging, 112
    printing selected, 255
    ready-made backdrop,
        351–352
    rotating, 161, 164–169,
        335–349
    scaling, 160–164, 334, 348, 349
    separating 3-D, 187
    shaders, 350
    skewing, 161, 164–169, 335
    spraying onto images, 308–310
    stacking order, 120–122
    Super Nudge, 112
    textures, 350
    transferring from Photo-Paint
        to CorelDraw, 264–269
    transforming, 334, 336–337

    ungrouping, 119
    welding, 385
Objects Browser window, 322,
    345
Objects roll-up, 337, 369–370
    Ctrl+F7 keyboard shortcut, 368
OCR (optical character
    recognition), 14, 388
OLE (object linking and
    embedding), 264–271
On CorelDraw Start-Up
    pop-up menu, 18
online services and download-
    ing photos, 11
Open (Ctrl+O) keyboard
    shortcut, 21, 32, 39, 265,
    275, 277, 377
Open an Image dialog box, 277
Open Drawing dialog box, 39, 41
open paths, 80–82
    closing, 95–96, 124
    extending, 84
    fills, 83
    independent, 95–96
    outlines, 132
Option dialog box, 64
Option Properties dialog box,
    207–208
Options (Ctrl+J) keyboard
    shortcut, 38, 55, 78, 112,
    153, 167, 197, 199, 214, 222,
    243, 281, 288, 296, 305, 317,
    322, 333
Options dialog box
    Advanced tab, 55
    Angle value, 85
    Auto-backup option, 55
    Auto-Save Every option, 288
    Automatic View Resize option,
        281
    Automatically Close Object
        option, 97
    Calligraphy option, 85
    Constrain Angle option, 167
    Corner Threshold option, 94
    Default Text Units pop-up
        menu, 209
    Expand and Shrink Paragraph
        Text Frames to Fit Text
        option, 197, 200, 243
    Fixed Width option, 85
    Freehand Tracking option, 94
    General tab, 18, 38, 112, 167,
        281, 305, 322, 334
    Horizontal option, 153

Marquee tab, 317, 333
Maximum Width option, 85
Memory tab, 296
Nudge option, 112, 222–223
On CorelDraw Start-Up pop-up
    menu, 18
Perform Automatic Spell
    Checking option, 199
Polygon as Star option, 64
polygon default setting, 63
Polygon option, 64
Presets option, 85
Pressure option, 85
Replace Text While Typing
    option, 215
Shape Cursor for Brush Tools
    option, 305
Sharpness option, 65
Show Errors Which Have Been
    Turned Off option, 199
Spelling tab, 199
Star option, 64
Start a new Document from
    the On CorelDraw Startup
    menu option, 38
Straight Line Threshold
    option, 94
Super Nudge option, 112
Text tab, 197, 209
Thickness option, 97
Toolbox panel, 65
Type Assist tab, 214–215
Undo Levels option, 78, 296
Vertical option, 153
Warn Me Before Saving
    option, 288
Outline (F12) keyboard
    shortcut, 135
Outline Pen dialog box,
    134–138 359
outline tool, 130
outlines, 130–135
    automatically replacing
        color, 145–146
    caps, 136–138
    color, 24, 131, 134
    corners, 136–138
    custom line widths,
        135–136
    fills and, 138–139
    transparent, 24, 132
oval mask tool, 313
ovals, 61–62, 67. See also
    ellipses, 70

• P •

page boundary, 23
page controls, 24
Page Setup dialog box,
    247–248
Page tabs, 241, 242
pages, 240–243
    grouping multiple for printing
        on one page, 252
    master layer, 243–247
    moving between, 241–242
    object alignment position, 116
    preview options, 257–259
    printing images centered, 256
    resizing, 247–248
    resizing drawing while
        printing, 255–256
paint tool, 290, 295–297,
    303–305, 339, 340
painting images 11, 303–305
paintings, 12–13
pan one-shot tool, 48
pan tool, 48
paper, 251–252
paragraph text, 192
    automatically growing or
        shrinking text block, 197
    automatically wrapping, 195
    converting to artistic text
        blocks, 203–204
    creation, 192, 195–196
    editing, 196–198
    evenly spacing lines between,
        225–226
    flowing between text blocks,
        199–201
    Format Text dialog box,
        210–212
    formatting attributes, 204–205
    frames, 211
    limitations, 198
    rotating, 197
    scaling text block, 196
    skewing, 197
    symbols at beginning of, 211
    too much text for text block,
        197
    wrapping around graphic
        special effect, 364–365
Paste (Ctrl+V) keyboard
    shortcut, 148, 204, 269,
    325, 332, 360, 381
pasteboard, 24, 150
path node edit tool, 313

paths, 81–82
    bending, 89
    breaking apart, 96–98
    changing default options, 138
    closed, 80–82
    closing, 83–84, 95–97
    concentric fills, 170
    corners, 89
    detaching text from, 237
    duplicating several at a time,
        151–153
    editing, 85–86
    editing text on, 236–237
    erasing part while drawing, 83
    extending open, 84
    fills, 124–125
    finding lost, 132
    fitting text to, 226–237
    free-form, 100
    gradients, 141
    intermediate shapes
        between, 170
    joining two independent
        open, 96
    nodes, 82, 93
    open, 80–82
    opening closed, 95
    outlines, 130–135
    rounding corners, 136
    rubber, 99
    segments, 82
    splitting open into indepen-
        dent paths, 95
    straight lines, 83
    tips for successful, 83–84
patterns
    CorelDream 3D, 342
    fills, 141–142
    images, 299
PCD file format, 392
PCX file format, 391
Pen roll-up, 132–135
pen tool, 130, 132–133
    F12 keyboard shortcut, 359
pencil tool, 27, 80, 82–84, 94, 130
    F5 keyboard shortcut, 80, 380
pentagons, 63
Perspective function, 169–172
Photo-Paint, 10–11, 273–274
    auto-save feature, 288
    automatically resizing
        window, 281
    canvas color, 285
    changing photo resolution and
        color, 286–287
    cloning objects, 325
    color palette, 290–291

combining images, 324–325
copying portions of images,
    307–308
correcting focus and contrast,
    325–331
custom backgrounds, 299
custom gradients, 301–303
default colors, 291
describing tool in status
    bar, 275
dragging images from
    Scrapbook, 278
drawing lines, 296–297
drawings, 13
editing screen shots, 14
Effects menu, 327–328
erasing images, 293–295
exiting, 267
file formats, 278
filling images, 299–301
free-floating objects,
    332–337
geometric shapes, 297–298
getting photos onto Photo CD
    or floppy disk, 10–11
grids, 282
guidelines, 282
image color, 290–291
interface, 274–275
keyboard shortcuts, 275
linking object to CorelDraw,
    270–271
manipulating portions of
    images, 312–322
matching colors, 292
Maximize button, 280
memory available to, 285
modifying images, 322–324
moving Property Bar, toolbar,
    or toolbox, 276
Navigator window, 281–282
new image, 282–283
number of colors, 284–285
opening images, 265, 277–278
painting, 11, 303–305
pixels, 12, 284
print preview, 288
Property Bar, 275
removing toolbar and
    Property Bar buttons, 276
replacing foreground color
    with background color,
    295
resolution, 283–286
reverting images to saved, 296
right-clicking and pop-up
    menus, 276

rulers, 282
scanning, 387
selecting commands from
    menus, 275
separating color channels, 387
special effects, 305–307
spraying objects onto images,
    308–310
starting, 274
text, 337–340
Tool Settings roll-up, 276
toolbar, 275–276
toolbox, 289–290
tools, 276
Tools menu, 282
transferring object to
    CorelDraw, 264–269
translucent background
    color, 295
viewing images, 279–282
versus CorelDraw, 12–13
Welcome screen, 274
windows, 280–281
zooming and scrolling
    images, 280–281
Photo-Paint Color Mode
    roll-up, 284–285
photos, 10–11
    color changes, 286–287
    colorizing grayscale, 307
    CorelDraw and, 13
    downloading, 11
    getting onto Photo CD or
        floppy disk, 10–11
    matching colors, 292
    opening, 277–278
    provided with CorelDraw 7, 16,
        277–278
    resolution changes, 286–287
    scanning, 11
    stock, 11
    viewing, 279–282
    zooming and scrolling, 280
Photos folder, 277
pick tool, 75, 312. *See* arrow tool
pies, 68–72
pixels, 12, 284
planet with ring around it
    special effect, 358–360
plates, 260
points, 130, 207–208
polygon tool, 30, 63, 65, 291, 297
polygons, 63–65, 67, 72–75
pop-up menus, 33
Position (Alt+F7) keyboard
    shortcut, 112

Position roll-up, 112–115
PostScript
    fills, 142
    fonts, 208
PowerClip feature, 170
Prepress toolbar, 258
Preserve Image (Ctrl+Q)
    keyboard shortcut, 332
preview mode (Ctrl+Alt+Shift+Y)
    keyboard shortcut, 346
Previous Option (Shift+Tab)
    keyboard shortcut, 34, 378
Previous Shape (Shift+Tab)
    keyboard shortcut, 76
Print (Ctrl+P) keyboard
    shortcut, 250–255, 259,
    288, 377, 386
Print dialog box, 251–255, 257,
    259, 288, 386
Print Options dialog box,
    255–259, 258
Print Preview dialog box, 255
print preview window, 257–260
Print Setup dialog box, 258
print style, saving, 259
printer properties dialog box,
    251–252
printers, 249–250
    color, 259
    imageable area guide, 258
    Photo-Paint resolution, 286
    quality of printing, 10
    selecting, 251, 258
printing, 253
    3D drawings, 353–354
    basic steps, 250
    centering images on page, 256
    certain pages, 254–255
    changing paper size and
        orientation, 251–252
    collating, 254
    color printer, 259
    color separations, 258–260
    drawing orientation, 252
    entire document, 253–254
    full–color artwork, 259–260
    grouping multiple to print on
        one page, 252
    halting, 254
    hiding master layers, 247
    images, 287–288
    multiple copies, 254
    page preview options, 257–259
    plates, 260
    reducing drawing to fit, 256
    resizing drawing on page,
        255–256

saving print style, 259
selected objects, 255
selecting printer, 251
Programs⇨CorelDraw 7⇨
    CorelDream 3D command,
    342
Property Bar, 22–23, 90, 130, 231
    Actual Size button, 47
    Additive button, 322
    Align button, 115
    anti-aliasing option, 297, 301
    Apply button, 303
    B button, 207
    Center Alignment button, 209
    cloning images, 307–308
    Color roll-up button, 292
    controls, 22
    Convert Text button, 203
    default layout, 23
    Depth option, 187
    dimmed buttons, 92
    Distance from path option, 231
    editing extrusions, 180,
        186–187
    editing nodes, 92
    Ending Angle option, 359
    Facing Pages option, 248
    Feather Mask button, 319
    Fill button, 298
    fill types, 143
    fitting text to path options, 228
    Font pop-up menu, 206
    Forced Full Alignment
        button, 209
    Format Text button, 210, 212
    formatting text, 204–207
    Fountain Fill option, 143
    From Color pop-up menu, 187
    Full Alignment button, 209
    Gradient Type icons, 144, 302
    Group button, 118, 154, 161
    Grow button, 321
    hand tool, 48
    Height option, 247–248
    hiding, 23
    Horizontal Size control,
        76–77
    I button, 207
    Landscape option, 248
    Left Alignment button, 209
    line options, 297
    Load Image List button, 308
    lock icon, 76
    mirror buttons, 162
    Mirror Horizontal button, 72
    moving, 23, 276

(continued)

Property Bar *(continued)*
  moving objects, 112–113
  No Alignment button, 209
  node editing buttons, 93, 177
  Normal button, 322
  Nudge box, 112
  Object Color icons, 187
  Object Positions option, 334
  object size controls, 161
  Opacity and merge mode
    controls options, 337
  Page Width button, 47
  Paper pop-up menu, 247
  Photo-Paint, 275
  polygon tool and controls, 65
  Portrait option, 248
  proportional sizing
    control, 162
  Radius option, 321
  rearranging or removing
    buttons, 23, 276
  Render to Mask option, 339
  Render to Object button, 332
  reshaping controls, 70
  resizing and reshaping, 23
  resizing and reshaping
    eraser, 295
  resizing and rotating artistic
    text block, 195
  resizing pages, 247–248
  Right Alignment button, 209
  roll-up icons, 187
  rotation angle option box, 166
  rounding corners, 68
  Roundness slider, 68
  Save Objects as Image List
    option, 310
  scale factor controls, 161
  Shade option, 187
  Show All Objects button, 47
  Show Page Button, 47
  Show/Hide Drop Cap
    button, 212
  Similar button, 321
  size and scale controls, 196
  Size pop-up menu, 208
  Snap to Grid button, 107
  Snap to Guidelines button, 110
  special effects brushes,
    305–307
  Starting Angle option, 359
  Stroke Mask button, 324
  Subtractive button, 322
  text alignment, 209
  text settings, 338–339
  To Back button, 121
  To Color pop-up menu, 187

To Front button, 121
Tolerance option, 295, 300,
  319, 321
transformations, 321, 335
Ungroup All button, 119
Ungroup button, 119
Units pop-up menu, 103–104
vanishing point controls, 186
Vertical Size control, 76–77
View Manager button, 47
Width option, 247–248
X option, 77, 113, 115, 153,
  194, 221
XOR Mask button, 322
Y option, 77, 113, 115, 153,
  194, 221
Zoom 100% icon, 279
Zoom 1:1 option, 280
Zoom In button, 46, 280
Zoom Level pop-up menu, 46,
  279–280
Zoom Out button, 46
Zoom to Fit button, 280
Zoom to Selected button, 47
zoom tools, 46

• *Q* •

quotation marks, 215

• *R* •

radial symmetry, 73
radio buttons, 33
Rat.CDR file, 40
Reapply Effect (Ctrl+F)
  keyboard shortcut,
  327–328
rectangle mask tool, 313
rectangle tool, 60–61, 291, 297,
  299
  F6 keyboard shortcut, 60, 380
rectangles, 60–61, 67–68, 297
rectangular mask icon, 265
rectangular mask tool, 313
redoing actions, 78
reflecting, 160–161
Remove (Ctrl+D) keyboard
  shortcut, 321
Render (Ctrl+R) keyboard
  shortcut, 354
rendering 3D drawings,
  353–354
Rendering Settings dialog
  box, 353
repeat brush stroke tool, 313
repeating pattern special effect,
  374–376

Replace Wizard dialog box,
  145–146
Resample dialog box, 286–287
resolution, 267, 283–284,
  286–287
restoring windows, 20
reverting images to saved, 296
RGB (red, green, blue) color
  model, 128–129
right-clicking, 26
roll-ups, 34–36
Rotate (Alt+F11) keyboard
  shortcut, 168
Rotate (Alt+F8) keyboard
  shortcut, 168
rotating, 160–161
  15-degree increments, 167
  extrusions, 181
  handles, 165
  objects, 161, 164–169, 335–337,
    348–349
  paragraph text, 197
  segments, 99
  shapes, 77
  text, 195
Rotation roll-up, 167–168
rubber paths, 99
rulers, 24, 102–105
  dragging guidelines from, 108
  Photo-Paint, 282
  print preview window, 258

• *S* •

Save (Ctrl+S) keyboard
  shortcut, 54–55, 250, 287,
  354, 377
Save an Image to Disk dialog
  box, 287–288, 310
Save dialog box, 354
Save Drawing dialog box, 54, 56
Scale & Mirror roll-up, 71–72,
  163–164
  Alt+F9 keyboard shortcut, 71,
    163, 362
scaling, 160
  objects, 161–164, 334–349
  segments, 99
  shapes, 76–77
  text blocks, 196
scanners, 11
Scene Wizard, 351–352
Scene⇨Camera Settings
  command, 388
Scene⇨Render Settings
  command, 353

Scene⇨Render⇨Low Res
Preview command, 353
scenes, 342, 351
Scrapbook roll-up, 42–43, 139,
142, 145, 278
screen
display modes, 50–51
items on, 19–23
screen shots of, 14
screen shots, 14
scroll bars, 24
segments, 82, 86–87, 89, 96–98
Perspective function, 172
selection handles, 75
selection outlines, 313–322
service bureaus, 11
Shaders Browser window,
342, 350
shadow for text special effect,
361–363
shape tool, 65, 67–70, 237,
380–381
F10 keyboard shortcut, 67,
70–71, 86, 220, 359, 380
number of path nodes, 82
reshaping drawing, 67, 87–90
rounding corners, 67–68
selecting multiple text nodes,
221–222
viewing nodes, 86
shapes, 59, 81–82
assigning depth, 179
blending color with shapes
below, 170
circles, 61–62, 297
converting to free-form
paths, 100
converting to object, 298
deleting, 77
duplicating, 71
ellipses, 297
filling, 125, 143
flipping, 77
free-form with straight
sides, 297
intermediate between paths,
170
moving, 77
nodes, 66–67, 70, 93
ovals, 61–62
polygons, 63–65
rectangles, 60–61, 297
redoing actions to, 78
reshaping, 66–72
rotating, 77
rounding corners, 67–68
scaling, 76–77

selecting, 64, 75–76
slanting, 77
squares, 60–61, 297
transparent fill, 125
undoing actions to, 77–78
Show submenu, 111
simple wireframe mode, 51
Skew roll-up, 167–169
skewing, 160–161
15-degree increments, 167
handles, 165
objects, 164–169, 335
paragraph text, 197
segments, 99
shapes, 77
text, 195
small caps, 210
smooth nodes, 87, 94, 98
Snap To Grid (Ctrl+Y) keyboard
shortcut, 107, 110
software requirements, 393
sound files included with
program, 16
special effects, 357
2D Effects submenu, 371–373
3D Effects submenu, 371–374
ghosted images, 367–370
morphing between two
shapes, 360–361
Photo-Paint, 305–307
planet with ring around it,
358–360
repeating pattern, 374–376
shadow for text, 361–363
shuffling colors in image, 370
text zooming across screen,
365–367
type bulging like balloon,
363–364
wrapping paragraph text
around graphic, 364–365
Special Fill roll-up, 139–142
Ctrl+F keyboard shortcut, 227
Spell Check (Ctrl+F12) keyboard
shortcut, 213
Spell Checker dialog box,
213–214
spell checking text, 213–214
squares, 60–61, 297
stacking order, rearranging,
120–122
standard eraser tool, 294–295
stars, 64–65, 67, 72–74
Start Arrow pop-up menu, 135
Start menu (Ctrl+Esc) keyboard
shortcut, 378

Start⇨Programs⇨CorelDraw 7⇨
Corel Photo-Paint 7
command, 265, 274
startup, automatically
performing Welcome
screen actions, 18
status bar, 25, 102, 111–110
artistic text block or paragraph text indicator, 204
Cone and Control, 156
corresponding to horizontal
ruler, 105
describing Photo-Paint
tools, 275
number of path nodes, 82
numerical cursor coordinates,
102
transformation percentage
points, 163
stencils, 170
sticky notes, 385
stock photos, 11
straight lines, 83
straight segments, curving, 98
stretching handles, 165
subscript, 210
Subtractive mode
(Ctrl+minus (-)) keyboard
shortcut, 322
SUNFLOWR.CPT file, 308
Super Nudge (Ctrl+arrow keys)
keyboard shortcut,
222, 322
superscript, 210
Switch Mode (Shift+F9)
keyboard shortcut, 51
Switch Program (Alt+Tab)
Alt-key combination, 378
Switch Tool
Ctrl+Spacebar keyboard
shortcut, 76, 193, 195, 362,
379–380
Spacebar keyboard shortcut, 76,
312, 379–380
symbols, 192, 216–217
Symbols roll-up, 216–217
Ctrl+F11 keyboard shortcut,
216

● *T* ●

tabs, 200, 211
target object, 116
taskbar
Alt+Esc keyboard shortcut,
378
minimizing windows to, 21

Technical Stuff icon, 5
ten file formats, 389–392
ten less-known features, 383–388
ten special effects, 357–376
ten time-saving shortcuts, 377–382
Terrazzo dialog box, 374–376
text, 191–192
  adding, 338–339
  alignment, 209
  all capital letters, 210
  alternative spellings, 199
  attaching to geometric object, 231
  automatically fixing typing errors, 214–216
  backing up before attaching to paths, 238
  baseline, 226
  capitalizing word following period, 214
  characters, 192, 223–224
  circle, 231–235
  condensed, 194
  creation of, 192
  detaching from path, 237
  drop caps, 212
  editing path, 236–237
  enlarging or reducing size, 207–209
  evenly spacing words, 224
  expanded, 194
  fitting to paths, 226–237
  flowing between pages, 243
  flowing between text blocks, 199–201
  formatting, 202–212
  images and, 337–340
  indents, 211
  insertion marker, 198–199
  justification, 209
  kerning, 222–223
  line spacing, 211, 225–226
  misspelled, 199
  modifying, 338–339
  multiple columns, 211
  names of days, 215
  painting inside, 339–340
  points, 207–208
  quotation marks, 215
  replacing abbreviations with spelled-out words, 215
  repositioning characters, 221–222
  returning character to original position, 222
  rotated, 195
  selecting, 202
  selecting typeface, 206
  skewed, 195
  small caps, 210
  spacing between letters and words, 211
  spell checking, 213–214
  subscript, 210
  superscript, 210
  symbols, 211, 216–217
  tabs, 211
  three-dimensional effects, 15
  two capital letters in a row, 215
  type styles, 207
  underlining, 210
  units of measurement, 209
  zooming across screen special effect, 365–367
text blocks. See also artistic text blocks
  affecting all text in, 206
  artistic, 192–195
  automatically growing or shrinking, 197
  flowing text between, 199–201
  formatting text, 202–212
  hyphenation, 211
  linked, 201
  moving, 194
  nodes and handles, 220
  paragraph text, 192
  scaling, 196
  selecting and dragging text nodes, 221–222
  spacing handles, 223–224, 226
  tabs, 200
  too much text for, 197
text effects, 219–220
  attaching text to geometric object, 231
  detaching text from path, 237
  editing path, 236–237
  editing text on path, 236
  evenly spacing characters, 223–224
  evenly spacing lines, 225–226
  fitting text to path, 223
  kerning, 222–223
  repositioning characters, 221–222
  selecting and dragging text nodes, 221–222
  text on circle, 231–235
text objects, 192
text tool, 192–193, 195, 199, 201–203, 206, 226–227, 243, 290, 337–339
  F8 keyboard shortcut, 193, 195, 338, 362, 364, 380
Text toolbar, 205
Text⇨Convert to Artistic Text command, 204
Text⇨Convert to Paragraph Text command, 204
Text⇨Edit Text command, 198, 236
Text⇨Fit Text to Path command, 227, 232
Text⇨Format Text command, 204, 206
Text⇨Straighten Text command, 222, 237
Text⇨Writing Tools⇨Spell Check command, 213
Text⇨Writing Tools⇨Type Assist command, 214
textures
  CorelDream 3D, 342
  custom, 15
  fills, 142
  images, 299
  objects, 350
three-dimensional text effects, 15
thumbnail views of drawings, 42–43
TIFF file format, 391
time-saving shortcuts, 377–382
Tip icon, 5
title bar, 20–21
To Back (Shift+Page Down) keyboard shortcut, 121
To Front (Shift+Page Up) keyboard shortcut, 121, 151, 153
toggle, 51
Tool Settings roll-up, 276, 290
  Add option, 304
  alternative brushes, 304–305
  anti-aliasing option, 297, 301, 303, 319
  Apply button, 303
  Blend brush, 307
  Brightness brush, 306
  brushes, 303
  cloning images, 307–308
  Color option, 304
  Contrast brush, 306
  Ctrl+F8 keyboard shortcut, 276, 280, 290

Edit button, 297
Eraser brush, 308
Feather option, 319
Flat Fill option, 298
Flip options, 336
Fountain Fill option, 297
gradients or textures, 301–302
Hue brush, 306
Hue Replacer brush, 306
Impressionism Clone brush, 308
line options, 297
Load Image List command, 308
No Fill option, 297
Normal clone brush, 307
Object Positions option, 334
Object Scale tab, 336
Paint pop-up menu, 304
paint tool options, 303–305
Pointillism Clone brush, 308
Radius option, 321
Render to Mask option, 339
Render to Object option, 298, 332
resizing and reshaping eraser, 295
Save Objects as Image List option, 310
Sharpen brush, 307
Smear brush, 306
Smudge brush, 306
special effects brushes, 305–307
Sponge brush, 307
Subtract option, 304
text settings, 338–339
Tint brush, 307
Tolerance option, 300, 319, 321
transformations, 321, 335
Undither brush, 307
Use Right Mouse Button for Zoom Out option, 280
toolbar, 21–22
buttons, 23, 276
CorelDream 3D, 343
default layout, 23
Draft View option, 50
hiding, 22, 276
moving, 23, 276
Open button, 21
Photo-Paint, 275
Preview icon, 346
resizing and reshaping, 23
Scrapbook roll-up icon, 142
Simple Wireframe option, 51
Wireframe option, 50

Zoom Level pop-up menu, 46, 280
Zoom to Selected icon, 345
Toolbars dialog box, 22, 31
toolbox, 23
CorelDream 3D, 343
enlarging/reducing tool icons, 31
flyout menu, 28–30
hidden tools, 28–30
moving, 30
Photo-Paint, 289–290
pop-up menu, 47
resizing, 30
returning to original location, 31
tools, 23, 26–29
cursors, 305
enlarging/reducing icons, 31
hidden, 28–30
options related to, 28–30
Photo-Paint, 276
Tools⇨Clipart command, 42
Tools⇨Object Data command, 386
Tools⇨Options command, 18, 38, 55, 78, 112, 153, 167, 197, 199, 222–223, 281, 288, 296, 305, 322
Tools⇨Symbols command, 216
tracking lines, 102
transferring objects, 147–151
transformations, 159–160
Contour function, 170
by degrees, 166–167
Envelope feature, 169, 173–178, 364
extruding, 169, 179–187
flipping, 160–164
free-floating objects, 334–337
grouping objects before, 161
intermediate shapes between paths, 170
Lens function, 170
Perspective function, 169–172
PowerClip feature, 170
rotate and skew handles, 165
rotating, 160–161, 164–169
scaling, 160–164
selection outlines, 321
skewing, 160–161, 164–169
stretch and mirror handles, 165
transparent fills and outlines, 24, 132
trapping colors, 386

TrueType fonts, 208
Type Assist, 214–216
type bulging like balloon special effect, 363–364
typefaces, 16, 206–207
Tyranno2.CDR file, 148

• *U* •

underlining text, 210
Undo
Alt+Backspace keyboard shortcut, 78, 110, 380
Ctrl+Shift+Z keyboard shortcut, 78, 380
Ctrl+Z keyboard shortcut, 78, 110, 151, 153, 296, 336, 380
undoing actions, 77–78, 295–296
Ungroup (Ctrl+U) keyboard shortcut, 119, 172, 180, 187
ungrouping
cloned group of objects, 157
objects, 119
units of measurement, 103
line widths, 134
Outline Pen dialog box, 136
text, 209
updating drawings, 55
user-created colors, 127–129, 131

• *V* •

vanishing point, 172, 180–181, 186
Version 7 icon, 5
View Grid (Ctrl+J) keyboard shortcut, 347
View⇨Color Palette command, 126
View⇨Color Palette⇨None command, 127
View⇨Default Quality⇨Better Preview command, 347
View⇨Default Quality⇨ Bounding Box command, 347
View⇨Default Quality⇨Preview command, 346
View⇨Default Quality⇨ Wireframe command, 347
View⇨Draft command, 50
View⇨Full Screen Preview command, 52
View⇨Grid command, 107, 347
View⇨Normal command, 51

View⇨Preview Selected Only
command, 53
View⇨Property Bar command,
23
View⇨Roll-Ups command, 35
View⇨Roll-Ups⇨Channels
command, 387
View⇨Roll-Ups⇨Color
command, 127, 131
View⇨Roll-Ups⇨Tool Settings
command, 276, 290
View⇨Roll-Ups⇨Tools⇨
Scrap-book command, 42,
142, 278
View⇨Rulers command, 102,
105
View⇨Simple Wireframe
command, 51
View⇨Status Bar command, 111
View⇨Toolbars command,
22–23, 276
View⇨Wireframe command,
50, 132
View⇨Zoom 100% command,
279
View⇨Zoom 1:1 command, 280
View⇨Zoom submenu, 280
virtual trackball tool, 348

• W •

Warning icon, 5
Welcome screen, 18, 274
WI file format, 390, 391
Window⇨Tile Horizontally
command, 157
Window⇨Tile Vertically
command, 157, 324
windows, 20–21, 281
Windows 95, 17–19
wireframe mode, 50–51, 346–347
Ctrl+Shift+Y keyboard
shortcut, 347
WMF file format, 390
work area, 342
working box, 342, 344
World Wide Web image
resolution, 286

• X •

XOR mode (Ctrl+asterisk (*))
keyboard shortcut, 322

• Y •

yellow, 128

• Z •

zero point, 102–103
Zoom 100% (Ctrl+1) keyboard
shortcut, 279, 379
Zoom All the Way Out (Shift+F4)
keyboard shortcut, 50
Zoom Enter Page (Shift+F4)
keyboard shortcut, 46, 379
Zoom Out (F3) keyboard
shortcuts, 46, 76, 172,
280–281, 345, 379
Zoom palette, 47–48, 50
Zoom See All (F4) keyboard
shortcut, 46
Zoom Selected Portion
(Shift+F2) keyboard
shortcut, 46, 345, 379
Zoom to Fit (F4) keyboard
shortcut, 280, 379
zoom tool, 44–46, 48, 279–281
F2 keyboard shortcut, 45, 280,
345, 379
zooming, 44–48

Pro WF

Windows Workflow in .NET 4

Bruce Bukovics

Apress®

Pro WF: Windows Workflow in .NET 4

ISBN-13 (pbk): 978-1-4302-2721-2

ISBN-13 (electronic): 978-1-4302-2722-9

Printed and bound in the United States of America 9 8 7 6 5 4 3 2 1

President and Publisher: Paul Manning
Lead Editor: Ewan Buckingham, Matt Moodie
Technical Reviewer: Matt Milner
Editorial Board: Clay Andres, Steve Anglin, Mark Beckner, Ewan Buckingham, Gary Cornell, Jonathan Gennick, Jonathan Hassell, Michelle Lowman, Matthew Moodie, Duncan Parkes, Jeffrey Pepper, Frank Pohlmann, Douglas Pundick, Ben Renow-Clarke, Dominic Shakeshaft, Matt Wade, Tom Welsh
Coordinating Editor: Jim Markham
Copy Editor: Kim Wimpsett
Production Support: Patrick Cunningham
Indexer: Brenda Miller
Artist: April Milne
Cover Designer: Anna Ishchenko

Distributed to the book trade worldwide by Springer Science+Business Media, LLC., 233 Spring Street, 6th Floor, New York, NY 10013. Phone 1-800-SPRINGER, fax (201) 348-4505, e-mail orders-ny@springer-sbm.com, or visit www.springeronline.com.

For information on translations, please e-mail rights@apress.com, or visit www.apress.com.

Apress and friends of ED books may be purchased in bulk for academic, corporate, or promotional use. eBook versions and licenses are also available for most titles. For more information, reference our Special Bulk Sales–eBook Licensing web page at www.apress.com/info/bulksales.

The source code for this book is available to readers at www.apress.com. You will need to answer questions pertaining to this book in order to successfully download the code.

For Teresa and Brennan

Contents at a Glance

About the Author xxxi

About the Technical Reviewer xxxii

Acknowledgments xxxiii

Introduction xxxiv

■Chapter 1: A Quick Tour of Windows Workflow Foundation 1

■Chapter 2: Foundation Overview 45

■Chapter 3: Activities 71

■Chapter 4: Workflow Hosting 111

■Chapter 5: Procedural Flow Control 163

■Chapter 6: Collection-Related Activities 195

■Chapter 7: Flowchart Modeling Style 229

■Chapter 8: Host Communication 265

■Chapter 9: Workflow Services 313

■Chapter 10: Workflow Services Advanced Topics 369

■Chapter 11: Workflow Persistence 415

■Chapter 12: Customizing Workflow Persistence 469

■Chapter 13: Transactions, Compensation, and Exception Handling 507

■Chapter 14: Workflow Tracking 565

■Chapter 15: Enhancing the Design Experience 629

For Teresa and Brennan

Contents at a Glance

About the Author xxxi

About the Technical Reviewer xxxii

Acknowledgments xxxiii

Introduction xxxiv

■Chapter 1: A Quick Tour of Windows Workflow Foundation 1

■Chapter 2: Foundation Overview 45

■Chapter 3: Activities 71

■Chapter 4: Workflow Hosting 111

■Chapter 5: Procedural Flow Control 163

■Chapter 6: Collection-Related Activities 195

■Chapter 7: Flowchart Modeling Style 229

■Chapter 8: Host Communication 265

■Chapter 9: Workflow Services 313

■Chapter 10: Workflow Services Advanced Topics 369

■Chapter 11: Workflow Persistence 415

■Chapter 12: Customizing Workflow Persistence 469

■Chapter 13: Transactions, Compensation, and Exception Handling 507

■Chapter 14: Workflow Tracking 565

■Chapter 15: Enhancing the Design Experience 629

■Chapter 16: Advanced Custom Activities 687

■Chapter 17: Hosting the Workflow Designer...753

■Chapter 18: WF 3.*x* Interop and Migration..801

■Appendix A: Glossary...849

■Appendix B: Comparing WF 3.x to WF 4 861

Index...869

Contents

About the Author xxxi

About the Technical Reviewers xxxii

Acknowledgments xxxiii

Introduction xxxiv

■Chapter 1: A Quick Tour of Windows Workflow Foundation 1

Why Workflow? 1

    Workflows Are Different 2

    Why Windows Workflow Foundation? 3

Your Development Environment 4

The Workflow Workflow 4

Hello Workflow 5

    Creating the Project 6

    Declaring the Workflow 8

    Adding the Sequence Activity 9

    Adding the WriteLine Activity 10

    Hosting the Workflow 12

    Running the Application 14

    Exploring the Xaml 15

Passing Parameters 17

    Declaring the Workflow 17

    Hosting the Workflow 20

Running the Application 21

Using Argument Properties 21

Making Decisions 22

Creating the Project 23

Implementing a Custom Activity 23

Defining Arguments 25

Defining Variables 26

Adding the Custom Activity 28

Adding the Switch<T> and Assign Activities 29

Hosting the Workflow 34

Running the Application 35

Debugging the Application 37

Unit Testing 39

Testing the Custom Activity 39

Testing the Workflow 41

Summary 43

■ Chapter 2: Foundation Overview 45

WF Features and Capabilities 45

Declarative Activity Model 45

Standard Activities 46

Custom Activities 46

Workflow Designer 47

Custom Activity Designers and Validation 47

Multiple Modeling Styles 47

Workflow Debugger 48

Workflow Services 48

Multiple Workflow Hosts 48

Workflow Extensions 49

Persistence 49

Bookmark Processing..49

Expressions 50

Transaction Support 50

Compensation and Exception Handling 50

Workflow Tracking..50

Designer Rehosting 51

WF 3.x Migration..51

Assemblies and Namespaces..51

System.Activities 51

System.Activities.DurableInstancing 52

System.Runtime.DurableInstancing 52

System.Activities.Presentation 53

System.ServiceModel.Activities 53

3.x Assemblies 54

Activity Life Cycle 55

Definition vs. Runtime Instance..55

Definition vs. Runtime Variables...56

Activity States...57

Expressions 57

Visual Basic Expressions 58

VB Primer for Workflow Developers 58

Expression Activities...62

Missing 4 Features 66

State Machine..67

Reuse of WCF Contracts 67

C# Expression Support 68

Tracking to SQL Server 68

Rules Engine..68

Dynamic Updates..68

Summary 68

■**Chapter 3: Activities** **71**

Understanding Activities...71

    Authoring Activities 72

    Kinds of Work 72

    Kinds of Data 74

    Activity Class Hierarchy 76

    Custom Activity Workflow...78

An Example Activity 78

Implementing an Activity in Code 78

    Creating the Project...79

    Implementing the Activity...79

    Implementing Unit Tests...81

    Testing the Activity 83

Declaring an Activity with Xaml...84

    Creating the Activity Class..84

    Defining Arguments...84

    Defining Variables...85

    Declaring the Activity 85

    Implementing Unit Tests...87

    Testing the Activity 88

Declaring an Activity with Code...88

    Creating the Activity Class..89

    Implementing the Activity...89

    Implementing Unit Tests...92

    Testing the Activity 93

Implementing an Asynchronous Activity..93

    Creating the Activity Class..94

Implementing the Activity..94

Implementing Unit Tests..96

Testing the Activity..97

Using Activities...97

Workflow Building Blocks...97

Activity Data Flow..99

Variable Scoping..100

Standard Activities Summary...101

Standard Activities..103

Control Flow..104

Flowchart..105

Messaging...106

Runtime..107

Primitives..107

Transactions and Compensation..108

Collection Management..109

Error Handling...109

Migration..110

Summary...110

■Chapter 4: Workflow Hosting..111

Understanding the WorkflowInvoker Class...111

Using the Static Methods...111

Using the Instance Methods...112

Using the WorkflowInvoker Static Methods...114

Declaring the HostingDemoWorkflow..114

Simple Hosting of the Workflow..117

Passing Arguments with Workflow Properties..118

Declaring a Timeout Value...119

Invoking a Generic Activity 120

Using the WorkflowInvoker Instance Methods 122

Using the InvokeAsync Method 122

Using the BeginInvoke Method..124

Understand the WorkflowApplication Class..126

Constructing a WorkflowApplication 127

Assigning Code to Delegate Members..127

Managing Extensions 129

Configuring and Managing Persistence...129

Executing a Workflow Instance 130

Managing Bookmarks..131

Manually Controlling a Workflow Instance 132

Using the WorkflowApplication Class 133

Hosting the Workflow with WorkflowApplication 133

Canceling a Workflow Instance 137

Aborting a WorkflowInstance 138

Terminating a WorkflowInstance...139

Using the BeginRun Method 140

Understanding the ActivityXamlServices Class 142

Using the ActivityXamlServices Class..143

Invoke Workflows from ASP.NET 145

Designing the ASP.NET Application 145

Hosting the Workflow 147

Testing the Application 149

Managing Multiple Workflow Instances..150

Implementing a Workflow Manager 150

Implementing the InstanceInfo Class 154

Designing the User Interface 154

Implementing the User Interface Code 156

Testing the Application 159

Using the WPF SynchronizationContext 160

Summary 161

Chapter 5: Procedural Flow Control 163

Understanding the Procedural Modeling Style 163

Making Decisions 164

Understanding the If Activity 164

Understanding the Switch<T> Activity 164

Understanding the While and DoWhile Activities 165

Using the While and DoWhile Activities 167

Implementing the InventoryLookup Activity 167

Declaring the GetItemInventory Workflow 169

Hosting the Workflow 172

Testing the Workflow 173

Using the DoWhile Activity 174

Understanding the Parallel Activity 176

Understanding Parallel Execution 176

Creating the ParallelDemo Project 179

Declaring the ParallelDemo Workflow 179

Hosting the Workflow 179

Testing the Workflow 180

Adding a Delay Activity 180

Testing the Revised Workflow 181

Using the Parallel Activity 182

Creating the GetItemLocation Project 182

Declaring the GetItemLocation Workflow 182

Hosting the Workflow 186

Testing the Workflow...187

Obtaining Asynchronous Execution with the Parallel Activity.......................189

Implementing the InventoryLookupAsync Activity...189

Modifying the GetItemLocation Workflow...191

Testing the Revised Workflow 192

Summary 194

Chapter 6: Collection-Related Activities..195

Understanding the ForEach<T> Activity...195

Understanding the Collection Activities...198

Using the ForEach<T> and Collection Activities 200

Creating the ActivityLibrary Project..200

Implementing Item Structures..200

Implementing the FindInCollection<T> Activity 201

Declaring the InventoryUpdate Workflow 203

Hosting the Workflow 209

Testing the Workflow...210

Using the ParallelForEach<T> Activity 211

Testing the Revised Workflow 212

Working with Dictionaries...213

Implementing the Dictionary-Related Activities 214

Declaring the InventoryUpdateDictionary Workflow..218

Hosting the Workflow 220

Testing the Workflow...221

Understanding the InvokeMethod Activity 222

Using the InvokeMethod Activity 223

Revising the ItemInventory Class 224

Modifying the Workflow..224

Testing the Workflow..226

Summary 228

■Chapter 7: Flowchart Modeling Style 229

Understanding the Flowchart Modeling Style..229

Using the Flowchart Modeling Style 230

Flowchart Activity 230

FlowDecision Activity 231

FlowSwitch<T> Activity 231

FlowStep Activity 232

Putting It All Together 232

The Flowchart Workflow.. 233

Making Simple Decisions 233

Implementing the ParseCalculatorArgs Activity 234

Creating the Console Project.. 235

Defining Arguments and Variables 235

Declaring the Workflow 236

Hosting the Workflow 239

Testing the Workflow.. 240

Declaring Looping Behavior 241

Implementing the InventoryLookup Activity 241

Creating the Console Project.. 243

Defining Arguments and Variables 243

Declaring the Workflow 243

Hosting the Workflow 247

Testing the Workflow.. 247

Declaring Custom Activities..248

Defining Arguments and Variables 248

Declaring the Activity 249

Implementing Unit Tests...251

Testing the Activity...253

Mixing the Two Styles...254

Implementing Item Structures...254

Implementing the FindInCollection\<T\> Activity..255

Creating the Console Project...256

Defining Arguments and Variables...256

Declaring the Workflow...257

Hosting the Workflow..261

Testing the Workflow..262

Summary..263

■Chapter 8: Host Communication...265

The Need for Long-Running Workflows...265

Understanding Bookmarks..266

Using Bookmarks...268

Implementing the GetString Activity...268

Implementing the ParseCalculatorArgs Activity...269

Creating the Console Project...270

Hosting the Workflow..273

Testing the Workflow..275

Understanding Workflow Extensions..276

Using Workflow Extensions..278

Declaring the Extension Interface..279

Implementing the HostEventNotifier Extension..279

Implementing the NotifyHost Activity...280

Declaring the BookmarkCalculatorExtension Workflow...281

Hosting the Workflow..283

Testing the Workflow..285

Using an Alternate Extension 286

    Implementing the HostQueueNotifier Extension 287

    Hosting the Workflow 288

    Testing the Workflow 289

Understanding the ActivityAction 290

Using the ActivityAction 293

    Implementing the NotifyHostWithAction Activity 293

    Declaring the BookmarkCalculatorAction Workflow 294

    Binding the Action Property 297

    Hosting the Workflow 297

    Testing the Workflow 300

    Using the InvokeAction Activity 300

Understanding the Pick Activity 302

Using the Pick Activity 303

    Implementing the WaitForBookmark Activity 303

    Creating the Console Project 304

    Defining Variables 304

    Declaring the ProblemReporting Workflow 304

    Hosting the Workflow 309

    Testing the Workflow 311

Summary 312

Chapter 9: Workflow Services **313**

Introducing Workflow Services 313

Understanding WCF 314

    Defining Service Contracts 315

    Configuring Endpoints and Bindings 316

    Hosting and Configuration 316

Understanding Workflow Services...317

  Messaging Activities.. 317

  Service Contracts and Message Types.. 322

  Correlation.. 324

  Declaration and Hosting Options 326

  Controlling Workflow Service Instances 327

Declaring a Workflow Service...327

  Tasks for a Request/Response Operation... 327

  Implementing the OrderProcessing Workflow Service 328

  Creating the ServiceLibrary Project 329

  Implementing Request and Response Classes... 329

  Declaring the Service Operation.. 332

  Populating the Response 337

  Configuring the Service 339

  Testing the Service.. 339

Publishing a Workflow Service to IIS 341

  Enhancing the Web.config... 341

  Publishing to IIS 342

Implementing a Client Application 342

  Adding a Service Reference 343

  Invoking the Service 343

  Reviewing the Configuration 346

  Testing the Client Application... 347

Implementing a Workflow Client...348

  Implementing Custom Activities... 349

  Adding a Service Reference 350

  Implementing the InitiateOrderProcessing Workflow 351

  Hosting the Workflow 359

  Testing the Client Application... 359

Self-hosting the Workflow Service 361

    Understanding the WorkflowServiceHost 361

    Tasks for Self-hosting a Service.. 362

    Implementing the ServiceHost Application.. 363

    Configuring the Service Host... 366

    Testing the Self-hosted Service 367

    Using the WorkflowClient Application 367

Summary 368

Chapter 10: Workflow Services Advanced Topics 369

Using Context-Based Correlation.. 369

    Guidelines for Context-Based Correlation 370

    Declaring the ShipOrder Workflow Service 371

    Modifying the OrderProcessing Service 379

    Hosting the ShipOrder Workflow Service 384

    Configuring the ServiceHost Application... 384

    Testing the Revised OrderProcessing Workflow.. 385

Using Content-Based Correlation.. 386

    Guidelines for Content-Based Correlation 386

    Modifying the ShipOrder Workflow Service... 386

    Configuring the ServiceHost Application... 388

    Testing the Revised Workflow Service 388

Implementing a Duplex Message Exchange Pattern 388

    Guidelines for the Duplex Message Exchange Pattern.. 389

    Declaring the CreditApproval Workflow Service.. 390

    Modifying the OrderProcessing Service 394

    Hosting the CreditApproval Workflow Service... 400

    Configuring the ServiceHost Application 400

    Testing the Revised Workflow Service 402

Using a Custom Workflow Extension 405

    Implementing the OrderUtilityExtension 406

    Implementing the GetOrderId Activity 406

    Modifying the OrderProcessing Workflow Service 407

    Adding the Extension 409

    Testing the Revised Workflow Service 409

Understanding Exceptions and Faults 409

Flowing Transactions into a Workflow Service 411

Using Standard Behaviors 412

Summary 414

■Chapter 11: Workflow Persistence 415

The Need for Workflow Persistence 415

Understanding Workflow Persistence 416

    Instance Stores 416

    Actions that Trigger Persistence 417

    Understanding Durable Delay 418

    Preventing Persistence 419

    Persisted Data and Extension Mechanisms 419

Understanding WorkflowApplication Persistence 419

Understanding the SqlWorkflowInstanceStore 421

Using the SqlWorkflowInstanceStore with WorkflowApplication 424

    Creating the ActivityLibrary Project 424

    Implementing the Item-Related Classes 425

    Implementing the Custom Extension 426

    Implementing Activities that use the Extension 428

    Implementing Bookmark-Related Activities 429

    Declaring the OrderEntry Workflow 431

    Hosting and Persisting the Workflow 435

Configuring the Application 440

Testing the Application 441

Understanding WorkflowServiceHost Persistence...443

Using the SqlWorkflowInstanceStore with WorkflowServiceHost 444

Declaring the OrderEntryService Workflow 445

Hosting the Workflow Service 452

Testing the ServiceHost Project 457

Implementing a Client Project 458

Configuring the Client Project.. 464

Testing the Client Project 465

Summary 467

Chapter 12: Customizing Workflow Persistence 469

Understanding the PersistenceParticipant Classes 469

The PersistenceParticipant Class 470

The PersistenceIOParticipant Class 471

Which Class to Use? 471

Using the PersistenceParticipant Class 472

Modifying the ItemSupportExtension Class.. 472

Testing the Revised Extension.. 474

Promoting Properties..474

Using Property Promotion...475

Modifying the ServiceHost... 475

Modifying the Client Application... 476

Configuring the Client Application 477

Testing the Revised Example 478

Understanding the Management Endpoint 479

Using the Management Endpoint..480

Modifying the ServiceHost Configuration 480

Modifying the Client Application 480

Configuring the Client Application 482

Testing the Revised Example 482

Implementing a Custom Instance Store 483

Understanding the InstanceStore Class 484

Understanding the Instance Persistence Commands 484

Understanding the InstancePersistenceContext Class 485

Implementing a File System–Based Instance Store 485

Implementing the FileSystemInstanceStoreIO Class 492

Modifying the ServiceHost Project 501

Testing the Custom Instance Store.. 502

Summary 505

Chapter 13: Transactions, Compensation, and Exception Handling 507

Understanding Default Exception Handling 507

Implementing the Example Workflow 508

Enabling LINQ Access to the AventureWorks Database 510

Implementing the GetOrderDetail Activity 511

Implementing the UpdateProductInventory Activity 514

Implementing the InsertTranHistory Activity 516

Implementing the ExternalUpdate Activity 517

Implementing the DisplayProductInventory Activity 518

Declaring the UpdateInventory Workflow 520

Declaring the DisplayInventory Workflow.. 523

Hosting the Workflow 526

Testing the Workflow.. 528

Understanding the TryCatch Activity 530

Using the TryCatch Activity...531

Declaring the UpdateInventoryTryCatch Workflow.. 532

Hosting the Workflow 535

Testing the Workflow.. 536

Catching Multiple Exceptions 537

Testing the Revised Workflow 539

Understanding the TransactionScope Activity 540

Using the TransactionScope Activity 541

Declaring the UpdateInventoryTran Workflow.. 542

Hosting the Workflow 545

Testing the Workflow.. 545

Using a Host Transaction 546

Hosting the Workflow 547

Testing the Workflow.. 548

Understanding Compensation..549

Using the CompensableActivity 551

Implementing the ExternalVoid Activity 551

Declaring the UpdateInventoryComp Workflow.. 552

Hosting the Workflow 555

Testing the Workflow.. 555

Manually Triggering Compensation 557

Declaring the UpdateInventoryManualComp Workflow 557

Hosting the Workflow 562

Testing the Workflow.. 562

Understanding the CancellationScope Activity 564

Summary 564

■Chapter 14: Workflow Tracking...565

Understanding Workflow Tracking 565

Uses of Workflow Tracking.. 566

Workflow Tracking Architecture 566

Tracking Records...568

Tracking Profiles..574

Tracking Participants...578

Using ETW Workflow Tracking..579

Providing AdventureWorks Access...579

Copying the Custom Activities...580

Declaring the Workflow..580

Hosting the Workflow...584

Enabling ETW Workflow Tracking..584

Testing the Workflow...586

Viewing the Tracking Data...586

Using Tracking Profiles..591

Including Selected Workflow Instance States...592

Including All Workflow Instance States..593

Adding Selected Activity States...594

Targeting Selected Activities...596

Adding Selected Scheduled Records..598

Including Custom Tracking Records...600

Developing a Custom Tracking Participant..604

Implementing the Tracking Record Serializer...605

Implementing the Custom Tracking Participant..608

Testing the Tracking Participant...611

Developing a Nonpersisting Tracking Participant...615

Implementing the Tracking Participant...615

Testing the Tracking Participant...615

Using Workflow Tracking with a Declarative Service Application.................618

Declaring the InventoryService Workflow...618

Configuring Tracking in the Web.config..620

Testing the Workflow Service...622

Loading Tracking Profiles from App.config..623

   Implementing a Tracking Profile Loader...623

   Defining the Tracking Profile in the App.config file 625

   Testing the Tracking Profile Loader...626

Summary 626

Chapter 15: Enhancing the Design Experience 629

Understanding Activity Designers 629

   ActivityDesigner..630

   ModelItem..630

   ExpressionTextBox 631

   ArgumentToExpressionConverter 631

   Understanding Expression Types 632

   WorkflowItemPresenter and WorkflowItemsPresenter...632

   Metadata Store and Designer Assignment 633

   The Custom Designer Workflow 634

Supporting Activity Properties 634

   Creating the Projects 634

   Implementing the CalcShipping Activity..635

   Viewing the Default Design Experience...636

   Declaring a Custom Designer 636

   Associating the Activity with the Designer 639

   Using the MetadataStore to Associate a Designer 640

   Adding an Icon..643

Supporting Expanded and Collapsed Modes 645

   Declaring the Collapsible Designer...645

   Changing the Designer Attribute 648

   Testing the Collapsible Designer 648

Supporting a Single Child Activity...649

   Implementing the MyWhile Activity 650

   Declaring a Custom Designer 650

   Testing the Designer.. 652

Supporting Multiple Child Activities..653

   Implementing the MySequence Activity 653

   Declaring a Custom Designer 654

   Testing the Designer.. 655

Supporting the ActivityAction Activity...657

   Implementing the MyActivityWithAction Activity.. 657

   Declaring a Custom Designer 659

   Testing the Designer.. 660

Understanding Validation..661

   Validation Attributes 662

   Validation Code... 662

   Constraints 662

Using Validation Attributes 663

   Using the RequiredArgument Attribute... 663

   Using the OverloadGroup Attribute 664

Adding Validation in Code..667

   Adding an Error... 667

   Adding a Warning 669

Using Constraints for Validation 669

   Implementing a Simple Constraint 670

   Validating Against Other Activities 672

Manually Executing Validation..679

   Implementing the Validation Tests 679

   Executing the Validation Tests 682

Implementing Activity Templates 683

    Implementing the Template.. 684

    Testing the Template 685

Summary 685

■ **Chapter 16: Advanced Custom Activities** **687**

Understanding Your Parental Responsibilities 687

    Configuring Activity Metadata 688

    Scheduling Child Execution 690

    Handling Child Completion 691

    Handling Bookmarks 692

    Handling a Cancellation Request 693

    Reacting to Abort and Terminate 693

Scheduling a Single Child 693

    Implementing the Custom Activity.. 694

    Implementing the Activity Designer.. 696

    Declaring a Test Workflow 697

    Implementing a Test Application 699

    Testing the Activity 701

Repeating Execution of a Single Child 702

    Implementing the Custom Activity.. 703

    Implementing the Activity Designer.. 705

    Declaring a Test Workflow 706

    Testing the Activity 707

Handling Exceptions 709

    Throwing an Exception 709

    Handling the Exception... 712

Scheduling Multiple Children...714

    Implementing the Custom Activity.. 714

Implementing the Activity Designer 717

Declaring a Test Workflow 719

Testing the Activity 721

Testing the Condition Logic 723

Scheduling Parallel Execution 725

Implementing the Custom Activity 725

Declaring a Test Workflow 728

Testing the Activity 731

Scheduling an ActivityAction 734

Implementing the Custom Activity 734

Implementing the Activity Designer 737

Declaring a Test Workflow 738

Testing the Activity 739

Using the DynamicActivity Class 741

The Example Scenario 741

Constructing a DynamicActivity 742

Testing the Activity 746

Using Execution Properties 747

Implementing the OrderScope Activity 748

Implementing the OrderAddItems Activity 749

Declaring a Test Workflow 750

Testing the Activities 751

Summary 752

■Chapter 17: Hosting the Workflow Designer 753

Understanding the Workflow Designer Components 753

Understanding the WorkflowDesigner Class 754

Understanding the ToolboxControl 755

Defining New Activities 756

Understanding the EditingContext 757

Providing Designer Metadata 760

The Self-hosting Designer Workflow 760

Implementing a Simple Workflow Designer 760

Creating the Application 761

Declaring the Window Layout 761

Implementing the Application 763

Testing the Application 769

Executing the Workflow 772

Modifying the Application 772

Testing the Application 773

Loading and Saving the Definition 775

Modifying the Application 775

Testing the Application 777

Displaying Validation Errors 777

Implementing the ValidationErrorService 777

Modifying the Application 778

Testing the Application 779

Adding Activities to the Toolbox 780

Modifying the Application 781

Testing the Application 785

Providing Designer Metadata 788

Referencing the Custom Designer 788

Modifying the Application 789

Testing the Application 789

Tracking the Selected Activity 790

Modifying the Application 791

Testing the Application 792

Modifying the Context Menu...793

    Modifying the Application... 794

    Testing the Application... 796

Locating the Arguments 796

    Modifying the Application... 797

    Testing the Application... 798

Summary 799

Chapter 18: WF 3.*x* Interop and Migration...801

Reviewing Migration Strategies..801

    Continuing with WF 3.x... 802

    Migrating to WF 4 804

    Preparing for Migration 804

Understanding the Interop Activity 806

    Limitations of the Interop Activity... 807

Invoking a WF 3.*x* Activity..807

    Implementing a WF 3.5 Activity.. 808

    Declaring a Test Workflow 811

    Testing the Workflow... 814

Invoking a WF 3.*x* Workflow 815

    Implementing a WF 3.5 Custom Activity.. 815

    Implementing the WF 3.5 Workflow 817

    Declaring a Test Workflow 822

    Testing the Workflow... 823

Using the ExternalDataExchangeService 823

    Implementing the Event Arguments 824

    Implementing the Data Exchange Service.. 825

    Generating the Communication Activities 826

    Declaring the WF 3.5 Workflow 826

Declaring a Test Workflow 830

Testing the Workflow.. 831

Executing Rules Using the Interop Activity **834**

Implementing the SalesItem Class 834

Declaring the WF 3.5 Workflow and Rules 835

Declaring a Test Workflow 838

Testing the Workflow.. 838

Executing Rules Using a Custom Activity **842**

Implementing a SalesItemWrapper 842

Implementing the ApplyRules Activity... 843

Declaring a Test Workflow 845

Testing the Workflow.. 847

Summary **847**

■Appendix A: Glossary...**849**

■Appendix B: Comparing WF 3.x to WF 4 ....**861**

WF 3.*x* to WF 4 Architectural Differences **861**

WF 3.*x* to WF 4 Activities **865**

Index...**869**

About the Author

■**Bruce Bukovics** has been a working developer for more than 25 years. During this time, he has designed and developed applications in such widely varying areas as banking, corporate finance, credit card processing, payroll processing, and retail systems.

He has firsthand developer experience with a variety of languages, including C, C++, Delphi, Java, Visual Basic, and C#. His design and development experience began back in the mainframe days and includes client/server, distributed n-tier, and service-oriented applications.

He considers himself a pragmatic programmer and test-driven development evangelist. He doesn't always stand on formality and is willing to look at alternate or unorthodox solutions to a problem if that's what it takes.

He is currently employed at Radiant Systems Inc. in Alpharetta, Georgia, as a senior software architect in the central technology group.

About the Technical Reviewer

■**Matt Milner** is a member of the technical staff at Pluralsight, where he focuses on connected systems technologies (WCF, Windows WF, BizTalk, AppFabric, and Windows Azure). Matt is also an independent consultant specializing in Microsoft .NET application design and development. As a writer, Matt has contributed to several journals and magazines, including MSDN Magazine where he authored the workflow content for the *Foundations* column. Matt regularly shares his love of technology by speaking at local, regional, and international conferences such as TechEd. Microsoft has recognized Matt as an MVP for his community contributions around connected systems technology.

Acknowledgments

As usual, a number of people deserve my appreciation. At the top of the list are my wife, Teresa, and my son, Brennen. While I was spending every available hour working on this book, you were both going about your day-to-day lives without me. I'm sorry about that. Thank you for being patient with me and supporting me while I finished this project. I love you both very much.

A big thank-you also goes out to Matt Milner, the technical reviewer for this book. Matt's job was basically to keep me honest. He reviewed each chapter and had the tedious job of executing all of my example code to ensure that it ran correctly. Matt also directed my attention to areas that I might have missed and provided valuable suggestions that improved the quality of this book.

The Apress team once again did an outstanding job—this is my fourth book with them. Matthew Moodie was the editor for my last book and once again stepped in to work with me on this one. He did another superb job providing guidance and suggestions that improved the overall quality of this book. Thanks also go to Ewan Buckingham who was there to provide his editorial guidance at just the right moments in the project.

James Markham was the coordinating editor on the project. That means he was the traffic cop who managed the schedules and directed files to and from the rest of the team. Great job, James; thank you for your work on this book. Thanks also go to Fran Parnell who served as the original coordinating editor before James transitioned to the team. I was very fortunate to have Kim Wimpsett as my copy editor once again. She worked on my last book, and I requested her early in this project. Thank you, Kim, for an excellent job. You once again corrected my many errors without dramatically changing my written voice. Production has my appreciation for their fine formatting work on this book.

For this book, I was fortunate to have access to additional Microsoft development resources that were not available to me for my previous books. Foremost among these resources was Ed Hickey. Ed was the Microsoft program coordinator for the Connect program that I joined and my central contact for all things Microsoft. On more than one occasion I contacted Ed with a problem, and he always followed through by contacting just the right Microsoft developer. Thank you, Ed.

I also need to thank the Microsoft (and non-Microsoft) folks who frequented the private Microsoft WF 4 forum. These folks addressed my questions, comments, suggestions, and bug reports and patiently tried to explain how WF 4 really worked without the benefit of any formal public documentation. I'm sure I've missed some names, but these folks went the extra mile to make sure that my questions were addressed: Scott Mason, Justin Brown, Nate Talbert, Ed Pinto, Matt Winkler, and Dave Cliffe. And thanks also go out to Maurice de Beijer who often pointed me in the right direction went I went astray. On more than one occasion, it seemed as though Maurice and I had the forum to ourselves and were asking similar questions.

I continue to receive many positive comments from readers of my previous WF books. Many of you write to me with questions that I try to answer, but others simply write to let me know how much they enjoyed one of my books. Thank you for your continued support. I hope you enjoy this latest edition.

Introduction

I started working with Windows Workflow Foundation (WF) in 2006 during the early beta and Community Technology Preview (CTP) stages. WF became a shipping Microsoft product named .NET Framework 3.0 in November 2006 along with Windows Presentation Foundation (WPF) and Windows Communication Foundation (WCF). I actually started to learn and use all three of these foundations at the same time in my day job.

While I was impressed with the flexibility and capabilities of WPF and WCF, I was somehow inexplicably drawn to Windows Workflow Foundation (WF). WF isn't just a new way to implement a user interface or a new way to communicate between applications and services. WF represents a completely new way to develop applications. It is declarative, visual, and infinitely flexible. It promotes a model that cleanly separates *what* to do from *when* to do it. This separation allows you to change the *when* without affecting the *what*. Business logic is implemented as a set of discrete, testable components that are assembled into workflows like building blocks.

Workflow isn't a new concept. But when Microsoft spends years developing a workflow foundation and provides it to us without cost, it is an event worth noting. Other workflow frameworks exist, but since it is included in the .NET Framework, WF is the de facto standard workflow framework for Windows applications.

This is the third edition of this book. The first two editions targeted the version of WF that shipped with the .NET Framework 3.0 and 3.5, respectively. This book targets the all-new version 4 of WF, which has been completely redesigned and rewritten. If you are using the 3.*x* version of WF, this is not the book for you—you need my book *Pro WF: Windows Workflow in .NET 3.5*, also published by Apress.

I originally wrote the first edition of this book because I was excited about WF. I was excited about the opportunities that it held for application developers like us. I'm even more excited today, since Microsoft has listened to the feedback and given us a completely new and greatly improved workflow framework.

My hope is that this book will help you use WF to build an exciting new generation of workflow-enabled applications.

Who Should Read This Book

This book is for all .NET developers who want to learn how to use Windows Workflow Foundation version 4 in their own applications. This book is not a primer on .NET or the C# language. To get the most out of the examples that I present in this book, you need a good working knowledge of the .NET Framework. All of the examples are presented in C#, so you should be proficient with C#.

An Overview of This Book

The material in this book is a WF 4 tutorial presented in 18 chapters, with each chapter building upon the ones before it. I've tried to organize the material so that you don't have to jump ahead in order to understand how something works. But since the chapters build upon each other, I do assume that you have read each chapter in order and understand the material that has already been presented.

The short sections that follow provide a brief summary of each chapter.

Chapter 1: A Quick Tour of Windows Workflow Foundation

This chapter provides a brief introduction to WF. In this chapter, you jump right in and develop your first workflow ("Hello Workflow"). You are introduced to some of the fundamental concepts of WF, such as how to pass parameters to a workflow and how to make decisions within a workflow.

Chapter 2: Foundation Overview

The goal of this chapter is to provide a high-level overview of WF in its entirety. This chapter doesn't teach you how to use each individual WF feature, but it does acquaint you with the design-time and runtime features that are available with WF. This chapter is a road map for the material that is covered in the remainder of the book.

Chapter 3: Activities

Activities are the building blocks of WF and where you place the business logic that is specific to your particular problem domain. In this chapter, you will learn how to develop your own custom activities using the base classes that ship with WF. This chapter also provides a high-level review of the standard activities that are provided with WF.

Chapter 4: Workflow Hosting

WF is not a stand-alone application. It is a framework for building your own workflow-enabled applications. This chapter demonstrates how to host and execute workflows in your own application. It describes how to use each of the hosting classes that are supplied with WF.

Chapter 5: Procedural Flow Control

WF includes support for two different workflow modeling styles out of the box: procedural and flowchart. The modeling style determines how the flow of control between individual activities is modeled. The focus of this chapter is the procedural modeling style. It uses familiar programming constructs to control the flow of execution.

Chapter 6: Collection-Related Activities

This chapter focuses on the activities that enable you to work with collections of data. WF includes standard activities that iterates over each element in a collection, executing the same activity for each element. Also included in WF are a set of activities that allow you to manipulate collections, adding and removing elements and so on.

Chapter 7: Flowchart Modeling Style

The other workflow modeling style that is supported by WF is the flowchart modeling style. This style of modeling workflows enables you to use direct links between activities to control the flow of execution. In this chapter, I review the activities that are provided with WF to support this modeling style. After explaining how to model a workflow using this style, I revisit several examples that were presented in earlier chapters. This is done to contrast how the two modeling styles (procedural and flowchart) can be used to solve similar business problems.

Chapter 8: Host Communication

This chapter focuses on direct communication between the host application and a workflow instance. The chapter provides an overview of long-running workflows and the bookmark mechanism used to implement them. The use of workflow extensions for sending data to a host application is also discussed. The classes that support a general-purpose callback mechanism are also demonstrated.

Chapter 9: Workflow Services

This chapter focuses on the Windows Communication Foundation (WCF) support that is provided with WF. Included with this support is the ability to declaratively author WCF services using WF as well as to invoke WCF services from within a workflow.

Chapter 10: Workflow Services Advanced Topics

This chapter continues coverage of the WCF support that is provided by WF. The chapter expands on this basic example from Chapter 9 by implementing additional workflow services that are consumed by the original workflow. Context-based and Content-based correlation is demonstrated, along with the duplex message exchange pattern. The chapter concludes with a discussion of exception and fault processing, flowing transactions into a workflow service, and the use of standard WF behaviors to fine-tune workflow service performance.

Chapter 11: Workflow Persistence

An important capability of WF is the ability to persist workflow instances (save and reload them at a later time). The chapter focuses on how to enable workflow persistence in your applications. The built-in support for persistence to a SQL Server database is demonstrated in this chapter.

Chapter 12: Customizing Workflow Persistence

This chapter focuses on ways to extend or customize workflow persistence and continues the discussion that began in Chapter 11. The chapter also provides an example that implements a custom instance store that persists workflow instances to the file system rather than to a database.

Chapter 13: Transactions, Compensation, and Exception Handling

This chapter focuses on the mechanisms provided by WF to support the handling of exceptions and to ensure the consistency of work that is performed within a workflow. Exception handling techniques, transactions and compensation are all demonstrated.

Chapter 14: Workflow Tracking

Workflow tracking is a built-in mechanism that automatically instruments your workflows. By simply adding a tracking participant to the workflow runtime, you are able to track and record status and event data related to each workflow and each activity within a workflow. This chapter shows you how to use the built-in support for tracking and how to use tracking profiles to filter the type of tracking data that is produced. The chapter also demonstrates how to develop your own custom tracking participants to process the tracking data.

Chapter 15: Enhancing the Design Experience

In this chapter, you learn how to create custom activity designers. These designer components provide the visible representation of an activity on the workflow designer canvas. The chapter also demonstrates several ways to implement validation logic for activities.

Chapter 16: Advanced Custom Activities

This chapter focuses on several advanced custom activity scenarios. Most of these scenarios are related to the execution of one or more children. The chapter demonstrates how to develop your own custom activities that execute one or more child activities or invoke a callback delegate. Also demonstrated are the techniques for providing the metadata that WF requires for each activity. The chapter concludes with an example that demonstrates the use of execution properties and bookmark options.

Chapter 17: Hosting the Workflow Designer

The workflow designer is not limited to use only within the Visual Studio environment. WF provides the classes necessary to host this same designer within your applications. This chapter is all about hosting this designer. After a brief overview of the major workflow designer components, you will implement a simple application that hosts the workflow designer. In subsequent sections, you will build upon the application, adding new functionality with each section.

Chapter 18: WF 3.*x* Interop and Migration

This chapter focuses on strategies for dealing with existing WF 3.0 or 3.5 applications (WF 3.*x*). The chapter begins with an overview of the migration strategies that are available to you followed by a demonstration of the Interop activity. This activity enables you to execute some WF 3.*x* activities within the WF 4 runtime environment.

Appendix A: Glossary

This is a glossary of commonly used WF terms.

Appendix B: Comparing WF 3.*x* to WF 4

This appendix highlights major differences between the previous version of WF (3.*x*) and WF 4.

What You Need to Use This Book

To execute the examples presented in this book, you'll need to install a minimum set of software components on a supported OS. The minimum requirements are the following:

- Visual Studio 2010 Professional, Premium, or Ultimate.

- The .NET 4 runtime (installed with Visual Studio 2010).

- SQL Server 2005 or 2008 Express edition. If you have one of the full licensed versions of SQL Server, that will work fine. SQL Server 2008 Express is installed with Visual Studio 2010.

Check with Microsoft for a current list of supported operating systems. The Microsoft .NET Framework Development Center (http://msdn.microsoft.com/en-us/netframework/default.aspx) is a good starting point to locate any miscellaneous files that you need.

Obtaining This Book's Source Code

I have found that the best way to learn and retain a new skill is through hands-on examples. For this reason, this book contains a lot of example source code. I've been frustrated on more than one occasion with technical books that don't print all of the source code in the book. The code may be available for download, but then you need to have a computer handy while you are reading the book. That doesn't work well at the beach. So, I've made it a point to present all of the code that is necessary to actually build and execute the examples.

When you are ready to execute the example code, you don't have to enter it yourself. You can download all of the code presented in this book from the Apress site at www.apress.com; go to the Source Code/Download section to find it. I've organized all of the downloadable code into separate folders and Visual Studio solutions for each chapter. I suggest that you use the same approach as you work through the examples in this book.

How to Reach Me

If you have questions or comments about this book or Windows Workflow, I'd love to hear from you. Just send your email to workflow@bukovics.com. To make sure your mail makes it past any spam filters, you might want to include the text *ProWF4* somewhere in the subject line.

CHAPTER 1

A Quick Tour of Windows Workflow Foundation

This chapter introduces you to Windows Workflow Foundation (WF). Instead of diving deeply into any single workflow topic, it provides you with a brief sampling of topics that are fully presented in other chapters.

You'll learn why workflows are important and why you might want to develop applications using them. You'll then jump right in and implement your very first functioning workflow. Additional hands-on examples are presented that demonstrate other features of Windows Workflow Foundation.

Why Workflow?

As developers, our job is to solve real business problems. The type and complexity of the problems will vary broadly depending on the nature of the business in which we work. But regardless of the complexity of any given problem, we tend to solve problems in the same way: we break the problem down into identifiable and manageable tasks. Those tasks are further divided into smaller tasks, and so on.

When we've finally reached a point where each task is the right size to understand and manage, we identify the individual steps needed to accomplish the task. The steps usually have an order associated with them. They represent a sequence of individual instructions that will yield the expected behavior only when they are executed in the correct order.

In the traditional procedural programming model, you implement a task in code using your chosen development language. First and foremost, the code performs some small unit of useful work. It might execute a query or update statement on a database, enforce validation rules, determine the next page to show to a user, queue a message on another system, and so on. But in addition to implementing the real work of the task, you also need to implement the "glue" code that determines the sequence of the individual steps. You need to make branching and looping decisions, check the value of variables, validate inputs, and produce outputs. And when the smallest of tasks are combined into larger composite tasks, there's even more code needed to control how all of those tasks will work together to accomplish some greater purpose.

A workflow is simply an ordered series of steps that accomplish some defined purpose according to a set of rules. By that definition, what I just described in the previous paragraphs is a *workflow*. It might be defined entirely in code, but it is no less a workflow. The point is that we already use workflows every day when we develop software. We might not consider affixing the *workflow* label to our work, but we do use workflow concepts even if we are not consciously aware of them.

Workflows Are Different

The workflow definition that I gave previously doesn't tell the whole story, of course. There must be more to it, and there is. To a developer, the word *workflow* typically conjures up images of a highly graphical environment where complex business rules are declared visually rather than entirely in code. Individual tasks are organized into an appropriate sequence, and branching and looping decisions are declared to control the flow of execution between tasks. It's an environment that allows you to easily visualize and model the tasks to solve a problem. And since you can visualize the tasks, it's easier to understand and change them.

But there's much more to workflows than just a visual development environment. Workflows represent an entirely different programming model—a declarative one. In a traditional procedural programming model, the code that performs the real work for a task may be entwined with the code that determines when to execute the task. If you need to change the conditions under which a task should execute, you may have to slog your way past a lot of code that is unrelated to your change. And when you apply your simple flow control change, you need to avoid inadvertent changes to the part of the code that performs the real work.

In contrast with this, a declarative workflow model promotes a clear separation between *what* to do (the real work that you're trying to accomplish) and *when* to do it. This separation allows you to change the *when* without affecting the *what*. With this model, the real work of the task is encapsulated in discrete activities. You can think of an activity as a unit of work with a defined set of inputs and outputs. In WF, you have the option of implementing activities in code or declaratively assembling them from other activities. But regardless of how the individual activities are authored, they are assembled like building blocks into complete workflows. The job of the workflow is to coordinate the work of one or more activities. Branching and looping decisions that control the flow of execution between activities are declared within the workflow—they are not hard-coded within each activity. With the workflow model, if you need to make that same flow control change, you simply change the workflow declaration. The activity code that performs the real work remains untouched.

General-purpose languages such as C# or Visual Basic can obviously be used to solve business problems. But one additional advantage of the workflow programming model is that it enables you to implement your own domain-specific language. In WF, this is accomplished by developing custom activities that model the problem domain. With such a language, you can express business rules using terms that are common to a specific problem domain. Experts in that domain are able to view a workflow and the activities that are declared within it. They can easily understand it, since it is declared in terminology that they understand.

For example, if your domain is banking and finance, you might refer to *accounts, checks, loans, debits, credits, customers, tellers, branches*, and so on. But if the problem domain is pizza delivery, those entities don't make much sense. Instead, you would model your problems using terms such as *menus, specials, ingredients, addresses, phone numbers, drivers, tips*, and so on. The workflow model allows you to define the problem using terminology that is appropriate for each problem domain.

Workflows allow you to easily model system and human interactions. A *system interaction* is how we as developers would typically approach a problem. You define the steps to execute and write code that controls the sequence of those steps. The code is always in total control.

Human interactions are those that involve real live people. The problem is that people are not always as predictable as your code. For example, you might need to model a mortgage loan application. The process might include steps that must be executed by real people in order to complete the process. How much control do you have over the order and timing of those steps? Does the credit approval always occur first, or is it possible for the appraisal to be done first? What about the property survey? Is it done before or after the appraisal? And what activities must be completed before you can schedule the loan closing? The point is that these types of problems are difficult to express using a purely procedural model because human beings are in control. The exact sequence of steps is not always predictable, and a large amount of code is required just to manage all of the possible execution paths. A human interaction problem such as this can typically be expressed more naturally and clearly in a workflow model.

Why Windows Workflow Foundation?

If workflows are important, then why use Windows Workflow Foundation? Microsoft has provided this foundation in order to simplify and enhance your .NET development. It is not a stand-alone application. It is a software foundation that is designed to enable the use of a declarative workflow model within your own applications. Regardless of the type of application you are developing, you can likely leverage something in WF.

If you are developing line-of-business applications, you can use WF to implement the business rules as a set of custom activities and workflows. If your application comprises a series of human interactions, you can model long-running workflows that are capable of coordinating the work that is done by humans with the application.

If you need a highly customizable application, you can use the declarative nature of WF to allow end-user customization of the workflows. And if you are just looking for a better way to encapsulate and organize your application logic, you can implement the logic as discrete custom activities. Since each activity has a defined set of inputs and outputs, it is easy to independently test each activity before it is assembled into a workflow.

The previous were all good reasons to use WF, and here are a few more of them:

- WF provides a flexible and powerful framework for developing workflows. You can spend your time and energy developing your own framework, visual workflow designer, and runtime environment. Or you can use a foundation that Microsoft provides and spend your valuable time solving real business problems.

- WF promotes a consistent way to develop your applications. One workflow looks very similar to the next. This consistency in the programming model and tools improves your productivity when developing new applications and improves your visibility when maintaining existing ones.

- WF supports multiple modeling styles. You can choose to model a workflow using familiar procedural constructs such as `if` statements and `while` loops. Or you can choose to model a workflow that uses flowchart concepts where looping and branching decisions are declared as direct links between activities. And for the ultimate in flexibility, you can even mix and match both styles within the same workflow.

- WF provides tight integration with Windows Communication Foundation (WCF). Standard activities are provided that enable you to consume WCF services from within a workflow or expose a workflow as a WCF service endpoint.

- WF supports workflow persistence. The ability to save and later reload the state of a running workflow is especially important when modeling human interactions and for other potentially long-running workflows.

- WF provides a complete workflow ecosystem. Microsoft provides the workflow runtime, a suite of standard activities, base classes for building your own activities, workflow persistence, and workflow tracking. Tooling support is also provided in the form of a workflow designer that is integrated with Visual Studio, which you can also host in your own applications.

- WF is included with .NET and Visual Studio and available for use in your applications without any additional licensing fees.

Your Development Environment

Windows Workflow Foundation was originally made available as part of .NET 3.0 and later enhanced in .NET 3.5. The tooling support for WF (workflow designer, templates, and debugger support) was originally provided as an add-in to Visual Studio 2005 and later built in to Visual Studio 2008.

Visual Studio 2010 and .NET 4 are the delivery vehicle for WF 4, which is the topic of this book. All of the examples in this book target WF 4, and all of the screen shots were captured from Visual Studio 2010. The one exception is the chapter on interop with WF 3.x. That chapter uses some activities that target the WF 3.x environment to demonstrate the interop capabilities in WF 4.

To run the examples in this book, you'll need the following:

- Visual Studio 2010 Professional, Premium, or Ultimate

- The .NET 4 runtime (installed with Visual Studio 2010)

- SQL Server Express 2008 (installed with Visual Studio 2010)

WF 4 represents a significant break from previous versions of WF. Microsoft has listened to the feedback that it received for WF 3.x and decided to take a clean-slate approach to improve WF 4. The result is that the entire framework has been rewritten from the ground up.

The good news is that WF 4 is a monumental improvement over its predecessors. Microsoft has gone to great lengths to simplify the development model, improve the performance, and reduce many of the pain points that were present with the previous versions of the framework.

The bad news is that the 3.x and 4 versions are not compatible with each other. A custom activity written for WF 3.x won't run under WF 4 unless it is first wrapped in an interop activity. But the entire WF 3.x framework continues to be shipped with .NET 4. And Visual Studio 2010 includes all of the designer, debugger, and template support for the WF 3.x version of the framework. So if you've already made a substantial investment in WF 3.x, you can continue to support and enhance those applications using the latest Microsoft offerings.

■ **Note** This book targets the 4 version of WF. If you're looking for a book on WF 3.0 or 3.5, please consider my previous workflow book, *Pro WF Windows Workflow in .NET 3.5*, published by Apress.

The Workflow Workflow

Before I begin the first example, I want to present what I call the *workflow workflow*. This is the mental checklist of steps that you follow when developing workflow applications. I'll present enhanced or more specialized revisions of this list throughout the book to add other steps that you should consider. But in its simplest form, developing workflow applications using WF can be summarized by these steps:

1. Select or implement the activities to perform some work.

2. Declare a workflow that coordinates the work of one or more activities.

3. Develop a workflow host application.

The first step is to select the activities that you need in order to perform some useful work. The work could be updating a database, sending a WCF message to another system, performing a calculation, and so on. The work to perform is entirely up to you and depends on the problem that you are attempting to solve. You might be able to use an out-of-the-box activity (or combination of activities) that is provided with WF to perform the work. Or, more than likely, you will need to implement your own custom activities that perform the work. Once your custom activities have been developed and tested, they form a library of reusable building blocks that can be used to build multiple workflows.

After you identify (or implement) the activities that do the real work, you can turn your attention to the workflow itself. Remember that the job of the workflow is to coordinate work, not to necessarily perform the work itself. During this step you declare the structure of the workflow by adding activities and flow control elements. The flow control elements may be other activities that define loops and make branching decisions. Or they may take the form of direct connections between activities that define the execution sequence.

Finally, you need a host application that can execute instances of your new workflow. Since WF is a set of foundation classes rather than a finished application, you are able to leverage WF in a wide variety of application types. You can use WF from WinForms, Windows Presentation Foundation (WPF), ASP.NET, Windows services, or even lowly console applications. You may need to expose your workflow as a Windows Communication Foundation service and consume it from other client applications. If so, you can host the workflow using a Microsoft-provided hosting environment such as Internet Information Services (IIS) or Windows Process Activation Service (WAS). Or you can choose to develop your own self-hosting application. Regardless of the type of application, the most basic job of the host is to start an instance of the workflow and wait until it completes. In subsequent chapters, you will learn about additional duties that the host application can perform.

Hello Workflow

At this point, you are ready to create your first workflow. In the world of technology in which we work, it has become customary to begin any new technical encounter with a "Hello World" example.

Not wanting to break with tradition, I present a "Hello Workflow" example in the pages that follow. If you follow along with the steps as I present them, you will have a really simple yet functional workflow application.

Here are the steps you will follow to implement the "Hello Workflow" example:

1. Create a new Workflow Console Application.

2. Add a `Sequence` activity to the workflow.

3. Add a `WriteLine` activity as a child of the `Sequence` activity.

4. Set the `Text` property of the `WriteLine` activity to the message that you'd like to display.

5. Review the boilerplate code that runs the workflow.

In this example, and in the other examples in this chapter, I present fundamental concepts that are the basis for working with all workflows, regardless of their complexity. If you already have experience working with Windows Workflow Foundation, you might feel compelled to skip this information. If so, go ahead, but you might want to give this chapter a quick read anyway.

Creating the Project

You create workflow projects in the same way as other project types in Visual Studio. After starting Visual Studio, select File ➤ New ➤ Project. A New Project dialog is presented that allows you to enter project parameters and to select the template to use for the new project.

After selecting Visual C# as the language, you'll see Workflow as one of the available project template categories. Visual Studio is capable of creating projects that target different versions of the .NET Framework. The.NET Framework to target is set at the top of the New Project dialog. The New Project dialog is target-aware, meaning that it presents only the templates that are available for the selected version of the framework. The Visual Studio Toolbox also filters the list of controls to those that are available in the selected version of the .NET Framework. You should select .NET Framework 4 for all of the examples in this book. The one exception will be when you are creating 3.5 workflow components in Chapter 18.

For this example, select Workflow Console Application as the template to use for the new project. This creates a Windows console application that includes an empty workflow definition file and the necessary boilerplate code to execute it. Enter `HelloWorkflow` as the project name, and also enter a solution name of `chapter 01`. Figure 1-1 shows the New Project dialog after I've entered all of the necessary information to create the new project. Click OK once you are ready to create the new project.

■ **Note** In the example code that accompanies this book, I use a separate solution for each chapter. All of the example projects for a chapter are added to the solution for that chapter. You might want to adopt the same strategy when you are entering these examples.

Figure 1-1. New Project dialog

The new project template creates two files that you'll need to modify in the steps that follow. The `Workflow1.xaml` file is the workflow definition, and the `Program.cs` file contains the code needed to run an instance of the workflow. The `Workflow1.xaml` file is an XML-based declarative definition of the workflow that is compiled into a Common Language Runtime (CLR) type during the build process.

The new project also includes references to the .NET assemblies that you need to execute a simple workflow. Foremost in the list of assembly references that you need is `System.Activities`. Within this assembly, the workflow-related classes and activities are organized into a number of namespaces. In your code, you need to reference only the namespaces that you are actually using.

■ **Note** The Workflow Console Application template creates a project that targets the .NET Framework 4 Client Profile. This is a subset of the full .NET Framework that omits server-oriented assemblies in order to reduce its size. If necessary, the target framework can be changed from the project properties page. This subset of the full framework is fine for most of the examples in this book. I'll draw your attention to the examples that require the full framework.

Declaring the Workflow

I said previously that workflows coordinate the work of one or more activities. So, declaring a workflow requires that you identify the activities to execute and arrange them in some logical sequence. You can do that entirely in code, or you can accomplish the same thing declaratively using the workflow designer. The designer supports dragging and dropping of activities onto the workflow canvas from the Visual Studio Toolbox.

In this project, the `Workflow1.xaml` file that was added for you contains a declarative XML-based representation of the workflow that can be maintained by the workflow designer. If it is not already open, double-click the `Workflow1.xaml` file in Solution Explorer to open it in the designer now. Figure 1-2 shows the workflow in the designer.

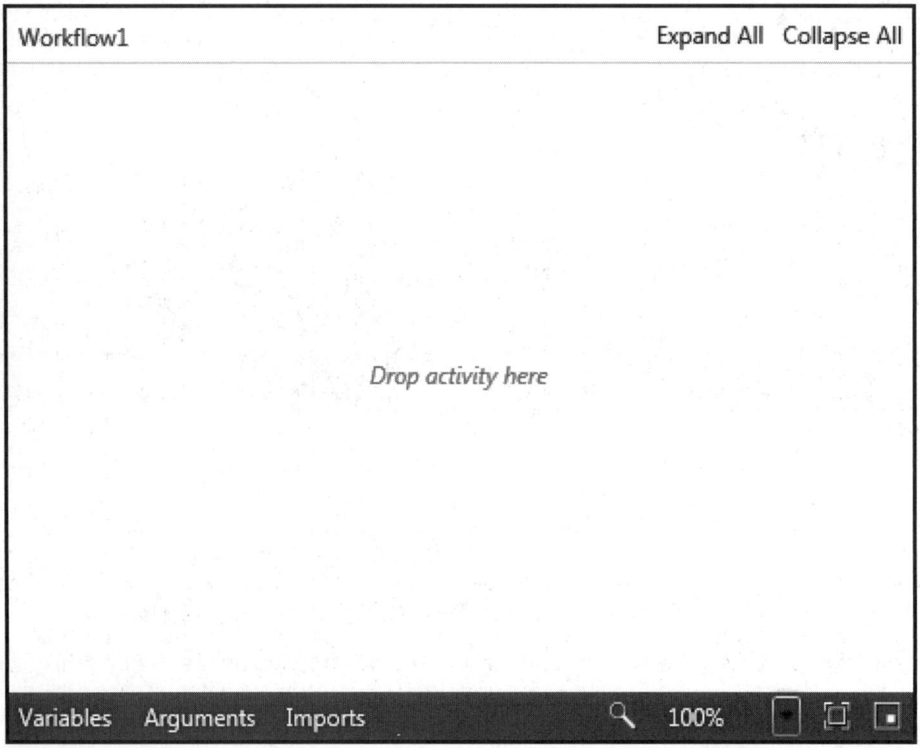

Figure 1-2. Empty Workflow1.xaml opened in the workflow designer

As you can see from Figure 1-2, the workflow is initially empty. At this point it represents an empty canvas, ready to accept workflow activities that you drag and drop from the Visual Studio Toolbox.

An activity represents a step in the workflow and is the fundamental building block of all WF workflows. Microsoft supplies a set of standard activities that you can use, but you will need to develop your own custom activities in order to accomplish any really meaningful work. Each activity is designed to serve a unique purpose and encapsulates the logic needed to fulfill that purpose.

Since most workflows require more than one activity to accomplish a task, you will usually begin by adding a container for those activities. The first activity that you add to a workflow (known as the *topmost* or *root* activity) is frequently the Sequence or Flowchart activity. These are two standard control flow activities that are provided with WF. They are both composite activities that allow you to add other activities as children. They both serve the same purpose: to provide a simple way to determine the sequence in which any child activities execute.

The examples in this chapter (and the next few chapters) are based on the Sequence activity, which uses a procedural style of flow control. The Flowchart activity represents a different and unique way to author workflows and is discussed in Chapter 7.

Adding the Sequence Activity

Begin the declaration of this workflow by dragging and dropping a Sequence activity from the Visual Studio Toolbox to the empty Workflow1.xaml file in the designer. The standard activities provided with WF are organized into several different categories according to the purpose for each activity. You should find the Sequence activity in the Control Flow category of the Toolbox, as shown in Figure 1-3.

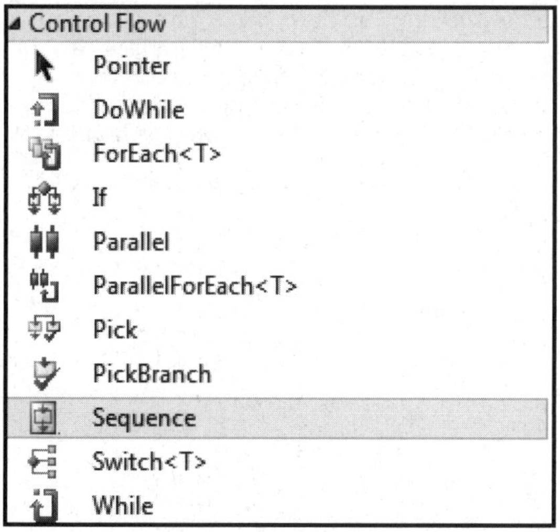

Figure 1-3. Toolbox with Sequence activity

A Sequence activity is considered a composite activity because it is a container for other child activities. In general, the primary responsibility of any composite activity is to run any child activities contained within it in some prescribed order. In the case of the Sequence activity, the prescribed order is a simple sequence: run the first child activity, followed by the second child activity, and so on. After you have added a series of activities to a Sequence activity, you can modify their execution order by simply dragging them to a new location relative to the other activities.

While you're taking a look at the workflow designer for the first time, you might want to also make note of several of its features. The Variables button allows you to define local variables to maintain state within the workflow or to pass data between activities. The Arguments button allows you to define input or output arguments for the workflow. This first example doesn't require the use of either of these features.

Also included is an Imports button. This allows you to add namespaces that you will frequently reference within the workflow. This is similar to adding a `using` statement in your C# code. It allows you to reference the class name without the need to specify the entire namespace-qualified name.

The lower-right corner of the designer includes controls that let you modify the designer display. You can zoom in or out to change the set of activities that are visible at one time. A Mini map control allows you to navigate large workflows using a scrollable thumbnail view of the entire workflow.

The designer also includes Expand and Collapse options located at the upper-right corner of the design surface. These options allow you to further refine the view of the activities shown within the designer by expanding or collapsing additional detail for each activity. You won't need to use these options for these first simple examples, but they are helpful when you are working with larger workflows.

Adding the WriteLine Activity

The objective of this example is to write the message "Hello Workflow" on the console. To accomplish that objective, you can use one of the standard activities named `WriteLine`. As the name implies, this activity can write any text that you want to the console. Optionally, it can write text to a `TextWriter` instead of directly to the console, but you don't need that functionality for this example. To add this activity to the workflow, open the Toolbox again, and find the `WriteLine` activity. It should be located in the Primitives category of the Toolbox.

Once you've located it, drag the `WriteLine` activity to the workflow designer, and drop it on the open `Sequence` activity. The workflow should now look like Figure 1-4.

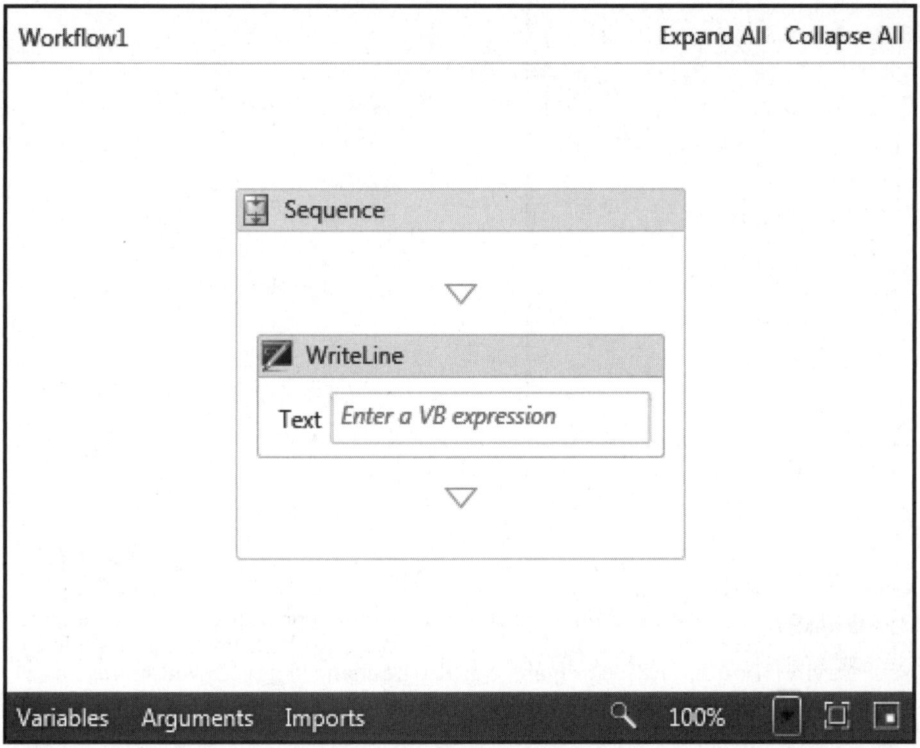

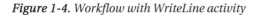

Figure 1-4. Workflow with WriteLine activity

To complete the workflow definition for this example, you need to set the Text property of the WriteLine activity. To accomplish this, highlight the WriteLine activity and then press F4 (assuming you still have the default key mappings) to open the Properties window. Enter the string literal "Hello Workflow" (including the double quotes) as the value for the Text property.

■ **Caution** String literals must be entered within double quotes. The Text property is actually expecting you to define a workflow expression that returns a string. An expression can be a simple string literal or something much more complex such as a call to a method. If you enter Hello World with no double quotes, the Expression Editor won't know that it's a string literal and will attempt to parse and interpret the string as a Visual Basic expression.

Figure 1-5 shows the completed Properties window for the WriteLine activity.

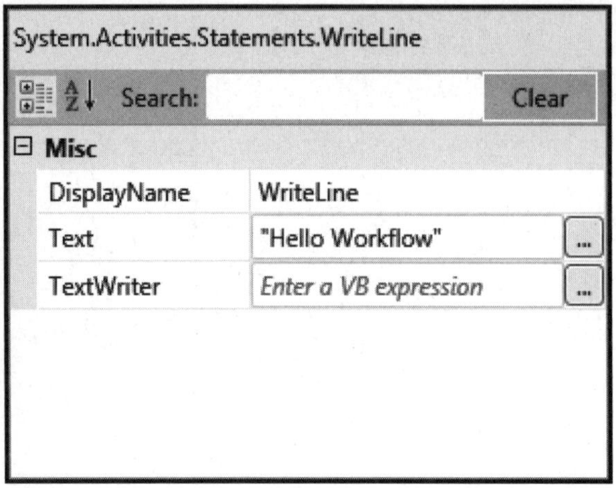

Figure 1-5. *Properties window for WriteLine activity*

As shown in Figure 1-5, the `WriteLine` activity also includes a property named `DisplayName`. This property is common to all activities and determines the name that is shown for the activity within the designer. Most of the time you can use the default name, but it is helpful to provide a more meaningful name when you are working with a larger workflow, especially when the workflow includes multiple instances of the same activity. The `DisplayName` property can also be changed directly within the designer.

Also note that the `Text` property for the `WriteLine` activity can be set directly within the designer. This eliminates the need to use the Properties window to set the properties that are used most often. Not all activities support this kind of property editing, but most try to support the most common properties directly in the designer.

Save all of your changes to the `Workflow1.xaml` file if you haven't already done so.

■ **Tip** This particular example really doesn't require the `Sequence` activity since it contains only a single `WriteLine` activity. You could have added the `WriteLine` activity directly to the empty `Workflow1.xaml` file, and the workflow would execute correctly with the same results. However, in most cases, you will declare workflows that require many activities, and you will need a container activity such as `Sequence` to organize and control their execution. For this reason, it is a good habit to always start with a `Sequence` or `Flowchart` activity.

Hosting the Workflow

Now that you've declared the example workflow, open the `Program.cs` file, and turn your attention to the code that runs an instance of the workflow. For the most part, you can use the boilerplate code that was produced by the new project template.

In the following code, I've made a few minor changes and reformatted the code to fit the format of this book. Since this is a console application, all of the code is contained within the static `Main` method.

```csharp
using System;
using System.Activities;

namespace HelloWorkflow
{
    class Program
    {
        static void Main(string[] args)
        {
            WorkflowInvoker.Invoke(new Workflow1());

            Console.WriteLine("Press any key to exit");
            Console.ReadKey();
        }
    }
}
```

■ **Note** The boilerplate code that was generated for you will likely contain additional `using` statements that are not shown here. To avoid confusion, I show only those `using` statements that are absolutely necessary. I try to follow this practice for all the examples in this book.

As you will see in later chapters of this book, there are a number of ways to execute a workflow. What you see here is absolutely the simplest way to execute a workflow. The `WorkflowInvoker` class provides a way to execute a workflow with the simplicity of calling a method. The static `Invoke` method requires an instance of the workflow that you want to execute. When the `Invoke` method is used like this, the workflow executes synchronously on the current thread. In this sense, the `Invoke` method is a blocking call that completes only once the workflow has completed.

■ **Note** Please refer to Chapter 4 for an in-depth discussion of other workflow hosting options.

Whenever I'm working with console applications, I add a couple of final calls to the `Console` class. These calls display a message on the console and pause the application until a key has been pressed. Without these lines, a console application that is run in the debugger (F5) will execute and then immediately finish, not providing you with a chance to see the results.

Running the Application

After building the project, you should be ready to test it. You can press F5 (or Ctrl-F5 to start without debugging). This assumes the default C# key mappings. Use the appropriate key combination for your development environment, or select Start Debugging from the Debug menu.

If everything works correctly, you should see these results on the console:

```
Hello Workflow

Press any key to exit
```

Congratulations! Your first encounter with Windows Workflow Foundation was successful.

Exploring the Xaml

Before moving on to the next example, you should take a few minutes to examine the `Workflow1.xaml` file that was used in the previous example. This is the file that contains the workflow definition that you modified via the workflow designer.

If you still have this file open in the designer, close it. Double-clicking the file opens it in the default view, which is the workflow designer. Instead, right-click the file and open it in Code View. This should open it using the XML editor. I've reformatted the contents of the file to fit the format of this book, and I've removed a few entries that are used internally by the debugger and designer. Your file should look similar to this:

```xml
<Activity mc:Ignorable="sap" x:Class="HelloWorkflow.Workflow1"
  mva:VisualBasic.Settings=
    "Assembly references and imported namespaces serialized as XML namespaces"
  xmlns="http://schemas.microsoft.com/netfx/2009/xaml/activities"
  xmlns:mc="http://schemas.openxmlformats.org/markup-compatibility/2006"
  xmlns:mv="clr-namespace:Microsoft.VisualBasic;assembly=System"
  xmlns:mva=
    "clr-namespace:Microsoft.VisualBasic.Activities;assembly=System.Activities"
  xmlns:s="clr-namespace:System;assembly=mscorlib"
  xmlns:s1="clr-namespace:System;assembly=System"
  xmlns:s2="clr-namespace:System;assembly=System.Xml"
  xmlns:s3="clr-namespace:System;assembly=System.Core"
  xmlns:sad="clr-namespace:System.Activities.Debugger;assembly=System.Activities"
  xmlns:sap="http://schemas.microsoft.com/netfx/2009/xaml/activities/presentation"
  xmlns:scg="clr-namespace:System.Collections.Generic;assembly=System"
  xmlns:scg1=
    "clr-namespace:System.Collections.Generic;assembly=System.ServiceModel"
  xmlns:scg2="clr-namespace:System.Collections.Generic;assembly=System.Core"
  xmlns:scg3="clr-namespace:System.Collections.Generic;assembly=mscorlib"
  xmlns:sd="clr-namespace:System.Data;assembly=System.Data"
  xmlns:sd1="clr-namespace:System.Data;assembly=System.Data.DataSetExtensions"
  xmlns:sl="clr-namespace:System.Linq;assembly=System.Core"
  xmlns:st="clr-namespace:System.Text;assembly=mscorlib"
  xmlns:x="http://schemas.microsoft.com/winfx/2006/xaml">
  <Sequence>
    <WriteLine Text="Hello Workflow" />
  </Sequence>
</Activity>
```

This file uses Extensible Application Markup Language (Xaml) to declare the workflow. Xaml is a serialization format that specifies object instances as XML elements and properties of those objects as XML attributes.

Most of this small Xaml file is occupied with Microsoft namespace definitions. These namespaces provide access to the schemas that define the various parts of the Xaml structure. During the build process, this file is compiled into a new CLR type. In the `Program.cs` file that we just reviewed, you saw that you were able to create an instance of this compiled workflow type like this:

```
WorkflowInvoker.Invoke(new Workflow1());
```

In this case, `Workflow1` is a new class that is defined by this Xaml file. The `Class` attribute on the first line of the Xaml file is what determines the fully qualified namespace and class name of the new compiled type:

```
<Activity mc:Ignorable="sap" x:Class="HelloWorkflow.Workflow1"
```

The root tag of `Activity` is significant, since it indicates that the base class for this new type is `Activity`. The `Activity` class is a base type provided with WF that all activities and workflows must ultimately derive from.

■ **Note** You will learn more about the `Activity` class hierarchy in Chapter 3.

This workflow used a `Sequence` activity that was the container for a single `WriteLine` activity. The `WriteLine` activity had a default `Text` property that you set to an appropriate message to write to the console. It's easy to see how the remaining XML nodes map to this structure that you declared using the workflow designer:

```
<Sequence>
  <WriteLine Text="Hello Workflow" />
</Sequence>
```

Please note that the workflow is fully declared within this Xaml file. Many of the other designers in Visual Studio create separate code-beside files that separate the designer-maintained code from the code that you maintain. Examples that use this mechanism include WinForms, WPF, and the 3.*x* version of WF. But with WF 4, the workflows are entirely declarative—there is no code-beside file. Unlike previous versions of WF, no procedural code is allowed within the workflow definition. All C# code has been pushed into custom activities where it really belongs.

Most of the time, you'll want to use the workflow designer to declare and maintain your workflows. It just makes sense to use the development tools that will make you most productive, and the designer provides that nice drag-and-drop development experience. But there will be times when you find it easier to manually edit the Xaml files directly. There's absolutely no problem in doing that. The designer doesn't add any magic entries that you can't do yourself. It simply provides a very nice visual way to manipulate these files.

To see this in action for yourself, you can modify the `HelloWorkflow` project by modifying the Xaml file directly. For a quick example of this, duplicate the `WriteLine` element, and change the message like this:

```
<Sequence>
  <WriteLine Text="Hello Workflow" />
  <WriteLine Text="I added this activity via Xaml" />
</Sequence>
```

If you haven't made a really dreadful cut-and-paste error, you should be able to build the project and run it to see these results:

```
Hello Workflow

I added this activity via Xaml

Press any key to exit
```

Passing Parameters

Workflows would have limited usefulness without the ability to receive input parameters. Passing parameters to a workflow is one of the basic mechanisms that permit you to affect the outcome of the workflow.

The preceding example writes a constant string literal to the console. To see how parameters are passed to a workflow, you'll implement another similar example that uses input parameters to format the string before it is written.

Here are the steps you will follow to implement this example:

1. Add a new workflow to the `HelloWorkflow` project.

2. Define a workflow input argument

3. Add a `Sequence` activity to the workflow.

4. Add a `WriteLine` activity to the `Sequence` activity.

5. Set the `Text` property to a message that includes the input argument.

6. Pass the input argument to the workflow when you are executing it.

■ **Note** Throughout the remainder of this book, I'll assume that you already know the basics of creating new projects and don't require the step-by-step commentary. However, I will let you know when there is something significant that you need to be aware of when creating the new project or adding a new item to an existing project.

Declaring the Workflow

For this example, you will add a new workflow to the existing `HelloWorkflow` project. Select the Add New Item option for the project, and then select the Workflow category. Select the Activity template, and name the new workflow `HelloWorkflowParameters`. The new item should open in designer view.

■ **Tip** Don't be confused by the terminology that is used here. You are adding a new workflow, but since all workflows are actually activities, the Add New Item template uses the term *Activity*.

The purpose of this example is to demonstrate how to pass data to the workflow. Any data that you want to pass to a workflow must first be declared as a workflow argument. To accomplish this, click the Arguments button to open the Argument Editor. You can find this button on the lower-left side of the designer. The list of arguments is initially empty, so you should select the Create Argument option to add a new one. Arguments have a name, direction (in, out, or both), argument type, and optional default value. You need to add a single argument with these parameters:

Name	Direction	Argument Type
ArgFirstName	In	String

The direction of In indicates that this is data that will be passed as an input argument to the workflow. Figure 1-6 shows the Argument Editor after I've entered the required input argument. Click the Arguments button once again closes the Argument Editor.

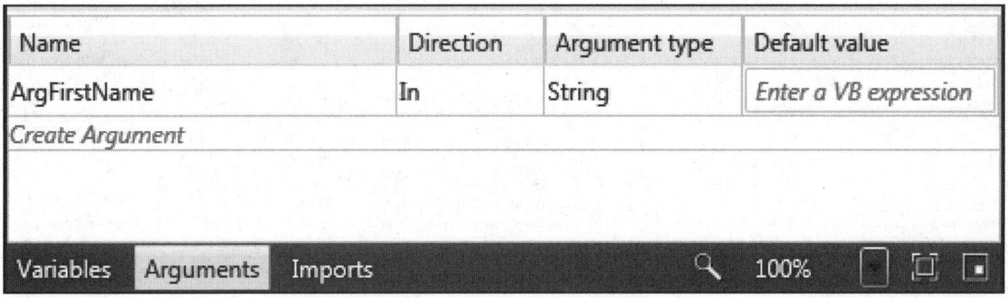

Name	Direction	Argument type	Default value
ArgFirstName	In	String	*Enter a VB expression*
Create Argument			

Variables **Arguments** Imports   🔍 100%

Figure 1-6. Argument Editor with required argument

■ **Note** You may notice that I included the *Arg* prefix in front of the argument name. This isn't a WF requirement or an attempt on my part to talk like a pirate (not that there's anything wrong with that). I simply did this to make it easier to spot the arguments as you proceed with the workflow declaration. In this example, you're working with only a single argument. However, in much larger workflows, you will be using a combination of input and output arguments and workflow variables. It's convenient to be able to look at the name and immediately know that it's an argument.

Now that the input argument has been defined, please follow these steps to finish the declaration of the workflow:

1. Add a `Sequence` activity to the empty workflow.

2. Add a `WriteLine` activity to the Sequence activity.

3. Set the `WriteLine.Text` property to a meaningful message. This time, instead of using only a string literal, you need to reference the `ArgFirstName` argument in the expression. After selecting the `WriteLine` activity, you can enter the string expression directly in the Properties window as you did in the previous example. Or you can click the ellipsis button next to the `Text` property to open the Expression Editor. The Expression Editor provides a bit more real estate for entering your expressions.

Figure 1-7 shows the Expression Editor after I've entered the string expression.

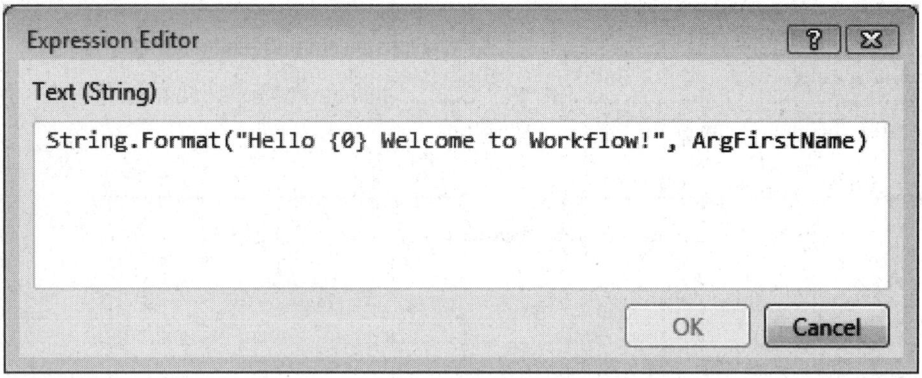

Figure 1-7. Expression Editor with string expression

As shown in Figure 1-7, I entered an expression that uses the `String.Format` method to concatenate several strings, including the value from the `ArgFirstName` argument:

```
String.Format("Hello {0} Welcome to Workflow!", ArgFirstName)
```

In this expression, `ArgFirstName` is not double-quoted, so it references the input argument that you defined instead of a string literal.

When you are entering an expression, you can use the IntelliSense support that is provided by the Expression Editor. For example, once you enter `String.` (including the period), you should see an IntelliSense window pop up to assist you in selecting the correct member from the `String` class. Likewise, when you start to enter `Arg`, you should be presented with a list of everything that is in scope that begins with those letters.

■ **Tip** When using IntelliSense within the Expression Editor, remember to use the Tab key to select the highlighted item in the list. Don't use the Enter key. Pressing the Enter key will add a carriage return, causing a line break after the selected item. Workflow expressions are entered using Visual Basic (VB) syntax, so the extra carriage return causes errors in the expression. If you really do need to continue an expression on multiple lines, you'll need to include the VB continuation character (_, an underscore) at the end of the line you want to continue.

When entering an expression, you actually have quite a bit of freedom to decide how it will be entered. In this particular case, the `Text` property of the `WriteLine` activity expects an expression that returns a string. It really doesn't matter how you build that string, as long as it resolves to a string. For example, you could have concatenated the string yourself instead of using the `String.Format` method.

■ **Note** For now, you really only have to be aware that expressions are entered in VB syntax, so you don't need to enter trailing semicolons and other bits of C# syntax. I provide more information on expressions in Chapter 2.

This completes the workflow definition. Structurally, the workflow should look like the previous example shown in Figure 1-4.

Hosting the Workflow

To complete this example, open the `Program.cs` file, and make just a few minor modifications to pass the input argument and to execute this new workflow. Here is a revised copy of the `Program.cs` file with the necessary changes:

```
using System;
using System.Activities;
using System.Collections.Generic;

namespace HelloWorkflow
{
    class Program
    {
        static void Main(string[] args)
        {
            WorkflowInvoker.Invoke(new HelloWorkflowParameters(),
                new Dictionary<String, Object>
                {
                    {"ArgFirstName", "Bruce"}
                });
```

```
        Console.WriteLine("Press any key to exit");
        Console.ReadKey();
      }
    }
}
```

Parameters are passed to a workflow in the form of a generic dictionary of objects keyed by a string (`Dictionary<String, Object>`). The string key must exactly match the argument name (including case), and the type of the object must match the expected argument type. This workflow requires only the single `ArgFirstName` argument, but multiple arguments would be passed in this same dictionary if they were required. An overload of the `WorkflowInvoker.Invoke` method is used that accepts the dictionary of parameters.

■ **Note** If you do manage to misspell a parameter name, you won't know it until you actually run the workflow. At that time, a `System.ArgumentException` will be raised, informing you that you tried to set a nonexistent argument. Likewise, if you pass data of an incorrect type (such as passing an integer when the argument is expecting a string), the same exception will be raised with a slightly different message.

Running the Application

After building the application, you should be able to run it and see these results, proving that the parameter correctly made its way into the workflow:

```
Hello Bruce Welcome to Workflow!

Press any key to exit
```

Using Argument Properties

Using a `Dictionary` to pass input arguments to a workflow is a flexible way to provide input. However, it doesn't provide you with much feedback during development. In particular, you have no compile-time checking of argument names or types.

To remedy this, the compiled workflow class also exposes any input arguments as public properties. The properties are defined as `InArgument<T>` for input arguments, where the generic parameter identifies the underlying type that you defined for the argument. The `InArgument<T>` class is one of a series of related classes used to define arguments (`InArgument<T>`, `OutArgument<T>`, `InOutArgument<T>`). To make it easier to set the value for an argument, the `InArgument<T>` class defines an assignment operator that allows you to directly assign a value of type T to the argument.

What all of this means is that a much more type-safe way to pass arguments to a workflow is to use these generated properties like this:

```
using System;
using System.Activities;
using System.Collections.Generic;

namespace HelloWorkflow
{
    class Program
    {
        static void Main(string[] args)
        {
            HelloWorkflowParameters wf = new HelloWorkflowParameters();
            wf.ArgFirstName = "Bruce";
            WorkflowInvoker.Invoke(wf);

            Console.WriteLine("Press any key to exit");
            Console.ReadKey();
        }
    }
}
```

Now you no longer have to wait until you run the workflow to determine whether the argument name is correct and that the value is of the correct type. If you run this revised code, you should see the same results as the previous example that used a `Dictionary` for argument input.

■ **Note** Although using the argument properties of a workflow does solve the problem of type safety, it does raise a potential performance problem. In the previous example that does not use argument properties, the workflow definition and the input arguments were passed to the `WorkflowInvoker` class as separate arguments. This means that you could potentially create a single instance of the workflow definition and use it over and over again to start multiple workflow instances. Each workflow instance could easily have a different set of arguments since they are passed separately from the definition. If you use argument properties, you would have to create a new instance of the workflow definition for each instance that you want to execute. With argument properties, you lose some of the performance advantage of reusing the workflow definition.

Making Decisions

This next example demonstrates a number of other WF concepts. You'll learn how to develop a simple custom activity, how to define and use workflow variables, how to obtain a result value from the workflow, and one way to make simple branching decisions. In the process, you'll be introduced to the `Assign`, `Switch<T>`, and `Throw` activities, which are three of the standard activities included with WF.

The sample application for this example is a simple command-line calculator. The goal is to be able to enter an expression such as `1 + 1` and have the workflow return the correct result. To accomplish this, you will implement a new custom activity to parse the expression into its respective parts (two numbers and an operation). You will then declare a calculator workflow that uses the new activity along with several standard activities to perform the calculation. The result is returned as an output argument of the workflow.

Here are the steps you will follow to implement this example:

1. Create a new Workflow Console Application.

2. Implement a custom activity to parse the arithmetic expression.

3. Define input and output workflow arguments.

4. Define workflow variables.

5. Add the custom activity to the workflow.

6. Add Switch<T> and Assign activities to perform the requested calculation.

7. Write the host application code to accept user input, and execute the workflow.

Creating the Project

Create a new project using the Workflow Console Application template. Name the project Calculator, and add it to the solution for this chapter. You can delete the Workflow1.xaml file that was generated for the project since it won't be used.

Add a new workflow to the project using the Activity template, naming it Calculator. Add a Sequence activity to the empty Calculator workflow.

Implementing a Custom Activity

To use this application, the user will enter an expression such as 1 + 1 or 3 * 5 that is passed to the workflow as a single string. In this step, you will develop a custom activity that will parse the string into its respective parts (two numbers and an operation string). Later, when you declare the workflow, the three parsed values will be assigned to workflow variables and used by other activities.

To create a new activity, select the Add New Item option for the Calculator project, and select the Code Activity template. You can find this new item template in the Workflow category, and it is used to create a new activity that is implemented in code rather than assembled from existing activities. Name the file for the new activity ParseCalculatorArgs.cs. The complete implementation for this activity is shown here:

```
using System;
using System.Activities;

namespace Calculator
{
```

The base class for this activity is CodeActivity. WF provides several base classes that you can derive from to implement your own activities. Your choice of base class depends on the requirements of the custom activity.

> ■ **Note** Chapter 3 discusses the activity base classes in greater detail.

`CodeActivity` is the simplest of the base classes and is the one that you want in this case. It provides minimal access to the workflow runtime and is designed as a simple way to execute your own code within the workflow model.

The activity defines a total of four arguments that are exposed as public properties: one input and three output. Arguments are defined using the generic `InArgument<T>` or `OutArgument<T>` class (depending on the intended direction). In both cases, the type parameter to the generic class specifies the type of the argument. The arguments determine the shape of this activity, just as the input parameters and the return value determine the shape of a C# method. They are the contract with any other WF classes that need to interact with this activity.

I've added `RequiredArgumentAttribute` to the input argument. This identifies that argument as being required and is used to produce an error indicator in the designer if this argument is not set. Adding this attribute isn't a requirement, but it is a good practice to identify required arguments. Anything that helps the consumers of your custom activities to avoid errors is worth the minimal effort.

```
public sealed class ParseCalculatorArgs : CodeActivity
{
    [RequiredArgument]
    public InArgument<String> Expression { get; set; }
    public OutArgument<Double> FirstNumber { get; set; }
    public OutArgument<Double> SecondNumber { get; set; }
    public OutArgument<String> Operation { get; set; }
```

The `Execute` method is where the real work of this activity takes place. This method is defined in the base class as virtual and is overridden here. The `CodeActivityContext` passed to the `Execute` method provides access to the execution context for this activity. The execution context determines the runtime environment that is available to this activity while it executes. This includes the set of variables in scope and that can be safely referenced by the activity.

Before doing anything else, the three output arguments are set to default values. The `FirstNumber` and `SecondNumber` arguments represent the two numbers that will be parsed from the expression and are set to zero. The `Operation` argument will be later set to the operation (+, -, *, /). The `Set` method is called when setting the value of an argument. This method requires you to pass the context object because it determines the current scope of the argument. You aren't simply setting the value for a global argument that you directly manage. You're setting the value for a single instance of an argument that is in scope during a single execution of this activity.

```
protected override void Execute(CodeActivityContext context)
{
    FirstNumber.Set(context, 0);
    SecondNumber.Set(context, 0);
    Operation.Set(context, "error");
```

In a similar manner, the value for the `Expression` argument is retrieved and stored in a local variable. This argument is the single string that contains the entire arithmetic expression to be parsed. The `Get` method of the argument is called to retrieve the value, passing the execution context object as was done with the `Set` method.

The remainder of the code is simple C# parsing logic that splits the expression into its respective parts. As the three parts of the expression are identified, the values are used to set the output arguments.

```csharp
String line = Expression.Get(context);
if (!String.IsNullOrEmpty(line))
{
    String[] arguments = line.Split(' ');
    if (arguments.Length == 3)
    {
        Double number = 0;
        if (Double.TryParse(arguments[0], out number))
        {
            FirstNumber.Set(context, number);
        }
        Operation.Set(context, arguments[1]);
        if (Double.TryParse(arguments[2], out number))
        {
            SecondNumber.Set(context, number);
        }
    }
}
}
```

At this point you should build the project to ensure that the code for this activity was entered correctly. Building the project also adds this activity to the Toolbox, making it available to you when declaring the workflow. Since the `Workflow1.xaml` file that was generated with the new project was deleted, you'll need to comment out or remove one line in the `Program.cs` file in order to successfully build the project.

Defining Arguments

Now that you've implemented the custom activity, it's time to declare the workflow. Open the `Calculator.xaml` file in the workflow designer if it isn't already open. The first order of business is to define the input and output arguments for the workflow. You do this just as you did in the previous example by clicking the Arguments button to open the Argument Editor. Enter these two arguments:

Name	Direction	Argument Type
ArgExpression	In	String
Result	Out	Double

The `ArgExpression` argument is the arithmetic expression that was entered by the user, and the `Result` is the return value from the workflow containing the result of the calculation. Figure 1-8 shows the Argument Editor after I've entered these arguments.

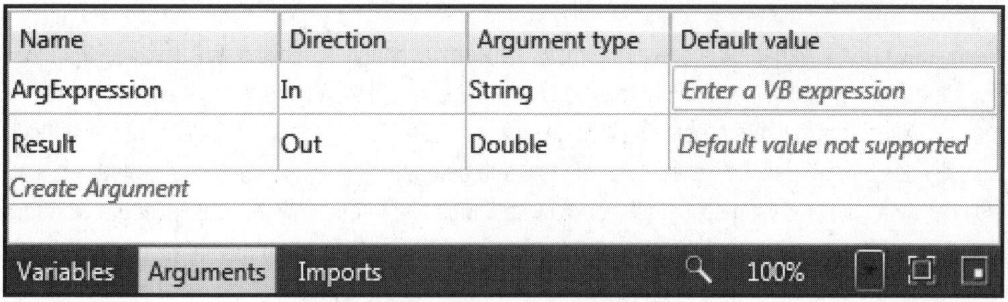

Name	Direction	Argument type	Default value
ArgExpression	In	String	*Enter a VB expression*
Result	Out	Double	*Default value not supported*
Create Argument			

| Variables | **Arguments** | Imports | 🔍 100% | ⬛ ⬜ ◻ |

Figure 1-8. Argument Editor with input and output arguments

■ **Note** You may have noticed that I didn't add the *Arg* prefix to the Result argument. That's because WF uses the argument name Result in certain types of activities as the name for a single output argument. I just happen to like that convention, so I kept it as Result. I also generally don't add the *Arg* prefix to arguments that I define in code, such as in this custom activity. I reserve the prefix for use within the workflow. These are my conventions—you should feel free to define ones that make sense for you.

Defining Variables

You saw that arguments define the shape of an activity and define its contract with other WF classes. And the arguments that you define for a workflow serve the same purpose on a larger scale. But what do you do when you need to maintain internal state within a workflow? That's a job for workflow variables. You define workflow variables when you have data that must be maintained throughout the life of the workflow or when you have transient data that is passed between activities. Variables are always internal to the workflow, in much the same way that private or local variables are internal to a C# class or method.

Workflow variables are entered by pressing the Variables button located in the lower-left corner of the workflow designer. Clicking this button opens the Variable Editor, which operates in a similar fashion as the Argument Editor. When defining variables, you don't need to define a direction since they are always internal. However, you do need to define the scope for each variable. All variables are scoped to a single activity. Just as in traditional C# programming, the scope of a variable determines its visibility, which in this case means which activities can reference the variable. If you decide to scope a variable at the root (topmost) activity of a workflow, it is visible to all activities. But you can also define variables for other composite activities in the workflow that are designed to accept variables. For example, you can define variables for the Sequence activity, but you can't define variables for the custom ParseCalculatorArgs that you developed earlier in this example.

The scoping of variables is important since it not only determines their visibility but also determines when they can be disposed of and garbage collected. Just as in a traditional C# program, a local variable that is defined within a method can be freed and garbage collected as soon as the method ends and the variable goes out of scope. In like manner, the memory used by workflow variables can be freed once the activity that defines them goes out of scope.

■ **Note** The scoping of workflow variables is one of the major conceptual changes between WF 3.*x* and WF 4. In WF 3.*x*, workflow variables were always scoped at the root workflow level. Although this made it easy to share variables between activities, it also led to problems since all data was essentially global. It was sometimes difficult to identify all the activities that referenced a particular variable and determine how their interactions modified the data. Since the global data was always in scope, all workflow variables had to be persisted whenever the workflow was persisted (written to disk when it was idle). The introduction of variable scope into the WF 4 model makes it much clearer how the variables are being used and by which activities. It also improves the performance when persisting workflows since only those variables that are currently in scope need to be persisted.

For this workflow, you need to define the variables listed here. You need these variables as a temporary storage location for the output arguments of the `ParseCalculatorArgs` activity. The variables will then be used as input to subsequent activities defined within the workflow.

Name	Variable Type	Scope
FirstNumber	Double	Sequence
SecondNumber	Double	Sequence
Operation	String	Sequence

To set the scope of a variable, you can either select the activity first or select it from the list in the Variable Editor. The Variable Editor should look like Figure 1-9 after you've entered the variables.

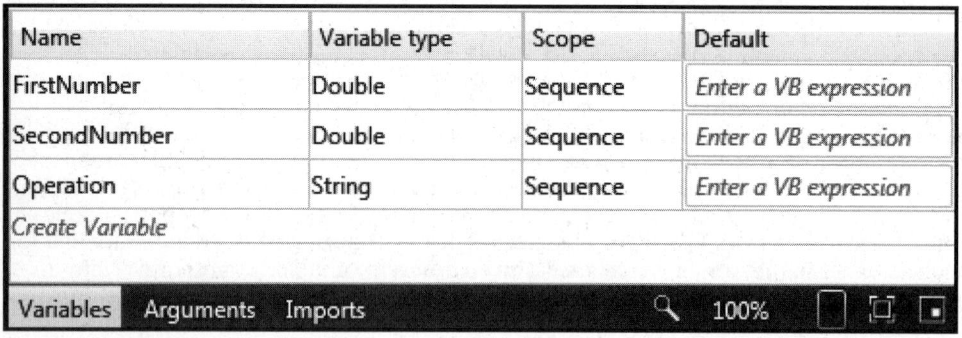

Name	Variable type	Scope	Default
FirstNumber	Double	Sequence	*Enter a VB expression*
SecondNumber	Double	Sequence	*Enter a VB expression*
Operation	String	Sequence	*Enter a VB expression*
Create Variable			

Variables   Arguments   Imports   🔍 100%   ☐ ⧉ ▪

Figure 1-9. Variable Editor

Adding the Custom Activity

Add an instance of the custom `ParseCalculatorArgs` activity that you developed earlier to the open `Sequence` activity. You should see this activity at the top of the Toolbox just like the standard activities that ship with WF. Figure 1-10 is the top of the Toolbox showing this custom activity.

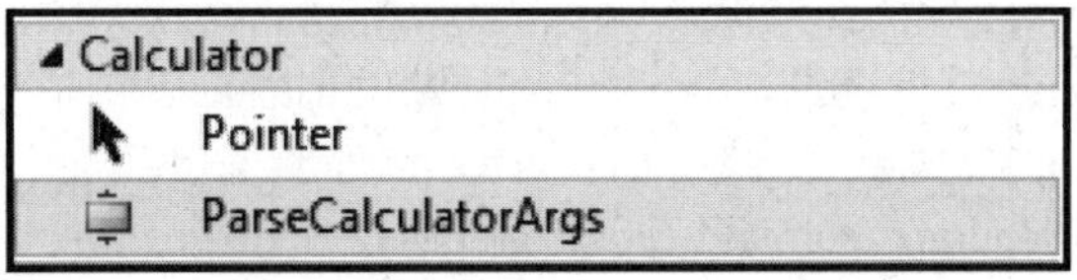

Figure 1-10. *Toolbox showing custom activity*

After dropping a single instance of this activity onto the `Sequence` activity, open the Properties window for the `ParseCalculatorArgs` activity. The four arguments that you defined for this activity are shown here as properties. Your job now is to wire up these properties to the workflow arguments and variables that you defined in the previous steps. Here are the property assignments that you need to make:

Property Name	Value	Description
Expression	ArgExpression	Assigned to the workflow InArgument
FirstNumber	FirstNumber	Assigned to the workflow Variable
Operation	Operation	Assigned to the workflow Variable
SecondNumber	SecondNumber	Assigned to the workflow Variable

In this particular case, most of the property names just happen to be the same as the argument or variable that you are assigning to each property. But that won't always be the case. This assigns the `InArgument` named `Expression` to the `InArgument` of the workflow named `ArgExpression`. The other properties are each defined as an `OutArgument` of the activity and are assigned to workflow variables. Those three variables will be used by subsequent steps in the workflow.

As you enter these argument or variable names, keep in mind that you are really entering workflow expressions. For example, the `Expression` property (an `InArgument` of the activity) is defined as a string. Since you are entering an expression, you can assign any value to this property as long as it resolves to a string. You could enter a literal string, or in this case, you are assigning the property to the value of the workflow argument named `ArgExpression`. When the activity executes and the code retrieves the value for the `InArgument` named `Expression` (using the `Get` method), the workflow expression that you entered here is evaluated. Since the expression is a reference to the workflow `InArgument`, the value of that argument is returned.

In a similar way, the other properties are assigned workflow expressions that will evaluate to the named workflow variables. Since the other properties are each defined as an `OutArgument` of the activity, you can't assign a literal value to them. They must be assigned to a workflow variable or `OutArgument`.

Figure 1-11 is the Properties window after I have entered expressions for all the activity properties.

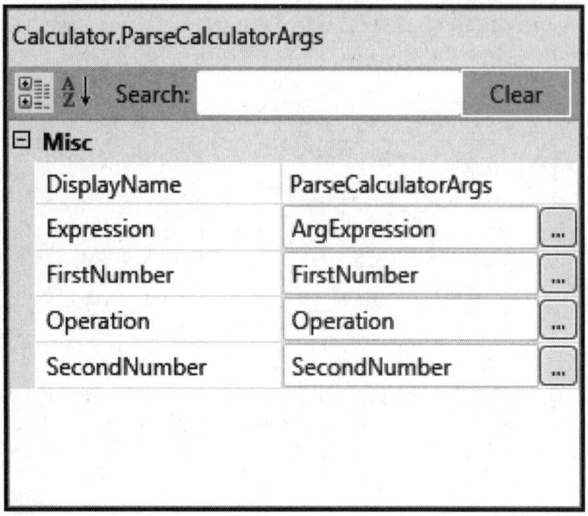

Figure 1-11. *ParseCalculatorArgs properties*

Adding the Switch<T> and Assign Activities

Now that the workflow has parsed the arithmetic expression, it's time to make decisions and perform some basic arithmetic. The only real decision that must be made is what type of arithmetic operation the user wants to perform.

You can make that decision in several ways within the workflow model, but the one that I've chosen to use for this example is the `Switch<T>` activity. This generic activity operates just like a `switch` statement in C#, allowing you to execute a different set of activities based on the value of a single expression.

Drag and drop an instance of the `Switch<T>` activity to the location just below the `ParseCalculatorArgs` activity. When you do, you will be prompted to select the type for this generic activity. The generic type must match the type of the expression that will be evaluated for branching. In this example, the branching decisions will be made on the value of the `Operation` workflow variable, which is a string. So, select String when you are prompted to select a generic type. Figure 1-12 is the type selection dialog after I made my selection.

Figure 1-12. Generic type selection dialog

The Switch<T> activity should already be expanded for your use, but you can double-click it to expand it if necessary. The Expression property is where you supply the workflow expression that you want to use for branching. Enter the Operation variable name for this property. You can enter it directly within the workflow designer, or you can switch to the Properties window and enter it there.

The Switch<T> activity allows you to enter any number of cases, each one containing the activities that you want to execute when that case is true. In this example, each case is one of the supported arithmetic operations (+, -, *, /). There is also a placeholder for a default case that is executed when none of the other cases is true.

To add the first case to support addition, click "Add new case" at the bottom of the activity. The left side of the case is where you enter the value to match, and the right side is the container for the activities to execute when the case is true. For this first case, enter + on the left side (where it is labeled "Input case here").

Since this first case is for addition, you need to add the FirstNumber and SecondNumber variables together and assign the sum to the Result argument of the workflow. You can accomplish this with another one of the standard activities included with WF, the Assign activity (found in the Primitives Toolbox category). This activity assigns an expression to a variable or argument. Drag and drop an instance of the Assign activity to the open addition case that you just added. The Assign activity has two properties. The Assign.To property is the variable or argument that receives the assignment. The Assign.Value property is the expression that will be assigned to the Assign.To property. Enter Result for the Assign.To property name. This is the workflow OutArgument that is used to return the result of the arithmetic operation. Enter this expression in the Assign.Value property:

```
FirstNumber + SecondNumber
```

This expression adds the two numbers and places the sum in the Result argument of the workflow. Your Switch<T> activity should look like Figure 1-13 at this point.

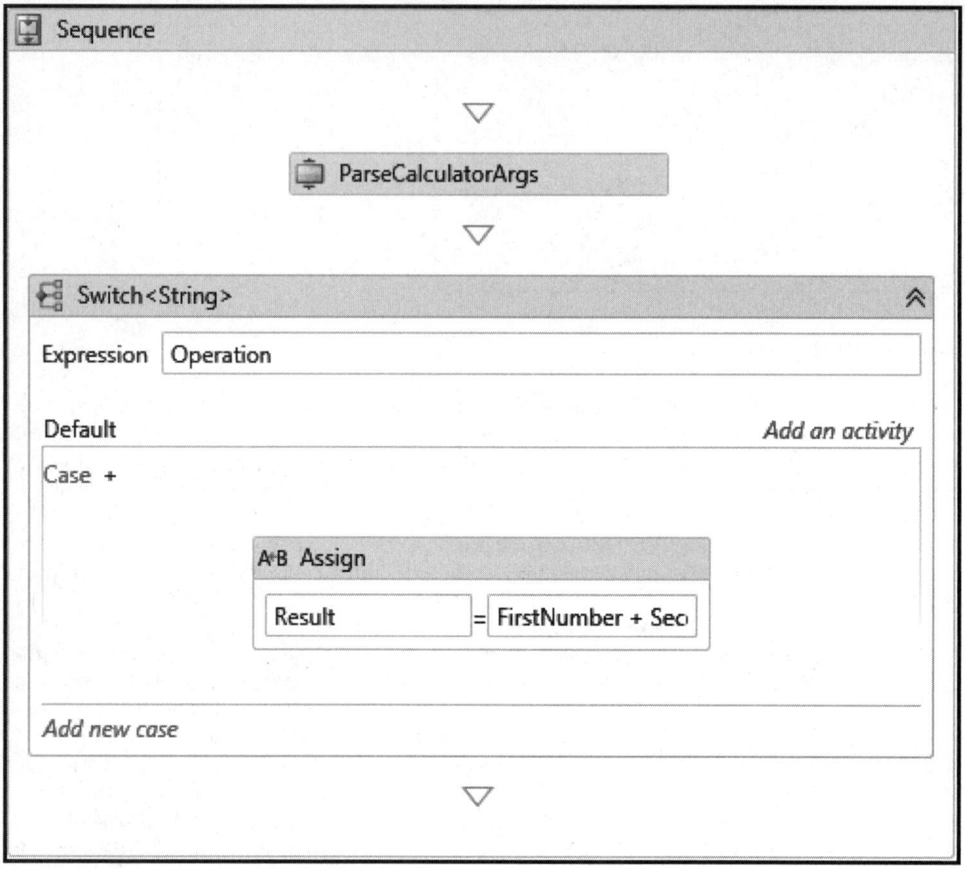

Figure 1-13. Switch activity with the addition case

Add three additional cases to the `Switch<T>` activity to handle subtraction, multiplication, and division. Add an `Assign` activity to each one to perform the requested operation. Here are the parameters that you should enter. Even though the case for addition has already been entered, the parameters for this case are included in this list for completeness.

Case	Assign To	Assign Value
+	Result	FirstNumber + SecondNumber
-	Result	FirstNumber - SecondNumber
*	Result	FirstNumber * SecondNumber
/	Result	FirstNumber / SecondNumber

■ **Note** In this example, you added a single `Assign` activity to each case within the `Switch<T>`. However, you're not limited to executing a single activity for each case. You could have added a `Sequence` activity to the case and then added multiple child activities to the `Sequence` activity. In this way, the workflow model allows you to compose multiple layers of child activities that are executed at the proper time.

You need to add one final activity to this workflow to complete it. The Default case of the `Switch<T>` activity is executed when none of the other cases is true. Instead of ignoring the error, go ahead and drop a `Throw` activity onto the right side of the Default case. The `Throw` activity is used to throw a .NET exception. Enter this expression in the `Exception` property of the `Throw` activity to raise an exception if the user enters an invalid operation:

```
New InvalidOperationException("Operation Invalid")
```

The `Switch<T>` activity should now look like Figure 1-14.

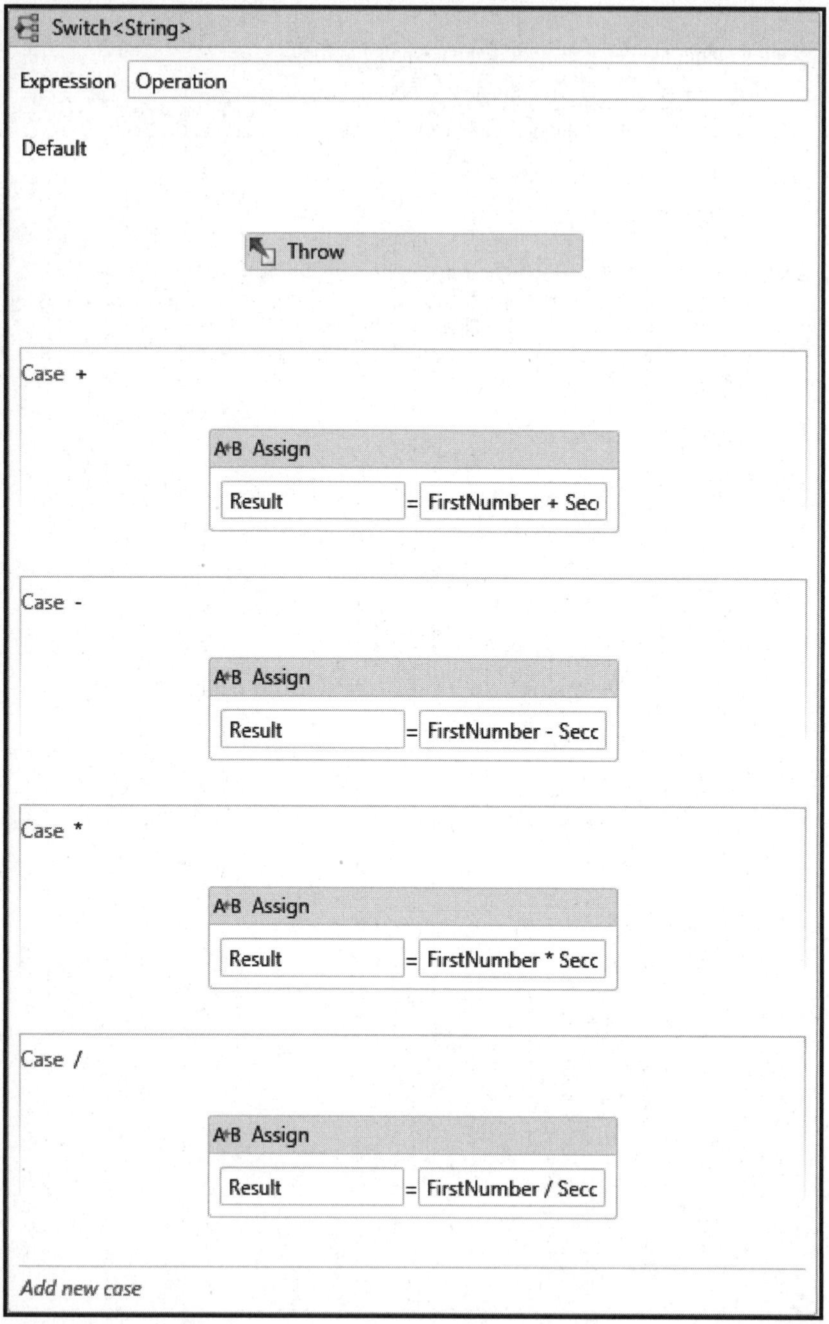

Figure 1-14. *Completed Switch activity*

When you're done working in the expanded view of the **Switch<T>** activity, you can return to the parent activity using the breadcrumb navigation at the top of the designer. Figure 1-15 shows the navigation bar that you should see at this point. Clicking Sequence will return you to the parent activity. Clicking Calculator will return all the way to the root activity of the workflow.

```
Calculator  >  Sequence  >  Switch<String>
```

Figure 1-15. Breadcrumb navigation

Hosting the Workflow

The code that you need to add to the **Program.cs** file is shown here. The code to start the workflow is similar to what you've already seen in the previous examples. The major difference from the previous hosting code is that the entire process of starting a workflow has been put into a **while** loop. At the top of the loop, the user is asked to enter an arithmetic expression or to enter the literal "quit" to exit the program. The string that is accepted from the console is passed to the workflow as the expression to solve.

```csharp
using System;
using System.Activities;
using System.Collections.Generic;

namespace Calculator
{
    class Program
    {
        static void Main(string[] args)
        {
            while (true)
            {
                Console.WriteLine("Enter an expression or 'quit' to exit");
                String expression = Console.ReadLine();
                if (!String.IsNullOrEmpty(expression))
                {
                    if (expression.Trim().ToLower() == "quit")
                    {
                        Console.WriteLine("Exiting program");
                        return;
                    }
                }

                Calculator wf = new Calculator();
                wf.ArgExpression = expression;
```

Output from the workflow is returned by the `Invoke` method in the form of a `IDictionary<String, Object>`. The output value for an argument is retrieved from the dictionary using its name. Only workflow arguments defined with a direction of out or in/out are returned in this collection. This code also wraps the `Invoke` method in a `try`/`catch` block in order to catch the exception that might be thrown by the workflow if an invalid expression is entered.

```
try
{
    IDictionary<String, Object> results =
        WorkflowInvoker.Invoke(wf);
    Console.WriteLine("Result = {0}", results["Result"]);
}
catch (InvalidOperationException exception)
{
    Console.WriteLine(exception.Message.ToString());
}
}
}
}
}
```

■ **Note** In this example, the work of polling the user for input and looping until they are done is handled by the host application. It could have also been handled within the workflow itself. However, at this point in the discussion I wanted to keep the example as simple as possible and not prematurely introduce additional workflow concepts related to host communication. Chapter 8 provides additional information on host communication and the interactions between the host application and the workflow instance.

Running the Application

After building the project, you should be ready to take it out for a test-drive. Make sure you set the `Calculator` project as the startup project. When you first run the program, you should be prompted to enter an arithmetic expression to solve. If you enter a valid expression such as `1 + 1`, you should receive the correct answer of "2" and be prompted to enter another expression:

```
Enter an expression or 'quit' to exit

1 + 1

Result = 2

Enter an expression or 'quit' to exit
```

Try all of the other operations (-, *, /) to make sure that they all work correctly. If you enter an invalid operation or an expression that is not in the correct format (two numbers and an operation separated by spaces), the Default case in the `Switch<T>` activity is executed, and an exception is thrown. The exception is caught by the host application, and the exception message is displayed:

```
Enter an expression or 'quit' to exit

bad expr

Operation Invalid

Enter an expression or 'quit' to exit
```

When you're done testing this application, you can enter the literal "quit" to exit the program. Here's a representative example of the results that you should see:

```
Enter an expression or 'quit' to exit

5 + 3

Result = 8

Enter an expression or 'quit' to exit

100 - 75

Result = 25

Enter an expression or 'quit' to exit

8 * 7.56

Result = 60.48

Enter an expression or 'quit' to exit

123 / 2

Result = 61.5

Enter an expression or 'quit' to exit

1+1
```

```
Operation Invalid

Enter an expression or 'quit' to exit

quit

Exiting program

Press any key to continue . . .
```

Debugging the Application

Before you leave this example, this is a good time to familiarize yourself with the debugging support provided by the development environment. As you might expect, all of the normal C# debugging is still available. You can set a breakpoint anywhere within the C# code, and the debugger will stop when it reaches that breakpoint. For example, you can set a breakpoint within the custom ParseCalculatorArgs activity and step through the code as the activity executes.

But the WF support in Visual Studio also provides additional ways to debug your workflows. You can also set breakpoints directly on an activity while you are in the workflow designer. For example, Figure 1-16 shows the workflow after I set a breakpoint on the Switch<T> activity.

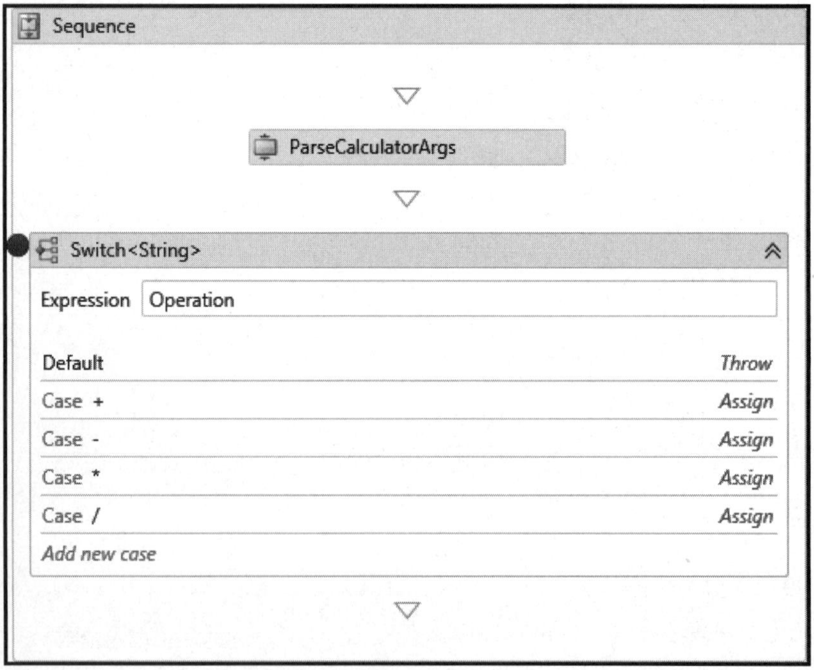

Figure 1-16. Workflow with breakpoint set

When I run the application with debugging (F5), execution breaks just before the activity begins execution. This is shown in Figure 1-17.

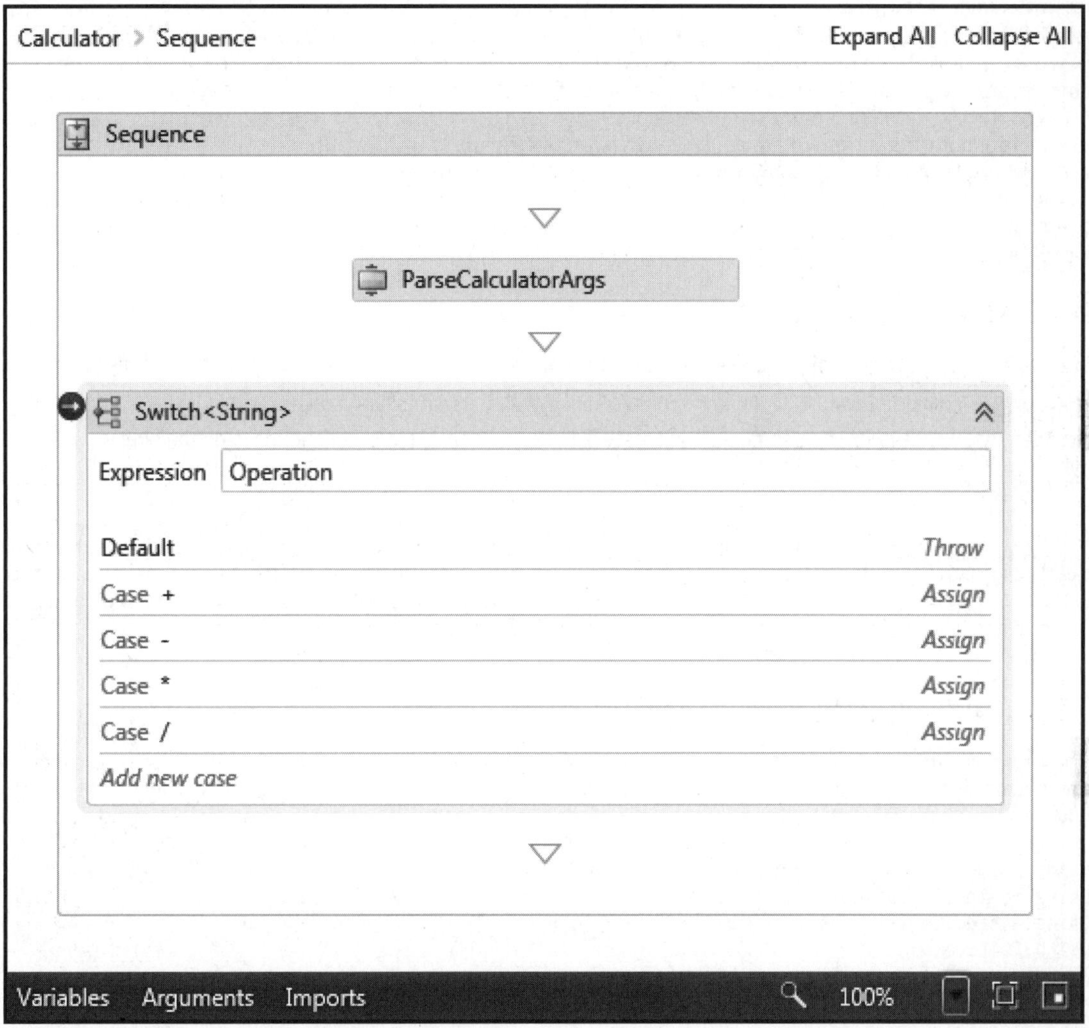

Figure 1-17. Workflow with breakpoint hit

Once the breakpoint is hit and execution has stopped, you have the usual set of debugging actions such as "step into" or "step over." You can also use the debugger when you are viewing the workflow Xaml in Code View. You can set breakpoints directly in the Xaml and use debugger actions to step through the activities once the breakpoint has been hit. In fact, breakpoints set in one view (for example in the workflow designer) are carried forward when you view the same workflow in the other view.

CHAPTER 1 ■ A QUICK TOUR OF WINDOWS WORKFLOW FOUNDATION

Unit Testing

One of the benefits of the workflow model is that it forces you to think about encapsulating your business logic into discrete components. It's good practice to do this even when you are developing nonworkflow applications. But everything in WF is built around the idea that you are coordinating units of work (encapsulated in activities) that have (ideally) already been tested. That's where unit testing comes into the picture. The same design features of WF that make it easy to coordinate these separate units of work also make it easy to test them.

Before completely leaving the calculator example, I want to briefly implement a few unit tests for the application. Unit tests in Visual Studio live in their own separate projects, so to begin, add a new project to the solution named `CalculatorTest`. Use the project template named Test Project that is in the Test category. The project template creates a sample `UnitTest1.cs` file for you. You can delete this file since it won't be needed.

■ **Note** The goal of these tests is to demonstrate how you can implement unit tests for your WF activities and workflows. My assumption is that you are already familiar with the unit testing support within Visual Studio. If you are interested in a tutorial or reference on unit testing, I suggest one of the excellent books on the subject.

The unit test project you added already has a reference to the Microsoft unit test framework, but you need to add an assembly reference to `System.Activities` to provide access to the WF classes. You should also add a project reference to the `Calculator` project since it contains the classes that you need to test. That project should be in the same solution as this test project.

Testing the Custom Activity

The first tests are for the custom `ParseCalculatorArgs` activity. Select Add New Test for the test project, and select Basic Unit Test as the item template. Name the new test class `ParseCalculatorArgsTest`. The code for this class follows:

```
using System;
using System.Activities;
using System.Collections.Generic;
using Calculator;
using Microsoft.VisualStudio.TestTools.UnitTesting;

namespace CalculatorTest
{
    [TestClass]
    public class ParseCalculatorArgsTest
    {
```

This first method tests for valid results using a valid parameter that is passed to the activity. The second method tests the negative condition by passing an invalid argument.

This test code illustrates one important new concept: you can execute individual activities just as easily as you can execute a complete workflow. To the workflow runtime, a workflow is really just another activity that has one or more child activities.

```
[TestMethod]
public void ValidExpressionTest()
{
    Dictionary<String, Object> parameters
        = new Dictionary<string, object>();
    parameters.Add("Expression", "1 + 2");

    IDictionary<String, Object> outputs = WorkflowInvoker.Invoke(
        new ParseCalculatorArgs(), parameters);

    Assert.IsNotNull(outputs, "outputs should not be null");
    Assert.AreEqual(3, outputs.Count, "outputs count is incorrect");
    Assert.AreEqual((Double)1, outputs["FirstNumber"],
        "FirstNumber is incorrect");
    Assert.AreEqual((Double)2, outputs["SecondNumber"],
        "SecondNumber is incorrect");
    Assert.AreEqual("+", outputs["Operation"],
        "Operation is incorrect");
}

[TestMethod]
public void InvalidExpressionTest()
{
    Dictionary<String, Object> parameters
        = new Dictionary<string, object>();
    parameters.Add("Expression", "badexpression");

    IDictionary<String, Object> outputs = WorkflowInvoker.Invoke(
        new ParseCalculatorArgs(), parameters);

    Assert.IsNotNull(outputs, "outputs should not be null");
    Assert.AreEqual(3, outputs.Count, "outputs count is incorrect");
    Assert.AreEqual("error", outputs["Operation"],
        "Operation is incorrect");
}
}
}
```

After building the project, you should be ready to execute the tests. There are several ways to do this, but I find that the easiest is to start the test from within the current source file. You can scroll up to the top of the file and right-click the class name (ParseCalculatorArgsTest). One of the options should be Run Tests, which runs all of the tests that are currently in scope. Since you selected the class name, it runs all of the tests for the class. Figure 1-18 shows the Test Results panel after I run these tests:

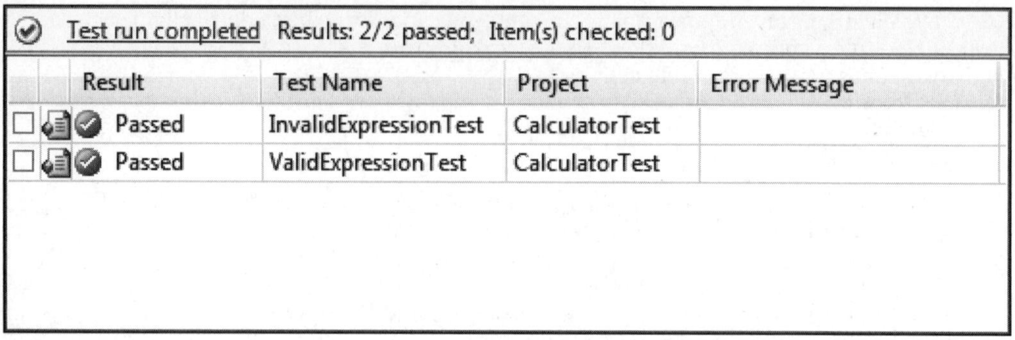

	Result	Test Name	Project	Error Message
☑	✔ Passed	InvalidExpressionTest	CalculatorTest	
☑	✔ Passed	ValidExpressionTest	CalculatorTest	

✔ Test run completed Results: 2/2 passed; Item(s) checked: 0

Figure 1-18. Successful unit tests for ParseCalculatorArgs

Testing the Workflow

The previous tests exercised only the **ParseCalculatorArgs** activity. Now that you have some reassurance that the activity works by itself, you can add a set of tests for the calculator workflow. Add another unit test class to the same project, and name it **CalculatorTest**. Here is the code for the **CalculatorTest.cs** file:

```
using System;
using System.Activities;
using System.Collections.Generic;
using Microsoft.VisualStudio.TestTools.UnitTesting;

namespace CalculatorTest
{
    [TestClass]
    public class CalculatorTest
    {
        [TestMethod]
        public void AddTest()
        {
            Dictionary<String, Object> parameters
                = new Dictionary<string, object>();
            parameters.Add("ArgExpression", "111 + 222");

            IDictionary<String, Object> outputs = WorkflowInvoker.Invoke(
                new Calculator.Calculator(), parameters);

            Assert.IsNotNull(outputs, "outputs should not be null");
            Assert.AreEqual(1, outputs.Count, "outputs count is incorrect");
            Assert.AreEqual((Double)333, outputs["Result"],
                "Result is incorrect");
        }
```

```csharp
[TestMethod]
public void SubtractTest()
{
    Dictionary<String, Object> parameters
        = new Dictionary<string, object>();
    parameters.Add("ArgExpression", "333 - 222");

    IDictionary<String, Object> outputs = WorkflowInvoker.Invoke(
        new Calculator.Calculator(), parameters);

    Assert.IsNotNull(outputs, "outputs should not be null");
    Assert.AreEqual(1, outputs.Count, "outputs count is incorrect");
    Assert.AreEqual((Double)111, outputs["Result"],
        "Result is incorrect");
}

[TestMethod]
public void MultiplyTest()
{
    Dictionary<String, Object> parameters
        = new Dictionary<string, object>();
    parameters.Add("ArgExpression", "111 * 5");

    IDictionary<String, Object> outputs = WorkflowInvoker.Invoke(
        new Calculator.Calculator(), parameters);

    Assert.IsNotNull(outputs, "outputs should not be null");
    Assert.AreEqual(1, outputs.Count, "outputs count is incorrect");
    Assert.AreEqual((Double)555, outputs["Result"],
        "Result is incorrect");
}

[TestMethod]
public void DivideTest()
{
    Dictionary<String, Object> parameters
        = new Dictionary<string, object>();
    parameters.Add("ArgExpression", "555 / 5");

    IDictionary<String, Object> outputs = WorkflowInvoker.Invoke(
        new Calculator.Calculator(), parameters);

    Assert.IsNotNull(outputs, "outputs should not be null");
    Assert.AreEqual(1, outputs.Count, "outputs count is incorrect");
    Assert.AreEqual((Double)111, outputs["Result"],
        "Result is incorrect");
}
}
}
```

This code is very similar to the previous tests. In this case, the focus is on testing the entire workflow rather than a single activity, so the WorkflowInvoker executes the workflow instead of the custom activity.

I've included separate test methods for each of the possible operations (add, subtract, multiply, and divide).

When you're ready, you can execute all the tests for the entire project from the Test menu. Select the Run option and then All Tests in Solution. If all goes well, your results should look like Figure 1-19.

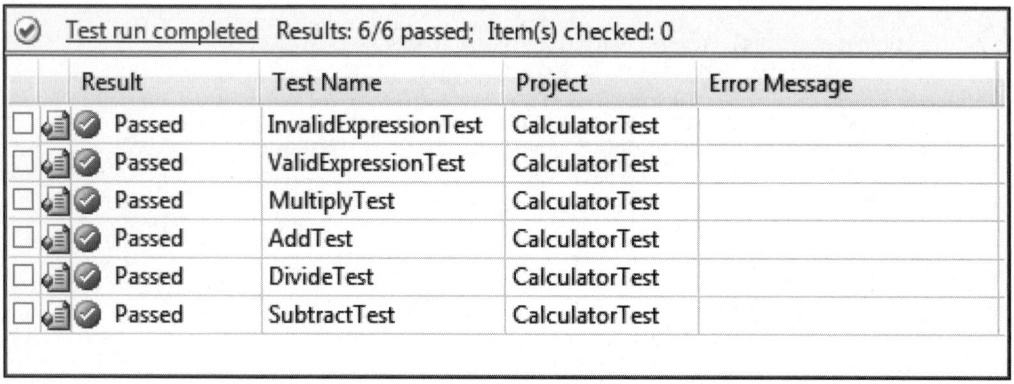

		Result	Test Name	Project	Error Message
⊘	Test run completed	Results: 6/6 passed; Item(s) checked: 0			
☐		Passed	InvalidExpressionTest	CalculatorTest	
☐		Passed	ValidExpressionTest	CalculatorTest	
☐		Passed	MultiplyTest	CalculatorTest	
☐		Passed	AddTest	CalculatorTest	
☐		Passed	DivideTest	CalculatorTest	
☐		Passed	SubtractTest	CalculatorTest	

Figure 1-19. Successful unit tests for the solution

■ **Note** In this example, I chose to fully implement the custom activity and the workflow first and perform the initial testing from the console application. The unit tests were developed afterward. The test-first school of thought is that you should develop your tests first before you have fully implemented the classes that you want to test. Initially the tests will fail, but that changes after the classes are fully implemented.

You can implement your applications and unit tests either way. Because workflow applications are built from a number of discrete activities, it is fairly easy to follow the test-first methodology if that is your choice. I chose to fully implement the application first because the focus of this book is on demonstrating WF concepts, not on unit testing. And quite frankly, it's more interesting to see a working application rather than a list of green check marks.

Summary

The purpose of this chapter was to provide you with a quick tour of Windows Workflow Foundation. You started by implementing your first workflow application. This simple example introduced you to the workflow designer, workflow activities, the Sequence and WriteLine activities, and the WorkflowInvoker class that you used to execute a workflow. This first example also introduced you to the Xaml format that is used to declare workflows. In the second example, you learned how to pass parameters using workflow arguments.

The calculator example demonstrated how to construct a simple custom activity and one way to declare branching decisions within a workflow. You learned how to define input and output arguments for the custom activity and how to use workflow variables to pass values between activities. This example also introduced you to the `Switch<T>`, `Assign`, and `Throw` standard activities.

After demonstrating some of the additional debugger fweatures that are available for WF, the chapter concluded with a set of unit tests for the calculator example.

In the next chapter, you'll learn more about the major components in Windows Workflow Foundation.

CHAPTER 2

∎∎∎

Foundation Overview

The purpose of this chapter is to provide a grand tour of Windows Workflow Foundation (WF). It includes a high-level description of the major features of WF. The chapter also provides some necessary background information that will help you get the most out of the remaining chapters. Because of the summary focus of this chapter, it doesn't contain much actual workflow code.

The chapter begins with a brief description of the features and capabilities that are included with WF. Following this, I provide an overview of the .NET assemblies and namespaces within them that are related to WF. Topics related to the activity life cycle are then discussed, followed by a short primer on workflow expressions. The chapter concludes with a list of the top features that are currently missing from WF 4.

WF Features and Capabilities

In this section, I briefly describe the most important features and capabilities of WF. The focus is on familiarizing you with the out-of-the-box features that are available when you build your own workflow-enabled applications.

Declarative Activity Model

Activities are the core building blocks of workflows. Each activity is narrowly designed to accomplish some type of useful work. Workflows are composed by assembling multiple activities into a useful pattern to accomplish some goal.

WF uses a declarative model to describe activities and workflows that I think is the single most important feature of WF. Individual activities and workflows are organized as a hierarchical tree of activities. Some activities are leaf nodes; others act as containers for child activities. Using this declarative model, you declare the activities that you want to execute in some prescribed sequence. The sequence and conditions under which the activities execute is based on their location in the tree. Changing the conditions under which an activity executes may be as simple as changing its location in the tree. The declarative model encourages a clear separation between the actual work to be accomplished (represented by the individual activities) and the mechanism that coordinates that work.

This is in contrast with the procedural model. In that model, you need to implement not only the code necessary to accomplish some useful work but also the control code to coordinate that work. Under this model, the lines are often blurred between the code that accomplishes the actual work and the coordinating code. The coordinating code is typically implemented as a series of imperative procedural statements that may be entwined with the code that performs the real work. Changing the sequence or conditions under which the work is executed is accomplished by changing the procedural code.

In WF, activities and workflows are really interchangeable components since they are built upon the same model. There is nothing distinctive about a workflow that prevents it from being used as an activity (a building block) in another workflow. Likewise, there is nothing that prevents you from directly executing a single activity as if it were a much larger workflow.

■ **Tip** The real deciding factor that distinguishes an activity from a workflow is how it is used. If the component is directly executed by an application, I call that a *workflow*. If it is used as a single building block within a larger workflow, I call that an *activity*. A single component may serve both roles: sometimes executed directly and other times used within a larger workflow.

Using the same underlying model for activities and workflows provides important advantages. It allows you to freely declare and assemble activities without regard for how they were originally used. When you declare your own custom activities, you don't need to predestine or restrict their future use based solely on their original use. For example, you might initially declare a workflow and execute it directly to meet your immediate needs. Later, you might discover that you also need to execute the steps in that workflow as part of a much larger workflow. Since an activity is a workflow and a workflow is an activity, you can now include the original workflow as an individual step in the new workflow.

This consistent model also allows you to more easily compose activities. You can start by declaring activities that complete small, granular units of work. You then compose those activities into slightly larger ones that coordinate a handful of activities. Those activities are then incrementally composed into larger activities and so on. Composition is now promoted as a first-class authoring style of this model.

WF always uses a declarative model, regardless of how the model is constructed. Most of the time, you will declare activities in Xaml, an XML-based markup syntax that supports the declaration of objects and properties. However, WF also supports the declaration of activities entirely in code. Even though it may be defined in code, the model is still a declarative one.

Standard Activities

One of the most significant WF deliverables is a standard activity library. This library consists of the most common essential building blocks that you will need to construct your own activities and workflows. Chapter 3 provides a summary of the standard activities that are included with WF.

Custom Activities

Although WF includes a set of standard activities, you are by no means limited to using only the activities that come with WF. In fact, you will find it difficult to harness the real power of WF without developing your own custom activities.

Custom activities can be implemented in procedural code or declaratively composed from other activities. Composition can take place in code or, more often, using Xaml.

WF provides several base classes that you can use to author your own custom activities. Each base class is tailored to a particular type of work. For example, the `CodeActivity` class provides a simple way to synchronously execute imperative code on the workflow thread. In contrast with this, the

`AsyncCodeActivity` class provides a way to execute work asynchronously on another thread. Here are the major categories of work that you can accomplish within an activity:

- Atomic unit of work

- Asynchronous unit of work

- Long-running unit of work

- Control flow activities

Activities that are implemented entirely in code are compiled into Common Language Runtime (CLR) types. Activities that are declared in Xaml are either compiled into CLR types or deserialized and executed directly from the file system.

Chapter 3 provides additional information on creating custom activities.

Workflow Designer

WF includes a workflow designer that is integrated into Visual Studio. This designer allows you to visually declare activities and workflows using a familiar drag-and-drop interface. Properties of each activity are set using the Properties window or, in some cases, directly on the design surface. Individual activities are selected from the Visual Studio Toolbox and dropped onto the workflow design canvas. The standard activities that are included with WF as well as any custom activities in referenced assemblies are included in the Toolbox.

Custom Activity Designers and Validation

Properties for each activity may be set using the standard Properties window within Visual Studio. In addition, individual activities may support in-place designers that allow you to set the most frequently used properties directly from the design surface.

Custom activity designers are not restricted to only the activities that are provided with WF. The classes that are needed to support an enhanced design experience are also available for use with your custom activities. Although you aren't required to create custom designers, doing so may greatly increase the productivity of the developers that use your activities.

You can also add validation rules to your custom activities. The purpose of validation rules is to catch potential errors as early as possible in the development process. For example, you can identify required properties for an activity by simply applying the `RequiredArgument` attribute to the properties. If a developer uses the activity but neglects to set a value for the required properties, they are immediately alerted to the problem with an error that is shown on the design surface. A build error would be generated if the project was built without setting values for the required properties. You can also implement more elaborate validation logic when it is necessary.

Chapter 15 discusses developing custom designers and adding validation to your activities.

Multiple Modeling Styles

WF includes support for two standard modeling styles out-of-the-box: procedural and flowchart. The modeling style determines how the flow of control between individual activities is modeled. Microsoft may provide other modeling styles in the future (for example, state machine), or you can implement activities that support your own modeling style. However, the two styles that are included with WF are both flexible enough to tackle most workflow tasks.

The procedural modeling style uses familiar programming constructs to control the flow of execution. Standard activities are included that mimic C# branching and looping keywords such as `if` and `while`. You control the flow of execution by placing child activities into the appropriate control activity. In contrast with this, the flowchart modeling style uses direct links between activities to control the flow of execution. The procedural modeling style could be thought of as rigid, structured, and precise, while the flowchart style is free-form. The two styles peacefully coexist and can be freely mixed within a single activity or workflow.

Workflow Debugger

The Visual Studio debugger provides an integrated solution for debugging your activities and workflows. Breakpoints can be set directly on the workflow designer surface or within a Xaml document for individual activities. Once the debugger stops at a breakpoint, you can step into or stop over activities, just as you would when you are debugging C# code. You can also seamlessly step into code from the workflow model.

Workflow Services

Workflow services are Windows Communication Foundation (WCF) services that are declaratively implemented as workflows. WCF clients directly access the workflow via one or more exposed endpoints. The workflow service is completely self-contained, defining the service contract as well as other parameters within the workflow itself. Common message exchange patterns of request/response, one-way, and duplex are supported.

WF also provides standard activities that allow you to consume WCF services from within an activity or workflow. This allows a workflow to take on the role of a WCF client and invoke services that may or may not be implemented as workflows.

Multiple WCF service operations can be implemented by a workflow. At least one operation must be designated as one that can create a new instance of the workflow. Other operations may work with an existing workflow instance. To route WCF messages to an existing workflow instance, correlation is used. WF supports two types of correlation:

- Context correlation uses tokens passed within the SOAP headers to identify the workflow instance to receive the message.

- Content correlation uses one or more data elements from the message itself to route the message.

Chapters 9 and 10 discuss workflow services in further detail.

Multiple Workflow Hosts

All workflows are executed by a workflow runtime that is provided with WF (although it might be more appropriate to call it an activity runtime). Your application code doesn't directly execute an activity – that task is reserved for the workflow runtime. The runtime is responsible for the execution of individual activities that have been scheduled for execution, thread management, persistence, tracking, bookmark processing, and so on.

Activities can be hosted within your application using one of the workflow host classes provided with WF. These classes are your public interface to the workflow runtime. The `WorkflowInvoker` class is the simplest way to execute an activity. It is designed to execute an activity with the simplicity of calling a C# method. The `WorkflowApplication` class is a full-featured workflow host that supports additional features such as asynchronous operation, persistence, and bookmark support for long-running workflows.

You also have several choices for hosting workflow services. They can be hosted in a Microsoft-provided environment such as IIS, or they can be self-hosted within your own application. The `WorkflowServiceHost` class is used when you want to self-host workflow services.

WF also provides the ability to directly use a Xaml file containing an activity definition without any intermediate build step. A workflow service Xamlx file can be loaded and used directly from the file system in a similar way. Once an activity definition has been deserialized, it can be hosted by any of the self-hosting classes in the same way as a definition that was compiled into a CLR type.

Chapter 4 further discusses the workflow hosting options. Chapter 9 covers hosting for workflow services.

Workflow Extensions

WF supports an extension mechanism that can provide additional functionality for activities and workflows. These custom workflow extensions are added to the host classes described in the previous section. Once an extension is added, the public methods of the extension can be invoked from a custom activity. A singleton instance of an extension can be shared by multiple workflow instances, or a new instance can be constructed for each workflow instance.

Workflow extensions are first demonstrated in Chapter 8.

Persistence

Workflow persistence is the ability to save and later reload the state of a workflow instance. This capability is important since it facilitates the development of long-running workflows that may take minutes, hours, or days to complete. While a workflow is waiting for some external input, its state is safely persisted, and it can be unloaded from memory. When the external input is available, the instance is reloaded into memory, and processing can continue.

WF includes support for persistence to a SQL Server database. This SQL Server support should meet your needs for most workflow applications. However, persistence is a pluggable component. You can use the SQL Server support, or you can develop your own custom class (an instance store) that supports persistence to some other medium. Custom workflow extensions can also participate in persistence, allowing you to inject additional data that is persisted along with the workflow instance.

Chapters 11 and 12 discuss workflow persistence.

Bookmark Processing

WF supports the ability to temporarily suspend execution of a workflow and resume execution at a later time. The general mechanism that supports this is called *bookmark processing*. Just as a real bookmark identifies your place in a real book, a WF bookmark identifies the point of execution in a workflow.

When a bookmark is created, the workflow signals that it is waiting for some external input. At this point, the activity yields control over the workflow thread, allowing it to be used elsewhere in the same workflow. If there is no other scheduled work to be performed within the workflow, the workflow becomes idle and is capable of being persisted and unloaded. When a bookmark is resumed, execution continues at the location of the bookmark. Additional data can be passed into the workflow instance when a bookmark is resumed.

This same general mechanism is used for conventional workflows and also for workflow services. In the case of workflow services, the receipt of a WCF message triggers the resumption of a bookmark.

Bookmark processing is first demonstrated in Chapter 8.

Expressions

One of the design goals of WF was to support a completely declarative design-time experience. This included the ability to set values for activity properties and workflow variables. What WF really required was a general-purpose mechanism to declaratively execute some code and return a value. The mechanism that was chosen was workflow expressions. In the broadest sense, expressions in WF include any activities that return a single value. Expressions allow you to declare code that assigns a value to a property, saves a value to a workflow variable, and so on. You can think of expressions as the small bits of glue code within the declarative model.

At design time, expressions are entered within the designer using the property editor or a separate expression editor dialog. They become part of the workflow model and are saved as part of the definition document (Xaml or Xamlx).

Expressions are discussed in more detail later in this chapter and are used throughout this book.

Transaction Support

Transactions allow you to ensure consistency when you are performing update operations against a resource such as a SQL Server database. WF provides the ability to declare a transaction within the workflow model using the `TransactionScope` activity. Child activities that are added to this activity all share the same transaction, and all succeed or fail as one unit of work. If you are using workflow services, you also have the ability to flow an existing external transaction into the workflow.

Chapter 13 covers transaction support. Chapter 10 discusses flowing a transaction into a workflow service.

Compensation and Exception Handling

Unhandled exceptions within an activity or workflow can be handled by the host application. WF also provides a declarative way to handle exceptions internally within a workflow. Handling the exception locally provides you with a better opportunity to possibly recover from the failure.

Compensation is the undoing of work that has already completed. WF provides a mechanism to optionally declare a set of activities to execute when compensation is triggered.

Chapter 13 covers compensation and exception handling.

Workflow Tracking

Workflow tracking is a built-in mechanism that provides automatic instrumentation of workflows. WF provides a fairly large amount of potential tracking information for each workflow. The tracking data includes the time when each activity was scheduled for execution, when it began execution, when it ended, each transition to a different status, and so on. You can define and apply a tracking profile to filter the information to just the right amount to meet your needs.

The most important feature of workflow tracking is that it is automatic. It is built into the workflow runtime infrastructure and can be enabled without changing your workflows at all.

Out of the box, WF provides a tracking participant that directs tracking data to the Event Tracing for Windows system (ETW). This data is viewable using the Windows Event Viewer. If you want to persist the tracking data in a more usable form, you can develop your own tracking participant.

Chapter 14 covers workflow tracking.

Designer Rehosting

The workflow designer that is integrated with Visual Studio allows developers to efficiently declare activities and workflows. WF provides the classes necessary to host this same designer within your applications. This is especially important when your application end users require the ability to customize the workflows that are used by the application. If this is the case, you might want to rehost the designer to provide them with the same highly productive environment that developers enjoy. The rehosted designer can also be useful in situations where you want to monitor the progress of running workflows.

Chapter 17 discusses rehosting the workflow designer.

WF 3.x Migration

WF 4 is not the first workflow framework produced by Microsoft. WF 3.0 was first introduced in 2007 and subsequently enhanced with WF 3.5 in 2008. If you have already invested in WF 3.x, rest assured that your investment has not been wasted. Visual Studio 2010 and .NET 4 includes support for the original 3.x version of WF. However, the 3.x WF components have been built to use the new 4 CLR. This enables continued development and maintenance of your 3.x workflow applications in a 4 CLR. In addition, WF 4 includes an `Interop` activity that allows you to execute your 3.x custom activities with the 4 runtime. You can use this mechanism as a migration tool when you decide to move to the new 4 environment.

Chapter 18 discusses migration strategies and 3.x interop.

Assemblies and Namespaces

In this section of the chapter, I outline the assemblies and namespaces within them that are related to WF. This information should provide you with a general road map to where you might find a particular class.

System.Activities

This assembly contains the most frequently used WF types, including the standard activities, support for VB expressions, classes for hosting workflows, workflow tracking, and so on. Here are the most important namespaces that can be found in this assembly:

Namespace	Notes
Microsoft.VisualBasic.Activities	Includes the classes that provide VB expressions support
Microsoft.VisualBasic.Activities.XamlIntegration	Converter and serialization classes for VB support
System.Activities	Base activity classes, bookmarks, arguments, activity contexts, variables, hosting classes
System.Activities.DurableInstancing	Workflow-related commands used for persistence
System.Activities.Expressions	Expression activities, InvokeFunc
System.Activities.Hosting	Classes used internally for self-hosting
System.Activities.Persistence	PersistenceParticipant and PersistenceIOParticipant used for extending persistence
System.Activities.Statements	The standard set of activities that you normally see in the Toolbox: Assign, If, While, Parallel, Pick, Sequence, Flowchart, and so on
System.Activities.Tracking	Tracking records, queries and states
System.Activities.Validation	Classes related to activity validation
System.Activities.XamlIntegration	Converters and serializers

System.Activities.DurableInstancing

This assembly contains classes that are related to workflow persistence. It has only a single namespace and doesn't contain a large number of classes, but it is very important if you need to use SQL Server persistence.

Namespace	Notes
System.Activities.DurableInstancing	Includes the SqlWorkflowInstanceStore class, which provides the standard SQL Server persistence

System.Runtime.DurableInstancing

This assembly isn't strictly defined as a WF assembly, but I'm including it since it contains classes that are vital for workflow persistence. It contains the base classes that allow multiple persistence mechanisms (instance stores) to be developed. The `SqlWorklfowInstanceStore` class (from the `System.Activities.DurableInstancing` assembly) uses the base classes provided in this assembly.

Namespace	Notes
System.Runtime.DurableInstancing	Includes base classes used when you need to develop your own instance store such as InstanceStore, InstanceView, and so on

System.Activities.Presentation

This assembly includes the classes that you will use to implement custom activity designers or to rehost the workflow designer.

Namespace	Notes
System.Activities.Presentation	Includes activity and workflow designer classes
System.Activities.Presentation.Converters	Converter classes used for activity designers
System.Activities.Presentation.Hosting	Includes classes used when rehosting the workflow designer
System.Activities.Presentation.Metadata	Classes related to associating a designer with an activity
System.Activities.Presentation.Model	Provides an intermediate layer between a design view and an instance of an activity being edited
System.Activities.Presentation.PropertyEditing	Classes to support activity property editing
System.Activities.Presentation.Services	Services that assist with tree navigation
System.Activities.Presentation.Toolbox	Includes classes that assist with toolbox management
System.Activities.Presentation.Validation	Classes used for activity validation
System.Activities.Presentation.View	Includes classes that map visual presentation elements to an underlying model

System.ServiceModel.Activities

This assembly contains the classes that support workflow services and WCF integration.

Namespace	Notes
System.ServiceModel	Includes classes related to service endpoints and correlation.
System.ServiceModel.Activities	The core set of classes that provide WCF support for WF. Included are the primary Send and Receive activities and the WorkflowServiceHost class used for self-hosting.
System.ServiceModel.Activities.Configuration	Includes configuration element classes that are used when you configure workflow services using an application configuration file.
System.ServiceModel.Activities.Description	Includes workflow-related WCF behaviors.
System.ServiceModel.Activities.Tracking	Includes workflow tracking records that are related to WCF messaging.
System.ServiceModel.Activities.Tracking.Configuration	Includes tracking classes that are related to profiles and configuration.
System.ServiceModel.XamlIntegration	Converters used with workflow services support.

3.x Assemblies

In addition to the assemblies that support WF 4, .NET 4 also includes the assemblies that support the previous versions of WF (3.0 and 3.5). These assemblies have a 4 version number and are built to use the .NET 4 runtime, but they contain the classes that were originally developed for versions 3.0 and 3.5.

I wanted to draw your attention to these assemblies for two reasons:

- To identify the assemblies that you will continue to use if you are developing or maintaining an application that uses the 3.x version of WF.

- To warn you to avoid referencing these assemblies if your intent is to build new applications using WF 4. Many of the class names between the 3.x and 4 versions of WF are the same or similar (although the namespaces are different). Referencing the wrong version of a class will likely result in a great deal of anguish and frustration.

I won't detail every namespace in these assemblies, since the 3.*x* version of WF is not the focus of this book. Here are the assemblies:

Assembly Name
System.Workflow.Activities
System.Workflow.ComponentModel
System.Workflow.Runtime
System.WorkflowServices

Activity Life Cycle

In this section, I briefly present topics that are related to the WF runtime environment. These topics provide background information that should be helpful as you work through the remaining chapters of this book.

Definition vs. Runtime Instance

The WF runtime makes a clear distinction between an activity definition and an activity instance. As a developer, you declare and maintain the activity definition. The definition is the declarative tree of activities that you modify with the workflow designer and that is saved as an Xaml file (or for workflow services a Xamlx file). The file containing the definition may be compiled into a CLR type, or it may be deserialized and used directly from the file system.

■ **Note** Although I'm using the term *activity* here, this also applies to a workflow that is composed of other activities. Remember that activities and workflows share the same model and are really different names for the same thing.

To instruct the workflow runtime to execute a particular activity, you pass it an instance of that activity's definition. But the instance of the definition that you construct isn't executed by the runtime. It is simply a template or guide to the runtime that defines the activity's structure. Using the activity definition as a guide, the workflow runtime creates an instance of the root activity and executes it. If that activity is a container for other child activities, the root activity schedules execution of each child activity and so on.

As each activity is executed, the runtime creates an instance of the `ActivityInstance` class for it. This internal structure is used to track the execution state of the activity as it is executed. It also maintains the variables and arguments that are in scope for the activity's execution. Once execution of an activity has been completed, the `ActivityInstance` that was acting as the runtime wrapper for the activity is no longer needed. The runtime places the `ActivityInstance` back into a pool of these objects for later reuse.

As you develop your own custom activities in code, you will frequently use the `ActivityContext` class (or more likely one of the classes that derive from it such as `CodeActivityContext`, `AsyncCodeActivityContext`, or `NativeActivityContext`). For example, in a custom activity that is derived from the base `CodeActivity` class, an instance of the `CodeActivityContext` is passed as an argument to the `Execute` method. This object is the developer's view into the `ActivityInstance` runtime structure. This explains why the context object is passed to the `Get` method of each argument or variable to retrieve its value. The context is needed to obtain the value that is currently in scope for the current execution of the activity.

■ **Note** Chapter 3 dicusses the use of the activity context, the `Execute` method and other topics related to authoring custom activities. Chapter 16 covers more advanced custom activity topics.

Definition vs. Runtime Variables

If an activity is executed multiple times (perhaps as the child of a looping activity such as the `While` activity), a single instance of the activity is created. However, a separate `ActivityInstance` is used for each execution through the loop. This runtime behavior has a significant impact on private variables that you define within a custom activity. If the activity defines a private variable using a CLR type, that variable becomes part of the activity definition. In this case, the value of the CLR variable is maintained between executions since there is a single instance of the variable. For example, an activity might include a counter variable that you increment each time the activity is executed. If the counter variable is defined as a CLR type (`Int32`), the ending value of the counter will contain the expected execution count.

On the other hand, you may choose to define private variables within an activity using the `Variable<T>` class that is provided with WF. This type of variable defines storage for a single runtime instance of the activity that is maintained by the `ActivityInstance` wrapper. The `ActivityContext` object must be used to retrieve the variable value that is currently in scope for each execution of the activity. Since a new `ActivityInstance` is used each time an activity is executed, the activity receives a fresh starting value of a `Variable<T>` with each execution. If the same counter variable was defined as a `Variable<Int32>`, the ending value would likely not be what you expect. Instead of an ending value containing the total execution count, it would likely end with a value of one (assuming that the variable begins with a value of zero each time the activity is executed).

■ **Warning** Be aware of the differences in behavior between CLR variables and `Variable<T>` when you implement custom activities in code.

Activity States

As activities are executed, the workflow runtime maintains their execution state. Here are the known activity states as defined by the `ActivityInstanceState` enum:

- Executing
- Closed
- Canceled
- Faulted

All activities begin in the `Executing` state. When they have completed all of their work, they normally transition to the `Closed` state, which means that they successfully completed their work. If an activity has scheduled the execution of any child activities, it remains in the `Executing` state until all children have transitioned to the `Closed` state. An activity also remains in the `Executing` state while it is waiting for the resumption of a bookmark, if it has been persisted, or if it is unloaded from memory. An activity in the `Closed` state cannot be resumed.

If cancellation of an activity has been requested (either by its parent activity or directly by the host application), the activity transitions to the `Canceled` state. Canceling an activity gracefully stops execution and allows any cancellation and compensation handlers to execute. Once it is canceled, execution of an activity cannot be resumed.

There are several ways that an activity can move to the `Faulted` state. Once an activity is in the `Faulted` state, it cannot be resumed. If an unhandled exception is thrown, the activity *may* move to the `Faulted` state. This depends on how the application handles the exception. If you are using the `WorkflowApplication` class to host the activity, you specify how exceptions are handled by assigning code to the `OnUnhandledException` delegate. The value that you return from this code determines how the unhandled exception is ultimately handled. If you return a value of `UnhandledExceptionAction.Terminate`, the activity transitions to the `Faulted` state.

If you are hosting a workflow service, you determine how unhandled exceptions are handled using the `WorkflowUnhandledExceptionBehavior` class. Setting the `Action` property of this behavior to a value of `WorkflowUnhandledExceptionAction.Terminate` will terminate the activity and cause it to transition to the `Faulted` state.

You can also manually terminate a running activity instance, which causes it to transition to the `Faulted` state. This can be accomplished using the `Terminate` method of the `WorkflowApplication` class. You can terminate workflow services by invoking the `Terminate` method of the `WorkflowControlEndpoint`.

Please refer to Chapters 9 and 13 for more information on exception handling. Chapter 13 also discusses compensation handlers.

Expressions

As I mentioned earlier in the chapter, expressions are the small bits of glue code within the declarative model. They are pervasive within WF. Most of the time, you use expressions to set activity properties (arguments really) or workflow variables. Expressions come in two flavors:

- Visual Basic expressions
- Expression activities

The Visual Basic expressions are what you will use most often since they are supported within the workflow designer. Expression activities are a set of individual activities that are included with WF. They are designed to be added individually to the workflow model or chained together with other expression activities to return a result. They are primarily used when you compose an activity in code from other activities.

Visual Basic Expressions

As you have already seen, expressions that you enter at design time use the Visual Basic (VB) syntax. This may seem strange, especially if you create C# projects. But Microsoft has indicated that it was easier to implement expressions in VB because it was able to leverage existing components that parse and interpret the expressions. Microsoft has promised that VB is the first language dialect that is supported for expressions, but it won't be the last. Ideally, it will offer a Visual Studio add-on that supports C# expressions.

VB expressions are represented by the `VisualBasicValue<TResult>` and `VisualBasicReference<TResult>` classes (found in the `Microsoft.VisualBasic.Activities` namespace). These are two very special expression activity classes. They accept a string expression as input (using VB syntax of course) and return the designated generic type. But when expressions are entered via the Properties window or the expression editor, they are serialized to the Xaml (or Xamlx) file within square brackets. The square brackets are shorthand for `VisualBasicValue<TResult>` or `VisualBasicReference<T>`.

For example, in one of the examples from Chapter 1, you set the `WriteLine.Text` property to this:

```
String.Format("Hello {0} Welcome to Workflow!", ArgFirstName)
```

This is a VB expression that returns a string. If you take a look at the Xaml file for that example, you should see that the expression was serialized with square brackets like this:

```
<WriteLine
    Text="[String.Format(&quot;Hello {0} Welcome to Workflow!&quot;, ArgFirstName)]" />
```

However, there are some exceptions to this square-brackets rule. If the expression that you enter is a simple primitive literal (`Int32`, `Boolean`, `Double`, and so on) or a string, it is serialized as a literal value without the brackets. For example, for the first Hello Workflow example in Chapter 1, you entered the literal "Hello Workflow" (including double quotes) for the `WriteLine.Text` property. This was serialized to Xaml like this:

```
<WriteLine Text="Hello Workflow" />
```

When this string literal is processed at runtime, it is wrapped in an instance of the `Literal<TResult>` class. This class is one of the expression activity classes that are provided with WF.

VB Primer for Workflow Developers

Since VB is the only language option for expressions (for now), you need to familiarize yourself with the VB syntax. In this section, I review a few VB language constructs and keywords and contrast them with C#.

My intent is not to teach you to become a productive VB developer. I think you probably need an entirely different book if that is your goal. Instead, I'll try to focus on the very small subset of the language that you are most likely to use when you write workflow expressions. If you need to use some

VB feature that I don't cover, your best bet is to head to the online MSDN documentation. And feel free to skip this section if are already intimately familiar with VB.

A Few Basic Rules

First, VB is not case sensitive. So whether you enter *And, and,* or *AND,* the VB expression should produce the same result. VB generally requires that you use a line continuation character (an underscore) if you need to continue a statement on another line. I say generally because the latest version of VB should be able to properly detect a statement continuation if the line break is at an unambiguous point. If the expression editor complains about a multiline VB statement, just add an underscore to the end of the prior line.

Many of the operators and keywords are the same (or very similar) between C# and VB. However, there are a few areas that are drastically different. One area that greatly differs between C# and VB is generic types. For example, in C# you might create an instance of a generic dictionary like this:

```
new Dictionary<string, int>()
```

But in VB, you need to use the `Of` keyword to create the same dictionary like this:

```
New Dictionary(Of string, int)
```

Note that the VB code does not require the parentheses "()" to execute the constructor. They are optional.

Another area that is very different between C# and VB is the use of the object initializer syntax. This syntax allows you to set property values during the construction of the object. For example, assume that you have a class defined like this in C#:

```
public class MyType
{
    public string Prop1 { get; set; }
    public int Prop2 { get; set; }
}
```

If you want to create an instance of this type and initialize the properties using C#, you might code something like this:

```
new MyType { Prop1 = "foo", Prop2 = 123 };
```

To initialize the same object in VB, you use the `With` keyword like this:

```
New MyType With { .Prop1 = "foo", .Prop2 = 123 }
```

Notice that each property name is also preceded by a period.

Operator and Keyword Comparison

In this table, I list some commonly used C# operators and keywords along with their VB equivalents:

Meaning	C# Operator	VB Operator
Equal to	==	=
Less than	<	<
Less than or equal to	<=	<=
Greater than	>	>
Greater than or equal to	>=	>=
Not equal to	!=	<>
Addition	+	+
Subtraction	-	-
Multiplication	*	*
Division	/	/
Modulus	%	Mod
Assignment	=	=
Assignment with Addition	+=	+=
Assignment with Subtraction	-=	-=
Assignment with Multiplication	*=	*=
Assignment with Division	/=	/=
Left shift	<<	<<
Right shift	>>	>>
Assignment with Concatenate	+=	&=
Concatenate Strings	+	&
Access Array Element	[]	()
Function Call	()	()

Meaning	C# Operator	VB Operator
Logical Not	!	Not
Logical And	&&	And
Logical Or	||	Or
Create new object	new	New
A reference that does not refer to an object	null	Nothing
Compare object types	x is MyType	TypeOf x is MyType
Generic types	<type>	(of type)

Data Type Comparison

This table lists some commonly used data types for C# and VB:

C# Type	VB Type
byte	Byte
bool	Boolean
short	Short
char	Char
int	Integer
long	Long
float	Single
double	Double
string	String
decimal	Decimal
DateTime	Date

Literal Data Types

This table lists the literal type characters that are used for C# and VB. These are the characters that you can optionally place after a numeric literal to force the data type of the literal.

Description	C# Type Literal	VB Type Literal
Integer		I
Short	S	S
Long	L	L
Decimal	M	D
Single	F	F
Double	D	R
Unsigned Short		US
Unsigned Integer	U	UI
Unsigned Long	UL	UL

Expression Activities

Most of the time you will use the built-in support for VB expressions. They are the easiest way to supply an expression where one is required. WF also includes a set of expression activity classes that you can use when you are composing an activity in code. These activities have designer support, so you won't find them in the Visual Studio Toolbox.

■ **Note** These expression activities are available for your use, but they are not the recommended way to enter expressions. I've covering them here to make you aware of their existence, not to recommend them above VB expressions.

These activities are located in the `System.Activities.Expressions` namespace. Here is a representative selection of these activities. This is not an exhaustive list of all expression activities, but it should be enough to give you a feel for the type of activities that are provided:

Activity	Description
Add	Perform addition on two values
And	Bitwise logical AND of two values
AndAlso	Logical AND of two values
As	Attempts to convert an operant to a given type
Cast	Converts an operant to given type
Divide	Computes the quotient of a division operation
Equal	Tests for equality between two values
GreaterThan	Test for one value that is greater than another
GreaterThanOrEqual	Test for one value that is greater than or equal to another
InvokeFunc	Invokes an ActivityFunc activity
LessThan	Test for one value that is less than another
LessThanOrEqual	Test for one value that is less than or equal to another
Multiply	Performs multiplication on two values
New	Creates a new instance of the specified type
NewArray	Creates an array of the specified type
Not	Logical negation of the value
NotEqual	Test for inequality of two values
Or	Bitwise logical OR of two values
OrElse	Logical OR of two values
Subtract	Perform subtraction on two values

All of these activities derive from the `CodeActivity<TResult>` activity, and as such they return a single value. This fits the definition of an expression that I gave earlier. As you can tell from the list of activities, these are primitive building blocks that you can use directly or combine with other activities to create more complex expressions. They are all generics, so you will need to provide one or more generic types when you use each activity. For example, the Add expression is defined as `Add<TLeft,TRight,TResult>`.

Using an Expression Activity

The most common way to use these activities is to include them during the composition of a custom code activity. For example, in this short example, you will implement a simple custom activity that adds two numbers. It doesn't add any real value over and above the `Add` activity that it uses, but it does illustrate how these expression activities might be used.

Create a Workflow Console application, and name it `ExpressionActivites`. You can remove the `Workflow1.xaml` file since it won't be used. Add a new Code Activity to the project, and name it `AddNumber`. Here is the code for this activity:

```
using System;
using System.Activities;
using System.Activities.Expressions;
using System.Activities.Statements;

namespace ExpressionActivities
{
    public sealed class AddNumbers : Activity<Int32>
    {
        public InArgument<Int32> NumberOne { get; set; }
        public InArgument<Int32> NumberTwo { get; set; }

        protected override Func<Activity> Implementation
        {
            get { return () => BuildImplementation(); }
        }

        private Activity BuildImplementation()
        {
            return new Sequence
            {
                Activities =
                {
                    new Assign
                    {
                        To = new OutArgument<Int32>(ac =>
                            this.Result.Get(ac)),
                        Value = new InArgument<Int32>
                        {
                            Expression = new Add<Int32,Int32,Int32>
                            {
                                Left = new InArgument<Int32>(ac =>
                                    NumberOne.Get(ac)),
```

```
                            Right = new InArgument<Int32>(ac =>
                                NumberTwo.Get(ac)),
                        }
                    }
                }
            };
        }
    }
}
```

■ **Note** Chapter 3 provides much more information on implementing and composing your own custom activities. Included in that chapter is another example of composition in code.

Here is the code that you need to add to the `Program.cs` file to execute this test:

```csharp
using System;
using System.Activities;
using System.Activities.Expressions;
using System.Collections.Generic;

namespace ExpressionActivities
{
    class Program
    {
        static void Main(string[] args)
        {
            Direct();
            Composition();

            Console.WriteLine("Press any key to exit");
            Console.ReadKey();
        }

        private static Int32 Composition()
        {
            Int32 result = WorkflowInvoker.Invoke<Int32>(
                new AddNumbers(),
                new Dictionary<String, Object>
                {
                    {"NumberOne", 1},
                    {"NumberTwo", 2}
                });

            Console.WriteLine("Result: {0}", result);
            return result;
        }
```

```
    private static Int32 Direct()
    {
        Int32 result = WorkflowInvoker.Invoke<Int32>(
            new Add<Int32, Int32, Int32>(),
            new Dictionary<String, Object>
            {
                {"Left", 1},
                {"Right", 2}
            });
        Console.WriteLine("Result: {0}", result);
        return result;
    }
  }
}
```

This code illustrates two ways that you can use one of these expression activities. First, it executes the `Add<TLeft,TRight,TResult>` expression directly using the `WorkflowInvoker` class. After all, it is an activity, so there's really no reason that you can't execute it directly like this. Second, it executes the custom `AddNumbers` activity that demonstrates how to use the expression activity during composition of a custom activity. Here are my results:

```
Result: 3

Result: 3

Press any key to exit
```

You are not limited to the set of expression activities that are provided with WF. You can always develop your own custom activities that meet your specialized needs. And if those activities derive from `CodeActivity<TResult>` and return a single value, they can be used as expressions.

Missing 4 Features

Version 4 represents a completely new version of WF. It is a complete redesign and rewrite from the previous versions (3.0 and 3.5). Depending on how you look at things, you could view this version in a couple of different ways.

- First, since it was completely redesigned and rewritten, you could think of it as version 1.0. In this case, you would expect that it is still rough around the edges and has a few missing features.

- Second, since it is the third version of WF, you could think of it as the mystical third version where Microsoft finally gets things just right.

The reality is somewhere in between the two extremes. In most ways, I consider it the mystical third version of WF that Microsoft got right. It attempts to correct most of the problems with the previous versions of WF, indicating that the Microsoft designers did indeed learn from past versions (and past mistakes). However, although the core architecture of WF 4 is greatly improved over previous versions, there are missing features. In this respect, it is more or less a 1.0 release.

The following are the most important features that I think WF 4 really should have but are not currently available. No doubt, Microsoft is already working on many of these features. As you begin to work with WF, you will likely develop your own list of features that you'd like to have. In the following short sections, I present my top list (in no particular order).

State Machine

The 3.*x* version of WF supports a state machine workflow type. A state machine represents a different way of thinking about a problem. Instead of attacking a problem procedurally by defining steps to execute, you define the states that can exist for a workflow. A workflow instance can exist in only one state at a time. Then you define operations that can be performed while the workflow is in each state. Finally, you define transitions between each state.

Microsoft has released guidance documents that describe how you can mimic the feel of a state machine using the flowchart modeling style in WF 4. But this is really a short-term solution. WF 4 needs a real state machine since some problems can more naturally be modeled with one. Microsoft is working on state machine support and has already delievered the first CTP of state machine activities as a post-4 add-on.

Reuse of WCF Contracts

WF 4 provides a fairly easy way to declare workflow services. These services are exposed as WCF endpoints and can be consumed by any WCF client. A core concept of WCF is the use of contracts. In traditional WCF development, you first define a contract using a C# interface. That interface identifies the service operations (methods) that are supported by your service, along with the arguments and return value (if any) for each operation. The interface is decorated with attributes that identify it as a WCF service contract and also affect characteristics of the service. You then develop a service class that implements the interface. Traditional WCF development definitely emphasizes a contract-first approach.

Although WF 4 eases the declaration of new services, it isn't built around the concept of using an explicit service contract. It is certainly not a contract-first approach to service development. In fact, the WCF contract that is generated for a workflow service is implied based on the properties and parameters that you set within the workflow. And there is currently no facility in WF to import and reuse WCF service contracts that you have already defined using C# interfaces.

Being a contract-first kind of developer myself, I feel that WF 4 could be improved if it supported these features:

- The ability to reference and import WCF contracts that are already defined. This might take the form of a utility that generates custom messaging activities based on a properly decorated C# interface.

- The ability to generate the source for a C# interface based on the implied WCF contract. The source should be autogenerated each time the implied contract changes. The generated interface could then be consumed by client applications that use a channel factory instead of adding service references.

C# Expression Support

WF 4 currently supports expressions entered in Visual Basic (VB) only. According to Microsoft, this limitation was necessary because of development time constraints. Although this is a workable solution, it is a bit awkward to create new C# projects but have to use VB for expressions. A much more consistent development environment would result if expressions were entered in the selected project language. And that includes C#. The expectation is that Microsoft will, in time, provide support for additional expressions languages.

Tracking to SQL Server

WF 4 includes a very flexible mechanism for workflow instrumentation. Workflow tracking automatically provides data that allows you to monitor the progress and performance of individual workflow instances. Out of the box, WF includes a tracking participant that persists the tracking data to the Event Tracking for Windows (ETW) subsystem. Although this works, it isn't always the optimal solution.

WF 3.*x* has its own version of a tracking system, and its default persistence medium is a SQL Server database. Although I think ETW tracking has its uses, it would be beneficial to have an out-of-the-box option to persist tracking data to a database. However, tracking to a database is available if you use AppFabric to manage your server environment.

Rules Engine

WF 3.*x* supports a general-purpose rules engine. The rules engine allows you to make assertions or statements of fact about your data. The rules are organized into a rule set and are executed one at a time against your data. WF 3.*x* supports forward-chaining of rules, meaning that a rule might be executed more than once if it was detected that data referenced by a rule had changed. There is no native equivalent support in WF 4. However, the 3.*x* rules engine can be executed using the `Interop` activity or from a custom activity.

Dynamic Updates

The 3.*x* version of WF supports the ability to dynamically update a workflow instance after it was started. When the workflow instance is in an idle state, you can add, change, or delete individual activities within the workflow. This update mechanism can potentially be used to help with versioning of long-running workflows. WF 4 does not have any support for dynamic updates to an active workflow instance.

Summary

The focus of this chapter was a brief summary of WF and coverage of a few topics that provide background information. The chapter began with a review of the major features and capabilities of WF. This was followed by a summary of the assemblies and namespaces that you will use for WF development. Topics related to the activity life cycle, activity states, workflow definitions vs. runtime instances, and differences in variable types were covered next.

WF uses VB as the language that you use when entering expressions. After an overview of expressions, the chapter included a short primer on VB. The goal was not to teach you how to develop applications in VB. Instead, it was intended to acquaint you with the elements of VB that you will most commonly use as a workflow developer. The chapter concluded with my list of the top features that are currently missing from WF 4.

In the next chapter, you will learn more about the most basic building block of WF: the activity.

CHAPTER 3

■ ■ ■

Activities

The focus of this chapter is the primary building block of all workflows: the activity. Activities are where you place the business logic that is specific to your particular problem domain. In this chapter, you will learn how to develop your own custom activities using the base classes that ship with Windows Workflow Foundation (WF). You can choose to create new activities in code completely from scratch, or you can declaratively assemble existing activities into a new custom activity. This chapter demonstrates both authoring styles.

This chapter also provides a high-level review of the standard activities that are provided with WF. You will become acquainted with the available activities, but you will not learn how to use them in detail. This is the one chapter that provides an overview of all the available activities. Many of the individual activities are difficult to understand unless they are discussed as part of a larger subject area. For this reason, the subsequent chapters in this book each focus on a specific subject area and provide additional detail on the activities that are relevant to that subject.

Understanding Activities

An activity is a discrete, reusable component that is designed to fulfill a defined purpose. WF includes a set of standard activities that you can leverage within your workflows. But those activities should really be viewed as just the starting point. You are encouraged to develop your own custom activities that solve your own specialized business problems. For instance, if you are developing a loan application, you might develop custom activities such as `SetupAccount`, `ReviewCredit`, and `LoanFunding`. For a point-of-sale system, you might need custom activities such as `ItemLookup`, `SellItem`, and `TenderTransaction`. Once you develop a custom activity, it joins your library of activities and is available for reuse in multiple workflows.

■ **Tip** The most important take-away point from this chapter is this: don't be afraid to develop your own custom activities. You might be tempted to try to solve all your workflow problems using only the out-of-the-box activities. Although that might be possible in some cases, doing so severely limits what you can do with WF. Develop your own custom activities to encapsulate the business rules that you need for your particular application.

Regardless of the activity's origin (standard or custom), the design-time experience of working with activities is the same. You start by dragging and dropping an activity onto a workflow or another activity. Then, using the Properties window in Visual Studio, you set properties that are specific to that activity. The properties may control some facet of runtime behavior, or they may be used to wire up the input and output arguments of the activity to variables or workflow arguments.

When you are developing your own custom activities, you should be aware of the dual audience for activities. First and foremost, activities are designed to perform some defined work. If they don't do anything useful when they are executed, they have no real value. While performing their work, they are expected to behave in a particular way in order to cooperate with other workflow activities and the workflow runtime. The workflow runtime and other activities are the *runtime audience* for the activity.

But activities also have a *design-time audience* that is equally important. The design-time audience includes the developers who use the activity as one of the building blocks for their workflows. An additional responsibility of an activity is to cooperate with the workflow designer in order to provide an appealing and productive design experience. An activity that is designed to fully support the design experience is easier to use and helps you become more productive. WF provides you with the ability to develop custom activities and to also develop custom designers for those activities.

■ **Note** Enhancing the design experience for custom activities is discussed in Chapter 15.

Authoring Activities

There are two approaches to authoring a new custom activity:

- You can declaratively compose a new activity by assembling existing activities.

- You can code a new custom activity from scratch.

Your choice of authoring style depends on your exact needs and the availability of other activities. If there are existing activities (either standard or custom) that you can reuse and compose into a new activity, then that is a viable approach. The process of declaratively creating a custom activity feels just like declaring a workflow—except that it's typically on a smaller scale.

If you decide to compose a new activity using existing activities, you have another choice to make. You can declare the activity in Xaml using the workflow designer, or you can assemble the tree of activities in code.

On the other hand, the activity may be easier to implement or more concise if you write it in code from scratch. Or the work that the activity must perform is highly specialized and isn't easily composed from other activities. Or, you may need to migrate an existing nonworkflow application to WF, and you may have large amounts of existing code that can be reused. In these situations, it's probably easier to develop the activity in code.

Kinds of Work

Developers love to categorize things (at least I do) because it helps them understand how things work. And activities can be categorized in several different ways. One way is to separate them into the *standard* activities that are included with WF and the *custom* activities that you build yourself. But you use activities the same way regardless of their origin, so this may not be the best way to understand them.

Since all activities perform some type of work, a better way to understand them is to define categories based on the general kind of work that they perform. Here is the list of work categories:

- Atomic Unit of Work

- Asynchronous Unit of Work

- Long Running Unit of Work

- Control Flow Activities

- Infrastructure

This list was primarily developed with custom activities in mind, but the list also applies equally well to the standard activities that ship with WF. In the sections that follow, I provide a short description of each of these categories.

Atomic Unit of Work

This kind of activity encapsulates the logic to perform an atomic unit of work synchronously on the workflow thread. It is the workhorse activity where you place most of the business logic associated with your application. You will probably implement more activities of this kind than any other.

The unit of work that it performs is atomic in the sense that it is completed entirely during a single execution of the activity. It doesn't need to suspend execution and wait for external input. It is short-lived and doesn't perform time-consuming operations such as long-running database queries, file I/O, or exchanging messages with another system. It executes synchronously on the workflow thread and doesn't create or use other threads.

WF provides a class named `CodeActivity` that you should use as the base class when you develop custom activities of this kind.

Asynchronous Unit of Work

This kind of activity is similar to the Atomic Unit of Work described earlier. It is designed to perform an atomic unit of work but is capable of doing so asynchronously on a separate thread. This makes it perfect for operations such as database queries and file I/O that benefit from executing on a separate thread.

However, although these activities can use a separate thread for part of their work, that work must still execute in a relatively short period of time. They are not designed for long-running operations that might take days to complete. The work they perform should still be atomic, completing entirely during a single execution of the activity.

WF provides the `AsyncCodeActivity` that you should use as the base class when you need to develop this kind of custom activity.

Long Running Unit of Work

This kind of activity is designed to perform work that may take a very long time to complete. The best example is any type of work that includes human interaction. The activity may perform part of its work and then have to wait for a response from a real human in order to continue.

While it is waiting, the activity is suspended and is not occupying the workflow thread. Depending on how the workflow is modeled, other activities may now have a chance to execute while this activity is waiting for external input. Or execution of the entire workflow may be suspended and the current state of the workflow persisted. This kind of activity can also be used for long-running database queries, file I/O, and messaging with other systems.

WF supports this long-running behavior using a concept called *bookmarks*. Just like a real bookmark that you would use in a book, the purpose of a workflow bookmark is to resume execution. When the activity is about to suspend execution and begin waiting, it creates a named bookmark. When the external input is available or the long-running task has completed, the named bookmark is used to resume execution of the activity.

WF provides the `NativeActivity` that you must use as your base class when you need to develop long-running activities.

■ **Note** The use of bookmarks in long-running activities is discussed in Chapter 8.

Control Flow Activities

Some activities don't perform atomic work at all. Sometimes the purpose of an activity is to be a container for other activities. An example of this is the `Sequence` activity provided with WF. It doesn't perform any work of its own, but it instead acts as a container for child activities. Its job is to schedule the execution of those child activities. Activities of this kind are also referred to as *composite* activities.

WF includes a number of activities that fall into this category. Many of them are used to implement the standard procedural execution patterns supported by WF (`Sequence`, `While`, `Parallel`, and so on). You may be excited at the prospect of developing new composite activities. I personally think it's much more fun to implement a bizarre new execution pattern than to code just one more database query. But the reality is that you probably won't spend most of your time developing new activities of this kind. When you do, you will need to use the `NativeActivity` as your base class.

■ **Note** Developing new control flow activities is discussed in Chapter 16.

Infrastructure

Included with WF are the activities that act as the glue that holds everything else together. These are the activities that support arguments, variables, expressions, and so on. You may find it necessary to develop your own extensions to the infrastructure already provided by WF, but that won't be a common situation.

Kinds of Data

The work that an activity does is only half the story. Each activity must also have data that it operates upon to be really useful. And just as there are several general kinds of work that an activity can perform, there are also a few general categories of data that an activity can use. Those categories can be best summarized in this way:

- Arguments
- Variables

Arguments

Arguments are the inputs and outputs of the activity and define the public contract that the activity supports. Input arguments are passed to the activity when it begins execution. Values for these arguments might be passed from the host application when the workflow is started. Or they might be populated with the current value of workflow variables (see the discussion next) that were set by another activity within the workflow.

Output arguments contain the results from the activity's work. These output arguments may be assigned to a variable or an output argument of the workflow. The `InArgument<T>` and `OutArgument<T>` generic classes are used to define arguments.

Variables

Variables define internal storage within an activity and are always considered private. Within an activity, they are used to store either transient results or longer-lasting state that must be maintained during the lifetime of the activity. They are also used within workflows to maintain state and as temporary storage to pass result data from one activity to another. Within a workflow, variables can be declared only for a select group of activities, typically composites that act as containers for child activities. Table 3-2 later in this chapter identifies the standard activities that support variables. When you use the workflow designer to define a variable for an activity, it is represented by the `Variable<T>` generic class.

If you are creating a new activity in C# code, there are two ways to define private variables. You can use the `Variable<T>` generic class to declare your variables, or you can use Common Language Runtime (CLR) data types as either private member or local variables. The difference between the two approaches is subtle but important. The `Variable<T>` class essentially defines storage for a single runtime instance of an activity. If the activity is executed multiple times (for example as a child of a looping activity such as the `While` activity), each execution will point to a fresh set of variables. The variables are sensitive to the current runtime context. On the other hand, a variable that is a normal CLR data type defines storage for the activity definition. If an activity using CLR variables is executed multiple times, the value of any CLR member variables is maintained between executions. A `Variable<T>` class must be used to pass values between existing activities that you are composing in code.

Just like variables that you might define in your everyday C# code, all activity variables have a defined scope. For example, a private member variable that is defined in a normal C# class is visible to all methods within the class and exists until the object instance is disposed. A variable that is defined within a single C# method exists only until the method ends. Likewise, variables that you declare for an activity have a defined scope. They are visible to the activity that declared them as well as any children of that activity. Once the activity where they were declared goes out of scope, they can be disposed.

■ **Caution** It is possible that the activity you are developing may be used in a wide variety of workflows. If any of those workflows are capable of being persisted, then the arguments and variables must be serializable. If you are working with nonserializable data, you can apply the `NonSerialized` attribute to indicate that they should not be persisted. Workflow persistence is discussed in Chapter 11.

Activity Class Hierarchy

As I briefly described earlier, several classes can be used as a base for your custom activities. Each class has a distinctive set of features that are designed to assist you in performing a particular kind of work. One of the major differences of these classes is in the amount of access to the workflow runtime that each of them provides.

For example, the `CodeActivity` provides the least amount of access to the workflow runtime. It is the most restrictive because of the simplicity of the work that it is designed to perform. It provides access to only the minimum set of runtime operations.

On the opposite end of the spectrum, the `NativeActivity` provides the maximum amount of access to the workflow runtime. It allows you to implement an activity that can take full advantage of all runtime features.

Table 3-1 summarizes the most important features of each base activity class.

Table 3-1. *Activity Class Features*

Class	Arguments/Variables	Extensions	Bookmarks	Async	Manage Children
CodeActivity	Yes	Yes	No	No	No
AsyncCodeActivity	Yes	Yes	No	Yes	No
NativeActivity	Yes	Yes	Yes	Yes	Yes

Here is an explanation of the columns in Table 3-1:

- *Arguments/Variables*: Yes means that the activity has access to argument and variable values.

- *Extensions*: Yes means that the activity can access and reference workflow extensions. Extensions are custom classes that you add to the workflow runtime to make their functionality available to activities. They are discussed in detail in Chapter 8.

- *Bookmarks*: Yes means that the activity is capable of creating and resuming bookmarks. Bookmarks are used when implementing long-running workflows.

- *Async*: Yes means that the activity is capable of asynchronous activity on a separate thread.

- *Manage Children*: Yes means the activity can schedule child activities and manage their execution.

All of these base classes come in two flavors: generic and nongeneric. The generic version takes a single generic type parameter that represents the return type of the activity. This can be likened to a C# method that returns a single value. When the generic class is used, an `OutArgument<T>` named `Result` is defined for you using the type that you specify. For example, if you base your activity on `CodeActivity<String>`, an `OutArgument<String>` named `Result` is available for your use just like any other argument.

The nongeneric version does not define the `Result` argument for you. This is similar to a C# method that returns void. Of course, you can easily declare an `OutArgument<T>` yourself. The reason for the generic version is simply as a productivity tool. It saves you the time of declaring that argument yourself. And it comes in especially handy when you require only a single **OutArgument** from the activity. Using the generic versions also tend to enforce consistency in your activities. If the activity has only a single **OutArgument**, you know that it will be named **Result**. If you need additional output arguments, you can define them yourself. Figure 3-1 illustrates the hierarchy of these classes.

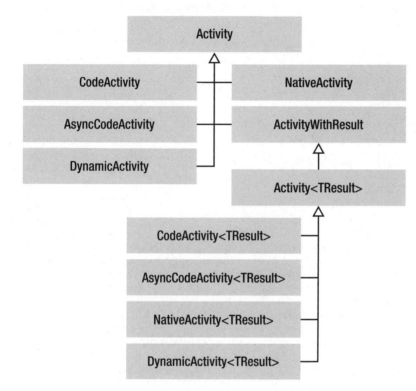

Figure 3-1. Activity class hierarchy

As shown in Figure 3-1, all of these classes derive from the **Activity** or **Activity<TResult>** class. Most of the time, you will use one of the derived classes when constructing your own activities in code. But you can also derive directly from **Activity** or **Activity<TResult>**. They are used as the base class only when you are declaratively assembling an activity out of existing activities.

■ **Note** WF also includes DynamicActivity and DynamicActivity<TResult> classes. These classes are used to load and execute activities directly from Xaml files without first compiling them into a CLR type.

Custom Activity Workflow

In general, here is the workflow (the steps) that you should follow when developing custom activities. Not all steps will be needed for each custom activity that you author.

1. Determine the authoring style that you will use. Will you declaratively compose the new activity from existing activities, or will you implement it entirely in code?

2. Determine the base class to use depending on the feature set that the activity requires.

3. Declare input and output arguments.

4. Declare private variables.

5. Implement the activity's logic. Develop the code or compose the set of existing activities that will perform the work of the activity.

6. Implement custom activity designers and other features to enhance the design experience.

An Example Activity

In the sections that follow, I demonstrate the process of developing a custom activity. I develop the same custom activity using several different authoring styles. As an example problem to solve, I've chosen an activity that calculates the shipping charges for an order. Although this is obviously a contrived example, it is a problem that can be readily understood. It's also easy to envision this type of activity being part of a larger e-commerce shopping cart workflow.

The business rules for this activity are fairly simple. The input arguments to the activity are the weight of the order, shipping method, and total currency amount of the order. The output argument is the calculated shipping amount. There are two shipping methods supported: normal and express. If the normal shipping method is requested, the shipping is calculated as the weight * 1.95. However, if the order total is greater than or equal to 75.00, the shipping is free. If the express shipping method is requested, the shipping is calculated as the weight * 3.50. The free shipping option does not apply to express shipping. Regardless of the shipping method, the minimum shipping amount is 12.95 unless the shipping is free.

This same custom activity will be implemented in these authoring styles:

- Entirely in code

- Composed declaratively from other activities in Xaml

- Composed declaratively from other activities in code

- Asynchronously in code

Implementing an Activity in Code

In this example, you will implement the custom activity to calculate shipping charges entirely in code. The `CodeActivity<TResult>` class will be the base class for this activity.

Creating the Project

To begin this example, create a new activity library project named **ActivityLibrary**. You should add it to a new solution named for this chapter. This same project can be used for all the remaining custom activity examples in this chapter. Use the Activity Library project template, which you can find in the Workflow category. This project template creates a file named **Activity1.xaml** that you can delete since it is not needed.

Implementing the Activity

To implement the custom activity in code, add a new source file named **CalcShipping.cs** to the project using the Code Activity new item template. This template is used when you want to develop a new custom activity entirely in code. Here is the C# code that you need in order to implement this new activity class:

```
using System;
using System.Activities;

namespace ActivityLibrary
{
```

The base class for this activity is **CodeActivity<Decimal>**. Remember that the generic type parameter that you provide to this class determines the type for the **Result OutArgument<T>** of the class. The only output from this class is the total shipping amount, so a type of **Decimal** makes sense.

Input arguments are defined for the weight of the order, the order total, and the shipping method. Several private member variables are also declared that are used later in the code. Many of these variables are used to define simple constant values. This was done to define these values in one place and eliminate any magic numbers within the calculation code itself. In a real-life example, you probably wouldn't hard-code these values directly in this activity. You might instead retrieve the values from a database based on the destination of the order or obtain them in some other way. But hard-coding them here suffices in order to keep this example as simple as possible.

```
    public sealed class CalcShipping : CodeActivity<Decimal>
    {
        public InArgument<Int32> Weight { get; set; }
        public InArgument<Decimal> OrderTotal { get; set; }
        public InArgument<String> ShipVia { get; set; }

        private Decimal _normalRate = 1.95M;
        private Decimal _expressRate = 3.50M;
        private Decimal _minimum = 12.95M;
        private Decimal _freeThreshold = 75.00M;
        private Boolean _isFreeShipping = false;
```

The **Execute** method is where you place the business logic for this activity. In this example, the code first determines whether the requested shipping method is normal or express. If it is normal, the order total is tested to determine whether it has reached the threshold necessary to receive free shipping. If not, the shipping amount is calculated using the established rate for the normal shipping method. If express shipping is requested, no check for free shipping is performed. Instead, the shipping amount is a simple calculation using the rate for express shipping. Finally, if necessary, a minimum shipping amount is applied.

All of this is implemented as straightforward C# code. The only aspect of this code that is slightly unusual is the use of the Get method when accessing the arguments. This method is passed the CodeActivityContext that is a parameter of the Execute method. This context object identifies the set of arguments that are active for this particular execution of the activity. Passing this context is necessary since it is possible for multiple instances of this activity to be created during the lifetime of workflow. And the argument (and variable) values may change with each execution. For example, if this activity is used within a looping structure such as a While activity, the argument and variable values may be different each time through the loop. The context object always identifies the arguments that are active for the current execution.

Since the generic version of CodeActivity is used as the base class, the Execute method returns the result value directly (the total shipping charge). The value that you return is used to populate the output argument named Result. If you have other output arguments that need to be set, you would use the Set method of each argument to set them to the correct value. The Set method is similar to the Get method in that it requires you to pass the CodeActivityContext as one of the arguments.

```csharp
protected override Decimal Execute(CodeActivityContext context)
{
    Decimal result = 0;
    switch (ShipVia.Get(context))
    {
        case "normal":
            if (OrderTotal.Get(context) >= _freeThreshold)
            {
                _isFreeShipping = true;
            }
            else
            {
                result = (Weight.Get(context) * _normalRate);
            }
            break;

        case "express":
            result = (Weight.Get(context) * _expressRate);
            break;
    }

    if ((result < _minimum) && (!_isFreeShipping))
    {
        result = _minimum;
    }

    return result;
}
```

After entering this code, you should be able to build the project.

Implementing Unit Tests

The focus of this chapter is on developing new custom activities, not declaring complete workflows. For that reason, the most straightforward way to test your new activity is to use the unit testing framework included with Visual Studio.

In the code that follows, you will first implement a set of shared test methods, followed by the actual unit tests that invoke those methods. The tests are implemented in this way in order to reuse the test methods for all versions of the example activity that you will author in this chapter.

To begin developing the unit tests, first add a new Test project to the solution and name it ActivityLibraryTest. Delete the UnitTest1.cs file that was added for you since it won't be needed. Add an assembly reference to System.Activities, and add a project reference to the ActivityLibrary project, which should be in the same solution.

Select Add New Test for the test project, and select Basic Unit Test as the item template. Name the new class SharedShippingTest. The code for this class follows:

```
using System;
using System.Activities;
using System.Collections.Generic;
using Microsoft.VisualStudio.TestTools.UnitTesting;

namespace ActivityLibraryTest
{
    public static class SharedShippingTest
    {
        #region shared test method
```

The code is organized into several static methods that each tests a single condition. I've included methods that test the normal shipping method, the minimum amount, free shipping, and express shipping. Although this is far from an exhaustive list of tests for this activity, it's enough to give you a taste of how this is done.

Notice that these methods do not include the TestMethod attribute that identifies them as a test method. These are the reusable static methods that will be called by other test methods (to be defined in the next step). It is for this reason that they are not identified as test methods.

Instead of creating the activity instance within each method, it is passed as an argument. This allows for maximum reuse of this code since the tests that invoke these methods can create the activity that they want to test.

```
        public static void NormalTest(Activity activity)
        {
            Dictionary<String, Object> parameters
                = new Dictionary<string, object>();
            parameters.Add("ShipVia", "normal");
            parameters.Add("Weight", 20);
            parameters.Add("OrderTotal", 50M);

            IDictionary<String, Object> outputs = WorkflowInvoker.Invoke(
                activity, parameters);
            Assert.AreEqual(39.00M, outputs["Result"], "Result is incorrect");
        }
```

```csharp
public static void NormalMinimumTest(Activity activity)
{
    Dictionary<String, Object> parameters
        = new Dictionary<string, object>();
    parameters.Add("ShipVia", "normal");
    parameters.Add("Weight", 5);
    parameters.Add("OrderTotal", 50M);

    IDictionary<String, Object> outputs = WorkflowInvoker.Invoke(
        activity, parameters);
    Assert.AreEqual(12.95M, outputs["Result"], "Result is incorrect");
}

public static void NormalFreeTest(Activity activity)
{
    Dictionary<String, Object> parameters
        = new Dictionary<string, object>();
    parameters.Add("ShipVia", "normal");
    parameters.Add("Weight", 5);
    parameters.Add("OrderTotal", 75M);

    IDictionary<String, Object> outputs = WorkflowInvoker.Invoke(
        activity, parameters);
    Assert.AreEqual(0.00M, outputs["Result"], "Result is incorrect");
}

public static void ExpressTest(Activity activity)
{
    Dictionary<String, Object> parameters
        = new Dictionary<string, object>();
    parameters.Add("ShipVia", "express");
    parameters.Add("Weight", 5);
    parameters.Add("OrderTotal", 50M);

    IDictionary<String, Object> outputs = WorkflowInvoker.Invoke(
        activity, parameters);
    Assert.AreEqual(17.50M, outputs["Result"], "Result is incorrect");
}

#endregion
    }
}
```

Now add another unit test class named CalcShippingTest to the same test project. The purpose of this class is to execute the static methods that you just defined. Here is the code for this file:

```
using System;
using ActivityLibrary;
using Microsoft.VisualStudio.TestTools.UnitTesting;

namespace ActivityLibraryTest
{
    [TestClass]
    public class CalcShippingTest
    {
        [TestMethod]
        public void NormalTest()
        {
            SharedShippingTest.NormalTest(new CalcShipping());
        }

        [TestMethod]
        public void NormalMinimumTest()
        {
            SharedShippingTest.NormalMinimumTest(new CalcShipping());
        }

        [TestMethod]
        public void NormalFreeTest()
        {
            SharedShippingTest.NormalFreeTest(new CalcShipping());
        }

        [TestMethod]
        public void ExpressTest()
        {
            SharedShippingTest.ExpressTest(new CalcShipping());
        }
    }
}
```

You should now be able to build the solution that includes this test project.

Testing the Activity

It's now time to run the unit tests and see whether the custom activity works correctly. You can scroll to the top of the CalcShippingTest.cs file and right-click the class name (CalcShippingTest). Select the Run Tests option to execute all the tests for the class. Figure 3-2 shows the Test Results panel after I run these tests:

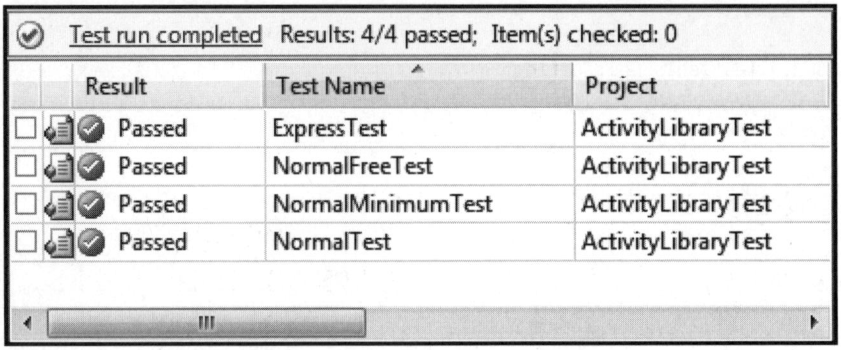

		Result	Test Name	Project
☐	📄✓	Passed	ExpressTest	ActivityLibraryTest
☐	📄✓	Passed	NormalFreeTest	ActivityLibraryTest
☐	📄✓	Passed	NormalMinimumTest	ActivityLibraryTest
☐	📄✓	Passed	NormalTest	ActivityLibraryTest

Test run completed   Results: 4/4 passed;   Item(s) checked: 0

Figure 3-2. *Successful unit tests for CalcShipping Activity*

Declaring an Activity with Xaml

In this example, you will declaratively create a custom activity by composing it from existing activities. The activity will implement the same set of business rules as the previous example and will be testable using the same set of static test methods.

Creating the Activity Class

To begin, add a new activity named `CalcShippingInXaml` to the `ActivityLibrary` project. Use the Activity add item template to create an empty activity. Since the activity is initially empty, you should go ahead and add a `Sequence` activity to it by dragging that activity to the design surface.

Defining Arguments

Arguments are added to the activity using the Arguments Editor. Click the Arguments button to open the editor, and add these arguments:

Name	Direction	Argument Type
Weight	In	Int32
OrderTotal	In	Decimal
ShipVia	In	String
Result	Out	Decimal

Defining Variables

This activity requires a number of variables. Click the Variables button to open the Variables Editor, and enter these variables:

Name	Variable Type	Scope	Default Value
IsFreeShipping	Boolean	Sequence	False
NormalRate	Decimal	Sequence	1.95D
ExpressRate	Decimal	Sequence	3.50D
Minimum	Decimal	Sequence	12.95D
FreeThreshold	Decimal	Sequence	75D

Notice that you are providing default values for all of these variables. Once again the variables are used as a convenient place to define all of the current rates and limits associated with this activity.

■ **Caution** Like many of the values that you enter in the designer, the default value is actually an expression. And because the Expression Editor expects the expressions to be entered in VB syntax, you need to use the VB suffix for the decimal type ("D") instead of the suffix used for C# ("M").

Declaring the Activity

The body of this activity will consist of a `Switch<T>` activity followed by an `If` activity. The `If` activity works just like a C# `if` statement. It provides properties for you to specify the condition to test (`If.Condition`), the activity to execute when the condition is true (`If.Then`), and the activity to execute when it is false (`If.Else`).

Other activities will be added as children of these two activities. The `Switch<T>` activity is used to branch execution on the requested shipping method (the `ShipVia` argument). The `Switch<T>` activity will need two cases, one for each of the possible shipping methods (normal and express). Within each case you will declare the activities needed to calculate the shipping charge for that shipping method. The `If` activity is used to apply the minimum shipping charge if necessary.

Follow these steps to declare the body of the activity:

1. Add a `Switch<T>` activity as a child of the `Sequence` activity. Use `String` as the generic type, and set the `Switch.Expression` property to the `ShipVia` argument.

2. Add a new case to the `Switch<T>` activity, and set the key to `normal`.

3. Add an `If` activity to the new case.

4. Enter an expression of `OrderTotal >= FreeThreshold` for the `If.Condition` property.

5. Add an `Assign` activity to the `If.Then` property. Set the `Assign.To` property to `IsFreeShipping` and the `Assign.Value` property to `True`.

6. Add an `Assign` activity to the `If.Else` property. Set the `Assign.To` property to `Result` and the `Assign.Value` property to an expression of `Weight * NormalRate`.

7. Add another case to the `Switch<T>` activity, and set the key to `express`.

8. Add an `Assign` activity to the new case. Set the `Assign.To` property to `Result` and the `Assign.Value` property to `Weight * ExpressRate`.

9. Add an `If` activity to the `Sequence`, directly under the `Switch<T>` activity.

10. Enter an expression of `Result < Minimum And Not IsFreeShipping` as the `If.Condition` property.

11. Add an `Assign` activity to the `If.Then` property. Set the `Assign.To` property to `Result` and the `Assign.Value` property to `Minimum`.

Figure 3-3 shows the `If` activity for the normal shipping method. Figure 3-4 shows the top-level view of the completed custom activity.

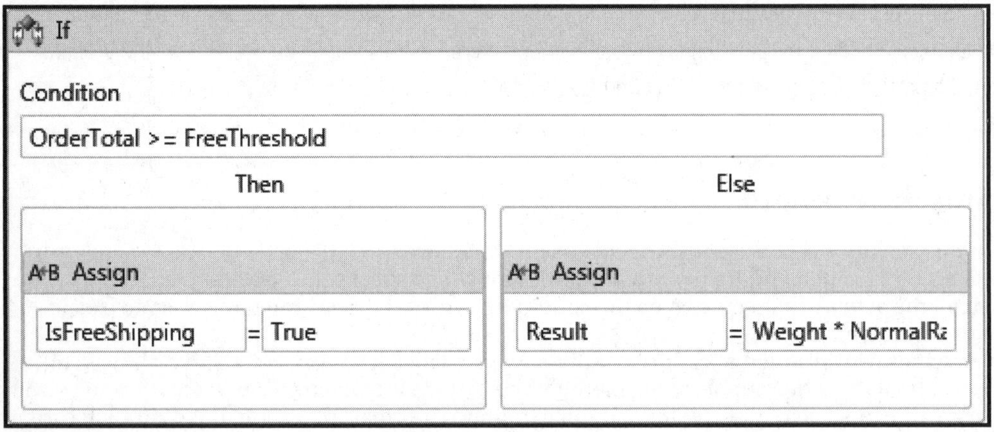

Figure 3-3. Normal shipping method if activity

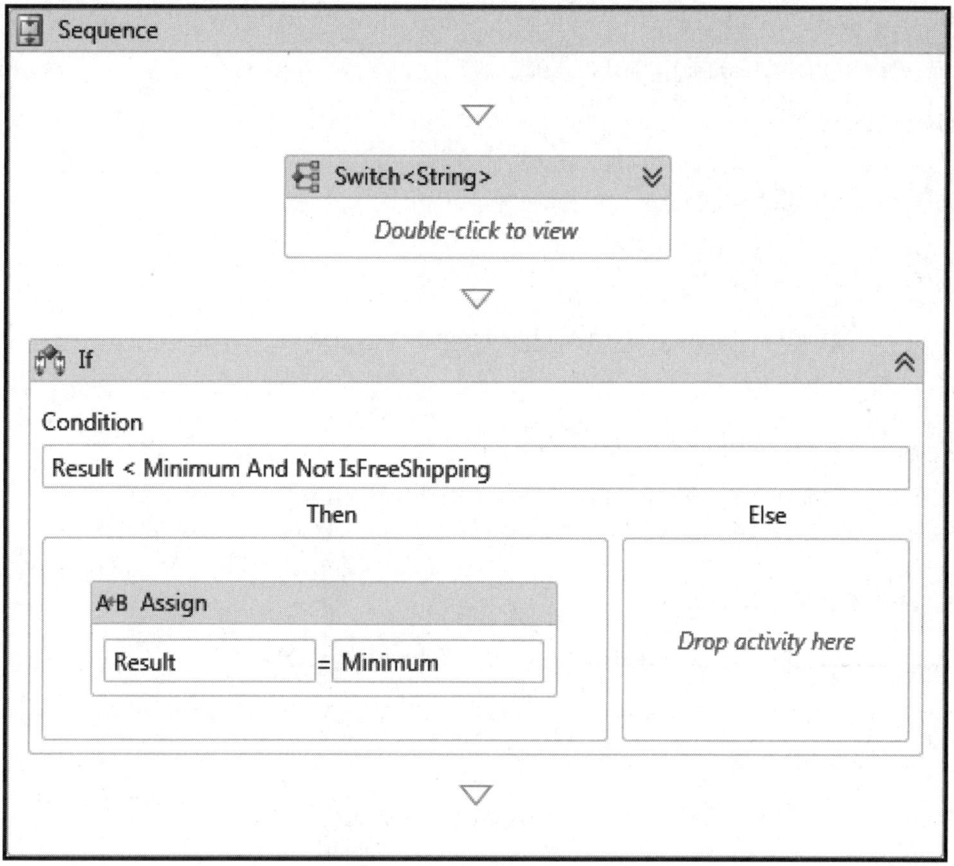

Figure 3-4. Completed CalcShippingInXaml activity

You should be able to build the project at this point.

Implementing Unit Tests

To test this activity, you can use the same set of static test methods that you implemented for the CalcShipping example presented earlier. However, you do need to add a new unit test class named CalcShippingInXamlTest to the ActivityLibraryTest project. The purpose of this class is to execute the static methods, passing an instance of the CalcShippingInXaml activity that you just declared. Here is the code for this file:

```
using System;
using ActivityLibrary;
using Microsoft.VisualStudio.TestTools.UnitTesting;

namespace ActivityLibraryTest
{
    [TestClass]
    public class CalcShippingInXamlTest
    {
        [TestMethod]
        public void XamlNormalTest()
        {
            SharedShippingTest.NormalTest(new CalcShippingInXaml());
        }

        [TestMethod]
        public void XamlNormalMinimumTest()
        {
            SharedShippingTest.NormalMinimumTest(new CalcShippingInXaml());
        }

        [TestMethod]
        public void XamlNormalFreeTest()
        {
            SharedShippingTest.NormalFreeTest(new CalcShippingInXaml());
        }

        [TestMethod]
        public void XamlExpressTest()
        {
            SharedShippingTest.ExpressTest(new CalcShippingInXaml());
        }
    }
}
```

Testing the Activity

After building the ActivityLibraryTest project, you should be ready to execute the unit tests. Scroll to the top of the CalcShippingInXamlTest.cs file, and right-click the class name (CalcShippingInXamlTest). Select the Run Tests option to execute all the tests for the class. The results should be similar to those shown in Figure 3-2 for the previous set of tests.

Declaring an Activity with Code

Just as you did in the previous example, you will declaratively create another custom activity by composing it from existing activities. The difference this time is that you will do everything in code. This example demonstrates a hybrid mix of the two authoring styles demonstrated previously. You use code to define the activity instead of Xaml, but you're not implementing all the logic from scratch. Instead, you assemble existing activities into a finished activity as you did in the Xaml example. The finished activity will implement the same set of business rules that you saw in the previous examples and will be testable using the same set of static test methods.

Creating the Activity Class

To begin, add a new activity named `CalcShippingInCode` to the `ActivityLibrary` project. Use the Code Activity add item template to create a code-based activity class.

Implementing the Activity

The code that you need to declare this activity is shown next. The first order of business is to change the base class from `CodeActivity` to `Activity<Decimal>`. The `Activity<TResult>` class is designed for the composition of an activity from a tree of other existing activities. If you look at the Xaml file from the previous example, you will see that the root node is `Activity`. The only difference is that you are using the generic version of this class.

The usual input arguments are defined as properties of the class. The majority of your work for this activity is done in a new private method named `BuildImplementation`.

```
using System;
using System.Activities;
using System.Activities.Statements;

namespace ActivityLibrary
{
    public sealed class CalcShippingInCode : Activity<Decimal>
    {
        public InArgument<Int32> Weight { get; set; }
        public InArgument<Decimal> OrderTotal { get; set; }
        public InArgument<String> ShipVia { get; set; }
```

During construction of the activity, the private `BuildImplementation` method is assigned to the `Implementation` property. This property is a delegate defined as `Func<Activity>`, meaning that it must be assigned to a method that takes no parameters and returns an `Activity`. The `Implementation` property is the extension point that allows you to provide an activity declaration that is implemented in code.

```
        public CalcShippingInCode()
        {
            this.Implementation = BuildImplementation;
        }

        private Activity BuildImplementation()
        {
```

Just as you did in the first example in this chapter, variables are defined with default values. The difference this time is the use of the `Variable<T>` class to define the variables. Previously, normal C# CLR types were used to define them. The `Variable<T>` class is used because the variables must be of a type that is supported by the workflow infrastructure. As you will see later in the code, instead of using the variables privately in C# code, they are passed as arguments to the various activities.

```
Variable<Boolean> isFreeShipping =
    new Variable<Boolean> { Name = "IsFreeShipping" };
Variable<Decimal> normalRate =
    new Variable<Decimal> { Name = "NormalRate", Default = 1.95M };
Variable<Decimal> expressRate =
    new Variable<Decimal> { Name = "ExpressRate", Default = 3.50M };
Variable<Decimal> minimum =
    new Variable<Decimal> { Name = "Minimum", Default = 12.95M };
Variable<Decimal> freeThreshold =
    new Variable<Decimal> { Name = "FreeThreshold", Default = 75.00M };
```

The work of composing a tree of existing activities now begins. The `Implementation` property requires a single `Activity` that forms the body of this custom activity. Therefore, the goal of this code is to return that single `Activity`.

At the top of this tree of activities is a `Sequence` activity, which contains a single `Switch<T>` activity and an `If` activity. The `Switch<T>` activity has two case instances and so on. This structure should be familiar to you since it is the same set of activities that you saw in the previous example. The only difference is that you're seeing it composed in code instead of in the workflow designer (or Xaml).

The variables that were just defined are added to the `Sequence.Variables` property.

```
return new Sequence
{
    Variables =
    {
        isFreeShipping, normalRate, expressRate, minimum, freeThreshold
    },

    Activities =
    {
```

The code that sets the `Switch.Expression` property illustrates an important pattern that should be followed. This property is typed as an `InArgument<String>`. You might be tempted to directly assign the `ShipVia` input argument to it, but that wouldn't work. Remember that when you are referencing arguments and variables in code from within an activity, you need to pass the activity context to the `Get` or `Set` method. This is necessary in order to retrieve the instance of the argument or variable that is appropriate for the current execution of the activity.

To satisfy this requirement, the code that sets the `Switch.Expression` property constructs a new `InArgument<T>` instance instead of directly assigning the `ShipVia` argument. It uses a constructor overload of the `InArgument<T>` class that is defined like this:
`InArgument(Expression<Func<ActivityContext, T>> expression)`. This constructor requires a `Func` that expects an `ActivityContext` as the only parameter and returns an instance of the generic type T. Using this constructor provides the activity context that is necessary to retrieve the argument or variable.

The code shown next uses the Lambda expression syntax to keep the code as concise as possible. For a very brief description of Lambda expressions, please refer to the "Understanding Lambda Expressions" sidebar in this chapter.

```
            new Switch<String>
            {
                Expression = new InArgument<String>(
                    ac => ShipVia.Get(ac)),
                Cases =
                {
                    {"normal", new If
                        {
                            Condition = new InArgument<Boolean>(ac =>
                              OrderTotal.Get(ac) >= freeThreshold.Get(ac)),
                            Then = new Assign<Boolean>
                            {
                                To = new OutArgument<Boolean>(ac =>
                                  isFreeShipping.Get(ac)),
                                Value = true
                            },
                            Else = new Assign<Decimal>
                            {
                                To = new OutArgument<Decimal>(ac =>
                                  this.Result.Get(ac)),
                                Value = new InArgument<Decimal>(ac =>
                                  Weight.Get(ac) * normalRate.Get(ac))
                            }
                        }
                    },
                    {"express", new Assign<Decimal>
                        {
                            To = new OutArgument<Decimal>(ac =>
                              this.Result.Get(ac)),
                            Value = new InArgument<Decimal>(ac =>
                              Weight.Get(ac) * expressRate.Get(ac))
                        }
                    }
                }
            },
            new If
            {
                Condition = new InArgument<bool>(ac =>
                  Result.Get(ac) < minimum.Get(ac) &&
                  (!isFreeShipping.Get(ac))),
                Then = new Assign
                {
                    To = new OutArgument<Decimal>(ac => Result.Get(ac)),
                    Value = new InArgument<Decimal>(ac => minimum.Get(ac))
                }
            }
        }
    }; //new Sequence
    }
    }
}
```

Clearly, this is not the easiest way to author new activities. If your plan is to compose your custom activity using existing activities, it is much easier and more intuitive to use the workflow designer or to compose the activity by hand directly in Xaml. But I've included this example to demonstrate that there is no real magic behind the scenes when you use Xaml or the workflow designer. Child activities are simply a collection of activities that you construct and add to the appropriate properties of other activities.

Implementing Unit Tests

This activity can be tested in the same way as the previous examples. Add a new unit test class named CalcShippingInCodeTest to the ActivityLibraryTest project. Here is the code that you need for this class:

```
using System;
using ActivityLibrary;
using Microsoft.VisualStudio.TestTools.UnitTesting;

namespace ActivityLibraryTest
{
    [TestClass]
    public class CalcShippingInCodeTest
    {
        [TestMethod]
        public void CodeNormalTest()
        {
            SharedShippingTest.NormalTest(new CalcShippingInCode());
        }

        [TestMethod]
        public void CodeNormalMinimumTest()
        {
            SharedShippingTest.NormalMinimumTest(new CalcShippingInCode());
        }

        [TestMethod]
        public void CodeNormalFreeTest()
        {
            SharedShippingTest.NormalFreeTest(new CalcShippingInCode());
        }

        [TestMethod]
        public void CodeExpressTest()
        {
            SharedShippingTest.ExpressTest(new CalcShippingInCode());
        }
    }
}
```

Testing the Activity

At this point, you can build the `ActivityLibraryTest` project and execute the tests as you have done previously. The test results should be consistent with Figure 3-2.

Understanding Lambda Expressions

Lambda expressions are simply a very concise way to define anonymous functions. They were introduced along with other C# language enhancements that were needed to support Language Integrated Query (LINQ).

The `=>` operator is the lambda operator and separates the input parameters (on the left side) from the anonymous function. When reading Lambda expressions, the `=>` operator is typically read as "goes to." For example, consider this delegate to a function that passes and returns an `Int32` value:

```
delegate Int32 MyIntDelegate(Int32 value);
```

To use this delegate, you could assign it to a class method with this same signature (passing an `Int32` and returning an `Int32`). Or you could assign an anonymous delegate with this same signature. Now with Lambda expressions, you have another way to assign code to execute with this delegate:

```
MyIntDelegate foo = o => o + 1;
```

This creates an instance of the previously defined delegate named `foo` and assigns it an anonymous function that simply adds 1 to the number that is passed as an argument. You could then execute the delegate like this:

```
Int32 theResult = foo(10);
```

After execution, `theResult` would have a value of 11. This is obviously a very brief overview of Lambda expressions; there is much more to learn. If you need additional information, please refer to the documentation provided in MSDN on Lambda expressions, or reach for your favorite C# book such as this Apress book: *Pro C# 2010 and the .NET 4 Platform, Fifth Edition* (Apress, 2010).

Implementing an Asynchronous Activity

The final version of the example activity is one that demonstrates asynchronous execution. The work of the activity will be performed on a separate thread.

Admittedly, this particular example (calculating the shipping charge) doesn't really lend itself to asynchronous operation. In its current form, it doesn't do any work (such as accessing a database or file) that would normally benefit from execution on a separate thread. However, rather than developing a completely different example, I think it's more important to see the same example activity implemented in an asynchronous way. That should make it easier to compare this to the other implementations already presented in this chapter.

Creating the Activity Class

To implement this example, add a new activity named `CalcShippingAsync` to the `ActivityLibrary` project. Use the Code Activity add item template to create a code-based activity class.

Implementing the Activity

The code for this activity is shown next. If begins by defining a simple class named `CalcShippingAsyncArgs`. This class is used later in the code to pass the calculation arguments to the thread that performs the calculations.

```
using System;
using System.Activities;

namespace ActivityLibrary
{
    internal class CalcShippingAsyncArgs
    {
        public Int32 Weight { get; set; }
        public Decimal OrderTotal { get; set; }
        public String ShipVia { get; set; }
    }
```

This time, an `AsyncCodeActivity<T>` is used as the base class. This base class provides the necessary functionality to execute work asynchronously on a separate thread. The usual set of input arguments are defined, followed by the private variables that define the rates and thresholds used during the calculation.

```
    public sealed class CalcShippingAsync : AsyncCodeActivity<Decimal>
    {
        public InArgument<Int32> Weight { get; set; }
        public InArgument<Decimal> OrderTotal { get; set; }
        public InArgument<String> ShipVia { get; set; }

        private Decimal _normalRate = 1.95M;
        private Decimal _expressRate = 3.50M;
        private Decimal _minimum = 12.95M;
        private Decimal _freeThreshold = 75.00M;
```

For this example, the work of calculating the shipping charges has been moved to a private method that is executed on a separate thread. Instead of the `Execute` method that you've seen in previous examples, the `AsyncCodeActivity` class defines `BeginExecute` and `EndExecute` methods that you must override. The `BeginExecute` method is invoked first and is your opportunity to retrieve argument and variable values and to begin the real work on a separate thread. Once the asynchronous work completes, the `EndExecute` method is invoked. This is your opportunity to set any output arguments and generally complete the work of the activity.

The code for the `BeginExecute` method retrieves the input argument values and creates an instance of the `CalcShippingAsyncArgs` class that was defined earlier. The `CalcShippingAsyncArgs` instance is constructed in order to pass the arguments to the worker thread. The arguments are retrieved here since they can be referenced only on the workflow thread.

Next, a `Func` delegate is defined that expects an instance of the arguments class and returns a `Decimal` result. This delegate is assigned a private `Calculate` method that performs the calculation of the shipping charges. A reference to this `Func` delegate is saved in the `UserState` property of the activity context. This allows the code in the `EndExecute` method to reference this delegate.

Finally, the delegate is executed on a separate thread using the `BeginInvoke` method. This executes the target of the delegate (in this case the private `Calculate` method) on a separate thread pool thread.

```
protected override IAsyncResult BeginExecute(
    AsyncCodeActivityContext context,
    AsyncCallback callback, object state)
{
    CalcShippingAsyncArgs parameters = new CalcShippingAsyncArgs
    {
        Weight = Weight.Get(context),
        OrderTotal = OrderTotal.Get(context),
        ShipVia = ShipVia.Get(context),
    };

    Func<CalcShippingAsyncArgs, Decimal> asyncWork = a => Calculate(a);
    context.UserState = asyncWork;
    return asyncWork.BeginInvoke(parameters, callback, state);
}
```

The actual calculations are similar to what you've already seen in the previous examples. The main difference is that properties of the `CalcShippingAsyncArgs` object are referenced rather than the input arguments of the activity.

```
private Decimal Calculate(CalcShippingAsyncArgs parameters)
{
    Decimal result = 0;
    Boolean isFreeShipping = false;

    System.Threading.Thread.Sleep(500);   //simulate a short delay

    switch (parameters.ShipVia)
    {
        case "normal":
            if (parameters.OrderTotal >= _freeThreshold)
            {
                isFreeShipping = true;
            }
            else
            {
                result = parameters.Weight * _normalRate;
            }
            break;

        case "express":
            result = parameters.Weight * _expressRate;
            break;
    }
```

```
            if ((result < _minimum) && (!isFreeShipping))
            {
                result = _minimum;
            }

            return result;
        }
```

When the `Calculate` method has completed, the `EndExecute` method is executed on a workflow thread. The code for this method completes the execution of the asynchronous delegate by calling the `EndInvoke` method. The `Decimal` result from `EndInvoke` is used as a return value for the `EndExecute` method. This value is used to populate the `Result` argument of the activity.

```
        protected override Decimal EndExecute(
            AsyncCodeActivityContext context, IAsyncResult result)
        {
            return ((Func<CalcShippingAsyncArgs, Decimal>)
                context.UserState).EndInvoke(result);
        }
    }
}
```

Implementing Unit Tests

To test this new activity, add a new unit test class named `CalcShippingAsyncTest` to the `ActivityLibraryTest` project. The code for this class is shown here:

```
using System;
using ActivityLibrary;
using Microsoft.VisualStudio.TestTools.UnitTesting;

namespace ActivityLibraryTest
{
    [TestClass]
    public class CalcShippingAsyncTest
    {
        [TestMethod]
        public void AsyncNormalTest()
        {
            SharedShippingTest.NormalTest(new CalcShippingAsync());
        }

        [TestMethod]
        public void AsyncNormalMinimumTest()
        {
            SharedShippingTest.NormalMinimumTest(new CalcShippingAsync());
        }
```

```
        [TestMethod]
        public void AsyncNormalFreeTest()
        {
            SharedShippingTest.NormalFreeTest(new CalcShippingAsync());
        }

        [TestMethod]
        public void AsyncExpressTest()
        {
            SharedShippingTest.ExpressTest(new CalcShippingAsync());
        }
    }
}
```

Testing the Activity

After building the solution, you can execute the tests defined in the `CalcShippingAsyncTest` class. The test results should be similar to those shown in Figure 3-2 for the first set of tests.

Using Activities

You've now seen that the same custom activity can be implemented in several different ways. All of these authoring styles are valid, and you will likely use most of them at one time or another. Regardless of the style that you use, the message is the same: developing custom activities is the best way to make full use of WF.

Now that you know more about authoring custom activities, you might have a better appreciation of how they act as the reusable building blocks that you compose into finished workflows. In the next few sections, I discuss a few short topics related to using activities within a workflow.

Workflow Building Blocks

The custom activities that you develop work alongside the standard activities provided with WF. Together they form a seamless stack of workflow building blocks. This is illustrated in Figure 3-5.

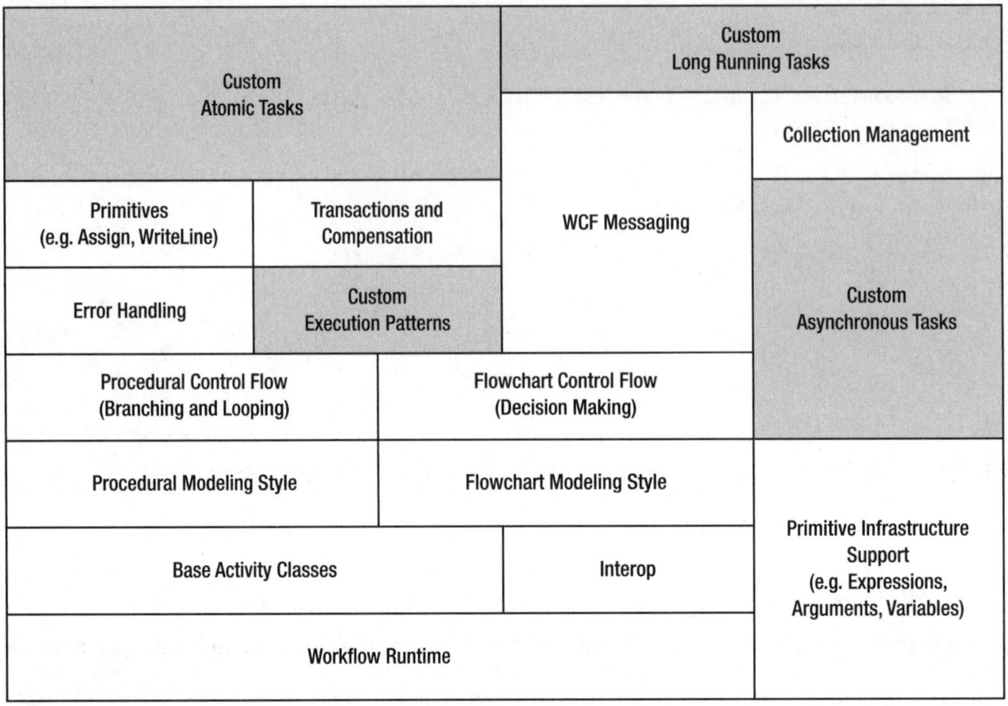

Custom Atomic Tasks		**Custom Long Running Tasks**	
			Collection Management
Primitives (e.g. Assign, WriteLine)	**Transactions and Compensation**	**WCF Messaging**	**Custom Asynchronous Tasks**
Error Handling	**Custom Execution Patterns**		
Procedural Control Flow (Branching and Looping)	**Flowchart Control Flow** (Decision Making)		
Procedural Modeling Style	**Flowchart Modeling Style**		**Primitive Infrastructure Support** (e.g. Expressions, Arguments, Variables)
Base Activity Classes	**Interop**		
Workflow Runtime			

Figure 3-5. *Activity stack*

As shown in Figure 3-5, the stack of WF building blocks begins at the bottom with a solid foundation. This foundation consists of the workflow runtime, the base activity classes along with other infrastructure classes such as those that support expressions, arguments, and variables. I've also included the classes that support interop with WF 3.*x* activities at this level.

Moving up in the stack, you find the classes that support workflow modeling styles such as procedural and flowchart. The control flow activities that are associated with each of these modeling styles are shown next. The control flow activities include the standard looping, branching, and decision-making activities. Also included in the stack are standard activities for error handling, transactions, compensation, and collection management. Activities that enable you to leverage WCF messaging as well as some miscellaneous primitives round out the standard activities.

Most of your custom activities will be built upon the foundation of standard activities beneath them. However, you may require custom activities that implement new execution patterns or fill in other missing blocks at any level of the stack.

The key point is that any given workflow requires a number of building blocks from these categories. Many of those blocks are supplied with WF, but many times you need to fill in those empty spaces yourself with custom activities.

■ **Note** Don't read too much into the relative sizes and positions of the blocks in Figure 3-5. My intent is not to suggest that certain categories contain more activities than others or are more important. The relative importance of the activities in any single category will vary based on the requirements of the workflow. I'm also not suggesting that any given block is directly dependent on those under it. Some blocks are clearly foundation pieces (Workflow Runtime and Infrastructure) and must be in place before other blocks are placed above them. But most blocks don't have a dependency on the blocks that are directly beneath them.

Activity Data Flow

You've already seen how data flows into a workflow or an activity via the arguments that you define. If output arguments from an individual activity are needed elsewhere in the workflow, they are passed to subsequent activities via variables. Since this is an authoring pattern that is repeated quite often, I thought it deserved another look before I move on to other topics. Figure 3-6 illustrates the relationship between arguments, variables, and activities.

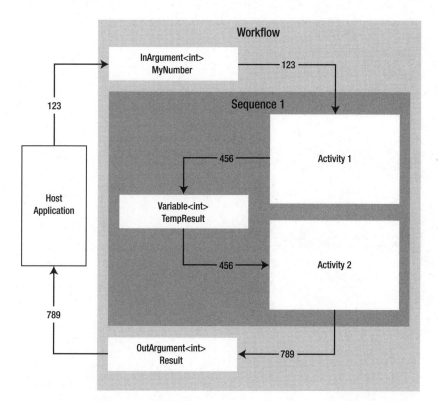

Figure 3-6. Activity data flow

As shown in Figure 3-6, data enters a workflow via an input argument. That initial data is used as input to the first activity that has output of its own. The output from the first activity is stored temporarily in a variable in order to make it available for use by a subsequent activity. Finally, the output from the second activity is assigned to an output argument and is made available to the host application that started the workflow.

The most important point is that the activities generally should not directly reference each other. Instead, variables are used as an intermediate storage location of any values that need to be used elsewhere in the workflow.

Variable Scoping

You have already seen that you must identify the scope of any variables that you define. A variable is visible to the activity that declared it as well as any children of that activity. Obviously this has implications when you are authoring workflows. You need to be conscious of how each variable will be used and which activities will require access to it. This is illustrated in Figure 3-7.

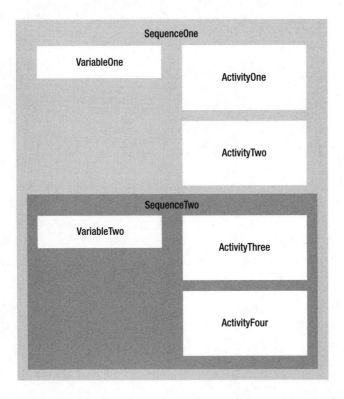

Figure 3-7. Variable scope

Figure 3-7 uses a set of four activities and two variables to illustrate how scoping of variables works. In this figure, `VariableOne` is defined at the outermost `Sequence` activity. It is visible to all child activities shown in the figure. On the other hand, `VariableTwo` is defined one level down in a child `Sequence` activity (`SequenceTwo`). Since it is scoped at a lower level, it is visible to only two of the activities (`ActivityThree` and `ActivityFour`).

Most importantly, variables go out of scope when the activity that owns them goes out of scope. In this example, once `ActivityThree` and `ActivityFour` have completed their execution, the work of their parent (`SequenceTwo`) is also complete. Once that occurs, `SequenceTwo` goes out of scope along with any variables (`VariableTwo`) that were defined within it.

Standard Activities Summary

Table 3-2 summarizes the standard activities that are provided with WF. The activities are presented in alphabetical sequence by activity name. A category is included that refers to the activity categories in the following section. The Allows Variables column indicates whether the activity supports the declaration of variables. The final column (Chapter) indicates the primary chapter in which you'll learn more about the activity.

Table 3-2. *Standard Activity Summary*

Activity Name	Category	Allows Variables	Chapter
AddToCollection	Collection		6
Assign	Primitives		1
CancellationScope	Transaction	Yes	13
ClearCollection	Collection		6
CompensableActivity	Transaction	Yes	13
Compensate	Transaction		13
Confirm	Transaction		13
CorrelationScope	Messaging		9
Delay	Primitives		5
DoWhile	Control Flow	Yes	5
ExistsInCollection	Collection		6
Flowchart	Control Flow	Yes	7

Continued

Activity Name	Category	Allows Variables	Chapter
FlowDecision	Control Flow		7
FlowSwitch	Control Flow		7
ForEach	Control Flow		6
If	Control Flow		5
InitializeCorrelation	Messaging		9
Interop	Migration		18
InvokeMethod	Primitives		8
Parallel	Control Flow	Yes	5
ParallelForEach	Control Flow		6
Persist	Runtime		10
Pick	Control Flow		8
PickBranch	Control Flow	Yes	8
Receive	Messaging		9
ReceiveAndSendReply	Messaging		9
RemoveFromCollection	Collection		6
Rethrow	Error Handling		13
Send	Messaging		9
SendAndReceiveReply	Messaging		9
Sequence	Control Flow	Yes	5
Switch	Control Flow		5
TerminateWorkflow	Runtime		

Activity Name	Category	Allows Variables	Chapter
Throw	Error Handling		13
TransactedReceiveScope	Messaging	Yes	9
TransactionScope	Transaction		13
TryCatch	Error Handling	Yes	13
While	Control Flow	Yes	5
WriteLine	Primitives		1

Standard Activities

In this section I review the standard activities provided with WF. The goal is to provide a short description of each activity without going into the details of how each activity is used. Detailed coverage of each activity is left to the other chapters in this book that target each functional area.

To better understand the purpose of each activity and how it relates to the others, I've organized them into these categories. These categories correspond to the Toolbox categories in which you will find these activities:

- Control Flow
- Flowchart
- Messaging
- Runtime
- Primitives
- Transactions
- Collection
- Error Handling
- Migration

The activities in each of these categories are discussed in the following sections.

■ **Note** You will notice that many of the activities allow you to declare a single activity as a child. Although support for only a single activity may seem like a major shortcoming, please remember that the single activity that you declare may itself be a container for other activities.

Control Flow

The activities in this category control the flow of execution within the workflow. The activities in this style use familiar programming constructs such as `if`, `while`, and `switch` for branching and looping. However, although they can be categorized as procedural control flow activities, they can also be used within workflows that also use flowchart activities.

Sequence

The `Sequence` activity is a simple container for other activities that implements a sequential execution pattern. Activities that are placed into this container are executed in the sequence in which they are defined.

If

The `If` activity is used to model an if-then-else condition within a workflow. You use it by supplying an expression that returns a Boolean value. If the value is true, the activity that you declare for the `If.Then` property is executed. Optionally, you can also declare an activity for the `If.Else` property. This activity is executed if the condition is false. If you need to implement an if-else-if pattern, you can nest one `If` activity in the `If.Else` property of another.

Although these properties accept only a single activity, that activity can be a container for other activities such a `Sequence` activity.

Switch<T>

The `Switch<T>` activity models the C# `switch` statement, which executes one of the declared cases. It is a generic activity; therefore, you must supply the type of the expression that will be evaluated. The expression to evaluate is set using the `Switch.Expression` property. Multiple cases may be defined that represent the possible values of the `Switch.Expression` property. The activity defined for a case is executed when the key value defined for the case matches the `Switch.Expression` property.

While

The `While` activity executes a child activity while a condition is true. The `While.Condition` property is used to define a Boolean expression. A single child activity is declared for the `While.Body` property. Since the condition may initially be false, it is possible that the child activity is never executed.

DoWhile

Like the `While` activity, the `DoWhile` continuously executes a child activity. However, the `DoWhile` evaluates the `DoWhile.Condition` property after execution of the activity declared for the `DoWhile.Body` property. This means that the child activity is always executed at least once. Execution of the child activity stops when the condition is no longer true.

Parallel

The `Parallel` activity schedules simultaneous execution of multiple child activities. The children are declared using the `Parallel.Branches` property. Execution of this activity completes when all child activities complete. An optional `Parallel.CompletionCondition` property allows you to declare a condition that causes execution to stop for all child activities. If this condition is true, child activities that are still executing are canceled.

ForEach<T>

The `ForEach<T>` activity executes a declared activity for each element in a collection. The activity to execute is set using the `ForEach.Body` property. The collection of values is set using the `ForEach.Values` property. `ForEach<T>` is a generic activity; therefore, the type of the elements in the collection must be set.

ParallelForEach<T>

The `ParallelForEach<T>` activity works like the `ForEach` activity. It executes an activity for each element in a collection. However, as the name implies, `ParallelForEach<T>` executes the child activity for each element in the collection in parallel. Parallel in this case means that execution of the child activity is immediately scheduled for all elements in the collection. Execution does not occur simultaneously on multiple threads unless all the child activities are implemented as asynchronous activities.

Pick and PickBranch

The `Pick` activity executes one of the declared branches based on the receipt of an event. It is similar in concept to the `Switch` activity, but instead of branching based on the value of an expression, execution of a single branch is determined by the receipt of an event.

To use the `Pick` activity, you declare multiple instances of the `PickBranch` activity as children. Each `PickBranch` has a `Trigger` and `Action` property. You set the `PickBranch.Trigger` property to an activity that waits for a continuation event via resumption of a bookmark. The `PickBranch.Action` property is used to declare the activity you want to execute when the trigger event is received.

Flowchart

The activities in this category are used to declare workflows using the flowchart style of modeling. This modeling style controls the flow of execution using direct links between node activities. This is in contrast with the procedural style of modeling, which uses more traditional programming constructs for looping and branching.

Flowchart

The `Flowchart` activity is the basis for the flowchart modeling style. It maintains the collection of child nodes that have been declared as well as a starting point for the flowchart.

FlowDecision

The FlowDecision activity models a simple decision within a workflow that uses the flowchart modeling style. The FlowDecision has a Condition property that allows you to set an expression to evaluate. Two outcomes are possible: the condition is either true or false. Flowchart nodes (paths to other activities) can be defined for one or both of the outcomes.

FlowSwitch and FlowSwitch<T>

The FlowSwitch activity implements the logic in a Switch activity for the flowchart modeling style. A single FlowSwitch.Expression property is used to define the expression to evaluate. Multiple cases are declared, with each one associated with the string representation of one possible value of the expression. Execution continues with the case that evaluates to true. The generic version of this activity identifies the type of the Expression property and supports the definition of cases using the actual values for the type instead of string values.

Messaging

The activities in this category are used to interact with other applications using Windows Communication Foundation (WCF).

ReceiveAndSendReply

This activity template is used to model the service side of a request/response message exchange pattern. The template contains a correlated Receive and SendReply activity. The purpose of this combination of activities is to model a WCF service using a workflow that receives a request and then sends a reply.

SendAndReceiveReply

This activity template models the requesting side of a request/response message exchange pattern. The template contains a correlated Send and ReceiveReply activity. The Send activity sends a request to a WCF endpoint and then waits for a response.

Send

The Send activity is used to send a request to a WCF endpoint. It is a single activity that initiates the request but doesn't contain the logic necessary to wait for a response. It is suitable for one-way communication (request only) with another system. If you require a request/response message exchange pattern, the SendAndReceiveReply template should be used instead.

Receive

The Receive activity models the receipt of a one-way message from a WCF client. If a request/response message exchange pattern is needed, the ReceiveAndSendReply template should be used instead.

CorrelationScope

The `CorrelationScope` activity is used to provide management of correlation between messaging activities. The messaging activities to manager are added as children of this activity.

InitializeCorrelation

The `InitializeCorrelation` activity is used to manually initialize correlation prior to sending or receiving a message. Normally, correlation is automatically initialized when a message is sent or received.

TransactedReceiveScope

The `TransactedReceiveScope` is used when you need to flow a transaction into a workflow via WCF messaging.

Runtime

Activities in this category are related to miscellaneous runtime operations.

Persist

The `Persist` activity is used to declaratively request that the workflow persist its current state.

TerminateWorkflow

The `TerminateWorkflow` activity is used to declaratively terminate execution of the workflow.

Primitives

These activities provide miscellaneous functionality that spans multiple categories.

Assign

The `Assign` activity allows you to set a variable or argument to a new value. The value is specified as an expression so it can be a literal value or it can reference other arguments or variables.

Delay

The `Delay` activity is used to set a timer within a workflow. When the timer expires, the `Delay` activity completes and execution of the remainder of the workflow can continue.

InvokeMethod

The `InvokeMethod` enables you to call a public method on an object instance or class.

WriteLine

The `WriteLine` activity writes a string to the console. You can optionally set the `WriteLine.TextWriter` property to direct the string to that writer instead of the console.

Transactions and Compensation

The activities in this category are used to manage the consistency of any work that is accomplished by a workflow. Transactions are used to guarantee the atomicity and consistency of short-lived units of work. Compensation is the process of undoing work that has already been completed.

TransactionScope

The `TransactionScope` activity protects the work that is done by a child activity with a transaction. A new transaction is created (if necessary) when this activity begins execution, and it is committed when it completes. Any child activities can enlist their work in the active transaction so that all the work is committed at the same time.

CompensableActivity

The `CompensableActivity` is a container for child activities that require compensation. The activity supports a `CompensableActivity.Body` property that is used to set the activity that requires compensation. Properties are also supported that allow you to set the activity to execute when compensation, cancellation, or confirmation is required. Compensation is the undoing of completed work. A confirmation activity would be used to confirm the successful completion of the work.

Compensate

The `Compensate` activity allows you to explicitly begin the compensation process for an activity.

Confirm

The `Confirm` activity allows you to explicitly begin the confirmation process.

CancellationScope

The `CancellationScope` activity allows you to declare an activity to execute if the main activity is canceled. The main activity is declared using the `CancellationScope.Body` property, while the cancellation activity is declared using `CancellationScope.CancelHandler`.

Collection Management

The activities in this category allow you to declaratively use and manage data in collections.

AddToCollection

The `AddToCollection` activity adds a new item to a collection. This is a generic activity, so you need to specify the type of the items in the collection. The `AddToCollection.Collection` property identifies the collection, and the `AddToCollection.Item` property is the new item to be added to the collection.

RemoveFromCollection

The `RemoveFromCollection` activity is similar in usage to `AddToCollection`. Instead of adding a new item to a collection, this activity removes the item.

ExistsInCollection

The `ExistsInCollection` activity is used to determine whether a given item is found in a collection.

ClearCollection

The `ClearCollection` activity clears all items from a collection.

Error Handling

Activities in this category are associated with error handling within a workflow.

TryCatch

The `TryCatch` activity models the familiar `try`/`catch` pattern that is supported in C#. A single activity to execute is declared using the `TryCatch.Try` property. One or more exceptions to catch are defined using the `TryCatch.Catches` property. Each catch declaration includes an activity to execute when the exception is caught. If the activity declared for the `TryCatch.Try` property throws an unhandled exception, the appropriate activity associated with the caught exception is executed. A `TryCatch.Finally` property is used to define an activity to execute after the `Try` and any `Catches` activities are executed.

Throw and Rethrow

The `Throw` activity allows you to declaratively raise an exception within a workflow. It is similar in usage as the C# `throw` statement. The `Rethrow` activity can be used only within the activity declared for the `TryCatch.Catch` property. It rethrows the exception that was caught.

Migration

Activities in this category are related to migration from an earlier version of WF.

Interop

The `Interop` activity is used for interoperability with activities that were developed for the 3.*x* version of WF. This activity acts as a wrapper for the 3.*x* activity, allowing it to execute in the latest version of WF. You declare the 3.*x* activity to execute using the `Interop.Body` property.

Summary

The purpose of this chapter was to help you become better acquainted with workflow activities. You learned about the different categories of work that activities can perform. This chapter also discussed the use of arguments and variables.

You learned that there are several authoring styles that you can use to develop your own custom activities. You can create a new activity in code completely from scratch, or you can assemble it using existing activities. Both of these authoring styles were demonstrated in a series of examples. The examples implemented the same custom activity using each of the available authoring styles.

Following the examples that demonstrated how to create custom activities, the chapter presented a brief overview of the standard activities that are included with WF.

In the next chapter, you will learn more about the options available for hosting workflows in your applications.

CHAPTER 4

■ ■ ■

Workflow Hosting

This chapter focuses on hosting and executing workflows. Regardless of the type of host application, the `WorkflowInvoker` and `WorkflowApplication` classes are used to execute your workflows. The chapter describes how to use each class and then demonstrates features of each class with a number of short examples.

The `WorkflowInvoker` and `WorkflowApplication` classes require that you create an instance of the workflow type that you want to execute. Windows Workflow Foundation (WF) also provides the ability to load and execute a workflow directly from a Xaml document. The `ActivityXamlServices` class provides this functionality and is described and demonstrated in this chapter.

Invoking a workflow from an ASP.NET web application is a common scenario that is demonstrated later in the chapter. Finally, the chapter concludes with an example that demonstrates how to execute and manage multiple instances of a workflow from a Windows Presentation Foundation (WPF) application.

■ **Note** Workflows that use Windows Communication Foundation (WCF) messaging can be self-hosted using the `WorkflowServiceHost` class. Chapter 9 discusses the use of this class.

Understanding the WorkflowInvoker Class

The `WorkflowInvoker` class is the simplest way to execute a complete workflow or a single activity. It allows you to execute an activity on the current thread with the simplicity of calling a method. This simplicity is primarily due to the use of the current thread for execution. This eliminates the need for thread synchronization code between the current thread and a separate workflow thread. It also eliminates the need for the class to support a wide range of state notification members and events.

But even with this simplicity, the class supports a number of variations and options for workflow and activity execution, which are described in the following sections.

Using the Static Methods

One way to use the `WorkflowInvoker` class is via a set of static `Invoke` methods. To use one of these methods, you create an instance of the workflow that you want to execute and pass it as an argument to the appropriate method. If the workflow requires input arguments, you pass them as a dictionary using one of the overloads of the Invoke method. Any output arguments are returned from the method as another dictionary. Other Invoke method overloads allow you to pass combinations of the workflow to execute, input arguments, and a timeout value.

Here are the variations of the static Invoke method that target the execution of workflows:

```
public static IDictionary<string, object> Invoke(Activity workflow);
public static IDictionary<string, object> Invoke(Activity workflow,
    IDictionary<string, object> inputs);
public static IDictionary<string, object> Invoke(Activity workflow,
    TimeSpan timeout);
public static IDictionary<string, object> Invoke(Activity workflow,
    IDictionary<string, object> inputs, TimeSpan timeout);
```

The timeout value determines the maximum amount of time that you want to allow the workflow to execute. If the elapsed time for execution of the workflow exceeds the specified timeout value, the workflow instance is terminated, and a System.TimeoutException is thrown.

The class also includes a set of static Invoke methods that target the execution of a single activity. The activity must derive from one of the generic activity base classes (Activity<TResult>, CodeActivity<TResult>, AsyncCodeActivity<TResult>, NativeActivity<TResult>) that return an output argument named Result. These Invoke methods accept a single generic argument that identifies the return type of the activity. Here are the method overloads:

```
public static TResult Invoke<TResult>(Activity<TResult> workflow);
public static TResult Invoke<TResult>(Activity<TResult> workflow,
    IDictionary<string, object> inputs);
public static TResult Invoke<TResult>(Activity<TResult> workflow,
    IDictionary<string, object> inputs, TimeSpan timeout);
public static TResult Invoke<TResult>(Activity<TResult> workflow,
    IDictionary<string, object> inputs,
    out IDictionary<string, object> additionalOutputs, TimeSpan timeout);
```

These methods simplify execution of a single activity since they eliminate the need to retrieve the output from a dictionary. The final method overload in the list does provide a way to retrieve additional output arguments.

Using the Instance Methods

In addition to the static Invoke method, you can create an instance of the WorkflowInvoker class and execute the workflow using instance methods. Using the instance methods provides you with a few additional options such as the ability to add workflow extensions to the instance before execution begins (using the Extensions property).

■ **Note** Workflow extensions are covered in Chapter 8.

After creating an instance of the `WorkflowInvoker` class, you call one of these `Invoke` methods to begin execution:

```
public IDictionary<string, object> Invoke();
public IDictionary<string, object> Invoke(IDictionary<string, object> inputs);
public IDictionary<string, object> Invoke(TimeSpan timeout);
public IDictionary<string, object> Invoke(IDictionary<string, object> inputs,
    TimeSpan timeout);
```

The `WorkflowInvoker` class is designed to execute a workflow or activity on the current thread; however, it does support a set of asynchronous methods:

```
public void InvokeAsync();
public void InvokeAsync(IDictionary<string, object> inputs);
public void InvokeAsync(object userState);
public void InvokeAsync(TimeSpan timeout);
public void InvokeAsync(IDictionary<string, object> inputs, object userState);
public void InvokeAsync(IDictionary<string, object> inputs, TimeSpan timeout);
public void InvokeAsync(TimeSpan timeout, object userState);
public void InvokeAsync(IDictionary<string, object> inputs, TimeSpan timeout,
    object userState);
```

When you use one of the `InvokeAsync` methods, you must add a handler to the `InvokeCompleted` event in order to retrieve any output arguments.

But contrary to their name, these methods don't actually begin execution of the workflow or activity on a separate thread. The `InvokeAsync` methods differ from the `Invoke` methods only in how they handle resumption of workflows that become idle.

To illustrate the difference in behavior between the `Invoke` and `InvokeAsync` methods, imagine a workflow that does some processing but also includes a `Delay` activity. If you start the workflow using either method, the workflow begins execution on the current thread. If you started it using the `Invoke` method, the workflow will resume execution on the same host thread after the delay expires. In contrast with this behavior, if you started the workflow using one of the `InvokeAsync` methods, execution after the delay will resume on a background thread from the thread pool.

If the workflow you are executing never becomes idle, there is no noticeable difference between `Invoke` and `InvokeAsync`. For full asynchronous operation, you need to use the `WorkflowApplication` class, which is discussed later in this chapter.

The `WorkflowInvoker` class also provides a set of `BeginInvoke` and `EndInvoke` methods. These methods operate in a similar way as the `InvokeAsync` method, but they support the familiar .NET asynchronous pattern.

On the surface, the differences between `InvokeAsync` and `BeginInvoke` are subtle. However, under the covers they do operate differently. The `InvokeAsync` method uses the current synchronization context, whereas `BeginInvoke` does not. This means that you can manually set the `Current` property of the `SynchronizationContext` class to a different synchronization context object, and this will change the behavior of `InvokeAsync`. For example, you might want to use a synchronization context designed for Windows Presentation Foundation, Windows Forms, or ASP.NET applications if the workflows that you are executing needed to directly interact with those frameworks.

Using the WorkflowInvoker Static Methods

In the series of short examples that follow, I will demonstrate some of the most common ways to use the `WorkflowInvoker` class. The same example workflow (along with one custom activity) will be used for all of the examples in this chapter. Since the goal is to demonstrate the various ways to host workflows, the workflow itself is very simple and totally contrived. It accepts a single integer as an input argument and returns a string containing the integer.

The workflow includes a `Delay` activity to introduce a short delay in processing. This is necessary in order to demonstrate the behavior when the workflow becomes idle in subsequent examples. The short delay also provides an opportunity to manually manage the workflow instance by canceling it and so on.

The workflow also writes messages that identify the current managed thread. Using these messages, you can determine when the workflow is using the host thread and when it is executing asynchronously on its own thread.

You will complete these tasks to implement this example:

1. Declare the `HostingDemoWorkflow`.

2. Implement the code to host the workflow.

Declaring the HostingDemoWorkflow

This example workflow will be used throughout the remainder of this chapter for several examples. For this reason, it should be declared in an activity library that can be referenced by other projects.

Create a new project using the Activity Library project template. Name the project `ActivityLibrary`, and add it to a new solution that you create for this chapter. You can delete the `Activity1.xaml` file since it won't be used.

Add a new workflow to the project using the Add Item Activity template, and name it `HostingDemoWorkflow`. Using the workflow designer, add these arguments to the workflow:

Name	Direction	Argument Type
ArgNumberToEcho	In	Int32
ArgTextWriter	In	TextWriter
Result	Out	String

The `ArgNumberToEcho` argument is the integer that is echoed back in the `Result` string argument. The `ArgTextWriter` argument is used to override the default `WriteLine` activity behavior that writes messages to the console. If an optional `TextWriter` property is provided, the `WriteLine` activity writes the messages to the `TextWriter` instead of the console. This feature is used later in the chapter.

Please follow these steps to complete the declaration of the workflow:

1. Add a `Sequence` activity to the empty workflow as the root activity.

2. Add a `WriteLine` activity to the `Sequence` activity. Set the `Text` property to `String.Format("Workflow: Started - Thread:{0}", System.Threading.Thread.CurrentThread.ManagedThreadId)`. Set the `TextWriter` property to `ArgTextWriter`.

3. Add another `WriteLine` activity below the previous one. Set the `Text` property to `"Workflow: About to delay"` and the `TextWriter` property to `ArgTextWriter`.

4. Add a `Delay` activity below the previous `WriteLine`. Set the `Duration` property to `TimeSpan.FromSeconds(3)` to provide a three-second delay.

5. Add another `WriteLine` activity below the `Delay`. Set the `Text` property to `"Workflow: Continue after delay"` and the `TextWriter` property to `ArgTextWriter`.

6. Add an `Assign` activity below the `WriteLine`. Set the `Assign.To` property to `Result` and the `Assign.Value` property to `String.Format("Result is {0}", ArgNumberToEcho)`.

7. Add a final `WriteLine` activity below the `Assign` activity. Set the `Text` property to `String.Format("Workflow: Completed - Thread:{0}", System.Threading.Thread.CurrentThread.ManagedThreadId)`. Set the `TextWriter` property to `ArgTextWriter`.

The completed workflow should look like Figure 4-1.

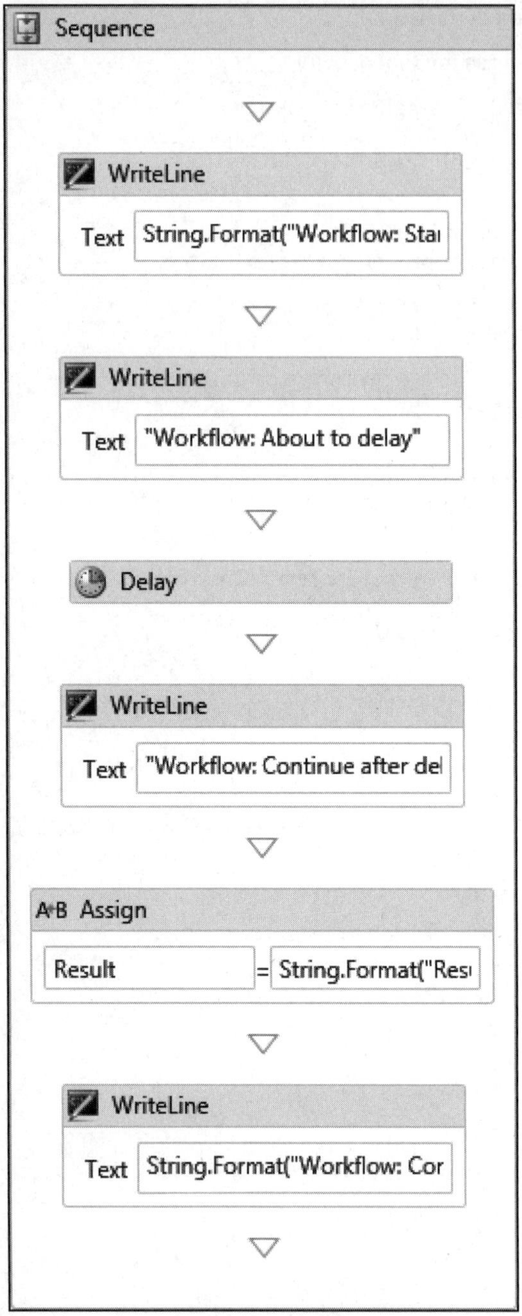

Figure 4-1. HostingDemoWorkflow

Simple Hosting of the Workflow

To host the workflow, create a new project using the Workflow Console Application template. Name the project InvokerHost, and add it to the solution for this chapter. You can delete the Workflow1.xaml file that was added for you since it won't be used. Add a project reference to the ActivityLibrary project, which is in the same solution.

Here is the code for the Program.cs file:

```
namespace InvokerHost
{
    using System;
    using System.Activities;
    using System.Collections.Generic;
    using System.Threading;

    using ActivityLibrary;

    class Program
    {
        static void Main(string[] args)
        {
            Console.WriteLine("Host: About to run workflow - Thread:{0}",
                System.Threading.Thread.CurrentThread.ManagedThreadId);

            try
            {
                IDictionary<String, Object> output = WorkflowInvoker.Invoke(
                    new HostingDemoWorkflow(),
                    new Dictionary<String, Object>
                    {
                        {"ArgNumberToEcho", 1001},
                    });

                Console.WriteLine("Host: Workflow completed - Thread:{0} - {1}",
                    System.Threading.Thread.CurrentThread.ManagedThreadId,
                    output["Result"]);
            }
            catch (Exception exception)
            {
                Console.WriteLine("Host: Workflow exception:{0}:{1}",
                    exception.GetType(), exception.Message);
            }
        }
    }
}
```

This hosting code displays the current managed thread before and after the workflow is executed. This allows you to compare the thread ID with the value that is displayed by the workflow itself. An instance of the workflow to execute and a single argument with the number to echo are passed to the static `Invoke` method of the `WorkflowInvoker` class. The `Result` output argument is returned in a dictionary by the `Invoke` method.

After building the solution and running the `InvokerHost` project, you should see results similar to these:

```
Host: About to run workflow - Thread:1

Workflow: Started - Thread:1

Workflow: About to delay

Workflow: Continue after delay

Workflow: Completed - Thread:1

Host: Workflow completed - Thread:1 - Result is 1001
```

As expected, the results indicate that the workflow executed on the current host thread.

■ **Note** The actual managed thread ID that you see in your results may be different from what is shown here. The important point is that the same thread ID (regardless of the actual value) is displayed by the host and the workflow instance.

Passing Arguments with Workflow Properties

In the previous example, a `Dictionary<String,Object>` was used to pass an argument to the workflow. A simpler and more type-safe way to pass arguments to a workflow is to set the public properties that are generated for each input argument. For example, the same workflow could be executed like this with the same results:

```
namespace InvokerHost
{
...
    class Program
    {
        static void Main(string[] args)
        {
...
            try
            {
                HostingDemoWorkflow wf = new HostingDemoWorkflow();
                wf.ArgNumberToEcho = 1001;
                IDictionary<String, Object> output = WorkflowInvoker.Invoke(wf);
...
            }
...
        }
    }
}
```

The choice as to which mechanism to use for passing input arguments really depends on your needs. If you need to create and execute a single instance of a workflow, then I personally favor using the argument properties. On the other hand, if you need to execute multiple instances of a particular workflow with different sets of parameters, you're better off passing the arguments as a dictionary. During the construction of a workflow instance, metadata about the workflow is detected and cached. This is a relatively expensive operation that you should try to avoid. Using a dictionary for arguments allows you to reuse a single instance of the workflow definition, passing a different set of arguments each time the workflow is executed.

■ **Tip** You can pass input arguments to the workflow using the argument properties that are provided. However, even though properties are also generated for the output arguments, you can't use them to obtain values when the workflow has completed. The reason for this difference is that the workflow instance passed to `WorkflowInvoker` (or `WorkflowApplication`) really represents the definition of the workflow. It is merely a template from which a runnable workflow instance is constructed and executed by the workflow runtime. Setting input argument properties makes sense since they become part of the workflow definition. Retrieving output arguments would require you to reference the actual workflow instance that was executed. Output arguments are not propagated back to the workflow definition.

Declaring a Timeout Value

One of the overloads of the static `Invoke` method allows you to specify a timeout value. This is used to limit the amount of time that the workflow is allowed to execute. If the workflow exceeds the `TimeSpan` value that you specify, the workflow is terminated, and an exception is thrown.

To see this in action, you only have to make a slight modification to the previous hosting code. Here is a partial listing of the `Program.cs` file showing the lines of code that require a change:

```
namespace InvokerHost
{
...
    class Program
    {
        static void Main(string[] args)
        {
...
            try
            {
                HostingDemoWorkflow wf = new HostingDemoWorkflow();
                wf.ArgNumberToEcho = 1001;
                IDictionary<String, Object> output = WorkflowInvoker.Invoke(
                    wf, TimeSpan.FromSeconds(1));
...
            }
...
        }
    }
}
```

In this example, the `TimeSpan` is set to one second. Since the workflow includes a `Delay` activity that is set to three seconds, the workflow should exceed the maximum timeout value and throw an exception. When you run the project again, the results should look like this:

```
Host: About to run workflow - Thread:1

Workflow: Started - Thread:1

Workflow: About to delay

Host: Workflow exception:System.TimeoutException:The operation did not complete

within the allotted timeout of 00:00:01. The time allotted to this operation may

have been a portion of a longer timeout.
```

Invoking a Generic Activity

The `WorkflowInvoker` class also makes it easy to execute an activity that derives from one of the generic base activity classes. The advantage to using one of these specialized `Invoke` methods is that the result is returned directly from the method rather than as a dictionary. This enables you to more easily incorporate execution of activities within your procedural C# code.

Implementing the HostingDemoActivity

To complete this example, you need a simple activity to execute. The activity must derive from one of the generic activity base classes: `Activity<TResult>`, `CodeActivity<TResult>`, `AsyncCodeActivity<T>`, or `NativeActivity<TResult>`. Add a new code activity to the `ActivityLibrary` project, and name it `HostingDemoActivity`. Here is the complete code for this activity:

```
using System;
using System.Activities;

namespace ActivityLibrary
{
    public sealed class HostingDemoActivity : CodeActivity<String>
    {
        public InArgument<Int32> NumberToEcho { get; set; }

        protected override string Execute(CodeActivityContext context)
        {
            return String.Format("Result is {0} - Thread:{1}",
                NumberToEcho.Get(context),
                System.Threading.Thread.CurrentThread.ManagedThreadId);
        }
    }
}
```

In similar fashion to the `HostingDemoWorkflow`, this activity defines a single input argument that is echoed back to the caller in a result string.

Executing the Activity

To execute an activity using the `WorkflowInvoker` class, you need to use one of the `Invoke` methods that accept a generic type parameter. The type that you specify must correspond to the return type of the activity. In the case of the `HostingDemoActivity` that you just implemented, the return type is a string.

You can modify the `Program.cs` file in the `InvokerHost` project as shown here:

```
namespace InvokerHost
{
    using System;
    using System.Activities;
    using System.Collections.Generic;
    using System.Threading;

    using ActivityLibrary;

    class Program
    {
        static void Main(string[] args)
        {
            Console.WriteLine("Host: About to run Activity - Thread:{0}",
                System.Threading.Thread.CurrentThread.ManagedThreadId);
```

```
        try
        {
            HostingDemoActivity activity = new HostingDemoActivity();
            activity.NumberToEcho = 1001;
            String result = WorkflowInvoker.Invoke<String>(activity);

            Console.WriteLine(
                "Host: Activity completed - Thread:{0} - {1}",
                System.Threading.Thread.CurrentThread.ManagedThreadId,
                result);
        }
        catch (Exception exception)
        {
            Console.WriteLine("Host: Activity exception:{0}:{1}",
                exception.GetType(), exception.Message);
        }
    }
}
}
```

The call to the generic version of the Invoke method simplifies the code by eliminating the dictionary of output arguments.

When I run the revised InvokerHost project, the results look like this:

```
Host: About to run Activity - Thread:1

Host: Activity completed - Thread:1 - Result is 1001 - Thread:1
```

Using the WorkflowInvoker Instance Methods

The WorkflowInvoker class also provides instance methods that allow you to execute a workflow or a single activity. One of the more interesting instance methods is InvokeAsync. This method allows you to begin execution of the workflow using the host thread but to then switch to a thread from the thread pool when the workflow resumes after becoming idle.

Similar functionality is also available using the BeginInvoke and EndInvoke methods. These methods implement the standard .NET asynchronous pattern.

Using the InvokeAsync Method

To demonstrate the InvokeAsync method, you can modify the Program.cs file in the InvokerHost project. Here is the updated code:

```
namespace InvokerHost
{
    using System;
    using System.Activities;
    using System.Collections.Generic;
    using System.Threading;

    using ActivityLibrary;

    class Program
    {
```

This example requires the use of a thread synchronization object such as the `AutoResetEvent` shown here. The object allows the host thread to wait until the workflow execution completes on a different thread.

```
        private static AutoResetEvent waitEvent = new AutoResetEvent(false);

        static void Main(string[] args)
        {
            Console.WriteLine("Host: About to run workflow - Thread:{0}",
                System.Threading.Thread.CurrentThread.ManagedThreadId);

            try
            {
```

After creating a new instance of the `WorkflowInvoker` class, a handler is added to the `InvokeCompleted` event. This event is the notification that the workflow has completed and enables retrieval of the output arguments.

```
                WorkflowInvoker instance = new WorkflowInvoker(
                    new HostingDemoWorkflow());
                instance.InvokeCompleted +=
                    delegate(Object sender, InvokeCompletedEventArgs e)
                    {
                        Console.WriteLine(
                            "Host: Workflow completed - Thread:{0} - {1}",
                            System.Threading.Thread.CurrentThread.ManagedThreadId,
                            e.Outputs["Result"]);
                        waitEvent.Set();
                    };

                instance.InvokeAsync(new Dictionary<String, Object>
                    {
                        {"ArgNumberToEcho", 1001},
                    });

                Console.WriteLine("Host: Workflow started - Thread:{0}",
                    System.Threading.Thread.CurrentThread.ManagedThreadId);
                waitEvent.WaitOne();
            }
```

```
        catch (Exception exception)
        {
            Console.WriteLine("Host: Workflow exception:{0}:{1}",
                exception.GetType(), exception.Message);
        }
    }
  }
}
```

After building the solution, you should be ready to run the **InvokeHost** project. Here are my results:

```
Host: About to run workflow - Thread:1

Workflow: Started - Thread:1

Workflow: About to delay

Host: Workflow started - Thread:1

Workflow: Continue after delay

Workflow: Completed - Thread:3

Host: Workflow completed - Thread:3 - Result is 1001
```

Notice that the workflow displays a different managed thread ID when it resumes after the short delay. Prior to the delay, the workflow was executing on the host thread. The switch to a separate thread occurred only when the workflow became idle. When that occurred, the workflow relinquished control over the original thread.

Using the BeginInvoke Method

The other way to use the **WorkflowInvoker** asynchronous functionality is to the use the **BeginInvoke** method. This method, along with the **EndInvoke** method, follows the standard .NET asynchronous pattern. The *begin* method returns an **IAsyncResult** object that must be passed to the *end* method to complete the processing.

To see this in action, modify the **Program.cs** once more. Here is the revised code:

```
namespace InvokerHost
{
    using System;
    using System.Activities;
    using System.Collections.Generic;
    using System.Threading;

    using ActivityLibrary;
```

```
class Program
{
    private static AutoResetEvent waitEvent = new AutoResetEvent(false);

    static void Main(string[] args)
    {
        Console.WriteLine("Host: About to run workflow - Thread:{0}",
            System.Threading.Thread.CurrentThread.ManagedThreadId);

        try
        {
```

This code is similar to the example that used the InvokeAsync method. One difference is that the InvokeCompleted event is no longer used. Instead, the output argument is retrieved by the call to EndInvoke.

The call to BeginInvoke specifies that the private BeginInvokeCallback method should be invoked when the workflow completes. The WorkflowInvoker instance is passed as the asynchronous state parameter to the BeginInvoke method.

```
            WorkflowInvoker instance = new WorkflowInvoker(
                new HostingDemoWorkflow { ArgNumberToEcho = 1001 });
            IAsyncResult ar = instance.BeginInvoke(
                BeginInvokeCallback, instance);

            Console.WriteLine(
                "Host: Workflow started - Thread:{0}",
                System.Threading.Thread.CurrentThread.ManagedThreadId);
            waitEvent.WaitOne();
        }
        catch (Exception exception)
        {
            Console.WriteLine("Host: Workflow exception:{0}:{1}",
                exception.GetType(), exception.Message);
        }
    }

    /// <summary>
    /// Callback when BeginInvoke is used
    /// </summary>
    /// <param name="ar"></param>
    private static void BeginInvokeCallback(IAsyncResult ar)
    {
```

To complete the asynchronous process, the code calls the EndInvoke method, passing it the IAsyncResult object that was passed to the callback method. The EndInvoke method returns the dictionary of output arguments and completes the asynchronous pattern. This callback method also sets the AutoResetEvent in order to release the host thread from its wait.

```
        IDictionary<String, Object> output =
            ((WorkflowInvoker)ar.AsyncState).EndInvoke(ar);

        Console.WriteLine(
            "Host: BeginInvokeCallback Invoked - Thread:{0} - {1}",
            System.Threading.Thread.CurrentThread.ManagedThreadId,
            output["Result"]);

        waitEvent.Set();
    }
  }
}
```

The results are similar to the example that used the **InvokeAsync** method:

```
Host: About to run workflow - Thread:1

Workflow: Started - Thread:1

Workflow: About to delay

Host: Workflow started - Thread:1

Workflow: Continue after delay

Workflow: Completed - Thread:4

Host: BeginInvokeCallback Invoked - Thread:4 - Result is 1001
```

Understand the WorkflowApplication Class

WF also provides a `WorkflowApplication` class that you can use to invoke workflows. The `WorkflowInvoker` class deliberately limits its functionality in order to provide a simple way to execute workflows and activities. In contrast with this, the `WorkflowApplication` class eliminates all self-imposed limits, but at the cost of a great deal more complexity. If there is a scenario that WF supports, it is supported by the `WorkflowApplication` class.

The most prominent feature that distinguishes the `WorkflowApplication` class from `WorkflowInvoker` is its use of a separate thread for workflow execution. Because the workflow executes asynchronously, the `WorkflowApplication` class supports additional members that notify the host application of changes in the execution state of the workflow (idled, completed, unloaded, and so on). The host application may also need to use some type of thread synchronization object if it is required to wait until the workflow completes before processing can continue.

The question remains, why use `WorkflowApplication` if using it requires additional complexity? The answer is that it enables scenarios that are not available with `WorkflowInvoker`.

For example, long-running workflows require the asynchronous execution, persistence, bookmark management, and instance control methods that are supported by the `WorkflowApplication` class. The instance control methods enable you to take direct control over a workflow instance by canceling, aborting, terminating, or unloading it. Communication between the host application and a workflow instance can be accomplished using the bookmark resumption methods that are supported by the `WorkflowApplication` class. And custom workflow extensions make additional functionality available to workflow instances.

When hosting workflows using the `WorkflowApplication` class, you can generally follow these steps. Not all the steps will be necessary for all workflows that you host.

1. Construct a `WorkflowApplication` instance.

2. Assign code to the delegate members that you want to handle.

3. Add workflow extensions.

4. Configure persistence.

5. Start execution of the workflow instance.

6. Resume bookmarks as necessary.

7. Manually control the workflow instance as necessary.

In the sections that follow, I describe the most important members that are supported by the `WorkflowApplication` class. This is not an exhaustive list of all members of the class.

Constructing a WorkflowApplication

The vast majority of the members for this class are instance members. Therefore, you will almost always start by creating an instance of the `WorkflowApplication` class. You create a new instance by passing the constructor an instance of the workflow that you want to execute. You can optionally use a version of the constructor that also accepts a dictionary of input arguments.

Assigning Code to Delegate Members

A number of notification delegate members are provided by the `WorkflowApplication` class. At first glance, these members look and feel like C# events, but they really aren't. Instead, they are defined using the `Action<>` or `Func<>` general-purpose generic delegates. Any code that you assign to one of these members is executed by `WorkflowApplication` at the appropriate time in the life cycle of the workflow instance. For example, the `Completed` delegate is executed when the workflow has completed, the `Idle` delegate is executed when the workflow becomes idle, and so on.

Since they are defined as delegates, you can choose to assign code to them in a number of ways. You can create and assign an anonymous method, define a Lambda expression, or even reference an old-fashioned, named method.

You may wonder why delegates are used instead of C# events. One reason is that some of these members require that you return a result from the handling code. An example of this is the `OnUnhandledException` member, which requires that you return an `UnhandledExceptionAction` from the handler. If a multicast C# event was used instead, there might be multiple handlers assigned to the event. It would then become difficult to determine which return value to use and which one to ignore. Also, C# events always pass the sender of the event as the first parameter. In this case, the sender would be the `WorkflowApplication` instance. However, there are no valid operations that you can perform on the `WorkflowApplication` instance while you are handling one of these events. So, the inclusion of the sender parameter doesn't make sense.

Here is a summary of the most important delegates supported by the `WorkflowApplication` class:

Member	Definition	Description
Completed	Action<WorkflowApplicationCompletedEventArgs>	Executed when the workflow instance completes, successfully or not.
Idle	Action<WorkflowApplicationIdleEventArgs>	Executed when the workflow instance becomes idle.
PersistableIdle	Func<WorkflowApplicationIdleEventArgs, PersistableIdleAction>	Executed when the workflow instance becomes idle and a persistence instance store has been assigned. If an instance store is not assigned to the WorkflowApplication, the Idle member is executed instead of this member.
Unloaded	Action<WorkflowApplicationEventArgs>	Executed when the workflow instance has been unloaded from memory.
Aborted	Action<WorkflowApplicationAbortedEventArgs>	Executed when the workflow instance has been manually aborted.
OnUnhandledException	Func<WorkflowApplicationUnhandledExceptionEventArgs, UnhandledExceptionAction>	Executed when an unhandled exception is thrown during the execution of the workflow instance. An UnhandledExceptionAction value must be returned from the handler code to specify how the exception should be handled.

■ **Note** Chapter 13 covers error and exception handling. In particular, additional information on the use of the OnUnhandledException member is provided in that chapter.

Managing Extensions

Workflow extensions are ordinary C# classes that you implement to provide needed functionality to workflow instances. Exactly what functionality they provide is completely up to you. Custom activities can be developed that retrieve and use an extension.

■ **Note** Chapter 8 discusses the use of workflow extensions for two-way communication between the host application and a workflow instance.

If used, an extension must be added to the WorkflowApplication prior to starting the workflow instance (prior to the Run method). Here are the most important WorkflowApplication members that are related to extension management:

Member	Description
AddExtension	A generic method used to add an extension to the WorkflowApplication instance. The generic type specifies the type of the extension.
Extensions	A property that returns the collection of extensions.
GetExtension	A generic method used to retrieve a single extension. The generic type specifies the type of the extension to retrieve.
GetExtensions	A generic method used to retrieve all extensions matching the specified generic type.

Configuring and Managing Persistence

Several of the members of the WorkflowApplication class are related to workflow persistence. Here are the most important members that fall into this category:

Member	Description
InstanceStore	A property used to set the instance store for the WorkflowApplication instance. The instance store provides the functionality necessary to persist the workflow instance.
Persist	A method used to manually persist a workflow instance from the host application.
BeginPersist	A method similar to the Persist method but implemented using the .NET asynchronous pattern.
Load	A static method used to manually load a persisted workflow instance from the instance store.
BeginLoad	An asynchronous pattern version of the Load method.

■ **Note** Chapter 11 covers workflow persistence.

Executing a Workflow Instance

After you have constructed a `WorkflowApplication` instance, assigned code to any notification delegates that interest you, added any workflow extensions, and configured persistence, you need a way to actually execute the workflow instance. That's the job of the `Run` method, or the `BeginRun` and `EndRun` pair of methods that use the .NET asynchronous pattern. Here is a summary of these methods:

Member	Description
Run	Executes the workflow instance that was passed to the WorkflowApplication during its construction. An overload of this method allows you to specify a maximum timeout value for the Run method to complete. This method is also used to resume execution of a workflow instance.
BeginRun	Executes the workflow instance using the standard .NET asynchronous pattern. This method returns an IAsyncResult which you then pass to the EndRun method.
EndRun	Completes the asynchronous operation to start execution of a workflow instance.
SynchronizationContext	A property that allows you to optionally set the SynchronizationContext object to use for scheduling workflow execution.

> ■ **Warning** The WorkflowApplication class supports an overload of the Run method that allows you to specify a TimeSpan value. You might initially think that this value is used in the same way as the TimeSpan that is passed to the WorkflowInvoker.Invoke method. It isn't. The TimeSpan passed to the WorkflowInvoker.Invoke method determines the maximum elapsed time that you want to allow for the execution of the workflow. The TimeSpan passed to WorkflowApplication.Run determines the maximum time allowed for the Run method to complete—not for the entire workflow to complete. Remember that Run simply starts execution of the workflow instance on another thread. It is possible that the Run method may take longer than expected because of contention with another operation that is occurring on the same workflow runtime thread (for example, a persistence operation). This should be a highly unlikely scenario when you are first starting a workflow instance, but it is possible if you are calling Run to resume execution of an instance.

The WorkflowApplication class uses a SynchronizationContext instance for scheduling workflow execution. By default, the synchronization context that is used executes workflow instances asynchronously on a thread pool thread. In most situations, this is the desired behavior. However, you can optionally set the SynchronizationContext property prior to running the workflow instance if you need to use a different context. For example, if you are executing workflows in a WPF application, you could utilize the context that schedules work on the WPF user interface thread (DispatcherSynchronizationContext). WinForms also provides a synchronization context that is designed to execute work on the user interface thread. If you are really ambitious (or have special workflow scheduling needs), you can even implement your own SynchronizationContext.

Be aware that using a nondefault synchronization context potentially has a significant impact on the workflow runtime. For example, if you use the synchronization context that uses the WPF user interface thread, all workflow instances will be synchronously executed on that thread. The default WorkflowApplication behavior of asynchronously executing workflows on a thread pool thread will be completely replaced.

Managing Bookmarks

A bookmark represents a resumption point within a workflow instance. You can create a custom activity that creates a new bookmark to indicate that it is waiting for input. When this occurs, the activity relinquishes control of the workflow thread since it is waiting for some external stimulus. If no other work has been scheduled within the workflow, the entire workflow instance becomes idle—waiting for input. The WorkflowApplication class provides several methods that enable you to resume a bookmark and pass any data that the workflow requires to continue processing.

Here are the most important members related to bookmark processing:

Member	Description
ResumeBookmark	This method is used to resume execution of a workflow at the named bookmark. Any needed data can be passed to the workflow along with the bookmark. There are several overloads of this method that allow you to specify the bookmark in different ways (a string name or a Bookmark object), pass a timeout value, and so on.
BeginResumeBookmark	This method works like ResumeBookmark, except that it follows the asynchronous pattern and returns an IAsyncResult object.
GetBookmarks	This method allows you to retrieve a collection of available bookmarks for the workflow instance.

■ **Note** Chapter 8 discusses the use of bookmarks for host-to-workflow communication.

Manually Controlling a Workflow Instance

The final category of `WorkflowApplication` members allows you to manually control a workflow instance. Here are the most important members that fall into this category:

Member	Description
Cancel	A method that schedules cancellation of the workflow instance
BeginCancel	An asynchronous version of the Cancel method
Terminate	A method used to terminate execution of the workflow instance
BeginTerminate	An asynchronous version of the Terminate method
Unload	A method that unloads the workflow instance from memory
BeginUnload	An asynchronous version of the Unload method
Abort	A method used to immediately abort execution of the workflow instance.

The differences between `Cancel`, `Terminate`, and `Abort` can sometimes be confusing. All of these methods have the same net result of stopping the execution of a workflow instance. But that's where the similarities really end.

- *Canceling* a workflow is the most graceful way to stop execution of an instance. It triggers any optional cancellation and compensation logic that you have declared within the workflow model, and it leaves the workflow in the canceled state. A canceled workflow cannot be resumed.

- *Terminating* a workflow does not trigger cancelation and compensation logic. The workflow instance is left in the faulted state and cannot be resumed. When a workflow instance has been terminated, any code that you have assigned to the `Completed` delegate member is executed.

- *Aborting* a workflow is an ungraceful and immediate teardown of the workflow instance. However, if an aborted workflow has been previously persisted, it can be loaded and resumed from its last persistence point. The aborting of the workflow simply throws away everything since the last persistence point.

Which option should you use to stop execution of a workflow? That depends on your reason for stopping the workflow. First and foremost, do you plan on resuming the workflow later, reloading it from its last persistence point? If so, you should call the `Abort` method since it is the only option that allows the workflow to be reloaded and restarted. You would use this method when there was a recoverable problem during the execution of the workflow. After aborting the workflow, you can correct the issue and resume execution. On the other hand, if you simply want to stop execution of the workflow and have no plans to restart it later, you can call the `Cancel` or `Terminate` method. Call `Cancel` if you have cancellation or compensation logic that you want to execute. Call `Terminate` if you want to more quickly stop execution without running any cancellation or compensation logic.

■ **Warning** The instance control methods such as `Cancel`, `Terminate`, and `Unload` cannot be invoked from within code that is assigned to one of the notification delegates. For example, it is not permissible to call `Cancel` from code assigned to the `Idle` member. If you do, an `InvalidOperationException` will be thrown.

Using the WorkflowApplication Class

In the examples that follow, you will execute the same `HostingDemoWorkflow` that you declared and used earlier in the chapter. However, you will use the `WorkflowApplication` class to execute the workflow instead of the `WorkflowInvoker` class.

Hosting the Workflow with WorkflowApplication

Create a new Workflow Console Application, and name it `ApplicationHost`. Add the new project to the solution that was created for this chapter, and delete the `Workflow1.xaml` file. Add a project reference to the `ActivityLibrary` project in the same solution.

Revise the `Program.cs` file with this code to host the workflow:

```
namespace ApplicationHost
{
    using System;
    using System.Activities;
    using System.Collections.Generic;
    using System.Threading;
    using ActivityLibrary;

    class Program
    {
        static void Main(string[] args)
        {
            AutoResetEvent waitEvent = new AutoResetEvent(false);
```

An instance of the workflow to execute is first constructed and passed to the `WorkflowApplication` constructor. Any input arguments are also passed to the constructor in a dictionary. Optionally, you can set the input arguments directly using the generated properties of the workflow type.

```
            WorkflowApplication wfApp = new WorkflowApplication(
                new HostingDemoWorkflow(),
                new Dictionary<String, Object>
                {
                    {"ArgNumberToEcho", 1001},
                });
```

Once a `WorkflowApplication` instance has been constructed, code is assigned to the status notification delegates. The `Completed` member is important since this is the mechanism by which the host application is notified of the completion of the workflow instance.

Notice that the code uses the `CompletionState` property of the event arguments to determine the final outcome of the workflow instance. This is necessary since the `Completed` member is executed for several different completion states, not only for a successful completion. The `Closed` completion state means that the workflow completed normally and the output arguments are available for retrieval.

The `AutoResetEvent` is set to a signaled state regardless of the completion state of the workflow. This releases the host application from waiting for the workflow instance to complete.

Not all of these completion states or delegate members are required for this first example. However, several of them will be used during subsequent examples.

```
            wfApp.Completed = delegate(WorkflowApplicationCompletedEventArgs e)
            {
                switch (e.CompletionState)
                {
                    case ActivityInstanceState.Closed:
                        Console.WriteLine("Host: {0} Closed - Thread:{1} - {2}",
                            wfApp.Id,
                            System.Threading.Thread.CurrentThread.ManagedThreadId,
                            e.Outputs["Result"]);
                        break;
```

```
            case ActivityInstanceState.Canceled:
                Console.WriteLine("Host: {0} Canceled - Thread:{1}",
                    wfApp.Id,
                    System.Threading.Thread.CurrentThread.ManagedThreadId);
                break;
            case ActivityInstanceState.Executing:
                Console.WriteLine("Host: {0} Executing - Thread:{1}",
                    wfApp.Id,
                    System.Threading.Thread.CurrentThread.ManagedThreadId);
                break;
            case ActivityInstanceState.Faulted:
                Console.WriteLine(
                    "Host: {0} Faulted - Thread:{1} - {2}:{3}",
                    wfApp.Id,
                    System.Threading.Thread.CurrentThread.ManagedThreadId,
                    e.TerminationException.GetType(),
                    e.TerminationException.Message);
                break;
            default:
                break;
        }
        waitEvent.Set();
};
```

The code assigned to the `OnUnhandledException` member is executed when an unhandled exception is thrown during workflow execution. The code for the **Aborted** member is executed if the workflow instance is manually aborted.

```
wfApp.OnUnhandledException =
    delegate(WorkflowApplicationUnhandledExceptionEventArgs e)
    {
        Console.WriteLine(
            "Host: {0} OnUnhandledException - Thread:{1} - {2}",
            wfApp.Id,
            System.Threading.Thread.CurrentThread.ManagedThreadId,
            e.UnhandledException.Message);
        waitEvent.Set();
        return UnhandledExceptionAction.Cancel;
    };

wfApp.Aborted = delegate(WorkflowApplicationAbortedEventArgs e)
{
    Console.WriteLine("Host: {0} Aborted - Thread:{1} - {2}:{3}",
        wfApp.Id,
        System.Threading.Thread.CurrentThread.ManagedThreadId,
        e.Reason.GetType(), e.Reason.Message);
    waitEvent.Set();
};
```

```
        wfApp.Idle = delegate(WorkflowApplicationIdleEventArgs e)
        {
            Console.WriteLine("Host: {0} Idle - Thread:{1}",
                wfApp.Id,
                System.Threading.Thread.CurrentThread.ManagedThreadId);
        };
```

The code assigned to the PersistableIdle delegate is never executed for any of the examples in this chapter but is included for completeness. This delegate is used only when the WorkflowApplication instance has been configured to use workflow persistence.

```
        wfApp.PersistableIdle = delegate(WorkflowApplicationIdleEventArgs e)
        {
            Console.WriteLine("Host: {0} PersistableIdle - Thread:{1}",
                wfApp.Id,
                System.Threading.Thread.CurrentThread.ManagedThreadId);
            return PersistableIdleAction.Unload;
        };

        wfApp.Unloaded = delegate(WorkflowApplicationEventArgs e)
        {
            Console.WriteLine("Host: {0} Unloaded - Thread:{1}",
                wfApp.Id,
                System.Threading.Thread.CurrentThread.ManagedThreadId);
        };
```

After preparing the WorkflowApplication instance, execution of the workflow begins with a call to the Run method. Since the workflow execution takes place on a separate thread, the host uses the AutoResetEvent to suspend the primary thread until the workflow has completed.

```
        try
        {
            Console.WriteLine("Host: About to run {0} - Thread:{1}",
                wfApp.Id,
                System.Threading.Thread.CurrentThread.ManagedThreadId);

            wfApp.Run();
            waitEvent.WaitOne();
        }
        catch (Exception exception)
        {
            Console.WriteLine("Host: {0} exception:{1}:{2}",
                wfApp.Id, exception.GetType(), exception.Message);
        }
    }
  }
}
```

At this point you should build the solution and be able to run the **ApplicationHost** project. Here are my results:

```
Host: About to run 5dc6752a-70b1-4d32-a1b1-3303428041df - Thread:1

Workflow: Started - Thread:3

Workflow: About to delay

Host: 5dc6752a-70b1-4d32-a1b1-3303428041df Idle - Thread:3

Workflow: Continue after delay

Workflow: Completed - Thread:3

Host: 5dc6752a-70b1-4d32-a1b1-3303428041df Closed - Thread:3 - Result is 1001

Host: 5dc6752a-70b1-4d32-a1b1-3303428041df Unloaded - Thread:3
```

Notice that right from the very start, the workflow instance reports a different managed thread ID. This confirms that a separate thread is being used for workflow execution. After the short delay, the same workflow thread is used to resume and complete the workflow.

■ **Note** In this example, the same workflow thread was used to continue execution of the workflow after the short delay. However, use of the same thread is not guaranteed. In this example, the same thread pool thread just happened to be available and was used.

Also notice that the host receives notification when the workflow was Idle, Closed, and Unloaded. These notifications were executed on the workflow thread, not the host thread.

And finally, notice that the workflow instance is uniquely identified with a **Guid**. This is not critically important for this example where only a single workflow instance is executed. However, if your host application is managing multiple workflow instances, this instance ID is the primary means by which one instance is distinguished from another.

Canceling a Workflow Instance

If you need to cancel an executing workflow instance, you can invoke the **Cancel** method. To demonstrate this, make the minor changes to the **Program.cs** file in the **ApplicationHost** project shown here in bold:

```
namespace ApplicationHost
{
...
    class Program
    {
        static void Main(string[] args)
        {
...
            try
            {
...
                wfApp.Run();
                //Wait just a bit then cancel the workflow
                Thread.Sleep(1000);
                wfApp.Cancel();
                waitEvent.WaitOne();
            }
...
        }
    }
}
```

This test starts execution of the workflow and then waits one second before canceling the instance. Here are my results when I run this test:

```
Host: About to run fc749e0f-f3e0-4435-95cd-ce7e56d4470a - Thread:1

Workflow: Started - Thread:4

Workflow: About to delay

Host: fc749e0f-f3e0-4435-95cd-ce7e56d4470a Idle - Thread:4

Host: fc749e0f-f3e0-4435-95cd-ce7e56d4470a Canceled - Thread:4

Host: fc749e0f-f3e0-4435-95cd-ce7e56d4470a Unloaded - Thread:4
```

Your only notification that the workflow was canceled comes from code assigned to the Completed delegate. When an instance is canceled, the CompletionState is equal to ActivityInstanceState.Canceled.

Aborting a WorkflowInstance

To abort a workflow instance, you invoke the Abort method like this:

```
namespace ApplicationHost
{
...
    class Program
    {
        static void Main(string[] args)
        {
...
            try
            {
...
                wfApp.Run();
                //Wait just a bit then abort the workflow
                Thread.Sleep(1000);
                wfApp.Abort("My aborted reason");
                waitEvent.WaitOne();
            }
...
        }
    }
}
```

Now when I run the ApplicationHost project, I see these results:

```
Host: About to run 977d3ec8-4d42-488c-b6fb-014925d0ee43 - Thread:1

Workflow: Started - Thread:4

Workflow: About to delay

Host: 977d3ec8-4d42-488c-b6fb-014925d0ee43 Idle - Thread:4

Host: 977d3ec8-4d42-488c-b6fb-014925d0ee43 Aborted - Thread:4 -

System.Activities.WorkflowApplicationAbortedException:My aborted reason
```

This time the code assigned to the Aborted notification delegate is executed instead of the Completed member. The exception that is thrown contains the abort reason that was provided to the Abort method. Since the workflow was aborted, you no longer receive the Unloaded notification.

Terminating a WorkflowInstance

The final way to stop execution of a workflow instance is to terminate it. As you might have already guessed, you accomplish this by calling the Terminate method like this:

```
namespace ApplicationHost
{
...
    class Program
    {
        static void Main(string[] args)
        {
...
            try
            {
...
                wfApp.Run();
                //Wait just a bit then terminate the workflow
                Thread.Sleep(1000);
                wfApp.Terminate("My termination reason");
                waitEvent.WaitOne();
            }
...
        }
    }
}
```

The results when I run the ApplicationHost project now look like this:

```
Host: About to run b7c2e287-0234-4bf2-b68b-d43dcfb6f286 - Thread:1

Workflow: Started - Thread:4

Workflow: About to delay

Host: b7c2e287-0234-4bf2-b68b-d43dcfb6f286 Idle - Thread:4

Host: b7c2e287-0234-4bf2-b68b-d43dcfb6f286 Faulted - Thread:1 -

System.Activities.WorkflowApplicationTerminatedException:My termination reason

Host: b7c2e287-0234-4bf2-b68b-d43dcfb6f286 Unloaded - Thread:1
```

When you call Terminate on an instance, the code assigned to the Completed delegate is executed. The CompletionState is set to a value of ActivityInstanceState.Faulted to indicate that the workflow instance was terminated. The termination reason that you passed to the Terminate method is used as the exception message.

Using the BeginRun Method

The WorkflowApplication also supports the .NET asynchronous pattern with the BeginRun and EndRun methods. Since the WorkflowApplication is designed to execute workflows asynchronously on another thread, I think the usefulness of this pattern for this class is limited. However, it is available if you want to asynchronously begin the process of running the workflow (which will then run asynchronously).

To demonstrate the `BeginRun` method, modify the `Program.cs` file in the `ApplicationHost` project as shown here:

```
namespace ApplicationHost
{
…
    class Program
    {
        static void Main(string[] args)
        {
…
            try
            {
…
                wfApp.BeginRun(delegate(IAsyncResult ar)
                {
                    Console.WriteLine(
                        "Host: {0} BeginRunCallback - Thread:{1}",
                        wfApp.Id,
                        System.Threading.Thread.CurrentThread.ManagedThreadId);
                    ((WorkflowApplication)ar.AsyncState).EndRun(ar);
                }, wfApp);
                waitEvent.WaitOne();
            }
…
        }
    }
}
```

The call to this overload of the `BeginRun` method takes two parameters. The first is a method that implements the `AsyncCallback` delegate, and the second is an asynchronous state object. In this example, an anonymous method is used for the callback, and the `WorkflowApplication` instance itself is passed as the asynchronous state object.

The callback invokes the `EndRun` method of the `WorkflowApplication` instance, passing the `IAsyncResult` object that was passed to the callback.

Here are my results when I executed the **ApplicationHost** project with this revised code:

```
Host: About to run b9b63d47-b5a8-4430-a680-b171dbad4547 - Thread:1

Workflow: Started - Thread:4

Workflow: About to delay

Host: b9b63d47-b5a8-4430-a680-b171dbad4547 Idle - Thread:4

Host: b9b63d47-b5a8-4430-a680-b171dbad4547 BeginRunCallback - Thread:1

Workflow: Continue after delay

Workflow: Completed - Thread:3

Host: b9b63d47-b5a8-4430-a680-b171dbad4547 Closed - Thread:3 - Result is 1001

Host: b9b63d47-b5a8-4430-a680-b171dbad4547 Unloaded - Thread:3
```

Understanding the ActivityXamlServices Class

One of the most significant benefits of using Xaml to declare workflows is the portability and flexibility that it affords. For the most part, the workflows that you create with Visual Studio are saved as Xaml documents. The build process then compiles these files into managed types that are constructed and referenced just like any other .NET CLR type.

These compiled workflows are fine for many applications. However, since the workflow definitions are baked into a .NET assembly, they are no longer easily modified and used. If a change is necessary, you need to fire up Visual Studio, make the necessary changes to the Xaml file (probably using the Workflow designer), and then rebuild the project. The net result of that process is a revised .NET assembly that contains the compiled workflow definition.

WF also provides you with the ability to read and process a Xaml document directly, instead of using a compiled .NET type. The **ActivityXamlServices** class is the key to this functionality. The static **Load** method reads a Xaml document and returns a **DynamicActivity** object that represents the workflow. The **DynamicActivity** class derives from the base **Activity** class and is designed for situations such as this where a new activity instance is dynamically created. The activity instance is then passed to the **WorkflowInvoker** or **WorkflowApplication** class just like a normally compiled workflow or activity. There are several overloaded versions of the **Load** method that provide some flexibility in how the Xaml document is read. You can pass a **Stream**, **TextReader**, **XmlReader**, **XamlReader**, or simply the path to a Xaml file.

What this functionality provides is flexibility and portability. The workflow declaration can be maintained outside of Visual Studio (you can self-host the workflow designer) and persisted in a way that makes sense for your application. For example, you can persist Xaml documents in a database, in SharePoint, or as a file somewhere in the file system.

Using the ActivityXamlServices Class

To demonstrate the use of the `ActivityXamlServices` class, you will create a new application that loads and executes the `HostingDemoWorkflow` that you developed earlier in the chapter. However, unlike the other examples in this chapter, the workflow declaration will be loaded directly from the Xaml file instead of constructing an instance of the `HostingDemoWorkflow` compiled type.

Create a new Workflow Console Application, and name it `InvokerHostXaml`. Add the new project to the solution that was created for this chapter, and delete the `Workflow1.xaml` file. Unlike previous examples, you do not need to add a reference to any other projects in the solution. In particular, you don't need a reference to the `ActivityLibrary` project since you won't be referencing the compiled version of the workflow.

Here is the completed code that you need for the `Program.cs` in this new project:

```
namespace InvokerHostXaml
{
    using System;
    using System.Activities;
    using System.Activities.XamlIntegration;
    using System.Collections.Generic;

    class Program
    {
        static void Main(string[] args)
        {
            Console.WriteLine("\n>>>> From Xaml <<<<");
            RunFromXaml();
        }

        private static void RunFromXaml()
        {
            Console.WriteLine("Host: About to run workflow - Thread:{0}",
                System.Threading.Thread.CurrentThread.ManagedThreadId);

            try
            {
```

I'm using a relative path from this new project to the `ActivityLibrary` project where the Xaml file should be located. This assumes that both of these projects are in the same solution and that you've used the recommended name for the project containing the Xaml file (`ActivityLibrary`). If you used a different project name, you'll need to revise this file path.

There is no magic to loading the Xaml file from the `ActivityLibrary` project. I'm simply doing that because I happen to know that the file exists at that location and to eliminate the need to make a copy of the Xaml file. If you prefer, you can copy the Xaml file into the `\bin\debug` directory of the new `InvokerHostXaml` project and load it from that location.

```
            String fullFilePath =
                @"..\..\..\ActivityLibrary\HostingDemoWorkflow.xaml";
            Activity activity = ActivityXamlServices.Load(fullFilePath);
            //activity is a DynamicActivity
            if (activity == null)
            {
                throw new NullReferenceException(String.Format(
                    "Unable to deserialize {0}", fullFilePath));
            }
```

The result of loading the Xaml file is an **Activity** object. After verifying that the Xaml file was deserialized correctly, this object is passed to the **WorkflowInvoker** class in the same manner as the examples earlier in this chapter. Please note that there is no requirement to use the **WorkflowInvoker** class. You could have also used the **WorkflowApplication** class to execute the workflow.

```
            IDictionary<String, Object> output = WorkflowInvoker.Invoke(
                activity, new Dictionary<String, Object>
                {
                    {"ArgNumberToEcho", 1001},
                });

            Console.WriteLine("Host: Workflow completed - Thread:{0} - {1}",
                System.Threading.Thread.CurrentThread.ManagedThreadId,
                output["Result"]);
        }
        catch (Exception exception)
        {
            Console.WriteLine("Host: Workflow exception:{0}:{1}",
                exception.GetType(), exception.Message);
        }
    }
  }
}
```

After building the solution, you should be able to run the **InvokerHostXaml** project. Here are my results, which are consistent with previous examples in this chapter:

```
Host: About to run workflow - Thread:1

Workflow: Started - Thread:1

Workflow: About to delay

Workflow: Continue after delay

Workflow: Completed - Thread:1

Host: Workflow completed - Thread:1 - Result is 1001
```

Invoke Workflows from ASP.NET

WF provides two options when you need to invoke a workflow from an ASP.NET web application:

- You can invoke a WCF workflow service from the ASP.NET application.

- You can host the workflow directly within the ASP.NET application.

When deciding which mechanism to use, the default answer should be to invoke a separately hosted workflow service via WCF. Doing so enforces a clear separation between the web tier containing the presentation logic and the business tier that is implemented as workflow services. And independently hosted workflow services provide more opportunities for scalability, load balancing, and overall management of the runtime environment. Workflow services can also use additional WF features such as persistence that are important for long-running workflows.

However, you do have the option of directly invoking a workflow from an ASP.NET application. You normally wouldn't choose this option to execute the bulk of your workflow business logic. You should generally limit the use of this approach to short-lived workflows—the kind that you would normally execute just like a C# method. Since you need to execute the workflow on the ASP.NET thread, you are generally limited to using the `WorkflowInvoker` class. And this class doesn't support persistence and isn't designed for the management of long-running workflows.

The short example that follows demonstrates how easy it can be to invoke a workflow directly from within an ASP.NET application.

■ **Note** Chapter 9 covers the use of WCF workflow services.

In this example, you will construct a very simple ASP.NET application that invokes the same `HostingDemoWorkflow` that has been used throughout this chapter.

Designing the ASP.NET Application

To begin this example, create a new web application using the Empty ASP.NET Web Application template. Name the application `WebInvokerHost`, and add it to the existing solution for this chapter.

Add a new Web Form to the project. You can use the default name of `WebForm1.aspx`. Add the following web controls to the form:

Control	ID	Text	Notes
Label	Label1	"Enter Test Number:"	
TextBox	TextBox1		Content: 1001
Button	Button1	"Run Workflow"	OnClick=Button1_Click
Label	Label2		
TextBox	TextBox2		ReadOnly=True, TextMode=MultiLine

Here is the completed markup for the WebForm1.aspx page:

```
<%@ Page Language="C#" AutoEventWireup="true" CodeBehind="WebForm1.aspx.cs"
    Inherits="WebInvokerHost.WebForm1" %>

<!DOCTYPE html PUBLIC "-//W3C//DTD XHTML 1.0 Transitional//EN"
    "http://www.w3.org/TR/xhtml1/DTD/xhtml1-transitional.dtd">
<html xmlns="http://www.w3.org/1999/xhtml">
<head runat="server">
    <title></title>
</head>
<body>
    <form id="form1" runat="server">
    <div>
        <asp:Label ID="Label1" runat="server"
            Text="Enter Test Number:"></asp:Label>
        <br />
        <asp:TextBox ID="TextBox1" runat="server"
            Width="84px">1001</asp:TextBox>
        <br />
        <asp:Button ID="Button1" runat="server"
            OnClick="Button1_Click" Text="Run Workflow" />
        <br />
        <asp:Label ID="Label2" runat="server"></asp:Label>
        <br />
        <br />
        <asp:TextBox ID="TextBox2" runat="server" Height="128px"
            ReadOnly="True" TextMode="MultiLine"
            Width="456px" Wrap="False"></asp:TextBox>
        <br />
        <br />
    </div>
    </form>
</body>
</html>
```

TextBox1 is used to enter the test number that is echoed back from the workflow as the result string. Button1 triggers execution of the workflow and requires an event handler for the OnClick event. You can add an event handler by double-clicking the control in the designer. Label2 displays the string result. TextBox2 is a read-only, multiline control that displays all the logging messages that are produced by the hosting code and the workflow.

Figure 4-2 shows how I've positioned these controls. Feel free to improve on my meager efforts at user interface design.

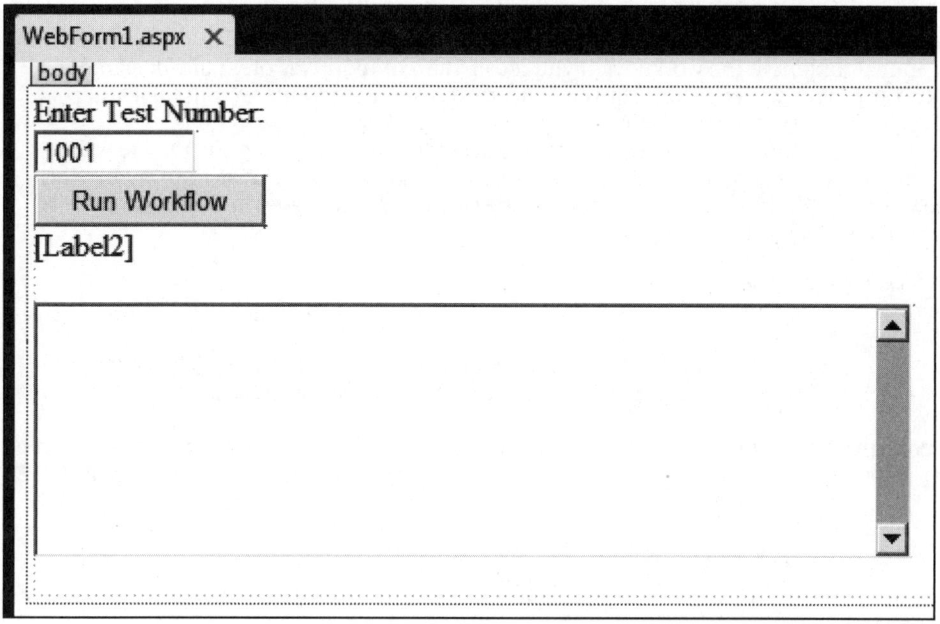

Figure 4-2. *WebForm1.aspx*

Hosting the Workflow

Before you can add the code needed to host the workflow, you need to add two references to the project. Add a project reference to the ActivityLibrary project that should be in the same solution. Also add a .NET reference to System.Activities.

Open WebForm1 in Code View to enter the code necessary to execute the workflow. For simplicity, I've placed all the code in the button event handler. Here is the WebForm1.aspx.cs file containing all the code that you need for this example:

```
using System;
using System.Activities;
using System.Collections.Generic;
using System.IO;
using ActivityLibrary;
```

```
namespace WebInvokerHost
{
    public partial class WebForm1 : System.Web.UI.Page
    {
        protected void Button1_Click(object sender, EventArgs e)
        {
            Int32 testNumber = 0;
            if (Int32.TryParse(TextBox1.Text, out testNumber))
            {
```

After retrieving and parsing the test number, the code creates a `StringWriter`. This is passed as the `ArgTextWriter` input argument to the workflow. If you recall, the workflow was originally declared to assign the `TextWriter` property of each `WriteLine` activity to this argument. Throughout the earlier examples in this chapter, this argument was not supplied and was therefore always null.

However, in this example, you want to display these messages on the web page instead of writing them to the console. Since this code supplies a value for this argument, all `WriteLine` messages in the workflow will be written to the `StringWriter` instead of the console. All messages in this hosting code also write to this same `StringWriter`.

```
                StringWriter writer = new StringWriter();
                try
                {
                    writer.WriteLine("Host: About to run workflow - Thread:{0}",
                        System.Threading.Thread.CurrentThread.ManagedThreadId);
```

The actual code to execute the workflow looks similar to the previous examples in this chapter. The `WorkflowInvoker` class is used in order to execute the workflow synchronously using the current ASP.NET thread.

```
                    HostingDemoWorkflow wf = new HostingDemoWorkflow();
                    IDictionary<String, Object> output =
                        WorkflowInvoker.Invoke(wf, new Dictionary<String, Object>
                        {
                            {"ArgNumberToEcho", 1001},
                            {"ArgTextWriter", writer},
                        });

                    Label2.Text = (String)output["Result"];

                    writer.WriteLine(
                        "Host: Workflow completed - Thread:{0} - {1}",
                        System.Threading.Thread.CurrentThread.ManagedThreadId,
                        output["Result"]);
                }
                catch (Exception exception)
                {
                    writer.WriteLine("Host: Workflow exception:{0}:{1}",
                        exception.GetType(), exception.Message);
                }
```

```
              //dump the contents of the writer
              TextBox2.Text = writer.ToString();
          }
      }
   }
}
```

Testing the Application

Before you test the application, you should set `WebForm1.aspx` as the startup page to simplify the testing. To accomplish this, select `WebForm1.aspx` in the Solution Explorer, right-click, and choose Set as Start Page.

You should now be ready to build the solution and run the web application. When you run it without debugging (Ctrl-F5), the ASP.NET development server will start in order to host the application. Your default browser should also start and present the default page (`WebForm1.aspx`) for your viewing pleasure. Figure 4-3 shows the page on my system after I entered a new test number and clicked the Run Workflow button.

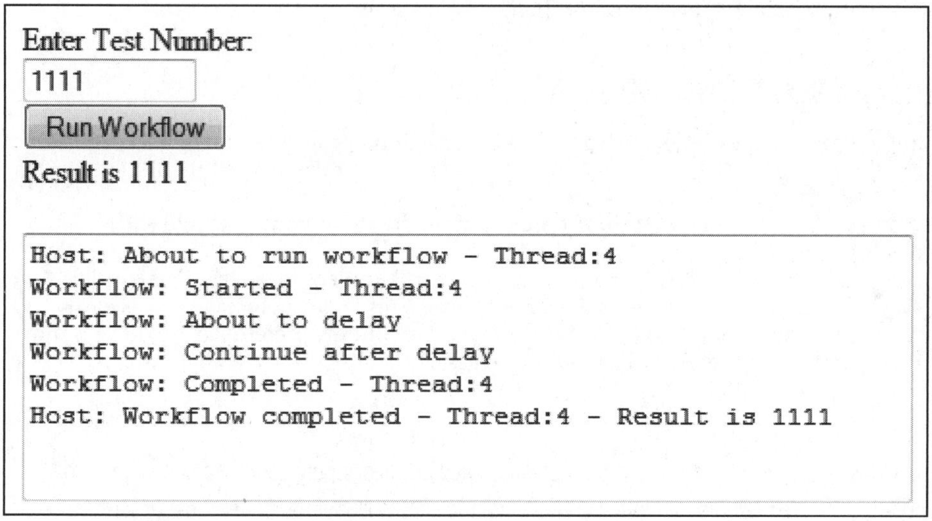

Enter Test Number:

```
1111
```

[Run Workflow]

Result is 1111

```
Host: About to run workflow - Thread:4
Workflow: Started - Thread:4
Workflow: About to delay
Workflow: Continue after delay
Workflow: Completed - Thread:4
Host: Workflow completed - Thread:4 - Result is 1111
```

Figure 4-3. *WebInvokerHost application*

Since the `WorkflowInvoker` class was used to execute the workflow, the same managed thread ID is shown for the hosting code as well as the workflow instance.

Managing Multiple Workflow Instances

As you have seen, WF supports several flexible ways to execute workflows. Because of this flexibility, you have the ability to incorporate workflows into many different application types.

But WF does not include an out-of-the-box manager for multiple workflow instances. If your application requires the ability to start and manage multiple instances of a workflow, you need to develop that code yourself.

■ **Tip** WF does provide the `WorkflowServiceHost` class, which allows you to manage multiple WCF-based workflow instances. However, those instances can be started only via WCF. You can find more information on the `WorkflowServiceHost` class in Chapter 9.

In the example that follows, you will develop a simple Windows Presentation Foundation application that hosts multiple instances of the `HostingDemoWorkflow`. The user interface allows you to start new instances of the workflow and to monitor their current status.

Implementing a Workflow Manager

To begin this example, create a new project using the WPF Application project template. You can find this template under the Windows category. Name this project `WpfHost`, and add it to the solution for this chapter.

Add a project reference to the `ActivityLibrary` project in the same solution. Also add a .NET reference to `System.Activities`.

Before you turn your attention to the WPF application, you will implement a class that handles some of the dirty work of managing multiple workflow instances. This code could have just as easily been added directly to the `MainWindow` class of the WPF application. But my preference is to always move nonvisual state management code such as this to its own class.

■ **Note** This workflow manager class is tailored to the needs of this particular application and is designed to demonstrate one possible way to manage multiple workflow instances. It is likely that it won't necessarily meet the exact needs of your particular application. However, it should be helpful as a starting point when you need to develop your own workflow applications.

Add a new C# class to the `WpfHost` project, and name it `WorkflowManager`. This is a normal C# class, not a workflow-related class. This class will track the state of multiple workflow instances for the application. Here is the complete code for the `WorkflowManager.cs` file:

```
using System;
using System.Activities;
using System.Collections.Generic;

namespace WpfHost
{
    public class WorkflowManager
    {
```

This class uses a private dictionary of WorkflowApplication instances to track each workflow instance. The key to the dictionary is the workflow instance ID, which is a Guid.

```
        private Dictionary<Guid, WorkflowApplication> _wfApps
            = new Dictionary<Guid, WorkflowApplication>();
```

A generic Run method is designed to start a workflow instance using the parameters that have been passed to the method. The generic type identifies the workflow type to create and execute.

After creating an instance of the requested workflow type, a WorkflowApplication is created and added to the private dictionary of workflow instances. Handlers for the most important members (Completed, Idle, Aborted, and OnUnhandledException) are then added. Finally, the workflow instance is started with a call to the WorkflowApplication.Run method.

```
        public Guid Run<T>(IDictionary<String, Object> parameters)
            where T : Activity, new()
        {
            Guid id = Guid.Empty;

            T activity = new T();
            WorkflowApplication wfApp = null;
            if (parameters != null)
            {
                wfApp = new WorkflowApplication(activity, parameters);
            }
            else
            {
                wfApp = new WorkflowApplication(activity);
            }
            id = wfApp.Id;

            _wfApps.Add(wfApp.Id, wfApp);

            wfApp.Completed = AppCompleted;
            wfApp.Idle = AppIdle;
            wfApp.Aborted = AppAborted;
            wfApp.OnUnhandledException = AppException;
```

```
            if (Started != null)
            {
                Started(id, parameters);
            }

            wfApp.Run();
            return id;
        }
```

A set of public delegates is supported by this class. Each one is used to notify the host application of a state change for a particular workflow instance.

```
        public Action<Guid, IDictionary<string, object>> Started { get; set; }
        public Action<Guid, IDictionary<string, object>> Completed { get; set; }
        public Action<Guid> Idle { get; set; }
        public Action<Guid, String, String> Incomplete { get; set; }

        public Int32 GetActiveCount()
        {
            lock (_wfApps)
            {
                return _wfApps.Count;
            }
        }
    }
```

The code to handle the various WorkflowApplication delegate members is shown next. The AppCompleted method handles the Completed calls from each WorkflowApplication instance. The code notifies the host application of the new state and removes the instance from the private dictionary.

```
        private void AppCompleted(WorkflowApplicationCompletedEventArgs e)
        {
            switch (e.CompletionState)
            {
                case ActivityInstanceState.Closed:
                    if (Completed != null)
                    {
                        Completed(e.InstanceId, e.Outputs);
                    }
                    RemoveInstance(e.InstanceId);
                    break;
                case ActivityInstanceState.Canceled:
                    if (Incomplete != null)
                    {
                        Incomplete(e.InstanceId, "Canceled",
                            String.Empty);
                    }
                    RemoveInstance(e.InstanceId);
                    break;
                case ActivityInstanceState.Faulted:
                    if (Incomplete != null)
                    {
```

```
                    Incomplete(e.InstanceId, "Faulted",
                        e.TerminationException.Message);
                }
                RemoveInstance(e.InstanceId);
                break;
            default:
                break;
        }
    }
}
```

The code that handles the Idle and Aborted notifications from each WorkflowApplication instance notifies the host application. In the case of the Aborted notification, the instance is removed from the dictionary.

```
private void AppIdle(WorkflowApplicationIdleEventArgs e)
{
    if (Idle != null)
    {
        Idle(e.InstanceId);
    }
}

private void AppAborted(WorkflowApplicationAbortedEventArgs e)
{
    if (Incomplete != null)
    {
        Incomplete(e.InstanceId, "Aborted", e.Reason.Message);
    }
    RemoveInstance(e.InstanceId);
}
```

Unhandled exceptions are managed in a similar way as the other notifications. The host application is notified of the problem, and the instance is removed from the dictionary.

```
private UnhandledExceptionAction AppException(
    WorkflowApplicationUnhandledExceptionEventArgs e)
{
    if (Incomplete != null)
    {
        Incomplete(e.InstanceId, "Exception",
            e.UnhandledException.Message);
    }
    RemoveInstance(e.InstanceId);
    return UnhandledExceptionAction.Cancel;
}
```

A private `RemoveInstance` method is used by the other methods to remove a `WorkflowApplication` instance from the private dictionary.

```
private void RemoveInstance(Guid id)
{
    lock (_wfApps)
    {
        if (_wfApps.ContainsKey(id))
        {
            _wfApps[id].Completed = null;
            _wfApps[id].Idle = null;
            _wfApps[id].Aborted = null;
            _wfApps[id].OnUnhandledException = null;
            _wfApps.Remove(id);
        }
    }
}
```

Implementing the InstanceInfo Class

Add a new C# class to the `WpfHost` project, and name it `InstanceInfo`. This is a normal C# class, not a workflow class. The purpose of this class is to define a structure that is used by the `MainWindow` class to display a status line for each workflow instance. Here is the complete code for the `InstanceInfo.cs` file:

```
using System;

namespace WpfHost
{
    public class InstanceInfo
    {
        public Guid Id { get; set; }
        public Int32 TestNumber { get; set; }
        public String Result { get; set; }
        public String Status { get; set; }
    }
}
```

Designing the User Interface

Next, open the `MainWindow.xaml` file of the `WpfHost` project in the designer. Add the following controls to the form:

Control	Name	Text/Content	Notes
Button	button1	"Start Workflow"	Click=button1_Click
Button	button2	"Clear"	Click=button2_Click
DataGrid	dataGrid1		IsReadOnly=True, AutoGenerateColumns=True

Figure 4-4 shows the layout of the controls on `MainForm.xaml`.

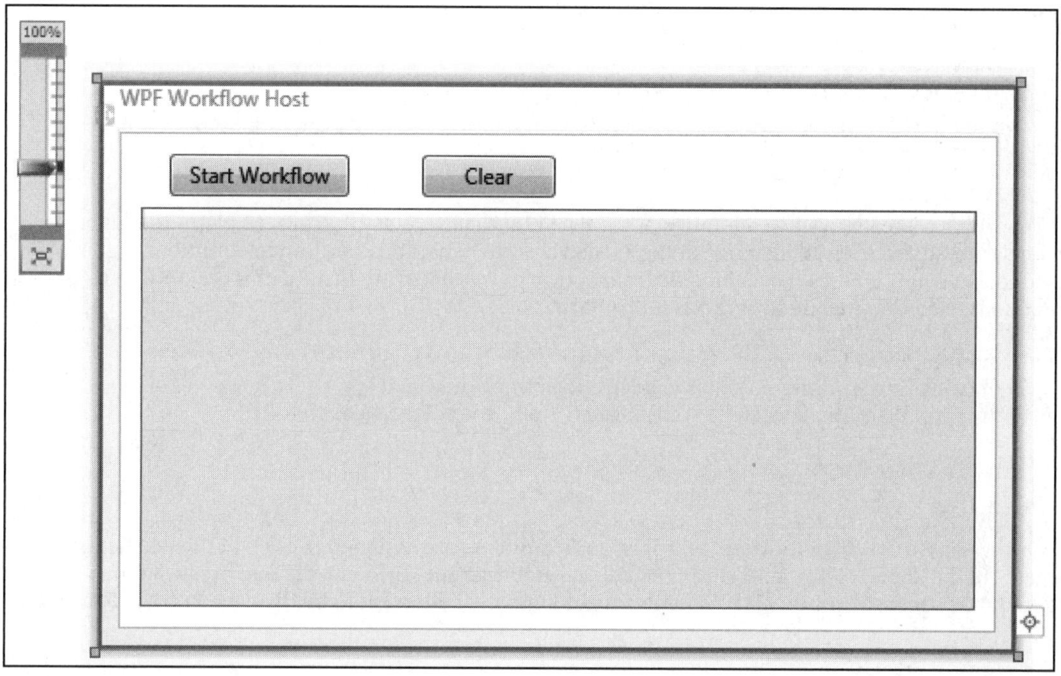

Figure 4-4. WpfHost MainWindow.xaml

■ **Note** As long as the `AutoGenerateColumns` property of the `DataGrid` is enabled, the individual columns of the grid will be generated based on the data source for the grid (the `ItemsSource` property). The initial column widths will be based on the first row of data.

Add `Click` event handlers for the two buttons as listed in the previous table. Also add a handler for the `Closing` event of the window. You can use the default name of `Window_Closing` for the handler.

Implementing the User Interface Code

You can now turn your attention to the code needed to handle the user interface events and to populate the DataGrid with status information for each workflow instance. Here is the complete code that you need for the MainWindow.xaml.cs file:

```
using System;
using System.Collections.Generic;
using System.Linq;
using System.Windows;
using ActivityLibrary;

namespace WpfHost
{
    /// <summary>
    /// Interaction logic for MainWindow.xaml
    /// </summary>
    public partial class MainWindow : Window
    {
```

The window creates a single instance of the WorkflowManager class that you implemented in a previous step. It also uses an instance of the Random class to generate a random test number that is passed to each workflow instance. Finally, a collection of InstanceInfo instances is created. This collection is used to populate the entries in the DataGrid.

```
        private WorkflowManager _manager = new WorkflowManager();
        private Random _rnd = new Random(Environment.TickCount);
        private List<InstanceInfo> _instances = new List<InstanceInfo>();

        public MainWindow()
        {
```

During construction of the main window, code handlers are assigned to each of the notification delegates of the WorkflowManager class. The collection of InstanceInfo objects is assigned to the DataGrid.ItemsSource property. This enables the data in the collection to be displayed on the DataGrid.

```
            InitializeComponent();

            _manager.Started = Started;
            _manager.Completed = Completed;
            _manager.Idle = Idle;
            _manager.Incomplete = Incomplete;
            dataGrid1.ItemsSource = _instances;
        }
```

Each time button1 is clicked, a new instance of the workflow is created and run. The actual work of preparing and starting the workflow is deferred to the WorkflowManager class.

```
private void button1_Click(object sender, RoutedEventArgs e)
{
    Int32 testNumber = _rnd.Next(9999);

    //start a workflow instance
    Guid id = _manager.Run<HostingDemoWorkflow>(
        new Dictionary<String, Object>
        {
            {"ArgNumberToEcho", testNumber},
        });
}
```

The code for **button2** is used to clear the current list of instances from the **DataGrid**.

```
private void button2_Click(object sender, RoutedEventArgs e)
{
    _instances.Clear();
    dataGrid1.Items.Refresh();
}
```

Each of the notification handlers works in a similar way. They create a new instance of the **InstanceInfo** class and set the appropriate properties. The class is then passed to the private **UpdateDisplay** method that updates the collection of instances with the new data.

Notice that the **UpdateDisplay** method is invoked using the WPF dispatcher. This ensures that the user interface thread is used. This is necessary since these methods are triggered by a workflow instance state change that executes on the workflow thread, not the user interface thread. You can only update WPF controls from the user interface thread.

```
private void Started(Guid id, IDictionary<string, object> parameters)
{
    Application.Current.Dispatcher.BeginInvoke(
        new Action<InstanceInfo>(UpdateDisplay), new InstanceInfo
        {
            Id = id,
            TestNumber = (Int32)parameters["ArgNumberToEcho"],
            Result = String.Empty,
            Status = "Started"
        });
}

private void Completed(Guid id, IDictionary<string, object> outputs)
{
    Application.Current.Dispatcher.BeginInvoke(
        new Action<InstanceInfo>(UpdateDisplay), new InstanceInfo
        {
            Id = id,
            Result = outputs["Result"] as String,
            Status = "Completed"
        });
}
```

```
private void Idle(Guid id)
{
    Application.Current.Dispatcher.BeginInvoke(
        new Action<InstanceInfo>(UpdateDisplay), new InstanceInfo
        {
            Id = id,
            Status = "Idle"
        });
}

private void Incomplete(Guid id, String reason, String message)
{
    Application.Current.Dispatcher.BeginInvoke(
        new Action<InstanceInfo>(UpdateDisplay), new InstanceInfo
        {
            Id = id,
            Result = message,
            Status = reason
        });
}

private void UpdateDisplay(InstanceInfo info)
{
    InstanceInfo currInfo = null;
    currInfo =
        (from i in _instances
         where i.Id == info.Id
         select i).SingleOrDefault();
    if (currInfo != null)
    {
        currInfo.Status = info.Status;
        currInfo.Result = info.Result;
    }
    else
    {
        _instances.Add(info);
        currInfo = info;
    }

    dataGrid1.Items.Refresh();
    dataGrid1.ScrollIntoView(currInfo);
}
```

The handler for the window's Closing event retrieves the active count of workflows from the WorkflowManager instance. If the count is zero, then the window is allowed to close. If it is greater than zero, the user is asked whether they want to execute the application while one or more workflows are still executing.

```
        private void Window_Closing(
            object sender, System.ComponentModel.CancelEventArgs e)
        {
            Int32 count = _manager.GetActiveCount();
            if (count != 0)
            {
                if (MessageBox.Show(String.Format(
                    "{0} workflows are still executing.  Continue?", count),
                    "Workflow Executing",
                    MessageBoxButton.YesNo, MessageBoxImage.Warning)
                        != MessageBoxResult.Yes)
                {
                    e.Cancel = true;
                }
            }
        }
    }
}
```

Testing the Application

After building the solution, you should be ready to run the `WpfHost` application. Figure 4-5 shows a representative view of the application after I have started a few workflow instances.

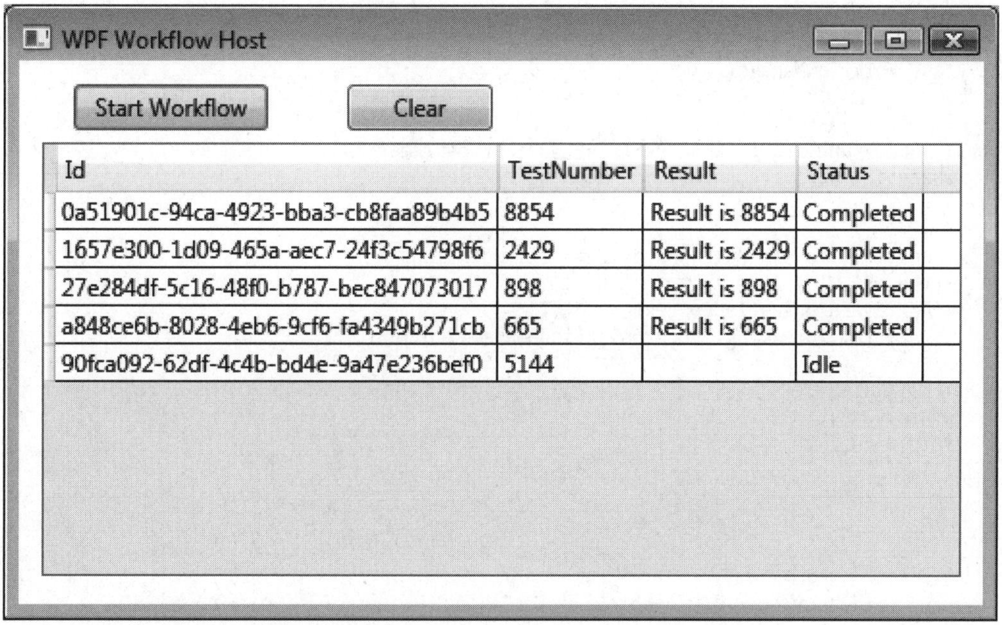
WPF Workflow Host
Start Workflow
Clear
Id
TestNumber
Result
Status
0a51901c-94ca-4923-bba3-cb8faa89b4b5
8854
Result is 8854
Completed
1657e300-1d09-465a-aec7-24f3c54798f6
2429
Result is 2429
Completed
27e284df-5c16-48f0-b787-bec847073017
898
Result is 898
Completed
a848ce6b-8028-4eb6-9cf6-fa4349b271cb
665
Result is 665
Completed
90fca092-62df-4c4b-bd4e-9a47e236bef0
5144
Idle

Figure 4-5. *WpfHost application*

As each workflow is started, the `DataGrid` will be updated. The Status column for each instance always begins with "Started" but immediately changes to "Idle" as the workflow moves into that state. After a short delay, each instance then changes to a "Completed" status.

Using the WPF SynchronizationContext

Since this example uses WPF, this is a good opportunity to demonstrate the use of the optional `SynchronizationContext` property of the `WorkflowApplication` class. By setting this property to the current synchronization context, the WPF context will be used for the scheduling of all workflows.

■ **Note** Setting the `SynchronizationContext` isn't something that you will normally need to do. It is necessary only in advanced threading scenarios where you want to provide a nondefault threading and execution model for the workflow runtime to use.

To see this in action, you need to make this small change to the `WorkflowManager.cs` code:

```
using System;
using System.Activities;
using System.Collections.Generic;

namespace WpfHost
{
    public class WorkflowManager
    {
…
        public Guid Run<T>(IDictionary<String, Object> parameters)
            where T : Activity, new()
        {
…
            //Add this to schedule and execute all workflows on
            //the WPF UI thread.
            wfApp.SynchronizationContext =
                System.Threading.SynchronizationContext.Current;


            wfApp.Run();
            return id;
        }
…
    }
}
```

Prior to running the workflow, the `SynchronizationContext` property is set to the current synchronization context. Since the `Run<T>` method is invoked on the WPF user interface thread, the current synchronization context is the one used by WPF (`DispatcherSynchronizationContext`).

You shouldn't see any observable difference in the results after making this change, other than the user interface may feel a bit sluggish. That's because the workflows are now executing on the WPF user interface thread. Now that the workflows are executing on the user interface thread, there is no need for the calls to the `Application.Current.Dispatcher.BeginInvoke` method. You could safely replace those calls with a direct call to the private `UpdateDisplay` method.

Summary

This chapter focused on hosting and executing workflows. The `WorkflowInvoker` and `WorkflowApplication` classes are provided with WF and are used to execute workflows. `WorkflowInvoker` is the simplest way to execute a workflow since it executes synchronously on the current thread. `WorkflowApplication` provides the ability to execute workflows asynchronously on a separate thread, resume bookmarks, configure persistence, and manually control running workflows. The chapter presented a number of short examples that demonstrated the most important features of these two classes.

Workflows are normally compiled into .NET types that are instantiated before they are executed. However, WF also provides the `ActivityXamlServices` class, which allows you to load a workflow instance directly from the Xaml declaration rather than a compiled type. The chapter included an example that demonstrated how to use this class.

Another example demonstrated how to invoke a workflow from within an ASP.NET Web Forms application. The final example demonstrated one way to execute and manage multiple instances of a workflow from a WPF application. An option to use the WPF synchronization context for scheduling and execution of the workflows was also presented.

In the next chapter, you will learn about the core procedural flow control activities that are provided with WF.

CHAPTER 5

■ ■ ■

Procedural Flow Control

The focus of this chapter is a core set of procedural flow control activities that are included with Windows Workflow Foundation (WF). These are some of the most frequently used activities that implement branching and looping. The `If` and `Switch<T>` activities are first discussed, followed by examples that demonstrate the `While` and `DoWhile` activities. The `Parallel` activity is then discussed, followed by several examples that demonstrate its use.

Understanding the Procedural Modeling Style

WF includes support for two different workflow modeling styles out of the box: procedural and flowchart. The modeling style determines how the flow of control between individual activities is modeled. Microsoft may provide other modeling styles in the future (for example, state machine), or you can implement activities that support your own modeling style. However, the two styles that are included with WF are both flexible enough to tackle most workflow tasks.

The procedural modeling style (the focus of this chapter) uses familiar programming constructs to control the flow of execution. Standard activities are included that mimic C# branching and looping keywords such as `if` and `while`. You control the flow of execution by placing child activities into the appropriate control activity. In contrast with this, the flowchart modeling style uses direct links between activities to control the flow of execution. The procedural modeling style could be thought of as rigid, structured, and precise while the flowchart style is free-form.

■ **Note** Chapter 7 discusses the activities that are used to implement the flowchart modeling style.

The modeling styles are implemented as activities along with the designer support for those activities. They are not implemented as fixed workflow or project types that must be selected up front and are difficult to change later. This enables you to mix and match the two styles by simply including the activities for either style. Your choice for the original root activity does not force you to exclusively use that modeling style for the entire workflow or activity.

Making Decisions

I think that the most common requirement of any programming language is the ability to make branching decisions. It would be difficult to write any useful code if you couldn't test a condition and then do something based on the results of the test. WF supports two commonly used decision-making constructs that I discuss next: `If` and `Switch<T>`.

Understanding the If Activity

The `If` activity allows you to model an if-then-else condition. You use it by supplying a Boolean value, usually in the form of an expression. You can reference arguments, variables, and literal values in the expression. You can also declare an activity that you want to execute if the condition evaluates to true and another activity to execute if the condition is false. You can decide to declare one or both of these activities depending on your needs. Here are the most important properties of the `If` activity:

Property	Type	Required	Description
Condition	InArgument<Boolean>	Yes	The condition that you want to evaluate
Then	Activity	No	The activity to execute if the condition is true
Else	Activity	No	The activity to execute if the condition is false

■ **Tip** Many activities, including this one, allow you to declare a single activity as a child. While support for only a single activity may seem like a major shortcoming, please remember that the single activity that you declare may itself be a container for other activities. For example, the activity that you declare for the `If.Then` property may be a `Sequence` activity containing its own child activities.

The `If` activity is pervasive and can be seen in examples that are presented later in this chapter (as well as throughout this book). You can also refer to the examples in Chapter 3 that use this activity.

Understanding the Switch<T> Activity

If you need to make a branching decision based on a single Boolean condition, the `If` activity does the trick. However, often you're not dealing with a binary true or false decision. You might need the ability to take one of several branches depending on a single value. For example, if you were declaring a calculator workflow, you would need to branch the flow of execution based on the requested operation (add, subtract, multiply, divide, and so on). You could model that using several instances of the `If` activity, but it's a much cleaner design to use a `Switch<T>` activity.

The `Switch<T>` activity models the C# `switch` statement. You use this activity by setting a single value to evaluate using the `Switch.Expression` property. Since this is a generic activity, you must also supply a type for the activity. The type you specify determines the type for the `Switch.Expression` property. When the activity is executed, the `Switch.Expression` property is evaluated, and the current value of the property is used to branch execution to one of the defined cases. Each case is uniquely identified with a value of the specified type.

Using the calculator example, the `Switch<T>` activity might be constructed with a type of string as the generic type parameter. The individual cases might use string literals of **add**, **subtract**, **multiply**, and **divide** as their key values. If a case has been defined for the current value of the `Switch.Expression` property, the activity defined for that case is executed. You can also define an activity for a default case. This default activity is executed when a matching key is not found for any of the other cases.

Here are the most important properties of the `Switch<T>` activity:

Property	Type	Required	Description
Expression	InArgument<T>	Yes	The value used to determine which case to execute.
Cases	IDictionary<T, Activity>	Yes	One activity is declared for each potential case. Each case is uniquely identified with a key of the generic type.
Default	Activity	No	An optional activity that is executed if the Expression value doesn't match any of the Cases.

You have already seen the `Switch<T>` activity used in Chapter 1 and Chapter 3. Please refer to the examples in those chapters to see the `Switch<T>` activity in action.

Understanding the While and DoWhile Activities

Looping is also a common workflow construct. There are many times when you need the ability to repeatedly execute an activity while a condition is true. Two of the procedural activities that support looping are `While` and `DoWhile`.

The `While` activity repeatedly executes a child activity while a condition is true. You use it by first providing a Boolean value for the `While.Condition` property. This is usually done by providing an expression that evaluates to a Boolean value. The `While.Body` property is where you declare the activity that you want to repeatedly execute.

The `While` activity checks the condition at the top of the loop, before the `While.Body` activity is executed. Therefore, if the condition is initially false, it is possible that the activity specified for `While.Body` is never executed.

The `While` activity is also one of the activities that supports the declaration of variables. Here are the most important properties of the `While` activity:

Property	Type	Required	Description
Condition	Activity<Boolean>	Yes	The condition to be evaluated. Execution of the child activity continues while this condition evaluates to true.
Body	Activity	Yes	The child activity that is executed while the condition is true.

Like the `While` activity, the `DoWhile` activity repeatedly executes a child activity. The difference between the two activities is when the condition is evaluated. The `While` activity evaluates the condition at the beginning of each cycle. In contrast with this, the `DoWhile` activity evaluates the condition at the end of each cycle.

Because of this difference, the child activity that is declared for the `DoWhile.Body` property is always executed at least once. After it is executed, the `DoWhile.Condition` property is evaluated. If it evaluates to true, another cycle of execution begins, and the `DoWhile.Body` activity is executed once again. If the condition evaluates to false, no further execution of the activity takes place, and the work of the `DoWhile` activity is completed.

Like the `While` activity, `DoWhile` supports the definition of variables. Here are the most important properties of the `DoWhile` activity:

Property	Type	Required	Description
Condition	Activity<Boolean>	Yes	The condition to be evaluated at the end of each cycle. Execution of the child activity stops once this condition evaluates to false.
Body	Activity	Yes	The child activity that is executed until the condition is false.

■ **Note** These activities construct a single instance of the activity that you specify for the Body property and reuse it for each iteration. The variable and argument values may change with each iteration, but the activity is constructed only once.

In the following section, I present an example that demonstrates the use of the `While` activity. Later, the example will be modified to replace all instances of the `While` activity with the `DoWhile` activity to achieve the same results.

Using the While and DoWhile Activities

To demonstrate the use of these activities, I've chosen an inventory lookup scenario. Prior to placing an order for an item, the inventory for the item must be checked to determine whether sufficient inventory exists to fill the order. However, the inventory may be distributed across multiple warehouses, and each one may need to be checked to determine whether the entire order can be filled. The While activity is used to loop through all warehouses until the requested item quantity can be filled or all warehouses have been checked.

Here are the steps that you will follow to implement this example:

1. Implement a custom InventoryLookup activity.

2. Declare the GetItemInventory workflow.

3. Implement the code to execute the workflow.

Implementing the InventoryLookup Activity

To begin this example, create a new project named ActivityLibrary using the Activity Library template. Add it to a new solution that is named for this chapter. You can delete the Activity1.xaml file since it won't be needed.

■ **Tip** For most of the examples in this book, you can delete the activity or workflow file that is created for you when you add a new project. In this example, the file to delete is named Activity1.xaml since this is an activity library. If you prefer, you can choose to rename the file to the name that I specify for a new activity or workflow. In my opinion, it just seems easier to add a new item rather than to rename the existing one. In addition, renaming the source file is not sufficient to actually change the name. The Xaml file contains a class name that must also be changed.

This example uses a custom activity to simulate the lookup of the warehouse inventory. To create this activity, add a new custom activity to the ActivityLibrary project that you just created, and name it InventoryLookup. Use the Code Activity new item template. Here is the code that you need to implement this activity:

```
using System;
using System.Activities;
using System.Collections.Generic;

namespace ActivityLibrary
{
```

This activity uses the CodeActivity<TResult> generic class as its base. A type of Int32 is provided to set the type of the Result property to OutArgument<Int32>. Three additional input arguments are defined. The ItemId will identify the item to look up. The WarehouseId determines which warehouse the activity should use when retrieving the current inventory. The RequestedQty is the quantity being requested for the item.

After declaring the arguments, a dictionary of test data is created. Normally the inventory data would be retrieved from a database or perhaps from another system via messaging. But in this case, a set of hard-coded test data suffices to demonstrate this particular scenario. Separate test data is loaded for each warehouse that is identified with a simple sequential integer. The actual test data consists of an item identifier and the current quantity on hand for that item.

```
public class InventoryLookup : CodeActivity<Int32>
{
    public InArgument<Int32> ItemId { get; set; }
    public InArgument<Int32> WarehouseId { get; set; }
    public InArgument<Int32> RequestedQty { get; set; }

    private Dictionary<Int32, Dictionary<Int32, Int32>> _warehouses
        = new Dictionary<Int32, Dictionary<Int32, Int32>>();

    public InventoryLookup()
    {
        //load some test data
        _warehouses.Add(1, new Dictionary<int, int>
        {
            {100, 5},
            {200, 0},
            {300, 0},
        });

        _warehouses.Add(2, new Dictionary<int, int>
        {
            {100, 10},
            {200, 0},
            {300, 0},
        });

        _warehouses.Add(3, new Dictionary<int, int>
        {
            {100, 50},
            {200, 75},
            {300, 0},
        });
    }
```

The Execute method contains the code to look up the inventory for the requested item. After locating the correct warehouse, the inventory for the item is retrieved and compared to the requested quantity. The lower of the requested quantity or the available inventory is returned in the Result property.

```
    protected override int Execute(CodeActivityContext context)
    {
        Int32 availableInventory = 0;
        Int32 warehouseId = WarehouseId.Get(context);
        Dictionary<Int32, Int32> warehouse = null;
        if (_warehouses.TryGetValue(warehouseId, out warehouse))
        {
            Int32 itemId = ItemId.Get(context);
            if (warehouse.TryGetValue(itemId, out availableInventory))
            {
                Int32 requestedQty = RequestedQty.Get(context);
                if (availableInventory > requestedQty)
                {
                    availableInventory = requestedQty;
                }
            }
        }
        return availableInventory;
    }
  }
}
```

Build the solution before you continue to the next step. This ensures that the custom activity builds without any problems and is added to the Visual Studio Toolbox.

Declaring the GetItemInventory Workflow

To declare the example workflow and an application to test it, add a new project named GetItemInventory to the solution. Use the Workflow Console Application template. You can delete the Workflow1.xaml file that was generated for you since it won't be needed. Add a project reference to the ActivityLibrary project, which should be in the same solution.

Add a new workflow named GetItemInventory to the project using the Activity template. The job of this workflow is to execute the custom InventoryLookup activity repeatedly until the requested quantity is found for the requested item. Start the workflow declaration by adding these arguments to the workflow:

Name	Direction	Argument Type
ArgItemId	In	Int32
ArgQuantity	In	Int32
ArgQuantityFound	Out	Int32

The workflow also requires four variables that are scoped at different levels. You can't enter all of these variables now, since many of them are scoped by activities that are yet to be added. In the step-by-step instructions that follow, I'll tell you when to add each variable. But I've included this summary of all the variables that you will need to add:

Name	Variable Type	Scope	Default Value
TotalFound	Int32	Sequence	
WarehouseId	Int32	While	1
MaxWarehouseId	Int32	While	3
WarehouseQty	Int32	WhileSequence	

Please follow these steps to declare the remainder of the workflow:

1. Add a `Sequence` activity as the root activity of the workflow.

2. Add a new `Int32` variable to the `Sequence` activity named `TotalFound`.

3. Add a `While` activity as a child of the `Sequence` activity.

4. Add the two `Int32` variables that are scoped at the `While` activity level: `WarehouseId` and `MaxWarehouseId`. `WarehouseId` should have a default value of `1`, and `MaxWarehouseId` has a default value of `3`.

5. Set the `While.Condition` property to this expression: `TotalFound < ArgQuantity And WarehouseId <= MaxWarehouseId`.

6. Add a `Sequence` activity to the `While.Body` property. Change the `Sequence.DisplayName` property to `WhileSequence`. This makes it easier to distinguish this `Sequence` activity from the topmost root activity of the workflow.

7. Add the final variable named `WarehouseQty` to the `WhileSequence` activity.

8. Add an `InventoryLookup` activity to the `WhileSequence` activity. Set the `ItemId` property to `ArgItemId`, `RequestedQty` to `ArgQuantity - TotalFound`, `Result` to `WarehouseQty`, and `WarehouseId` to `WarehouseId`. Figure 5-1 shows the Properties window for this activity after the properties have been set.

9. Add an `Assign` activity directly under the `InventoryLookup` activity. Set the `Assign.To` property to `TotalFound` and the `Assign.Value` property to `TotalFound + WarehouseQty`.

10. Add another `Assign` activity under the previous one. Set the `Assign.To` property to `WarehouseId` and the `Assign.Value` property to `WarehouseId + 1`. Figure 5-2 shows the completed `WhileSequence` activity.

11. After navigating back to the root `Sequence` activity, add an `Assign` activity directly under the `While` activity. Set the `Assign.To` property to `ArgQuantityFound` and the `Assign.Value` property to `TotalFound`. Figure 5-3 is the completed top-level view of the workflow.

■ **Note** The solution will likely not build at this point since the code in the `Program.cs` file is referencing the `Workflow1.xaml` file that you deleted. That will be remedied in the next step.

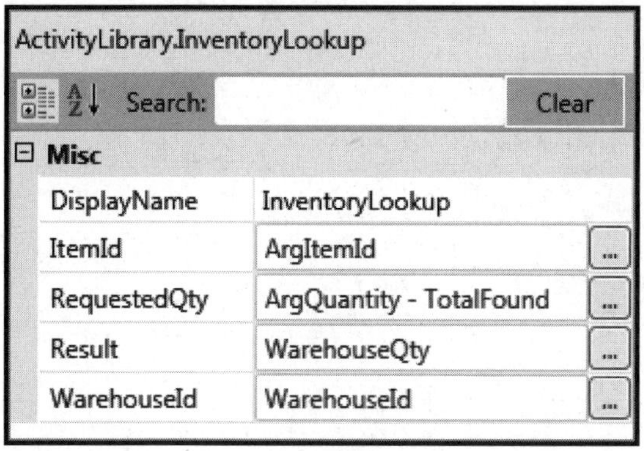

Figure 5-1. InventoryLookup properties

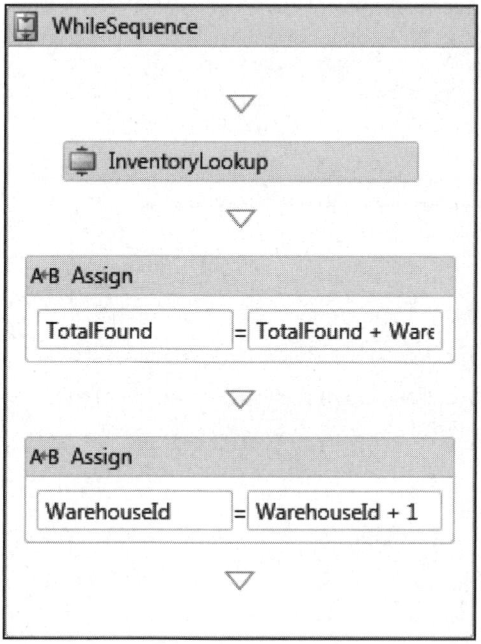

Figure 5-2. Completed WhileSequence activity

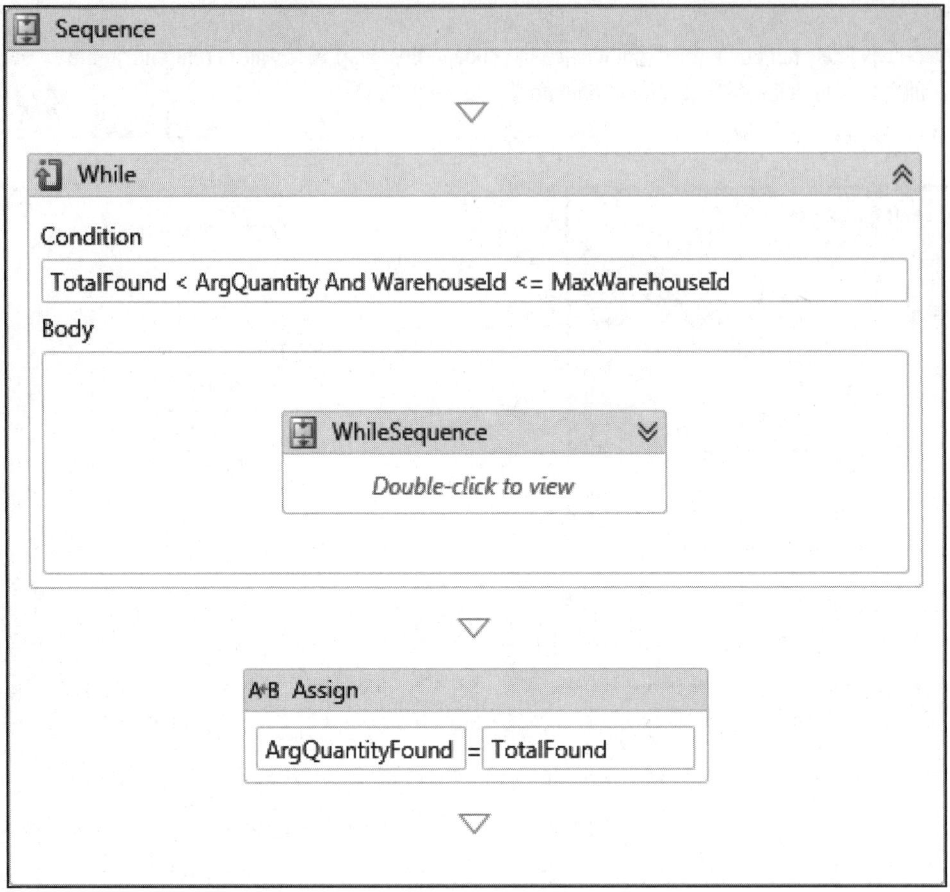

Figure 5-3. Completed GetItemInventory workflow

Hosting the Workflow

Next you will implement the code to host and execute this workflow. Open the `Program.cs` file in the `GetItemInventory` project, and replace it with the following code:

```
using System;
using System.Activities;
using System.Collections.Generic;

namespace GetItemInventory
{
    class Program
    {
        static void Main(string[] args)
        {
```

The workflow is executed a number of times, each time with a different combination of itemId and requested quantity. After each test completes, the actual quantity found is written to the console.

```
            RunWorkflow(new GetItemInventory(), 100, 2);
            RunWorkflow(new GetItemInventory(), 100, 8);
            RunWorkflow(new GetItemInventory(), 100, 20);
            RunWorkflow(new GetItemInventory(), 100, 100);
            RunWorkflow(new GetItemInventory(), 200, 10);
            RunWorkflow(new GetItemInventory(), 300, 15);

            Console.WriteLine("Press any key to exit");
            Console.ReadKey();
        }

        private static void RunWorkflow(Activity wf,
            Int32 itemId, Int32 quantity)
        {
            IDictionary<String, Object> output = WorkflowInvoker.Invoke(
                wf, new Dictionary<string, object>
                {
                    {"ArgItemId", itemId},
                    {"ArgQuantity", quantity}
                });

            Console.WriteLine("Item: {0} Requested: {1} Found: {2}",
                itemId, quantity, output["ArgQuantityFound"]);
        }
    }
}
```

Testing the Workflow

You should now be able to build the solution and verify that everything builds correctly. After running this example code, I see these results:

```
Item: 100 Requested: 2 Found: 2

Item: 100 Requested: 8 Found: 8

Item: 100 Requested: 20 Found: 20

Item: 100 Requested: 100 Found: 65

Item: 200 Requested: 10 Found: 10

Item: 300 Requested: 15 Found: 0

Press any key to exit
```

The results show that the looping logic of the `While` activity works correctly. For example, the requested quantity of 8 for the second test case couldn't be filled by only the first warehouse because it has a quantity of only 5 available. A combination of the first two warehouses was necessary. A requested quantity of 100 for that same item could not be filled. Instead, the total quantity available for all warehouses was shown (65).

Using the DoWhile Activity

To see the `DoWhile` activity in action, you could create another workflow using the instructions that were given for the `While` activity example in the previous section. But all that you really need to do is to replace all `While` activity references with `DoWhile`. It's not really worth the effort to use the workflow designer for that. The easiest way to do this is to make a copy of the `GetItemInventory.xaml` file and edit the copy outside of the designer.

You can follow these steps:

1. Make a copy of the `GetItemInventory.xaml` file in the same `GetItemInventory` project. Name the copy `GetItemInventoryDoWhile.xaml`.

2. Open the copied `GetItemInventoryDoWhile.xaml` in Code View, which should open the XML editor.

3. Edit the `x:Class` attribute of the root element to provide the new name for the activity: `x:Class="GetItemInventory.GetItemInventoryDoWhile"`. Make sure you don't change the namespace, which should remain as `GetItemInventory`.

4. Change all `While` activity references to `DoWhile`. If you decide to do a global change, make sure you don't change the `x:Class` attribute that you already changed.

■ **Caution** This particular workflow works equally well using either the While or DoWhile activity. However, you can't make the assumption that these two activities are completely interchangeable in all cases. For example, if you changed the default value of the WarehouseId variable, the expression in the Condition property, or the location of the Assign activity that increments the WarehouseId, the two activities might not produce the same results.

Here's an abbreviated list of the revised GetItemInventoryDoWhile.xaml file:

```
<Activity x:Class="GetItemInventory.GetItemInventoryDoWhile">
…
  <Sequence>
…
    <DoWhile>
      <DoWhile.Variables>
        <Variable x:TypeArguments="x:Int32" Name="WarehouseId" />
        <Variable x:TypeArguments="x:Int32" Default="3" Name="MaxWarehouseId" />
      </DoWhile.Variables>
      <DoWhile.Condition>
          [TotalFound &lt; ArgQuantity And WarehouseId &lt;= MaxWarehouseId]
      </DoWhile.Condition>
…
    </DoWhile>
…
  </Sequence>
</Activity>
```

That's all that you should have to change in the workflow declaration. You also need to modify the class name that the code creates in the Program.cs file. Change the statements that create a GetItemInventory instance to create a GetItemInventoryDoWhile instance instead. When you execute the application, you should see the same results as you saw for the While example.

■ **Note** Instead of creating a copy of the existing workflow, you could have modified the original workflow to use DoWhile instead of While. However, I wanted to use this opportunity to show you just how easy it is to copy and modify an existing workflow. In this example, it made sense to change the value of the x:Class attribute using the XML editor since you were making other changes to the file. But be aware that you can also change the class name of an activity or workflow using the Properties window. To accomplish this, open the Xaml file in designer view, and make sure that none of the individual activities is highlighted. You should see the Name property in the Properties window. The value of this property contains the namespace and class name. Changing this value modifies the x:Class attribute within the Xaml file.

Understanding the Parallel Activity

The `Parallel` activity is used to schedule two or more child activities for execution at the same time. You declare the activities to execute using the `Parallel.Branches` property. Each child activity that you add to this property represents a separate branch of execution. The branch activities can be composite activities such as `Sequence` that contain other children. The `Parallel` activity is also one of the standard activities that support the definition of variables.

Here are the most important properties of the Parallel activity:

Property	Type	Required	Description
Branches	Collection<Activity>	Yes	A collection of activities that will be scheduled for parallel execution. Each activity represents a separate branch of execution.
CompletionCondition	Activity<Boolean>	No	An optional condition that is evaluated after any of the branches complete. If the condition evaluates to true, the remaining branches are canceled.

The `Parallel` activity continues to execute until all of its branches have completed their work. However, it supports an optional `CompletionCondition` property that can be used to short-circuit the normal completion logic. This is a Boolean condition that is evaluated each time a branch completes. If the condition evaluates to true, all remaining branches are canceled, and the `Parallel` activity immediately completes.

Understanding Parallel Execution

At first glance, you might think that the `Parallel` activity is an easy way to simultaneously execute any activities. The truth is that while the `Parallel` activity is very useful, it doesn't work exactly as you might expect.

The `Parallel` activity doesn't really execute multiple branches simultaneously on *multiple threads*. Each workflow instance executes on a single thread, so true parallel execution of multiple activities isn't possible unless the activities are written to support asynchronous execution. Instead of true parallel execution, the `Parallel` activity is designed to interleave work that is defined in multiple child activities. It *schedules* all the branches for immediate execution, and scheduling an activity for execution is not the same as immediately executing it. If one of the branches of execution become idle (for example, an activity is waiting for some external input), execution can resume with another branch that is not idle.

All activities are executed by the workflow runtime, not directly by their parent activity. The job of a composite activity such as `Parallel` or `Sequence` is to schedule their children for execution. Scheduling for execution means telling the workflow runtime a particular activity should be executed. The runtime queues those requests and executes them one at a time.

The scheduling algorithm that each composite activity implements is what makes it unique. For example, the `Sequence` activity is designed to execute each child activity in the defined order. It schedules the first child for execution and then waits for it to complete. When the first child has completed, the second child is scheduled for execution and so on. In contrast with this, the `Parallel` activity immediately schedules all branch activities for execution. It doesn't wait for the first branch to complete before it schedules the next.

This means that the actual order in which the child activities are executed greatly depends on the kind of work that they perform. For example, consider the `Parallel` activity illustrated in Figure 5-4.

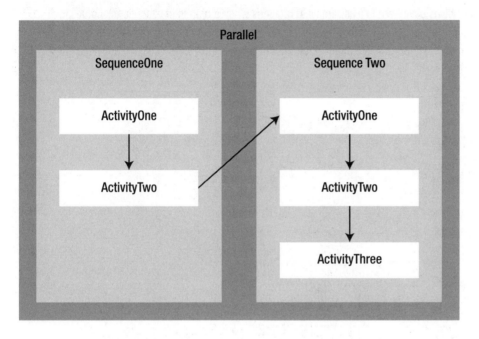

Figure 5-4. Parallel activity

In this illustration, a `Parallel` activity has two child `Sequence` activities defined. The `SequenceOne` activity has two child activities, and `SequenceTwo` has three. When the `Parallel` activity begins to execute, it immediately schedules the two `Sequence` activities for execution. As the arrows indicate, the `SequenceOne` activity begins execution by scheduling its first child activity (`ActivityOne`) for execution. When it completes, `ActivityTwo` is scheduled for execution. When `ActivityTwo` completes, the work of `SequenceOne` is complete, and `SequenceTwo` (which was already scheduled for execution) begins execution. `SequenceTwo` can begin execution only once `SequenceOne` yields control over the workflow thread. In this example, that occurs only once `SequenceOne` has completed the processing of all of its children. Once it begins execution, `SequenceTwo` continues to schedule its remaining children for execution until all of them have been processed.

In this example, the `Parallel` activity didn't provide any real benefit. Because the work that was performed by these child activities never caused them to yield control of the workflow thread (become idle), no real parallel (interleaved) behavior can be observed. The `Sequence` activities don't relinquish control of the workflow thread until they have completed their work or are idle and waiting for input.

In contrast with this, Figure 5-5 illustrates the same set of activities with the addition of a `Delay` activity in `SequenceOne`. A `Delay` activity does exactly what you might expect based on its name. It introduces a configurable amount of delay to the execution. The most important feature of the `Delay` activity is that it causes the current branch of execution to relinquish control of the workflow thread. In essence, it informs the workflow runtime that it's idle for a short period of time and that the runtime can go ahead and execute any other work that has been scheduled.

■ **Note** The `Delay` activity is used here to illustrate what happens when a branch of execution becomes idle. There are other activities that can cause a workflow to become idle. As a rule of thumb, any time a workflow is waiting on some external input, it is idle. Examples of other activities are the WCF messaging activities that are discussed in Chapter 9.

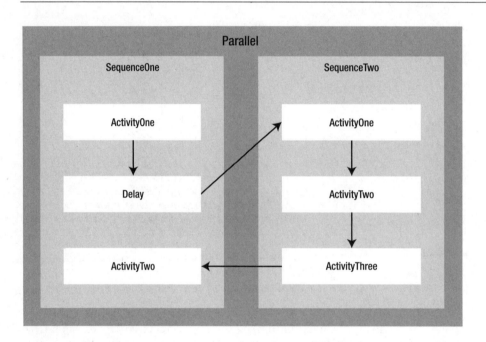

Figure 5-5. *Parallel activity with Delay*

As shown in Figure 5-5, the execution path is very different once the `Delay` activity is introduced. After executing `ActivityOne`, a short delay for `SequenceOne` begins when the `Delay` activity is executed. Since `SequenceOne` is now considered idle, control of the workflow thread is relinquished, and execution continues with the activities in `SequenceTwo`. Once all the activities in `SequenceTwo` have completed their work, execution returns to the remaining activity in `SequenceOne`.

In this example, the `Parallel` activity made a difference. Because the `SequenceOne` branch became idle, execution continued with the other branch of the `Parallel` activity. Without the `Parallel` activity, the entire workflow would have been idle for a short period of time when the `Delay` activity was executed.

■ **Caution** The actual execution sequence within a `Parallel` activity is not guaranteed. Because an execution branch may be required to wait for an external event, the actual execution sequence is unpredictable.

Creating the ParallelDemo Project

The purpose of this short example is to demonstrate the `Parallel` activity behavior that was just discussed. This example uses a `Parallel` activity that has two branches of execution, each defined by a `Sequence` activity. Each `Sequence` activity contains a set of `WriteLine` activities that each write a message to the console.

To implement this example, create a new project named `ParallelDemo`, and add it to the solution for this chapter. Use the Workflow Console Application template for the new project. For this example, you can use the `Workflow1.xaml` file that was created with the project.

Declaring the ParallelDemo Workflow

Follow these steps to declare the activities for this workflow:

1. Add a `Parallel` activity as the root of the workflow.

2. Add two `Sequence` activities as branches of the `Parallel` activity.

3. Add two `WriteLine` activities to the `Sequence` activity on the left side. Set the `Text` property of the two activities to `"Seq 1 Activity 1"` and `"Seq 1 Activity 2"`, respectively.

4. Add three `WriteLine` activities to the `Sequence` activity on the right side. Set the `Text` property to `"Seq 2 Activity 1"`, `"Seq 2 Activity 2"`, and `"Seq 2 Activity 3"`, respectively.

Figure 5-6 is the top-level view of the `Workflow1` workflow.

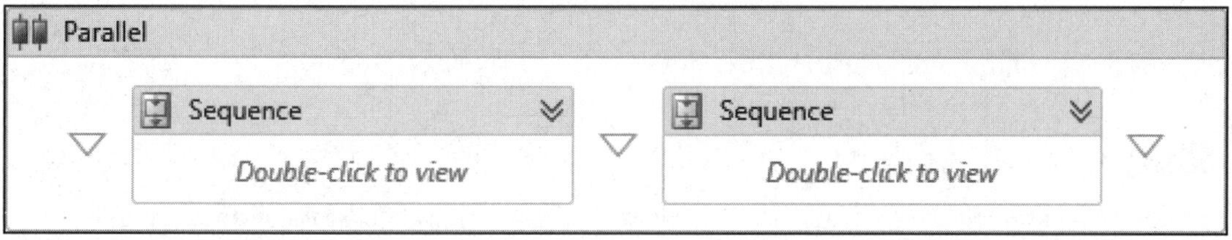

Figure 5-6. Workflow1

Hosting the Workflow

Here is the code for the `Program.cs` file in the `ParallelDemo` project that you need in order to execute this workflow. The code is similar to the default code that is generated when you create a new project.

```
using System;
using System.Activities;

namespace ParallelDemo
{
    class Program
    {
        static void Main(string[] args)
        {
            WorkflowInvoker.Invoke(new Workflow1());

            Console.WriteLine("Press any key to exit");
            Console.ReadKey();
        }
    }
}
```

Testing the Workflow

After building the `ParallelDemo` project, you should be able to run it and see these results:

```
Seq 1 Activity 1

Seq 1 Activity 2

Seq 2 Activity 1

Seq 2 Activity 2

Seq 2 Activity 3

Press any key to exit
```

These results mirror those illustrated in Figure 5-4.

Adding a Delay Activity

To complete the example, you will add a `Delay` activity to the workflow. Please follow these steps to modify the `Workflow1` workflow:

1. Open the `Workflow1` workflow in the designer, and navigate to the `Sequence` activity on the left side.

2. Add a `Delay` activity between the first and second `WriteLine` activities.

3. The `Delay.Duration` property is used to set the amount of delay and is defined as a `TimeSpan`. Set this property to `TimeSpan.FromSeconds(1)` to create a one-second delay.

Figure 5-7 shows the `Sequence` activity on the left side after the `Delay` has been added.

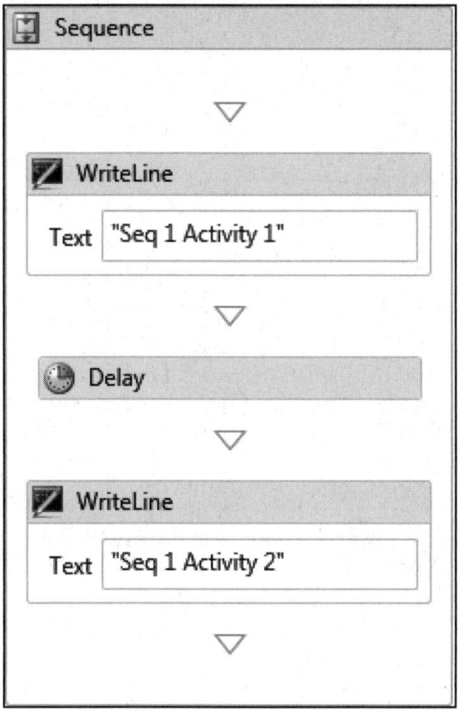

Figure 5-7. Workflow1 with Delay

Testing the Revised Workflow

Build and run the project to see these results:

```
Seq 1 Activity 1

Seq 2 Activity 1

Seq 2 Activity 2

Seq 2 Activity 3

Seq 1 Activity 2

Press any key to exit
```

These results correspond to the illustration in Figure 5-5.

Using the Parallel Activity

Now that you have an understanding of how the `Parallel` activity works, it's time to use it in a slightly more realistic example. In this example, you will revisit the `InventoryLookup` custom activity that you implemented earlier in the chapter. You will create a new workflow that uses the `InventoryLookup` within a `Parallel` activity instead of a `While` activity.

The purpose of this workflow also changes slightly. Earlier in the chapter, the purpose of the `GetItemInventory` workflow was to determine whether the requested quantity was available for an item using any combination of warehouses. In this new example, the purpose is to find a single warehouse that can satisfy the requested quantity for an item. The assumption in this scenario is that the order must be shipped from a single warehouse.

Creating the GetItemLocation Project

Begin this example by creating a new project named `GetItemLocation`. Use the Workflow Console Application project template, and add the new project to the solution for this chapter. Delete the `Workflow1.xaml` file, and add a project reference to the `ActivityLibrary` project, which should be in the same solution. Add a new workflow named `GetItemLocation` to the project using the Activity add item template.

Declaring the GetItemLocation Workflow

This workflow uses three branches of execution within a `Parallel` activity. Each branch is represented by a `Sequence` activity that contains the activities to query a single warehouse. Each `Sequence` activity contains an `InventoryLookup` instance and an `If` activity. The `If.Then` property contains another `Sequence` that has two `Assign` activity instances. The `Parallel` activity is used to query the inventory for an item from all three warehouses in parallel. The first warehouse that can fill the requested quantity for the item wins.

Begin the workflow declaration by adding these arguments:

Name	Direction	Argument Type
ArgItemId	In	Int32
ArgQuantity	In	Int32
ArgQuantityFound	Out	Int32
ArgWarehouseIdFound	Out	Int32

In the steps that follow, you will declare the first branch of execution and then copy it to create a total of three branches. Please follow these steps to declare the workflow:

1. Add a `Parallel` activity as the root of the workflow.

2. Add a single `Sequence` activity to the `Parallel` activity. Change the `Sequence.DisplayName` property to `Warehouse1`.

3. Add two `Int32` variables to the `Warehouse1 Sequence` activity. The first variable is named `WarehouseQty` and does not require a default value. The second variable is named `WarehouseId` and should have a default value of `1`. The scope for both variables is the `Warehouse1` activity.

4. Add a `WriteLine` activity to the `Sequence` activity. Set the `Text` property to `String.Format("Warehouse {0} InventoryLookup", WarehouseId)`.

5. Add an `InventoryLookup` activity under the `WriteLine` activity. Set the properties of the `InventoryLookup` to the values shown here:

Property Name	Value
ItemId	ArgItemId
RequestedQty	ArgQuantity
Result	WarehouseQty
WarehouseId	WarehouseId

183

6. Add another `WriteLine` activity under the `InventoryLookup` activity. Set the `Text` property to `String.Format("Warehouse {0} If", WarehouseId)`.

7. Add an `If` activity under the `WriteLine` activity. Set the `If.Condition` to `WarehouseQty = ArgQuantity And ArgQuantityFound = 0`.

8. Add a `Sequence` activity to the `If.Then` property.

9. Add an `Assign` activity to the `Sequence` activity. Set the `Assign.To` property to `ArgQuantityFound` and the `Assign.Value` property to `WarehouseQty`.

10. Add another `Assign` activity to the `Sequence` activity. Set the `Assign.To` property to `ArgWarehouseIdFound` and the `Assign.Value` property to `WarehouseId`.

11. Navigate back to the `Parallel` activity. Copy the `Warehouse1 Sequence` activity and paste the copy as a second branch to the `Parallel` activity. Change the `DisplayName` property of the copied `Sequence` activity to `Warehouse2`.

12. The copied `Sequence` activity should have its own set of copied variables that are now scoped by `Warehouse2`. Change the default value of the `WarehouseId` variable from `1` to `2`.

13. Make another copy of the `Warehouse1 Sequence` activity, and add it as a third branch to the `Parallel` activity. Change the `DisplayName` to `Warehouse3`, and change the `WarehouseId` variable from `1` to `3`.

14. Set the `Parallel.CompletionCondition` property to `ArgQuantityFound = ArgQuantity`. This condition is evaluated each time a branch of execution completes. If the condition is true, all other branches of execution are canceled. In this case, when the requested quantity has been found, there is no need to check the other warehouses.

Figure 5-8 is the completed `Warehouse1 Sequence` activity. The other branches under the `Parallel` activity should look structurally the same.

Figure 5-8. Warehouse1 Sequence activity

Hosting the Workflow

To host this workflow, modify the `Program.cs` file in the `GetItemLocation` project to look like this:

```
using System;
using System.Activities;
using System.Collections.Generic;

namespace GetItemLocation
{
    class Program
    {
        static void Main(string[] args)
        {
            RunWorkflow(new GetItemLocation(), 100, 2);
            RunWorkflow(new GetItemLocation(), 100, 8);
            RunWorkflow(new GetItemLocation(), 100, 20);
            RunWorkflow(new GetItemLocation(), 100, 100);
            RunWorkflow(new GetItemLocation(), 200, 10);
            RunWorkflow(new GetItemLocation(), 300, 15);

            Console.WriteLine("Press any key to exit");
            Console.ReadKey();
        }

        private static void RunWorkflow(Activity workflow,
            Int32 itemId, Int32 quantity)
        {
            IDictionary<String, Object> output = WorkflowInvoker.Invoke(
                workflow, new Dictionary<string, object>
                {
                    {"ArgItemId", itemId},
                    {"ArgQuantity", quantity}
                });

            Console.WriteLine(
                "Item: {0} Requested: {1} Found: {2} Warehouse: {3}",
                    itemId, quantity, output["ArgQuantityFound"],
                    output["ArgWarehouseIdFound"]);
        }
    }
}
```

Just as you did previously for the `While` activity example, the workflow is executed a number of times. Each time a different combination of itemId and requested quantity are passed as input arguments.

Testing the Workflow

You should now be able to successfully build the `GetItemLocation` project and run it. When I execute it, I see these results:

```
Warehouse 1 InventoryLookup

Warehouse 1 If

Item: 100 Requested: 2 Found: 2 Warehouse: 1

Warehouse 1 InventoryLookup

Warehouse 1 If

Warehouse 2 InventoryLookup

Warehouse 2 If

Item: 100 Requested: 8 Found: 8 Warehouse: 2

Warehouse 1 InventoryLookup

Warehouse 1 If

Warehouse 2 InventoryLookup

Warehouse 2 If

Warehouse 3 InventoryLookup

Warehouse 3 If

Item: 100 Requested: 20 Found: 20 Warehouse: 3

Warehouse 1 InventoryLookup

Warehouse 1 If

Warehouse 2 InventoryLookup

Warehouse 2 If

Warehouse 3 InventoryLookup

Warehouse 3 If
```

```
Item: 100 Requested: 100 Found: 0 Warehouse: 0

Warehouse 1 InventoryLookup

Warehouse 1 If

Warehouse 2 InventoryLookup

Warehouse 2 If

Warehouse 3 InventoryLookup

Warehouse 3 If

Item: 200 Requested: 10 Found: 10 Warehouse: 3

Warehouse 1 InventoryLookup

Warehouse 1 If

Warehouse 2 InventoryLookup

Warehouse 2 If

Warehouse 3 InventoryLookup

Warehouse 3 If

Item: 300 Requested: 15 Found: 0 Warehouse: 0

Press any key to exit
```

The results are a bit noisy because of the WriteLine activities. But they do serve a purpose. They show that each Sequence activity under the Parallel activity was executed to full completion before moving on the next Sequence activity. This example doesn't exhibit any parallel behavior because none of the activities yields control of the workflow thread. Knowing how the Parallel activity works, these are the results that you should have expected. The results for each requested item and quantity are also correct.

Please note that the first test execution processed only the first warehouse. This is due to the CompletionCondition that was set for the Parallel activity. Since the first warehouse satisfied the requested quantity for the item, there was no need to continue processing with the other warehouses. Likewise, the second test execution was satisfied by the second warehouse, and processing stopped before the third warehouse was processed.

This workflow obviously doesn't take full advantage of the Parallel activity. The problem is that the InventoryLookup activity isn't implemented to perform its work asynchronously. That problem is solved in the next example.

Obtaining Asynchronous Execution with the Parallel Activity

If you do want true asynchronous parallel execution, you need an activity that was written to perform its work asynchronously. In this example, you will revisit the **InventoryLookup** activity. You will rewrite the activity using the **AsyncCodeActivity<TResult>** base class to take advantage of the capabilities of the **Parallel** activity. The goal is to perform the same work as before but to allow the query against all three warehouses to take place simultaneously.

Implementing the InventoryLookupAsync Activity

Add a new activity to the **ActivityLibrary** project using the Code Activity new item template. Name this new activity **InventoryLookupAsync**. The code that you need for this new activity is shown next.

■ **Tip** Much of the code for this activity can be copied from the original **InventoryLookup** activity that was presented earlier in the chapter.

```
using System;
using System.Activities;
using System.Collections.Generic;

namespace ActivityLibrary
{
```

The code first defines an internal class that is used to pass the arguments to a worker thread. The activity class itself is derived from the **AsyncCodeActivity<TResult>** base class and specifies **Int32** as the type for the **Result OutArgument**. As was the case with the original version of this activity, a set of test data is populated during construction of the class.

```
    internal class InventoryLookupAsyncArgs
    {
        public Int32 ItemId { get; set; }
        public Int32 WarehouseId { get; set; }
        public Int32 RequestedQty { get; set; }
    }

    public class InventoryLookupAsync : AsyncCodeActivity<Int32>
    {
        public InArgument<Int32> ItemId { get; set; }
        public InArgument<Int32> WarehouseId { get; set; }
        public InArgument<Int32> RequestedQty { get; set; }

        private Dictionary<Int32, Dictionary<Int32, Int32>> _warehouses
            = new Dictionary<Int32, Dictionary<Int32, Int32>>();
```

```
public InventoryLookupAsync()
{
    //load some test data
    _warehouses.Add(1, new Dictionary<int, int>
    {
        {100, 5},
        {200, 0},
        {300, 0},
    });

    _warehouses.Add(2, new Dictionary<int, int>
    {
        {100, 10},
        {200, 0},
        {300, 0},
    });

    _warehouses.Add(3, new Dictionary<int, int>
    {
        {100, 50},
        {200, 75},
        {300, 0},
    });
}
```

The BeginExecute method follows the same pattern that you first saw in Chapter 3. An instance of the InventoryLookupAsyncArgs class is populated with the input arguments since they can only be retrieved on the workflow thread. A Func delegate is defined that takes an instance of the arguments class and returns an Int32. This delegate is assigned to a private Lookup method of this class that matches the delegate definition. After assigning the delegate to the UserState property of the activity context, the delegate is asynchronously executed with a call to the BeginInvoke method.

```
protected override IAsyncResult BeginExecute(
    AsyncCodeActivityContext context,
    AsyncCallback callback, object state)
{
    InventoryLookupAsyncArgs parameters = new InventoryLookupAsyncArgs
    {
        ItemId = ItemId.Get(context),
        WarehouseId = WarehouseId.Get(context),
        RequestedQty = RequestedQty.Get(context),
    };

    Func<InventoryLookupAsyncArgs, Int32> asyncWork =
        args => Lookup(args);
    context.UserState = asyncWork;
    return asyncWork.BeginInvoke(parameters, callback, state);
}
```

The Lookup method is executed on a thread pool thread. It uses the arguments to look up the inventory for the requested item and quantity. The available inventory for the requested item is returned from the method.

```
private Int32 Lookup(InventoryLookupAsyncArgs args)
{
    Int32 availableInventory = 0;
    Dictionary<Int32, Int32> warehouse = null;
    if (_warehouses.TryGetValue(args.WarehouseId, out warehouse))
    {
        if (warehouse.TryGetValue(args.ItemId, out availableInventory))
        {
            if (availableInventory > args.RequestedQty)
            {
                availableInventory = args.RequestedQty;
            }
        }
    }
    return availableInventory;
}
```

The EndExecute method is invoked when the asynchronous work (the Lookup method) completes. This is your opportunity to complete the asynchronous processing of the delegate with a call to EndInvoke. The available inventory is returned from the EndInvoke method and is, in turn, returned from EndExecute. The value that is returned from this method is used to set the Result OutArgument of the activity.

```
protected override int EndExecute(
    AsyncCodeActivityContext context, IAsyncResult result)
{
    return ((Func<InventoryLookupAsyncArgs, Int32>)
        context.UserState).EndInvoke(result);
}
}
}
```

Modifying the GetItemLocation Workflow

To test this new asynchronous version of the custom activity, you need to make only a few changes to the existing GetItemLocation workflow (in the GetItemLocation project). You simply need to change all InventoryLookup activity references to InventoryLookupAsync. The easiest way to do this is by directly editing the Xaml file instead of using the designer. Please follow these steps:

1. Open the GetItemLocation.xaml file in Code View. This should open the XML editor rather than the designer.

2. Change all InventoryLookup references to InventoryLookupAsync. This will change the actual activity declarations as well as the string literals for three of the WriteLine activities.

Testing the Revised Workflow

After building the solution, you should be ready to execute the `GetItemLocation` project. Here are my results:

```
Warehouse 1 InventoryLookupAsync

Warehouse 2 InventoryLookupAsync

Warehouse 3 InventoryLookupAsync

Warehouse 1 If

Item: 100 Requested: 2 Found: 2 Warehouse: 1

Warehouse 1 InventoryLookupAsync

Warehouse 2 InventoryLookupAsync

Warehouse 3 InventoryLookupAsync

Warehouse 1 If

Warehouse 2 If

Item: 100 Requested: 8 Found: 8 Warehouse: 2

Warehouse 1 InventoryLookupAsync

Warehouse 2 InventoryLookupAsync

Warehouse 3 InventoryLookupAsync

Warehouse 1 If

Warehouse 2 If

Warehouse 3 If

Item: 100 Requested: 20 Found: 20 Warehouse: 3

Warehouse 1 InventoryLookupAsync

Warehouse 2 InventoryLookupAsync

Warehouse 3 InventoryLookupAsync
```

```
Warehouse 1 If

Warehouse 2 If

Warehouse 3 If

Item: 100 Requested: 100 Found: 0 Warehouse: 0

Warehouse 1 InventoryLookupAsync

Warehouse 2 InventoryLookupAsync

Warehouse 3 InventoryLookupAsync

Warehouse 1 If

Warehouse 2 If

Warehouse 3 If

Item: 200 Requested: 10 Found: 10 Warehouse: 3

Warehouse 1 InventoryLookupAsync

Warehouse 2 InventoryLookupAsync

Warehouse 3 InventoryLookupAsync

Warehouse 1 If

Warehouse 2 If

Warehouse 3 If

Item: 300 Requested: 15 Found: 0 Warehouse: 0

Press any key to exit
```

The results indicate that the warehouse that was chosen for each item and quantity are the same as the previous results. But clearly there is a significant difference in how those results were obtained. In this test, all three instances of the InventoryLookupAsync activity were started immediately, even though they were in three separate branches under the Parallel activity. Once the asynchronous work of each InventoryLookupAsync activity was completed, the corresponding If activity within the same branch was executed.

Since the work of looking up the inventory for a warehouse was executing asynchronously on another thread, the workflow thread was available to process other branches of execution. In this case, the combination of the `Parallel` activity and an activity that is capable of asynchronous work accomplishes much more than either activity can by itself.

As you saw in the original version of this workflow, the `CompletionCondition` of the `Parallel` activity was used to cancel additional processing once a satisfactory warehouse was found.

■ **Tip** You will receive the most significant benefit from the `Parallel` activity when its child activities yield control of the workflow thread. The child activities could be asynchronous activities that perform work on a separate thread, or they could be other activities that become idle because they are waiting for external input.

Summary

This chapter focused on the procedural activities that are most frequently used for branching and looping. The `If` and `Switch<T>` activities were discussed first. They are used to make decisions that affect the flow of execution within a workflow. The `While` and `DoWhile` activities implement looping patterns and were demonstrated next. The chapter concluded with a discussion of the `Parallel` activity, which supports parallel scheduling and interleaved execution of multiple branches. The `Delay` activity allows you to introduce a short delay into the execution of a workflow. This activity was used in the `Parallel` activity examples.

In the next chapter, you will learn about additional procedural activities that are used for data driven flow control and collection management.

CHAPTER 6

■ ■ ■

Collection-Related Activities

This chapter focuses on the activities that enable you to work with collections of data. Windows Workflow Foundation (WF) includes a ForEach<T> activity that iterates over each element in a collection, executing the same activity for each element. WF also includes a parallel version of this activity and a set of activities that allow you to manipulate collections, adding and removing elements and so on. After a brief summary of these activities, this chapter presents an example that demonstrates their use.

The standard activities provided with WF are designed to work with simple collections, not dictionaries. To demonstrate one way to work with dictionaries, this chapter presents a set of custom activities. It then presents the original example workflow again using a dictionary instead of a collection.

Finally, the chapter ends with a discussion and demonstration of the InvokeMethod activity. This activity allows you to declaratively invoke an instance or static method.

Understanding the ForEach<T> Activity

The first collection-related activity that I'll cover is ForEach<T>. Conceptually, it is designed to operate in a similar way to the foreach C# keyword. The foreach keyword allows you to iterate over the elements in a collection, executing the same block of code for each element. In a similar way, the ForEach<T> activity iterates over a collection (defined as either an argument or a variable) and executes a child activity for each element in the collection.

Here are the most important properties of the ForEach<T> activity:

Property	Type	Required	Description
Values	InArgument<IEnumerable<T>>	Yes	The input collection to be processed
Body	ActivityAction<T>	Yes	An ActivityAction<T> that points to the activity that you want to execute for each element

To use the generic ForEach<T> activity, you first specify the generic type that identifies the type of elements in the collection. You then set the ForEach.Values property to an argument or variable that is a collection of the correct type. Finally, you add an activity to the ForEach.Body property. This activity will be executed once for each element in the collection. Of course, this activity can be a composite activity like Sequence that contains other child activities to execute.

The activity that you specify for the `Body` property has access to a named argument that represents the element to process. For more information on the plumbing that WF uses to make this work, please see the "Supplying Arguments with an `ActivityAction`" sidebar in this chapter.

■ **Note** When the `ForEach<T>` activity executes, a single instance of the `Body` activity is constructed. That same instance is used to process all elements in the collection.

WF also includes a `ParallelForEach<T>` activity, which is used in the same way as `ForEach<T>` with one big exception. The `ForEach<T>` activity processes one element from the collection at a time. It schedules execution of the activity specified in the `ForEach.Body` property for each element. Execution of the `Body` activity isn't scheduled for the next element until execution for the first element has completed.

In contrast with this, the `ParallelForEach<T>` activity immediately processes all the elements in the collection by scheduling execution of the `Body` activity for each of them. This means that depending on the type of work done by the `Body` activity, you may experience simultaneous execution of the `Body` activity.

The following are the most important properties of the `ParallelForEach<T>` activity:

Property	Type	Required	Description
Value	InArgument<IEnumerable<T>>	Yes	The input collection to be processed
Body	ActivityAction<T>	Yes	An ActivityAction<T> that points to the activity that you want to execute for each element
CompletionCondition	Activity<bool>	No	An optional condition that is evaluated after completion of each iteration

The `ParallelForEach<T>` activity also includes an optional `CompletionCondition` property. Normally, the `ParallelForEach<T>` activity completes when all elements in the collection have been processed. By supplying a Boolean condition for this property, you can short-circuit the normal completion logic. If defined, this condition is evaluated each time the `Body` activity is completed for one of the elements. If the condition evaluates to true, no additional processing takes place for the other elements. Any work that has already been scheduled is canceled.

Supplying Arguments with an ActivityAction

The ForEach<T> and ParallelForEach<T> activities define the Body property as an ActivityAction<T> instead of referencing an activity directly. An ActivityAction<T> works in a similar way to the C# Action<T> delegate. An Action<T> allows you to define a delegate that takes a single parameter and does not return a value. By assigning code to this delegate (via a named method, anonymous method, or Lambda expression), you can indirectly execute the code via execution of the delegate. The generic argument (T) identifies the type of the parameter that is passed to the code as an argument.

The ActivityAction<T> serves a similar purpose. It enables indirect execution of another activity, making available a single argument of type T. WF includes a number of ActivityAction classes, with each one supporting a different number of arguments that are made available to the target activity. The ForEach<T> and ParallelForEach<T> activities use the version of ActivityAction that support a single argument.

The ForEach<T> and ParallelForEach<T> activities use an ActivityAction<T> in order to provide a named argument that can be consumed by the target activity. The named argument represents the current element in the collection that is being processed. Without the ActivityAction<T>, the target activity wouldn't have a way to reference each individual element as it is processed.

For example, here is a selected portion of Xaml from one of the examples that you will see later in this chapter:

```
<ForEach x:TypeArguments="a:ItemInventory"
    DisplayName="PrintInventory" Values="[ArgInventory]">
  <ActivityAction x:TypeArguments="a:ItemInventory">
    <ActivityAction.Argument>
      <DelegateInArgument x:TypeArguments="a:ItemInventory" Name="item" />
    </ActivityAction.Argument>
    <WriteLine
        Text="[String.Format(&quot;Item {0} beginning inventory: {1}&quot;,
            item.ItemId, item.QuantityOnHand)]" />
  </ActivityAction>
</ForEach>
```

In this example, an ActivityAction<T> with a single named argument of type ItemInventory is defined under the ForEach<T> activity. The argument is named item. The actual child activity that you want to execute (WriteLine in this case) is able to reference the current element in an expression using this named argument. The argument (item) is available only within the scope of this particular ForEach<T> activity and cannot be used elsewhere. The good news is that most of this complexity is handled for you by the workflow designer.

You will see the ForEach<T> and ParallelForEach<T> activities in action later in the chapter. But before I can present the first example, you need to learn about the other collection-related activities.

Understanding the Collection Activities

The ForEach<T> and ParallelForEach<T> activities allow you to iterate over the elements in a collection. WF also includes a set of standard activities that enable you to perform common operations on a collection. Here is a quick recap of the available activities and their purpose:

Activity	Description
AddToCollection<T>	Adds a new element to a collection
RemoveFromCollection<T>	Removes an existing element from a collection
ExistsInCollection<T>	Tests whether an element exists in a collection
ClearCollection<T>	Removes all elements from a collection

All of these activities are generics, requiring you to specify the type of object that is contained within the collection. These activities reference the target collection using the Collection property. This property is typed as InArgument<ICollection<T>>; therefore, any collection that implements the ICollection<T> generic interface can be used. The collection that you reference can be a variable or argument.

Here are the most important properties of the AddToCollection<T> activity:

Property	Type	Required	Description
Collection	InArgument<ICollection<T>>	Yes	The collection to manipulate
Item	InArgument<T>	Yes	The new element to add to the collection

The AddToCollection.Item property is used to supply the new element that you want to add to the collection. It can reference a variable or argument, or you can construct the new object directly in an expression.

The RemoveFromCollection<T> activity supports a similar set of properties:

Property	Type	Required	Description
Collection	InArgument<ICollection<T>>	Yes	The collection to manipulate
Item	InArgument<T>	Yes	The existing element to remove from the collection
Result	OutArgument<Boolean>	No	True if the specified element was found and removed from the collection

In addition to the `Collection` and `Item` properties, the `RemoveFromCollection` activity also includes a Boolean `Result` property. This property can be checked to determine whether the remove operation was successful.

The `ExistsInCollection<T>` doesn't update the collection but is instead used to determine whether an element exists in the collection. These are the most important properties supported by the `ExistsInCollection` activity:

Property	Type	Required	Description
Collection	InArgument<ICollection<T>>	Yes	The collection to test
Item	InArgument<T>	Yes	The element to locate in the collection
Result	OutArgument<Boolean>	No	True if the specified element was found in the collection

Finally, the `ClearCollection<T>` activity can be used to remove all elements from a collection. Here is the most important property for this activity:

Property	Type	Required	Description
Collection	InArgument<ICollection<T>>	Yes	The collection to clear

■ **Tip** Missing from this set of activities is the ability to find and retrieve an existing element from a collection. The `ExistsInCollection<T>` activity can be used to determine whether an element exists in the collection, but it doesn't provide a way to retrieve the element when it does exist. This may not be important if you are working with a collection of simple intrinsic types, but it seems like a glaring omission if you are working with more complex types and need the ability to retrieve or update an existing object in a collection. To solve this, you will implement a custom `FindInCollection<T>` activity in the example that follows.

These activities make it very easy to declaratively work with collections. However, be aware of the potential performance implications of using activities such as `ExistsInCollection<T>` and `RemoveFromCollection<T>`. The actual mechanism used to locate the specified element in the collection depends on the implementation of the particular collection. Of course, these same performance concerns also apply when you are working with collections directly in code. For example, if your collection is a `List<T>`, a default comparer is used to locate the element in the collection. This will likely mean iterating over the entire collection to find the element that you want to process. In a very large collection, that may result in a performance penalty.

The examples that are presented in the next few sections demonstrate how to use several of these collection-related activities.

Using the ForEach<T> and Collection Activities

The example that follows demonstrates the use of the `ForEach<T>` activity along with several of the collection-related activities that were just discussed. The scenario for this example is an inventory update workflow. The workflow is passed two collections as arguments. The first collection contains the available inventory for several items and is the collection that is updated by the workflow. The second collection contains individual item sales. The quantity for each item sold is used to reduce the available inventory for that item.

The workflow also handles the peculiar situation where an item has been sold but is not in the collection representing the available inventory. In cases like this, the updated inventory is a negative amount.

Here are the steps that you will follow to implement this example:

1. Implement simple C# classes to represent the item inventory and sales history.

2. Implement a new custom activity to locate and retrieve an element in a collection.

3. Declare a workflow to update a collection of item inventory elements.

4. Host and test the workflow.

Creating the ActivityLibrary Project

To begin this example, create a new project named `ActivityLibrary` using the Activity Library template. Add it to a new solution that is named for this chapter. You can delete the `Activity1.xaml` file since it won't be needed. This project will be used throughout this chapter and will house several custom activities as well as classes to define the item inventory and sales structures.

Implementing Item Structures

Add a new C# class to the `ActivityLibrary` project, and name it `ItemInventory`. This should be a normal C# class, not a workflow activity or class. This class defines the item inventory structure for a single sales item. A collection of these objects will be updated by the example workflow. Here is the code that you need for this class:

```
using System;

namespace ActivityLibrary
{
    public class ItemInventory : IEquatable<ItemInventory>
    {
        public Int32 ItemId { get; set; }
        public Int32 QuantityOnHand { get; set; }

        public bool Equals(ItemInventory other)
        {
```

```
        if (other == null)
        {
            return false;
        }
        else
        {
            return (this.ItemId == other.ItemId);
        }
    }
  }
}
```

I've chosen to have this class implement the **IEquatable** interface. This interface represents a type-safe way to check for the equality of two objects of the same type. If an object implements this interface, the **Equals** method that is defined by the interface is used by the collection-related activities to determine object equality.

If you don't provide this interface or override the default **Object.Equals** method, the default behavior is a reference equality check (both objects referencing the same instance). For this example, you need the ability to determine whether two of these objects are the same based on the value of their **ItemId**.

You also need to implement a class that defines the individual sales that are applied to the inventory collection. Add another C# class to the same project, and name it **SalesHistory**. Here is the code you need for this class:

```csharp
using System;

namespace ActivityLibrary
{
    public class SalesHistory
    {
        public Int32 ItemId { get; set; }
        public Int32 Quantity { get; set; }
    }
}
```

Implementing the FindInCollection<T> Activity

This example requires the ability to find and update an existing **ItemInventory** object in a collection. You can use the **ExistsInCollection<T>** activity to determine whether the object is in the collection, but it doesn't provide a way to retrieve the object when it does exist. To remedy this situation, you will implement a custom activity that locates a requested object and returns it as a output argument that can be assigned to a workflow variable.

Add a new custom activity to the **ActivityLibrary** project, and name it **FindInCollection**. This is a code-based activity, so use the Code Activity new item template. Here is the code for this new activity:

```
using System;
using System.Activities;
using System.Collections.Generic;

namespace ActivityLibrary
{
    public class FindInCollection<T> : CodeActivity<Boolean>
    {
```

I follow the pattern established by the standard collection activities and define properties named Collection and Item. The Item property is the element that you want to find in the collection. The FoundItem property is an output argument that will reference the element that was found in the collection. The activity uses the generic form of CodeActivity as its base, so it also supports a Boolean Result property. This property is set to true if the requested element is found in the collection.

Note that I've added the RequiredArgument attribute to two of the properties. This presents an error to the developer if they fail to set values for these properties in the workflow designer.

```
        [RequiredArgument]
        public InArgument<ICollection<T>> Collection { get; set; }
        [RequiredArgument]
        public InArgument<T> Item { get; set; }
        public OutArgument<T> FoundItem { get; set; }

        protected override Boolean Execute(CodeActivityContext context)
        {
            Boolean result = false;
            FoundItem.Set(context, default(T));
            ICollection<T> collection = Collection.Get(context);
            T item = Item.Get(context);

            if (collection != null)
            {
                foreach (T entry in collection)
                {
```

The check for equality first determines whether the object implements the IEquatable interface. If it does, it calls the IEquatable.Equals method defined by that interface. If not, the standard Equals method that is defined by the Object class is invoked to test equality.

```
                    if (entry is IEquatable<T>)
                    {
                        if (((IEquatable<T>)entry).Equals(item))
                        {
                            FoundItem.Set(context, entry);
                            result = true;
                            break;
                        }
                    }
```

```
            else if (entry.Equals(item))
            {
                FoundItem.Set(context, entry);
                result = true;
                break;
            }
        }
    }
        return result;
    }
    }
}
```

If you haven't done so already, you should build the **ActivityLibrary** project to ensure that everything builds correctly and that this activity is made available in the Toolbox.

Declaring the InventoryUpdate Workflow

Add a new project named **InventoryUpdate** to the solution using the Workflow Console Application template. You can delete the **Workflow1.xaml** file that was generated for you since it won't be needed. Add a project reference to the **ActivityLibrary** project that should be in the same solution. You will be using a number of types that are defined in the **ActivityLibrary** namespace, so you might want to add this namespace to the Imports list for the workflow. Doing this avoids the need to fully qualify the types contained in this namespace.

Add a new workflow named **InventoryUpdate** to the project using the Activity template. This workflow will process two collections that are passed as arguments. The **ArgSales** argument is a collection of **SalesHistory** objects representing new sales that should be used to reduce the available inventory. The **ArgInventory** collection represents the available inventory for multiple items. Start the workflow declaration by adding these arguments to the workflow:

Name	Direction	Argument Type
ArgSales	In	IList<SalesHistory>
ArgInventory	In	IList<ItemInventory>

You can follow these steps to declare the remainder of workflow:

1. Add a **Sequence** activity to the empty workflow, and then add a **ForEach<T>** activity to the **Sequence** activity. Select **ActivityLibrary.ItemInventory** as the generic type for this activity. The purpose of this activity is to display the starting values for the inventory collection, so change the **DisplayName** property to **PrintInventory**. Set the **ForEach.Values** property to **ArgInventory**. Note that the default name of **item** will be used for the argument that represents each element in the collection. This argument can be referenced by any child activities.

2. Add a WriteLine as the child of the ForEach activity, and set its Text property to String.Format("Item {0} beginning inventory: {1}", item.ItemId, item.QuantityOnHand). Figure 6-1 shows the completed ForEach activity.

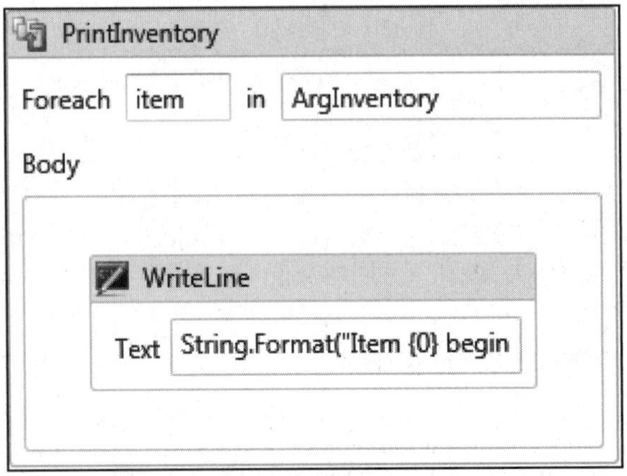

Figure 6-1. *PrintInventory activity*

3. Add another ForEach<T> activity to the Sequence activity, directly under the first ForEach activity (PrintInventory). This is the main ForEach<T> activity that will process updates to the inventory. Set the generic type to ActivityLibrary.SalesHistory. Set the ForEach.Values property to ArgSales.

4. Add a Sequence activity as the child of the ForEach. Add a Boolean variable to the Sequence activity that you just added, and name it IsItemExists.

5. Add a WriteLine activity to the Sequence activity (the one that is the child of the ForEach<T> activity) to display the individual sales transactions as they are processed. Set the Text property to String.Format("Sales item: {0} quantity: {1}", item.ItemId, item.Quantity).

6. Add an ExistsInCollection<T> activity under the WriteLine activity. Set the generic type to ActivityLibrary.ItemInventory. Set the Collection property to ArgInventory, the Result property to IsItemExists, and the Item property to this expression: New ActivityLibrary.ItemInventory With {.ItemId = item.ItemId}. This expression creates a new ItemInventory object using the ItemId from the current sales element. The new object is necessary only because an object of this type must be passed to the activity to determine whether the object already exists in the collection.

7. Add an If activity directly under the ExistsInCollection<T> activity. Set the Condition property to IsItemExists. Add Sequence activities to the If.Then and If.Else properties. Change the DisplayName of the If.Then Sequence activity to ExistsSequence and the DisplayName of the If.Else Sequence activity to NotExistsSequence to make it easier to distinguish these activities from others of the same type.

8. Add a new variable to the ExistsSequence activity named FoundItem with a type of ActivityLibrary.ItemInventory. This variable will reference the existing element in the collection that has been found.

9. Add an instance of the custom FindInCollection<T> activity to the ExistsSequence activity. Set the generic type to ActivityLibrary.ItemInventory. Set the Collection property to ArgInventory, the FoundItem property to FoundItem, and the Item property to New ActivityLibrary.ItemInventory() With {.ItemId = item.ItemId}.

10. Add an Assign activity directly below the FindInCollection<T> activity. This activity will reduce the inventory of the existing element that was just found. Set the Assign.To property to FoundItem.QuantityOnHand and the Assign.Value property to FoundItem.QuantityOnHand - item.Quantity.

11. Navigate to the NotExistsSequence activity that was added to the If.Else property. Add an AddToCollection<T> activity to this Sequence activity. Set the generic type to ActivityLibrary.ItemInventory. Set the Collection property to ArgInventory and the Item property to New ActivityLibrary.ItemInventory() With {.ItemId = item.ItemId, .QuantityOnHand = (0 - item.Quantity)}. This adds a new ItemInventory object to the collection with a negative available quantity.

Figure 6-2 shows the child Sequence activity of the ForEach<T> activity, while Figure 6-3 shows the main ForEach<T> activity. Figure 6-4 is a top-level view of the entire workflow.

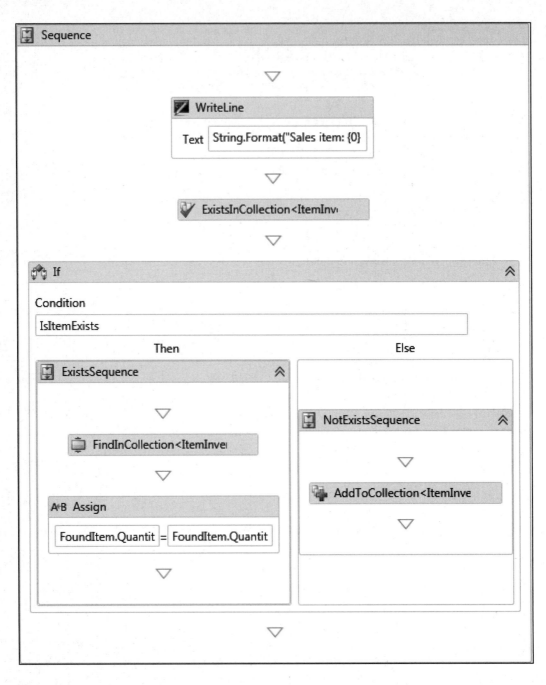

Figure 6-2. ForEach Sequence activity

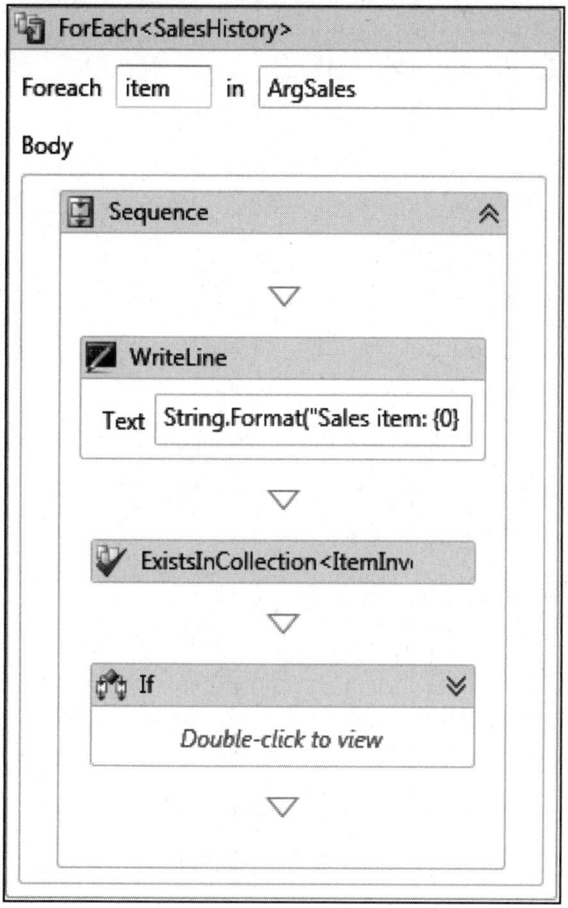

Figure 6-3. ForEach activity

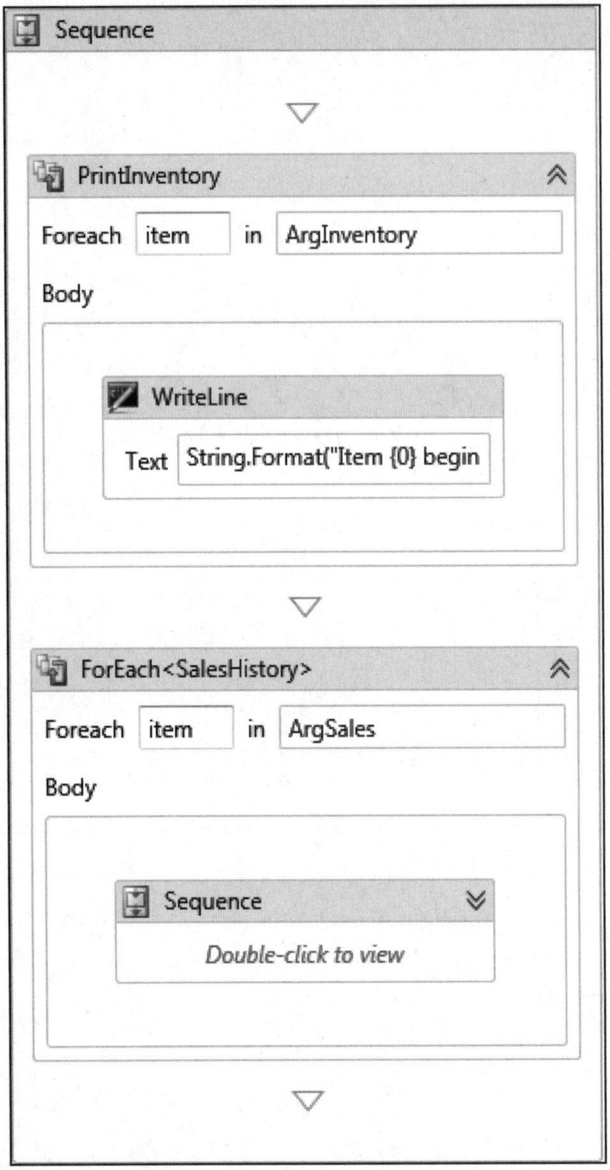

Figure 6-4. *InventoryUpdate workflow*

Hosting the Workflow

To host the workflow, open the `Program.cs` file in the `InventoryUpdate` project, and modify it to look like this:

```
using System;
using System.Activities;
using System.Collections.Generic;
using ActivityLibrary;

namespace InventoryUpdate
{
    class Program
    {
        static void Main(string[] args)
        {
            Console.WriteLine("Test InventoryUpdate...");
            RunWorkflow(new InventoryUpdate());

            Console.WriteLine("Press any key to exit");
            Console.ReadKey();
        }
```

The code to run the workflow creates two collections, one containing the available inventory by item and another containing individual item sales. Note that the sales history contains multiple sales for two of the items (`ItemId` 100 and 300). The final inventory for these two items should be reduced by all the sales history objects for each item. Also note that `ItemId` 300 doesn't currently exist in the collection of available inventory. Therefore, any sales posted against that item should result in a negative amount for the available inventory. Both of these collections are passed as arguments to the workflow.

```
        private static void RunWorkflow(Activity workflow)
        {
            List<SalesHistory> salesHist = new List<SalesHistory>
            {
                new SalesHistory{ItemId = 100, Quantity = 5},
                new SalesHistory{ItemId = 200, Quantity = 25},
                new SalesHistory{ItemId = 100, Quantity = 7},
                new SalesHistory{ItemId = 300, Quantity = 75},
                new SalesHistory{ItemId = 100, Quantity = 30},
                new SalesHistory{ItemId = 300, Quantity = 26},
            };

            List<ItemInventory> inventory = new List<ItemInventory>
            {
                new ItemInventory{ItemId = 100, QuantityOnHand = 100},
                new ItemInventory{ItemId = 200, QuantityOnHand = 200},
            };

            WorkflowInvoker.Invoke(workflow,
                new Dictionary<string, object>
                {
```

```
                {"ArgSales", salesHist},
                {"ArgInventory", inventory}
        });
```

After running the workflow, the ending item inventory is displayed in order to determine whether the workflow applied the updates correctly.

```
        foreach (ItemInventory item in inventory)
        {
            Console.WriteLine("Item {0} ending inventory: {1}",
                item.ItemId, item.QuantityOnHand);
        }
    }
  }
}
```

Testing the Workflow

You should now be able to build the solution and run the **InventoryUpdate** project. Here are my results when I run this project:

```
Test InventoryUpdate...

Item 100 beginning inventory: 100

Item 200 beginning inventory: 200

Sales item: 100 quantity: 5

Sales item: 200 quantity: 25

Sales item: 100 quantity: 7

Sales item: 300 quantity: 75

Sales item: 100 quantity: 30

Sales item: 300 quantity: 26

Item 100 ending inventory: 58

Item 200 ending inventory: 175

Item 300 ending inventory: -101

Press any key to exit
```

The results indicate that the updates were correctly applied to the available inventory. Since the inventory collection did not originally contain an object for item 300, a new instance was added with a negative inventory value.

Using the ParallelForEach<T> Activity

The `ParallelForEach<T>` activity works in a similar way as the `ForEach<T>` activity and supports the same properties. Therefore, the easiest way to see the `ParallelForEach<T>` activity in action is to modify the `InventoryUpdate` workflow from the previous example.

■ **Note** The instructions for this example assume that you are modifying the workflow from the previous example. If you prefer being able to compare the results from the two workflows side by side, you can make a copy of the `InventoryUpdate` workflow, rename it, and modify the copy.

Follow these steps to modify the `InventoryUpdate` workflow:

1. Open the `InventoryUpdate.xaml` file in Code View. This should open the file in the XML editor instead of the workflow designer. This file is located in the `InventoryUpdate` project.

2. The top level of this workflow contains two `ForEach<T>` activities. The first one displays the beginning inventory, and the second one processes the sales history and applies it to the inventory. Locate each `ForEach<T>` activity under the root `Sequence` activity, and change the activity name to `ParallelForEach`. Make sure you also change the closing element name for each activity.

Here is an abbreviated copy of the revised Xaml file showing the location of the `ParallelForEach<T>` activities:

```
<Activity>
…
  <Sequence>
    <ParallelForEach x:TypeArguments="a:ItemInventory"
        DisplayName="PrintInventory" Values="[ArgInventory]">
…
    </ParallelForEach>
    <ParallelForEach x:TypeArguments="a:SalesHistory"
        DisplayName="ParallelForEach&lt;SalesHistory&gt;" Values="[ArgSales]">
…
    </ParallelForEach>
  </Sequence>
</Activity>
```

If you close the workflow in the XML editor and open it in the designer, it should look like Figure 6-5.

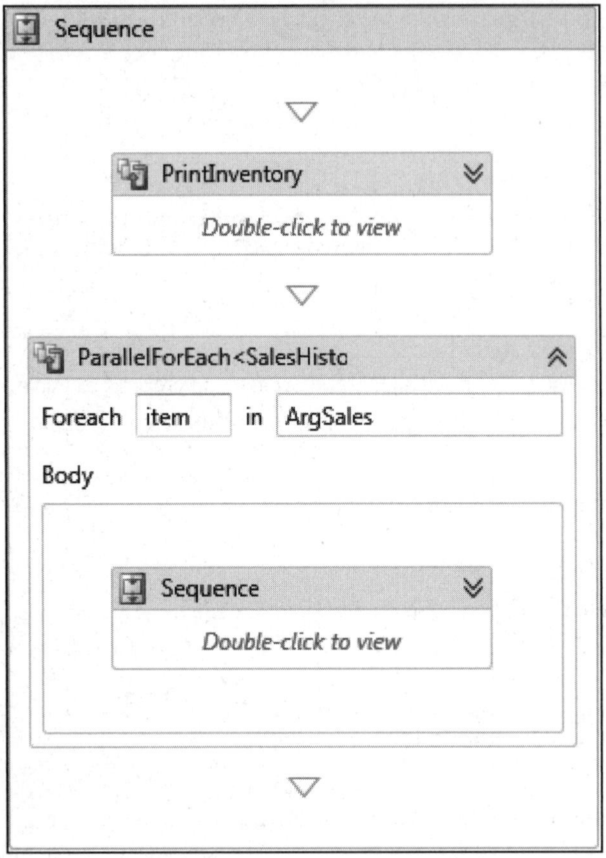

Figure 6-5. InventoryUpdate workflow using ParallelForEach

Testing the Revised Workflow

After building the solution, you should be ready to run the `InventoryUpdate` project. Here are the results that I see when the `ParallelForEach` activity is used:

```
Test InventoryUpdate...

Item 200 beginning inventory: 200

Item 100 beginning inventory: 100

Sales item: 300 quantity: 26
```

```
Sales item: 100 quantity: 30

Sales item: 300 quantity: 75

Sales item: 100 quantity: 7

Sales item: 200 quantity: 25

Sales item: 100 quantity: 5

Item 100 ending inventory: 58

Item 200 ending inventory: 175

Item 300 ending inventory: -101

Press any key to exit
```

The only difference between these results and those from the original version of the workflow is the sequence of the "beginning inventory" and "Sales item" lines. The difference in sequence is because of the way the `ParallelForEach<T>` activity immediately schedules execution of the child activity for all elements in the collection. The `ForEach<T>` activity schedules execution for the next element only after the current one has finished processing.

■ **Tip** Remember that the actual sequence in which the children of parallel activities are executed greatly depends on the type of work that they perform. In this case, none of the work was asynchronous or would have otherwise caused the workflow to become idle. If this was not the case, the actual execution sequence would have been much different. Please refer to the discussion of the `Parallel` activity in Chapter 5 for more information.

Working with Dictionaries

The standard WF activities provide good support for working with simple collections. However, they don't directly address the more specialized needs when you are working with dictionaries. The primary reason you would use a dictionary instead of a simple collection is the requirement to quickly locate any particular element based on its unique key. Of course, you can search for a particular element in a simple collection, but that search is likely implemented by iterating through all the elements. That can quickly become a performance problem if the collection contains thousands of elements.

Fortunately, it is fairly easy to implement a set of custom activities that work with dictionaries instead of simple collections. In this section, I present a set of custom activities that work in a similar way as the standard collection-related activities. After implementing the activities, I present a revised version of the `InventoryUpdate` workflow that uses a dictionary.

■ **Tip** The goal of this section is not to present a set of production-ready dictionary-related activities. I'm sure you will be able to easily improve on my code. These activities are presented to once again drive home the point that you should create your own custom activities. You should never feel that you are limited to using only the out-of-the-box activities provided with WF. If Microsoft hasn't provided an activity that meets your needs, just build it yourself.

Here are the steps that you will follow to implement this example:

1. Implement a set of custom dictionary-related activities.

2. Declare a workflow to update a dictionary of item inventory elements instead of a simple collection.

3. Host and test the workflow.

■ **Note** The downloadable code for this book includes a set of simple unit tests for these custom activities. I've omitted those tests from the book to keep the focus of this chapter on implementing and using the activities.

Implementing the Dictionary-Related Activities

Here is a quick recap of the custom dictionary-related activities that you will implement:

Activity	Description
AddToDictionary<TKey, TValue>	Adds a new element to a dictionary
RemoveFromDictionary<TKey, TValue>	Removes an existing element from a dictionary
ExistsInDictionary<TKey, TValue>	Tests whether an element exists in a dictionary
FindInDictionary<TKey, TValue>	Finds and returns an element from a dictionary
ClearDictionary<TKey, TValue>	Removes all elements from a dictionary

You will add all of these activities to the `ActivityLibrary` project that you created earlier in the chapter. They are all implemented in code, so you should use the Code Activity add item template when adding them to the `ActivityLibrary` project. Since the activities are very similar to each other, you'll find that copying part of the code from the first activity is a great way to implement the others.

Implementing AddToDictionary<TKey, TValue>

Here is the code to implement the AddToDictionary<TKey, TValue> activity:

```
using System;
using System.Activities;
using System.Collections.Generic;

namespace ActivityLibrary
{
    public class AddToDictionary<TKey, TValue> : CodeActivity
    {
        [RequiredArgument]
        public InArgument<IDictionary<TKey, TValue>> Dictionary { get; set; }
        [RequiredArgument]
        public InArgument<TKey> Key { get; set; }
        [RequiredArgument]
        public InArgument<TValue> Item { get; set; }

        protected override void Execute(CodeActivityContext context)
        {
            IDictionary<TKey, TValue> dictionary = Dictionary.Get(context);
            TKey key = Key.Get(context);
            TValue item = Item.Get(context);
            if (dictionary != null)
            {
                dictionary.Add(key, item);
            }
        }
    }
}
```

Notice that in addition to the Item argument, which was also implemented in the standard collection-related activities, a Key argument is included. This is needed since a dictionary requires you to set a unique key for each element. You'll see this additional argument in most of these custom activities.

Implementing RemoveFromDictionary<TKey, TValue>

Here is the code to implement the RemoveFromDictionary<TKey, TValue> activity:

```
using System;
using System.Activities;
using System.Collections.Generic;

namespace ActivityLibrary
{
    public class RemoveFromDictionary<TKey, TValue> : CodeActivity<Boolean>
    {
        [RequiredArgument]
        public InArgument<IDictionary<TKey, TValue>> Dictionary { get; set; }
```

```
    [RequiredArgument]
    public InArgument<TKey> Key { get; set; }

    protected override Boolean Execute(CodeActivityContext context)
    {
        Boolean result = false;
        IDictionary<TKey, TValue> dictionary = Dictionary.Get(context);
        TKey key = Key.Get(context);
        if (dictionary != null)
        {
            if (dictionary.ContainsKey(key))
            {
                result = dictionary.Remove(key);
            }
        }
        return result;
    }
  }
}
```

Implementing ExistsInDictionary<TKey, TValue>

Here is the code to implement the ExistsInDictionary<TKey, TValue> activity:

```
using System;
using System.Activities;
using System.Collections.Generic;

namespace ActivityLibrary
{
    public class ExistsInDictionary<TKey, TValue> : CodeActivity<Boolean>
    {
        [RequiredArgument]
        public InArgument<IDictionary<TKey, TValue>> Dictionary { get; set; }
        [RequiredArgument]
        public InArgument<TKey> Key { get; set; }

        protected override Boolean Execute(CodeActivityContext context)
        {
            Boolean result = false;
            IDictionary<TKey, TValue> dictionary = Dictionary.Get(context);
            TKey key = Key.Get(context);
            if (dictionary != null)
            {
                result = dictionary.ContainsKey(key);
            }
            return result;
        }
    }
}
```

Implementing FindInDictionary<TKey, TValue>

Here is the code to implement the FindInDictionary<TKey, TValue> activity:

```
namespace ActivityLibrary
{
    using System;
    using System.Activities;
    using System.Collections.Generic;

    public class FindInDictionary<TKey, TValue> : CodeActivity<Boolean>
    {
        [RequiredArgument]
        public InArgument<IDictionary<TKey, TValue>> Dictionary { get; set; }
        [RequiredArgument]
        public InArgument<TKey> Key { get; set; }
        public OutArgument<TValue> FoundItem { get; set; }

        protected override Boolean Execute(CodeActivityContext context)
        {
            Boolean result = false;
            FoundItem.Set(context, default(TValue));
            IDictionary<TKey, TValue> dictionary = Dictionary.Get(context);
            TKey key = Key.Get(context);
            if (dictionary != null)
            {
                if (dictionary.ContainsKey(key))
                {
                    FoundItem.Set(context, dictionary[key]);
                    result = true;
                }
            }
            return result;
        }
    }
}
```

Implementing ClearDictionary<TKey, TValue>

Here is the code to implement the ClearDictionary<TKey, TValue> activity:

```
using System;
using System.Activities;
using System.Collections.Generic;

namespace ActivityLibrary
{
    public class ClearDictionary<TKey, TValue> : CodeActivity
    {
        [RequiredArgument]
```

```
    public InArgument<IDictionary<TKey, TValue>> Dictionary { get; set; }

    protected override void Execute(CodeActivityContext context)
    {
        IDictionary<TKey, TValue> dictionary = Dictionary.Get(context);
        if (dictionary != null)
        {
            dictionary.Clear();
        }
    }
  }
}
```

■ **Note** Since a dictionary is technically also a collection, you can use the standard `ClearCollection<T>` activity to clear it. However, I've included the `ClearDictionary<TKey, TValue>` activity to round out a uniform set of dictionary-related activities. As an alternate implementation of the `ClearDictionary<TKey, TValue>` activity, you could use composition to wrap the `ClearCollection<T>` activity.

Declaring the InventoryUpdateDictionary Workflow

After building the solution to ensure that everything builds correctly, you are ready to implement a workflow that uses these new activities. The structure of this workflow will be similar to the `InventoryWorkflow` that you declared earlier in the chapter, and many of the steps needed to declare the workflow will be the same. The difference is that the collection of `ItemInventory` objects has been replaced with a dictionary of these objects. The collection-related activities that were previously used to manipulate this collection have now been replaced with the new dictionary-related activities that you just implemented. Most of the dictionary-related activities require an additional `Key` argument.

Instead of creating a new project, add a new workflow named `InventoryUpdateDictionary` to the existing `InventoryUpdate` project using the Activity add item template. Add these arguments to the workflow:

Name	Direction	Argument Type
ArgSales	In	IList<SalesHistory>
ArgInventory	In	IDictionary<Int32, ItemInventory>

Follow these steps to declare the remainder of workflow:

1. Add a `Sequence` activity to the empty workflow, and then add a `ForEach<T>` activity to the `Sequence` activity. Select `ActivityLibrary.ItemInventory` as the generic type for this activity. Change the `DisplayName` property to `PrintInventory`. Set the `ForEach.Values` property to `ArgInventory.Values`. Notice that you are iterating over the `Values` property of the `ArgInventory` dictionary instead of the dictionary itself. The `Values` property of a dictionary is exposed as a simple collection.

2. Add a `WriteLine` as the child of the `ForEach` activity, and set its `Text` property to `String.Format("Item {0} beginning inventory: {1}", item.ItemId, item.QuantityOnHand)`. The `PrintInventory` activity should look just like the one that you declared for the previous example that is shown in Figure 6-1.

3. Add another `ForEach<T>` activity to the `Sequence` activity, directly under the first `ForEach<T>` activity. This is the main `ForEach<T>` activity that will process updates to the inventory. Set the generic type to `ActivityLibrary.SalesHistory`. Set the `ForEach.Values` property to `ArgSales`.

4. Add a `Sequence` activity as the child of the `ForEach<T>`. Add a Boolean variable to the `Sequence` activity named `IsItemExists`.

5. Add a `WriteLine` activity to the `Sequence` activity to display the individual sales transactions as they are processed. Set the `Text` property to `String.Format("Sales item: {0} quantity: {1}", item.ItemId, item.Quantity)`.

6. Add an `ExistsInDictionary<TKey,TValue>` activity under the `WriteLine` activity. Set the generic types to `Int32` and `ActivityLibrary.ItemInventory`. Set the `Result` property to `IsItemExists`, the `Dictionary` property to `ArgInventory`, and the `Key` property to `item.ItemId`. This passes the `ItemId` of the current sales element to the activity for direct lookup based on the unique key.

7. Add an `If` activity directly under the `ExistsInDictionary<TKey,TValue>` activity. Set the `Condition` property to `IsItemExists`. Add `Sequence` activities to the `If.Then` and `If.Else` properties. Change the `DisplayName` of the `If.Then` `Sequence` activity to `ExistsSequence` and the `DisplayName` of the `If.Else` `Sequence` to `NotExistsSequence`.

8. Add a new variable to the `ExistsSequence` activity with a name of `FoundItem` and a type of `ActivityLibrary.ItemInventory`. This variable will reference the existing element in the collection that has been found.

9. Add an instance of the `FindInDictionary<TKey,TValue>` activity to the `ExistsSequence`. Set the generic types to `Int32` and `ActivityLibrary.ItemInventory`. Set the `Dictionary` property to `ArgInventory`, the `FoundItem` property to `FoundItem`, and the `Key` property to `item.ItemId`.

10. Add an `Assign` activity directly below the `FindInDictionary<TKey,TValue>` activity. This activity will update the inventory of the existing element that was just found. Set the `Assign.To` property to `FoundItem.QuantityOnHand` and the `Assign.Value` property to `FoundItem.QuantityOnHand - item.Quantity`.

11. Navigate to the NotExistsSequence activity that was added to the If.Else property. Add a generic AddToDictionary<TKey,TValue> activity to the Sequence activity. Set the generic types to Int32 and ActivityLibrary.ItemInventory. Set the Dictionary property to ArgInventory, the Key property to item.ItemId, and the Item property to New ActivityLibrary.ItemInventory() With {.ItemId = item.ItemId, .QuantityOnHand = (0 - item.Quantity)}.

Hosting the Workflow

To host this new workflow, you can revise the Program.cs file in the InventoryUpdate project. Instead of changing the existing code that executes the InventoryUpdate workflow, you can add a method that runs the new InventoryUpdateDictionary workflow and passes it a dictionary argument instead of a simple collection. Here is the revised code for the Program.cs file:

```
namespace InventoryUpdate
{
    class Program
    {
        static void Main(string[] args)
        {
...
```

Add these lines to execute the new workflow after the existing call to the RunWorkflow method:

```
            Console.WriteLine("\nTest InventoryUpdateDictionary...");
            RunDictionaryWorkflow(new InventoryUpdateDictionary());
...
        }
...
```

Add this new method to run the new workflow that uses a dictionary instead of a collection. You can copy the existing RunWorkflow method and change the definition of the inventory variable to a dictionary.

```
        private static void RunDictionaryWorkflow(Activity workflow)
        {
            List<SalesHistory> salesHist = new List<SalesHistory>
            {
                new SalesHistory{ItemId = 100, Quantity = 5},
                new SalesHistory{ItemId = 200, Quantity = 25},
                new SalesHistory{ItemId = 100, Quantity = 7},
                new SalesHistory{ItemId = 300, Quantity = 75},
                new SalesHistory{ItemId = 100, Quantity = 30},
                new SalesHistory{ItemId = 300, Quantity = 26},
            };
```

```
        Dictionary<Int32, ItemInventory> inventory
            = new Dictionary<int, ItemInventory>
        {
            { 100, new ItemInventory{ItemId = 100, QuantityOnHand = 100}},
            { 200, new ItemInventory{ItemId = 200, QuantityOnHand = 200}},
        };

        WorkflowInvoker.Invoke(workflow,
            new Dictionary<string, object>
            {
                {"ArgSales", salesHist},
                {"ArgInventory", inventory}
            });

        foreach (ItemInventory item in inventory.Values)
        {
            Console.WriteLine("Item {0} ending inventory: {1}",
                item.ItemId, item.QuantityOnHand);
        }
    }
  }
}
```

Testing the Workflow

After building the solution, you can run the **InventoryUpdate** project. It will first execute the current
version of the **InventoryUpdate** workflow (which should be the one that uses the **ParallelForEach<T>**
activity), followed by the new **InventoryUpdateDictionary** workflow. Here are the results that I see when
I run the revised project:

```
Test InventoryUpdate...

Item 200 beginning inventory: 200

Item 100 beginning inventory: 100

Sales item: 300 quantity: 26

Sales item: 100 quantity: 30

Sales item: 300 quantity: 75

Sales item: 100 quantity: 7

Sales item: 200 quantity: 25

Sales item: 100 quantity: 5
```

```
Item 100 ending inventory: 58

Item 200 ending inventory: 175

Item 300 ending inventory: -101


Test InventoryUpdateDictionary...

Item 100 beginning inventory: 100

Item 200 beginning inventory: 200

Sales item: 100 quantity: 5

Sales item: 200 quantity: 25

Sales item: 100 quantity: 7

Sales item: 300 quantity: 75

Sales item: 100 quantity: 30

Sales item: 300 quantity: 26

Item 100 ending inventory: 58

Item 200 ending inventory: 175

Item 300 ending inventory: -101

Press any key to exit
```

Understanding the InvokeMethod Activity

In the previous examples, the updates to the item inventory were accomplished using an expression that was entered in an `Assign` activity like this: `FoundItem.QuantityOnHand - item.Quantity`. Although this is a fine solution, WF also supports other mechanisms to accomplish the same goal. For example, WF allows you to declaratively invoke a public method on an object using the `InvokeMethod` activity. You can also use this activity to invoke a public static method that is defined for a type.

> ■ **Note** The `InvokeMethod` activity isn't directly related to the processing of data in collections and, as such, doesn't really follow the theme of this chapter. However, the examples in this chapter present an opportunity for improvement by using this activity, so I've presented this activity here.

Here are the most important properties of the `InvokeMethod` activity:

Property	Type	Required	Description
TargetObject	InArgument	See discussion	Identifies the object that implements the public instance method to be invoked
TargetType	Type	See discussion	The type that implements the static public method to be invoked
MethodName	String	Yes	The name of the public instance or status method to be invoked
Parameters	Collection<Argument>	No	A collection of parameters that are passed as arguments to the method
GenericTypeArguments	Collection<Type>	No	The generic type arguments for the method if it is a generic method
Result	OutArgument	No	The return value of the method if there is one
RunAsynchronously	Boolean	No	Set to true to execute the method asynchronously

The properties that you set for the `InvokeMethod` activity vary depending on whether you are invoking an instance or static method. If you are invoking an instance method, you must set the `TargetObject` property and the `MethodName`. If you are invoking a static method, you must set the `TargetType` and the `MethodName`. The `TargetObject` must not be set when you are invoking a static method. In either case, you set values for the arguments that are passed to the method using the `Parameters` property. Method arguments must be added to the `Parameters` collection in the same order as they are defined in the method signature. If the method is a generic method, you also need to identify types for each generic type defined by the method.

Using the InvokeMethod Activity

To demonstrate the `InvokeMethod` activity, you will revise the `InventoryUpdateDictionary` workflow that you declared in the previous example. Instead of reducing the inventory for an item using an expression, you will invoke a new method that you add to the ItemInventory class. And instead of creating a new ItemInventory object in an expression, you will invoke a new static factory method to create the object.

Revising the ItemInventory Class

Before you can invoke the new methods, they must be added to the ItemInventory class that you previously implemented (located in the ActivityLibrary project). Here are the additional methods that you should add to this class:

```
using System;

namespace ActivityLibrary
{
    public class ItemInventory : IEquatable<ItemInventory>
    {
...

        public void ReduceInventory(Int32 adjustment)
        {
            QuantityOnHand -= adjustment;
        }

        public static ItemInventory Create(Int32 itemId, Int32 quantity)
        {
            return new ItemInventory
            {
                ItemId = itemId,
                QuantityOnHand = quantity
            };
        }
    }
}
```

Build the solution before proceeding with the next steps.

Modifying the Workflow

Open the InventoryUpdateDictionary workflow in the designer, and follow these steps:

1. Navigate to the If activity that determines whether an existing inventory element should be updated or a new one is added.

2. Navigate to the Sequence activity under the If.Then property (named ExistsSequence). Delete the Assign activity that immediately follows the FindInDictionary activity since it is no longer needed.

3. Add an InvokeMethod activity where the Assign activity was located. Set the TargetObject property to FoundItem and the MethodName property to ReduceInventory. Add a single InArgument to the Parameters collection, using a type of Int32 and a value of item.Quantity. Figure 6-6 shows the revised ExistsSequence activity with the InvokeMethod activity.

Figure 6-6. Revised ExistsSequence

4. Navigate to the `NotExistsSequence` activity under the `If.Else` property. Add a new variable to this `Sequence` activity. Name the variable `NewItem` with a type of `ActivityLibrary.ItemInventory`.

5. Add an `InvokeMethod` activity as the first activity in the `Sequence` activity. Set the `TargetType` to `ActivityLibrary.ItemInventory` and the `MethodName` to `Create`. Set the `Result` property to `NewItem`. Add two `InArguments` to the `Parameters` property. The first argument is an `Int32` and has a value of `item.ItemId`. The second argument is also an `Int32` and has a value of `0 - item.Quantity`.

6. Make one change to the properties of the `AddToDictionary` activity. Set the expression for the `Item` property to `NewItem`. This will add the `ItemInventory` object that was constructed by the `InvokeMethod` activity to the collection. Figure 6-7 shows the revised `NotExistsSequence` with the `InvokeMethod` activity.

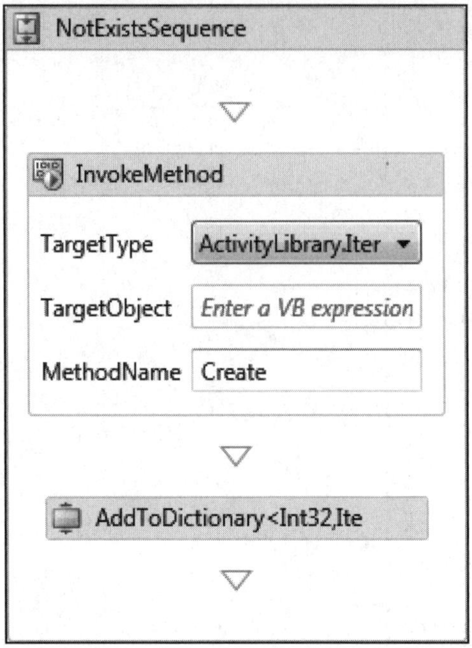

Figure 6-7. Revised NotExistsSequence

Testing the Workflow

After rebuilding the solution, you should be ready to test the revised workflow. When I run the InventoryUpdate project, I see the same results as before:

```
Test InventoryUpdate...

Item 200 beginning inventory: 200

Item 100 beginning inventory: 100

Sales item: 300 quantity: 26

Sales item: 100 quantity: 30

Sales item: 300 quantity: 75

Sales item: 100 quantity: 7

Sales item: 200 quantity: 25
```

```
Sales item: 100 quantity: 5

Item 100 ending inventory: 58

Item 200 ending inventory: 175

Item 300 ending inventory: -101


Test InventoryUpdateDictionary...

Item 100 beginning inventory: 100

Item 200 beginning inventory: 200

Sales item: 100 quantity: 5

Sales item: 200 quantity: 25

Sales item: 100 quantity: 7

Sales item: 300 quantity: 75

Sales item: 100 quantity: 30

Sales item: 300 quantity: 26

Item 100 ending inventory: 58

Item 200 ending inventory: 175

Item 300 ending inventory: -101

Press any key to exit
```

In this particular case, I think the use of the **InvokeMethod** activity makes a lot of sense. This is especially true when creating a new **ItemInventory** instance. Although you can construct a simple object like this using an expression, it seems more intuitive to implement a factory method to create new object instances. Doing so allows you to hide any initialization details in the code rather than having to deal with them in an expression.

Summary

The focus of this chapter was the activities that enable you to work with collections of data. The `ForEach<T>` and `ParallelForEach<T>` activities iterate over the elements in a collection, while the collection-related activities such as `AddToCollection<T>` and `ExistsInCollection<T>` work with the elements in the collection. The use of these activities was demonstrated in a series of example workflows and activities.

This chapter also presented a set of custom activities that are designed to work with dictionaries of data instead of simple collections. Using a dictionary provides potential performance improvements over a simple collection, especially when individual elements from a large collection must be located and updated.

The chapter concluded with a demonstration of the `InvokeMethod` activity. This activity allows you to invoke an instance method on an object or a static method defined for a type.

In the next chapter, you will learn about the flowchart modeling style and the activities that are provided to implement this style.

CHAPTER 7

Flowchart Modeling Style

The focus of this chapter is the flowchart modeling style. This style of modeling workflows enables you to use direct links between activities to control the flow of execution. In this chapter, I first review the activities that are provided with Windows Workflow Foundation (WF) to support this modeling style. After explaining how to model a workflow using this style, I revisit several examples that were presented in earlier chapters. This is done to contrast how the two modeling styles (procedural and flowchart) can be used to solve similar business problems.

Understanding the Flowchart Modeling Style

The modeling style that you choose determines how the flow of control between individual activities is modeled. WF provides activities that support two different workflow modeling styles: procedural and flowchart. The procedural modeling style uses familiar programming constructs to control the flow of execution and was discussed in Chapter 5.

The focus of this chapter is the flowchart modeling style. This style uses direct links between activities to control the flow of execution. This is in contrast with the control flow activities (`If`, `While`, `DoWhile`, `Switch`, and so on) that are used by the procedural modeling style to make branching and looping decisions.

As you will see when you work through the examples in this chapter, the two modeling styles can easily coexist, allowing you to mix and match the two styles throughout a workflow or activity. The flowchart modeling style is implemented as a set of activities rather than a particular project or workflow type. You can start with the flowchart modeling style by adding a `Flowchart` activity as the root of the workflow and then add procedural control flow activities where it makes sense. Likewise, you can start with a procedural activity such as `Sequence` and introduce the flowchart model in selected portions of the workflow or activity.

Both modeling styles have their place in the WF world. The procedural modeling style is rigid and structured and enables you to solve problems using programming constructs that are familiar to most developers. The flowchart modeling style is free-form and flexible and enables you to solve problems using concepts and constructs that are more easily understood by business analysts and application stakeholders. Developers also benefit from using the flowchart modeling style since it mimics the thought process that developers often use when they first attack a problem.

Using the Flowchart Modeling Style

The flowchart modeling behavior is implemented in this set of activities:

Activity	Description
Flowchart	The activity that enables the flowchart modeling style
FlowDecision	An activity that tests a Boolean condition and allows branching to other activities when the condition is true or false
FlowSwitch<T>	An activity that enables branching to different activities based on the value of a single expression
FlowStep	An activity that represents the individual steps in the flowchart

These activities are discussed in the following sections.

Flowchart Activity

This is the primary activity that must be used to enable the flowchart modeling style. It is the canvas that acts as a container for the other flowchart activities. It also supports the definition of variables.

This activity can be added as the root of a workflow or custom activity. But it can also be added to workflows that start with procedural activities. For example, your workflow may contain an activity such as the `While` activity that supports a single child activity. By adding a `Flowchart` activity as the child activity, you enable the use of the flowchart modeling style for that portion of the workflow model. This mixing and matching of styles is demonstrated in the final example of this chapter.

Here are the most important properties of the `Flowchart` activity:

Property	Type	Required	Description
StartNode	FlowNode	Yes	Identifies the starting node in the flowchart
Nodes	Collection<FlowNode>	No	The collection of steps in the flowchart

All flowcharts are made up of individual nodes. Each node represents a step in the workflow or custom activity. The `StartNode` property identifies the first node to execute and is required. When you first add a `Flowchart` activity, the `StartNode` property is already set for you to a default starting point, shown at the top of the activity in the designer view. You can change this to a different node, but you will rarely need to do this.

The `Nodes` property is a collection of `FlowNode` activities. The `FlowNode` class is the abstract base class for `FlowDecision`, `FlowSwitch<T>`, and `FlowStep`, which are discussed in the sections that follow.

FlowDecision Activity

The `FlowDecision` activity enables you to branch the flow of control based on a Boolean condition. You can branch to two different activities depending on whether the condition evaluates to true or false. You use this activity to make branching decisions based on a simple true or false condition.

Here are the most important properties of the `FlowDecision` activity:

Property	Type	Required	Description
Condition	Activity<Boolean>	Yes	The Boolean condition to evaluate
True	FlowNode	No	Execution passes to this activity when the condition is true
False	FlowNode	No	Execution passes to this activity when the condition is false

You can choose to declare an activity to execute when the condition is true, false, or both. Execution within a flowchart always follows the direct links between activities. If you haven't defined a path of execution for a particular condition, the work of the flowchart is complete. For example, if you don't define an execution path for the `FlowDecision.False` property and the condition evaluates to false, no additional activities in the flowchart are executed.

FlowSwitch<T> Activity

The `FlowSwitch<T>` generic activity works like the `Switch<T>` activity and the `switch` statement in C#. It allows you to specify a single expression and multiple branches based on the potential values of the expression. You use this activity when you need to make branching decisions based on an expression that can have several possible values.

Here are the most important properties of the `FlowSwitch<T>` activity:

Property	Type	Required	Description
Expression	Activity<Object>	Yes	The expression to evaluate
Cases	IDictionary<Object, FlowNode>	Yes	A collection of potential values for the expression and the nodes to branch to for each value
Default	FlowNode	No	A default branch of execution to be used if the expression does not match any of the values defined in the Cases property

The `FlowSwitch<T>.Cases` property defines the possible values for the expression. The `FlowSwitch<T>` is a generic activity and requires you to specify the type of value that you want to compare. Each case value that you enter must be of the specified generic type. If the value of the expression matches one of the case values, execution passes to the `FlowNode` defined for that value. You can optionally declare a default execution path to use when the expression doesn't match any of the defined values.

FlowStep Activity

The `FlowStep` activity is the glue used to declare transitions between nodes in the flowchart. These are the most important properties of the `FlowStep`:

Property	Type	Required	Description
Action	Activity	Yes	The activity to execute
Next	FlowNode	Yes	The next node in the flowchart that will be executed after the current Action activity

This activity is the container for nonflowchart activities and enables them to be used within a flowchart. For example, you can add one of the procedural activities such as a `Sequence` activity to a flowchart. To execute the nonflowchart activity, a `FlowStep` is first added, and the nonflowchart activity is added to the `FlowStep.Action` property.

You won't see the `FlowStep` activity in the Toolbox or see it explicitly shown on the design surface. Within the designer, each `FlowStep` is represented by the connecting lines between the individual activities.

Putting It All Together

After reviewing the flowchart activities along with their available properties, you might feel that declaring a flowchart is a cumbersome process. It isn't. To the contrary, the flowchart designer frees you from having to worry about most of these properties. In particular, you don't have to explicitly add `FlowStep` activities yourself; the flowchart designer takes care of that for you. As far as you are concerned, you're simply dropping activities on the Flowchart canvas and dragging links between them.

When you are working with a flowchart, you declare the flow of control by dragging and dropping a direct connection between two activities. You do this by hovering over one of the activities, causing the connection points to appear in the designer. Connecting two activities is as easy as clicking one of the connectors and dragging a connection to the target activity. As you drag the connection with your mouse, a connection line is shown to highlight the link that you are about to make between the activities. When you reach the target activity, its connection points are shown. Dropping the connection on one of the connection points links the two activities.

The same procedure is followed when you connect flowchart activities such as `FlowDecision` and `FlowSwitch<T>` to other activities. However, the connections from these activities each have a special meaning. In the case of the `FlowDecision`, the connection on one side of the activity represents the path of execution when the condition is true and the other side when the condition is false. When you are connecting a `FlowSwitch<T>` to other activities, each connection represents one of the possible values (a case) for the expression.

Flowcharts are designed to be free-form, but you should keep in mind a few general rules when you are working with them:

- All nodes must have at least one connection. A node in the flowchart without any connections can never be executed. This results in a build error.

- The `Flowchart` activity completes its work when it follows a path of execution without a connection to any other activities (a dead end).

- You can connect nonflowchart activities together in a flowchart. You are not limited to using only the flowchart activities (`FlowDecision`, `FlowSwitch<T>`).

■ **Tip** It is possible to construct a flowchart workflow entirely in code. However, the real benefit in using the flowchart modeling style is the ease in which you can visually declare the flow of control using direct connections between activities. The flowchart designer makes this ease of use possible. The flowchart modeling style is decidedly less friendly when you are using it in code. Therefore, although you can use the flowchart modeling style in code, I highly recommended using the workflow designer.

The Flowchart Workflow

In general, here are the steps that you should follow when declaring a workflow or custom activity using the flowchart modeling style:

1. Add a `Flowchart` activity to enable the use of the flowchart modeling style.

2. Declare input and output arguments.

3. Declare private variables.

4. Add nonflowchart activities to perform the required work, setting properties as necessary.

5. Add flowchart activities (`FlowDecision` and `FlowSwitch<T>`) as needed to make branching and looping decisions.

6. Add direct connections between activities to determine the path of execution.

Making Simple Decisions

To introduce you to the flowchart modeling style, you will revisit the command-line calculator example from Chapter 1. Implementing the same example will allow you to more easily contrast the two modeling styles. The example application prompts the user to enter an expression such as "1 + 1" or "3 * 5" that is passed to the workflow as a single string.

The goal of this example is to declare a workflow that calculates the result for simple arithmetic expressions (add, subtract, multiply, divide). In Chapter 1, the workflow was declared using the procedural modeling style. A `Sequence` activity was used as the root of the workflow, and a `Switch<T>` activity was used to control the flow of execution depending on the requested arithmetic operation.

In this chapter, the workflow will use the `Flowchart` activity as the root. You will use the `FlowSwitch<T>` activity to control the flow of execution. In both versions of this workflow, an `Assign` activity is used to return the calculated result for each operation. Both versions use the same custom activity to parse the arithmetic expression.

Implementing the ParseCalculatorArgs Activity

An arithmetic expression such as "1 + 1" is passed to the workflow as a single string. To process the expression, it must first be parsed into the two individual numbers and a string arithmetic operation. As you did in Chapter 1, you will implement a custom activity that parses the expression.

To implement the custom activity, create a new project named **ActivityLibrary** using the Activity Library template. Add it to a new solution that is named for this chapter. Delete the **Activity1.xaml** file since it is not needed. Add a new activity named **ParseCalculatorArgs** to the project using the Code Activity Add Item template. Here is the code that you need to implement this custom activity:

■ **Tip** The implementation for this activity is the same as the one in Chapter 1, so you should be able to make a copy of that code and use it for this example. The only minor difference is the namespace definition, since in Chapter 1, this activity was implemented directly in the console application. Please refer to Chapter 1 for a full description of this particular custom activity.

```
using System;
using System.Activities;

namespace ActivityLibrary
{
    public sealed class ParseCalculatorArgs : CodeActivity
    {
        [RequiredArgument]
        public InArgument<String> Expression { get; set; }
        public OutArgument<Double> FirstNumber { get; set; }
        public OutArgument<Double> SecondNumber { get; set; }
        public OutArgument<String> Operation { get; set; }

        protected override void Execute(CodeActivityContext context)
        {
            FirstNumber.Set(context, 0);
            SecondNumber.Set(context, 0);
            Operation.Set(context, "error");

            String line = Expression.Get(context);
            if (!String.IsNullOrEmpty(line))
            {
                String[] arguments = line.Split(' ');
                if (arguments.Length == 3)
                {
                    Double number = 0;
                    if (Double.TryParse(arguments[0], out number))
                    {
                        FirstNumber.Set(context, number);
                    }
                    Operation.Set(context, arguments[1]);
```

```
            if (Double.TryParse(arguments[2], out number))
            {
                SecondNumber.Set(context, number);
            }
        }
      }
    }
  }
}
```

Build the solution to ensure that this activity builds correctly. This also adds the activity to the Toolbox for later use in the workflow.

Creating the Console Project

Create a new project using the Workflow Console Application template. Name the project `FlowchartCalculator`, and add it to the current solution for this chapter. Delete the `Workflow1.xaml` file since it won't be needed. Add a project reference to the `ActivityLibrary` project, which should be in the same solution. Add a new workflow named `FlowchartCalculator` to the project using the `Activity` add item template. Add a `Flowchart` activity to the empty workflow.

Defining Arguments and Variables

The workflow requires a similar set of arguments and variables that you defined in the original version that you implemented in Chapter 1.

Name	Direction	Argument Type
ArgExpression	In	String
Result	Out	Double

The `ArgExpression` argument is the arithmetic expression that was entered by the user, and the `Result` is the return value from the workflow containing the result of the calculation.

Here are the variables that you need to define. All of them are scoped by the root `Flowchart` activity.

Name	Variable Type	Scope
FirstNumber	Double	Flowchart
SecondNumber	Double	Flowchart
Operation	String	Flowchart

Declaring the Workflow

Please follow these steps to declare the remainder of the workflow:

1. Add an instance of the `ParseCalculatorArgs` custom activity to the `Flowchart` activity. Set the `Expression` property to `ArgExpression`, the `FirstNumber` property to `FirstNumber`, the `SecondNumber` property to `SecondNumber`, and the `Operation` property to `Operation`.

2. Connect the starting point of the workflow to the top of the `ParseCalculatorArgs` activity. To accomplish this, hover over the starting point until a connection point appears. Drag and drop a connection from the starting point to a connection point at the top of the `ParseCalculatorArgs` activity. Dragging connections from one activity to another may take a bit of practice.

3. Add a `FlowSwitch<T>` activity to the workflow, selecting `System.String` as the generic type. Set the `FlowSwitch.Expression` property to `Operation`. This causes the `FlowSwitch<T>` to branch the flow of execution based on the parsed arithmetic operation (+, -, *, /). Add a connection from the `ParseCalculatorArgs` activity to the top of the `FlowSwitch<T>`.

4. Add an `Assign` activity to the workflow to handle the addition operation. Set the `Assign.To` property to `Result` and the `Assign.Value` property to `FirstNumber + SecondNumber`.

5. Add a connection from the `FlowSwitch<T>` to the `Assign` activity. Set the `Case` property to +. This identifies the value of the `FlowSwitch<T>.Expression` property that is associated with this path of execution. Make sure that the `Default` property on the connection is not checked.

■ **Warning** Even though you are entering a string literal for the Case property, you do not need to enclose it in double quotes. That's because this instance of the FlowSwitch<T> activity has its generic type set to System.String. Therefore, the Case values in this particular instance are assumed to be strings. The Case values must always be of the correct type as defined by the FlowSwitch<T>.

6. Repeat the last two steps for the other arithmetic operations (subtract, multiply, and divide). You will need to add three Assign activities, one for each operation. You will also need connections from the FlowSwitch<T> activity to each of the Assign activities. Make sure that the value used for the Case property of each connection (-, *, /) matches the calculation that you define for each Assign activity.

7. Add a Throw activity to the workflow. This activity will throw an exception if the parsed operation is invalid. Set the Throw.Exception property to New InvalidOperationException("Operation Invalid") to create the exception.

8. Connect the FlowSwitch<T> to the Throw activity. For this connection, do not specify a value for the Case property. Instead, set the Default property to true by setting the check box. This indicates that this is the default execution path if the FlowSwitch<T>.Expression property doesn't match any of the defined cases.

This completes the workflow definition. Your workflow should look similar to Figure 7-1. Don't worry if the activities are laid out in different positions. Build the solution to ensure that all required properties have been set.

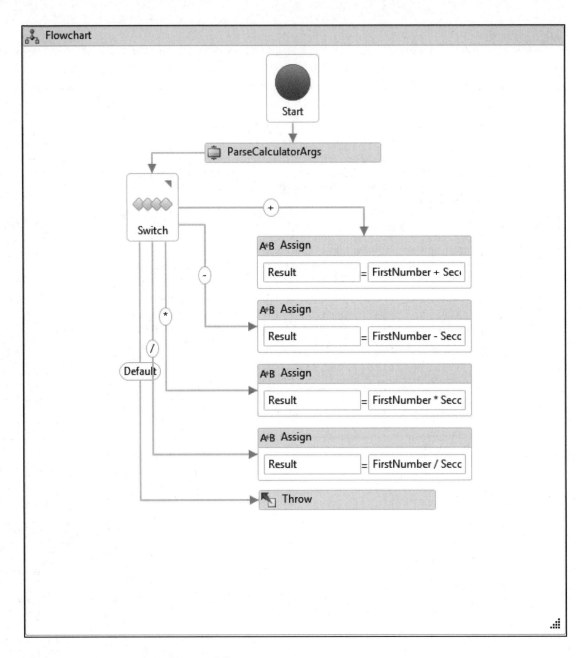

Figure 7-1. *FlowchartCalculator workflow*

■ **Note** You may have noticed that the visual layout of the activities in the flowchart is preserved when you reopen the workflow. If you take a look at the Xaml file for a flowchart workflow, you'll notice that the layout information is persisted along with the workflow declaration. There's no need for an additional layout file as was the case with 3.*x* workflows such as the state machine.

Hosting the Workflow

To implement the code to host the calculator workflow, open the **Program.cs** file in the **FlowchartCalculator** project, and revise it to look like this:

■ **Tip** The code should be similar to what you implemented to host the calculator example in Chapter 1. You should be able to copy that code and modify the namespace and the workflow name.

```
using System;
using System.Activities;
using System.Collections.Generic;

namespace FlowchartCalculator
{
    class Program
    {
        static void Main(string[] args)
        {
            while (true)
            {
                Console.WriteLine("Enter an expression or 'quit' to exit");
                String expression = Console.ReadLine();
                if (!String.IsNullOrEmpty(expression))
                {
                    if (expression.Trim().ToLower() == "quit")
                    {
                        Console.WriteLine("Exiting program");
                        return;
                    }
                }

                FlowchartCalculator wf = new FlowchartCalculator();
                wf.ArgExpression = expression;
```

```
            try
            {
                IDictionary<String, Object> results =
                    WorkflowInvoker.Invoke(wf);
                Console.WriteLine("Result = {0}", results["Result"]);
            }
            catch (InvalidOperationException exception)
            {
                Console.WriteLine(exception.Message.ToString());
            }
        }
    }
}
}
```

Testing the Workflow

After building the solution, you should be ready to test the calculator. Here is the output when I ran the application and entered a few representative test expressions:

```
Enter an expression or 'quit' to exit

5 + 3

Result = 8

Enter an expression or 'quit' to exit

100 - 75

Result = 25

Enter an expression or 'quit' to exit

8 * 7.56

Result = 60.48

Enter an expression or 'quit' to exit

123 / 2

Result = 61.5

Enter an expression or 'quit' to exit

1+1
```

```
Operation Invalid

Enter an expression or 'quit' to exit

quit

Exiting program

Press any key to continue . . .
```

The results should be consistent with the original version of this workflow that you declared in Chapter 1. Which implementation is better? In this particular case, they feel about equal to me; it really comes down to personal preference. One modeling style doesn't have any clear advantage over the other.

Declaring Looping Behavior

The previous example demonstrated how to make simple branching decisions using the flowchart modeling style. In this next example, I will demonstrate how to declare looping behavior in a flowchart workflow.

Once again, you will revisit an example workflow from one of the previous chapters. This time, the inventory lookup example from Chapter 5 will be implemented as a flowchart. The purpose of that example workflow was to find the requested inventory for a sales item. The inventory may be distributed across multiple warehouses, and each warehouse may need to be checked to determine whether the requested quantity for the item is available. In the original version, a `While` activity was used to loop through all warehouses until the requested item quantity is found or all warehouses have been checked.

In the new flowchart version of this workflow, direct connections between activities are used to model the looping behavior. A `FlowDecision` activity is used to determine when to exit the loop. This workflow also uses a `Sequence` activity to encapsulate a group of child activities. In a very small way, this demonstrates the mixing and matching ability of the two workflow styles.

Implementing the InventoryLookup Activity

This example uses a custom activity named `InventoryLookup` to simulate the lookup of the warehouse inventory for an item. You can copy the code for this activity directly from Chapter 5 and add it to the `ActivityLibrary` project. Here is the code that you need for this activity:

```
using System;
using System.Activities;
using System.Collections.Generic;

namespace ActivityLibrary
{
    public class InventoryLookup : CodeActivity<Int32>
    {
        public InArgument<Int32> ItemId { get; set; }
        public InArgument<Int32> WarehouseId { get; set; }
```

```csharp
public InArgument<Int32> RequestedQty { get; set; }

private Dictionary<Int32, Dictionary<Int32, Int32>> _warehouses
    = new Dictionary<Int32, Dictionary<Int32, Int32>>();

public InventoryLookup()
{
    //load some test data
    _warehouses.Add(1, new Dictionary<int, int>
    {
        {100, 5},
        {200, 0},
        {300, 0},
    });

    _warehouses.Add(2, new Dictionary<int, int>
    {
        {100, 10},
        {200, 0},
        {300, 0},
    });

    _warehouses.Add(3, new Dictionary<int, int>
    {
        {100, 50},
        {200, 75},
        {300, 0},
    });
}

protected override int Execute(CodeActivityContext context)
{
    Int32 availableInventory = 0;
    Int32 warehouseId = WarehouseId.Get(context);
    Dictionary<Int32, Int32> warehouse = null;
    if (_warehouses.TryGetValue(warehouseId, out warehouse))
    {
        Int32 itemId = ItemId.Get(context);
        if (warehouse.TryGetValue(itemId, out availableInventory))
        {
            Int32 requestedQty = RequestedQty.Get(context);
            if (availableInventory > requestedQty)
            {
                availableInventory = requestedQty;
            }
        }
    }
    return availableInventory;
}
```

Creating the Console Project

Add a new project named `GetItemInventory` to the solution. Use the Workflow Console Application template for the project, and delete the `Workflow1.xaml` file since it won't be used. Add a new workflow named `GetItemInventoryFlowchart` to the project using the Activity add item template. Add a project reference to the `ActivityLibrary` project that is in the same solution. Add a `Flowchart` as the root activity of the workflow.

Defining Arguments and Variables

Here are the arguments that you should define for the `GetItemInventoryFlowchart` workflow:

Name	Direction	Argument Type
ArgItemId	In	Int32
ArgQuantity	In	Int32
ArgQuantityFound	Out	Int32

Here is a summary of the variables that you'll need to add to the workflow. The first three variables are scoped by the root `Flowchart` activity and can be added immediately. The final variable is scoped by a `Sequence` activity and can be added as soon as you add that activity to the workflow. Note that some of the variables have default values that must be entered.

Name	Variable Type	Scope	Default Value
TotalFound	Int32	Flowchart	
WarehouseId	Int32	Flowchart	1
MaxWarehouseId	Int32	Flowchart	3
WarehouseQty	Int32	Sequence	

Declaring the Workflow

You can follow these steps to declare the remainder of the workflow:

1. Add a `FlowDecision` activity to the `Flowchart` activity. Connect the starting point of the workflow to the top of the `FlowDecision`. Set the `FlowDecision.Condition` property to `TotalFound < ArgQuantity And WarehouseId <= MaxWarehouseId`. This condition determines whether the workflow should continue to loop to process additional warehouses. When the condition is true, looping should continue. When the condition is false, either the requested quantity has been found or all warehouses have been processed and the workflow should end.

2. Add a **Sequence** activity to the workflow. This will be a container for a set of child activities that are always executed in order without any branching decisions between them.

■ **Note** As an alternative, you could have placed the individual child activities directly on the root **Flowchart** activity instead of using a **Sequence** activity. You would then link the individual activities with connections. But placing them in a separate **Sequence** container has two advantages. First, since there are no branching decisions to be made between these activities, it logically groups them together as one unit of work, which keeps the top-level view of the flowchart much cleaner. Second, the **Sequence** activity also provides a place to define an additional scoped variable. Without the **Sequence** activity as a variable container, all of the variables would be essentially global, scoped at the root **Flowchart** level.

---

3. Define the **WarehouseQty** variable that is scoped at the **Sequence** activity level.

4. The connection points on the left and right sides of the **FlowDecision** activity represent the execution path when the condition is either true or false. If the condition is true, you want to execute the **Sequence** activity. To accomplish this, drag a connection from the left side (the true side) of the **FlowDecision** to the top of the **Sequence** activity. You will add the child activities to the **Sequence** activity in just a few more steps.

5. After the **Sequence** activity executes, you always want to test the **FlowDecision** condition again. To accomplish this, drag a connection from the side of the **Sequence** activity to the top of the **FlowDecision** activity. You've just created a flowchart loop.

6. Add an **Assign** activity to the workflow. The purpose of this activity is to set the **ArgQuantityFound** output argument to the actual quantity that was found. Set the **Assign.To** property to **ArgQuantityFound** and the **Assign.Value** property to **TotalFound**.

7. Drag a connection from the right side of the **FlowDecision** activity (the false connection) to the **Assign** activity. This will cause execution of the **Assign** activity once the condition is false and the workflow exits the loop.

8. Expand the **Sequence** activity, and add an instance of the custom **InventoryLookup** activity. Set the **ItemId** property to **ArgItemId**, the **RequestedQty** property to **ArgQuantity - TotalFound**, the **WarehouseId** property to **WarehouseId**, and the **Result** property to **WarehouseQty**.

9. Add an **Assign** activity directly under the **InventoryLookup** activity. Set the **Assign.To** property to **TotalFound** and the **Assign.Value** property to **TotalFound + WarehouseQty**.

10. Add another **Assign** activity under the first one. Set the **Assign.To** property to **WarehouseId** and the **Assign.Value** property to **WarehouseId + 1**.

Figure 7-2 is the completed **Sequence** activity, and Figure 7-3 is the top-level workflow view.

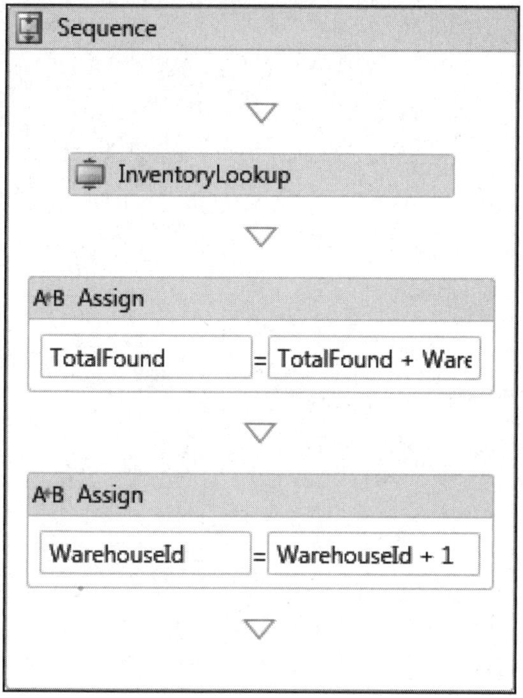

Figure 7-2. Sequence activity

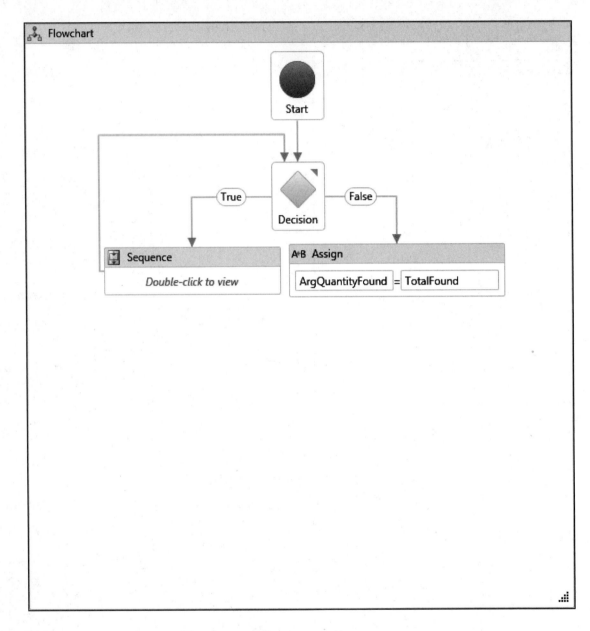

Figure 7-3. GetItemInventoryFlowchart workflow

Hosting the Workflow

Modify the `Program.cs` file in the `GetItemInventory` project so that it contains this code to run the workflow:

```
namespace GetItemInventory
{
    using System;
    using System.Activities;
    using System.Collections.Generic;

    class Program
    {
        static void Main(string[] args)
        {
            Console.WriteLine("GetItemInventoryFlowchart tests...");

            RunWorkflow(new GetItemInventoryFlowchart(), 100, 8);
            RunWorkflow(new GetItemInventoryFlowchart(), 100, 20);
            RunWorkflow(new GetItemInventoryFlowchart(), 100, 100);
            RunWorkflow(new GetItemInventoryFlowchart(), 200, 10);
            RunWorkflow(new GetItemInventoryFlowchart(), 300, 15);

            Console.WriteLine("Press any key to exit");
            Console.ReadKey();
        }

        private static void RunWorkflow(Activity workflow,
            Int32 itemId, Int32 quantity)
        {
            IDictionary<String, Object> output = WorkflowInvoker.Invoke(
                workflow, new Dictionary<string, object>
                {
                    {"ArgItemId", itemId},
                    {"ArgQuantity", quantity}
                });

            Console.WriteLine("Item: {0} Requested: {1} Found: {2}",
                itemId, quantity, output["ArgQuantityFound"]);
        }
    }
}
```

Testing the Workflow

After building the solution, you should be ready to run the `GetItemInventory` project. Here are the results that I see when I run this program:

```
GetItemInventoryFlowchart tests...

Item: 100 Requested: 8 Found: 8

Item: 100 Requested: 20 Found: 20

Item: 100 Requested: 100 Found: 65

Item: 200 Requested: 10 Found: 10

Item: 300 Requested: 15 Found: 0

Press any key to exit
```

These results should be similar to those that you received for the procedural workflow version of this example in Chapter 5.

Declaring Custom Activities

As you might expect, the flowchart modeling style is not limited to workflows. You can also use this style to model custom activities. In this next example, you will revisit the custom `CalcShipping` activity that you implemented in Chapter 3. In that chapter, you implemented this same custom activity in several different ways (in code, declarative Xaml, and so on).

The purpose of the activity is to calculate shipping charges for an order. The input arguments to the activity are the weight of the order, shipping method, and total currency amount of the order. The output argument is the calculated shipping amount. There are two shipping methods supported: normal and express. If the normal shipping method is requested, the shipping is calculated as the weight * 1.95. However, if the order total is greater than or equal to 75.00, the shipping is free. If the express shipping method is requested, the shipping is calculated as the weight * 3.50. The free shipping option does not apply to express shipping. Regardless of the shipping method, the minimum shipping amount is 12.95 unless the shipping is free.

The original procedural version of this activity used the `Switch<T>` and `If` activities. The new flowchart version will use the `FlowDecision` and `FlowSwitch<T>`.

Defining Arguments and Variables

To begin this example, use the Activity template to add a new custom activity to the `ActivityLibrary` project named `CalcShippingFlowchart`. Add a `Flowchart` activity as the root activity. Here are the arguments that you should add to the activity:

Name	Direction	Argument Type
ArgWeight	In	Int32
ArgOrderTotal	In	Decimal
ArgShipVia	In	String
Result	Out	Decimal

The activity also requires a set of variables. Most of these variables define constant values that are used during the calculation of the shipping charges. Here are the variables that you should add to the activity, along with their default values:

Name	Variable Type	Scope	Default Value
IsFreeShipping	Boolean	Flowchart	False
NormalRate	Decimal	Flowchart	1.95D
ExpressRate	Decimal	Flowchart	3.50D
Minimum	Decimal	Flowchart	12.95D
FreeThreshold	Decimal	Flowchart	75D

Declaring the Activity

Please follow these steps to declare the remainder of the custom activity:

1. Add a `FlowSwitch<T>` activity to the root `Flowchart` activity, setting the generic type to `System.String`. This activity will branch the path of execution based on the shipping method (the `ArgShipVia` argument). Set the `Expression` property to `ArgShipVia`. Drag a connection from the starting point of the activity to the top of the `FlowSwitch<T>`.

2. Add an `Assign` activity to calculate the shipping charges for express shipping. Set the `Assign.To` property to `Result` and the `Assign.Value` property to `ArgWeight * ExpressRate`.

3. Drag a connection from the `FlowSwitch<T>` activity to the `Assign` activity you just added. Set the `Case` property of the connection to `express` to indicate that this is the path of execution for the express shipping method.

4. Add a `FlowDecision` activity to determine whether the order total qualifies for free shipping. Set the `Condition` property to `ArgOrderTotal >= FreeThreshold`.

5. Drag a connection from the `FlowSwitch<T>` activity to the `FlowDecision` that you just added. Set the `Case` property of the connection to `normal` since this path is followed when the normal shipping method has been selected.

6. Add another `Assign` activity below the `FlowDecision` to calculate the normal shipping amount. Set the `Assign.To` property to `Result` and the `Assign.Value` property to `ArgWeight * NormalRate`.

7. Drag a connection from the right side of the `FlowDecision` (the false side) to the `Assign` activity that you just added. The condition that you entered for the `FlowDecision` determines whether the order total qualifies for free shipping. If it does (the left side of the `FlowDecision`), the activity has completed its work, and no further processing is needed. If the condition is false (the right side), processing should continue by executing the `Assign` activity.

8. Add another `FlowDecision` activity to determine whether a minimum shipping amount should be applied. Set the `Condition` property to `Result < Minimum`. Drag connections from both `Assign` activities to the top of this `FlowDecision` activity.

9. Add one final `Assign` activity to apply the minimum shipping amount if necessary. Set the `Assign.To` property to `Result` and the `Assign.Value` property to `Minimum`.

10. Drag one final connection from the left side of most recent `FlowDecision` (the true side) to the `Assign` activity that you just added. This will apply the minimum shipping amount if the current shipping amount is below the minimum.

Figure 7-4 shows the completed custom activity.

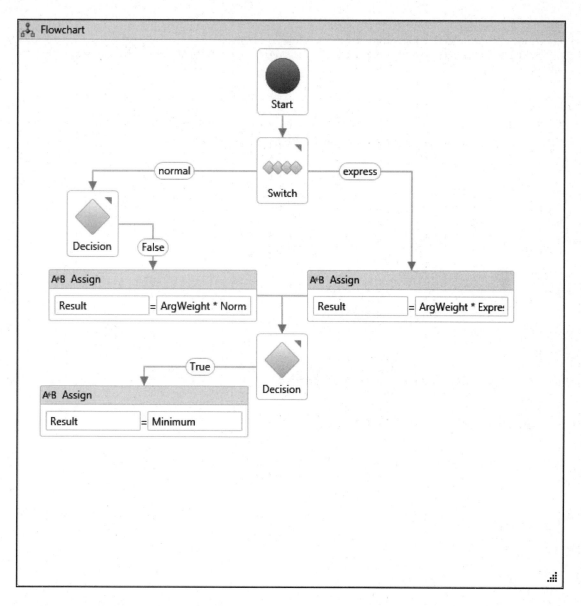

Figure 7-4. CalcShippingFlowchart activity

Implementing Unit Tests

As you did in Chapter 3 when you implemented the procedural versions of this activity, you can test the activity with a series of simple unit tests. Create a new unit test project named `ActivityLibraryTest`, and add it to the solution. Add an assembly reference to System.Activities and a project reference to the ActivityLibrary project, which should be in the same solution.

Add a new test class named CalcShippingFlowchartTest to the project. Here is code that you need to add to this class:

■ **Tip** These are the same basic tests that you implemented in Chapter 3. However, in that chapter the actual tests were organized as shared static methods that were reused for the multiple versions of the activity.

```
using System;
using System.Activities;
using System.Collections.Generic;
using ActivityLibrary;
using Microsoft.VisualStudio.TestTools.UnitTesting;

namespace ActivityLibraryTest
{
    [TestClass]
    public class CalcShippingFlowchartTest
    {
        [TestMethod]
        public void NormalTest()
        {
            Dictionary<String, Object> parameters
                = new Dictionary<string, object>();
            parameters.Add("ArgShipVia", "normal");
            parameters.Add("ArgWeight", 20);
            parameters.Add("ArgOrderTotal", 50M);

            IDictionary<String, Object> outputs = WorkflowInvoker.Invoke(
                new CalcShippingFlowchart(), parameters);
            Assert.AreEqual(39.00M, outputs["Result"], "Result is incorrect");
        }

        [TestMethod]
        public void NormalMinimumTest()
        {
            Dictionary<String, Object> parameters
                = new Dictionary<string, object>();
            parameters.Add("ArgShipVia", "normal");
            parameters.Add("ArgWeight", 5);
            parameters.Add("ArgOrderTotal", 50M);

            IDictionary<String, Object> outputs = WorkflowInvoker.Invoke(
                new CalcShippingFlowchart(), parameters);
            Assert.AreEqual(12.95M, outputs["Result"], "Result is incorrect");
        }
```

```
[TestMethod]
public void NormalFreeTest()
{
    Activity activity = new CalcShippingFlowchart();
    Dictionary<String, Object> parameters
        = new Dictionary<string, object>();
    parameters.Add("ArgShipVia", "normal");
    parameters.Add("ArgWeight", 5);
    parameters.Add("ArgOrderTotal", 75M);

    IDictionary<String, Object> outputs = WorkflowInvoker.Invoke(
        new CalcShippingFlowchart(), parameters);
    Assert.AreEqual(0.00M, outputs["Result"], "Result is incorrect");
}

[TestMethod]
public void ExpressTest()
{
    Dictionary<String, Object> parameters
        = new Dictionary<string, object>();
    parameters.Add("ArgShipVia", "express");
    parameters.Add("ArgWeight", 5);
    parameters.Add("ArgOrderTotal", 50M);

    IDictionary<String, Object> outputs = WorkflowInvoker.Invoke(
        new CalcShippingFlowchart(), parameters);
    Assert.AreEqual(17.50M, outputs["Result"], "Result is incorrect");
}
}
}
```

Testing the Activity

After building the solution, you should be ready to execute the unit tests. Figure 7-5 shows the successful test results.

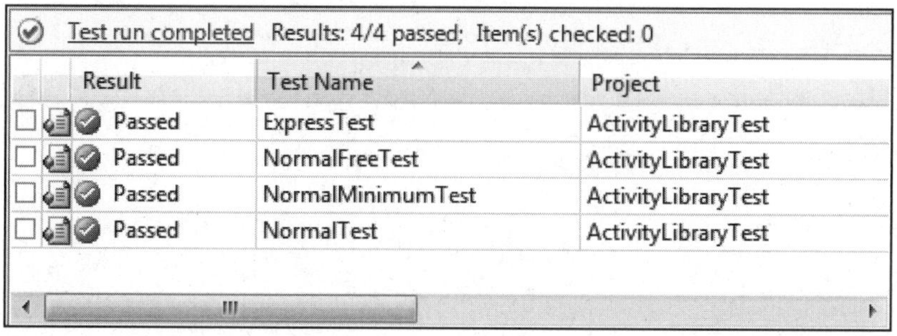

	Result	Test Name	Project
Test run completed	Results: 4/4 passed; Item(s) checked: 0		
☐	Passed	ExpressTest	ActivityLibraryTest
☐	Passed	NormalFreeTest	ActivityLibraryTest
☐	Passed	NormalMinimumTest	ActivityLibraryTest
☐	Passed	NormalTest	ActivityLibraryTest

Figure 7-5. CalcShippingFlowchart activity test results

Mixing the Two Styles

In this final example, you will mix the procedural and flowchart modeling styles in a single workflow. The workflow that you will implement comes from Chapter 6: the InventoryUpdate workflow. The purpose of the workflow is to apply a collection of item sales to another collection containing the current inventory for each item.

The original version of this workflow used the ForEach<T> activity to iterate over the collections. It also used several of the collection-related activities (AddToCollection<T>, ExistsInCollection<T>) to apply the updates to the item inventory.

The new flowchart version still uses the ForEach<T> activity to iterate over the collections. However, the child activity of the ForEach<T> will be a Flowchart instead of a Sequence containing other procedural activities.

Implementing Item Structures

This example uses two classes to define the sales and inventory data for each item. Add both of these classes to the ActivityLibrary project. These are the same classes that you implemented in Chapter 6. You should be able to copy them to the ActivityLibrary project for this chapter without any changes.

Here is the code for the ItemInventory class:

```
using System;

namespace ActivityLibrary
{
    public class ItemInventory : IEquatable<ItemInventory>
    {
        public Int32 ItemId { get; set; }
        public Int32 QuantityOnHand { get; set; }

        public bool Equals(ItemInventory other)
        {
            if (other == null)
            {
                return false;
            }
            else
            {
                return (this.ItemId == other.ItemId);
            }
        }

        public void ReduceInventory(Int32 adjustment)
        {
            QuantityOnHand -= adjustment;
        }
```

```
        public static ItemInventory Create(Int32 itemId, Int32 quantity)
        {
            return new ItemInventory
            {
                ItemId = itemId,
                QuantityOnHand = quantity
            };
        }
    }
}
```

Here is the code for the **SalesHistory** class:

```
using System;

namespace ActivityLibrary
{
    public class SalesHistory
    {
        public Int32 ItemId { get; set; }
        public Int32 Quantity { get; set; }
    }
}
```

Implementing the FindInCollection<T> Activity

This example also requires a custom activity that is similar to the other collection-related activities included with WF. The **FindInCollection<T>** activity locates an existing element in a collection and provides a reference to the found element in order to update it. The code for this activity can also be copied from Chapter 6. Here is the code for the **FindInCollection<T>** activity that you should add to the **ActivityLibrary** project:

```
using System;
using System.Activities;
using System.Collections.Generic;

namespace ActivityLibrary
{
    public class FindInCollection<T> : CodeActivity<Boolean>
    {
        [RequiredArgument]
        public InArgument<ICollection<T>> Collection { get; set; }
        [RequiredArgument]
        public InArgument<T> Item { get; set; }
        public OutArgument<T> FoundItem { get; set; }
```

```
protected override Boolean Execute(CodeActivityContext context)
{
    Boolean result = false;
    FoundItem.Set(context, default(T));
    ICollection<T> collection = Collection.Get(context);
    T item = Item.Get(context);

    if (collection != null)
    {
        foreach (T entry in collection)
        {
            if (entry is IEquatable<T>)
            {
                if (((IEquatable<T>)entry).Equals(item))
                {
                    FoundItem.Set(context, entry);
                    result = true;
                    break;
                }
            }
            else if (entry.Equals(item))
            {
                FoundItem.Set(context, entry);
                result = true;
                break;
            }
        }
    }
    return result;
}
```

Creating the Console Project

Add a new project named **InventoryUpdate** to the solution. Use the Workflow Console Application template for the project. You can delete the **Flowchart1.xaml** file since it won't be used. Add a new workflow to the project, and name it **InventoryUpdateFlowchart**. Add a project reference to the **ActivityLibrary** project in the same solution. Go ahead and add a **Flowchart** activity as the root of the workflow.

Defining Arguments and Variables

The workflow requires these two input arguments:

Name	Direction	Argument Type
ArgSales	In	IList<SalesHistory>
ArgInventory	In	IList<ItemInventory>

Here are the variables that you will need to define for this workflow. The first variable can be added immediately to the root **Flowchart** activity. The remaining variables will be added to a second **Flowchart** activity that is the child of one of the **ForEach** activities.

Name	Variable Type	Scope	Note
IsItemExists	Boolean	Flowchart	
FoundItem	ActivityLibrary.ItemInventory	ProcessSalesFC	Defined for the Flowchart under the ForEach activity named ProcessSales
NewItem	ActivityLibrary.ItemInventory	ProcessSalesFC	Defined for the Flowchart under the ForEach activity named ProcessSales

Declaring the Workflow

Please follow these steps to complete the declaration of the workflow:

1. Add a **ForEach<T>** activity to the workflow. This activity will print the beginning inventory for all items in the **ArgInventory** collection. Set the generic type to **ActivityLibrary.ItemInventory**. Change the **DisplayName** property to **PrintInventory** to more easily identify the purpose of this activity. Set the **ForEach.Values** property to **ArgInventory**. Drag a connection from the workflow starting point to the top of this activity.

2. Expand the **ForEach<T>** activity, and add a **WriteLine** activity as the only child. Set the **WriteLine.Text** property to **String.Format("Item {0} beginning inventory: {1}", item.ItemId, item.QuantityOnHand)**.

3. After navigating back to the top level of the workflow, add another **ForEach<T>** activity directly under the first **ForEach<T>** activity. This activity will process all item sales in the **ArgSales** collection. Set the generic type to **ActivityLibrary.ItemSales**, and change the **DisplayName** property to **ProcessSales**. Set the **ForEach.Values** property to **ArgSales**. Drag a connection between the two **ForEach** activities.

4. Expand the **ForEach<T>** activity that you just added, and add a **Flowchart** as the **ForEach.Body**. Change the **DisplayName** property of this new **Flowchart** to **ProcessSalesFC**. This enables you to declare the logic that processes each element of the **ArgSales** collection using the flowchart modeling style.

5.   Now that the `ProcessSalesFC` activity has been added to the `ForEach.Body`, add the remaining variables to this `Flowchart` activity (variables `FoundItem` and `NewItem`).

6.   Add a `WriteLine` to the `ProcessSalesFC` that you just added (the child of the `ForEach<T>` activity). Set the `WriteLine.Text` property to `String.Format("Sales item: {0} quantity: {1}", item.ItemId, item.Quantity)`. Drag a connection from the starting point of the ProcessSalesFC `Flowchart` to the top of the `WriteLine`.

7.   Add an `ExistsInCollection<T>` activity under the `WriteLine`. Set the generic type to `ActivityLibrary.ItemInventory`. Set the `Collection` property to `ArgInventory`, the `Result` property to `IsItemExists`, and the `Item` property to `New ActivityLibrary.ItemInventory With {.ItemId = item.ItemId}`. Drag a connection from the `WriteLine` activity to this activity.

8.   Add a `FlowDecision` activity under the `ExistsInCollection<T>` activity. Set the `FlowDecision.Condition` property to `IsItemExists`. Drag a connection from the `ExistsInCollection<T>` to this activity.

9.   Add a `FindInCollection<T>` activity below the `FlowDecision` and to the left. Set the generic type to `ActivityLibrary.ItemInventory`. Set the `Collection` property to `ArgInventory`, the `FoundItem` property to `FoundItem`, and the `Item` property to `New ActivityLibrary.ItemInventory With {.ItemId = item.ItemId}`.

10. Drag a connection from the left side of the `FlowDecision` (representing true) to the `FindInCollection<T>` activity.

11. Add an `InvokeMethod` activity under the `FindInCollection<T>` activity. Set the `TargetObject` property to `FoundItem` and the `MethodName` property to `ReduceInventory`. Add a single `Int32` parameter with a value of `item.quantity`. Drag a connection from the `FindInCollection<T>` activity to the `InvokeMethod` activity.

12. Add an `InvokeMethod` activity below and to the right of the `FlowDecision`. Set the `TargetType` property to `ActivityLibrary.ItemInventory` and the `MethodName` to `Create`. Add two `Int32` parameters. The first has a value of `item.ItemId` and the second has a value of `0 - item.Quantity`. Set the `Result` property to `NewItem`.

13. Drag a connection from the right side of the `FlowDecison` (representing false) to the `InvokeMethod` activity that you just added on the right side.

14. Add an `AddToCollection<T>` activity just below the last `InvokeMethod` that you added. Set the generic type to `ActivityLibrary.ItemInventory`. Set the `Collection` property to `ArgInventory` and the `Item` property to `NewItem`.

This completes the workflow declaration. Figure 7-6 is the completed `ProcessSalesFC` activity under the `ProcessSales ForEach<T>` activity. Figure 7-7 is the top-level view of the completed workflow.

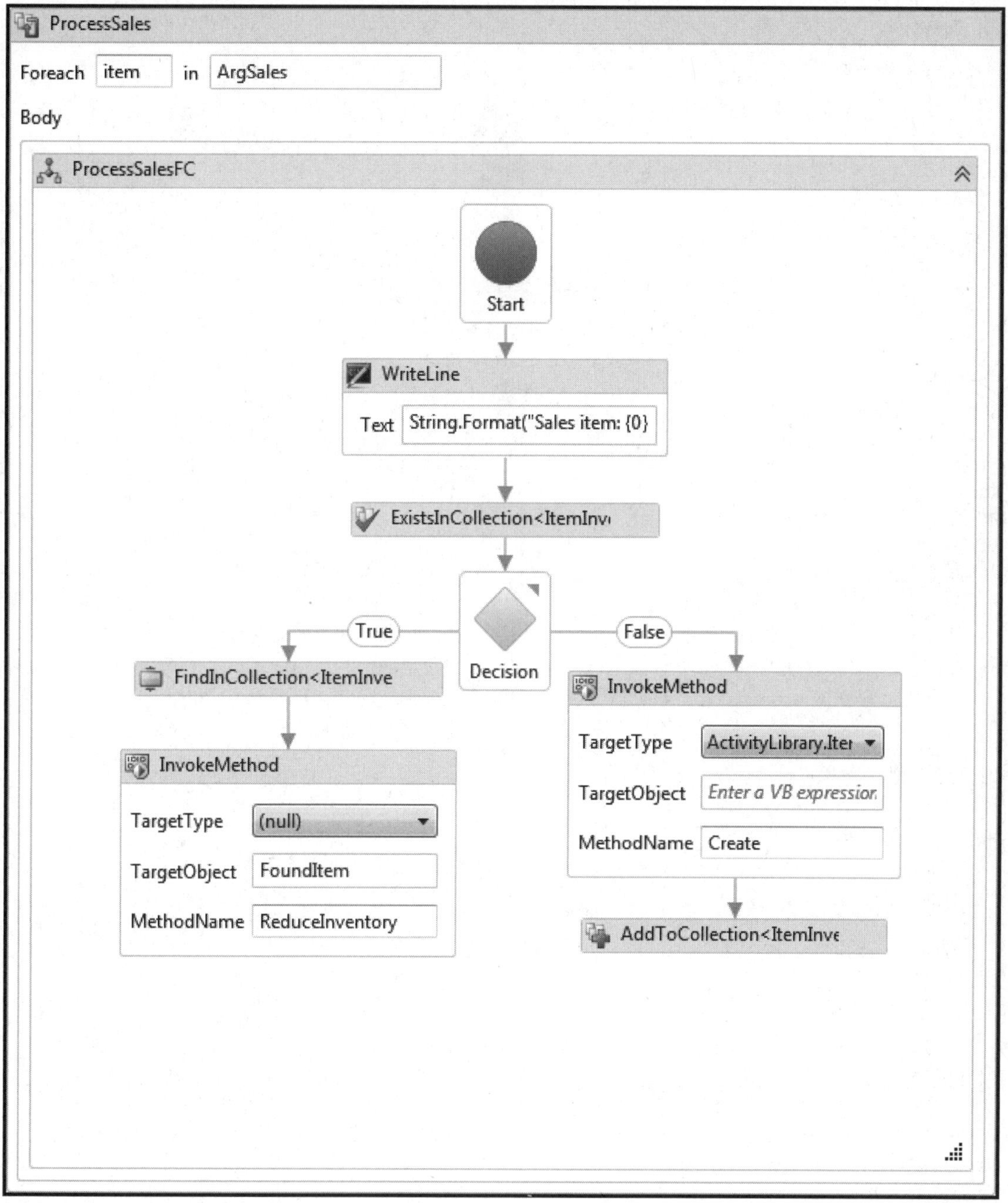

ProcessSales

Foreach [item] in [ArgSales]

Body

ProcessSalesFC

Start

WriteLine

Text │ String.Format("Sales item: {0}

ExistsInCollection<ItemInv

True ◇ *False*
Decision

FindInCollection<ItemInve

InvokeMethod

TargetType │ (null) ▼

TargetObject │ FoundItem

MethodName │ ReduceInventory

InvokeMethod

TargetType │ ActivityLibrary.Iter ▼

TargetObject │ *Enter a VB expression*

MethodName │ Create

AddToCollection<ItemInve

Figure 7-6. ProcessSalesFC flowchart

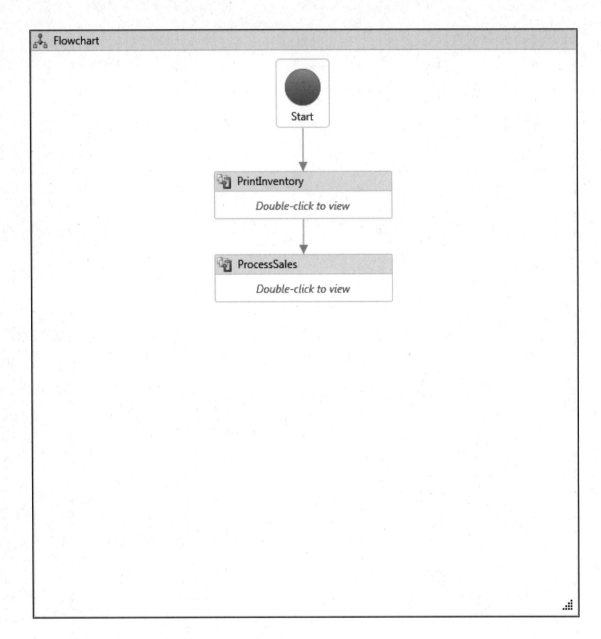

Figure 7-7. InventoryUpdateFlowchart workflow

Hosting the Workflow

To test the workflow, you can modify the `Program.cs` file in the `InventoryUpdate` project. Here is the revised code for this file:

```csharp
namespace InventoryUpdate
{
    using System;
    using System.Linq;
    using System.Activities;
    using System.Activities.Statements;
    using System.Collections.Generic;
    using ActivityLibrary;

    class Program
    {
        static void Main(string[] args)
        {
            Console.WriteLine("Test InventoryUpdateFlowchart...");
            RunWorkflow(new InventoryUpdateFlowchart());
        }

        private static void RunWorkflow(Activity workflow)
        {
            List<SalesHistory> salesHist = new List<SalesHistory>
            {
                new SalesHistory{ItemId = 100, Quantity = 5},
                new SalesHistory{ItemId = 200, Quantity = 25},
                new SalesHistory{ItemId = 100, Quantity = 7},
                new SalesHistory{ItemId = 300, Quantity = 75},
                new SalesHistory{ItemId = 100, Quantity = 30},
                new SalesHistory{ItemId = 300, Quantity = 26},
            };

            List<ItemInventory> inventory = new List<ItemInventory>
            {
                new ItemInventory{ItemId = 100, QuantityOnHand = 100},
                new ItemInventory{ItemId = 200, QuantityOnHand = 200},
            };

            WorkflowInvoker.Invoke(workflow,
                new Dictionary<string, object>
                {
                    {"ArgSales", salesHist},
                    {"ArgInventory", inventory}
                });
```

```
        foreach (ItemInventory item in inventory)
        {
            Console.WriteLine("Item {0} ending inventory: {1}",
                item.ItemId, item.QuantityOnHand);
        }
    }
  }
}
```

Testing the Workflow

After building the solution, you should be ready to run the InventoryUpdate project. Here are the results when I run the program:

```
Test InventoryUpdateFlowchart...

Item 100 beginning inventory: 100

Item 200 beginning inventory: 200

Sales item: 100 quantity: 5

Sales item: 200 quantity: 25

Sales item: 100 quantity: 7

Sales item: 300 quantity: 75

Sales item: 100 quantity: 30

Sales item: 300 quantity: 26

Item 100 ending inventory: 58

Item 200 ending inventory: 175

Item 300 ending inventory: -101

Press any key to continue . . .
```

These results are consistent with the results from the procedural version of this workflow in Chapter 6.

This example demonstrated the ability to mix and match the procedural and flowchart styles in the same workflow. Use the style that makes sense and feels like a better fit for the problem you are trying to solve. Some problems, because of the way branching or looping decisions must be declared, may be difficult to model using the procedural style. For those problems, you will likely start with the flowchart style. But remember that even if you start with the procedural style, you can model portions of the workflow in the flowchart style by simply adding a `Flowchart` activity.

Summary

This chapter focused on the flowchart modeling style. This modeling style is free-form and flexible and allows you to control the flow of execution with direct connections between activities. In contrast with this, the procedural modeling style uses branching and looping activities to declare a model that is highly structured. Since it uses familiar flowchart constructs, this model is more easily understood by business analysts and application stakeholders.

This chapter began with a review of the WF activities that support the flowchart style. This was followed by a short explanation of how to model workflows and activities using the flowchart style. The remainder of the chapter revisited several examples that were presented in earlier chapters. When they were originally presented, these examples were modeled using the procedural style. By revisiting the same examples in this chapter, you can directly contrast the two styles to solve similar business problems.

In the next chapter, you will learn how to implement local communication between the host application and a workflow instance.

CHAPTER 8

■ ■ ■

Host Communication

The focus of this chapter is direct communication between the host application and a workflow instance. The chapter begins with an overview of long-running workflows and the bookmark mechanism used to implement them. Bookmarks provide a way to temporarily suspend execution of a workflow instance while it is waiting for external input. They also provide a way to pass data to a waiting instance as the bookmark is resumed.

But bookmarks only permit data to be passed into a workflow instance, not in the other direction to the host application. The use of workflow extensions for sending data to a host application is discussed and demonstrated next.

The `ActivityAction` and `ActivityFunc` activities are a general-purpose extensibility mechanism. They allow you to execute activities that are provided outside the workflow declaration. The chapter continues with a discussion and demonstration of using an `ActivityAction` as a way to communicate between a workflow instance and the host application.

The chapter ends with coverage of the `Pick` and `PickBranch` activities. These activities allow you to model workflows that can create and wait for multiple bookmarks at the same time.

■ **Note** This chapter discusses bookmark concepts and focuses on ways to implement direct communication between a workflow instance and the application that hosts it. Another mechanism for communication is Windows Communication Foundation (WCF) messaging, which is covered in Chapter 9.

The Need for Long-Running Workflows

Some workflows operate solely on the arguments that are passed to them when they are started. They may perform calculations, make decisions based on those arguments, and then return a result. However, workflows of this type are likely in the minority. To solve real problems, many workflows require some interaction with other systems or resources. The interaction may take the form of a WCF message to another application, a query to a database or other resource, or direct interaction with the application that is hosting the workflow. These interactions enable the running workflow to work with additional data that has been received (or retrieved) after it has begun execution.

These interactions always involve a degree of uncertainty. This is especially true if you are communicating with another application. The actual work that is done by the other application, and the length of time it will take, may be completely out of your control. If you are communicating directly with the host application, you may have much better control over the performance requirements of the interaction.

But you have little or no control if the interaction involves real human beings. For example, you may be processing a mortgage loan workflow that requires multiple approvals from the credit department, account managers, and loan officers to complete the workflow. Each of these approvals must come from a real human being. The workflow will likely signal that it is waiting for these external inputs, but then it must wait until they are received before it can continue processing.

When an activity in a workflow does need to reach out and touch some other system, you have a choice. You can choose to handle the interaction just like any other atomic unit of work, or you can implement a long-running activity. The correct choice is to model the interaction with a long-running activity. But why is this so? Remember that activities within a workflow are executed on a single workflow thread. If that thread is occupied waiting for external input, it can't be used for any other purpose. You're wasting a valuable resource (a workflow thread) that could be used to execute other activities in the same workflow (perhaps to process other external input as it is received). Equally important, you've locked the workflow in memory—it can't be unloaded since the thread is occupied waiting for external input. The workflow runtime doesn't know that you're waiting for external input and that external input might take minutes, hours, or days before it is received.

In contrast with this, a long-running activity is designed to yield control of the workflow thread when it requires some external interaction. When the interaction is complete, the activity continues processing. While the workflow is waiting for external input, it can use the workflow thread to process other activities (if it was modeled to take advantage of parallel processing), or the entire workflow can become idle. When it is idle, it is no longer occupying a workflow thread, and it is a candidate to be persisted and unloaded from memory. Long-running activities are implemented using a concept called *bookmarks*, which are discussed in the next section.

▦ **Note** Chapter 11 covers workflow persistence.

To recap, you should keep these two guidelines in mind when an activity is required to interact with an external application or resource:

- Make no assumptions concerning the duration of the interaction. By default, you should assume that the interaction will be long-running.

- Don't occupy a workflow thread for the interaction. Use a long-running activity that is designed to yield control of the workflow thread.

Understanding Bookmarks

WF supports long-running activities using a concept called *bookmarks*. A WF bookmark serves the same purpose as a real bookmark that you would use in a book. It marks your place when you need to temporarily do something else. When you are ready to continue reading a book, you locate the bookmark and resume reading at the exact point where you stopped. In a similar manner, a WF bookmark enables you to resume processing of the activity at the point where you stopped.

To use bookmarks, an activity must derive from `NativeActivity` (or the generic version `NativeActivity<TResult>`). This is the only base activity class that supports the ability to create and resume bookmarks. You create a bookmark within the `Execute` method of the activity. This method is passed a `NativeActivityContext` object that supports the `CreateBookmark` method. There are several overloads of this method that allow you to create a bookmark in slightly different ways. Bookmarks must be uniquely named within a workflow since the string name is used by the host application to resume execution at the bookmark. Optionally, you can specify a callback that is executed when the bookmark is resumed. The callback must match the `BookmarkCallback` delegate signature. You can use this callback to retrieve any data that was passed from the host application when the bookmark was resumed. The data is likely the external input that the workflow requires in order to continue processing.

Any custom activity that creates a bookmark must also override the virtual `CanInduceIdle` property. This Boolean property returns a value indicating whether the activity is capable of causing the workflow to become idle.

When the host application is ready to resume a bookmark, it uses the `ResumeBookmark` method of the `WorkflowApplication` instance. This method accepts the string name of the bookmark to resume along with any data that you want to pass back to the waiting activity. The `WorkflowInvoker` class does not support the resumption of bookmarks.

Figure 8-1 illustrates this interaction between the long-running activity and the hosts application.

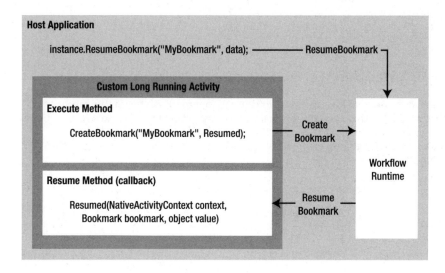

Figure 8-1. Bookmark processing overview

■ **Note** Don't confuse long-running bookmark processing with asynchronous processing. Asynchronous processing operates on a separate thread, but it is assumed that it will complete without waiting for external stimulus. It is also assumed that an asynchronous activity will complete in a relatively short period of time, while a long-running activity may take an extraordinarily long period of time before it is resumed.

Using Bookmarks

To demonstrate how to use a bookmark, you will revisit a familiar example: the command-line calculator. You first saw this example in Chapter 1 but last worked with it in Chapter 7 when you implemented it using the flowchart modeling style. In that example, the host application passed the arithmetic expression to process as an argument when the workflow was started.

In this example, you will revise the workflow and the host application to use bookmarks. A new custom activity will be developed that creates a bookmark in order to wait for input from the host application. The host application uses the named bookmark to pass the arithmetic expression to the waiting workflow.

You will complete these tasks to implement this example:

1. Implement a custom `GetString` activity that uses bookmark processing to retrieve the arithmetic expression.

2. Copy the `ParseCalculatorArgs` activity from Chapter 7.

3. Declare the `BookmarkCalculator` workflow.

4. Implement the host application code to resume the bookmark.

Implementing the GetString Activity

This new custom activity will demonstrate how to create and use a bookmark. To begin this example, create a new project named `ActivityLibrary` using the Activity Library template. Add it to a new solution that is named for this chapter. Delete the `Activity1.xaml` file since it is not needed.

Add a new activity named `GetString` to the project using the Code Activity add item template. Here is the complete code to implement this activity:

```
using System;
using System.Activities;

namespace ActivityLibrary
{
    public sealed class GetString : NativeActivity<String>
    {
```

The code in the `Execute` method immediately creates a new bookmark, assigning it a name of `GetString`. It registers a callback method named `Resumed` that will be invoked when the host application resumes the bookmark.

When the new bookmark is created, this informs the workflow runtime that the activity is not yet complete but that it requires some external stimulus in order to continue processing. This allows the runtime to use the workflow thread for other work while this activity is waiting for resumption of the bookmark.

```
        protected override void Execute(NativeActivityContext context)
        {
            context.CreateBookmark("GetString", Resumed);
        }
```

When the bookmark is resumed, the **Resumed** method is invoked since it was identified as the callback method. Any data passed from the host application is passed in the **value** parameter to this method. In this example, the activity is expecting this data to be a string containing the arithmetic expression. The value of that expression is used to set the **Result** property of this activity.

```
private void Resumed(NativeActivityContext context,
    Bookmark bookmark, object value)
{
    if (value != null && value is String)
    {
        Result.Set(context, value as String);
    }
}
```

The **CanInduceIdle** property is overridden in order to indicate that the activity is capable of causing the workflow to become idle.

```
protected override bool CanInduceIdle
{
    get { return true; }
}
    }
}
```

Implementing the ParseCalculatorArgs Activity

This example workflow also uses the **ParseCalculatorArgs** activity that you used in Chapter 7. You can copy the code that you used in that chapter to the **ActivityLibrary** project without any changes. Here is the code for this activity:

```
using System;
using System.Activities;

namespace ActivityLibrary
{
    public sealed class ParseCalculatorArgs : CodeActivity
    {
        [RequiredArgument]
        public InArgument<String> Expression { get; set; }
        public OutArgument<Double> FirstNumber { get; set; }
        public OutArgument<Double> SecondNumber { get; set; }
        public OutArgument<String> Operation { get; set; }

        protected override void Execute(CodeActivityContext context)
        {
            FirstNumber.Set(context, 0);
            SecondNumber.Set(context, 0);
            Operation.Set(context, "error");
```

```
            String line = Expression.Get(context);
            if (!String.IsNullOrEmpty(line))
            {
                String[] arguments = line.Split(' ');
                if (arguments.Length == 3)
                {
                    Double number = 0;
                    if (Double.TryParse(arguments[0], out number))
                    {
                        FirstNumber.Set(context, number);
                    }
                    Operation.Set(context, arguments[1]);
                    if (Double.TryParse(arguments[2], out number))
                    {
                        SecondNumber.Set(context, number);
                    }
                }
            }
        }
    }
}
```

Creating the Console Project

Create a new project to host the calculator workflow. Name the project `BookmarkCalculator`, and use the Workflow Console Application template. Add the new project to the current solution for this chapter. Delete the `Workflow1.xaml` file that was created for you since you won't use it. Add a project reference to the `ActivityLibrary` project, which should be in the same solution.

The workflow for this example is almost exactly the same as the one you implemented in Chapter 7. The most efficient way to implement this example is to copy the `FlowchartCalculator.xaml` file from the `FlowchartCalculator` project in Chapter 7. Name the copied workflow `BookmarkCalculator.xaml`, and add it to the `BookmarkCalculator` project that you just created. Open the copied `BookmarkCalculator.xaml` file in Code View, which should open the XML editor. Change both the namespace and the workflow name in the root element to `BookmarkCalculator`. Here is an abbreviated copy of the modified Xaml file showing the changes:

```
<Activity x:Class="BookmarkCalculator.BookmarkCalculator">
…
</Activity>
```

■ **Note** I prefer to rename activities and workflows directly in the Xaml file as I indicated here. However, you can also change the namespace and workflow name in designer view. If you make sure that the workflow itself is highlighted (rather than one of the activities within it), you should be able to change the namespace and name in the Properties window.

After closing the XML editor, rebuild the solution and then open the workflow in Design View. Follow these steps to modify the workflow:

1. Delete the `ArgExpression` argument that is defined for this workflow. This was previously used to pass the arithmetic expression to the workflow but will no longer be needed.

2. Add a new string variable named `Expression` to the workflow, scoped by the root `Flowchart` activity.

3. Add an instance of the new `GetString` activity to the top of the workflow. Set the `GetString.Result` property to `Expression`. This will populate the new `Expression` variable with the value that is passed to the activity when its bookmark is resumed.

4. Modify one of the property values of the `ParseCalculatorArgs` activity. Change the `Expression` property from `ArgExpression` to `Expression` to use the value of the new variable instead of the argument that was previously used.

5. Modify the flowchart connections so that the `GetString` activity is now executed first, followed by the `ParseCalculatorArgs` activity. Previously, the `ParseCalculatorArgs` Activity was executed first.

Figure 8-2 shows the revised workflow.

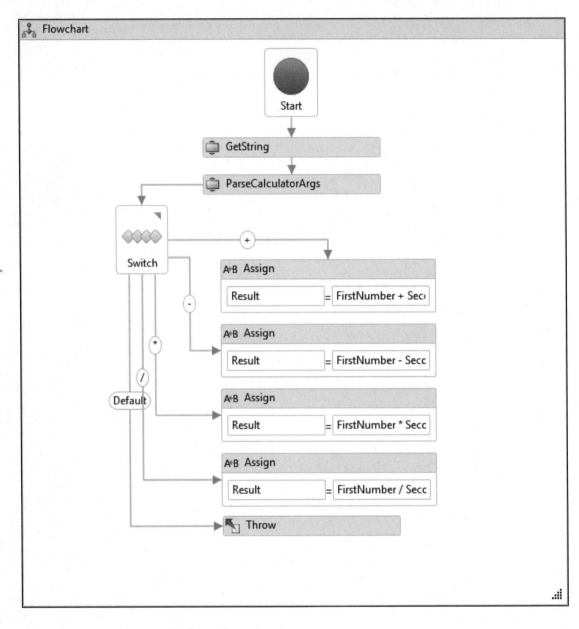

Figure 8-2. BookmarkCalculator workflow

Hosting the Workflow

To host this revised workflow, you need to make significant changes to the `Program.cs` file compared to previous versions of the calculator example. The major changes are the use of `WorkflowApplication` instead of `WorkflowInvoker` and the code to validate and resume a bookmark. Here is the complete `Program.cs` file that you need for this example:

```
using System;
using System.Activities;
using System.Linq;
using System.Threading;

namespace BookmarkCalculator
{
    class Program
    {
        static void Main(string[] args)
        {
            Boolean isRunning = true;
            while (isRunning)
            {
                try
                {
```

The `WorkflowApplication` class is used to host the workflow instead of `WorkflowInvoker` that was used in the previous calculator examples. Since this invokes the workflow on a separate thread, an `AutoResetEvent` is created in order to notify the host application when the workflow completes. After creating a `WorkflowApplication` instance for the workflow, handlers are added to the `Completed`, `Idle`, and `OnUnhandledException` delegates. The handler code for the `Completed` delegate retrieves and displays the workflow result.

```
                    AutoResetEvent syncEvent = new AutoResetEvent(false);
                    WorkflowApplication wfApp =
                        new WorkflowApplication(new BookmarkCalculator());

                    wfApp.Completed = delegate(
                        WorkflowApplicationCompletedEventArgs e)
                    {
                        if (e.CompletionState == ActivityInstanceState.Closed)
                        {
                            Console.WriteLine("Result = {0}", e.Outputs["Result"]);
                        }
                        syncEvent.Set();
                    };
```

The code that is assigned to the `Idle` delegate is executed when the workflow becomes idle. This helps to confirm that the workflow thread isn't occupied while the workflow is waiting for the resumption of the bookmark.

```
wfApp.Idle = delegate(WorkflowApplicationIdleEventArgs e)
{
    Console.WriteLine("Workflow is idle");
};

wfApp.OnUnhandledException = delegate(
    WorkflowApplicationUnhandledExceptionEventArgs e)
{
    Console.WriteLine(e.UnhandledException.Message.ToString());
    return UnhandledExceptionAction.Terminate;
};

wfApp.Run();
```

After starting the workflow instance, the code prompts the user to enter an arithmetic expression. If the user indicates that they want to quit the application, the `Cancel` method is called on the `WorkflowApplication` instance. Otherwise, the `ResumeBookmark` method of the `WorkflowApplication` is called, passing the bookmark name and the arithmetic expression as arguments.

Prior to calling the `ResumeBookmark` method, the bookmark is validated using a private `IsBookmarkValid` method.

```
            Console.WriteLine("Enter an expression or 'quit' to exit");
            String expression = Console.ReadLine();

            if ((String.IsNullOrEmpty(expression)) ||
                (!String.IsNullOrEmpty(expression) &&
                 expression.Trim().ToLower() == "quit"))
            {
                wfApp.Cancel();
                Console.WriteLine("Exiting program");
                isRunning = false;
            }
            else if (IsBookmarkValid(wfApp, "GetString"))
            {
                wfApp.ResumeBookmark("GetString", expression);
            }

            syncEvent.WaitOne();
        }
        catch (Exception exception)
        {
            Console.WriteLine("Error: {0}", exception.Message);
        }
    }
}
```

The `IsBookmarkValid` method is used to validate a bookmark prior to calling the `ResumeBookmark` method. A bookmark may be validated by calling the `GetBookmarks` method of the `WorkflowApplication` instance. This method returns a collection of `BookmarkInfo` objects, one for each bookmark that is currently active. Calling `ResumeBookmark` with an invalid bookmark name will cause an exception to be thrown.

```
        private static Boolean IsBookmarkValid(
            WorkflowApplication wfApp, String bookmarkName)
        {
            Boolean result = false;
            var bookmarks = wfApp.GetBookmarks();
            if (bookmarks != null)
            {
                result =
                    (from b in bookmarks
                     where b.BookmarkName == bookmarkName
                     select b).Any();
            }
            return result;
        }
    }
}
```

■ **Note** If your application is multithreaded, you may need to guard against a race condition where another thread has already resumed a bookmark. Standard .NET locking and thread synchronization techniques should be used within a multithreaded application to protect against this.

Testing the Workflow

After building the solution, you should be ready to run the **BookmarkCalculator** project and exercise the application. Here are some representative results when I run the project:

```
Enter an expression or 'quit' to exit

Workflow is idle

5 + 3

Result = 8

Workflow is idle

Enter an expression or 'quit' to exit

100 - 75

Result = 25

Workflow is idle
```

```
Enter an expression or 'quit' to exit

8 * 7.56

Result = 60.48

Workflow is idle

Enter an expression or 'quit' to exit

123 / 2

Result = 61.5

Workflow is idle

Enter an expression or 'quit' to exit

1+1

Operation Invalid

Workflow is idle

Enter an expression or 'quit' to exit

quit

Exiting program

Press any key to continue . . .
```

Understanding Workflow Extensions

The previous example illustrated the use of bookmarks to resume processing and to pass data from the host application to a running workflow instance. However, it didn't address communication in the opposite direction: from the workflow instance to the host application. You will frequently need to communicate in both directions.

For example, in the `BookmarkCalculator` project that you just completed, the host application immediately resumes the bookmark after the expression is read from the console. It can safely do this because it has intimate knowledge that the workflow has created the bookmark and is awaiting input. The design could be improved if the workflow could notify the host application when it is waiting for input.

You can enable communication between a workflow instance and the host application in a number of ways. One way to accomplish this is to implement WCF messaging at the host and invoke the WCF services from the workflow. Although that is a viable (and perhaps even preferred) approach, a much simpler solution is to use a *workflow extension*.

■ **Note** Chapter 9 covers the use of WCF messaging.

Workflow extensions are ordinary C# classes that you implement to provide needed functionality to workflow instances. Exactly what functionality they provide is completely up to you. For example, Microsoft provides an out-of-the-box extension that you can use for event tracking (EtwTrackingParticipant).

Extensions are added to a WorkflowApplication instance using the Add method of the Extensions property. Extensions can be added after the WorkflowApplication instance is created but before you begin execution of the workflow. You can also add extensions using the WorkflowInvoker class in a similar manner. Once an extension is added to an instance, it can be retrieved by a custom code activity using the GetExtension method of the activity context. Once the extension has been retrieved, the activity can then invoke any public methods or properties of the extension.

■ **Note** Even though the WorkflowInvoker class supports extensions, it doesn't support the ability to resume a bookmark. That makes sense since WorkflowInvoker runs the workflow just as if it were a method on the host thread. Because of this, the WorkflowInvoker class is not a suitable way to host a workflow if a bookmark must be resumed from the host application.

A workflow extension solves the problem of workflow-to-host communication because it is accessible by both the host and any workflow instances that have the extension. You can think of it as a communication bridge between the host and a workflow instance. A custom activity can invoke a method on the extension to provide a simple signal (with or without additional data) that can be consumed by the host. The signal itself can be implemented in a number of ways. You can use a C# event, a delegate, a queue, a thread synchronization object such as an AutoResetEvent, and so on.

The GetExtension method of the activity context accepts a single Type parameter that identifies the extension that you want to retrieve. You can specify the extension class, an interface that it implements, or an abstract class that it derives from. The only requirement is that the Type you provide to GetExtension uniquely identifies the extension to retrieve. The advantage to using an interface or abstract class is that it decouples the extension implementation from the contract that is referenced by the custom activity. This allows you to swap out the extension implementation without changing the custom activity. You'll see an example of this later in the chapter. You can retrieve and use an extension regardless of the base class of your custom code activity (CodeActivity, AsyncCodeActivity, or NativeActivity).

A different instance of an extension can be added to each workflow instance, or a single extension instance can be shared by multiple workflow instances. You might need to share an instance when the extension provides access to common state data that must be shared by multiple workflows.

■ **Caution** If a single extension instance is designed to be shared by multiple workflow instances, you need to ensure that any public methods invoked by the workflow instances are thread-safe. Remember that each workflow instance executes on its own thread, so the danger of multiple threads accessing the same method is real.

WF provides the `IWorkflowInstanceExtension` interface that your extensions can optionally implement. This interface provides your extension class with the ability to reference the current workflow instance and to also add additional extensions to the instance. Here are the members that your extension class must implement if you choose to use this interface:

Member Name	Description
SetInstance	Called by the workflow runtime to provide the extension with a WorkflowInstance object that represents the current workflow instance
GetAdditionalExtensions	Called by the workflow runtime to retrieve additional extensions that are added to the workflow instance

The `SetInstance` method is useful if the extension has the need to reference or otherwise identify the current workflow instance. For example, if an extension needs the workflow instance ID it can be obtained from the object that is passed with the `SetInstance` method. The `GetAdditionalExtensions` method provides an extension with the opportunity to create and return additional extensions, acting as an extension factory. If a single instance of an extension is shared by multiple workflow instances, these methods are called for each workflow instance.

Using Workflow Extensions

In the example that follows, you will enhance the `BookmarkCalculator` application that you implemented in the previous example. The goal for this example is to notify the host application when the workflow is waiting for input. To accomplish this, you will implement a simple workflow extension and a custom activity that uses it. The extension supports a single public method that raises an event. The event is handled by the host and signals that the workflow is waiting for input. The host code will be modified to wait for the signal before attempting to resume the bookmark.

You will complete these tasks to implement this example:

1. Declare an interface that defines the extension method that is used by a custom activity.

2. Implement an extension class that provides a notification to the host application using a C# event.

3. Implement a custom activity that calls the `Notify` method on the extension.

4. Modify the `BookmarkCalculator` workflow to use the new custom activity.

5. Implement the code to host the workflow and react to the notification.

Declaring the Extension Interface

To begin this example, you need to declare a C# interface that defines the public extension method. I prefer to use an interface to define the contract of an extension since it allows you to swap out the extension implementation if necessary.

Add a new C# interface to the `ActivityLibrary` project for this chapter, and name it `IHostNotification`. Here is the code for this interface:

```
using System;

namespace ActivityLibrary
{
    public interface IHostNotification
    {
        void Notify(String message, String bookmarkName);
    }
}
```

■ **Note** I'm using the `ActivityLibrary` project for this interface and the extension that you will implement in the next section. You could argue that these new types really don't belong in this project since they are not WF activities. If you prefer, you can place them in a different project, as long as it is referenced by all the other projects in this example. In this example, I'm simply using the `ActivityLibrary` project as a convenience.

Implementing the HostEventNotifier Extension

Next, add a new C# class to the `ActivityLibrary` project, and name it `HostEventNotifier`. This is the workflow extension that implements the `IHostNotification` interface you just declared. Here is the code that you need to implement this class:

```
using System;
using System.Threading;

namespace ActivityLibrary
{
    public class HostEventNotifier : IHostNotification
    {
```

The class defines a public C# event that will be handled by the host application. When the `Notify` method is invoked by a custom activity (implemented in the next section), the event is raised.

Most importantly, the event is raised on a different thread. For convenience, I'm using the thread pool for this purpose. The assumption is that the host application will take a considerable amount of time before it responds to this notification. You don't want to occupy the workflow thread while you're waiting for the host to process this event. Raising the event on a different thread allows the `Notify` method to return immediately.

Since the host may take an unknown amount of time to respond, you could argue that it would be better to use a dedicated thread rather than the thread pool. Thread pool threads are another limited resource that you generally shouldn't use for long-running tasks. Although I generally agree with that thinking, I used the thread pool since it was easier to implement. I didn't want to divert your attention to aspects of the code that don't directly contribute to the example.

```
public event EventHandler<HostNotifyEventArgs> Notification;

public void Notify(string message, String bookmarkName)
{
    if (Notification != null)
    {
        ThreadPool.QueueUserWorkItem(delegate(Object state)
        {
            Notification(this,
                new HostNotifyEventArgs(state as String, bookmarkName));
        }, message);
    }
}
```

The HostNotifyEventArgs class defines the event arguments that are used when the event is raised. In this example, the string message and the bookmark name are passed as properties of this class. In your code, you could easily pass any other data that is meaningful to your application.

```
public class HostNotifyEventArgs : EventArgs
{
    public String Message { get; private set; }
    public String BookmarkName { get; private set; }
    public HostNotifyEventArgs(String message, String bookmarkName)
        : base()
    {
        Message = message;
        BookmarkName = bookmarkName;
    }
}
```

Implementing the NotifyHost Activity

The next step is to implement a new custom activity that will retrieve and use the extension that you just implemented. Add a new activity named NotifyHost to the ActivityLibrary project using the Code Activity add item template. Here is the code for this activity:

```
using System;
using System.Activities;

namespace ActivityLibrary
{
    public sealed class NotifyHost : CodeActivity
    {
```

```
public InArgument<string> Message { get; set; }
public InArgument<string> BookmarkName { get; set; }
```

The code in the Execute method first retrieves the extension, identifying it by the interface that it implements rather than by the concrete class name. Once the extension is retrieved, the Notify method is invoked, passing the value of the string Message and BookmarkName arguments.

```
protected override void Execute(CodeActivityContext context)
{
    IHostNotification extension =
        context.GetExtension<IHostNotification>();
    if (extension != null)
    {
        extension.Notify(Message.Get(context),
            BookmarkName.Get(context));
    }
}
```

You should build the solution at this point to make sure that everything builds correctly. This also makes the new custom activity available in the Toolbox.

Declaring the BookmarkCalculatorExtension Workflow

The workflow for this example is almost exactly like the BookmarkCalculator workflow from the previous example. In fact, the only real change is the addition of the new NotifyHost activity.

Create a new project named BookmarkCalculatorEvent using the Workflow Console Application template, and delete the Workflow1.xaml file. Add the new project to the current solution for this chapter. Add a project reference to the ActivityLibrary project.

You can follow these steps to prepare the revised workflow:

1. Copy the BookmarkCalculator.xaml file from the BookmarkCalculator project (the previous example) to this new project. Name the copied workflow BookmarkCalculatorExtension.xaml to indicate that this version uses the workflow extension.

2. Open the copied workflow in the XML editor, and revise the namespace and workflow names at the top of the Xaml file.

3. Reopen the workflow in the designer, and add an instance of the NotifyHost activity to the top of the workflow.

4. Set the NotifyHost.Message property to "Enter an expression or 'quit' to exit". Set the NotifyHost.BookmarkName property to "GetString".

5. Modify the flowchart connections so that the NotifyHost activity is executed first, followed by the GetString activity.

Figure 8-3 is the modified workflow.

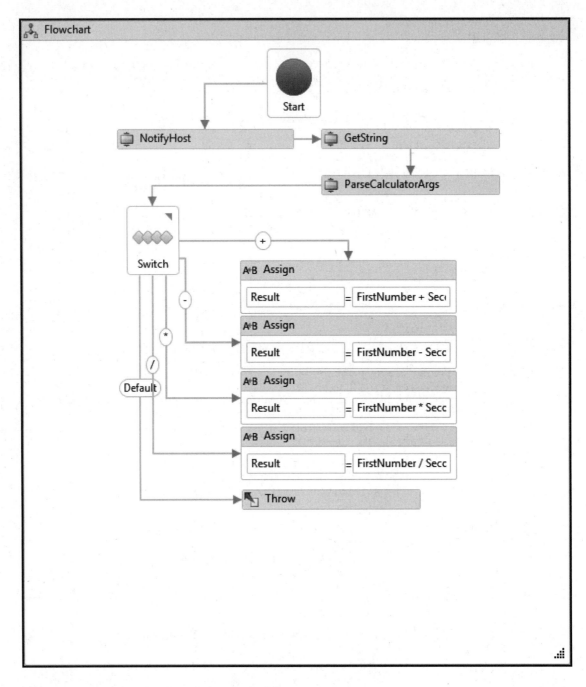

Figure 8-3. *BookmarkCalculatorExtension workflow*

Hosting the Workflow

The code to host this revised workflow is similar to the code in the **BookmarkCalculator** project. The primary differences are the code to create and add the workflow extension and to react to the event when it is raised by the workflow. Here is the complete code that you need for the **Program.cs** file of the **BookmarkCalculatorEvent** project:

```
using System;
using System.Activities;
using System.Linq;
using System.Threading;
using ActivityLibrary;

namespace BookmarkCalculatorEvent
{
    class Program
    {
        static void Main(string[] args)
        {
            Boolean isRunning = true;
            while (isRunning)
            {
                try
                {
                    AutoResetEvent syncEvent = new AutoResetEvent(false);

                    WorkflowApplication wfApp =
                        new WorkflowApplication(new BookmarkCalculatorExtension());

                    wfApp.Completed = delegate(
                        WorkflowApplicationCompletedEventArgs e)
                    {
                        if (e.CompletionState == ActivityInstanceState.Closed)
                        {
                            Console.WriteLine("Result = {0}", e.Outputs["Result"]);
                        }
                        syncEvent.Set();
                    };

                    wfApp.Idle = delegate(WorkflowApplicationIdleEventArgs e)
                    {
                        Console.WriteLine("Workflow is idle");
                    };

                    wfApp.OnUnhandledException = delegate(
                        WorkflowApplicationUnhandledExceptionEventArgs e)
                    {
                        Console.WriteLine(e.UnhandledException.Message.ToString());
                        return UnhandledExceptionAction.Terminate;
                    };
```

Just prior to running the workflow instance, the custom extension is created and added to the `WorkflowApplication` instance using the `Extensions.Add` method. The code that resumes the bookmark has been moved into a handler for the `Notification` event of the extension. When the event is raised by the workflow, the host displays the prompt string that is received with the event, reads a line from the console, and then resumes the bookmark.

```
HostEventNotifier extension = new HostEventNotifier();
extension.Notification += delegate(
    Object sender, HostNotifyEventArgs e)
{
    Console.WriteLine(e.Message);
    String expression = Console.ReadLine();

    if ((String.IsNullOrEmpty(expression)) ||
        (!String.IsNullOrEmpty(expression) &&
         expression.Trim().ToLower() == "quit"))
    {
        wfApp.Cancel();
        Console.WriteLine("Exiting program");
        isRunning = false;
    }
    else if (IsBookmarkValid(wfApp, e.BookmarkName))
    {
        wfApp.ResumeBookmark(e.BookmarkName, expression);
    }
};

wfApp.Extensions.Add(extension);
wfApp.Run();
syncEvent.WaitOne();
}
catch (Exception exception)
{
    Console.WriteLine("Error: {0}", exception.Message);
}
}
}

private static Boolean IsBookmarkValid(
    WorkflowApplication wfApp, String bookmarkName)
{
    Boolean result = false;
    var bookmarks = wfApp.GetBookmarks();
    if (bookmarks != null)
    {
        result =
            (from b in bookmarks
             where b.BookmarkName == bookmarkName
             select b).Any();
    }
```

```
            return result;
        }
    }
}
```

■ **Tip** In this example, the host application was passed the bookmark name with the event arguments. This helps reduce the need for the host application to have intimate knowledge of the workflow's inner workings. Instead of maintaining the string literal for the bookmark name in the workflow and the host application, it is now only defined in the workflow. This design could be improved even further by modifying the GetString activity to retrieve the bookmark name from an argument. This would remove the definition of the bookmark name from all code and push it all the way to the workflow declaration.

Testing the Workflow

At this point you can build the solution and run the BookmarkCalculatorEvent project. Here are my results, which are similar to the previous example:

```
Workflow is idle

Enter an expression or 'quit' to exit

5 + 3

Result = 8

Workflow is idle

Enter an expression or 'quit' to exit

100 - 75

Result = 25

Workflow is idle

Enter an expression or 'quit' to exit

8 * 7.56

Result = 60.48
```

```
Workflow is idle

Enter an expression or 'quit' to exit

123 / 2

Result = 61.5

Workflow is idle

Enter an expression or 'quit' to exit

1 + 1

Result = 2

Workflow is idle

Enter an expression or 'quit' to exit

quit

Exiting program

Press any key to continue . . .
```

Using an Alternate Extension

One of the key benefits of workflow extensions is the ability to swap out the implementation without changing the workflows that use the extension. You'll realize this benefit only if the custom activity that uses the extension retrieves it using an interface or base class.

To demonstrate this benefit, you can modify the previous example to use a different workflow extension. This new extension will provide an alternate communication mechanism between the workflow instance and the host application. The previous application used a C# event to notify the host when the workflow was waiting for a bookmark to be resumed. In this alternate example, you will implement the communication using the Queue class instead of an event. Depending on the exact needs of your application, this might actually provide a better communication mechanism. The benefit of a queue is that the host can determine when to process a message from the queue rather than reacting to an event immediately as it is raised. The queue also provides a way to throttle the processing of multiple messages, which might be important if you are hosting multiple workflow instances.

You will complete these tasks to implement this example:

1. Implement a new HostQueueNotifier extension class.

2. Modify the host application code to use the new extension class and retrieve notification messages using a queue.

Implementing the HostQueueNotifier Extension

To implement the new extension, add a new C# class to the **ActivityLibrary** project, and name it **HostQueueNotifier**. Here is the complete code for this class:

```
using System;
using System.Collections.Generic;
using System.Threading;

namespace ActivityLibrary
{
    public class HostQueueNotifier : IHostNotification
    {
```

The extension has two public properties that will be used by the host application. The **MessageQueue** property is the queue containing the messages to be processed. The **MessageAvailableEvent** property is an **AutoResetEvent** that provides a signaling mechanism to notify the host that a new message is available for processing.

```
        public Queue<HostNotifyMessage> MessageQueue { get; private set; }
        public AutoResetEvent MessageAvailableEvent { get; private set; }

        public HostQueueNotifier()
        {
            MessageQueue = new Queue<HostNotifyMessage>();
            MessageAvailableEvent = new AutoResetEvent(false);
        }
```

The **Notify** method is similar to the **HostEventNotifier** that you implemented in the previous example. The primary difference is that the code adds a message to a queue rather than raising an event. This implementation does not need to use a separate thread to add the message since the host application will retrieve the message from the queue using its own thread. The workflow thread has completed its work once the message is added to the queue.

```
        public void Notify(string message, String bookmarkName)
        {
            lock (MessageQueue)
            {
                MessageQueue.Enqueue(
                    new HostNotifyMessage(message, bookmarkName));
                MessageAvailableEvent.Set();
            }
        }
    }
}
```

```
public class HostNotifyMessage
{
    public String Message { get; private set; }
    public String BookmarkName { get; private set; }
    public HostNotifyMessage(String message, String bookmarkName)
    {
        Message = message;
        BookmarkName = bookmarkName;
    }
}
}
```

Hosting the Workflow

The only remaining task is to modify the code in the BookmarkCalculatorEvent host application. You need to add the new HostQueueNotifier extension to the workflow instance instead of the HostEventNotifier used in the previous example. You also need to update the code to retrieve the notification from the queue instead of immediately reacting to the event.

Here are the revised sections of code in the Program.cs file:

```
namespace BookmarkCalculatorEvent
{
    class Program
    {
        static void Main(string[] args)
        {
            Boolean isRunning = true;
            while (isRunning)
            {
                try
                {
...

                    HostQueueNotifier extension = new HostQueueNotifier();
                    wfApp.Extensions.Add(extension);
                    wfApp.Run();
```

After starting the workflow instance, the host application waits for the MessageAvailableEvent property of the extension (an AutoResetEvent) to be signaled. A signal means that a new message has arrived in the queue. This code assumes that only one message arrives for each signal, but this could easily be modified to process multiple messages from the queue if your application requires that.

```
                    if (extension.MessageAvailableEvent.WaitOne())
                    {
                        HostNotifyMessage msg = null;
                        lock (extension.MessageQueue)
                        {
```

```
                    if (extension.MessageQueue.Count > 0)
                    {
                        msg = extension.MessageQueue.Dequeue();
                    }
                }

                if (msg != null)
                {
                    Console.WriteLine(msg.Message);
                    String expression = Console.ReadLine();
                    if ((String.IsNullOrEmpty(expression)) ||
                        (!String.IsNullOrEmpty(expression) &&
                         expression.Trim().ToLower() == "quit"))
                    {
                        wfApp.Cancel();
                        Console.WriteLine("Exiting program");
                        isRunning = false;
                    }
                    else if (IsBookmarkValid(wfApp, msg.BookmarkName))
                    {
                        wfApp.ResumeBookmark(
                            msg.BookmarkName, expression);
                    }
                }
            }

            syncEvent.WaitOne();
        }
        catch (Exception exception)
        {
            Console.WriteLine("Error: {0}", exception.Message);
        }
    }
}
...
    }
}
```

Testing the Workflow

You should now be able to build the solution and run the `BookmarkCalculatorEvent` project that you just modified. The results that you see should be consistent with the previous example.

This example illustrates a couple of points. First, workflow extensions are a flexible way to provide additional functionality to workflow instances. Second, there are multiple ways to provide communication between a workflow instance and the host application.

Understanding the ActivityAction

Since the overall theme of this chapter is communication between the host application and workflow instances, there is one additional mechanism that I will present: the `ActivityAction` class. This class (along with the closely related `ActivityFunc` class) provides a general-purpose extensibility point for workflows that can be used for much more than simple communication. This section and the subsequent example will focus only on its use as a communication mechanism.

The `ActivityAction` class provides a way to defer the choice of activity to execute until runtime. It declares a planned hole that must be filled at runtime before the workflow can be executed. Within the workflow model, an `InvokeAction` activity can be declared that executes an `ActivityAction` activity with a defined signature. Just like a C# method, the signature consists of the number and type of input parameters. At design time, the `InvokeActivity` is not aware of the exact type of activity that it is invoking. It is only aware of the signature of that activity. The activity to execute is supplied externally at runtime from outside the workflow model. When the `InvokeAction` is executed, the `ActivityAction` that is assigned to it is executed. In turn, the `ActivityAction` identifies a handler activity that is executed.

■ **Tip** Remember that the `ActivityAction` isn't the final activity that you're attempting to execute. The real goal is to execute the activity that is assigned to the `ActivityAction.Handler` property.

The general concept is no different from a C# delegate or event (or even late binding in the COM world). In all of these cases, the invoking code is working with a method signature, not the actual concrete method. The assignment of the concrete method to execute is made at runtime, not design time. You can think of the `ActivityAction` and `ActivityFunc` classes as the way to declaratively execute a delegate to an activity.

■ **Note** If you require only a simple way to notify the host of an event, one of the previous implementations that used a workflow extension and an event or queue is a much simpler approach. The `ActivityAction` mechanism is a powerful, yet somewhat complicated, way to implement host communication.

The `ActivityAction` class is used when you need to execute an activity that does not return a result. The `ActivityFunc` class works in a similar manner, but it supports execution of an activity with a result value.

The `ActivityAction` and `ActivityFunc` classes are really a family of related generic classes designed to support a varying number of input arguments. For example, `ActivityAction<T>` supports a single input argument, while `ActivityAction<T1,T2>` supports two input arguments. Likewise, `ActivityFunc<T, TResult>` supports a single input and output argument, while `ActivityFunc<T1, T2, TResult>` supports two input arguments and one output argument. WF provides variations of these classes to support up to 16 input arguments.

Within the workflow model, you declaratively use the `InvokeAction` or `InvokeFunc` activity to execute an `ActivityAction` or `ActivityFunc`, respectively. Just like the activities they execute, there are variations of these classes that support up to 16 input arguments. The version of `InvokeAction` or `InvokeFunc` that you use must match the signature of the `ActivityAction` or `ActivityFunc` that you want to execute. For example, you would need to use an `InvokeAction<T1, T2, T3>` to execute an `ActivityAction<T1, T2, T3>`.

■ **Note** The `InvokeAction` and `InvokeFunc` classes are activities, but they lack enhanced designer support and are not currently added to the Toolbox by default. Therefore, before you use them, you need to first add them to the Visual Studio Toolbox. The alternative is to implement a declarative custom activity in code that includes these activities.

If you are implementing a custom activity that derives from `NativeActivity` (or `NativeActivity<TResult`), you have an additional way to execute an `ActivityAction` or `ActivityFunc`. The `NativeActivityContext` provides a set of overloaded methods named `ScheduleAction` and `ScheduleFunc`. Just like everything else associated with these classes, there are overloads that allow you to pass up to 16 typed input arguments. These methods do essentially the same thing as `InvokeAction` and `InvokeFunc` but do so entirely in code instead of declaratively.

Here is a representative sample of the most important properties of `ActivityAction`. It is only a representative sample since there are so many variations of this class to support a varying number of input arguments. The properties for an `ActivityAction<T>` that supports a single input argument would look like this:

Property	Type	Required	Description
Handler	Activity	Yes	The activity that is executed
Argument	DelegateInArgument<T>	Yes	A single input argument

If you are using the `ActivityAction<T1,T2,T3>` version, which supports three arguments, the properties would look like this:

Property	Type	Required	Description
Handler	Activity	Yes	The activity that is executed
Argument1	DelegateInArgument<T1>	Yes	The first input argument
Argument2	DelegateInArgument<T2>	Yes	The second input argument
Argument3	DelegateInArgument<T3>	Yes	The third input argument

The `ActivityFunc` class supports a similar set of properties. Here are the most important properties for the `ActivityFunc<T, TResult>` that supports a single input and output argument:

Property	Type	Required	Description
Handler	Activity	Yes	The activity that is executed.
Result	DelegateOutArgument<TResult>	Yes	The result output argument
Argument	DelegateInArgument<T>	Yes	The single input argument

If you use the `ActivityFunc<T1, T2, T3, TResult>` that supports three input arguments and one output argument, the properties would look like this:

Property	Type	Required	Description
Handler	Activity	Yes	The activity that is executed
Result	DelegateOutArgument<TResult>	Yes	The result output argument
Argument1	DelegateInArgument<T1>	Yes	The first input argument
Argument2	DelegateInArgument<T2>	Yes	The second input argument
Argument3	DelegateInArgument<T3>	Yes	The third input argument

The `ActivityAction` mechanism is flexible and can be implemented and used in several different ways. Figure 8-4 illustrates one way to use it that corresponds to the way it is used in the following example.

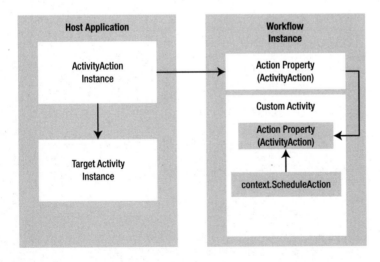

Figure 8-4. ActivityAction usage

In Figure 8-4, a custom code activity is developed that executes an `ActivityAction`. This custom activity has a public property of type `ActivityAction` named `Action`. The activity code uses the `ScheduleAction` method of the activity context to schedule execution of the `ActivityAction` that is assigned to the `Action` property. The workflow also declares an `Action` property of the same type (`ActivityAction`). The value of this property is bound to the `Action` property of the custom activity.

At runtime, the host application creates an instance of an `ActivityAction`. The `Action` property of the workflow instance is set to this activity. The `ActivityAction` references an instance of another activity that is the real target activity to be executed.

Putting it all together, when the workflow is started, the custom activity executes and schedules execution of the `ActivityAction` that was assigned to the workflow by the host application. The `ActivityAction` executes the activity that was constructed by the host application and assigned to the `ActivityAction.Handler` property.

Using the ActivityAction

In the example that follows, you will implement yet another version of the `BookmarkCalculator` application. This time, you will use an `ActivityAction` as a communication mechanism between the workflow instance and the host application.

The host application code will create an `ActivityAction` and assign it to a property of the workflow. That property will, in turn, be bound to a similar property of a custom activity. The custom activity will schedule execution of the `ActivityAction` that was set for the property. In this example, the `ActivityAction` that is created by the host application will use `InvokeMethod` to execute a method in the host class.

You will complete these tasks to complete this example:

1.   Implement a new `NotifyHostWithAction` custom activity.

2.   Declare the `BookmarkCalculatorAction` workflow.

3.   Manually modify the workflow Xaml file to bind the workflow property to the custom activity.

4.   Implement the code to host the workflow.

Implementing the NotifyHostWithAction Activity

Add a new Code Activity to the `ActivityLibrary` project, and name it `NotifyHostWithAction`. This new custom activity schedules execution of the `ActivityAction` that is exposed as a property. Here is the complete code for this class:

```
using System;
using System.Activities;

namespace ActivityLibrary
{
```

Two string input arguments are defined. The first is used to provide a prompt that is passed to the target activity, and the second is used to pass the bookmark name that should be resumed by the host application. The Action property is the ActivityAction to be executed. It defines two string arguments, which correspond to the two input arguments of this custom activity (Prompt and BookmarkName).

It is critical to note that the ActivityAction to be executed is declared as a normal C# property instead of a workflow argument. This is necessary since the InvokeAction activity must work with a direct reference to an ActivityAction instance.

Also note that the ContentProperty attribute has been applied to this class. This attribute identifies the property that is associated with the contents of this activity when it is declared in a Xaml document. The contents value is the one that is declared without specifying the property name as an attribute. You will use this feature when you manually modify the Xaml file for the workflow that uses this activity.

```
[System.Windows.Markup.ContentProperty("Action")]
public sealed class NotifyHostWithAction : NativeActivity
{
    public InArgument<String> Prompt { get; set; }
    public InArgument<String> BookmarkName { get; set; }
    public ActivityAction<String, String> Action { get; set; }

    protected override void Execute(NativeActivityContext context)
    {
```

The NativeActivityContext provides the ScheduleAction method, which is used to schedule execution of the ActivityAction that is assigned to the Action property. The overload of this method that supports two input arguments is used to pass the two string arguments.

```
        if (Action != null)
        {
            context.ScheduleAction(Action,
                Prompt.Get(context), BookmarkName.Get(context));
        }
    }
}
```

Declaring the BookmarkCalculatorAction Workflow

Create a new project named BookmarkCalculatorAction using the Workflow Console Application template. Add the new project to the solution for this chapter, and add a project reference to the ActivityLibrary project in the same solution.

Delete the Workflow1.xaml file that was created with the project since it won't be needed. Instead, copy the BookmarkCalculatorExtension.xaml file from the previous example to this new project. Name the copied file BookmarkCalculatorAction.xaml. Open the Xaml file in the XML editor (Code View), and change the namespace and class entries at the top of the file to correspond with the new name. Rebuild the solution before proceeding with the remaining steps.

Open the workflow in Design View, and follow these steps to complete the declaration of the workflow:

1. Open the argument editor for the workflow, and add a new property named `Action` with a type of `ActivityAction<String,String>`. Most importantly, make sure that you specify the type of argument as Property. This must not be an input or output argument.

2. Remove the `NotifyHost` activity from the workflow since it is no longer needed.

3. Replace the `NotifyHost` with an instance of the new `NotifyHostWithAction` activity. Set the `Prompt` property to `"Enter an expression or 'quit' to exit"` and the `BookmarkName` property to `"GetString"`. The `Action` property cannot be directly set within the designer and will be handled in the next section.

4. Drag a connection from the start of the flowchart to the `NotifyHostWithAction` activity so this activity is executed first. Drag another connection from this activity to the `GetString` activity.

The workflow should look like Figure 8-5.

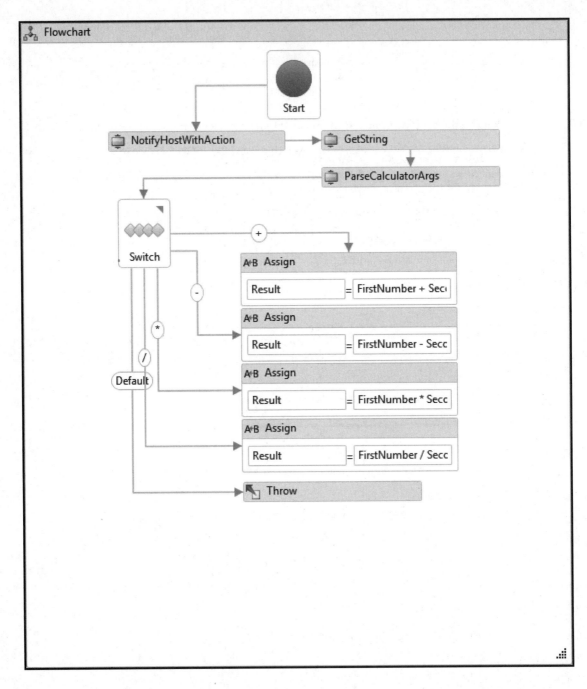

Figure 8-5. BookmarkCalculatorAction workflow

Binding the Action Property

There is one remaining step before the workflow declaration is complete. The `Action` property of the `NotifyHostWithAction` activity must reference the `Action` property of the workflow. To accomplish this, a `PropertyReference` must be used. This is a specialized type of activity that enables the binding of two properties to each other. However, the use of the `PropertyReference` is not supported by the workflow designer. You'll need to manually edit the Xaml file to add this binding element.

After saving your changes, close the Design View for the workflow, and reopen it using the XML editor (Code View). Find the reference to the `NotifyHostWithAction` activity in the file. Add the `PropertyReference` element shown here, which binds the `Action` property of the activity to the `Action` property of the workflow. Here is the revised `NotifyHostWithAction` element:

```
<a:NotifyHostWithAction Prompt="Enter an expression or 'quit' to exit"
    BookmarkName="GetString" >
    <PropertyReference x:TypeArguments="ActivityAction(x:String,x:String)"
        PropertyName="Action" />
</a:NotifyHostWithAction>
```

The property name (`Action`) of the activity is not specified since this property was identified as the `ContentProperty` in the activity.

■ **Warning** One unfortunate by-product of this manual change is that the workflow designer doesn't know how to handle it. You can open the workflow in the designer and make additional changes, but when the workflow is saved, an additional entry containing `<x:Null />` is added under the `PropertyReference`. Ideally, Microsoft will eventually provide a better way to add and maintain a `PropertyReference`. If you do need to open this workflow in the designer, you will need to remove the offending `<x:Null />` line after you save your changes.

Hosting the Workflow

The code that hosts the workflow must supply an `ActivityAction` to the `Action` property of the workflow after it has been constructed. The `ActivityAction` is really just a generalized way to execute another activity, so another activity must be created and assigned to the `ActivityAction.Handler` property. For this example, an `InvokeMethod` activity is created and assigned to the `ActivityAction` as the activity to execute. The `InvokeMethod` will execute a static method of the `Program` class to handle the notification from the workflow.

Here is the complete code for the `Program.cs` file in the `BookmarkCalculatorAction` project:

```
using System;
using System.Activities;
using System.Activities.Statements;
using System.Linq;
using System.Threading;

namespace BookmarkCalculatorAction
{
```

```
class Program
{
    private static Boolean isRunning = true;
    private static WorkflowApplication wfApp;

    static void Main(string[] args)
    {
        while (isRunning)
        {
            try
            {
                AutoResetEvent syncEvent = new AutoResetEvent(false);
                BookmarkCalculatorAction wf = new BookmarkCalculatorAction();
```

After constructing an instance of the workflow, an `ActivityAction<T1,T2>` activity is constructed and assigned to the `Action` property of the workflow. An `InvokeMethod` activity is created and assigned to the `ActivityAction.Handler` property. The properties of the `InvokeMethod` activity are set to execute the static `ReceivedNotification` method of this class, which is defined to accept two string arguments. The string argument values that are passed into the `ActivityAction<T1,T2>` are passed as parameters to this static method. The `InArgument` constructor that provides access to the activity context is used to retrieve the current value of each argument.

```
wf.Action = new ActivityAction<String, String>
{
    Argument1 = new DelegateInArgument<String>(),
    Argument2 = new DelegateInArgument<String>(),
    Handler = new InvokeMethod
    {
        TargetType = typeof(Program),
        MethodName = "ReceivedNotification",
        Parameters =
        {
            new InArgument<String>(
                ac => wf.Action.Argument1.Get(ac)),
            new InArgument<String>(
                ac => wf.Action.Argument2.Get(ac))
        }
    }
};

wfApp = new WorkflowApplication(wf);
wfApp.Completed = delegate(
    WorkflowApplicationCompletedEventArgs e)
{
    if (e.CompletionState == ActivityInstanceState.Closed)
    {
        Console.WriteLine("Result = {0}", e.Outputs["Result"]);
    }
    syncEvent.Set();
};
```

```
                wfApp.Idle = delegate(WorkflowApplicationIdleEventArgs e)
                {
                    Console.WriteLine("Workflow is idle");
                };

                wfApp.OnUnhandledException = delegate(
                    WorkflowApplicationUnhandledExceptionEventArgs e)
                {
                    Console.WriteLine(e.UnhandledException.Message.ToString());
                    return UnhandledExceptionAction.Terminate;
                };

                wfApp.Run();
                syncEvent.WaitOne();
            }
            catch (Exception exception)
            {
                Console.WriteLine("Error: {0}", exception.Message);
            }
        }
    }

    private static Boolean IsBookmarkValid(
        WorkflowApplication wfApp, String bookmarkName)
    {
        Boolean result = false;
        var bookmarks = wfApp.GetBookmarks();
        if (bookmarks != null)
        {
            result =
                (from b in bookmarks
                 where b.BookmarkName == bookmarkName
                 select b).Any();
        }
        return result;
    }
```

The static `ReceivedNotification` method is the target of the `InvokeMethod` activity that was constructed earlier in the code. It is invoked when the `NotifyHostWithAction` activity is executed from within the workflow. The string prompt and bookmark name arguments that are passed as parameters to this method originated as the `Prompt` and `BookmarkName` properties of the `NotifyHostWithAction` activity.

This method has now become an externally defined extension of the workflow instance that is executed on the workflow thread. Because you shouldn't occupy the workflow thread for longer than is necessary, the actual work of this method is performed using the thread pool. An `Action<T1,T2>` delegate is used as a convenient way to execute this code on a thread pool thread. The code to resume the bookmark is similar to the previous examples.

```
public static void ReceivedNotification(
    String prompt, String bookmarkName)
{
    Action<String, String> asyncWork = (msg, bm) =>
    {
        Console.WriteLine(msg);
        String expression = Console.ReadLine();

        if ((String.IsNullOrEmpty(expression)) ||
            (!String.IsNullOrEmpty(expression) &&
             expression.Trim().ToLower() == "quit"))
        {
            wfApp.Cancel();
            Console.WriteLine("Exiting program");
            isRunning = false;
        }
        else if (IsBookmarkValid(wfApp, bm))
        {
            wfApp.ResumeBookmark(bm, expression);
        }
    };

    asyncWork.BeginInvoke(prompt, bookmarkName,
        ar => { ((Action<String, String>)ar.AsyncState).EndInvoke(ar); },
        asyncWork);
}
}
}
```

Testing the Workflow

You should be able to build the entire solution and run the BookmarkCalculatorAction project. The results should be consistent with the previous calculator examples.

Using an ActivityAction is the most complex way to provide a simple notification to the host application. The real power of this approach is in the flexibility that it provides. In this example, you executed a simple static method of the host class. But this extension point is extremely flexible, and you could have just as easily executed another type of activity that contained additional business logic. This mechanism allows you to defer the decision as to which activity to execute until runtime when the workflow is executed. The ultimate in declarative late binding!

Using the InvokeAction Activity

As an alternative to developing the custom NotifyHostWithAction activity, you can use the InvokeAction activity to declaratively execute an ActivityAction. If you want to see this in action, you can follow these steps to modify the BookmarkCalculatorAction workflow that you declared for the previous example:

1. You first need to add the `InvokeAction<T1,T2>` activity to the Visual Studio Toolbox if it is not already there. To accomplish this, follow the steps outlined in the "Adding Activities to the Toolbox" sidebar.

2. Open the `BookmarkCalculatorAction` workflow in the designer.

3. Delete the `NotifyHostWithAction` activity from the workflow.

4. Add an instance of the `InvokeAction<T1,T2>` activity to the workflow to replace the `NotifyHostWithAction` activity that you just deleted. Select `System.String` as the type for the `T1` and `T2` generic parameters. Set the `Argument1` property to `"Enter an expression or 'quit' to exit"` and the `Argument2` property to `"GetString"`.

5. Drag a connection from the start of the flowchart to the `InvokeAction<String,String>` activity so this activity is executed first. Drag another connection from this activity to the `GetString` activity.

Structurally, the workflow looks the same as the previous example shown in Figure 8-5. The only difference is that the `NotifyHostWithAction` activity has been replaced with an `InvokeAction<String,String>`.

After saving your changes, close and reopen the workflow in the XML editor. Locate the `InvokeAction` in the Xaml file, and add the same `PropertyReference` that you previously added to the `NotifyHostWithAction` activity. Here is the updated `InvokeAction` element with the `PropertyReference`:

```
<InvokeAction x:TypeArguments="x:String, x:String"
    Argument1="Enter an expression or 'quit' to exit"
    Argument2="GetString">
  <PropertyReference x:TypeArguments="ActivityAction(x:String, x:String)"
      PropertyName="Action" />
</InvokeAction>
```

Since you haven't made any changes to the overall signature of the workflow, there are no changes necessary to the host application code. After building the project, you should be able to execute the `BookmarkCalculatorAction` project and see the same consistent results.

Adding Activities to the Toolbox

WF provides a number of activity classes that are not added to the Visual Studio Toolbox by default. It is likely that these activities were not added to the Toolbox because they are primarily designed to be used by custom code activities or they lack enhanced designer support. Regardless of the reason, it is a simple matter to add these missing activities to the Visual Studio Toolbox. The steps that follow add an `InvokeAction` activity to the Toolbox, but you can follow similar steps to the add other activities that you want to routinely use.

1. Right-click the Toolbox, and select the Add Tab option. Provide the new tab with a meaningful name such as Additional Activities.

2. Right-click the new tab, and select the Choose Items option. After a brief wait, you should be presented with a multitabbed dialog box.

3. Select the System.Activities Components tab where you will find the workflow activities.

4. Check the activities that you want to add to the Toolbox. In the example for this chapter, you need to locate and add the `InvokeAction<T1,T2>` activity.

Understanding the Pick Activity

In the previous examples, the workflow waited for a single bookmark to be resumed. Another frequently used pattern is to wait for multiple bookmarks at the same time. Each bookmark may be associated with a different type of external event. When one of the events is received (its bookmark is resumed), the other bookmarks are canceled.

Since this is a frequently used pattern, Microsoft provides the `Pick` and `PickBranch` activities that you can use to implement it in your workflows. The `Pick` activity is the container for a collection of `PickBranch` activities. Each `PickBranch` activity represents one possible path of execution that is triggered by the resumption of a unique bookmark.

Here is the most important property of the `Pick` activity:

Property	Type	Required	Description
Branches	Collection<PickBranch>	Yes	A collection of PickBranch activities

And here are the most important properties of the `PickBranch` activity:

Property	Type	Required	Description
Trigger	Activity	Yes	The activity that creates a bookmark. The resumption of this bookmark triggers execution of the activity defined for the Action property.
Action	Activity	Yes	The activity that is executed when the bookmark has been resumed.

The `Pick` activity immediately schedules execution of all of its `PickBranch` activities. Each `PickBranch` immediately schedules execution of its `Trigger` activity. The job of the `Trigger` activity is to create a bookmark. When one of the bookmarks is resumed, the `Trigger` activity of that `PickBranch` completes, and execution of the `Action` activity for that `PickBranch` is scheduled. Once one of the `Trigger` activities completes, all other `PickBranch` `Trigger` activities are canceled.

It is worth noting that the `PickBranch` activity supports variables. This allows you to define private workflow variables that are scoped to a single path of execution and are not shared with other branches.

■ **Note** You can use any custom activity that creates a bookmark as the `Trigger` of a `PickBranch`. In addition to custom activities, you can also use the WCF messaging activities provided with WF. These activities use bookmarks as the underlying mechanism to handle incoming WCF messages. The `Delay` activity can also be used as a trigger.

Using the Pick Activity

To demonstrate the use of the `Pick` and `PickBranch` activities, I've chosen a simple problem reporting workflow. Each workflow instance represents a problem that has been reported and must be researched and resolved. The workflow supports a small set of bookmarks that mimic status changes to the problem as it is being reviewed and corrected. Just as you saw in an earlier example, the workflow uses an extension to raise an event that is handled by the host application. The event is used to notify the host that the status has changed and that the workflow is waiting for resumption of one of the bookmarks. The workflow really doesn't accomplish any useful work, other than to notify the host of the status changes as they occur.

To add a small twist to this example, I've chosen to filter the set of bookmarks that are created based on the current status. A set of `If` activity instances is used to perform the filtering. The workflow starts with a status of Triage, assuming that a problem is first reviewed to determine whether further investigation is necessary. From this status, the workflow can progress to the Active status or directly to Closed. From the Active status, it can move to the Resolved status. And finally, from Resolved, it can move to Closed.

You will complete these tasks to implement this example:

1. Implement a custom `WaitForBookmark` activity.

2. Implement the `ProblemReporting` workflow.

3. Implement a host application that allows you to enter a new status to resume one of the available bookmarks.

Implementing the WaitForBookmark Activity

This example uses a simple custom activity to create a bookmark. The activity doesn't perform any real work other than to create the named bookmark. But it satisfies the requirements of this example and allows each `PickBranch` to be externally triggered with a different named bookmark.

To implement this activity, add a new Code Activity to the `ActivityLibrary` project, and name it `WaitForBookmark`. Here is the code for this activity:

```
using System;
using System.Activities;

namespace ActivityLibrary
{
```

```
public sealed class WaitForBookmark : NativeActivity
{
    [RequiredArgument]
    public InArgument<String> BookmarkName { get; set; }
```

Unlike the previous activities that created a bookmark, this activity does not provide a callback to execute when the bookmark is resumed. The callback is needed when you need to retrieve data that is passed when the bookmark is resumed. In this case, no additional data will be passed with the bookmark. The bookmark is created as a trigger mechanism only.

```
    protected override void Execute(NativeActivityContext context)
    {
        context.CreateBookmark(BookmarkName.Get(context));
    }

    protected override bool CanInduceIdle
    {
        get { return true; }
    }
}
}
```

Rebuild the solution to ensure that the `WaitForBookmark` activity builds successfully and is added to the Toolbox.

Creating the Console Project

Create a new Workflow Console Application project, and name it `ProblemReporting`. Add the new project to the current solution for this chapter, and delete the `Workflow1.xaml` file that was created. Add a project reference to the `ActivityLibrary` project in the same solution. Add a new workflow named `ProblemReporting` to the project, and add a `Flowchart` as the root activity of the workflow.

Defining Variables

The `ProblemReporting` workflow requires a single variable that maintains the current status. You can add this variable immediately since it is scoped by the root `Flowchart` activity. Here is the variable that you should add:

Name	Variable Type	Scope	Default
Status	String	Flowchart	"Triage"

Please note that the variable requires a default string value.

Declaring the ProblemReporting Workflow

You should follow these steps to complete the workflow declaration:

1. Add a `NotifyHost` activity to the top of the root `Flowchart` activity. This activity was implemented and used in the previous examples in this chapter. Set the `NotifyHost.Message` property to `String.Format("New status: {0}", Status)`.

2. Add a connection from the starting point of the flowchart to the `NotifyHost` activity.

3. Add a `Pick` activity directly below the `NotifyHost`. Add a connection from the `NotifyHost` to the `Pick` activity. The `Pick` activity initially has two `PickBranch` activities. You will need a total of three `PickBranch` activities, so you can add an additional one now. You may need to drill down into the `Pick` activity by double-clicking it before you can add a new branch.

4. Add an `If` activity as the `Trigger` of the leftmost `PickBranch`. Set the `If.Condition` property to `Status = "Triage"`. The purpose of the `If` activity is to use the value of the `Status` variable to determine whether the bookmark should be created.

5. Add a `WaitForBookmark` activity to the `If.Then` property. Set the `WaitForBookmark.BookmarkName` property to `"Active"`.

6. Add a `Delay` activity to the `If.Else` property. Set the `Delay.Duration` property to `TimeSpan.MaxValue`. The `Delay` activity is needed to balance both sides of the `If` activity. Even if the `WaitForBookmark` is not executed (the condition is false), you still need to execute an activity that creates a bookmark. The `Delay` activity with its `Duration` set to the maximum possible value satisfies that requirement.

7. Add an `Assign` activity to the `Action` of the leftmost `PickBranch`. Set the `Assign.To` property to `Status` and the `Assign.Value` property to `"Active"`. This completes the first `PickBranch`, which is shown in Figure 8-6.

8. The second and third `PickBranch` instances have the same structure as the first. Add an `If` activity to the `PickBranch.Target` and an `Assign` activity to the `PickBranch.Action`. Add a `WaitForBookmark` to the `If.Then` and a `Delay` to the `If.Else`. Instead of declaring these branches step by step, you can choose to copy and paste the first `PickBranch` and then delete the unused default `PickBranch` instances.

9. Set the property values for all the activities in the second and third `PickBranch` instances. Please refer to the property values in the following tables. Figure 8-7 shows the completed `Pick` activity with three `PickBranch` instances.

Second Pickbranch Property Values

Activity	Property	Value
If	Condition	Status = "Active"
WaitForBookmark	BookmarkName	"Resolved"
Delay	Duration	TimeSpan.MaxValue
Assign	To	Status
Assign	Value	"Resolved"

Third Pickbranch Property Values

Activity	Property	Value
If	Condition	Status = "Triage" Or Status = "Resolved"
WaitForBookmark	BookmarkName	"Closed"
Delay	Duration	TimeSpan.MaxValue
Assign	To	Status
Assign	Value	"Closed"

10. Return to the top level of the flowchart, and add a `FlowDecision` directly below the `Pick` activity. Add a connection from the bottom of the `Pick` activity to the top of the `FlowDecision`.

11. Set the `FlowDecision.Condition` property to `Status = "Closed"`. Drag a connection from the right side of the `FlowDecision` (the false side) to the side of the `NotifyHost` activity. This causes the workflow to loop until the `Status` is equal to `"Closed"`. Figure 8-8 shows the completed top-level view of the workflow.

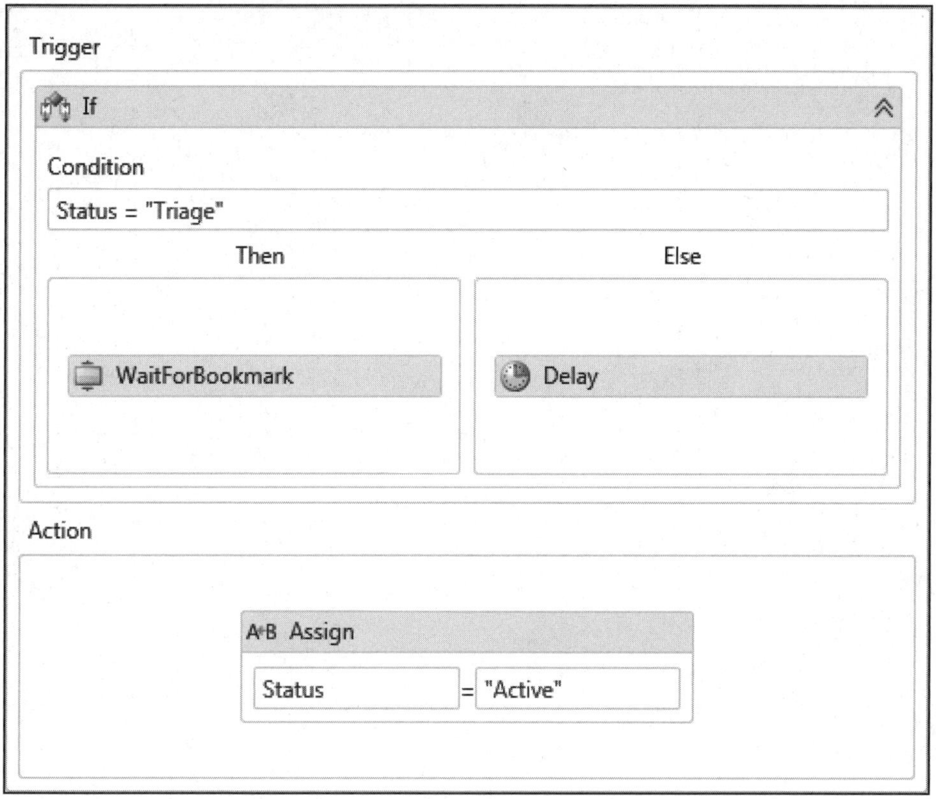

Figure 8-6. First PickBranch

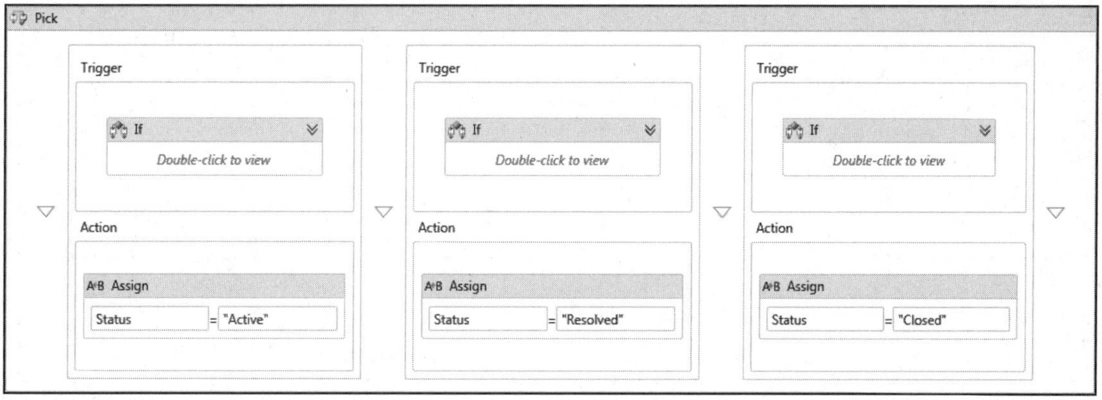

Figure 8-7. Completed Pick activity

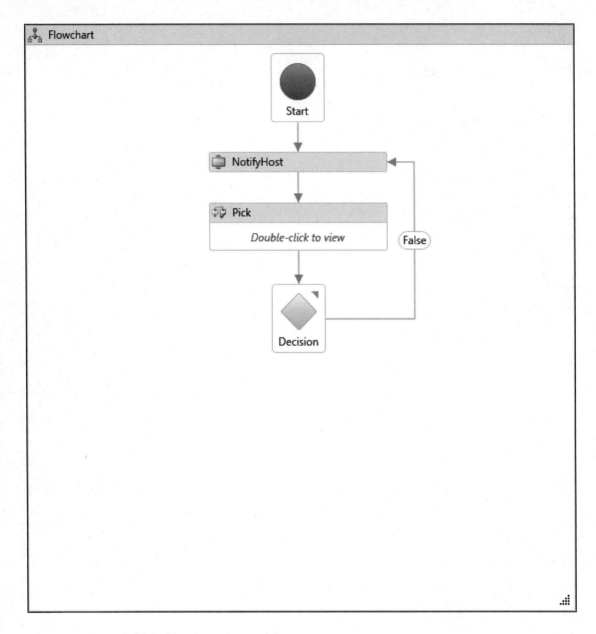

Figure 8-8. Completed ProblemReporting workflow

Hosting the Workflow

The code to host the workflow uses the HostEventNotifier extension developed earlier in the chapter. Here is the completed Program.cs file in the ProblemReporting project:

```
using System;
using System.Activities;
using System.Activities.Hosting;
using System.Linq;
using System.Threading;
using ActivityLibrary;

namespace ProblemReporting
{
    class Program
    {
        static void Main(string[] args)
        {
            try
            {
                AutoResetEvent syncEvent = new AutoResetEvent(false);

                WorkflowApplication wfApp =
                    new WorkflowApplication(new ProblemReporting());

                wfApp.Completed = delegate(
                    WorkflowApplicationCompletedEventArgs e)
                {
                    syncEvent.Set();
                };

                wfApp.Idle = delegate(WorkflowApplicationIdleEventArgs e)
                {
                    Console.WriteLine("Workflow is idle");
                };

                wfApp.OnUnhandledException = delegate(
                    WorkflowApplicationUnhandledExceptionEventArgs e)
                {
                    Console.WriteLine(e.UnhandledException.Message.ToString());
                    return UnhandledExceptionAction.Terminate;
                };

                HostEventNotifier extension = new HostEventNotifier();
                extension.Notification += delegate(
                    Object sender, HostNotifyEventArgs e)
                {
                    Console.WriteLine(e.Message);
```

When an event is received from the workflow, the collection of all available bookmarks is displayed on the console. This prompts the user with a list of available actions.

```csharp
                var bookmarks = wfApp.GetBookmarks();
                if (bookmarks != null && bookmarks.Count > 0)
                {
                    Console.WriteLine("Select one of these available actions:");
                    foreach (BookmarkInfo bookmark in bookmarks)
                    {
                        Console.WriteLine("->{0}", bookmark.BookmarkName);
                    }
                }

                Boolean isWaitingForChoice = true;
                while (isWaitingForChoice)
                {
                    String newAction = Console.ReadLine();
                    if (IsBookmarkValid(wfApp, newAction))
                    {
                        isWaitingForChoice = false;
                        wfApp.ResumeBookmark(newAction, null);
                    }
                    else
                    {
                        Console.WriteLine("Incorrect choice!");
                    }
                }
            };

            wfApp.Extensions.Add(extension);
            wfApp.Run();
            syncEvent.WaitOne();
        }
        catch (Exception exception)
        {
            Console.WriteLine("Error: {0}", exception.Message);
        }
    }

    private static Boolean IsBookmarkValid(
        WorkflowApplication wfApp, String bookmarkName)
    {
        Boolean result = false;
        var bookmarks = wfApp.GetBookmarks();
        if (bookmarks != null)
        {
            result =
                (from b in bookmarks
                 where b.BookmarkName == bookmarkName
                 select b).Any();
        }
```

```
            return result;
        }
    }
}
```

Testing the Workflow

After building the solution, run the `ProblemReporting` project. Here is a representative sample of my results:

```
Workflow is idle

New status: Triage

Select one of these available actions:

->Active

->Closed

Active

Workflow is idle

New status: Active

Select one of these available actions:

->Resolved

Resolved

Workflow is idle

New status: Resolved

Select one of these available actions:

->Closed

Closed
```

From these results you can see that the list of available actions (bookmarks) varies depending on the current status. For example, when the workflow first begins, the status is Triage, and the available actions are Active and Closed. This was accomplished using the `If` activity as the trigger for each `PickBranch`. If you used the `WaitForBookmark` directly as the trigger, all bookmarks would be available regardless of the current status.

Summary

This chapter focused on the various ways to implement direct communication between the host application and a running workflow instance. The chapter began with a discussion of the bookmark mechanism. Bookmarks are the WF mechanism that support long-running workflows. Long-running workflows are temporarily suspended while they are waiting for external input. Bookmarks also allow you to pass data back to the workflow as the bookmark is resumed. The first example of the chapter revisited the command-line calculator and revised it to use the bookmark mechanism.

Workflow extensions are a general-purpose mechanism used to provide additional functionality to workflow instances and were covered next. They can serve a wide variety of purposes, but their use as a communication mechanism for sending data back to the host application was demonstrated in the next few examples. The `ActivityAction` activity was also demonstrated as a possible way to send data from a running workflow instance to the host application.

One common workflow pattern is to wait for multiple external events, continuing with the execution of the workflow when one of the events is received. The `Pick` and `PickBranch` activities are used to support this pattern and were demonstrated in the final sections of the chapter.

In the next chapter, you will learn how to implement message-based communication using the WCF integration features of WF.

CHAPTER 9

■ ■ ■

Workflow Services

This chapter focuses on theWindows Communication Foundation (WCF) support that is provided by Windows Workflow Foundation (WF). This broad category of WCF support falls under the moniker of *workflow services*. Included with this support is the ability to declaratively author WCF services using WF as well as to invoke WCF services from within a workflow.

The chapter begins with a brief introduction of workflow services and WCF followed by an in-depth discussion of the WF classes and activities that you will use to declare and invoke WCF services. The centerpiece example of this chapter is an order processing service that simulates an ecommerce transaction. The example begins with a relatively simple request/response service operation. This first basic example is used to demonstrate how to initially test the service, how to publish the service to Internet Information Services (IIS), how to develop a self-hosting application for the service, and how to implement nonworkflow and workflow client applications that invoke the service.

In Chapter 10, you will expand on this basic example by implementing additional workflow services that are consumed by this original workflow.

Introducing Workflow Services

WF provides the ability to author workflows that use WCF to communicate. Using WF, you can author WCF services that are fully implemented as declarative workflows. These services can be hosted by a centralized Microsoft environment such as IIS or WAS, or they can be self-hosted by an application that you develop yourself. Once hosted, these services can be consumed by any WCF client. Depending on the WCF bindings that you use, the services can also be consumed by web service clients. As is true for all WCF services, the WCF client is unaware of the implementation details of the service. In the case of WF workflow services, the client is not necessarily aware that it is communicating with a workflow instance.

In addition to authoring new WCF services, you can also use WF to consume existing WCF or web services. WF provides standard activities that allow you to declaratively send messages to WCF services as well as handle any response that is part of the service contract. The services that you consume need not be implemented using WF—they can also be implemented in traditional procedural languages.

Before diving deeply into the WF support for WCF services, the next section provides a brief overview of WCF. It should provide you with just enough WCF background information to allow you to effectively consume and author services in WF. If you are an experienced WCF developer, you will already be familiar with the concepts that are presented.

> ■ **Note** The goal of the next section is to provide an overview of how WCF works from the standpoint of traditional non-WF applications. The basic concepts that are discussed also apply to services that are implemented using WF. However, some of the tasks needed to implement a service are not necessary when you are implementing a service with WF.

Understanding WCF

In this section, I provide a brief overview of the key WCF concepts. Understanding just a few WCF concepts will provide the background that you'll need to implement and use WF workflow services.

> ■ **Note** WCF is a rich and complex Microsoft foundation that is at least as substantial as WF. In an effort to keep the focus of this book on WF, I've kept this overview as concise and high-level as possible. The information that I present here barely scratches the surface of WCF, and entire books have been written on the subject. If you plan on making extensive use of workflow services, you might want to purchase one of the many good WCF books, such as *Pro WCF: Practical Microsoft SOA Implementation* from Apress, that provide more in-depth coverage.

WCF is the enabling Microsoft technology for building service-oriented applications that was introduced in .NET 3.0. It provides a unified programming model for applications that are providers or consumers of contract-based services. WCF is really a superset of previous communication technologies including web services, Microsoft Message Queuing (MSMQ), and plain old sockets. It doesn't replace any of these technologies, since they are all still available for use in your applications. But it does replace multiple communication APIs with a single one that can simultaneously target different transport mechanisms.

When using WCF, you implement an application using a single unified model and API. WCF decouples the transport mechanism from the service contract. This allows you to change the transport mechanism without affecting application code.

At its core, WCF is a framework for sending messages between systems. It is not a distributed component-based framework like remoting or Distributed COM (DCOM). When you are working with WCF (including when you are working with workflow services), this is an important distinction to keep in mind. When you use WCF to consume a service, you are exchanging a request message and (if applicable) a response message. The exact type and number of objects that are instantiated by the service provider to handle your request are not under your direct control (and really shouldn't be your concern). In contrast with this, mechanisms like .NET remoting give you the ability to directly create instances of objects on a remote system. With remoting, you have intimate knowledge of the type of each object that you create as well as complete control over the object lifetime.

Defining Service Contracts

All WCF services define a service contract that identifies one or more operations. In a non-WF service implementation, the service contract usually takes the form of a C# interface that is decorated with the `ServiceContract` attribute. Each service method defined in the interface is decorated with the `OperationContract` attribute to identify it as a service operation.

■ **Note** When declaring WCF services using WF, the service contract and operation are inferred from properties of the messaging activities. There is no need to explicitly define the service contract using a C# interface.

Service operations can pass or return simple built-in types (for example, integers or strings) or complex types that you define. You define each complex type as you normally would a C# class. However, the class can be decorated with the `DataContract` attribute to identify it as part of the *data contract* for an operation. The data contract simply describes the data that is transmitted between the client and server and serialized by the `DataContractSerializer` (the default serializer used by WCF).

Data contracts are defined on an opt-in basis. When defining a data contract, you must explicitly select the members that you want to include in the contract. You do this by applying the `DataMember` attribute to a member of the class. Since you explicitly identify the members that are serialized as part of the data contract, you can choose to include any combination of public and private members.

WCF is all about messages, and it supports several well-established message exchange patterns:

- *Request/response*: With this message exchange pattern, a client sends a request message to the service and then expects (and waits for) a response message. This is the most common message exchange pattern since it nicely maps to service operations that accept parameters and return a result.

- *One-way*: Operations that use this pattern do not return a response message. They are considered fire-and-forget operations since the client receives no direct feedback concerning the success or failure of the operation.

- *Duplex*: With this message exchange pattern, a client initiates contact with a service and provides the service with a direct callback address to the client. The service uses the callback address to send messages (most typically one way) back to the client.

After defining all the necessary contracts, a service class is developed that provides an implementation for all the operations of the service contract. The service itself takes the form of a normal C# class that implements the service interface. Additional attributes such as the `ServiceBehavior` attribute can be applied to the service class to control aspects of the runtime service behavior.

■ **Note** When you are using WF to implement a service, there is no need for a service class. The implementation of the WCF service is fully provided in a declarative way by a workflow service definition.

Configuring Endpoints and Bindings

A WCF *endpoint* identifies a location where messages are sent. Each WCF service is exposed as one or more endpoints. For instance, the same service can be simultaneously exposed to web service clients using HTTP and to local clients using TCP. In both cases, the same service implementation is used, but it is exposed as two separate endpoints, each with their own set of capabilities and behaviors.

Each endpoint is composed of an address, a binding, and the contract. The *address* is a Uniform Resource Identifier (URI) that identifies the location that clients use to invoke operations on the service contract. The address takes different forms depending on the transport being used for the endpoint. For instance, a service that is exposed to web service clients using HTTP might specify the address like this:

```
http://www.myserverhost.com:8000/MyServices/SampleService1
```

The same service exposed to TCP clients might use an address such as this:

```
net.tcp://myserverhost:9876/MyServices/SampleService1
```

The *contract* that is associated with the endpoint is the service contract that was discussed in the previous section. It defines all the operations that are available from the service.

The *binding* describes how the messages are exchanged between systems using this endpoint. It is a named stack containing the transport, encoding, and protocols that control the way WCF processes inbound and outbound messages on an endpoint. At a minimum, the binding identifies the *transport protocol* (for example, HTTP, TCP, MSMQ) and the *encoding* (for example, Text, Binary). The encoding determines the form that serialized messages take across the wire.

In addition, a binding can include a number of other capabilities or protocols that are provided with WCF or developed on your own. For example, a binding can also specify the type of security that is used (or not used), security credentials, reliable sessions, transaction support, throttling behavior (to limit the size of messages processed), and so on.

WCF includes a number of system-provided bindings that you can use, configure, or extend (for example, `BasicHttpBinding`, `WSHttpBinding`, `NetTcpBinding`). Each system-provided binding comes with a default set of capabilities and behaviors that are enabled, but the defaults can usually be configured to meet your needs. And you always have the option of building your own stack of capabilities and behaviors to create a custom binding that meets your exact needs.

Hosting and Configuration

WCF services can be self-hosted by your own .NET application, by Internet Information Services (IIS), Windows Process Activation Service (WAS), or Windows Server AppFabric.

To configure and host a service, you need to tie together all the elements that were just reviewed. These elements include the service implementation (the service class), the contract (the interface), an endpoint (address and transport), and a binding (capabilities and behaviors). The configuration of the service can be accomplished using application configuration files (`App.config` or `Web.config`) or in code if you are self-hosting.

Clients can consume the service in a couple of ways. One option is to create a set of client proxy classes based on the service metadata. To accomplish this, you must configure the service so that it exposes the service metadata. This metadata provides a complete description of the service contract (along with any data contracts used by the service) in a standard format. This metadata is then consumed by clients (or utilities) to understand how to use the service. In the Microsoft WCF world, the `svcutil.exe` utility (ServiceModel Metadata Utility) generates the necessary client proxy classes from the exposed metadata.

In addition to using a generated proxy, a client application can also make use of the WCF `ChannelFactory` class to invoke the service. To do this, the `ChannelFactory` references the interface that defines the service contract.

Understanding Workflow Services

In this section, I provide the background information that you need to know in order to implement and use workflow services. In Chapter 10, I expand on this basic information to discuss more specialized topics. I begin with an overview of the messaging activities that are included with WF.

Messaging Activities

WF provides a set of standard messaging activities that you use to implement a workflow service or to declaratively consume a WCF service within a workflow. These activities are used to implement a workflow service:

- `Receive`
- `SendReply`

And these activities are used when you need to consume a WCF service from within a client workflow:

- `Send`
- `ReceiveReply`

All the standard WCF message exchange patterns (request/response, one-way, duplex) can be implemented using this standard set of messaging activities. Each of these activities is briefly discussed in the sections that follow.

Receive Activity

The `Receive` activity defines a single service operation that can be consumed by WCF client applications. If a workflow implements multiple service operations, you would declare a separate `Receive` activity for each operation. The request parameters for each operation are defined using the `Receive.Content` property.

Here are the most important properties of the `Receive` activity:

Property	Type	Required	Description
Content	ReceiveContent	No	Defines the contents that must be passed with the request message
OperationName	String	Yes	Identifies the name of the operation
ServiceContractName	XName	Yes	Identifies the service contract name for the operation
CanCreateInstance	Boolean	Yes	True if this operation is capable of creating a new workflow instance
KnownTypes	Collection<Type>	No	A collection of additional types that may be serialized during the operation
CorrelatesWith	InArgument<CorrelationHandle>	No	A correlation handle used to logically associate this operation with another messaging activity
CorrelatesOn	MessageQuerySet	No	Defines a query that is used during content correlation
CorrelationInitializers	Collection<CorrelationInitializer>	No	A collection of initializers that are used to create correlation handles

If you are modeling a request/response operation, a `Receive` activity would be paired with a `SendReply` activity to send the response message. Any business logic that is necessary to implement the service operation would be declared between the `Receive` and `SendReply` activities.

If you are modeling a one-way operation, there is no need for additional messaging activities to implement the operation. Once the client application makes the one-way request, there is no expectation of a response.

Valid service contract names include a namespace and a contract name (typically specified as an interface name). For example, `http://bukovics.com/IMyService` is a fully qualified service contract name. If you don't specify a namespace, `http://tempuri.org` is assumed. The `ServiceContactName` property is defined as an `XName`, which provides the means to define the namespace and contract name of the service contract.

The `CanCreateInstance` property is especially significant. If it is your intent to create a new workflow instance each time the operation is invoked, you need to set this property to true. Otherwise, the service operation can be invoked only on an existing workflow instance.

The `KnownTypes` property allows you to optionally specify additional types that may need to be serialized during the operation. This property is typically used when the content for the operation defines a base type that has multiple derived types. You would specify the derived types using the `KnownTypes` property. This informs the serializer that these additional types might be passed as part of the content.

The correlation-related properties are used to manually control correlation for the service operation. Please refer to the sections on correlation in Chapter 10 for more information on how to use these properties.

SendReply Activity

The `SendReply` activity provides the implementation for the second half of a request/response operation. It can never be used by itself. It can be paired only with a `Receive` activity to send the response for the service operation.

Here are the most important properties of the `SendReply` activity:

Property	Type	Required	Description
Content	SendContent	No	Defines the message contents that are passed with the response
Request	Receive	Yes	Identifies the Receive activity that is associated with this SendReply activity
CorrelationInitializers	Collection<CorrelationInitializer>	No	A collection of initializers that are used to create correlation handles

The `Request` property identifies the `Receive` activity that initiated the operation (the request). This property is set for you when a `ReceiveAndSendReply` activity template is added to the workflow. The workflow designer and property editor does not provide a way to manually set this property.

ReceiveAndSendReply Activity Template

A request/response operation requires a coordinated pair of activities (`Receive`, `SendReply`) to complete the operation. Because this is a common messaging pattern, an activity template is provided that preconfigures this combination of activities.

When you add a `ReceiveAndSendReply` activity template to a workflow, three activities are actually added. A `Sequence` activity is added as the container for a `Receive` and `SendReply` activity. The `SendReply.Request` property references the `Receive` activity to logically link the two activities.

Send Activity

The `Send` activity is used to declaratively invoke a service from within a workflow or custom activity. The service that you are invoking may have been implemented using WF, but that is not a requirement.

Here are the most important properties of the `Send` activity:

Property	Type	Required	Description
Content	SendContent	No	Defines the message contents that are passed to the service with the request
OperationName	String	Yes	Identifies the name of the operation being invoked
ServiceContractName	XName	Yes	Identifies the service contract name for the operation being invoked
Endpoint	Endpoint	No	Identifies the endpoint where the message is sent
EndpointAddress	InArgument<Uri>	No	Identifies the address where the message is sent
EndpointConfigurationName	String	No	The name of a configured endpoint that identifies where the message is sent

Property	Type	Required	Description
KnownTypes	Collection<Type>	No	A collection of additional types that may be serialized during the operation
CorrelatesWith	InArgument<CorrelationHandle>	No	A correlation handle used to logically associate this operation with another messaging activity
CorrelationInitializers	Collection<CorrelationInitializer>	No	A collection of initializers that are used to create correlation handles

If you are invoking a request/response operation, a **Send** activity would be paired with a **ReceiveReply** activity to receive the response from the service. If you are invoking a one-way operation, the **Send** activity is used by itself without any additional messaging activities.

The three endpoint-related properties provide three different ways to specify the endpoint of the operation that you are invoking. Only one of these properties needs to be specified for any single **Send** activity.

ReceiveReply Activity

The **ReceiveReply** activity receives the response from a request/response operation. It cannot be used by itself and must be paired with a **Send** activity.

Here are the most important properties of the ReceiveReply activity:

Property	Type	Required	Description
Content	ReceiveContent	No	Defines the message contents that are received as a response from the service operation
Request	Send	Yes	Identifies the Send activity that is associated with this ReceiveReply activity
CorrelationInitializers	Collection<CorrelationInitializer>	No	A collection of initializers that are used to create correlation handles

SendAndReceiveReply Activity Template

The SendAndReceiveReply activity template is used to declare the activities that consume a request/response operation. When you add a SendAndReceiveReply activity template to a workflow, a set of Sequence, Send, and ReceiveReply activities are added. The template sets the ReceiveReply.Request property to logically relate the activity to the Send activity that initiates the request.

Service Contracts and Message Types

To invoke a WCF service operation, a message is sent to an endpoint for the service. If the operation uses the request/response message exchange pattern, another message is returned to the original caller as the response. WCF (and WF workflow services) supports two ways to describe these messages:

- Data contract. A high-level, opt-in approach to defining the data that is exchanged in a service message.

- Message contract. A single class that describes the low-level shape of the message header and body.

These two message types have slightly different characteristics, but in general, you can use either type. A *data contract* uses classes that are decorated with the DataContract attribute. Individual members of the class that you want to include in the message are decorated with the DataMember attribute. One or more of these classes can be included as individual parameters that are passed with the message. The parameters can also be primitive types (such as a string, float, or integer) or a collection of objects or values. A data contract can be likened to a method of a C# class that is passed multiple arguments. Internally, WCF does some wrapping of the individual parameters to create a single message.

In contrast with this, a *message contract* uses a single argument to represent the entire message. That argument can be a primitive type, or it can be a C# class that defines the individual properties of the message. Since a message contract is limited to a single argument, it avoids the additional layers of wrapping when the message is created. This usually results in a more concise XML representation of the message. A message contract also provides more control over the shape of the resulting message. For example, you can apply attributes to the properties of the message class that determine which properties are sent as message headers (`MessageHeader` attribute) versus the message body (`MessageBodyMember` attribute).

When you declare a new service operation, you determine the message type using the `Content` property of the `Receive` activity. The Content Definition dialog that you use to set this property presents you with a choice of Message or Parameters. This can be seen in Figure 9-1 shown later in this chapter. If you select the Message option, you are declaring a WCF message contract and are limited to a single argument that completely defines the message. If that single argument is a class, you can optionally decorate it with the `MessageContract`, `MessageHeader`, and `MessageBodyMember` attributes to fine-tune the exact shape of the message. If you select the Parameters content option, you are declaring a WCF data contract that supports single or multiple arguments. If an argument is a class, you can optionally decorate it with the `DataContract` and `DataMember` attributes to control which members are included in the message.

If the operation returns a response, the `Content` property of the `SendReply` activity determines the message type of the response.

■ **Warning** A class that is decorated with the `MessageContract` attribute and other attributes related to message contracts cannot be used if you select the Parameters content option. However, the inverse is not true. A class that is decorated with the `DataContract` and `DataMember` attributes can be used for either content type (Message or Parameters).

When you are the consumer of a service operation, the `Content` property of the `Send` and `ReceiveReply` activities must match the signature of the operation being invoked. For example, if the service operation you are invoking uses a data contract, then you must do the same when you set the `Content` property of these activities.

Controlling Serialization of Complex Types

Regardless of the message type, complex types such as a C# class can be included in the message. By default, all public fields and properties of the class are serialized (using the `DataContractSerializer`) and included in the message.

However, you can determine which members are included and how they are serialized by applying a set of attributes to the class. Applying the `DataContract` attribute to the class allows you to control aspects of the contract, such as specifying a namespace used to scope the type. When you apply the `DataContract` attribute to a class, you must also apply the `DataMember` attribute to each member that you want to include. These attributes change the default behavior that includes all public fields and properties into opt-in serialization instead. Only the members that have a `DataMember` attribute applied to them are included in the message.

Controlling Message Contracts

If you are declaring a message contract, you can control aspects of the contract by applying the MessageContract attribute to the class. You then apply the MessageBodyMember or MessageHeader attribute to each field or property that you want to include in the message. One advantage to using a message contract is that it allows you to selectively control the signing and encryption of individual members of the message class. This is controlled by additional properties on the attributes.

Inferred Contracts

The contract for a conventional WCF service is declared using a C# interface that has been decorated with ServiceContract and OperationContract attributes. However, there is current no facility provided with WF to import or otherwise reuse existing contracts that are defined in C# interfaces. Perhaps this is something that Microsoft will address with a post-4 release of .NET. Instead, all contracts for workflow services are inferred based on the properties of the Receive and SendReply activities.

These properties of the Receive activity combine to form the service contract:

- ServiceContractName. The namespace and name of the contract.

- OperationName. The name of the operation.

- Content. The number, type and sequence of parameters that define a message or data contract.

If you are defining a request/response operation, the Content property of the SendReply activity determines the parameters that constitute the response portion of the contract.

Correlation

Correlation is really an overloaded term in WF. There are two ways that correlation is used with workflow services:

- Associating one messaging activity with another in the same workflow

- A way to route messages to the correct workflow instance

Associating Activities

In the first case, correlation is used to logically relate one messaging activity with another. For example, if you are using the duplex message exchange pattern, two workflows can independently exchange messages with each other. Each workflow has a Receive activity that is used to receive messages from the other workflow and a Send activity that sends a message to the other workflow. To logically relate the two messages (sent and received), correlation is used within each workflow.

■ **Note** Chapter 10 presents a workflow example that uses the duplex message exchange pattern.

On the other hand, if you are implementing a request/reply message exchange pattern, the activities that declare the service (`Receive` and `SendReply`) are already logically related to each other via the `Request` property of the `SendReply`. In this case, there is usually no need for additional correlation. However, it may be necessary to implement correlation when a workflow has multiple, parallel messaging activities that are active at the same time.

Identifying Workflow Instances

The second use of correlation is to ensure that messages are routed to the correct workflow instance. For example, you might declare a stateful workflow that implements multiple operations. One operation would be used to create a new workflow instance (a `Receive` activity with the `CanCreateInstance` property set to true), while the other operations use the existing instance. Correlation is used to route the operations to the correct workflow instance.

Correlation for the purpose of identifying the correct workflow instance can be accomplished using *context-based* or *content-based* correlation. Context-based correlation requires a WCF binding that supports the exchange of context information in the SOAP headers or HTTP cookies. For example, the `WSHttpContextBinding`, `NetTcpContextBinding`, or `BasicHttpContextBinding` can be used for this purpose.

Content-based correlation uses data within the message itself to route the message. For example, each message may contain an account or order number that can be used to logically relate each operation to the others. This identifying value could be used to route each message to the correct workflow instance. Content-based correlation has the advantage that it does not require one of the special bindings that supports context exchange.

■ **Note** In Chapter 10 you will see both correlation types in action. You will declare a workflow that first uses context-based correction and then modify it to use content-based correlation.

Controlling Correlation

Within a workflow, you can correlate messaging activities using one of these mechanisms:

- Initialize and reference a `CorrelationHandle`.

- Place the messaging activities in a `CorrelationScope` activity.

To use a `CorrelationHandle`, you first define it as a workflow variable. One messaging activity initializes the handle, while the other messaging activities reference it. The initialization is accomplished using one of the available correlation initializers provided with WF. All of these initializer classes derive from the abstract `CorrelationInitializer` class. Each initializer serves a slightly different correlation scenario:

- `RequestReplyCorrelationInitializer`. Used for correlation in request/response operations.

- `ContextCorrelationInitializer`. Used for context-based correlation.

- **QueryCorrelationInitializer**. Used for content-based correlation.

- **CallbackCorrelationInitializer**. Used with a duplex message exchange pattern to correlate a message with the calling service.

If you simply need to correlate two or more messaging activities with each other, you can choose to use a **CorrelationScope** activity. This is a container for one or more activities. The correlation is managed for you by placing the messaging activities that you want to correlate in the **CorrelationScope**. This eliminates the need to manually define and manage a **CorrelationHandle**.

Declaration and Hosting Options

WF provides two packaging options for workflows that use the WCF messaging activities:

- As a Xaml workflow

- As a Xamlx workflow service

A *Xaml workflow* is the same type of workflow that you have been using throughout this book. You can use messaging activities such **Receive** and **SendReply** in the workflow to declare a service operation. An instance of the workflow would typically be created when a client invokes the service operation (assuming that the **CanCreateInstance** property of the **Receive** activity is set to true). Xaml workflows can also act as a client and invoke a WCF service using the **Send** and **ReceiveReply** activities.

A *Xamlx workflow service* is designed to provide additional properties that simplify hosting by one of the Microsoft hosting environments (IIS, WAS, Windows Server AppFabric). If you plan to use one of these environments, it is recommended that you declare your workflows as Xamlx workflow services.

The top-level node of a Xamlx file is an instance of a **WorkflowService** class instead of an **Activity**. This class provides these properties:

Property	Type	Required	Description
Name	XName	Yes	The service name
ConfigurationName	String	Yes	Identifies the section within a Web.config or App.config file that defines the WCF properties for the service
Body	Activity	Yes	The workflow service definition

In addition to declaring service operations (using **Receive** and **SendReply**), a Xamlx workflow service can take on the role of the client and invoke other services using **Send** and **ReceiveReply**.

When it comes to hosting your Xamlx workflow services, you have these options available to you:

- Self-hosted in your application using the **WorkflowServiceHost** class

- Hosted in IIS/WAS

■ **Note** Xaml workflows that contain messaging activities can be self-hosted using the `WorkflowServiceHost` class, or they can be deployed to IIS and hosted with the addition of an .SVC file. However, it is recommended that you use Xamlx workflow services if you are planning on using a Microsoft-provided hosting environment. Doing so simplifies the deployment of your workflow services since the additional SVC file is not required. Hosting of workflow services is discussed and demonstrated later in this chapter.

Controlling Workflow Service Instances

A new workflow service instance is created each time an operation is invoked (assuming that the `CanCreateInstance` property is set to true). For many operations, the lifetime of the instance is short-lived. The workflow performs the necessary work to complete the operation, returns a response to the caller (if necessary), and is removed from memory.

However, long-running workflow services are also possible. These services may declare multiple operations that are invoked over a span of minutes, hours, or days. While they are waiting for the next service operation to be invoked, these instances are safely persisted in a durable store such as a SQL Server database.

To help with the management of these long-running workflow service instances that are hosted by `WorkflowServiceHost`, WF provides a standard WCF management endpoint (`WorkflowControlEndpoint`). This endpoint supports operations that manage existing service instances such as `Cancel`, `Suspend`, and `Terminate`. A client proxy class (`WorkflowControlClient`) is also provided that simplifies the calls to this control endpoint.

■ **Note** You can't effectively use the control endpoint unless you are working with long-running workflow instances that have been persisted. For this reason, use of the `WorkflowControlEndpoint` and the `WorkflowControlClient` is discussed in Chapter 12, which covers the larger topic of workflow persistence.

Declaring a Workflow Service

In this section, you will declare the first of several workflow services in this chapter. This first workflow forms the foundation for the subsequent examples in this chapter. In the sections that follow this one, you will declare additional service operations that will be invoked by this workflow service.

Tasks for a Request/Response Operation

This first service operation uses the request/response message exchange pattern. A client invokes the operation by sending it a request message and then waits for a response message. In general, you can follow these steps to implement a service operation using this pattern:

1. Use the WCF Workflow Service Application new project template to create a project that is suitable for workflow services.

2. Use the WCF Workflow Service add item template to add Xamlx files to the project if needed for additional services.

3. Set the `Name` and `ConfigurationName` properties of the workflow.

4. Add a `ReceiveAndSendReply` activity template to the workflow.

5. At a minimum, set the `ServiceContractName`, `OperationName`, and `Content` properties of the `Receive` activity. It is permissible to omit setting the `Content` property if the request does not require any input parameters.

6. Set the `Receive.CanCreateInstance` property to true to create a new instance of the workflow each time this operation is invoked.

7. At a minimum, set the `Content` property of the `SendReply` activity. It is permissible to leave this property unset if the response does not return any data.

8. Add additional activities between the `Receive` and `SendReply` to implement the business logic of the service operation.

9. Modify the `Web.config` (or `App.config` if self-hosting) to include the necessary WCF entries for the new service (endpoints, bindings, behaviors, and so on).

10. Deploy the workflow to a Microsoft hosting environment such as IIS or implement a self-hosting application.

■ **Note** A new WCF Workflow Service includes a `ReceiveAndSendReply` activity template by default. You can choose to modify the properties of the existing `Receive` and `SendReply` activities or delete them and add a new `ReceiveAndSendReply` activity template to the empty workflow.

Implementing the OrderProcessing Workflow Service

The business scenario for this example is an order processing workflow service. If you think of the typical ecommerce site with a shopping cart, you'll quickly get the idea. The request that is sent to this order processing service contains some basic customer information (their name, address, email, and so on), the items that they have ordered, and credit card information that is used for payment processing. This main workflow controls the overall process of assigning an order number, authorizing the credit card purchase, instructing the warehouse to ship the items, and determining a shipping date. The response from the workflow includes the order number, a ship date, and a credit card authorization code.

The initial version of this workflow will complete the service operation internally by populating the response with default values. Subsequent versions will enhance this example by invoking other service operations to perform the individual order processing tasks.

You will complete these tasks to implement this example:

1. Create a new WCF Workflow Service Application project, and add a new WCF Workflow Service to the project.

2. Implement C# classes that represent the request and response for the service operation.

3. Add a `ReceiveAndSendReply` activity template to the workflow service, add the necessary workflow variables, and configure the individual messaging activities.

4. Add additional activities to populate the response with valid values before it is returned to the caller.

5. Review the `Web.config` file, and test the workflow service using the ASP.NET Development Server and WCF Test Client.

Creating the ServiceLibrary Project

To begin this example, create a new project using the WCF Workflow Service Application project template. Name the new project `ServiceLibrary`. Delete the `Service1.xamlx` file that is created with the new project since it won't be used. The `Web.config` file that is created for the project will be used, so do not delete it.

Add a new WCF Workflow Service to the project, and name it `OrderProcessing.xamlx`.

■ **Tip** I recommend that you start Visual Studio with elevated administrator privileges (the Run as Administrator option in Vista and Windows 7). Doing so avoids any security issues that you would otherwise encounter opening ports, publishing to IIS, and so on.

Implementing Request and Response Classes

The message content type, which supports only a single argument, will be used for this service operation; therefore, C# classes must be implemented for the request and response messages. Add a new C# class to the `ServiceLibrary` project, and name it `OrderProcessingRequest`. Here is the implementation for this class:

```
using System;
using System.Collections.Generic;

namespace ServiceLibrary
{
    public class OrderProcessingRequest
    {
```

```
            public OrderProcessingRequest()
            {
                Items = new List<Item>();
            }

            public String CustomerName { get; set; }
            public String CustomerAddress { get; set; }
            public String CustomerEmail { get; set; }
            public Decimal TotalAmount { get; set; }
            public String CreditCard { get; set; }
            public String CreditCardExpiration { get; set; }
            public List<Item> Items { get; set; }
        }
    }
```

This class defines the properties that are passed to the service operation as a request message. The `Item` type referenced in the final property defines a single item to be sold along with the quantity to be ordered of that item. Add a new class named `Item` to the `ServiceLibrary` project to implement this type:

```
using System;

namespace ServiceLibrary
{
    public class Item
    {
        public Int32 ItemId { get; set; }
        public Int32 Quantity { get; set; }
    }
}
```

Finally, add a new class named `OrderProcessingResponse` to the `ServiceLibrary` to define the response from the service operation:

```
using System;

namespace ServiceLibrary
{
    public class OrderProcessingResponse
    {
        public Int32 OrderId { get; set; }
        public DateTime ShipDate { get; set; }
        public String CreditAuthCode { get; set; }
        public Boolean IsSuccessful { get; set; }
    }
}
```

Controlling the Data or Message Contract

As you can see, these are all ordinary C# classes that don't require any additional attributes. By default, all the public properties are serialized and become part of the message. Optionally, you could explicitly control the serialization by adding instances of the DataContract and DataMember attributes to the classes. For example, here is the OrderProcessingRequest class after the data contract attributes have been added:

```
using System;
using System.Collections.Generic;
using System.Runtime.Serialization;

namespace ServiceLibrary
{
    [DataContract]
    public class OrderProcessingRequest
    {
        public OrderProcessingRequest()
        {
            Items = new List<Item>();
        }

        [DataMember]
        public String CustomerName { get; set; }
        [DataMember]
        public String CustomerAddress { get; set; }
        [DataMember]
        public String CustomerEmail { get; set; }
        [DataMember]
        public Decimal TotalAmount { get; set; }
        [DataMember]
        public String CreditCard { get; set; }
        [DataMember]
        public String CreditCardExpiration { get; set; }
        [DataMember]
        public List<Item> Items { get; set; }
    }
}
```

These attributes allow you to explicitly determine which properties are included with the message as well as to override the name or sequence of each property. If you add the DataContract attribute to the class, only those properties that include the DataMember attribute will be included.

Alternatively, since the OrderProcessingRequest class is designed to represent the entire message contract, you can choose to apply the MessageContract, MessageBodyMember, and MessageHeader attributes to the class. Collectively, these attributes provide a fine degree of control over the exact shape of the serialized message. For example, here is the same request class decorated with these message contract attributes:

```
using System;
using System.Collections.Generic;
using System.ServiceModel;
```

```
namespace ServiceLibrary
{
    [MessageContract]
    public class OrderProcessingRequest
    {
        public OrderProcessingRequest()
        {
            Items = new List<Item>();
        }

        [MessageBodyMember]
        public String CustomerName { get; set; }
        [MessageBodyMember]
        public String CustomerAddress { get; set; }
        [MessageBodyMember]
        public String CustomerEmail { get; set; }
        [MessageBodyMember]
        public Decimal TotalAmount { get; set; }
        [MessageHeader]
        public String CreditCard { get; set; }
        [MessageHeader]
        public String CreditCardExpiration { get; set; }
        [MessageBodyMember]
        public List<Item> Items { get; set; }
    }
}
```

The placement of the MessageHeader or MessageBodyMember attributes determine whether each property is included in the header or body of the message.

■ **Note** The lack of these message contract attributes doesn't prevent a class from being used as a message contract. A service operation uses a WCF message contract if you select the Message option when you set the Receive.Content property. The single type that you designate for the Message option can be any of the variations that were just reviewed (no attributes, data contract attributes, or message contract attributes). If you use data contract attributes on the class, it simply means that you are refining elements of the data contract serialization for the class, but it is still considered a WCF message contract since that is the option you chose for the Receive.Content property.

Declaring the Service Operation

Now that the request and response classes have been defined, you can turn your attention to the workflow service. Rebuild the solution at this point to ensure that the classes that you have defined build successfully. After opening the OrderProcessing.xamlx workflow in the designer, you can follow the steps outlined next to declare a new ProcessOrder service operation.

■ **Note** The instructions that follow and the test results that are shown assume that the original version of the request and response classes (without any additional attributes) have been used.

The workflow requires two variables, but you won't be able to add them immediately. The step-by-step instructions will indicate when the variables can be added. Here is a recap of the variables required by the workflow:

Name	Variable Type	Scope	Default
Request	ServiceLibrary.OrderProcessingRequest	Sequence	
Response	ServiceLibrary.OrderProcessingResponse	Sequence	New OrderProcessingResponse()

Please follow these steps:

1. Select the `Sequence` activity that was included with the new workflow service, and delete it. This also deletes the two messaging activities that are children of the `Sequence` activity. I've included this step since I find that it's easier to drag a new activity template to the empty workflow to modify the property values of the one that is added by default.

2. While the empty workflow is selected, set the `Name` and `ConfigurationName` properties to `OrderProcessing`. This sets the name for the service and also identifies the section within the `Web.config` (or `App.config`) file that defines WCF settings for this service.

3. Add a `ReceiveAndSendReply` activity template (found in the Messaging category of the Toolbox) to the empty workflow. The template adds a `Sequence` activity with a `Receive` and `SendReply` activity (named `SendReplyToReceive`) as children.

4. Add the two workflow variables indicated in the previous table. Both of them are scoped by the `Sequence` activity. Please note that the `Response` variable requires a default value to construct a new instance of the response object.

5. Open the Content Definition dialog for the `Receive` activity by selecting Content on the activity or by clicking the ellipsis for the `Content` property in the Properties window. Once the dialog is opened, select the Message option if it is not already selected. Then set the Message data value to `Request` in order to reference the variable that you defined. When a new message is received for this operation, the value of that message will be used to populate the properties of the `Request` variable. The Message Type property does not need to be set. The type is inferred from the Message data value. Figure 9-1 shows the Content Definition dialog.

■ **Note** The Message Type is normally inferred from the Message data value that you specify. However, the Message Type property determines the data type that is published as part of the service description. You might need to explicitly set the Message Type if the data value that you set is a derived type but you want to expose a service description with the base type. If you set it, the Message Type must be the same type as the Message data value or its base class.

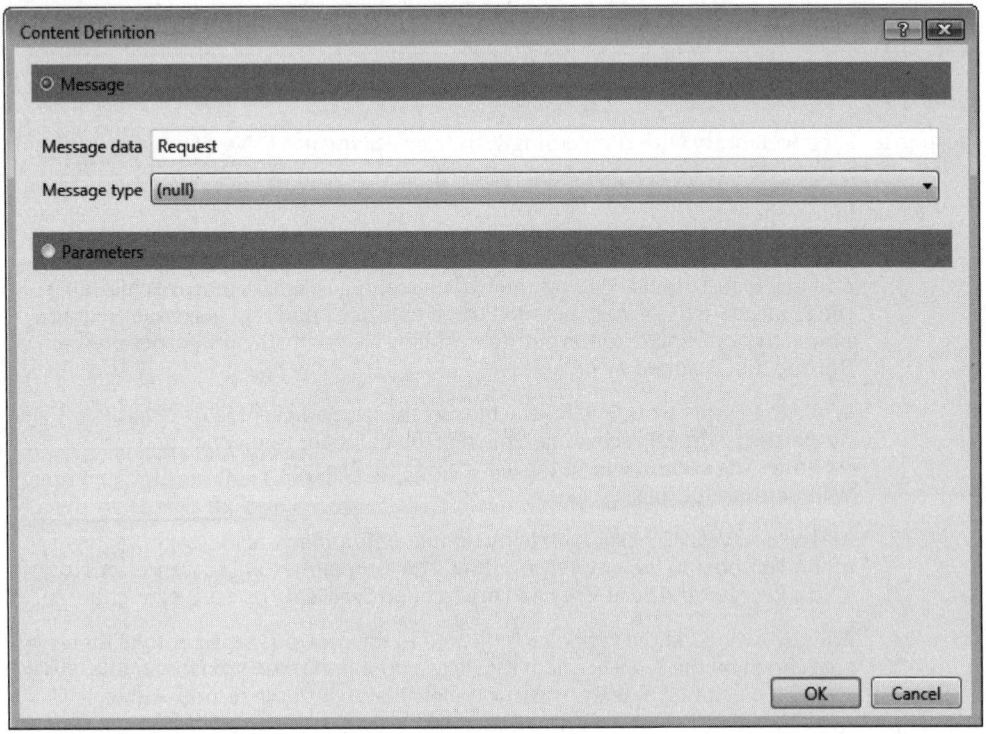

Figure 9-1. Receive activity content definition

6. Set other properties of the `Receive` activity. Set the `ServiceContractName` property to `{http://tempuri.org/}IOrderProcessing` and the `OperationName` property to `ProcessOrder`. Set the `CanCreateInstance` property to true (checked). Figure 9-2 shows the completed properties for the `Receive` activity.

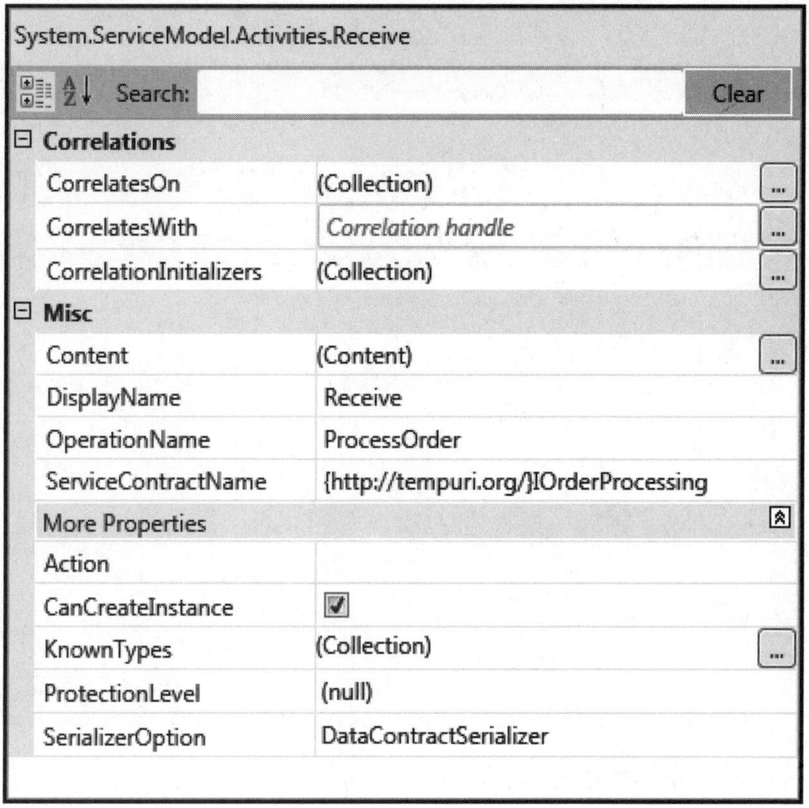

System.ServiceModel.Activities.Receive		
▦ A↓ Search:		Clear

⊟ Correlations

CorrelatesOn	(Collection)	…
CorrelatesWith	*Correlation handle*	…
CorrelationInitializers	(Collection)	…

⊟ Misc

Content	(Content)	…
DisplayName	Receive	
OperationName	ProcessOrder	
ServiceContractName	{http://tempuri.org/}IOrderProcessing	

More Properties		⊠
Action		
CanCreateInstance	☑	
KnownTypes	(Collection)	…
ProtectionLevel	(null)	
SerializerOption	DataContractSerializer	

Figure 9-2. Receive properties

7. Select the SendReplyToReceive activity (a SendReply), and set the Content
    property in a similar way. Select Message for the content type, and set the
    Message data to the Response variable. Figure 9-3 shows the Content
    Definition dialog for this activity.

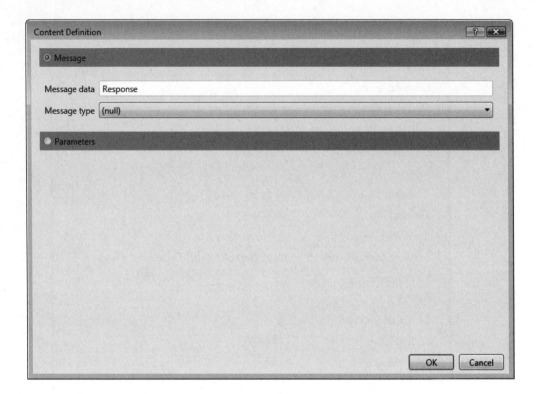

Figure 9-3. SendReplyToReceive content definition

■ **Note** The ReceiveAndSendReply activity template also creates a CorrelationHandle variable named
__handle1. This handle is initialized with a RequestReplyCorrelationInitializer by the Receive activity, but
it is not referenced anywhere in the workflow and is not needed for this example. The activity template includes it
for you to use when correlating other messaging activities with this Receive activity. For this example, you can
choose to keep this handle or remove it. If you choose to remove it, make sure that you also remove the
correlation initializer from the Receive activity (see the CorrelationInitializers property).

Populating the Response

You have now declared the service operation, but the workflow doesn't contain any real business logic. For this initial version of the workflow, you will add a set of `Assign` activities that populate the properties of the `Response` variable with valid values without actually implementing any business logic. In subsequent examples, you will replace these `Assign` activities with other activities that invoke additional service operations or use a workflow extension.

Add four new `Assign` activities to the workflow. All of these activities should be placed between the `Receive` and `SendReplyToReceive` activities. Set the properties for each of these `Assign` activities using the values shown here. Use one set of `Assign.To` and `Assign.Value` values for each `Assign` activity:

Assign.To Property	Assign.Value Property
Response.OrderId	New Random().Next(Int32.MaxValue)
Response.CreditAuthCode	New Random().Next(100000).ToString()
Response.ShipDate	Date.Now.AddDays(3).Date
Response.IsSuccessful	True

Figure 9-4 shows the completed `OrderProcessing` workflow service.

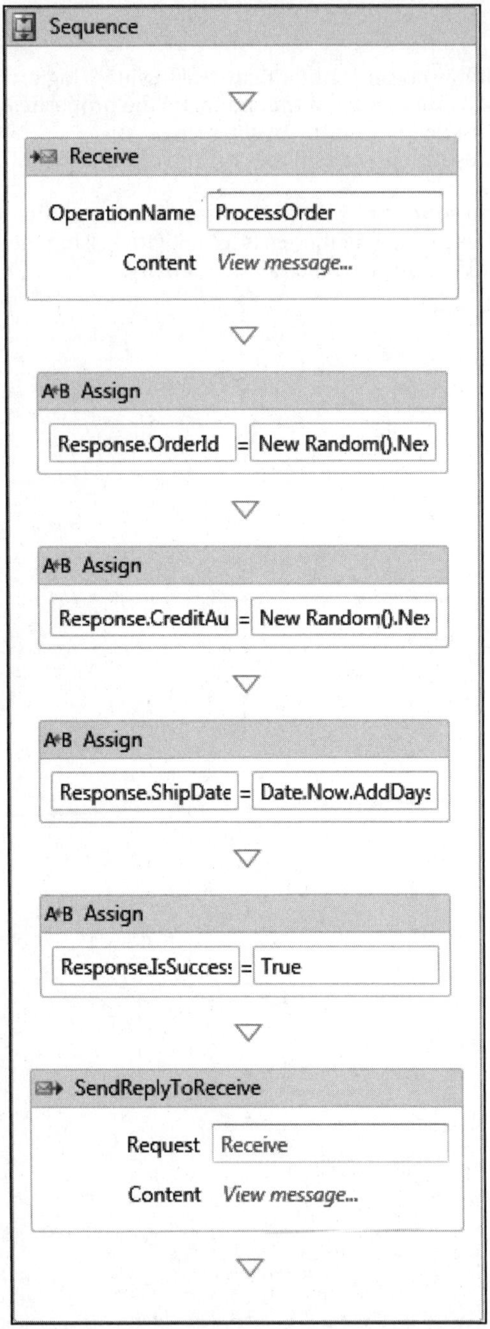

Figure 9-4. *OrderProcessing workflow*

Configuring the Service

This first example does not require any changes to the default `Web.config` file that was created with the `ServiceLibrary` project. Here are the contents of the default `Web.config` file with only a few cosmetic formatting changes to fit the format of this book:

```xml
<?xml version="1.0" encoding="utf-8" ?>
<configuration>
  <system.web>
    <compilation debug="true" targetFramework="4" />
  </system.web>
  <system.serviceModel>
    <behaviors>
      <serviceBehaviors>
        <behavior>
          <serviceMetadata httpGetEnabled="true"/>
          <serviceDebug includeExceptionDetailInFaults="false"/>
        </behavior>
      </serviceBehaviors>
    </behaviors>
  </system.serviceModel>
  <system.webServer>
    <modules runAllManagedModulesForAllRequests="true"/>
  </system.webServer>
</configuration>
```

Testing the Service

After building the solution, you should be ready to test this new service operation. Please follow these steps to test the service:

1. Open the project properties for the project, and select the Web tab; make sure the Start Action is set to Current Page. This causes the currently selected page to be opened in the WCF Test Client. Make sure the Use Visual Studio Development Server option is set, and choose the Specific Port option. Set the port number to 8080. Setting a specific port isn't strictly necessary, but it will ensure that your results match those shown here.

2. Make sure the `OrderProcessing.xamlx` file is highlighted in the Solution Explorer, and press the Ctrl-F5 combination to start without debugging.

3. After a brief wait, the ASP.NET Development Server should start, followed by the WCF Test Client.

4. If all goes well, the WCF Test Client should be able to retrieve the metadata for the service and allow you to invoke the service operation. Enter test data for the request and then invoke the operation. Figure 9-5 shows the request data that I used along with the results of my test.

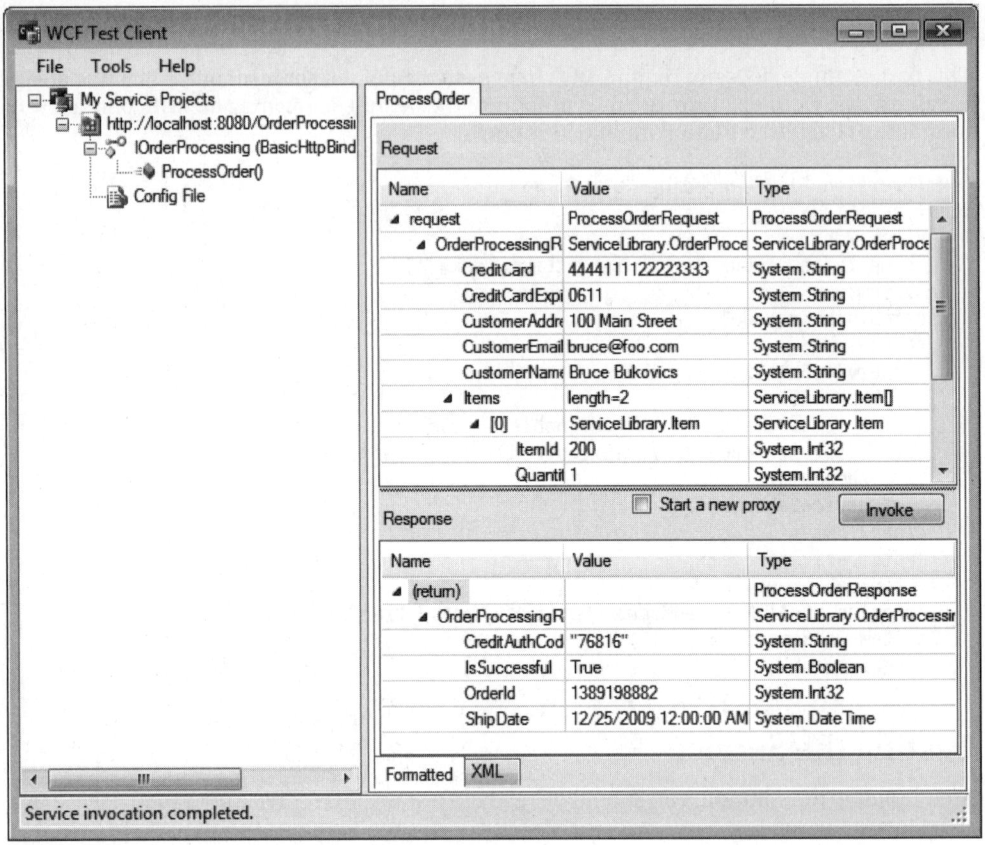

Figure 9-5. ProcessOrder using WCF Test Client

You may notice that the `BasicHttpBinding` was used for the service. This is the default binding that is used by services that use the HTTP protocol scheme and that are not explicitly defined in the `Web.config` file.

■ **Note** Since many of the response properties are populated with random numbers, your results will be similar to the results shown here but will not match them exactly.

Publishing a Workflow Service to IIS

The ASP.NET Development server is fine for the initial development and testing of the workflow service, but it is not suitable as a permanent hosting environment. In this section, you will walk through the steps needed to publish the OrderProcessing workflow service to IIS.

Enhancing the Web.config

When you publish a project to IIS, the Web.config file for the project is deployed along with any required assembly files. Therefore, it is appropriate to make any adjustments to the Web.config file before publishing. To make things slightly more interesting, I've made a few slight modifications to the Web.config file for the ServiceLibrary project. Here is the modified file:

```
<?xml version="1.0" encoding="utf-8" ?>
<configuration>
  <system.web>
    <compilation debug="true" targetFramework="4" />
  </system.web>
  <system.serviceModel>
    <services>
      <service name="OrderProcessing">
        <endpoint contract="IOrderProcessing" binding="wsHttpBinding"
          bindingConfiguration="OrderProcessingBinding" />
      </service>
    </services>
    <bindings>
      <wsHttpBinding>
        <binding name="OrderProcessingBinding">
          <security mode="Message">
            <message clientCredentialType="Windows"
            algorithmSuite="TripleDesRsa15"
            establishSecurityContext="true"
            negotiateServiceCredential="true" />
          </security>
        </binding>
      </wsHttpBinding>
    </bindings>
    <behaviors>
      <serviceBehaviors>
        <behavior>
          <serviceMetadata httpGetEnabled="true"/>
          <serviceDebug includeExceptionDetailInFaults="false"/>
        </behavior>
      </serviceBehaviors>
    </behaviors>
  </system.serviceModel>
  <system.webServer>
    <modules runAllManagedModulesForAllRequests="true"/>
  </system.webServer>
</configuration>
```

Instead of relying on the default WCF settings, the file now explicitly defines the OrderProcessing service. The single endpoint defines the contract (IOrderProcessing), the binding (wsHttpBinding), and a binding configuration (OrderProcessingBinding). The name specified here for the service (OrderProcessing) must match the value that you used when you set the ConfigurationName property of the workflow service.

The binding configuration provides values for a few security-related properties. These binding values are not absolutely necessary for this service. I've included them only to demonstrate how binding properties can be set within a configuration file.

■ **Tip** You can hand-code the WCF configuration settings, or you can use the WCF Service Configuration Editor. This tool should be available as one of the standard options in the Visual Studio Tools menu. You can also start it outside of Visual Studio from the command line. The executable name is svcconfigeditor.exe, and it is distributed with the Windows SDK.

Publishing to IIS

Assuming that IIS has been installed and configured on your development machine, you can follow these steps to publish the OrderProcessing service to IIS:

1. Right-click the ServiceLibrary project in the Solution Explorer, and select the Publish option. Select File System as the Publish Method. Create a new folder named ProWF under the Inetpub\wwwroot folder. Select the new ProWF folder as the Target Location. This should publish all the files needed to host the service to the new folder.

2. Open the IIS management console plug-in. I start this by right-clicking Computer and selecting the Manage option. You can also start the IIS Manager by running the executable InetMgr.exe directly.

3. Find the ProWF folder under the Default Web Site, right-click it, and select the Convert to Application option. You should also verify that the ASP .NET 4 application pool is selected for this application.

The OrderProcessing service should now be published and ready for use. To test the service under IIS, you can start the WCF Test Client (WcfTestClient.exe) and add the service located at this URL: http://localhost/ProWF/OrderProcessing.xamlx. When you invoke the service, you should see similar results as your previous test using the ASP.NET Development Server.

Implementing a Client Application

In this section, you will implement a Windows console application that invokes the OrderProcessing workflow service. The purpose of this short example is to demonstrate how to invoke a WCF service from a nonworkflow application.

■ **Note** The section following this one demonstrates how to invoke a WCF service from a workflow.

Adding a Service Reference

Create a new project using the Windows Console Application template (not a workflow project). Name the new project ConsoleClient, and add it to the solution that you created for this chapter. The first order of business is to add a service reference to the OrderProcessing workflow service. Adding a service references generates a set of classes that you can use to invoke the service. Please follow these steps to add the service reference:

1. Right-click the new ConsoleClient project, and select the Add Service Reference option. This opens a dialog that allows you to select, configure, and add a service reference.

2. Click the Discover button to search for any services in the same solution. You should see the OrderProcessing.xamlx service displayed in the list of available services.

3. Select the OrderProcessing.xamlx service, and change Namespace to OrderProcessing. Before clicking OK, click the Advanced button. Change the Collection type option from the default of System.Array to System.Collections.Generic.List. This causes the generated client proxy code to use a generic class for any collections instead of a simple array.

4. After making the changes indicated in the previous steps, click OK to generate the service reference. The ASP.NET Development Server should start to enable the service metadata to be retrieved. Once started, the server should continue running until you stop it, close the solution, or shut down Visual Studio.

Invoking the Service

Once the service reference has been created, the code to actually invoke the service is fairly simple. Here is the code that should be added to the Program.cs file of the ConsoleClient project:

```
using System;
using System.Collections.Generic;
using System.ServiceModel;
using System.ServiceModel.Channels;
using ConsoleClient.OrderProcessing;

namespace ConsoleClient
{
    class Program
    {
        static void Main(string[] args)
        {
```

In this example code, I've chosen to execute the workflow service twice: the first time using a set of generated proxy classes and the second time using a generated interface. Both mechanisms are a valid way to access the service.

```
CallViaProxy();
CallViaInterface();

Console.WriteLine("Press any key to exit");
Console.ReadKey();
}
```

The service is first invoked using a set of generated proxy classes. This is the simplest way to invoke the service since the proxy classes hide most of the WCF-specific details. To invoke the service, you first create an instance of the request class and populate it with appropriate values. You then create an instance of the client proxy class and invoke the method named for the service operation (ProcessOrder), passing it the request object. The result is a response object containing the output from the service operation.

By default, the proxy class retrieves the WCF endpoint and binding configuration from the App.config file. This configuration file was also added to the project when you added the service reference.

Proper WCF etiquette requires that you call the Close method of the proxy class when you are finished with it. This closes the WCF channel to the server in a graceful and controlled manner.

```
static void CallViaProxy()
{
    OrderProcessingClient client = null;
    try
    {
        Console.WriteLine("About to invoke OrderProcessing service");
        client = new OrderProcessingClient();

        OrderProcessingRequest request = new OrderProcessingRequest();
        request.CreditCard = "4444111111111111";
        request.CreditCardExpiration = "0611";
        request.CustomerName = "Joe Consumer";
        request.CustomerAddress = "100 Main Street";
        request.CustomerEmail = "joe@foo.com";
        request.TotalAmount = 75.00M;
        request.Items = new List<Item>
        {
            new Item { ItemId = 1234, Quantity = 1 },
            new Item { ItemId = 2345, Quantity = 3 },
        };

        OrderProcessingResponse response = client.ProcessOrder(request);

        Console.WriteLine("Response IsSuccessful: {0}",
            response.IsSuccessful);
        Console.WriteLine("Response OrderId: {0}",
            response.OrderId);
```

```
            Console.WriteLine("Response ShipDate: {0:D}",
                response.ShipDate);
            Console.WriteLine("Response CreditAuthCode: {0}",
                response.CreditAuthCode);
        }
        catch (Exception exception)
        {
            Console.WriteLine("Unhandled exception: {0}", exception.Message);
        }
        finally
        {
            client.Close();
        }
    }
```

The second way to invoke a service operation is to use a generated interface. To use the interface, the `CreateChannel` method of the `ChannelFactory<TChannel>` generic class is invoked. The call to this method returns an object that implements the service interface. There are several overloads of the `CreateChannel` method. The one used here specifies the binding and endpoint address. The `ProcessOrder` method of the returned object can then be invoked in a similar way as was done in the previous code.

```
    static void CallViaInterface()
    {
        IOrderProcessing client = null;
        try
        {
            Console.WriteLine("About to invoke OrderProcessing service");

            WSHttpBinding binding = new WSHttpBinding(
                "WSHttpBinding_IOrderProcessing");
            EndpointAddress epAddr = new EndpointAddress(
                "http://localhost:8080/OrderProcessing.xamlx");

            client = ChannelFactory<IOrderProcessing>.CreateChannel(
                binding, epAddr);

            OrderProcessingRequest request = new OrderProcessingRequest();
            request.CreditCard = "4444111111111111";
            request.CreditCardExpiration = "0611";
            request.CustomerName = "Joe Consumer";
            request.CustomerAddress = "100 Main Street";
            request.CustomerEmail = "joe@foo.com";
            request.TotalAmount = 75.00M;
            request.Items = new List<Item>
            {
                new Item { ItemId = 1234, Quantity = 1 },
                new Item { ItemId = 2345, Quantity = 3 },
            };
```

```
                    ProcessOrderResponse poResponse = client.ProcessOrder(
                        new ProcessOrderRequest(request));

                    OrderProcessingResponse response =
                        poResponse.OrderProcessingResponse;

                    Console.WriteLine("Response IsSuccessful: {0}",
                        response.IsSuccessful);
                    Console.WriteLine("Response OrderId: {0}",
                        response.OrderId);
                    Console.WriteLine("Response ShipDate: {0:D}",
                        response.ShipDate);
                    Console.WriteLine("Response CreditAuthCode: {0}",
                        response.CreditAuthCode);
                }
                catch (Exception exception)
                {
                    Console.WriteLine("Unhandled exception: {0}", exception.Message);
                }
                finally
                {
                    ((IChannel)client).Close();
                }
            }
        }
    }
```

Reviewing the Configuration

When you added a service reference to the `ConsoleClient` project, an `App.config` file was also added to the project. This file contains the WCF configuration settings that are appropriate for the service that you referenced. You should be able to use the generated settings without any changes. Your `App.config` file should look similar to this:

```xml
<?xml version="1.0" encoding="utf-8" ?>
<configuration>
  <system.serviceModel>
    <bindings>
      <wsHttpBinding>
        <binding name="WSHttpBinding_IOrderProcessing" closeTimeout="00:01:00"
          openTimeout="00:01:00" receiveTimeout="00:10:00" sendTimeout="00:01:00"
          bypassProxyOnLocal="false" transactionFlow="false"
          hostNameComparisonMode="StrongWildcard"
          maxBufferPoolSize="524288" maxReceivedMessageSize="65536"
          messageEncoding="Text"
          textEncoding="utf-8" useDefaultWebProxy="true" allowCookies="false">
          <readerQuotas maxDepth="32" maxStringContentLength="8192"
            maxArrayLength="16384"
            maxBytesPerRead="4096" maxNameTableCharCount="16384" />
```

```
      <reliableSession ordered="true" inactivityTimeout="00:10:00"
        enabled="false" />
      <security mode="Message">
        <transport clientCredentialType="Windows" proxyCredentialType="None"
          realm="" />
        <message clientCredentialType="Windows"
          negotiateServiceCredential="true"
          algorithmSuite="TripleDesRsa15" />
      </security>
    </binding>
  </wsHttpBinding>
</bindings>
<client>
  <endpoint address="http://localhost:8080/OrderProcessing.xamlx"
    binding="wsHttpBinding"
    bindingConfiguration="WSHttpBinding_IOrderProcessing"
    contract="OrderProcessing.IOrderProcessing"
    name="WSHttpBinding_IOrderProcessing">
  </endpoint>
</client>
</system.serviceModel>
</configuration>
```

■ **Note** This `App.config` file and the code in `Program.cs` contain endpoint addresses that reference the `OrderProcessing` service that is hosted by the ASP.NET Development Server. It is assumed that you are using the recommended port (8080) for the service. If not, you'll need to adjust the settings shown here to match your development environment.

Testing the Client Application

After building the `ConsoleClient` application, you should be ready to execute it. Before you do, you'll need to make sure that the ASP.NET Development Server is running and is hosting the `ServiceLibrary` project. If it is not already running, you can set the `ServiceLibrary` project as the startup project and press Ctrl-F5 to start it without debugging. Once it starts, you can set the `ConsoleClient` project as the startup project and execute it. Optionally, you can change the startup project option to start multiple projects (`ServiceLibrary` and `ConsoleClient`).

Here are my results when I execute the `ConsoleClient` project:

```
About to invoke OrderProcessing service

Response IsSuccessful: True

Response OrderId: 1320239653

Response ShipDate: Friday, December 25, 2009

Response CreditAuthCode: 61478

About to invoke OrderProcessing service

Response IsSuccessful: True

Response OrderId: 696000473

Response ShipDate: Friday, December 25, 2009

Response CreditAuthCode: 32410

Press any key to exit
```

Implementing a Workflow Client

The previous client application populated the request class with a fixed set of values and then invoked the service operation entirely in code. In this example, you will develop a client workflow that declaratively invokes the service operation. To make the example slightly more interesting, the workflow will prompt the user (via the console) to enter the values that are needed for the request.

To begin this example, create a new project named `WorkflowClient` using the Workflow Console Application template, and add it to the existing solution for this chapter. You can delete the `Workflow1.xaml` file since it won't be used.

■ **Tip** The workflow for this client application contains a large number of activities, most of which are not directly related to the WCF messaging activities. The nonmessaging activities demonstrate one way to interact with a real human being to obtain input. Because of the size of this workflow, you may want to download the code for this particular example and review it instead of constructing the application from scratch.

Implementing Custom Activities

This example uses a custom activity that provides a way to prompt the user with a message and then wait for input from the console. To implement this activity, add a new Code Activity to the WorkflowClient project, and name it ReadLineWithPrompt. Here is the code for this activity:

```csharp
using System;
using System.Activities;
using System.Reflection;

namespace WorkflowClient
{
    public class ReadLineWithPrompt<TResult> : AsyncCodeActivity<TResult>
    {
```

This generic activity defines a single input argument named Prompt that allows you to specify the message that is displayed to the user on the console. The generic type identifies the return type of the activity. In the example workflow that uses this activity, you will use return types of String and Int32.

```csharp
        public InArgument<string> Prompt { get; set; }

        protected override IAsyncResult BeginExecute(
            AsyncCodeActivityContext context,
            AsyncCallback callback, object state)
        {
```

After displaying the prompt message, the code to read input from the console (WaitForConsoleInput) is asynchronously executed.

```csharp
            Console.WriteLine(Prompt.Get(context));
            Func<TResult> getInput = () => { return WaitForConsoleInput(); };
            context.UserState = getInput;
            return getInput.BeginInvoke(callback, state);
        }

        private TResult WaitForConsoleInput()
        {
            TResult value = default(TResult);
            String stringInput = Console.ReadLine();
```

If the generic type is String, the work of this activity is done and no conversion of the input data is required. If it is some other type, reflection is used to execute the static Parse method. The assumption of this activity is that only types that support the Parse method will be used as the generic type.

```csharp
            if (typeof(TResult) == typeof(String))
            {
                value = (TResult)(Object)(stringInput);
            }
```

```csharp
            else
            {
                MethodInfo parse = typeof(TResult).GetMethod(
                    "Parse", BindingFlags.Static | BindingFlags.Public,
                    null, new Type[] { typeof(String) }, null);
                if (parse != null)
                {
                    try
                    {
                        value = (TResult)parse.Invoke(
                            null, new Object[] { stringInput });
                    }
                    catch
                    {
                        //ignore any parsing errors
                    }
                }
                else
                {
                    throw new InvalidOperationException(
                        "Parse method not supported");
                }
            }

            return value;
        }

        protected override TResult EndExecute(
            AsyncCodeActivityContext context, IAsyncResult ar)
        {
            return ((Func<TResult>)context.UserState).EndInvoke(ar);
        }
    }
}
```

Before moving on to the next step, you should build the solution to ensure that this custom activity builds correctly. This also adds the activity to the Toolbox to make it available for your use. If you receive an error that the Workflow1 type is missing, you can delete the offending code in the Program.cs file.

Adding a Service Reference

Just as was the case with the previous client application, the WorkflowClient project requires a service reference to the OrderProcessing workflow service. However, adding a service reference to a workflow project generates a custom activity for each service operation instead of the proxy classes that you used in the previous example. These generated activities enable you to easily invoke a WCF service operation declaratively within a workflow.

You can follow the same set of steps to add a service reference that you completed for the previous client application. After the service reference has been added to the project, build the solution to ensure that everything builds correctly. This also adds the generated messaging activity to the Toolbox, making it available for your use.

Implementing the InitiateOrderProcessing Workflow

Add a new workflow to the `WorkflowClient` project using the Activity add item template. Name the new workflow `InitiateOrderProcessing`. The goal of this workflow is to invoke the `ProcessOrder` service operation. It begins by prompting the user to enter property values for the service request. Once the request has been populated with the user's input, the `ProcessOrder` operation is invoked. When the operation has completed, the properties of the service response are displayed on the console.

■ **Tip** This workflow references a number of types that were generated by adding the service reference. To make it easier to quickly work with these types, you may want to add the `WorkflowClient.OrderProcessing` namespace to the Imports list of the workflow. To do this, click the Imports button on the design canvas, and enter the namespace at the top of the list. Adding a namespace to this list is similar in concept to adding a `using` statement to the top of a C# class. It allows you to access the types defined within the namespace without the need to fully quality them with the namespace.

Here is a recap of the workflow variables that you will add to the workflow. The instructions that follow will tell you when to add the variables.

Name	Variable Type	Scope	Default
Request	OrderProcessingRequest	Flowchart	New OrderProcessingRequest()
Response	OrderProcessingResponse	Flowchart	
Item	Item	EnterItemsFC	
Items	List<Item>	EnterItemsFC	New List(Of Item)

Please follow these steps to declare the workflow:

1. Add a Flowchart activity to the empty workflow.

2. Add the Request and Response variables that are scoped by this topmost Flowchart activity.

3. Add another Flowchart as the child of the topmost Flowchart activity. Change the DisplayName of this new Flowchart to EnterCustInfoFC to more easily distinguish from other Flowchart activities. Drag a connection from the starting point of the Flowchart to the top of the EnterCustInfoFC activity that you just added.

4. After opening the EnterCustInfoFC activity, add a set of five ReadLineWithPrompt activities. Set the generic type for all of them to String. Connect the activities so that they are all executed in sequence. The purpose of these activities is to prompt the user to enter values for the customer-related properties of the request. Please refer to the following table for a list of the properties that should be set for each of these activities. The completed EnterCustInfoFC activity should look like Figure 9-6.

Prompt	Result
"Enter the customer name"	Request.CustomerName
"Enter the customer email"	Request.CustomerEmail
"Enter the customer address"	Request.CustomerAddress
"Enter credit card number"	Request.CreditCard
"Enter credit card expiration date (mmyy)"	Request.CreditCardExpiration

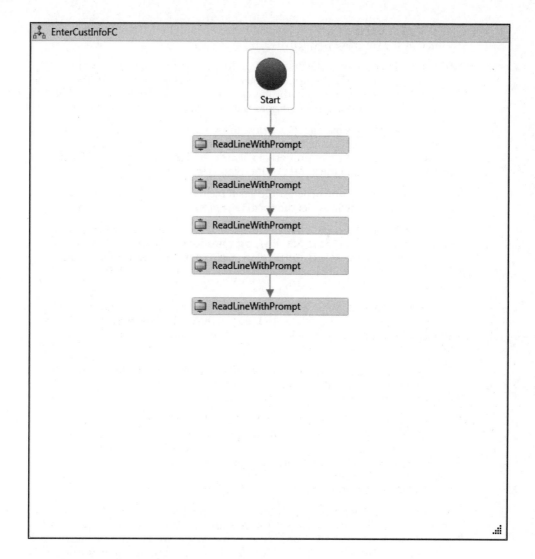

Figure 9-6. EnterCustInfoFC flowchart

5.   Return to the topmost Flowchart, and add another Flowchart activity as a child. Change the DisplayName of this new activity to EnterItemsFC. Drag a connection from the bottom of the EnterCustInfoFC to this new activity.

6. Open the `EnterItemsFC` activity, and add the Item and Items variables that are scoped by the `EnterItemsFC` activity.

7. Add an `Assign` activity as the first child of the `EnterItemsFC` activity. Connect the starting point of the flowchart to the top of the `Assign` activity. Set the `Assign.To` property to Item and the `Assign.Value` property to `New Item()`. This initializes the Item variable and prepares it for the steps that follow this one.

8. Add a `ReadLineWithPrompt` activity below the `Assign`. Set the generic type to `Int32`. Drag a connection between the bottom of the `Assign` and the top of this new activity. Set the `Prompt` property to `"Enter an item ID (enter 0 if done entering items)"` and the `Result` property to `Item.ItemId`.

9. Add a `FlowDecision` control below the `ReadLineWithPrompt`. Add a connection between the two activities. Set the `Condition` property to `Item.ItemId <> 0`.

10. Add a `ReadLineWithPrompt` activity below and to the left of the `FlowDecision`. Set the generic type to `Int32`. Set the `Prompt` property to `"Enter the quantity of the item"` and the `Result` property to `Item.Quantity`. Drag a connection from the true side of the `FlowDecision` (the left side) to the top of the `ReadLineWithPrompt`.

11. Add an `AddToCollection<T>` activity below the last `ReadLineWithPrompt` activity. Set the generic type of the activity to Item. Set the `Collection` property to Items and the `Item` property to Item. This adds the newly constructed Item object to the collection.

12. Drag a connection from the side of the `AddToCollection<T>` activity to the side of the `Assign` activity at the top of the flowchart. This causes the flowchart to loop back to the top to allow entry of another item.

13. Turning your attention to the false side of the `FlowDecision`, add an `Assign` activity to the right and below the `FlowDecision`. Set the `Assign.To` property to `Request.Items` and the `Assign.Value` property to Items. This populates the Items property of the Request variable with the collection of items that has been constructed by this flowchart. Drag a connection from the false side of the `FlowDecision` to the top of this `Assign` activity.

14. Add another `Assign` activity below the one that you just added. Set the `Assign.To` property to `Request.TotalAmount` and the `Assign.Value` property to `Items.Count * 1.99D`. Add a connection between the two `Assign` activities. This completes the `EnterItemsFC` flowchart activity, which is shown in Figure 9-7.

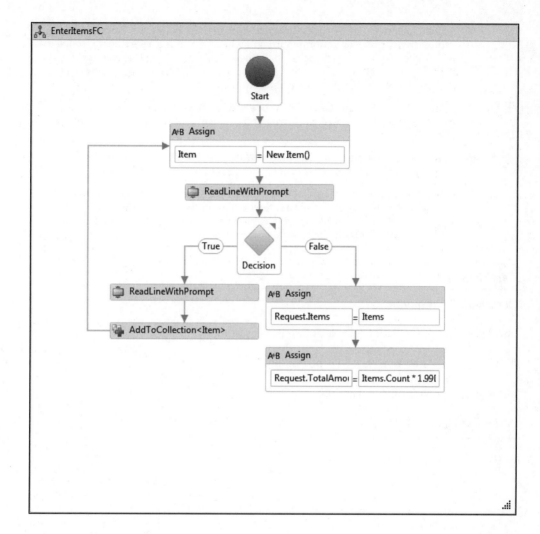

Figure 9-7. EnterItemsFC flowchart

15. Return to the topmost `Flowchart` activity, and add a `WriteLine` activity below the `EnterItemsFC`. Set the `Text` property to `"Invoking ProcessOrder service method"`. Add a connection from the `EnterItemsFC` to this activity.

16. Add an instance of the ProcessOrder custom activity below the WriteLine. This is the activity that was generated for you when you added a service reference to the project. Set the OrderProcessingRequest property to Request and the OrderProcessingResponse property to Response. Add a connection between this activity and the WriteLine that is directly above it.

17. Add another WriteLine below the ProcessOrder activity. Set the Text property to "Back from ProcessOrder". Connect it to the ProcessOrder activity directly above it.

18. Add another Flowchart activity below the WriteLine. Change its DisplayName to DisplayResponseFC and connect it to the WriteLine that is directly above it.

19. Open the DisplayResponseFC activity, and add a set of five WriteLine activities. Connect all of the activities so that they are executed in order. Set the Text property of each WriteLine activity as indicated in the following table. Figure 9-8 shows the completed DisplayResponseFC activity.

Text Property
"ProcessOrder response:"
String.Format("IsSuccessful: {0}", Response.IsSuccessful)
String.Format("ShipDate: {0:D}", Response.ShipDate)
String.Format("OrderId: {0}", Response.OrderId)
String.Format("CreditAuthCode: {0}", Response.CreditAuthCode)

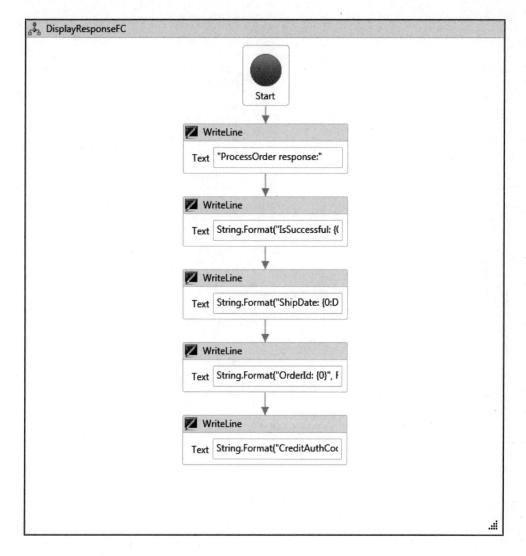

Figure 9-8. *DisplayResponseFC flowchart*

Figure 9-9 shows the completed `InitiateOrderProcessing` workflow.

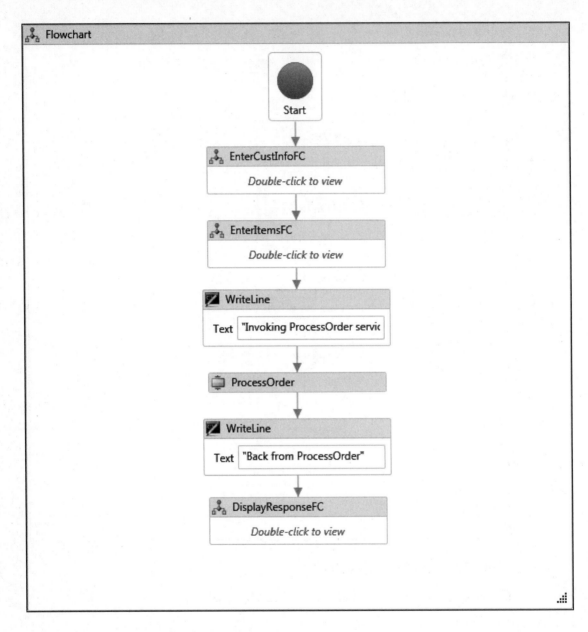

Figure 9-9. InitiateOrderProcessing workflow

Hosting the Workflow

The final task for this example is to add the code that executes the `InitiateOrderProcessing` workflow. Here is the code for the `Program.cs` file of the `WorkflowClient` project:

```
using System;
using System.Activities;
using System.Collections.Generic;
using System.Threading;

namespace WorkflowClient
{
    class Program
    {
        static void Main(string[] args)
        {
            ExecuteClientWorkflow();
            Console.WriteLine("Press any key to exit");
            Console.ReadKey();
        }

        private static void ExecuteClientWorkflow()
        {
            WorkflowApplication wfApp = new WorkflowApplication(
                new InitiateOrderProcessing());

            AutoResetEvent waitEvent = new AutoResetEvent(false);
            wfApp.Completed = (a) =>
            {
                waitEvent.Set();
            };

            wfApp.OnUnhandledException = (e) =>
            {
                Console.WriteLine("OnUnhandledException: {0}",
                    e.UnhandledException.Message);
                return UnhandledExceptionAction.Cancel;
            };

            wfApp.Run();
            waitEvent.WaitOne(90000);
        }
    }
}
```

Testing the Client Application

Adding the service reference to the project should have also added an `App.config` file containing the necessary WCF configuration settings. The contents of this `App.config` file should look exactly like the previous client application.

To test the application, you need to also start the **ServiceLibrary** project using the ASP.NET Development Server. The easiest way to do this is to change the startup project option to start multiple projects (**ServiceLibrary** and **WorkflowClient**). After pressing Ctrl-F5 (run without debugging), you should be prompted to enter the customer and order information. When you have finished entering one or more items with their quantity, you can just press Enter without entering a value or enter a value of **0**. This is the signal to the workflow that entry of the request properties is complete and that it should invoke the **ProcessOrder** service operation.

Here is a representative example of my results:

```
Enter the customer name

Bruce Bukovics

Enter the customer email

bruce@foo.com

Enter the customer address

100 Main Street

Enter credit card number

4444111122223333

Enter credit card expiration date (mmyy)

0611

Enter an item ID (enter 0 if done entering items)

200

Enter the quantity of the item

1

Enter an item ID (enter 0 if done entering items)

300

Enter the quantity of the item

2

Enter an item ID (enter 0 if done entering items)
```

```
Invoking ProcessOrder service method

Back from ProcessOrder

ProcessOrder response:

IsSuccessful: True

ShipDate: Sunday, December 27, 2009

OrderId: 351417896

CreditAuthCode: 38789

Press any key to exit
```

Self-hosting the Workflow Service

Up to this point, you have used the ASP.NET Development Server and IIS to host the workflow service. You can also choose to self-host the service in an application that you develop. The advantage to self-hosting is that it is typically easier to deploy your application since you don't require a dependency on IIS. Self-hosting also presents you with additional opportunities to fine-tune the hosting environment in code.

Understanding the WorkflowServiceHost

The WorkflowServiceHost class that is included with WF provides the ability to self-host a workflow service in your own application. You construct this class by passing an instance of an **Activity** (a Xaml workflow) or **WorkflowService** (a Xamlx workflow service) in the constructor. You then provide binding and endpoint information for the service (either in code or using entries in an **App.config** file). Finally, you call the **Open** method to enable the service to begin processing messages. During the shutdown processing of your application, you call the **Close** method to gracefully transition the service host to a state that no longer processes incoming messages.

■ **Warning** Be aware that .NET 4 actually includes two types with the same WorkflowServiceHost name. The one that is capable of hosting .NET 4 workflow services is in namespace System.ServiceModel.Activities. The one that is located in the System.ServiceModel namespace is used for hosting WF 3.x workflows.

The WorkflowServiceHost class derives from the ServiceHostBase class, which in turn, derives from the base CommunicationObject class. Because of this class hierarchy, the WorkflowServiceHost inherits a large number of members that are defined by these base classes. Here are the most important members of the WorkflowServiceHost class:

Member	Description
AddServiceEndpoint	A method used to add a WCF endpoint for the service. There are several overloads of this method that provide alternate ways to specify the contract, binding, and endpoint address.
AddBaseAddress	Adds a base address to the service.
WorkflowExtensions	A property of type WorkflowInstanceExtensionManager that allows you to add workflow extensions to the service.
DurableInstancingOptions	A property that is used during the configuration of an instance store for workflow persistence.
Open	Transitions the service host to a state that accepts incoming service requests. BeginOpen and EndOpen asynchronous methods are also provided to open the service to requests.
Close	Gracefully transitions the service host to a closed state. BeginClose and EndClose asynchronous methods are also provided.
Opening	An event that is raised when the service is in the process of opening.
Opened	An event that is raised when the service has successfully opened.
Closing	An event that is raised when the service begins the process of closing.
Closed	An event that is raised when the service has successfully closed.
Faulted	An event that is raised when the service has transitioned into the Faulted state.

■ **Note** Chapter 11 discusses the use of persistence with workflow services along with other persistence topics.

Tasks for Self-hosting a Service

In general, you can follow these steps to self-host a workflow service:

1. Create an instance of the `Activity` or `WorkflowService` that you want to host.

2. Use the `Activity` or `WorkflowService` instance to construct a `WorkflowServiceHost` instance.

3. Add any workflow extensions (if required).

4. Configure persistence options (if required).

5. Provide a binding and endpoint for the service (either in code or via `App.config` entries).

6. Open the workflow service to enable it to receive requests.

7. Close the workflow service to gracefully transition the service to a closed state before exiting the application.

Implementing the ServiceHost Application

To see the `WorkflowServiceHost` in action, you will implement a simple console application that hosts the `OrderProcessing` workflow service. Create a new project using the Workflow Console Application template. Name the new project `ServiceHost`, and add it to the existing solution for this chapter. Delete the `Workflow1.xaml` file since it won't be used.

By default, the Workflow Console Application project template targets the .NET Framework 4 Client Profile. This profile does not include the server-related types needed to host a workflow service. For this reason, you need to open the project properties and change the Target framework to .NET Framework 4 (the full framework).

You also need to add a project reference to the `ServiceLibrary` project. You will be loading the workflow service definition directly from the Xamlx file instead of referencing the compiled types in the `ServiceLibrary` project. However, you do need to reference the `ServiceLibrary` assembly in order to deserialize the types that are used by the workflow service such as the request and response classes. Adding the project reference causes the `ServiceLibrary` assembly to be copied into the output folder for the `ServiceHost` project. This is strictly a runtime dependency—not a design-time dependency.

Here is the complete `Program.cs` file that contains the code needed to host the service:

```
using System;
using System.Collections.Generic;
using System.IO;
using System.ServiceModel.Activities;
using System.Xaml;

namespace ServiceHost
{
    class Program
    {
        private static List<WorkflowServiceHost> _hosts =
            new List<WorkflowServiceHost>();

        static void Main(string[] args)
        {
            try
            {
```

A private `CreateServiceHost` method is called to create a `WorkflowServiceHost` instance for the requested workflow service. The code was organized in this way to make it easier to host the additional services that you will develop in Chapter 10. Each service host that has been created is then opened. For this example, that's a single host. Code in the finally block closes any service hosts that have been opened.

This code assumes that the necessary WCF configuration entries for this service will be provided by an **App.config** file. Alternatively, you could call the **AddServiceEndpoint** method to add an endpoint directly in the code.

```
CreateServiceHost("OrderProcessing.xamlx");

foreach (WorkflowServiceHost host in _hosts)
{
    host.Open();
    foreach (var ep in host.Description.Endpoints)
    {
        Console.WriteLine("Contract: {0}",
            ep.Contract.Name);
        Console.WriteLine("    at {0}",
            ep.Address);
    }
}

Console.WriteLine("Press any key to stop hosting and exit");
Console.ReadKey();
}
catch (Exception exception)
{
    Console.WriteLine("Service Exception: {0}", exception.Message);
}
finally
{
    Console.WriteLine("Closing services...");
    foreach (WorkflowServiceHost host in _hosts)
    {
        host.Close();
    }
    Console.WriteLine("Services closed");
    _hosts.Clear();
}
}
```

The **CreateServiceHost** method first loads the service definition directly from the named Xamlx file. The root node of a Xamlx file is actually a **WorkflowService** instead of an **Activity**. It is for this reason that the code defines the output from the **LoadService** method as a **WorkflowService** and uses it to construct the **WorkflowServiceHost** instance.

The **WorkflowService** object includes the additional **Name** and **ConfigurationName** properties that associate the workflow service with configuration entries in the **App.config** file. Alternatively, you could reference the **WorkflowService.Body** property if you only want to use the **Activity** definition instead of the entire **WorkflowService** definition. You would do this if you wanted to provide your own **Name** and **ConfigurationName** values for the service.

```
    private static WorkflowServiceHost CreateServiceHost(String xamlxName)
    {
        WorkflowService wfService = LoadService(xamlxName);
        WorkflowServiceHost host = new WorkflowServiceHost(wfService);

        _hosts.Add(host);

        return host;
    }
```

The private LoadService method deserializes a WorkflowService instance from the named Xamlx file. For this example, the Xamlx file is assumed to be found in a relative path under the ServiceLibrary project. This relative path was used as a convenience since that is the source location of the Xamlx file. This code assumes that these projects are located in the same solution. You will need to adjust this path if the Xamlx files are in a different location. To deserialize the Xamlx file, the static XamlServices.Load method is called.

```
    private static WorkflowService LoadService(String xamlxName)
    {
        String fullFilePath = Path.Combine(
            @"..\..\..\ServiceLibrary", xamlxName);
        WorkflowService service =
            XamlServices.Load(fullFilePath) as WorkflowService;
        if (service != null)
        {
            return service;
        }
        else
        {
            throw new NullReferenceException(String.Format(
                "Unable to load service definition from {0}", fullFilePath));
        }
    }
}
}
}
```

■ **Tip** Please remember that the XamlServices.Load method requires runtime access to the types in the ServiceLibrary assembly. In particular, any types referenced by the Xamlx file such as the request and response classes must be available in order to deserialize the workflow service. If you receive an exception that the Xamlx file cannot be deserialized, it is most likely caused by a missing ServiceLibrary.dll assembly. If you make sure that this assembly is in the same \bin\debug folder as ServiceHost.exe, the deserialization should work correctly.

Configuring the Service Host

Before you can run the ServiceHost project, you need to provide WCF configuration entries in the App.config file. Here is a complete App.config file that provides the necessary settings:

```xml
<?xml version="1.0"?>
<configuration>
  <system.serviceModel>
    <services>
      <service name="OrderProcessing">
        <host>
          <baseAddresses>
            <add baseAddress="http://localhost:9000/"/>
          </baseAddresses>
        </host>
        <endpoint contract="IOrderProcessing"
          address="http://localhost:9000/OrderProcessing"
          binding="wsHttpBinding"
          bindingConfiguration="OrderProcessingBinding" />
      </service>
    </services>

    <bindings>
      <wsHttpBinding>
        <binding name="OrderProcessingBinding">
          <security mode="Message">
            <message clientCredentialType="Windows"
              algorithmSuite="TripleDesRsa15"
              establishSecurityContext="true"
              negotiateServiceCredential="true" />
          </security>
        </binding>
      </wsHttpBinding>
    </bindings>

    <behaviors>
      <serviceBehaviors>
        <behavior>
          <serviceDebug includeExceptionDetailInFaults="True"
            httpHelpPageEnabled="True"/>
          <serviceMetadata httpGetEnabled="True"/>
        </behavior>
      </serviceBehaviors>
    </behaviors>
  </system.serviceModel>

  <startup>
    <supportedRuntime version="v4" sku=".NETFramework,Version=v4"/>
  </startup>
</configuration>
```

This configuration file defines the OrderProcessing service with an endpoint address of http://localhost:9000/OrderProcessing. The port number of 9000 was chosen somewhat at random because it's just a nice round number that is easy to remember. The name specified for the service (OrderProcessing) matches the ConfigurationName property that is set within the Xamlx file. A binding configuration is also included which has the similar set of properties that you have used in previous examples.

Testing the Self-hosted Service

After building the solution, you should be ready to test the ServiceHost project. Select this project as the startup project, and press Ctrl-F5 to run the project without debugging. After a short wait, you should see these results:

```
Contract: IOrderProcessing

    at http://localhost:9000/OrderProcessing

Press any key to stop hosting and exit
```

The workflow service is now hosted and is awaiting client requests. You can use the WCF Test Client to perform an initial test of the service. You should be able to point to the base service address of http://localhost:9000/ to retrieve the metadata for the service.

■ **Tip** These instructions assume that you have started Visual Studio with elevated administrator privileges. If you run the ServiceHost.exe application outside of Visual Studio, you will also need to run it with these increased privileges. If you don't, you will receive an error indicating that you do not have the authority to open the designated port. Alternatively, you can use the netsh scripting utility to add the current machine user to the access list for the desired port. Please refer to the "Configuring HTTP and HTTPS" topic in the WCF online documentation for more information.

Using the WorkflowClient Application

At this point you should also change the configuration for the WorkflowClient application to reference this self-hosted service. Previously, the WorkflowClient application referenced the service that was hosted by the ASP.Net Development Server (port 8080). To reference the self-hosted service, change this port number to 9000. The .xamlx extension has also been removed from the endpoint address. Here is an abbreviated version of the App.config file showing the section that requires a change:

```xml
<?xml version="1.0" encoding="utf-8" ?>
<configuration>
  <system.serviceModel>
...
    <client>
      <endpoint address="http://localhost:9000/OrderProcessing"
        binding="wsHttpBinding"
        bindingConfiguration="WSHttpBinding_IOrderProcessing"
        contract="OrderProcessing.IOrderProcessing"
        name="WSHttpBinding_IOrderProcessing">
      </endpoint>
    </client>
  </system.serviceModel>
</configuration>
```

After making this configuration change, you should be able to execute the `WorkflowClient` application and reference the self-hosted service. Make sure that the `ServiceHost` project is also running. Your results should be consistent with the previous test for this application.

Summary

The focus of this chapter was the WCF and workflow services support provided with WF. The chapter presented a brief introduction of workflow services and WCF followed by an in-depth review of the WF messaging-related activities and classes.

The chapter presented a workflow service that declared a relatively simple request/response operation. This example service was used to demonstrate how to publish a workflow service to IIS as well as how to implement an application that self-hosted the service. Two client applications were developed. One was a nonworkflow application and the other invoked the workflow service declaratively from another workflow.

In the next chapter, you will build upon the example service that you began in this chapter to learn about correlation and other message exchange patterns.

■ ■ ■

CHAPTER 10

Workflow Services Advanced Topics

This chapter continues coverage of the Windows Communication Foundation (WCF) support that is provided by Windows Workflow Foundation (WF). Chapter 9 began the discussion with an introduction to workflow services and WCF in general. In that chapter, you declared a simple request/response service operation, hosted it using Internet Information Services (IIS), developed a self-hosting application, and developed two client applications to test it.

The chapter expands on this basic example from Chapter 9 by implementing additional workflow services that are consumed by the original workflow. One additional service demonstrates how to use context-based and content-based correlation to route messages to the correct service instance. Another example service uses the duplex message exchange pattern to invoke callback operations of the calling service. The final example demonstrates how to use workflow extensions with services.

The chapter concludes with a discussion of exception and fault processing, flowing transactions into a workflow service, and the use of standard WF behaviors to fine-tune workflow service performance.

■ **Note** This chapter assumes that the examples presented in Chapter 9 are used as the starting point for this chapter. In particular, the `ServiceLibrary`, `ServiceHost`, and `WorkflowClient` projects that were first developed in Chapter 9 will be used in this chapter. Any new workflows or activities that you develop in this chapter should be added to one of these existing projects.

Using Context-Based Correlation

In this section, you will declare a workflow service that relies upon context-based correlation to route messages to the correct workflow instance. The `ProcessOrder` operation that you declared and used in Chapter 9 is a simple request/response operation. When a client application invokes the operation, a new instance of the workflow service is created (because of the `Receive.CanCreateInstance` property with a value of true). When the service sends a reply to the caller (using the `SendReply` activity), the workflow is complete, and the instance is disposed.

In contrast with this, you will now declare a workflow service (named `ShipOrder`) that is stateful and supports multiple operations. This new workflow extends the previous example scenario by implementing a set of service operations related to the shipment of the order. These operations will be invoked by the `ProcessOrder` operation of the `OrderProcessing` workflow service.

Here are the operations that you will declare in the `ShipOrder` workflow service:

Operation	Type	Creates Instance	Description
BeginOrder	Request/Response	Yes	Invoked to start a series of operations for a new order that is to be shipped.
AddItem	One-way	No	A one-way operation that adds a new item ID and quantity to the order. This operation is called repeatedly until all items in the order have been processed.
CompleteOrder	Request/Response	No	Ends the series of operations by shipping the order.

The `BeginOrder` operation is the only one that is capable of creating a new instance of the workflow service. It is invoked first, followed by one or more calls to the `AddItem` operation. Finally, the `CompleteOrder` operation is invoked to signal that entry of the order is complete and that it can be shipped. The response from the `CompleteOrder` operation provides the expected date of shipment.

Correlation is required when multiple operations must all use the same workflow instance. Correlation ensures that the messages for each operation are routed to the correct instance. As I mentioned in Chapter 9, there are two ways to implement this type of correlation: *context-based* and *content-based*.

In the example that follows, you will implement the `ShipOrder` workflow service using context-based correlation. This form of correlation relies upon a WCF binding that supports the exchange of context information in the SOAP headers (`WSHttpContextBinding`, `NetTcpContextBinding`, `BasicHttpContextBinding`). Context-based correlation is the easiest of the two correlation types to implement. Later, you will revise the `ShipOrder` workflow service to use content-based correlation.

Guidelines for Context-Based Correlation

In general, you can follow these guidelines when using context-based correlation:

- At least one service operation must have the `Receive.CanCreateInstance` property set to true in order to create a new instance of the workflow.

- Service operations that are designed to interact with an existing workflow instance should have their `CanCreateInstance` properties set to false.

- All service operations that are designed to create a new workflow instance must use the request/response message exchange pattern. The response is necessary to return context information to the caller that is used in subsequent operations.

- A binding that supports the exchange of context information must be used.

Declaring the ShipOrder Workflow Service

The basic structure of this workflow service will be a flowchart with a `Pick` activity. The `Pick` activity has three `PickBranch` activities, one for each operation that is supported. The flowchart will continuously loop until the `CompleteOrder` operation has been invoked. Each time through the loop, the `Pick` activity is executed again, preparing the workflow to accept any of the three operations.

Add a new WCF Workflow Service to the `ServiceLibrary` project, and name it `ShipOrder`. Delete the top-level `Sequence` activity (along with its child messaging activities) since it won't be used. Set the `Name` and `ConfigurationName` properties of the workflow service to `ShipOrder`.

Here is a recap of the workflow variables that you will add to the workflow. Follow the instructions to see when you can add them to the workflow.

Name	Variable Type	Scope	Default
IsDone	Boolean	Flowchart	
Items	List<ServiceLibrary.Item>	Flowchart	New List(Of ServiceLibrary.Item)()
OrderId	Int32	Flowchart	
CustomerName	String	Flowchart	
Item	ServiceLibrary.Item	Branch2 (AddItem branch)	
ShipDate	DateTime	Sequence (CompleteOrder branch)	

Follow these steps to complete the declaration of this workflow:

1. Add a `Flowchart` activity to the empty workflow.

2. Add the four variables that are scoped by the `Flowchart`: `IsDone`, `Items`, `OrderId`, and `CustomerName`.

3. Add a `Pick` activity as a child of the `Flowchart`. Connect the starting point of the flowchart to the top of the `Pick` activity.

4. Add a `FlowDecision` below the `Pick` activity. Set the `Condition` property to `IsDone`. Connect the `Pick` activity to the top of the `FlowDecision`. Drag a connection from the false side of the `FlowDecision` (the right side) to the side of the `Pick` activity. This causes the workflow to execute the `Pick` activity until the `IsDone` variable is true.

5. Open the `Pick` activity, and add a third `PickBranch` (the `Pick` activity starts with two branches).

6. Add a `ReceiveAndSendReply` activity template to the `Trigger` property of the leftmost `PickBranch`. Use the values shown in the following tables to set the properties and parameters of the `Receive` activity. For this operation, the content type is set to `Parameters`.

BeginOrder Receive Properties

Property	Value
OperationName	BeginOrder
ServiceContractName	{http://tempuri.org/}IShipOrder
CanCreateInstance	True

BeginOrder Receive Parameters

Parameter Name	Type	Value
orderId	Int32	OrderId
customerName	String	CustomerName

7. The `SendReplyToReceive` activity does not require any changes. No individual parameters are returned with the response.

8. Add a `WriteLine` activity between the `Receive` and `SendReplyToReceive` activities. Set the `Text` property to `String.Format("BeginOrder OrderId: {0}, Cust: {1}", OrderId, CustomerName)`. Figure 10-1 shows the completed `PickBranch` for the `BeginOrder` operation.

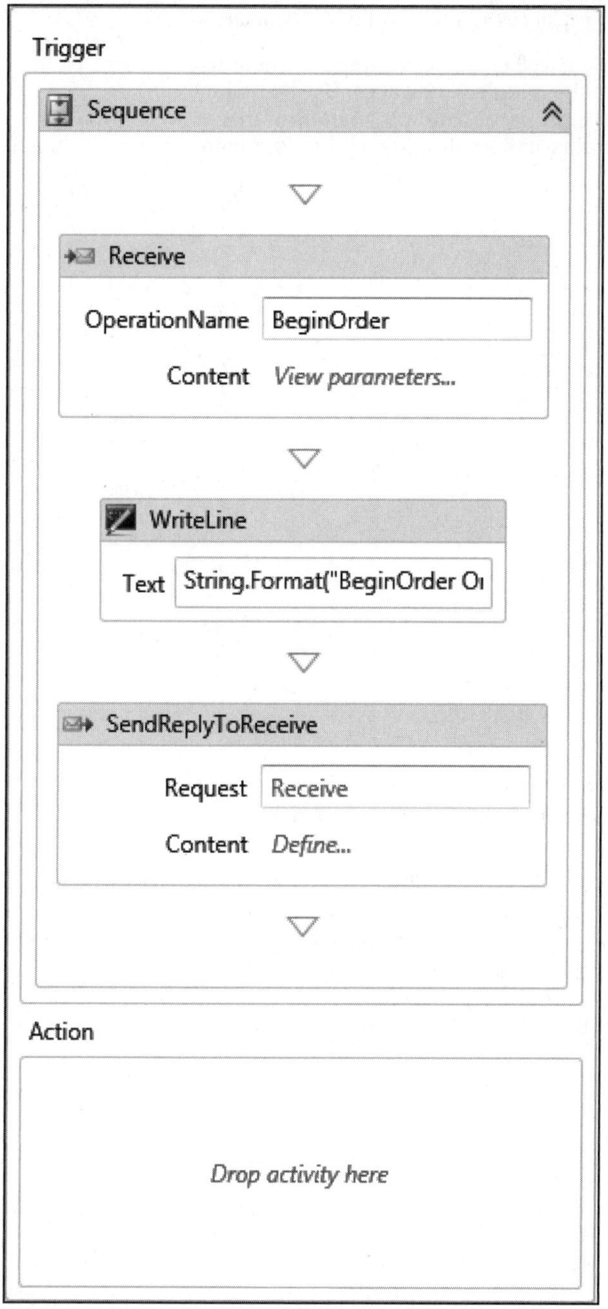

Figure 10-1. *BeginOrder PickBranch*

9. Add the Item variable that is scoped by Branch2 to the middle PickBranch.

10. Add a Receive activity (not a ReceiveAndSendReply activity template as you usually do) to the Trigger property of the middle PickBranch. Use the values shown in the following tables to set the properties and parameters of this Receive activity. The content type for this activity should be set to Parameters.

AddItem Receive Properties

Property	Value
OperationName	AddItem
ServiceContractName	{http://tempuri.org/}IShipOrder
CanCreateInstance	False

AddItem Receive Parameters

Parameter Name	Type	Value
orderId	Int32	OrderId
item	ServiceLibrary.Item	Item

11. Add a Sequence activity to the Action portion of the middle PickBranch. Add an AddToCollection<T> activity to the Sequence. Set the generic type to ServiceLibrary.Item. Set the Collection property to Items and the Item property to Item. This adds the newly received Item object to a collection of items for the order.

12. Add a WriteLine activity to the Sequence activity, directly below the AddToCollection<T> activity. Set the Text property to String.Format("AddItem OrderId:{0}, ItemId:{1}, Qty:{2}", OrderId, Item.ItemId, Item.Quantity). Figure 10-2 shows the completed PickBranch for the AddItem operation.

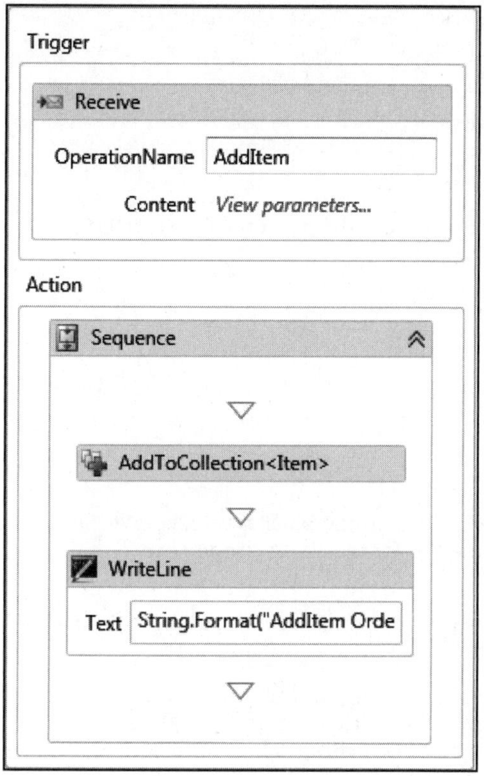

Figure 10-2. AddItem PickBranch

13. Add a `ReceiveAndSendReply` activity template to the `Trigger` property of the rightmost `PickBranch`.

14. Add the `ShipDate` variable to the `Sequence` activity that was just added with the `ReceiveAndSendReply`.

15. Set the properties and parameters of the `Receive` activity to the values shown in the following tables.

CompleteOrder Receive Properties

Property	Value
OperationName	CompleteOrder
ServiceContractName	{http://tempuri.org/}IShipOrder
CanCreateInstance	False

CompleteOrder Receive Parameters

Parameter Name	Type	Value
orderId	Int32	OrderId

16. Set the parameters of the `SendReplyToReceive` activity (for the `CompleteOrder` operation) to the values shown in this table.

CompleteOrder SendReplyToReceive Parameters

Parameter Name	Type	Value
shipDate	DateTime	ShipDate

17. Add an `Assign` activity between the `Receive` and the `SendReplyToReceive`. Set the `Assign.To` property to `ShipDate` and the `Assign.Value` property to `Date.Now.AddDays(Items.Count).Date`.

18. Add another `Assign` activity below the previous one. Set the `Assign.To` property to `IsDone` and the `Assign.Value` to True.

19. Add a `WriteLine` activity below the `Assign` activity, and set the `Text` property to `String.Format("CompleteOrder OrderId:{0}, ShipDate:{1:D}", OrderId, ShipDate)`. Figure 10-3 shows the completed `PickBranch` for the `CompleteOrder` operation.

■ **Tip** It is interesting to note that the SendReply activity that is associated with the BeginOrder operation (SendReplyToReceive) does not return any parameters. Because of this, you might feel that you can change this to a one-way operation and remove the SendReply completely. Even though no parameters are returned with the reply, the SendReply serves a vital purpose. It returns the context information in the SOAP headers that is used by the subsequent operations to locate the correct workflow instance. If you are using context-based correlation, the first operation must use the request/response message exchange pattern in order to return the context information.

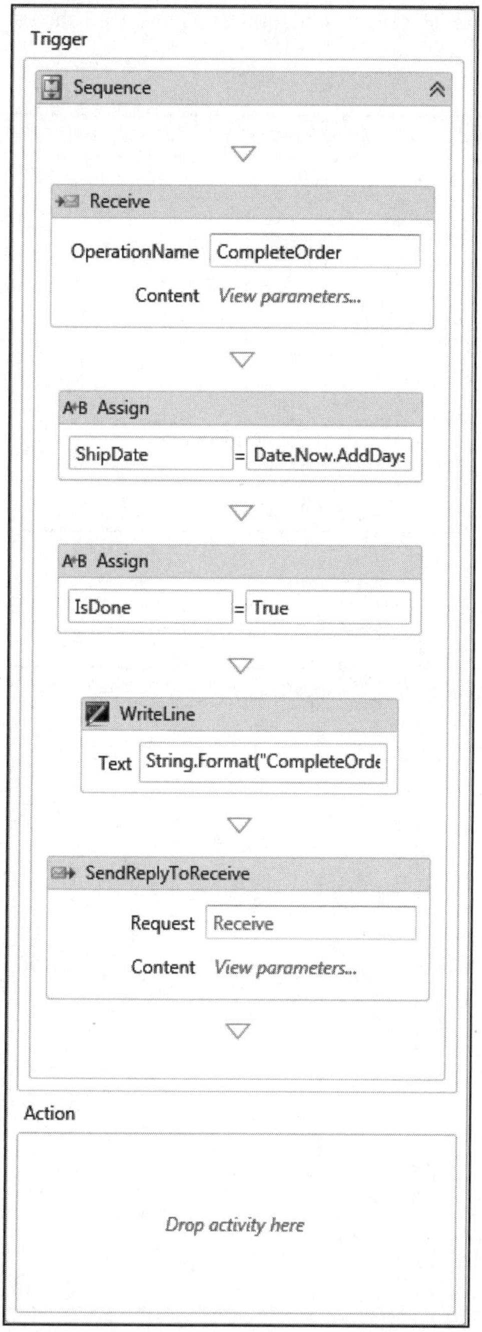

Figure 10-3. *CompleteOrder PickBranch*

Figure 10-4 shows the completed `Pick` activity with all three `PickBranch` instances. Figure 10-5 shows the completed top-level of the `ShipOrder` workflow.

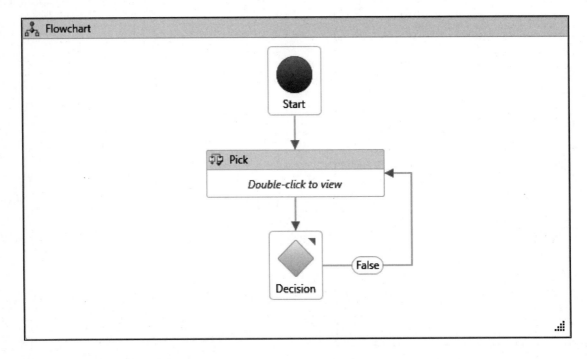

Figure 10-4. Pick activity

Figure 10-5. ShipOrder workflow

In the next section, you will modify the `OrderProcessing` workflow to invoke operations of the `ShipOrder` workflow. For simplicity in testing, both workflow services will be hosted by the `ServiceHost` application.

If you like, you can first test this new workflow service directly using the WCF Test Client. However, if you do, be aware that you need to add entries to the `Web.config` file to use `wsHttpContextBinding` for this service. If you don't use a binding that supports context exchange, the operations will not work correctly.

Modifying the OrderProcessing Service

You will now modify the `OrderProcessing` workflow to invoke the operations of the new `ShipOrder` service. This is the workflow service that you implemented in Chapter 9. After opening the `OrderProcessing` workflow in the designer, you can follow these steps to make the modification:

1. Delete the third `Assign` statement that assigns a value to `Response.ShipDate`. In its place, add a `Flowchart` activity. Change the `DisplayName` of the new activity to `ShipOrderFC`.

2. After opening the new `ShipOrderFC` activity, add a `SendAndReceiveReply` activity template to the empty flowchart. Change the `DisplayName` of the `Sequence` activity that is added with the template to `BeginOrderSequence`. Drag a connection from the starting point of the flowchart to this new `Sequence` activity.

3. Set the properties of the `Send` activity to invoke the `BeginOrder` operation. Use the values from the following tables to set the properties and parameters. The value for the `EndpointConfigurationName` must match a client configuration section that you will add to the `App.config` file for the `ServiceHost` project. The settings in the configuration file identify the endpoint and other settings that allow this workflow service to invoke the `ShipOrder` operations.

BeginOrder Send Properties

Property	Value
OperationName	BeginOrder
ServiceContractName	{http://tempuri.org/}IShipOrder
EndpointConfigurationName	ClientShipOrder

BeginOrder Send Parameters

Parameter Name	Type	Value
orderId	Int32	Response.OrderId
customerName	String	Request.CustomerName

4. There are no properties or parameters that need to be set for the
   ReceiveReplyForSend activity.

5. Add a ForEach<T> activity below the BeginOrderSequence activity. Set the
   generic type to ServiceLibrary.Item. Set the Values property to Request.Items.
   Add a connection from the BeginOrderSequence activity to the top of this
   activity.

6. Add an If activity as a child of the ForEach<T> activity. Set the If.Condition
   property to item IsNot Nothing. This prevents the processing of collection
   entries that are null.

7. Add a Send activity to the If.Then property. The purpose of this activity is to
   invoke the AddItem service operation. Set the properties and parameters for the
   Send activity according to the values shown in the following tables.

AddItem Send Properties

Property	Value
OperationName	AddItem
ServiceContractName	{http://tempuri.org/}IShipOrder
EndpointConfigurationName	ClientShipOrder

AddItem Send Parameters

Parameter Name	Type	Value
orderId	Int32	Response.OrderId
item	ServiceLibrary.Item	item

8. Add another SendAndReceiveReply activity template below the ForEach<T> that
   you just added. Connect the bottom of the ForEach<T> to the top of the
   Sequence activity that was added. Change the DisplayName of the Sequence
   activity to CompleteOrderSequence.

9. Use the values in the following tables to set the properties and parameters for
   the Send activity that was just added.

CompleteOrder Send Properties

Property	Value
OperationName	CompleteOrder
ServiceContractName	{http://tempuri.org/}IShipOrder
EndpointConfigurationName	ClientShipOrder

CompleteOrder Send Parameters

Parameter Name	Type	Value
orderId	Int32	Response.OrderId

10. Set the content parameters for the `ReceiveReplyForSend` activity for the
    `CompleteOrder` operation using the values shown in the following table.

CompleteOrder ReceiveReply Parameters

Parameter Name	Type	Value
shipDate	DateTime	Response.ShipDate

Figure 10-6 shows the completed `ShipOrderFC` activity. Figure 10-7 shows the updated
`OrderProcessing` workflow.

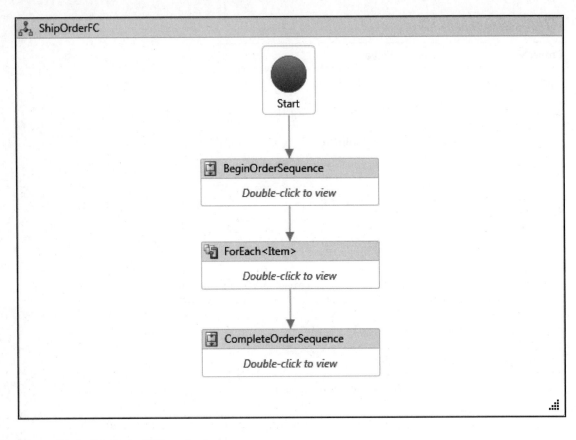

Figure 10-6. ShipOrderFC flowchart

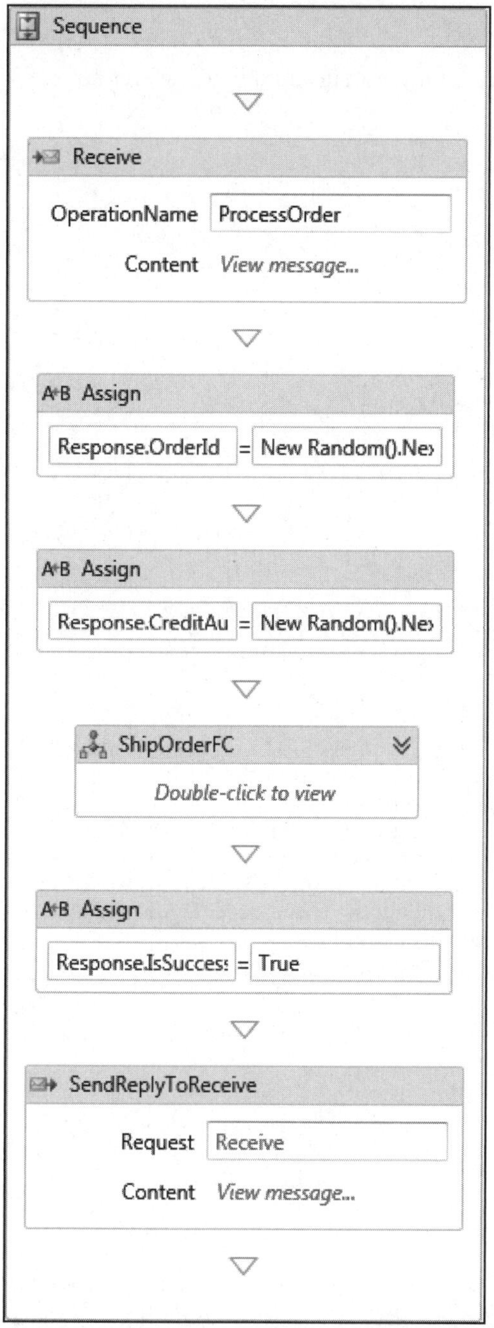

Figure 10-7. Revised OrderProcessing workflow

Hosting the ShipOrder Workflow Service

To host the new ShipOrder workflow service, you have to make only a small addition to the Program.cs file of the ServiceHost project, as shown here:

```
namespace ServiceHost
{
    class Program
    {
...
        static void Main(string[] args)
        {
            try
            {
                CreateServiceHost("OrderProcessing.xamlx");
                CreateServiceHost("ShipOrder.xamlx");
...
            }
...
        }
...
    }
}
```

Configuring the ServiceHost Application

The App.config file for the ServiceHost project also requires a few changes. First, you need to add a service entry for the ShipOrder workflow service. Make sure that this service uses the wsHttpContextBinding since context information must be exchanged.

Second, you need to add a client section that identifies the endpoint and binding for the ShipOrder workflow service. These settings are used for client applications that need to access the operations within the ShipOrder workflow service. The client in this case is actually the OrderProcessing workflow. The client endpoint name shown here (ClientShipOrder) must match the EndpointConfigurationName property that was set for the Send activities in the OrderProcessing workflow.

Here is an abbreviated App.config file showing the new entries that need to be added:

```
<?xml version="1.0"?>
<configuration>
  <system.serviceModel>
    <services>
...
      <service name="ShipOrder">
        <host>
          <baseAddresses>
            <add baseAddress="http://localhost:9031/"/>
          </baseAddresses>
        </host>
```

```
      <endpoint contract="IShipOrder"
        address="http://localhost:9031/ShipOrder"
        binding="wsHttpContextBinding" />
    </service>
  </services>
...
  <client>
    <endpoint name="ClientShipOrder"
     contract="IShipOrder" binding="wsHttpContextBinding"
     address="http://localhost:9031/ShipOrder" />
  </client>
...
 </system.serviceModel>
...
</configuration>
```

Testing the Revised OrderProcessing Workflow

After building the solution, you should be ready to test the revised `OrderProcessing` workflow and the `ShipOrder` workflow that it invokes. You'll need to run both the `ServiceHost` and `WorkflowClient` projects, so you need to once again make sure that the multiple project startup option is set. Here are my results for the `ServiceHost` project:

```
Contract: IOrderProcessing

    at http://localhost:9000/OrderProcessing

Contract: IShipOrder

    at http://localhost:9031/ShipOrder

Press any key to stop hosting and exit

BeginOrder OrderId: 124395128, Cust: Bruce Bukovics

AddItem OrderId:124395128, ItemId:200, Qty:1

AddItem OrderId:124395128, ItemId:300, Qty:2

CompleteOrder OrderId:124395128, ShipDate:Saturday, December 26, 2009
```

The additional lines are generated by the `WriteLine` activities of the `ShipOrder` workflow. The results for the `WorkflowClient` project should be consistent with previous tests.

Using Content-Based Correlation

In the previous example, you used context-based correlation to invoke the operations of the ShipOrder workflow service from the OrderProcessing workflow. The context information that routed the messages to the correct workflow instance was transmitted by the WCF infrastructure in the SOAP headers.

In this example, you will revise the ShipOrder workflow service to use content-based correlation instead. As the name implies, content-based correlation uses data in the message itself to route the message to the correct instance. You may have noted that all the operations of the ShipOrder workflow service conveniently include an orderId parameter. Since the value of this parameter is unique and is consistent for all calls to the service operations, it can be used for content-based correlation. If necessary, you can also use the values from multiple parameters to control correlation.

The value of the selected parameter is retrieved from each request using an XPath query. Fortunately, the workflow designer enables you to very simply define the query using a drop-down list of available parameters.

Guidelines for Content-Based Correlation

In general, you can follow these guidelines when using content-based correlation:

- At least one service operation must have the CanCreateInstance property set to true in order to create a new instance of the workflow.

- Service operations that are designed to interact with an existing workflow instance should have their CanCreateInstance properties set to false.

- All operations that you want to correlate must include a parameter that can be used to consistently and uniquely identify a workflow instance.

- A single CorrelationHandle variable should be shared by all service operations that you want to correlate.

- Each operation that is capable of creating a new workflow instance should initialize the shared CorrelationHandle using a QueryCorrelationInitializer.

- All operations that must correlate with an existing workflow instance should reference the shared CorrelationHandle using the CorrelatesWith property. They should also retrieve the data used for correlation from the current message by setting the CorrelatesOn property.

Modifying the ShipOrder Workflow Service

In the steps that follow, you will modify the ShipOrder workflow service to use content-based correlation. Open the ShipOrder.xamlx file in the designer, and follow these steps to make the necessary modifications:

1. Add a new variable that is scoped by the topmost Flowchart activity. The variable is named SharedHandle, and the type is CorrelationHandle. This handle must be placed at the top-level of the workflow in order to be shared by all of the service operations.

2. Locate the Receive activity for the BeginOrder operation. Modify the CorrelationInitializers property by clicking the ellipsis in the Properties window. Delete any correlation initializers that may already exist for the activity. Add a new QueryCorrelationInitializer by selecting Query correlation initializer from the list of available initializers. Enter SharedHandle as the handle variable to be initialized. In the XPath Queries section, select the orderId parameter from the drop-down list. This initializes the SharedHandle using the contents of the orderId request parameter. Figure 10-8 shows the completed Add Correlation Initializers dialog.

3. Locate the Receive activity for the AddItem operation. Set the CorrelatesWith property to the SharedHandle variable. The CorrelatesWith property specifies the handle that was initialized during the first service operation. The CorrelatesOn property uses an XPath query to retrieve the data to be used for correlation from the request message. Select the orderId parameter as the CorrelatesOn XPath query.

4. Locate the Receive activity for the CompleteOrder operation. Set the CorrelatesWith and CorrelatesOn properties in the same way as you did for the AddItem operation.

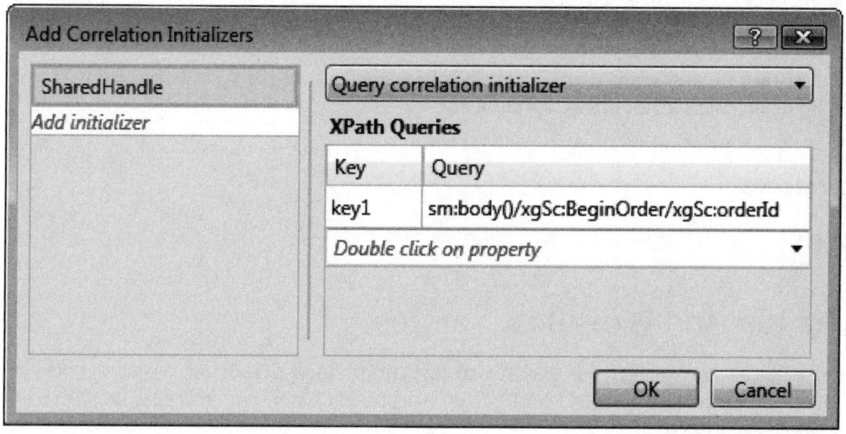

Figure 10-8. Query correlation initializer

Configuring the ServiceHost Application

Since the service contract for the ShipOrder workflow service did not change, there are no changes that are necessary to the OrderProcessing workflow.

However, you can make a minor change to the App.config file for the ServiceHost project. The original context-based version of the ShipOrder workflow service used wsHttpContextBinding since a binding that supported context exchange was required. That requirement is no longer valid, and you can change this workflow service to use basicHttpBinding instead. Here is an abbreviated App.config file showing the section that has changed:

```xml
<?xml version="1.0"?>
<configuration>
  <system.serviceModel>
    <services>
...
      <service name="ShipOrder">
        <host>
          <baseAddresses>
            <add baseAddress="http://localhost:9031/"/>
          </baseAddresses>
        </host>
        <endpoint contract="IShipOrder"
          address="http://localhost:9031/ShipOrder"
          binding="basicHttpBinding" />
      </service>
    </services>
...
    <client>
      <endpoint name="ClientShipOrder"
        contract="IShipOrder" binding="basicHttpBinding"
        address="http://localhost:9031/ShipOrder" />
    </client>
...
  </system.serviceModel>
...
</configuration>
```

Testing the Revised Workflow Service

After building the solution, you should be ready to test the revised ShipOrder workflow service. After running the ServiceHost and WorkflowClient projects in the normal way, the results should be consistent with the previous test.

Implementing a Duplex Message Exchange Pattern

The duplex pattern is another message exchange pattern that is supported by WF. In this pattern, two-way communication is established between two WCF services. The first service invokes a one-way operation on the second service. After completing its work, the second service invokes a one-way operation (a callback) on the first service. The endpoint address for the callback was provided by the infrastructure with the initial operation.

The assumption when using this pattern is that the second service operation may take some extended amount of time to complete. That's the primary reason why a more typical request/response pattern isn't used.

In this section, you will once again extend the original order processing scenario by implementing the CreditApproval workflow service. This new service will be invoked by the OrderProcessing workflow to simulate authorization of a credit card as payment for the order. The CreditApproval service uses the duplex message exchange pattern to call back to the OrderProcessing workflow with the result of the credit authorization.

Here is a summary of the operation that you will declare in the CreditApproval workflow as well as additional operations that you will add to the OrderProcessing workflow:

Workflow	Operation	Type	Creates Instance	Description
CreditApproval	Authorize	One-way	Yes	Invoked to authorize credit card information for payment of the order.
OrderProcessing	CreditApproved	One-way	No	Callback to signal that the credit card has been approved.
OrderProcessing	CreditDenied	One-way	No	Callback to signal that the credit card has been denied.

Guidelines for the Duplex Message Exchange Pattern

In general, you can follow these guidelines when implementing the duplex message exchange pattern:

- Use a binding that supports context exchange. More specifically, you need to use a binding that supports the ClientCallbackAddress property of the ContextBindingElement.

- Declare one or more service operations that are capable of creating a new service instance.

- Any service operations that create a new instance should initialize a CorrelationHandle with the CallbackCorrelationInitializer.

- Callback operations into the original calling workflow should use the CorrelatesWith property to reference the CorrelationHandle that was previously initialized.

- The calling workflow service must declare one or more operations that are invoked as a callback.

- Do not use the original ServiceContractName for callback operations. A different ServiceContractName should be used for all callback operations since these operations require additional binding settings.

- Define a unique endpoint for the callback operations.

- The binding configuration used by the first workflow to invoke the second must include the `ClientCallbackAddress` property. This property must reference the unique endpoint that was established for the callback operations.

Declaring the CreditApproval Workflow Service

Add a new WCF Workflow Service to the `ServiceLibrary` project, and name it `CreditApproval`. Delete the top-level `Sequence` activity (along with its child messaging activities). Set the `Name` and `ConfigurationName` properties of the workflow service to `CreditApproval`.

Here is a recap of the workflow variables that you will add to the workflow:

Name	Variable Type	Scope
TotalAmount	Decimal	Flowchart
CreditCard	String	Flowchart
CreditCardExpiration	String	Flowchart
CreditAuthCode	String	Flowchart
CallbackHandle	CorrelationHandle	Flowchart

Follow these steps to complete the declaration of this workflow:

1. Add a `Flowchart` activity to the empty workflow, and add all of the variables.

2. Add a `Receive` activity to the flowchart. Use the values in the following tables to set the properties and content parameters of this activity. Connect the starting point of the flowchart to the top of this `Receive` activity.

Authorize Receive Properties

Property	Value
OperationName	Authorize
ServiceContractName	{http://tempuri.org/}ICreditApproval
CanCreateInstance	True

Authorize Receive Parameters

Parameter Name	Type	Value
totalAmount	Decimal	TotalAmount
creditCard	String	CreditCard
creditCardExpiration	String	CreditCardExpiration

3. Remove any initializers that may already exist for the `Receive` activity. Add a `CallbackCorrelationInitializer` to the `Receive` activity. Set the `CorrelationHandle` for the initializer to the `CallbackHandle` variable. This is an important step since it initializes the `CallbackHandle` with the correlation data that is needed to call back into the original calling workflow. Figure 10-9 shows the Add Correlation Initializers dialog.

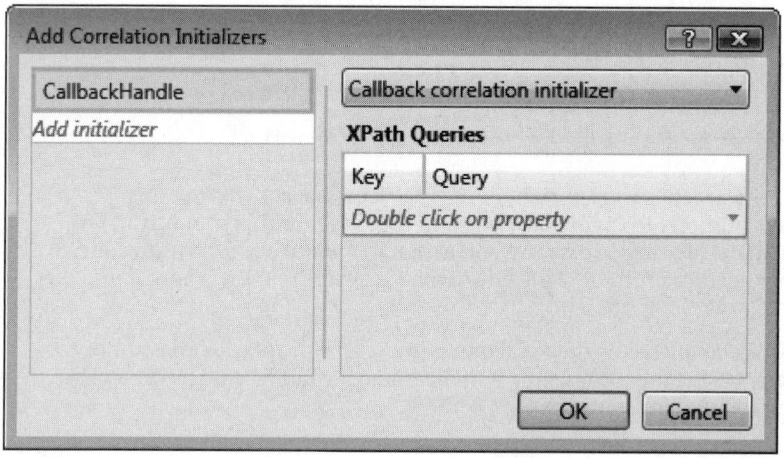

Figure 10-9. Receive activity callback correlation initializer

4. Add a `WriteLine` to the flowchart, and set the `Text` property to `String.Format("Simulate credit auth for {0} {1} {2}", CreditCard, CreditCardExpiration, TotalAmount)`. Connect the `Receive` activity to this new `WriteLine` activity.

5. Add a `Delay` activity to the flowchart. Set the `Duration` property to `TimeSpan.FromSeconds(4)`. This adds a short delay to simulate the credit authorization process. Connect the `WriteLine` activity to the `Delay` activity.

6. Add a `FlowDecision` activity to the flowchart. Set the `Condition` property to `String.IsNullOrEmpty(CreditCard) Or String.IsNullOrEmpty(CreditCardExpiration)`. This adds a simple rule that is used to determine whether to approve or deny the credit request.

7. Add a `Send` activity to the left side of the `FlowDecision`. The purpose of this activity is to call back to the calling workflow to deny the credit request. Set the properties of this activity using the values in the following table. The `CorrelatesWith` property is important since it references the `CallbackHandle` that was previously initialized. The `Endpoint.Binding` property identifies the type of binding that will be used for this callback operation. Add a connection from the left side of the `FlowDecision` (the true side) to this activity.

CreditDenied Send Properties

Property	Value
OperationName	CreditDenied
ServiceContractName	{http://tempuri.org/}IOrderProcessingCallback
CorrelatesWith	CallbackHandle
Endpoint.Binding	WSHttpContextBinding

8. Add an `Assign` activity to the right of the `FlowDecision` activity. Set the `Assign.To` property to `CreditAuthCode` and the `Assign.Value` property to `New Random().Next(100000).ToString()` to assign a random authorization code. Add a connection from the right side of the `FlowDecision` (the false side) to this activity.

9. Add a `Send` activity below the `Assign` activity. Set the properties and content parameters using the values shown in the following tables. Add a connection from the `Assign` activity to this `Send` activity.

CreditApproved Send Properties

Property	Value
OperationName	CreditApproved
ServiceContractName	{http://tempuri.org/}IOrderProcessingCallback
CorrelatesWith	CallbackHandle
Endpoint.Binding	WSHttpContextBinding

CreditApproved Send Parameters

Parameter Name	Type	Value
creditAuthCode	String	CreditAuthCode

Figure 10-10 shows the completed `CreditApproval` workflow.

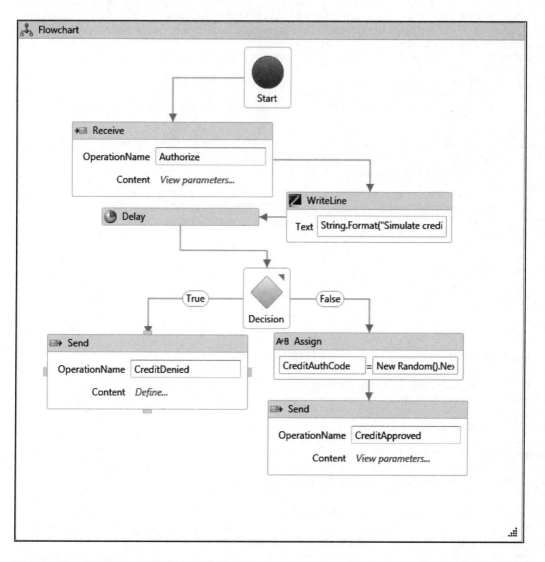

Figure 10-10. CreditApproval workflow

Modifying the OrderProcessing Service

The next step in this example is to modify the `OrderProcessing` workflow service to invoke the `Authorize` operation of the `CreditApproval` workflow service. The `CreditApproved` and `CreditDenied` operations must also be added to the `OrderProcessing` workflow.

You will invoke the `Authorize` operation using a `Send` activity. You will also add two `Receive` activities, one for the `CreditApproved` and one for the `CreditDenied` operation. These are the two callback operations that are invoked by the `CreditApproval` workflow. These activities all need to be correlated with each other. You can do this manually with a `CorrelationHandle` that is shared by all the activities. Or alternatively, you can place all of these activities into a `CorrelationScope` activity. This activity manages the correlation of its child activities and removes the need to manage a `CorrelationHandle` yourself. For this example, I've chosen the `CorrelationScope` approach.

Please follow these steps to modify the `OrderProcessing` workflow:

1. Locate the `Assign` activity that sets the `Response.CreditAuthCode` to a random number. Delete this activity, and replace it with a `CorrelationScope` activity. Change the `DisplayName` of the `CorrelationScope` activity to `GetCreditApproval` to better identify its purpose.

2. Add a `Sequence` activity to the body of the `CorrelationScope` activity, followed by an `Assign` activity. Set the `Assign.To` property to `Response.CreditAuthCode` and the `Assign.Value` property to `Nothing`.

3. Add a `Send` activity under the `Assign` activity. The purpose of this activity is to invoke the `Authorize` operation of the `CreditApproval` workflow service. Use the values shown in the following tables to set the properties of the `Send` activity.

Authorize Send Properties

Property	Value
OperationName	Authorize
ServiceContractName	{http://tempuri.org/}ICreditApproval
EndpointConfigurationName	ClientCreditApproval

Authorize Send Parameters

Parameter Name	Type	Value
totalAmount	Decimal	Request.TotalAmount
creditCard	String	Request.CreditCard
creditCardExpiration	String	Request.CreditCardExpiration

4. Add a Pick activity directly below the Send activity. After the Send activity
    invokes the Authorize operation, the workflow must wait for either the
    CreditApproved or CreditDenied callback operation to be invoked. The Pick
    activity allows you to conveniently model both of those operations. Figure 10-
    11 shows the GetCreditApproval activity after adding the Pick activity.

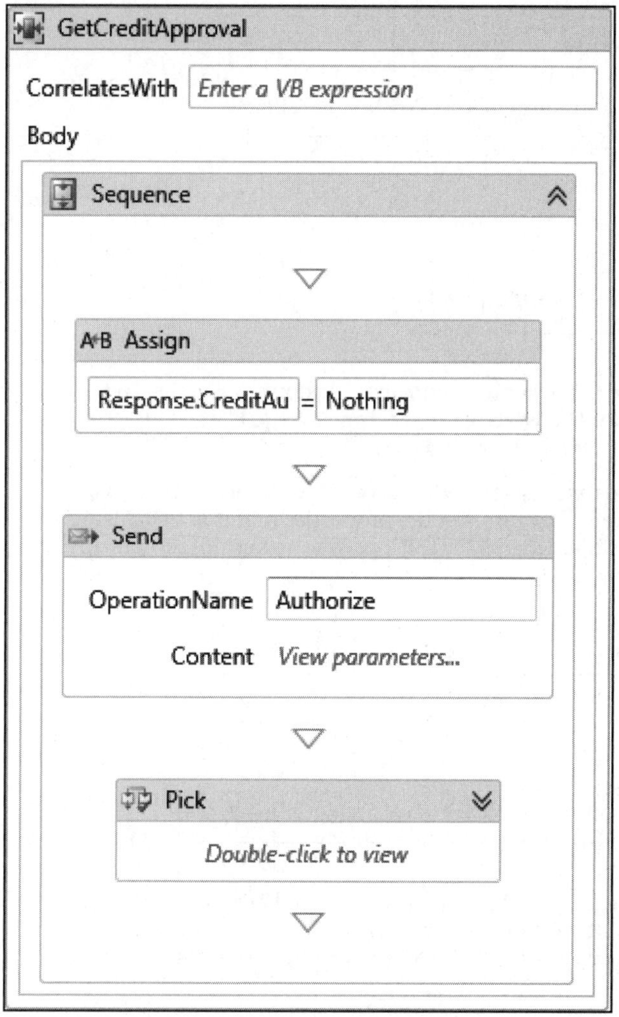

Figure 10-11. GetCreditApproval CorrelationScope activity

5. Add a Receive activity to the Trigger of the first PickBranch. This activity declares the CreditApproved operation. Set the properties and parameters of this activity using the values shown in the following tables.

CreditApproved Receive Properties

Property	Value
OperationName	CreditApproved
ServiceContractName	{http://tempuri.org/}IOrderProcessingCallback

CreditApproved Receive Parameters

Parameter Name	Type	Value
creditAuthCode	String	Response.CreditAuthCode

6. Add a WriteLine activity to the Action of the first PickBranch. Set the Text property to String.Format("Credit approved for {0}: {1}", Response.OrderId, Response.CreditAuthCode).

7. Add a Receive activity to the Trigger of the second PickBranch. This activity declares the CreditDenied operation. Set the properties of this activity using the values shown in the following table. This operation does not require any content parameters.

CreditDenied Receive Properties

Property	Value
OperationName	CreditDenied
ServiceContractName	{http://tempuri.org/}IOrderProcessingCallback

8. Add a WriteLine activity to the Action of the second PickBranch. Set the Text property to String.Format("Credit denied for {0}", Response.OrderId). Figure 10-12 shows the completed Pick activity with the two branches.

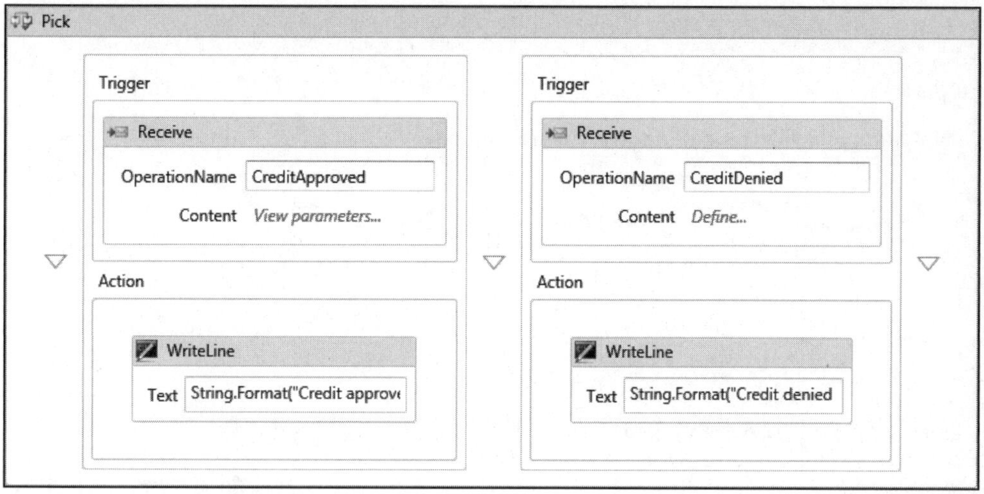

Figure 10-12. *GetCreditApproval Pick activity*

9. Return to the topmost level of the workflow, and add an `If` activity under the `GetCreditApproval` activity. Set the `If.Condition` property to `Not String.IsNullOrEmpty(Response.CreditAuthCode)`. If the condition is true, it means that the credit card was approved; otherwise, it was denied.

10. Add a `Sequence` activity to the `If.Then` property. Move the `ShipOrderFC` activity and the final `Assign` activity (the one that sets the `Response.IsSuccessful` property) from the top level of the workflow to this new `Sequence` activity. This is necessary since you want to ship the order and indicate success only if the credit was approved. Figure 10-13 shows the completed `If` activity.

Figure 10-14 shows the revised `OrderProcessing` workflow.

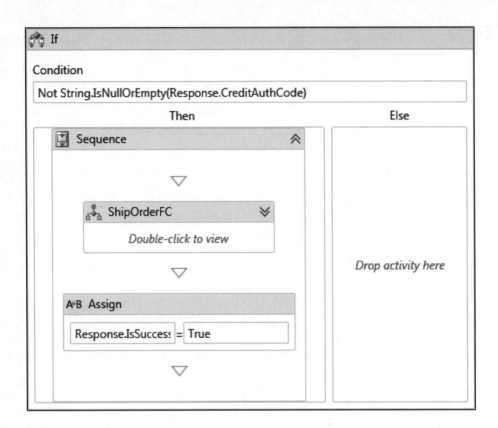

Figure 10-13. If activity with ShipOrderFC

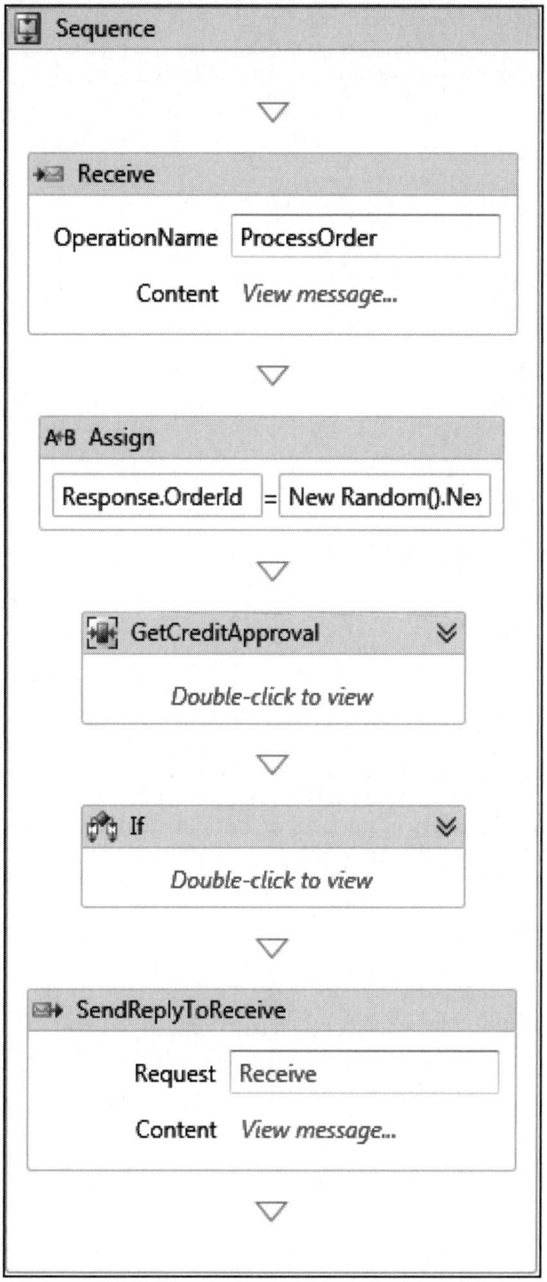

Sequence

▽

Receive

OperationName | ProcessOrder

Content | *View message...*

▽

A→B Assign

Response.OrderId | = | New Random().Ne›

▽

GetCreditApproval ≫

Double-click to view

▽

If ≫

Double-click to view

▽

SendReplyToReceive

Request | Receive

Content | *View message...*

▽

Figure 10-14. Revised OrderProcessing workflow

Hosting the CreditApproval Workflow Service

To host the new **CreditApproval** workflow service, once again modify the **Program.cs** file of the **ServiceHost** project, as shown here:

```
namespace ServiceHost
{
    class Program
    {
...
        static void Main(string[] args)
        {
            try
            {
                CreateServiceHost("OrderProcessing.xamlx");
                CreateServiceHost("ShipOrder.xamlx");
                CreateServiceHost("CreditApproval.xamlx");
...
            }
...
        }
...
    }
}
```

Configuring the ServiceHost Application

Before testing these revisions, you need to make several changes to the **App.config** file for the **ServiceHost** project. You need to add a service endpoint for the new **CreditApproval** workflow service. You also need to add a new endpoint to the **OrderProcessing** service, since it now supports a new set of callback operations. Finally, you need to configure a client section and binding configuration that allows the **OrderProcessing** service to invoke the **CreditApproval** service.

■ **Tip** Probably the most important section of this **App.config** is the definition of the binding that is used by the **OrderProcessing** service to access the **CreditApproval** service. That named binding configuration (**ClientCreditApprovalBinding**) includes an entry that sets the **clientCallbackAddress** property to the new callback endpoint. Without this entry, the **CreditApproval** workflow will be unable to successfully invoke the callback operations (**CreditApproved** or **CreditDenied**).

Here is a complete revised copy of the `App.config` file including all of the previous changes:

```xml
<?xml version="1.0"?>
<configuration>
  <system.serviceModel>
    <services>
      <service name="OrderProcessing3">
        <host>
          <baseAddresses>
            <add baseAddress="http://localhost:9000/"/>
          </baseAddresses>
        </host>
        <endpoint contract="IOrderProcessing"
          address="http://localhost:9000/OrderProcessing"
          binding="wsHttpBinding"
          bindingConfiguration="OrderProcessingBinding" />
        <endpoint contract="IOrderProcessingCallback"
          address="http://localhost:9000/OrderProcessingCallback"
          binding="wsHttpContextBinding" />
      </service>
      <service name="ShipOrderContent">
        <host>
          <baseAddresses>
            <add baseAddress="http://localhost:9031/"/>
          </baseAddresses>
        </host>
        <endpoint contract="IShipOrder"
          address="http://localhost:9031/ShipOrder"
          binding="basicHttpBinding" />
      </service>
      <service name="CreditApproval">
        <host>
          <baseAddresses>
            <add baseAddress="http://localhost:9033/"/>
          </baseAddresses>
        </host>
        <endpoint contract="ICreditApproval"
          address="http://localhost:9033/CreditApproval"
          binding="wsHttpContextBinding" />
      </service>
    </services>

    <bindings>
      <wsHttpBinding>
        <binding name="OrderProcessingBinding">
          <security mode="Message">
            <message clientCredentialType="Windows"
              algorithmSuite="TripleDesRsa15"
              establishSecurityContext="true"
              negotiateServiceCredential="true" />
```

```
            </security>
          </binding>
        </wsHttpBinding>
        <wsHttpContextBinding>
          <binding name="ClientCreditApprovalBinding"
            clientCallbackAddress="http://localhost:9000/OrderProcessingCallback"/>
        </wsHttpContextBinding>
      </bindings>

      <client>
        <endpoint name="ClientShipOrder"
          contract="IShipOrder" binding="basicHttpBinding"
          address="http://localhost:9031/ShipOrder" />
        <endpoint name="ClientCreditApproval"
          contract="ICreditApproval" binding="wsHttpContextBinding"
          bindingConfiguration="ClientCreditApprovalBinding"
          address="http://localhost:9033/CreditApproval" />
      </client>

      <behaviors>
        <serviceBehaviors>
          <behavior>
            <serviceDebug includeExceptionDetailInFaults="True"
              httpHelpPageEnabled="True"/>
            <serviceMetadata httpGetEnabled="True"/>
          </behavior>
        </serviceBehaviors>
      </behaviors>

    </system.serviceModel>

    <startup>
      <supportedRuntime version="v4" sku=".NETFramework,Version=v4"/>
    </startup>
</configuration>
```

Testing the Revised Workflow Service

You can now build the solution and start the ServiceHost and WorkflowClient projects in the usual way. According to the simple rules of the CreditApproval workflow, the credit card will be approved if the CreditCard and CreditCardExpiration contain some value (the workflow really doesn't care what you enter for those parameters). If either parameter is null or an empty string, the credit card is denied.

The results from the WorkflowClient should be consistent with previous tests. The output from the ServiceHost now includes additional information. Here is the output from the ServiceHost when the credit card has been approved:

```
Contract: IOrderProcessing

    at http://localhost:9000/OrderProcessing

Contract: IOrderProcessingCallback

    at http://localhost:9000/OrderProcessingCallback

Contract: IShipOrder

    at http://localhost:9031/ShipOrder

Contract: ICreditApproval

    at http://localhost:9033/CreditApproval

Press any key to stop hosting and exit

Simulate credit auth for 4444111122223333 0611 3.98

Credit approved for 1279593577: 30475

BeginOrder OrderId: 1279593577, Cust: Bruce Bukovics

AddItem OrderId:1279593577, ItemId:200, Qty:1

AddItem OrderId:1279593577, ItemId:300, Qty:2

CompleteOrder OrderId:1279593577, ShipDate:Saturday, December 26, 2009
```

And here are my results when the credit is denied:

```
Contract: IOrderProcessing

    at http://localhost:9000/OrderProcessing

Contract: IOrderProcessingCallback

    at http://localhost:9000/OrderProcessingCallback

Contract: IShipOrder

    at http://localhost:9031/ShipOrder

Contract: ICreditApproval
```

```
    at http://localhost:9033/CreditApproval

Press any key to stop hosting and exit

Simulate credit auth for 4444111122223333  3.98

Credit denied for 1141076803
```

If the credit is denied, the output from the WorkflowClient project is also slightly different. For example:

```
Enter the customer name

Bruce Bukovics

Enter the customer email

bruce@foo.com

Enter the customer address

100 Main Street

Enter credit card number

4444111122223333

Enter credit card expiration date (mmyy)


Enter an item ID (enter 0 if done entering items)

200

Enter the quantity of the item

1

Enter an item ID (enter 0 if done entering items)

300

Enter the quantity of the item
```

```
2

Enter an item ID (enter 0 if done entering items)

0

Invoking ProcessOrder service method

Back from ProcessOrder

ProcessOrder response:

IsSuccessful: False

ShipDate: Monday, January 01, 0001

OrderId: 1141076803

CreditAuthCode:

Press any key to exit
```

Using a Custom Workflow Extension

WF allows you to develop custom workflow extensions and then make them available to workflows at runtime. These custom extensions can provide any additional functionality that you see fit to implement. You can use these extensions with nonmessaging workflows, and WF also enables you to use them with workflow services.

■ **Note** Chapter 8 discussed the use of custom workflow extensions in a nonmessaging workflow.

To make a workflow extension available to workflow services, you use the `WorkflowExtensions` property of the `WorkflowServiceHost`. You have the choice of adding a single extension instance that is shared by all workflow service instances or creating a new extension instance for each service instance. The `WorkflowExtensions` property (actually a `WorkflowInstanceExtensionManager` object) provides two overloads of the `Add` method that support these two instancing scenarios.

In this section, you will modify the OrderProcessing workflow to use a workflow extension to generate the order ID instead of generating it internally.

Implementing the OrderUtilityExtension

The first order of business is to implement the workflow extension. Add a new C# class to the ServiceLibrary project, and name it OrderUtilityExtension. Here is the complete code for this extension:

```
using System;

namespace ServiceLibrary
{
    public class OrderUtilityExtension
    {
        private Random random = new Random(Environment.TickCount);

        public Int32 GetOrderId()
        {
            return random.Next(Int32.MaxValue);
        }
    }
}
```

The code doesn't really change the way an order ID is generated. It is assigned a random number just as is currently done within the OrderProcessing workflow. However, this simple example is enough to demonstrate how to access an extension from a workflow service.

Implementing the GetOrderId Activity

You also need a custom activity that retrieves the extension and invokes the GetOrderId method of the extension. Add a new Code Activity to the ServiceLibrary project, and name it GetOrderId. Here is the complete code for this activity:

```
using System;
using System.Activities;

namespace ServiceLibrary
{
    public sealed class GetOrderId : CodeActivity<Int32>
    {
        protected override int Execute(CodeActivityContext context)
        {
            OrderUtilityExtension extension =
                context.GetExtension<OrderUtilityExtension>();
```

```
        if (extension != null)
        {
            return extension.GetOrderId();
        }
        else
        {
            return 0;
        }
    }
  }
}
```

Modifying the OrderProcessing Workflow Service

To use the new extension within the OrderProcessing workflow service, you need to replace the Assign activity that sets the OrderId to a random number with an instance of the new GetOrderId activity.

After building the solution, open the OrderProcessing workflow service, and locate the Assign activity that populates the Response.OrderId property. Delete the activity, and replace it with an instance of the new GetOrderId activity. Set the GetOrderId.Result property to Response.OrderId. Figure 10-15 shows the revised workflow.

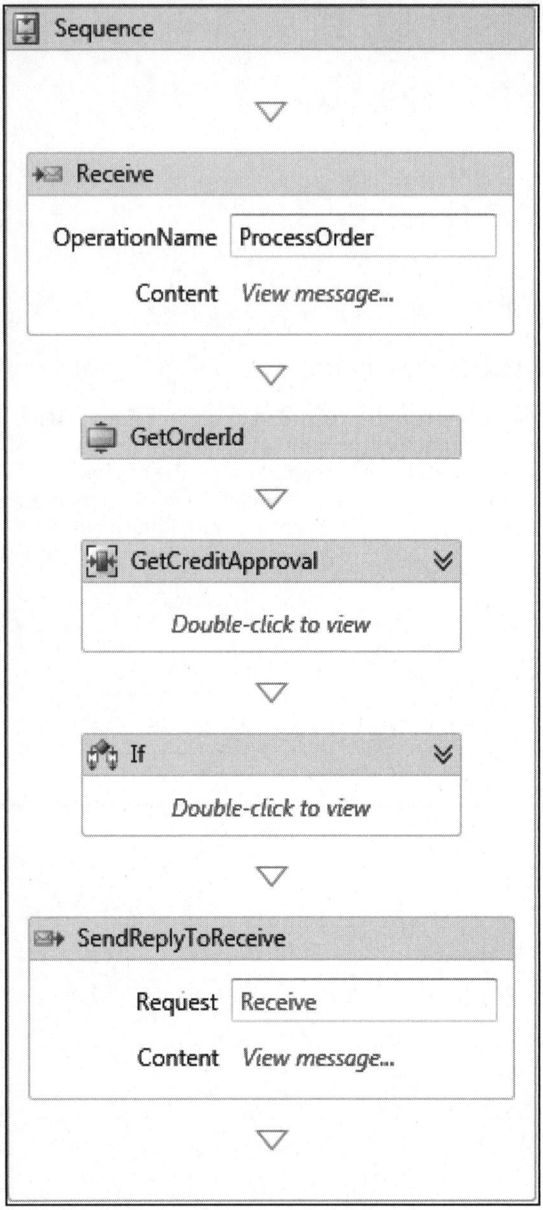

Figure 10-15. *Revised OrderProcessing workflow*

Adding the Extension

To add the extension and make it available to workflow instances, you need to modify the `Program.cs` file of the `ServiceHost` project. Here is an abbreviated copy of the `Program.cs` file showing only the method that requires the change:

```
namespace ServiceHost
{
    class Program
    {
...
        private static WorkflowServiceHost CreateServiceHost(String xamlxName)
        {
            WorkflowService wfService = LoadService(xamlxName);
            WorkflowServiceHost host = new WorkflowServiceHost(wfService);

            host.WorkflowExtensions.Add(new ServiceLibrary.OrderUtilityExtension());

            _hosts.Add(host);

            return host;
        }
...
    }
}
```

In this revised code, the `WorkflowExtensions.Add` method is called to add the new extension after creating the `WorkfowServiceHost`. This code adds a single instance of the extension that is shared by all workflow service instances. This should work fine for this particular extension.

However, you may need to create a new instance of an extension for each workflow service instance. If this is the case, you could use an overload of the `Add` method like this:

```
host.WorkflowExtensions.Add<ServiceLibrary.OrderUtilityExtension>(
    () => new ServiceLibrary.OrderUtilityExtension());
```

This version of the `Add` method requires a `Func<T>` (a delegate that returns an instance of type T). The code satisfies the requirements of the method with a Lambda expression. The expression creates a new instance of the extension each time it is invoked.

Testing the Revised Workflow Service

After building the solution, you should be able to test these changes by running the `ServiceHost` and `WorkflowClient` projects. The results should be consistent with the previous test.

Understanding Exceptions and Faults

You have seen that the contract for a service operation is defined by the properties of the `Receive` activity. If the operation uses the request/response pattern, the `SendReply` activity defines the response portion of the contract. In addition, any unhandled exceptions that are thrown by a service operation essentially become part of their contracts.

If an unhandled exception is thrown by a service operation, the exception is converted to a SOAP fault and transmitted as a response to the caller. Assuming that the caller is also a .NET application, the SOAP fault is converted back to a managed exception for consumption by the calling code. This transformation from managed exception to SOAP fault and back to an exception is handled by the WCF infrastructure automatically. On the client side, all SOAP faults are transformed into a `FaultException`.

■ **Note** Detailed fault information such as a stack trace is provided to the client only if the `ServiceDebugBehavior` has been added to the WCF service behaviors and the `IncludeExceptionDetailInFaults` property of this behavior is set to true. All of the `Web.Config` and `App.config` examples in this chapter and the previous one include this behavior.

However, it is sometimes beneficial to explicitly define and send a SOAP fault. You might want to define a fault class that contains just the right amount of data that is appropriate for the client application to receive and process. This is often better (and safer) than simply returning the unhandled exception. The exception might expose implementation details that you shouldn't really expose to the caller.

If the service operation is declared as a workflow service, you can explicitly send a fault using the standard `SendReply` or `Send` activity. You first define a class that contains the properties that you want to return as a fault (for example `MyServiceFault`). Think of this *expected fault* as just another type of response that can be returned from your service.

You then catch the original exception within the workflow service using the `TryCatch` activity. Just like a C# try/catch block of code, this activity allows you to catch an exception and handle it declaratively with other WF activities.

■ **Note** Chapter 13 discusses the `TryCatch` activity and other topics related to exception handling.

Once the original exception has been caught, you construct an instance of your custom fault class and populate it with the values that you want to return. You send the fault to the caller wrapped in a `FaultException<T>` instance. The generic type of this class must be the fault type that you defined. For example, if you are declaring a request/response operation, you might set the content of the `SendReply` activity to `New FaultException<MyServiceFault>(myFault)`. This assumes that a variable named `myFault` has already been populated with the values that you want to return.

Remember that the fault is an alternate type of response that can be returned to the caller. It doesn't replace the normal response. For this reason, the service operation will require two `SendReply` activities: one for the normal response and one for the fault. Both of these activities must be associated with the same `Receive` activity (identified by the `SendReply.Request` property).

■ **Tip** The WF designer does not allow you to manually set the `SendReply.Request` property. Therefore, the easiest way to create the additional `SendReply` needed to send a fault is to copy the original `SendReply` that returns the normal response. You can make a copy of this activity and paste it into the appropriate `Catch` of the `TryCatch` activity. Alternatively, you can right-click the `Receive` activity and select the option to create a `SendReply` activity. The new activity is created directly below the `Receive` activity. You can then move it to the proper location within the workflow.

If you send your own fault as a response, the client code should catch (using **TryCatch**) a `FaultException<T>` instead of the more general `FaultException`. For example, it is preferable to catch `FaultException<MyServiceFault>` instead of `FaultException`. The nongeneric `FaultException` does not provide access to the detail fault object, while the generic version does.

■ **Warning** Any custom fault types that you want to handle on the client side must be added to the `KnownTypes` property of the `Send` activity that invoked the service operation. Doing this identifies the custom fault type as an expected type that should be serialized. If you fail to do this, the custom fault will be returned only as the general `FaultException` instead of the generic `FaultException<T>`. Additionally, there is currently no support for the `KnownTypes` property if you are using a generated `Send` activity (one that was generated by adding a service reference to the workflow project). For this reason, you will need to use the standard `Send` activity if you are expecting custom fault types as a response.

Flowing Transactions into a Workflow Service

A transaction guarantees the atomicity of work that is performed using a resource manager (such as SQL Server). It ensures that individual updates are committed as a single unit of work or rolled back completely if there is a problem.

WF provides two activities that enable you to use transactions within a workflow. The `TransactionScope` activity provides support for transactions that are created within the current process.

■ **Note** Chapter 13 discusses the `TransactionScope` activity.

The `TransactedReceiveScope` activity is similar to the `TransactionScope`, but it is designed to work with WCF messaging activities. And unlike the `TransactionScope` activity, `TransactedReceiveScope` allows you to flow a transaction that was created by the calling application into the service operation. Here are the most important properties of this activity:

Property	Type	Required	Description
Request	Receive	Yes	The Receive activity that requires a transaction
Body	Activity	No	The activity that completes the implementation of the service operation
AbortInstanceOnTransactionFailure	Boolean	No	True to abort the workflow if the transaction is aborted

You use a `TransactedReceiveScope` by placing a `Receive` activity that requires a transaction into the `Request` property. The other activities that are needed to implement the service operation are placed into the `Body`. The `Body` property must include the `SendReply` activity if you are modeling a request/response operation.

If the client has an open ambient transaction when the service operation is invoked, the transaction will flow to the service, and any work that you perform will be performed under the transaction. When the service operation successfully completes, the transaction remains open and must be completed by the calling client application. If the service operation throws an unhandled exception, any work performed under the transaction is rolled back.

If a transaction is not provided by the client application, a new local transaction is created for the service operation. The behavior of the activity then becomes similar to that of the `TransactionScope` activity. If the service operation successfully completes, the locally created transaction is committed; otherwise, it is rolled back.

■ **Tip** To flow a transaction into a service, you must use a binding that supports this behavior. For example, `WSHttpBinding`, `WSHttpContextBinding`, and `NetTcpBinding` support flowing a transaction. `BasicHttpBinding` does not. Additionally, you need to set the `TransactionFlow` property of the binding to true in order to enable the flowing of transactions to the called service.

Using Standard Behaviors

WF provides two standard behaviors that enable you to control aspects of the runtime environment for workflow services.

The `WorkflowUnhandledExceptionBehavior` determines what action will be taken when a workflow service throws an unhandled exception. The `Action` property is defined as enum type `WorkflowUnhandledExceptionAction` with these possible values:

- **Abandon**. The workflow service is immediately abandoned. No additional execution is scheduled.

- **Cancel**. The workflow service is scheduled for cancellation. This option allows the workflow service to gracefully transition to the Canceled state.

- **Terminate**. The workflow service is scheduled for termination. Termination moves the workflow service into the Faulted state, which prevents it from being resumed or restarted.

- **AbandonAndSuspend**. Same as **Abandon**, but the last persisted state for the instance is suspended. Suspending an instance prevents messages from being delivered to the persisted instance.

The `WorkflowIdleBehavior` determines when idle workflow service instances are unloaded and persisted. The `TimeToPersist` property is a `TimeSpan` value that determines how long the instance must be idle before it is persisted. The `TimeToUnload` property determines how long the instance must be idle before it is unloaded from memory.

Taken together, these properties enable you to fine-tune how quickly you persist and unload workflow service instances. The default value for `TimeToUnload` is one minute, which means that an instance will be persisted and unloaded one minute after it becomes idle. If you want to be more aggressive in persisting and removing idle instances from memory, you can reduce the default value for this property. A value of zero means that an idle instance will be persisted and unloaded immediately when it becomes idle.

The `TimeToPersist` property must be less than the `TimeToUnload` value; otherwise, it is ignored. It is used to persist an idle instance more quickly without immediately removing it from memory. An idle instance is first persisted according to the value that you set for the `TimeToPersist` property. Then, once the `TimeToUnload TimeSpan` has been reached, the idle instance is removed from memory.

You can add these behaviors in code using the `Description.Behaviors` property of the `WorkflowServiceHost`. Or you can configure these behaviors with entries in the `Web.config` or `App.config` file, as shown here:

```
<behaviors>
  <serviceBehaviors>
    <behavior>
      <serviceMetadata httpGetEnabled="true"/>
      <serviceDebug includeExceptionDetailInFaults="false"/>

      <workflowIdle timeToPersist="0" timeToUnload="0"/>
      <workflowUnhandledException action ="Cancel"/>

    </behavior>
  </serviceBehaviors>
</behaviors>
```

Summary

The focus of this chapter was several advanced topics related to the WCF and workflow services support provided with WF. This chapter was a continuation of the WCF and workflow services coverage that was first presented in Chapter 9.

The examples in this chapter build upon the workflow service example that was started in Chapter 9. Examples in this chapter demonstrated context-based and content-based correlation, the duplex message exchange pattern, and workflow extensions.

The chapter concluded with a discussion of a few miscellaneous topics related to workflow services. These topics included exception and fault handling, flowing transactions into a workflow service, and the use of standard behaviors provided by WF.

In the next chapter you will learn about workflow persistence.

CHAPTER 11

■■■

Workflow Persistence

One of the most important capabilities of Windows Workflow Foundation (WF) is the ability to persist workflow instances (save and reload them at a later time). Without persistence, the lifetime of your workflows is limited. When the host application is shut down, any workflow instances simply cease to exist. Without workflow persistence, the development of long-running workflow applications would be difficult, if not completely impossible.

The chapter begins with an overview of the workflow persistence support in WF. The discussion includes information on how to enable persistence when you are using the `WorkflowApplication` class to host your workflows. Other sections describe how persistence is used with workflow services that are hosted by the `WorkflowServiceHost` class. Coverage of the `SqlWorkflowInstanceStore`, which supports persistence to a SQL Server database, is also included.

The chapter includes hands-on examples that demonstrate persistence with `WorkflowApplication` and `WorkflowServiceHost`.

■ **Note** Chapter 12 continues with the example projects that you develop in this chapter to extend and customize workflow persistence.

The Need for Workflow Persistence

Up to this point, you have seen workflows that perform only short-lived tasks. You have seen that multiple instances of a workflow can be started by an application, but each workflow exists only in memory. Although these in-memory workflows are very useful and can be used to accomplish many tasks, they are limited. When the host application is stopped, the workflow instances cease to exist. Their lifetime is tightly bound to a single host application.

Workflow persistence means to save the state of a workflow instance to a durable store such as a SQL database or file. Once persisted, the workflow can be removed from memory and reloaded at a later time. Here are some of the reasons to use persistence with your workflows:

- *Human interaction tasks*: Workflows that are designed to interact with humans are typically long running. They may take minutes, hours, days, or weeks to complete. It isn't practical to keep such a workflow alive in memory for that length of time. Persistence of the workflow provides a way to unload it while it is waiting for the next human event and then reload it when the event is received.

- *Scalability*: In-memory workflows are limited to execution within a single application host. To provide scalability, some applications may require multiple hosts, perhaps running on multiple servers. A persisted workflow can be loaded and executed on a different server than the one that started it.

- *Resource consumption*: Without a persistence mechanism, workflows must stay in memory. They have nowhere else to go. If a workflow is waiting for an external input, it is actually idle. With a persistence mechanism in place, the idled workflow can be persisted and unloaded from memory. Once the external stimulus is received, the workflow is loaded back into memory, and processing can continue. Swapping workflows in and out of memory like this frees resources, making them available for workflows that are actively executing.

- *Application flexibility*: An in-memory workflow can be executed only by the application that started it. Perhaps you have a web-based application that starts a workflow, but you also want to use more traditional smart-client applications (for example, Windows Forms) to work with the workflow. Persisting the workflow allows it to be reloaded by an entirely different class of application.

Not every application requires persistence. If you require only short-lived workflows that execute within a single application, you can probably do without persistence. On the other hand, if your workflows model long-running tasks that are designed around human interactions or if you need the flexibility to tune the performance of your application, then you likely need persistence.

Understanding Workflow Persistence

Workflow persistence is supported by the primary self-hosting classes (`WorkflowApplication` and `WorkflowServiceHost`) included with WF. Persistence is not supported by `WorkflowInvoker` since this class wasn't designed to handle long-running workflows. You can also use persistence when you use one of the Microsoft-provided hosting environments such as IIS to host workflow services.

Instance Stores

You enable persistence by creating and configuring an *instance store* and providing this store to the workflow host. The instance store implements the logic needed to save a workflow instance and reload it based on requests from the workflow host. The host uses a standard persistence API to communicate with the instance store, but it's not aware of exactly how the workflow instances are persisted.

This pluggable architecture provides a great deal of flexibility. It allows you to change the way workflow instances are stored by simply providing a different instance store. They might be securely stored in a SQL Server database or as XML files stored in the file system.

All instance stores must derive from the base `InstanceStore` class (in the `System.Runtime.DurableInstancing` namespace). WF includes a ready-to-use instance store (`System.Activities.DurableInstancing.SqlWorkflowInstanceStore`) that persists workflow instances to a SQL Server database. The only prerequisite for its use is to first create a SQL Server database with the required schema.

Most of the time, you will want to use the `SqlWorkflowInstanceStore` since it is fully integrated with other WF components and is designed as a general-purpose persistence mechanism. However, you can also develop a custom instance store if you have specialized needs that are not addressed by `SqlWorkflowInstanceStore`. For example, your application might require the use of a different SQL database engine (for example Oracle or MySQL), a smaller footprint (SQL Server Compact Edition), or a completely different type of data store (XML files stored in the file system).

■ **Warning** Remember that persisting workflow instances as files in the file system is inherently unsecure. Any instance data that is serialized to the files can be easily viewed with a text editor. For this reason, a secured environment like a database is recommended when you are working with any data that might be considered confidential. If you need to persist directly to files, you might want to consider encrypting the data during persistence.

Actions that Trigger Persistence

The most important feature of WF persistence is that persistence of workflow instances is generally automatic once an instance store has been added to the workflow host. You don't need to add anything to your workflow definitions to take advantage of workflow persistence. For the most part, the responsibility for persisting workflow instances at the proper time falls on the workflow host classes that are provided with WF.

When an instance store has been provided, a workflow instance is persisted (and possibly unloaded) in these situations:

- Automatically when the workflow instance is idle

- Explicitly when a `Persist` activity is executed

- Explicitly when the `WorkflowApplication.Persist` method is invoked

- Automatically at the completion of a `TransactionScope` or `TransactedReceiveScope`

The `Persist` activity allows you to declaratively request persistence at a particular point in the workflow. In most cases you can rely upon the automatic persistence behavior instead of using this activity. You only need to consider using the `Persist` activity when you need to save the workflow state at times that are outside of the normal persistence behavior. For example, you might want to declare a `Persist` activity immediately following a CPU-intensive calculation that would be expensive to execute again. The workflow instance could then be reloaded using this snapshot of the workflow state, thus avoiding a repeat of the expensive calculations.

An unloaded workflow instance remains in a persisted and unloaded state until it is reloaded by one of these actions:

- Automatically when a correlated service operation is invoked on an unloaded workflow service instance.

- Explicitly when the `WorkflowApplication.Load` method is invoked.

- Automatically when a `Delay` activity expires. Note: Please see the "Understanding Durable Delay" section for more information on the limitations of this functionality.

■ **Note** WF does provide options to control some aspects of persistence. For example, the `WorkflowApplication` host allows you to determine whether an idle workflow instance is persisted and unloaded from memory or is simply persisted. The available options vary by the type of workflow host and are covered later in the chapter when each type of workflow host is discussed.

Understanding Durable Delay

Workflow instances that contain a `Delay` activity are capable of being automatically reloaded when the elapsed time of the `Delay` activity expires. However, this capability is dependent on exactly how the workflow instance is hosted. These conditions must be met in order to utilize this feature:

- You must use IIS as your hosting environment or self-host the workflow service using the `WorkflowServiceHost` class.

- You must load the `SqlWorkflowInstanceStoreBehavior`, which provides the instance store.

- The hosting environment (IIS or self-hosting application) must remain active while an unexpired delay is active.

What this means is that a functional durable delay is really limited to workflow services. The `WorkflowApplication` class does not support automatic reloading of workflows with an expired delay.

■ **Note** You can execute workflows that have a `Delay` activity using the `WorkflowApplication` class. However, you can't unload them from memory and expect that they will be automatically reloaded when the delay expires.

If you are using the `WorkflowApplication` class to host workflows with a `Delay` activity, your choices are as follows:

- Don't unload the workflow instances.

- Develop a custom instance store that supports the ability to reload workflow instances with an expired delay.

- Manage the reloading of instances in your host application.

- Switch to `WorkflowServiceHost` and start new workflow instances with a WCF operation.

Preventing Persistence

WF persistence also supports the concept of no-persist zones. These are zones of execution in which the persistence of a workflow instance is suspended. One such zone is automatically created by the execution of an `AsyncCodeActivity`. WF doesn't have visibility into the asynchronous work that you might perform within an `AsyncCodeActivity`. Since it can't determine whether it is safe to persist the workflow instance, it temporarily suspends persistence while an `AsyncCodeActivity` is executing. Once the workflow exits the no-persist zone, the normal persistence behavior is resumed.

You can also manually create a no-persist zone within a code activity using the `NoPersistHandle` class. For example, you could write code like this:

```
NoPersistHandle handle = new NoPersistHandle();
handle.Enter(context);
//
//do work without persistence here
//
handle.Exit(context);
```

The context that is passed to the `Enter` and `Exit` methods is typed as `NativeActivityContext`. This means that you can use the `NoPersistHandle` class only within a custom code activity that derives from `NativeActivity` or `NativeActivity<TResult>`.

Persisted Data and Extension Mechanisms

When a workflow instance is persisted, all data that is currently in scope is persisted. This includes any workflow arguments and variables that are in scope. In addition to this application data, WF also saves runtime data related to the current state of the instance, including any active bookmarks. Some amount of metadata for the instance is also saved. This is needed in order to identify the workflow definition associated with the instance.

All serializable application data that is in scope is persisted. Any data that you do not want to persist should be marked with the `NonSerialized` attribute. As an alternative, you can use the `DataContract` and `DataMember` attributes to explicitly indicate the members of a class that should be serialized. The presence of these attributes on a class triggers an opt-in serialization to take place of only those members with the `DataMember` attribute.

Custom workflow extensions can also participate in persistence. To enable this, the extension must derive from the `PersistenceParticipant` class. By overriding members of this class, the extension can inject additional data to be persisted. If you are using the `SqlWorkflowInstanceStore`, you can also invoke its `Promote` method to save selected values to a queryable table in the database. The values are associated with the workflow instance, so they can be used to look up a particular workflow instance based on one or more key values.

Understanding WorkflowApplication Persistence

The `WorkflowApplication` class is one of the host classes that support persistence (the other being the `WorkflowServiceHost` class). To enable persistence with the `WorkflowApplication` class, you need to follow these steps:

1. Create and configure an instance store.

2. Set the `WorkflowApplication.InstanceStore` property to the newly created instance store.

3. Assign code to the `PersistableIdle` delegate member to return a `PersistableIdleAction` value.

After following these steps, the workflow instance is capable of being persisted. The instance store that you assign to the `InstanceStore` property can be the standard one that supports persistence to a SQL Server database (`SqlWorkflowInstanceStore`) or a custom instance store that you develop yourself. If you use the `SqlWorkflowInstanceStore`, there are additional properties that you can set to control aspects of its behavior. Please refer to the section following this one for more information on this instance store.

Like the other eventlike members of `WorkflowApplication`, the `PersistableIdle` member is actually a delegate that is defined like this:

```
Func<WorkflowApplicationIdleEventArgs, PersistableIdleAction> PersistableIdle
```

This member is similar to the `Idle` member that is executed whenever the workflow instance becomes idle. The main difference between the two members is that `PersistableIdle` is executed only when the workflow instance is capable of being persisted. For example, if you haven't assigned an instance store to the `InstanceStore` property, the `PersistableIdle` member will never be executed. Also, if the current workflow is idle but is in a no-persist zone (perhaps it is executing an `AsyncCodeActivity`), the `PersistableIdle` member is not executed. When it is executed, the code assigned to the `PersistableIdle` member is executed immediately following any code assigned to the `Idle` member.

The `PersistableIdle` delegate member requires that you return a valid `PersistableIdleAction` value from any assigned code. The value that you return determines the persistence action that should take place. The valid values for this `enum` are as follows:

- `None`. The instance is not persisted and not unloaded from memory.

- `Unload`. The instance is persisted and then unloaded from memory.

- `Persist`. The instance is persisted but is not unloaded from memory.

There are two ways to resume execution of a persisted instance. The `ResumeBookmark` method can be invoked if the workflow instance became idle because it was waiting for resumption of a bookmark. This is the most common way to resume execution of an instance and the one that is demonstrated in the first example of this chapter. Alternatively, if the workflow instance was aborted, the `Run` method can be invoked to resume execution at the last persistence point. Resumption of a workflow is not possible if it was terminated or canceled.

However, if the workflow instance was persisted and unloaded from memory, you must first call the `Load` method to load it back into memory. This method requires that you pass the workflow instance ID (a `Guid`) that uniquely identifies the instance.

The `WorkflowApplication` class also supports the `Persist` method. This method can be invoked by the host application to manually force persistence of the instance. You typically won't need to use this method, but it is available for your use in situations where the host application needs to directly initiate persistence. Asynchronous versions of the `Load` and `Persist` methods are also supported (`BeginLoad`, `EndLoad`, `BeginPersist`, `EndPersist`).

Understanding the SqlWorkflowInstanceStore

The `SqlWorkflowInstanceStore` is an instance store that is designed to persist workflow instances to a SQL Server database. To use it, you can follow these simple steps:

1. Prepare the SQL Server database using the SQL scripts provided with .NET Framework 4.

2. In your host application, create an instance of the instance store, passing the constructor a connection string to the database that you prepared.

3. Optionally set other properties of the instance store.

4. Optionally execute the `CreateWorkflowOwnerCommand` command to register the host application with the instance store. This step is required only when you are using this instance store with `WorkflowApplication`. The `DeleteWorkflowOwnerCommand` should be issued when the application is no longer using the instance store.

The database preparation step is an initial task that is performed only once. Please refer to the "SQL Server Instance Store Preparation" sidebar in this chapter for the steps needed to prepare the database.

Here are the optional properties of the `SqlWorkflowInstanceStore` that you can set to control aspects of its behavior:

Property	Type	Description
HostLockRenewalPeriod	TimeSpan	The maximum amount of time in which the instance store must extend a lock on a workflow instance.
InstanceEncodingOption	InstanceEncodingOption	A value that determines whether the instance store compresses instance data. Values are None or GZip.
InstanceCompletionAction	InstanceCompletionAction	Determines the action to take when a workflow instance is completed. Possible values are DeleteNothing and DeleteAll. A value of DeleteAll instructs the instance store to delete all data for a workflow instance when it completes. A value of DeleteNothing causes the persisted workflow instance data to remain persisted after the instance has completed.

Continued

Property	Type	Description
InstanceLockedExceptionAction	InstanceLockedExceptionAction	Determines the action to take when the instance store attempts to lock an instance that is already locked by another host. Possible values are None, BasicRetry, and AggressiveRetry. A value of None indicates that the instance store does not retry the lock. A value of BasicRetry causes the instance store to retry the lock with a simple linear retry delay. A value of AggressiveRetry initially uses a shorter retry delay and then increases the delay for subsequent retry attempts.
RunnableInstancesDetectionPeriod	TimeSpan	The interval in which the instance store runs a task to detect any runnable workflow instances.

If you are sharing a single `SqlWorkflowInstanceStore` with multiple `WorkflowApplication` instances in a single host application, you need to execute the `CreateWorkflowOwnerCommand` against the instance store. Doing so registers the host application as an instance store owner and enables saving and loading of workflow instances. The code to accomplish this isn't exactly intuitive, but it is demonstrated in the first example of this chapter. In addition, you also need to execute the `DeleteWorkflowOwnerCommand` against the instance store once the host application no longer requires it.

The requirement to manually execute `CreateWorkflowOwnerCommand` and `DeleteWorkflowOwnerCommand` applies only to the `WorkflowApplication` class. The `WorkflowServiceHost` class takes care of this bit of housekeeping for you.

If you are self-hosting workflow services using the `WorkflowServiceHost` class, you should use the `SqlWorkflowInstanceStoreBehavior` class to enable persistence instead of the `SqlWorkflowInstanceStore` class. The `SqlWorkflowInstanceStoreBehavior` class is added to the `WorkflowServiceHost` as a standard WCF behavior. It supports the same set of properties that were described in the previous table.

The `SqlWorkflowInstanceStore` supports locking of workflow instances. This allows you to deploy a server farm of workflow hosts that all work with the same persistence database. As a host loads a previously persisted instance, it checks for an existing lock on the instance. If it isn't already locked by another host, it obtains the lock, thus preventing another host from working with the instance.

This instance store also supports durable delays. A delay is considered durable if an unloaded workflow instance is automatically reloaded when the delay expires. The workflow instance does not have to remain resident in memory for the delay to work properly. When a workflow containing a `Delay` activity is persisted and unloaded, the instance store monitors the scheduled time for the delay to expire.

When the delay does expire, the instance store signals to the workflow host that the instance should be reloaded. This allows processing to continue after the Delay activity.

While the `SqlWorkflowInstanceStoreBehavior` supports this type of delay, there are limitations to its design. This functionality is supported only for workflow services that are hosted by IIS or self-hosted using the `WorkflowServiceHost` class. Workflows that are hosted by the `WorkflowApplication` class are not automatically reloaded when their delay expires.

SQL Server Instance Store Preparation

The `SqlWorkflowInstanceStore` requires a SQL Server database with a known schema and set of stored procedures. Microsoft provides the SQL scripts that are needed to prepare the database. You simply need to create the database and execute the scripts. You can follow these steps:

1. If you haven't done so already, install a copy of SQL Server 2008 Express on your development machine. SQL Server 2008 Express should have been installed during the installation of Visual Studio, but if you prefer, you can also use the full version of SQL Server if you have a licensed copy of that available. SQL Server Management Studio Express is packaged with SQL Server Express but may not be installed by default. This is the application that you will use to create the database and execute the SQL scripts. As an alternative, you can use the `sqlcmd` command-line utility to execute the steps that follow. Please refer to the `sqlcmd` documentation for an explanation of the command-line arguments that you'll need to use.

2. After starting SQL Server Management Studio Express, create a new database named `InstanceStore`. You can use the default settings for the new database.

3. Navigate to the folder containing the SQL scripts. The scripts should be located under this folder: `%SystemRoot%\Microsoft.Net\Framework\v4.0.30319\ SQL\en`. The `%SystemRoot%` folder should correspond to your Windows directory. The last node of the path (en) signifies the installed language and may be different on your machine.

4. Execute the `SqlWorkflowInstanceStoreSchema.sql` script against the new `InstanceStore` database to create the database schema.

5. Execute the `SqlWorkflowInstanceStoreLogic.sql` script against the same database to create the stored procedures that are used by `SqlWorkflowInstanceStore`.

After completing these steps, the `InstanceStore` database should be ready for use.

Using the SqlWorkflowInstanceStore with WorkflowApplication

This first example demonstrates how to use the `SqlWorkflowInstanceStore` when you are using the `WorkflowApplication` class as the workflow host. The scenario for this example (as well as the other examples in this chapter and Chapter 12) is an e-commerce shopping cart workflow. Each workflow instance represents an order. Consumers add one or more items to the order and then retrieve all the items once the order is complete. As each item is added to the order, the price and current inventory of the item is retrieved.

This example aptly illustrates the need for workflow persistence. The consumer controls the number of new items added as well as the frequency between new items. While the workflow is waiting for the consumer to make their next selection, the workflow is effectively idle and can be persisted to an instance store and unloaded from memory. When the next item is added, the workflow instance is reloaded and the appropriate bookmark resumed.

■ **Note** Most of the tasks that you will complete for this example are related to the implementation of the example workflow itself. A relatively small amount of the work is actually directly related to workflow persistence.

You will complete these tasks to implement this example:

1. Implement simple C# classes that are related to sales items.

2. Implement a custom extension.

3. Implement custom activities that reference the extension.

4. Implement bookmark-related custom activities.

5. Declare the `OrderEntry` workflow.

6. Implement the code to host the workflow including the creation of the instance store.

Creating the ActivityLibrary Project

Create a new project using the Activity Library template. Name the new project `ActivityLibrary`, and delete the `Activity1.xaml` file since it won't be used. Add the project to a new solution that is named for this chapter. Add these additional .NET assembly references to the project:

- `System.Runtime.DurableInstancing`
- `System.Runtime.Serialization`

■ **Note** Some of the references that you will add to projects in this chapter are not immediately required. I generally provide you with a list of all the references up front to simplify the instructions. In this project, the reference to System.Runtime.DurableInstancing is not actually required for this first example but will be needed for subsequent examples.

Implementing the Item-Related Classes

You need to define two classes that are related to sellable items. The Item class represents a sellable item that a consumer adds to the shopping cart. The ItemDefinition class is used to define a price and available inventory for each sellable item.

Add a new C# class to the ActivityLibrary project, and name it Item. Here is the implementation for the Item class:

```
using System;

namespace ActivityLibrary
{
    public class Item
    {
        public Int32 ItemId { get; set; }
        public Int32 Quantity { get; set; }
        public Decimal UnitPrice { get; set; }
        public Decimal TotalPrice { get; set; }
    }
}
```

Add another C# class named ItemDefinition to the same project. Here is the implementation for this class:

```
using System;

namespace ActivityLibrary
{
    public class ItemDefinition
    {
        public Int32 ItemId { get; set; }
        public Int32 QtyAvailable { get; set; }
        public Decimal Price { get; set; }
    }
}
```

Implementing the Custom Extension

This example uses a custom workflow extension to provide price lookup and inventory management functionality. To implement this extension, first add a new C# interface to the **ActivityLibrary** project, and name it **IItemSupport**. Here is the definition of this interface:

```csharp
using System;
using System.Collections.Generic;

namespace ActivityLibrary
{
    public interface IItemSupport
    {
        Decimal GetItemPrice(Int32 itemId);
        Boolean UpdatePendingInventory(
            Int32 orderId, Int32 itemId, Int32 quantity);
        List<ItemDefinition> GetItemDefinitions();
    }
}
```

Now add a new C# class to the **ActivityLibrary** project, and name it **ItemSupportExtension**. This class implements the **IItemSupport** interface and provides the necessary item-related functionality that will be used by the workflow.

■ **Note** The use of a custom extension is not absolutely necessary to complete this particular example. The example could have easily been implemented in another way without the use of an extension. But using an extension provides an opportunity to later illustrate how an extension can participate in workflow persistence. This is demonstrated in Chapter 12 when this extension is enhanced.

Here is the implementation of this class:

```csharp
using System;
using System.Collections.Generic;
using System.Linq;

namespace ActivityLibrary
{
    public class ItemSupportExtension : IItemSupport
    {
        private Dictionary<Int32, ItemDefinition> _items =
            new Dictionary<Int32, ItemDefinition>();
        private Int32 _orderId;

        #region IItemSupport Members
```

```
public Decimal GetItemPrice(int itemId)
{
    Decimal price = 0;
    ItemDefinition def = null;
    if (_items.TryGetValue(itemId, out def))
    {
        price = def.Price;
    }
    return price;
}

public bool UpdatePendingInventory(
    Int32 orderId, int itemId, int quantity)
{
    Boolean result = false;
    ItemDefinition def = null;
    lock (_items)
    {
        if (_items.TryGetValue(itemId, out def))
        {
            if (quantity <= def.QtyAvailable)
            {
                Int32 origQuantity = def.QtyAvailable;
                def.QtyAvailable -= quantity;
                Console.WriteLine(
                    "Update: ItemId={0}, QtyBefore={1}, QtyAfter={2}",
                    def.ItemId, origQuantity, def.QtyAvailable);
                _orderId = orderId;
                result = true;
            }
        }
    }
    return result;
}

public List<ItemDefinition> GetItemDefinitions()
{
    return _items.Values.ToList();
}

#endregion

#region Host Members

public void AddItemDefinition(Int32 itemId, Decimal price,
    Int32 qtyAvailable)
{
```

```
            if (!_items.ContainsKey(itemId))
            {
                ItemDefinition def = new ItemDefinition
                {
                    ItemId = itemId,
                    Price = price,
                    QtyAvailable = qtyAvailable
                };
                _items.Add(def.ItemId, def);
            }
        }
    }

    #endregion
    }
}
```

Implementing Activities that use the Extension

You also need to implement two custom activities that invoke methods of the workflow extension. The first custom activity invokes the GetItemPrice method of the extension to retrieve the configured price for an item. To implement this activity, add a new Code Activity to the ActivityLibrary project, and name it GetItemPrice. Here is the complete implementation for this activity:

```
using System;
using System.Activities;

namespace ActivityLibrary
{
    public sealed class GetItemPrice : CodeActivity<Decimal>
    {
        [RequiredArgument]
        public InArgument<Int32> ItemId { get; set; }

        protected override Decimal Execute(CodeActivityContext context)
        {
            Decimal price = 0;
            IItemSupport extension = context.GetExtension<IItemSupport>();
            if (extension != null)
            {
                price = extension.GetItemPrice(ItemId.Get(context));
            }
            return price;
        }
    }
}
```

You also need another custom activity that invokes the `UpdatePendingInventory` method of the extension. This method determines whether there is sufficient inventory available to satisfy the request. If there is, the current inventory is decremented by the requested quantity for the item. Add another Code Activity to the `ActivityLibrary` project, and name it `CheckInventory`. Here is the implementation of this activity:

```
using System;
using System.Activities;

namespace ActivityLibrary
{
    public sealed class CheckInventory : CodeActivity<Boolean>
    {
        public InArgument<Int32> OrderId { get; set; }
        [RequiredArgument]
        public InArgument<Int32> ItemId { get; set; }
        [RequiredArgument]
        public InArgument<Int32> Quantity { get; set; }

        protected override Boolean Execute(CodeActivityContext context)
        {
            Boolean result = false;
            IItemSupport extension = context.GetExtension<IItemSupport>();
            if (extension != null)
            {
                result = extension.UpdatePendingInventory(OrderId.Get(context),
                    ItemId.Get(context), Quantity.Get(context));
            }
            return result;
        }
    }
}
```

Implementing Bookmark-Related Activities

This first example uses bookmarks to communicate between the host application and the workflow instance. To facilitate this, you need two custom activities that create bookmarks and handle the input of data as each bookmark is resumed. Add a new Code Activity to the `ActivityLibrary` project, and name it `WaitForAddItem`. This is the activity that supports the addition of new items to the shopping cart. Here is the implementation for this activity:

```
using System.Activities;

namespace ActivityLibrary
{
    public sealed class WaitForAddItem : NativeActivity<Item>
    {
        protected override void Execute(NativeActivityContext context)
        {
            context.CreateBookmark("AddItem", Resumed);
        }

        private void Resumed(NativeActivityContext context,
            Bookmark bookmark, object value)
        {
            if (value is Item)
            {
                Result.Set(context, value as Item);
            }
        }

        protected override bool CanInduceIdle
        {
            get { return true; }
        }
    }
}
```

You also need an activity that allows the user to signal that all items have been entered and that the order is now complete. Add another Code Activity to the **ActivityLibrary** project, and name it **WaitForOrderComplete**. Here is the implementation of this activity:

```
using System.Activities;

namespace ActivityLibrary
{
    public sealed class WaitForOrderComplete : NativeActivity
    {
        protected override void Execute(NativeActivityContext context)
        {
            context.CreateBookmark("OrderComplete");
        }

        protected override bool CanInduceIdle
        {
            get { return true; }
        }
    }
}
```

You should build the solution at this point. This ensures that it builds correctly and adds the custom activities to the Visual Studio Toolbox.

Declaring the OrderEntry Workflow

Create a new Workflow Console project, and name it `OrderEntry`. Add this project to the solution that you created for this chapter and delete the `Workflow1.xaml` file since it won't be used. Add these references to the project:

- `ActivityLibrary` (project reference)

- `System.Activities.DurableInstancing`

- `System.Configuration`

- `System.Runtime.DurableInstancing`

- `System.Runtime.Serialization`

Add a new Activity to the project, and name it `OrderEntry`. Add this output argument to the workflow:

Name	Direction	Argument Type
Items	Out	List<ActivityLibrary.Item>

Here is a recap of the workflow variables that are used by the workflow. Please follow the step-by-step instructions to determine when each variable can be added:

Name	Variable Type	Scope
IsDone	Boolean	While
Item	ActivityLibrary.Item	AddItem
IsInventoryOK	Boolean	AddItem

Follow these steps to complete the workflow definition:

1. Add a `Sequence` activity as the root activity of the workflow.

2. Add an `Assign` activity to the `Sequence` activity. Set the `Assign.To` property to `Items` and the `Assign.Value` property to `New List(Of ActivityLibrary.Item)`. This initializes the output argument.

3. Add a While activity below the Assign activity. Add the IsDone variable that is scoped by the While activity.

4. Set the While.Condition property to Not IsDone. This causes the activities within the While activity to repeat until the IsDone variable is set to true.

5. Add a Pick activity as the body of the While activity. The Pick activity should already have two PickBranch instances. The PickBranch on the left side will handle the requests to add an item to the order, and the PickBranch on the right side handles completion of the order.

6. Change the DisplayName of the PickBranch on the left to AddItem. Add the variables that are scoped by the AddItem activity (Item and IsInventoryOK).

7. Add a WaitForAddItem activity as the trigger of the AddItem PickBranch. Set the Result property of this activity to Item.

8. Add a Sequence activity to the Action portion of the PickBranch. Add a CheckInventory activity to this new Sequence activity. Set the ItemId property to Item.ItemId, the Quantity property to Item.Quantity, and the Result property to IsInventoryOK.

9. Add an If activity directly under the CheckInventory activity. Set the If.Condition property to IsInventoryOK.

10. Add a Sequence activity to the If.Then property. Add a GetItemPrice activity to the new Sequence activity. Set the ItemId property to Item.ItemId and the Result property to Item.UnitPrice.

11. Add an Assign activity under the GetItemPrice activity. Set the Assign.To property to Item.TotalPrice and the Assign.Value property to Item.UnitPrice * Item.Quantity.

12. Add an AddToCollection activity under the Assign activity. Set the generic type to ActivityLibrary.Item. Set the Collection property to Items and the Item property to Item.

13. Add a WriteLine activity to the If.Else property. Set the Text property to String.Format("Quantity of {0} for Item {1} is unavailable", Item.Quantity, Item.ItemId). Figure 11-1 shows the completed AddItem PickBranch.

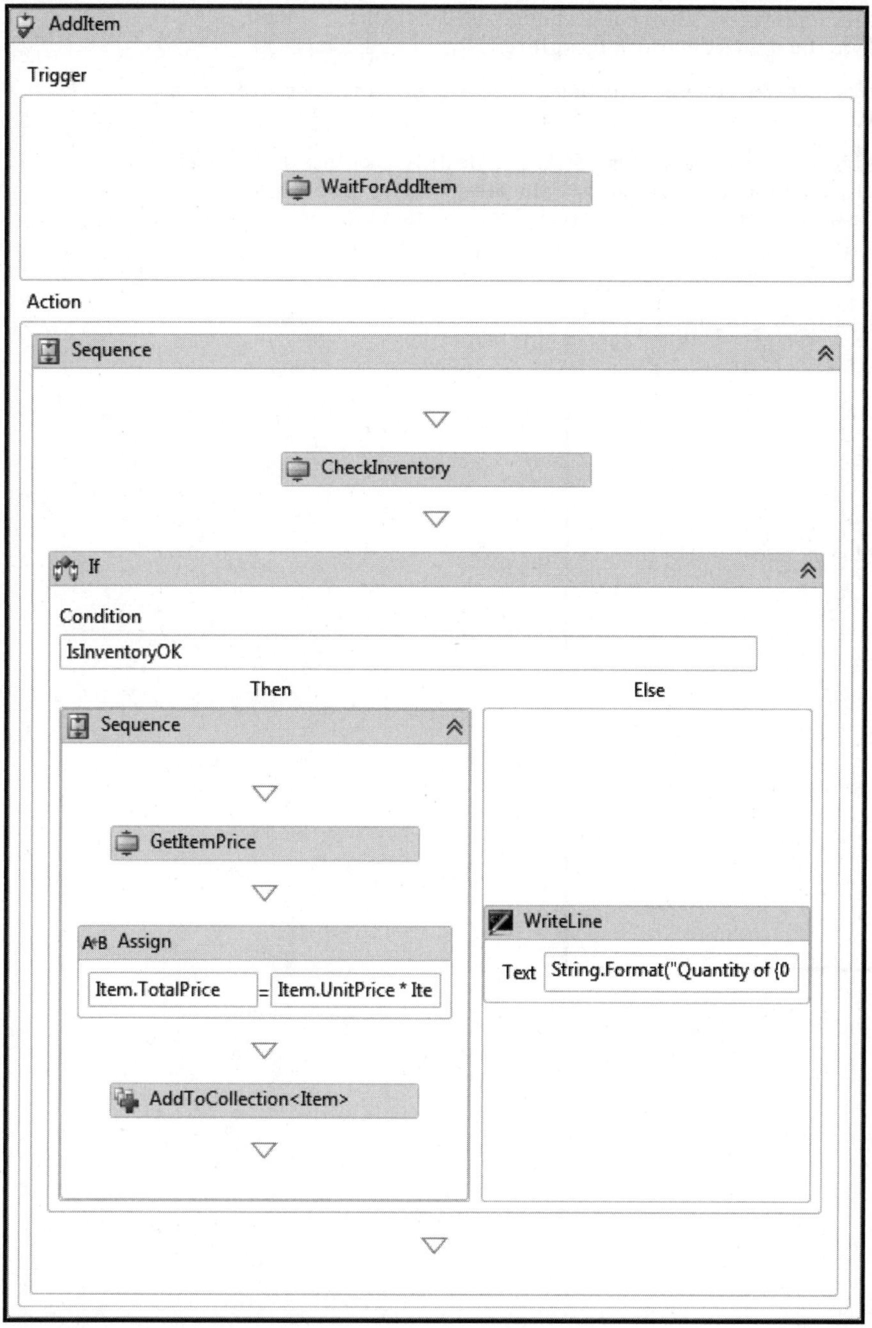

Figure 11-1. AddItem PickBranch

14. Navigate back to the Pick activity, and change the DisplayName of the PickBranch on the right side to OrderComplete.

15. Add a WaitForOrderComplete activity to the trigger of the OrderComplete PickBranch.

16. Add an Assign activity to the Action portion of the OrderComplete PickBranch. Set the Assign.To property to IsDone and the Assign.Value property to True. Figure 11-2 shows the completed OrderComplete PickBranch.

Figure 11-3 shows the completed top level of the workflow.

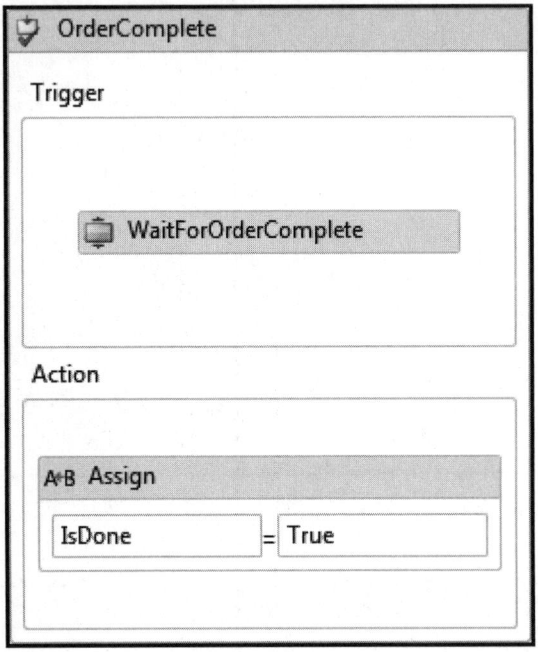

Figure 11-2. OrderComplete PickBranch

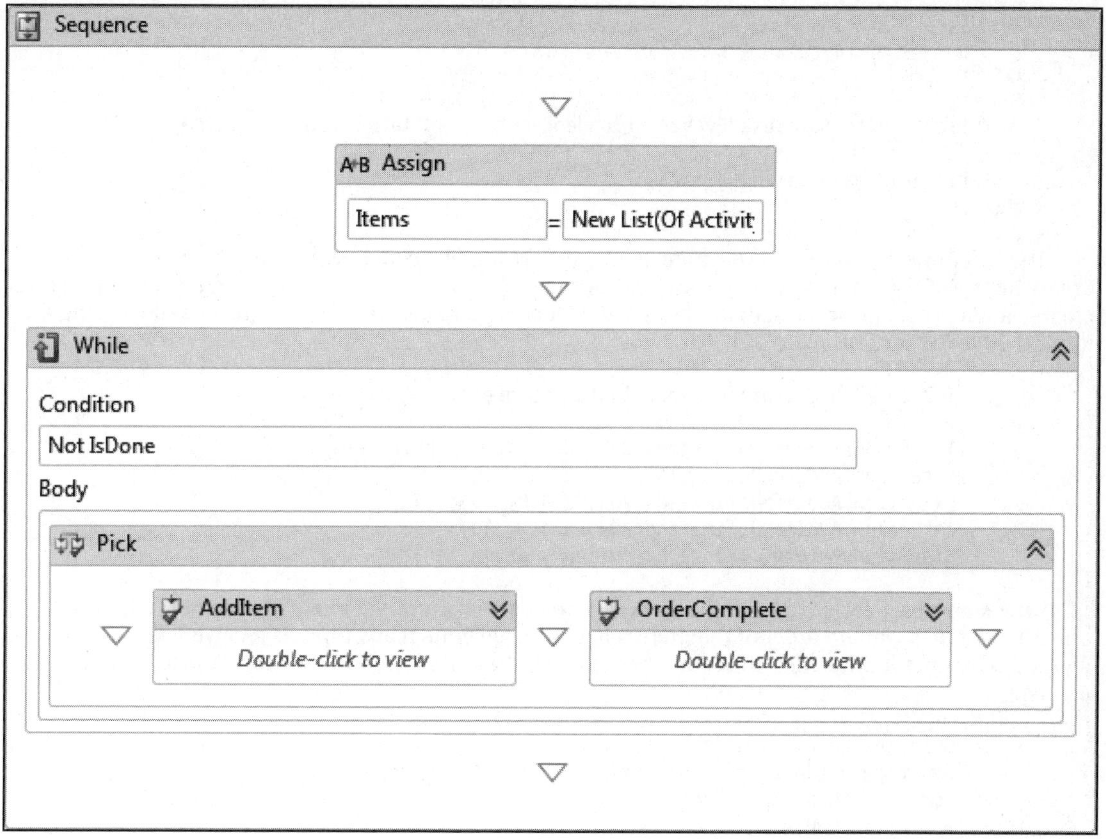

Figure 11-3. Completed OrderEntry workflow

Hosting and Persisting the Workflow

This example uses the `WorkflowApplication` class to host the workflow. The following host code should be added to the `Program.cs` file of the `OrderEntry` project:

```
using System;
using System.Activities;
using System.Activities.DurableInstancing;
using System.Collections.Generic;
using System.Configuration;
using System.Runtime.DurableInstancing;
using System.Threading;
using ActivityLibrary;
```

```
namespace OrderEntry
{
    class Program
    {
        static private AutoResetEvent _unloadedEvent = new AutoResetEvent(false);

        static void Main(string[] args)
        {
```

The first order of business is to create an instance store. The code executes the private CreateInstanceStore method (shown later in the code) to accomplish this. The custom extension is then created and populated with test data. The test data loaded here allows testing of the workflow using the item IDs shown here (101, 202, and 303).

```
            InstanceStore store = CreateInstanceStore();

            ItemSupportExtension extension = new ItemSupportExtension();
            extension.AddItemDefinition(101, 1.23M, 10);
            extension.AddItemDefinition(202, 2.34M, 20);
            extension.AddItemDefinition(303, 3.45M, 30);
            DisplayInventory("Before Execution", extension);
```

After starting a new instance of the workflow, the user is prompted to enter an item ID and the quantity that they want to order of that item (all on a single line). If any input is received, the AddItem method is executed. Otherwise, the order is assumed to be complete, and the OrderComplete method is invoked.

```
            Guid instanceId = Guid.Empty;
            StartNewInstance(ref instanceId, store, extension);
            Boolean isRunning = true;
            while (isRunning)
            {
                Console.WriteLine(
                    "Enter ItemId and Quantity (Ex: 101 1) or [Enter] to quit");
                String input = Console.ReadLine();
                if (!String.IsNullOrEmpty(input))
                {
                    AddItem(instanceId, store, extension, input);
                }
                else
                {
                    OrderComplete(instanceId, store, extension);
                    isRunning = false;
                }
            }

            DisplayInventory("After Execution", extension);

            Console.WriteLine("Press any key to exit");
            Console.ReadKey();
```

Before exiting the application, the `DeleteWorkflowOwnerCommand` is executed against the instance store. This notifies the instance store that this application is no longer an owner of workflow instances and that any locks that might have been placed by this owner can be removed.

```
store.Execute(store.CreateInstanceHandle(),
    new DeleteWorkflowOwnerCommand(), TimeSpan.FromSeconds(10));
}
```

The `StartNewInstance` method is used to create a new instance of the workflow. It is passed a reference to the instance store and the extension. The `SetupInstance` method is invoked to create the `WorkflowApplication` and set any properties, including the `InstanceStore`. After creating a new `WorkflowApplication`, the `Run` method is invoked. At this point, the workflow should immediately become idle since it is waiting for one of the bookmarks to be resumed.

```
private static void StartNewInstance(
    ref Guid instanceId, InstanceStore store, IItemSupport extension)
{
    WorkflowApplication wfApp = SetupInstance(
        ref instanceId, store, extension);
    wfApp.Run();
    _unloadedEvent.WaitOne(5000);
}
```

The `AddItem` method parses the input from the user and determines whether the correct number and type of arguments were entered (an item ID and quantity). If so, a `WorkflowApplication` instance is created and the `AddItem` bookmark is resumed, passing an instance of the `Item` class that represents the item and quantity that were just ordered.

```
private static void AddItem(Guid instanceId, InstanceStore store,
    IItemSupport extension, String input)
{
    Int32 itemId = 0;
    Int32 quantity = 0;
    String[] parts = input.Split(' ');
    if (parts.Length != 2)
    {
        Console.WriteLine("Incorrect number of arguments entered!");
        return;
    }
    Int32.TryParse(parts[0], out itemId);
    Int32.TryParse(parts[1], out quantity);
    if (itemId == 0 || quantity == 0)
    {
        Console.WriteLine("Arguments in incorrect format!");
        return;
    }
```

```
        WorkflowApplication wfApp = SetupInstance(
            ref instanceId, store, extension);
        Item item = new Item
        {
            ItemId = itemId,
            Quantity = quantity
        };

        wfApp.ResumeBookmark("AddItem", item);
        _unloadedEvent.WaitOne(5000);
    }
```

The `OrderComplete` method is executed when the user presses Enter without any input. This signals completion of the current order. After creating a `WorkflowApplication` instance and assigning code to the `Completed` property, the `OrderComplete` bookmark is resumed. When the workflow completes, the `Items` output argument is used to display the line items that were added to the order.

```
    private static void OrderComplete(
        Guid instanceId, InstanceStore store, IItemSupport extension)
    {
        WorkflowApplication wfApp = SetupInstance(
            ref instanceId, store, extension);
        wfApp.Completed = (e) =>
        {
            Console.WriteLine("{0} Is Completed", e.InstanceId);
            List<Item> items = e.Outputs["Items"] as List<Item>;
            Console.WriteLine("\nOrdered Items:");
            foreach (Item i in items)
            {
                Console.WriteLine(
                    "ItemId={0}, Quantity={1}, UnitPrice={2}, Total={3}",
                    i.ItemId, i.Quantity, i.UnitPrice, i.TotalPrice);
            }
        };

        wfApp.ResumeBookmark("OrderComplete", null);
        _unloadedEvent.WaitOne(5000);
    }
```

The `SetupInstance` method is responsible for the creation of a `WorkflowApplication` instance. In addition to assigning code to the standard set of delegates, it also sets the `InstanceStore` and adds the custom workflow extension. If the method is passed a nonempty `instanceId`, the `Load` method is invoked to load the designated workflow instance from the instance store.

The code assigned to the `PersistableIdle` member returns a value of `PersistableIdleAction.Unload`. This instructs the `WorkflowApplication` to persist the idle workflow instance and then unload it from memory.

```
private static WorkflowApplication SetupInstance(
    ref Guid instanceId, InstanceStore store, IItemSupport extension)
{
    WorkflowApplication wfApp =
        new WorkflowApplication(new OrderEntry());

    wfApp.Idle = (e) =>
    {
        Console.WriteLine("{0} Is Idle", e.InstanceId);
    };
    wfApp.PersistableIdle = (e) =>
    {
        Console.WriteLine("{0} Is PersistableIdle", e.InstanceId);
        return PersistableIdleAction.Unload;
    };
    wfApp.Unloaded = (e) =>
    {
        Console.WriteLine("{0} Is Unloaded", e.InstanceId);
        _unloadedEvent.Set();
    };
    wfApp.OnUnhandledException = (e) =>
    {
        Console.WriteLine("{0} OnUnhandledException: {1}",
            e.InstanceId, e.UnhandledException.Message);
        return UnhandledExceptionAction.Cancel;
    };

    wfApp.InstanceStore = store;
    wfApp.Extensions.Add(extension);

    if (instanceId == Guid.Empty)
    {
        instanceId = wfApp.Id;
    }
    else
    {
        wfApp.Load(instanceId);
    }
    return wfApp;
}
```

The `CreateInstanceStore` method creates an instance of the `SqlWorkflowInstanceStore`. It retrieves the SQL Server connection string from the `App.config` file for this project. This method also executes the `CreateWorkflowOwnerCommand` against the instance store. The `InstanceView` that is returned is used to set the `DefaultInstanceOwner` property of the instance store. Doing this registers the application as an instance owner and allows multiple `WorkflowApplication` instances to use the same instance store.

```
    private static InstanceStore CreateInstanceStore()
    {
        string connectionString = ConfigurationManager.ConnectionStrings
            ["InstanceStore"].ConnectionString;
        InstanceStore store =
            new SqlWorkflowInstanceStore(connectionString);
        InstanceView view = store.Execute(
            store.CreateInstanceHandle(),
            new CreateWorkflowOwnerCommand(),
            TimeSpan.FromSeconds(30));
        store.DefaultInstanceOwner = view.InstanceOwner;
        return store;
    }

    private static void DisplayInventory(String desc, IItemSupport extension)
    {
        Console.WriteLine("\nItem inventory {0}:", desc);
        foreach (ItemDefinition item in extension.GetItemDefinitions())
        {
            Console.WriteLine("ItemId={0}, QtyAvailable={1}",
                item.ItemId, item.QtyAvailable);
        }
        Console.WriteLine("");
    }
  }
}
```

Configuring the Application

The code in **Program.cs** retrieves the SQL Server connection string from the **App.config** file. If the project doesn't already have an **App.config** file, add one now. Here are the contents of the file:

```
<?xml version="1.0" encoding="utf-8" ?>
<configuration>
  <connectionStrings>
    <add name="InstanceStore"
        connectionString="Data Source=localhost\SQLExpress;
            Initial Catalog=InstanceStore;Integrated Security=True;
            Asynchronous Processing=True"
        providerName="System.Data.SqlClient" />
  </connectionStrings>
</configuration>
```

If you have not already done so, you should now prepare the SQL Server database. You can follow the steps outlined in the "SQL Server Instance Store Preparation" sidebar.

The connection string shown here assumes that the persistence database is named **InstanceStore** and is located on your local development machine. You will need to make the necessary adjustments to this connection string if this is not the case.

Testing the Application

After building the solution, you should be able to run the OrderEntry project. When you are prompted for an item and quantity, enter the item ID and quantity on a single line, separated by a space. Valid item IDs are 101, 202, and 303. Here are representative results when I test this project:

```
Item inventory Before Execution:

ItemId=101, QtyAvailable=10

ItemId=202, QtyAvailable=20

ItemId=303, QtyAvailable=30


5576faf5-91da-4710-ae34-397ab3844ce8 Is Idle

5576faf5-91da-4710-ae34-397ab3844ce8 Is PersistableIdle

5576faf5-91da-4710-ae34-397ab3844ce8 Is Unloaded

Enter ItemId and Quantity (Ex: 101 1) or [Enter] to quit

101 1

Update: ItemId=101, QtyBefore=10, QtyAfter=9

5576faf5-91da-4710-ae34-397ab3844ce8 Is Idle

5576faf5-91da-4710-ae34-397ab3844ce8 Is PersistableIdle

5576faf5-91da-4710-ae34-397ab3844ce8 Is Unloaded

Enter ItemId and Quantity (Ex: 101 1) or [Enter] to quit

202 2

Update: ItemId=202, QtyBefore=20, QtyAfter=18

5576faf5-91da-4710-ae34-397ab3844ce8 Is Idle
```

```
5576faf5-91da-4710-ae34-397ab3844ce8 Is PersistableIdle

5576faf5-91da-4710-ae34-397ab3844ce8 Is Unloaded

Enter ItemId and Quantity (Ex: 101 1) or [Enter] to quit


5576faf5-91da-4710-ae34-397ab3844ce8 Is Completed


Ordered Items:

ItemId=101, Quantity=1, UnitPrice=1.23, Total=1.23

ItemId=202, Quantity=2, UnitPrice=2.34, Total=4.68

5576faf5-91da-4710-ae34-397ab3844ce8 Is Unloaded


Item inventory After Execution:

ItemId=101, QtyAvailable=9

ItemId=202, QtyAvailable=18

ItemId=303, QtyAvailable=30


Press any key to exit
```

Please make note of the messages that are written by the WorkflowApplication delegates. They indicate that as soon as the workflow starts, the Idle delegate is executed followed by the PersistableIdle. Since the code assigned to the PersistableIdle member returns a value of PersistableIdleAction.Unload, the workflow is persisted to the instance store and unloaded. This same behavior occurs after each item is added to the order. Finally, when I press Enter without entering an item and quantity, the workflow is completed, and the collection of Item objects that were added is retrieved as an output argument.

Note that the available inventory for each item is displayed at the beginning and end of the application and that the ending inventory has been reduced by the requested quantity for each item.

■ **Note** This particular workflow does not attempt to handle orphaned workflow instances. This situation would occur when a new workflow instance is created but never completed. An example in Chapter 12 demonstrates how you can monitor for the existence of persisted instances. You can then use the `WorkflowControlEndpoint` to cancel or terminate orphaned instances. Another way to handle orphaned workflow instances would be to add a `Delay` activity to an additional `PickBranch` in the workflow. The `Delay` activity could then be used to trigger completion of the workflow after some defined period of inactivity. However, both of these solutions really require the use of `WorklfowServiceHost` as the workflow host.

Understanding WorkflowServiceHost Persistence

You enable persistence with the `WorkflowServiceHost` in a similar way as you do with the `WorkflowApplication` class. Here are the steps that you follow when working with the `WorkflowServiceHost` class:

1. Create and configure an instance store behavior.

2. Add the newly created instance store behavior to the `Description.Behaviors` property of the `WorkflowServiceHost`.

3. Optionally, add a `WorkflowIdleBehavior` to control persistence behavior.

The `WorkflowServiceHost` class supports direct assignment of an instance store but also supports instance store creation using a WCF behavior. Generally, when you are working with the `WorkflowServiceHost` and using the SQL Service instance store that is supplied with WF, you will configure and add a behavior rather than directly assigning the instance store.

The `SqlWorkflowInstanceStoreBehavior` supports the same set of properties that I described for the `SqlWorkflowInstanceStore` class. A constructor is also available that allows you to pass the SQL Server connection string. After constructing and configuring the behavior, you add it to the `Description.Behaviors` property of the `WorkflowServiceHost`. This must be done prior to calling the `Open` method of the `WorkflowServiceHost`.

You can also add an instance of the `SqlWorkflowInstanceStore` class to a `WorkflowServiceHost` via the `DurableInstancingOptions` property. This member supports an `InstanceStore` property that can be set to a newly constructed instance store.

The `WorkflowServiceHost` does not support the `PersistableIdle` property as the `WorkflowApplication` class does. Therefore, you don't have a direct way to specify whether an individual idle workflow instance should be persisted, unloaded, or otherwise left alone. Instead, WF does provide the `WorkflowIdleBehavior`. This WCF behavior supports these two properties:

Property	Type	Description
TimeToUnload	TimeSpan	A time span that determines when idle workflow instances are persisted and unloaded. Set this to TimeSpan.MaxValue to disable unloading of idle instances. Set to zero to immediately persist and unload idle instances. The default is one minute.
TimeToPersist	TimeSpan	If set, this value must be less than the TimeToUnload property. This value determines when idle workflow instances are persisted (but not unloaded). Setting this property allows you to persist instances more quickly without immediately unloading them from memory. After they are persisted, they are unloaded from memory according to the value of the TimeToUnload property.

After constructing and configuring a `WorkflowIdleBehavior`, you add it to the `WorkflowServiceHost` using the `Description.Behaviors` property.

You can also configure these behaviors using entries in the `Web.config` file. This is the mechanism used to configure workflow persistence when you are using IIS or another Microsoft-provided hosting environment to host your workflow services.

When you use the `SqlWorkflowInstanceStore` with the `WorkflowServiceHost`, there is no need to manually execute `CreateWorkflowOwnerCommand` and `DeleteWorkflowOwnerCommand` against the instance store. Unlike the `WorkflowApplication` class where you must execute these commands yourself, the `WorkflowServiceHost` takes care of those housekeeping tasks for you.

Using the SqlWorkflowInstanceStore with WorkflowServiceHost

In this example, you will implement the same shopping cart scenario using a workflow service. The workflow will reuse most of the custom classes, activities, and the extension that you developed for the previous example. The workflow will implement three service operations: `StartOrder`, `AddItem`, and `OrderComplete`. The `StartOrder` operation is capable of starting a new workflow instance. The other operations are designed to work with an existing instance. To accomplish this, content correlation is used. The assumption is that while the workflow is waiting for the next service operation to be invoked, it is safely persisted in the SQL Server instance store.

The initial goal of this workflow is to demonstrate how to use persistence with the `WorkflowServiceHost`. But this same example workflow will also be used throughout the remainder of this chapter and Chapter 12 to illustrate other persistence-related topics.

You will complete these tasks to implement this example:

1. Declare the `OrderEntryService` workflow service.

2. Implement and configure an application that hosts the workflow service.

3. Implement a console application that acts as a client of the workflow service.

Declaring the OrderEntryService Workflow

Create a new project using the WCF Workflow Service Application project template. Name the new problem `ServiceLibrary`, and add it to the solution for this chapter. You can delete the `Service1.xamlx` file since it won't be used. Add these references to the project:

- `ActivityLibrary` (project reference)

- `System.Runtime.DurableInstancing`

Add a new WCF Workflow Service to the project, and name it `OrderEntryService`. Delete the `Sequence` activity that is added for you along with all of its child messaging activities. Check the properties for the workflow, and verify that the `Name` and `ConfigurationName` are both set to `OrderEntryService`.

Here are the workflow variables that are used by the workflow. Please follow the step-by-step instructions to determine when each variable can be added:

Name	Variable Type	Scope	Default Value
IsDone	Boolean	While	
Items	List<ActivityLibrary.Item>	While	New List(Of ActivityLibrary.Item)
OrderId	Int32	While	
SharedHandle	CorrelationHandle	While	
Item	ActivityLibrary.Item	AddItem	
IsInventoryOK	Boolean	AddItem	

Please follow these steps to complete the workflow definition:

1. Add a `While` activity as the root activity of the workflow. Define the variables that are scoped by the `While` activity: `IsDone`, `Items`, `OrderId`, and `SharedHandle`. Note that the Items variable requires a Default Value. Set the `While.Condition` property to `Not IsDone`.

2. Add a `Pick` activity to the `Body` of the `While` activity. The `Pick` activity should initially have two `PickBranch` instances. Add another one to bring the total to three.

3. Set the `DisplayName` of the leftmost `PickBranch` to `StartOrder`. This branch will contain the activities needed to declare the `StartOrder` service operation. Add a `ReceiveAndSendReply` activity template to the trigger of the `StartOrder` `PickBranch`. Set the properties and parameters of the `Receive` activity to the values shown in the following tables.

StartOrder Receive Properties

Property	Value
OperationName	StartOrder
ServiceContractName	{http://tempuri.org/}IOrderEntry
CanCreateInstance	True

StartOrder Receive Parameters

Parameter Name	Type	Value
orderId	Int32	OrderId

4. Modify the CorrelationInitializers property of the Receive activity by clicking the ellipsis in the Properties window. Delete any correlation initializers that may already exist for the activity. Add a new QueryCorrelationInitializer by selecting Query correlation initializer from the list of available initializers. Enter SharedHandle as the handle variable to be initialized. In the XPath Queries section, select the orderId parameter from the drop-down list. This initializes the SharedHandle using the contents of the orderId request parameter. The SendReplyToReceive activity does not require you to set any properties or parameters. Figure 11-4 shows the completed StartOrder PickBranch.

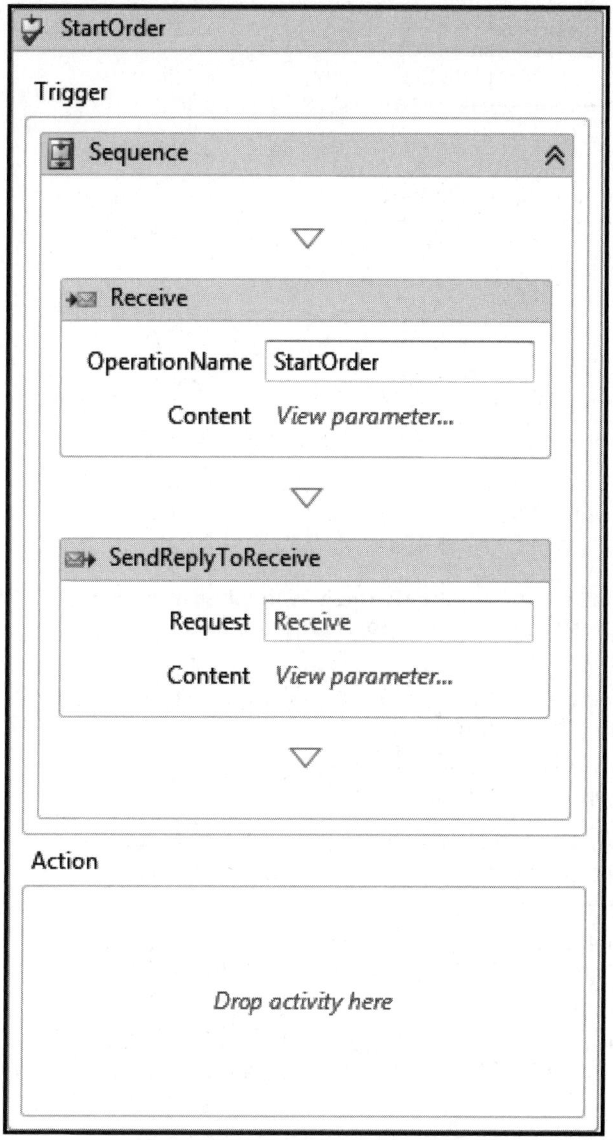

Figure 11-4. StartOrder PickBranch

5. Set the DisplayName of the middle PickBranch to AddItem. Define the two
    variables that are scoped by the AddItem activity: Item and IsInventoryOK.

6. Add a ReceiveAndSendReply activity template to the trigger of the AddItem
    activity. Set the properties ad parameters of the Receive activity to the values
    shown in the following tables.

AddItem Receive Properties

Property	Value
OperationName	AddItem
ServiceContractName	{http://tempuri.org/}IOrderEntry
CanCreateInstance	False

AddItem Receive Parameters

Parameter Name	Type	Value
orderId	Int32	OrderId
item	ActivityLibrary.Item	Item

7. Set the `CorrelatesWith` property of the `Receive` activity to the `SharedHandle` variable. Set the `CorrelatesOn` property to the `orderId` parameter.

8. Add a `CheckInventory` activity below the `Receive` activity. Set the `ItemId` property to `Item.ItemId`, the `OrderId` property to `OrderId`, `Quantity` to `Item.Quantity`, and `Result` to `IsInventoryOK`.

9. Add an `If` activity below the `CheckInventory` activity. Set the `If.Condition` property to `IsInventoryOK`.

10. Add a `Sequence` activity to the `If.Then` property. Add a `GetItemPrice` activity to the new `Sequence` activity. Set the `ItemId` property to `Item.ItemId` and the `Result` to `Item.UnitPrice`.

11. Add an `Assign` activity below the `GetItemPrice` activity. Set the `Assign.To` property to `Item.TotalPrice` and the `Assign.Value` property to `Item.UnitPrice * Item.Quantity`.

12. Add an `AddToCollection` activity below the `Assign`. Set the generic type to `ActivityLibrary.Item`. Set the `Collection` property to `Items` and the `Item` property to `Item`.

13. Add a `WriteLine` activity to the `If.Else` property. Set the `Text` property to `String.Format("Quantity of {0} for Item {1} is unavailable", Item.Quantity, Item.ItemId)`.

14. Make sure that the `SendReplyToReceive` activity hasn't been deleted and is still within the trigger section of the `PickBranch`. You do not need to set any properties for this activity. Figure 11-5 shows the complete `AddItem` `PickBranch`.

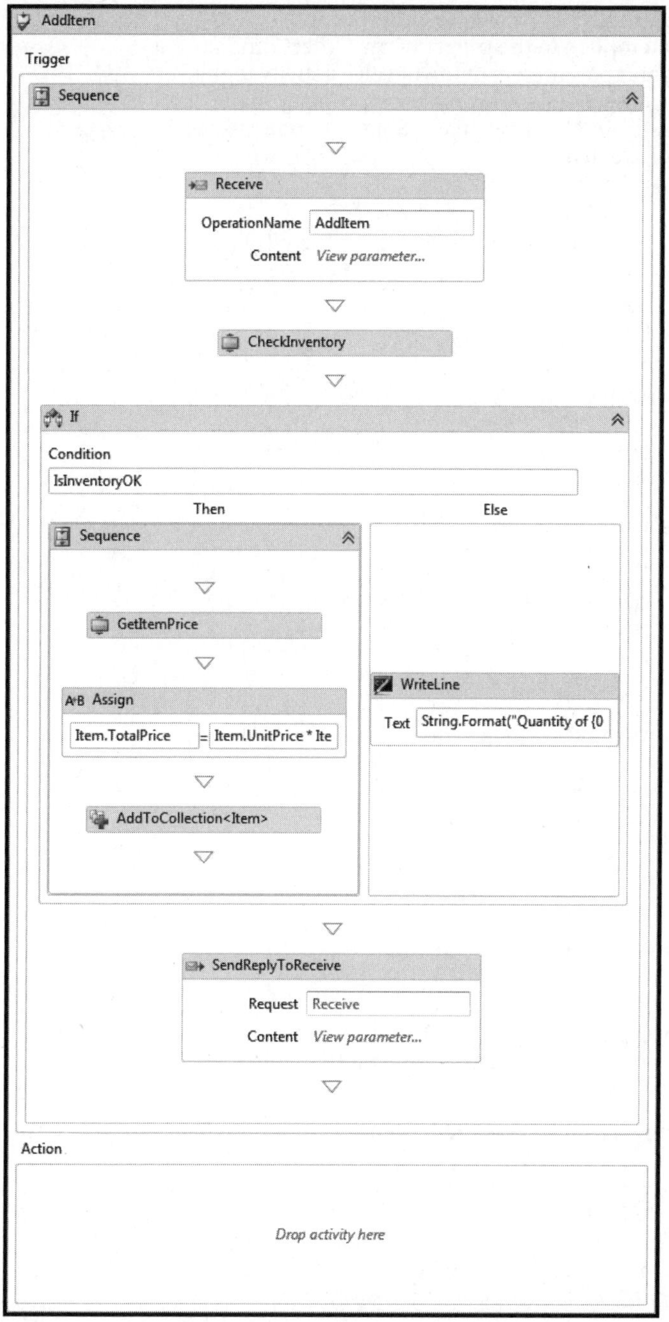

Figure 11-5. AddItem PickBranch

15. Set the DisplayName of the rightmost PickBranch to OrderComplete. Add a ReceiveAndSendReply activity template to the trigger of the OrderComplete PickBranch. Set the properties and parameters of the Receive activity to the values shown in the following tables. Set the CorrelatesOn property to the orderId parameter and the CorrelatesWith property to SharedHandle just as you did with the AddItem Receive activity.

OrderComplete Receive Properties

Property	Value
OperationName	OrderComplete
ServiceContractName	{http://tempuri.org/}IOrderEntry
CanCreateInstance	False

OrderComplete Receive Parameters

Parameter Name	Type	Value
orderId	Int32	OrderId

16. Set the parameters for the SendReplyToReceive activity to the values shown in this table.

OrderComplete SendReplyToReceive Parameters

Parameter Name	Type	Value
items	List<ActivityLibrary.Item>	Items

17. Add an Assign activity to the Action property of the OrderComplete PickBranch. Set the Assign.To property to IsDone and the Assign.Value property to True.

Figure 11-6 shows the completed `OrderComplete PickBranch`. Figure 11-7 shows the topmost view of the completed workflow.

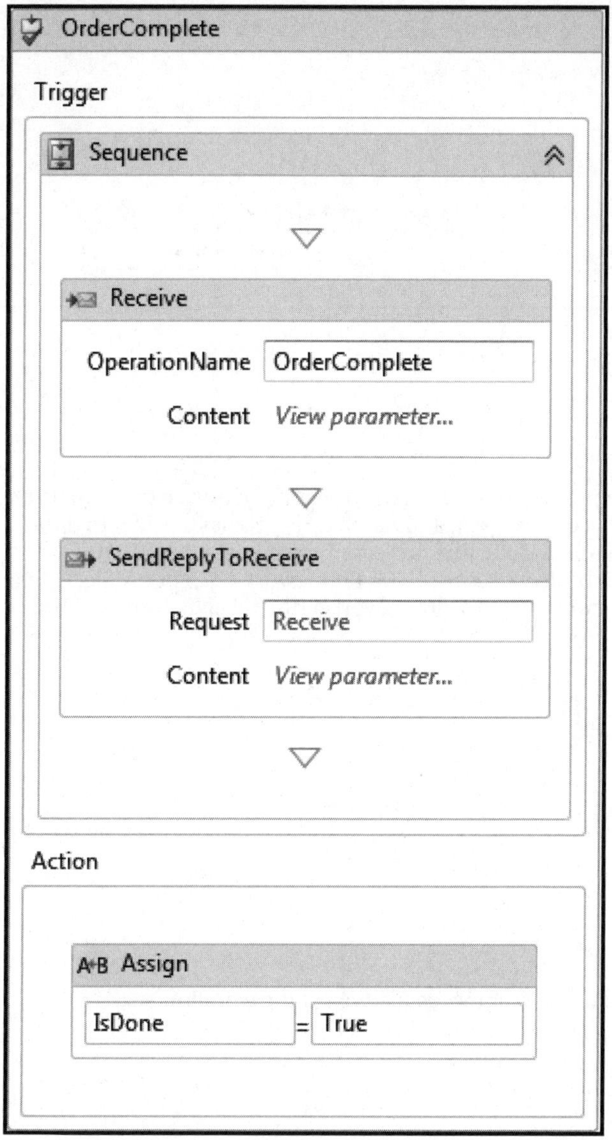

OrderComplete

Trigger

Sequence ⌃

▽

Receive

OperationName | OrderComplete

Content | *View parameter...*

▽

SendReplyToReceive

Request | Receive

Content | *View parameter...*

▽

Action

A+B Assign

IsDone | = | True

Figure 11-6. OrderComplete PickBranch

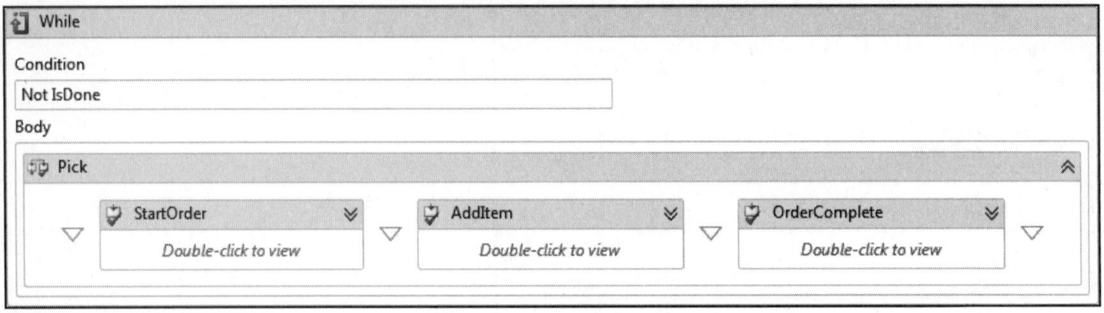

Figure 11-7. Complete OrderEntryService workflow

Hosting the Workflow Service

The next step in this example is to implement a project to self-host the `OrderEntryService` that you just declared. Create a new Workflow Console Application project, and name it `ServiceHost`. Add it to the solution for this chapter, and delete the `Workflow1.xaml` file that is created since it won't be used.

By default, a Workflow Console Application project uses the .NET Framework 4 Client profile. Open the project settings, and change the target framework to .NET Framework 4 (the full .NET profile). Add these additional references to the project:

- `ActivityLibrary`

- `System.Activities.DurableInstancing`

- `System.Configuration`

- `System.Runtime.DurableInstancing`

- `System.Runtime.Serialization`

Implementing the Service Host

Here is the complete code that you need to add to the `Program.cs` file to host the workflow service:

```
using System;
using System.Activities.DurableInstancing;
using System.Collections.Generic;
using System.Configuration;
using System.IO;
using System.Runtime.DurableInstancing;
using System.ServiceModel.Activities;
using System.ServiceModel.Activities.Description;
using System.Xaml;
using System.Xml.Linq;
using ActivityLibrary;
```

```
namespace ServiceHost
{
    class Program
    {
        private static List<WorkflowServiceHost> _hosts =
            new List<WorkflowServiceHost>();

        static void Main(string[] args)
        {
            try
            {
```

In a similar way as you saw with the WorkflowApplication example earlier in this chapter, an instance of the custom extension is created and populated with test item definitions. The private CreateServiceHost method is invoked to load and configure the WorkflowServiceHost. Finally, the Open method of the service host is called to enable it to receive incoming messages.

```
                ItemSupportExtension extension =
                    new ActivityLibrary.ItemSupportExtension();

                extension.AddItemDefinition(101, 1.23M, 10);
                extension.AddItemDefinition(202, 2.34M, 20);
                extension.AddItemDefinition(303, 3.45M, 30);
                DisplayInventory("Before Execution", extension);

                CreateServiceHost("OrderEntryService.xamlx", extension);

                foreach (WorkflowServiceHost host in _hosts)
                {
                    host.Open();
                    foreach (var ep in host.Description.Endpoints)
                    {
                        Console.WriteLine("Contract: {0}",
                            ep.Contract.Name);
                        Console.WriteLine("    at {0}",
                            ep.Address);
                    }
                }

                Console.WriteLine("Press any key to stop hosting and exit");
                Console.ReadKey();

                DisplayInventory("After Execution", extension);
            }
            catch (Exception exception)
            {
                Console.WriteLine("Service Exception: {0}", exception.Message);
            }
            finally
            {
                Console.WriteLine("Closing services...");
```

```
                foreach (WorkflowServiceHost host in _hosts)
                {
                    host.Close();
                }
                Console.WriteLine("Services closed");
                _hosts.Clear();
            }
    }
```

The `CreateServiceHost` method loads the workflow service directly from the Xamlx file. It uses the loaded `WorkflowService` to construct a `WorkflowServiceHost` instance. An instance of the `SqlWorkflowInstanceStoreBehavior` class is then constructed and configured. The property values used here are similar to those that were used in the `WorkflowApplication` example earlier in the chapter. Once it has been configured, the instance store behavior is added to the service host using the `Description.Behaviors` property.

```
        private static WorkflowServiceHost CreateServiceHost(
            String xamlxName, IItemSupport extension)
        {
            WorkflowService wfService = LoadService(xamlxName);
            WorkflowServiceHost host = new WorkflowServiceHost(wfService);

            string connectionString = ConfigurationManager.ConnectionStrings
                ["InstanceStore"].ConnectionString;
            SqlWorkflowInstanceStoreBehavior storeBehavior =
                new SqlWorkflowInstanceStoreBehavior(connectionString);
            storeBehavior.InstanceCompletionAction =
                InstanceCompletionAction.DeleteAll;
            storeBehavior.InstanceLockedExceptionAction =
                InstanceLockedExceptionAction.BasicRetry;
            storeBehavior.InstanceEncodingOption =
                InstanceEncodingOption.GZip;
            storeBehavior.HostLockRenewalPeriod =
                TimeSpan.FromMinutes(1);
            host.Description.Behaviors.Add(storeBehavior);
```

An instance of the `WorkflowIdleBehavior` class is also constructed and added to the service host. The `TimeToUnload` property is set to zero to force workflow instances to be immediately persisted and unloaded from memory as soon as they become idle. You probably don't need to be this aggressive in a real application, but this does allow you to see actual persistence and unloading behavior when you test this example.

```
            WorkflowIdleBehavior idleBehavior = new WorkflowIdleBehavior()
            {
                TimeToUnload = TimeSpan.FromSeconds(0)
            };
```

```
        host.Description.Behaviors.Add(idleBehavior);
        if (extension != null)
        {
            host.WorkflowExtensions.Add(extension);
        }

        _hosts.Add(host);

        return host;
    }
```

The private `LoadService` method deserializes a `WorkflowService` instance from the named Xamlx file. The file is assumed to be located in a relative path under the `ServiceLibrary` project. This code assumes that these projects are located in the same solution. You will need to adjust this path if the Xamlx files are in a different location.

```
    private static WorkflowService LoadService(String xamlxName)
    {
        String fullFilePath = Path.Combine(
            @"..\..\..\ServiceLibrary", xamlxName);
        WorkflowService service =
            XamlServices.Load(fullFilePath) as WorkflowService;
        if (service != null)
        {
            return service;
        }
        else
        {
            throw new NullReferenceException(String.Format(
                "Unable to load service definition from {0}", fullFilePath));
        }
    }

    private static void DisplayInventory(String desc, IItemSupport extension)
    {
        Console.WriteLine("\nItem inventory {0}:", desc);
        foreach (ItemDefinition item in extension.GetItemDefinitions())
        {
            Console.WriteLine("ItemId={0}, QtyAvailable={1}",
                item.ItemId, item.QtyAvailable);
        }
        Console.WriteLine("");
    }
  }
}
```

Configuring the Service Host

If the `ServiceHost` project does not already have an `App.config` file, add one now. The `App.config` file requires WCF-related entries to define an endpoint for the workflow service and to also specify the SQL

Server connection string for the instance store. Here is the complete **App.config** file that you need to execute this example:

```xml
<?xml version="1.0"?>
<configuration>
  <connectionStrings>
    <add name="InstanceStore"
        connectionString="Data Source=localhost\SQLExpress;
          Initial Catalog=InstanceStore;Integrated Security=True;
          Asynchronous Processing=True"
        providerName="System.Data.SqlClient" />
  </connectionStrings>
  <system.serviceModel>
    <services>
      <service name="OrderEntryService">
        <host>
          <baseAddresses>
            <add baseAddress="http://localhost:9000/"/>
          </baseAddresses>
        </host>
        <endpoint contract="IOrderEntry"
          address="http://localhost:9000/OrderEntry"
          binding="wsHttpBinding" />
      </service>
    </services>
    <behaviors>
      <serviceBehaviors>
        <behavior>
          <serviceMetadata httpGetEnabled="true"/>
          <serviceDebug includeExceptionDetailInFaults="false"/>
        </behavior>
      </serviceBehaviors>
    </behaviors>
    <serviceHostingEnvironment multipleSiteBindingsEnabled="true" />
  </system.serviceModel>
  <startup>
    <supportedRuntime version="v4.0" sku=".NETFramework,Version=v4.0"/>
  </startup>
</configuration>
```

This configuration file uses port 9000 for hosting the workflow service. Feel free to change this port number if necessary, but you'll also need to make a similar change to the configuration of the client project (developed next).

Loading the Instance Store from the Configuration File

The SqlWorkflowInstanceStoreBehavior can also be loaded from entries in the **App.config** file instead of entirely in code. For example, here is the section of the **App.config** file containing the additional entries to load the instance store:

```xml
<?xml version="1.0"?>
<configuration>
...
  <system.serviceModel>
...
    <behaviors>
      <serviceBehaviors>
        <behavior>
...
          <sqlWorkflowInstanceStore
            connectionStringName="InstanceStore"
            instanceCompletionAction="DeleteAll"
            instanceLockedExceptionAction="BasicRetry"
            instanceEncodingOption="GZip"
            hostLockRenewalPeriod="00:01:00" />
        </behavior>
      </serviceBehaviors>
    </behaviors>
...
</configuration>
```

If you load the instance store behavior from the configuration file like this, you can remove all references to the `SqlWorkflowInstanceStoreBehavior` in the hosting code. The same set of entries can be added to the `Web.config` file when you host your workflow services in IIS.

■ **Note** The remaining examples in this chapter and Chapter 12 assume that you are loading the instance store in code (as shown in the `Program.cs` file) rather than from the configuration file.

Testing the ServiceHost Project

After building the solution, you should be able to execute the `ServiceHost` project to ensure that the code to host the workflow service is working properly.

■ **Tip** Before you run any WCF-related projects, you will need to start Visual Studio with elevated administrator privileges (the Run as Administrator option in Vista and Windows 7). Doing so avoids any security issues that you would otherwise encounter opening ports.

When I run the ServiceHost project, I see these results:

```
Item inventory Before Execution:

ItemId=101, QtyAvailable=10

ItemId=202, QtyAvailable=20

ItemId=303, QtyAvailable=30


Contract: IOrderEntry

    at http://localhost:9000/OrderEntry

Press any key to stop hosting and exit


Item inventory After Execution:

ItemId=101, QtyAvailable=10

ItemId=202, QtyAvailable=20

ItemId=303, QtyAvailable=30


Closing services...

Services closed

Press any key to continue . . .
```

Admittedly, the results are not very exciting since you don't yet have a client application that uses this service. You will develop a client application in the next section.

Implementing a Client Project

In this section, you will develop a Windows console client application that exercises the OrderEntryService workflow. Create a new Windows console project named OrderEntryConsoleClient, and add it to the solution for this chapter. Add these references to the project:

- System.Configuration

- System.Runtime.Serialization

- System.ServiceModel.Activities

Add a service reference to the OrderEntryService that you declared and hosted in the previous sections. To accomplish this, you need to first run the ServiceHost project in order to retrieve the metadata for the service. While the ServiceHost project is running, select the Add Service Reference option for the OrderEntryConsoleClient project. You can use an address of http://localhost:9000 for the service (unless you decided to use a different port when you configured the ServiceHost project). Don't immediately accept all of the default options for the service reference. Change the namespace to OrderEntryReference, and change the collection type to System.Collections.Generic.List (found under the Advanced options).

Next, add the code to the Program.cs file to interact with the user and to invoke the service operations of the workflow. Here is the complete Program.cs file:

```
using System;
using System.Collections.Generic;
using System.Configuration;
using System.Data.SqlClient;
using System.ServiceModel.Activities;
using OrderEntryConsoleClient.OrderEntryReference;

namespace OrderEntryConsoleClient
{
    class Program
    {
```

The initial version of this client application allows the user to start new workflow instances (new orders), add items to the order, and complete the order. In Chapter 12, you will build upon this client to also support querying for existing workflow instances and canceling them. To simplify the later examples, I've included some of the code that is related to this additional functionality in this initial version of the code. For example, the queriedInstances variable shown here at the top of the class is not used until the additional functionality is fully implemented.

```
        static private Int32 lastOrderId = 0;
        static private Dictionary<Int32, Guid> queriedInstances =
            new Dictionary<int, Guid>();
```

The Main method of the class prompts the user for the command that they want to execute and then invokes the appropriate private method to handle that command.

```csharp
static void Main(string[] args)
{
    Boolean isDone = false;
    while (!isDone)
    {
        Console.WriteLine(
          "Commands: start | add | complete | query | cancel | exit");
        String command = Console.ReadLine();
        if (String.IsNullOrEmpty(command))
        {
            command = "exit";
        }
        switch (command.ToLower())
        {
            case "start":
                Start();
                break;
            case "add":
                Add();
                break;
            case "complete":
                Complete();
                break;
            case "query":
                Query();
                break;
            case "cancel":
                Cancel();
                break;
            case "exit":
                Console.WriteLine("Exiting application...");
                isDone = true;
                break;
            default:
                Console.WriteLine("Invalid command");
                break;
        }
    }
}

static Int32 GetOrderId(Boolean isPromptForEntry)
{
    if (lastOrderId == 0 || isPromptForEntry)
    {
        Console.WriteLine("Enter an OrderId (int) for the order");
        String input = Console.ReadLine();
        Int32 value = 0;
        if (String.IsNullOrEmpty(input))
        {
            Console.WriteLine("A value must be entered");
            return value;
        }
```

```
        Int32.TryParse(input, out value);

        if (value == 0)
        {
            Console.WriteLine("OrderId must not be zero");
            return value;
        }

        lastOrderId = value;
    }

    return lastOrderId;
}
```

The **Start** method is invoked to start a new order. This calls the **StartOrder** service operation, which creates a new workflow instance.

```
static void Start()
{
    try
    {
        Int32 orderId = GetOrderId(true);
        if (orderId == 0)
        {
            return;
        }

        OrderEntryReference.OrderEntryClient client =
            new OrderEntryReference.OrderEntryClient();
        client.StartOrder(orderId);
        lastOrderId = orderId;
        Console.WriteLine("New order {0} started", orderId);
    }
    catch (Exception exception)
    {
        lastOrderId = 0;
        Console.WriteLine("Start Unhandled exception: {0}",
            exception.Message);
    }
}
```

The **Add** method parses the item ID and quantity that was entered and invokes the **AddItem** service operation. This adds the requested item and quantity to the existing order. You may recall that the **Receive** activity for the **AddItem** operation has its **CanCreateInstance** property set to false. This means that this operation cannot create a new workflow instance but must instead correlate with an existing instance based on the order ID.

```csharp
static void Add()
{
    try
    {
        Int32 orderId = GetOrderId(false);
        if (orderId == 0)
        {
            return;
        }

        Console.WriteLine(
            "Enter ItemId and Quantity (Ex: 101 1)");
        String input = Console.ReadLine();

        Int32 itemId = 0;
        Int32 quantity = 0;
        String[] parts = input.Split(' ');
        if (parts.Length != 2)
        {
            Console.WriteLine("Incorrect number of arguments entered!");
            return;
        }
        Int32.TryParse(parts[0], out itemId);
        Int32.TryParse(parts[1], out quantity);
        if (itemId == 0 || quantity == 0)
        {
            Console.WriteLine("Arguments in incorrect format!");
            return;
        }

        Item item = new Item
        {
            ItemId = itemId,
            Quantity = quantity
        };

        OrderEntryReference.OrderEntryClient client =
            new OrderEntryReference.OrderEntryClient();
        client.AddItem(orderId, item);
        Console.WriteLine("Ordered {0} of ItemId {1} for OrderId {2}",
            item.Quantity, item.ItemId, orderId);
    }
    catch (Exception exception)
    {
        lastOrderId = 0;
        Console.WriteLine("Add Unhandled exception: {0}",
            exception.Message);
    }
}
```

The Complete method invokes the OrderComplete operation of the existing workflow instance. Once the response is received, the collection of Item objects that were ordered is displayed.

```
static void Complete()
{
    try
    {
        Int32 orderId = GetOrderId(false);
        if (orderId == 0)
        {
            return;
        }

        OrderEntryReference.OrderEntryClient client =
            new OrderEntryReference.OrderEntryClient();
        List<Item> items = client.OrderComplete(orderId);
        lastOrderId = 0;
        Console.WriteLine("Order {0} Is Completed", orderId);
        if (items != null && items.Count > 0)
        {
            Console.WriteLine("\nOrdered Items:");
            foreach (Item i in items)
            {
                Console.WriteLine(
                    "ItemId={0}, Quantity={1}, UnitPrice={2}, Total={3}",
                    i.ItemId, i.Quantity, i.UnitPrice, i.TotalPrice);
            }
        }
    }
    catch (Exception exception)
    {
        lastOrderId = 0;
        Console.WriteLine("Complete Unhandled exception: {0}",
            exception.Message);
    }
}
```

I've included the empty Query and Cancel private methods in this initial version of the client code. You will add the implementation for these methods in later examples that are presented in Chapter 12.

```
static void Query()
{
}

static void Cancel()
{
}
    }
}
```

Configuring the Client Project

A fully configured `App.config` file should have been added to the project when you added a service reference. You should be able to use this file as is without any changes. Your `App.config` file should look similar to this:

```xml
<?xml version="1.0" encoding="utf-8" ?>
<configuration>
  <system.serviceModel>
    <bindings>
      <wsHttpBinding>
        <binding name="WSHttpBinding_IOrderEntry" closeTimeout="00:01:00"
            openTimeout="00:01:00" receiveTimeout="00:10:00"
            sendTimeout="00:01:00"
            bypassProxyOnLocal="false" transactionFlow="false"
            hostNameComparisonMode="StrongWildcard"
            maxBufferPoolSize="524288" maxReceivedMessageSize="65536"
            messageEncoding="Text" textEncoding="utf-8" useDefaultWebProxy="true"
            allowCookies="false">
          <readerQuotas maxDepth="32" maxStringContentLength="8192"
              maxArrayLength="16384"
              maxBytesPerRead="4096" maxNameTableCharCount="16384" />
          <reliableSession ordered="true" inactivityTimeout="00:10:00"
              enabled="false" />
          <security mode="Message">
            <transport clientCredentialType="Windows"
                proxyCredentialType="None" realm="" />
            <message clientCredentialType="Windows"
                negotiateServiceCredential="true"
                algorithmSuite="Default" />
          </security>
        </binding>
      </wsHttpBinding>
    </bindings>
    <client>
      <endpoint address="http://localhost:9000/OrderEntry"
          binding="wsHttpBinding"
          bindingConfiguration="WSHttpBinding_IOrderEntry"
          contract="OrderEntryReference.IOrderEntry"
          name="WSHttpBinding_IOrderEntry">
      </endpoint>
    </client>
  </system.serviceModel>
</configuration>
```

Testing the Client Project

After rebuilding the solution, you should be ready to these the **OrderEntryService** using the newly constructed client project. For this test, you need to start both the **ServiceHost** and **OrderEntryConsoleClient** projects. The easiest way to accomplish this is to set the startup project option to start multiple projects and select both of these projects.

Here is a representative sample of my results when I run the client project:

```
Commands: start | add | complete | query | cancel | exit

start

Enter an OrderId (int) for the order

1

New order 1 started


Commands: start | add | complete | query | cancel | exit

add

Enter ItemId and Quantity (Ex: 101 1)

101 1

Ordered 1 of ItemId 101 for OrderId 1


Commands: start | add | complete | query | cancel | exit

add

Enter ItemId and Quantity (Ex: 101 1)

202 2

Ordered 2 of ItemId 202 for OrderId 1
```

```
Commands: start | add | complete | query | cancel | exit

complete

Order 1 Is Completed


Ordered Items:

ItemId=101, Quantity=1, UnitPrice=1.23, Total=1.23

ItemId=202, Quantity=2, UnitPrice=2.34, Total=4.68


Commands: start | add | complete | query | cancel | exit


Exiting application...

Press any key to continue . . .
```

In this sample, I started order number 1 and then added two items to the order: Item 101 with a quantity of 1 and item 202 with a quantity of 2. Finally, I completed the order. Here is the corresponding output from the **ServiceHost** project:

```
Item inventory Before Execution:

ItemId=101, QtyAvailable=10

ItemId=202, QtyAvailable=20

ItemId=303, QtyAvailable=30


Contract: IOrderEntry

    at http://localhost:9000/OrderEntry

Press any key to stop hosting and exit
```

```
Update: ItemId=101, QtyBefore=10, QtyAfter=9

Update: ItemId=202, QtyBefore=20, QtyAfter=18


Item inventory After Execution:

ItemId=101, QtyAvailable=9

ItemId=202, QtyAvailable=18

ItemId=303, QtyAvailable=30


Closing services...

Services closed

Press any key to continue . . .
```

Although this works as expected, much more interesting results can be observed if you close and restart the projects in the middle of a test. For example, run the projects once again and start another order, adding one or two items to the order. Now, instead of immediately completing the order, close the projects and then restart them. You can now use the add command to add additional items to the same order (identified by the order ID) and then use the complete command to finish the order. You should see that the order contains all of the items that you entered, regardless of whether they were entered before or after the projects were restarted. This demonstrates that the current state of the workflow was safely persisted while the projects were restarted.

However, with this example, the current inventory values are maintained in memory and are not persisted. That will be remedied in Chapter 12 when you extend this example using a custom `PersistenceParticipant` class.

Summary

The focus of this chapter was workflow persistence. The chapter included coverage of persistence using the `SqlWorkflowInstanceStore` with the `WorkflowApplication` and `WorkflowServiceHost` classes. Both of these self-hosting classes were used in examples.

In the next chapter, you will learn how to extend the build-in workflow persistence and how to create your own custom instance store.

CHAPTER 12

Customizing Workflow Persistence

This chapter continues the discussion of workflow persistence that began in Chapter 11. In that chapter, you learned the basics of workflow persistence using the `SqlWorkflowInstanceStore`. By following the examples presented in that chapter, you should now know how to enable persistence for applications that are hosted by the `WorkflowApplication` class as well as workflow services hosted by IIS or self-hosted by the `WorkflowServiceHost` class.

This chapter focuses on ways to extend or customize workflow persistence. It builds upon the examples that were presented in Chapter 11. Additional examples in this chapter extend persistence using the `PersistenceParticipant` class and demonstrate the promotion of properties to make them externally queryable. Another example demonstrates how to use the `WorkflowControlEndpoint` to manage active workflow instances.

The chapter concludes with an example that implements a custom instance store. The instance store persists workflow instances to the file system rather than to a database.

■ **Note** This chapter assumes that you are using the examples presented in Chapter 11 as the starting point for this chapter. In particular, the `ActivityLibrary`, `ServiceLibrary`, `ServiceHost`, and `OrderEntryConsoleClient` projects that were first developed in Chapter 11 will be used in this chapter.

Understanding the PersistenceParticipant Classes

You can customize workflow persistence in two primary ways. First, you can implement your own instance store. This option provides you with complete flexibility as to how persistence is implemented. However, this is also the most labor-intensive option. Second, WF provides the `PersistenceParticipant` class that enables you to participate in workflow persistence without the need to implement your own instance store. By deriving a custom workflow extension from the abstract `PersistenceParticipant` class, you can inject additional data that is persisted along with the workflow instance.

■ **Note** Developing your own instance store is demonstrated later in this chapter.

The PersistenceParticipant Class

Here are the most important members of the `PersistenceParticipant` class:

Member	Description
CollectValues	A virtual method that is invoked to collect additional data to be persisted
PublishValues	A virtual method that is invoked to load additional data that was previously persisted
MapValues	A virtual method that is invoked to provide visibility into the data that was collected by all persistence participants

You can follow these steps to use this extension mechanism:

1. Develop a custom workflow extension that derives from the `PersistenceParticipant` class (found in the `System.Activities.Persistence` namespace).

2. Override the virtual `CollectValues` method to inject additional data to be persisted.

3. Optionally, override the virtual `PublishValues` method to load additional data that was previously persisted.

4. Optionally, override the virtual `MapValues` method to review data to be persisted that was collected from all persistence participants.

The `CollectValues` and `PublishValues` methods complement each other. The `CollectValues` method is invoked when a workflow instance is persisted and is your opportunity to add data to be persisted. The method signature defines two out arguments of type `IDictionary` that must be populated by your code. One dictionary is used for read-write values and the other for write-only values. The difference between the two collections is that read-write values are expected to make a round-trip. They are persisted and then loaded when the workflow instance is loaded. The write-only values are persisted but not loaded. By specifying them as write-only values, you are indicating that they are not vital to the successful execution of the workflow. They might be queried and used by other nonworkflow portions of the application.

The `PublishValues` method is invoked during the process of loading a workflow instance that was previously persisted. The method is passed an `IDictionary` of read-write values that were previously persisted. This is your opportunity to retrieve each named value from the collection and load it back into memory.

Each value that you persist or load is uniquely identified with a string name that you must provide. The name is defined as an `XName` so it includes a full namespace.

The other virtual method that you can choose to override is `MapValues`. The purpose of this method is not as straightforward as the other methods. To better understand its purpose, you need to understand that persistence is accomplished in stages. In the first stage, the `CollectValues` method is invoked for all persistence participants that are currently loaded. At the end of this stage, all data to be persisted has been collected. In the second stage, the MapValues method is invoked to provide you with an opportunity to make additional persistence decisions based on the superset of data that was collected from all participants. The MapValues method is passed two IDictionary arguments (one for read-write values and another for write-only values) and returns a new IDictionary instance. The IDictionary of values that you must return is added to the previously collected data as write-only values. In the third stage of persistence, the SaveWorkflowCommand is executed against the instance store to persist the workflow instance and any additional data that was collected.

The PersistenceIOParticipant Class

WF also provides the PersistenceIOParticipant class, which derives from PersistenceParticipant. Here are the most important additional members of this class:

Member	Description
BeginOnSave	Invoked to asynchronously save additional data during the persistence operation
EndOnSave	Invoked to end the BeginOnSave asynchronous operation
BeginOnLoad	Invoked to asynchronously load additional data
EndOnLoad	Invoked to end the BeginOnLoad operation

The additional methods provided by the PersistenceIOParticipant class enable you to save and load data during the standard persistence operations, but to use a storage mechanism that is separate from the instance store. For example, you want to use the standard SqlWorkflowInstanceStore for the primary workflow persistence. But in additional to the standard workflow persistence, you also need to save a subset of the instance data to an XML file or to a table in another application database. The PersistenceIOParticipant class allows you to accomplish this by overriding the methods listed previously.

Which Class to Use?

You can follow these general guidelines to help you determine which base class to use:

- Use PersistenceParticipant when you need to persist and reload additional data with each workflow instance.

- Use PersistenceParticipant when you need to persist additional write-only data.

- Use PersistenceIOParticipant when you want to persist and reload workflow instance data using an instance store but you also need to persist (and possibly reload) data from a separate data store.

Using the PersistenceParticipant Class

To demonstrate how to use the PersistenceParticipant class, you will modify the custom extension that you implemented in Chapter 11. One of the design problems with the previous examples is that the ItemSupportExtension maintains a running count of available inventory for each item. As each new item is added to an order, the available inventory is decremented by the requested quantity. In the previous examples, the inventory is reset to the starting values when the applications are recycled. It would be better if the current inventory values were persisted and then reloaded along with the workflow instance.

In this example, you will modify the ItemSupportExtension class to persist the inventory values. You will add the PersistenceParticipant class as the base class and override the CollectValues and PublishValues methods.

■ **Note** Even with these changes, this is not an optimal solution to this particular test scenario. Saving the available inventory with each workflow instance works great if you work with only a single instance at any one time. In a more realistic scenario where you might have hundreds or thousands of orders executing at any one time, the inventory would naturally be persisted in a database. However, this contrived example should be adequate to demonstrate the persistence concepts that are the focus of this chapter.

Modifying the ItemSupportExtension Class

You originally implemented the ItemSupportExtension class in Chapter 11. It is located in the ActivityLibrary project. Here is an abbreviated copy of the class showing the changes that you need to make:

```
using System;
using System.Activities.Persistence;
using System.Collections.Generic;
using System.Linq;
using System.Xml.Linq;

namespace ActivityLibrary
{
    public class ItemSupportExtension : PersistenceParticipant, IItemSupport
    {
…
        private XName _itemsName = XName.Get(
            "ItemDefinitions", "ActivityLibrary.ItemSupportExtension");
        private XName _orderIdName = XName.Get(
            "OrderId", "ActivityLibrary.ItemSupportExtension");
…
        #region PersistenceParticipant members
```

The code in the CollectValues method adds the entire collection of ItemDefinition objects (the _items variable) as a read-write value. This is the collection containing the available inventory values for each item. Additionally, the value of the _orderId variable is added to the write-only collection. Since it is added to the write-only collection, this value is serialized and persisted along with the instance store but is not reloaded. It will be used in the next example to demonstrate the use of the Promote method of the SQL Server instance store.

```
protected override void CollectValues(
    out IDictionary<System.Xml.Linq.XName, object> readWriteValues,
    out IDictionary<System.Xml.Linq.XName, object> writeOnlyValues)
{
    readWriteValues = new Dictionary<System.Xml.Linq.XName, object>();
    lock (_items)
    {
        readWriteValues.Add(_itemsName, _items);
    }

    if (_orderId > 0)
    {
        writeOnlyValues = new Dictionary<System.Xml.Linq.XName, object>();
        writeOnlyValues.Add(_orderIdName, _orderId);
        _orderId = 0;
    }
    else
    {
        writeOnlyValues = null;
    }
}
```

The PublishValues method retrieves the value of the collection of ItemDefinition objects that was previously persisted and assigns it to the _items member variable.

```
protected override void PublishValues(
    IDictionary<System.Xml.Linq.XName, object> readWriteValues)
{
    object value = null;
    if (readWriteValues.TryGetValue(_itemsName, out value))
    {
        if (value is Dictionary<Int32, ItemDefinition>)
        {
            lock (_items)
            {
                _items = value as Dictionary<Int32, ItemDefinition>;
            }
        }
    }
}

    #endregion
    }
}
```

Testing the Revised Extension

After rebuilding the solution, you can test the enhanced extension class by running the **ServiceHost** and **OrderEntryConsoleClient** projects as you did for the previous example. Start a new order, add a few items, and then close the projects without completing the order. Then restart the projects and complete the order.

You should see that the final ending inventory that is displayed has been reduced by the items that you added to the order. This confirms that the collection of **ItemDefinition** objects was persisted and loaded along with the workflow instance. Previously, the inventory values were reset to their original values when the **ServiceHost** project was restarted.

■ **Caution** The ServiceHost project loads a singleton instance of the ItemSupportExtension that is shared by all workflow instances. When you are adding your own extensions, you can also use the override of the WorkflowExtensions.Add method that allows you to assign a delegate. The delegate is executed for each workflow instance, allowing you to construct a new instance of the extension for each workflow instance.

Be careful if you use this approach with an extension that derives from the PersistenceParticipant class. If the extension implements an interface that you defined (IItemSupport in this example), you might be tempted to specify the interface as the generic type when you add the extension like this: host.WorkflowExtensions. Add<IItemSupport>(() => return new ItemSupportExtension()). If you do this, the extension will not be recognized as a persistence participant, and the persistence methods (CollectValues, MapValues, PublishValues) will not be invoked. Instead, you need to specify the concrete type name as the generic type like this: host.WorkflowExtensions.Add<ItemSupportExtension>(() => return new ItemSupportExtension()).

Promoting Properties

When you extend workflow persistence by providing your own **PersistenceParticipant**-derived class, the additional data that you inject is serialized and saved in the instance store along with the workflow instance. This means that the data is completely opaque and not easily available for consumption by any process except for workflow persistence. You can't easily query it or use it to look up the workflow instance ID that is associated with it.

However, many times you might want to extend workflow persistence specifically to provide a lookup mechanism. For example, in the workflow service examples that were presented in Chapter 11, each workflow instance was associated with an order ID number. You might need the ability to look up the workflow instance ID that is associated with a particular order ID.

To address this need, the `SqlWorkflowInstanceStore` class supports the concept of property promotion. Promotion instructs the instance store to save the properties that you identify to another table in the persistence database. The fully qualified name of this table is `System.Activities.DurableInstancing.InstancePromotedProperties`. There is also a view provided with the same name (`InstancePromotedProperties`). The table contains a number of variant columns (named `Value1`, `Value2`, and so on) that can store most simple data types (integers, strings, and so on) and columns that can store binary data. The workflow instance ID is one of the columns in the table. Therefore, once the properties are persisted in this manner, they are queryable and available for your use. If you query for some known value (for example an order ID), you will be able to identify the workflow instance ID associated with that value.

Promotion is enabled by calling the `Promote` method of the `SqlWorkflowInstanceStore` class. The method is defined with this signature:

```
public void Promote(string name, IEnumerable<XName> promoteAsVariant,
    IEnumerable<XName> promoteAsBinary)
```

The name parameter should be a meaningful name that you apply to the promotion. It is also saved to the database along with the individual properties that you specify in the collection. The `promoteAsVariant` parameter is a collection of properties that you want to store in the variant columns. Each one is uniquely identified by a namespace-qualified name that must exactly match the name you used in your custom `PersistenceParticipant` class to persist the values. The properties that you specify are persisted in the variant columns in the order in which they are defined. So, the first property goes into the `Value1` column, the second in `Value2`, and so on. The second collection is for properties that you want to save as binary data.

■ **Note** The promoted data exists for the same duration as the workflow instance itself. When the workflow instance completes and is removed from the database, the promoted data is also removed.

Using Property Promotion

To demonstrate property promotion, you will make a few small changes to the previous example to promote the order ID property. Since the order ID is used for content correlation, it makes sense that someone might want to query for this value.

You will complete these tasks to implement this example:

1. Modify the `ServiceHost` project to promote the order ID.

2. Modify the `OrderEntryConsoleClient` project to query for the promoted values.

3. Add the SQL Server connection string to the `App.config` file of the `OrderEntryConsoleClient` project.

Modifying the ServiceHost

Modify the `Program.cs` file of the `ServiceHost` project to promote the `OrderId` property. Here is an abbreviated listing of the code showing the new code that you need to add:

```
namespace ServiceHost
{
    class Program
    {
...

        private static WorkflowServiceHost CreateServiceHost(
            String xamlxName, IItemSupport extension)
        {
...

            List<XName> variables = new List<XName>()
            {
                XName.Get("OrderId", "ActivityLibrary.ItemSupportExtension")
            };
            storeBehavior.Promote("OrderEntry", variables, null);

            host.Description.Behaviors.Add(storeBehavior);
...

        }
    }
}
```

■ **Tip** Notice that the property name and namespace specified here exactly match the name used in the
ItemSupportExtension class to save the order ID.

Modifying the Client Application

You will now modify the OrderEntryConsoleClient project to query the table containing the promoted
values. This provides the client application with the ability to display a list of all active and incomplete
workflow instances along with their order IDs.

Here is an abbreviated listing of the Program.cs file of the OrderEntryConsoleClient project with the
implementation of the private Query method:

```
namespace OrderEntryConsoleClient
{
    class Program
    {
...

        static void Query()
        {
            String sql =
             @"Select Value1, InstanceId from
                [System.Activities.DurableInstancing].[InstancePromotedProperties]
                where PromotionName = 'OrderEntry'
                order by Value1";
```

```
        try
        {
            queriedInstances.Clear();
            string connectionString = ConfigurationManager.ConnectionStrings
                ["InstanceStore"].ConnectionString;
            using (SqlConnection conn = new SqlConnection(connectionString))
            {
                conn.Open();
                SqlCommand cmd = new SqlCommand(sql, conn);
                using (SqlDataReader reader = cmd.ExecuteReader())
                {
                    Console.WriteLine("Promoted OrderId values:");
                    while (reader.Read())
                    {
                        Int32 orderId = (Int32)reader["Value1"];
                        Guid instanceId = (Guid)reader["InstanceId"];

                        Console.WriteLine("OrderId={0}, InstanceId={1}",
                            orderId, instanceId);
                        if (!queriedInstances.ContainsKey(orderId))
                        {
                            queriedInstances.Add(orderId, instanceId);
                        }
                    }
                }
            }
        }
        catch (Exception exception)
        {
            lastOrderId = 0;
            Console.WriteLine("Query Unhandled exception: {0}",
                exception.Message);
        }
    }
...
    }
}
```

The code not only displays the results of the query on the console, but it also saves the data in a dictionary. This dictionary will be used in a subsequent example to cancel an active workflow instance.

Configuring the Client Application

The query code assumes that the SQL Server connection string is defined in the App.config file, so you'll need to add it to the existing file:

```xml
<?xml version="1.0" encoding="utf-8" ?>
<configuration>
  <connectionStrings>
    <add name="InstanceStore"
        connectionString="Data Source=localhost\SQLExpress;
            Initial Catalog=InstanceStore;Integrated Security=True;
            Asynchronous Processing=True"
        providerName="System.Data.SqlClient" />
  </connectionStrings>
...
</configuration>
```

Testing the Revised Example

After rebuilding the project, you should be ready to run the **ServiceHost** and **OrderEntryConsoleClient** projects. To test this new functionality, I started two new orders, adding an item to each order. I then executed the query command, which successfully listed the workflow instance IDs along with the order ID that is associated with each instance. Here is a representative sample of my results:

```
Commands: start | add | complete | query | cancel | exit

start

Enter an OrderId (int) for the order

1

New order 1 started


Commands: start | add | complete | query | cancel | exit

add

Enter ItemId and Quantity (Ex: 101 1)

101 1

Ordered 1 of ItemId 101 for OrderId 1
```

```
Commands: start | add | complete | query | cancel | exit

start

Enter an OrderId (int) for the order

2

New order 2 started


Commands: start | add | complete | query | cancel | exit

add

Enter ItemId and Quantity (Ex: 101 1)

202 2

Ordered 2 of ItemId 202 for OrderId 2


Commands: start | add | complete | query | cancel | exit

query

Promoted OrderId values:

OrderId=1, InstanceId=0ce418f4-74a4-49d0-85cb-886d9139d120

OrderId=2, InstanceId=4b6a0ade-9afe-435e-ba5d-99dee801e5fc


Commands: start | add | complete | query | cancel | exit
```

Understanding the Management Endpoint

WF provides a standard WCF management endpoint (WorkflowControlEndpoint) that can be added to a service. This endpoint is designed to assist with the management of long-running workflow services, such as the one that you have been using in this chapter and in Chapter 11. This endpoint supports operations that manage existing service instances such as Cancel, Suspend, Terminate, Abandon, Unsuspend, and Run.

To enable this endpoint, you simply need to add it to the `WorkflowServiceHost` instance. This can be accomplished in code or via entries in the `App.config` file for the project. You can also add these same entries to a `Web.config` file if you are using IIS to host your workflow services.

To consume the management endpoint, WF also provides a client proxy class named `WorkflowControlClient`. It eliminates the need for you to create your own client proxy for the management endpoint.

Using the Management Endpoint

To demonstrate a realistic use of the managed endpoint and client class, you will modify the previous example to allow cancellation of an active workflow instance. The client application will use the results of the query (implemented in the last example) to identify the workflow instance ID to cancel.

You will complete these tasks to implement this example:

1. Add the `WorkflowControlEndpoint` to the `ServiceHost` configuration file.

2. Modify the `OrderEntryConsoleClient` project to use the `WorkflowControlClient`.

3. Define the management endpoint in the client configuration file.

Modifying the ServiceHost Configuration

Since the `ServiceHost` project is already defining all endpoints via the `App.config` file, it makes sense to add the `WorkflowControlEndpoint` in the same manner. Here are the additional entries that you need to make to the `App.config` file of the `ServiceHost` project:

```
<?xml version="1.0"?>
<configuration>
...
  <system.serviceModel>
    <services>
      <service name="OrderEntryService">
...
        <endpoint kind="workflowControlEndpoint"
          address="http://localhost:9000/OrderEntryControl"
          binding="wsHttpBinding" />
      </service>
    </services>
...
  </system.serviceModel>
...
</configuration>
```

Modifying the Client Application

The `OrderEntryConsoleClient` project will now be modified to cancel an active workflow instance using the `WorkflowControlClient` class. Here is the implementation for the private `Cancel` method in the `Program.cs` file of this project:

```
namespace OrderEntryConsoleClient
{
    class Program
    {
...
        static void Cancel()
        {
            try
            {
                Console.WriteLine("Enter an OrderId to cancel");
                String input = Console.ReadLine();
                Int32 orderIdToCancel = 0;
                if (String.IsNullOrEmpty(input))
                {
                    Console.WriteLine("A value must be entered");
                    return;
                }
                Int32.TryParse(input, out orderIdToCancel);
                if (orderIdToCancel == 0)
                {
                    Console.WriteLine("OrderId must not be zero");
                    return;
                }
```

The workflow instance ID to cancel is obtained from the private queriedInstances dictionary. This dictionary is populated by a call to the Query method.

```
                Guid instanceId = Guid.Empty;
                if (!queriedInstances.TryGetValue(orderIdToCancel,
                    out instanceId))
                {
                    Console.WriteLine("Instance not found");
                    return;
                }

                using (WorkflowControlClient client =
                    new WorkflowControlClient("ClientControlEndpoint"))
                {
                    client.Cancel(instanceId);
                }
            }
            catch (Exception exception)
            {
                lastOrderId = 0;
                Console.WriteLine("Cancel Unhandled exception: {0}",
                    exception.Message);
            }
        }
    }
}
```

Configuring the Client Application

The client project now requires the address of the management control endpoint that is hosted by the ServiceHost project. Add these lines to the App.config file of the OrderEntryConsoleClient project:

```xml
<?xml version="1.0" encoding="utf-8" ?>
<configuration>
...
  <system.serviceModel>
...
    <client>
...
      <endpoint name="ClientControlEndpoint"
        contract="System.ServiceModel.Activities.IWorkflowInstanceManagement"
        address="http://localhost:9000/OrderEntryControl"
        binding="wsHttpBinding" />
    </client>
  </system.serviceModel>
</configuration>
```

Testing the Revised Example

After rebuilding the solution, start the ServiceHost and OrderEntryConsoleClient projects once again. To test this new functionality, you need to have one or two active workflow instances. If you didn't complete the instances from the previous test, you can use them. Otherwise, you'll need to add at least one instance with at least one item. Use the query command to prepare a list of active instances. Then you can use the cancel command to cancel one of the instances. Finally, execute the query command one more time to verify that the canceled instance is actually gone.

Here are my results, which assume that the instances from the previous example were not completed and are still active:

```
Commands: start | add | complete | query | cancel | exit

query

Promoted OrderId values:

OrderId=1, InstanceId=0ce418f4-74a4-49d0-85cb-886d9139d120

OrderId=2, InstanceId=4b6a0ade-9afe-435e-ba5d-99dee801e5fc


Commands: start | add | complete | query | cancel | exit

cancel
```

```
Enter an OrderId to cancel

1


Commands: start | add | complete | query | cancel | exit

query

Promoted OrderId values:

OrderId=2, InstanceId=4b6a0ade-9afe-435e-ba5d-99dee801e5fc


Commands: start | add | complete | query | cancel | exit

complete

Enter an OrderId (int) for the order

2

Order 2 Is Completed


Ordered Items:

ItemId=202, Quantity=2, UnitPrice=2.34, Total=4.68


Commands: start | add | complete | query | cancel | exit
```

Implementing a Custom Instance Store

As you have already seen, WF includes an instance store (`SqlWorkflowInstanceStore`) that uses a SQL Server database for persistence. This instance store should really be your default answer when you need to add workflow persistence to an application. In most garden-variety scenarios, the instance store that is provided with WF should meet your needs.

However, WF does provide the necessary classes to develop your own instance store. In this section of the chapter, you will develop a custom instance store that persists workflow instances to the file system instead of a database.

I chose to persist to the file system for a couple of reasons. First, WF already has an instance store that uses a SQL Server database, and I wanted to demonstrate something that was significantly different from what you get out of the box. Second, using the file system keeps things as simple as possible. It eliminates the SQL (or LINQ), connection strings, transaction management, and so on. It allows me to present code that focuses on the required interaction with WF rather than with SQL Server.

Understanding the InstanceStore Class

To implement a custom instance store, you must derive from the `InstanceStore` class (located in the `System.Runtime.DurableInstancing` namespace). This class defines a number of members, but here are the virtual members that you must override:

Member	Description
TryCommand	Invoked to synchronously execute a command
BeginTryCommand	Invoked to begin asynchronous execution of a command
EndTryCommand	Completes asynchronous execution of a command

The WF runtime communicates with an instance store through a set of command classes (listed in the next section). Your custom instance store is responsible for handling these commands.

The `BeginTryCommand` and `EndTryCommand` methods are invoked by the persistence framework to execute commands asynchronously. The commands that are passed to `BeginTryCommand` are the result of automatic persistence operations (for example, when a workflow instance becomes idle). On the other hand, the `TryCommand` method is invoked in response to some direct action by you. For example, when you execute `CreateWorkflowOwnerCommand` or `DeleteWorkflowOwnerCommand` against an instance store, those commands are passed to `TryCommand`, not to `BeginTryCommand`.

What this means is that you must provide an implementation for the synchronous and asynchronous versions of these methods. However, as you will see in the example code, the `TryCommand` can simply pass the command to `BeginTryCommand` to satisfy this requirement.

Understanding the Instance Persistence Commands

All persistence commands derive from the base `InstancePersistenceCommand` class. Here is a brief summary of each command and its purpose:

Command	Description
LoadWorkflowCommand	Loads a workflow instance based on its unique instance ID
LoadWorkflowByInstanceKeyCommand	Loads a workflow instance based on a correlation key
SaveWorkflowCommand	Persists a workflow instance
CreateWorkflowOwnerCommand	Registers a host application as a lock owner
DeleteWorkflowOwnerCommand	Deletes the host application as a lock owner

Some of these command classes contain additional properties that you will definitely need to use in your instance store. For example, the `SaveWorkflowCommand` contains the workflow instance data that you need to persist. And the `LoadWorkflowByInstanceKeyCommand` contains the lookup key (a correlation key) that you must use to retrieve the workflow instance.

■ **Note** The properties of these commands are more easily understood by seeing them in actual use. For this reason, I'll skip the usual list of properties for each class to keep this discussion moving along.

Understanding the InstancePersistenceContext Class

The `InstancePersistenceContext` class is similar in purpose to the `ActivityContext` that you reference within custom activities. The `ActivityContext` provides access to the workflow runtime environment. In a similar way, the `InstancePersistenceContext` provides access to the runtime environment for persistence. It provides properties and methods that you use to interact with the WF persistence runtime.

An `InstancePersistenceContext` object is passed as an argument to the `TryCommand` and `BeginTryCommand` methods of the `InstanceStore` class along with the command to execute.

One of the more important properties of the `InstancePersistenceContext` class is the `InstanceView` property. It provides access to an `InstanceView` object, which is a snapshot of a single workflow instance.

The `InstanceView` contains properties that describe the workflow instance that the current command executes against. For example, this class has an `InstanceId` property that uniquely identifies the workflow instance. You will frequently need to navigate to this `InstanceId` property of the `InstanceView` when you need to know the ID of the workflow instance to load or save.

Implementing a File System–Based Instance Store

The custom instance store that you are about to develop is separated into two classes. The `FileSystemInstanceStore` class is derived from the base `InstanceStore` class and is responsible for the handling of persistence commands and interacting with the WF persistence API. It defers all the actual file system I/O to a second class named `FileSystemInstanceStoreIO`. This separation should make it easier to distinguish between the code that responds to the persistence commands (which you will need to implement regardless of the storage medium) and the I/O code that is specific to the chosen storage medium (the file system).

To begin the implementation of the instance store, add a new class to the `ActivityLibrary` project named `FileSystemInstanceStore`. Here is the annotated code for this class:

```
using System;
using System.Activities.DurableInstancing;
using System.Collections.Generic;
using System.Runtime.DurableInstancing;
using System.Threading;
using System.Xml.Linq;

namespace ActivityLibrary
{
    public class FileSystemInstanceStore : InstanceStore
    {
        private Guid _ownerId = Guid.NewGuid();
        private Guid _lockToken = Guid.NewGuid();
        private FileSystemInstanceStoreIO _dataStore;

        public FileSystemInstanceStore()
        {
            _dataStore = new FileSystemInstanceStoreIO();
        }

        #region InstanceStore overrides
```

The `BeginTryCommand` is invoked to asynchronously process a persistence command. The code uses a `switch` statement to branch the processing based on the type of command that is received. The code to process each command follows a consistent pattern. The only real difference is the private method that is invoked to process each command.

To easily process the commands asynchronously, a `Func` delegate is declared that executes the correct private method. The `BeginInvoke` method of the delegate is used to begin asynchronous execution of the code that is assigned to the delegate. The `Func` delegate is declared to return an `Exception`. This is necessary in order to pass any unhandled exception from the asynchronous thread to the original thread. The callback code that is assigned to the `BeginInvoke` method first calls `EndInvoke` on the delegate. This completes the asynchronous operation. It then passes the `Exception` (if any) to the original callback that was provided as an argument to the `BeginTryCommand` method. Execution of the original callback triggers execution of the `EndTryCommand` method.

```
        protected override IAsyncResult BeginTryCommand(
            InstancePersistenceContext context,
            InstancePersistenceCommand command,
            TimeSpan timeout, AsyncCallback callback, object state)
        {
        Console.WriteLine("BeginTryCommand: {0}", command.GetType().Name);

        switch (command.GetType().Name)
        {
            case "CreateWorkflowOwnerCommand":
```

```
    Func<Exception> createFunc = () =>
    {
        return ProcessCreateWorkflowOwner(context,
            command as CreateWorkflowOwnerCommand);
    };

    return createFunc.BeginInvoke((ar) =>
        {
            Exception ex = createFunc.EndInvoke(ar);
            callback(new InstanceStoreAsyncResult(ar, ex));
        }, state);

case "LoadWorkflowCommand":
    Func<Exception> loadFunc = () =>
    {
        return ProcessLoadWorkflow(context,
            command as LoadWorkflowCommand);
    };

    return loadFunc.BeginInvoke((ar) =>
        {
            Exception ex = loadFunc.EndInvoke(ar);
            callback(new InstanceStoreAsyncResult(ar, ex));
        }, state);

case "LoadWorkflowByInstanceKeyCommand":
    Func<Exception> loadByKeyFunc = () =>
    {
        return ProcessLoadWorkflowByInstanceKey(context,
            command as LoadWorkflowByInstanceKeyCommand);
    };

    return loadByKeyFunc.BeginInvoke((ar) =>
        {
            Exception ex = loadByKeyFunc.EndInvoke(ar);
            callback(new InstanceStoreAsyncResult(ar, ex));
        }, state);

case "SaveWorkflowCommand":
    Func<Exception> saveFunc = () =>
    {
        return ProcessSaveWorkflow(context,
            command as SaveWorkflowCommand);
    };

    return saveFunc.BeginInvoke((ar) =>
        {
            Exception ex = saveFunc.EndInvoke(ar);
            callback(new InstanceStoreAsyncResult(ar, ex));
        }, state);

default:
```

```
        return base.BeginTryCommand(
            context, command, timeout, callback, state);
    }
}
```

The `EndTryCommand` method is paired with the execution of the `BeginTryCommand` method. Execution of this method is triggered by invoking the original callback argument that was passed to the `BeginTryCommand`.

A private `InstanceStoreAsyncResult` class is passed to this method by the `Func` delegate callback code. This private class was needed to pass the unhandled exception (if any) along the standard `IAsyncResult` properties. If an `Exception` was passed, it is rethrown here in order to throw it on the correct thread.

```
protected override bool EndTryCommand(IAsyncResult ar)
{
    if (ar is InstanceStoreAsyncResult)
    {
        Exception exception = ((InstanceStoreAsyncResult)ar).Exception;
        if (exception != null)
        {
            throw exception;
        }
    }

    return true;
}
```

The `TryCommand` method defers execution of the command to the `BeginTryCommand`. Since `BeginTryCommand` executes the command asynchronously, `TryCommand` has to wait for the command to complete before returning.

```
protected override bool TryCommand(
    InstancePersistenceContext context,
    InstancePersistenceCommand command, TimeSpan timeout)
{
    ManualResetEvent waitEvent = new ManualResetEvent(false);
    IAsyncResult asyncResult = BeginTryCommand(
        context, command, timeout, (ar) =>
    {
        waitEvent.Set();
    }, null);

    waitEvent.WaitOne(timeout);
    return EndTryCommand(asyncResult);
}

#endregion

#region Command processing
```

The `ProcessCreateWorkflowOwner` command is executed to associate a host application as an instance owner. The `BindInstanceOwner` method of the context is executed to satisfy the requirements of this command.

```
private Exception ProcessCreateWorkflowOwner(
    InstancePersistenceContext context,
    CreateWorkflowOwnerCommand command)
{
    try
    {
        context.BindInstanceOwner(_ownerId, _lockToken);
        return null;
    }
    catch (InstancePersistenceException exception)
    {
        Console.WriteLine(
            "ProcessCreateWorkflowOwner exception: {0}",
            exception.Message);
        return exception;
    }
}
```

The `ProcessLoadWorkflow` method is invoked to load a workflow instance when a `LoadWorkflowCommand` is received. This command may be sent to load an existing workflow instance that was previously persisted or to initialize a new instance.

If an existing instance is to be loaded, the instance ID to load is obtained from the `InstanceView.InstanceId` property of the context. This value, along with the context, is passed to a private `SharedLoadWorkflow` method.

```
private Exception ProcessLoadWorkflow(
    InstancePersistenceContext context,
    LoadWorkflowCommand command)
{
    try
    {
        if (command.AcceptUninitializedInstance)
        {
            context.LoadedInstance(InstanceState.Uninitialized,
                null, null, null, null);
        }
        else
        {
            SharedLoadWorkflow(context, context.InstanceView.InstanceId);
        }
        return null;
    }
    catch (InstancePersistenceException exception)
    {
        Console.WriteLine(
            "ProcessLoadWorkflow exception: {0}",
            exception.Message);
```

```
        return exception;
    }
}
```

The `ProcessLoadWorkflowByInstanceKey` method is invoked in response to the receipt of a `LoadWorkflowByInstanceKeyCommand`. This command is used to retrieve an existing workflow instance based on an instance key. This is not the workflow instance ID. It is a correlation key that must be used to look up the actual workflow instance ID. A single workflow instance may have multiple instance keys.

```
private Exception ProcessLoadWorkflowByInstanceKey(
    InstancePersistenceContext context,
    LoadWorkflowByInstanceKeyCommand command)
{
    try
    {
        Guid instanceId = _dataStore.GetInstanceAssociation(
            command.LookupInstanceKey);
        if (instanceId == Guid.Empty)
        {
            throw new InstanceKeyNotReadyException(
                String.Format("Unable to load instance for key: {0}",
                    command.LookupInstanceKey));
        }
        SharedLoadWorkflow(context, instanceId);
        return null;
    }
    catch (InstancePersistenceException exception)
    {
        Console.WriteLine(
            "ProcessLoadWorkflowByInstanceKey exception: {0}",
            exception.Message);
        return exception;
    }
}
```

The `SharedLoadWorkflow` method is common code that is executed by the `ProcessLoadWorkflow` and `ProcessLoadWorkflowByInstanceKey` methods. It loads the instance and instance metadata for the workflow instance. After loading the data, the `LoadedInstance` method of the context is invoked to provide this data to the persistence API.

```
private void SharedLoadWorkflow(InstancePersistenceContext context,
    Guid instanceId)
{
    if (instanceId != Guid.Empty)
    {
        IDictionary<XName, InstanceValue> instanceData = null;
        IDictionary<XName, InstanceValue> instanceMetadata = null;
        _dataStore.LoadInstance(instanceId,
            out instanceData, out instanceMetadata);
```

```
        if (context.InstanceView.InstanceId == Guid.Empty)
        {
            context.BindInstance(instanceId);
        }
        context.LoadedInstance(InstanceState.Initialized,
            instanceData, instanceMetadata, null, null);
    }
    else
    {
        throw new InstanceNotReadyException(
            String.Format("Unable to load instance: {0}", instanceId));
    }
}
```

The `ProcessSaveWorkflow` is invoked to persist a workflow instance. It has a number of tasks that it must complete. First, if the `CompleteInstance` property of the command is true, it means that the command is signaling the completion of the workflow instance. This means that the data that was previously persisted can be deleted. Second, if instance data or instance metadata is available, it is persisted. Finally, if there are any instance keys to associate with the instance, they are persisted. The instance keys are correlation keys that are later used to retrieve the correct workflow instance.

```
private Exception ProcessSaveWorkflow(
    InstancePersistenceContext context,
    SaveWorkflowCommand command)
{
    try
    {
        if (command.CompleteInstance)
        {
            _dataStore.DeleteInstance(
                context.InstanceView.InstanceId);
            _dataStore.DeleteInstanceAssociation(
                context.InstanceView.InstanceId);
            return null;
        }

        if (command.InstanceData.Count > 0 ||
            command.InstanceMetadataChanges.Count > 0)
        {
            if (!_dataStore.SaveAllInstanceData(
                context.InstanceView.InstanceId, command))
            {
                _dataStore.SaveAllInstanceMetaData(
                    context.InstanceView.InstanceId, command);
            }
        }
```

```
            if (command.InstanceKeysToAssociate.Count > 0)
            {
                foreach (var entry in command.InstanceKeysToAssociate)
                {
                    _dataStore.SaveInstanceAssociation(
                        context.InstanceView.InstanceId, entry.Key, false);
                }
            }
            return null;
        }
        catch (InstancePersistenceException exception)
        {
            Console.WriteLine(
                "ProcessSaveWorkflow exception: {0}", exception.Message);
            return exception;
        }
    }

    #endregion

    #region Private types

    private class InstanceStoreAsyncResult : IAsyncResult
    {
        public InstanceStoreAsyncResult(
            IAsyncResult ar, Exception exception)
        {
            AsyncWaitHandle = ar.AsyncWaitHandle;
            AsyncState = ar.AsyncState;
            IsCompleted = true;
            Exception = exception;
        }

        public bool IsCompleted { get; private set; }
        public Object AsyncState { get; private set; }
        public WaitHandle AsyncWaitHandle { get; private set; }
        public bool CompletedSynchronously { get; private set; }
        public Exception Exception { get; private set; }
    }

    #endregion
    }
}
```

Implementing the FileSystemInstanceStoreIO Class

Add another class to the `ActivityLibrary` project, and name it `FileSystemInstanceStoreIO`. This class is referenced by the `FileSystemInstanceStore` class and implements the logic to persist workflow instances to the file system. Here is the code for this class:

```
using System;
using System.Activities.DurableInstancing;
using System.Collections.Generic;
using System.IO;
using System.Linq;
using System.Runtime.DurableInstancing;
using System.Runtime.Serialization;
using System.Text;
using System.Xml;
using System.Xml.Linq;

namespace ActivityLibrary
{
    internal class FileSystemInstanceStoreIO
    {
        private String _dataDirectory = String.Empty;

        public FileSystemInstanceStoreIO()
        {
            CreateDataDirectory();
        }

        #region Save Methods
```

The SaveAllInstanceData method is designed to persist the instance data of a workflow instance.
The instance data can be found in the InstanceData property of the SaveWorkflowCommand that is passed
to this method. This property is a collection of named elements that are individually serialized by calling
the private SaveSingleEntry method. All of this instance data is saved to a single XML file that uses the
workflow instance ID Guid as the file name.

```
        public Boolean SaveAllInstanceData(Guid instanceId,
            SaveWorkflowCommand command)
        {
            Boolean isExistingInstance = false;
            try
            {
                String fileName = String.Format("{0}.xml", instanceId);
                String fullPath = Path.Combine(_dataDirectory, fileName);
                isExistingInstance = File.Exists(fullPath);

                XElement root = new XElement("Instance");
                root.Add(new XAttribute("InstanceId", instanceId));
                XDocument xml = new XDocument(root);

                NetDataContractSerializer serializer =
                    new NetDataContractSerializer();
```

```
            XElement section = new XElement("InstanceData");
            root.Add(section);
            foreach (var entry in command.InstanceData)
            {
                SaveSingleEntry(serializer, section, entry);
            }
            SaveInstanceDocument(fullPath, xml);
        }
        catch (IOException exception)
        {
            Console.WriteLine(
                "SaveAllInstanceData Exception: {0}", exception.Message);
            throw exception;
        }
        return isExistingInstance;
    }
```

The `SaveAllInstanceMetaData` method is similar to the `SaveAllInstanceData` method just above this. The difference is that this method saves workflow instance metadata rather than the instance data. The metadata includes elements such as the workflow type that are needed by the infrastructure.

The metadata is saved to a separate file from the instance data. This separate file is necessary because of the differences in the way instance data and metadata are saved. Each time instance data is saved, it is a complete replacement of the previously saved instance data. However, metadata is made available as changes instead of a complete replacement. Each time metadata changes are available to be saved, they should be merged with any previously saved metadata.

However, this custom instance store takes a few shortcuts and saves the metadata only the first time a workflow instance is saved. No subsequent changes to metadata are actually saved. This is sufficient to produce a working instance store since no metadata changes actually occur in these examples. Saving the metadata to a separate file allows this code to completely replace the instance data without the need to merge previously saved metadata.

```
        public void SaveAllInstanceMetaData(Guid instanceId,
            SaveWorkflowCommand command)
        {
            try
            {
                String fileName = String.Format("{0}.meta.xml", instanceId);
                String fullPath = Path.Combine(_dataDirectory, fileName);

                XElement root = new XElement("Instance");
                root.Add(new XAttribute("InstanceId", instanceId));
                XDocument xml = new XDocument(root);

                NetDataContractSerializer serializer =
                    new NetDataContractSerializer();
```

```
            XElement section = new XElement("InstanceMetadata");
            root.Add(section);
            foreach (var entry in command.InstanceMetadataChanges)
            {
                SaveSingleEntry(serializer, section, entry);
            }
            SaveInstanceDocument(fullPath, xml);
        }
        catch (IOException exception)
        {
            Console.WriteLine(
                "SaveAllMetaData Exception: {0}", exception.Message);
            throw exception;
        }
    }
```

The SaveSingleEntry method serializes an individual data element. This shared code is invoked when instance data and metadata are saved. Each data element is represented by an InstanceValue object along with a fully qualified name. The InstanceValue class includes an Options property that is serialized along with the key and the actual data.

```
    private void SaveSingleEntry(NetDataContractSerializer serializer,
        XElement section, KeyValuePair<XName, InstanceValue> entry)
    {
        if (entry.Value.IsDeletedValue)
        {
            return;
        }

        XElement entryElement = new XElement("Entry");
        section.Add(entryElement);
        Serialize(serializer, entryElement, "Key", entry.Key);
        Serialize(serializer, entryElement, "Value", entry.Value.Value);
        Serialize(serializer, entryElement, "Options", entry.Value.Options);
    }
```

The SaveInstanceDocument method physically writes a completed XML document to a file.

```
    private static void SaveInstanceDocument(String fullPath, XDocument xml)
    {
        using (FileStream stream =
            new FileStream(fullPath, FileMode.Create))
        {
            XmlWriterSettings settings = new XmlWriterSettings();
            settings.Encoding = Encoding.UTF8;
```

```
                using (XmlWriter writer = XmlWriter.Create(stream, settings))
                {
                    writer.WriteRaw(xml.ToString());
                }
            }
        }
```

```
#endregion
```

```
#region Load Methods
```

The `LoadInstance` method retrieves and deserializes a workflow instance. The instance data and metadata for the workflow instance are both retrieved. This method invokes the `LoadSingleEntry` method to deserialize each individual data element.

```
public Boolean LoadInstance(Guid instanceId,
    out IDictionary<XName, InstanceValue> instanceData,
    out IDictionary<XName, InstanceValue> instanceMetadata)
{
    Boolean result = false;
    try
    {
        instanceData = new Dictionary<XName, InstanceValue>();
        instanceMetadata = new Dictionary<XName, InstanceValue>();

        String fileName = String.Format("{0}.xml", instanceId);
        String fullPath = Path.Combine(_dataDirectory, fileName);
        if (!File.Exists(fullPath))
        {
            return result;
        }

        NetDataContractSerializer serializer =
            new NetDataContractSerializer();

        //load instance data
        XElement xml = XElement.Load(fullPath);
        var entries =
            (from e in xml.Element("InstanceData").Elements("Entry")
             select e).ToList();
        foreach (XElement entry in entries)
        {
            LoadSingleEntry(serializer, instanceData, entry);
        }
```

```
            //load instance metadata
            fileName = String.Format("{0}.meta.xml", instanceId);
            fullPath = Path.Combine(_dataDirectory, fileName);
            xml = XElement.Load(fullPath);
            entries =
                (from e in xml.Element(
                     "InstanceMetadata").Elements("Entry")
                  select e).ToList();
            foreach (XElement entry in entries)
            {
                LoadSingleEntry(serializer, instanceMetadata, entry);
            }

            result = true;
        }
        catch (IOException exception)
        {
            Console.WriteLine(
                "LoadInstance Exception: {0}", exception.Message);
            throw exception;
        }
        return result;
    }
```

The LoadSingleEntry method deserializes a single data element. It is used to deserialize instance data and metadata elements. Notice that the InstanceValue options that were previously persisted with the data element are checked in this method. If the value of the option indicates that the data is WriteOnly, it is not loaded. Data that is flagged with the WriteOnly option should be persisted but not loaded.

```
    private void LoadSingleEntry(NetDataContractSerializer serializer,
        IDictionary<XName, InstanceValue> instanceData, XElement entry)
    {
        XName key =
            (XName)Deserialize(serializer, entry.Element("Key"));
        Object value =
            Deserialize(serializer, entry.Element("Value"));
        InstanceValue iv = new InstanceValue(value);
        InstanceValueOptions options =
            (InstanceValueOptions)Deserialize(
                serializer, entry.Element("Options"));
        if (!options.HasFlag(InstanceValueOptions.WriteOnly))
        {
            instanceData.Add(key, iv);
        }
    }

    #endregion

    #region Delete Methods
```

The DeleteInstance method is used to remove the instance and metadata files for an instance. It is invoked when a workflow instance is completed and can be removed from the file system.

```
public void DeleteInstance(Guid instanceId)
{
    String fileName = String.Format("{0}.xml", instanceId);
    String fullPath = Path.Combine(_dataDirectory, fileName);
    if (File.Exists(fullPath))
    {
        File.Delete(fullPath);
    }

    fileName = String.Format("{0}.meta.xml", instanceId);
    fullPath = Path.Combine(_dataDirectory, fileName);
    if (File.Exists(fullPath))
    {
        File.Delete(fullPath);
    }
}

#endregion

#region Association Methods
```

The SaveInstanceAssociation method saves a file that associates an instance key with an instance ID. The instance key represents a correlation key that is later used to look up the correct workflow instance ID. The association between the key and the instance ID is maintained by the file name itself. The first node of the name is the instance key, and the second node is the instance ID. This mechanism may be simple, but it does support multiple instance keys for an instance ID.

```
public void SaveInstanceAssociation(Guid instanceId,
    Guid instanceKeyToAssociate, Boolean isDelete)
{
    try
    {
        String fileName = String.Format("Key.{0}.{1}.xml",
            instanceKeyToAssociate, instanceId);
        String fullPath = Path.Combine(_dataDirectory, fileName);
        if (!isDelete)
        {
            if (!File.Exists(fullPath))
            {
                File.Create(fullPath);
            }
        }
        else
        {
```

```
                if (File.Exists(fullPath))
                {
                    File.Delete(fullPath);
                }
            }
        }
        catch (IOException exception)
        {
            Console.WriteLine(
                "PersistInstanceAssociation Exception: {0}",
                exception.Message);
            throw exception;
        }
    }
```

The `GetInstanceAssociation` method retrieves an instance ID based on an instance key that was provided. It does this by finding any files with the requested instance key and parsing the file name to determine the instance ID.

```
    public Guid GetInstanceAssociation(Guid instanceKey)
    {
        Guid instanceId = Guid.Empty;
        try
        {
            String[] files = Directory.GetFiles(_dataDirectory,
                String.Format("Key.{0}.*.xml", instanceKey));
            if (files != null && files.Length > 0)
            {
                String[] nodes = files[0].Split('.');
                if (nodes.Length == 4)
                {
                    instanceId = Guid.Parse(nodes[2]);
                }
            }
        }
        catch (IOException exception)
        {
            Console.WriteLine(
                "GetInstanceAssociation Exception: {0}",
                exception.Message);
            throw exception;
        }
        return instanceId;
    }
```

The `DeleteInstanceAssociation` method removes a specific instance key. This method is invoked when a workflow instance is completed.

```csharp
public void DeleteInstanceAssociation(Guid instanceKey)
{
    try
    {
        String[] files = Directory.GetFiles(_dataDirectory,
            String.Format("Key.*.{0}.xml", instanceKey));
        if (files != null && files.Length > 0)
        {
            foreach (String file in files)
            {
                File.Delete(file);
            }
        }
    }
    catch (IOException exception)
    {
        Console.WriteLine(
            "DeleteInstanceAssociation Exception: {0}",
            exception.Message);
        throw exception;
    }
}

#endregion

#region Private methods

private void CreateDataDirectory()
{
    _dataDirectory = Path.Combine(
        Environment.CurrentDirectory, "InstanceStore");
    if (!Directory.Exists(_dataDirectory))
    {
        Directory.CreateDirectory(_dataDirectory);
    }
}

private XElement Serialize(NetDataContractSerializer serializer,
    XElement parent, String name, Object value)
{
    XElement element = new XElement(name);
    using (MemoryStream stream = new MemoryStream())
    {
        serializer.Serialize(stream, value);
        stream.Position = 0;
        using (StreamReader reader = new StreamReader(stream))
        {
            element.Add(XElement.Load(stream));
        }
    }
```

```
            parent.Add(element);
            return element;
        }

        private Object Deserialize(NetDataContractSerializer serializer,
            XElement element)
        {
            Object result = null;
            using (MemoryStream stream = new MemoryStream())
            {
                using (XmlDictionaryWriter writer =
                    XmlDictionaryWriter.CreateTextWriter(stream))
                {
                    foreach (XNode node in element.Nodes())
                    {
                        node.WriteTo(writer);
                    }

                    writer.Flush();
                    stream.Position = 0;
                    result = serializer.Deserialize(stream);
                }
            }
            return result;
        }

        #endregion
    }
}
```

You should rebuild the solution at this point to verify that all the code for the custom instance store builds correctly.

Modifying the ServiceHost Project

To test the new instance store, you can modify the ServiceHost project to load it instead of the SqlWorkflowInstanceStoreBehavior. You need to completely replace the existing CreateServiceHost method with a new implementation that uses the custom instance store instead of the SqlWorkflowInstanceStore. If you like, you can make a copy of the method under a different method name before you completely replace it. This allows you to later swap back to using the SqlWorkflowInstanceStore. Here are the changes that you need to make to the Program.cs file of the ServiceHost project:

```
namespace ServiceHost
{
    class Program
    {
...
        private static WorkflowServiceHost CreateServiceHost(
            String xamlxName, IItemSupport extension)
        {
            WorkflowService wfService = LoadService(xamlxName);
            WorkflowServiceHost host = new WorkflowServiceHost(wfService);

            InstanceStore store = new FileSystemInstanceStore();
            host.DurableInstancingOptions.InstanceStore = store;

            WorkflowIdleBehavior idleBehavior = new WorkflowIdleBehavior()
            {
                TimeToUnload = TimeSpan.FromSeconds(0)
            };
            host.Description.Behaviors.Add(idleBehavior);

            if (extension != null)
            {
                host.WorkflowExtensions.Add(extension);
            }

            _hosts.Add(host);

            return host;
        }
...
    }
}
```

Testing the Custom Instance Store

You can now rebuild the solution and run the ServiceHost and OrderEntryConsoleClient projects to test the new instance store. The observable results that you see from the client application should be consistent with your previous tests that used the SqlWorkflowInstanceStoreBehavior. Here is a representative set of results from the client application:

```
Commands: start | add | complete | query | cancel | exit

start

Enter an OrderId (int) for the order

1
```

New order 1 started

Commands: start | add | complete | query | cancel | exit

add

Enter ItemId and Quantity (Ex: 101 1)

101 1

Ordered 1 of ItemId 101 for OrderId 1

Commands: start | add | complete | query | cancel | exit

add

Enter ItemId and Quantity (Ex: 101 1)

202 2

Ordered 2 of ItemId 202 for OrderId 1

Commands: start | add | complete | query | cancel | exit

complete

Order 1 Is Completed

Ordered Items:

ItemId=101, Quantity=1, UnitPrice=1.23, Total=1.23

ItemId=202, Quantity=2, UnitPrice=2.34, Total=4.68

Commands: start | add | complete | query | cancel | exit

And here are the results from the **ServiceHost** using the new instance store:

```
Item inventory Before Execution:

ItemId=101, QtyAvailable=10

ItemId=202, QtyAvailable=20

ItemId=303, QtyAvailable=30


BeginTryCommand: CreateWorkflowOwnerCommand

Contract: IOrderEntry

    at http://localhost:9000/OrderEntry

Contract: IWorkflowInstanceManagement

    at http://localhost:9000/OrderEntryControl

Press any key to stop hosting and exit

BeginTryCommand: LoadWorkflowCommand

BeginTryCommand: SaveWorkflowCommand

BeginTryCommand: SaveWorkflowCommand

BeginTryCommand: LoadWorkflowByInstanceKeyCommand

Update: ItemId=101, QtyBefore=10, QtyAfter=9

BeginTryCommand: SaveWorkflowCommand

BeginTryCommand: LoadWorkflowByInstanceKeyCommand

Update: ItemId=202, QtyBefore=20, QtyAfter=18

BeginTryCommand: SaveWorkflowCommand

BeginTryCommand: LoadWorkflowByInstanceKeyCommand

BeginTryCommand: SaveWorkflowCommand
```

```
Item inventory After Execution:

ItemId=101, QtyAvailable=9

ItemId=202, QtyAvailable=18

ItemId=303, QtyAvailable=30


Closing services...

BeginTryCommand: DeleteWorkflowOwnerCommand

Services closed
```

The XML files that are maintained by the instance store are saved to the `\bin\debug\InstanceStore` folder under the `ServiceHost` project. This assumes that you are building and running a debug version of the project. If you take a look in this folder before you complete an order, you should see files similar to these:

```
4db8abc8-b7f6-40b4-910c-12e2970d1551.xml

4db8abc8-b7f6-40b4-910c-12e2970d1551.meta.xml

Key.07f41faa-52f0-ce5f-8f26-85b7e0299515.4db8abc8-b7f6-40b4-910c-12e2970d1551.xml
```

The first file is the instance data, the second is the metadata, and the third file is the association file for a correlation key. Once you complete an order, the custom instance store deletes these files.

Summary

The focus of this chapter was extending and customizing workflow persistence. The chapter built upon the examples that were first presented in Chapter 11.

The chapter included coverage of mechanisms to extend the standard SQL Server persistence that is supported by WF. Included was an example that used the `PersistenceParticipant` class to persist additional data when an instance was persisted. The ability to promote selected properties in order to make them externally queryable was also demonstrated.

Although it is not directly related to the topic of persistence, use of the `WorkflowControlEndpoint` was demonstrated. This endpoint supports the management of active workflow instances.

The chapter concluded with the implementation of a custom instance store. This instance store uses the file system for persistence rather than a database.

In the next chapter, you will learn how WF implements transaction support, compensation, and error handling.

CHAPTER 13

Transactions, Compensation, and Exception Handling

This chapter focuses on the mechanisms provided by Windows Workflow Foundation (WF) to support the handling of exceptions and to ensure the consistency of work that is performed within a workflow.

The chapter begins with an overview of the default exception handling logic. Following that introduction, a preliminary example is developed that is used to illustrate the concepts throughout the chapter. Enhancements to the example workflow include using the `TryCatch` activity to handle exceptions, using the `TransactionScope` activity to provide transaction support, and using the `CompensableActivity` to execute compensation logic.

Understanding Default Exception Handling

WF builds upon the standard exception handling provided for all .NET applications. Within any C# code, for example within a custom activity or workflow extension, exceptions can be handled in the normal way using a `try`/`catch` code block. If the exception is handled within the code, no further action within the WF runtime environment is necessary.

However, your C# code can elect to not handle an exception, allowing it to bubble up to a higher level in the call stack until either it is handled or it reaches the top of the call stack. WF provides the `TryCatch` activity (discussed later in this chapter), which allows you to declaratively handle the exception within the workflow model. If the exception reaches the top of the activity call stack without being handled, it is an unhandled exception.

In a normal C# application, an unhandled exception usually causes the application to terminate. In a WF application, an unhandled exception causes the workflow to terminate, but this does not necessarily cause the entire application to terminate. It depends on how you are hosting the workflow.

If you are using the `WorkflowInvoker` class to execute a workflow, the unhandled exception will reach the host application where it is either handled or not. If you don't handle it with a `try`/`catch` block of code in the host application, then the application will terminate. This makes sense since the `WorkflowInvoker` class is used to execute a workflow just like an ordinary C# method.

If you are using the `WorkflowApplication` class to execute a workflow, the unhandled exception is handled internally by the workflow runtime. By default, the workflow instance will terminate, but it won't take down the entire application.

The `WorkflowApplication` class provides the `OnUnhandledException` member that allows you to be notified when an unhandled exception occurs. This member is defined as a `Func<`

WorkflowApplicationUnhandledExceptionEventArgs, UnhandledExceptionAction>, so the code that is assigned to this member is expected to return an UnhandledExceptionAction value. The UnhandledExceptionAction value determines how the unhandled exception is handled. These are the possible values for UnhandledExceptionAction:

- **Terminate**. The root activity of the workflow is scheduled for termination, and then the workflow is resumed. This is the default action if you don't assign a handler for the OnUnhandledException delegate. Termination moves the workflow into the Faulted state, which prevents it from being resumed or restarted.

- **Cancel**. The root activity is scheduled for cancellation, and then the workflow is resumed. This option allows the workflow to gracefully transition to the Canceled state.

- **Abort**. The workflow is immediately aborted. No additional execution is scheduled.

If you return Terminate or Cancel, any code assigned to the WorkflowApplication.Complete delegate is executed when the workflow instance has completed. If Abort is returned, any code assigned to the Aborted delegate is executed.

■ **Note** Chapter 10 covers exception handling when you are using the WorkflowServiceHost class.

Implementing the Example Workflow

The first example in this chapter is designed to demonstrate the default processing for an unhandled exception. The remaining examples in this chapter will be variations of the same workflow, each one modified slightly to demonstrate a different aspect of exception handling, transactions, or compensation. But regardless of the actual implementation, the example scenario that you will model is the same: applying updates to product inventory.

The example workflows reference tables in the AdventureWorks SQL Server sample database. This database was chosen because it presents a fairly representative example of a SQL Server database and it is readily available for download from Microsoft. Using an existing database eliminates the need to create the database schema and populate it with sample data before it can be used.

The inventory update scenario that you will implement is fairly simple. The workflow will be passed an integer sales order ID, which identifies the single order to be processed. Any rows in the SalesOrderDetail table that match the specified sales order ID are retrieved. Each row in this table contains the quantity sold for an individual product in the order. These rows are used to drive updates to the ProductInventory table. Each row in this table represents the current inventory for a product at a given location. The current quantity in inventory for the product is reduced by the quantity of each SalesOrderDetail row. A new row is also added to the TransactionHistory table for each product being processed for the order.

It should be noted that this process could be executed for all rows in the SalesOrderDetail table. But the results from such a large update would be difficult to validate. It is much easier to validate the results when only a single sales order ID is processed.

The ultimate goal is to apply all updates to the database as a single atomic unit of work. If the ProductInventory table is updated, the inserts to the TransactionHistory table must also occur. If an exception occurs during the processing, any updates that have already been applied should be rolled back. To enforce consistency of the database updates, a `TransactionScope` activity will be introduced later in the chapter.

To add a wrinkle to the process, this contrived scenario calls for an external system to also be notified when each product is processed. This notification might be a Windows Communication Foundation (WCF) message to the warehouse to ship the product, an e-mail to a sales representative, or a low-level socket call to a legacy billing system. Regardless of the real purpose of the external system or the mechanism used to communicate, the examples in this chapter will use a simple custom activity to simulate this external system notification. This is sufficient to demonstrate the problem when external systems are included in the process. The problem that arises is that external systems also need to be notified when a problem occurs. And the notification to an external system typically can't participate in a database transaction. This is where compensation comes to the rescue. The `CompensableActivity` will be introduced later in the chapter to solve this issue.

■ **Note** The examples in this chapter are designed to demonstrate the exception handling, transaction, and compensation mechanisms provided with WF. The `AdventureWorks` database is used as a convenience because it is a readily available source of test data. No attempt has been made to accurately reproduce the business functionality of the sample Adventure Works application.

Before you begin the development of this first example, you'll need to download and install the `AdventureWorks` sample database. Please refer to the "Preparing the AdventureWorks Sample Database" sidebar in this chapter for instructions.

You will complete these tasks to implement this example:

1. Generate LINQ to SQL classes for the `AdventureWorks` database.

2. Implement the `GetOrderDetail` activity to retrieve `SalesOrderDetail` rows from the database.

3. Implement the `UpdateProductInventory` activity to update the `ProductInventory` table.

4. Implement the `InsertTransactionHistory` activity to insert rows into the `TransactionHistory` table.

5. Implement the `ExternalUpdate` activity to simulate the notification to an external system for an order.

6. Implement the `DisplayProductInventory` activity to display the current state of selected rows in the database.

7. Declare the `UpdateInventory` workflow.

8. Declare the `DisplayInventory` workflow.

9. Host the workflows in a console application.

Preparing the AdventureWorks Sample Database

The AdventureWorks database is a sample that is freely available from Microsoft for download. It contains a sample schema along with data for a fictitious bicycle manufacturer. Microsoft provides several versions of this database for download. Even though I used SQL Server 2008 Express during the development of this book, I used the older version of the AdventureWorks database that was originally designed for SQL Server 2005. I used the older version simply because it requires a much smaller set of SQL Server software to use it.

The SQL Server 2008 version of the database requires that you first install the version of SQL Server with Advanced Services. The Advanced Services version installs the full-text search capabilities of SQL Server that are required by the 2008 version of the database. Because none of my examples requires the full-text search capabilities, I decided to use the older 2005 version, which is still available. If you decide to use the 2008 version of AdventureWorks, be aware that it also comes in two flavors. There is one version that is backwardly compatible with the 2005 version and another version that includes 2008-only features. The version that is backwardly compatible with the 2005 version is the one that you need to run the examples in this book. The 2008-only version has breaking schema changes that may not match the schema expected by the examples in this book.

Microsoft does tend to move things around on its various web sites, so the best way to locate a copy of the database is to search for *Microsoft SQL Server AdventureWorks* using your favorite search engine. That should point you to the official Microsoft site where the downloads are located.

Once downloaded, you can follow the current instructions to install the database on your development machine or server. These are the general steps to prepare the database:

1. Download the AdventureWorks sample database.

2. Run the MSI that installs the database into its own `\program files\` folder.

3. Use SQL Server Management Studio Express (included with SQL Server 2008 Express) to attach the AdventureWorks database to your SQL Server instance.

Once installed, you should be able to proceed with the implementation of the examples in this chapter.

Enabling LINQ Access to the AventureWorks Database

The examples in this chapter all use LINQ to SQL to access the AdventureWorks database. LINQ (Language INtegrated Query) is used for a couple of reasons. First, LINQ is a great tool for querying and updating tables in your database. Once you generate a data context for the tables that you want to reference, all operations are done in a type-safe way. No more hand-coding of SQL statements, hoping that you didn't misspell a column or parameter name. Second, the examples all need to pass a collection of rows from one activity to another using workflow variables. The LINQ data context that is generated in the following steps produces a set of strongly typed classes that are perfect for this purpose.

■ **Note** The examples in this chapter use simple LINQ statements that should be easily understood even if you have no previous exposure to LINQ. However, if these examples whet your appetite for more LINQ, I'd recommend the book Pro LINQ: Language Integrated Query in C# 2010 by Joseph C. Rattz Jr. and Adam Freeman, also published by Apress.

To begin, create a new project named AdventureWorksAccess using the C# Class Library project template. This is an ordinary class library, not a workflow-related project. Add this project to a new solution named for this chapter.

You can follow these steps to prepare the LINQ to SQL data context for the AdventureWorks database:

1. Add a new LINQ to SQL class to the project, and name it AdventureWorks.dbml. You can find the template for this new item under the Data category. After adding the file, the Design View should be shown. The designer canvas is used to add the tables that you want to use via LINQ to SQL and is initially empty.

2. From within Visual Studio, open the Server Explorer window. Right-click Data Connections, and select Add Connection.

3. Select Microsoft SQL Server as the database type and Windows Authentication for the credentials unless you've configured SQL Server to use SQL Server authentication. In that case, you'll need to provide a username and password. The server name should be the location of the server that is hosting the AdventureWorks database. In my case, I'm using a local instance of SQL Server Express, so the server name is localhost\SQLExpress. You'll need to supply a different server name if you are not using a local SQL Server instance.

4. Once the server name has been entered, select the AdventureWorks database on the server. Expand the Tables category for the database. Select and drag all of the tables to the empty designer canvas.

5. After a few relatively brief moments (depending on the speed of your machine), the canvas will redisplay with all the tables in the database.

You can now save the AdventureWorks.dbml file and build the project. You won't need to add anything else to this project. This project will be referenced by the other projects that you will create in the subsequent steps.

The process of generating the LINQ to SQL classes also adds an App.config file to the project. You will copy this file to another project in a later step.

Implementing the GetOrderDetail Activity

This example uses a series of custom activities to execute the LINQ queries and updates. Create a new project that will be used for all the custom activities in this chapter. Name the new project ActivityLibrary, and use the Activity Library template. Add this new project to the solution that you created for this chapter. Delete the Activity1.xaml file since will not be used.

Add a project reference to the AdventureWorksAccess project that you created in the previous step. You'll also need to add a .NET assembly reference to System.Data.Linq and System.Transactions.

Add a new custom activity named **GetOrderDetail** to the project using the Code Activity template. The purpose of this activity is to retrieve selected **SalesOrderDetail** rows from the database and return them as a collection that can be consumed by other activities.

This activity is implemented as an asynchronous activity using **AsyncCodeActivity** as its base class. This allows the actual LINQ query to execute on a separate background thread, freeing the primary workflow thread for other work. Although this is not a strict requirement, it is generally good practice to execute database queries and updates on a separate thread. Your workflows won't always take full advantage of the parallel processing that this enables. But implementing the custom activity to use asynchronous processing keeps your options open. It allows you to model the workflow to effectively use parallel processing in those situations where it would be beneficial.

Here is the code for the **GetOrderDetail** activity:

```
using System;
using System.Activities;
using System.Collections.Generic;
using System.Linq;
using AdventureWorksAccess;

namespace ActivityLibrary
{
    public sealed class GetOrderDetail : AsyncCodeActivity
    {
```

The **SalesOrderId** argument identifies the single sales order ID that you want to process. The **OrderDetail** output argument will contain the list of **SalesOrderDetail** rows that are retrieved. The **SalesOrderDetail** class was one of the classes that was generated when you prepared the **AdventureWorksAccess** project. This class mirrors the definition of the **SalesOrderDetail** table in the database and contains an individual property for each column in the table.

```
        public InArgument<Int32> SalesOrderId { get; set; }
        public OutArgument<List<SalesOrderDetail>> OrderDetail { get; set; }

        protected override IAsyncResult BeginExecute(
            AsyncCodeActivityContext context, AsyncCallback callback,
            object state)
        {
```

The LINQ query is executed on a separate thread using a **Func** generic delegate. The delegate is defined as requiring a single **Int32** as its only input parameter and returning a **List<SalesOrderDetail>** as the result. The target of the delegate is set to the **RetrieveOrderDetail** private method of this class. After creating an instance of the delegate, the **BeginInvoke** method is called to begin the processing on a thread pool thread. Notice that the input argument (**SalesOrderId**) is accessed here in the main workflow thread since it cannot be accessed from a worker thread.

```
            Func<Int32, List<SalesOrderDetail>> asyncWork =
                orderId => RetrieveOrderDetail(orderId);
            context.UserState = asyncWork;
            return asyncWork.BeginInvoke(
                SalesOrderId.Get(context), callback, state);
        }
```

The `EndExecute` method is invoked on the workflow thread when the asynchronous work (the `RetrieveOrderDetail` method) completes. When this occurs, the `EndInvoke` method is called on the `Func` delegate, which was passed in the `context.UserState`. The call to `EndInvoke` returns the result from the `Func` delegate, which in this case is a `List<SalesOrderDetail>`. This result value is used to set the `OrderDetail` output argument.

```
protected override void EndExecute(
    AsyncCodeActivityContext context, IAsyncResult result)
{
    List<SalesOrderDetail> orderDetail =
        ((Func<Int32, List<SalesOrderDetail>>)
            context.UserState).EndInvoke(result);
    if (orderDetail != null)
    {
        OrderDetail.Set(context, orderDetail);
    }
}
```

The `RetrieveOrderDetail` method is where the actual LINQ query is executed on a worker thread. The `AdventureWorksDataContext` was one of the classes generated in the `AdventureWorksAccess` project and provides access to the tables in the database. The LINQ query syntax is then used to retrieve the rows that match the specified `SalesOrderId`.

You might notice that the code doesn't specify a connection string for the database. The default constructor for the `AdventureWorksDataContext` class retrieves the database connection string from the `app.config` file. A sample `app.config` file containing the connection string was generated for the `AdventureWorksAccess` project. In a later step, you will copy this `app.config` to the console application that hosts the example workflow.

```
private List<SalesOrderDetail> RetrieveOrderDetail(Int32 salesOrderId)
{
    List<SalesOrderDetail> result = new List<SalesOrderDetail>();
    using (AdventureWorksDataContext dc =
        new AdventureWorksDataContext())
    {
        var salesDetail =
            (from sd in dc.SalesOrderDetails
             where sd.SalesOrderID == salesOrderId
             select sd).ToList();

        if (salesDetail != null && salesDetail.Count > 0)
        {
            result = salesDetail;
        }
    }
    return result;
}
```

Implementing the UpdateProductInventory Activity

Add a new custom activity named UpdateProductInventory to the ActivityLibrary project. This activity uses the properties from a single SalesOrderDetail row to update the ProductInventory table. Just like the GetOrderDetail activity that you just implemented, this activity is also coded to use asynchronous processing. Here is the code for this activity:

```
using System;
using System.Activities;
using System.Linq;
using System.Transactions;
using AdventureWorksAccess;

namespace ActivityLibrary
{
    public sealed class UpdateProductInventory : AsyncCodeActivity
    {
```

This activity has a single input argument containing a SalesOrderDetail object. This object represents a single row in the SalesOrderDetail table.

```
        public InArgument<SalesOrderDetail> SalesDetail { get; set; }

        protected override IAsyncResult BeginExecute(
            AsyncCodeActivityContext context,
            AsyncCallback callback, object state)
        {
```

The code to asynchronously execute the LINQ update is similar to what you have already seen in the GetOrderDetail activity. One major difference is that this code creates a DependentTransaction. Although this initial example doesn't use a transaction, subsequent examples do, so it's easier to implement the code to properly handle the transaction now rather than to revisit it later.

If you implemented this activity using the CodeActivity class and executed the LINQ update on the workflow thread, you wouldn't need to create a DependentTransaction. In fact, the next activity that you'll implement is implemented this way so you can see the contrast between the two coding styles.

In this activity, the DependentTransaction is needed because ambient transactions do not automatically flow to worker threads. If an ambient transaction exists (Transaction.Current is not null), the DependentClone method is called to create a DependentTransaction. The BlockCommitUntilComplete option is used when creating the DependentTransaction. This option causes the original transaction to block during commit processing until the DependentTransaction has signaled that its work is complete. This allows the worker thread to coordinate its work with the original thread.

The DependentTransaction that is created is passed to the private UpdateInventory method along with the SalesOrderDetail object.

```
            DependentTransaction dependentTran = null;
            if (Transaction.Current != null)
            {
                dependentTran = Transaction.Current.DependentClone(
                    DependentCloneOption.BlockCommitUntilComplete);
            }
```

```
    Action<DependentTransaction, SalesOrderDetail> asyncWork =
        (dt, sale) => UpdateInventory(dt, sale);
    context.UserState = asyncWork;
    return asyncWork.BeginInvoke(
        dependentTran, SalesDetail.Get(context), callback, state);
}

protected override void EndExecute(
    AsyncCodeActivityContext context, IAsyncResult result)
{
    ((Action<DependentTransaction, SalesOrderDetail>)
        context.UserState).EndInvoke(result);
}

private void UpdateInventory(DependentTransaction dt,
    SalesOrderDetail salesDetail)
{
    try
    {
        using (AdventureWorksDataContext dc =
            new AdventureWorksDataContext())
        {
```

The UpdateInventory method is invoked on the worker thread. A TransactionScope is created using the DependentTransaction (if it exists). Remember that a DependentTransaction is created in the previous code only if an ambient transaction already exists. If it doesn't, a null value is passed to this method, and a new TransactionScope is created using the Suppress option. This suppresses creation of a transaction and allows this activity to be used with or without a transaction.

```
            //use the dependent transaction if there is one,
            //or suppress the creation of a new transaction
            using (TransactionScope scope = (dt != null ?
                new TransactionScope(dt) :
                new TransactionScope(TransactionScopeOption.Suppress)))
            {
```

The existing ProductInventory row is retrieved. If the row exists, the Quantity and ModifiedDate properties are updated. The call to SubmitChanges is the signal for LINQ to submit all changes to the database. Following this call, the local TransactionScope is completed, indicating that any changes should be committed to the database. But since the local TransactionScope is using the DependentTransaction (or no transaction at all), the actual commit is deferred until the original transaction is committed.

```
                var inventoryRow =
                    (from pi in dc.ProductInventories
                     where pi.ProductID == salesDetail.ProductID
                        && pi.LocationID == 7 //finished goods storage
                     select pi).SingleOrDefault();
```

```
                    if (inventoryRow != null)
                    {
                        inventoryRow.Quantity -= salesDetail.OrderQty;
                        inventoryRow.ModifiedDate = DateTime.Now;
                        Console.WriteLine(
                            "Product {0}: Reduced by {1}",
                            inventoryRow.ProductID, salesDetail.OrderQty);
                        dc.SubmitChanges();
                    }

                    scope.Complete();
                }
            }
        }
        finally
        {
```

Regardless of the success or failure of the LINQ operation, the `DependentTransaction` must be marked as complete. This is the signal to the original transaction that this worker thread has completed its work using the `DependentTransaction`. If this isn't done, the original transaction will block its thread when it is committed.

```
            //the DependentTransaction must be completed otherwise
            //the ambient transaction will block on complete
            if (dt != null)
            {
                dt.Complete();
                dt.Dispose();
            }
        }
    }
  }
}
```

Implementing the InsertTranHistory Activity

Add another custom activity to the `ActivityLibrary` project using the Code Activity template. Name this activity `InsertTranHistory`. Its purpose is to insert a row into the `TransactionHistory` table for each product that is processed.

Unlike the two previous activities, this one is implemented using the synchronous `CodeActivity` as the base class. This was done to illustrate the differences in the code between the asynchronous and synchronous activities that update the database.

Here is the complete code for this activity:

```
using System;
using System.Activities;
using System.Linq;
using AdventureWorksAccess;
using System.Transactions;
```

```
namespace ActivityLibrary
{
    public sealed class InsertTranHistory : CodeActivity
    {
        public InArgument<SalesOrderDetail> SalesDetail { get; set; }

        protected override void Execute(CodeActivityContext context)
        {
```

You'll immediately notice how much simpler this code is compared to the previous asynchronous activities. The code uses the properties of the SalesOrderDetail that is passed as an input argument to insert a new TransactionHistory row in the database.

Even though this activity is applying an update to the database (like the UpdateProductInventory activity just reviewed), there is no need for a DependentTransaction. A DependentTransaction is necessary only if the actual LINQ update is taking place on a worker thread. All of this code executes on the workflow thread, and any ambient transaction that exists when it is executed will be used.

```
            SalesOrderDetail salesDetail = SalesDetail.Get(context);

            using (AdventureWorksDataContext dc =
                new AdventureWorksDataContext())
            {
                var historyRow = new TransactionHistory();
                historyRow.ProductID = salesDetail.ProductID;
                historyRow.ModifiedDate = DateTime.Now;
                historyRow.Quantity = salesDetail.OrderQty;
                historyRow.TransactionDate = salesDetail.ModifiedDate;
                historyRow.TransactionType = 'S';
                historyRow.ReferenceOrderID = salesDetail.SalesOrderID;
                historyRow.ReferenceOrderLineID
                    = salesDetail.SalesOrderDetailID;

                dc.TransactionHistories.InsertOnSubmit(historyRow);
                dc.SubmitChanges();
                Console.WriteLine(
                    "Product {0}: Added history for Qty of {1} ",
                    salesDetail.ProductID, salesDetail.OrderQty);
            }
        }
    }
}
```

Implementing the ExternalUpdate Activity

You also need a custom activity to simulate a notification to an external system for the order. Add a new custom activity to the ActivityLibrary project using the Code Activity template. Name the new activity ExternalUpdate.

Unlike the previous activities, this one doesn't really produce any useful results. It simply writes messages to the console to let us know that it is executing. After all, it is just a simulation. Here is the code that you'll need to implement this class:

```
using System;
using System.Activities;
using System.Collections.Generic;
using AdventureWorksAccess;

namespace ActivityLibrary
{
    public sealed class ExternalUpdate : CodeActivity
    {
        public InArgument<Int32> SalesOrderId { get; set; }
        public InArgument<List<SalesOrderDetail>> OrderDetail { get; set; }

        protected override void Execute(CodeActivityContext context)
        {
            String operation = "record new sale";
            Console.WriteLine(
                "Order Id {0}: Notifying external system to {1}",
                SalesOrderId.Get(context), operation);
            foreach (SalesOrderDetail detail in OrderDetail.Get(context))
            {
                Console.WriteLine(
                    "Product {0}: {1}", detail.ProductID, operation);
            }
        }
    }
}
```

Implementing the DisplayProductInventory Activity

Since the example workflow updates the AdventureWorks database, you also need a way to independently verify the results of the update. To accomplish this, you will implement another custom activity that queries the database and displays the current state of selected rows on the console. This custom activity will be used in a second workflow that is executed during each round of tests.

Add a new Code Activity to the ActivityLibrary project, and name it DisplayProductInventory. Here is the complete code for this new activity:

```
using System;
using System.Activities;
using System.Linq;
using AdventureWorksAccess;

namespace ActivityLibrary
{
    public sealed class DisplayProductInventory : AsyncCodeActivity
    {
```

The Description property is used to display a message along with the current state of the database rows. The message will indicate whether this execution of the activity is displaying the state of the database before or after the inventory update test.

```
public InArgument<String> Description { get; set; }
public InArgument<SalesOrderDetail> SalesDetail { get; set; }

protected override IAsyncResult BeginExecute(
    AsyncCodeActivityContext context, AsyncCallback callback,
    object state)
{
    Action<SalesOrderDetail, String> asyncWork =
        (sale, desc) => DisplayInventory(sale, desc);
    context.UserState = asyncWork;
    return asyncWork.BeginInvoke(
        SalesDetail.Get(context), Description.Get(context),
        callback, state);
}

protected override void EndExecute(
    AsyncCodeActivityContext context, IAsyncResult result)
{
    ((Action<SalesOrderDetail, String>)
        context.UserState).EndInvoke(result);
}

private void DisplayInventory(SalesOrderDetail salesDetail, String desc)
{
```

The LINQ queries are similar to what you have already seen in previous activities. A selected ProductInventory row is retrieved along with a TransactionHistory row for the same product.

The plan is to run multiple tests against this same database using slightly different versions of the example workflow. Therefore, this code can't simply test for the existence of a TransactionHistory row to determine whether the history was successfully added. History rows from previous test runs could already exist, thus skewing the results. For this reason, the query for the TransactionHistory table uses the ModifiedDate column of the table to filter the results, only looking for rows that were added within the last three seconds.

```
using (AdventureWorksDataContext dc =
    new AdventureWorksDataContext())
{
    var inventoryRow =
        (from pi in dc.ProductInventories
         where pi.ProductID == salesDetail.ProductID
            && pi.LocationID == 7 //finished goods storage
         select pi).SingleOrDefault();

    Boolean historyRowFound =
        (from th in dc.TransactionHistories
         where th.ProductID == salesDetail.ProductID
          && (DateTime.Now - th.ModifiedDate < new TimeSpan(0, 0, 3))
         select th).Any();
```

```
        if (inventoryRow != null)
        {
            Console.WriteLine("Product {0}: {1} - {2} - {3}",
                inventoryRow.ProductID, inventoryRow.Quantity, desc,
                (historyRowFound ? "History Row Found" : "No History"));
        }
    }
  }
 }
}
```

Declaring the UpdateInventory Workflow

Before you continue with this example, you should build the solution. This ensures that all of the custom activities build correctly and are available for your use in the Toolbox.

Create a new project to host the example workflow. Name the project `UpdateInventory`, and use the Workflow Console Application template. Add the new project to the solution for this chapter, and delete the `Workflow1.xaml` file since it won't be used. Add these references to the project:

- Project reference to the `AdventureWorksAccess` project

- Project reference to the `ActivityLibrary` project

- .NET assembly reference to `System.Data.Linq`

- .NET assembly reference to `System.Transactions`

Add a new workflow to the project using the Activity template, and name it `UpdateInventory`. Begin the declaration of the workflow by adding a `Flowchart` activity to the empty workflow and then adding these arguments:

Name	Direction	Argument Type
ArgSalesOrderId	In	Int32
ArgIsDemoException	In	Boolean

The workflow also requires this single variable:

Name	Variable Type	Scope
OrderDetail	List<SalesOrderDetail>	Flowchart

Please follow these steps to complete the declaration of the workflow:

1. Add a GetOrderDetail activity to the flowchart. Set the OrderDetail property to OrderDetail and the SalesOrderId property to ArgSalesOrderId. This activity will retrieve the SalesOrderDetail rows for the requested ArgSalesOrderId and place the result in the OrderDetail variable. Drag a connection from the start of the flowchart to the top of this activity.

2. Add an ExternalUpdate activity to the flowchart below the GetOrderDetail. Set the OrderDetail property to OrderDetail and the SalesOrderId property to ArgSalesOrderId. Drag a connection between the GetOrderDetail activity and this activity.

3. Add a ForEach<T> activity below the ExternalUpdate activity. Set the generic type to AdventureWorksAccess.SalesOrderDetail, and set the Values property to the OrderDetail variable. Change the DisplayName to ApplyUpdates to better identify the purpose of this activity. Drag a connection from the ExternalUpdate activity to this activity.

4. Expand the ApplyUpdates activity (the ForEach<T> that you just added), and add an UpdateProductInventory activity as the only child. Set the SalesDetail property to item. Figure 13-1 shows the completed ApplyUpdates activity.

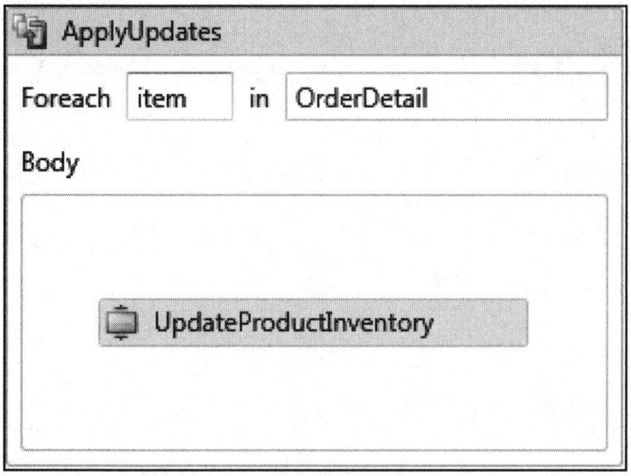

Figure 13-1. ApplyUpdates ForEach activity

5. Navigate to the root `Flowchart` activity, and add a `FlowDecision` below the `ApplyUpdates` activity. Drag a connection from the `ApplyUpdates` to the top of the `FlowDecision`. Set the `FlowDecision.Condition` property to `ArgIsDemoException`. The purpose of the `FlowDecision` is to model a contrived exception that can be triggered externally by setting the `ArgIsDemoException` argument to true. This allows the workflow to be executed first without any exception and then with a forced exception in order to compare the results.

6. Add a `Throw` activity below and to the left of the `FlowDecision`. Drag a connection from the left side of the `FlowDecision` (the true side) to the `Throw` activity. Set the `Throw.Exception` property to `New DivideByZeroException("Throw a demo exception!")`.

7. Add a generic `ForEach<T>` activity below and to the right of the `FlowDecision` activity. Set the generic type to `AdventureWorksAccess.SalesOrderDetail`, and set the `Values` property to the `OrderDetail` variable. Change the `DisplayName` property to `InsertHistory`. Drag a connection from the right side of the `FlowDecision` (the false side) to the new `ForEach` activity.

8. Expand the `InsertHistory` activity, and add an `InsertTranHistory` activity as the only child. Set the `SalesDetail` property to `item`. Figure 13-2 shows the completed `InsertHistory` activity.

Figure 13-3 shows the completed workflow.

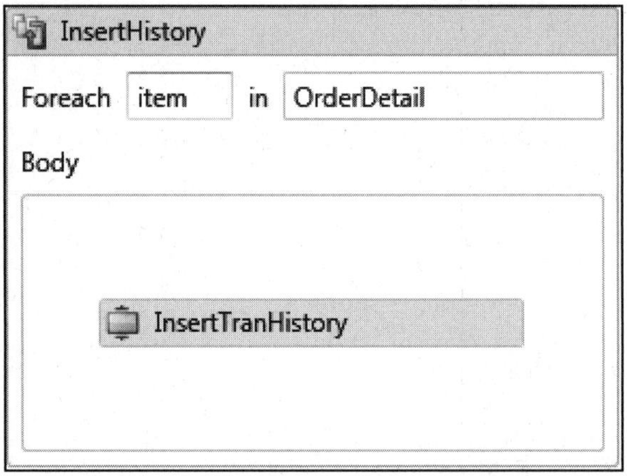

Figure 13-2. InsertHistory ForEach activity

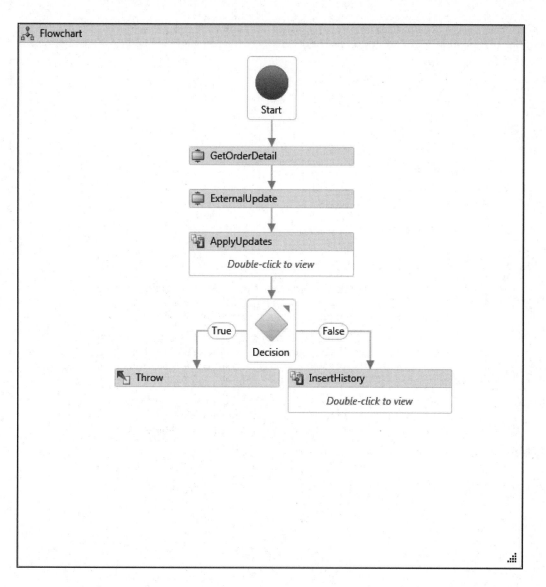

Figure 13-3. UpdateInventory workflow

Declaring the DisplayInventory Workflow

A second workflow is needed to verify the results of each test. This workflow uses the `DisplayProductInventory` custom activity that you implemented in a previous step to display the current state of the database.

Add a new workflow to the `UpdateInventory` project, and name it `DisplayInventory`. Start the declaration of this workflow by adding a `Flowchart` activity as the root and then adding these arguments:

Name	Direction	Argument Type
ArgSalesOrderId	In	Int32
ArgDescription	In	String

The workflow also requires this single variable:

Name	Variable Type	Scope
OrderDetail	List<SalesOrderDetail>	Flowchart

Please follow these steps to complete the declaration of the workflow:

1.   Add a `GetOrderDetail` activity to the flowchart. Set the `OrderDetail` property to `OrderDetail` and the `SalesOrderId` property to `ArgSalesOrderId`. Drag a connection from the start of the flowchart to the top of this activity.

2.   Add a `ForEach<T>` activity under the `GetOrderDetail` activity. Set the generic type to `AdventureWorksAccess.SalesOrderDetail` and the `Values` property to `OrderDetail`. Change the `DisplayName` property to `Display`. Drag a connection from the bottom of the `GetOrderDetail` to this activity.

3.   Expand the `Display` activity, and add a `DisplayProductInventory` activity. Set the `SalesDetail` property to `item` and the `Description` property to `ArgDescription`. You can see the completed `Display` activity in Figure 13-4.

Figure 13-5 shows the completed workflow.

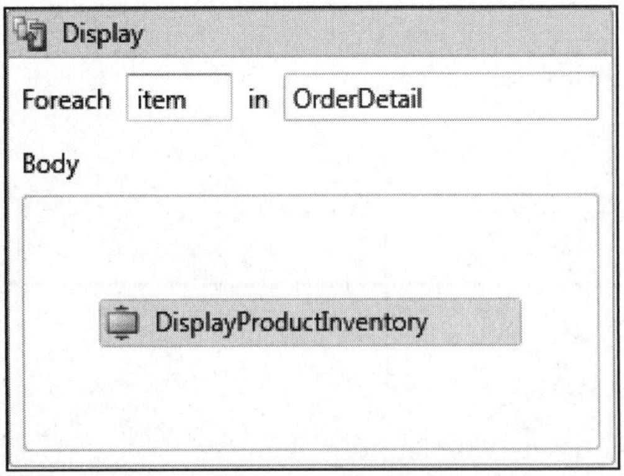

Figure 13-4. *Display ForEach activity*

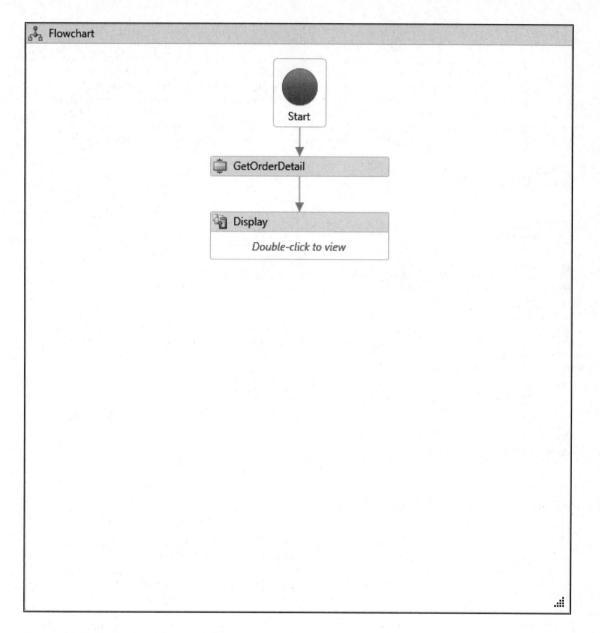

Figure 13-5. DisplayInventory workflow

Hosting the Workflow

The LINQ queries in the custom activities all use the default constructor for the generated data context class. This means that they will attempt to retrieve the database connection string from an `app.config` file. An `app.config` file containing the correct entries was created for you in the `AdventureWorksAccess` project when you first generated the LINQ classes. You should be able to copy the `app.config` file from that project and add the copy to the `UpdateInventory` project. If the `UpdateInventory` project already has an `app.config` file, you can safely replace its contents. Here is the `app.config` file that I'm using on my machine. Yours may be slightly different depending on your server name and database credentials.

```xml
<?xml version="1.0" encoding="utf-8" ?>
<configuration>
  <configSections>
  </configSections>
  <connectionStrings>
    <add name=
      "AdventureWorksAccess.Properties.Settings.AdventureWorksConnectionString"
        connectionString="Data Source=localhost\SQLExpress;
            Initial Catalog=AdventureWorks;Integrated Security=True"
        providerName="System.Data.SqlClient" />
  </connectionStrings>
</configuration>
```

Modify the `Program.cs` file in the `UpdateInventory` project to host the workflow. Here is the complete `Program.cs` file:

```csharp
using System;
using System.Activities;
using System.Collections.Generic;
using System.Threading;

namespace UpdateInventory
{
    class Program
    {
        static void Main(string[] args)
        {
```

The code to execute the workflow has been pushed off into a private `RunWorkflow` method. This allows you to easily run multiple instances of the example workflow with different parameters for each execution. For this example, the first execution passes false as the last parameter, and the second execution passes true. This parameter is passed to the workflow as the `ArgIsDemoException` argument. This means that the first execution should complete successfully while the second execution should throw an exception.

As you work through the remaining examples in this chapter, you will modify these lines in the `Main` method to execute enhanced versions of the example workflow.

The magic 43687 number is an order ID that can be found in the `AdventureWorks` database. It has no special meaning other than it provides a small amount of test data that can be used to exercise the example workflow.

```
Console.WriteLine("UpdateInventory without exception");
        RunWorkflow(new UpdateInventory(), 43687, false);
        Thread.Sleep(4000);

        Console.WriteLine("\nUpdateInventory with exception");
        RunWorkflow(new UpdateInventory(), 43687, true);
        Thread.Sleep(4000);
    }

    private static void RunWorkflow(Activity wf,
        Int32 orderId, Boolean isDemoException)
    {
        try
        {
```

Before the example workflow is executed, the private `DisplayInventory` method is invoked. This method (defined toward the end of this listing) executes the `DisplayInventory` workflow that displays the current state of the database. It is also executed after the example workflow has completed. This allows you to compare the values before and after the execution of the example workflow to identify any changes that have been made to the data.

```
            DisplayInventory(orderId, "Starting");
            AutoResetEvent syncEvent = new AutoResetEvent(false);
            WorkflowApplication wfApp =
                new WorkflowApplication(wf, new Dictionary<String, Object>
                    {
                        {"ArgSalesOrderId", orderId},
                        {"ArgIsDemoException", isDemoException}
                    });

            wfApp.Completed = delegate(
                WorkflowApplicationCompletedEventArgs e)
            {
                syncEvent.Set();
            };
```

Note that the handler for the `OnUnhandledException` delegate returns the `Cancel` action. This is necessary to execute any compensation logic that has been declared. It isn't necessary for this first example but will be required later in the chapter when you are working through the compensation examples.

```
            wfApp.OnUnhandledException = delegate(
                WorkflowApplicationUnhandledExceptionEventArgs e)
            {
                Console.WriteLine("OnUnhandledException: {0}",
                    e.UnhandledException.Message);
                return UnhandledExceptionAction.Cancel; //needed to compensate
            };

            wfApp.Run();
```

```
            syncEvent.WaitOne();
            DisplayInventory(orderId, "Ending");
        }
        catch (Exception exception)
        {
            Console.WriteLine("Exception: {0}", exception.Message);
        }
    }
}
```

Here is the private `DisplayInventory` method that is invoked before and after each workflow test. To simplify the execution of the `DisplayInventory` workflow, the `WorkflowInvoker` class is used.

```
        private static void DisplayInventory(Int32 orderId, String desc)
        {
            WorkflowInvoker.Invoke(
                new DisplayInventory(), new Dictionary<String, Object>
                {
                    {"ArgSalesOrderId", orderId},
                    {"ArgDescription", desc}
                });
        }
    }
}
```

Testing the Workflow

You should now be ready to build the solution and run the `UpdateInventory` project. Here are my results when I run the project:

```
UpdateInventory without exception

Product 768: 67 - Starting - No History

Product 765: 56 - Starting - No History

Order Id 43687: Notifying external system to record new sale

Product 768: record new sale

Product 765: record new sale

Product 768: Reduced by 1

Product 765: Reduced by 2

Product 768: Added history for Qty of 1

Product 765: Added history for Qty of 2
```

```
Product 768: 66 - Ending - History Row Found

Product 765: 54 - Ending - History Row Found


UpdateInventory with exception

Product 768: 66 - Starting - No History

Product 765: 54 - Starting - No History

Order Id 43687: Notifying external system to record new sale

Product 768: record new sale

Product 765: record new sale

Product 768: Reduced by 1

Product 765: Reduced by 2

OnUnhandledException: Throw a demo exception!

Product 768: 65 - Ending - No History

Product 765: 52 - Ending - No History
```

These results assume that this test was run against a fresh copy of the AdventureWorks database with no previous tests having been run against the data.

The starting inventory for the two products in the selected order was displayed prior to the execution of the workflow (quantity of 67 and 56, respectively). The "No History" message indicates that no history rows exist for these two products in the TransactionHistory table.

The first execution of the UpdateInventory workflow should have completed without any exception. The console entries show that a notification to an external system was simulated, followed by the updates to the ProductInventory table (reducing the quantity by one and two units, respectively) and by the insertion of TransactionHistory rows.

The DisplayInventory workflow was again executed to display the new state of the database. This time the results show that the inventory was correctly reduced (from 67 to 66 and from 56 to 54) and that the history rows were now found.

It's not really a problem if your results are slightly different than these. In particular, if the beginning and ending inventory counts are different, it may mean that you have a slightly different version of the AdventureWorks database. What is important is the relative difference in inventory counts between the starting and ending values and the presence or absence of history rows.

The second execution of the UpdateInventory workflow should have generated an exception. The results show that the external system was notified and the inventory was reduced, but the history rows were not inserted due to the exception. As expected, the OnUnhandledException code in the host program was invoked to handle the exception.

This second workflow instance that threw an unhandled exception highlights several problems that will be solved in subsequent examples:

1. The exception was unhandled by the workflow, deferring the responsibility of handling the exception to the host application. Handling the exception within the workflow may provide a better opportunity to correct the problem.

2. The ProductInventory table was updated, but the TransactionHistory table was not, leaving the database in an inconsistent state. To ensure consistency, the workflow should roll back the updates to the ProductInventory table or make sure that the inserts to the TransactionHistory table always succeed.

3. The external system was notified of the order for the two products, but not notified when the update failed due to the exception. If the update is executed again, the external system will once again be notified, possibly causing duplicate processing of the order. Optimally, the external system should be notified of the failure and instructed to ignore the previous sales notification.

Understanding the TryCatch Activity

The mechanism that WF provides to declaratively catch and process an exception is the TryCatch activity. This activity is used in a similar way to the try and catch C# keywords. Here are the most important properties of the TryCatch activity:

Property	Type	Required	Description
Try	Activity	Yes	The activity to be executed and protected by the TryCatch activity
Catches	Collection<Catch>	Yes	A collection of Catch activities with each one associated with an exception type to catch
Finally	Activity	No	An optional activity to execute regardless of the success or failure of the Try activity

You use the TryCatch activity by declaring the activity that you want to execute in the Try property. You then declare one or more exceptions that you want to catch using the Catches property. Each exception is defined as a Catch<TException> activity, which supports these properties:

Property	Type	Required	Description
ExceptionType	Type	Yes	Identifies the type of exception to catch.
Action	ActivityAction<TException>	No	Identifies the activity to execute if this exception is caught. The ActivityAction is used to provide the target activity with access to the thrown exception.

The TryCatch logic will always attempt to find the correct Catch<TException> regardless of the sequence in which the Catches are defined. This is in contrast with a C# try/catch block that requires you to order the individual exceptions from most specific to most general. For example, in a C# try/catch block, if you want to catch DivideByZeroException (the derived class) and ArithmeticException (the base class), you must declare the most specific exception first (DivideByZeroException). Although the TryCatch activity does process the Catches in the order in which they are specified, in most cases the sequence doesn't matter. The TryCatch activity first looks for an exact match using the exception type. If an exact match is found, no additional searching is necessary. If an exact match is not found, the logic looks for the closest candidate exception type using the IsAssignableFrom and IsSubclassOf methods of the Type class.

You can also specify an optional activity to execute using the Finally property. If declared, the activity is executed immediately following the Try activity and any Catches. The TryCatch activity also supports the declaration of variables.

■ **Warning** Under normal circumstances, any activity that you specify for the Finally property is executed following the Try activity and any Catches. However, if the Try activity throws an unhandled exception (one that is not caught by any of the Catches), the Finally activity might not execute. It depends on how the unhandled exception is ultimately handled. If the workflow is canceled (a graceful shutdown of the workflow), then the Finally activity is executed. But if the workflow is aborted or terminated, the Finally activity is never executed.

Using the TryCatch Activity

In this example, you will modify a copy of the UpdateInventory workflow from the previous example to add a TryCatch activity. The TryCatch activity will catch the exception locally within the workflow rather than allowing it to bubble up to the host application as an unhandled exception.

You will complete these tasks to implement this example:

1. Make a copy of the UpdateInventory workflow.

2. Modify the copied workflow to use a TryCatch activity.

3. Modify the host application to execute the new workflow.

Declaring the UpdateInventoryTryCatch Workflow

To begin this example, make a copy of the UpdateInventory.xaml file, and name the copy UpdateInventoryTryCatch.xaml. You can place the copy in the same UpdateInventory project as the original workflow. Open the copied UpdateInventoryTryCatch.xaml file in the XML editor (Code View), and modify the workflow name. Here is an abbreviated example of the Xaml file showing the changes that you need to make:

```
<Activity x:Class="UpdateInventory.UpdateInventoryTryCatch" />
...
</Activity>
```

Once you've renamed the workflow, you can save the changes and open the workflow in the designer view. Please follow these steps to modify the UpdateInventoryTryCatch workflow:

1. Add a TryCatch activity to the flowchart.

2. Expand the TryCatch, and add a Flowchart activity to the Try property. Adding a Flowchart allows you to easily cut and paste selected activities from the top-level Flowchart to the TryCatch activity. Change the DisplayName of the new Flowchart to TCFlowchart to more easily distinguish it from the top-level Flowchart of the workflow.

3. Return to the top-level Flowchart, and select a group of four activities: ApplyUpdates, FlowDecision, Throw, and InsertHistory. Right-click and select the Cut option for these activities.

4. Expand the TryCatch activity and the TCFlowchart under it. Select the Paste option to add the four activities that you moved from the top-level Flowchart. These four activities should have been copied with their connections intact. But you will need to drag a new connection from the starting point of the TCFlowchart to the top of the ApplyUpdates activity. Figure 13-6 shows the completed TCFlowchart activity.

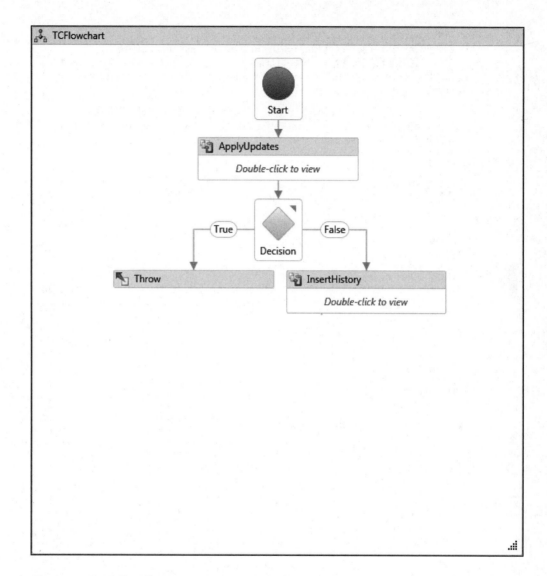

Figure 13-6. TCFlowchart activity

5. Return to the `TryCatch`, and select the Add new catch option. You will be
    prompted to select the type of exception that you want to catch. Choose
    `System.ArithmeticException`.

6. Add a WriteLine activity to the newly added catch for System.ArithmeticException. Set the WriteLine.Text property to String.Format("Caught ArithmeticException: {0}", exception.Message) to display the exception message on the console. Figure 13-7 shows the completed TryCatch activity.

7. Return to the top-level Flowchart, and drag a new connection from the ExternalUpdate to the top of the TryCatch. Figure 13-8 shows the completed top-level of the workflow.

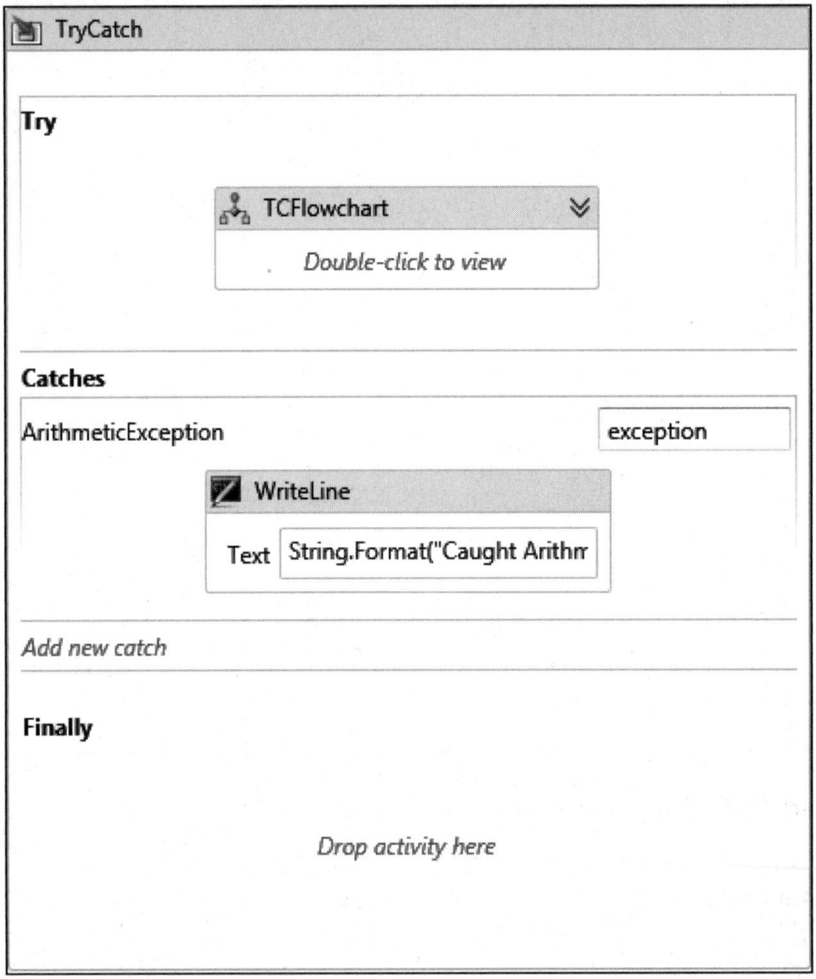

Figure 13-7. TryCatch activity

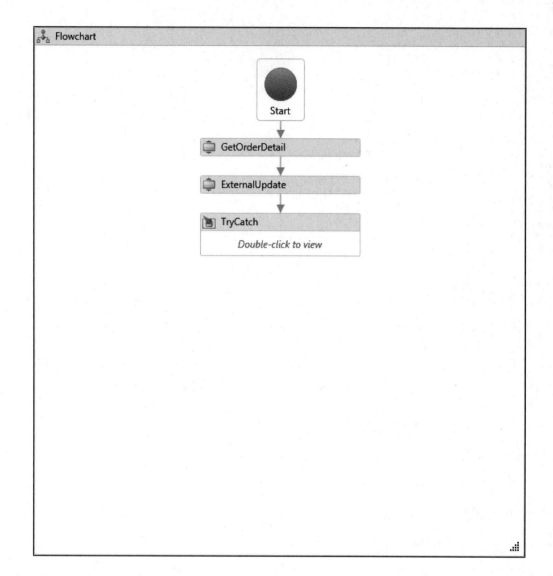

Figure 13-8. UpdateInventoryTryCatch workflow

Hosting the Workflow

To execute this new workflow, you only have to revise a few lines in the `Program.cs` file. Replace the lines in the `Main` method that executed the `UpdateInventory` workflow with these lines:

```
using System;
using System.Activities;
using System.Collections.Generic;
using System.Threading;

namespace UpdateInventory
{
    class Program
    {
        static void Main(string[] args)
        {
            Console.WriteLine("UpdateInventoryTryCatch with exception");
            RunWorkflow(new UpdateInventoryTryCatch(), 43687, true);
            Thread.Sleep(4000);
        }
        …
    }
}
```

Testing the Workflow

After building the solution, you should be able to run the UpdateInventory project. Here are my results:

```
UpdateInventoryTryCatch with exception

Product 768: 65 - Starting - No History

Product 765: 52 - Starting - No History

Order Id 43687: Notifying external system to record new sale

Product 768: record new sale

Product 765: record new sale

Product 768: Reduced by 1

Product 765: Reduced by 2

Caught ArithmeticException: Throw a demo exception!

Product 768: 64 - Ending - No History

Product 765: 50 - Ending - No History
```

The results indicate that the exception was caught by the `TryCatch` activity rather than the host application. These results assume that the workflow was executed immediately following the previous test. If you executed the previous example workflow more than once, the current inventory numbers for each product will be different.

Catching Multiple Exceptions

The previous example caught a single exception (`ArithmeticExpression`), but you can also declare a catch for multiple exceptions. In this example, you will revise the `UpdateInventoryTryCatch` workflow to catch an additional exception (`DivideByZeroException`). Catching multiple exceptions allows you to declare a different set of activities to handle each type of exception.

However, catching the exception doesn't really solve any of the problems that are present with this workflow. In particular, the `ProductInventory` and `TransactionHistory` tables are still inconsistent after execution of the workflow. One solution is to modify the workflow so that the updates to the `TransactionHistory` table always occur, even when an exception has been thrown. In this example, you will use the `Finally` property of the `TryCatch` to accomplish this.

Please follow these steps to modify the existing `UpdateInventoryTryCatch` workflow:

1. Expand the `TryCatch` activity, and add a new catch. Select `System.DivideByZeroException` as the type of exception to catch. The sequence of the new catch relative to the previous one does not matter.

2. Add a `WriteLine` to the new catch. Set the `WriteLine.Text` property to `String.Format("Caught DivideByZeroException: {0}", exception.Message)`.

3. Expand the `TCFlowchart` activity, and cut the `InsertHistory` activity from the `Flowchart` (removing it from `TCFlowchart`).

4. Return to the `TryCatch`, and paste the `InsertHistory` activity that you cut into the `TryCatch.Finally` property. This will cause the `InsertHistory` activity to be executed even when an exception occurs. Figure 13-9 shows the modified `TryCatch` activity.

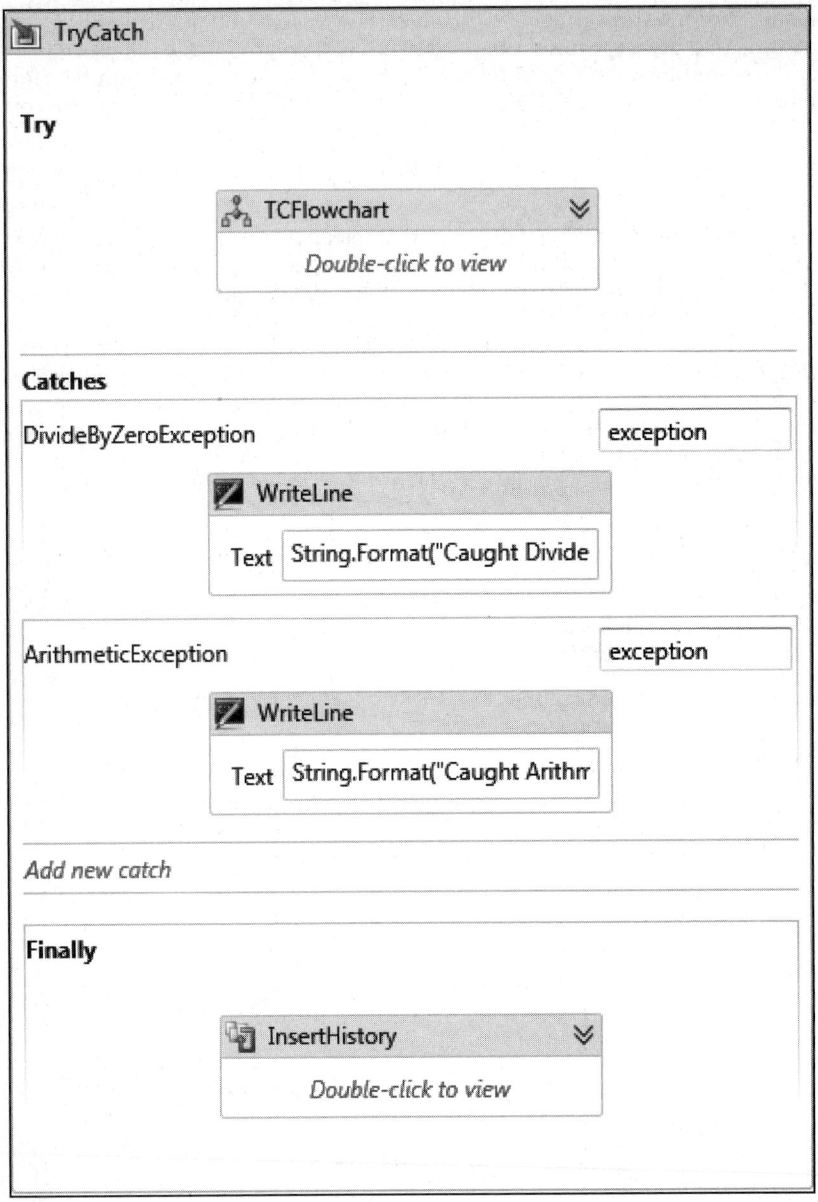

Figure 13-9. Revised TryCatch activity

■ **Note** The workflow designer does not currently provide a way to reorder the individual catches in a `TryCatch` activity. Therefore, you'll need to edit the Xaml file directly if you want to change the order. Most of the time the order of the individual catches does not matter. But the catches are processed in the sequence in which they are defined. If the `TryCatch` activity doesn't find an exact match on exception type, the logic to find the closest match may be affected by the sequence.

Testing the Revised Workflow

After modifying the workflow, you should be ready to build the solution and run the `UpdateInventory` project. Here are my results:

```
UpdateInventoryTryCatch with exception

Product 768: 64 - Starting - No History

Product 765: 50 - Starting - No History

Order Id 43687: Notifying external system to record new sale

Product 768: record new sale

Product 765: record new sale

Product 768: Reduced by 1

Product 765: Reduced by 2

Caught DivideByZeroException: Throw a demo exception!

Product 768: Added history for Qty of 1

Product 765: Added history for Qty of 2

Product 768: 63 - Ending - History Row Found

Product 765: 48 - Ending - History Row Found
```

After the latest changes, the exception is now caught by the `DivideByZeroException` handler instead of the one for the more general `ArithmeticException`. Moving the `InsertHistory` activity to the `Finally` property of the `TryCatch` activity caused it to be executed regardless of the success or failure of the previous steps.

In this particular case, the results are closer to being correct since the ProductInventory and TransactionHistory tables were both updated. However, it's not likely that this is the best way to solve this particular problem. If an exception occurred in a real, live workflow, it was probably thrown for a very valid reason. Assuming that the exception meant that something really, really bad occurred, you probably don't want to continue with additional updates. On the contrary, you probably want to reverse course and roll back the updates that have already occurred. If that is your intent, then the TransactionScope activity (discussed next) is the answer.

Understanding the TransactionScope Activity

The TransactionScope activity is similar to the System.Transactions.TransactionScope class that you might use in your nonworkflow C# code. That class is typically used by defining a C# using block around a TransactionScope instance. The code that you want to execute within a transaction is placed inside the block. At the end of the block, you call the Complete method on the TransactionScope instance. This indicates that all updates that have been applied during the lifetime of the transaction should now be committed. If execution exits the block prematurely due to an exception, the TransctionScope is disposed, and the transaction, along with any work performed using the transaction, is rolled back.

When using the TransactionScope activity, you place the activity that you want to execute within a transaction in the Body property. If the activity completes without throwing an unhandled exception, the transaction is committed. If an unhandled exception is thrown, the transaction is rolled back.

Here are the most important properties of the TransactionScope activity:

Property	Type	Required	Description
Body	Activity	Yes	The activity that you want to execute within a transaction.
Timeout	InArgument<TimeSpan>	No	A TimeSpan that defines the maximum allowed time for the transaction to complete. If the lifetime of the transaction exceeds this value, the transaction is aborted.
IsolationLevel	System.Transactions. IsolationLevel	No	Determines the isolation level to use for the transaction.
AbortInstanceOn-TransactionFailure	Boolean	No	If set to false, the transaction will be rolled back on a failure, but the workflow instance can continue execution. This allows any exception to be handled higher up the activity stack. Set to true to abort the workflow instance on a failure of the transaction.

The IsolationLevel property determines the amount of access that other transactions have to the data being updated (termed *volatile data* in the Microsoft documentation). Here are the valid values for the IsolationLevel property, listed in order from most to least restrictive:

Value	Description
Serializable	Volatile data can be read by other transactions but not modified. New data cannot be added.
RepeatableRead	Volatile data can be read by the other transactions but not modified. New data can be added.
ReadCommitted	Volatile data cannot be read by other transactions until this transaction is committed.
ReadUncommitted	Volatile data can be read and modified.
Snapshot	Volatile data can be read. Modifications of data are allowed but with restrictions.
Chaos	Volatile data from transactions that are more isolated are not overwritten.
Unspecified	The isolation level being used is different from what was originally specified, but it also cannot be determined.

■ **Note** The `TransactionScope` activity does not support the `TransactionOption` property that is supported by the `System.Transactions.TransactionScope` class. This option allows you to specify the type of transaction requested by the `TransactionScope` instance. In particular, the `TransactionOption.RequiresNew` option, which forces a new transaction to be created, is not supported. The `TransactionScope` activity uses the `TransactionOption.Required` option.

WF also includes a `TransactedReceiveScope` activity. This activity is designed to be used in workflows that use WCF messaging activities. It allows you to flow a transaction into a workflow that uses WCF messaging. Please refer to Chapter 9 for more information on the WCF messaging activities.

Using the TransactionScope Activity

In this example, you will use the `TransactionScope` activity to ensure the consistency of the database updates. The updates to the `ProductInventory` and the inserts to the `TransactionHistory` will all succeed together as one unit of work, or they will be rolled back. In either case, the database will always be left in a consistent state.

You will complete these tasks to implement this example:

1. Make a copy of the UpdateInventory workflow.

2. Modify the copied workflow to use a TransactionScope activity.

3. Modify the host application to execute the new workflow.

Declaring the UpdateInventoryTran Workflow

This workflow is a revision of the original UpdateInventory workflow that you declared in the first example of this chapter (not a copy of the previous TryCatch example). Make a copy of the UpdateInventory.xaml file, and name the copy UpdateInventoryTran.xaml, placing the copy in the same UpdateInventory project as the original. As you did previously, open the copied Xaml file in the XML editor, and change the workflow name to UpdateInventoryTran.

After saving the changes, reopen the workflow in the designer view. You can follow these steps to modify the UpdateInventoryTran workflow:

1. Add a TransactionScope activity to the workflow. Check the properties for the activity, and make sure that the AbortInstanceOnTransactionFailure property is set to false.

2. Expand the TransactionScope activity that you just added, and add a Flowchart activity as its only child. Change the DisplayName of the new Flowchart activity to TSFlowchart to more easily distinguish it from the top-level Flowchart.

3. Return to the top-level Flowchart, and select a group of four activities: ApplyUpdates, FlowDecision, Throw, and InsertHistory. Right-click and select the Cut option for these activities.

4. Expand the TransactionScope and the TSFlowchart under it. Use the Paste option to add the four activities that you just cut from the top-level Flowchart. Verify that the original connections between these activities are still intact. Drag a new connection from the start of the TSFlowchart to the top of the ApplyUpdates activity. The structure of the TSFlowchart should look just like the TCFlowchart shown in Figure 13-6. Figure 13-10 shows the finished TransactionScope activity.

5. Return to the top-level Flowchart, and drag a connection between the ExternalUpdate activity and the TransactionScope. Figure 13-11 shows the top level of the workflow.

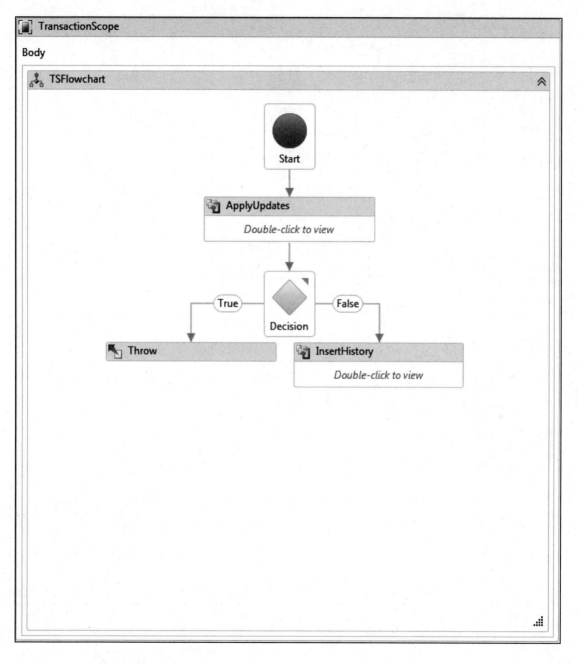

Figure 13-10. TransactionScope activity

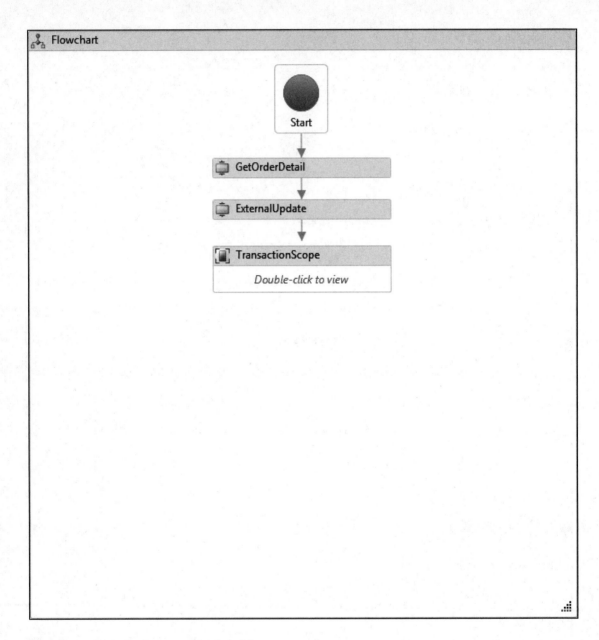

Figure 13-11. UpdateInventoryTran workflow

Hosting the Workflow

Modify the `Program.cs` file to execute this new workflow instead of the previous one. For this test, you will execute the workflow twice—first without an exception to ensure that everything works correctly and then with an exception. Here are the affected lines of code in the `Main` method:

```
using System;
using System.Activities;
using System.Collections.Generic;
using System.Threading;

namespace UpdateInventory
{
    class Program
    {
        static void Main(string[] args)
        {
            Console.WriteLine("UpdateInventoryTran without exception");
            RunWorkflow(new UpdateInventoryTran(), 43687, false);
            Thread.Sleep(4000);

            Console.WriteLine("\nUpdateInventoryTran with exception ");
            RunWorkflow(new UpdateInventoryTran(), 43687, true);
            Thread.Sleep(4000);
        }
...
    }
}
```

Testing the Workflow

When you build the solution and run the `UpdateInventory` project, your results should be similar to these:

```
UpdateInventoryTran without exception

Product 768: 63 - Starting - No History

Product 765: 48 - Starting - No History

Order Id 43687: Notifying external system to record new sale

Product 768: record new sale

Product 765: record new sale

Product 768: Reduced by 1
```

```
Product 765: Reduced by 2

Product 768: Added history for Qty of 1

Product 765: Added history for Qty of 2

Product 768: 62 - Ending - History Row Found

Product 765: 46 - Ending - History Row Found

UpdateInventoryTran with exception

Product 768: 62 - Starting - No History

Product 765: 46 - Starting - No History

Order Id 43687: Notifying external system to record new sale

Product 768: record new sale

Product 765: record new sale

Product 768: Reduced by 1

Product 765: Reduced by 2

OnUnhandledException: Throw a demo exception!

Product 768: 62 - Ending - No History

Product 765: 46 - Ending - No History
```

As expected, the workflow that executed without an exception worked perfectly. The updates and inserts to the database were placed within a TransactionScope, causing them to be executed under the same transaction. Since the TransactionScope completed normally (no unhandled exception was thrown), the transaction was committed.

The second workflow triggered an unhandled exception. When the exception was thrown, the TransactionScope rolled back the uncommitted updates that were made by the UpdateProductInventory activity. You'll notice that the results show the same starting and ending values for each product, proving that a rollback occurred. The updates failed due to the unhandled exception, but the database is now left in a consistent state.

Using a Host Transaction

The TransactionScope activity is the mechanism for declaratively protecting portions of a workflow with a transaction. However, you can execute the entire workflow under a transaction if the host provides one. This works only when you use the `WorkflowInvoker` class to execute a workflow. That class executes the workflow on the current host thread, just like a method call.

Hosting the Workflow

To illustrate how to execute the entire workflow under a host-provided transaction, you will add a new private method to the `Program.cs` file and use it to execute the original `UpdateInventory` activity. For this test, you don't want to use the version of the workflow that contains a `TransactionScope` since that won't necessarily prove that the host transaction is being used.

Here are the affected portions of the `Program.cs` file in the `UpdateInventory` project:

```
using System;
using System.Activities;
using System.Collections.Generic;
using System.Threading;

namespace UpdateInventory
{
    class Program
    {
        static void Main(string[] args)
        {
```

Replace all the code in the `Main` method with these lines to execute the original workflow. Notice that the new `RunWorkflowWithTran` private method is used instead of the `RunWorkflow` method that you have been using.

```
            Console.WriteLine("UpdateInventory with Host Tran and exception");
            RunWorkflowWithTran(new UpdateInventory(), 43687, true);
            Thread.Sleep(4000);
        }
...
```

Add this new private method to execute the workflow using the `WorkflowInvoker` class. Prior to the workflow execution, a `TransactionScope` object is constructed to create the transaction. Notice that this is the standard C# class provided in the `System.Transactions` assembly, not the WF activity that you used in the previous example.

A C# `using` block is used to automatically dispose of the `TransactionScope` instance. After invoking the workflow, the `TransactionScope.Complete` method is called to commit any work that was performed under the transaction.

```
        private static void RunWorkflowWithTran(Activity wf,
            Int32 orderId, Boolean isDemoException)
        {
            try
            {
                DisplayInventory(orderId, "Starting");

                using (System.Transactions.TransactionScope scope =
                    new System.Transactions.TransactionScope())
```

```
                {
                    WorkflowInvoker.Invoke(wf, new Dictionary<String, Object>
                        {
                            {"ArgSalesOrderId", orderId},
                            {"ArgIsDemoException", isDemoException}
                        });

                    scope.Complete();
                }
            }
            catch (Exception exception)
            {
                Console.WriteLine("Exception: {0}", exception.Message);
            }
            finally
            {
                DisplayInventory(orderId, "Ending");
            }
        }
    }
}
```

Testing the Workflow

After building the solution, you can run the revised UpdateInventory project. Here are my results:

```
UpdateInventory with Host Tran and exception

Product 768: 62 - Starting - No History

Product 765: 46 - Starting - No History

Order Id 43687: Notifying external system to record new sale

Product 768: record new sale

Product 765: record new sale

Product 768: Reduced by 1

Product 765: Reduced by 2

Exception: Throw a demo exception!

Product 768: 62 - Ending - No History

Product 765: 46 - Ending - No History
```

The results indicate that the host-created transaction was used, since the database is now back in a consistent state after the unhandled exception. Also notice that the exception that was thrown by the workflow was caught by the `try`/`catch` block of C# code, just as if you had called a method.

Executing the workflow under a transaction (using the `TransactionScope` or providing one from the host application) solved the database consistency problems with the workflow. Now, all updates and inserts to the database are executed as a single unit of work. They all succeed or fail together.

However, one problem still remains with this workflow. The external system is notified of the sale for each product, but it is not notified when a problem occurs. That problem is solved by the use of compensation, which is discussed in the next section.

Understanding Compensation

A transaction is used to ensure consistency for short-lived units of work. You can extend the life of a transaction for a few seconds (or even longer if it is really necessary), but they are certainly not designed to span minutes, hours, days, or weeks. And they are generally not suitable when you are interacting with an external system.

Like transactions, compensation is a way to ensure consistency. But there are differences in the approach that the two mechanisms take. Transactions ensure consistency by preventing inconsistent updates from being committed. Compensation ensures consistency by undoing work that has already been completed.

To support compensation, WF provides the `CompensableActivity`. This activity allows you to declare an activity that is capable of being compensated (using the `Body` property). The `CompensableActivity` also provides multiple handler properties that allow you to declare activities to execute under several situations that might occur later in the workflow.

Here are the most important properties of the `CompensableActivity`:

Property	Type	Required	Description
Body	Activity	Yes	The activity whose work may need to be compensated or confirmed
CompensationHandler	Activity	No	The activity to execute when compensation is triggered (either automatically or manually)
ConfirmationHandler	Activity	No	The activity to execute when confirmation is triggered (either automatically or manually)
CancellationHandler	Activity	No	The activity to execute when the CompensableActivity has been canceled
Result	CompensationToken	No	A token that identifies this CompensableActivity and is used to manually trigger compensation or confirmation

The `CompensableActivity` also supports something called *confirmation*. If compensation is the undoing of work that was previously completed, then confirmation can be thought of as confirming that the work was completed and can no longer be compensated. Once it is confirmed, the work is past the point of no return and can no longer be undone. For example, if the product has been shipped from the warehouse, the order can no longer be canceled.

If an activity is declared for one of the handler properties, it is executed automatically when necessary. Compensation and confirmation can also be manually triggered from within the workflow model using the `Compensate` and `Confirm` activities. These activities both support a single property:

Property	Type	Required	Description
Target	InArgument<CompensationToken>	Yes	Identifies the CompensableActivity to manually compensate or confirm

This table summarizes the conditions under which each of the handler activities of the `CompensableActivity` are executed if they are declared:

Handler Property	Conditions
CompensationHandler	The activity has completed (but has not been manually confirmed), and the workflow is later canceled.
	The activity has completed (but has not been manually confirmed), and the Compensate activity is used to manually trigger compensation.
ConfirmationHandler	The activity has completed, and the workflow completes normally.
	The activity has completed, and the Confirm activity is used to manually trigger confirmation.
CancellationHandler	The activity is still active (has not completed), and the activity is canceled.

The `CompensableActivity` also supports the definition of workflow variables. In addition to being used by the `Body` activity, the variables are also in scope for any handler activities that have been declared.

■ **Tip** It is important to note that automatic compensation occurs only when the workflow is canceled. If it is terminated or aborted, compensation does not occur.

Using the CompensableActivity

In the example workflow, an inconsistency exists since the external system was notified of the sale but was not notified when an exception occurred. In this example, you will revise the UpdateInventoryTran workflow to use a CompensableActivity. This enables the declaration of compensation logic to notify the external system that the inventory update failed.

You will complete these tasks to implement this example:

1. Implement a new ExternalVoid custom activity.

2. Copy the UpdateInventoryTran workflow.

3. Modify the copied workflow.

4. Host and execute the workflow.

Implementing the ExternalVoid Activity

The ExternalUpdate activity that you implemented at the beginning of the chapter simulates communication with an external system. That activity notifies the external system that a new sale has been processed. Since this is the activity that you need to compensate, it makes sense to implement another activity that reverses the notification.

Add a new Code Activity to the ActivityLibrary, and name it ExternalVoid. This activity will mimic a call to an external system to notify it that the previous sale should be voided. Here is the code to implement this activity:

```
using System;
using System.Activities;
using System.Collections.Generic;
using AdventureWorksAccess;

namespace ActivityLibrary
{
    public sealed class ExternalVoid : CodeActivity
    {
        public InArgument<Int32> SalesOrderId { get; set; }
        public InArgument<List<SalesOrderDetail>> OrderDetail { get; set; }

        protected override void Execute(CodeActivityContext context)
        {
            String operation = "void previous sale";
            Console.WriteLine(
                "Order Id {0}: Notifying external system to {1}",
                SalesOrderId.Get(context), operation);
```

```
        foreach (SalesOrderDetail detail in OrderDetail.Get(context))
        {
            Console.WriteLine("Product {0}: {1}",
                detail.ProductID, operation);
        }
      }
    }
}
```

Build the solution before proceeding with the next step. This ensures that the new activity is added to the Toolbox.

Declaring the UpdateInventoryComp Workflow

This workflow is a revision of the UpdateInventoryTran workflow that includes the TransactionScope activity. Make a copy of the UpdateInventoryTran.xaml file, naming the copy UpdateInventoryComp.xaml. Place the copy in the same UpdateInventory project as the original. Remember to open the copied Xaml file in the XML editor and change the workflow name to UpdateInventoryComp.

Please follow these steps to modify the UpdateInventoryComp workflow using the workflow designer:

1. Add a CompensableActivity to the workflow.

2. Select and cut the ExternalUpdate activity from the top-level Flowchart activity. Expand the CompensableActivity, and paste the ExternalUpdate activity into the Body property.

3. Add an ExternalVoid activity to the CompensationHandler of the CompensableActivity. Set the ExternalVoid.OrderDetail property to OrderDetail and the SalesOrderId property to ArgSalesOrderId.

4. Add a WriteLine activity to the ConfirmationHandler of the CompensableActivity. Set the WriteLine.Text property to "Confirmation Handler Executed". Figure 13-12 shows the completed CompensableActivty.

5. Navigate back to the top-level of the workflow and drag a connection between the GetOrderDetail and the CompensableActivity. Then connect the CompensableActivity to the TransactionScope.

Figure 13-13 shows the completed top-level of the workflow. There are no changes required to the TransactionScope or any of the activities under it.

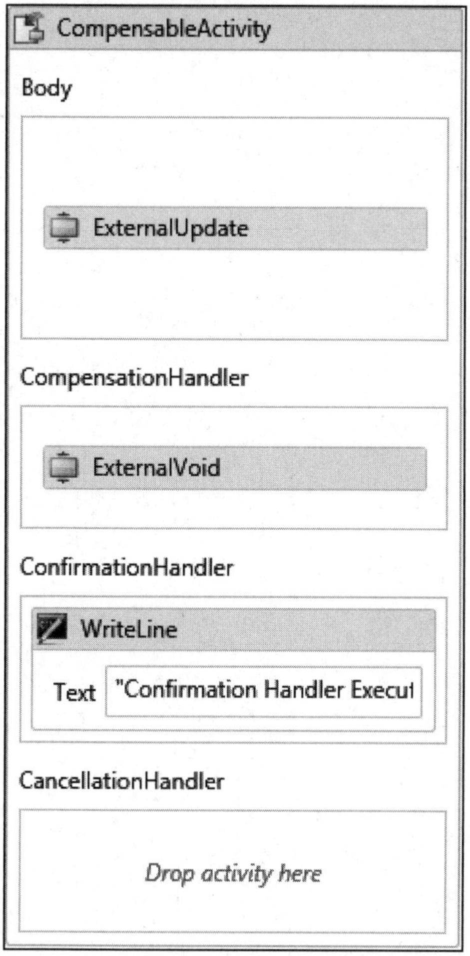

Figure 13-12. CompensableActivity

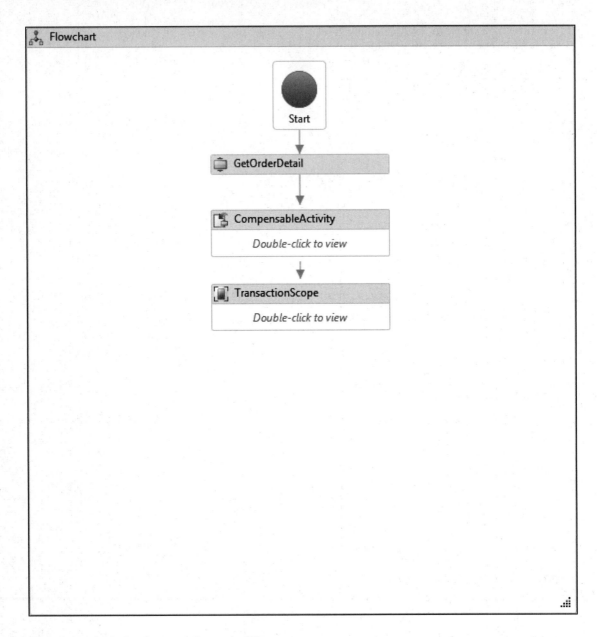

Figure 13-13. UpdateInventoryComp workflow

Hosting the Workflow

Modify the `Program.cs` file of the `UpdateInventory` project to execute the `UpdateInventoryComp` workflow. Here is the affected portion of the `Program.cs` file:

```
using System;
using System.Activities;
using System.Collections.Generic;
using System.Threading;

namespace UpdateInventory
{
    class Program
    {
        static void Main(string[] args)
        {
            Console.WriteLine("UpdateInventoryComp without exception ");
            RunWorkflow(new UpdateInventoryComp(), 43687, false);
            Thread.Sleep(4000);

            Console.WriteLine("\nUpdateInventoryComp with exception ");
            RunWorkflow(new UpdateInventoryComp(), 43687, true);
            Thread.Sleep(4000);
        }
...
    }
}
```

Testing the Workflow

If you build the solution and run the `UpdateInventory` project, you should see results similar to these:

```
UpdateInventoryComp without exception

Product 768: 62 - Starting - No History

Product 765: 46 - Starting - No History

Order Id 43687: Notifying external system to record new sale

Product 768: record new sale

Product 765: record new sale

Product 768: Reduced by 1

Product 765: Reduced by 2
```

```
Product 768: Added history for Qty of 1

Product 765: Added history for Qty of 2

Confirmation Handler Executed

Product 768: 61 - Ending - History Row Found

Product 765: 44 - Ending - History Row Found

UpdateInventoryComp with exception

Product 768: 61 - Starting - No History

Product 765: 44 - Starting - No History

Order Id 43687: Notifying external system to record new sale

Product 768: record new sale

Product 765: record new sale

Product 768: Reduced by 1

Product 765: Reduced by 2

OnUnhandledException: Throw a demo exception!

Order Id 43687: Notifying external system to void previous sale

Product 768: void previous sale

Product 765: void previous sale

Product 768: 61 - Ending - No History

Product 765: 44 - Ending - No History
```

The first workflow was executed without an exception and completed normally. The only additional element that this version of the workflow introduced was the execution of the confirmation handler. In this example, it merely displayed a message on the console, but it could have invoked any other logic necessary to confirm the original execution of the ExternalUpdate activity.

Notice that the confirmation handler was executed after all other activities were completed (including the TransactionScope and all of its children). This makes sense since the confirmation logic shouldn't automatically execute until the entire workflow has succeeded.

The second workflow was executed with an unhandled exception. As you saw in the UpdateInventoryTran example, the database was left in a consistent state, thanks to the

TransactionScope. But in addition to this, the compensation logic was automatically triggered, and the ExternalVoid activity was executed. The previous call to the external system was hypothetically reversed by the ExternalVoid activity.

Now this workflow performs a proper cleanup of itself when an exception is thrown. The database is consistent, and the external system is properly notified of the problem.

Manually Triggering Compensation

The previous example demonstrated how the automatic compensation logic works. You may also need to manually trigger compensation within a workflow. Since the automatic logic relies upon the workflow being canceled, you will need to use manual compensation if you catch and handle an exception condition internally without canceling the entire workflow.

To manually control compensation, you use the Compensate activity. You can also use the related Confirm activity to manually trigger confirmation. You would need to manually confirm a business process once it reached a point where compensation was no longer possible or necessary. Both of these activities require a CompensationToken as an argument. This token is returned in the CompensableActivity.Result property and should be saved in a variable so it can be referenced by a Compensate or Confirm activity.

■ **Note** You also need to manually trigger compensation for nested CompensableActivity instances. The parent activity uses the Compensate activity to trigger compensation for the child instance.

You will complete these tasks to implement this example:

1. Declare the UpdateInventoryManualComp workflow.

2. Host and execute the workflow.

Declaring the UpdateInventoryManualComp Workflow

Make a copy of the UpdateInventoryComp.xaml file, and name the new copy UpdateInventoryManualComp.xaml. Place the copy in the same UpdateInventory project as the original, and modify the workflow name within the Xaml file as you have in previous examples.

Please follow these steps in the workflow designer to modify the UpdateInventoryManualComp workflow:

1. Add a new variable to the top-level Flowchart activity of the workflow. Name the variable Token with a type of CompensationToken. This variable will be used to store the CompensationToken that is returned by the CompensableActivity.

2. Add a TryCatch activity to the workflow. Expand the TryCatch activity, and add a Flowchart activity to the TryCatch.Try property. Change the DisplayName of the Flowchart to TCFlowchart.

3. Add a catch to the TryCatch activity for System.ArithmeticException. Add a Sequence activity to the handler of the new catch.

4. Add a WriteLine activity to the Sequence activity. Set the WriteLine.Text property to String.Format("Caught ArithmeticException: {0}", exception.Message).

5. Add a Compensate activity immediately following the WriteLine in the Sequence activity. Set the Compensate.Target property to Token to reference the new variable.

6. Return to the top-level of the workflow, and select the CompensableActivity and the TransactionScope activity at the same time. Select the Cut option and then expand the TryCatch and the TCFlowchart activities. Paste the two activities that you cut into the TCFlowchart activity. Drag a connection from the start of the TCFlowchart to the top of the CompensableActivity that you just added. Figure 13-14 shows the completed TCFlowchart activity, and Figure 13-15 shows the completed TryCatch.

7. Select the CompensableActivity, and set the Result property to Token. This will store the CompensationToken in the variable for use by the Compensate activity.

8. Return to the top-level Flowchart of the workflow, and drag a connection from the bottom of the GetOrderDetail to the top of the TryCatch.

The top-level of the workflow should look like Figure 13-16. The structure of the TransactionScope, TSFlowchart, and CompensableActivity are unchanged in this workflow.

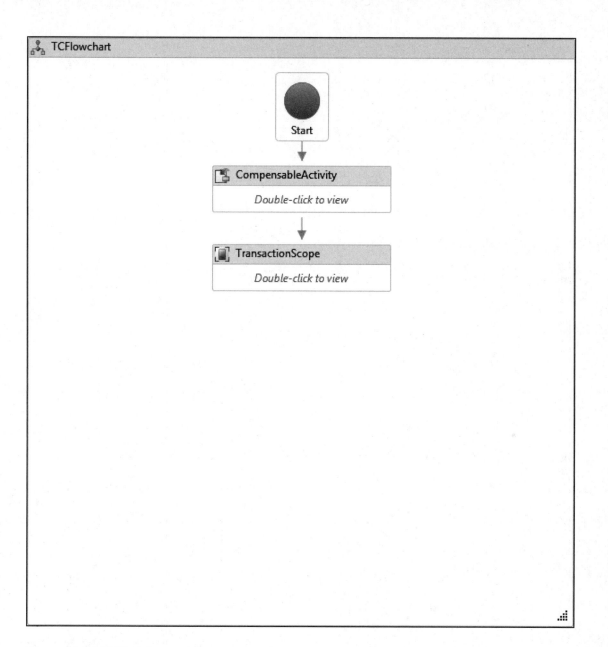

Figure 13-14. TCFlowchart activity

```
┌─────────────────────────────────────────────────────────────┐
│ 🖼 TryCatch                                                  │
│  ┌───────────────────────────────────────────────────────┐  │
│  │ Try                                                    │  │
│  │                                                        │  │
│  │         ┌─────────────────────────────────┐           │  │
│  │         │ 🔗 TCFlowchart              ≫   │           │  │
│  │         │      Double-click to view        │           │  │
│  │         └─────────────────────────────────┘           │  │
│  │                                                        │  │
│  └───────────────────────────────────────────────────────┘  │
│  ┌───────────────────────────────────────────────────────┐  │
│  │ Catches                                                │  │
│  │ ArithmeticException                 ┌───────────────┐  │  │
│  │                                     │ exception     │  │  │
│  │                                     └───────────────┘  │  │
│  │      ┌─────────────────────────────────────────┐      │  │
│  │      │ 🖥 Sequence                        ≪    │      │  │
│  │      │                  ▽                       │      │  │
│  │      │   ┌───────────────────────────────────┐ │      │  │
│  │      │   │ ▨ WriteLine                       │ │      │  │
│  │      │   │  Text │String.Format("Caught Arithn│ │      │  │
│  │      │   └───────────────────────────────────┘ │      │  │
│  │      │                  ▽                       │      │  │
│  │      │   ┌───────────────────────────────────┐ │      │  │
│  │      │   │ 🖹 Compensate                     │ │      │  │
│  │      │   └───────────────────────────────────┘ │      │  │
│  │      │                  ▽                       │      │  │
│  │      └─────────────────────────────────────────┘      │  │
│  │ Add new catch                                          │  │
│  │ Finally                                                │  │
│  │                                                        │  │
│  │                 Drop activity here                     │  │
│  │                                                        │  │
│  └───────────────────────────────────────────────────────┘  │
└─────────────────────────────────────────────────────────────┘
```

Figure 13-15. TryCatch activity

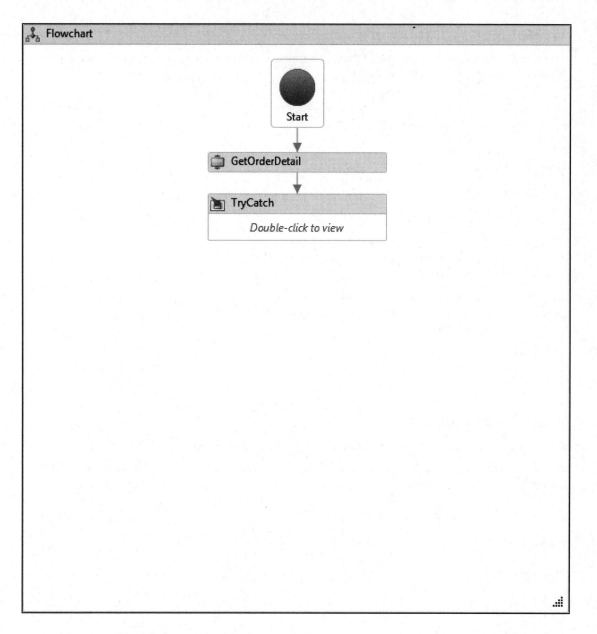

Figure 13-16. UpdateInventoryManualComp *workflow*

Hosting the Workflow

Modify the `Program.cs` file of the `UpdateInventory` project to execute the `UpdateInventoryManualComp` workflow as shown in this code fragment:

```
using System;
using System.Activities;
using System.Collections.Generic;
using System.Threading;

namespace UpdateInventory
{
    class Program
    {
        static void Main(string[] args)
        {
            Console.WriteLine("UpdateInventoryManualComp without exception ");
            RunWorkflow(new UpdateInventoryManualComp(), 43687, false);
            Thread.Sleep(4000);

            Console.WriteLine("\nUpdateInventoryManualComp with exception ");
            RunWorkflow(new UpdateInventoryManualComp(), 43687, true);
            Thread.Sleep(4000);
        }
...
    }
}
```

Testing the Workflow

After building the solution, run the `UpdateInventory` project. Here are my results:

```
UpdateInventoryManualComp without exception

Product 768: 61 - Starting - No History

Product 765: 44 - Starting - No History

Order Id 43687: Notifying external system to record new sale

Product 768: record new sale

Product 765: record new sale

Product 768: Reduced by 1

Product 765: Reduced by 2
```

```
Product 768: Added history for Qty of 1

Product 765: Added history for Qty of 2

Confirmation Handler Executed

Product 768: 60 - Ending - History Row Found

Product 765: 42 - Ending - History Row Found

UpdateInventoryManualComp with exception

Product 768: 60 - Starting - No History

Product 765: 42 - Starting - No History

Order Id 43687: Notifying external system to record new sale

Product 768: record new sale

Product 765: record new sale

Product 768: Reduced by 1

Product 765: Reduced by 2

Caught ArithmeticException: Throw a demo exception!

Order Id 43687: Notifying external system to void previous sale

Product 768: void previous sale

Product 765: void previous sale

Product 768: 60 - Ending - No History

Product 765: 42 - Ending - No History
```

The results are consistent with the previous example. The only difference is that the exception that is thrown by the second workflow is now caught by the **TryCatch** activity. In this case, the workflow wasn't canceled externally by the host application, so the **Compensate** activity was used to manually trigger compensation.

Understanding the CancellationScope Activity

There is one additional activity that is loosely related to the overall topic of this chapter. The CancellationScope activity allows you to assign a handler activity to be executed when an activity is canceled. You would use this activity when you have special processing that is necessary when the activity is canceled.

For example, you might have a long-running activity that is interacting with an external system and is waiting for input. You might pair this activity with a Delay activity, declaring them in separate PickBranch instances within a Pick activity. The Delay would serve as a safeguard to cancel the activity when too much time has elapsed waiting for the receipt of external input. When your long-running activity is canceled, you may want to execute some additional cleanup logic. That additional logic could be declared using the CancellationScope activity.

Here are the most important properties of the CancellationScope activity:

Property	Type	Required	Description
Body	Activity	Yes	The activity that requires cancellation logic
CancellationHandler	Activity	No	The activity to execute when the Body activity is canceled

The CancellationScope is also one of the activities that supports the definition of workflow variables.

Summary

This chapter focused on exception handling and the mechanisms that WF provides to ensure the consistency of work that is performed. After reviewing the default handling for unhandled exceptions, the TryCatch activity was used to handle exceptions declaratively within the workflow.

The TransactionScope activity was then introduced and demonstrated. This activity provides transaction support for activities that can make use of it, such as activities that update a resource like as a database.

Compensation is the process of undoing work that was previously completed. The CompensableActivity, along with the Compensate and Confirm activities, were used to execute declared compensation logic. The chapter concluded with a brief overview of the CancellationScope activity.

In the next chapter, you will learn how to use workflow tracking to instrument your workflows.

■ ■ ■

CHAPTER 14

Workflow Tracking

Workflow tracking is a built-in mechanism that automatically instruments your workflows. By simply adding a tracking participant to the workflow runtime, you are able to track and record status and event data related to each workflow and each activity within a workflow.

The chapter begins with an overview of the workflow tracking functionality included with Windows Workflow Foundation (WF). Following the overview, a more detailed discussion of tracking records, profiles, and participants is presented.

The chapter contains numerous examples that demonstrate how to use the ETW (Event Tracing for Windows) tracking participant that is included with WF. A series of examples is presented that demonstrate how tracking profiles can be used to filter the type of tracking data that is passed to a tracking participant. The creation of custom tracking records is also demonstrated.

The ability to develop your own tracking participant is important since it allows you to directly consume the tracking records in any way that is needed by your application. Two different custom tracking participants are implemented in this chapter.

The chapter concludes with a demonstration of how to configure workflow tracking for declarative workflow services and how to load the tracking configuration from an `App.config` file.

Understanding Workflow Tracking

Visibility is one of the key benefits to using WF. So far, you've seen evidence of this visibility at design time. Using the workflow designer, you visually declare what steps a workflow should execute, the sequence of each step, and the conditions that must be true for each step to execute. You can later view the workflow model that you designed and quickly discern the relationships between activities. This design-time visibility eases the initial development and, more importantly, future maintenance of the workflow.

Visibility at runtime is also an important key benefit of using WF. Since workflows execute within the confines of the workflow runtime engine, they truly operate in a black box. This boundary between the host application and the runtime environment increases the need for some way to monitor the progress of the individual activities within a workflow. Without a built-in mechanism to monitor their execution, you would have to instrument each workflow using your own mechanism.

WF provides such a built-in tracking mechanism. Workflow tracking can monitor each workflow throughout its entire life cycle, tracking important events along the way. Tracking data can be gathered for the workflow as a whole or for individual activities within the workflow. You can even extract argument or variable values from running workflows. And best of all, this tracking mechanism is automatically available without any changes to your activities or workflows.

Uses of Workflow Tracking

As I already mentioned, visibility is the key reason to use workflow tracking. The ability to peek inside the workflow runtime and monitor the progress of a running workflow can be useful in a number of scenarios:

- During development to test and validate the workflow behavior.

- Monitoring the status of workflows in a production environment.

- Performance monitoring for the continuous improvement of production workflow applications.

- Extraction of workflow data for integration with other applications.

Workflow Tracking Architecture

The WF tracking mechanism was designed using a flexible publish and subscribe architecture. The workflow runtime publishes raw *tracking records* that can be consumed by one or more *tracking participants*. It uses a class derived from the abstract `TrackingProvider` class to manage the publishing and filtering of tracking records. Each tracking participant can use the data as it sees fit to meet the needs of that particular participant. Custom participants might be developed to persist tracking data in various forms (to the file system, to a SQL Server database, and so on), to provide simple status notifications to the host application or to pass the relevant data to another application.

    Tracking profiles act as filters for the raw tracking data that is passed to each participant. Each profile contains one or more tracking queries that specify the type of tracking records to include. The tracking queries also allow you to further limit the flow of data based on attributes of each tracking record. For example, you might want to limit the tracking data to a limited set of execution states (Executing, Closed, and so on) for each activity. And you can also filter the tracking data by activity name. Figure 14-1 shows an overview of the WF tracking architecture.

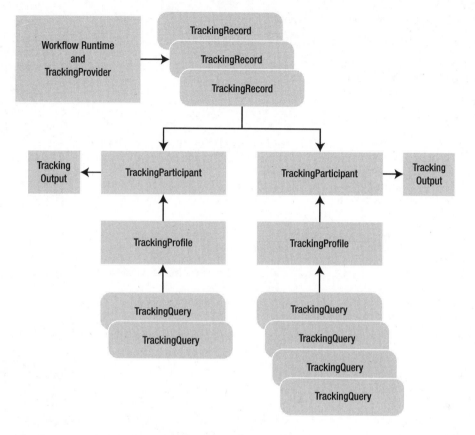

Figure 14-1. Tracking overview

In the sections that follow, I provide additional information on the three major components of workflow tracking: tracking records, profiles, and participants. But before diving into these details, it is important to know that it is actually very easy to utilize workflow tracking in your application. You can generally follow these steps:

1. Determine the reason that you want to use tracking. Do you want to monitor live workflows, improve performance, transmit data to another application, and so on?

2. Based on the reason for wanting to use tracking, select a tracking participant. If necessary, develop a custom tracking participant that meets your specific needs.

3. Create an instance of the tracking participant.

4. Create a tracking profile, and add it to the tracking participant.

5. Add the tracking participant to the workflow instance prior to running the instance.

6. View or otherwise consume the tracking data.

Tracking Records

The tracking data that is produced by the workflow runtime takes the form of a tracking record. WF includes a large variety of different tracking record definitions, with each one containing the additional properties needed to track a particular type of workflow event.

But the base class for all tracking data is the `TrackingRecord` class. This class includes the properties that are common to all tracking records. Here are the most important properties of the `TrackingRecord` class:

Property	Type	Description
InstanceId	Guid	Uniquely identifies the workflow instance
EventTime	DateTime	The date and time of the event
RecordNumber	Int64	A sequential record number for a workflow instance
Level	System.Diagnostics.TraceLevel	Determines the severity of the tracking record (Info, Warning, Error, and so on)
Annotations	IDictionary<String, String>	A collection of optional annotations that are used to describe the data or the event

Figure 14-2 shows the relationship between the other tracking records that are provided with WF.

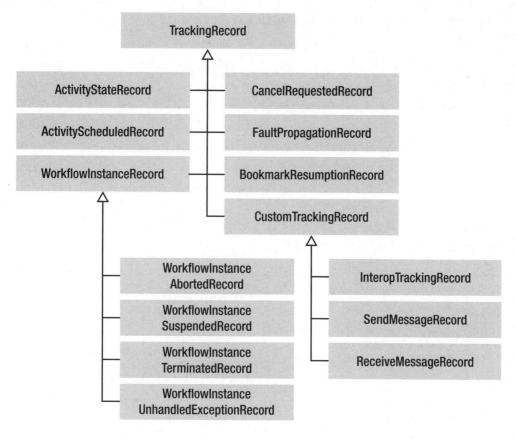

Figure 14-2. Tracking record hierarchy

In the sections that follow, I provide a short description of each of these tracking records. This will provide you with a good overview of the type of data that is made available to you by workflow tracking.

WorkflowInstanceRecord

A `WorkflowInstanceRecord` contains additional data related to the workflow instance as a whole. One of these records is produced when the workflow state has changed. Like all of the tracking records, `WorkflowInstanceRecord` is derived from `TrackingRecord`, so all the properties listed for `TrackingRecord` are also supported. Here are the most important additional properties of this class:

Property	Type	Description
ActivityDefinitionId	String	Contains the workflow name
State	String	Describes the workflow instance state

The `State` property identifies the workflow state and is one of the string values that are defined in the `WorkflowInstanceStates` class:

- Aborted
- Canceled
- Completed
- Deleted
- Idle
- Persisted
- Resumed
- Started
- Suspended
- Terminated
- UnhandledException
- Unloaded
- Unsuspended

WF also provides these four specialized classes that derive from `WorkflowInstanceRecord`:

Class	Description
WorkflowInstanceAbortedRecord	Produced when a workflow instance has been aborted
WorkflowInstanceSuspendedRecord	Produced when a workflow instance has been suspended
WorkflowInstanceTerminatedRecord	Produced when a workflow instance has been terminated
WorkflowInstanceUnhandledExceptionRecord	Produced when a workflow instance throws an unhandled exception

The first three of these classes provide an additional string property named `Reason`. This property is used to identify the reason the workflow instance was aborted, suspended, or terminated. The `WorkflowInstanceUnhandledExceptionRecord` provides these two additional properties:

Property	Type	Description
FaultSource	ActivityInfo	Contains data that identifies the activity that caused the exception
UnhandledException	Exception	The unhandled exception

The `ActivityInfo` class defines basic properties that identify an activity. This class is used in several of the other tracking records whenever a specific activity is identified. Here are the properties supported by the `ActivityInfo` class:

Property	Type	Description
Id	String	A number that uniquely identifies the activity within the workflow
InstanceId	String	Identifies the activity instance within the workflow
Name	String	The display name of the activity
TypeName	String	The type name of the activity, including namespace

ActivityStateRecord

An `ActivityStateRecord` is produced each time the state of an individual activity changes. The most important additional properties of the `ActivityStateRecord` are as follows:

Property	Type	Description
Activity	ActivityInfo	Identifies the activity
State	String	The new state of the activity
Arguments	IDictionary<String, Object>	A collection of input and output arguments for the activity
Variables	IDictionary<String, Object>	A dictionary of named variables that have been collected for the activity

The **State** property is one of the states defined by the **ActivityState** class:

- Executing
- Canceled
- Faulted
- Closed

ActivityScheduledRecord

A **ActivityScheduledRecord** is produced when execution of a child activity is scheduled by its parent. The most important additional properties of this class are as follows:

Property	Type	Description
Activity	ActivityInfo	Identifies the activity that is scheduling execution of one of its children
Child	ActivityInfo	Identifies the child activity being scheduled

BookmarkResumptionRecord

A **BookmarkResumptionRecord** is produced to record the data related to the resumption of a bookmark. The additional properties for this class include the following:

Property	Type	Description
BookmarkName	String	The name of the bookmark being resumed
BookmarkScope	Guid	Identifies the scope of the bookmark
Owner	ActivityInfo	Identifies the activity that created the bookmark and is being resumed
Payload	Object	Any additional data that was passed to the activity when the bookmark was resumed

CancelRequestedRecord

A **CancelRequestedRecord** is produced when a child activity is canceled by its parent. The most important additional properties for this class are as follows:

Property	Type	Description
Activity	ActivityInfo	The activity that is scheduling the cancellation of the child activity
Child	ActivityInfo	The child activity being canceled

FaultPropagationRecord

A FaultPropagationRecord is produced when an exception is thrown within the workflow. The additional properties for this class include the following:

Property	Type	Description
Fault	Exception	The exception that was thrown
FaultSource	ActivityInfo	Identifies the activity that threw the exception
FaultHandler	ActivityInfo	Identifies the activity that ultimately handled the exception
IsFaultSource	Boolean	True if the originator of the exception and the activity that handled it are the same activity

CustomTrackingRecord

The CustomTrackingRecord is produced when you explicitly add code to a custom activity to produce it. It allows you to track any meaningful events or data within your custom activities. The additional properties provided by this class are as follows:

Property	Type	Description
Activity	ActivityInfo	Identifies the activity that produced the custom tracking data
Name	String	A name that you assign to the tracking data to identify it
Data	IDictionary<String, Object>	A collection of named data that you added to the record

The `CustomTrackingRecord` class is the parent of these three specialized classes that derive from it:

Class	Description
InteropTrackingRecord	Produced when the Interop activity is used to execute WF 3.*x* activities
SendMessageRecord	Produced when an activity sends a WCF message
ReceiveMessageRecord	Produced when an activity receives a WCF message

The `InteropTrackingRecord` class provides this additional property:

Property	Type	Description
TrackingRecord	TrackingRecord	The underlying TrackingRecord produced by the Interop activity

The `SendMessageRecord` class provides this additional property:

Property	Type	Description
E2EActivityId	Guid	A unique ID that identifies the end-to-end activity associated with this tracking record

The `ReceiveMessageRecord` class provides these additional properties:

Property	Type	Description
MessageId	Guid	Unique identifier for the message
E2EActivityId	Guid	A unique ID that identifies the end-to-end activity associated with this tracking record

Tracking Profiles

Tracking profiles are used to filter the tracking records that are passed to a tracking participant and are defined using the `TrackingProfile` class. Without a tracking profile, all possible tracking records are passed to the participant. This might result in a much larger set of tracking data than is really necessary for your particular needs. By using a tracking profile, you can tune the type and amount of tracking data that is passed to the tracking participant.

Here are the most important properties of the `TrackingProfile` class:

Property	Type	Description
Name	String	A descriptive name for the tracking profile
ActivityDefinitionId	String	Identifies the activity that this profile should be applied to
Queries	Collection<TrackingQuery>	A collection of TrackingQuery objects that collectively determine which tracking records to include in the profile

There are several tracking query classes that derive from the `TrackingQuery` class. Each one contains additional properties that target queries against a different type of `TrackingRecord`:

Tracking Query Class	Target Tracking Record Class
WorkflowInstanceQuery	WorkflowInstanceRecord
ActivityStateQuery	ActivityStateRecord
ActivityScheduledQuery	ActivityScheduledRecord
BookmarkResumptionQuery	BookmarkResumptionRecord
CancelRequestedQuery	CancelRequestedRecord
FaultPropagationQuery	FaultPropagationRecord
CustomTrackingQuery	CustomTrackingRecord

Each tracking profile that you create can consist of any combination of these tracking query objects. Multiple instances of the same query type are supported. For example, you might need to select tracking data for only a small set of activities by name. To accomplish this, you might need to include an `ActivityStateQuery` (or one of the other queries) for each named activity.

Tracking profiles are generally created in code and added to a tracking participant. Alternatively, for declarative workflow services, they can be defined in the `Web.config` file and read directly at runtime.

■ **Note** WF does not directly read tracking profiles from an `App.config` file for nonmessaging workflows. However, with a small amount of code, you can read a tracking profile from an `App.config` and pass it to a tracking participant. This is demonstrated in one of the examples presented later in this chapter.

In the sections that follow, I provide a brief overview of each query type and a list of their most important properties. You will quickly see a direct correlation between a tracking query and the tracking record that it targets.

The values that you specify for a query are used to limit the tracking records that are sent to the tracking participant. If you specify a value for more than one property of a query, all of the values must match the tracking record in order for the record to be included. For example, entering an `ActivityName` and a `State` value for an `ActivityStateQuery` requires that the tracking record be produced by the named activity and that the state match the one that you specified.

You can specify * (all) as a wildcard value for the query properties. For example, the `WorkflowInstanceQuery` includes a `States` property, which is a collection of `WorkflowInstanceStates`. To specify a value for this property, you can explicitly list the states that you want to include in the profile. Alternatively, you can specify * to include all possible states.

WorkflowInstanceQuery

A `WorkflowInstanceQuery` is used to select instances of the `WorkflowInstanceRecord` class within a profile. Here is the additional property that this query class provides:

Property	Type	Description
States	Collection<String>	A collection of one or more WorkflowInstanceStates that you want to include in the profile. Each value in the collection must be one of the valid states.

ActivityStateQuery

An `ActivityStateQuery` is used to select instances of the `ActivityStateRecord`. Here are the additional properties for this class:

Property	Type	Description
ActivityName	String	Used to restrict the selection to a single named activity.
States	Collection<String>	A collection of one or more ActivityStates that you want to include in the profile. Each value in the collection must be one of the valid states.
Arguments	Collection<String>	A collection of one or more named arguments of the activity that you want to include in the profile.
Variables	Collection<String>	A collection of one or more named in-scope variables of the activity that you want to include in the profile.

ActivityScheduledQuery

An `ActivityScheduledQuery` is used to select instances of the `ActivityScheduledRecord`. Here are the additional properties supported by this class:

Property	Type	Description
ActivityName	String	Used to restrict the selection to a single named parent activity that is scheduling execution of a child activity.
ChildActivityName	String	Used to restrict the selection to a single named child activity that is being scheduled.

BookmarkResumptionQuery

A `BookmarkResumptionQuery` is used to select instances of the `BookmarkResumptionRecord`. Here is the additional property provided by this class:

Property	Type	Description
Name	String	Used to restrict the selection to the named bookmark

CancelRequestedQuery

A `CancelRequestedQuery` is used to select instances of the `CancelRequestedRecord`. The additional properties for this class are as follows:

Property	Type	Description
ActivityName	String	Used to restrict the selection to a single named parent activity that is canceling a child activity
ChildActivityName	String	Used to restrict the selection to a single named child activity that is being canceled

FaultPropagationQuery

A `FaultPropagationQuery` is used to select instances of the `FaultPropagationRecord`. The additional properties for this class are as follows:

Property	Type	Description
FaultSourceActivityName	String	Used to restrict the selection to a single named activity that is throwing an exception
FaultHandlerActivityName	String	Used to restrict the selection to a single named activity that is handling the exception

CustomTrackingQuery

A `CustomTrackingQuery` is used to select instances of the `CustomTrackingRecord`. Additional properties for this class include the following:

Property	Type	Description
ActivityName	String	Used to restrict the selection to a single named activity.
Name	String	Used to restrict the selection to the named custom tracking record. The name specified here must match the name that you supply when the tracking record is produced in code.

Tracking Participants

Tracking participants are the components in the tracking system that receive and work with the tracking records. The records that they receive are first filtered by the tracking profile.

WF includes the `TrackingParticipant` class that all tracking participants must use as their base class. When you need to develop your own tracking participant, you derive from this base class and provide an implementation for the abstract `Track` method.

■ **Note** An example later in this chapter demonstrates how to implement a custom tracking participant.

Out of the box, WF includes a tracking participant (the `EtwTrackingParticipant` class) that records tracking records using the Event Tracing for Windows system. ETW is a greatly enhanced version of the standard Windows event logging system. Just like the standard event logging, ETW logs can be viewed with the Windows Event Viewer management console plug-in.

Using ETW Workflow Tracking

The easiest way to demonstrate workflow tracking is to use the ETW tracking participant that is included with WF. This allows you to immediately see the type of tracking data that is produced by the workflow runtime without the need to first develop your own tracking participant. The tracking data that is produced is viewable using the Windows Event Viewer management console plug-in.

But before you can view tracking data, you need to implement a workflow to track. To satisfy this need, you will declare a workflow that builds upon the examples in Chapter 13. In that chapter, you implemented a series of workflows that update inventory data in the AdventureWorks sample database. For the examples in this chapter, you will declare a greatly simplified workflow that updates the same inventory data. You will reuse the custom activities that you developed for Chapter 13 but will declare a new workflow. The workflow for this chapter does not require the activities that generated a test exception or the transaction or compensation activities.

You will complete these tasks to implement this example:

1. Reference the AdventureWorksAccess project from Chapter 13.

2. Copy selected custom activities from Chapter 13.

3. Implement a new example workflow.

4. Use an ETW tracking participant within the workflow hosting code.

5. Enable the collection of workflow tracking data within the ETW system.

6. View the tracking data after execution of the workflow.

Providing AdventureWorks Access

The custom activities that you will copy in the next step reference the AdventureWorks database tables using LINQ to SQL classes. In Chapter 13, LINQ to SQL classes were generated from the database schema and added to a project named AdventureWorksAccess.

For the examples in this chapter, you can directly reuse that project without any changes. In the steps that follow, the assumption is that you are reusing the existing project by adding it to a new solution for this chapter. Please follow these steps:

1. Create a new empty Visual Studio solution named for this chapter.

2. Use the Add Existing Project option to add the AdventureWorksAccess project from Chapter 13 to the solution for this chapter.

3. Build the solution to make sure it builds correctly.

Copying the Custom Activities

Add a new project to the solution for this chapter using the Activity Library workflow project template, and name the project ActivityLibrary. You can delete the Activity1.xaml file that is generated since it won't be used. Add these references to the ActivityLibrary project if they are not already added for you:

- AdventureWorksAccess (project reference)
- System.Transactions
- System.Data.Linq
- System.Xml.Linq

Make a copy of three of the custom activities from the ActivityLibrary project in Chapter 13, adding each copy to the newly created ActivityLibrary project for this chapter. You'll want to make a copy rather than simply referencing the existing code since you will be modifying one of these activities in an example later in this chapter. Here are the custom activity source files to copy:

- GetOrderDetail.cs
- InsertTranHistory.cs
- UpdateProductInventory.cs

Please refer to Chapter 13 for a complete listing and discussion of these activities. Build the solution before proceeding to the next step. This ensures that everything builds correctly and also adds these custom activities to the Visual Studio Toolbox.

Declaring the Workflow

Unlike most of the examples in this book, you will add this example workflow to the ActivityLibrary instead of implementing it in the host application. Doing this allows you to repackage the workflow for use within a declarative workflow service later in the chapter.

Add a new workflow to the ActivityLibrary project using the Activity Add New Item template. Name the workflow UpdateInventory. The steps needed to declare this workflow are similar to those that you followed in Chapter 13. However, many of the steps are no longer needed for this simplified version of the workflow.

Begin by adding a Flowchart activity to the empty workflow. Add this single argument to the workflow:

Name	Direction	Argument Type
ArgSalesOrderId	In	Int32

The workflow also requires this single variable:

Name	Variable Type	Scope
OrderDetail	List<AdventureWorksAccess.SalesOrderDetail>	Flowchart

Please follow these steps to complete the declaration of the UpdateInventory workflow:

1. Add a GetOrderDetail activity to the flowchart. Set the OrderDetail property to OrderDetail and the SalesOrderId property to ArgSalesOrderId. This activity will retrieve the SalesOrderDetail rows for the requested ArgSalesOrderId and place the result in the OrderDetail variable. Drag a connection from the start of the flowchart to the top of this activity.

2. Add a ForEach<T> activity below the GetOrderDetail activity. Set the generic type to AdventureWorksAccess.SalesOrderDetail, and set the Values property to the OrderDetail variable. Change the DisplayName to ApplyUpdates to better identify the purpose of this activity. Drag a connection from the GetOrderDetail activity to this activity.

3. Expand the ApplyUpdates activity (the ForEach<T> that you just added), and add an UpdateProductInventory activity as the only child. Set the SalesDetail property to item. Figure 14-3 shows the completed ApplyUpdates activity.

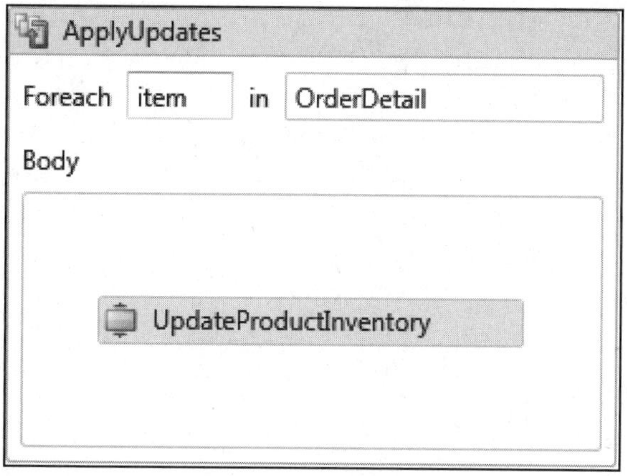

Figure 14-3. ApplyUpdates activity

4. Return to the root **Flowchart** activity, and add another **ForEach<T>** activity below the **ApplyUpdates** activity. Set the generic type to **AdventureWorksAccess.SalesOrderDetail**, and set the **Values** property to the **OrderDetail** variable. Change the **DisplayName** property to **InsertHistory**. Drag a connection from the **ApplyUpdates** activity to this new **ForEach<T>** activity.

5. Expand the **InsertHistory** activity, and add an **InsertTranHistory** activity as the only child. Set the **SalesDetail** property to **item**. Figure 14-4 shows the completed **InsertHistory** activity.

Figure 14-5 shows the completed workflow.

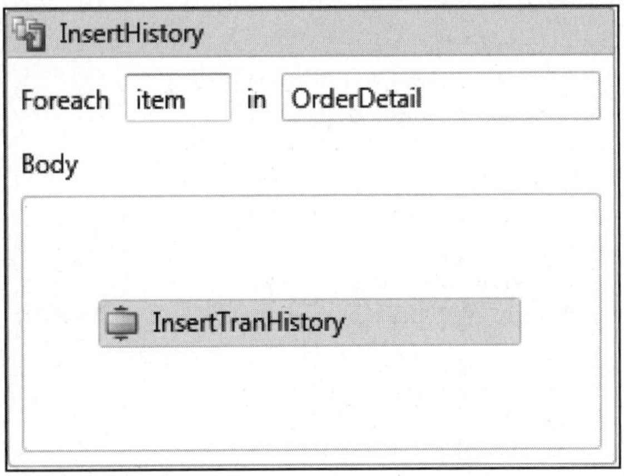

Figure 14-4. InsertHistory activity

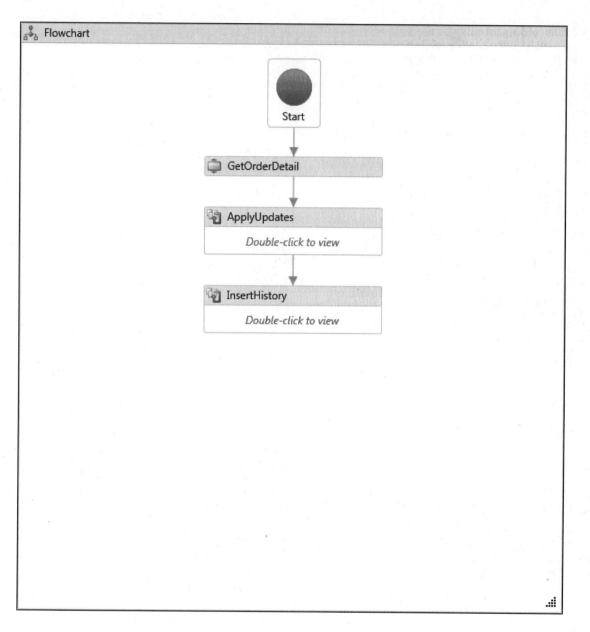

Figure 14-5. Complete UpdateInventory workflow

Hosting the Workflow

To host the workflow, create a new Workflow Console Application project named UpdateInventoryTracking, and add it to the solution for this chapter. Delete the Workflow1.xaml file that is generated with the new project since it won't be used. Add these references to the new project:

- AdventureWorksAccess (project reference)
- ActivityLibrary (project reference)

Revise the Program.cs file to use the EtwTrackingParticipant for tracking when the UpdateInventory workflow is executed. Here is the code that you need for the Program.cs file:

```
namespace UpdateInventoryTracking
{
    using System;
    using System.Activities;
    using System.Activities.Tracking;
    using System.Collections.Generic;
    using ActivityLibrary;

    class Program
    {
        static void Main(string[] args)
        {
            UpdateInventory wf = new UpdateInventory();
            wf.ArgSalesOrderId = 43687;
            WorkflowInvoker instance = new WorkflowInvoker(wf);
            instance.Extensions.Add(new EtwTrackingParticipant());
            instance.Invoke();
        }
    }
}
```

In this first example, a new instance of the EtwTrackingParticpant is created and added to the Extensions property of the WorkflowInvoker instance. Since a tracking profile has not been added to the EtwTrackingParticipant, no filtering of tracking records will be performed. This means that all potential tracking records will be produced. In subsequent examples, you will modify this code by adding a tracking profile to control the type of tracking data that is produced.

The same sales order ID that was used for the examples in Chapter 13 is also used here. This example uses a WorkflowInvoker for simplicity. You can also add a tracking participant to a WorkflowApplication instance in a similar way.

Enabling ETW Workflow Tracking

If you build the solution and run the UpdateInventoryTracking project now, the workflow should execute correctly and update the AdventureWorks database. However, no tracking data will be produced because, by default, the ETW log that controls workflow tracking data is not enabled. To enable workflow tracking, you need to follow these steps:

1. Open the Windows Event Viewer management console plug-in. The easiest way to open this application is to do so directly by entering `eventvwr.msc` on the command line.

2. Navigate to the category that is used for workflow tracking. All workflow tracking records are managed and found under the Applications and Services Logs category. Expand this category, and you should see a category named Microsoft. Under it is another subcategory named Windows.

3. Right-click the Windows category (under Microsoft), and select the View option. Make sure that the Show Analytic and Debug Logs option is selected. If this option is disabled, you won't be able to view and manage the workflow tracking data.

4. The workflow tracking data is located two category levels under the Windows category. First you need to expand the Application Server-Applications category, and under it you should find the Analytic category. The workflow tracking records are managed under the Analytic category.

Figure 14-6 shows a partial view of the Event Viewer category tree that was just described.

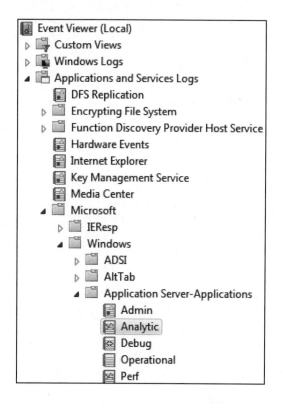

Figure 14-6. Log tree view within Event Viewer

To enable ETW workflow tracking on systems running Vista or later, you need to right-click the Analytic category, and select the Enable Log option. The option to enable the log is also available in a control panel on the right side of the Event Viewer. This panel also contains options to disable, save, and clear the log.

Once this log is enabled, it will continue to record workflow tracking data when an `EtwTrackingParticipant` instance is added as an extension to a workflow instance.

■ **Tip** Once you have enabled logging, leave the Windows Event Viewer open since you will be using it to view the workflow tracking records.

Testing the Workflow

Now that you have enabled ETW logging, you should be able to run the `UpdateInventoryTracking` project and produce working tracking records. Here are the results when I run the project, proving that the workflow itself is operating as expected:

```
Product 768: Reduced by 1

Product 765: Reduced by 2

Product 768: Added history for Qty of 1

Product 765: Added history for Qty of 2
```

Viewing the Tracking Data

To view the tracking data, you can return to the Windows Event Viewer and refresh the Analytic log under the Application Server-Applications category. Figure 14-7 shows the log after running the `UpdateInventoryTracking` project.

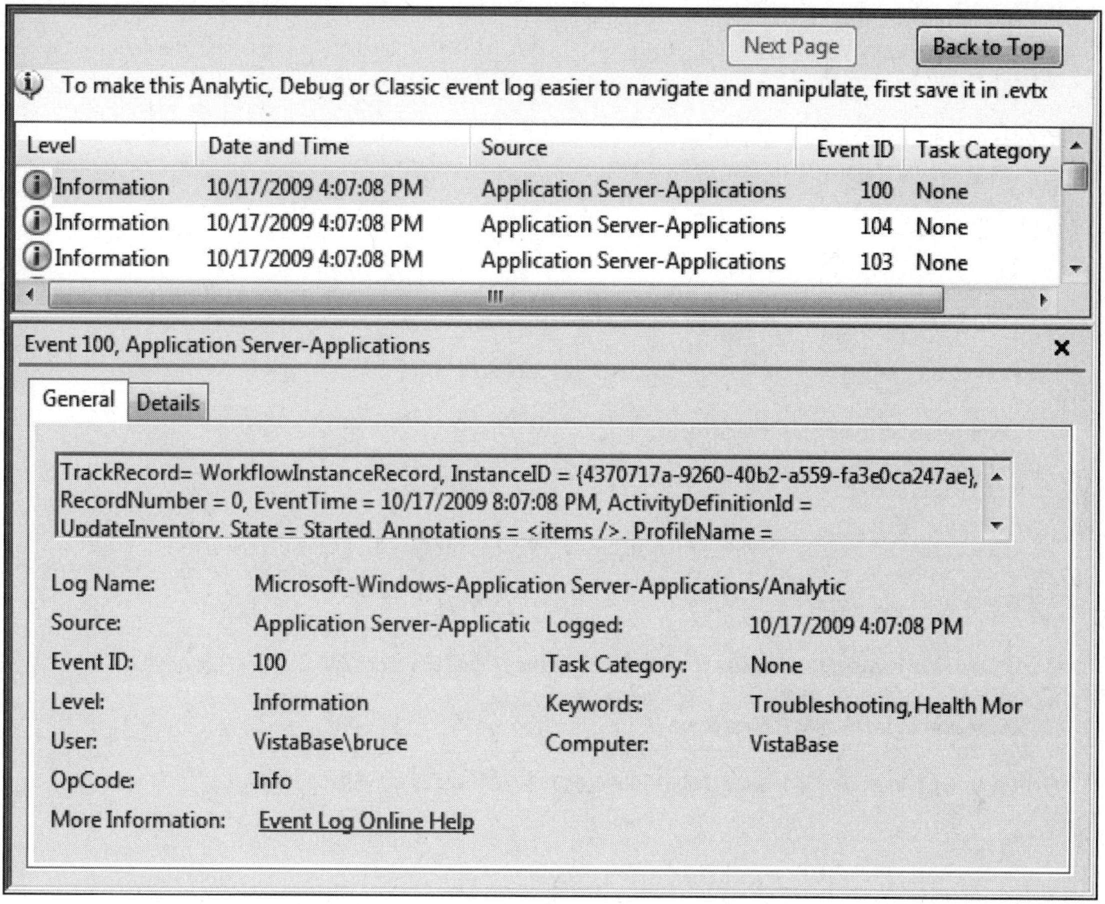

Figure 14-7. Sample Analytic log

The log viewer allows you to examine the values for each tracking record by double-clicking an entry in the list or by selecting the detail tab found in the lower half of the form. Once you select the detail tab, you can view the tracking record in basic or XML format.

Here is an example of the first tracking record after I saved it to an XML file:

```
<Event xmlns='http://schemas.microsoft.com/win/2004/08/events/event'>

  <System>

    <Provider Name='Microsoft-Windows-Application Server-Applications'

      Guid='{c651f5f6-1c0d-492e-8ae1-b4efd7c9d503}'/>
```

```
    <EventID>100</EventID>

    <Version>0</Version>

    <Level>4</Level>

    <Task>0</Task>

    <Opcode>0</Opcode>

    <Keywords>0x20000000000e0040</Keywords>

    <TimeCreated SystemTime='2009-10-22T00:41:24.010Z'/>

    <EventRecordID>0</EventRecordID>

    <Correlation/>

    <Execution ProcessID='3280' ThreadID='12' ProcessorID='0' KernelTime='245'

        UserTime='168'/>

    <Channel>Microsoft-Windows-Application Server-Applications/Analytic</Channel>

    <Computer>VistaBase</Computer>

    <Security UserID='S-1-5-21-2006389094-1177327066-4125713969-1000'/>

</System>

<EventData>

  <Data Name='InstanceId'>{B5A38A3C-FD82-4833-8D11-4DB46012A4C6}</Data>

  <Data Name='RecordNumber'>0</Data>

  <Data Name='EventTime'>2009-10-22T00:41:23.801Z</Data>

  <Data Name='ActivityDefinitionId'>UpdateInventory</Data>

  <Data Name='State'>Started</Data>

  <Data Name='Annotations'>&lt;items /&gt;</Data>

  <Data Name='ProfileName'></Data>

  <Data Name='HostReference'></Data>
```

```
    <Data Name='AppDomain'>UpdateInventoryTracking.exe</Data>

  </EventData>

  <RenderingInfo Culture='en-US'>

    <Message>TrackRecord= WorkflowInstanceRecord,

        InstanceID = {B5A38A3C-FD82-4833-8D11-4DB46012A4C6}, RecordNumber = 0,

        EventTime = 2009-10-22T00:41:23.801Z,

        ActivityDefinitionId = UpdateInventory, State = Started,

        Annotations = &lt;items /&gt;, ProfileName = </Message>

    <Level>Information</Level>

    <Task></Task>

    <Opcode>Info</Opcode>

    <Channel>Analytic</Channel>

    <Provider></Provider>

    <Keywords>

      <Keyword>WF Tracking</Keyword>

      <Keyword>End-to-End Monitoring</Keyword>

      <Keyword>Health Monitoring</Keyword>

      <Keyword>Troubleshooting</Keyword>

    </Keywords>

  </RenderingInfo>

</Event>
```

This saved entry is organized into three major XML elements. The System element contains the data that is common to all ETW log entries. The EventData element contains the workflow tracking data, and the RenderingInfo element contains an interpreted version of the raw data. The RenderingInfo element was generated by selecting "Display information for this language" when I saved the log entries to an XML file. In this case, it was rendered for U.S. English.

By examining this data, you quickly determine that it is a `WorkflowInstanceRecord` for the `UpdateInventory` workflow and that the current workflow state is `Started`. In the table that follows, I outline the complete set of workflow tracking records that were produced for this simple example:

Record Type	Description
WorkflowInstanceRecord	State=Started
ActivityScheduledRecord	Scheduling execution of the UpdateInventory workflow
ActivityStateRecord	Name=UpdateInventory, State=Executing
ActivityScheduledRecord	Scheduling execution of the Flowchart activity
ActivityStateRecord	Name=Flowchart, State=Executing
ActivityScheduledRecord	Scheduling execution of the GetOrderDetail activity
ActivityStateRecord	Name=GetOrderDetail, State=Executing
WorkflowInstanceRecord	State=Idle
ActivityStateRecord	Name=GetOrderDetail, State=Closed
ActivityScheduledRecord	Scheduling execution of the ApplyUpdates activity
ActivityStateRecord	Name=ApplyUpdates, State=Executing
ActivityScheduledRecord	Scheduling execution of the UpdateProductInventory activity
ActivityStateRecord	Name=UpdateProductInventory, State=Executing
WorkflowInstanceRecord	State=Idle
ActivityStateRecord	Name=UpdateProductInventory, State=Closed
ActivityScheduledRecord	Scheduling execution of the UpdateProductInventory activity
ActivityStateRecord	Name=UpdateProductInventory, State=Executing
WorkflowInstanceRecord	State=Idle
ActivityStateRecord	Name=UpdateProductInventory, State=Closed
ActivityStateRecord	Name= ApplyUpdates, State=Closed

Record Type	Description
ActivityScheduledRecord	Scheduling execution of the InsertHistory activity
ActivityStateRecord	Name= InsertHistory, State=Executing
ActivityScheduledRecord	Scheduling execution of the InsertTranHistory activity
ActivityStateRecord	Name= InsertTranHistory, State=Executing
ActivityStateRecord	Name= InsertTranHistory, State=Closed
ActivityScheduledRecord	Scheduling execution of the InsertTranHistory activity
ActivityStateRecord	Name= InsertTranHistory, State=Executing
ActivityStateRecord	Name= InsertTranHistory, State=Closed
ActivityStateRecord	Name= InsertHistory, State=Closed
ActivityStateRecord	Name= Flowchart, State=Closed
ActivityStateRecord	Name= UpdateInventory, State=Closed
WorkflowInstanceRecord	State=Completed, indicating the completion of the workflow

I've obviously had to omit most of the detail that was produced for each of these records. But if you take the time to view these records on your own system, you'll gain a better appreciation of the type of data that is produced for each record type. Particularly interesting is the fact that many of these records include a serialized form of the arguments that are passed to each activity.

■ **Tip** It may be helpful to clear the ETW log before you run each subsequent example in this chapter. Doing this allows you to more easily locate the records from the most recent test. Before a log can be cleared, it must first be disabled.

Using Tracking Profiles

In the examples that follow, you will construct a tracking profile to filter the tracking records that are produced by the UpdateInventory workflow. The tracking profile will be built incrementally, allowing you to see the results as each change is made to the profile. It will begin with a single tracking query but will be enhanced in subsequent examples to include additional tracking records.

Including Selected Workflow Instance States

This first version of the tracking profile will select only WorkflowInstanceRecords that have a state of Started or Completed. A simple profile like this can be used to track when each workflow begins and ends—but that's just about all that it provides. Modify the Program.cs file of the UpdateInventoryTracking project to look like this:

```
namespace UpdateInventoryTracking
{
    using System;
    using System.Activities;
    using System.Activities.Tracking;
    using System.Collections.Generic;
    using ActivityLibrary;

    class Program
    {
        static void Main(string[] args)
        {
            UpdateInventory wf = new UpdateInventory();
            wf.ArgSalesOrderId = 43687;
            WorkflowInvoker instance = new WorkflowInvoker(wf);

            EtwTrackingParticipant tp = new EtwTrackingParticipant();
            tp.TrackingProfile = new TrackingProfile
            {
                Name = "MyTrackingProfile",
                Queries =
                {
                    new WorkflowInstanceQuery
                    {
                        States =
                        {
                            WorkflowInstanceStates.Started,
                            WorkflowInstanceStates.Completed,
                        }
                    }
                }
            };

            instance.Extensions.Add(tp);
            instance.Invoke();
        }
    }
}
```

If you build the solution and run the `UpdateInventoryTracking` project, you should see only these tracking records produced:

Record Type	Description
WorkflowInstanceRecord	State=Started
WorkflowInstanceRecord	State=Completed

Including All Workflow Instance States

Instead of selecting only one or two workflow instance states, you might want to see all state changes for the workflow. To accomplish this, you can modify the profile to look like this:

```
namespace UpdateInventoryTracking
{
...
    class Program
    {
        static void Main(string[] args)
        {
...
            tp.TrackingProfile = new TrackingProfile
            {
                Name = "MyTrackingProfile",
                Queries =
                {
                    new WorkflowInstanceQuery
                    {
                        States = {"*"}
                    }
                }
            };
...
        }
    }
}
```

By specifying the wildcard symbol (*), you should see all possible workflow state changes. When you run the project again, the tracking results should look like this:

Record Type	Description
WorkflowInstanceRecord	State=Started
WorkflowInstanceRecord	State=Idle
WorkflowInstanceRecord	State=Idle
WorkflowInstanceRecord	State=Idle
WorkflowInstanceRecord	State=Completed

The three `Idle` state changes are caused by the asynchronous execution of the `GetOrderDetail` and `UpdateProductInventory` custom activities.

Adding Selected Activity States

You might also want to know when all activities within the workflow begin and end. To accomplish this, you can modify the profile to include an `ActivityStateQuery` like this:

```
namespace UpdateInventoryTracking
{
…
    class Program
    {
        static void Main(string[] args)
        {
…
            tp.TrackingProfile = new TrackingProfile
            {
                Name = "MyTrackingProfile",
                Queries =
                {
                    new WorkflowInstanceQuery
                    {
                        States = {"*"}
                    },
                    new ActivityStateQuery
                    {
```

```
                    States =
                    {
                        ActivityStates.Executing,
                        ActivityStates.Closed
                    }
                }
            }
        };
...
        }
    }
}
```

This time, when you run the `UpdateInventoryTracking` project, the results should look like this:

Record Type	Description
WorkflowInstanceRecord	State=Started, indicating the start of the workflow
ActivityStateRecord	Name=UpdateInventory, State=Executing
ActivityStateRecord	Name=Flowchart, State=Executing
ActivityStateRecord	Name=GetOrderDetail, State=Executing
WorkflowInstanceRecord	State=Idle
ActivityStateRecord	Name=GetOrderDetail, State=Closed
ActivityStateRecord	Name=ApplyUpdates, State=Executing
ActivityStateRecord	Name=UpdateProductInventory, State=Executing
WorkflowInstanceRecord	State=Idle
ActivityStateRecord	Name=UpdateProductInventory, State=Closed
ActivityStateRecord	Name=UpdateProductInventory, State=Executing
WorkflowInstanceRecord	State=Idle
ActivityStateRecord	Name=UpdateProductInventory, State=Closed
ActivityStateRecord	Name= ApplyUpdates, State=Closed
ActivityStateRecord	Name= InsertHistory, State=Executing

Continued

Record Type	Description
ActivityStateRecord	Name= InsertTranHistory, State=Executing
ActivityStateRecord	Name= InsertTranHistory, State=Closed
ActivityStateRecord	Name= InsertTranHistory, State=Executing
ActivityStateRecord	Name= InsertTranHistory, State=Closed
ActivityStateRecord	Name= InsertHistory, State=Closed
ActivityStateRecord	Name= Flowchart, State=Closed
ActivityStateRecord	Name= UpdateInventory, State=Closed
WorkflowInstanceRecord	State=Completed

Targeting Selected Activities

In the previous tracking profiles, you saw how to limit the kind of tracking records that are produced for all activities. You can also construct a tracking profile that targets one or more named activities. You may find this useful during the initial development of the workflow or for a targeted approach to performance tuning once the workflow is in production.

The profile that follows retrieves the activity state data for only a selected list of activities. It also demonstrates how to extract named arguments for an activity and how to add an annotation to a query.

```
namespace UpdateInventoryTracking
{
…
    class Program
    {
        static void Main(string[] args)
        {
…
            tp.TrackingProfile = new TrackingProfile
            {
                Name = "MyTrackingProfile",
                Queries =
                {
                    new WorkflowInstanceQuery
                    {
```

```
                        States =
                        {
                            WorkflowInstanceStates.Started,
                            WorkflowInstanceStates.Completed,
                        }
                    },
```

The two queries that follow use the wildcard indicator for the `Arguments` property. This causes all arguments for the activity to be extracted and included in the tracking record.

```
                new ActivityStateQuery
                {
                    ActivityName = "UpdateInventory",
                    States = { ActivityStates.Executing },
                    Arguments = { "*" }
                },
                new ActivityStateQuery
                {
                    ActivityName = "InsertTranHistory",
                    States = {"*"}
                },
```

The next two queries both reference the same named activity. The first one targets the `Executing` state, while the second specifies the `Closed` state. For the `Executing` state, the `SalesDetail` argument is extracted and included in the tracking record. This particular query also demonstrates the use of an annotation. An annotation is simply additional text that is included in the tracking record to provide a meaningful description for the activity, argument, or state.

```
                new ActivityStateQuery
                {
                    ActivityName = "UpdateProductInventory",
                    States = { ActivityStates.Executing },
                    Arguments = { "SalesDetail" },
                    QueryAnnotations =
                    {
                        {"Threading Model", "Asynchronous update"}
                    }
                },
                new ActivityStateQuery
                {
                    ActivityName = "UpdateProductInventory",
                    States = { ActivityStates.Closed }
                }
            }
        };
...
    }
  }
}
```

When you run the project, the tracking results should look like this:

Record Type	Description
WorkflowInstanceRecord	State=Started, indicating the start of the workflow
ActivityStateRecord	Name=UpdateInventory, State=Executing
ActivityStateRecord	Name=UpdateProductInventory, State=Executing
ActivityStateRecord	Name=UpdateProductInventory, State=Closed
ActivityStateRecord	Name=UpdateProductInventory, State=Executing
ActivityStateRecord	Name=UpdateProductInventory, State=Closed
ActivityStateRecord	Name= InsertTranHistory, State=Executing
ActivityStateRecord	Name= InsertTranHistory, State=Closed
ActivityStateRecord	Name= InsertTranHistory, State=Executing
ActivityStateRecord	Name= InsertTranHistory, State=Closed
WorkflowInstanceRecord	State=Completed

Adding Selected Scheduled Records

In this next example, the previous profile is enhanced to also include the `ActivityScheduledRecord` when a specific named child activity is scheduled.

```
namespace UpdateInventoryTracking
{
...
    class Program
    {
        static void Main(string[] args)
        {
...
            tp.TrackingProfile = new TrackingProfile
            {
                Name = "MyTrackingProfile",
                Queries =
                {
```

```
                    new WorkflowInstanceQuery
                    {
                        States =
                        {
                            WorkflowInstanceStates.Started,
                            WorkflowInstanceStates.Completed,
                        }
                    },
                    new ActivityStateQuery
                    {
                        ActivityName = "UpdateInventory",
                        States = { ActivityStates.Executing },
                        Arguments = { "*" }
                    },
                    new ActivityStateQuery
                    {
                        ActivityName = "InsertTranHistory",
                        States = {"*"}
                    },
                    new ActivityStateQuery
                    {
                        ActivityName = "UpdateProductInventory",
                        States = { ActivityStates.Executing },
                        Arguments = { "SalesDetail" },
                        QueryAnnotations =
                        {
                            {"Threading Model", "Asynchronous update"}
                        }
                    },
                    new ActivityStateQuery
                    {
                        ActivityName = "UpdateProductInventory",
                        States = { ActivityStates.Closed }
                    },
                    new ActivityScheduledQuery
                    {
                        ChildActivityName = "UpdateProductInventory"
                    }
                }
            };
    ...
        }
    }
}
```

The results are similar to the previous example but they now include the selected scheduled records:

Record Type	Description
WorkflowInstanceRecord	State=Started, indicating the start of the workflow
ActivityStateRecord	Name=UpdateInventory, State=Executing
ActivityScheduledRecord	Name=ApplyUpdates, ChildActivityName=UpdateProductInventory
ActivityStateRecord	Name=UpdateProductInventory, State=Executing
ActivityStateRecord	Name=UpdateProductInventory, State=Closed
ActivityScheduledRecord	Name=ApplyUpdates, ChildActivityName=UpdateProductInventory
ActivityStateRecord	Name=UpdateProductInventory, State=Executing
ActivityStateRecord	Name=UpdateProductInventory, State=Closed
ActivityStateRecord	Name= InsertTranHistory, State=Executing
ActivityStateRecord	Name= InsertTranHistory, State=Closed
ActivityStateRecord	Name= InsertTranHistory, State=Executing
ActivityStateRecord	Name= InsertTranHistory, State=Closed
WorkflowInstanceRecord	State=Completed

Including Custom Tracking Records

WF also allows you to create custom tracking records within your custom activities. These tracking records can be used to track any meaningful event or data that is not already provided by one of the standard tracking records.

Creating Custom Tracking Records

To demonstrate how to create custom tracking records, you will modify the `GetOrderDetail` custom activity that can be found in the `ActivityLibrary` project. This is one of the custom activities that you copied from the example code in Chapter 13. You will need to add a `using` statement for the `System.Activities.Tracking` namespace in order to complete the changes.

■ **Note** You can find a full description of this activity in Chapter 13.

Modify the `GetOrderDetail.cs` file to include the additional tracking code shown here:

```
using System;
using System.Activities;
using System.Collections.Generic;
using System.Linq;
using AdventureWorksAccess;

using System.Activities.Tracking;

namespace ActivityLibrary
{
    public sealed class GetOrderDetail : AsyncCodeActivity
    {
        public InArgument<Int32> SalesOrderId { get; set; }
        public OutArgument<List<SalesOrderDetail>> OrderDetail { get; set; }

        protected override IAsyncResult BeginExecute(
            AsyncCodeActivityContext context, AsyncCallback callback,
            object state)
        {
            Func<Int32, List<SalesOrderDetail>> asyncWork =
                orderId => RetrieveOrderDetail(orderId);
            context.UserState = asyncWork;
            return asyncWork.BeginInvoke(
                SalesOrderId.Get(context), callback, state);
        }

        protected override void EndExecute(
            AsyncCodeActivityContext context, IAsyncResult result)
        {
            List<SalesOrderDetail> orderDetail =
                ((Func<Int32, List<SalesOrderDetail>>)
                    context.UserState).EndInvoke(result);
```

After the query against the `AdventureWorks` database has completed, a custom tracking record is created. In this example, the row count from the query is included as additional tracking data. The `Track` method of the activity context is used to record the custom tracking data.

```
            if (orderDetail != null)
            {
                OrderDetail.Set(context, orderDetail);

                //add custom tracking
                CustomTrackingRecord trackRec =
                    new CustomTrackingRecord("QueryResults");
```

```
                    trackRec.Data.Add("Count", orderDetail.Count);
                    context.Track(trackRec);
                }
            }

        private List<SalesOrderDetail> RetrieveOrderDetail(Int32 salesOrderId)
        {
            List<SalesOrderDetail> result = new List<SalesOrderDetail>();
            using (AdventureWorksDataContext dc =
                new AdventureWorksDataContext())
            {
                var salesDetail =
                    (from sd in dc.SalesOrderDetails
                      where sd.SalesOrderID == salesOrderId
                      select sd).ToList();

                if (salesDetail != null && salesDetail.Count > 0)
                {
                    result = salesDetail;
                }
            }
            return result;
        }
    }
}
```

Modifying the Profile

Next, you need to modify the previous tracking profile to also include custom tracking records. Here is the revised profile:

```
namespace UpdateInventoryTracking
{
...
    class Program
    {
        static void Main(string[] args)
        {
...
            tp.TrackingProfile = new TrackingProfile
            {
                Name = "MyTrackingProfile",
                Queries =
                {
                    new WorkflowInstanceQuery
                    {
```

```
                    States =
                    {
                        WorkflowInstanceStates.Started,
                        WorkflowInstanceStates.Completed,
                    }
                },
                new ActivityStateQuery
                {
                    ActivityName = "UpdateInventory",
                    States = { ActivityStates.Executing },
                    Arguments = { "*" }
                },
                new ActivityStateQuery
                {
                    ActivityName = "InsertTranHistory",
                    States = {"*"}
                },
                new ActivityStateQuery
                {
                    ActivityName = "UpdateProductInventory",
                    States = { ActivityStates.Executing },
                    Arguments = { "SalesDetail" },
                    QueryAnnotations =
                    {
                        {"Threading Model", "Asynchronous update"}
                    }
                },
                new ActivityStateQuery
                {
                    ActivityName = "UpdateProductInventory",
                    States = { ActivityStates.Closed }
                },
                new ActivityScheduledQuery
                {
                    ChildActivityName = "UpdateProductInventory"
                },
                new CustomTrackingQuery
                {
                    ActivityName = "*",
                    Name = "*"
                }
            }
        };
...
        }
    }
}
```

The results are similar to the previous example with the addition of the custom tracking record:

Record Type	Description
WorkflowInstanceRecord	State=Started, indicating the start of the workflow
ActivityStateRecord	Name=UpdateInventory, State=Executing
CustomTrackingRecord	ActivityName=GetOrderDetail, Count=2
ActivityScheduledRecord	Name=ApplyUpdates, ChildActivityName=UpdateProductInventory
ActivityStateRecord	Name=UpdateProductInventory, State=Executing
ActivityStateRecord	Name=UpdateProductInventory, State=Closed
ActivityScheduledRecord	Name=ApplyUpdates, ChildActivityName=UpdateProductInventory
ActivityStateRecord	Name=UpdateProductInventory, State=Executing
ActivityStateRecord	Name=UpdateProductInventory, State=Closed
ActivityStateRecord	Name= InsertTranHistory, State=Executing
ActivityStateRecord	Name= InsertTranHistory, State=Closed
ActivityStateRecord	Name= InsertTranHistory, State=Executing
ActivityStateRecord	Name= InsertTranHistory, State=Closed
WorkflowInstanceRecord	State=Completed

Developing a Custom Tracking Participant

The out-of-the-box ETW tracking participant provides an easy way to view and manage workflow tracking data. However, ETW may not always be the right choice for workflow tracking. You may want to persist the tracking data in a format of your own choosing, perhaps writing it to the file system or to a SQL Server database. Or, you may not need to persist the tracking data at all. You might want to use workflow tracking as a communication mechanism and pass the data to another application in real time.

To provide you with the flexibility you need, WF supports an easy way to implement your own custom tracking participant. The steps to accomplish this are indeed very simple:

1. Develop a new class that derives from the base `TrackingParticipant` class provided with WF.

2. Provide an implementation for the abstract `Track` method.

The Track method is invoked by the WF runtime each time one of the workflow tracking records is available and ready to be processed. If a tracking profile was provided, the records have already been filtered by the time the Track method is invoked. In your implementation of the Track method, you have the flexibility to handle the tracking records in any way that makes sense for your application. The TrackingParticipant class also defines BeginTrack and EndTrack virtual methods. You can override these methods to implement asynchronous processing of tracking records.

Once the custom tracking participant has been developed, it is added to the workflow instance as an extension, in exactly the same way as the standard EtwTrackingParticipant class.

To demonstrate how to develop a custom tracking participant, you will implement a tracking participant that persists tracking records to the file system as separate XML files. You will then use this participant to record the tracking records that are produced by the UpdateInventory workflow.

Implementing the Tracking Record Serializer

The XML files that are persisted by the custom tracking participant will contain a serialized form of each tracking record. The actual serialization is done using a bit of reflection and some LINQ to XML code. I chose this approach because my goal was to write one set of code that would be able to easily serialize the most important data from all of the possible workflow tracking records. I wanted to avoid writing hard-coded logic to handle each and every tracking record individually.

■ **Note** My first attempt at implementing a quick way to serialize the tracking records was to turn to the XmlSerializer class. However, I quickly discovered that the tracking records lack a parameterless constructor, which is a requirement when using the XmlSerializer. The next best approach was to write the code that you see here to perform my own XML serialization.

The XML serialization code is implemented in its own class, separate from the tracking participant. Add a new class (a normal C# class, not a workflow class) to the ActivityLibrary project, and name it TrackingRecordSerializer. Here is the implementation for this class:

```
using System;
using System.Activities.Tracking;
using System.Collections.Generic;
using System.Reflection;
using System.Xml.Linq;

namespace ActivityLibrary
{
    public static class TrackingRecordSerializer
    {
```

The Serialize method is the only public member of this class. It is invoked from the tracking participant (implemented in the next step) as each record is being processed. The method creates the outermost root elements of the XML document and then calls a private SerializeObject method to handle the serialization of the record.

```
public static String Serialize(TrackingRecord tr)
{
    if (tr == null)
    {
        return String.Empty;
    }

    XElement root = new XElement(tr.GetType().Name);
    XDocument xml = new XDocument(root);

    SerializeObject(root, tr);
    return xml.ToString();
}
```

The private SerializeObject method controls the serialization of each property of the tracking record. A design assumption of this class is that I only want to serialize public properties of each object. Special handling is provided for IDictionary properties. This was necessary in order to handle several of the tracking record properties (Annotations, Arguments, Variables). You will need to enhance this code if the data that you are tracking includes other collection types such as IList.

```
private static void SerializeObject(
    XElement parent, Object o)
{
    PropertyInfo[] properties = o.GetType().GetProperties();
    foreach (PropertyInfo property in properties)
    {
        if (IsPropertyWeWant(property))
        {
            if (property.PropertyType.IsGenericType)
            {
                if (property.PropertyType.Name == "IDictionary`2")
                {
                    SerializeDictionary(property, parent, o);
                }
            }
            else
            {
                Object value = property.GetValue(o, null);
                parent.Add(new XElement(property.Name, value));
            }
        }
    }
}
```

The IsPropertyWeWant method is invoked for each property before it is serialized. In its current form, it is designed to omit certain LINQ-related properties. This was necessary for this particular example because the LINQ to SQL classes that were generated for the AdventureWorksAccess project include several of these special association properties that you wouldn't normally want to serialize.

```
private static bool IsPropertyWeWant(PropertyInfo property)
{
    if (property.IsDefined(
        typeof(System.Data.Linq.Mapping.AssociationAttribute), true))
    {
        return false;
    }
    else
    {
        return true;
    }
}
```

The SerializeDictionary and SerializeKeyValuePair methods are used when serializing an IDictionary. The goal of this code is to perform a serialization of the properties for each entry in the dictionary.

```
private static void SerializeDictionary(
    PropertyInfo property, XElement parent, Object o)
{
    XElement element = new XElement(property.Name);
    parent.Add(element);

    Object value = property.GetValue(o, null);
    if (value is IDictionary<String, String>)
    {
        foreach (var kvPair in (IDictionary<String, String>)value)
        {
            SerializeKeyValuePair(element, kvPair.Key, kvPair.Value);
        }
    }
    else if (value is IDictionary<String, Object>)
    {
        foreach (var kvPair in (IDictionary<String, Object>)value)
        {
            SerializeKeyValuePair(element, kvPair.Key, kvPair.Value);
        }
    }
}

private static void SerializeKeyValuePair(
    XElement element, Object key, Object value)
{
    if (value == null)
    {
        return;
    }

    Type type = value.GetType();
    if (type.IsPrimitive || type == typeof(String))
    {
```

```
                    element.Add(new XElement("item",
                        new XAttribute("key", key),
                        new XAttribute("value", value)));
                }
                else
                {
                    XElement valueElement = new XElement("value");
                    //recursive call to serialize the value object
                    SerializeObject(valueElement, value);
                    element.Add(new XElement("item",
                        new XAttribute("key", key), valueElement));
                }
            }
        }
    }
}
```

■ **Note** Please remember that this serialization code is not a requirement for implementing your own custom tracking participant. It is required by this particular example since I made the design decision to serialize the tracking records to XML.

Implementing the Custom Tracking Participant

Now that the serialization logic has been implemented, you can turn your attention to the tracking participant itself. This tracking participant uses an in-memory queue and a separate thread to serialize and persist each tracking record.

Add a new C# class to the **ActivityLibrary**, and name it **FileTrackingParticipant**. Here is the complete implementation for this class:

```
using System;
using System.Activities.Tracking;
using System.Collections.Generic;
using System.IO;
using System.Text;
using System.Threading;
using System.Xml;

namespace ActivityLibrary
{
    public class FileTrackingParticipant : TrackingParticipant
    {
        private Queue<TrackingRecord> _records = new Queue<TrackingRecord>();
        private AutoResetEvent _recordsToProcess = new AutoResetEvent(false);
        private Thread _processingThread;
        private Boolean _isThreadRunning;
```

```
public FileTrackingParticipant()
{
    _processingThread = new Thread(ProcessingThreadProc);
    _isThreadRunning = true;
    _processingThread.Start();
}
```

The Track method is invoked for each record that is produced by the WF runtime. In this implementation, the records are immediately added to an in-memory queue. An AutoResetEvent is set in order to signal to the processing thread that one or more records are available to be processed. This approach isn't absolutely necessary, since you could more easily serialize and persist the tracking record directly in the Track method. However, using a queue and a separate thread allows the Track method to complete more quickly and offloads the real work to a separate thread.

```
protected override void Track(TrackingRecord record, TimeSpan timeout)
{
    lock (_records)
    {
        _records.Enqueue(record);
    }
    _recordsToProcess.Set();
}
```

Since this class immediately creates and starts a separate thread, a method was needed to stop the thread once all processing was complete. This Stop method will be called by the workflow host application.

```
public void Stop()
{
    _isThreadRunning = false;
    _processingThread.Join(5000);
}

private void ProcessingThreadProc()
{
    while (_isThreadRunning)
    {
        if (_recordsToProcess.WaitOne(2000))
        {
            Int32 count = 0;
            lock (_records)
            {
                count = _records.Count;
            }
```

```
                while (count > 0)
                {
                    TrackingRecord record = null;
                    lock (_records)
                    {
                        record = _records.Dequeue();
                        count = _records.Count;
                    }

                    if (record != null)
                    {
                        PersistRecord(record);
                    }
                }
            }
        }
    }
```

The private `PersistRecord` method is invoked by the processing thread for each tracking record. Each record is written to a separate file, with the file name being generated from the `EventTime` and `RecordNumber` of each tracking record. A call to the static `Serialize` method of the `TrackingRecordSerializer` class is made to serialize each record to XML.

```
    private void PersistRecord(TrackingRecord tr)
    {
        try
        {
            String path = Path.Combine(
                Environment.CurrentDirectory, "tracking");
            String fileName = String.Format("{0}.{1}",
                tr.EventTime.ToString("yyyyMMdd.HHmmss.fffffff"),
                tr.RecordNumber);
            String fullPath = Path.Combine(path, fileName + ".xml");

            if (!Directory.Exists(path))
            {
                Directory.CreateDirectory(path);
            }

            using (FileStream stream =
                new FileStream(fullPath, FileMode.Create))
            {
                XmlWriterSettings settings = new XmlWriterSettings();
                settings.Encoding = Encoding.UTF8;
                using (XmlWriter writer = XmlWriter.Create(stream, settings))
                {
                    writer.WriteRaw(TrackingRecordSerializer.Serialize(tr));
                }
            }
        }
```

```
            catch (IOException exception)
            {
                Console.WriteLine(
                    "PersistRecord Exception: {0}", exception.Message);
            }
        }
    }
}
```

Testing the Tracking Participant

To test the new tracking participant, you can modify the `Program.cs` file of the `UpdateInventoryTracking` project to use the new `FileTrackingParticipant` like this:

```
namespace UpdateInventoryTracking
{
    using System;
    using System.Activities;
    using System.Activities.Tracking;
    using System.Collections.Generic;
    using ActivityLibrary;

    class Program
    {
        static void Main(string[] args)
        {
            FileTrackingParticipant tp = new FileTrackingParticipant();

            UpdateInventory wf = new UpdateInventory();
            wf.ArgSalesOrderId = 43687;
            WorkflowInvoker instance = new WorkflowInvoker(wf);

            tp.TrackingProfile = new TrackingProfile
            {
                Name = "MyTrackingProfile",
                Queries =
                {
                    new WorkflowInstanceQuery
                    {
                        States =
                        {
                            WorkflowInstanceStates.Started,
                            WorkflowInstanceStates.Completed,
                        }
                    },
                    new ActivityStateQuery
                    {
                        ActivityName = "UpdateInventory",
                        States = { ActivityStates.Executing },
                        Arguments = { "*" }
                    },
```

```
                new ActivityStateQuery
                {
                    ActivityName = "InsertTranHistory",
                    States = {"*"}
                },
                new ActivityStateQuery
                {
                    ActivityName = "UpdateProductInventory",
                    States = { ActivityStates.Executing },
                    Arguments = { "SalesDetail" },
                    QueryAnnotations =
                    {
                        {"Threading Model", "Asynchronous update"}
                    }
                },
                new ActivityStateQuery
                {
                    ActivityName = "UpdateProductInventory",
                    States = { ActivityStates.Closed }
                },
                new ActivityScheduledQuery
                {
                    ChildActivityName = "UpdateProductInventory"
                },
                new CustomTrackingQuery
                {
                    ActivityName = "*",
                    Name = "*"
                }
            }
        };

        instance.Extensions.Add(tp);
        instance.Invoke();

        tp.Stop();
    }
  }
}
```

The only significant changes are the creation of the `FileTrackingParticipant` instead of the `EtwTrackingParticipant` and the call to the `Stop` method once the workflow has completed.

When you run the `UpdateInventoryProject`, you should see that a `\tracking` subfolder has been created under the `\bin\debug` folder for the project and that the new folder contains a number of XML files. Here is a list of the files created when I run this test:

```
20091021.204148.8879005.0.xml

20091021.204148.8879005.2.xml

20091021.204149.0594477.6.xml

20091021.204149.0644637.8.xml

20091021.204149.0654669.9.xml

20091021.204149.1457229.11.xml

20091021.204149.1487325.12.xml

20091021.204149.1497357.13.xml

20091021.204149.1988925.15.xml

20091021.204149.2029053.18.xml

20091021.204149.2430333.19.xml

20091021.204149.2470461.21.xml

20091021.204149.2771421.22.xml

20091021.204149.2801517.24.xml
```

If you take a look at the files that were generated, you'll see that they do indeed contain the tracking records. For example, the contents of the `20091021.204149.0654669.9.xml` file look like this:

```
<?xml version="1.0" encoding="utf-8"?><ActivityStateRecord>

  <Activity>Name=UpdateProductInventory, ActivityId = 1.9, ActivityInstanceId = 5,
TypeName=ActivityLibrary.UpdateProductInventory</Activity>

  <State>Executing</State>

  <Variables />

  <Arguments>

    <item key="SalesDetail">

      <value>
```

```
            <SalesOrderID>43687</SalesOrderID>

            <SalesOrderDetailID>256</SalesOrderDetailID>

            <CarrierTrackingNumber>61FA-475A-AC</CarrierTrackingNumber>

            <OrderQty>1</OrderQty>

            <ProductID>768</ProductID>

            <SpecialOfferID>1</SpecialOfferID>

            <UnitPrice>419.4589</UnitPrice>

            <UnitPriceDiscount>0.0000</UnitPriceDiscount>

            <LineTotal>419.458900</LineTotal>

            <rowguid>9bfb4b65-3927-4084-ba66-2678173a69d0</rowguid>

            <ModifiedDate>2001-07-01T00:00:00</ModifiedDate>

        </value>

      </item>

  </Arguments>

  <InstanceId>eaf2cd93-cd29-46ce-908d-c9d7226b1806</InstanceId>

  <RecordNumber>9</RecordNumber>

  <EventTime>2009-10-21T20:41:49.0654669-04:00</EventTime>

  <Level>Info</Level>

  <Annotations>

    <item key="Threading Model" value="Asynchronous update" />

  </Annotations>

</ActivityStateRecord>
```

Developing a Nonpersisting Tracking Participant

In the previous example, you developed a custom tracking participant that serialized and persisted each tracking record to an XML file. However, it is important to note that persistence is not a requirement of a tracking participant. You might not require persistence of tracking data and instead want to consume it immediately within your application.

In this short example, you will develop a much simpler custom tracking participant that forwards the tracking records to the host application for processing.

Implementing the Tracking Participant

This custom tracking participant defines a public delegate that is used to pass the tracking records to the host application. The host application can assign code to the delegate in order to handle the tracking data.

Add a new C# class to the `ActivityLibrary` project, and name it `EventTrackingParticipant`. Here is the complete code for this class:

```
using System;
using System.Activities.Tracking;

namespace ActivityLibrary
{
    public class EventTrackingParticipant : TrackingParticipant
    {
        public Action<TrackingRecord> Received { get; set; }

        protected override void Track(TrackingRecord record, TimeSpan timeout)
        {
            if (Received != null)
            {
                Received.BeginInvoke(record, BeginInvokeCallback, Received);
            }
        }

        private void BeginInvokeCallback(IAsyncResult ar)
        {
            ((Action<TrackingRecord>)ar.AsyncState).EndInvoke(ar);
        }
    }
}
```

Testing the Tracking Participant

To test this new tracking participant, you can modify the `Program.cs` file of the `UpdateInventoryTracking` project as shown here:

```
namespace UpdateInventoryTracking
{
    using System;
    using System.Activities;
    using System.Activities.Tracking;
    using System.Collections.Generic;
    using ActivityLibrary;

    class Program
    {
        static void Main(string[] args)
        {
            EventTrackingParticipant tp =
                new EventTrackingParticipant();
            tp.Received = tr =>
                Console.WriteLine("{0:D2} {1:HH:mm:ss.ffffff} {2}",
                    tr.RecordNumber,
                    tr.EventTime,
                    tr.GetType().Name);

            UpdateInventory wf = new UpdateInventory();
            wf.ArgSalesOrderId = 43687;
            WorkflowInvoker instance = new WorkflowInvoker(wf);

            instance.Extensions.Add(tp);
            instance.Invoke();
        }
    }
}
```

Before executing the workflow, code is assigned to the `Received` delegate of the custom
`EventTrackingParticipant` class. In this example, the assigned code simply writes a line to the console
for each tracking record that it receives. However, you could easily use this data to update a progress
indicator in the application, notify an external application of the workflow's progress, and so on. A
tracking profile is not provided for this example, so all possible tracking records should be processed.

When I run the `UpdateInventoryTracking` project, I see these results:

```
00 20:41:57.741140 WorkflowInstanceRecord

01 20:41:57.741140 ActivityScheduledRecord

02 20:41:57.741140 ActivityStateRecord

04 20:41:57.752175 ActivityStateRecord

05 20:41:57.752175 ActivityScheduledRecord

03 20:41:57.741140 ActivityScheduledRecord
```

```
06 20:41:57.755185 ActivityStateRecord

07 20:41:57.756188 WorkflowInstanceRecord

08 20:41:57.819390 CustomTrackingRecord

09 20:41:57.819390 ActivityStateRecord

10 20:41:57.820393 ActivityScheduledRecord

11 20:41:57.821396 ActivityStateRecord

12 20:41:57.821396 ActivityScheduledRecord

13 20:41:57.823402 ActivityStateRecord

14 20:41:57.824406 WorkflowInstanceRecord

Product 768: Reduced by 1

15 20:41:57.862527 ActivityStateRecord

16 20:41:57.863530 ActivityScheduledRecord

Product 765: Reduced by 2

17 20:41:57.863530 ActivityStateRecord

18 20:41:57.863530 WorkflowInstanceRecord

19 20:41:57.890617 ActivityStateRecord

20 20:41:57.895633 ActivityStateRecord

21 20:41:57.896636 ActivityScheduledRecord

22 20:41:57.897639 ActivityStateRecord

23 20:41:57.897639 ActivityScheduledRecord

Product 768: Added history for Qty of 1

24 20:41:57.899646 ActivityStateRecord

25 20:41:57.921716 ActivityStateRecord

26 20:41:57.921716 ActivityScheduledRecord
```

```
Product 765: Added history for Qty of 2

27 20:41:57.922719 ActivityStateRecord

28 20:41:57.937767 ActivityStateRecord

29 20:41:57.938770 ActivityStateRecord

30 20:41:57.938770 ActivityStateRecord

31 20:41:57.938770 ActivityStateRecord

32 20:41:57.938770 WorkflowInstanceRecord
```

■ **Note** Remember that you can use multiple tracking participants at the same time. If you want to see this in action yourself, you can add the `EtwTrackingParticipant` or the `FileTrackingParticipant` to this example and run it again.

Using Workflow Tracking with a Declarative Service Application

As you might expect, workflow tracking can also be enabled for workflows that use WCF messaging. This includes declarative services that are hosted by IIS. The workflow tracking concepts are the same for declarative service applications. The one major difference is the way tracking is enabled and how profiles are defined. Unless a messaging workflow is self-hosted using the `WorkflowServiceHost`, you don't have an opportunity to construct a tracking participant and profile in code. Instead, workflow tracking must be declared in the `Web.config` file.

In this next example, you will construct a declarative service that packages the `UpdateInventory` activity as a WCF-enabled workflow that can be hosted by IIS.

Declaring the InventoryService Workflow

Begin this example by adding a new WCF Workflow Service Application to the solution for this chapter. Name the new application `UpdateInventoryService`. You can delete the `Service1.xamlx` file since it won't be used. Add these references to the project:

- `AdventureWorksAccess` (project reference)
- `ActivityLibrary` (project reference)

Add a new WCF Workflow Service to the project, and name it `InventoryService`. You can now open the `InventoryService.xamlx` file in the workflow designer, and follow these steps to complete the declaration of the workflow:

1. Delete the root `Sequence` activity that was generated for you. I find it easier to start from scratch instead of modifying the template-generated service.

2. Add a new `ReceiveAndSendReply` activity template to the empty workflow.

3. Add an `Int32` variable named `SalesOrderId` that is scoped by the `Sequence` activity.

4. Set the properties for the `Receive` activity. Set the `CanCreateInstance` property to true, set the `OperationName` to `Update`, and change the `ServiceContractName` to `IInventoryService`. Define the content for the activity by adding a single `Int32` parameter named `salesOrderId` with the value set to the `SalesOrderId` variable that you previously defined. Add `System.Int32` to the collection of `KnownTypes` if it is not already included.

5. Set the properties for the `SendReplyToReceive` activity. Define the content for the activity by adding a single `Boolean` parameter named result. Return a value of `True` for this parameter.

6. Drag an instance of the `UpdateInventory` activity from the Toolbox to the location between the `Receive` and `Send` activities. This activity is the complete workflow that you have been using throughout this chapter. However, in this case, you are executing it as an activity within this declarative service workflow. Set the `ArgSalesOrderId` property to the `SalesOrderId` variable.

Figure 14-8 is the completed `InventoryService` workflow.

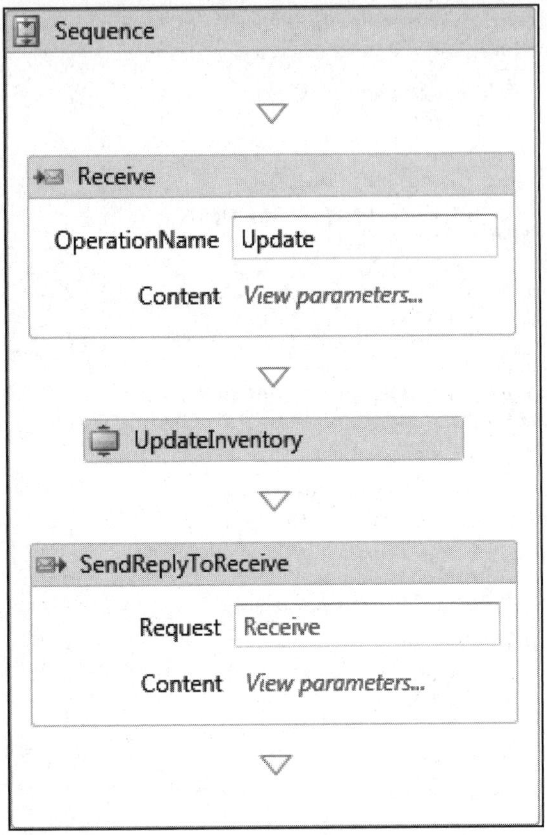

Figure 14-8. InventoryService.xamlx

Configuring Tracking in the Web.config

For an application like this that is not self-hosted, the tracking participant and profile must be configured in the `Web.config` file. For this example, you will define a tracking profile that is similar to those that you have previously defined in this chapter. The `UpdateInventoryService` project should already have a `Web.config` file. You simply need to update it with the entries shown here:

```
<?xml version="1.0" encoding="utf-8" ?>
<configuration>
  <system.web>
  </system.web>
```

The tracking participant is defined as a service behavior. This is also where the tracking profile (defined next in the file) is referenced.

```
<system.serviceModel>
  <behaviors>
    <serviceBehaviors>
      <behavior>
        <etwTracking profileName="MyTrackingProfile"/>
        <serviceDebug includeExceptionDetailInFaults="False" />
        <serviceMetadata httpGetEnabled="True"/>
      </behavior>
    </serviceBehaviors>
  </behaviors>
```

The definition of the tracking profile follows a format that is logically the same as the profiles that you defined in code. The profile consists of one or more queries that each support their own particular set of properties.

```
<tracking>
  <profiles>
    <trackingProfile name="MyTrackingProfile">
      <workflow activityDefinitionId="*">
        <workflowInstanceQueries>
          <workflowInstanceQuery>
            <states>
              <state name="Started"/>
              <state name="Completed"/>
            </states>
          </workflowInstanceQuery>
        </workflowInstanceQueries>
        <activityStateQueries>
          <activityStateQuery activityName="UpdateInventory">
            <states>
              <state name="Executing"/>
            </states>
            <arguments>
              <argument name="*"/>
            </arguments>
          </activityStateQuery>
          <activityStateQuery activityName="UpdateProductInventory">
            <states>
              <state name="Executing"/>
              <state name="Closed"/>
            </states>
            <arguments>
              <argument name="SalesDetail"/>
            </arguments>
            <annotations>
              <annotation name="Threading Model" value="Asynchronous update"/>
            </annotations>
          </activityStateQuery>
```

```
        </activityStateQueries>
        <activityScheduledQueries>
          <activityScheduledQuery childActivityName="UpdateProductInventory"/>
        </activityScheduledQueries>
        <customTrackingQueries>
          <customTrackingQuery activityName="*" name="*"/>
        </customTrackingQueries>
        <faultPropagationQueries>
          <faultPropagationQuery faultSourceActivityName ="*"
            faultHandlerActivityName="*"/>
        </faultPropagationQueries>
      </workflow>
    </trackingProfile>
   </profiles>
  </tracking>
 </system.serviceModel>
</configuration>
```

Testing the Workflow Service

You can follow these steps to test workflow tracking for the workflow service:

1. Since this example is using the EtrTrackingParticipant, make sure that the Analytic log has been enabled.

2. Run the UpdateInventoryService project without debugging (Ctrl-F5). This starts the ASP.NET development server. You should see an icon for the development server in the system tray.

3. Running the project should also start your default browser, opened to the project directory.

4. Right-click the InventoryService.xamlx link in the browser, and copy the link location.

5. Start the WcfTestClient utility (distributed with Visual Studio and found under the \Common7\IDE folder). Select the Add Service option from the File menu, and paste the link location that you copied from the browser. At this point, the WcfTestClient retrieves the metadata that defines the workflow service.

6. Once the metadata for the service has been retrieved, you should see the Update operation on the left side of the client. Double-click the Update operation, and enter 43687 as the salesOrderId parameter. Click the Invoke button to execute the workflow service.

Figure 14-9 shows the WcfTestClient after the workflow service has been invoked.

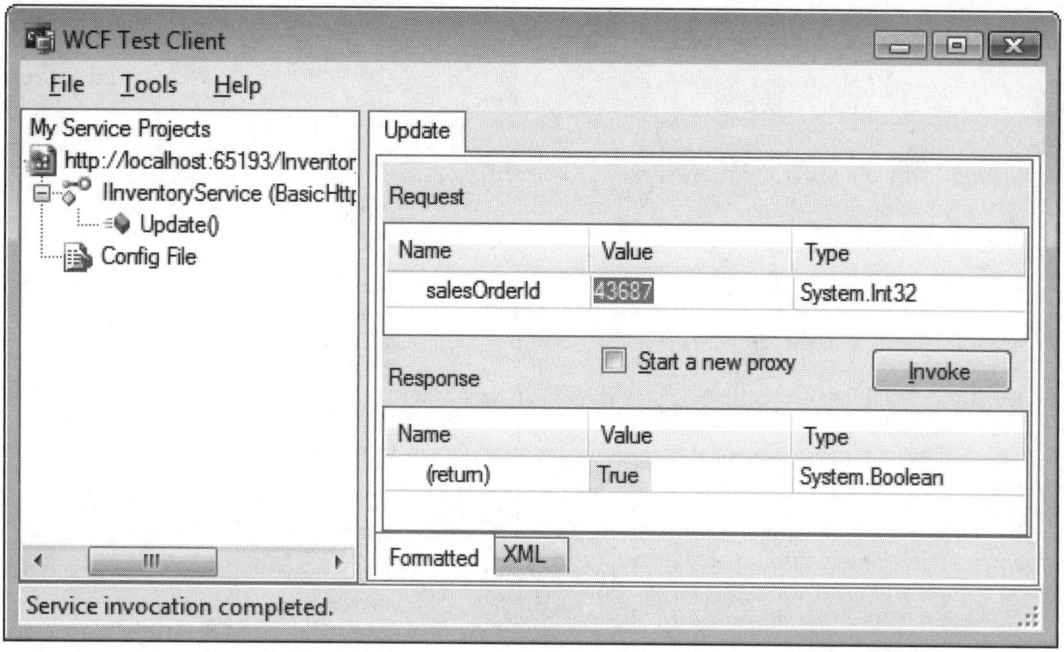

Figure 14-9. Invoking InventoryService.xamlx with WcfTestClient

You should now be able to view the ETW workflow tracking records using the Windows Event Viewer as you did earlier in the chapter. The results should be similar to the previous examples. However, the log will also include additional WCF-related entries in addition to the workflow tracking records.

Loading Tracking Profiles from App.config

The ability to configure tracking profiles in the `Web.config` file is convenient since it avoids the need to modify and rebuild profiles that are defined in code. However, although this works for declarative service workflows, WF does not provide an out-of-the-box way to load tracking profiles from an `App.config` file for non-WCF workflows. But with a small amount of code, you can load tracking profiles from the `App.config` file.

In the short example that follows, you will develop a class that loads a named tracking profile from an `App.config` file. You will then define a tracking profile in an `App.config` file and use this class to load it.

Implementing a Tracking Profile Loader

Add a new C# class to the `ActivityLibrary` project, and name it `TrackingProfileLoader`. This class uses the `ConfigurationManager` class, which requires that you add a reference to the `System.Configuration` assembly to the project.

Here is the complete implementation of this class:

```
using System;
using System.Activities.Tracking;
using System.Configuration;
using System.Linq;
using System.ServiceModel.Activities.Tracking.Configuration;

namespace ActivityLibrary
{
    public class TrackingProfileLoader
    {
        public TrackingProfile Profile { get; set; }

        public TrackingProfileLoader(String profileName)
        {
            LoadConfig(profileName);
        }
```

After retrieving the tracking section from the `App.config` file, the named tracking profile is located and made available from a public `Profile` property.

```
        private void LoadConfig(String profileName)
        {
            TrackingSection ts =
                (TrackingSection)ConfigurationManager.GetSection(
                    "system.serviceModel/tracking");
            if (ts != null && ts.TrackingProfiles != null)
            {
                TrackingProfile profile =
                    (from tp in ts.TrackingProfiles
                     where tp.Name == profileName
                     select tp).SingleOrDefault();
                if (profile != null)
                {
                    Profile = profile;
                }
            }

            if (Profile == null)
            {
                throw new ArgumentException(String.Format(
                    "Tracking Profile {0} not found in app.config",
                    profileName));
            }
        }
    }
}
```

Defining the Tracking Profile in the App.config file

If the UpdateInventoryTracking application doesn't already have an App.config file, add one now. Modify the App.config file so that it has all of the entries shown here:

```xml
<?xml version="1.0" encoding="utf-8" ?>
<configuration>
  <startup>
  </startup>
  <system.serviceModel>
    <tracking>
      <profiles>
        <trackingProfile name="MyTrackingProfile">
          <workflow activityDefinitionId="*">
            <workflowInstanceQueries>
              <workflowInstanceQuery>
                <states>
                  <state name="Started"/>
                  <state name="Completed"/>
                </states>
              </workflowInstanceQuery>
            </workflowInstanceQueries>
            <activityStateQueries>
              <activityStateQuery activityName="UpdateProductInventory">
                <states>
                  <state name="Executing"/>
                </states>
                <arguments>
                  <argument name="SalesDetail"/>
                </arguments>
                <annotations>
                  <annotation name="Threading Model" value="Asynchronous update"/>
                </annotations>
              </activityStateQuery>
            </activityStateQueries>
            <customTrackingQueries>
              <customTrackingQuery activityName="*" name="*"/>
            </customTrackingQueries>
          </workflow>
        </trackingProfile>
      </profiles>
    </tracking>
  </system.serviceModel>
</configuration>
```

Testing the Tracking Profile Loader

You can now modify the `Program.cs` file in the `UpdateInventoryTracking` project to use the new `TrackingProfileLoader` class as shown here:

```
namespace UpdateInventoryTracking
{
    using System;
    using System.Activities;
    using System.Activities.Tracking;
    using System.Collections.Generic;
    using ActivityLibrary;

    class Program
    {
        static void Main(string[] args)
        {
            TrackingProfileLoader config =
                new TrackingProfileLoader("MyTrackingProfile");

            FileTrackingParticipant tp = new FileTrackingParticipant();
            tp.TrackingProfile = config.Profile;

            UpdateInventory wf = new UpdateInventory();
            wf.ArgSalesOrderId = 43687;
            WorkflowInvoker instance = new WorkflowInvoker(wf);

            instance.Extensions.Add(tp);
            instance.Invoke();

            tp.Stop();
        }
    }
}
```

In this example, the code uses the `FileTrackingParticipant` that was developed earlier in the chapter. However, you could just as easily use the `EtwTrackingParticipant` if you prefer. When you run the `UpdateInventoryTracking` project, you should see several new records created in the `\bin\debug\tracking` folder for the project.

Summary

This chapter focused on workflow tracking. Workflow tracking is the built-in mechanism that allows you to automatically instrument your workflows. This chapter demonstrated how to use the `EtwTrackingParticipant` that is included with WF. This tracking participant enables viewing and management of the tracking records using the Windows Event Viewer.

A number of examples explored the use of tracking profiles to filter the type and amount of tracking data that is passed to a tracking participant. Included in these examples was a demonstration of how to create custom tracking records from within a custom activity.

Two different custom tracking participants were implemented in examples in this chapter. The first one persisted tracking records to XML files, and the second was used to pass tracking records directly to the host application.

The use of workflow tracking with declarative workflow services was demonstrated in another example. The chapter concluded with a custom class that allows you to read a tracking profile from an `App.config` file for non-WCF applications.

In the next chapter, you will learn how to enhance the design experience by developing your own custom activity designers.

CHAPTER 15

■ ■ ■

Enhancing the Design Experience

One of the responsibilities of an activity is to cooperate with the workflow designer in order to provide an appealing and productive design experience. This chapter focuses on the mechanisms provided with Windows Workflow Foundation (WF) that make the design-time experience easier to use and less error-prone. Rather than focus on a particular runtime feature of WF, this chapter is all about helping the developers who use your custom activities at design time.

This chapter begins with an overview of the classes that you will use to create custom activity designers. Several designer scenarios are then presented in a series of examples. The first example exposes the properties of an activity directly on the design surface. Subsequent examples demonstrate custom designers that allow you to add one or multiple children to an activity. Another designer targets activities that support the `ActivityAction` class as a property.

Custom activity designers are really only half of the design-time story. The second half is activity validation. WF provides several ways that you can enforce validation logic for your activities. In a series of examples, validation attributes, code, and constraints are demonstrated. WF also allows you to manually perform activity validation outside the design experience. This is demonstrated in another example.

The chapter concludes with an example that creates an activity template. Activity templates allow you to create combinations of activities or preconfigured activities that are added to the design surface just like a normal activity.

Understanding Activity Designers

The workflow designer is built upon Windows Presentation Foundation (WPF). Therefore, any custom activity designers that you develop are implemented as WPF controls. In a similar way to WF, WPF uses Xaml files to declaratively define the user interface. WPF is an incredibly rich and complex foundation that is comprised of a seemingly endless array of classes. Fortunately, WF provides a set of specialized classes that handle most of the heavy lifting for you. Before diving into the mechanics of creating a custom activity designer, this section acquaints you with the presentation-related WF classes that you will use along with a few designer concepts.

■ **Note** Helping you learn WPF is beyond the scope of this book. If you are new to WPF, you may want to refer to one of the many good references on WPF. I recommend *Illustrated WPF* (Apress, 2009).

ActivityDesigner

The `ActivityDesigner` class (found in the `System.Activities.Presentation` namespace) is the base class to use when you create a new designer. This class, in turn, derives from the `WorkflowViewElement` class. The `WorkflowViewElement` class is the common base class for all editable UI elements that appear on the design canvas. Currently, the `ActivityDesigner` is the only type derived from this class that is available for your use. The `WorkflowViewElement` class is derived from the WPF `ContentControl` class.

When you create a new designer, the `ActivityDesigner` class is the root element of the Xaml file. The `x:Class` attribute specifies the name of the resulting designer class that you are defining. This is similar to the way that workflow Xaml files are defined.

■ **Note** You are permitted to develop your own base class and to use it as the root of a designer Xaml file. You might want to do this if you need to develop several designers that share similar functionality. However, that base class must ultimately derive from the `ActivityDesigner` class.

The `ActivityDesigner` class supports a large number of properties and members (most of which are inherited from the `WorkflowViewElement` class). Most of these members are related to their use as a WPF UI element and are used for event handling and management of the visual aspects of the control (location, size, style, resources, and so on). However, there are a few workflow-related properties that you will use. Here are the most important ones:

Property	Type	Description
ModelItem	ModelItem	Represents the activity that is currently being edited
Icon	DrawingBrush	The icon that is shown for the activity on the design canvas
Collapsible	Boolean	True if the activity can be shown in either an expanded or collapsed mode
ShowExpanded	Boolean	True if the activity should be shown in the expanded mode

ModelItem

Within the `ActivityDesigner` class, the `ModelItem` property represents the activity that the designer is currently editing. This property is actually an instance of the `ModelItem` class (found in the `System.Activities.Presentation.Model` namespace) class. This object sits between the visual elements that present an activity to the developer and the in-memory representation of the activity. As you will soon see when you develop your first custom designer, the visual elements of the designer bind to properties of the `ModelItem` object. When a change is made to an activity, the change is made via a WPF binding to the `ModelItem`. The changes are eventually propagated to the source Xaml file when any pending changes are saved.

ExpressionTextBox

As you have already seen, expressions are pervasive in WF. It would be difficult (if not impossible) to declare a meaningful workflow without them. Because of this, WF includes a UI element that is specifically designed to support the entry of expressions. The `ExpressionTextBox` class (found in the `System.Activities.Presentation.View` namespace) is a WPF `ContentControl` that you will use when you want to expose one or more activity properties on the design surface. Here are the most important properties of this class:

Property	Type	Description
Expression	ModelItem	Used to bind the expression to a property of the activity.
ExpressionType	Type	Identifies the CLR return type of the expression (String, Int32, Boolean, and so on).
OwnerActivity	ModelItem	Identifies the activity that is currently being edited.
HintText	String	Text that is displayed to the developer before an expression has been entered.
UseLocationExpression	Boolean	True if the Expression property is bound to an L-value expression (representing a memory location). False if the Expression property is bound to a value expression.

ArgumentToExpressionConverter

The `ExpressionTextBox` is the visual UI element that allows a developer to enter an expression. It supports expression syntax checking, IntelliSense, and all of the other Visual Basic expression goodness. However, it requires the use of a separate value converter (`ArgumentToExpressionConverter`) to actually convert the expression to a form that can be saved to the Xaml file. This converter (found in the `System.Activities.Presentation.Converters` namespace) is typically added to the designer as a static resource. Once it is added as a resource, it is referenced in the WPF binding to the `ExpressionTextBox.Expression` property.

When you use this converter to bind an expression, you must also provide a `ConverterParameter` value that determines the type of conversion that should take place. A `ConverterParameter` value of `In` indicates that a value expression is being edited. A value of `Out` indicates that an L-value expression is being edited. Additional information on these expression types is presented in the next section.

Understanding Expression Types

Expressions generally come in two flavors: L-value and value expressions. You can think of the "L" in L-value as referring to locator, location, or left. The type of expression that you are editing will determine the property values that you should use for the `ExpressionTextBox` and the `ArgumentToExpressionConverter`.

The best way to illustrate the difference between the two types of expressions is to review the `Assign` activity. This activity supports two properties that are set via expressions in the designer: `To` and `Value`. The `Assign.Value` property (an `InArgument`) represents the value that you want to assign to the `Assign.To` property. The `Assign.Value` property is a value expression. It equates to a value that you could use on the right side of an assignment statement. The `Assign.To` property (an `OutArgument`) is an L-value expression. It represents a location in memory that you might use on the left side of an assignment statement. You can assign values to an L-value expression, but a value expression is read-only.

Using the `Assign` activity as an example, the L-value expression is defined as an `OutArgument`, and the value expression is an `InArgument`. You will find that this is generally the case.

Follow these guidelines if you are binding an `ExpressionTextBox` to a value expression (`InArgument`):

- Set the `ConverterParameter` to a value of `In`.

- Set the `UseLocationExpression` property to False (the default).

Follow these guidelines if you are binding to an L-value expression (`OutArgument`):

- Set the `ConverterParameter` to a value of `Out`.

- Set the `UseLocationExpression` property to True.

WorkflowItemPresenter and WorkflowItemsPresenter

The `WorkflowItemPresenter` (found in the `System.Activities.Presentation` namespace) is another WPF `ContentControl` that is provided with WF. You use this UI element for activities that support a single child activity. Examples of activities that fall into this category are the `While` and `DoWhile` activities. This control supports the standard drag-and-drop interface that allows a developer to easily add an activity. Here are the most important properties of this UI element:

Property	Type	Description
Item	ModelItem	The child activity that is being added to the activity
HintText	String	A descriptive hint that is displayed in the drop target area

The `WorkflowItemsPresenter` serves a similar purpose; however, it supports multiple child activities. The best known example of this type of activity is the `Sequence` activity. It supports a similar set of properties:

Property	Type	Description
Items	ModelItemCollection	The collection of child activities
ItemsPanel	ItemsPanelTemplate	A template that describes the layout of the multiple child activities
SpacerTemplate	DataTemplate	A template that describes the separator between each child activity
HeaderTemplate	DataTemplate	A template that describes an area prior to the first child activity
FooterTemplate	DataTemplate	A template that describes the area following the last child activity
HintText	String	A descriptive hint for the drop target area

■ **Note** The `WorkflowItemPresenter` and `WorkflowItemsPresenter` classes are demonstrated later in the chapter.

Metadata Store and Designer Assignment

WF uses a metadata store to associate a particular designer with an activity. An instance of this in-memory store is automatically created when the workflow designer is loaded. The association between an activity and the designer that it should use can be added to the metadata store in two ways:

- The `System.ComponentModel.Designer` attribute can be added to the activity. This attribute specifies the designer that should be used each time the activity is shown on the design canvas.

- The static `AddAttributeTable` method of the `MetadataStore` class can be called to add the association.

The advantage to the first option (using the `Designer` attribute) is that it is extremely simple to implement. However, the downside is that the designer is directly coupled to the activity at build time. Although this works well in many (if not most) situations, it doesn't provide you with the flexibility that you might need if you choose to self-host the workflow designer in your own application. More specifically, it doesn't allow you to dynamically swap out different designers based on the current editing context, the user's security level, and so on.

The second option (using the `MetadataStore` class) allows you to effectively perform late-binding of the designer with the activity. With this option, the activity is no longer hard-coded to always use a particular designer. You can choose the proper designer at runtime as the workflow designer is initialized.

The Custom Designer Workflow

In general, you should follow these steps when creating a new customer activity designer:

1. Create a separate project to house activity designers.

2. Create a new activity designer class that is derived from `ActivityDesigner`.

3. If necessary, add support for multiple viewing modes (expanded and collapsed).

4. Implement the visual elements and controls of the designer in Xaml.

5. Add bindings for each `ModelItem` property that you want to maintain in the designer.

6. Optionally, add a custom icon to the designer.

7. Add entries to the metadata store that associate the designer with the activities that should use it.

Supporting Activity Properties

A common use of a custom designer is to expose activity properties directly on the design surface. You've already seen this behavior in many of the standard activities. By exposing the most frequently used properties on the design surface, you improve the usability of the activity. Instead of switching to the Properties window, the developer can usually set property values more quickly on the design surface.

In this first example, you will develop a custom activity and a designer that supports the entry of property values.

Creating the Projects

To begin this example, create a new Activity Library workflow project. Name the project `ActivityLibrary`, and add it to a new solution that is named for this chapter. All the projects in this chapter can be added to this same solution. The purpose of this project is to house the custom activities that you will develop in this chapter.

You can keep the `Activity1.xaml` file that is created with the new project. At this point, add a `Sequence` activity as the root of the `Activity1.xaml` file, and save this change. To test each example, you need to actually drag and drop the custom activity onto the design surface. The `Activity1.xaml` file can be used as a scratch pad for your testing. Once you finish with an example and are satisfied with the results, you can delete the individual activities that you added and prepare for the next example.

Create a second project, this time using the Activity Designer Library new project template. Name the project `ActivityDesignerLibrary`, and add it to the solution. You can delete the `ActivityDesigner1.xaml` file that is created with this project. This project will be used for all the custom designers that you will develop. You generally want to place the designers into a separate assembly instead of placing them in the same assembly as the activities. This allows maximum flexibility and keeps your options open when it comes to associating an activity with a designer. It also provides an opportunity to potentially reuse a designer for multiple activities in multiple assemblies.

The ActivityDesignerLibrary project should already include the usual set of assembly references that are used for workflow projects (System.Activities and so on). In addition, it should also reference these assemblies that are related to WPF and activity designers:

- PresentationCore

- PresentationFramework

- System.Activities.Presentation

- WindowsBase

Add this same list of additional assembly references to the ActivityLibrary project. In addition, add a project reference to the ActivityDesignerLibrary project. These additional references are needed because the ActivityLibrary project will be referencing the custom designers directly via the Designer attribute. Without these additional references, the ActivityLibrary project will not successfully build.

Implementing the CalcShipping Activity

This first example uses a slightly modified version of the CalcShipping activity that you developed in Chapter 3. Add a new Code Activity to the ActivityLibrary project, and name it CalcShipping. Here is the code for this activity:

```
using System;
using System.Activities;

namespace ActivityLibrary
{
    public sealed class CalcShipping : CodeActivity<Decimal>
    {
        public InArgument<Int32> Weight { get; set; }
        public InArgument<Decimal> OrderTotal { get; set; }
        public InArgument<String> ShipVia { get; set; }

        protected override Decimal Execute(CodeActivityContext context)
        {
            throw new NotImplementedException();
        }
    }
}
```

■ **Note** You will quickly notice that I haven't provided an implementation for the Execute method. Since this chapter is all about the design experience, you won't actually be executing any of these activities. So, there's no need for a full implementation.

Viewing the Default Design Experience

Before you go any further, build the solution to make sure that everything builds correctly. This also adds the new custom activity to the Visual Studio Toolbox.

As a point of reference, you can remind yourself what the default designer looks like before you implement a custom one. Open the `Activity1.xaml` file in the `ActivityLibrary` project, and add the `CalcShipping` activity to the root `Sequence` activity. Figure 15-1 shows the default designer for this activity.

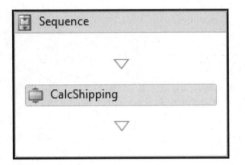

Figure 15-1. CalcShipping with standard designer

Declaring a Custom Designer

To declare a custom designer, add a new Activity Designer item to the `ActivityDesignLibrary` project. Name the new designer `CalcShippingDesigner`. Custom designers have Xaml extensions since they are WPF markup.

Here is the default markup when you first create a new designer:

```
<sap:ActivityDesigner x:Class="ActivityDesignerLibrary.CalcShippingDesigner"
    xmlns="http://schemas.microsoft.com/winfx/2006/xaml/presentation"
    xmlns:x="http://schemas.microsoft.com/winfx/2006/xaml"
    xmlns:sap="clr-namespace:System.Activities.Presentation;
        assembly=System.Activities.Presentation"
    xmlns:sapv="clr-namespace:System.Activities.Presentation.View;
        assembly=System.Activities.Presentation">
    <Grid>

    </Grid>
</sap:ActivityDesigner>
```

As you can see, the root element is `ActivityDesigner`. The `x:Class` attribute identifies the namespace and class name that will be assigned to the resulting type.

■ **Note** Each namespace in the designer markup must be entered on a single line. Because the length of many of these namespaces exceeds the maximum width allowed for this book, I've arbitrarily split the namespaces into multiple lines. When you enter them, make sure that the entire namespace is entered on a single line. This applies to all of the designer markup shown in this chapter.

For this example, the plan is to provide access to the four arguments of the activity directly on the design surface. Note, the fourth argument is the standard-named `Result` argument.

The contents of this file should be replaced with the markup shown here. The first change that you might notice is the addition of two new namespaces. The `xmlns:s` attribute references `mscorlib` since you will need to reference types from the `System` namespace. The `xmlns:sapc` attribute references the `System.Activities.Presentation.Converters` namespace. That namespace provides access to the `ArgumentToExpressionConverter`.

Also please note that I am setting the `Collapsible` property to `False`. If this is set to `True`, the expand/collapse indicator is shown in the upper-right corner of the activity. Since this first version of the designer does not support expand/collapse functionality, I wanted to avoid any confusion by hiding this indicator.

```
<sap:ActivityDesigner x:Class="ActivityDesignerLibrary.CalcShippingDesigner"
    xmlns:s="clr-namespace:System;assembly=mscorlib"
    xmlns="http://schemas.microsoft.com/winfx/2006/xaml/presentation"
    xmlns:x="http://schemas.microsoft.com/winfx/2006/xaml"
    xmlns:sap="clr-namespace:System.Activities.Presentation;
        assembly=System.Activities.Presentation"
    xmlns:sapv="clr-namespace:System.Activities.Presentation.View;
        assembly=System.Activities.Presentation"
    xmlns:sapc="clr-namespace:System.Activities.Presentation.Converters;
        assembly=System.Activities.Presentation"
    Collapsible="False" >
```

The `ArgumentToExpressionConverter` is now added as a static resource. This is necessary in order to reference this converter later in the markup.

```
<sap:ActivityDesigner.Resources>
    <ResourceDictionary>
        <sapc:ArgumentToExpressionConverter
            x:Key="ArgumentToExpressionConverter" />
    </ResourceDictionary>
</sap:ActivityDesigner.Resources>
```

Next, a grid is declared with two columns and four rows. The first column is for the label that describes each property. The second column will be used for the `ExpressionTextBox` for each property. And since there are four properties, there are four rows.

```
<Grid>
    <Grid.ColumnDefinitions>
        <ColumnDefinition />
        <ColumnDefinition />
    </Grid.ColumnDefinitions>
    <Grid.RowDefinitions>
        <RowDefinition />
        <RowDefinition />
        <RowDefinition />
        <RowDefinition />
    </Grid.RowDefinitions>
</Grid.RowDefinitions>
```

The markup is organized by row, with each row supporting a different property. The `TextBlock` is used to display text that identifies the property by name. Following it, an `ExpressionTextBox` is declared. The `OwnerActivity` is bound to the `ModelItem` property of the `ActivityDesigner`. As I mentioned at the beginning of the chapter, the `ModelItem` property provides a reference to the activity that is currently being edited.

The `Expression` property is bound to the `ModelItem.Weight` property. In this case, `Weight` is the name of the property in the custom activity. The binding `Mode` is set to `TwoWay`. This allows the `ExpressionTextBox` to be populated with an existing value as well as to enter a new value. The `ArgumentToExpressionConverter` is then specified as the converter to use for the expression. The `ConverterParameter` is set to `In`. This indicates that this is a value expression. Finally, the `ExpressionType` is set to the `Int32`, which is the CLR type for this property.

```
<TextBlock Text="Weight" Grid.Row ="0" Grid.Column="0"
    HorizontalAlignment="Left" VerticalAlignment="Center" />
<sapv:ExpressionTextBox HintText="Total weight"
    Grid.Row ="0" Grid.Column="1" MaxWidth="150" MinWidth="150" Margin="5"
    OwnerActivity="{Binding Path=ModelItem}"
    Expression="{Binding Path=ModelItem.Weight, Mode=TwoWay,
        Converter={StaticResource ArgumentToExpressionConverter},
        ConverterParameter=In }"
    ExpressionType="s:Int32" />
```

The next two properties are handled in a similar way. All these properties are value properties.

```
<TextBlock Text="OrderTotal" Grid.Row ="1" Grid.Column="0"
    HorizontalAlignment="Left" VerticalAlignment="Center" />
<sapv:ExpressionTextBox HintText="Order Total"
    Grid.Row ="1" Grid.Column="1" MaxWidth="150" MinWidth="150" Margin="5"
    OwnerActivity="{Binding Path=ModelItem}"
    Expression="{Binding Path=ModelItem.OrderTotal, Mode=TwoWay,
        Converter={StaticResource ArgumentToExpressionConverter},
        ConverterParameter=In }"
    ExpressionType="s:Decimal" />

<TextBlock Text="ShipVia" Grid.Row ="2" Grid.Column="0"
    HorizontalAlignment="Left" VerticalAlignment="Center" />
<sapv:ExpressionTextBox HintText="Shipping Method"
    Grid.Row ="2" Grid.Column="1" MaxWidth="150" MinWidth="150" Margin="5"
    OwnerActivity="{Binding Path=ModelItem}"
```

```
    Expression="{Binding Path=ModelItem.ShipVia, Mode=TwoWay,
        Converter={StaticResource ArgumentToExpressionConverter},
        ConverterParameter=In }"
    ExpressionType="s:String" />
```

The final property is the `Result` property. This is an L-value expression since it represents a storage location in memory. The markup is similar to the previous properties, but it does have some subtle differences. The `ConverterParameter` for this property is set to `Out`. This is the direction that must be used for an L-value expression. Also, the `UseLocationExpression` property is now included and is set to `True`.

```
    <TextBlock Text="Result" Grid.Row ="3" Grid.Column="0"
        HorizontalAlignment="Left" VerticalAlignment="Center" />
    <sapv:ExpressionTextBox HintText="Result"
        Grid.Row ="3" Grid.Column="1" MaxWidth="150" MinWidth="150" Margin="5"
        OwnerActivity="{Binding Path=ModelItem}"
        Expression="{Binding Path=ModelItem.Result, Mode=TwoWay,
            Converter={StaticResource ArgumentToExpressionConverter},
            ConverterParameter=Out }"
        UseLocationExpression="True"
        ExpressionType="s:Decimal" />

    </Grid>
</sap:ActivityDesigner>
```

■ **Tip** In this chapter, I list the markup for each designer since that is the most concise and accurate way to represent each designer. Although I actually prefer to work with the Xaml directly, you may prefer to set some of these properties using the Properties window of the WPF designer.

Associating the Activity with the Designer

There are two ways to associate an activity with a designer. The easiest (and most direct) way to accomplish this is to add the `System.ComponentModel.Designer` attribute to the activity. Here is the revised `CalcShipping` activity class definition with the addition of the `Designer` attribute:

```
using System;
using System.Activities;
using System.ComponentModel;

namespace ActivityLibrary
{
    [Designer(typeof(ActivityDesignerLibrary.CalcShippingDesigner))]
    public sealed class CalcShipping : CodeActivity<Decimal>
    {
...
    }
}
```

After rebuilding the solution, you should be able to test the new designer. Open the `Activity1.xaml` file, and add an instance of the `CalcShipping` activity to the `Sequence` activity. If you saved the file after adding the previous `CalcShipping` instance, there's no need to add a new one. You can see my results in Figure 15-2. To test the ability to enter expressions, I've added a few workflow arguments of the correct types and used them in expressions. Feel free to test each property to see whether it correctly enters and saves each expression.

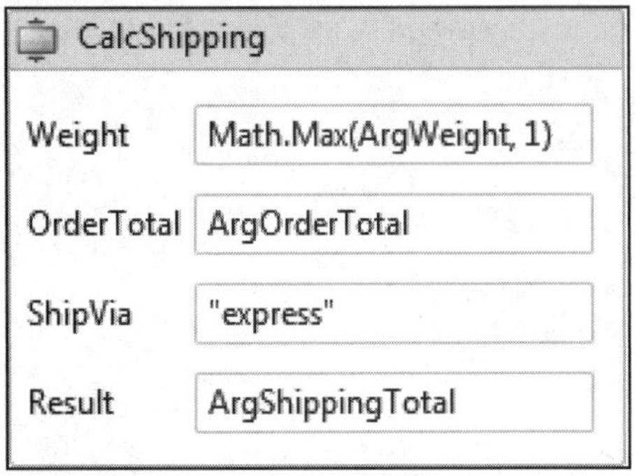

Figure 15-2. *CalcShipping with custom designer*

Using the MetadataStore to Associate a Designer

The second way to associate an activity to a designer is to use the `MetadataStore` class. This has the advantage of decoupling the activity from the designer, allowing you to specify a different designer depending on the circumstances. This capability is more important if you are self-hosting the workflow designer. However, the disadvantage to this approach is that there are a number of steps involved, and they must all be followed correctly in order to achieve the correct results.

To demonstrate this approach, you will associate the same `CalcShipping` activity to the custom designer that you developed.

■ **Warning** To complicate this process even more, there are subtle differences depending on whether you are using the activity within the Visual Studio environment or you are self-hosting the designer in your own application. The instructions given here assume that you are using Visual Studio. You can find information on self-hosting the workflow designer in Chapter 17. The instructions given in this section are important only if you want the designer to be self-discovered by Visual Studio.

Creating the Design Project

Visual Studio uses a special naming convention for assemblies that contain activity designers. The assembly containing the designers must be in the form of `[ActivityProjectName].VisualStudio.Design` or [ActivityProjectName].Design. Replace [ActivityProjectName] with the name of the assembly containing the activities. If you don't place the activity designers in this specially named assembly, Visual Studio won't find them. Visual Studio first searches for the [ActivityProjectName].Design assembly and loads it if it is found. It then looks for the version with VisualStudio in its name. An assembly containing VisualStudio in its name overrides any metadata settings that might have already been loaded.

To illustrate this, create a new Activity Design Library project named ActivityLibrary. VisualStudio.Design. Add this project to the solution for this chapter. Add a project reference to the ActivityLibrary project.

Make a copy of the CalcShippingDesigner.xaml file that is currently located in the ActivityDesignerLibrary project. You also need to copy the CalcShippingDesigner.Xaml.cs file. Add the copied files to the new ActivityLibrary.VisualStudio.Design project. Make sure you open the Xaml and .cs files for the designer and change the namespace to match the new project name.

■ **Note** If you are self-hosting the workflow designer, you need to omit the VisualStudio node of the project name. For example, you would name the project containing the designer (and the metadata that is discussed in the next step) ActivityLibrary.Design. This means that you may need to package your custom designers two different ways if they are used in both environments.

Adding the Metadata Class

Once Visual Studio loads the correct assembly containing the designer, it looks for a class that implements the IRegisterMetadata interface (found in the System.Activities.Presentation.Metadata namespace). This interface defines a Register method that is executed to add any necessary metadata entries.

To satisfy this requirement, add a new C# class named Metadata to the ActivityLibrary. VisualStudio.Design project. Here is the code that you need for this class:

```
using System;
using System.Activities.Presentation.Metadata;
using System.ComponentModel;

namespace ActivityLibrary.VisualStudio.Design
{
    public class Metadata : IRegisterMetadata
    {
        public void Register()
        {
            AttributeTableBuilder atb =
                new AttributeTableBuilder();
            atb.AddCustomAttributes(typeof(CalcShipping),
                new DesignerAttribute(typeof(CalcShippingDesigner)));
            MetadataStore.AddAttributeTable(atb.CreateTable());
        }
    }
}
```

The code first creates an instance of the `AttributeTableBuilder` class. Added to this class is a new `Designer` attribute indicating the designer to use for the `CalcShipping` activity. The `CreateTable` method of the `AttributeTableBuilder` is then executed, and the result is passed to the static `AddAttributeTable` method of the `MetadataStore` class.

Removing the Design Attribute

To perform a meaningful test, you need to comment out the `Designer` attribute from the `CalcShipping` class (located in the `ActivityLibrary` project). Otherwise, you are still relying on this attribute to designate the designer that will be used within Visual Studio. Here is the line that you should temporary comment out:

```
[Designer(typeof(ActivityDesignerLibrary.CalcShippingDesigner))]
```

You should rebuild the solution before proceeding to the next step.

Testing the Designer

To test the designer, create a new Workflow Console project named `TestMetadata`. Add a reference to the `ActivityLibrary` project.

For the custom designer to be located, the `Activity.VisualStudio.Design.dll` must be in the same folder as the `ActivityLibrary.dll`. Assuming that you are building for debug, copy this file from the `\bin\debug` folder of the project to the `\bin\debug` folder of the `ActivityLibrary` project.

Open the `Activity1.xaml` file in the new `TestMetadata` project, and drop a `CalcShipping` instance on the design canvas. If all goes well, you should see the custom designer. If not, the most likely cause is that the `Activity.VisualStudio.Design.dll` file is not located in the correct folder.

Warning: Consistency Is Important

You really need to choose one of the mechanisms to associate an activity with a designer and use it consistently. It is difficult to easily switch between the two approaches because of the assembly references that are used in each approach.

If you choose to use the `Designer` attribute approach, the assembly containing the activity references the assembly containing the designer. However, if you choose to go with the metadata store approach, the assembly containing the designer and the metadata references the assembly containing the activity. You can't use both approaches since that would result in a circular assembly reference, which would, of course, be very bad and not permitted.

Throughout the remainder of this chapter, I will be using the `Designer` attribute to associate an activity with a designer. This allows you to more quickly see the results of each designer.

Adding an Icon

Since you are able to determine the placement of controls within the designer, you might expect to also be able to change the icon that is displayed on the designer surface. To accomplish this, you need to follow these steps:

1. Add the image to the designer project.

2. Set the Build Action option for the image to Resource.

3. Add entries to the designer Xaml to reference the image.

To demonstrate this, you will now modify the `CalcShippingDesigner` that is in the `ActivityDesignerLibrary` project.

■ **Note** Throughout the remainder of this chapter, you will be working with designers in the `ActivityDesignerLibrary` project once again. The `ActivityLibrary.VisualStudio.Design` project was used only to demonstrate the use of the `MetadataStore` and won't be used again. If you commented out the `Designer` attributed for the `CalcShipping` activity, please uncomment it at this point.

Adding the Image to the Project

Instead of designing a custom image (and demonstrating my total lack of artistic ability), I've chosen one of the sample images that ships with Visual Studio. Please follow these steps to add the `CalculatorHS.png` image to the designer project:

1. Locate the `VS2010ImageLibrary.zip` file that is deployed with Visual Studio. The file should be located in the `\Program Files\Microsoft Visual Studio 10.0\Common7\VS2010ImageLibrary\1033` folder. The last node of the path (1033) may be different on your machine if you are using a non-English version of Windows.

2. Unzip the `VS2010ImageLibrary.zip` file into a temporary directory.

3. Locate the `CalculatorHS.png` file, which should be located in the `\VS2010ImageLibrary\Actions\png_format\Office and VS` relative folder after unzipping the image library.

4. Copy the `CalculatorHS.png` file to the `ActivityDesignerLibrary` project folder.

5. Add the `CalculatorHS.png` file to the project, and change the Build Action option for the file to Resource.

Adding the Image to the Designer

Open the `CalcShippingDesigner` (in the `ActivityDesignerLibrary` project), and switch to the Xaml view.
Add these entries to the markup to assign the new image to the `Icon` property of the `ActivityDesigner`.
The new entries should be located as shown in this example markup:

```
<sap:ActivityDesigner>

    <sap:ActivityDesigner.Resources>
...
    </sap:ActivityDesigner.Resources>

    <sap:ActivityDesigner.Icon>
        <DrawingBrush>
            <DrawingBrush.Drawing>
                <ImageDrawing>
                    <ImageDrawing.Rect>
                        <Rect Location="0,0"  Size="16,16" />
                    </ImageDrawing.Rect>
                    <ImageDrawing.ImageSource>
                        <BitmapImage UriSource="CalculatorHS.png" />
                    </ImageDrawing.ImageSource>
                </ImageDrawing>
            </DrawingBrush.Drawing>
        </DrawingBrush>
    </sap:ActivityDesigner.Icon>

    <Grid>
...
    </Grid>
</sap:ActivityDesigner>
```

Testing the Designer Icon

After rebuilding the solution, you should be able to test the revised designer. Open the `Activity1.xaml`
file in the `ActivityLibrary` project, and add an instance of the `CalcShipping` activity (or simply view the
instance that is already there). Figure 15-3 shows my results after adding the icon.

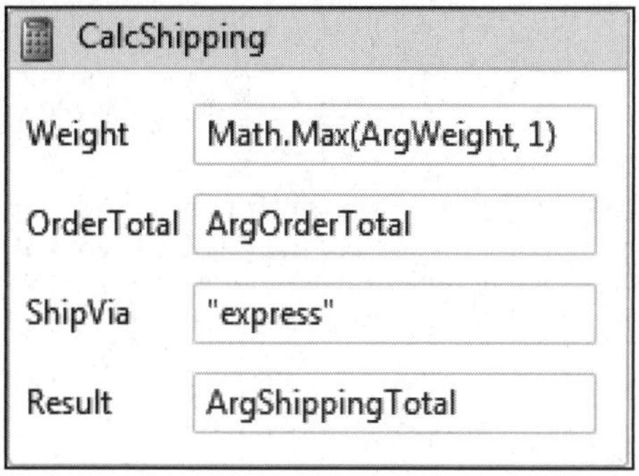

Figure 15-3. CalcShipping with custom icon

Supporting Expanded and Collapsed Modes

Many of the designers for the standard activities support two viewing modes: expanded and collapsed. The expanded mode allows you to work with all the visual elements that you have added to the designer. For example, the `CalcShippingDesigner` that you developed in the previous sections would look the same in the expanded view. You would be able to view and edit all of the properties that you have added to the designer. In collapsed mode, the activity shrinks to a much smaller single bar, hiding the properties.

In this example, you will create a new designer for the `CalcShipping` activity that supports the expanded and collapsed modes.

Declaring the Collapsible Designer

A good portion of this designer will contain the same markup as the original `CalcShippingDesigner` that you implemented in the previous sections. However, much of the markup has been moved around to accommodate the two viewing modes.

The easiest way to create this designer is to make a copy of the `CalcShippingDesigner.xaml` and `CalcShippingDesigner.xaml.cs` files (in the `ActivityDesignerLibrary` project). Name the copied files CalcShippingCollapsibleDesigner, and add them it to the same project. Make sure that you rename the class name within the Xaml file and the `CalcShippingCollapsibleDesigner.cs` file that is associated with it.

Here is the complete markup for this new designer:

```
<sap:ActivityDesigner x:Class="ActivityDesignerLibrary.CalcShippingCollapsibleDesigner"
    xmlns:s="clr-namespace:System;assembly=mscorlib"
    xmlns="http://schemas.microsoft.com/winfx/2006/xaml/presentation"
    xmlns:x="http://schemas.microsoft.com/winfx/2006/xaml"
    xmlns:sap="clr-namespace:System.Activities.Presentation;
        assembly=System.Activities.Presentation"
    xmlns:sapv="clr-namespace:System.Activities.Presentation.View;
        assembly=System.Activities.Presentation"
    xmlns:sapc="clr-namespace:System.Activities.Presentation.Converters;
        assembly=System.Activities.Presentation"
```

This version of the designer sets the `Collapsible` property to `True`. This allows the collapse/expand icon to be shown in the upper-right corner of the designer.

```
Collapsible="True" >
```

In addition to the `ArgumentToExpressionConverter`, the designer now requires several other resources. Two named data templates are defined. One is used to define the look of the designer when it is collapsed (named `ShowAsCollapsed`), and the other defines the look when the designer is expanded (`ShowAsExpanded`). Most of the markup from the previous version of the designer has been moved into the `ShowAsExpanded` data template.

```xml
<sap:ActivityDesigner.Resources>
    <sapc:ArgumentToExpressionConverter
            x:Key="ArgumentToExpressionConverter" />

    <DataTemplate x:Key="ShowAsCollapsed">
        <TextBlock>Expand to edit properties</TextBlock>
    </DataTemplate>
    <DataTemplate x:Key="ShowAsExpanded">
        <Grid>
            <Grid.ColumnDefinitions>
                <ColumnDefinition />
                <ColumnDefinition />
            </Grid.ColumnDefinitions>
            <Grid.RowDefinitions>
                <RowDefinition />
                <RowDefinition />
                <RowDefinition />
                <RowDefinition />
            </Grid.RowDefinitions>

            <TextBlock Text="Weight" Grid.Row ="0" Grid.Column="0"
                HorizontalAlignment="Left" VerticalAlignment="Center" />
            <sapv:ExpressionTextBox HintText="Total weight"
                Grid.Row ="0" Grid.Column="1" MaxWidth="150"
                MinWidth="150" Margin="5"
                OwnerActivity="{Binding Path=ModelItem}"
                Expression="{Binding Path=ModelItem.Weight, Mode=TwoWay,
                    Converter={StaticResource ArgumentToExpressionConverter},
                    ConverterParameter=In }"
                ExpressionType="s:Int32" />

            <TextBlock Text="OrderTotal" Grid.Row ="1" Grid.Column="0"
                HorizontalAlignment="Left" VerticalAlignment="Center" />
            <sapv:ExpressionTextBox HintText="Order Total"
                Grid.Row ="1" Grid.Column="1" MaxWidth="150"
                MinWidth="150" Margin="5"
                OwnerActivity="{Binding Path=ModelItem}"
```

```
                Expression="{Binding Path=ModelItem.OrderTotal, Mode=TwoWay,
                    Converter={StaticResource ArgumentToExpressionConverter},
                    ConverterParameter=In }"
                ExpressionType="s:Decimal" />

            <TextBlock Text="ShipVia" Grid.Row ="2" Grid.Column="0"
                HorizontalAlignment="Left" VerticalAlignment="Center" />
            <sapv:ExpressionTextBox HintText="Shipping Method"
                Grid.Row ="2" Grid.Column="1" MaxWidth="150"
                MinWidth="150" Margin="5"
                OwnerActivity="{Binding Path=ModelItem}"
                Expression="{Binding Path=ModelItem.ShipVia, Mode=TwoWay,
                    Converter={StaticResource ArgumentToExpressionConverter},
                    ConverterParameter=In }"
                ExpressionType="s:String" />

            <TextBlock Text="Result" Grid.Row ="3" Grid.Column="0"
                HorizontalAlignment="Left" VerticalAlignment="Center" />
            <sapv:ExpressionTextBox HintText="Result"
                Grid.Row ="3" Grid.Column="1" MaxWidth="150"
                MinWidth="150" Margin="5"
                OwnerActivity="{Binding Path=ModelItem}"
                Expression="{Binding Path=ModelItem.Result, Mode=TwoWay,
                    Converter={StaticResource ArgumentToExpressionConverter},
                    ConverterParameter=Out }"
                UseLocationExpression="True"
                ExpressionType="s:Decimal" />
        </Grid>
    </DataTemplate>
```

The designer uses a style (another resource) to determine which data template to show at any point in time. The style has a trigger that is bound to the ShowExpanded property of the designer. When this property is False, the ShowAsCollapsed data template is shown. When it is True, the ShowAsExpanded data template is used.

```
    <Style x:Key="StyleWithCollapse" TargetType="{x:Type ContentPresenter}">
        <Setter Property="ContentTemplate"
            Value="{DynamicResource ShowAsExpanded}"/>
        <Style.Triggers>
            <DataTrigger Binding="{Binding Path=ShowExpanded}" Value="False">
                <Setter Property="ContentTemplate"
                    Value="{DynamicResource ShowAsCollapsed }"/>
            </DataTrigger>
        </Style.Triggers>
    </Style>
</sap:ActivityDesigner.Resources>
```

```
<sap:ActivityDesigner.Icon>
    <DrawingBrush>
        <DrawingBrush.Drawing>
            <ImageDrawing>
                <ImageDrawing.Rect>
                    <Rect Location="0,0"  Size="16,16" />
                </ImageDrawing.Rect>
                <ImageDrawing.ImageSource>
                    <BitmapImage UriSource="CalculatorHS.png" />
                </ImageDrawing.ImageSource>
            </ImageDrawing>
        </DrawingBrush.Drawing>
    </DrawingBrush>
</sap:ActivityDesigner.Icon>
```

The remainder of the designer simply uses a WPF `ContentPresenter` control that is associated with the style that was defined earlier. The style and the data templates do all of the heavy lifting to display the designer in the correct viewing mode.

```
<Grid>
    <ContentPresenter Style="{DynamicResource StyleWithCollapse}"
        Content="{Binding}" />
</Grid>
</sap:ActivityDesigner>
```

Changing the Designer Attribute

You need to change the `Designer` attribute that is attached to the `CalcShipping` activity to use the new designer. Here is the revised attribute:

```
[Designer(typeof(ActivityDesignerLibrary.CalcShippingCollapsibleDesigner))]
public sealed class CalcShipping : CodeActivity<Decimal>
```

Testing the Collapsible Designer

You should now be able to rebuild the solution and test the revised designer. Open the `Activity1.xaml` file in the designer, and add or view the `CalcShipping` activity. Figure 15-4 shows the expanded designer, and Figure 15-5 shows the same designer in collapsed mode.

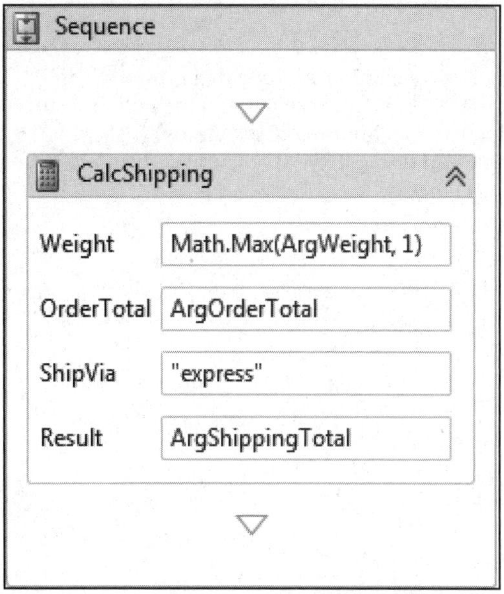

Figure 15-4. CalcShipping with collapsible designer

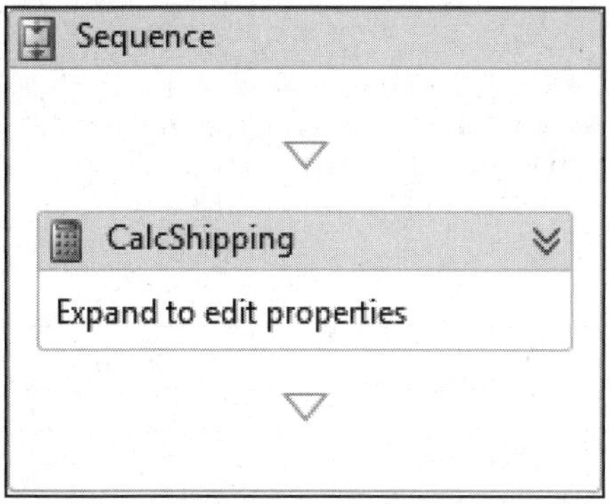

Figure 15-5. Collapsed CalcShipping

Supporting a Single Child Activity

In this example, you will develop a designer for a custom activity that supports a single child activity. To accomplish this, the `WorkflowItemPresenter` control will be used.

Implementing the MyWhile Activity

An example of a standard activity that supports a single child is the `While` activity. So in honor of the `While` activity, you will implement an activity with a similar look. As is the case with all the activities in this chapter, you won't actually implement the logic needed to replicate the `While` activity.

Add a new Code Activity to the `ActivityLibrary` project, and name it `MyWhile`. Here is the code for this activity:

```
using System;
using System.Activities;
using System.ComponentModel;

namespace ActivityLibrary
{
    [Designer(typeof(ActivityDesignerLibrary.MyWhileDesigner))]
    public sealed class MyWhile : NativeActivity
    {
        [Browsable(false)]
        public Activity Body { get; set; }
        public Activity<Boolean> Condition { get; set; }

        protected override void Execute(NativeActivityContext context)
        {
            throw new NotImplementedException();
        }
    }
}
```

The activity has two properties. The `Body` property is the child activity that will be maintained using the `WorkflowItemPresenter` control. The `Condition` property represents a Boolean condition that must be true in order to schedule execution of the `Body` activity. Also note that the `Body` property is decorated with the `Browsable` attribute with a value of `False`. This removes the property from the Properties window in Visual Studio.

■ **Note** To save a bit of time, I've already included the `Designer` attribute that assigns the custom designer. Keep in mind that this code won't actually build until you've implemented the designer in the next step.

Declaring a Custom Designer

Add a new Activity Designer to the `ActivityDesignerLibrary` project. Name the new designer `MyWhileDesigner`. Here is the markup for this new designer:

```xml
<sap:ActivityDesigner x:Class="ActivityDesignerLibrary.MyWhileDesigner"
    xmlns:s="clr-namespace:System;assembly=mscorlib"
    xmlns="http://schemas.microsoft.com/winfx/2006/xaml/presentation"
    xmlns:x="http://schemas.microsoft.com/winfx/2006/xaml"
    xmlns:sap="clr-namespace:System.Activities.Presentation;
        assembly=System.Activities.Presentation"
    xmlns:sapv="clr-namespace:System.Activities.Presentation.View;
        assembly=System.Activities.Presentation"
    xmlns:sapc="clr-namespace:System.Activities.Presentation.Converters;
        assembly=System.Activities.Presentation"
    Collapsible="False" >

<Grid>
    <Grid.ColumnDefinitions>
        <ColumnDefinition />
        <ColumnDefinition />
    </Grid.ColumnDefinitions>
    <Grid.RowDefinitions>
        <RowDefinition />
        <RowDefinition />
    </Grid.RowDefinitions>

    <TextBlock Text="Condition" Grid.Row ="0" Grid.Column="0"
        HorizontalAlignment="Left" VerticalAlignment="Center" />

    <sapv:ExpressionTextBox HintText="Enter a condition"
        Grid.Row ="0" Grid.Column="1" MaxWidth="150" MinWidth="150" Margin="5"
        OwnerActivity="{Binding Path=ModelItem}"
        ExpressionType="{x:Type TypeName=s:Boolean}"
        Expression="{Binding Path=ModelItem.Condition, Mode=TwoWay}" />
```

The only new element to this designer is the inclusion of the WorkflowItemPresenter. The Item property of the WorkflowItemPresenter is bound to the Body property of the custom activity. As you can see, the binding for this control is actually much simpler than the ExpressionTextBox. Although this is not a requirement, I decided to wrap this control in a thin WPF Border. This draws attention to the drop area for the child activity.

```xml
<Border Grid.Row ="1" Grid.Column="0" Grid.ColumnSpan="2" Margin="5"
    MinHeight="40" BorderBrush="LightGray"  BorderThickness="1" >
    <sap:WorkflowItemPresenter HintText="Drop an activity here"
        Item="{Binding Path=ModelItem.Body, Mode=TwoWay}" />
</Border>

</Grid>
</sap:ActivityDesigner>
```

> ■ **Note** This example also introduces a slight variation on the `ExpressionTextBox`. You may notice that the `ExpressionTextBox` that is bound to the `Condition` property does not specify the `ArgumentToExpressionConverter`. The converter is omitted because the control is bound to a property that is defined as `Activity<Boolean>`, not to an `InArgument<T>` or `OutArgument<T>`. This works because the output from the `ExpressionTextBox` is always a `VisualBasicValue<T>` or `VisualBasicReference<T>`, both of which are actually activities.

Testing the Designer

You should now be able to successfully rebuild the solution and try this new activity. Open the `Activity1.xaml` file, and add an instance of the `MyWhile` activity to the root `Sequence` activity. Figure 15-6 shows the activity after I added a child `Sequence` activity (with its own children) to the activity. I've also exercised the `Condition` property using a variable that I added to the workflow.

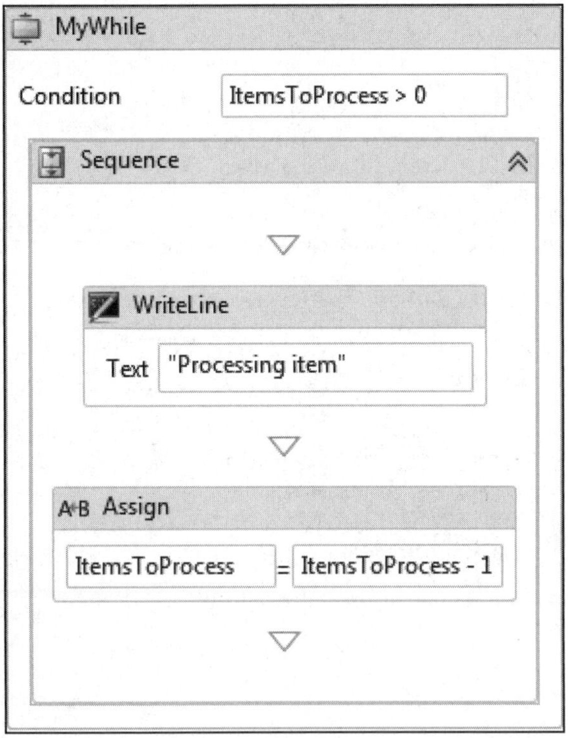

Figure 15-6. MyWhile with custom designer

Supporting Multiple Child Activities

The custom activity and designer you will develop in this example are similar to the previous example. However, in this example the custom activity supports a collection of child activities, similar in concept to the Sequence activity. The designer uses the WorkflowItemsPresenter control to permit the declaration of the child activities.

Implementing the MySequence Activity

To implement the custom activity for this example, add a new Code Activity to the ActivityLibrary project, and name it MySequence. Here is the code for this activity:

```
using System;
using System.Activities;
using System.Collections.ObjectModel;
using System.ComponentModel;
using System.Windows.Markup;

namespace ActivityLibrary
{
    [Designer(typeof(ActivityDesignerLibrary.MySequenceDesigner))]
    [ContentProperty("Activities")]
    public class MySequence : NativeActivity
    {
        [Browsable(false)]
        public Collection<Activity> Activities { get; set; }
        public Activity<Boolean> Condition { get; set; }
        [Browsable(false)]
        public Collection<Variable> Variables { get; set; }

        public MySequence()
        {
            Activities = new Collection<Activity>();
            Variables = new Collection<Variable>();
        }

        protected override void Execute(NativeActivityContext context)
        {
            throw new NotImplementedException();
        }
    }
}
```

The properties of this activity are fairly straightforward and probably what you might expect to see. The Activities property is a collection of Activity objects and is the property used to add the child activities. As you saw in the previous example, this activity also includes a Condition property. It also has a Variables property that is typed as Collection<Variable>. If you include a property with this exact name (Variables) with this exact type, it is automatically supported by the variable editor of the designer.

As I did with the previous example, I've already included the `Designer` attribute that references the custom designer. So, this code won't build until you implement the designer.

Declaring a Custom Designer

Add a new Activity Designer to the `ActivityDesignerLibrary` project, and name it `MySequenceDesigner`. Since this activity might have a large number of children, the designer supports the expanded and collapsed viewing modes. Here is the markup for this designer:

```
<sap:ActivityDesigner x:Class="ActivityDesignerLibrary.MySequenceDesigner"
    xmlns:s="clr-namespace:System;assembly=mscorlib"
    xmlns="http://schemas.microsoft.com/winfx/2006/xaml/presentation"
    xmlns:x="http://schemas.microsoft.com/winfx/2006/xaml"
    xmlns:sap="clr-namespace:System.Activities.Presentation;
        assembly=System.Activities.Presentation"
    xmlns:sapv="clr-namespace:System.Activities.Presentation.View;
        assembly=System.Activities.Presentation"
    xmlns:sapc="clr-namespace:System.Activities.Presentation.Converters;
        assembly=System.Activities.Presentation"
    Collapsible="True" >
```

Just for fun, I decided to display the count of child activities when the designer is in collapsed mode. This is accomplished by binding the `Text` property of the `TextBlock` control to the `Activities.Count` property of the activity.

```
<sap:ActivityDesigner.Resources>
    <DataTemplate x:Key="ShowAsCollapsed">
        <TextBlock Foreground="Gray">
            <TextBlock.Text>
                <MultiBinding StringFormat="Expand for {0} Activities">
                    <Binding Path="ModelItem.Activities.Count" />
                </MultiBinding>
            </TextBlock.Text>
        </TextBlock>
    </DataTemplate>
    <DataTemplate x:Key="ShowAsExpanded">
        <Grid>
            <Grid.ColumnDefinitions>
                <ColumnDefinition />
                <ColumnDefinition />
            </Grid.ColumnDefinitions>
            <Grid.RowDefinitions>
                <RowDefinition />
                <RowDefinition />
            </Grid.RowDefinitions>

            <TextBlock Text="Condition" Grid.Row ="0" Grid.Column="0"
            HorizontalAlignment="Left" VerticalAlignment="Center" />
            <sapv:ExpressionTextBox HintText="Enter a condition"
            Grid.Row ="0" Grid.Column="1"
```

```
MaxWidth="150" MinWidth="150" Margin="5"
OwnerActivity="{Binding Path=ModelItem}"
ExpressionType="{x:Type TypeName=s:Boolean}"
Expression="{Binding Path=ModelItem.Condition, Mode=TwoWay}" />
```

As you might expect, the `WorkflowItemsPresenter` control is bound to the `Activities` property of the custom activity. However, unlike the `WorkflowItemPresenter`, this control provides you with the ability to fine-tune additional aspects of its presentation. In this example, the markup displays a `LightGray` rectangle as the spacer, which is shown between each child activity. The `ItemsPanel` property defines the layout and orientation of the child activities. In this case, I went with the traditional top-down vertical orientation.

```
<sap:WorkflowItemsPresenter HintText="Drop activities here"
Grid.Row ="1" Grid.Column="0" Grid.ColumnSpan="2"
Margin="5" MinHeight="100"
Items="{Binding Path=ModelItem.Activities}">
    <sap:WorkflowItemsPresenter.SpacerTemplate>
        <DataTemplate>
            <Rectangle Width="140" Height="3"
            Fill="LightGray" Margin="7" />
        </DataTemplate>
    </sap:WorkflowItemsPresenter.SpacerTemplate>
    <sap:WorkflowItemsPresenter.ItemsPanel>
        <ItemsPanelTemplate>
            <StackPanel Orientation="Vertical" />
        </ItemsPanelTemplate>
    </sap:WorkflowItemsPresenter.ItemsPanel>
</sap:WorkflowItemsPresenter>
</Grid>
</DataTemplate>
<Style x:Key="StyleWithCollapse" TargetType="{x:Type ContentPresenter}">
    <Setter Property="ContentTemplate"
        Value="{DynamicResource ShowAsExpanded}"/>
    <Style.Triggers>
        <DataTrigger Binding="{Binding Path=ShowExpanded}" Value="False">
            <Setter Property="ContentTemplate"
                Value="{DynamicResource ShowAsCollapsed}"/>
        </DataTrigger>
    </Style.Triggers>
</Style>
</sap:ActivityDesigner.Resources>
<Grid>
    <ContentPresenter Style="{DynamicResource StyleWithCollapse}"
        Content="{Binding}"/>
</Grid>

</sap:ActivityDesigner>
```

Testing the Designer

After rebuilding the solution, you can open the `Activity1.xaml` file and add an instance of the `MySequence` activity. Once added, you should be able to add multiple child activities and set the `Condition` property to a valid Boolean condition. Figure 15-7 shows the expanded view of the designer, and Figure 15-8 shows the designer collapsed. Note that the collapsed version correctly shows the count of child activities.

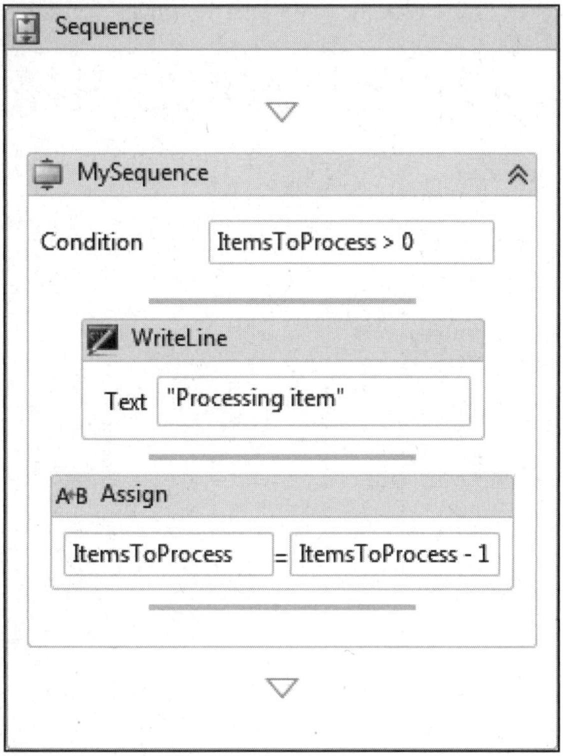

Figure 15-7. MySequence with custom designer

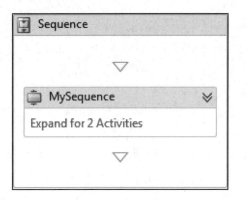

Figure 15-8. Collapsed MySequence

Although not shown in these figures, this activity does support the entry of variables. You should be able to open the variable editor and add one or more variables that are scoped by this activity.

Supporting the ActivityAction Activity

The `ActivityAction` activity is used for callback-like processing from an activity. It defines a planned hole that must be filled with an activity to execute. The `ActivityAction` class is really a family of related generic classes designed to support a varying number of input arguments. For example, `ActivityAction<T>` supports a single input argument, while `ActivityAction<T1,T2>` supports two input arguments.

The `ActivityAction` class presents an additional activity designer challenge since any arguments must be presented as arguments within the designer. To illustrate this, take a look at the standard `ForEach<T>` activity. This activity iterates over the items in a collection, executing a single child activity for each item. To allow the child activity to access each item in the collection, an `ActivityAction<T>` is used. The generic type assigned to this class defines the type of each item in the collection. But the real purpose of using the `ActivityAction<T>` class is to provide an argument that represents the current item in the collection. This argument, with a default name of `item`, is made available to the child activity so that it can reference each item.

■ **Note** You used an `ActivityAction` for communication between the workflow and the host application in Chapter 8. You might want to refer to that chapter for more information on the `ActivityAction` class. For more information on the `ForEach<T>` activity, please refer to Chapter 6.

To demonstrate the additional designer requirements when an `ActivityAction` is in the picture, you will implement an activity and designer that use an `ActivityAction`.

Implementing the MyActivityWithAction Activity

Add a new Code Activity to the `ActivityLibrary` project, and name it `MyActivityWithAction`. Here is the code for this custom activity:

```
using System;
using System.Activities;
using System.Collections.Generic;
using System.ComponentModel;

namespace ActivityLibrary
{
    [Designer(typeof(ActivityDesignerLibrary.MyActivityWithActionDesigner))]
    public class MyActivityWithAction : NativeActivity
    {
```

This activity defines an `ActivityAction<String>` property named `Notify`. In addition, it defines an input argument named `Strings`, which, as you might guess, contains a collection of strings. The assumption is that this activity will iterate over the collection of strings and invoke the `ActivityAction` for each string. This allows any activity that is assigned as the handler for the `ActivityAction` to do something with each string.

```
        [Browsable(false)]
        public ActivityAction<String> Notify { get; set; }

        [RequiredArgument]
        public InArgument<List<String>> Strings { get; set; }
```

One crucial step to make this work is to initialize the `ActivityAction` as shown in the constructor of this activity. This code creates a named `DelegateInArgument` and assigns it to the `Argument` property of the `ActivityAction`. The `Name` property that you assign here (`message` in this example) is the name of the argument that is made available to the activity that is assigned to this `ActivityAction`.

```
        public MyActivityWithAction()
        {
            Notify = new ActivityAction<String>
                {
                    Argument = new DelegateInArgument<String>
                    {
                        Name = "message"
                    }
                };
        }
```

In this example, the code overrides the `CacheMetadata` method to manually define the properties of this activity. Notice that `AddDelegate` is used for the `Notify` property since it is an `ActivityAction`.

```
    protected override void CacheMetadata(NativeActivityMetadata metadata)
    {
        metadata.AddDelegate(Notify);
        metadata.AddArgument(new RuntimeArgument(
            "Strings", typeof(List<String>), ArgumentDirection.In));
    }

    protected override void Execute(NativeActivityContext context)
    {
        throw new NotImplementedException();
    }
  }
}
```

Declaring a Custom Designer

Add a new Activity Designer to the **ActivityDesignerLibrary** project, and name it **MyActivityWithActionDesigner**. Here is the complete markup for this designer:

```xml
<sap:ActivityDesigner x:Class="ActivityDesignerLibrary.MyActivityWithActionDesigner"
    xmlns:s="clr-namespace:System;assembly=mscorlib"
    xmlns="http://schemas.microsoft.com/winfx/2006/xaml/presentation"
    xmlns:x="http://schemas.microsoft.com/winfx/2006/xaml"
    xmlns:sap="clr-namespace:System.Activities.Presentation;
        assembly=System.Activities.Presentation"
    xmlns:sapv="clr-namespace:System.Activities.Presentation.View;
        assembly=System.Activities.Presentation"
    xmlns:sapc="clr-namespace:System.Activities.Presentation.Converters;
        assembly=System.Activities.Presentation"
    Collapsible="False" >

    <sap:ActivityDesigner.Resources>
        <ResourceDictionary>
            <sapc:ArgumentToExpressionConverter
                x:Key="ArgumentToExpressionConverter" />
        </ResourceDictionary>
    </sap:ActivityDesigner.Resources>

    <Grid>
        <Grid.ColumnDefinitions>
            <ColumnDefinition />
            <ColumnDefinition />
        </Grid.ColumnDefinitions>
        <Grid.RowDefinitions>
            <RowDefinition />
            <RowDefinition />
        </Grid.RowDefinitions>
```

```
<TextBlock Text="Strings" Grid.Row ="0" Grid.Column="0"
    HorizontalAlignment="Left" VerticalAlignment="Center" />

<sapv:ExpressionTextBox HintText="List of Strings"
    Grid.Row ="0" Grid.Column="1" MaxWidth="150" MinWidth="150" Margin="5"
    OwnerActivity="{Binding Path=ModelItem}"
    Expression="{Binding Path=ModelItem.Strings, Mode=TwoWay,
        Converter={StaticResource ArgumentToExpressionConverter},
        ConverterParameter=In }" />
```

A `WorkflowItemPresenter` is used to allow the addition of an activity that will be executed by the `ActivityAction`. Notice that this control is bound to the `Notify.Handler` property, not to the `Notify` property directly. The `Handler` property of an `ActivityAction` represents the real target activity to be executed.

```
<Border Grid.Row ="1" Grid.Column="0" Grid.ColumnSpan="2" Margin="5"
    MinHeight="40" BorderBrush="LightGray"  BorderThickness="1" >
    <sap:WorkflowItemPresenter HintText="Drop an activity action handler here"
        Item="{Binding Path=ModelItem.Notify.Handler, Mode=TwoWay}" />
</Border>

    </Grid>
</sap:ActivityDesigner>
```

Testing the Designer

To test the new custom activity and designer, rebuild the solution, and open the `Activity1.xaml` file in the designer. Add an instance of the `MyActivityWithAction` activity. Now add a `Sequence` activity as the child of the `MyActivityWithAction` activity, and then a `WriteLine` as the child of the `Sequence`. Start typing the argument name `message` in the `Text` property of the `WriteLine` activity. As you type, you should see the `message` argument in the IntelliSense list. This proves that this argument, which was created within the activity, is now available for your consumption within the designer. Figure 15-9 shows my test of this activity and designer.

Figure 15-9. MyActivityWithAction

■ **Note** Implementing a custom activity that uses an `ActivityAction` is one of the scenarios discussed in Chapter 16.

Understanding Validation

In addition to developing a custom designer, you can also provide validation for your custom activities. The most common type of validation checks for missing arguments, but you can also implement additional kinds of validation. For example, if your activity supports child activities, you can add validation logic that limits the types of activities that are allowed as children. Or you can limit the type of parent activity that uses your activity as a child.

Regardless of the kind of validation that you implement, the goal of validation is to assist the developer at design time by identifying error and warning conditions. A custom activity that provides this type of validation enhances the design experience by providing cues to the proper use of the activity. The developer doesn't have to wait until the workflow is executed to find out that a required argument was not provided. They are notified of problems at design time via visual designer cues.

If validation logic is directly associated with an activity, it is executed automatically each time an activity is used within the workflow designer. In addition, you can manually validate an activity using the `ActivityValidationServices` class. The static `Validate` method of this class allows you to execute the validation logic from within your own application, completely outside the designer environment. You might want to execution the validation logic if your application provides the end users with an opportunity to customize activities and workflows. If the activity definitions are outside of your application's direct control, it's a good idea to validate them before you attempt to execute them.

WF provides three mechanisms that you can use for activity validation:

- Validation attributes
- Validation code within the activity itself
- Constraints

Each of these validation mechanisms is briefly discussed in the sections that follow.

Validation Attributes

Using validation attributes is the easiest way to introduce basic validation to a custom activity. WF includes these two attributes (both found in the `System.Activities` namespace):

- `RequiredArgument`
- `OverloadGroup`

Both of these attributes are designed to be applied to public properties of your activity. You have already seen the `RequiredArgument` attributed used with some of the custom activities in previous chapters. Applying this attribute to a property indicates that it is required. When this attribute is applied, the developer must provide a value for the property; otherwise, the activity is flagged as failing validation.

A property that has the `RequiredArgument` attribute applied is always required. In contrast with this, the `OverloadGroup` attribute allows you to define multiple named groups of properties that must be supplied. The properties within a named group must be supplied, but other properties may be optional.

The `OverloadGroup` attribute is best understand in the context of an example, so I'll defer further discussion of it until it is used in an example later in this chapter.

Validation Code

You also have the option of implementing validation code within the activity itself. Any validation code is placed in an override of the `CacheMetadata` virtual method. The purpose of this method is to create a complete description of the activity prior to its execution. The description includes any arguments, variables, delegates, and children that are referenced during execution.

Constraints

WF also provides a mechanism to provide validation logic that resides outside the activity. This mechanism is called a *constraint* and is implemented by the `Constraint<T>` class. This class is derived from the abstract `Constraint` class, which ultimately derives from the base `Activity` class. So, constraints are actually a specialized type of activity, and you compose them in code as you would other activities.

■ **Note** The `Constraint<T>` class is sealed, so you can't derive your own constraint class from it. Instead, all constraints are composed by assigning a tree of activities to their `Body` property.

Once it is implemented, a constraint can be applied to an activity in two ways. First, you can add a constraint directly to an activity using its `Constraints` property. This can be done in the constructor of the activity. Second, you can add constraints if you are using the `ActivityValidationServices` class to manually validate an activity. An overload of the `Validate` method of this class allows you to pass an instance of the `ValidationSettings` class. This class supports an `AdditionalConstraints` property that can be used to add constraints prior to validation.

Using Validation Attributes

In this section of the chapter, you will use the `RequiredArgument` and `OverloadGroup` attributes to add basic validation to an activity.

Using the RequiredArgument Attribute

To see the `RequiredArgument` attribute in action, you can revise the `CalcShipping` activity that you used in the earlier examples in this chapter. This activity is located in the `ActivityLibrary` project. Here is the revised code that adds this attribute to the input arguments:

```
using System;
using System.Activities;
using System.ComponentModel;

namespace ActivityLibrary
{
    [Designer(typeof(ActivityDesignerLibrary.CalcShippingCollapsibleDesigner))]
    public sealed class CalcShipping : CodeActivity<Decimal>
    {
        [RequiredArgument]
        public InArgument<Int32> Weight { get; set; }

        [RequiredArgument]
        public InArgument<Decimal> OrderTotal { get; set; }

        [RequiredArgument]
        public InArgument<String> ShipVia { get; set; }

        protected override Decimal Execute(CodeActivityContext context)
        {
            throw new NotImplementedException();
        }
    }
}
```

After rebuilding the solution, you should be able to open the `Activity1.xaml` file and add a new instance of the `CalcShipping` activity to the root `Sequence` activity. As the activity is added, you should almost immediately see the errors shown in Figure 15-10.

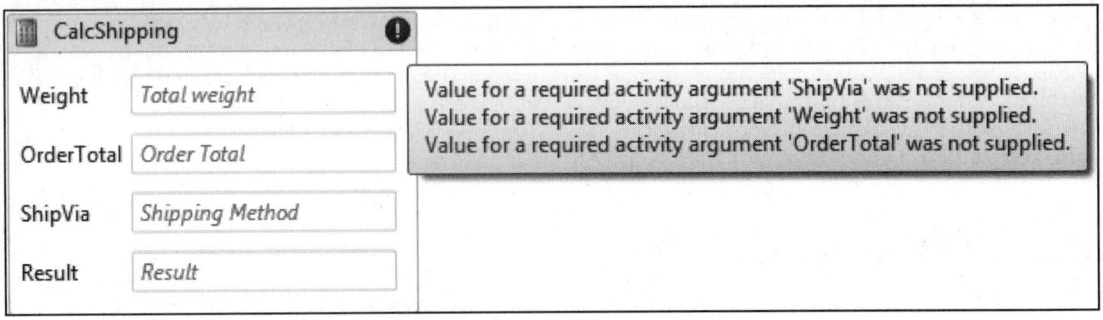

Figure 15-10. CalcShipping with requirement arguments

Providing values for each property should eliminate the errors

Using the OverloadGroup Attribute

To see the `OverloadGroup` activity in action, you need to first implement a new example activity. To demonstrate this attribute, you need an activity that has multiple sets of mutually exclusive properties. Add a new Code Activity named `TitleLookup` to the `ActivityLibrary` project. Here is the code for this activity:

```
using System;
using System.Activities;

namespace ActivityLibrary
{
    public sealed class TitleLookup : CodeActivity
    {
        [RequiredArgument]
        [OverloadGroup("ByKeyword")]
        [OverloadGroup("ByTitle")]
        public InArgument<String> Category { get; set; }

        [RequiredArgument]
        [OverloadGroup("ByKeyword")]
        public InArgument<String> Keyword { get; set; }

        [RequiredArgument]
        [OverloadGroup("ByTitle")]
        public InArgument<String> Author { get; set; }

        [RequiredArgument]
        [OverloadGroup("ByTitle")]
        public InArgument<String> Title { get; set; }
```

```
        [RequiredArgument]
        [OverloadGroup("ByISBN")]
        public InArgument<String> ISBN { get; set; }

        protected override void Execute(CodeActivityContext context)
        {
            throw new NotImplementedException();
        }
    }
}
```

The activity uses the OverloadGroup attribute to organize the input arguments into three separate groups. If this contrived activity is used to find a book, it is completely reasonable that you might support several ways to perform the lookup. In this example, the OverloadGroup attribute is used with three different named groups:

- ByKeyword

- ByTitle

- ByISBN

The ByKeyword group is assigned to the Category and Keyword properties. The RequiredArgument attribute has also been applied to these properties. This combination of attributes means that one of the groups is required and that you cannot provide a value for properties in another group. Likewise, the ByTitle group is assigned to the Category, Author, and Title properties. Notice that the Category property participates in both groups. Finally, the ByISBN group is applied only to the ISBN property. At design time, these groups are used to ensure that a valid combination of properties have values, as well as to prohibit values for properties that should not have them.

After rebuilding the solution, open the Activity1.xaml file, and add an instance of this new activity to the root Sequence activity. To test the validation, you can enter values for the Author, Category, and Keyword properties, as shown in Figure 15-11.

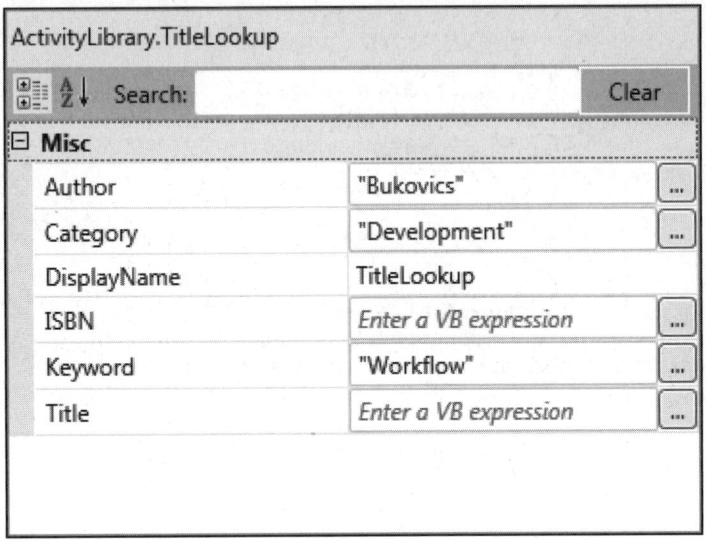

Figure 15-11. *TitleLookup properties*

When you do this, you should see the error shown in Figure 15-12.

Figure 15-12. *TitleLookup validation errors*

By entering values for the Category and Keyword properties, you satisfy the requirements of the ByKeyword OverloadGroup. But by also including a value for the Author property, the activity fails validation because this property is part of a different group. Clearing the value for the Author property clears the error. Feel free to try other combinations of properties to further test the validation.

Adding Validation in Code

To demonstrate how to add validation logic within the activity itself, you will now revisit the MySequence activity that was used earlier in the chapter. This activity supports multiple children, so it makes sense to validate that at least one child has been assigned to the Activities property. One way to accomplish this is by adding validation code to the CacheMetadata method of the activity.

■ **Note** In the section following this one, you will also implement a version of this activity that uses a constraint to perform the same type of validation. To make it clear that these are separate versions of the activity and are not built upon each other, I've chosen to make a copy of the previous MySequence activity rather than to modify it.

Adding an Error

Make a copy of the MySequence activity (in the ActivityLibrary project), and name the copy MySequenceWithValidation. Here is the code that includes the validation logic:

```
using System;
using System.Activities;
using System.Activities.Validation;
using System.Collections.ObjectModel;
using System.ComponentModel;
using System.Windows.Markup;

namespace ActivityLibrary
{
    [Designer(typeof(ActivityDesignerLibrary.MySequenceDesigner))]
    [ContentProperty("Activities")]
    public class MySequenceWithValidation : NativeActivity
    {
        [Browsable(false)]
        public Collection<Activity> Activities { get; set; }
        public Activity<Boolean> Condition { get; set; }
        [Browsable(false)]
        public Collection<Variable> Variables { get; set; }

        public MySequenceWithValidation()
        {
            Activities = new Collection<Activity>();
            Variables = new Collection<Variable>();
        }
```

After executing the base CacheMetadata method, the code performs a simple check to determine whether the count of child activities is equal to zero. If it is, the AddValidationError method of the metadata object is called to signal an error condition.

667

```
protected override void CacheMetadata(NativeActivityMetadata metadata)
{
    base.CacheMetadata(metadata);
    if (Activities.Count == 0)
    {
        metadata.AddValidationError(
            "At least one child activity must be added");
    }
}

protected override void Execute(NativeActivityContext context)
{
    throw new NotImplementedException();
}
}
}
```

Build the solution and add an instance of the new MySequenceWithValidation activity to the Activity1.xaml file. Figure 15-13 demonstrates the error that should appear when no children have been assigned to the activity.

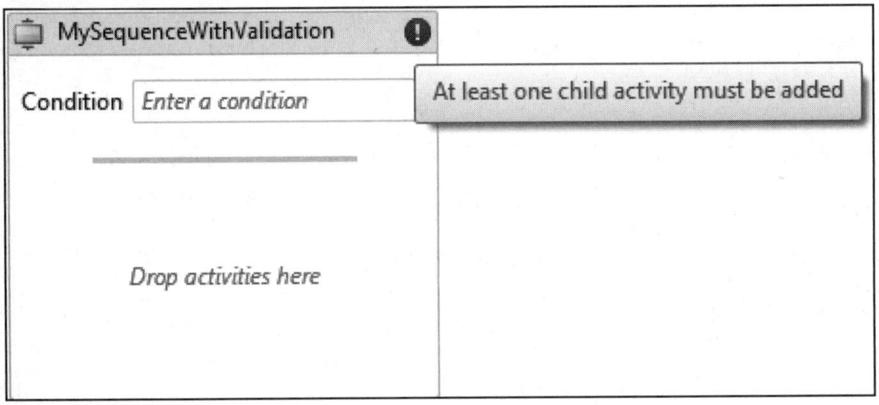

Figure 15-13. MySequenceWithValidation with error

Once you've added at least one child activity, the error should be cleared.

■ **Warning** Remember that you are validating the design-time properties of the activity. You do not have access to any of the runtime property values for the activity.

Adding a Warning

With just a slight modification to the code, you can turn this error into a warning instead. Instead of calling the version of the `AddValidationError` method shown in the original code, you can use an override that accepts a `ValidationError` object. When you construct this object, you can pass a Boolean value that determines whether the validation failure is considered an error or a warning. Here is the revised section of code:

```
protected override void CacheMetadata(NativeActivityMetadata metadata)
{
    base.CacheMetadata(metadata);
    if (Activities.Count == 0)
    {
        metadata.AddValidationError(
            new ValidationError(
                "At least one child activity must be added",
                true, "Activities"));
    }
}
```

After rebuilding the solution again, you should see that the previous error is now considered a warning, as shown in Figure 15-14.

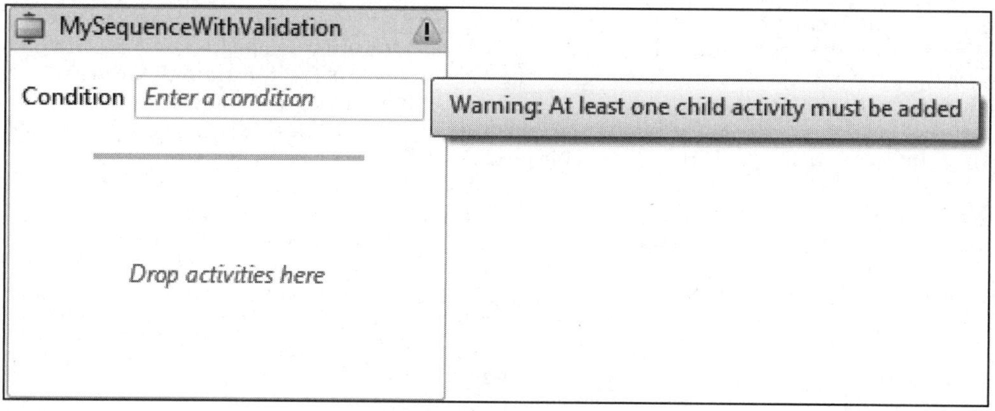

Figure 15-14. MySequenceWithValidation with warning

Using Constraints for Validation

To demonstrate the use of a constraint for validation, you will create yet another version of the `MySequence` activity. You will develop a series of constraints that demonstrate various types of validation that can be implemented with constraints.

Implementing a Simple Constraint

The first constraint that you will implement validates that at least one child activity has been added to the activity. This is the same validation logic that you implemented as imperative code within the activity in the previous example. Add a new C# class to the **ActivityLibrary** project. Name the new class **ChildActivityRequiredConstraint**. Constraints need to reference the activity type that they are constraining. For this reason, it makes sense to house the constraints in the same assembly as their activity type. Here is the code for this constraint class:

```
using System;
using System.Activities;
using System.Activities.Validation;

namespace ActivityLibrary
{
    public static class ChildActivityRequiredConstraint
    {
        public static Constraint GetConstraint()
        {
```

The **Constraint\<T>** class is sealed, so you can't derive your own class from it. Instead, you need to construct a constraint using composition as demonstrated in this example. Note that each constraint must know the type of activity that it is designed to constrain (specified as the generic type). This is necessary in order to provide access to any properties that might be unique to the activity. Depending on your needs, you can compose constraints that narrowly target a single activity (such as this one) or more broadly constrain the design-time behavior of an entire related family of activities.

In this example, an **ActivityAction** is assigned to the **Body** property of the constraint. The **ActivityAction** is defined to pass two arguments: the instance of the activity that you are validating (in this case a **MySequenceWithConstraint**) and a **ValidationContext** object. A **DelegateInArgument** is assigned to the **Argument1** property of the **ActivityAction**. This provides access to the activity that is being validated.

An **AssertValidation** activity is assigned to the **Handler** property of the **ActivityAction**. This is where the real work is of this constraint is accomplished. The **Assertion** property is a Boolean **InArgument** that asserts that the count of the **Activities** property is greater than zero. If the assertion is true, the activity passes validation. If the assertion is false, the text that is provided for the **Message** property is displayed as an error.

```
DelegateInArgument<MySequenceWithConstraint> element =
    new DelegateInArgument<MySequenceWithConstraint>();
return new Constraint<MySequenceWithConstraint>
{
    Body = new ActivityAction<MySequenceWithConstraint, ValidationContext>
    {
        Argument1 = element,
        Handler = new AssertValidation
        {
            IsWarning = false,
            Assertion = new InArgument<bool>(
                env => (element.Get(env).Activities.Count > 0)),
```

```
                    Message = new InArgument<string>(
                        "At least one child activity must be added"),
                }
            }
        };
    }
  }
}
```

■ **Note** The constraint won't build at this point since it is referencing a new version of the MySequence activity that you haven't implemented yet. That is the next step in this example.

To create an activity that will use the constraint, make another copy of the original MySequence activity (in the ActivityLibrary project). Name the copy MySequenceWithConstraint. Here is the code for this version of the activity:

```
using System;
using System.Activities;
using System.Collections.ObjectModel;
using System.ComponentModel;
using System.Windows.Markup;

namespace ActivityLibrary
{
    [Designer(typeof(ActivityDesignerLibrary.MySequenceDesigner))]
    [ContentProperty("Activities")]
    public class MySequenceWithConstraint : NativeActivity
    {
        [Browsable(false)]
        public Collection<Activity> Activities { get; set; }
        public Activity<Boolean> Condition { get; set; }
        [Browsable(false)]
        public Collection<Variable> Variables { get; set; }

        public MySequenceWithConstraint()
        {
            Activities = new Collection<Activity>();
            Variables = new Collection<Variable>();
```

The constraint is adding in the constructor of the activity. The static GetConstraint method that was defined in the constraint class is invoked, and the result (an instance of the constraint) is passed to the Constraints.Add method of the activity.

```
        this.Constraints.Add(
            ChildActivityRequiredConstraint.GetConstraint());
    }

    protected override void Execute(NativeActivityContext context)
    {
        throw new NotImplementedException();
    }
  }
}
```

Rebuild the solution, and test the new MySequenceWithConstraint activity by adding it to the Activity1.xaml file. Other than the difference in the display name of the activity, the results should be the same as you saw in Figure 15-13.

Validating Against Other Activities

Constraints also allow you to execute validation logic against other activities. For example, you can validate that only certain types of activities are allowed (or forbidden) as children. Or, you can mandate that your activity must be the child of a specific parent (or not).

To help you to perform validation in these scenarios, WF includes a set of activities that you can use within a constraint:

- GetParentChain returns a collection of parents of the current activity.

- GetChildSubtree returns all children of the current activity.

- GetWorkflowTree returns the entire tree of activities in the current workflow.

All of these activities function in the same basic way. They all support a ValidationContext property that must be set to the current ValidationContext of the constraint. This object is provided as an argument to the ActivityAction that you assign to the Constraint.Body property. These activities return a collection of Activity objects that represent the requested activities.

Checking the Children

To demonstrate these activities, add another C# class to the ActivityLibrary project, and name it LimitedChildActivitiesConstraint. The purpose of this constraint is to restrict the type of activities that you can add as children to the MySequenceWithConstraint activity. Here is the code for this constraint:

```
using System;
using System.Activities;
using System.Activities.Statements;
using System.Activities.Validation;
using System.Collections.Generic;
```

```
namespace ActivityLibrary
{
    public static class LimitedChildActivitiesConstraint
    {
        public static Constraint GetConstraint()
        {
```

A collection of allowed types is first populated. This list represents the activities that will be allowed as children of the activity. In this contrived example, only the Sequence, WriteLine, and Assign activities are allowed. The code also defines two namespaces that are to be allowed. This was necessary if you want to allow expressions (which you most certainly do).

```
            List<Type> allowedTypes = new List<Type>
            {
                typeof(Sequence),
                typeof(WriteLine),
                typeof(Assign)
            };

            List<String> allowedNamespaces = new List<String>
            {
                "Microsoft.VisualBasic.Activities",
                "System.Activities.Expressions"
            };

            Variable<Boolean> result =
                new Variable<Boolean>("result", true);
            DelegateInArgument<MySequenceWithConstraint> element =
                new DelegateInArgument<MySequenceWithConstraint>();
            DelegateInArgument<ValidationContext> vc =
                new DelegateInArgument<ValidationContext>();
            DelegateInArgument<Activity> child =
                new DelegateInArgument<Activity>();

            return new Constraint<MySequenceWithConstraint>
            {
                Body = new ActivityAction
                    <MySequenceWithConstraint, ValidationContext>
                {
                    Argument1 = element,
                    Argument2 = vc,
                    Handler = new Sequence
                    {
                        Variables = { result },
                        Activities =
                        {
```

The real work of this constraint takes place here in a ForEach<T> activity. The collection of activities that the ForEach<T> iterates over is retrieved from the GetChildSubtree activity. Each activity in the returned collection is checked against the list of allowed types and namespaces. If it isn't in one of those lists, a Boolean variable (named result) is set to false.

An `AssertValidation` activity is used to check the value of the `result` variable. If it is false, the validation error is presented.

```
new ForEach<Activity>
{
    Values = new GetChildSubtree
    {
        ValidationContext = vc
    },
    Body = new ActivityAction<Activity>
    {
        Argument = child,
        Handler = new If()
        {
            Condition = new InArgument<Boolean>(ac =>
                allowedTypes.Contains(
                    child.Get(ac).GetType()) ||
                allowedNamespaces.Contains(
                    child.Get(ac).GetType().Namespace)),
            Else = new Assign<Boolean>
            {
                To = result,
                Value = false
            }
        }
    }
},
new AssertValidation
{
    Assertion = new InArgument<Boolean>(result),
    Message = new InArgument<String>(
        "Only Sequence, WriteLine, Assign allowed"),
    PropertyName = new InArgument<String>(
        (env) => element.Get(env).DisplayName)
}
        }
    }
};
    }
  }
}
```

Checking the Parents

Just to make this example more interesting, go ahead and add another constraint class to the `ActivityLibrary` project. This time name the new class `WhileParentConstraint`. The purpose of this constraint is to prevent the `While` activity from being the parent of the constrained activity. Note that this particular constraint targets the base `Activity` class. This allows the constraint to be used to constrain any activity. Here is the code for this constraint:

```
using System;
using System.Activities;
using System.Activities.Statements;
using System.Activities.Validation;
using System.Collections.Generic;

namespace ActivityLibrary
{
    public static class WhileParentConstraint
    {
        public static Constraint GetConstraint()
        {
            List<Type> prohibitedParentTypes = new List<Type>
            {
                typeof(While),
            };

            Variable<Boolean> result =
                new Variable<Boolean>("result", true);
            DelegateInArgument<Activity> element =
                new DelegateInArgument<Activity>();
            DelegateInArgument<ValidationContext> vc =
                new DelegateInArgument<ValidationContext>();
            DelegateInArgument<Activity> child =
                new DelegateInArgument<Activity>();

            return new Constraint<Activity>
            {
                Body = new ActivityAction
                    <Activity, ValidationContext>
                {
                    Argument1 = element,
                    Argument2 = vc,
                    Handler = new Sequence
                    {
                        Variables = { result },
                        Activities =
                        {
```

This constraint is similar in structure to the previous one. The major difference is that the GetParentChain activity is used instead of GetChildSubtree. This returns a collection of all parent activities instead of all children.

```
                            new ForEach<Activity>
                            {
                                Values = new GetParentChain
                                {
                                    ValidationContext = vc
                                },
                                Body = new ActivityAction<Activity>
                                {
```

```
                                  Argument = child,
                                  Handler = new If()
                                  {
                                      Condition = new InArgument<Boolean>(ac =>
                                          prohibitedParentTypes.Contains(
                                              child.Get(ac).GetType())),
                                      Then = new Assign<Boolean>
                                      {
                                          To = result,
                                          Value = false
                                      }
                                  }
                              }
                          },
                          new AssertValidation
                          {
                              Assertion = new InArgument<Boolean>(result),
                              Message = new InArgument<String>(
                                "Parent While activity not allowed"),
                              PropertyName = new InArgument<String>(
                                  (env) => element.Get(env).DisplayName)
                          }
                      }
                  }
              }
          }
      };
  }
      }
  }
```

Adding the Constraints

To use these new constraints, you need to add them in the constructor of the `MySequenceWithConstraint` activity. Here is the affected code:

```
public MySequenceWithConstraint()
{
    Activities = new Collection<Activity>();
    Variables = new Collection<Variable>();

    this.Constraints.Add(
        ChildActivityRequiredConstraint.GetConstraint());
    this.Constraints.Add(
        LimitedChildActivitiesConstraint.GetConstraint());
    this.Constraints.Add(
        WhileParentConstraint.GetConstraint());
}
```

Testing the Constraints

After rebuilding the solution, you should be ready to test the new constraints. Open the `Activity1.xaml` file and add a new instance of the `MySequenceWithConstraint` activity. To test for valid children of this activity, add a `WriteLine` (which is valid), followed by a `Delay` activity as children. Set the `Delay.Duration` property to clear the `RequiredArgument` error due for that property. You should now see the error shown in Figure 15-15.

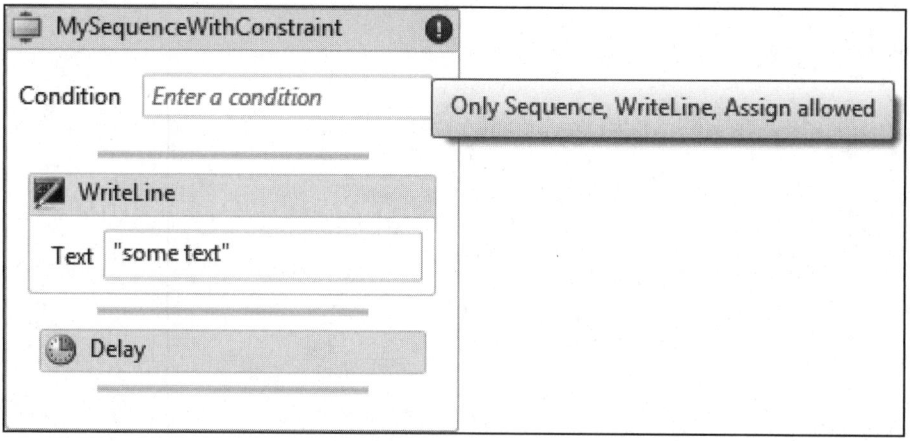

Figure 15-15. MySequenceWithConstraint with invalid child

To prove that the entire tree of children is inspected, add a `Sequence` activity (which is allowed) to the activity and then move the `Delay` activity into it. The `Delay` activity should continue to be flagged as a validation error, as shown in Figure 15-16.

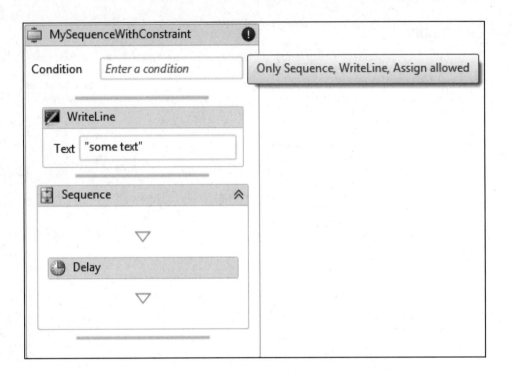

Figure 15-16. MySequenceWithConstraint with invalid grandchild

Removing the Sequence activity containing the Delay activity should clear the error. To test the parent validation, add a While activity to the root Sequence of the Activity1.xaml file, and move the MySequenceWithConstraint activity into it as a child. Enter True for the While.Condition property to clear that particular validation error. You should now see the error shown in Figure 15-17.

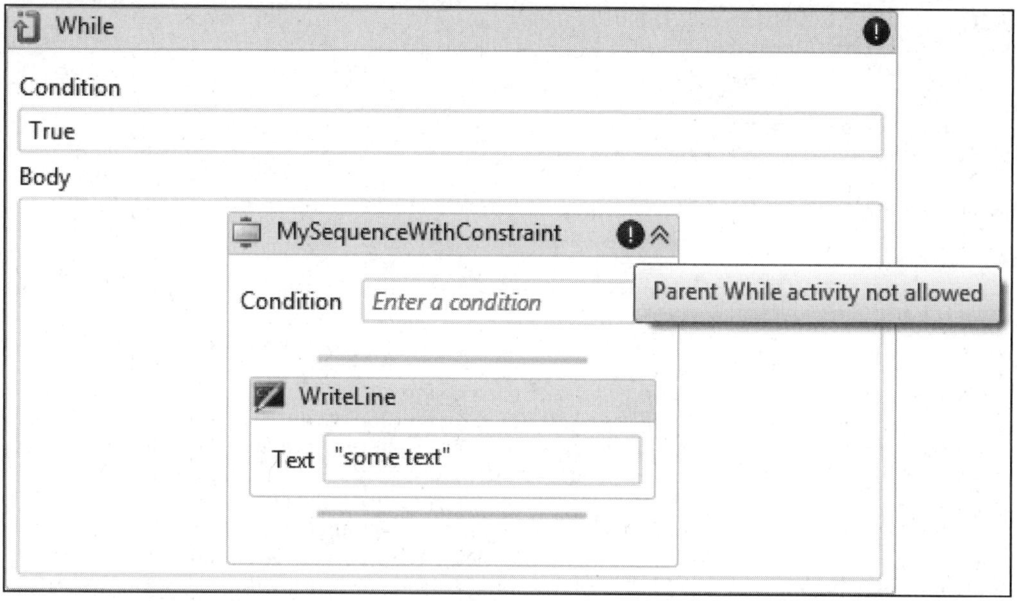

Figure 15-17. MySequenceWithConstraint with invalid parent

Manually Executing Validation

Most of the time, you will use the validation logic that is already associated with a particular activity (attributes, code validation, or constraints). This is especially true for the standard activities that ship with WF, but this is also the case for custom activities that you develop. Generally, you bake the validation into the activity so that it is automatically executed each and every time the activity is used.

However, you can also choose to manually validate an activity. And when you do so, you have the option of associating additional constraints with activities that may not already have them. This is useful in an environment where you are self-hosting the workflow designer in your own application. If you are self-hosting, it is likely that you want to tightly control what a user can do with a particular workflow. You might want to place additional restrictions on the user as to what activities they can use and so on. Performing manual validation on an activity provides you with an opportunity to enforce any additional constraints that you want to add.

In this short example, you will manually execute validation on a series of activities that are constructed entirely in code. Some of the test activities are designed to pass validation while others deliberately fail.

Implementing the Validation Tests

Create a new Workflow Console project, and name it `WorkflowValidation`. Add this new project to the solution for this chapter. Add a project reference to the `ActivityLibrary` project. You can delete the `Worklfow1.xaml` file since it won't be used. All the code for this example goes into the `Program.cs` file of the project. Here is the complete code that you need for this example:

```
using System;
using System.Activities;
using System.Activities.Statements;
using System.Activities.Validation;
using System.Collections.Generic;
using ActivityLibrary;

namespace WorkflowValidation
{
    class Program
    {
        static void Main(string[] args)
        {
```

The code executes a series of validation tests, with each test using a slightly different activity. The actual validation is accomplished by calling the static **Validate** method of the **ActivityValidationServices** class. Two different overloads of this method are used. One overload passes only the activity to be validated. This overload demonstrates the ability to manually execute the validation logic that has already been associated with an activity (or its children).

The second overload of the **Validate** method allows you to pass an instance of the **ValidationSettings** object. This class provides an **AdditionalConstraints** property that can be used to inject additional constraints. The constraints that you add are used only during the call to the **Validate** method; they are not permanently added to the activity.

```
            Console.WriteLine("\nMySequenceWithError");
            ShowValidationResults(ActivityValidationServices.Validate(
                MySequenceWithError()));

            Console.WriteLine("\nMySequenceNoError");
            ShowValidationResults(ActivityValidationServices.Validate(
                MySequenceNoError()));
```

This validation test adds the **WhileParentConstraint** to the **WriteLine** activity. You implemented this constraint earlier in the chapter. It prohibits the use of the **While** activity as the parent of the activity with the constraint. Since this constraint is being added to the **WriteLine** activity, the **WriteLine** activity cannot be used as a child of the **While** activity (at least for the duration of the call to the **Validate** method).

```
            Console.WriteLine("\nWhileAndWriteLineError");
            ValidationSettings settings = new ValidationSettings();
            settings.AdditionalConstraints.Add(
                typeof(WriteLine), new List<Constraint>
                {
                    WhileParentConstraint.GetConstraint()
                });
            ShowValidationResults(ActivityValidationServices.Validate(
                WhileAndWriteLine(), settings));
```

```
        Console.WriteLine("\nWhileAndWriteLineNoError");
        ShowValidationResults(ActivityValidationServices.Validate(
            WhileAndWriteLine()));
    }
```

The MySequenceWithError method constructs an activity that includes an instance of the MySequenceWithConstraint activity. This custom activity was developed in the previous sections of this chapter. This activity defines a set of constraints that are added during construction. One of those is a requirement that at least one child be added to the activity. Therefore, the activity that is constructed by this method should fail validation.

```
    private static Activity MySequenceWithError()
    {
        return new Sequence
        {
            Activities =
            {
                new MySequenceWithConstraint
                {
                    Activities =
                    {
                        //no child activities is an error
                    }
                }
            }
        };
    }
```

The MySequenceNoError method also constructs an activity that uses the MySequenceWithConstraint activity. However, this activity does include the required child activity; therefore, it should pass validation.

```
    private static Activity MySequenceNoError()
    {
        return new Sequence
        {
            Activities =
            {
                new MySequenceWithConstraint
                {
                    Activities =
                    {
                        new WriteLine()
                    }
                }
            }
        };
    }
```

The `WhileAndWriteLine` method constructs an activity that includes a **Sequence**, a **While**, and a **Writeline** —all standard activities. The activity that is constructed by this method is used for validation tests that inject additional constraints that are used during validation.

```
private static Activity WhileAndWriteLine()
{
    return new Sequence
    {
        Activities =
        {
            new While
            {
                Condition = true,
                Body = new WriteLine()
            }
        }
    };
}

private static void ShowValidationResults(ValidationResults vr)
{
    Console.WriteLine("Total Errors: {0} - Warnings: {1}",
        vr.Errors.Count, vr.Warnings.Count);
    foreach (ValidationError error in vr.Errors)
    {
        Console.WriteLine("  Error: {0}", error.Message);
    }
    foreach (ValidationError warning in vr.Warnings)
    {
        Console.WriteLine("  Warning: {0}", warning.Message);
    }
}
```

Executing the Validation Tests

Build the `WorkflowValidation` project, and run it without debugging (Ctrl-F5). Here are my results:

MySequenceWithError

Total Errors: 1 - Warnings: 0

  Error: At least one child activity must be added

```
MySequenceNoError

Total Errors: 0 - Warnings: 0



WhileAndWriteLineError

Total Errors: 1 - Warnings: 0

  Error: Parent While activity not allowed



WhileAndWriteLineNoError

Total Errors: 0 - Warnings: 0

Press any key to continue . . .
```

From these results, you can see that the tests that used the `MySequenceWithConstraint` activity returned the expected results. When a child activity was present, the activity passed validation. When the child activity was missing, the validation error was generated.

The test that added the additional constraint to the `WriteLine` activity also worked as expected. This demonstrates how you can add constraints to activities that don't originally use them.

Implementing Activity Templates

In addition to activities, WF also supports the concept of activity templates. An activity template is presented as a single activity in the Visual Studio Toolbox, but when added to the design surface, it may generate multiple activities. Or it may generate a single activity with property values that have been preconfigured for a given purpose.

Several of the standard activities that are supplied with WF are actually activity templates. For example, `ReceiveAndSendReply` (used for WCF messaging) is actually an activity template. When added to the design surface, it generates instances of the `Receive` and `SendReply` activities that are preconfigured to work with each other. The `SendAndReceiveReply` is also an activity template and works in a similar way.

Another example of a standard activity template is the `ForEachWithBodyFactory<T>` class. This template is associated with the `ForEach<T>` tool that you see in the standard WF Toolbox. When you drag and drop a `ForEach<T>` activity to the workflow designer, you are actually adding this template. The need for this template arises because a `ForEach<T>` activity also requires an `ActivityAction<T>` instance to be added to allow you to add your own child activity. The activity template is the mechanism that is used to add the `ForEach<T>` and an associated child `ActivityAction<T>`. You might want to follow Microsoft's example when you create custom activities that require an `ActivityAction<T>`.

WF provides the `IActivityTemplateFactory` interface (found in the `System.Activities.Presentation` namespace), which you can use to develop your own activity templates. You can use this mechanism any time you need to combine multiple activities into a single package for use at design time. This mechanism can also be used to preconfigure activity property values. Although you can certainly compose multiple activities into a single custom activity, adding those activities with an activity template allows you to alter the structure at design time.

To implement an activity template, you simply need to create a class that implements the IActivityTemplateFactory interface. This interface defines a single Create method that returns a single Activity. The Activity that you return is the preconfigured activity or root of an activity tree containing the activities that you want to add to the design surface.

Implementing the Template

In this example, you will create an activity template that preconfigures an instance of the MySequenceWithConstraint activity. For demonstration purposes, the template populates this activity with a child Sequence activity. And the Sequence activity contains a WriteLine activity with a default message for its Text property.

To create an activity template, add a new C# class to the ActivityLibrary project, and name it MySequenceTemplate. Here is the code that you need to implement this class:

```csharp
using System;
using System.Activities;
using System.Activities.Presentation;
using System.Activities.Statements;

namespace ActivityLibrary
{
    public class MySequenceTemplate : IActivityTemplateFactory
    {
        public Activity Create(System.Windows.DependencyObject target)
        {
            return new MySequenceWithConstraint
            {
                DisplayName = "MySequenceTemplate",
                Activities =
                {
                    new Sequence
                    {
                        Activities =
                        {
                            new WriteLine
                            {
                                Text = "Template generated text"
                            }
                        }
                    }
                }
            };
        }
    }
}
```

Testing the Template

Rebuild the solution, and then open the `Activity1.xaml` file in the `ActivityLibrary` project. You should see that `MySequenceTemplate` has been added to the Toolbox, just like all the other custom activities. When you drag and drop an instance of this template onto the designer surface, you should see the preconfigured collection of activities. Figure 15-18 shows the results that I see when I use this template.

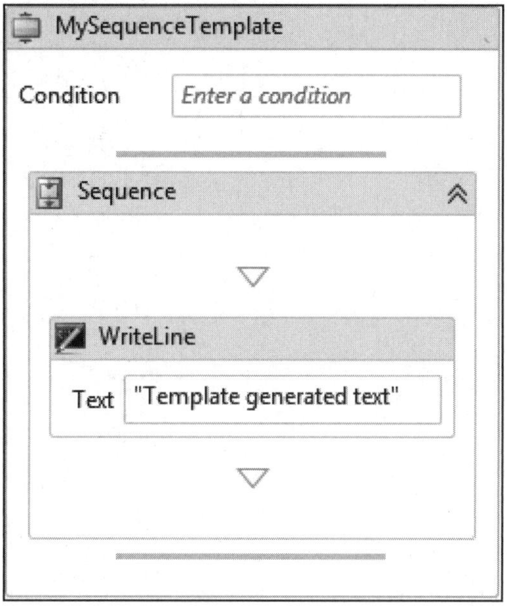

Figure 15-18. *MySequenceTemplate*

Summary

This chapter focused on enhancing the design-time experience. WF provides you with the ability to create an appealing and productive environment using custom designers and activity validation.

The chapter began with an overview of the classes that are used to develop custom activity designers. Example activity designers were presented that expose the activity properties on the design surface, support dragging and dropping a single or multiple child activities, and support the special needs of an `ActivityAction` property. The chapter also demonstrated how to construct an activity template.

Several examples were presented that demonstrated the three types of activity validation (attributes, code, and constraints). Manually executed validation and the injection of additional constraints was also demonstrated in another example.

In the next chapter, you will learn more about building advanced custom activities.

CHAPTER 16

■ ■ ■

Advanced Custom Activities

This chapter focuses on several advanced custom activity scenarios. Most of these scenarios are related to the execution of one or more children. The chapter begins with a general overview of the process that you must follow to schedule the execution of children. Your responsibilities as a parent activity are also reviewed. A simple activity that schedules a single child for execution is then demonstrated.

Following this first example, the chapter presents an activity that repeats execution of a single child while a condition is true. This example also explores the options that are available to you for handling an exception that is thrown by a child activity.

Other examples in this chapter demonstrate how to execute multiple children sequentially, or using a parallel execution pattern. An activity that supports an `ActivityAction` is also demonstrated. Dynamically constructing an activity using the `DynamicActivity` class is demonstrated next.

The chapter concludes with an example that demonstrates the use of execution properties and bookmark options.

Understanding Your Parental Responsibilities

A central theme of this chapter is the development of custom composite activities. These are parent activities that support the execution of one or more children (either child activities or delegates). Regardless of the real purpose for the parent activity, it has several responsibilities that you should consider. These responsibilities include the following:

- Configuring activity metadata
- Scheduling the execution of any children
- Reacting to the completion (successful or not) of children
- Creating bookmarks and reacting to their resumption
- Handling a cancellation request
- Reacting when the activity is aborted or terminated

These responsibilities are explored in the following sections.

■ **Note** The `NativeActivity` or `NativeActivity<TResult>` is the only base activity class that allows you to schedule and manage child activities. For this reason, the discussion and subsequent examples in this chapter pertain to custom activities that derive from one of these base classes.

Configuring Activity Metadata

The workflow runtime doesn't just blindly execute an activity. It instead employs a mechanism that provides a full description of the activity prior to its execution. This metadata about an activity includes a description of all child activities, arguments, variables, and delegates that will be used by the activity when it is executed. The metadata forms a contract between the activity and the workflow runtime and is used to validate the activity prior to its execution and to manage the relationships and dependencies between activities.

One of the responsibilities of any custom activity is to provide this metadata. For most simple custom activities, the metadata is automatically detected using reflection. However, the runtime may not always be able to accurately detect the metadata. For this reason, it is important to understand how to manually configure the metadata for an activity.

Automatically Configuring Metadata

In an activity derived from `NativeActivity` or `NativeActivity<TResult>`, the metadata is represented by an instance of the `NativeActivityMetadata` struct. This object is passed to the virtual `CacheMetadata` method of the activity. If you want to use the default metadata behavior (automatic detection using reflection), you can simply use the base version of the `CacheMetadata` method. If you need (or want) to configure the metadata yourself, you should override this method and provide your own implementation.

One common reason to override the `CacheMetadata` method is when your activity requires members that are not part of the activity's public signature. This includes private members such as variables and child activities that are used only during the implementation of the activity. Since they are private, they are not automatically detected by the default `CacheMetadata` method.

The default implementation of `CacheMetadata` inspects the members of the activity and automatically configures metadata for these public members based on their CLR type:

- Argument members
- Variable members
- Activity members
- `ActivityDelegate` members

The `CacheMetadata` method is executed only once as the activity is constructed but before it is executed. This makes sense since using reflection to create the metadata is relatively expensive. You wouldn't want to perform this logic each time the activity is executed.

Manually Configuring Metadata

To manually configure the metadata for an activity, you override the virtual `CacheMetadata` method in your activity and provide your own implementation. An instance of the `NativeActivityMetadata` struct is passed to this method, and it provides a number of methods that you can use to add metadata for the activity.

Here are the most commonly used methods of the `NativeActivityMetadata` struct:

Method	Description
AddArgument	Adds an Argument. The argument is described using an instance of the `RuntimeArgument` class.
AddChild	Adds a child `Activity`. Child activities added with this method can be provided publicly by the consumer of this activity.
AddDelegate	Adds an `ActivityDelegate`. Commonly used classes that derive from `ActivityDelegate` include `ActivityAction<T>` and `ActivityFunc<T>`. Delegates added with this method can be provided publicly by the consumer of this activity.
AddImplementationChild	Adds a child `Activity` that is an implementation detail of this activity. This child activity can only be provided internally by this activity and cannot be set publicly.
AddImplementationDelegate	Adds an `ActivityDelegate` that is an implementation detail of this activity. This delegate can only be provided internally and cannot be set publicly.
AddVariable	Adds a publicly accessible `Variable`. This variable becomes part of the public contract for this activity and can be accessed by child activities and delegates that were added with the `AddChild` and `AddDelegate` methods.
AddImplementationVariable	Adds a `Variable` that is an implementation detail of this activity. Variables added using this method can only be accessed by other implementation details that were added with the `AddImplementationChild` and `AddImplementationDelegate` methods.
AddImportedChild	A child activity that can be referenced by this activity but cannot be scheduled for execution by it.
AddImportedDelegate	A delegate that can be referenced by this activity but cannot be scheduled for execution by it.

As you review the list of methods that are supported by the `NativeActivityMetadata` struct, you will likely see a pattern. Most of the members are organized into two distinct categories: publicly accessible members and implementation details. Examples of publicly accessible members are the `Body` property of the `While` activity or the `Activities` property of the `Sequence` activity. These properties are publicly accessible since you (the consumer of the activity) provides values for them at design time. On the other hand, implementation details are private members that are used internally during the execution of the activity. They are not assigned values at design time by the consumer of the activity.

Why would you want to manually configure metadata for an activity? There are two good reasons:

- To gain better performance

- To provide implementation details

As far as performance is concerned, reflection is used if you rely upon the automatic metadata detection. Reflection is also relatively slow, especially compared to explicitly adding the metadata yourself. And the automatic metadata detection can detect only those members that are publicly available. Any private members that are considered implementation details must be added manually.

Scheduling Child Execution

Scheduling the execution of children implies some type of execution pattern. The pattern that you implement and the internal scheduling decisions that you make really define how your custom activity is used.

For example, you might implement an activity that supports the execution of a single child activity. Do you execute this activity just one time? Do you repeat the execution a number of times? How do you determine when to stop execution? Do you evaluate a `Boolean` condition to determine when to stop execution of the child? Do you check that condition before or after each execution? If you support multiple children, what execution pattern will you implement? Do you schedule execution of one child at a time (similar to the `Sequence` activity)? Do you schedule execution of all children immediately (similar to the `Parallel` activity)? The execution pattern that you implement is the one that meets your particular needs.

Regardless of the pattern that you implement, you use methods provided by the `NativeActivityContext` object that is passed to the `Execute` method to schedule execution of a child activity or delegate. The `NativeActivityContext` class provides a very large number of methods, but here are the methods that you will most frequently use:

Method	Description
ScheduleActivity	Schedules the exection of an `Activity`.
ScheduleActivity<TResult>	Schedules the execution of an `Activity<TResult>` that returns a single result.
ScheduleAction	Schedules the execution of an `ActivityAction` delegate. Overloads of this method are provided that support from zero to sixteen parameters.
ScheduleFunc	Schedules the execution of an `ActivityFunc` delegate. Overloads of this method are provided that support from zero to sixteen parameters.
ScheduleDelegate	Schedules the execution of an `ActivityDelegate`.

As each child is scheduled for execution it is added to a queue of work items for the workflow. The workflow runtime always executes the work item at the top (head) of the queue. You might expect that all new work items are added to the bottom (tail) of the queue. However, this is not always the case. Scheduling execution of a child adds it to the top of the queue, not the bottom. Microsoft has indicated that this was done to keep related activities closer together to, among other things, ease debugging. When you request cancellation of an activity, that also goes to the top of the queue. On the other hand, when you resume a bookmark, it is added to the bottom of the queue, as is an asynchronous callback. This was done to allow the activities that are closely related to complete before the resumption of the bookmark is processed. So, the internal queue of work items sometimes acts as a stack instead.

An `ActivityInstance` object is returned each time you schedule execution of a child. This object is a thin wrapper for the runtime instance of the scheduled child. It provides these properties:

Property	Type	Description
Activity	Activity	The activity that this `ActivityInstance` represents
Id	String	A unique identifier for this `ActivityInstance`
IsCompleted	Boolean	True if the scheduled child has completed
State	ActivityInstanceState	Identifies the current state of child

The `ActivityInstanceState` enum defines these possible execution states:

- Executing
- Closed
- Canceled
- Faulted

Handling Child Completion

The current activity is considered complete only when all of its scheduled children have also completed (or have been canceled). When you schedule the execution of a child, you can optionally specify these callback delegates that notify you of the completion of a child:

- CompletionCallback
- FaultCallback

One or both of these delegates are specified as arguments to the scheduling method (`ScheduleActivity`, `ScheduleAction`, and so on). The code that you assign to the `CompletionCallback` delegate is executed when the child completes normally. The code assigned to the `FaultCallback` is executed when an unhandled exception has occurred during execution of the child. Both delegates are passed an `ActivityInstance` object that identifies the child that has completed or faulted.

One common execution pattern is to execute one or more children while some condition is true (for example, the `While` activity). If this is the scenario that you are implementing, the `CompletionCallback` is your opportunity to test the condition as each child completes.

Handling Child Faults

The FaultCallback delegate is passed the unhandled exception along with a special limited version of the activity context (a NativeActivityFaultContext object). This allows you to optionally handle the exception in the parent activity instead of allowing it to propagate up the activity stack. How you choose to handle the exception is obviously up to you to decide.

If you decide to handle the exception in the parent activity, you call the HandleFault method of the NativeActivityFaultContext object to indicate that the exception has been handled. You also need to cancel further execution of the child that caused the fault. This can be accomplished with a call to the CancelChild method of the context object.

■ **Note** Handling a child fault is one of the scenarios that is demonstrated later in this chapter.

Handling Bookmarks

You have already seen bookmarks used as a communication mechanism between the host application and a workflow instance. Bookmarks can also be used for communication between activities within the same workflow. When used in this way, the bookmark is created by the parent activity and resumed by one or more child activities.

A bookmark that is designed to be resumed by a child activity is created using the CreateBookmark method of the activity context. This is the same method used to create the bookmarks that you saw in earlier chapters. However, by default, the creation of a bookmark blocks further execution of the activity that created it. Execution normally continues when the bookmark has been resumed. This default behavior may not be appropriate when you are using bookmarks between a parent and child.

To remedy this, you can optionally specify a BookmarkOptions value when you create a bookmark. This enum specifies several values that may be combined when you create a bookmark. Here are the possible values for the BookmarkOptions enum:

- **None**. This is the default if no options are specified. This creates a blocking bookmark that can be resumed only once.

- **MultipleResume**. This option creates a bookmark that can be resumed multiple times.

- **NonBlocking**. This option creates a nonblocking bookmark. When a bookmark of this type is created, execution of the activity that created the bookmark is not blocked and can complete without the bookmark ever being resumed.

■ **Note** You will implement an example that uses these bookmark options later in the chapter.

Handling a Cancellation Request

Cancellation is a request for a graceful shutdown. It doesn't mean that you must immediately abandon all work that you have already completed. It does mean that further execution of the activity (and its children) should cease in a controlled way as soon as possible. All activities should gracefully handle a cancellation request, but this is especially important for activities that schedule execution of one or more children. It is the responsibility of the parent activity to pass the cancellation request downstream to any children that are executing or are scheduled and waiting to be executed.

An activity is notified of a cancellation request by the virtual `Cancel` method. The base implementation of this method cancels all children that have been scheduled. You should override this method and provide your own implementation if you want to fine-tune the cancellation logic. For example, you may need to individually cancel your children in a particular controlled sequence. Or you may use the cancellation request as an opportunity to save any partially completed work.

To cancel a child, you can call one of these methods of the `NativeActivityContext` object:

- `CancelChild`. Cancels a single child (identified by an `ActivityInstance` object)

- `CancelChildren`. Cancels all children that you have scheduled and either executing or waiting to be executed

Reacting to Abort and Terminate

An activity is notified that it has been aborted by a call to the virtual `Abort` method of the base class. The default behavior of the base class also notifies any children. You can override this method if you need to provide your own implementation. But in general, the default implementation should be sufficient. The `Abort` method is passed a special `NativeActivityAbortContext` object. This class includes an additional `Reason` property (an `Exception`) that identifies the reason that the activity is being aborted.

If you need to manually abort the execution of a child, you can invoke the `AbortChildInstance` method of the `NativeActivityContext` object.

The `Abort` method is invoked when the entire workflow (or just the single activity) is aborted or terminated. There is a subtle difference between the two requests, but in both cases, execution should immediately cease. If a workflow or activity is terminated, it is left in the faulted state, and it cannot be resumed. On the other hand, if it is aborted, it can be resumed from the last persistence point (if one exists).

Scheduling a Single Child

In this first example, you will develop a relatively simple custom activity that schedules the execution of a single child activity. You will need to complete these tasks for this example:

1. Implement a custom activity.

2. Implement a custom designer for the activity.

3. Declare a workflow to test the activity.

4. Implement a test application to execute the workflow.

Implementing the Custom Activity

Create a new project using the Workflow Activity Library project template. Name the project `ActivityLibrary`, and add it to a new solution that is named for this chapter. This project will be used for all the custom activities and most of the test workflows that you develop in this chapter. You can delete the `Activity1.xaml` file that is created along with the new project since it won't be used.

At this time, you should also create another new project using the Workflow Activity Designer project template. Name this project `ActivityLibrary.Design`. To test the custom activities that support one or more children, you need to be able to add the children. To accomplish that using the workflow designer, each custom activity will need to use a custom activity designer. Delete the `ActivityDesigner1.xaml` file since it is not needed.

Add these assembly and project references to the `ActivityLibrary` project:

- ActivityLibrary.Design (project reference)
- PresentationCore
- PresentationFramework
- System.Activities.Presentation
- WindowsBase

Add a new Code Activity to the `ActivityLibrary` project, and name it `MySimpleParent`. The only real purpose of this activity is to schedule execution of a single child activity. As such, it doesn't really add any value, but it does demonstrate the code that you need to schedule a execution of a child. Here is the complete code for the `MySimpleParent` activity:

```
using System;
using System.Activities;
using System.ComponentModel;

namespace ActivityLibrary
{
```

The new activity derives from the `NativeActivity` class since this is the only base activity class that allows you to schedule the execution of other activities. I've also included the `Designer` attribute that specifies the custom activity designer to be used for this activity. Since you haven't implemented the designer yet (that's in the next step), the code won't build at this point.

```
[Designer(typeof(ActivityLibrary.Design.MySimpleParentDesigner))]
public class MySimpleParent : NativeActivity
{
```

The activity supports a single public activity named `Body`. This property represents the child activity that will be scheduled for execution. Note that I included the `Browsable` attribute with a value of false for this property. This removes the property from the Properties window since the custom designer will provide a way to drag and drop the child activity.

In this particular case, you could have relied upon the automatic behavior of the base `CacheMetadata` method. Since the `Body` property is public and is typed as an `Activity`, the automatic detection logic would have added this property to the metadata. But I instead provided an override for the `CacheMetadata` method to demonstrate how to add the metadata for this child yourself. In general, you should configure the metadata yourself since you are intimately aware of how each member and property will be used.

I've also included code to write to the console each time one of these methods is executed. This will help you to better understand when each method is executed during the lifetime of the activity.

```
[Browsable(false)]
public Activity Body { get; set; }

protected override void CacheMetadata(NativeActivityMetadata metadata)
{
    Console.WriteLine("CacheMetadata");
    metadata.AddChild(Body);
}
```

The real work of the activity takes place in the Execute method. The ScheduleActivity method of the activity context is executed to schedule execution of the activity that was assigned to the Body property. I've specified that the OnComplete method should be executed when the child activity completes execution. In this example, the OnComplete method displays only the fact that the child has completed along with the state of the completed activity.

```
protected override void Execute(NativeActivityContext context)
{
    Console.WriteLine("Execute Scheduled Body");
    ActivityInstance instance =
        context.ScheduleActivity(Body, OnComplete);
    Console.WriteLine("Execute: ID: {0}, State: {1}",
        instance.Id, instance.State);
}

private void OnComplete(NativeActivityContext context,
    ActivityInstance completedInstance)
{
    Console.WriteLine("OnComplete: State:{0}, IsCompleted:{1}",
        completedInstance.State, completedInstance.IsCompleted);
}
```

The code includes an override of the Cancel and Abort methods. The override code writes a message to the console to let you know when these methods have been invoked. The Cancel method uses the CancelChildren method of the activity context to cancel its single child. The Abort method executes the default logic by invoking the base version of Abort.

```
protected override void Cancel(NativeActivityContext context)
{
    Console.WriteLine("Cancel");
    context.CancelChildren();
}
```

```
        protected override void Abort(NativeActivityAbortContext context)
        {
            base.Abort(context);
            Console.WriteLine("Abort: Reason: {0}", context.Reason.Message);
        }
    }
}
```

Implementing the Activity Designer

Add a new Activity Designer to the `ActivityLibrary.Design` project, and name it
`MySimpleParentDesigner`. This designer allows you to drag and drop a single child activity onto the
`MySimpleParent` activity. Here is the complete markup for this designer:

```
<sap:ActivityDesigner x:Class="ActivityLibrary.Design.MySimpleParentDesigner"
    xmlns:s="clr-namespace:System;assembly=mscorlib"
    xmlns="http://schemas.microsoft.com/winfx/2006/xaml/presentation"
    xmlns:x="http://schemas.microsoft.com/winfx/2006/xaml"
    xmlns:sap="clr-namespace:System.Activities.Presentation;
        assembly=System.Activities.Presentation"
    xmlns:sapv="clr-namespace:System.Activities.Presentation.View;
        assembly=System.Activities.Presentation"
    xmlns:sapc="clr-namespace:System.Activities.Presentation.Converters;
        assembly=System.Activities.Presentation"
    Collapsible="False" >
    <StackPanel>
        <Border Margin="5"
            MinHeight="40" BorderBrush="LightGray"  BorderThickness="1" >
            <sap:WorkflowItemPresenter HintText="Drop an activity here"
                Item="{Binding Path=ModelItem.Body, Mode=TwoWay}" />
        </Border>
    </StackPanel>
</sap:ActivityDesigner>
```

■ **Note** As was the case when you first encountered custom activity designers in Chapter 15, each namespace in
the designer markup must be entered on a single line. Because the length of many of these namespaces exceeds
the maximum width allowed for this book, I've arbitrarily split the namespaces into multiple lines. When you enter
them, make sure that the entire namespace is entered on a single line. This applies to all the designer markup
shown in this chapter.

Please refer to Chapter 15 for more details on creating your own custom activity designers.

Rebuild the solution to ensure that the activity and its custom designer build correctly. This also
adds the custom activity to the Visual Studio Toolbox.

Declaring a Test Workflow

To test the MySimpleParent activity, you will declare a simple test workflow. Add a new Activity to the ActivityLibrary project, and name it MySimpleParentTest. Please follow these steps to declare this workflow:

1. Add a Sequence activity as the root of the workflow. This particular example doesn't really require this activity. But in subsequent examples, the Sequence activity is used to provide scope for any variables that might be used in the workflow. So, you should get in the habit of adding the Sequence as the root activity for these examples.

2. Add an instance of the MySimpleParent activity to the Sequence activity.

3. Add a Sequence activity as the single child of MySimpleParent.

4. Add a set of three WriteLine activities to the Sequence activity that you just added (the child of the MySimpleParent activity). Set the Text property of the WriteLine activities to "one", "two", and "three", respectively.

5. Add a Delay activity between the "one" and "two" WriteLine activities. Set the Delay.Duration property to TimeSpan.FromSeconds(1) to add a one-second delay. A Delay is introduced into this workflow to demonstrate what happens when you cancel, terminate, or abort the workflow. Without the Delay activity, the workflow would likely complete before the host application has a chance to interact with it.

You can see the completed workflow in Figure 16-1.

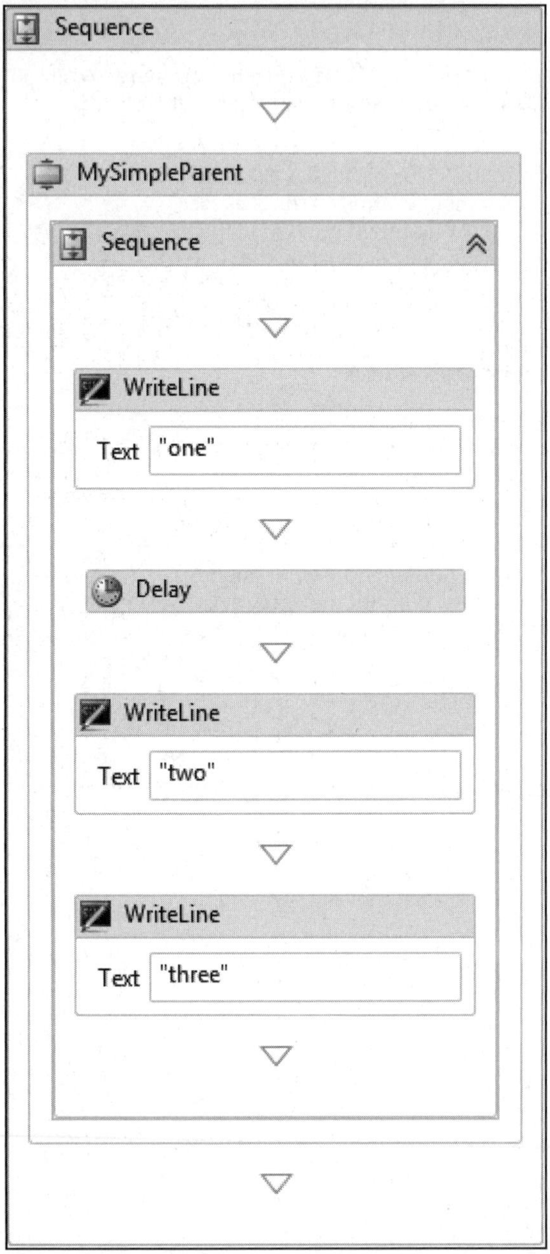

Figure 16-1. *MySimpleParentTest workflow*

Implementing a Test Application

To execute the MySimpleParentTest workflow, create a new Workflow Console application project named TestApplication. Add this new project to the same solution as the other projects for this chapter. Delete the Workflow1.xaml file since it won't be used. Add these references to the project:

- ActivityLibrary
- ActivityLibrary.Design

The goal of this project is to execute the MySimpleParentTest a total of four times to test several different situations. First it will execute the workflow normally to full completion. Then it will execute the workflow again, but it will call the Cancel method of the WorkflowApplication class to request cancellation after a short pause. The third test calls the Abort method, and the final test calls Terminate.

Here is the code for the Program.cs file to execute these tests:

```
using System;
using System.Activities;
using System.Threading;
using ActivityLibrary;

namespace TestApplication
{
    class Program
    {
        static void Main(string[] args)
        {
            try
            {
                RunActivity(new MySimpleParentTest());

                Console.WriteLine("Press any key to exit");
                Console.ReadKey();
            }
            catch (Exception exception)
            {
                Console.WriteLine(
                    "caught unhandled exception: {0}", exception.Message);
            }
        }

        private static void RunActivity(Activity activity)
        {
            RunActivity(activity, TestType.Normal);
            RunActivity(activity, TestType.Cancel);
            RunActivity(activity, TestType.Abort);
            RunActivity(activity, TestType.Terminate);
        }
```

```csharp
private static void RunActivity(Activity activity, TestType testType)
{
    Console.WriteLine("\n{0} {1}", activity.DisplayName, testType);

    AutoResetEvent waitEvent = new AutoResetEvent(false);
    WorkflowApplication wfApp = new WorkflowApplication(activity);
    wfApp.Completed = (e) =>
    {
        Console.WriteLine("WorkflowApplication.Completed");
        waitEvent.Set();
    };

    wfApp.Aborted = (e) =>
    {
        Console.WriteLine("WorkflowApplication.Aborted");
        waitEvent.Set();
    };

    wfApp.OnUnhandledException = (e) =>
    {
        Console.WriteLine("WorkflowApplication.OnUnhandledException: {0}",
            e.UnhandledException.Message);
        return UnhandledExceptionAction.Cancel;
    };

    wfApp.Run();

    switch (testType)
    {
        case TestType.Cancel:
            Thread.Sleep(100);
            wfApp.Cancel();
            break;

        case TestType.Abort:
            Thread.Sleep(100);
            wfApp.Abort("Abort was called");
            break;

        case TestType.Terminate:
            Thread.Sleep(100);
            wfApp.Terminate("Terminate was called");
            break;
        default:
            break;
    }

    waitEvent.WaitOne(TimeSpan.FromSeconds(60));
}
```

```
        private enum TestType
        {
            Normal,
            Cancel,
            Abort,
            Terminate
        }
    }
}
```

■ **Note** This test application will also be used to test other examples in this chapter. The only change necessary for these other tests is to change the name of the workflow that is constructed and passed to the `RunActivity` method.

Testing the Activity

After building the solution, you should be able to run the `TestApplication` project. Here are my test results:

MySimpleParentTest Normal

CacheMetadata

Execute Scheduled Body

Execute: ID: 4, State: Executing

one

two

three

OnComplete: State:Closed, IsCompleted:True

WorkflowApplication.Completed

MySimpleParentTest Cancel

Execute Scheduled Body

Execute: ID: 4, State: Executing

one

Cancel

OnComplete: State:Canceled, IsCompleted:True

WorkflowApplication.Completed

```
MySimpleParentTest Abort
Execute Scheduled Body
Execute: ID: 4, State: Executing
one
Abort: Reason: Abort was called
WorkflowApplication.Aborted


MySimpleParentTest Terminate
Execute Scheduled Body
Execute: ID: 4, State: Executing
one
Abort: Reason: Terminate was called
WorkflowApplication.Completed
Press any key to exit
```

Notice that the CacheMetadata method is executed only once. This is the case since the code creates only a single instance of the MySimpleParentTest workflow and executes it four times. The normal test produced the expected results, with all three of the WriteLine activities being executed. The Cancel, Abort, and Terminate tests resulted in only the first WriteLine activity being executed. This is the correct behavior since the workflow was canceled (or aborted or terminated) while the Delay activity was executing. After the Delay completed its work, the requested action to stop execution was processed.

In this example, the child of the MySimpleParent activity is actually a Sequence activity. So, the request to cease processing was passed down from the MySimpleParent activity to the Sequence activity, who in turn passed it to its children.

Repeating Execution of a Single Child

This example is similar to the previous one, but it introduces a few new features. First, the activity supports a new Condition property. This property represents a Boolean condition that must be true in order to execute the child activity. Second, the single child activity is executed repeatedly while the Condition property evaluates to true. This means that the Condition must be executed prior to starting each iteration of the child activity.

You will need to complete these tasks for this example:

1. Implement a custom activity.

2. Implement a designer for the activity.

3. Declare a test workflow.

Implementing the Custom Activity

Add a new Code Activity to the `ActivityLibrary` project, and name it `MyWhile` (in honor of the standard `While` activity). Here is the complete implementation of this activity:

```
using System;
using System.Activities;
using System.ComponentModel;

namespace ActivityLibrary
{
    [Designer(typeof(ActivityLibrary.Design.MyWhileDesigner))]
    public class MyWhile : NativeActivity
    {
```

This activity has a `Body` property that represents the child activity to be executed. A `Condition` property is also included, which represents the `Boolean` condition to be evaluated before the `Body` activity is scheduled for execution. Note that the `Condition` property is defined as `Activity<Boolean>`. This is necessary since the `Condition` activity will be scheduled for execution just like any other activity. The `Boolean` result from the activity is used to determine whether or not the `Body` activity should be executed.

The `Body` and `Condition` activities are both added to the metadata as children.

```
        [Browsable(false)]
        public Activity Body { get; set; }
        [RequiredArgument]
        public Activity<Boolean> Condition { get; set; }

        protected override void CacheMetadata(NativeActivityMetadata metadata)
        {
            Console.WriteLine("CacheMetadata");
            metadata.AddChild(Body);
            metadata.AddChild(Condition);
        }
```

The first order of business in the `Execute` method is to schedule execution of the `Condition`. The execution pattern that this code implements checks the condition before executing the `Body`. The `OnConditionComplete` callback will be invoked when the `Condition` activity completes.

```
        protected override void Execute(NativeActivityContext context)
        {
            if (Condition != null)
            {
                Console.WriteLine("Execute Scheduled Condition");
                context.ScheduleActivity<Boolean>(Condition, OnConditionComplete);
            }
        }
```

The `OnConditionComplete` callback is executed when the `Condition` activity has completed. The `Boolean` result of the activity is checked to determine whether the `Body` activity should be scheduled. If the result is false, then the work of this activity is complete. If the value is true, the `Body` is scheduled for execution. Note that a different completion callback delegate is specified (OnComplete), along with a method to call if an unhandled exception occurs.

Also note that the IsCancellationRequested property of the context is checked before scheduling the Body. Since this activity is designed to repeatedly execute a child activity, this behavior must be short-circuited if cancellation has been requested.

```
private void OnConditionComplete(NativeActivityContext context,
    ActivityInstance completedInstance, Boolean result)
{
    Console.WriteLine(
        "OnConditionComplete: State:{0}, IsCompleted:{1}: Result:{2}",
        completedInstance.State, completedInstance.IsCompleted, result);
    if (!context.IsCancellationRequested)
    {
        if (result && (Body != null))
        {
            Console.WriteLine("OnConditionComplete Scheduled Body");
            context.ScheduleActivity(Body, OnComplete, OnFaulted);
        }
    }
}
```

The OnComplete method is executed each time the Body activity completes. If the activity has not been canceled, the Condition activity is once again executed. After all, the assumption is that the Condition will eventually evaluate to false in order to stop the execution and complete this activity.

```
private void OnComplete(NativeActivityContext context,
    ActivityInstance completedInstance)
{
    Console.WriteLine("OnComplete: State:{0}, IsCompleted:{1}",
        completedInstance.State, completedInstance.IsCompleted);
    if (!context.IsCancellationRequested)
    {
        if (Condition != null)
        {
            Console.WriteLine("OnComplete Scheduled Condition");
            context.ScheduleActivity<Boolean>(
                Condition, OnConditionComplete, OnFaulted);
        }
    }
}
```

For this example, the OnFaulted method simply writes a message to the console. In a subsequent example, you will enhance this method to handle an unhandled exception that was generated by the child activity. The Cancel and Abort methods are similar to the previous example.

```
private void OnFaulted(NativeActivityFaultContext faultContext,
    Exception propagatedException, ActivityInstance propagatedFrom)
{
    Console.WriteLine("OnFaulted: {0}", propagatedException.Message);
}
```

```csharp
    protected override void Cancel(NativeActivityContext context)
    {
        Console.WriteLine("Cancel");
        if (context.IsCancellationRequested)
        {
            Console.WriteLine("IsCancellationRequested");
            context.CancelChildren();
        }
    }

    protected override void Abort(NativeActivityAbortContext context)
    {
        base.Abort(context);
        Console.WriteLine("Abort Reason: {0}", context.Reason.Message);
    }

    }
}
```

Implementing the Activity Designer

Add a new Activity Designer to the `ActivityLibrary.Design` project, and name it `MyWhileDesigner`. Here is the complete markup for this custom designer:

```xml
<sap:ActivityDesigner x:Class="ActivityLibrary.Design.MyWhileDesigner"
    xmlns:s="clr-namespace:System;assembly=mscorlib"
    xmlns="http://schemas.microsoft.com/winfx/2006/xaml/presentation"
    xmlns:x="http://schemas.microsoft.com/winfx/2006/xaml"
    xmlns:sap="clr-namespace:System.Activities.Presentation;
        assembly=System.Activities.Presentation"
    xmlns:sapv="clr-namespace:System.Activities.Presentation.View;
        assembly=System.Activities.Presentation"
    xmlns:sapc="clr-namespace:System.Activities.Presentation.Converters;
        assembly=System.Activities.Presentation"
Collapsible="False" >

    <Grid>
        <Grid.ColumnDefinitions>
            <ColumnDefinition />
            <ColumnDefinition />
        </Grid.ColumnDefinitions>
        <Grid.RowDefinitions>
            <RowDefinition />
            <RowDefinition />
        </Grid.RowDefinitions>
```

```
    <TextBlock Text="Condition" Grid.Row ="0" Grid.Column="0"
        HorizontalAlignment="Left" VerticalAlignment="Center" />

    <sapv:ExpressionTextBox HintText="Enter a condition"
        Grid.Row ="0" Grid.Column="1" MaxWidth="150" MinWidth="150" Margin="5"
        OwnerActivity="{Binding Path=ModelItem}"
        ExpressionType="{x:Type TypeName=s:Boolean}"
        Expression="{Binding Path=ModelItem.Condition, Mode=TwoWay}" />

    <Border Grid.Row ="1" Grid.Column="0" Grid.ColumnSpan="2" Margin="5"
        MinHeight="40" BorderBrush="LightGray"  BorderThickness="1" >
        <sap:WorkflowItemPresenter HintText="Drop an activity here"
            Item="{Binding Path=ModelItem.Body, Mode=TwoWay}" />
    </Border>

    </Grid>
</sap:ActivityDesigner>
```

You should rebuild the solution before proceeding with the next step.

Declaring a Test Workflow

Add a new Activity to the ActivityLibrary project, and name it MyWhileTest. This workflow will be used to test the MyWhile custom activity. Please follow these steps to declare the test workflow:

1.   Add a Sequence activity as the root of the workflow.

2.   Add an Int32 variable named count that is scoped by the Sequence activity.

3.   Add an instance of the MyWhile activity as a child of the Sequence activity. Set the Condition property to count < 3.

4.   Add another Sequence activity as the only child of the MyWhile activity.

5.   Add an Assign activity as a child of the last Sequence that you added (the child of the MyWhile activity). Set the Assign.To property to count and the Assign.Value property to count + 1.

6.   Add a WriteLine activity below the Assign activity. Set the WriteLine.Text property to String.Format("Count = {0}", count).

7.   Add a Delay activity after the WriteLine activity. Set the Delay.Duration property to TimeSpan.FromSeconds(1).

Figure 16-2 shows the completed MyWhileTest workflow.

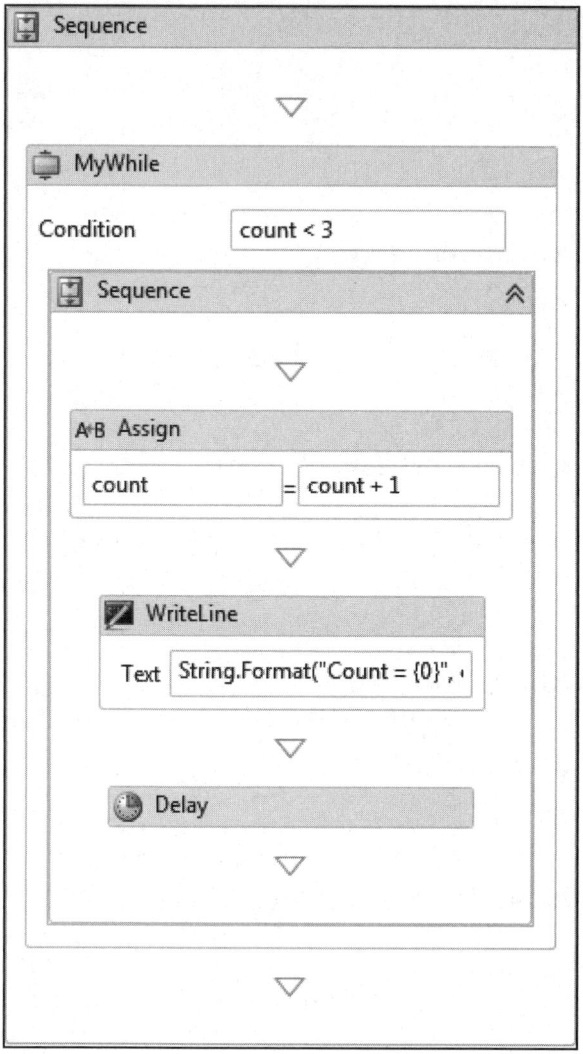

Figure 16-2. MyWhileTest workflow

Testing the Activity

You can use the same `TestApplication` project that you used in the previous example to also test this
new workflow. To do this, you need to make one small change to the `Program.cs` file in the
`TestApplciation` project. Change the type of the workflow that is created and passed to the `RunActivity`
method to `MyWhileTest` like this:

```
RunActivity(new MyWhileTest());
```

After building the solution, you should be able to run the **TestApplication** project. Here are my results:

```
MyWhileTest Normal

CacheMetadata

Execute Scheduled Condition

OnConditionComplete: State:Closed, IsCompleted:True: Result:True

OnConditionComplete Scheduled Body

Count = 1

OnComplete: State:Closed, IsCompleted:True

OnComplete Scheduled Condition

OnConditionComplete: State:Closed, IsCompleted:True: Result:True

OnConditionComplete Scheduled Body

Count = 2

OnComplete: State:Closed, IsCompleted:True

OnComplete Scheduled Condition

OnConditionComplete: State:Closed, IsCompleted:True: Result:True

OnConditionComplete Scheduled Body

Count = 3

OnComplete: State:Closed, IsCompleted:True

OnComplete Scheduled Condition

OnConditionComplete: State:Closed, IsCompleted:True: Result:False

WorkflowApplication.Completed


MyWhileTest Cancel

Execute Scheduled Condition

OnConditionComplete: State:Closed, IsCompleted:True: Result:True

OnConditionComplete Scheduled Body

Count = 1

Cancel

IsCancellationRequested

OnComplete: State:Canceled, IsCompleted:True

WorkflowApplication.Completed
```

```
MyWhileTest Abort

Execute Scheduled Condition

OnConditionComplete: State:Closed, IsCompleted:True: Result:True

OnConditionComplete Scheduled Body

Count = 1

Abort Reason: Abort was called

WorkflowApplication.Aborted


MyWhileTest Terminate

Execute Scheduled Condition

OnConditionComplete: State:Closed, IsCompleted:True: Result:True

OnConditionComplete Scheduled Body

Count = 1

Abort Reason: Terminate was called

WorkflowApplication.Completed

Press any key to exit
```

Handling Exceptions

One of the options available to a parent activity is to handle any unhandled exceptions from its children. This is not a requirement, but it is an option if you would prefer to handle the exception rather than allowing it to rise up the activity stack unhandled.

To demonstrate how a parent activity can handle an exception, you can make a small change to the MyWhile activity that you developed in the previous example.

Throwing an Exception

Before you handle the exception, you should first experience the default behavior when an exception is thrown by a child activity. Open the MyWhileTest workflow in the designer, and add a Throw activity after the existing Delay activity. Set the Throw.Exception property to New NullReferenceException("Exception was thrown"). Figure 16-3 shows the revised MyWhileTest workflow.

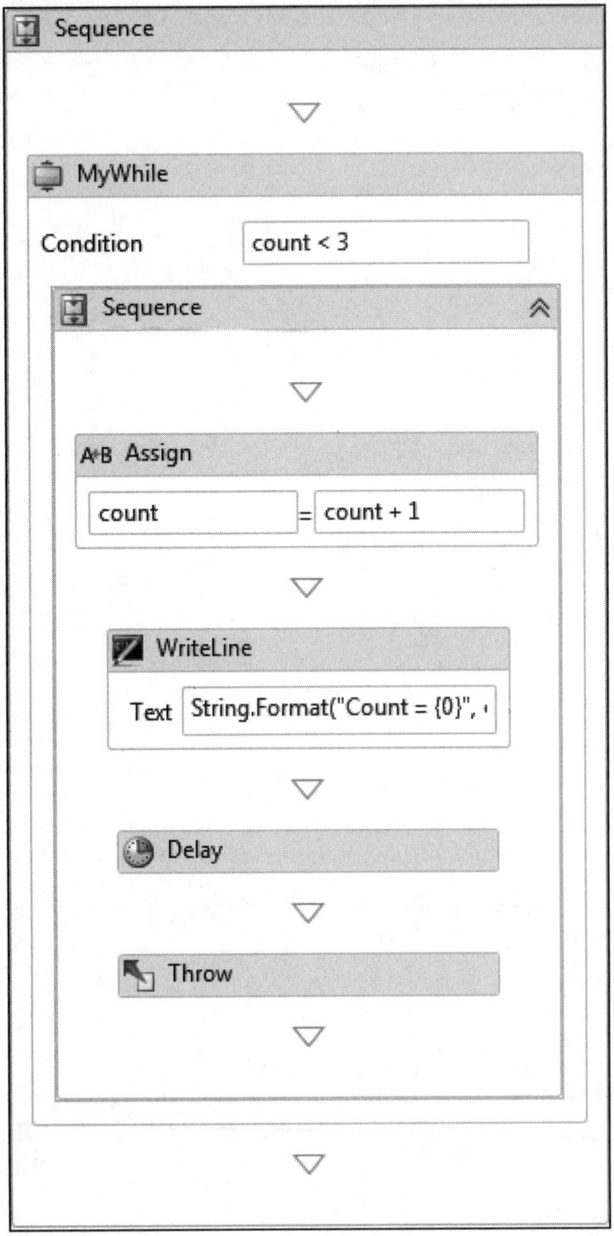

Figure 16-3. MyWhileTest workflow with Throw activity

Rebuild the solution, and run the **TestApplication** project to see the results when an exception is thrown by a child activity. Here are my results:

MyWhileTest Normal

CacheMetadata

Execute Scheduled Condition

OnConditionComplete: State:Closed, IsCompleted:True: Result:True

OnConditionComplete Scheduled Body

Count = 1

OnFaulted: Exception was thrown

WorkflowApplication.OnUnhandledException: Exception was thrown

Cancel

IsCancellationRequested

OnComplete: State:Canceled, IsCompleted:True

WorkflowApplication.Completed

MyWhileTest Cancel

Execute Scheduled Condition

OnConditionComplete: State:Closed, IsCompleted:True: Result:True

OnConditionComplete Scheduled Body

Count = 1

Cancel

IsCancellationRequested

OnComplete: State:Canceled, IsCompleted:True

WorkflowApplication.Completed

MyWhileTest Abort

Execute Scheduled Condition

OnConditionComplete: State:Closed, IsCompleted:True: Result:True

OnConditionComplete Scheduled Body

Count = 1

Abort Reason: Abort was called

WorkflowApplication.Aborted

```
MyWhileTest Terminate

Execute Scheduled Condition

OnConditionComplete: State:Closed, IsCompleted:True: Result:True

OnConditionComplete Scheduled Body

Count = 1

Abort Reason: Terminate was called

WorkflowApplication.Completed

Press any key to exit
```

As expected, execution of the workflow stopped at the end of the first iteration when the exception was thrown.

Handling the Exception

To handle the exception in the parent MyWhile activity, make a small addition to the OnFaulted method:

```
private void OnFaulted(NativeActivityFaultContext faultContext,
    Exception propagatedException, ActivityInstance propagatedFrom)
{
    Console.WriteLine("OnFaulted: {0}", propagatedException.Message);

    faultContext.HandleFault();
    faultContext.CancelChild(propagatedFrom);
    Console.WriteLine("OnFaulted: Exception was handled");
}
```

The call to the HandleFault method handles the fault and prevents it from being passed up the activity tree as an unhandled exception. After handling the fault, the child activity that caused the fault is canceled.

Rebuild the solution, and rerun the TestApplication project. You should now see these revised results, indicating that the unhandled fault has now been handled. Since the exception is now handled, the parent activity was never canceled:

```
MyWhileTest Normal

CacheMetadata

Execute Scheduled Condition

OnConditionComplete: State:Closed, IsCompleted:True: Result:True

OnConditionComplete Scheduled Body

Count = 1

OnFaulted: Exception was thrown
```

OnFaulted: Exception was handled

OnComplete: State:Canceled, IsCompleted:True

OnComplete Scheduled Condition

OnConditionComplete: State:Closed, IsCompleted:True: Result:True

OnConditionComplete Scheduled Body

Count = 2

OnFaulted: Exception was thrown

OnFaulted: Exception was handled

OnComplete: State:Canceled, IsCompleted:True

OnComplete Scheduled Condition

OnConditionComplete: State:Closed, IsCompleted:True: Result:True

OnConditionComplete Scheduled Body

Count = 3

OnFaulted: Exception was thrown

OnFaulted: Exception was handled

OnComplete: State:Canceled, IsCompleted:True

OnComplete Scheduled Condition

OnConditionComplete: State:Closed, IsCompleted:True: Result:False

WorkflowApplication.Completed

MyWhileTest Cancel

Execute Scheduled Condition

OnConditionComplete: State:Closed, IsCompleted:True: Result:True

OnConditionComplete Scheduled Body

Count = 1

Cancel

IsCancellationRequested

OnComplete: State:Canceled, IsCompleted:True

WorkflowApplication.Completed

MyWhileTest Abort

Execute Scheduled Condition

```
OnConditionComplete: State:Closed, IsCompleted:True: Result:True

OnConditionComplete Scheduled Body

Count = 1

Abort Reason: Abort was called

WorkflowApplication.Aborted


MyWhileTest Terminate

Execute Scheduled Condition

OnConditionComplete: State:Closed, IsCompleted:True: Result:True

OnConditionComplete Scheduled Body

Count = 1

Abort Reason: Terminate was called

WorkflowApplication.Completed

Press any key to exit
```

Scheduling Multiple Children

Another common scenario is to schedule multiple child activities, instead of a single one. In this example, you will implement a custom activity that accomplishes this. The custom activity will support multiple child activities and will execute each of them just once in sequence. Prior to scheduling the execution of each child, a `Condition` property is checked to determine whether execution should continue.

Implementing the Custom Activity

Add a new Code Activity to the `ActivityLibrary` project, and name it `MySequence`. Here is the code for this activity:

```
using System;
using System.Activities;
using System.Collections.ObjectModel;
using System.ComponentModel;

namespace ActivityLibrary
{
    [Designer(typeof(ActivityLibrary.Design.MySequenceDesigner))]
    public class MySequence : NativeActivity
    {
```

This class includes an **Activities** property to support multiple child activities. In addition to this, a **Condition** property is also included, which is used to determine whether each child activity is executed. This class also uses a private variable to track the index to the next child activity to be scheduled.

```
[Browsable(false)]
public Collection<Activity> Activities { get; set; }
[RequiredArgument]
public Activity<Boolean> Condition { get; set; }

private Variable<Int32> activityIndex =
    new Variable<int>("ActivityIndex", 0);

public MySequence()
{
    Activities = new Collection<Activity>();
}
```

The **CacheMetadata** method is similar to what you have already seen in previous examples. However, since you are working with a collection of child activities, the **SetChildrenCollection** method is invoked to set the **Activities** collection as the collection of child activities. In addition, the **AddImplementationVariable** method is used to add the private variable to the metadata. Using this method indicates that this variable is an implementation detail that the activity will use during its execution. I could have used a CLR type for the index instead of a variable. But using a workflow variable is the preferred approach since it is then managed by the workflow runtime (made part of the activity context) and properly scoped for a single execution of this activity.

```
protected override void CacheMetadata(NativeActivityMetadata metadata)
{
    Console.WriteLine("CacheMetadata");
    metadata.SetChildrenCollection(Activities);
    metadata.AddChild(Condition);
    metadata.AddImplementationVariable(activityIndex);
}
```

The **Execute** method begins by executing the **Condition** activity. The Boolean result from this activity is checked in the **OnConditionComplete** callback method.

```
protected override void Execute(NativeActivityContext context)
{
    if (Condition != null)
    {
        Console.WriteLine("Execute Scheduled Condition");
        context.ScheduleActivity<Boolean>(Condition, OnConditionComplete);
    }
}
```

The **OnConditionComplete** method is executed when the **Condition** activity has completed. If the result of the **Condition** is false, no further process takes place, and the work of this activity is complete. The **activityIndex** variable is used to track the index of the next child activity to execute. If there are activities in the collection that are yet to be executed, the next child activity in the collection is scheduled, and the index is incremented.

```
    private void OnConditionComplete(NativeActivityContext context,
        ActivityInstance completedInstance, Boolean result)
    {
        Console.WriteLine(
            "OnConditionComplete:  State:{0}, IsCompleted:{1}: Result:{2}",
            completedInstance.State, completedInstance.IsCompleted, result);
        if (!context.IsCancellationRequested)
        {
            if (result)
            {
                Int32 index = activityIndex.Get(context);
                if (index < Activities.Count)
                {
                    Console.WriteLine(
                        "OnConditionComplete Scheduled activity: {0}",
                            Activities[index].DisplayName);
                    context.ScheduleActivity(
                        Activities[index], OnComplete, OnFaulted);
                    index++;
                    activityIndex.Set(context, index);
                }
            }
        }
    }

    private void OnComplete(NativeActivityContext context,
        ActivityInstance completedInstance)
    {
        Console.WriteLine("OnComplete:  State:{0}, IsCompleted:{1}",
            completedInstance.State, completedInstance.IsCompleted);
        if (!context.IsCancellationRequested)
        {
            if (Condition != null)
            {
                Console.WriteLine("OnComplete Scheduled Condition");
                context.ScheduleActivity<Boolean>(
                    Condition, OnConditionComplete, OnFaulted);
            }
        }
    }

    private void OnFaulted(NativeActivityFaultContext faultContext,
        Exception propagatedException, ActivityInstance propagatedFrom)
    {
        Console.WriteLine("OnFaulted: {0}", propagatedException.Message);
    }
```

```
    protected override void Cancel(NativeActivityContext context)
    {
        Console.WriteLine("Cancel");
        if (context.IsCancellationRequested)
        {
            Console.WriteLine("IsCancellationRequested");
            context.CancelChildren();
        }
    }

    protected override void Abort(NativeActivityAbortContext context)
    {
        base.Abort(context);
        Console.WriteLine("Abort Reason: {0}", context.Reason.Message);
    }
    }
}
```

Implementing the Activity Designer

Add a new Activity Designer to the `ActivityLibrary.Design` project, and name it `MySequenceDesigner`. Here is the markup for this designer:

```
<sap:ActivityDesigner x:Class="ActivityLibrary.Design.MySequenceDesigner"
    xmlns:s="clr-namespace:System;assembly=mscorlib"
    xmlns="http://schemas.microsoft.com/winfx/2006/xaml/presentation"
    xmlns:x="http://schemas.microsoft.com/winfx/2006/xaml"
    xmlns:sap="clr-namespace:System.Activities.Presentation;
        assembly=System.Activities.Presentation"
    xmlns:sapv="clr-namespace:System.Activities.Presentation.View;
        assembly=System.Activities.Presentation"
    xmlns:sapc="clr-namespace:System.Activities.Presentation.Converters;
        assembly=System.Activities.Presentation"
    Collapsible="True" >

    <sap:ActivityDesigner.Resources>
        <DataTemplate x:Key="ShowAsCollapsed">
            <TextBlock Foreground="Gray">
                <TextBlock.Text>
                    <MultiBinding StringFormat="Expand for {0} Activities">
                        <Binding Path="ModelItem.Activities.Count" />
                    </MultiBinding>
                </TextBlock.Text>
            </TextBlock>
        </DataTemplate>
        <DataTemplate x:Key="ShowAsExpanded">
            <Grid>
                <Grid.ColumnDefinitions>
                    <ColumnDefinition />
                    <ColumnDefinition />
                </Grid.ColumnDefinitions>
```

```xml
                    <Grid.RowDefinitions>
                        <RowDefinition />
                        <RowDefinition />
                    </Grid.RowDefinitions>

                    <TextBlock Text="Condition" Grid.Row ="0" Grid.Column="0"
                    HorizontalAlignment="Left" VerticalAlignment="Center" />
                    <sapv:ExpressionTextBox HintText="Enter a condition"
                    Grid.Row ="0" Grid.Column="1"
                    MaxWidth="150" MinWidth="150" Margin="5"
                    OwnerActivity="{Binding Path=ModelItem}"
                    ExpressionType="{x:Type TypeName=s:Boolean}"
                    Expression="{Binding Path=ModelItem.Condition, Mode=TwoWay}" />

                    <sap:WorkflowItemsPresenter HintText="Drop activities here"
                    Grid.Row ="1" Grid.Column="0" Grid.ColumnSpan="2"
                    Margin="5" MinHeight="100"
                    Items="{Binding Path=ModelItem.Activities}">
                        <sap:WorkflowItemsPresenter.SpacerTemplate>
                            <DataTemplate>
                                <Rectangle Width="140" Height="3"
                                Fill="LightGray" Margin="7" />
                            </DataTemplate>
                        </sap:WorkflowItemsPresenter.SpacerTemplate>
                        <sap:WorkflowItemsPresenter.ItemsPanel>
                            <ItemsPanelTemplate>
                                <StackPanel Orientation="Vertical" />
                            </ItemsPanelTemplate>
                        </sap:WorkflowItemsPresenter.ItemsPanel>
                    </sap:WorkflowItemsPresenter>
                </Grid>
            </DataTemplate>
        <Style x:Key="StyleWithCollapse" TargetType="{x:Type ContentPresenter}">
            <Setter Property="ContentTemplate"
                Value="{DynamicResource ShowAsExpanded}"/>
            <Style.Triggers>
                <DataTrigger Binding="{Binding Path=ShowExpanded}" Value="False">
                    <Setter Property="ContentTemplate"
                        Value="{DynamicResource ShowAsCollapsed}"/>
                </DataTrigger>
            </Style.Triggers>
        </Style>
    </sap:ActivityDesigner.Resources>
    <Grid>
        <ContentPresenter Style="{DynamicResource StyleWithCollapse}"
            Content="{Binding}"/>
    </Grid>

</sap:ActivityDesigner>
```

Rebuild the solution before proceeding with the next step.

Declaring a Test Workflow

To test the MySequence activity, add a new Activity to the ActivityLibrary project, and name it MySequenceTest. Please follow these steps to declare this workflow:

1. Add a Sequence activity as the root of the workflow.

2. Add an Int32 variable named count that is scoped by the Sequence activity.

3. Add an instance of the new MySequence activity as a child of the Sequence activity. Set the Condition property of this activity to count < 3.

4. Add three WriteLine activities as children of the MySequence activity. Set the Text property of the WriteLine activities to "one", "two", and "three", respectively.

5. Add a Delay activity below the first WriteLine activity. Set the Delay.Duration property to TimeSpan.FromSeconds(1).

6. Add an Assign activity after the Delay activity. Set the Assign.To property to count and the Assign.Value property to 1. The Assign activity doesn't affect the outcome of this first test and really isn't needed. But in a subsequent test, you will assign a different value to the count variable to prematurely end the processing.

Figure 16-4 shows the completed MySequenceTest workflow.

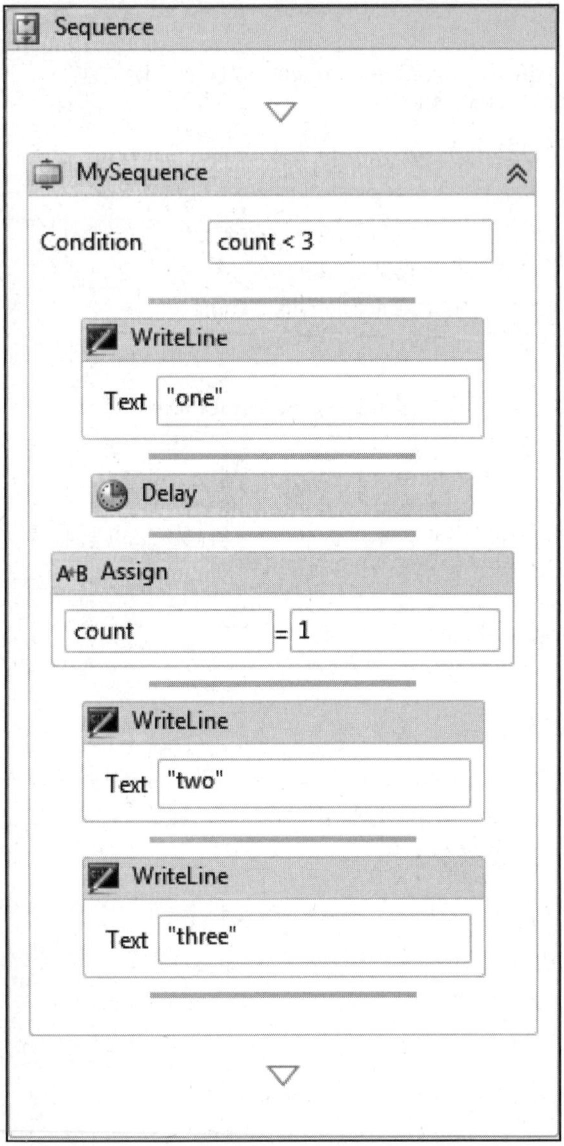

Figure 16-4. MySequenceTest workflow

Testing the Activity

You will once again use the **TestApplication** project to test this new activity. Modify the **Program.cs** file (as you did previously) to create an instance of the **MySequenceTest** workflow for the test. After rebuilding the solution, you can now run the **TestApplication**.

Your results should show that the condition is first executed and the Boolean result checked. The first **WriteLine** activity is then scheduled for execution. Following that, the condition is scheduled for execution again, and the result checked. The **Delay** activity is then scheduled for execution and then completed. This pattern continues until all the child activities have been processed. The abort, cancel, and terminate tests demonstrate that the activity is capable of correctly handling these requests.

Here are my results:

```
MySequenceTest Normal

CacheMetadata

Execute Scheduled Condition

OnConditionComplete:  State:Closed, IsCompleted:True: Result:True

OnConditionComplete Scheduled activity: WriteLine

one

OnComplete:  State:Closed, IsCompleted:True

OnComplete Scheduled Condition

OnConditionComplete:  State:Closed, IsCompleted:True: Result:True

OnConditionComplete Scheduled activity: Delay

OnComplete:  State:Closed, IsCompleted:True

OnComplete Scheduled Condition

OnConditionComplete:  State:Closed, IsCompleted:True: Result:True

OnConditionComplete Scheduled activity: Assign

OnComplete:  State:Closed, IsCompleted:True

OnComplete Scheduled Condition

OnConditionComplete:  State:Closed, IsCompleted:True: Result:True

OnConditionComplete Scheduled activity: WriteLine

two

OnComplete:  State:Closed, IsCompleted:True

OnComplete Scheduled Condition

OnConditionComplete:  State:Closed, IsCompleted:True: Result:True

OnConditionComplete Scheduled activity: WriteLine

three
```

```
OnComplete:   State:Closed, IsCompleted:True
OnComplete Scheduled Condition
OnConditionComplete:  State:Closed, IsCompleted:True: Result:True
WorkflowApplication.Completed


MySequenceTest Cancel
Execute Scheduled Condition
OnConditionComplete:  State:Closed, IsCompleted:True: Result:True
OnConditionComplete Scheduled activity: WriteLine
one
OnComplete:   State:Closed, IsCompleted:True
OnComplete Scheduled Condition
OnConditionComplete:  State:Closed, IsCompleted:True: Result:True
OnConditionComplete Scheduled activity: Delay
Cancel
IsCancellationRequested
OnComplete:   State:Canceled, IsCompleted:True
WorkflowApplication.Completed


MySequenceTest Abort
Execute Scheduled Condition
OnConditionComplete:  State:Closed, IsCompleted:True: Result:True
OnConditionComplete Scheduled activity: WriteLine
one
OnComplete:   State:Closed, IsCompleted:True
OnComplete Scheduled Condition
OnConditionComplete:  State:Closed, IsCompleted:True: Result:True
OnConditionComplete Scheduled activity: Delay
Abort Reason: Abort was called
WorkflowApplication.Aborted
```

```
MySequenceTest Terminate

Execute Scheduled Condition

OnConditionComplete:  State:Closed, IsCompleted:True: Result:True

OnConditionComplete Scheduled activity: WriteLine

one

OnComplete:  State:Closed, IsCompleted:True

OnComplete Scheduled Condition

OnConditionComplete:  State:Closed, IsCompleted:True: Result:True

OnConditionComplete Scheduled activity: Delay

Abort Reason: Terminate was called

WorkflowApplication.Completed

Press any key to exit
```

Testing the Condition Logic

To test the logic that checks the Boolean `Condition` property, you can make a small modification to the `MySequenceTest` workflow. Locate the `Assign` activity, and change the `Assign.Value` property to a number that is 3 or greater. This should cause the `Condition` to fail and further processing of child activities to cease.

If you build and run the `TestApplication` project, you should see these results, indicating that the `Condition` logic is working correctly:

```
MySequenceTest Normal

CacheMetadata

Execute Scheduled Condition

OnConditionComplete:  State:Closed, IsCompleted:True: Result:True

OnConditionComplete Scheduled activity: WriteLine

one

OnComplete:  State:Closed, IsCompleted:True

OnComplete Scheduled Condition

OnConditionComplete:  State:Closed, IsCompleted:True: Result:True

OnConditionComplete Scheduled activity: Delay

OnComplete:  State:Closed, IsCompleted:True

OnComplete Scheduled Condition

OnConditionComplete:  State:Closed, IsCompleted:True: Result:True
```

```
OnConditionComplete Scheduled activity: Assign
OnComplete:  State:Closed, IsCompleted:True
OnComplete Scheduled Condition
OnConditionComplete:  State:Closed, IsCompleted:True: Result:False
WorkflowApplication.Completed


MySequenceTest Cancel
Execute Scheduled Condition
OnConditionComplete:  State:Closed, IsCompleted:True: Result:True
OnConditionComplete Scheduled activity: WriteLine
one
OnComplete:  State:Closed, IsCompleted:True
OnComplete Scheduled Condition
OnConditionComplete:  State:Closed, IsCompleted:True: Result:True
OnConditionComplete Scheduled activity: Delay
Cancel
IsCancellationRequested
OnComplete:  State:Canceled, IsCompleted:True
WorkflowApplication.Completed


MySequenceTest Abort
Execute Scheduled Condition
OnConditionComplete:  State:Closed, IsCompleted:True: Result:True
OnConditionComplete Scheduled activity: WriteLine
one
OnComplete:  State:Closed, IsCompleted:True
OnComplete Scheduled Condition
OnConditionComplete:  State:Closed, IsCompleted:True: Result:True
OnConditionComplete Scheduled activity: Delay
Abort Reason: Abort was called
WorkflowApplication.Aborted
```

```
MySequenceTest Terminate

Execute Scheduled Condition

OnConditionComplete:  State:Closed, IsCompleted:True: Result:True

OnConditionComplete Scheduled activity: WriteLine

one

OnComplete:  State:Closed, IsCompleted:True

OnComplete Scheduled Condition

OnConditionComplete:  State:Closed, IsCompleted:True: Result:True

OnConditionComplete Scheduled activity: Delay

Abort Reason: Terminate was called

WorkflowApplication.Completed

Press any key to exit
```

Scheduling Parallel Execution

This example demonstrates how to schedule the execution of multiple children so that they can take advantage of parallel workflow processing. Remember that true parallel processing of multiple activities isn't directly supported by WF. All activities execute on a single thread that is assigned to a workflow instance. But by scheduling all children immediately, other children may be given the opportunity to execute when one of the children becomes idle. This mimics the type of parallel processing that is supported by the standard Parallel activity.

Implementing the Custom Activity

Add a new Code Activity to the ActivityLibrary project, and name it MyParallel. This activity is similar in structure to the MySequence activity from the previous example. However, it differs in the execution pattern that it implements (parallel vs. sequential). It also demonstrates one way to track individual ActivityInstance objects for each scheduled child activity. This isn't a requirement for this activity, but it does help to identify the activities that have been scheduled and have not yet completed. This is important in an activity such as this one that immediately schedules all children for execution.

Here is the code for this new activity:

```
using System;
using System.Activities;
using System.Collections.Generic;
using System.Collections.ObjectModel;
using System.ComponentModel;

namespace ActivityLibrary
{
```

The public interface to this activity is the same as the MySequence activity that you developed in the previous example. For this reason, you can use the same MySequenceDesigner that you developed for the MySequence activity.

In addition to the Activities and Condition properties, this activity also defines a private Variable named scheduledChildren. This is a dictionary of ActivityInstance objects keyed by a string and is used to track the children that have been scheduled but have not yet completed.

```
[Designer(typeof(ActivityLibrary.Design.MySequenceDesigner))]
public class MyParallel : NativeActivity
{
    [Browsable(false)]
    public Collection<Activity> Activities { get; set; }
    [RequiredArgument]
    public Activity<Boolean> Condition { get; set; }

    private Variable<Dictionary<String, ActivityInstance>> scheduledChildren =
        new Variable<Dictionary<String, ActivityInstance>>();

    public MyParallel()
    {
        Activities = new Collection<Activity>();
    }

    protected override void CacheMetadata(NativeActivityMetadata metadata)
    {
        Console.WriteLine("CacheMetadata");
        if (Activities != null && Activities.Count > 0)
        {
            foreach (Activity activity in Activities)
            {
                metadata.AddChild(activity);
            }
        }

        metadata.AddChild(Condition);
        metadata.AddImplementationVariable(scheduledChildren);
    }
```

Following the pattern that you used in previous examples, the Execute method schedules the Condition activity for execution. This activity checks the Boolean Condition only once, before any child activities have been scheduled.

```
    protected override void Execute(NativeActivityContext context)
    {
        if (Condition != null)
        {
            Console.WriteLine("Execute Scheduled Condition");
```

```
        scheduledChildren.Set(
            context, new Dictionary<String, ActivityInstance>());

        context.ScheduleActivity<Boolean>(Condition, OnConditionComplete);
    }
}
```

When the Condition activity completes, a go/no-go decision is made based on the result. If processing is to continue, then all child activities are immediately scheduled for execution. The ActivityInstance object that is returned from the ScheduleActivity method is added to the scheduledChildren dictionary. This object is essentially a handle or proxy to the activity that has been scheduled.

Notice that the code iterates through the collection of activities in reverse order. This is necessary to begin execute of each activity in the original sequence. Remember that the workflow runtime executes work items (in this case scheduled activities) from the top of the queue of work items. But the ScheduleActivity method also places new activities on the top of the queue. So in this case, the queue is actually acting like a stack. For this reason, new items must be pushed onto the stack in reverse order.

```
        private void OnConditionComplete(NativeActivityContext context,
            ActivityInstance completedInstance, Boolean result)
        {
            Console.WriteLine(
                "OnConditionComplete:  State:{0}, IsCompleted:{1}: Result:{2}",
                completedInstance.State, completedInstance.IsCompleted, result);
            if (!context.IsCancellationRequested)
            {
                if (result)
                {
                    if (Activities != null && Activities.Count > 0)
                    {
                        for (Int32 i = Activities.Count - 1; i >= 0; i--)
                        {
                            Console.WriteLine(
                                "OnConditionComplete Scheduled activity: {0}",
                                    Activities[i].DisplayName);
                            ActivityInstance instance = context.ScheduleActivity(
                                Activities[i], OnComplete, OnFaulted);
                            scheduledChildren.Get(context).Add(
                                instance.Id, instance);
                        }
                    }
                }
            }
        }
```

The OnComplete method is executed each time a child activity has completed. The code removes the completed activity from the scheduledChildren dictionary.

```
        private void OnComplete(NativeActivityContext context,
            ActivityInstance completedInstance)
        {
```

```
            Console.WriteLine(
                "OnComplete: Activity: {0}, State:{0}, IsCompleted:{1}",
                completedInstance.Activity.DisplayName,
                completedInstance.State, completedInstance.IsCompleted);

            scheduledChildren.Get(context).Remove(completedInstance.Id);
        }
        private void OnFaulted(NativeActivityFaultContext faultContext,
            Exception propagatedException, ActivityInstance propagatedFrom)
        {
            Console.WriteLine("OnFaulted: {0}", propagatedException.Message);
        }
```

Instead of invoking the CancelChildren method as your saw in previous examples, the Cancel method in this class calls the CancelChild method for each individual activity that has not yet completed. This was done to demonstrate that you can use either method to cancel the children. In this case, the code provides additional runtime information by displaying the name of each child that is canceled.

```
        protected override void Cancel(NativeActivityContext context)
        {
            Console.WriteLine("Cancel");
            if (context.IsCancellationRequested)
            {
                Console.WriteLine("IsCancellationRequested");

                foreach (ActivityInstance instance in
                    scheduledChildren.Get(context).Values)
                {
                    Console.WriteLine(
                        "Cancel scheduled child: {0}",
                            instance.Activity.DisplayName);
                    context.CancelChild(instance);
                }
            }
        }

        protected override void Abort(NativeActivityAbortContext context)
        {
            base.Abort(context);
            Console.WriteLine("Abort Reason: {0}", context.Reason.Message);
        }
    }
}
```

Please rebuild the solution before proceeding to the next step.

Declaring a Test Workflow

Add a new Activity to the ActivityLibrary project, and name it MyParallelTest. The MyParallel activity that you add to this workflow will contain three parallel branches of execution. Each branch is represented by a separate Sequence activity. You can follow these steps to declare the workflow that tests the MyParallel activity:

1. Add a Sequence activity as the root of the workflow.

2. Add an Int32 variable named count that is scoped by the Sequence activity.

3. Add an instance of the new MyParallel activity as a child of the Sequence activity. Set the Condition property of this activity to count < 3.

4. Add a Sequence activity as a child of the MyParallel activity. This activity represents the first parallel branch of execution so change the DisplayName property to Sequence1.

5. Add two WriteLine activities and a Delay activity to the Sequence1 activity that you just added (the child of the MyParallel activity). Move the Delay activity between the two WriteLine activities. The inclusion of the Delay should cause the activity to become idle. When this occurs, execution should immediately continue with the next branch of execution. Set the Delay.Duration to TimeSpan.FromSeconds(1). Set the Text property of the first WriteLine to "one-one" and the second WriteLine to "one-two". Figure 16-5 shows this first branch of execution.

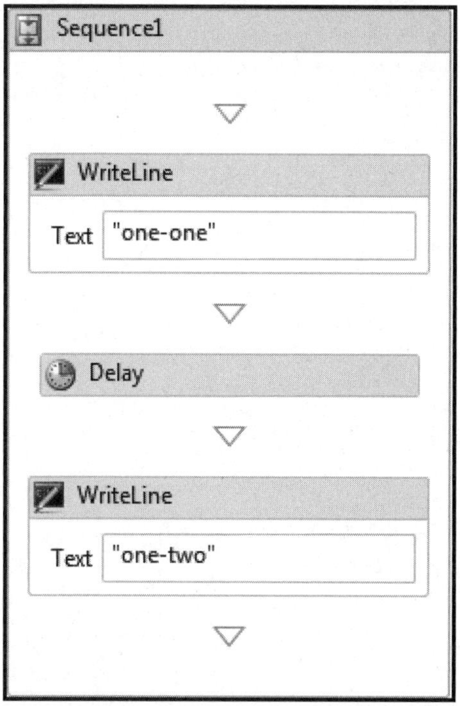

Figure 16-5. MyParallelTest Sequence1

6. Copy the Sequence1 activity that you just defined, and paste the copy as the next child of the MyParallel activity. Change the DisplayName of this activity to Sequence2 to indicate that it is the second branch of parallel execution. There are no changes that you need to make to the internal structure of this Sequence activity; however, you do need to change the Text property of the two WriteLine activities. Change the Text to "two-one" and "two-two", respectively, to indicate that this is the second branch of execution.

7. Copy the Sequence2 activity and paste the copy as the next (and final) child of the MyParallel activity. Change the DisplayName of this activity to Sequence3. Change the Text property of the WriteLine activities to "three-one" and "three-two", respectively.

8. Delete the Delay activity from the Sequence3 activity. This will test the execution of this final branch without any opportunity for it to become idle. Figure 16-6 shows the Sequence3 activity.

The top-level structure of the workflow (collapsed) should look like Figure 16-7.

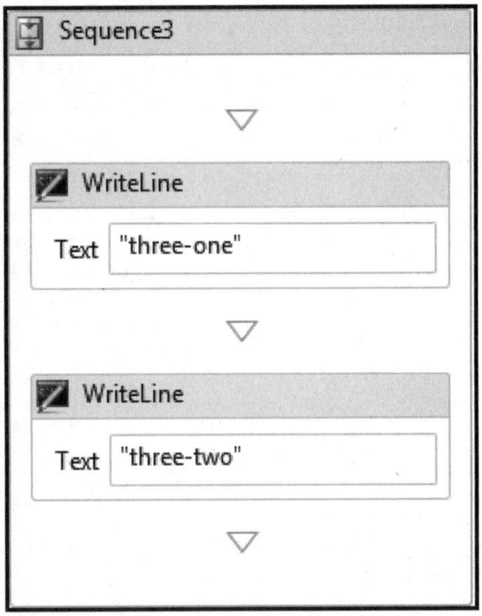

Figure 16-6. MyParallelTest Sequence3

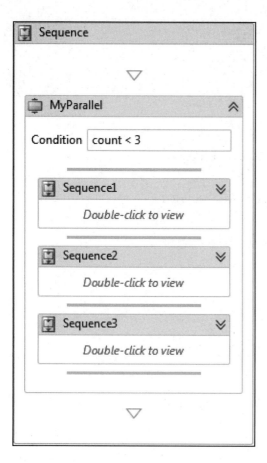

Figure 16-7. MyParallelTest workflow

Testing the Activity

To test the MyParallel activity using the TestApplication project, change the type of the workflow that is created in the Program.cs file to MyParallelTest. After rebuilding the solution, you should be able to run the project and see these results:

```
MyParallelTest Normal

CacheMetadata

Execute Scheduled Condition

OnConditionComplete:  State:Closed, IsCompleted:True: Result:True

OnConditionComplete Scheduled activity: Sequence3
```

```
OnConditionComplete Scheduled activity: Sequence2
OnConditionComplete Scheduled activity: Sequence1
one-one
two-one
three-one
three-two
OnComplete: Activity: Sequence3, State:Sequence3, IsCompleted:Closed
one-two
OnComplete: Activity: Sequence1, State:Sequence1, IsCompleted:Closed
two-two
OnComplete: Activity: Sequence2, State:Sequence2, IsCompleted:Closed
WorkflowApplication.Completed


MyParallelTest Cancel
Execute Scheduled Condition
OnConditionComplete:  State:Closed, IsCompleted:True: Result:True
OnConditionComplete Scheduled activity: Sequence3
OnConditionComplete Scheduled activity: Sequence2
OnConditionComplete Scheduled activity: Sequence1
one-one
two-one
three-one
three-two
OnComplete: Activity: Sequence3, State:Sequence3, IsCompleted:Closed
Cancel
IsCancellationRequested
Cancel scheduled child: Sequence2
Cancel scheduled child: Sequence1
OnComplete: Activity: Sequence1, State:Sequence1, IsCompleted:Canceled
OnComplete: Activity: Sequence2, State:Sequence2, IsCompleted:Canceled
WorkflowApplication.Completed
```

```
MyParallelTest Abort
Execute Scheduled Condition
OnConditionComplete:  State:Closed, IsCompleted:True: Result:True
OnConditionComplete Scheduled activity: Sequence3
OnConditionComplete Scheduled activity: Sequence2
OnConditionComplete Scheduled activity: Sequence1
one-one
two-one
three-one
three-two
OnComplete: Activity: Sequence3, State:Sequence3, IsCompleted:Closed
Abort Reason: Abort was called
WorkflowApplication.Aborted

MyParallelTest Terminate
Execute Scheduled Condition
OnConditionComplete:  State:Closed, IsCompleted:True: Result:True
OnConditionComplete Scheduled activity: Sequence3
OnConditionComplete Scheduled activity: Sequence2
OnConditionComplete Scheduled activity: Sequence1
one-one
two-one
three-one
three-two
OnComplete: Activity: Sequence3, State:Sequence3, IsCompleted:Closed
Abort Reason: Terminate was called
WorkflowApplication.Completed
Press any key to exit
```

If you examine the results for the first test (the one that ran normally to completion), you'll see that the results are what you might expect for an activity that implements a parallel execution pattern. The first branch began execution and the "one-one" text was written to the console. But when the Delay activity executed, that branch became idle and execution began with the next scheduled activity, which was the second branch of execution. That's why the "two-one" is displayed next in the results.

Execution continued with the second branch until it also executed a `Delay` activity. This caused execution to move to the third branch of execution. This branch executed to completion since it didn't include a `Delay` activity. When it completed, execution returned to the last half of the first and second branches in order to complete the workflow.

The results for the cancel test show that the cancellation took place after the third branch completed. At this point, the remaining branches (one and two) were canceled, and no further processing took place. The abort and terminate tests were similar to the cancel test, except that no cancellation logic was executed.

Scheduling an ActivityAction

The `ActivityAction` activity is used for callback-like processing from an activity. It defines a planned extension point that must be provided with an activity to execute. The `ActivityAction` class is really a family of related generic classes designed to support a varying number of input arguments. For example, `ActivityAction<T>` supports a single input argument, while `ActivityAction<T1,T2>` supports two input arguments.

■ **Note** The activity that you will develop in this example supports an `ActivityAction<T>` with a single argument. You can also implement an activity that supports one of the other `ActivityAction` classes with additional arguments. The most important change to support additional arguments is to use an overload of the `ScheduleAction` method that matches the type of `ActivityAction` that you are scheduling. In a similar way, you would need to use one of the `ScheduleFunc` methods if you are executing an `ActivityFunc` instead of an `ActivityAction`. You can also use the `ScheduleDelegate` method to schedule an `ActivityDelegate` (the base class of `ActivityAction` and `ActivityFunc`) without regard to the number of arguments that it defines.

One example where an `ActivityAction<T>` class is used is with the standard `ForEach<T>` activity. That activity iterates over the items in a collection and invokes a single child activity for each item. The `ActivityAction<T>` enables you to pass a named argument to the child activity that represents the current item in the collection. This allows the child activity to make decisions or perform processing for each item.

In the example that follows, you will implement an activity that iterates over a collection of strings. For each string, an `ActivityAction<String>` is scheduled for execution, allowing the handler for the `ActivityAction<String>` to use the string value as it is invoked.

Implementing the Custom Activity

Add a new Code Activity to the `ActivityLibrary` project, and name it `MyActivityWithAction`. Here is the code for this new activity:

```
using System;
using System.Activities;
using System.Collections.Generic;
using System.ComponentModel;

namespace ActivityLibrary
{
```

The code defines a property named `Notify` that is an `ActivityAction<String>`. In this case, the generic type (`String`) defines the type of argument that is passed to the `Handler` property of the `ActivityAction`. The `Handler` property defines the activity that is the real target activity to be executed.

The `Strings` property defines a collection of strings. The code iterates over this collection and invokes the `ActivityAction<String>` for each item in the collection. A private `Variable` named `NextIndex` is also defined to track the next element of the `Strings` collection to be processed.

```
[Designer(typeof(ActivityLibrary.Design.MyActivityWithActionDesigner))]
public class MyActivityWithAction : NativeActivity
{
    [Browsable(false)]
    public ActivityAction<String> Notify { get; set; }
    [RequiredArgument]
    public InArgument<List<String>> Strings { get; set; }

    private Variable<Int32> NextIndex = new Variable<Int32>();
```

The `Notify` property is initialized during construction of the activity. A `DelegateInArgument<String>` is assigned to the `Argument` property of the `ActivityAction<String>` and the `Name` property of the argument is set to `message`. This is the name of the argument that can be referenced by the target activity that is executed by the `ActivityAction<String>`.

```
    public MyActivityWithAction()
    {
        Notify = new ActivityAction<String>
            {
                Argument = new DelegateInArgument<String>
                {
                    Name = "message"
                }
            };
    }
```

The code in the `CacheMetadata` method calls the `AddDelegate` method to add the `ActivityAction<String>` to the meteadata. The `AddArgument` method is also called to add the `Strings` argument.

```
protected override void CacheMetadata(NativeActivityMetadata metadata)
{
    Console.WriteLine("CacheMetadata");
    metadata.AddDelegate(Notify);
    metadata.AddArgument(new RuntimeArgument(
        "Strings", typeof(List<String>), ArgumentDirection.In));
    metadata.AddImplementationVariable(NextIndex);
}
```

The Execute method and the OnComplete callback both invoke a private method named ScheduleNextItem to schedule execution of the ActivityAction<String>.

```
protected override void Execute(NativeActivityContext context)
{
    if (Notify != null)
    {
        ScheduleNextItem(context);
    }
}

private void OnComplete(NativeActivityContext context,
    ActivityInstance completedInstance)
{
    Console.WriteLine("OnComplete:  State:{0}, IsCompleted:{1}",
        completedInstance.State, completedInstance.IsCompleted);

    if (!context.IsCancellationRequested)
    {
        ScheduleNextItem(context);
    }
}
```

The ScheduleNextItem method first determines whether there are remaining items to be processed in the Strings collection. If there are, the next item is passed to the ScheduleAction<String> method as the Notify property (the ActivityAction<String>) is scheduled. The NextIndex variable is incremented to prepare for the next iteration.

```
private void ScheduleNextItem(NativeActivityContext context)
{
    List<String> collection = Strings.Get(context);
    Int32 index = NextIndex.Get(context);
    if (index < collection.Count)
    {
        Console.WriteLine(
            "ScheduleNextItem ScheduleAction: Handler: {0}, Value: {1}",
            Notify.Handler.DisplayName, collection[index]);
        context.ScheduleAction<String>(
            Notify, collection[index], OnComplete);
        NextIndex.Set(context, index + 1);
    }
}
```

```
        protected override void Cancel(NativeActivityContext context)
        {
            Console.WriteLine("Cancel");
            if (context.IsCancellationRequested)
            {
                Console.WriteLine("IsCancellationRequested");
                context.CancelChildren();
            }
        }

        protected override void Abort(NativeActivityAbortContext context)
        {
            base.Abort(context);
            Console.WriteLine("Abort Reason: {0}", context.Reason.Message);
        }
    }
}
```

Implementing the Activity Designer

Add a new Activity Designer to the ActivityLibrary.Design project, and name it
MyActivityWithActionDesigner. Here is the markup for this custom designer:

```
<sap:ActivityDesigner x:Class="ActivityLibrary.Design.MyActivityWithActionDesigner"
    xmlns:s="clr-namespace:System;assembly=mscorlib"
    xmlns="http://schemas.microsoft.com/winfx/2006/xaml/presentation"
    xmlns:x="http://schemas.microsoft.com/winfx/2006/xaml"
    xmlns:sap="clr-namespace:System.Activities.Presentation;
        assembly=System.Activities.Presentation"
    xmlns:sapv="clr-namespace:System.Activities.Presentation.View;
        assembly=System.Activities.Presentation"
    xmlns:sapc="clr-namespace:System.Activities.Presentation.Converters;
        assembly=System.Activities.Presentation"
    Collapsible="False" >

    <sap:ActivityDesigner.Resources>
        <ResourceDictionary>
            <sapc:ArgumentToExpressionConverter
                x:Key="ArgumentToExpressionConverter" />
        </ResourceDictionary>
    </sap:ActivityDesigner.Resources>

    <Grid>
        <Grid.ColumnDefinitions>
            <ColumnDefinition />
            <ColumnDefinition />
        </Grid.ColumnDefinitions>
        <Grid.RowDefinitions>
            <RowDefinition />
            <RowDefinition />
        </Grid.RowDefinitions>
```

```
        <TextBlock Text="Strings" Grid.Row ="0" Grid.Column="0"
            HorizontalAlignment="Left" VerticalAlignment="Center" />

        <sapv:ExpressionTextBox HintText="List of Strings"
            Grid.Row ="0" Grid.Column="1" MaxWidth="150" MinWidth="150" Margin="5"
            OwnerActivity="{Binding Path=ModelItem}"
            Expression="{Binding Path=ModelItem.Strings, Mode=TwoWay,
                Converter={StaticResource ArgumentToExpressionConverter},
                ConverterParameter=In }" />

        <Border Grid.Row ="1" Grid.Column="0" Grid.ColumnSpan="2" Margin="5"
            MinHeight="40" BorderBrush="LightGray"  BorderThickness="1" >
            <sap:WorkflowItemPresenter
                HintText="Drop an activity action handler here"
                Item="{Binding Path=ModelItem.Notify.Handler, Mode=TwoWay}" />
        </Border>

    </Grid>
</sap:ActivityDesigner>
```

You should rebuild the solution before you continue with the next step.

Declaring a Test Workflow

Add a new Activity named **MyActivityWithActionTest** to the **ActivityLibrary** project. This workflow tests the new activity using a collection of string values. Please follow these steps to complete the workflow:

1. Add a **Sequence** activity as the root of the workflow.

2. Define a new variable that is scoped by the **Sequence** activity. Name the variable **myStringList**, and set the type to **List<String>**. Set the initial value of the variable to a collection of strings like this: **New List(Of String) From {"One", "Two", "Three", "Four"}**.

3. Add an instance of the new **MyActivityWithAction** activity to the **Sequence** activity. Set the **Strings** property to the **myStringList** variable that you defined.

4. Add a **Sequence** activity as the single child of the **MyActivityWithAction** activity.

5. Add a **WriteLine** and **Delay** activity as children of the **Sequence** activity that you just added. Set the **Delay.Duration** property to **TimeSpan.FromSeconds(1)**. Set the **WriteLine.Text** property to **message**. This is the argument that you defined in the constructor of the **MyActivityWithAction** class.

The final **MyActivityWithActionTest** workflow should look like Figure 16-8.

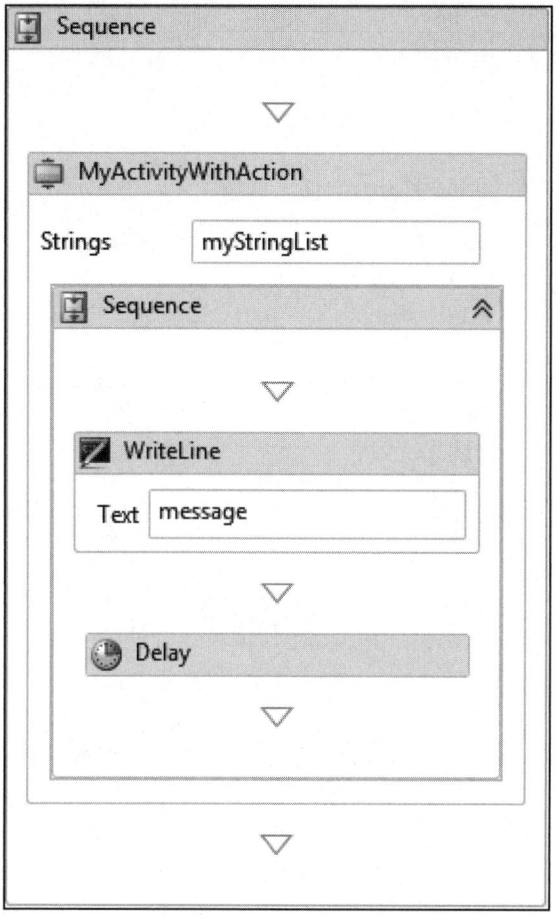

Figure 16-8. *MyActivityWithActionTest workflow*

Testing the Activity

As usual, you should change the type of workflow that is created in the **Program.cs** file to the new workflow (**MyActivityWithActionTest**). After rebuilding the solution, you should be able to run the **TestApplication** project and see these results:

```
MyActivityWithActionTest Normal

CacheMetadata

ScheduleNextItem ScheduleAction: Handler: Sequence, Value: One

One
```

```
OnComplete:  State:Closed, IsCompleted:True
ScheduleNextItem ScheduleAction: Handler: Sequence, Value: Two
Two
OnComplete:  State:Closed, IsCompleted:True
ScheduleNextItem ScheduleAction: Handler: Sequence, Value: Three
Three
OnComplete:  State:Closed, IsCompleted:True
ScheduleNextItem ScheduleAction: Handler: Sequence, Value: Four
Four
OnComplete:  State:Closed, IsCompleted:True
WorkflowApplication.Completed


MyActivityWithActionTest Cancel
ScheduleNextItem ScheduleAction: Handler: Sequence, Value: One
One
Cancel
IsCancellationRequested
OnComplete:  State:Canceled, IsCompleted:True
WorkflowApplication.Completed


MyActivityWithActionTest Abort
ScheduleNextItem ScheduleAction: Handler: Sequence, Value: One
One
Abort Reason: Abort was called
WorkflowApplication.Aborted


MyActivityWithActionTest Terminate
ScheduleNextItem ScheduleAction: Handler: Sequence, Value: One
One
Abort Reason: Terminate was called
WorkflowApplication.Completed
Press any key to exit
```

Using the DynamicActivity Class

The DynamicActivity class is one of the classes that derive from the base Activity class. It is available in normal and generic (DynamicActivity<TResult>) versions. It is used in scenarios where you dynamically create activities without creating new CLR types. You first saw this class used back in Chapter 4. In that chapter, you used the ActivityXamlServices class to load a workflow definition directly from a Xaml file. The net result of loading that file was a DynamicActivity instance. Once this object was constructed, it was executed just like any other activity.

I've included the DynamicActivity in this chapter because it has other uses that are somewhat specialized. Not only is it used when you deserialize Xaml files directly, but you can also use it to dynamically construct an activity entirely in code. Think of a situation where you might want to define a workflow with a structure that is different depending on runtime decisions that you make. The DynamicActivity allows you to do this. This is in contrast with a more general-purpose workflow that you declare that might make those same decisions internally based on input arguments.

In many ways, the process of constructing a DynamicActivity is similar to composing a new custom activity entirely in code. You first saw this approach to authoring in Chapter 3 when you developed multiple versions of the CalcShipping custom activity. One of those versions (named CalcShippingInCode) was constructed in code by assembling other activities.

But while the process is similar, there are some differences and restrictions when you use the DynamicActivity class:

- The example in Chapter 3 creates a new compiled CLR type containing the workflow definition.

- A DynamicActivity is not used to create a CLR type. It is used only to construct an in-memory activity definition.

- A DynamicActivity can define arguments and variables, but it cannot directly access runtime services such as scheduling child activities.

The Example Scenario

You are about to construct another version of the CalcChipping activity that you first developed in Chapter 3. This example will construct a DynamicActivity entirely in code and then execute it several times to test it. The test values are the same ones that you used in Chapter 3.

■ **Note** Please refer to Chapter 3 for a description of the design goals, arguments, and variables that are used for this custom activity.

However, instead of constructing an activity that makes all of its own decisions internally, you will dynamically construct two completely different workflows depending on runtime properties. In essence, some of the decision making has been moved out of the workflow and into the code that dynamically constructs it. This was intentionally done to demonstrate how you might want to combine the use of the DynamicActivity class with runtime decision-making.

Initialization Syntax vs. Procedural Code

You will quickly notice that the code that I use to construct the DynamicActivity is dramatically different from other examples in this book. Most of the examples in this book use the initialization syntax, which allows you to instantiate a tree of objects. This coding style uses indentation levels and appealing bracket placements to visually draw attention to the relationships between objects in the tree.

In contrast with this, I've chosen to implement this example using good old fashioned procedural code. I did this for two reasons. First, I realized that I haven't used this style much (if at all) in this book, and I wanted to demonstrate that this was still a very viable approach. After all, there is no magic to the initialization syntax. You can accomplish the same objects using procedural code. Second, I thought that the scenario I was presenting lent itself to this style of construction. I am moving some of the decisions out of the workflow and into the code that constructs it, so it is logical to make those decisions procedurally.

Most importantly, this style of constructing an activity is not a requirement for using the DynamicActivity class. You can most certainly construct a DynamicActivity using the initialization syntax that you've already seen in this book.

Constructing a DynamicActivity

Create a new Workflow Console project named TestDynamicActivity. Add this new project to the same solution that you have used for other projects in this chapter. You can delete the Workflow1.xaml file since it will not be used. All the code for this example goes into the Program.cs file. Here is a complete listing of this file:

```
using System;
using System.Activities;
using System.Activities.Statements;
using System.Collections.Generic;

namespace TestDynamicActivity
{
    class Program
    {
```

The DynamicActivity is constructed and executed four times. Each time, it is executed with a slightly different set of input arguments. The string ("normal" or "express") that is passed to the CreateDynamicActivity method is used to make runtime decisions that affect the structure of the workflow. The test methods such as NormalTest are defined at the end of this code listing.

```
        static void Main(string[] args)
        {
            NormalTest(CreateDynamicActivity("normal"));
            NormalMinimumTest(CreateDynamicActivity("normal"));
            NormalFreeTest(CreateDynamicActivity("normal"));
            ExpressTest(CreateDynamicActivity("express"));
```

```
        Console.WriteLine("Press any key to exit");
        Console.ReadKey();
    }

    private static Activity CreateDynamicActivity(String shipVia)
    {
        Boolean isNormal = (shipVia == "normal");
```

A DynamicActivity<Decimal> is first constructed and assigned a name. The generic version of this activity is used since the workflow is expected to return a Decimal result value. Several input arguments and variables are then constructed.

```
        DynamicActivity<Decimal> a = new DynamicActivity<Decimal>();
        a.DisplayName = "DynamicCalcShipping";

        InArgument<Int32> Weight = new InArgument<int>();
        InArgument<Decimal> OrderTotal = new InArgument<decimal>();

        Variable<Boolean> isFreeShipping =
            new Variable<Boolean> { Name = "IsFreeShipping" };

        Variable<Decimal> rate = null;
        if (isNormal)
        {
            rate = new Variable<Decimal> { Name = "Rate", Default = 1.95M };
        }
        else
        {
            rate = new Variable<Decimal> { Name = "Rate", Default = 3.50M };
        }

        Variable<Decimal> minimum =
            new Variable<Decimal> { Name = "Minimum", Default = 12.95M };
        Variable<Decimal> freeThreshold =
            new Variable<Decimal> { Name = "FreeThreshold", Default = 75.00M };
```

Properties are defined by adding instances of the DynamicActivityProperty class to the Properties member of the DynamicActivity. Each property defines a Name, a Type, and a Value. Each Value is assigned to one of the input arguments that was already constructed.

```
        a.Properties.Add(new DynamicActivityProperty
        {
            Name = "Weight",
            Type = typeof(InArgument<Int32>),
            Value = Weight
        });
```

```
a.Properties.Add(new DynamicActivityProperty
{
    Name = "OrderTotal",
    Type = typeof(InArgument<Decimal>),
    Value = OrderTotal
});
```

The Implementation property is where the body of the activity is constructed. A root **Sequence** activity is first added to the workflow. This allows the variables that were constructed above to be added to the **Sequence** activity.

Following this, the main structure of the workflow is constructed. The structure differs greatly depending on the requested shipping method that was passed to this method ("**normal**" or "**express**").

```
a.Implementation = () =>
{
    Sequence root = new Sequence();
    root.Variables.Add(isFreeShipping);
    root.Variables.Add(rate);
    //root.Variables.Add(expressRate);
    root.Variables.Add(minimum);
    root.Variables.Add(freeThreshold);

    if (isNormal)
    {
        //normal if statement to test free threshold
        If normalIf = new If();
        normalIf.Condition = new InArgument<Boolean>(ac =>
            OrderTotal.Get(ac) >= freeThreshold.Get(ac));

        //meets free threshold
        Assign<Boolean> isFreeAssign = new Assign<Boolean>();
        isFreeAssign.To = new OutArgument<Boolean>(ac =>
            isFreeShipping.Get(ac));
        isFreeAssign.Value = true;
        normalIf.Then = isFreeAssign;

        //not free, so calc using normal rate
        Assign<Decimal> calcNormalAssign = new Assign<Decimal>();
        calcNormalAssign.To = new OutArgument<Decimal>(ac =>
            a.Result.Get(ac));
        calcNormalAssign.Value = new InArgument<Decimal>(ac =>
            Weight.Get(ac) * rate.Get(ac));
        normalIf.Else = calcNormalAssign;
        root.Activities.Add(normalIf);
    }
```

```
        else
        {
            //calc using express rate
            Assign<Decimal> expressAssign = new Assign<Decimal>();
            expressAssign.To = new OutArgument<Decimal>(ac =>
                a.Result.Get(ac));
            expressAssign.Value = new InArgument<Decimal>(ac =>
                Weight.Get(ac) * rate.Get(ac));
            root.Activities.Add(expressAssign);
        }

        //test for minimum charge
        If testMinIf = new If();
        testMinIf.Condition = new InArgument<bool>(ac =>
            a.Result.Get(ac) < minimum.Get(ac) &&
                (!isFreeShipping.Get(ac)));
        Assign minAssign = new Assign();
        minAssign.To = new OutArgument<Decimal>(ac => a.Result.Get(ac));
        minAssign.Value = new InArgument<Decimal>(ac => minimum.Get(ac));
        testMinIf.Then = minAssign;

        root.Activities.Add(testMinIf);

        return root;
    };

    return a;
}
```

Rounding out the code is a set of four methods that test the new workflow. Each method passes a slightly different set of input arguments that are designed to test a different scenario.

```
private static void NormalTest(Activity activity)
{
    Dictionary<String, Object> parameters
        = new Dictionary<string, object>();
    parameters.Add("Weight", 20);
    parameters.Add("OrderTotal", 50M);

    IDictionary<String, Object> outputs = WorkflowInvoker.Invoke(
        activity, parameters);
    Console.WriteLine("Normal Result: {0}", outputs["Result"]);
}

private static void NormalMinimumTest(Activity activity)
{
    Dictionary<String, Object> parameters
        = new Dictionary<string, object>();
    parameters.Add("Weight", 5);
    parameters.Add("OrderTotal", 50M);
```

```
        IDictionary<String, Object> outputs = WorkflowInvoker.Invoke(
            activity, parameters);
        Console.WriteLine("NormalMinimum Result: {0}", outputs["Result"]);
    }

    private static void NormalFreeTest(Activity activity)
    {
        Dictionary<String, Object> parameters
            = new Dictionary<string, object>();
        parameters.Add("Weight", 5);
        parameters.Add("OrderTotal", 75M);

        IDictionary<String, Object> outputs = WorkflowInvoker.Invoke(
            activity, parameters);
        Console.WriteLine("NormalFree Result: {0}", outputs["Result"]);
    }

    private static void ExpressTest(Activity activity)
    {
        Dictionary<String, Object> parameters
            = new Dictionary<string, object>();
        parameters.Add("Weight", 5);
        parameters.Add("OrderTotal", 50M);

        IDictionary<String, Object> outputs = WorkflowInvoker.Invoke(
            activity, parameters);
        Console.WriteLine("Express Result: {0}", outputs["Result"]);
    }
  }
}
```

Testing the Activity

After building the TestDynamicActivity project, you should be ready to run it. Here are the results of my test:

```
Normal Result: 39.00

NormalMinimum Result: 12.95

NormalFree Result: 0

Express Result: 17.50

Press any key to exit
```

If you compare these test results to those from Chapter 3, you should see that they are the same expected results.

It is likely that you won't need to use the `DynamicActivity` class like this very often. Most of the time, you will use it when deserializing Xaml files in preparation for their execution. But this class is available for those special occasions when dynamic construction of an activity tree is just what you need.

Using Execution Properties

Most of the time, you will develop custom activities that define properties for any inputs and outputs. These properties define the public contract of the activity and allow you to alter the activity's behavior by setting the appropriate property values. Activities such as this generally provide the flexibility to be used beside other disparate activities in the workflow model. As long as you provide the correct property values, the activity produces the correct results.

However, you can also develop families of activities that are designed to work together to solve a common problem. Instead of receiving all their input arguments via public properties, activities can also retrieve their input arguments using an execution property mechanism. In this scenario, one activity acts as a container for other related activities in the family. This parent activity acts as a scoping mechanism, providing execution property values that are retrieved and consumed by any children within its scope. Activities such as this are not designed to execute outside of their scoping parent since the parent must provide the necessary execution property values.

Execution properties are managed using the `Properties` member of the `NativeActivityContext` object. This property is an instance of the `ExcecutionProperties` class, which supports members to add and retrieve execution property values. Here are the most important members of this class:

Member	Description
Add	Adds a named property to the collection of properties
Find	Locates and retrieves a named property
Remove	Removes a named property from the collection

Execution properties participate in persistence along with your activity. If your activity is persisted, any serializable execution properties that you have added are persisted and restored when the activity is later loaded back into memory.

To demonstrate how you might use execution properties, you will implement two custom activities that are designed to closely work together. The example scenario is an order-processing workflow that might use several activities that all require an `OrderId` argument. You could implement these activities the normal way and declare an `OrderId` argument on each activity. But as an alternative, you will develop an `OrderScope` activity that is designed to manage the state of an order. This activity defines an `OrderId` argument and passes the value of this argument to any children using an execution property. The child activity that you will develop (named `OrderAddItems` in this example) retrieves the `OrderId` from the execution properties rather than from a public input argument.

To make this example slightly more interesting, the `OrderScope` activity creates a nonblocking bookmark that is also passed as an execution property. The `OrderAddItems` activity retrieves the bookmark and resumes it for each item that it adds to the order. This demonstrates the use of the `BookmarkOptions` enum that was briefly discussed earlier in the chapter.

Implementing the OrderScope Activity

Add a new Code Activity to the `ActivityLibrary` project, and name it `OrderScope`. Here is the code for this new activity:

```
using System;
using System.Activities;
using System.ComponentModel;

namespace ActivityLibrary
{
```

This activity reuses the designer that you originally developed for the `MySimpleParent` activity earlier in the chapter. It supports a single `Body` property that represents the child activity to be scheduled. This activity also defines an input `OrderId` argument and an output `OrderTotal` argument. You could also use a `NativeActivity<T>` to define this activity and use the built-in `Result` argument for the order total. However, in some cases, I prefer to have a meaningful name instead of using the `Result` argument.

```
[Designer(typeof(ActivityLibrary.Design.MySimpleParentDesigner))]
public class OrderScope : NativeActivity
{
    [Browsable(false)]
    public Activity Body { get; set; }
    [RequiredArgument]
    public InArgument<Int32> OrderId { get; set; }
    public OutArgument<Decimal> OrderTotal { get; set; }
```

The `Execute` method uses the `Add` method of the `context.Properties` member to add the value of the `OrderId` argument as an execution property. It also creates a bookmark that is used to pass the cost of each item back to this activity. The assumption is that as items are added to the order, this activity is notified via this bookmark, and the total cost of the order is accumulated.

The bookmark that is created uses the `NonBlocking` and `MultipleResume` options. The `NonBlocking` option means that this activity can complete without ever receiving the bookmark. The `MultipleResume` option indicates that the bookmark can be resumed multiple times.

Any execution properties that are added in this way are visible to any child activities. However, they are not visible to any parent or sibling activities. They are truly scoped by this activity. After adding the execution properties, the `Body` activity is scheduled for execution in the usual way.

```
protected override void Execute(NativeActivityContext context)
{
    Int32 orderId = OrderId.Get(context);
    context.Properties.Add("OrderId", orderId);

    Bookmark bm = context.CreateBookmark(
        "UpdateOrderTotalBookmark", OnUpdateOrderTotal,
        BookmarkOptions.NonBlocking | BookmarkOptions.MultipleResume);
    context.Properties.Add(bm.Name, bm);

    context.ScheduleActivity(Body);
}
```

```
        private void OnUpdateOrderTotal(NativeActivityContext context,
            Bookmark bookmark, object value)
        {
            if (value is Decimal)
            {
                OrderTotal.Set(context,
                    OrderTotal.Get(context) + (Decimal)value);
                Console.WriteLine(
                    "OrderScope.OnUpdateOrderTotal Value: {0}, Total: {1}",
                    (Decimal)value, OrderTotal.Get(context));
            }
        }

        protected override bool CanInduceIdle
        {
            get { return true; }
        }
    }
}
```

Implementing the OrderAddItems Activity

Add another Code Activity to the ActivityLibrary project, and name it OrderAddItems. This activity is designed to be used as a child of the OrderScope activity and simulates adding sales items to the order. Here is the complete code for this activity:

```
using System;
using System.Activities;
using System.Collections.Generic;

namespace ActivityLibrary
{
```

This activity supports a single Items input argument. This argument is defined as a List<Int32> and will contain a list of item IDs that are to be added to the order.

```
    public class OrderAddItems : NativeActivity
    {
        [RequiredArgument]
        public InArgument<List<Int32>> Items { get; set; }

        protected override void Execute(NativeActivityContext context)
        {
```

The code in the Execute method first retrieves the two properties that were passed from the OrderScope activity. It then iterates over the item IDs in the input argument and resumes the bookmark for each item, passing a demonstration price.

```
    Int32 orderId = (Int32)context.Properties.Find("OrderId");
    Console.WriteLine("OrderAddItems process OrderId: {0}", orderId);
    Bookmark bm = (Bookmark)context.Properties.Find(
        "UpdateOrderTotalBookmark");

    if (bm == null)
    {
        throw new NullReferenceException(
            "UpdateOrderTotalBookmark was not provided by parent scope");
    }

    List<Int32> items = Items.Get(context);
    if (items != null && items.Count > 0)
    {
        foreach (Int32 itemId in items)
        {
            Decimal price = ((Decimal)itemId / 100);
            context.ResumeBookmark(bm, price);
        }
    }
}
        }
    }
}
```

Please rebuild the solution before proceeding to the next step.

Declaring a Test Workflow

Add a new Workflow Console Application to the solution for this chapter. Name the new project
TestOrderScope. Unlike most other examples, you will use the **Workflow1.xaml** file, so don't delete it. Add
a project reference to the **ActivityLibrary** project. Open the **Workflow1.xaml** file in the workflow
designer, and follow these steps to declare a test workflow:

1. Add a **Sequence** activity as the root of the workflow.

2. Define a **Decimal** variable named **Total** that is scoped by the **Sequence** activity.

3. Add an instance of the **OrderScope** activity to the **Sequence** activity. Set the
   OrderScope.OrderId property to **1001** and the **OrderTotal** to the **Total** variable
   that you just defined.

4. Add an instance of the **OrderAddItems** activity as the child of the **OrderScope**
   activity. Set the **Items** property to **New List(Of Int32) From {123, 456, 789}**
   to provide a few test items to process.

5. Add a **WriteLine** below the **OrderScope**. Set the **Text** property to
   String.Format("Final total: {0}", Total) to display the final total that was
   accumulated for the order.

The completed workflow should look like Figure 16-9.

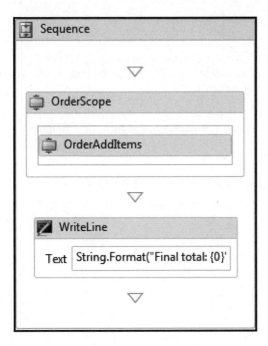

Figure 16-9. Workflow1

Testing the Activities

After building the **TestOrderScope** project, you can run it. Your results should look like mine:

```
OrderAddItems process OrderId: 1001

OrderScope.OnUpdateOrderTotal Value: 1.23, Total: 1.23

OrderScope.OnUpdateOrderTotal Value: 4.56, Total: 5.79

OrderScope.OnUpdateOrderTotal Value: 7.89, Total: 13.68

Final total: 13.68

Press any key to continue . . .
```

Summary

This chapter focused on several advanced custom activity scenarios, most of which were related to executing one or more children. The chapter began with an overview of how to schedule children for execution and other topics related to the responsibilities of a parent activity.

The first example of the chapter was a relatively simple activity that executed a single child. Following this, other examples were presented that demonstrated how to repeatedly execute an activity, how to execute and test Boolean conditions, how to execute multiple children, and how to implement a parallel execution pattern. Exception handling for child activities was also discussed and demonstrated.

The final sections of the chapter focused on the use of the `DynamicActivity` class, execution properties, and bookmark options.

In the next chapter, you will learn how to host the workflow designer in your own applications.

■ ■ ■

CHAPTER 17

Hosting the Workflow Designer

Most of the time you will author new activities and workflows using the workflow designer that is integrated into Visual Studio. However, you may need to enable end users of your application to also design activities and workflows. You can allow them to load and customize existing Xaml files or to create new ones.

The workflow designer is not limited to use only within the Visual Studio environment. WF provides the classes necessary to host this same designer within your applications. This chapter is all about hosting this designer. After a brief overview of the major workflow designer components, you will implement a simple application that hosts the workflow designer. In subsequent sections, you will build upon the application, adding new functionality with each section.

Understanding the Workflow Designer Components

The workflow designer functionality is provided in a set of classes that is located in the `System.Activities.Presentation` namespace and its associated child namespaces. Here are the additional child namespaces that you are likely to use when you host the designer:

Namespace	Notes
System.Activities.Presentation.Metadata	Classes related to associating an activity designer with an activity
System.Activities.Presentation.Model	Provides an intermediate layer between a design view and an instance of the activity being edited
System.Activities.Presentation.Services	Services that provide functionality that can be shared between the designer and the host application
System.Activities.Presentation.Toolbox	Includes classes that assist with Toolbox management
System.Activities.Presentation.Validation	Classes used for activity validation
System.Activities.Presentation.View	Includes classes that provide the visual presentation of the designer and associated components

The workflow designer is architected in layers, with components in each layer interacting with those above or beneath it. It might be helpful to keep these layers in mind as you explore the classes that you will use to host the designer.

- Visual: This includes the visual controls that a developer uses to interact with the activity definition. The visual components interact with the ModeItem tree.

- ModelItem tree: This is a tree of ModelItem objects that sit between the visual elements and the in-memory representation of the activity definition. They track changes to the underlying definition.

- Activity definition: This is the in-memory tree of activities that have been defined.

- MetadataStore: An in-memory store of attributes that is used to associate activities with their designers.

In the sections that follow, I review the most important classes that you are likely to encounter when you develop your own designer host application.

Understanding the WorkflowDesigner Class

To host the workflow designer, you create an instance of the WorkflowDesigner class. Here are the most important members of this class:

Member	Description
View	A UIElement property that is the visual representation of the designer canvas.
PropertyInspectorView	A UIElement property that is the visual representation of the property inspector.
Text	A string property that provides access to the Xaml representation of the model.
Context	An instance of an EditingContext object that provides access to the shared designer data and services.
ContextMenu	An instance of a ContextMenu object that defines the context menu of the designer canvas.
ModelChanged	An event that is raised when the design model has changed.
Load	A method that loads an activity or workflow definition into the designer. There are several available overloads of this method.
Save	A method that saves the currently loaded model to a file.
Flush	Updates the Text property with the current internal state of the model.

After creating the `WorkflowDesigner` instance, you add the control referenced by the `View` property to a WPF window in order to display the designer canvas. This property is a `UIElement`, which is a WPF control that can be placed directly on a window or within another control. In a like manner, the `PropertyInspectorView` property references a WPF control that you can also add to your WPF application. It provides the property grid, which allows you to change property values for the currently selected activity in the designer. The two controls are automatically linked, so there's no need for additional code to set the current selection for the property grid.

To initialize the designer with a definition, you use one of the overloads of the `Load` method. One overload of this method allows you to specify the file name of the Xaml file containing the definition. With another overload, you pass an object that represents the definition. This object could be a single activity or an entire tree of activities that you constructed in code. You can also set the `Text` property to the Xaml string representing the definition and then invoke the `Load` method without any parameters. This last option is useful if you are persisting the definition in a database or another medium instead of directly in the file system.

To save the current definition, you can invoke the `Save` method, passing the name of the file to use when saving. But that method is useful only if you are saving the definition directly to the file system. You can also retrieve the Xaml string from the `Text` property and save it yourself (to the file system, to a database, and so on).

■ **Tip** Remember to invoke the `Flush` method before you access the `Text` property; otherwise, you may not retrieve the latest version of the definition.

Understanding the ToolboxControl

The `WorkflowDesigner` class provides the designer canvas and a coordinated properties grid. It doesn't automatically provide a Toolbox containing the activities that can be dropped onto the canvas. However, WF does provide these classes that allow you to easily construct your own Toolbox:

- `ToolboxControl`: A WPF `UIElement` that visually represents the Toolbox

- `ToolboxCategory`: Defines a single activity category in the Toolbox

- `ToolboxItemWrapper`: Defines a single tool entry in the Toolbox

These classes are located in the `System.Activities.Presentation.Toolbox` namespace. To create a Toolbox, you first create an instance of the `ToolboxControl` and add it to the WPF window. You then create the categories and individual items that you want to show in the Toolbox. Since you are implementing your own designer host application, you have complete freedom as to the set of activities that you show, as well as how you organize them into categories. You don't have to include all of the standard activities or use the standard categories.

Each Toolbox category is represented by an instance of the `ToolboxCategory` class. After creating a new instance, you use the `Add` method of this class to add the individual items in that category. Each item is represented by an instance of the `ToolboxItemWrapper` class. Several constructor overloads are provided for this class, allowing you to specify varying degrees of information for each tool.

You must provide the type of the item and a display name. The item type is the type of `Activity` that you want to add when someone drags this tool to a workflow definition. You can optionally specify a bitmap file name if you want to customize the image that is shown for the item in the Toolbox.

■ **Note** If you don't provide a bitmap file name for a `ToolboxItemWrapper`, the tool will be shown with a default image. This applies to the standard activities as well as any custom activities that you develop. It would be convenient to have the ability to load a bitmap from a resource that is packaged with the assembly. Unfortunately, this class only supports loading a bitmap image directly from a file. It doesn't support loading an image that you obtained in some other way.

The images that are associated with the standard activities in Visual Studio are not available. For some reason, Microsoft chose to package these images in Visual Studio assemblies rather than in an assembly that is easily redistributable. So, for logistical or licensing reasons, you can't directly use the images that are associated with the standard WF activities.

Defining New Activities

To use the workflow designer, it must always have a root object. Loading an existing Xaml definition satisfies this requirement since the definition contains one or more activities with a single root activity.

But what do you load into the designer if you want to create a new activity? The answer to this question is not as obvious as you might think. You might look at a Xaml file and notice that the root is the **Activity** element. So, your first attempt might be to create an instance of an empty **Activity** class and load that into the designer. The problem is that the **Activity** class is abstract and doesn't have a public constructor. The same applies to frequently used child classes like **CodeActivity** and **NativeActivity**. You can create an instance of other activities, such as the **Sequence** class, and load them directly into the designer. But then every new activity that you design has the **Sequence** activity as its root. And the **Sequence** activity supports the entry of variables but doesn't support any way to define arguments.

To solve this problem, you need to load an instance of a special class named **ActivityBuilder** (found in the **System.Activities** namespace). This class is designed for the sole purpose of defining new activities. When loaded into the designer, this class provides an empty canvas, waiting for you to add your chosen root activity. It also supports the definition of arguments. Here are the most important properties of this class:

Property	Type	Required	Description
Implementation	Activity	Yes	Contains the tree of activities that will form the new activity
Name	String	Yes	A name for the new activity that sets the x:Class attribute
Properties	KeyedCollection<String, DynamicActivityProperty>	No	Contains property values for the new activity
Attributes	Collection<Attribute>	No	Contains attributes for the new activity
Constraints	Collection<Constraint>	No	Contains constraints for the new activity

I said that this class supports the definition of arguments, but from the list of supported properties, it may not be obvious where they are defined. Arguments are maintained in the `Properties` collection as `DynamicActivityProperty` instances. You will use this property later in the chapter to display a list of defined arguments.

■ **Warning** The `Name` property of the `ActivityBuilder` class is used to set the `x:Class` attribute. This defines the class name that is compiled into a CLR type when you are using Visual Studio. Since you are not compiling a definition into a CLR type, you might think that you don't need to provide a value for this property. However, you should always provide a value for the `Name` property. If you don't, you will be unable to successfully provide default values for any arguments. If you attempt to define default argument values, you will be unable to load or run the serialized Xaml. The best practice is to always provide a value for the `Name` property. The initial value that you provide can be changed in the designer.

Understanding the EditingContext

The `WorkflowDesigner` supports a `Context` property that is an instance of the `EditingContext` class. This object is your interface to the current internal state of the designer. It allows you to access state that is shared between the designer and the host application. For example, you can use the `Context` property to identify the activity that is currently selected in the designer. It also provides access to services that have been loaded into the designer. These services provide functionality that is shared between the designer and the host application or by individual activity designers. Here are the most important properties of this class:

Property	Type	Description
Items	ContextItemManager	Provides access to a collection of `ContextItem` objects that maintain shared state
Services	ServiceManager	Provides access to a collection of services that provide shared functionality

Context.Items

The `ContextItemManager` (the `Context.Items` property) provides access to individual objects that derive from the base `ContextItem` class. Here are the most important members of this class:

Member	Description
Contains	A method that allows you to determine whether or not a particular type of ContextItem exists
GetValue	A method used to retrieve an existing ContextItem based on its type
SetValue	A method to set a ContextItem to the value that you specify
Subscribe	A method that allows you to subscribe to callback notifications
Unsubscribe	Allows you to unsubscribe to previously subscribed notifications

Each object in the `Context.Items` collection serves a different purpose and maintains a different type of shared state. Here are the standard objects that are available—you won't necessarily need to access all of these objects in a typical designer application:

ContextItem Type	Description
System.Activities.Presentation.Hosting.AssemblyContextControlItem	Manages a list of local and referenced assemblies
System.Activities.Presentation.Hosting.ImportedNamespaceControlItem	Manages a list of imported namespaces
System.Activities.Presentation.Hosting.ReadOnlyState	Indicates whether the designer is currently in read-only mode
System.Activities.Presentation.Hosting.WorkflowCommandExtensionItem	Provides access to the designer commands that handle input gestures
System.Activities.Presentation.View.Selection	Provides access to the selected activities within the designer
System.Activities.Presentation.WorkflowFileItem	Provides information about the file (if any) associated with the current definition

Context.Services

The `Context.Services` property is an instance of a `ServiceManager` object. This object provides access to a set of standard services that are automatically loaded when you create an instance of the designer. As you will see later in the chapter, you can also add your own custom services to provide optional functionality. The `ServiceManager` class provides these members:

Member	Description
Contains	A method used to determine whether a service (identified by its Type) exists
GetService	A method used to retrieve an instance of a service
Publish	Used to add a new service, making it available for use by the designer or the host application
Subscribe	Allows you to subscribe to callback notifications
Unsubscribe	Allows you to unsubscribe to previously subscribed notifications

Here are some of the standard services that are available when you self-host the designer:

Service Type	Description
System.Activities.Presentation.Model.AttachedPropertiesService	Provides attached property functionality
System.Activities.Presentation.UndoEngine	Provides undo/redo functionality
System.Activities.Presentation.Validation.ValidationService	Provides activity validation
System.Activities.Presentation.Services.ModelService	A service that provides access to the ModelItem tree
System.Activities.Presentation.Model.ModelTreeManager	Provides access to the root ModelItem object
System.Activities.Presentation.Services.ViewService	Provides mapping of the visual elements to the underlying ModelItem instances
System.Activities.Presentation.View.VirtualizedContainerService	Provides virtualization functionality to only render those objects that are actually being viewed
System.Activities.Presentation.View.ViewStateService	Stores view states for ModelItem instances

Providing Designer Metadata

As you learned in Chapter 15, there are two ways to associate a designer with a particular activity:

- You can apply the `Designer` attribute directly to the activity.

- You can use the `MetadataStore` class at runtime.

If you opted for the second option when you implemented your custom activities and designers, you need to use the `MetadataStore` class to associate each activity with its designer. If you are using the standard WF activities (this is very likely), you also need to use the `DesignerMetadata` class (located in the `System.Activities.Core.Presentation` namespace). This class supports a single `Register` method that associates each standard WF activity with its designer. You only need to invoke this method once during the lifetime of your application.

You can also use the `MetadataStore` class to associate custom designers with the standard activities. Providing your own metadata entries overrides the defaults that are provided when you invoke the `DesignerMetadata.Register` method.

The Self-hosting Designer Workflow

If you are developing an application to host the workflow designer, you obviously need to create or maintain activity definitions outside Visual Studio. And your application will be designed to satisfy the particular requirements of your end users. That means your application will likely look much different from the one that I might implement (or the one that is presented in the remainder of this chapter). But in general, you might want to consider these steps when you decide to self-host the workflow designer:

1. Design a WPF application that can support the designer visual components.

2. Create an instance of the `WorkflowDesigner` class and add the object referenced by the `View` property to a WPF window to display the main designer canvas.

3. Add the object referenced by the `PropertyInspectorView` property to a WPF window to provide property grid functionality.

4. Register metadata for the standard and custom activities.

5. Create and manage a Toolbox containing activities that can be dropped onto the designer canvas.

6. Add logic to initialize a new activity definition. Also add logic to save and load activity definitions to a file or other persistence medium.

7. Add logic to react to the currently selected item by providing context menus, context Toolbox support, and so on.

8. Provide custom validation logic and display validation errors.

Implementing a Simple Workflow Designer

In the remainder of this chapter, you will implement a WPF application that hosts the workflow designer. The example application will begin with minimal functionality that will be enhanced in the sections that follow this one. Each section builds upon the code that was developed in the previous section.

■ **Note** The examples in this chapter all build upon each other and assume that you are implementing the code for each section in order. Each section presents only the necessary changes to the existing code. If you prefer to jump directly to the finished product, I suggest you download the sample code for this book from the Apress site.

Creating the Application

Create a new project using the WPF Application project template. Name the project `DesignerHost`, and add it to a new solution that is named for this chapter. Add these assembly references to the project:

- `System.Activities`

- `System.Activities.Presentation`

- `System.Activities.Core.Presentation`

All the components and code that you will add to this application will go into the `MainWindow` class that was added by the new project template. The `MainWindow.xaml` file contains the WPF markup for the window, and the `MainWindow.xaml.cs` file contains the C# code.

Declaring the Window Layout

Before you can implement any code for the application, you need to lay out the controls of the `MainWindow` class. Double-click the `MainWindow.xaml` file in the Solution Explorer to open it in Design View. Design View in this case is a split screen that includes a WPF designer and an XML editor showing the Xaml markup. Here is the complete markup that you need to add to this file:

```
<Window x:Class="DesignerHost.MainWindow"
        xmlns="http://schemas.microsoft.com/winfx/2006/xaml/presentation"
        xmlns:x="http://schemas.microsoft.com/winfx/2006/xaml"
        Title="Workflow Designer Host" Height="600" Width="800"
        Closing="Window_Closing">
    <Grid>
```

I've included a handler for the `Closing` event of the window (shown in the previous code). You will add code to this handler to test for any unsaved changes to the current definition. The window is organized into three columns and three rows. The leftmost column will be used for a Toolbox of activities, and the rightmost column is for the properties grid. The middle column is reserved for the workflow designer canvas. The first row is used for a menu, while the second row is the main area for the designer, Toolbox, and properties grid. The third row is reserved for a message area.

```
<Grid.ColumnDefinitions>
    <ColumnDefinition Width="2*" />
    <ColumnDefinition Width="5*"/>
    <ColumnDefinition Width="2*"/>
</Grid.ColumnDefinitions>
<Grid.RowDefinitions>
    <RowDefinition Height="25" />
    <RowDefinition />
    <RowDefinition Height="75" />
</Grid.RowDefinitions>
```

A menu is defined that allows the user to select the main operations of the application. Handlers are defined for all the menu items, so you'll need to include code for these event handlers even though you won't fully implement them immediately.

```
<Menu Width="Auto" Grid.Row="0">
    <MenuItem Header="File" Name="menuFile">
        <MenuItem Header="New" Name="menuNew"
            Click="menuNew_Click" />
        <MenuItem Header="Open..." Name="menuOpen"
            Click="menuOpen_Click" />
        <MenuItem Header="Save" Name="menuSave"
            Click="menuSave_Click" />
        <MenuItem Header="Save As..." Name="menuSaveAs"
            Click="menuSaveAs_Click" />
        <Separator />
        <MenuItem Header="Add Reference..." Name="menuAddReference"
            Click="menuAddReference_Click"  />
        <Separator />
        <MenuItem Header="Run..." Name="menuRun"
            Click="menuRun_Click" />
        <Separator/>
        <MenuItem Header="Exit" Name="menuExit"
            Click="menuExit_Click" />
    </MenuItem>
</Menu>
```

I've included a `Border` control as a placeholder for each of the three main designer areas. This provides a subtle visual separation between the controls and also simplifies the code that populates these areas with the designer controls. The markup also includes a `ListBox` control that occupies the final row (the message area).

The markup also includes `GridSplitter` controls between the three main sections. These controls allow you to drag the gray bar between the sections to resize the Toolbox or the properties grid.

```
<Border Name="toolboxArea" Grid.Column="0" Grid.Row="1"
    Margin="2"  BorderThickness="1" BorderBrush="Gray"  />
<GridSplitter Grid.Column="0" Grid.Row="1" Width="5"
    ResizeDirection="Columns" HorizontalAlignment="Right"
    VerticalAlignment="Stretch" Background="LightGray" />
```

```xml
<Border Name="designerArea" Grid.Column="1" Grid.Row="1"
    Margin="2" BorderThickness="1" BorderBrush="Gray" />

<Border Name="propertiesArea" Grid.Column="2" Grid.Row="1"
    Margin="2" BorderThickness="1" BorderBrush="Gray"  />
<GridSplitter Grid.Column="2" Grid.Row="1" Width="5"
    ResizeDirection="Columns" HorizontalAlignment="Left"
    VerticalAlignment="Stretch"  Background="LightGray" />

<ListBox Name="messageListBox" Grid.Column="0" Grid.Row="2"
    Grid.ColumnSpan="3" SelectionMode="Single"/>

    </Grid>
</Window>
```

The project won't build at this point since the markup is referencing event handlers that you haven't implemented. You'll turn your attention to the code next.

Implementing the Application

Open the `MainWindow` class in Code View. This should open the `MainWindow.xaml.cs` file in the code editor. Here is the initial implementation of this class:

```csharp
using System;
using System.Activities;
using System.Activities.Core.Presentation;
using System.Activities.Core.Presentation.Factories;
using System.Activities.Presentation;
using System.Activities.Presentation.Metadata;
using System.Activities.Presentation.Model;
using System.Activities.Presentation.Services;
using System.Activities.Presentation.Toolbox;
using System.Activities.Presentation.Validation;
using System.Activities.Presentation.View;
using System.Activities.Statements;
using System.Activities.XamlIntegration;
using System.Collections.Generic;
using System.ComponentModel;
using System.IO;
using System.Linq;
using System.Reflection;
using System.Text;
using System.Windows;
using System.Windows.Controls;
using System.Windows.Documents;
using Microsoft.Win32;
```

The code includes a number of namespaces that you won't initially need. However, you will need them by the time you complete this chapter, so go ahead and include all of them now.

```
namespace DesignerHost
{
    public partial class MainWindow : Window
    {
        private WorkflowDesigner wd;
        private ToolboxControl toolboxControl;
        private String currentXamlPath;
        private String originalTitle;
        private Boolean isModified = false;

        private HashSet<Type> loadedToolboxActivities =
            new HashSet<Type>();

        public MainWindow()
        {
            InitializeComponent();

            originalTitle = this.Title;
```

During construction of the window, the metadata for the standard activities is registered using the
DesignerMetadata class. A Toolbox containing a subset of the standard activities is then constructed.
Finally, an instance of the designer is initialized with a call to the private InitializeDesigner method,
and a new empty workflow is loaded by calling the StartNewWorkflow method.

```
            //register designers for the standard activities
            DesignerMetadata dm = new DesignerMetadata();
            dm.Register();

            //toolbox
            toolboxControl = CreateToolbox();
            toolboxArea.Child = toolboxControl;

            InitializeDesigner();
            StartNewWorkflow();
        }
```

The InitializeDesigner method creates a new instance of the designer and wires it up to the
designated areas on the window. An event handler is added to the ModelChanged event of the designer.
This will notify you whenever any changes are made to the current definition. As you will see later in the
code, the InitializeDesigner method is called each time you need to clear the designer and begin a new
activity definition. It is not possible to actually clear the designer or load a new definition once one has
already been loaded.

```
        private void InitializeDesigner()
        {
            //cleanup the previous designer
            if (wd != null)
            {
                wd.ModelChanged -= new EventHandler(Designer_ModelChanged);
            }
```

```
        //designer
        wd = new WorkflowDesigner();
        designerArea.Child = wd.View;

        //property grid
        propertiesArea.Child = wd.PropertyInspectorView;

        //event handler
        wd.ModelChanged += new EventHandler(Designer_ModelChanged);
    }
```

The StartNewWorklfow handles the task of preparing the designer with a new ActivityBuilder instance. Loading this object presents the user with a clean canvas that they can use to define their own activity.

```
    private void StartNewWorkflow()
    {
        wd.Load(new ActivityBuilder
        {
            Name = "Activity1"
        });
        currentXamlPath = null;
        isModified = false;
    }

    private void menuNew_Click(object sender, RoutedEventArgs e)
    {
        if (IsCloseAllowed())
        {
            InitializeDesigner();
            StartNewWorkflow();
            UpdateTitle();
        }
    }
```

The handlers for the Save, SaveAs, and Open menu items will be fully implemented later in the chapter. However, they must be defined as shown here in order to successfully build the project:

```
    private void menuSave_Click(object sender, RoutedEventArgs e)
    {
    }

    private void menuSaveAs_Click(object sender, RoutedEventArgs e)
    {
    }

    private void menuOpen_Click(object sender, RoutedEventArgs e)
    {
    }
```

```
private void menuExit_Click(object sender, RoutedEventArgs e)
{
    if (IsCloseAllowed())
    {
        isModified = false;
        this.Close();
    }
}

private void Window_Closing(object sender, CancelEventArgs e)
{
    if (!IsCloseAllowed())
    {
        e.Cancel = true;
    }
}
```

The Run and Add Reference menu item handlers will also be implemented later in the chapter. The Run handler will contain logic that allows you to execute the current definition using the WorkflowInvoker class. The Add Reference handler will be used to load additional activities from a referenced assembly.

The handler for the ModelChanged event simply updates the title to indicate that there are unsaved changes.

```
private void menuRun_Click(object sender, RoutedEventArgs e)
{
}

private void menuAddReference_Click(object sender, RoutedEventArgs e)
{
}

private void Designer_ModelChanged(object sender, EventArgs e)
{
    isModified = true;
    UpdateTitle();
}
```

The CreateToolbox method creates a Toolbox containing a small subset of the standard activities. There's nothing special about the activities that I've chosen. Once you've completed the examples in this chapter, feel free to change the list of activities that are loaded to your preferred set of activities.

Each set of activities is organized into a named category. Each defined category is then passed to the CreateToolboxCategory private method to construct a ToolboxCategory object. These categories are then added to an instance of the ToolboxControl.

```
private ToolboxControl CreateToolbox()
{
    Dictionary<String, List<Type>> activitiesToInclude =
        new Dictionary<String, List<Type>>();
```

```
activitiesToInclude.Add("Basic", new List<Type>
{
    typeof(Sequence),
    typeof(If),
    typeof(While),
    typeof(Assign),
    typeof(WriteLine)
});

activitiesToInclude.Add("Flowchart", new List<Type>
{
    typeof(Flowchart),
    typeof(FlowDecision),
    typeof(FlowSwitch<>)
});
```

You may notice that instead of adding the ForEach<T> activity, the code references a class named ForEachWithBodyFactory<T>. The ParallelForEach<T> activity has also been replaced with a different class name (ParallelForEachWithBodyFactory<T>). These are the classes that are actually included in the Visual Studio Toolbox. They are activity templates that add the primary activity (for example ForEach<T>) and also add an ActivityAction<T> as a child of the primary activity. The ActivityAction<T> is needed to provide access to the argument that represents each item in the collection.

```
activitiesToInclude.Add("Collections", new List<Type>
{
    typeof(ForEachWithBodyFactory<>),
    typeof(ParallelForEachWithBodyFactory<>),
    typeof(ExistsInCollection<>),
    typeof(AddToCollection<>),
    typeof(RemoveFromCollection<>),
    typeof(ClearCollection<>),
});

activitiesToInclude.Add("Error Handling", new List<Type>
{
    typeof(TryCatch),
    typeof(Throw),
    typeof(TransactionScope)
});

ToolboxControl tb = new ToolboxControl();
foreach (var category in activitiesToInclude)
{
    ToolboxCategory cat = CreateToolboxCategory(
        category.Key, category.Value, true);
    tb.Categories.Add(cat);
}

return tb;
}
```

The `CreateToolboxCategory` method is invoked to create a new `ToolboxCategory` instance. The code creates `ToolboxItemWrapper` instances for each activity that was defined for the category. The `null` value that is passed to the `ToolboxItemWrapper` constructor is where you would pass the file name of a bitmap to associate with the toolbox item. Since the code passes `null`, a default image will be shown.

```
private ToolboxCategory CreateToolboxCategory(
    String categoryName, List<Type> activities, Boolean isStandard)
{
    ToolboxCategory tc = new ToolboxCategory(categoryName);

    foreach (Type activity in activities)
    {
        if (!loadedToolboxActivities.Contains(activity))
        {
            //cleanup the name of generic activities
            String name;
            String[] nameChunks = activity.Name.Split('`');
            if (nameChunks.Length == 1)
            {
                name = activity.Name;
            }
            else
            {
                name = String.Format("{0}<>", nameChunks[0]);
            }

            ToolboxItemWrapper tiw = new ToolboxItemWrapper(
                activity.FullName, activity.Assembly.FullName,
                    null, name);
            tc.Add(tiw);

            if (isStandard)
            {
                loadedToolboxActivities.Add(activity);
            }
        }
    }

    return tc;
}

private void UpdateTitle()
{
    String modified = (isModified ? "*" : String.Empty);
    if (String.IsNullOrEmpty(currentXamlPath))
    {
        this.Title = String.Format("{0} - {1}{2}",
            originalTitle, "unsaved", modified);
    }
    else
    {
```

```
            this.Title = String.Format("{0} - {1}{2}",
                originalTitle,
                System.IO.Path.GetFileName(currentXamlPath), modified);
        }
    }

    private Boolean IsCloseAllowed()
    {
        Boolean result = true;

        if (isModified)
        {
            if (MessageBox.Show(this,
                "Are you sure you want to lose unsaved changes?",
                "Unsaved Changes",
                MessageBoxButton.YesNo, MessageBoxImage.Warning)
                    == MessageBoxResult.No)
            {
                result = false;
            }
        }

        return result;
    }
  }
}
```

Testing the Application

You should now be able to build the project and run it. Figure 17-1 shows the initial view of the DesignerHost project when it is first started. Feel free to give the designer a try by dropping a few activities onto the canvas.

Figure 17-1. *Initial view of DesignerHost*

With the relatively small amount of code that you added, the application already has these capabilities:

- A fully functional workflow designer canvas including expand and collapse, zoom controls, and so on

- An integrated, context-sensitive properties grid

- A functional custom Toolbox

- Add, delete, move, cut, copy, and paste activities

- The ability to set property values including expressions

- The ability to validate the definition and highlight errors

- The ability to add variables and arguments

- The ability to clear the designer and start a new definition (the New menu option)

Figure 17-2 shows the designer after I added `Sequence`, `Assign`, and `WriteLine` activities. To enter the expressions for the `Assign` properties, I first added an `Int32` variable named `count` that is scoped by the `Sequence` activity.

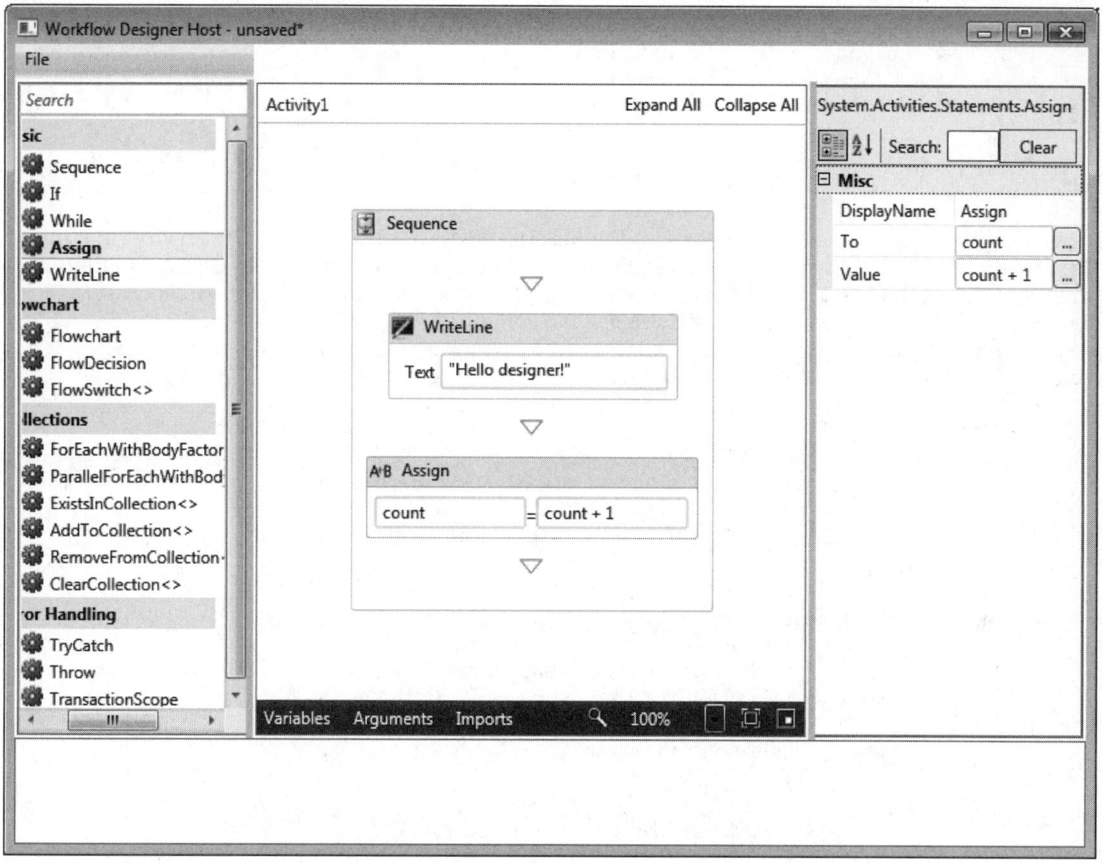

Figure 17-2. DesignerHost with activities

■ **Note** One thing that is missing is IntelliSense when you are entering expressions. Unfortunately, Microsoft didn't provide an easy way to implement this in your own application.

Executing the Workflow

In this section, you will enhance the application to support the execution of the current workflow definition. This allows the user to declare a workflow and immediately execute it as a preliminary test.

Modifying the Application

To add this functionality, you need to provide an implementation for the menuRun_Click event handler. Here is the code that you need to add to this method:

```
private void menuRun_Click(object sender, RoutedEventArgs e)
{
    try
    {
```

The code first calls the Flush method on the WorkflowDesigner object. Doing this ensures that the WorkflowDesigner.Text property contains Xaml that includes all of the most recent changes to the definition. The ActivityXamlServices class is used to deserialize the Xaml into a DynamicActivity instance that can be passed to the WorkflowInvoker class for execution.

Prior to execution, the standard Console is routed to a StringWriter. This allows the code to intercept and display the results that would normally go to the console.

```
                wd.Flush();
                Activity activity = null;
                using (StringReader reader = new StringReader(wd.Text))
                {
                    activity = ActivityXamlServices.Load(reader);
                }

                if (activity != null)
                {
                    StringBuilder sb = new StringBuilder();
                    using (StringWriter writer = new StringWriter(sb))
                    {
                        Console.SetOut(writer);
                        try
                        {
                            WorkflowInvoker.Invoke(activity);
                        }
                        catch (Exception exception)
                        {
                            MessageBox.Show(this,
                                exception.Message, "Exception",
                                MessageBoxButton.OK, MessageBoxImage.Error);
                        }
```

```
            finally
            {
                MessageBox.Show(this,
                    sb.ToString(), "Results",
                    MessageBoxButton.OK, MessageBoxImage.Information);
            }
        }

        StreamWriter standardOutput =
            new StreamWriter(Console.OpenStandardOutput());
        Console.SetOut(standardOutput);
    }
}
catch (Exception exception)
{
    MessageBox.Show(this,
        exception.Message, "Outer Exception",
        MessageBoxButton.OK, MessageBoxImage.Error);
}
}
```

Testing the Application

You can now rebuild and run the `DesignerHost` project. You can perform a preliminary test by just dropping a `WriteLine` activity onto the canvas and setting the `Text` property to a string of your choosing. If you select the Run option from the menu, you should see the expected results.

To perform a slightly more ambitious test that also includes a variable and an argument, I declared a simple workflow using these steps:

1. Add a `While` activity.

2. Declare an `Int32` variable named `count` that is scoped by the `While` activity.

3. Add an `Int32` input argument named `ArgMax`. Set the default value of this argument to 5.

4. Set the `While.Condition` property to `count < ArgMax`.

5. Add a `Sequence` to the `While.Body`.

6. Add an `Assign` activity to the `Sequence` activity. Set the `Assign.To` property to `count` and the `Assign.Value` property to `count + 1`.

7. Add a `WriteLine` immediately below the `Assign` activity. Set the `Text` property to `"Count is" + count.ToString()`.

Figure 17-3 shows the completed workflow definition. Figure 17-4 shows the results when I select the Run option from the menu.

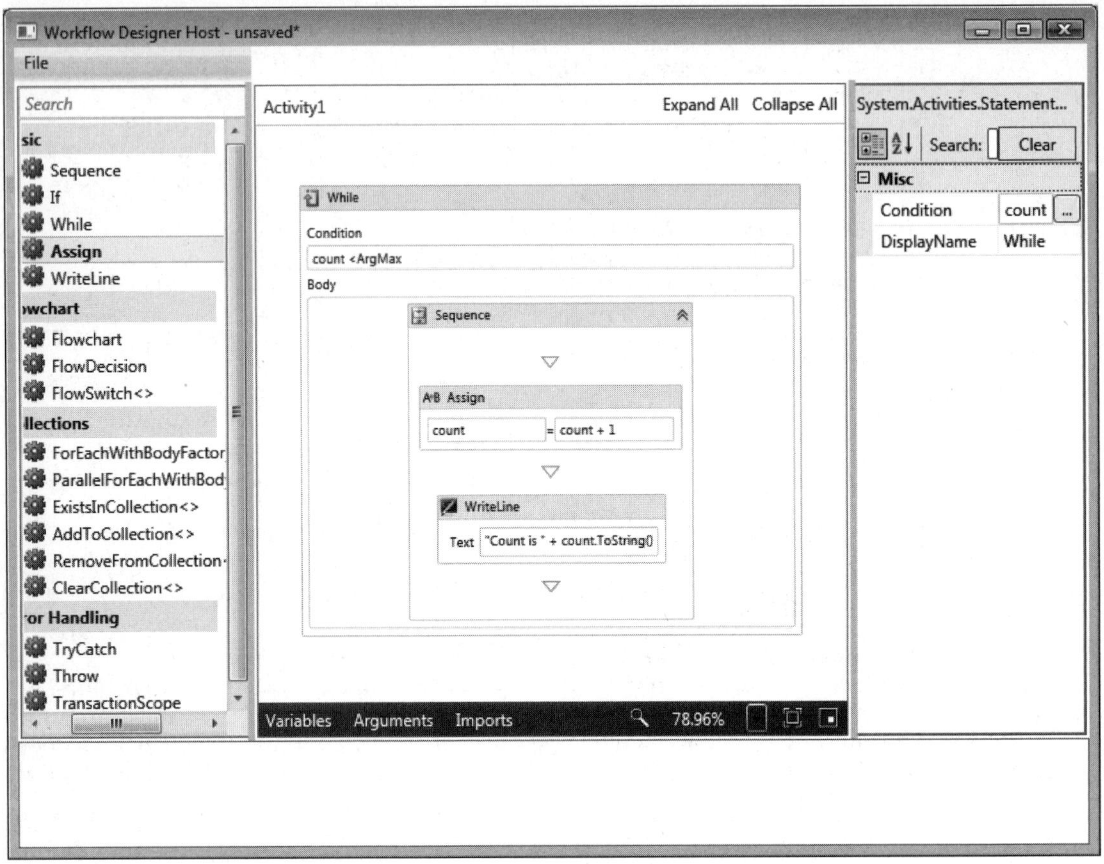

Figure 17-3. About to run a workflow

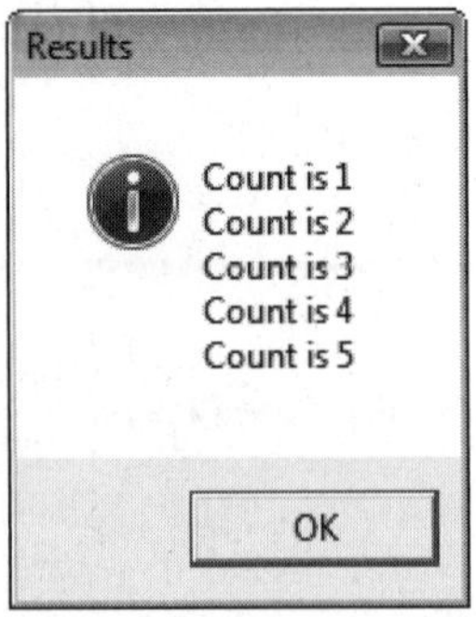

Figure 17-4. Workflow results

Loading and Saving the Definition

The next enhancement you will make is to add support for loading and saving the definition. The Save and SaveAs menu options will be implemented to save the definition to a Xaml file. The Open menu option will allow you to locate an existing Xaml file and load it into the designer.

Modifying the Application

You will make changes to the event handlers for the Save, SaveAs, and Open menu items that were defined but originally did not contain any code. The code that you add to these handlers will invoke new private methods that perform the actual I/O operations. Here is the code that you need to add to the three event handlers:

```
private void menuSave_Click(object sender, RoutedEventArgs e)
{
    if (String.IsNullOrEmpty(currentXamlPath))
    {
        menuSaveAs_Click(sender, e);
    }
    else
    {
        wd.Flush();
        SaveXamlFile(currentXamlPath, wd.Text);
        isModified = false;
        UpdateTitle();
    }
}

private void menuSaveAs_Click(object sender, RoutedEventArgs e)
{
    SaveFileDialog dialog = new SaveFileDialog();
    dialog.AddExtension = true;
    dialog.CheckPathExists = true;
    dialog.DefaultExt = ".xaml";
    dialog.Filter = "Xaml files (.xaml)|*xaml|All files|*.*";
    dialog.FilterIndex = 0;
    Boolean? result = dialog.ShowDialog(this);
    if (result.HasValue && result.Value)
    {
        wd.Flush();
        currentXamlPath = dialog.FileName;
        SaveXamlFile(currentXamlPath, wd.Text);
        isModified = false;
        UpdateTitle();
    }
}
```

```
private void menuOpen_Click(object sender, RoutedEventArgs e)
{
    if (!IsCloseAllowed())
    {
        return;
    }

    OpenFileDialog dialog = new OpenFileDialog();
    dialog.AddExtension = true;
    dialog.CheckPathExists = true;
    dialog.DefaultExt = ".xaml";
    dialog.Filter = "Xaml files (.xaml)|*xaml|All files|*.*";
    dialog.FilterIndex = 0;
    Boolean? result = dialog.ShowDialog(this);
    if (result.HasValue && result.Value)
    {
        String markup = LoadXamlFile(dialog.FileName);
        if (!String.IsNullOrEmpty(markup))
        {
            InitializeDesigner();
            wd.Text = markup;
            wd.Load();
            isModified = false;
            currentXamlPath = dialog.FileName;
            UpdateTitle();
        }
        else
        {
            MessageBox.Show(this,
                String.Format(
                    "Unable to load xaml file {0}", dialog.FileName),
                "Open File Error",
                MessageBoxButton.OK, MessageBoxImage.Error);
        }
    }
}
```

Here are the new private methods that you need to add to the `MainWindow` class:

```
private String LoadXamlFile(String path)
{
    String markup = null;
    try
    {
        using (FileStream stream = new FileStream(path, FileMode.Open))
        {
            using (StreamReader reader = new StreamReader(stream))
            {
                markup = reader.ReadToEnd();
            }
        }
    }
```

```
        catch (Exception exception)
        {
            Console.WriteLine("LoadXamlFile exception: {0}:{1}",
                exception.GetType(), exception.Message);
        }
        return markup;
    }

    private void SaveXamlFile(String path, String markup)
    {
        try
        {
            using (FileStream stream = new FileStream(path, FileMode.Create))
            {
                using (StreamWriter writer = new StreamWriter(stream))
                {
                    writer.Write(markup);
                }
            }
        }
        catch (Exception exception)
        {
            Console.WriteLine("SaveXamlFile exception: {0}:{1}",
                exception.GetType(), exception.Message);
        }
    }
```

Testing the Application

You can now rebuild the project and run it. All of the existing functionality should work in the same way as it did previously. However, you should now be able to use the Save, SaveAs, and Open operations to save your work and load existing Xaml files.

Displaying Validation Errors

The design canvas displays red error indicators on any activity that has a validation error. This works well, but you might also want to list all validation errors in one place. You can accomplish this by developing a custom service that implements the IValidationErrorService interface.

This interface (found in the System.Activities.Presentation.Validation namespace) defines a single ShowValidationErrors method that you must implement in your class. This method is passed a list of ValidationErrorInfo objects. Each object is an error or warning that has been detected. Once your custom service is registered with the EditingContext, the ShowValidationErrors method will be invoked to notify you of any errors or warnings.

Implementing the ValidationErrorService

Add a new C# class to the DesignerHost project, and name it ValidationErrorService. The plan is to display any validation errors and warnings in the ListBox that were added to the bottom of the window.

To accomplish this, the constructor of this class is passed a reference to this **ListBox**. Here is the complete code that you need for this class:

```csharp
using System;
using System.Activities.Presentation.Validation;
using System.Collections.Generic;
using System.Windows.Controls;

namespace DesignerHost
{
    public class ValidationErrorService : IValidationErrorService
    {
        private ListBox lb;

        public ValidationErrorService(ListBox listBox)
        {
            lb = listBox;
        }

        public void ShowValidationErrors(IList<ValidationErrorInfo> errors)
        {
            lb.Items.Clear();
            foreach (ValidationErrorInfo error in errors)
            {
                if (String.IsNullOrEmpty(error.PropertyName))
                {
                    lb.Items.Add(error.Message);
                }
                else
                {
                    lb.Items.Add(String.Format("{0}: {1}",
                        error.PropertyName,
                        error.Message));
                }
            }
        }
    }
}
```

Modifying the Application

To use the new service in the **DesignerHost** application, you first need to add a member variable for the service to the top of the **MainWindow** class like this:

```csharp
namespace DesignerHost
{
    public partial class MainWindow : Window
    {
        private ValidationErrorService errorService;
```

Next, create a new instance of this service in the constructor of the `MainWindow` class. This must be done before the call to the `InitializeDesigner` method as shown here:

```
public MainWindow()
{
    InitializeComponent();
...

    errorService = new ValidationErrorService(this.messageListBox);

    InitializeDesigner();
    StartNewWorkflow();
}
```

Finally, you need to add code to the `InitializeDesigner` method to publish this new service to the `EditingContext` of the designer. Calling the `Publish` method makes this new service available to the designer. You can add the call to the `Publish` method to the end of the `InitializeDesigner` method as shown here:

```
private void InitializeDesigner()
{
...

    wd.Context.Services.Publish<IValidationErrorService>(errorService);
}
```

Testing the Application

Rebuild the project and run it to test the new functionality. To see the new service in action, you simply need to add an activity and generate a validation error. For example, you can add a `Sequence` activity and an `Assign` activity as its child. Since the `Assign.To` and `Assign.Value` properties require values, this should immediately generate the errors that are shown at the bottom of Figure 17-5. Correcting any validation errors clears the `ListBox`.

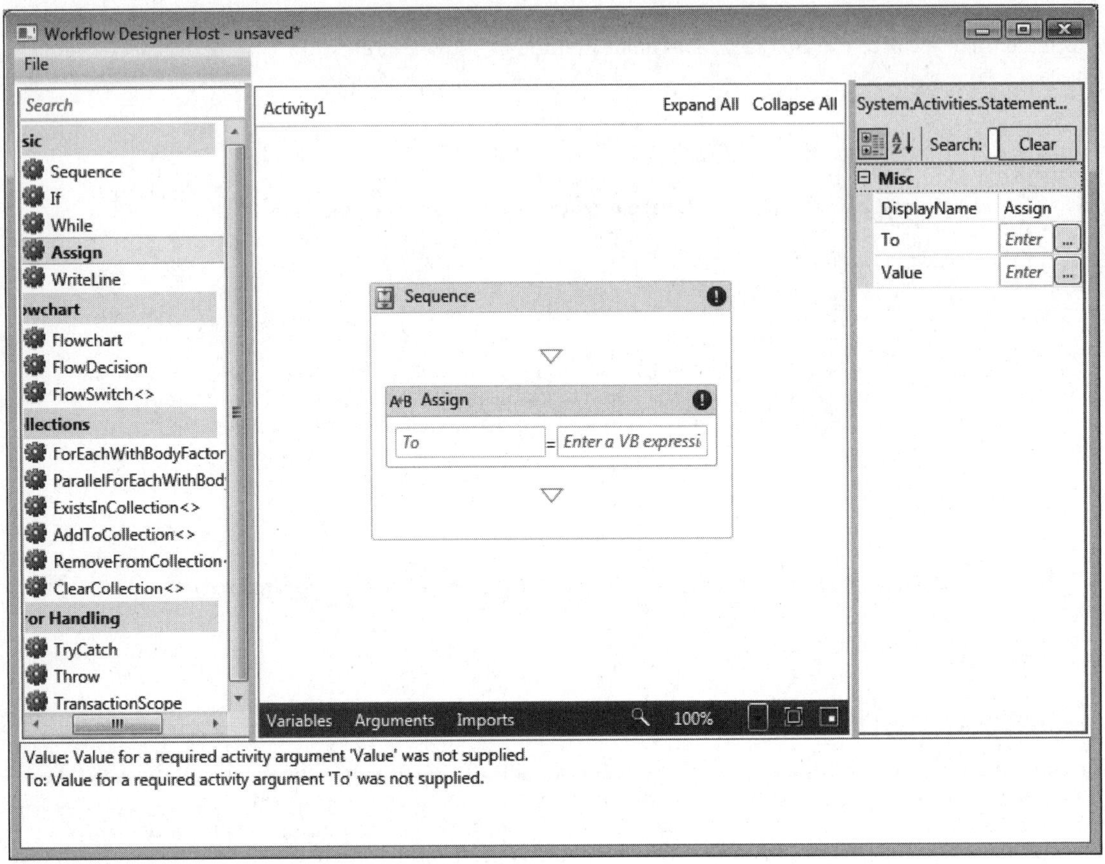

Figure 17-5. Workflow with validation errors

Adding Activities to the Toolbox

The designer application currently supports a subset of the standard activities in the Toolbox. In this section, you will enhance the application to support additional activities. You will add code to the Add Reference menu item handler that allows the user to select an assembly containing additional activities. Any activities that are found in the assembly are added to the Toolbox, making them available for use in the designer.

Additionally, you will enhance the code that loads an existing Xaml file to look for any activities that are not already in the Toolbox. Any new activities will be added to a new category and shown at the top of the Toolbox. This provides the user with access to any activities that are already in use in the loaded definition.

Modifying the Application

Begin by declaring two new member variables at the top of the `MainWindow` class. The `autoAddedCategory` will be reused each time a Xaml file is loaded to support any new activities that are found in the definition. The `referencedCategories` dictionary will be used to track the Toolbox categories for any assemblies that are manually referenced.

```
namespace DesignerHost
{
    public partial class MainWindow : Window
    {
...
        private ToolboxCategory autoAddedCategory;
        private Dictionary<String, ToolboxCategory> referencedCategories =
            new Dictionary<String, ToolboxCategory>();
```

Next, add code to the `StartNewWorkflow` method to call a new private method. You will implement this new method later in the code. This new method will remove the Toolbox category that contains automatically added activities.

```
        private void StartNewWorkflow()
        {
...
            RemoveAutoAddedToolboxCategory();
        }
```

Modify the event handler for the Open menu item (`menuOpen_Click`) to call a new method named `AutoAddActivitiesToToolbox`. This method will inspect the newly loaded definition looking for activities that are not already in the Toolbox. The call to this method should be added after the designer has been initialized with the new definition. I've included the entire method to show you the context of where this line should be added:

```
        private void menuOpen_Click(object sender, RoutedEventArgs e)
        {
            if (!IsCloseAllowed())
            {
                return;
            }

            OpenFileDialog dialog = new OpenFileDialog();
            dialog.AddExtension = true;
            dialog.CheckPathExists = true;
            dialog.DefaultExt = ".xaml";
            dialog.Filter = "Xaml files (.xaml)|*xaml|All files|*.*";
            dialog.FilterIndex = 0;
            Boolean? result = dialog.ShowDialog(this);
```

```
        if (result.HasValue && result.Value)
        {
            String markup = LoadXamlFile(dialog.FileName);
            if (!String.IsNullOrEmpty(markup))
            {
                InitializeDesigner();
                wd.Text = markup;
                wd.Load();
                isModified = false;
                currentXamlPath = dialog.FileName;
                UpdateTitle();

                AutoAddActivitiesToToolbox();
            }
            else
            {
                MessageBox.Show(this,
                    String.Format(
                        "Unable to load xaml file {0}", dialog.FileName),
                    "Open File Error",
                    MessageBoxButton.OK, MessageBoxImage.Error);
            }
        }
    }
```

You need to provide an implementation for the Add Reference menu item handler that was previously empty:

```
private void menuAddReference_Click(object sender, RoutedEventArgs e)
{
    OpenFileDialog dialog = new OpenFileDialog();
    dialog.AddExtension = true;
    dialog.CheckPathExists = true;
    dialog.DefaultExt = ".dll";
    dialog.Filter = "Assemblies (.dll)|*dll|All files|*.*";
    dialog.FilterIndex = 0;
    Boolean? result = dialog.ShowDialog(this);

    if (result.HasValue && result.Value)
    {
        AddReferencedActivitiesToToolbox(dialog.FileName);
    }
}
```

Finally, you need to add these new private methods to the MainWindow class. The AutoAddActivitiesToToolbox method finds any activities in the newly loaded definition that are not already in the Toolbox. There are two namespaces that are ignored during this process. If a new activity is found but is in one of these namespaces, it is not added to the Toolbox. These are the namespaces that are used for expression support, and you generally don't want to add these activities to the Toolbox.

```
private void AutoAddActivitiesToToolbox()
{
    ModelService ms = wd.Context.Services.GetService<ModelService>();
    IEnumerable<ModelItem> activities =
        ms.Find(ms.Root, typeof(Activity));

    List<String> namespacesToIgnore = new List<string>
    {
        "Microsoft.VisualBasic.Activities",
        "System.Activities.Expressions"
    };

    HashSet<Type> activitiesToAdd = new HashSet<Type>();
    foreach (ModelItem item in activities)
    {
        if (!loadedToolboxActivities.Contains(item.ItemType))
        {
            if (!namespacesToIgnore.Contains(item.ItemType.Namespace))
            {
                if (!activitiesToAdd.Contains(item.ItemType))
                {
                    activitiesToAdd.Add(item.ItemType);
                }
            }
        }
    }

    RemoveAutoAddedToolboxCategory();

    if (activitiesToAdd.Count > 0)
    {
        ToolboxCategory autoCat = CreateToolboxCategory(
            "Auto", activitiesToAdd.ToList<Type>(), false);
        CreateAutoAddedToolboxCategory(autoCat);
    }
}

private void RemoveAutoAddedToolboxCategory()
{
    if (autoAddedCategory != null)
    {
        toolboxControl.Categories.Remove(autoAddedCategory);
        autoAddedCategory = null;
    }
}
```

```
private void CreateAutoAddedToolboxCategory(ToolboxCategory autoCat)
{
    //add this category to the top of the list
    List<ToolboxCategory> categories = new List<ToolboxCategory>();
    categories.Add(autoCat);
    categories.AddRange(toolboxControl.Categories);
    toolboxControl.Categories.Clear();
    foreach (var cat in categories)
    {
        toolboxControl.Categories.Add(cat);
    }

    autoAddedCategory = autoCat;
}
```

The `AddReferencedActivitiesToToolbox` method loads the specified assembly and looks for any activities. Any activities that are found are added to a new Toolbox category that is named for the assembly.

```
private void AddReferencedActivitiesToToolbox(String assemblyFileName)
{
    try
    {
        HashSet<Type> activitiesToAdd = new HashSet<Type>();

        Assembly asm = Assembly.LoadFrom(assemblyFileName);
        if (asm != null)
        {
            if (referencedCategories.ContainsKey(asm.GetName().Name))
            {
                return;
            }

            Type[] types = asm.GetTypes();
            Type activityType = typeof(Activity);

            foreach (Type t in types)
            {
                if (activityType.IsAssignableFrom(t))
                {
                    if (!activitiesToAdd.Contains(t))
                    {
                        activitiesToAdd.Add(t);
                    }
                }
            }
        }
```

```
        if (activitiesToAdd.Count > 0)
        {
            ToolboxCategory cat = CreateToolboxCategory(
                asm.GetName().Name, activitiesToAdd.ToList<Type>(), false);
            toolboxControl.Categories.Add(cat);
            referencedCategories.Add(asm.GetName().Name, cat);
        }
    }
    catch (Exception exception)
    {
        MessageBox.Show(this,
            exception.Message, "Exception",
            MessageBoxButton.OK, MessageBoxImage.Error);
    }
}
```

Testing the Application

You should now be ready to rebuild the project and run it. To test the new functionality, you need one or more custom activities. You can use the custom activities that you developed in Chapter 16 for this purpose. Copy these assemblies that you implemented and built in Chapter 16 to the **\bin\debug** folder of the **DesignerHost** project. This assumes that you are currently building for debug.

- `ActivityLibrary.dll`

- `ActivityLibrary.Design.dll`

■ **Note** Please refer to Chapter 16 for detailed information on these custom activities.

Now use the Add Reference menu option of the designer application to add a reference to the **ActivityLibrary.dll** that you just copied. You need to reference the assembly that is in the same folder as the **DesignerHost** project; otherwise, .NET won't be able to resolve the reference correctly. After adding the reference to the assembly, you should see a list of custom activities appear at the bottom of the Toolbox. This is shown in Figure 17-6 under the **ActivityLibrary** category.

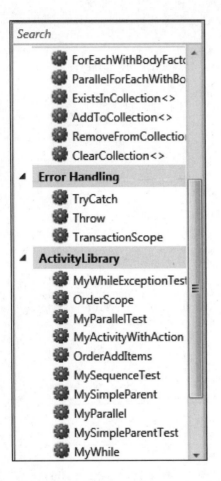

Figure 17-6. Toolbox with custom activities

You should now be able to drag the custom activities to the canvas. For example, you can follow these steps to produce the workflow shown in Figure 17-7.

1. Add a `MySequence` activity to the empty workflow. Set the `Condition` property to `True`.

2. Add an `OrderScope` activity as a child of the `MySequence` activity. Set the `OrderId` property to `1`.

3. Add an `OrderAddItems` activity as a child of the `OrderScope`. Set the `Items` property to `new System.Collections.Generic.List( Of Int32) From {1, 2, 3}`.

4. Save the workflow definition to a file named `CustomActivityTest.xaml`. You are saving the definition so you can load it to test the automatic activity detection that occurs when loading an existing definition.

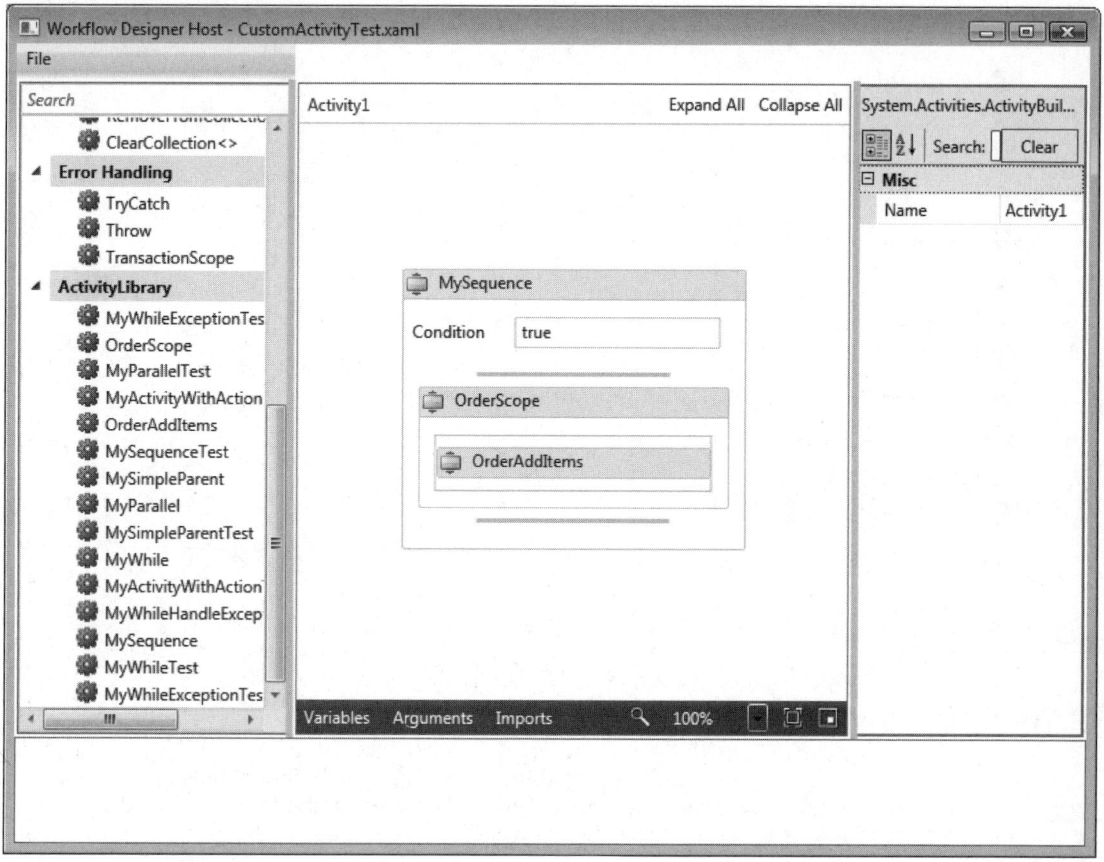

Figure 17-7. *Workflow using custom activities*

To test the automatic activity detection, close and restart the `DesignerHost` project. Doing so ensures that any custom activities that were previously loaded are now cleared. Now open the workflow file that you previously saved (`CustomActivityTest.xaml`). You should now see that the Auto category in the Toolbox has been populated with the custom activities that you referenced in the workflow, as shown in Figure 17-8.

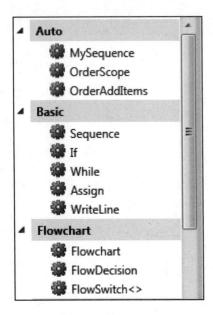

Figure 17-8. Auto Toolbox category

Providing Designer Metadata

The `DesignerHost` application currently relies upon the standard activity designer metadata that was provided by the `DesignerMetadata` class. When you called the `Register` method of this class, the associations between the standard activities and their designers were added to the in-memory `MetadataStore` object.

In this section, you will modify the application to override the default designer for the `While` activity. In Chapter 16, you developed a custom `MyWhile` activity that just happens to match the signature of the standard `While` activity. You will now instruct the workflow designer to use the custom designer that you developed for this activity with the standard `While` activity.

The point of all of this is not to provide a better designer for the `While` activity. The standard designer for this activity works just fine. The point is to demonstrate how you can override the designer for any activity, even those that you didn't author yourself. This demonstrates one of the key benefits of hosting the workflow designer yourself: you have much greater control over the design experience.

Referencing the Custom Designer

The custom designer that you will use is packaged in the `ActivityLibrary.Design` assembly that you developed in Chapter 16. You can update the `DesignerHost` project with a reference to this project in two ways. You can browse to this assembly (which should now be in your `\bin\debug` folder) and add a direct assembly reference. Or, you can add the existing `ActivityLibrary.Design` and `ActivityLibrary` projects from Chapter 16 to your solution for this chapter and build them as part of the solution. You would then need to modify the `DesignerHost` project with a project reference to the `ActivityLibrary.Design` project.

Modifying the Application

To override the designer that is used for the While activity, you need to add this small amount of code to the end of the MainWindow constructor:

```
public MainWindow()
{
...
    //override designer for the standard While activity
    AttributeTableBuilder atb = new AttributeTableBuilder();
    atb.AddCustomAttributes(typeof(While), new DesignerAttribute(
        typeof(ActivityLibrary.Design.MyWhileDesigner)));
    MetadataStore.AddAttributeTable(atb.CreateTable());
}
```

Testing the Application

Rebuild the solution, and run the DesignerHost project. Add a While activity to the empty designer canvas. You should see the custom designer that you developed in Chapter 16 instead of the standard designer, as shown in Figure 17-9. For your reference, Figure 17-3 shows the standard designer for the While activity.

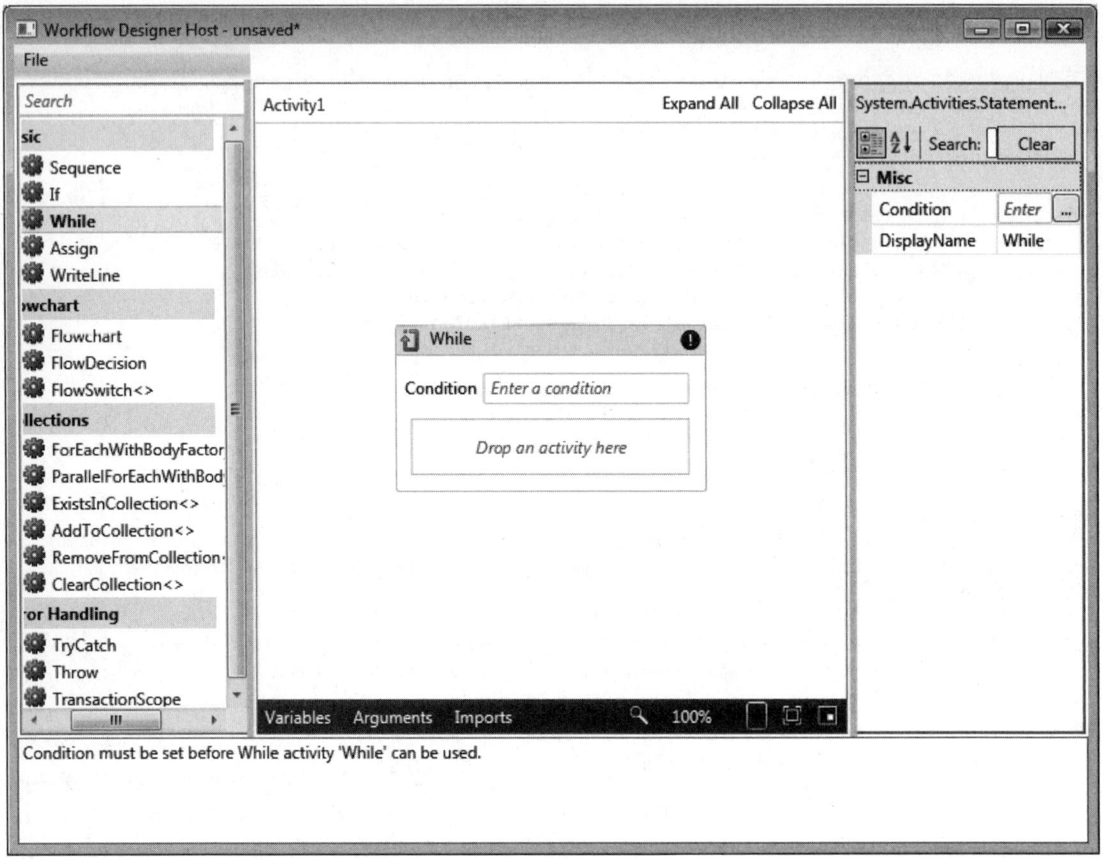

Figure 17-9. While activity with custom designer

Tracking the Selected Activity

In many cases, you may need to know which activity is currently selected and make decisions based on that selection. In this section, you will enhance the `DesignerHost` application to adjust the Toolbox based on the currently selected activity.

The current code includes the three flowchart-related activities in the list of standard activities that are added to the Toolbox. However, the `FlowDecision` and `FlowSwitch<T>` make sense only if the currently selected activity is a `Flowchart` activity. These two activities can be added directly to a `Flowchart` activity only. The code that you will add in this section adds or removes the Toolbox items for the `FlowDecision` and `FlowSwitch<T>` activities depending on the currently selected activity in the designer.

Modifying the Application

First, add the declaration for these new member variables to the top of the `MainWindow` class:

```
namespace DesignerHost
{
    public partial class MainWindow : Window
    {
...

        private ToolboxCategory flowchartCategory;
        private List<ToolboxItemWrapper> flowchartActivities =
            new List<ToolboxItemWrapper>();
```

Add new code to the end of the `InitializeDesigner` method. The new code adds a subscription to the `Selection` object in the `EditingContext`. Each time this object changes, the private `OnItemSelected` method will be executed.

```
        private void InitializeDesigner()
        {
...

            wd.Context.Items.Subscribe<Selection>(OnItemSelected);
        }
```

Add the new `OnItemSelected` method. This method determines whether the currently selected activity is a `Flowchart`. If it is, the other flowchart-related activities are added to the flowchart category of the Toolbox. If the selection is not a `Flowchart` activity, the activities are removed from the category.

```
        private void OnItemSelected(Selection item)
        {
            ModelItem mi = item.PrimarySelection;
            if (mi != null)
            {
                if (flowchartCategory != null && wd.ContextMenu != null)
                {
                    if (mi.ItemType == typeof(Flowchart))
                    {
                        //add the flowchart-only activities
                        foreach (var tool in flowchartActivities)
                        {
                            if (!flowchartCategory.Tools.Contains(tool))
                            {
                                flowchartCategory.Tools.Add(tool);
                            }
                        }
                    }
```

```
                else
                {
                    //remove the flowchart-only activities
                    foreach (var tool in flowchartActivities)
                    {
                        flowchartCategory.Tools.Remove(tool);
                    }
                }
            }
        }
    }
```

You also need to add code to the existing CreateToolbox method. The new code saves the flowchart category and the FlowDecision and FlowSwitch<T> Toolbox items in the new member variables. This allows the code in the OnItemSelected method (shown previously) to easily modify the category object.

```
        private ToolboxControl CreateToolbox()
        {
...
            ToolboxControl tb = new ToolboxControl();
            foreach (var category in activitiesToInclude)
            {
                ToolboxCategory cat = CreateToolboxCategory(
                    category.Key, category.Value, true);
                tb.Categories.Add(cat);

                if (cat.CategoryName == "Flowchart")
                {
                    flowchartCategory = cat;
                    foreach (var tool in cat.Tools)
                    {
                        if (tool.Type == typeof(FlowDecision) ||
                            tool.Type == typeof(FlowSwitch<>))
                        {
                            flowchartActivities.Add(tool);
                        }
                    }
                }
            }

            return tb;
        }
```

Testing the Application

Rebuild and run the DesignerHost project. To test the new functionality, add a Flowchart as the root of the workflow. All the flowchart-related activities are shown in the Toolbox. Now add a WriteLine to the Flowchart you just added. Notice that when the WriteLine activity is selected, the FlowDecision and FlowSwitch<T> activities are removed from the Toolbox, as shown in Figure 17-10.

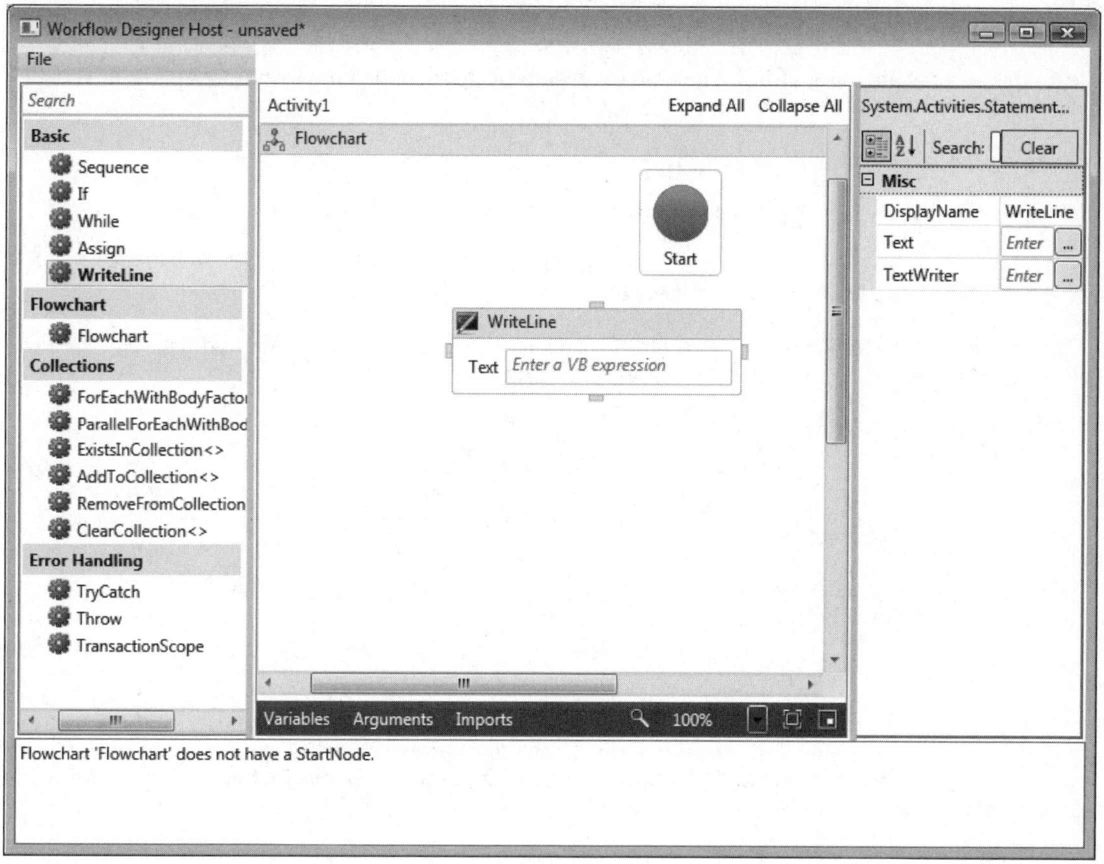

Figure 17-10. Flowchart with context-sensitive Toolbox

If you select the root Flowchart activity, all the flowchart-related activities are added back to the Toolbox.

Modifying the Context Menu

Since the application is now capable of reacting to the currently selected activity, it makes sense to enhance the context menu. The goal of the changes that you are about to make is to add a new context menu item when a Flowchart activity is selected. The new context menu will allow the user to add a FlowDecision activity to the Flowchart. When any other type of activity is selected, the context menu item will be removed. These changes also demonstrate how you can programmatically add activities to the model.

Modifying the Application

Begin this set of changes by adding a new member variable to the top of the `MainWindow` class, as shown here:

```
namespace DesignerHost
{
    public partial class MainWindow : Window
    {
...

        private MenuItem miAddFlowDecision;
```

Next, modify the `MainWindow` constructor to call a new `CreateContextMenu` method. This call should be done before the call to the `InitializeDesigner` method, as shown here:

```
        public MainWindow()
        {
...

            //create a context menu item
            CreateContextMenu();

...

            InitializeDesigner();
            StartNewWorkflow();

...

        }
```

Modify the `OnItemSelected` method that you recently added. If the selected activity is a `Flowchart`, the code adds the new context menu item to the `ContextMenu` property of the `WorkflowDesigner`. If any other activity type has been selected, the context menu item is removed. I've highlighted the new code in the listing that follows:

```
        private void OnItemSelected(Selection item)
        {
            ModelItem mi = item.PrimarySelection;
            if (mi != null)
            {
                if (flowchartCategory != null && wd.ContextMenu != null)
                {
                    if (mi.ItemType == typeof(Flowchart))
                    {
```

```
                    //add the flowchart-only activities
                    foreach (var tool in flowchartActivities)
                    {
                        if (!flowchartCategory.Tools.Contains(tool))
                        {
                            flowchartCategory.Tools.Add(tool);
                        }
                    }

                    if (!wd.ContextMenu.Items.Contains(miAddFlowDecision))
                    {
                        wd.ContextMenu.Items.Add(miAddFlowDecision);
                    }
                }
                else
                {
                    //remove the flowchart-only activities
                    foreach (var tool in flowchartActivities)
                    {
                        flowchartCategory.Tools.Remove(tool);
                    }
                    wd.ContextMenu.Items.Remove(miAddFlowDecision);
                }
            }
        }
    }
```

Finally, add these two new methods to the MainWindow class. The CreateContextMenu is invoked to create the context menu item. It assigns the AddFlowDecision_Click handler to the Click event of this new menu item. The code in the event handler first verifies that the currently selected activity is a Flowchart. If it is, a new FlowDecision activity instance is created and added to the Nodes property of the Flowchart activity.

```
private void CreateContextMenu()
{
    miAddFlowDecision = new MenuItem();
    miAddFlowDecision.Header = "Add FlowDecision";
    miAddFlowDecision.Name = "miAddFlowDecision";
    miAddFlowDecision.Click +=
        new RoutedEventHandler(AddFlowDecision_Click);
}

private void AddFlowDecision_Click(object sender, RoutedEventArgs e)
{
    ModelItem selected =
        wd.Context.Items.GetValue<Selection>().PrimarySelection;
    if (selected != null)
    {
        if (selected.ItemType == typeof(Flowchart))
        {
            ModelProperty mp = selected.Properties["Nodes"];
```

```
            if (mp != null)
            {
                mp.Collection.Add(new FlowDecision());
            }
        }
    }
}
```

Testing the Application

After rebuilding the DesignerHost project, you can run it and test the new functionality. Add a Flowchart as the root activity. Right-click to open the context menu for this activity. You should see the new Add FlowDecision menu item. If you select this menu item, a new FlowDecision activity should be added to the Flowchart. Figure 17-11 shows the new context menu item.

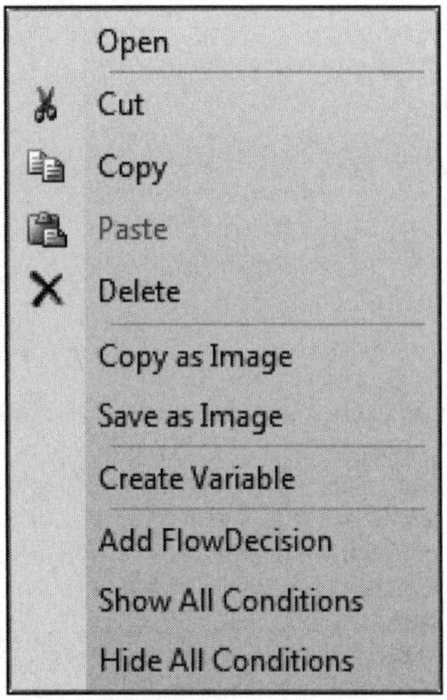

Figure 17-11. Flowchart with context menu

Once the FlowDecision has been added, select it and right-click to open the context menu. The Add FlowDecision menu item should now be removed.

Locating the Arguments

At some point, you may need to inspect the input and output arguments for the workflow definition. Their location within the activity model is not necessarily intuitive. They are actually located in the Properties collection of the root activity. To retrieve them, you first retrieve the ModelService from the EditingContext of the designer. You can then use the Root property of the ModelService to navigate to the `Properties` collection. This is a collection of `DynamicActivityProperty` objects. Each input or output argument is in this collection along with any other properties.

To demonstrate this, you will modify the handler for the Run menu item to display any arguments that have default values assigned to them.

Modifying the Application

The only necessary change is to add code to the `menuRun_Click` event handler to access the arguments. Here is the enhanced code for this handler with the new code highlighted:

```
private void menuRun_Click(object sender, RoutedEventArgs e)
{
    try
    {
        wd.Flush();
        Activity activity = null;
        using (StringReader reader = new StringReader(wd.Text))
        {
            activity = ActivityXamlServices.Load(reader);
        }

        if (activity != null)
        {
            //list any defined arguments
            messageListBox.Items.Clear();
            ModelService ms =
                wd.Context.Services.GetService<ModelService>();
            ModelItemCollection items =
                ms.Root.Properties["Properties"].Collection;
            foreach (var item in items)
            {
                if (item.ItemType == typeof(DynamicActivityProperty))
                {
                    DynamicActivityProperty prop =
                        item.GetCurrentValue() as DynamicActivityProperty;
                    if (prop != null)
                    {
                        Argument arg = prop.Value as Argument;
```

```
                                if (arg != null)
                                {
                                    messageListBox.Items.Add(String.Format(
                                        "Name={0} Type={1} Direction={2} Exp={3}",
                                        prop.Name, arg.ArgumentType,
                                        arg.Direction, arg.Expression));
                                }
                            }
                        }
                    }
                }

    ...
            }
```

Testing the Application

Rebuild and run the `DesignerHost` project to see the new functionality in action. To demonstrate this, you can use the same set of activities that you used in a previous example. Please follow these steps to define the test workflow:

1. Add a `While` activity.

2. Declare an `Int32` variable named `count` that is scoped by the `While` activity.

3. Add an `Int32` input argument named `ArgMax`. Set the default value of this argument to 5.

4. Set the `While.Condition` property to `count < ArgMax`.

5. Add a `Sequence` to the `While.Body`.

6. Add an `Assign` activity to the `Sequence` activity. Set the `Assign.To` property to `count` and the `Assign.Value` property to `count + 1`.

7. Add a `WriteLine` immediately below the `Assign` activity. Set the `Text` property to `"Count is" + count.ToString()`.

Now, select the Run menu item to execute the workflow using the default value of 5 for the `ArgMax` argument. In addition to the correct results from the execution of the workflow, you should also see the details of the input argument shown in the ListBox at the bottom of the window, as shown in Figure 17-12.

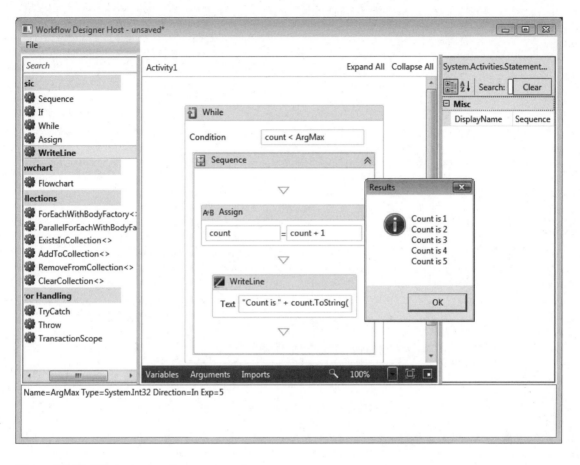

Figure 17-12. Displaying runtime arguments

Summary

This chapter focused on hosting the workflow designer in your own application. The chapter began with a simple application that hosted the major designer components. This same example application was enhanced in subsequent sections of this chapter.

You enhanced this application with the ability to load, save, and run workflow definitions as well as display validation errors. Other enhancements included the ability to reference activities in other assemblies and to automatically populate the Toolbox with activities that are found in loaded definitions. You saw how to override the activity designer that is assigned to standard activities and to locate any arguments in the workflow model. The application was also enhanced to provide a context-sensitive menu and Toolbox.

In the next chapter, you will learn how to execute some WF 3.*x* activities in the WF 4 environment.

■ ■ ■

CHAPTER 18

WF 3.*x* Interop and Migration

This chapter focuses on strategies for dealing with existing WF 3.0 or 3.5 applications (WF 3.*x*). The chapter begins with an overview of the migration strategies that are available to you. Following this, the `Interop` activity is discussed and demonstrated. This activity enables you to execute some WF 3.*x* activities within the WF 4 runtime environment.

Several specific migration scenarios are demonstrated next. The use of the WF 3.*x* `ExternalDataExchangeService` with WF 4 workflows is demonstrated followed by two examples that use the WF 3.*x* rules engine.

■ **Note** This chapter presents information that should interest existing WF 3.*x* developers and WF 4 developers who want to use the WF 3.*x* rules engine. This chapter does not present any new information that relates to the development of new native WF 4 applications.

Reviewing Migration Strategies

When Microsoft set out to develop WF 4, it had a few simple goals in mind. Included was the simplification of the object model and the overall development experience. Microsoft wanted to make WF easier to understand and to work with. Another stated goal was the improvement of design-time and runtime performance. When you compare WF 4 to WF 3.*x*, you're likely to agree with me that Microsoft achieved these goals.

However, in order to meet the design goals for WF 4, Microsoft decided to start with a clean slate, designing WF 4 as an entirely new framework. This was the cleanest way for the Microsoft developers to address what they thought were fundamental issues with the original WF 3.*x* design. The downside to this decision is that WF 4 and WF 3.*x* are not compatible with each other. Activities and workflows developed for one framework cannot be executed natively by the other.

If you have existing WF 3.*x* applications, it's not likely that you can simply scrap them and start over. Unless the applications are trivial, you have likely invested a substantial amount of time, energy, and development funds in their design, implementation, testing, and deployment.

You now have a decision to make regarding these applications:

- Will you continue to use WF 3.*x*?

- Will you migrate to WF 4?

These options are discussed in more depth in the following sections.

Continuing with WF 3.x

The good news is that the 3.*x* version of WF has not disappeared. .NET 4 includes all the original assemblies that support WF 3.*x*. Since they are part of .NET 4, they have all been built to use the .NET 4 Common Language Runtime (CLR). Here are the assemblies that constitute WF 3.*x*:

- `System.Workflow.Activities`

- `System.Workflow.ComponentModel`

- `System.Workflow.Runtime`

- `System.WorkflowServices`

Visual Studio 2010 also includes all the original tooling support for WF 3.*x*. The workflow designer can be used to maintain existing activities and workflows or to create new ones.

In short, Microsoft still supports WF 3.*x*. If this version of WF is currently meeting your needs, you can continue to use it. And you can upgrade to Visual Studio 2010 knowing that you will be able to maintain your existing WF 3.*x* applications.

■ **Note** The version numbers can sometimes be very confusing. Please refer to the "WF vs. Framework vs. CLR Versioning" sidebar for further information on this subject.

Targeting the Correct Version

Visual Studio 2010 allows you to target these versions of WF:

Target	WF Version	CLR Version
.NET Framework 3.0	3.0	2.0
.NET Framework 3.5	3.5	2.0
.NET Framework 4	4	4

I've omitted the client variations of each target since they don't affect the overall version of WF that is available to you. Depending on the configuration of your development machine, you may not initially have all these targets available to you. If you have never installed previous versions of the .NET

Framework, you may only have .NET Framework 4 available as a target. If you need to target one of the other versions, you can select the "Install other frameworks" option in the target selector.

If you are maintaining an existing WF application or developing a new one, you need to always be mindful of choosing the correct target framework. For instance, if you need to build your existing WF 3.*x* application with version 2.0 of the CLR, you need to choose version 3.0 or 3.5 as the target framework. If you choose to rebuild your existing WF 3.*x* application using version 4 of the CLR, you need to select .NET Framework 4 as the target. Your existing WF projects will initially target version 3.0 or 3.5 of the framework, but you can change this from the project settings page.

If you create a new project that targets .NET Framework 4, the assumption is that you want to use WF 4, not WF 3.*x*. In this case, the only new item templates available to you are those for WF 4. How do you create new projects that use WF 3.*x* but use the latest CLR (version 4)? You have to cheat the system just a bit. I've found that these steps do the trick:

1. Create a new project that targets .NET Framework 3.5.

2. Select the appropriate new project template under the Workflow category such as Sequential Workflow Console Application or Workflow Activity Library. This creates a project with the correct project type for WF 3.*x* development.

3. At this point, the new project targets the CLR version 2.0. Open the project properties, and change the target framework to .NET Framework 4.

4. After the project is reloaded, version 4 of the CLR should now be used.

Now when you add a new WF item to the project, the Workflow category includes the WF 3.*x* and WF 4 components. You simply have to make sure you always add the correct WF 3.*x* item type to the project.

WF vs. Framework vs. CLR Versioning

I've been referring to the 3.0 and 3.5 versions of WF collectively as WF 3.*x*. Each version of WF originally corresponded to the version of the .NET Framework that deployed it. The 3.0 version of WF was originally deployed with .NET Framework 3.0. And likewise, WF 3.5 was deployed with .NET Framework 3.5. However, both of these versions of the .NET Framework use the 2.0 version of the Common Language Runtime (CLR, or just "the runtime").

This implies that the version of WF and the CLR that it uses are independent. Given this fact, it should be possible to rebuild the WF 3.*x* assemblies using a newer version of the CLR. This is exactly what has been done with the latest version of the .NET Framework. .NET Framework 4 includes a new CLR (version 4) that all assemblies in the framework are built against and now use. This includes the assemblies that constitute the previous 3.*x* version of WF. These assemblies are built against the latest CLR (version 4) and are themselves labeled as version 4. However, they include the original types that made up WF 3.*x*.

To clarify my terminology, when I refer to WF 3.*x*, I'm referring to the types that constitute that version of WF. These are the types packaged in the `System.Workflow*` family of assemblies (`System.Workflow.Activities`, `System.Workflow.Runtime`, and so on). I'm not necessarily referring to the version of the .NET Framework or the CLR.

To further complicate the matter, Visual Studio 2010 allows you to choose the version of the .NET
Framework that you are targeting for each project. So, it is possible to target version 3.0, 3.5, or 4 of the
framework. And your choice of project and item templates changes depending on the targeted framework.
For example, if you create a new project and target .NET Framework 4, the Workflow category of the Add
New Project dialog contains only the templates for WF 4 (the subject of this book). Likewise, if you target
.NET Framework 3.5, the Workflow category of the same dialog includes the WF 3.5 templates.

Migrating to WF 4

Your other choice is to migrate your existing WF 3.x application to natively use WF 4. You might be able
to migrate the entire application to WF 4 all at once. But that's feasible only if the application is fairly
small or if you have ample development resources available to convert the entire application.

The more likely scenario is that you will migrate the application to WF 4 incrementally rather than
all at once. To assist with this migration, WF 4 includes the `Interop` activity (found in the Migration
category of the Toolbox). This activity is a wrapper for a WF 3.x activity or workflow that allows you to
execute the wrapped component using the WF 4 runtime. As you might expect, the `Interop` activity is
limited in the type of WF 3.x components it is capable of handling. This activity, including its limitations,
is discussed in a subsequent section of this chapter.

The `Interop` activity is just one part of your overall migration strategy. Generally, your approach will
be twofold:

1.   Use the `Interop` activity to wrap as many WF 3.x activities as you can.

2.   Implement the remainder of the WF 3.x application as native WF 4 activities.

This approach to migration may seem like an oversimplification (and perhaps it is). But these are
really your only two choices. You need to continue to execute existing WF 3.x components by wrapping
them, or you implement that logic again as new WF 4 activities. Wrapping WF 3.x activities with the
`Interop` activity provides you with the time you need to eventually migrate those WF 3.x activities to
native WF 4 activities. During the migration period, the application remains in a usable state.

Preparing for Migration

If you have an existing WF 3.x application, there are best practices that you can follow now with a view to
your eventual WF 4 migration. Following these practices now will make your life easier when you do
need to migrate. Here are Microsoft's recommended best practices for WF 3.x applications:

Avoid the CodeActivity

As you have already seen, WF 4 does not support code-beside logic within an activity or workflow. The
WF 3.x `CodeActivity` is an easy way to add imperative code to a workflow. But it forces you to add that
code directly to the workflow class – preventing it from being reused and also causing future migration
headaches.

If you don't follow any other best practice, please follow this one. Move any imperative code into
custom activities. When you migrate to WF 4, the code in these custom activities can be moved directly
into WF 4 activities based on the WF 4 `CodeActivity` class. Or very likely they can be easily wrapped by
the `Interop` activity.

■ **Tip** The WF 3.*x* CodeActivity is evil; you must avoid it. Use custom activities instead.

Avoid Custom Events

This best practice is similar to the prohibition against the CodeActivity. In WF 3.*x* you might implement a custom activity that supports a custom event. When you use that custom activity in a workflow, the event handler is added to the code-beside file of the workflow. Since WF 4 doesn't support code-beside, you'll need to develop a different event notification strategy. The best approach is to use a delegate mechanism that can be handled without code-beside.

Avoid Binding Activities to Other Activities

WF 3.*x* allows you to bind the dependency properties of one activity to those of another. In essence, the output from one activity can be funneled directly to another without any intermediate storage. This is convenient since it avoids the need for an additional variable to hold the value.

Although this is a perfectly valid WF 3.*x* approach, it creates a fairly large migration issue. In WF 4, variables and arguments are first-class constructs and can be easily declared within the workflow model. When you need to pass a value from one activity to another, a variable is used. Activities typically don't reference each other directly. The use of variables in WF 4 makes it clearer exactly when a given value is in scope and which activities reference it.

Instead of binding to another activity directly, your WF 3.*x* workflows should define variables in the workflow class and bind to them in order to pass values. This is closer to the WF 4 model and will be easier to migrate.

Avoid Activity.Initialize and Activity.Uninitialize

These methods are used in WF 3.*x* to initialize an activity prior to execution or uninitialize it after execution. The problem is that there is no corresponding set of methods (or activity execution state) in WF 4. To easily migrate your WF 3.*x* application, you need to avoid adding code to these methods.

Use a String WorkflowQueue Name

Your WF 3.*x* application may use a WorkflowQueue directly for communication. In WF 4, you will use a bookmark instead of a WorkflowQueue. Bookmarks are always named with a string, but the WorkflowQueue allows you to use any type that implements the IComparable interface. This includes a string, but it could also include other types. If you are using another type to name your WorkflowQueue, you'll need to change to a string name since this is all that the WF 4 bookmark mechanism supports.

Use EnqueueOnIdle Instead of Enqueue

The WF 3.*x* WorkflowInstance class supports two methods that allow you to enqueue a message on a workflow queue: Enqueue and EnqueueOnIdle. The Enqueue method posts the message immediately, while EnqueueOnIdle waits until the workflow is idle before posting the message. To ease migration to WF 4, you need to use `EnqueueOnIdle` since this more closely resembles the WF 4 behavior. In WF 4, bookmarks are resumed only when the workflow is idle.

Understanding the Interop Activity

The `Interop` activity is the wrapper that allows you to execute WF 3.x activities or workflows. It supports these properties:

Property	Type	Description
ActivityType	Type	Identifies the WF 3.x activity or workflow that is wrapped
ActivityProperties	IDictionary<String, Argument>	A dictionary of named arguments that represent the public properties of the wrapped activity
ActivityMetaProperties	IDictionary<String, Object>	A dictionary of named objects that represent metadata of the wrapped activity

After adding an `Interop` activity to your WF 4 activity or workflow, you select the WF 3.x type that you want to wrap. The selected type must derive from `System.Workflow.ComponentModel.Activity` and must be referenced by the current project. The selected type must also be public with a default (parameterless) constructor. It cannot be an abstract type. Once you select a type to wrap, the `ActivityProperties` collection is populated with arguments that represent each public property of the wrapped activity. Each argument is presented in the Properties window as a normal WF4 activity property.

Each WF 3.x property is actually represented by two WF 4 arguments in the collection. One argument uses the same name as the WF 3.x property and is an input argument. A second argument is generated with the literal "Out" appended to the property name. This second argument is an output argument for the WF 3.x property. Two arguments are needed since WF 3.x doesn't distinguish between input and output arguments the way WF 4 does. Collectively, these properties allow you to pass values into and out of the WF 3.x activity. You wire up values to the arguments as you normally would in the WF 4 world using expressions.

The `ActivityMetaProperties` collection is also populated with any metadata properties of the wrapped activity. For example, the name property of the WF 3.x activity would be available in this collection along with other properties that define the activity.

■ **Note** The `Interop` activity is available only if you select the full .NET Framework 4 as the target for the project. If your project targets the .NET Framework 4 Client Profile, you will need to change the target before you can use the `Interop` activity.

Limitations of the Interop Activity

You can use the Interop activity to wrap most individual WF 3.*x* activities and workflows. However, there are limitations:

- The InvokeWorkflowActivity cannot be wrapped. You can wrap an entire WF 3.*x* workflow, but it cannot use InvokeWorkflowActivity to invoke another workflow.

- The SuspendActivity cannot be wrapped.

- You can't directly wrap WF 3.*x* standard activities. The Interop activity is designed to wrap custom activities. If you need the functionality that is provided by a WF 3.*x* standard activity that is not available in WF 4, you need to implement a custom WF 3.*x* activity to expose this functionality. Your other option is to implement the logic natively in WF 4.

- The Send and Receive activities cannot be wrapped. Use the native WCF messaging activities that are available in WF 4 instead.

- The web service activities (WebServiceInputActivity, WebServiceOutputActivity, WebServiceFaultActivity) cannot be wrapped. Use the native WF 4 WCF messaging activities.

- WF 3.*x* compensation activities cannot be wrapped. Use the native WF 4 compensation activities.

- The HandleExternalEventActivity and CallExternalMethodActivity cannot be directly wrapped. However, you can use custom activities that have been generated using the Workflow Communication Activity utility (WCA.exe).

- Persistence is accomplished using the WF 4 instance store mechanism, not the WF 3.*x* mechanism. This means that you must prepare and configure a WF 4 instance store instead of configuring a WF 3.*x* persistence service and adding it to the WorkflowRuntime.

- The WF 3.*x* tracking mechanism is not available. When you use the Interop activity, any tracking data that is generated by the wrapped activity is exposed as an InteropTrackingRecord in the WF 4 tracking system.

Invoking a WF 3.*x* Activity

In this example, you will see how to use the Interop activity to wrap a simple WF 3.5 custom activity. The activity simulates the calculation of shipping charges for an order and is based on an example from my Pro WF 3.5 book. It supports several input and output properties so it aptly demonstrates how these properties are exposed as arguments of the Interop activity.

   You will complete these steps to complete the example:

1. Implement a WF 3.5 custom activity.

2. Implement a WF 4 workflow that uses the Interop activity to execute the WF 3.5 activity.

3. Use the WorkflowInvoker to execute the test workflow.

Implementing a WF 3.5 Activity

Begin this example by creating a WF 3.5 activity library. This project will be used for all of the WF 3.5 activities and workflows that you will implement in this chapter. When you create a new WF 3.5 project, you need to select .NET Framework 3.5 as the target. When you select the Workflow category of new project templates, you should see a list of WF 3.5 project templates. Select the Workflow Activity Library template, and name the new project ActivityLibrary35. Add this new project to a new solution that is named for this chapter. You can delete the Activity1.cs file that is created since it won't be used.

■ **Note** If you don't see .NFT Framework 3.5 as one of the available target options, it means that this version of the framework is not installed on your development machine. If this is the case, you can select the More Frameworks option in the list to download and install the framework.

Add a new Activity to the ActivityLibrary35 project, and name it CalcShipping35. Here is the full listing of the CalcShipping35.cs file that contains the implementation of this WF 3.5 activity:

```
using System;
using System.ComponentModel;
using System.Workflow.ComponentModel;

namespace ActivityLibrary35
{
    public partial class CalcShipping35 : Activity
    {
        public static DependencyProperty WeightProperty =
            DependencyProperty.Register(
                "Weight", typeof(Int32), typeof(CalcShipping35));

        [Description("Weight")]
        [Category("CalcShipping35 Category")]
        [Browsable(true)]
        [DesignerSerializationVisibility(DesignerSerializationVisibility.Visible)]
        public Int32 Weight
        {
            get
            {
                return ((Int32)(base.GetValue(CalcShipping35.WeightProperty)));
            }
            set
            {
                base.SetValue(CalcShipping35.WeightProperty, value);
            }
        }
    }
```

```
public static DependencyProperty OrderTotalProperty =
    DependencyProperty.Register(
        "OrderTotal", typeof(Decimal), typeof(CalcShipping35));

[Description("OrderTotal")]
[Category("CalcShipping35 Category")]
[Browsable(true)]
[DesignerSerializationVisibility(DesignerSerializationVisibility.Visible)]
public Decimal OrderTotal
{
    get
    {
        return ((Decimal)(base.GetValue(
            CalcShipping35.OrderTotalProperty)));
    }
    set
    {
        base.SetValue(CalcShipping35.OrderTotalProperty, value);
    }
}

public static DependencyProperty ShipViaProperty =
    DependencyProperty.Register(
        "ShipVia", typeof(string), typeof(CalcShipping35));

[Description("ShipVia")]
[Category("CalcShipping35 Category")]
[Browsable(true)]
[DesignerSerializationVisibility(DesignerSerializationVisibility.Visible)]
public string ShipVia
{
    get
    {
        return ((string)(base.GetValue(CalcShipping35.ShipViaProperty)));
    }
    set
    {
        base.SetValue(CalcShipping35.ShipViaProperty, value);
    }
}

public static DependencyProperty ResultProperty =
    DependencyProperty.Register(
        "Result", typeof(Decimal), typeof(CalcShipping35));
```

```
[Description("Result")]
[Category("CalcShipping35 Category")]
[Browsable(true)]
[DesignerSerializationVisibility(DesignerSerializationVisibility.Visible)]
public Decimal Result
{
    get
    {
        return ((Decimal)(base.GetValue(CalcShipping35.ResultProperty)));
    }
    set
    {
        base.SetValue(CalcShipping35.ResultProperty, value);
    }
}

private Decimal _normalRate = 1.95M;
private Decimal _expressRate = 3.50M;
private Decimal _minimum = 12.95M;
private Decimal _freeThreshold = 75.00M;
private Boolean _isFreeShipping = false;

public CalcShipping35()
{
    InitializeComponent();
}
```

The code first defines a set of dependency properties. These are the input and output properties that will be exposed as arguments of the Interop activity. Following the properties, a set of private variables is defined that is used in the calculations of the activity. The Execute method is where the order total and shipping charges are calculated.

```
protected override ActivityExecutionStatus Execute(
    ActivityExecutionContext executionContext)
{
    Result = 0;
    switch (ShipVia)
    {
        case "normal":
            if (OrderTotal >= _freeThreshold)
            {
                _isFreeShipping = true;
            }
            else
            {
                Result = (Weight * _normalRate);
            }
            break;
```

```
        case "express":
            Result = (Weight * _expressRate);
            break;
    }

    if ((Result < _minimum) && (!_isFreeShipping))
    {
        Result = _minimum;
    }

    return ActivityExecutionStatus.Closed;
        }
    }
}
```

At this point you should build the project to ensure that it successfully builds.

■ **Note** If you are reading this chapter, my assumption is that you are already intimately familiar with the 3.*x* version of WF. If this is not the case, you really don't need to be working through the examples in this chapter. Since the goal of this book is to teach you version 4 of WF (not version 3.*x*), I'm not going to provide an in-depth explanation of the 3.*x* code or activities. If you need assistance in understanding the 3.*x* examples, you might want to take a look at my *Pro WF: Windows Workflow in .NET 3.5* book from Apress.

Declaring a Test Workflow

To create a workflow that uses the WF 3.*x* activity that you just implemented, create a new WF 4 Activity Library, and name it `ActivityLibrary`. Add it to the same solution as the `ActivityLibrary35` project. Remember that you'll need to change the target framework back to .NET Framework 4 when you create this new project. Also, please remember to change the project properties to use the full framework (.NET Framework 4), not the client profile of the framework. The `Interop` activity is available only with the full version of the framework. You can delete the `Activity1.xaml` file since it won't be used.

Add these references to the new project:

- `ActivityLibrary35` (project reference)

- `System.Workflow.ComponentModel`

Add a new Activity to the `ActivityLibrary` project that you just created, and name it `CalcShipping35Interop`. Follow these steps to complete the declaration of this activity:

1. Add a `Sequence` activity as the root of the activity.

2. Add these variables that are all scoped by the `Sequence` activity. Note that most of them require default values:

Name	Variable Type	Scope	Default Value
weight	Int32	Sequence	20
orderTotal	Decimal	Sequence	50D
shipVia	String	Sequence	"normal"
shippingTotal	Decimal	Sequence	

3. Add an `Interop` activity as a child of the `Sequence` activity. The `Interop` activity can be found in the Migration category of the Toolbox. After adding the activity, click the "click to browse" area of the activity to select the 3.5 activity that you want to wrap. Select the `ActivityLibrary35.CalcShipping35` type.

4. View the Properties window for the `Interop` activity. You should notice that input and output arguments have been generated for all public properties of the 3.5 activity that you are wrapping. Set the `OrderTotal` property to `orderTotal`, the `ShipVia` property to `shipVia`, the `Weight` property to `weight`, and the `ResultOut` property to `shippingTotal`. Figure 18-1 shows the completed property settings for the `Interop` activity.

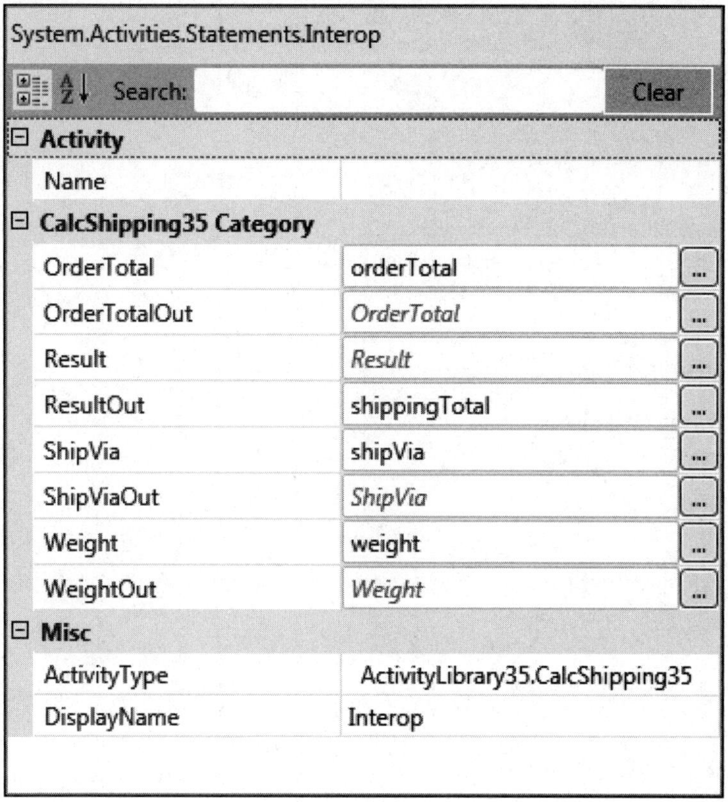

System.Activities.Statements.Interop	
Activity	
Name	
CalcShipping35 Category	
OrderTotal	orderTotal
OrderTotalOut	*OrderTotal*
Result	*Result*
ResultOut	shippingTotal
ShipVia	shipVia
ShipViaOut	*ShipVia*
Weight	weight
WeightOut	*Weight*
Misc	
ActivityType	ActivityLibrary35.CalcShipping35
DisplayName	Interop

Figure 18-1. Interop activity properties

5. Add a WriteLine activity below the Interop activity. This activity will display the results of the calculation. Set the Text property to String.Format("ShipVia: {0} Weight:{1} Total:{2} Shipping: {3}", shipVia, weight, orderTotal, shippingTotal).

Figure 18-2 shows the completed workflow.

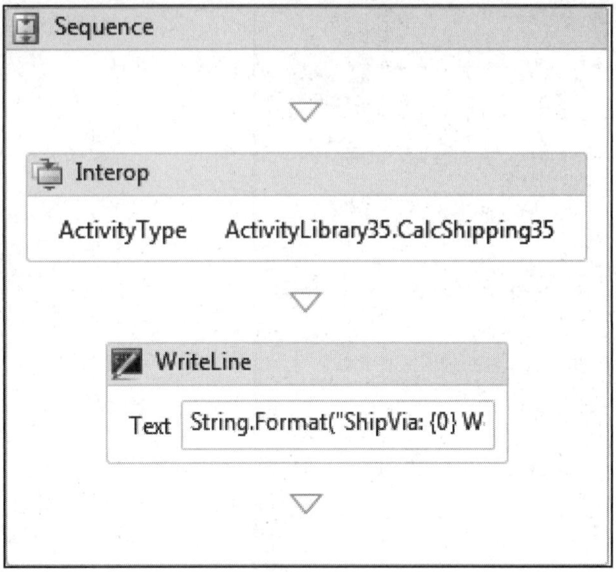

Figure 18-2. CalcShipping35Interop workflow

Rebuild the solution to ensure that it builds correctly.

Testing the Workflow

To test the workflow, you will use a simple console application. Create a new Workflow Console Application named RunWorkflow, and add it to the solution for this chapter. Delete the Worklfow1.xaml file since it won't be used.

After the new project is created, open the project properties, and change the target framework from .NET Framework 4 Client Profile to .NET Framework 4. This is needed in order to resolve the assembly references that are required by the Interop activity.

Add these references to the project:

- ActivityLibrary (project reference)

- ActivityLibrary35 (project reference)

- System.Workflow.ComponentModel

■ **Note** The ActivityLibrary35 project is not needed in order to build this project. But all of the referenced assemblies must be in the \bin\debug folder in order to run the project. Adding the ActivityLibrary35 project as a reference is simply a convenience since this copies the assembly into the \bin\debug folder.

Change the `Program.cs` file of the `RunWorkflow` project to execute the `CalcShipping35Interop` workflow that you declared in the previous step. Here is a listing of the revised Program.cs file:

```
using System;
using System.Activities;
using ActivityLibrary;

namespace RunWorkflow
{
    class Program
    {
        static void Main(string[] args)
        {
            WorkflowInvoker.Invoke(new CalcShipping35Interop());
        }
    }
}
```

After rebuilding the solution, you should be able to run the `RunWorkflow` project. Here are my results, which indicate that the WF 3.5 activity executed and produced the expected results:

```
ShipVia: normal Weight:20 Total:50 Shipping: 39.00
```

Invoking a WF 3.x Workflow

In this example, you will implement a WF 3.5 workflow and execute it using the WF 4 `Interop` activity. The workflow uses the `CalcShipping35` activity that you implemented in the first example, along with another new custom activity. You will complete these steps to implement this example:

1. Implement another WF 3.5 custom activity.

2. Implement a WF 3.5 workflow.

3. Declare a WF 4 workflow that uses the `Interop` activity to execute the WF 3.5 workflow.

Implementing a WF 3.5 Custom Activity

Add a new WF 3.5 Activity to the `ActivityLibrary35` project, and name it `LookupItem35`. The purpose of this activity is to simulate the retrieval of the price and weight for a sales item. These values are needed by the `CalcShipping35` activity to correctly calculate the shipping charges.

Here is a complete listing of the LookupItem35.cs file:

```csharp
using System;
using System.ComponentModel;
using System.Workflow.ComponentModel;

namespace ActivityLibrary35
{
    public partial class LookupItem35 : Activity
    {
        public static DependencyProperty ItemIdProperty =
            DependencyProperty.Register(
                "ItemId", typeof(Int32), typeof(LookupItem35));

        [Description("ItemId")]
        [Category("LookupItem35 Category")]
        [Browsable(true)]
        [DesignerSerializationVisibility(DesignerSerializationVisibility.Visible)]
        public Int32 ItemId
        {
            get
            {
                return ((Int32)(base.GetValue(LookupItem35.ItemIdProperty)));
            }
            set
            {
                base.SetValue(LookupItem35.ItemIdProperty, value);
            }
        }

        public static DependencyProperty WeightProperty =
            DependencyProperty.Register(
                "Weight", typeof(Int32), typeof(LookupItem35));

        [Description("Weight")]
        [Category("LookupItem35 Category")]
        [Browsable(true)]
        [DesignerSerializationVisibility(DesignerSerializationVisibility.Visible)]
        public Int32 Weight
        {
            get
            {
                return ((Int32)(base.GetValue(LookupItem35.WeightProperty)));
            }
            set
            {
                base.SetValue(LookupItem35.WeightProperty, value);
            }
        }
```

```
public static DependencyProperty PriceProperty =
    DependencyProperty.Register(
        "Price", typeof(Decimal), typeof(LookupItem35));

[Description("Price")]
[Category("LookupItem35 Category")]
[Browsable(true)]
[DesignerSerializationVisibility(DesignerSerializationVisibility.Visible)]
public Decimal Price
{
    get
    {
        return ((Decimal)(base.GetValue(LookupItem35.PriceProperty)));
    }
    set
    {
        base.SetValue(LookupItem35.PriceProperty, value);
    }
}

public LookupItem35()
{
    InitializeComponent();
}

protected override ActivityExecutionStatus Execute(
    ActivityExecutionContext executionContext)
{
    Weight = ItemId * 5;
    Price = (Decimal)ItemId * 3.95M;
    return ActivityExecutionStatus.Closed;
}
    }
}
```

Build the project to ensure that it builds correctly.

Implementing the WF 3.5 Workflow

Add a Sequential Workflow (with code separation) to the ActivityLibrary35 project. Name the new workflow CalcItemTotal35. This project type generates a CalcItemTotal35.xoml containing the markup for the workflow and a CalcItemTotal35.xoml.cs code-beside file.

Defining Properties

Open the CalcItemTotal35.xoml.cs file, and add the workflow properties shown here:

```csharp
using System;
using System.ComponentModel;
using System.Workflow.Activities;
using System.Workflow.ComponentModel;

namespace ActivityLibrary35
{
    public partial class CalcItemTotal35 : SequentialWorkflowActivity
    {
        public static DependencyProperty ItemIdProperty =
            DependencyProperty.Register(
                "ItemId", typeof(Int32), typeof(CalcItemTotal35));

        [Description("ItemId")]
        [Category("CalcItemTotal35 Category")]
        [Browsable(true)]
        [DesignerSerializationVisibility(DesignerSerializationVisibility.Visible)]
        public Int32 ItemId
        {
            get
            {
                return ((Int32)(base.GetValue(CalcItemTotal35.ItemIdProperty)));
            }
            set
            {
                base.SetValue(CalcItemTotal35.ItemIdProperty, value);
            }
        }

        public static DependencyProperty ShipViaProperty =
            DependencyProperty.Register(
                "ShipVia", typeof(string), typeof(CalcItemTotal35));

        [Description("ShipVia")]
        [Category("CalcItemTotal35 Category")]
        [Browsable(true)]
        [DesignerSerializationVisibility(DesignerSerializationVisibility.Visible)]
        public string ShipVia
        {
            get
            {
                return ((string)(base.GetValue(CalcItemTotal35.ShipViaProperty)));
            }
            set
            {
                base.SetValue(CalcItemTotal35.ShipViaProperty, value);
            }
        }
```

```
public static DependencyProperty WeightProperty =
    DependencyProperty.Register(
        "Weight", typeof(Int32), typeof(CalcItemTotal35));

[Description("Weight")]
[Category("CalcItemTotal35 Category")]
[Browsable(true)]
[DesignerSerializationVisibility(DesignerSerializationVisibility.Visible)]
public Int32 Weight
{
    get
    {
        return ((Int32)(base.GetValue(CalcItemTotal35.WeightProperty)));
    }
    set
    {
        base.SetValue(CalcItemTotal35.WeightProperty, value);
    }
}

public static DependencyProperty PriceProperty =
    DependencyProperty.Register(
        "Price", typeof(Decimal), typeof(CalcItemTotal35));

[Description("Price")]
[Category("CalcItemTotal35 Category")]
[Browsable(true)]
[DesignerSerializationVisibility(DesignerSerializationVisibility.Visible)]
public Decimal Price
{
    get
    {
        return ((Decimal)(base.GetValue(CalcItemTotal35.PriceProperty)));
    }
    set
    {
        base.SetValue(CalcItemTotal35.PriceProperty, value);
    }
}
```

```
        public static DependencyProperty ResultProperty =
            DependencyProperty.Register(
                "Result", typeof(Decimal), typeof(CalcItemTotal35));

        [Description("Result")]
        [Category("CalcItemTotal35 Category")]
        [Browsable(true)]
        [DesignerSerializationVisibility(DesignerSerializationVisibility.Visible)]

        public Decimal Result
        {
            get
            {
                return ((Decimal)(base.GetValue(CalcItemTotal35.ResultProperty)));
            }
            set
            {
                base.SetValue(CalcItemTotal35.ResultProperty, value);
            }
        }

    }
}
```

Declaring the Workflow

Rebuild the project before continuing with the workflow declaration. Open the `CalcItemTotal35.xoml` file in the WF 3.5 workflow designer, and follow these steps to complete the declaration of this workflow:

1. Add an instance of the `LookupItem35` activity. Bind the `Weight`, `ItemId`, and `Price` properties of the activity to like-named properties of the workflow.

2. Add a `CodeActivity` below the `LookupItem35` activity. Change the activity name to `codeDisplayItem`. Double-click the activity to add a handler for the `ExecuteCode` event. You'll add code to this handler after you have completed the declaration of the workflow.

3. Add a `CalcShipping35` activity below the `CodeActivity`. Bind the `ShipVia`, `Result`, and `Weight` properties of the activity to like-named properties of the workflow. Bind the `OrderTotal` property of the activity to the `Price` total of the workflow. The completed workflow should look like Figure 18-3.

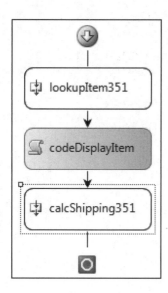

Figure 18-3. CalcItemTotal35 sequential workflow

4.   Switch to Code View, and add this code to the ExecuteCode handler of the
     CodeActivity:

```
private void codeDisplayItem_ExecuteCode(object sender, EventArgs e)
{
    Console.WriteLine(
        "Retrieved info for ItemId:{0} Weight:{1} Price:{2}",
            ItemId, Weight, Price);
}
```

You should build the project before continuing with the next step.

■ **Note** I said earlier that the CodeActivity is evil, but I am using it here for a few reasons. First, it's being used
as a debugging tool (writing a message to the console), and it doesn't execute any real business logic. Second, the
goal of this section is to invoke a complete WF 3.*x* workflow, not to reuse a single activity. In the context of
executing a workflow, the CodeActivity is slightly less evil, since the WF 3.*x* workflow is a completely self-
contained entity that is executed in its entirety. Third, the reality is that you likely have workflows that use the
CodeActivity, so I wanted to demonstrate that you can continue to execute them, as long as you do so as a
complete workflow.

Declaring a Test Workflow

Add a new WF 4 Activity to the **ActivityLibrary** project, and name it **CalcItemTotal35Interop**. This activity will execute the **CalcItemTotal35** workflow that you just completed. Please follow these steps to declare this activity:

1. Add a **Sequence** activity as the root of the activity.

2. Define these variables that are all scoped by the **Sequence** activity:

Name	Variable Type	Scope	Default Value
shipVia	String	Sequence	"normal"
itemId	Int32	Sequence	3
finalTotal	Decimal	Sequence	

3. Add an **Interop** activity to the **Sequence** activity. Select the **ActivityLibrary35.CalcItemTotal35** workflow as the type to wrap. Set the **ItemId** property to **itemId**, the **ShipVia** property to **shipVia**, and the **ResultOut** property to **finalTotal**.

4. Add a **WriteLine** activity below the **Interop** activity. Set the **Text** property to **String.Format("ItemId:{0} Total:{1}", itemId, finalTotal)**. Figure 18-4 shows the completed activity.

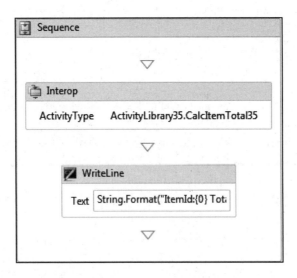

Figure 18-4. CalcItemTotal35Interop workflow

Testing the Workflow

You can use the RunWorkflow project that you used in the previous example to test this new workflow. The only required change is the name of the WF 4 activity to execute. Change the code to execute the CalcItemTotal35Interop activity, as shown here:

```
WorkflowInvoker.Invoke(new CalcItemTotal35Interop());
```

After rebuilding the solution, you can execute the RunWorkflow project. Here are the expected results:

```
Retrieved info for ItemId:3 Weight:15 Price:11.85

ItemId:3 Total:29.25
```

In this case, you were able to execute the WF 3.5 workflow without any problems at all. However, this workflow didn't exceed any of the limitations of the Interop activity that were previously discussed. You won't be as lucky with all WF 3.5 workflows.

Using the ExternalDataExchangeService

WF 3.*x* uses a mechanism called external data exchange to enable communication between a workflow instance and a host application. This same mechanism is not directly supported in WF 4. However, you can use the Interop activity to invoke WF 3.*x* workflows that do use this mechanism, with some restrictions.

To use this mechanism in WF 3.*x*, you define and implement a custom workflow service (sometimes called a *local service*) that adheres to a narrow set of requirements. One requirement is that the service must implement an interface that is decorated with the ExternalDataExchange attribute. The service that you implement is added to an instance of the ExternalDataExchangeService class that is itself added to the workflow runtime.

Within a WF 3.*x* workflow, you use the HandleExternalEventActivity and CallExternalMethodActivity activities to communicate via the service. The CallExternalMethodActivity invokes a method on the service object while the HandleExternalEventActivity waits for a service event to be raised. The host application can use the methods and events of the service to communicate with a running workflow instance.

The Interop activity can wrap WF 3.*x* workflows that use this mechanism, but with these restrictions:

- The HandleExternalEventActivity and CallExternalMethodActivity cannot be used directly. Instead, the WF 3.*x* workflow must use custom activities that are generated by the WCA.exe utility.

- You must use the WorkflowServiceHost to host the WF 4 activity. The WorkflowApplication class does not support interoperability with the WF 3.*x* ExternalDataExchangeService.

The WCA.exe utility has always been deployed with WF 3.*x* and is not new. It generates custom activities for any data exchange interfaces that are defined in a target assembly. These generated activities derive from the base `HandleExternalEventActivity` and `CallExternalMethodActivity` classes but are strongly typed for each data exchange interface. It is the strong typing of these custom activities that permits their use by the `Interop` activity.

The example that follows is taken from Chapter 7 of my *Pro WF: Windows Workflow in .NET 3.5* book from Apress. It uses this external data exchange mechanism to implement a guessing game application. The object of the game is to correctly guess a number between 1 and 10.

■ **Tip** Most of the steps that are presented next define the WF 3.*x* workflow and any types that it requires. Instead of manually following all of these steps, you might want to download the sample code from my *Pro WF: Windows Workflow in .NET 3.5* book. The original sample code for the book packages these types in a different set of projects, so you'll have to change namespaces and so on. But that may be easier than following all of these steps.

You will complete these steps to implement this example:

1. Implement event arguments that are used by events.

2. Implement a custom data exchange service.

3. Generate data exchange activities.

4. Declare the WF 3.5 workflow.

5. Declare a WF 4 test workflow.

6. Implement code to host the WF 4 workflow.

Implementing the Event Arguments

Add a new class named `GuessReceivedEventArgs` to the `ActivityLibrary35` project. This class defines the event arguments for the event that is handled by the WF 3.*x* workflow. Here is the complete code for this class:

```
using System;
using System.Workflow.Activities;

namespace ActivityLibrary35
{
    [Serializable]
    public class GuessReceivedEventArgs : ExternalDataEventArgs
    {
        public Int32 NextGuess { get; set; }
        public GuessReceivedEventArgs(Guid instanceId, Int32 nextGuess)
            : base(instanceId)
        {
            NextGuess = nextGuess;
        }
    }
}
```

Add another class named `MessageReceivedEventArgs` to the same project. This class defines event arguments for an event that will be handled by the host application.

```
using System;
using System.Workflow.Activities;

namespace ActivityLibrary35
{
    [Serializable]
    public class MessageReceivedEventArgs : ExternalDataEventArgs
    {
        public String Message { get; set; }
        public MessageReceivedEventArgs(Guid instanceId, String message)
            : base(instanceId)
        {
            Message = message;
        }
    }
}
```

Implementing the Data Exchange Service

Add a new interface to the `ActivityLibrary35` project named `IGuessingGame`. This interface defines the method and event that will be used by the workflow:

```
using System;
using System.Workflow.Activities;

namespace ActivityLibrary35
{
    [ExternalDataExchange]
    public interface IGuessingGame
    {
        void SendMessage(String message);
        event EventHandler<GuessReceivedEventArgs> GuessReceived;
    }
}
```

Add a class to the same project named `GuessingGameService`. This is the data exchange service that acts as the communications conduit between the host application and a workflow instance:

```
using System;
using System.Workflow.Runtime;

namespace ActivityLibrary35
{
    public class GuessingGameService : IGuessingGame
    {
        public void SendMessage(string message)
        {
```

```
        if (MessageReceived != null)
        {
            MessageReceivedEventArgs args
                = new MessageReceivedEventArgs(
                    WorkflowEnvironment.WorkflowInstanceId,
                    message);
            MessageReceived(this, args);
        }
    }

    public event EventHandler<GuessReceivedEventArgs> GuessReceived;

    public event EventHandler<MessageReceivedEventArgs> MessageReceived;

    public void OnGuessReceived(GuessReceivedEventArgs args)
    {
        if (GuessReceived != null)
        {
            GuessReceived(null, args);
        }
    }
  }
 }
}
```

Generating the Communication Activities

Build the `ActivityLibrary35` project before proceeding with the next step. You now need to execute the `WCA.exe` utility to generate custom communication activities for the method and event that are defined in the `IGuessingGame` interface. To accomplish this, follow these steps:

1. Open a Visual Studio 2010 command prompt.

2. Change the current directory to the ActivityLibrary35 project folder.

3. Enter and execute this command in the command prompt: `wca /collapseArgs bin\debug\ActivityLibrary35.dll`.

4. Two new source files should have been generated in the project folder: `IGuessingGame.Invokes.cs` and `IGuessingGame.Sinks.cs`. Add both of these files to the `ActivityLibrary35` project.

5. Add a reference to the `System.Drawing` assembly to the `ActivityLibrary35` project.

You should now rebuild the `ActivityLibrary35` project to ensure that everything builds successfully.

Declaring the WF 3.5 Workflow

Add a new Sequential Workflow named `GuessingGameWcaWorkflow` to the `ActivityLibrary35` project. Open the `GuessingGameWcaWorkflow.cs` file in Code View, and add the member variables and initialization code shown here:

```
sing System;
using System.Workflow.Activities;

namespace ActivityLibrary35
{
    public sealed partial class GuessingGameWcaWorkflow
        : SequentialWorkflowActivity
    {
        private Int32 _theNumber;

        public String Message { get; set; }
        public Boolean IsComplete { get; set; }

        public GuessingGameWcaWorkflow()
        {
            InitializeComponent();
            Random random = new Random();
            _theNumber = random.Next(1, 10);
            Message = "Please guess a number between 1 and 10.";
        }
    }
}
```

Now open the GuessingGameWcaWorkflow in designer view. You can follow these steps to complete the declaration of the workflow:

1. Add an instance of the SendMessage activity to the workflow. This is one of the communication activities that was generated from the IGuessingGame interface. Bind the Message property of the activity to the Message property of the workflow.

2. Add a WhileActivity below the SendMessage activity. Add a declarative rule condition named checkIsComplete that contains the following expression: !this.IsComplete. This condition will cause the child of the WhileActivity to repeat as long as the IsComplete workflow property is false.

3. The WhileActivity requires a single child activity, so add a ListenActivity to it. The ListenActivity creates two initial EventDrivenActivity instances as children. All of the remaining activities that you add will be children of one of these EventDrivenActivity instances. The EventDrivenActivity on the left will wait for the GuessReceived event, while the one on the right takes care of things if the event is never received.

4. Add a GuessReceived activity to the EventDrivenActivity on the left. Double-click the activity to add a handler for the Invoked event. Here is the code that you should add for this event handler:

```
private void guessReceived1_Invoked(object sender, ExternalDataEventArgs e)
{
    GuessReceivedEventArgs eventArgs
        = e as GuessReceivedEventArgs;
    if (eventArgs != null)
    {
        if (eventArgs.NextGuess < _theNumber)
        {
            Message = "Try a higher number.";
        }
        else if (eventArgs.NextGuess > _theNumber)
        {
            Message = "Try a lower number.";
        }
        else
        {
            Message = String.Format(
                "Congratulations! You correctly guessed {0}.", _theNumber);
            IsComplete = true;
        }
    }
}
```

5. Copy the SendMessage activity from the top of the workflow, and paste the copy below the GuessReceived activity that you just added. All the properties for this copied activity are the same.

6. Add a DelayActivity to the EventDrivenActivity on the right side. Set the TimeoutDuration to one minute (00:01:00).

7. Add a TerminateActivity directly below the DelayActivity. This will terminate the workflow if a guess has not been received within one minute.

Figure 18-5 shows the completed workflow.

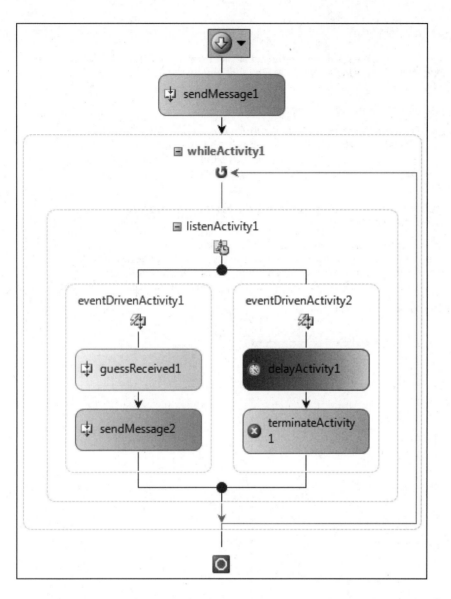

Figure 18-5. *GuessingGameWcaWorkflow*

Build the `ActivityLibrary35` project before continuing with the next steps.

Declaring a Test Workflow

Add a new Activity named GuessingGame35Interop to the ActivityLibrary project. This activity will use the Interop activity to execute the GuessingGameWcaWorkflow that you just defined. Please follow these steps to define this activity:

1. Add a Sequence activity as the root of the new activity.

2. Add a Receive activity to the Sequence activity. Since this workflow will be hosted by the WindowsServiceHost class, it requires a WCF messaging activity to start it. Set the CanCreateInstance property to True, the OperationName to "Start" and the ServiceContractName to " IServiceStarter". The activity does not require any content to be defined.

3. Add a WriteLine activity below the Receive activity. Set the Text property to "Guessing Game started".

4. Add an Interop activity below the WriteLine activity. Select ActivityLibrary35.GuessingGameWcaWorkflow as the type to be wrapped. There are no input or output parameters that you need to set for this workflow. All input and output is accomplished via the WF 3.5 data exchange service.

Figure 18-6 shows the completed activity.

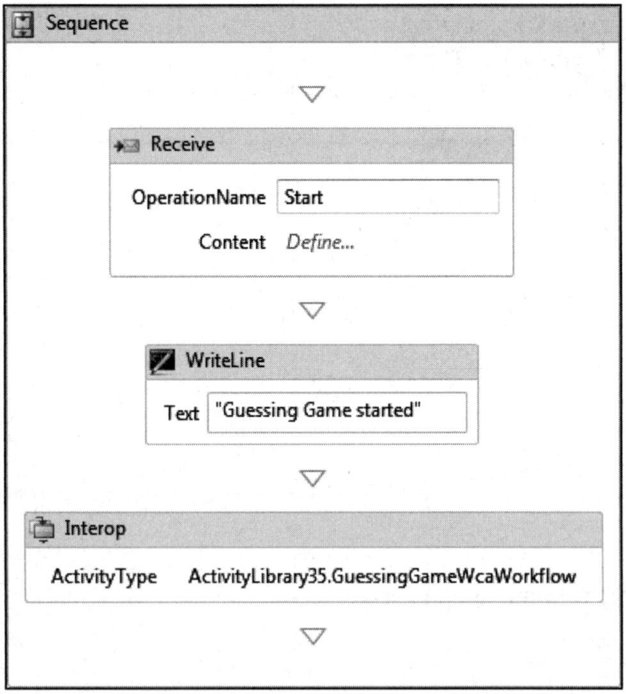

Figure 18-6. GuessingGame35Interop workflow

Testing the Workflow

Create a new Workflow Console application named `GuessingGame`, and add it to the solution for this chapter. Delete the `Workflow1.xaml` file since it won't be used. This application will host the `GuessingGame35Interop` workflow that you just defined using the `WorkflowServiceHost` class.

Open the project properties, and change the target framework for the project to .NET Framework 4 (the full framework). Add these references to the new project:

- `ActivityLibrary` (project reference)
- `ActivityLibrary35` (project reference)
- `System.Workflow.ComponentModel`
- `System.ServiceModelActivities`
- `System.Workflow.Activities`
- `System.Workflow.Runtime`
- `System.WorkflowServices`

Here is the code that you need to add to the `Program.cs` file to host the workflow:

```
using System;
using System.ServiceModel;
using System.ServiceModel.Activities.Description;
using System.Threading;
using ActivityLibrary;
using ActivityLibrary35;

namespace GuessingGame
{
    class Program
    {
        private static GuessingGameService ggService;
        private static AutoResetEvent waitEvent;

        [ServiceContract]
        public interface IServiceStarter
        {
            [OperationContract(IsOneWay = true)]
            void Start();
        }
```

The code creates an instance of a `WorkflowServiceHost` class to host the workflow. Note that this is the WF 4 version of this class. WF 3.*x* also has a class with the same name in a different namespace. A named pipes binding and URL are used since this workflow is accessed only locally from this application.

An instance of the WF 3.*x* `ExternalDataExchangeService` class is constructed, and an instance of the `GuessingGameService` is added to it. A handler for the `MessageReceived` event is added to the service. This event is the host application's notification that a message has been received from the workflow. The `ExternalDataExchangeService` is then added to the `WorkflowRuntimeEndpoint` as a service.

After opening the `WorkflowServiceHost`, a locally defined `IServiceStarter` interface is used to start an instance of the workflow.

```
static void Main(string[] args)
{
    System.ServiceModel.Activities.WorkflowServiceHost host = null;
    try
    {
        waitEvent = new AutoResetEvent(false);
        string baseAddr = "net.pipe://localhost/GuessingGame";

        host = new System.ServiceModel.Activities.WorkflowServiceHost(
                new GuessingGame35Interop(), new Uri(baseAddr));

        System.Workflow.Activities.ExternalDataExchangeService des =
            new System.Workflow.Activities.ExternalDataExchangeService();
        ggService = new GuessingGameService();
        ggService.MessageReceived +=
            new EventHandler<MessageReceivedEventArgs>(
                Service_MessageReceived);
        des.AddService(ggService);

        WorkflowRuntimeEndpoint endpoint = new WorkflowRuntimeEndpoint();
        endpoint.AddService(des);
        host.AddServiceEndpoint(endpoint);
        host.AddDefaultEndpoints();

        host.Open();

        IServiceStarter client =
            ChannelFactory<IServiceStarter>.CreateChannel(
                new NetNamedPipeBinding(), new EndpointAddress(baseAddr));
        client.Start();
        waitEvent.WaitOne(TimeSpan.FromMinutes(2));

        Console.WriteLine("Program exiting...");
    }
    catch (Exception exception)
    {
        Console.WriteLine("Unhandled exception: {0}",
            exception.Message);
    }
    finally
    {
        if (host != null)
        {
            host.Close();
        }
    }
}
```

The MessageReceived event handler is the host application's notification that a message has been received from the workflow instance. The code for this handler asynchronously executes the private HandleNewInput method. This method displays the message from the workflow on the console and then waits for input from the user. The input is assumed to be a guess, so it is parsed and passed to the waiting workflow instance via the GuessingGameService.OnGuessReceived method.

```
private static void Service_MessageReceived(
    object sender, MessageReceivedEventArgs e)
{
    Action<Guid, String> handler = HandleNewInput;
    handler.BeginInvoke(e.InstanceId, e.Message,
        ar => handler.EndInvoke(ar), handler);
}

private static void HandleNewInput(Guid instanceId, String message)
{
    Console.WriteLine(message);
    if (message.StartsWith("Congratulations"))
    {
        waitEvent.Set();
        return;
    }

    String input = Console.ReadLine();
    if (!String.IsNullOrEmpty(input))
    {
        Int32 guess = 0;
        if (Int32.TryParse(input, out guess))
        {
            ggService.OnGuessReceived(
                new GuessReceivedEventArgs(instanceId, guess));
        }
    }
    else
    {
        waitEvent.Set();
    }
}
```

After rebuilding the solution, you should be able to run the `GuessingGame` project. Here is a representative sample of my results:

```
Guessing Game started

Please guess a number between 1 and 10.

5

Try a lower number.

3

Try a lower number.

1

Congratulations! You correctly guessed 1.

Program exiting...
```

Executing Rules Using the Interop Activity

WF 3.x includes a rules engine that allows you to define and execute rule sets against application data. Within the workflow designer, the functionality to use the rules engine is exposed with the `PolicyActivity` class. WF 4 does not have a corresponding rules engine, but you can execute the WF 3.x engine using the `Interop` activity.

In this example, you will define a WF 3.x workflow that uses rules to calculate shipping and total charges for an order. The `Interop` activity will then be used to execute this WF 3.x workflow.

You will complete these steps to implement this example:

1. Implement a class to define test data.

2. Declare a WF 3.5 workflow that uses the `PolicyActivity` to execute a set of rules.

3. Define the `RuleSet` to be applied to the test data.

4. Declare a WF 4 workflow that uses the `Interop` activity to execute the WF 3.5 workflow.

5. Develop code to execute the WF 4 workflow.

Implementing the SalesItem Class

Add a new class to the `ActivityLibrary35` project named `SalesItem`. This simple class defines the data used to exercise the rules. Here is the code for this class:

```
using System;

namespace ActivityLibrary35
{
    [Serializable]
    public class SalesItem
    {
        public Int32 Quantity { get; set; }
        public Double ItemPrice { get; set; }
        public Double OrderTotal { get; set; }
        public Double Shipping { get; set; }
        public Boolean IsNewCustomer { get; set; }
    }
}
```

Build the project before continuing with the next step.

Declaring the WF 3.5 Workflow and Rules

Next, add a new Sequential Workflow named SellItemWorkflow to the ActivityLibrary35 project. This workflow will be used to apply a set of rules to the test data. Open the SellItemWorkflow in Code View, and define the SalesItem property as shown here:

```
using System;
using System.Workflow.Activities;

namespace ActivityLibrary35
{
    public sealed partial class SellItemWorkflow
        : SequentialWorkflowActivity
    {
        public SalesItem SalesItem { get; set; }

        public SellItemWorkflow()
        {
            InitializeComponent();
        }
    }
}
```

Now open the `SellItemWorkflow` in Designer View. You can follow these steps to complete the workflow declaration:

1. Add a `PolicyActivity` to the workflow.

2. Define a new `RuleSet` to be executed by the `PolicyActivity`. The `RuleSet` should be named `CalculateItemTotals` and includes three rules, as shown in this table:

Rule Name	Condition	Then Actions	Else Actions
CalcTotal	this.SalesItem.Quantity > 10	this.SalesItem.OrderTotal = this.SalesItem.Quantity * (this.SalesItem.ItemPrice * 0.95)	this.SalesItem.OrderTotal = this.SalesItem.Quantity * this.SalesItem.ItemPrice
CalcShipping	this.SalesItem.OrderTotal > 100.0	this.SalesItem.Shipping = 0	this.SalesItem.Shipping = this.SalesItem.Quantity * 0.95
NewCustomer	this.SalesItem.IsNewCustomer	this.SalesItem.OrderTotal = this.SalesItem.OrderTotal - 10.0	

Figure 18-7 shows the completed `RuleSet`, and Figure 18-8 shows the workflow. Build the solution before you proceed to the next step.

Rule Set Editor

Configure the rule set. Add and Remove rules from the list. For each rule, set condition and actions.

Rule Set

🔲 Add Rule | ✕ Delete   Chaining: [Full Chaining ▾]

Name	Priority	Reevaluation	Active	Rule Preview
CalcTotal	0	Always	True	IF this.SalesItem.Quantity > 10 THEN this.SalesItem.OrderTotal = t...
CalcShipping	0	Always	True	IF this.SalesItem.OrderTotal > 100.0 THEN this.SalesItem.Shippin...
NewCustomer	0	Always	True	IF this.SalesItem.IsNewCustomer THEN this.SalesItem.OrderTotal ...

Rule Definition

Name: [NewCustomer]   Priority: [0]   Reevaluation: [Always ▾]   ☑ Active

Condition (Example: this.Prop1>5 && this.Prop1<10):

```
this.SalesItem.IsNewCustomer
```

Then Actions (Examples: this.Prop2 = "Yes", Halt):

```
this.SalesItem.OrderTotal = this.SalesItem.OrderTotal - 10.0
```

Else Actions:

```

```

[OK]   [Cancel]

Figure 18-7. CalculateItemTotals RuleSet

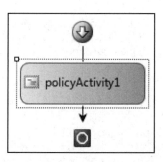

Figure 18-8. SellItemWorkflow

Declaring a Test Workflow

Add a new Activity to the `ActivityLibrary`, and name it `SellItem35Interop`. This WF 4 workflow will use the `Interop` activity to execute the `SellItemWorkflow` that you just defined. Please follow these steps to declare this workflow:

1. Define an `InOutArgument` named `ArgItem`. The argument type is `ActivityLibrary35.SalesItem`. This argument is used to pass a test instance of the `SalesItem` class to the workflow.

2. Add a `Sequence` activity as the root of the activity.

3. Add an `Interop` activity as a child of the `Sequence` activity. Select `ActivityLibrary35.SellItemWorkflow` as the type to be wrapped. Set the `SalesItem` argument of the `Interop` activity to `ArgItem`.

Figure 18-9 shows the completed workflow. Rebuild the solution before you continue with the next step.

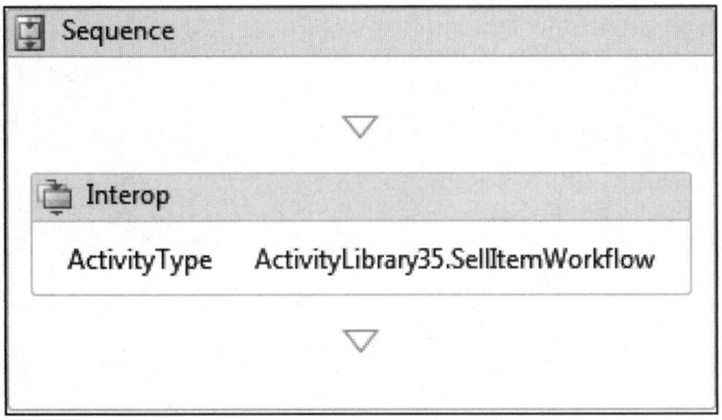

Figure 18-9. SellItem35Interop workflow

Testing the Workflow

To test the workflow, create a new Workflow Console application named `SellItem`. Add this new project to the solution for this chapter. Delete the `Workflow1.xaml` file since it won't be used. Change the target for the project to .NET Framework 4 instead of the Client Profile, which is the default. Add these references to the project:

- `ActivityLibrary` (project reference)

- `ActivityLibrary35` (project reference)

Add code to the `Program.cs` file to execute the `SellItem35Interop` several times. Each time the workflow is executed with a different set of test values designed to test the rules in the set. These are the same test values used for this example in my *Pro WF: Windows Workflow in .NET 3.5* book. Here is the complete code for the `Program.cs` file:

```csharp
using System;
using System.Activities;
using System.Collections.Generic;
using ActivityLibrary;

namespace SellItem
{
    class Program
    {
        static void Main(string[] args)
        {
            TestWorkflow(new SellItem35Interop());
        }

        private static void TestWorkflow(Activity activity)
        {
            ActivityLibrary35.SalesItem item = new ActivityLibrary35.SalesItem();

            //execute the workflow with parameters that will
            //result in a normal priced item and shipping
            Console.WriteLine("Executing SellItemWorkflow");
            item = new ActivityLibrary35.SalesItem();
            item.ItemPrice = 10.00;
            item.Quantity = 4;
            item.IsNewCustomer = false;
            ExecuteInteropWorkflow(activity, item);
            Console.WriteLine("Completed SellItemWorkflow\n\r");

            //execute the workflow again with parameters that
            //will cause a discounted price and shipping
            Console.WriteLine("Executing SellItemWorkflow (Discounts)");
            item = new ActivityLibrary35.SalesItem();
            item.ItemPrice = 10.00;
            item.Quantity = 11;
            item.IsNewCustomer = false;
            ExecuteInteropWorkflow(activity, item);
            Console.WriteLine("Completed SellItemWorkflow (Discounts)\n\r");

            //execute the workflow once more, this time with the
            //IsNewCustomer property set to true
            Console.WriteLine("Executing SellItemWorkflow (New Customer)");
            item = new ActivityLibrary35.SalesItem();
            item.ItemPrice = 10.00;
            item.Quantity = 11;
            item.IsNewCustomer = true;
            ExecuteInteropWorkflow(activity, item);
            Console.WriteLine("Completed SellItemWorkflow (New Customer)\n\r");
        }
```

```
        private static void ExecuteInteropWorkflow(Activity activity,
            ActivityLibrary35.SalesItem item)
        {
            DisplaySalesItem(item, "Before");
            WorkflowInvoker.Invoke(activity,
                new Dictionary<String, Object>
                {
                    {"ArgItem", item}
                });
            DisplaySalesItem(item, "After");
        }

        private static void DisplaySalesItem(
            ActivityLibrary35.SalesItem item, String message)
        {
            Console.WriteLine("{0}:", message);
            Console.WriteLine("  ItemPrice    = {0:C}", item.ItemPrice);
            Console.WriteLine("  Quantity     = {0}", item.Quantity);
            Console.WriteLine("  OrderTotal   = {0:C}", item.OrderTotal);
            Console.WriteLine("  Shipping     = {0:C}", item.Shipping);
            Console.WriteLine("  IsNewCustomer = {0}", item.IsNewCustomer);
        }
    }
}
```

After building the project, you can run it. Here are the correct results that you should see when you run this project:

```
Executing SellItemWorkflow

Before:

    ItemPrice    = $10.00

    Quantity     = 4

    OrderTotal   = $0.00

    Shipping     = $0.00

    IsNewCustomer = False

After:

    ItemPrice    = $10.00

    Quantity     = 4

    OrderTotal   = $40.00
```

```
  Shipping      = $3.80

  IsNewCustomer = False

Completed SellItemWorkflow


Executing SellItemWorkflow (Discounts)

Before:

  ItemPrice     = $10.00

  Quantity      = 11

  OrderTotal    = $0.00

  Shipping      = $0.00

  IsNewCustomer = False

After:

  ItemPrice     = $10.00

  Quantity      = 11

  OrderTotal    = $104.50

  Shipping      = $0.00

  IsNewCustomer = False

Completed SellItemWorkflow (Discounts)


Executing SellItemWorkflow (New Customer)

Before:

  ItemPrice     = $10.00

  Quantity      = 11

  OrderTotal    = $0.00
```

```
  Shipping      = $0.00

  IsNewCustomer = True

After:

  ItemPrice     = $10.00

  Quantity      = 11

  OrderTotal    = $94.50

  Shipping      = $10.45

  IsNewCustomer = True

Completed SellItemWorkflow (New Customer)
```

Executing Rules Using a Custom Activity

In addition to using the `PolicyActivity` to apply rules, WF 3.x also exposes the classes associated with the rules engine. This enables you to execute the rules engine directly from a WF 4 custom activity. This offers you an alternative to using the `Interop` activity to execute rules as you saw in the previous example.

In this example, you will develop a custom WF 4 activity that executes the WF 3.x rules engine in code instead of using the `Interop` activity. The same `RuleSet` that you defined for the previous example will also be used in this example.

You will complete these steps to implement this example:

1. Implement a `SalesItem` wrapper class.

2. Implement a new `ApplyRules` custom WF 4 activity.

3. Declare a test WF 4 workflow.

Implementing a SalesItemWrapper

First, add a new class named `SalesItemWrapper` to the `ActivityLibrary35` project. This simple wrapper class is needed only in order to use the same `RuleSet` as was used in the previous example. In that example, the rules were defined to reference the `SalesItem` property of the current target object. For example, the condition for the first rule is `this.SalesItem.Quantity > 10`.

This means that the rule expects an object with a `SalesItem` property. In the previous example, that object was the WF 3.5 workflow. In this example, the goal is to execute the same set of rules against an instance of the `SalesItem` class directly, without invoking the WF 3.5 workflow.

The `SalesItemWrapper` class solves this problem by standing in for the workflow and providing the `SalesItem` property that the rules expect. If you are defining sets of rules to be executed outside the WF 3.x environment, you will likely design them to operate upon the target object directly.

Here is the code for the `SalesItemWrapper` class:

```
using System;

namespace ActivityLibrary35
{
    [Serializable]
    public class SalesItemWrapper
    {
        public SalesItem SalesItem { get; set; }
    }
}
```

Implementing the ApplyRules Activity

Add a new Code activity to the `ActivityLibrary` project, and name it `ApplyRules`. This activity will retrieve a serialized `RuleSet` from a file and apply it to the target object. It will execute the WF 3.*x* rules engine directly instead of using the `Interop` activity.

This activity will need to reference the WF 3.*x* assembly that contains the rules engine, so you'll need to add the `System.Workflow.Activities` assembly to the `ActivityLibrary` project references.

Here is the code that you need to implement the `ApplyRules` activity:

```
using System;
using System.Activities;
using System.IO;
using System.Workflow.Activities.Rules;
using System.Workflow.ComponentModel.Compiler;
using System.Workflow.ComponentModel.Serialization;
using System.Xml;

namespace ActivityLibrary
{
```

This activity is implemented as an asynchronous generic activity. The generic type that you specify when you use this activity identifies the type of the target object that the rules will be applied against. In addition to an argument for the `Target` object, the `RulesFilePath` argument identifies the file containing the serialized rules. The `RuleSetName` argument specifies the `RuleSet` within the file that should be applied to the `Target` object. A collection of validation errors is made available as an output argument.

```
    public class ApplyRules<T> : AsyncCodeActivity
    {
        public InOutArgument<T> Target { get; set; }
        public InArgument<String> RulesFilePath { get; set; }
        public InArgument<String> RuleSetName { get; set; }
        public OutArgument<ValidationErrorCollection> Errors { get; set; }

        protected override IAsyncResult BeginExecute(
            AsyncCodeActivityContext context, AsyncCallback callback, object state)
        {
```

```
        T target = Target.Get(context);
        String path = RulesFilePath.Get(context);
        String setName = RuleSetName.Get(context);

        Func<T, String, String, ValidationErrorCollection> asyncWork =
            ApplyRuleSet;
        context.UserState = asyncWork;
        return asyncWork.BeginInvoke(target, path, setName, callback, state);
    }

    protected override void EndExecute(
        AsyncCodeActivityContext context, IAsyncResult result)
    {
        ValidationErrorCollection errors =
            ((Func<T, String, String, ValidationErrorCollection>)
                context.UserState).EndInvoke(result);
        if (errors != null)
        {
            Errors.Set(context, errors);
        }
    }
```

The private `ApplyRuleSet` method does the real work of this activity. It retrieves and deserializes the rule definition and then locates the specified `RuleSet`. If it exists, the `RuleSet` is validated and then executed against the target object. Any validation errors are returned in the output argument.

```
    private ValidationErrorCollection ApplyRuleSet(T target,
        String path, String setName)
    {
        ValidationErrorCollection errors = null;

        WorkflowMarkupSerializer serializer = new WorkflowMarkupSerializer();

        RuleSet rs = null;
        if (File.Exists(path))
        {
            using (XmlTextReader reader = new XmlTextReader(path))
            {
                RuleDefinitions rules =
                    serializer.Deserialize(reader) as RuleDefinitions;
                if (rules != null && rules.RuleSets.Contains(setName))
                {
                    rs = rules.RuleSets[setName];
                }
            }
        }

        if (rs == null)
        {
```

```
            throw new ArgumentException(String.Format(
                "Unable to retrieve RuleSet {0} from {1}", setName, path));
        }

        RuleValidation val = new RuleValidation(target.GetType(), null);
        if (!rs.Validate(val))
        {
            errors = val.Errors;
            return errors;
        }

        RuleEngine rulesEngine = new RuleEngine(rs, val);
        rulesEngine.Execute(target);
        return errors;
    }
  }
}
```

Build the `ActivityLibrary` project before continuing with the next step.

Declaring a Test Workflow

Add a new Activity to the `ActivityLibrary` project, and name it `SellItemApplyRules`. This workflow will use the new `ApplyRules` custom activity to execute the same set of rules that you used in the previous example against a `SalesItem` object. Please follow these steps to complete the declaration of this workflow:

1. Define an `InOutArgument` named `ArgItem`. The argument type is `ActivityLibrary35.SalesItem`.

2. Add a `Sequence` activity as the root of the activity.

3. Add these variables to the workflow that are scoped by the `Sequence` activity:

Name	Variable Type	Scope	Default Value
errors	System.Workflow.ComponentModel. Compiler.ValidationErrorCollection	Sequence	
salesItemWrapper	ActivityLibrary35.SalesItemWrapper	Sequence	New SalesItemWrapper With {.SalesItem = ArgItem}

4. Add an `ApplyRules` activity to the `Sequence` activity. Set the generic type to `ActivityLibrary.SalesItemWrapper`. Set the `RuleSetName` property to `"CalculateItemTotals"` and the `RulesFilePath` to `"..\..\..\ActivityLibrary35\SellItemWorkflow.rules"`. This should be the correct relative path to the rules file that you used in the previous example. Set the `Target` property to `salesItemWrapper` and the `Errors` property to `errors`.

5. Add an If activity below the ApplyRules activity. Set the If.Condition property to errors IsNot Nothing.

6. Add a ForEach<T> activity to the If.Then property. Select System.Workflow.ComponentModel.Compiler.ValidationError as the generic type.

7. Add a WriteLine activity as the child of the ForEach<T> activity. Set the Text property to item.ErrorText.

Figure 18-10 shows the completed workflow.

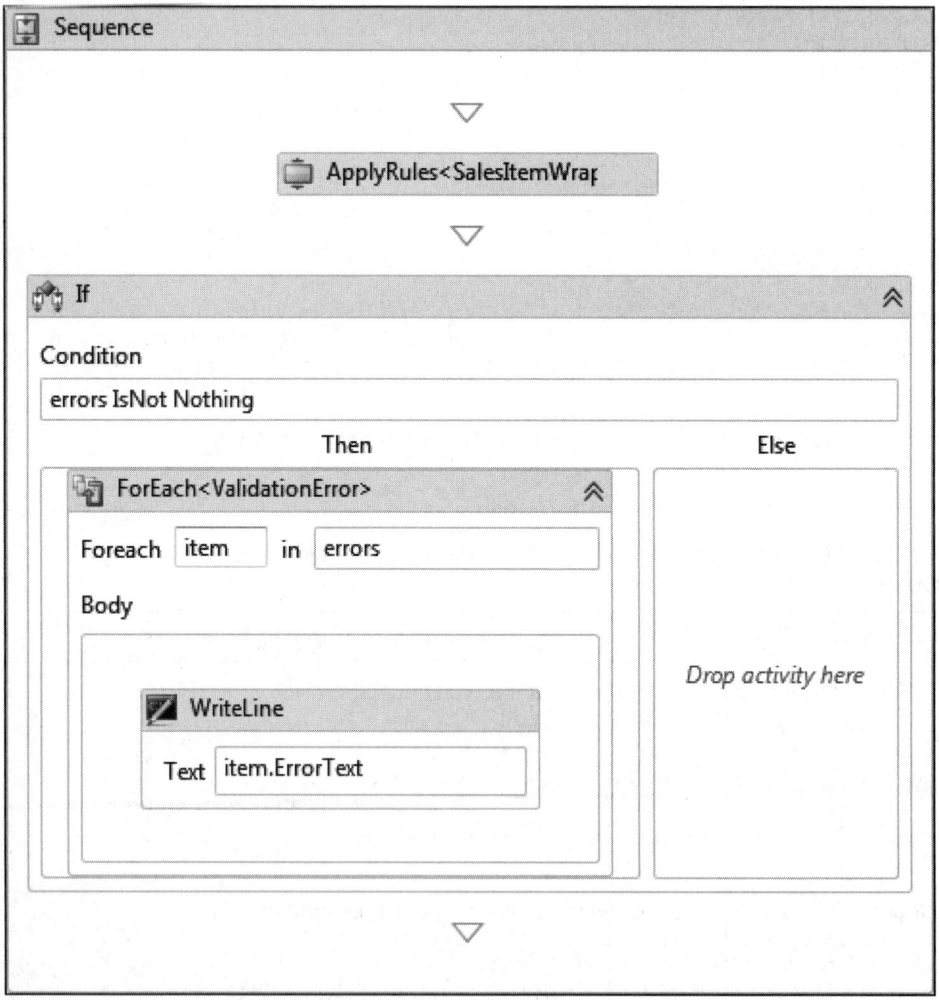

Figure 18-10. SellItemApplyRules workflow

Testing the Workflow

You can test the new workflow using the same `SellItem` project that you used for the previous example. You simply need to change the workflow type that is executed to `SellItemApplyRules` like this:

```
TestWorkflow(new SellItemApplyRules());
```

After building the solution, you should now be able to run the `SellItem` project. The results should look exactly like those from the previous example.

Summary

This chapter presented migration strategies for dealing with existing WF 3.0 or 3.5 applications. A brief overview of the migration strategies was presented followed by a discussion of the `Interop` activity. Several examples were presented that demonstrated how to use this activity to execute a single WF 3.x activity or an entire workflow. The `Interop` activity was also used to execute WF 3.x workflows that use the `ExternalDataExchangeService` for communication. The chapter concluded with two examples that demonstrate how to execute the WF 3.x rules engine from WF 4.

■ ■ ■

Glossary

aborting a workflow

An ungraceful and immediate teardown of a workflow instance. An aborted workflow that has been previously persisted can be loaded and resumed from its last persistence point. Aborting the workflow simply throws away everything since the last persistence point.

activity

The basic unit of composition within a workflow. An activity represents a single step in a tree of declared objects. Each activity can have its own set of input and output arguments and local variables and accomplishes some useful work.

Activity

The abstract base class for all other activity types in WF.

ActivityAction

A type-safe activity callback mechanism that allows you to pass 0–16 arguments with no return value. The target activity that is executed must match the argument signature of the `ActivityAction`. This class is derived from `ActivityDelegate`.

ActivityBuilder

A class that is designed to assist with the construction of activities. It enables the workflow designer to support the declaration of arguments and variables.

ActivityContext

A class that provides an activity with limited access to the WF runtime environment. The runtime environment includes the variables and arguments that are currently in scope for a single execution of an activity. This is the base class for the `CodeActivityContext` and `NativeActivityContext` classes that provide varying levels of access to the runtime environment.

ActivityDelegate

Represents a callback mechanism using an activity. This type allows you to define a type-safe callback for an activity. The callback activity to execute is specified at design time when the activity is used. This is the parent class of `ActivityAction` and `ActivityFunc`.

ActivityDesigner

A class that visually represents an activity on the workflow designer surface. You must derive from this class when you implement a custom designer for an activity.

ActivityFunc

A type-safe activity callback mechanism that allows you to pass 0–16 arguments with a return value. The `ActivityFunc` class is similar to the `ActivityAction` class except it supports a return value while `ActivityAction` does not. This class is derived from `ActivityDelegate`.

ActivityInstance

A class that represents the current runtime state of an activity.

arguments

Define the public inputs and outputs of an activity. The `Argument` class is the base for all arguments. Classes derived from this base (`InArgument`, `OutArgument`, `InOutArgument`) define and restrict the direction of data flowing into and out of an activity.

AsyncCodeActivity

An abstract base class that is used to implement an activity that performs work on a separate thread. This class is derived from the base `Activity` class.

asynchronous unit of work

A general category of work that an activity might perform. Activities in this category are designed to perform an atomic unit of work but are capable of doing so asynchronously on a separate thread. Although these activities can use a separate thread for part of their work, that work must execute in a relatively short period of time. They are not designed for long-running operations that might take days to complete. The work they perform should be atomic, completing entirely during a single execution of the activity.

atomic unit of work

A general category of work that an activity might perform. This kind of activity encapsulates the logic to perform a unit of work synchronously on the workflow thread. The unit of work that is performed is atomic in the sense that it is completed entirely during a single execution of the activity. It doesn't need to suspend execution and wait for external input. It is short-lived and doesn't perform time-consuming operations. It executes synchronously on the workflow thread and doesn't create or use other threads.

binding

In WCF, a binding describes how messages are exchanged between systems using an endpoint. It is a named stack containing the transport, encoding, and protocols that determine the way that WCF processes inbound and outbound messages on an endpoint.

bookmark

A general mechanism to temporarily suspend execution of an activity until external input is received. When the external input is available, the bookmark is resumed. Bookmarks can also be configured to not block execution of an activity and to be resumed multiple times.

CacheMetadata

A method of the `Activity` class that creates and validates a full description of the activity. The description includes the arguments, variables, child activities, child delegates, and other implementation details.

canceled activity state

The state that an activity transitions to when cancellation has been requested.

canceling a workflow

The most graceful way to stop execution of an instance. Canceling a workflow triggers any optional cancellation and compensation logic that you have declared within the workflow. It leaves the workflow in the canceled state. A canceled workflow cannot be resumed.

closed activity state

The state that an activity transitions to when it has successfully completed its work. An activity in the closed state cannot be resumed.

CLR

See Common Language Runtime.

CodeActivity

An abstract base class that is used to implement a custom activity. The work that is performed within the custom activity should be short-lived and execute synchronously on the workflow thread. This class is derived from the base `Activity` class.

Common Language Runtime

The managed runtime environment that permits cross-language .NET development.

compensation

The general mechanism by which work that has already been completed is undone.

composite activities

Activities that are designed to support one or more child activities or activity delegates.

composition

A way to implement new activities by combining existing child activities to serve a new specialized purpose.

confirmation

A mechanism to signal that an activity is past the point of execution where compensation is allowed or necessary.

constraints

Custom classes that externally perform validation on an activity.

content-based correlation

Correlation that is based on one or more selectable data elements within a message. This type of correlation uses application data to correlate messages rather than data that is provided by the infrastructure.

context-based correlation

Correlation that is based on fixed and well-known headers in the message that are provided by the infrastructure.

control flow activities

A general category of activities that allow you to make branching and looping decisions with a workflow.

correlation

A mechanism used to associate messages with the correct workflow service instance. Correlation is also used to associate multiple messaging activities with each other within a workflow.

data contract

In WCF, a data contract is one that permits the definition of messages with multiple parameters.

declarative model

An implementation model that defines the work to be performed using a tree of activities. The relationships between the activities determines the sequence and conditions under which each activity is executed. In a declarative model, imperative code is not used to control the flow of execute between activities.

duplex message exchange pattern

One of the WCF message exchange patterns supported by WF. When using this pattern, each side of the conversation can send out-of-band messages directly to the other side.

durable delay

Refers to a declared delay in a workflow that is persisted to storage during the delay period. When the delay expires, the workflow is reloaded from storage, and processing can continue. The delay is durable in the sense that it is not lost when the workflow is unloaded from memory.

DynamicActivity

An activity class that is used to dynamically construct activities at runtime rather than at design time. A `DynamicActivity` cannot be compiled into a CLR type. This class is derived from the base `Activity` class.

EditingContext

A class that is used by the `WorkflowDesigner` to manage internal designer state. Managed state includes services and context items.

endpoint

In WCF, a place where messages can be sent or received. All messages in WCF are exchanged between endpoints.

ETW

See Event Tracing for Windows.

Event Tracing for Windows

An enhanced Windows tracing facility that provides greater management and viewing of trace events.

executing activity state

The state that all activities begin in. This state indicates that an activity has not yet completed its work. An activity remains in the executing state when it becomes idle.

expressions

A general-purpose mechanism to declaratively execute some logic and return a value. Expressions in WF include any activities that return a single value. Expressions allow you to declare code that assigns a value to a property, saves a value to a workflow variable, and so on. Expressions are the small bits of glue code within the declarative workflow model.

extension

See workflow extension.

external data exchange

A WF 3.*x* mechanism that is used to facilitate communication between the host application and a workflow instance.

faulted activity state

The state that an activity transitions to when an unhandled exception has been thrown or when the activity has been terminated. An activity in the faulted state cannot be resumed.

flow chart modeling style

A style of workflow authoring that uses direct connections between activities to control the flow of execution. Looping and branching decisions are made using activity connections. This is in contrast with the procedural modeling style that adds activities as children of flow-control activities to control the flow of execution.

Flowchart

An activity that defines the flow chart modeling style. Child activities can be added to this activity, and direct connections can be defined between the activities to control the flow of execution.

FlowDecision

An activity that can be used as a child of the `Flowchart` activity to make branching decisions. This activity enables branching of the flow of execution based on the result of a Boolean condition.

FlowSwitch<T>

An activity that can be used as a child of the `Flowchart` activity to make branching decisions based on the value of an expression. A different flow of execution can be defined for each possible value of the expression.

human interaction

A general category of workflows that require interaction with humans. Workflows of this type are typically capable of long-running execution because of the unpredictability of the human interactions.

instance store

The persistence mechanism that is used by WF 4. Regardless of the actual persistence medium, all persistence is accomplished using a component known as an *instance store*.

InstanceStore

The base class that all instance store components must derive from.

Interop

An activity that is capable of wrapping an existing WF 3.*x* activity for execution in the WF 4 runtime environment.

Lambda expressions

An expression syntax that is used to define and execute anonymous functions.

Language Integrated Query

A set of extensions to the .NET Framework that provide native language support for queries. Support is currently available for C# and Visual Basic.

LINQ

See Language Integrated Query.

LINQ to SQL

LINQ extensions that provide the ability to query and manage data in a SQL database.

long-running unit of work

A general category of work that an activity might perform. This kind of activity is designed to perform work that may take a very long time to complete. It may perform part of its work and then wait until some external input is received. While it is waiting, the activity is idle and is not occupying the workflow thread. WF supports this long-running behavior using a concept called *bookmarks*.

MEP

See message exchange pattern.

message contract

In WCF, a message contract is one that supports only a single argument with a high degree of control over the shape of the actual message.

message exchange pattern

An established pattern for the exchange of messages between applications. Well-known patterns include One-way, Request/Response, and Duplex.

MetadataStore

A workflow designer runtime component that maps activity types to the designers that will be used for each activity.

modeling style

Describes the design metaphors that are used when you declare an activity or workflow. Two modeling styles that are available with WF are the procedural and flowchart modeling styles.

ModelItem

In the workflow designer, a `ModelItem` represents a single activity that is capable of being maintained. The workflow designer represents the activities in a design as a tree of `ModelItem` objects.

NativeActivity

An abstract base activity class that permits full and unrestricted access to all available functionality of the WF runtime. Included is the ability to schedule the execution of other activities and delegates and to create and resume bookmarks. This class is derived from the base `Activity` class.

one-way message exchange pattern

One of the message exchange patterns supported by WF. When using this pattern, messages are sent to an endpoint without any expectation of a response. One-way messages are also known as fire-and-forget messages since there is no direct confirmation that the message was received and acted upon.

parallel execution

Describes the ability of WF to interleave the execution of multiple scheduled activities.

persistence

The ability to save the current state of an activity or workflow to a durable store and reload it for execution at a later time. Activities are typically persisted when they are idle and waiting for external input. The activity is reloaded from the durable store when the external input is available.

PersistenceParticipant

The base class for any classes that extend the standard persistence mechanism. Classes that derive from this base class can participate in persistence by adding additional data elements to be saved and loaded.

procedural modeling style

A style of workflow authoring that uses familiar flow-control constructs such as `if`, `while`, and `switch` to control the flow of execution between activities. In this modeling style, the activities to execute are added as children of the flow-control activity.

request/response message exchange pattern

One of the message exchange patterns supported by WF. When using this pattern, messages are organized into pairs. After sending a request message to an endpoint, the requesting application waits for the receipt of a response message.

rules

In WF 3.x, rules are statements of fact concerning some data. WF 3.x includes a general rules engine that allows you to execute multiple rules (see `RuleSet`) against data.

RuleSet

In WF 3.x, this class defines multiple rules that are designed to be applied to data as a single set.

scheduling

The mechanism by which activities are executed. Child activities are not directly executed by their parent activity. Their execution is scheduled with the workflow runtime. The workflow runtime manages a queue of work items to determine the sequence in which activities are executed.

state machine

A WF 3.x modeling style that defines a workflow as a set of states and possible events. The events define interactions that the workflow is capable of handling while it is in each state. Transitions between states are also modeled.

system interaction

A general category of workflow that interacts with other parts of the application and does not require human interaction.

terminating a workflow

Stops execution of a workflow but does not trigger cancellation and compensation logic. The workflow instance is left in the faulted state and cannot be resumed.

tracking

A mechanism that enables instrumentation of workflows. Detailed tracking data is available for each activity in a workflow.

tracking participant

A component that is registered with the tracking system and receives a flow of tracking records.

tracking profile

A configurable profile that filters the tracking records that are passed to each tracking participant.

tracking record

The raw tracking data that is produced by the tracking system, filtered by a tracking profile, and consumed by one or more tracking participants.

transaction

A construct that guarantees the atomicity and integrity of work that is performed, especially to a database.

validation

In WF, validation ensures the correct usage of an activity. Arguments may be validated for correctness, and the relationships between the activity and other activities in the model may be examined.

variable

Defines a named storage location within an activity. Variables are typically used for the storage of intermediate results within a workflow. Variable values are scoped to a single execution of an activity.

variable scoping

Describes the characteristic of variables that limits their visibility and access to the activity that defined them and any child activities.

VB Expressions

Expressions that are implemented using Visual Basic syntax. See expressions.

WCF

See Windows Communication Foundation.

WF

See Windows Workflow Foundation.

WF 3.*x*

Refers to versions 3.0 and 3.5 of the Windows Workflow Foundation. This version of WF is not covered in this book.

WF 4

Refers to version 4.0 of the Windows Workflow Foundation and the subject of this book.

Windows Communication Foundation

A framework that is provided with the .NET Framework to enable message-based communication within or between applications.

Windows Workflow Foundation

A framework that is provided with the .NET Framework to enable developers to implement workflow-based applications.

workflow

An ordered series of steps that accomplish some defined purpose according to a set of rules.

workflow extension

A class that can provide functionality for one or more workflow instances and the host application. A custom workflow extension can provide any functionality that is required by your application. A single thread-safe instance of an extension can be shared by multiple workflow instances, or a new instance of an extension can be created for each workflow instance.

workflow services

WCF services that are implemented as a WF 4 workflow.

WorkflowApplication

A class that allows you to execute an activity with complete access to the features of the WF runtime. This class includes the ability to use features such as persistence, extensions, and bookmarks.

WorkflowDesigner

The class that encapsulates the workflow designer functionality. This is the primary class that enables rehosting of the workflow designer in your own application.

WorkflowInvoker

A class that provides a simplified way to execute an activity as if it were a method. The class provides limited runtime functionality.

WorkflowServiceHost

The class that enables self-hosting of WCF-based workflow services within your own application.

Xaml

A declarative XML-based markup language that is used by WF to declare activities and workflows.

Xamlx

A type of file that contains a Xaml declaration of a workflow service.

■ ■ ■

Comparing WF 3.x to WF 4

WF 3.x to WF 4 Architectural Differences

The following table summarizes the major architectural differences between WF 3.x and WF 4.

Category	WF 3.x	WF 4
Authoring styles	WF 3.x supports sequential or state machine workflows, but the two styles cannot be mixed. If you start with a sequential workflow, you can't mix state machine activities in the same workflow.	WF 4 supports procedural and flowchart modeling styles out of the box. Other modeling styles (such as state machine) may be provided in the future. Modeling styles are determined by the individual activities and are not restrictive based on the starting workflow type. Styles can be mixed within a single activity or workflow.
Code-beside	WF 3.x requires a code-beside file for property and variable definition and for event handling.	WF 4 does not require or support a code-beside file. Variables and arguments are fully declarative. Activity delegates can be used to execute callback functionality.
Conditions	WF 3.x supports Boolean conditions that are implemented in code or as declarative rule conditions.	WF 4 uses expressions to define Boolean conditions.
Confirmation	WF 3.x supports compensation but does not support confirmation.	WF 4 supports compensation and also supports confirmation. Confirmation is used to indicate that the workflow has progressed past the point where compensation is required or available as an option.

Continued

Category	WF 3.x	WF 4
Confirmation	WF 3.x supports compensation but does not support confirmation.	WF 4 supports compensation and also supports confirmation. Confirmation is used to indicate that the workflow has progressed past the point where compensation is required or available as an option.
Data model	WF 3.x manages data within an activity or workflow using private variables and public properties. The properties can be CLR types or dependency properties. Individual public property values can be used as input or output parameters or as temporary storage within a workflow.	WF 4 introduces an explicit data model that uses variables for storage within an activity and arguments for parameters.
Dynamic updates	WF 3.x supports the ability to dynamically alter the definition of a workflow after it has started execution.	WF 4 does not support dynamic updates to executing workflows.
Executing workflows	Workflows are executed using the `WorkflowRuntime` and `WorkflowInstance` classes.	The `WorkflowApplication` class is used to execute a workflow and provides access to all features of the workflow runtime. The `WorkflowInvoker` class provides a much simplified way to execute workflows with limited access to runtime features.
File Types	WF 3.x uses Xoml files for code separation activities and workflows. The Xoml file contains the declarative portion of the workflow and a separate code-beside file contains properties, variables, and event handler code.	WF 4 uses Xaml files for declarative activities and workflows. The Xaml file contains the complete declaration of an activity, so a separate code-beside file is not required. Xamlx files are used to declare workflow services.
Flowchart	WF 3.x does not support a free-form flowchart modeling style. Workflow types supported in WF 3.x include sequential and state machine.	WF 4 supports a Flowchart activity that allows free-form organization of the activity tree. The flow of control is managed using direct links between activities.
Flowed transactions	WF 3.x does not support flowing an external transaction into a workflow.	WF 4 supports flowing an external transaction into a workflow.

Category	WF 3.*x*	WF 4
Host communication	Workflow queues are used for communication between the host application and a workflow instance.	Bookmarks are used for communication between the host application and a workflow instance.
Parameter direction	In WF 3.*x*, parameters are defined as public properties. There is no explicit indication of the direction of the parameter (input or output).	In WF 4, parameters are declared as arguments. Each argument has an explicit direction (in, out, or in/out).
Parameters	Parameters to an activity or workflow must be defined as public CLR or dependency properties. These properties must be defined in code.	Parameters to an activity or workflow are declaratively added to the model as arguments. Arguments can also be added to code-based activities.
Passing values	Values may be passed between activities by directly binding a property of one activity to the property of another.	Use variables to define intermediate storage instead of directly binding the properties of one activity to another.
Rule engine	A general purpose rules engine is included with WF 3.*x*. This rules engine can be executed directly in code or from the workflow model using the `PolicyActivity`.	WF 4 does not include a rules engine. However, the WF 3.*x* engine can be invoked directly in code from a custom WF 4 activity. The WF 3.*x* `PolicyActivity` can be invoked using the `Interop` activity.
Runtime	A single instance of the `WorkflowRuntime` class can be created and used to execute multiple workflow instances. The `WorkflowServiceHost` class is used to manage multiple instances of workflows that use WCF services.	A separate instance of the `WorkflowApplication` class is created for each workflow instance. The `WorkflowServiceHost` class is used to manage multiple instances of workflow services.
Services	Custom services may be developed and added to the workflow runtime. This makes their functionality available to the host application and workflow instances.	Custom workflow extensions can be developed and added to the two full-featured hosting environments (`WorkflowApplication` and `WorkflowServiceHost`).

Continued

Category	WF 3.x	WF 4
Specialized base class	In WF 3.x, you can use one of the available base classes to develop custom activities in code. However, these base classes (for example `SequenceActivity` or `CompositeActivity`) all provide the same basic access to the workflow runtime. They each provide a varying feature set, but they are not designed to target a particular type of custom activity in the same way as the WF 4 base classes.	WF 4 provides multiple activity classes that can be used as the base class when you develop custom activities in code. Each base class is designed to meet the targeted needs of a particular type of custom activity and provides just enough access to the workflow runtime for that activity type. Example base classes are `CodeActivity`, `AsyncCodeActivity`, and `NativeActivity`.
State machine	WF 3.x supports a state machine workflow type that can be used to declare event-driven state machine workflows.	WF 4 does not support a state machine. However, the `Flowchart` activity provides the flexibility to declare many types of workflows that would previously require a state machine. True state machine functionality is promised by Microsoft after WF 4 is released.
Tracking	The default persistence mechanism for workflow tracking is a SQL Server database.	The default output medium for workflow tracking is Event Tracing for Windows (ETW). Persistence to a SQL Server database requires the development of a custom `InstanceStore`.
Variable scope	Variables that are defined for a workflow are always in scope. All member variables of the workflow class are global and accessible to all activities of the workflow.	Variables have scope and can be declared only for activities that support them. Defined variables are visible and accessible only to the activity that defined them and its children.
WCF contracts	WCF contracts can be defined as an interface in code and then referenced by WF 3.x activities. WF 3.x also supports workflow-first authoring of WCF operations.	WCF contracts are inferred from the properties of message-related activities within the workflow model. This is similar to the workflow-first WCF authoring style that is supported by WF 3.x. Contract-first authoring and reuse of existing WCF contract interfaces is not supported in WF 4.

Category	WF 3.x	WF 4
Workflow model base	Different base classes are used depending on the purpose of the WF component. Activities, sequential workflows, and state machine workflows are considered different components and are not interchangeable.	All WF components that are part of the workflow model have a consistent base class (`Activity`). An activity can be a single small component that is used by a larger workflow, or it can represent the entire workflow. Components are completely interchangeable, blurring the lines between what is an activity and what is a workflow.
Workflow service hosting	Workflow services that expose WCF endpoints can be self-hosted using the `WorkflowServiceHost` class.	A WF 4 version of the `WorkflowServiceHost` class is used to host workflow services. Note: Even though the class is named the same as its 3.x counterpart, this is a different class.
Workflow state	State within a workflow is maintained using member variables that are defined for the workflow class in code.	Workflow variables are used to maintain state within a workflow. Variables are declaratively added to the workflow model. Variables can also be added to custom activities in code.

WF 3.x to WF 4 Activities

The following table compares the list of WF 3.x and WF 4 standard activities. In cases where there isn't an exact match between WF 3.x and WF 4, I list the closest match that could be used to provide similar functionality or solve a similar problem.

WF 3.x Activity	WF 4 Activity
	AddToCollection
	Assign
CallExternalMethodActivity	
CancellationHandlerActivity	CancellationScope
	ClearCollection
CodeActivity	

Continued

WF 3.*x* Activity	WF 4 Activity
CompensatableSequenceActivity	CompensableActivity
CompensatableTransactionScopeActivity	CompensableActivity
CompensateActivity	Compensate
CompensationHandlerActivity	CompensableActivity
ConditionedActivityGroup	
	Confirm
	CorrelationScope
DelayActivity	Delay
	DoWhile
EventDrivenActivity	PickBranch
EventHandlersActivity	
EventHandlingScopeActivity	
	ExistsInCollection
FaultHandlerActivity	
FaultHandlersActivity	
	Flowchart
	FlowDecision
	FlowSwitch
HandleExternalEventActivity	
IfElseActivity	If
IfElseBranchActivity	If

WF 3.x Activity	WF 4 Activity
	InitializeCorrelation
	Interop
	InvokeMethod
InvokeWebServiceActivity	Send, SendAndReceiveReply
InvokeWorkflowActivity	
ListenActivity	Pick
ParallelActivity	Parallel
	ParallelForEach
	Persist
PolicyActivity	
ReceiveActivity	Receive, ReceiveAndSendReply
	RemoveFromCollection
ReplicatorActivity	ForEach
	Rethrow
SendActivity	Send, SendAndReceiveReply
SequenceActivity	Sequence
SetStateActivity	
StateActivity	
StateFinalizationActivity	
StateInitializationActivity	
SuspendActivity	

Continued

WF 3.*x* Activity	WF 4 Activity
	Switch
SynchronizationScopeActivity	
TerminateActivity	TerminateWorkflow
ThrowActivity	Throw
	TransactedReceiveScope
TransactionScopeActivity	TransactionScope
	TryCatch
WebServiceFaultActivity	SendReply
WebServiceInputActivity	Receive
WebServiceOutputActivity	SendReply
WhileActivity	While

Index

∎ Symbols

[ ] square brackets, 58

∎ A

Abort method, 132, 138, 693

Aborted delegate, WorkflowApplication class and, 128

aborting activities, 693

aborting workflows, 849

AbortInstanceOnTransactionFailure property (TransactionScope activity), 540

Action delegate (C#), 127, 197

Action property (PickBranch activity), 105

activities, 2–44, 71–110, 849. *See also* workflows

   aborting, 693

   activity definition vs. activity instance, 55

   activity properties and, 634–645

   activity templates for, 683–685

   adding to Visual Studio Toolbox, 301

   base classes and, 23, 76

   cancelling, 564, 693

   categories of work and, 47, 72

   child. *See* child activities

   collection-related, 195–228

   command-line calculator sample application illustrating. *See* command-line calculator (sample application)

   composite, 74

   creating, workflow designer and, 756

   custom. *See* custom activities

   data flow of, 99

   declarative activity model and, 45

   defined, 2

   executing individually, 40

   Hello Workflow sample application illustrating, 5–17

   life cycle of, 55

   metadata store for, 633, 640–642

   parent. *See* parent activities

   procedural, 163–194

   standard. *See* standard activities

   state and, 57

   as synonymous with workflows, understanding, 46, 55

   terminating, 693, 858

   understanding, 71–78

   using, 97

WF 3.*x*, executing from Interop activity, 801, 806–842

workflow declaration and, 8–12, 17

Activities assembly, 7

Activity class, 16, 77, 849

DynamicActivity class and, 142, 741–747

shipping charges calculator sample application and, 89

activity templates, 683–685, 767

ActivityAction activity, 290–302

activity templates and, 683

custom designers and, 657–661

scheduling, 734–740

ActivityAction class, 195, 290, 849

delegates and, 290

properties of, 291

supporting ActivityAction and, 657

scheduling ActivityAction and, 734

ActivityBuilder class, 756, 765, 849

ActivityContext class, 56, 485, 849

ActivityDefinitionId property (TrackingProfile class), 575

ActivityDelegate class, 850

ActivityDesigner class, 630, 850

ActivityFunc class, 290, 850

ActivityInfo class, 571

ActivityInstance class, 56, 691, 850

ActivityMetaProperties property (Interop activity), 806

ActivityProperties property (Interop activity), 806

ActivityScheduledQuery, 577

ActivityScheduledRecord, 572, 577, 598

ActivityState class, 572

ActivityStateQuery, 576, 594

ActivityStateRecord, 571, 576

ActivityType property (Interop activity), 806

ActivityValidationServices class, 661, 663, 680

ActivityXamlServices class, 142–144

AddBaseAddress method, 362

AddExtension method (WorkflowApplication class), 129

AddImplementationVariable method, 715

addition case, Switch activity and, 30

AdditionalConstraints property (ValidationSettings class), 663, 680

addresses, endpoints and, 316

AddServiceEndpoint method, 362

AddToCollection activity, 101, 109, 198

AddToDictionary activity, 214, 215

AddValidationError method, 667

AdventureWorks SQL Server sample database, 508–529

downloading/installing, 509

LINQ to SQL for accessing, 510

tracking workflows and, 579

Annotations property (TrackingRecord class), 568

annotations, to tracking records, 568, 597

anonymous functions, Lambda expressions and, 93

App.config file

credit approval sample workflow service and, 400

order processing sample workflow service and, 344, 346, 359

order shipment sample workflow service and, 384, 388

self-hosting workflow services and, 366

shopping cart sample workflow and, 440, 455, 464

tracking profiles read from, 575, 623–626

WorkflowControlEndpoint and, 480

applications, 35–37

debugging, 37

external, guidelines for workflow interaction with, 266

quitting, 36

running. *See* running applications

workflow persistence and, 416

Arg prefix, 18, 26

ArgExpression argument, 25, 235

Argument Editor, 18, 25

argument properties, 21

ArgumentException, 21

arguments, 75, 850

activity data flow and, 99

defining, 24, 25, 235

DesignerHost sample application, 796

dictionaries and, 118

properties and, 118

shipping charges calculator sample application and, 84

Arguments button (workflow designer), 10, 18

ArgumentToExpressionConverter class, 631, 637

arithmetic operations, Switch activity and, 29

ASP.NET web applications, invoking workflows from, 145–149

assemblies, 51

Assign activity, 29, 101, 107

expressions and, 632

vs. InvokeMethod activity, 222

AsyncCodeActivity class, 47, 73, 76, 850

inventory lookup sample and, 189

shipping charges calculator sample application and, 94

suspending persistence and, 419

AsyncCodeActivityContext class, 56

asynchronous unit of work, 73, 850

atomic unit of work, 73, 411, 850

Attributes property (ActivityBuilder class), 756

AutoResetEvent, 123, 125, 134, 273

■ B

base classes, 23, 76

generic/nongeneric versions of, 76

HostingDemoActivity sample and, 121

BasicHttpBinding, 340

BeginCancel method, WorkflowApplication class and, 132

BeginExecute method

inventory lookup sample and, 190

shipping charges calculator sample application and, 94

BeginInvoke method, 486

shipping charges calculator sample application and, 95

WorkflowInvoker class and, 113, 122, 124

BeginInvokeCallback method, 125

BeginLoad method (WorkflowApplication class), 130

BeginOnLoad method (PersistenceIOParticipant class), 471

BeginOnSave method (PersistenceIOParticipant class), 471

BeginPersist method (WorkflowApplication class), 130

BeginResumeBookmark method (WorkflowApplication class), 132

BeginRun method (WorkflowApplication class), 130, 140

BeginTerminate method (WorkflowApplication class), 132

BeginTrack method (TrackingParticipant class), 605

BeginTryCommand (InstanceStore class), 484, 486

BeginUnload method (WorkflowApplication class), 132

behaviors

workflow services and, 412

WorkflowServiceHost persistence and, 443

bindings, 851

endpoints and, 316

migration and, 805

properties and, 297

Web.config file and, 342

workflow services and, 316

Body property

CancellationScope activity, 108, 564

CompensableActivity, 108, 549

DoWhile activity, 104, 166

ForEach activity, 105, 195

ParallelForEach activity, 196

TransactionScope activity, 540

While activity, 104, 166

BookmarkCallback delegate, 267

BookmarkOptions enum, 692, 747

BookmarkResumptionQuery, 577

BookmarkResumptionRecord, 572, 577

bookmarks, 49, 266–276, 851

BookmarkResumptionQuery and, 577

BookmarkResumptionRecord and, 572

long-running unit of work and, 74

migration and, 805

nonblocking, 747, 748

parent/child activities and, 692

Pick/PickBranch activities and, 302–312

shopping cart sample workflow and, 429

workflow instances and, 131

Boolean conditions, evaluating/testing, 690, 702, 726

Branches property (Parallel activity), 105, 176

branching decisions

    decision-making constructs for, 164

    procedural modeling style and, 2, 3, 29

breakpoints, 37

building blocks, workflows and, 97

■C

C#

    expression support for, 68

    vs. Visual Basic, 58–62

C# events, vs. delegates, 128

CacheMetadata method, 658, 851

    configuring metadata and, 688

    validation code and, 662, 667

CallExternalMethodActivity

    ExternalDataExchangeService and, 823

    Interop activity and, 807, 823

Cancel method, 463

    child cancellations and, 693

    WorkflowApplication class, 132, 137

CancelChild method (NativeActivityContext class), 693, 728

CancelChild method (NativeActivityFaultContext class), 692

CancelChildren method (NativeActivityContext class), 693

CancelHandler property (CancellationScope activity), 108

Canceled state, 57, 851

cancellation requests, 693

CancellationHandler property

    CancellationScope activity, 564

    CompensableActivity, 549

CancellationScope activity, 101, 108, 564

CancelRequestedQuery, 577

CancelRequestedRecord, 572, 577

CanInduceIdle property, 267, 269

case sensitivity, Visual Basic and, 59

cases, arithmetic operations and, 30

Cases property (Switch activity), 165

Catches property (TryCatch activity), 109, 530

ChannelFactory class, 317

child activities, 9

    ActivityScheduledRecord and, 572, 598

    cancelling, 693

    CancelRequestedQuery and, 577

    CancelRequestedRecord and, 572

    exception handling for, 709–714

    execution completion and, 691

    execution properties and, 748

    execution repeated for, 702–709

    execution scheduling for, 690, 693–702, 714–725, 857

    Parallel activity and, 176, 194

parallel execution for, 725–734

Sequence activity and, 176

single/multiple, 649–657, 667–683

Switch activity and, 85

ClearCollection activity, 101, 109, 198, 218

ClearDictionary activity, 214, 217

client applications, implementing, 342–348

Close method (WorkflowServiceHost class), 362

Closed delegate, WorkflowApplication class and, 137

Closed event (WorkflowServiceHost class), 362

Closed state, 57, 851

Closing event (WorkflowServiceHost class), 362

CLR (Common Language Runtime). *See* runtime

CLR data types, variables and, 56, 75, 90

Code Activity template, 23

CodeActivity class, 23, 46, 64, 73, 851

access to the workflow runtime and, 76

migration and, 804

shipping charges calculator sample application and, 78

WF 3.*x* workflows and, 821

CodeActivityContext class, 24, 56

collapsed viewing mode, 645–649

collection activities, 198–211

collection category (of standard activities), 109

Collection property

AddToCollection activity, 109, 198

ClearCollection activity, 199

ExistsInCollection activity, 199

RemoveFromCollection activity, 198

collection-related activities, 195–228

CollectValues method (PersistenceParticipant class), 470

command-line calculator (sample application)

ActivityAction used with, 293–302

alternate extension used with, 286–289

bookmarks used with, 268–276

flowchart modeling style and, 233–241

hosting workflows and, 34

ParseCalculatorArgs activity for, 23, 27, 234, 236

procedural modeling style and, 22–43

running, 35

unit testing for, 39–43

workflow extensions used with, 276–286

Common Language Runtime. *See* runtime; CLR data types, variables and

communication, 265–312

CommunicationObject class, 361

CompensableActivity, 101, 108, 549–557

Compensate activity, 101, 108, 550, 557

compensation, 50, 549–563, 852

CompensableActivity and, 549–557

compensation handlers and, 57

triggering manually, 557–563

compensation activities (WF 3.*x*), Interop activity and, 807

CompensationHandler property (CompensableActivity), 549

Completed delegate, 127, 128, 273

CompletionCondition property

Parallel activity, 105, 176, 188, 194

ParallelForEach activity, 196

CompletionCallback callback delegate, 691

CompletionState property, 134

complex types, controlling serialization of, 323

composite activities, 9, 74, 852

composition, 852

Condition property, 106

Boolean conditions and, 702

child activity scheduling and, 714

DoWhile activity, 104, 166

If activity, 164

While activity, 104, 166

ConfigurationManager class, 623

configuring workflow services, 316

Confirm activity, 101, 108, 550

confirmation, 550, 852

ConfirmationHandler property (CompensableActivity), 549

consistency of database updates

compensation and, 549–557

TransactionScope activity for, 541–546, 549

Console class, 13

Constraint class, 662

Constraints property (ActivityBuilder class), 663, 756

constraints, for validation, 662, 669–679, 852

Content property, messaging activities and, 323, 324

content-based correlation, 325, 386–388, 852

ContentControl class, 630

ContentPresenter class, 648

context-based correlation, 369–385, 852

vs. content-based correlation, 325

guidelines for, 370

Context property (WorkflowDesigner class), 754, 757

ContextMenu property (WorkflowDesigner class), 754

control flow activities, 74, 852

control flow category (of standard activities), 104

correlation, 325, 370, 852

controlling, 325

workflow services and, 324

CorrelationHandle, 325

CorrelationInitializer class, 325

CorrelationScope activity, 101, 107, 326

CreateBookmark method (NativeActivityFaultContext class), 267, 692

CreateInstanceStore method, 436

CreateWorkflowOwnerCommand, 421, 422, 444, 485

credit approval (sample) workflow service, 388–405

    declaring, 390–393

    order processing sample workflow service modified for, 394–399

    testing, 402–405

custom activities, 23, 46, 71, 687–752

    adding to Sequence activity, 28

    asynchronous implementation for, 93–97

    authoring, ways of/steps for, 72, 78, 97

    cancelling, 564

    code authoring for, 78–84, 88–93

    custom tracking records and, 600–604

    CustomTrackingRecord for, 573

    designers for, 47, 629–634

    dictionary-related activities and, 213–222

    executing rules via, 842–847

    expression activities and, 64–66

    flowchart modeling style and, 248–253

    LINQ queries/updates and, 511–520

    migration and, 804

    order processing sample workflow service and, 349

    parents/children and, 687–725

    for shopping cart sample workflow, 428

    tracking workflows and, 580

    unit testing for, 39

    validation for, 661–683

    workflow building blocks and, 97

    workflow extensions and, 406

    Xaml authoring for, 84–88

CustomTrackingQuery, 578

CustomTrackingRecord, 573, 578

■ D

data

    categories of, activities and, 74

        data contracts and, 315, 322, 330, 852

        workflow persistence and, 419

data flow of activities, 99

data types, C# vs. Visual Basic, 61

DataContract attribute, 315, 322, 331, 419

DataMember attribute, 315, 322, 331, 419

debugging applications, 37, 48

decisions, 2, 22–38, 164, 233–241

declarative activity model, 45, 853

declarative workflow model, 2

declarative workflow services, tracking workflows and, 618–623

Default case, Switch activity and, 30, 32, 36

Default property (Switch activity), 165

definition, 55

Delay activity, 101, 107, 114

    adding to a workflow, 180

    Parallel activity and, 177

    SqlWorkflowInstanceStore persistence and, 422

    TimeSpan value and, 120

    workflow persistence and, 418

delegates

vs. C# events, 128

multiple instances of workflows and, 152

WorkflowApplication class and, 127

DeleteWorkflowOwnerCommand, 421, 422, 485

shopping cart sample workflow and, 437

WorkflowServiceHost and, 444

Designer attribute, 633, 639

commenting out for testing purposes, 642

using vs. metadata store, 642

DesignerHost (sample) application, 760–799

context menu, modifying for, 793–796

controls for, 761

currently selected activity, tracking, 790–793

implementing, 760–771

Save/SaveAs/Open operations and, 775–777

steps for implementing (list), 760

Toolbox for, 761–771, 780–788

DesignerMetadata class, 760, 764, 788

designers, 629–634

associating with activities, 633, 639–642

default, 636

expanded/collapsible, 645–649

shipping charges calculator sample application illustrating, 635–649

steps for creating (list), 634

design-time

custom activities and, 629–685

design-time audience and, 72

developers, activities and, 72

dictionaries

arguments and, 112, 118

dictionary-related activities for, 213–222

DisplayName property, 12

division case, Switch activity and, 31

domain-specific languages, workflow model and, 2

DoWhile activity, 101, 104, 165, 174, 632

downloads

AdventureWorks SQL Server sample database, 509

sample code for Pro WF (in .NET 3.5) book, 824

sample code for this book (Pro WF in .NET 4.0), 761

duplex message exchange pattern, 315, 388–405, 853

correlation and, 324

guidelines for, 389

durable delay, 853

DurableInstancingOptions property, 362

DynamicActivity class, 77, 142, 741–747, 853

DynamicActivityProperty class, 743

E

e-commerce shopping cart (sample) workflow. *See* shopping cart (sample) workflow

Else property (If activity), 104, 164

EditingContext class, 757, 853

EndExecute method

    inventory lookup sample and, 191

    shipping charges calculator sample application and, 94, 96

EndInvoke method, 486

    inventory lookup sample and, 191

    shipping charges calculator sample application and, 96

    WorkflowInvoker class, 113, 122, 124

EndOnLoad method (PersistenceIOParticipant class), 471

EndOnSave method (PersistenceIOParticipant class), 471

endpoints, 316, 479–483, 853

EndRun method (WorkflowApplication class), 130, 141

EndTrack method (TrackingParticipant class), 605

EndTryCommand (InstanceStore class), 484, 486

Enqueue method (WF 3.*x*), migration and, 805

EnqueueOnIdle (WF 3.*x*), migration and, 805

error handling category (of standard activities), 109

ETW (Event Tracing for Windows), 68, 565, 578, 853

ETW tracking participant, 579–591

EtwTrackingParticipant class, 277, 578

event logging, 578

Event Tracing for Windows (ETW), 68, 565, 578, 853

event tracking, EtwTrackingParticipant for, 277, 578

EventData element, tracking data and, 589

events

    custom, migration and, 805

    vs. queues, 286

EventTime property (TrackingRecord class), 568

examples. *See* samples

Executing state, 57

exception handling, 50, 57, 507–530

    ArgumentException and, 21

    FaultPropagationQuery for, 577

    FaultPropagationRecord for, 573

    multiple exceptions and, capturing, 537

    parents/children and, 692, 709–714

    Throw activity and, 32

    unhandled exceptions and, 507

    workflow services and, 409

Execute method, 266, 268

    command-line calculator sample application and, 24

    inventory lookup sample and, 168

    shipping charges calculator sample application and, 79, 94, 810

Executing state, 853

execution properties, 747–751

ExistsInCollection activity, 101, 109, 198, 201

ExistsInDictionary activity, 214, 216

expanded viewing mode, 645–649

expression activities, 62–66

Expression argument, 24, 28

Expression property

    FlowSwitch activity, 106

    Switch activity, 90, 104, 165

expressions, 50, 57–66, 854

    designer classes and, 631

    types of, 57, 632

    Visual Basic for, 57–62, 859

Expressions namespace, 63

ExpressionTextBox class, 631, 637, 651

Extensible Application Markup Language. *See* Xaml

Extensions property (WorkflowApplication class), 129

ExternalDataExchange attribute, 823

ExternalDataExchangeService, WF 3.*x* and, 823–834, 854

F

FaultCallback callback delegate, 691

Faulted event (WorkflowServiceHost class), 362

Faulted state, 57, 854

FaultPropagationQuery, 577

FaultPropagationRecord, 573, 577

file system

    file-based instance stores and, 485–492, 501

    workflow persistence and, 417, 484

FileSystemInstanceStore (sample) class, 485, 492

FileSystemInstanceStoreIO (sample) class, 485, 492–501

Finally property (TryCatch activity), 109, 530, 537

FindInCollection activity, 199, 201, 255

FindInDictionary activity, 214, 217

FirstNumber argument, 24–28, 30

flowchart activities, 230–263

Flowchart activity, 9, 101, 105, 230, 854

    command-line calculator sample application and, 233

    context menu and, 793–796

    Toolbox items and, 790–793

flowchart category (of standard activities), 105

flowchart modeling style, 3, 47, 163, 229–263, 854

    mixing with procedural modeling style, 229, 254–263

    using 230–233

FlowchartDecision activity, 230, 231

FlowchartStep activity, 230, 232

FlowchartSwitch activity, 230, 231

FlowDecision activity, 102, 106, 854

    context menu and, 793–796

    Toolbox items and, 790–793

FlowNode class, 230

FlowSwitch activity, 102, 106, 854

   context menu and, 793–796

   Toolbox items and, 790–793

Flush method (WorkflowDesigner class), 754, 772

ForEach activity, 102, 105, 195, 200–211, 254

   activity templates and, 683

   ActivityAction activity and, 734

   ActivityAction class and, 197, 657

foreach keyword (C#), 195

ForEachWithBodyFactory class, as activity template, 683, 767

Func delegate, 89, 95, 127, 486

G

GenericTypeArguments property (InvokeMethod activity), 223

generic types, C# vs. Visual Basic, 59

Get method, 24, 80

GetAdditionalExtensions method (IWorkflowInstanceExtension interface), 278

GetBookmarks method (WorkflowApplication class), 132

GetChildSubtree class, 672

GetExtension method (WorkflowApplication class), 129, 277

GetExtensions method (WorkflowApplication class), 129

GetParentChain class, 672, 675

GetWorkflowTree class, 672

globally unique identifiers GUIDs), workflow instances and, 137

glossary, 849–860

guessing game (sample) application, 824–834

GUIDs (globally unique identifiers), workflow instances and, 137

H

HandleExternalEventActivity

   ExternalDataExchangeService and, 823

   Interop activity and, 807, 823, 807, 823

HandleFault method (NativeActivityFaultContext class), 692, 712

Hello Workflow (sample application), 5–17

   adding new workflows to, 17

   hosting workflows and, 12, 20

   running, 14

host communication, 265–312

hosting workflow services, 49

   credit approval sample workflow service and, 400

   order processing sample workflow service and, 359

   order shipment sample workflow service and, 384

   self-hosting and, 361–368

   Xaml workflows and, 326

   Xamlx workflow services and, 326

hosting workflows, 48

   command-line calculator sample application and, 34, 239

Hello Workflow sample application and, 12, 20

HostingDemoActivity sample illustrating, 121

HostingDemoWorkflow sample illustrating, 117

WebInvokerHost and, 147

WorkflowApplication class and, 126–142

WorkflowInvoker class and, 111–126

Xaml workflows and, 326

HostingDemoActivity (sample), 121

HostingDemoWorkflow (sample)

ActivityXamlServices class and, 143

hosting the workflow, 117

multiple workflow instances and, 150

WorkflowApplication class and, 133

WorkflowInvoker class and, 114–120

workflows invoked from ASP.NET web applications and, 145

human interactions, 855

workflow model and, 2

workflow persistence and, 416

■ I

IActivityTemplateFactory interface, 683

IAsyncResult object, 124, 125

icons, 643

Idle delegate, 127, 128, 137, 273

Idle member, PersistableIdle member and, 420

IEquatable interface, 201, 202

If activity, 102, 104, 164

problem reporting sample workflow and, 303

shipping charges calculator sample application and, 85, 90

if keyword, 48

if statement (C#), 85

IIS (Internet Information Services), 316

publishing workflow services to, 341

workflow persistence and, 416

images, 643

imperative code, migration and, 804

Implementation property

Activity class, 89

ActivityBuilder class, 756

Imports button (workflow designer), 10

InArgument class, 21, 24, 75, 90

inferred contracts, 324

infrastructure, work categories and, 74

initialization syntax, vs. procedural code, 742

Initialize method/Uninitialize method (WF 3.x), migration and, 805

InitializeCorrelation activity, 102, 107

InitializeDesigner method, 764, 779

input arguments, 18, 75

input parameters, 17–22

instance methods, WorkflowInvoker class and, 112, 122–126

instance stores, 416, 483–505, 855

InstanceId property (TrackingRecord class), 568

InstanceInfo class (C#), 154, 156

InstancePersistenceCommand class, 484

InstancePersistenceContext class, 485

InstanceStore class, 416, 484, 485, 855

InstanceStore property, 130, 420, 443

InstanceView property
(InstancePersistenceContext
class), 485

IntelliSense, 19

Internet Information Services (IIS), 316

    publishing workflow services to, 341

    workflow persistence and, 416

Interop activity, 51, 102, 110, 806–842, 855

    ExternalDataExchangeService and,
843–834

    limitations of, 807

    migration and, 804

    rules, executing via, 834–842

    shipping charges calculator sample
application illustrating, 807–823,
834–842

    WF 3.*x* activities, executing from, 801,
806–842

Interop class, 806

InteropTrackingRecord class, 574, 807

inventory lookup (sample), 241

    hosting/testing, 172

    Parallel activity and, 182–194

    While/DoWhile activities and, 167–175

inventory update (sample), 200–213, 254–
263, 508–564

    custom activities for, 511–530

dictionary-related activities and, 218–
222

executing, 526

ForEach activity and, 200–211

InvokeMethod activity and, 223–227

ParallelForEach activity and, 211

tracking workflows and, 579–605, 611–
626

Invoke method, 13, 35, 111

InvokeAction activity, 290, 300

InvokeAction class, 290

InvokeAsync method (WorkflowInvoker
class), 113, 122

InvokeCompleted event, 123

InvokeFunc class, 290

InvokeMethod activity, 102, 108, 222–227

InvokeWorkflowActivity, Interop activity
and, 807

IsCancellationRequested property, 704

IsolationLevel property (TransactionScope
activity), 540

Item property

    AddToCollection activity, 109, 198

    RemoveFromCollection activity, 198

Items property

    EditingContext class, 757

    ExistsInCollection activity, 199

ItemSupportExtension (sample) custom
workflow extension, 426, 472–474

IValidationErrorService interface, 777

IWorkflowInstanceExtension interface, 278

■K

keywords, C# vs. Visual Basic, 59

■L

Lambda expressions, 90, 93, 855

Language INtegrated Query (LINQ), 93, 855, 510

Level property (TrackingRecord class), 568

LINQ (Language INtegrated Query), 93, 855, 510

LINQ to SQL, 510, 855

Literal class, 58

literal data types, C# vs. Visual Basic, 62

Load method

    resuming persistence after suspending, 420

    WorkflowApplication class and, 130, 417

    WorkflowDesigner class and, 754, 755

    Xaml and, 142

LoadWorkflowByInstanceKeyCommand, 485

LoadWorkflowCommand, 485

local services, 823

long-running unit of work, 73, 855

long-running workflows, 265, 327

    bookmarks for, 266–276

    cancelling, 564

    WorkflowControlEndpoint for, 479–483

looping decisions, 165

    procedural modeling style and, 2, 3, 34

    flowchart modeling style and, 241–248

L-value expressions, 632, 639

■M

management endpoints, 479–483

MapValues method (PersistenceParticipant class), 470

message-based communication. *See* workflow services

message contracts, 323, 330, 856

message exchange patterns, 315, 317, 856

MessageBodyMember attribute, 323, 324, 331

MessageContract attribute, 323, 324, 331

MessageHeader attribute, 323, 324, 331

MessageReceived event, ExternalDataExchangeService and, 831

messaging activities, 317–322, 324

messaging category (of standard activities), 106

metadata

    configuring automatically/manually, 688–690

    custom instance stores and, 490–498

    DesignerMetadata class and, 760, 764, 788

    MetadataStore class and, 633, 760, 856

metadata store, 633, 640–642

MetadataStore class, 633, 760, 856

MethodName property (InvokeMethod activity), 223

migration category (of standard activities), 110

migration strategies, 51, 801–806

ModelChanged event (WorkflowDesigner class), 754, 764

modeling styles. *See* flowchart modeling style; procedural modeling style

ModelItem class, 630, 856

ModelItem property (ActivityDesigner class), 630, 638

multiplication case, Switch activity and, 31

■N

Name property

ActivityBuilder class, 756

TrackingProfile class, 575

namespaces, 7, 10, 51

naming conventions

for assemblies, Visual Studio and, 640

for service contracts, 319

NativeActivity, 856

NativeActivity class, 74, 266, 291

access to the workflow runtime and, 76

configuring metadata and, 688

executing activities and, 694

NativeActivityContext class, 56, 267, 291

cancellation requests and, 693

child activity execution scheduling and, 690

execution properties and, 747

suspending persistence and, 419

NativeActivityFaultContext class, 692

NativeActivityMetadata struct, 689, 735

.NET Framework

examples in this book and, 6

projects and, 6

WF and, 4, 803

nonblocking bookmarks, 747, 748

nonflowchart activities, 232

nonpersisting tracking participants, 615–618

NonSerialized attribute, workflow persistence and, 419

nonworkflow applications, implementing, 342–348

NoPersistHandle class, suspending persistence via, 419

notification to external systems, 509, 517, 551

■O

object initialization, C# vs. Visual Basic, 59

Of keyword, 59

OnComplete method, 695, 704, 727

OnConditionComplete method, 703, 715

one-way message exchange pattern, 315, 856

OnFaulted method, 704, 712

OnUnhandledException delegate, 128, 135, 273

OnUnhandledException method, 507, 527, 529

Open method (WorkflowServiceHost class), 362

Opened event (WorkflowServiceHost class), 362

Opening event (WorkflowServiceHost class), 362

Operation argument, 24, 28

OperationContract attribute, 324

operators, C# vs. Visual Basic, 59

order processing (sample) workflow service, 313, 328–368

  classes for, 329–332

  client application for, 342–348

  configuring/testing, 339

  credit approval sample workflow service and, 388–405

  declaring, 332–336

  execution properties and, 747–751

  order shipment sample workflow service and, 369–388

  response for, populating, 337

  workflow client for, 348–361

  workflow extensions and, 405–409

order shipment (sample) workflow service, 369–388

  declaring, 371–379

  order processing sample workflow service modified for, 379–383

  testing, 385, 388

OrderEntry (sample) workflow

  configuring/testing and, 440

  declaring, 431

OrderEntryService (sample) workflow service

  client application and, 458

  configuring/testing, 464, 477

  declaring, 445

  promoting properties and, 476–479

OrderUtilityExtension (sample), 406–409

  order processing sample workflow service modified for, 407

  testing, 409

orphaned workflow instances, 443

OutArgument class, 21, 24, 75

output arguments, 18, 75

OverloadGroup validation attribute, 662, 664

P

Parallel activity, 102, 105, 176–188

  asynchronous execution via, 189

  child activities and, 176, 194

parallel execution, 176, 189, 725–734, 856

ParallelForEach activity, 102, 105, 211

  ActivityAction class and, 197

  vs. ForEach activity, 196

ParallelForEachWithBodyFactory activity, 767

parameters, passing to workflows, 17–22

Parameters property (InvokeMethod activity), 223

parent activities

  cancelling, 693

  constrained activities and, 674

exception handling for, 709–714

execution properties and, 748

responsibilities of, 687–693

validation and, 678

ParseCalculatorArgs (sample) activity

implementing in command-line calculator sample application, 234, 236, 269

unit testing for, 39

performance

argument properties and, 22

collection-related activities and, 199

Persist activity, 102, 107, 417

Persist method (WorkflowApplication class), 130, 417, 420

PersistableIdle delegate, WorkflowApplication class and, 128, 136

PersistableIdle member, 420, 438, 442

PersistableIdle property, WorkflowServiceHost and, 443

persistence, 3, 49, 415–467, 857

arguments/variables and, 75

configuring/managing, 129

customizing, 469–505

defined, 415

execution properties and, 747

file system and, 417, 484

how it works, 417

migration and, 807

nonpersisting tracking participants and, 615–618

persistence commands (list), 484

reasons for using, 415

resuming after suspending, 420

SqlWorkflowInstanceStore and, 421–467

suspending, 419

tracking participants and, 604–614

WorkflowApplication and, 419, 424–443

WorkflowServiceHost and, 443–467

PersistenceIOParticipant class, 471

PersistenceParticipant class, 419, 469, 472–474, 857

Pick activity, 102, 105, 302–312, 371, 378

PickBranch activity, 102, 105, 371, 378

PolicyActivity class, 834, 842

Presentation namespace, 753

primitives category (of standard activities), 107

problem reporting (sample) workflow, 303–312

procedural activities, 163–194, 230

procedural code, vs. initialization syntax, 742

procedural model, 1, 45

procedural modeling style, 3, 47, 163, 857

branching decisions and, 2, 3, 29

mixing with flowchart modeling style, 229, 254–263

Program.cs file, 7, 12, 20

projects

creating, 6

running, 15

Promote method
    (SqlWorkflowInstanceStore class)

promoting properties, 474–479

properties

    activity properties and, 634–645

    binding, 297

    execution properties and, 747–751

    promoting, 474–479

Properties property (ActivityBuilder class),
    756

Properties window, 11

PropertyInspectorView property
    (WorkflowDesigner class), 754, 755

PropertyReference activity, 297

proxy classes, client applications and, 316,
    344

PublishValues method
    (PersistenceParticipant class), 470

■ Q

Queries property (TrackingProfile class),
    575

Query method, 463

Queue class, 286

queues, 286

quitting applications, 36

■ R

Receive activity, 102, 106

    credit approval sample workflow
        service and, 394

    inferred contracts and, 324

    Interop activity and, 807

    SendReply activity and, 319

    WCF and, 317

ReceiveAndSendReply activity, 102, 106,
    683

ReceiveAndSendReply activity template,
    319

ReceiveMessageRecord, 574

ReceiveReply activity, 317, 321

RecordNumber property (TrackingRecord
    class), 568

referencedCategories dictionary, 781

reflection, activity metadata and, 690

Register method (DesignerMetadata class),
    760, 788

RemoveFromCollection activity, 102, 109,
    198

RemoveFromDictionary activity, 214, 215

RenderingInfo element, tracking data and,
    589

request/response message exchange
    pattern, 315, 857

    correlation and, 325

    order processing sample workflow
        service and, 327–368

RequiredArgument validation attribute,
    662, 663

RequiredArgumentAttribute, 24

resources, workflow persistence and, 416

resources for further reading

    Lambda expressions, 93

    LINQ, 511

    WCF, 314

WF 3.*x*, 811

WPF, 629

Result argument, 25

Result property

CompensableActivity, 549, 557

ExistsInCollection activity, 199

InvokeMethod activity, 223

RemoveFromCollection activity, 198

ResumeBookmark method, 267

resuming persistence after suspending, 420

WorkflowApplication class and, 132

Rethrow activity, 102, 109

root (topmost) activity, 9

rules engine, 68, 857

custom activities and, 842–847

Interop activity and, 834–842

RuleSet class, 836, 842, 857

Run method

resuming persistence after suspending, 420

WorkflowApplication class and, 130, 151

RunAsynchronously property (InvokeMethod activity), 223

running applications

command-line calculator sample application and, 35

Hello Workflow sample application and, 14, 21

runtime, 851

activity definition vs. activity instance, 55

ActivityAction class and, 290

DynamicActivity class and, 741

private variables and, 56

runtime category (of standard activities), 107

S

samples

command-line calculator. *See* command-line calculator (sample application)

credit approval workflow service, 388–405

DesignerHost application, 760–799

FileSystemInstanceStore class, 485

FileSystemInstanceStoreIO class, 485, 492–501

guessing game application, 824–834

Hello Workflow, 5–17

HostingDemoWorkflow. *See* HostingDemoWorkflow (sample)

inventory lookup, 167–175, 182–194, 241

inventory update. *See* inventory update (sample)

ItemSupportExtension custom workflow extension, 426, 472–474

order processing workflow service. *See* order processing (sample) workflow service

order shipment workflow service, 369–388

OrderEntry workflow, 431, 440

OrderEntryService workflow service, 445, 458, 464

OrderUtilityExtension, 406–409

problem reporting workflow, 303–312

sample code for this book, downloading, 761

shipping charges calculator. *See* shipping charges calculator (sample application)

shopping cart workflow, 424–467

Save method (WorkflowDesigner class), 754

SaveWorkflowCommand, 485

scalability, workflow persistence and, 416

ScheduleAction method (NativeActivityContext class), 291, 690, 734

ScheduleActivity method (NativeActivityContext class), 690, 695, 727

scheduledChildren dictionary, 726

ScheduleDelegate method (NativeActivityContext class), 690, 734

ScheduleFunc method (NativeActivityContext class), 291, 690, 734

scope, variables and, 26, 100

SecondNumber argument, 24–28, 30

self-hosting workflow services

steps for implementing, 361–368

testing/using, 367

WorkflowApplication class and, 416

WorkflowServiceHost class and, 416, 422

Send activity, 102, 106, 317, 320

Interop activity and, 807

ReceiveReply activity and, 321

SendAndReceiveReply activity, 102, 106, 683

SendAndReceiveReply activity template, 322

SendMessageRecord, 574

SendReply activity, 317, 319, 324

Sequence activity, 9, 102, 104

adding activities to, 9, 28

child activities and, 176

command-line calculator sample application and, 233

custom designers and, 653

Parallel activity and, 179

shipping charges calculator sample application and, 90

testing constraints and, 677

serializing tracking records to XML, 605–608

service contracts, 315

endpoints and, 316

naming conventions for, 319

service operations, order processing sample workflow service and, 327–368

ServiceContract attribute, 324

ServiceHostBase class, 361

ServiceModel Metadata Utility (svcutil.exe utility), 316

Services property (EditingContext class), 757

Set method, 24, 80

SetChildrenCollection method, 715

SetInstance method (IWorkflowInstanceExtension interface), 278

shipping charges calculator (sample application), 78–97

    custom activity asynchronous implementation for, 93–97

    custom activity code authoring for, 78–84, 88–93

    custom activity designers and, 635–649

    custom activity Xaml authoring for, 84–88

    DynamicActivity and, 741–747

    flowchart modeling style and, 248–253

    project for, 79

    unit testing for, 81–84, 87, 92, 96, 251

    validation and, 663

    WF 3.*x* activities and, 807–823

    WF 3.*x* workflows and, 815–823, 834–842

shopping cart (sample) workflow, 424–467

    configuring/testing, 440, 464

    item-related classes for, 425

    tasks for implementing (list), 424, 444

    workflow implementation for, 424–443

    workflow service implementation for, 444–467

ShowValidationErrors method, 777

SOAP fault handling, workflow services and, 409

SqlWorkflowInstanceStore, 421–467

    Delay activity and, 422

    properties of, 421

    SQL Server preparation for, 423

    using with WorkflowApplication, 424–443

    using with WorkflowServiceHost, 444–467

SqlWorkflowInstanceStore class, 53, 416, 443

    property promotion and, 474–479

    workflow persistence and, 420

SqlWorkflowInstanceStoreBehavior class, 454, 456

    Delay activity and, 423

    workflow persistence and, 422

    WorkflowServiceHost persistence and, 443

square brackets [ ], serializing expressions and, 58

standard activities, 3, 46, 71, 101–110

    categories of, 103–110

    Interop activity and, 807

    list of, 101

    WF 3.*x* vs. WF 4 (table), 865–868

    workflow building blocks and, 97

standard flow activities, 9

state

    activities and, 57

    ActivityState class and, 572

ActivityStateQuery and, 576

ActivityStateRecord and, 571

tracking profiles and, 592–596

tracking workflows and, 569

state machine, 67, 857

static methods, WorkflowInvoker class and, 111, 114–122

String class, 19

string literals, 11

subtraction case, Switch activity and, 31

SuspendActivity, Interop activity and, 807

svcconfigeditor.exe (WCF Service Configuration Editor), 342

svcutil.exe utility (ServiceModel Metadata Utility), 316

Switch activity, 29, 102, 104, 164

FlowchartSwitch activity and, 231

shipping charges calculator sample application and, 85, 90

switch statement (C#), 29, 104, 165, 231

SynchronizationContext class, InvokeAsync method and, 113

SynchronizationContext property (WorkflowApplication class), 130, 160

System element, tracking data and, 589

system interactions, 2, 858

system-provided bindings, WCF and, 316

■ **T**

Target property (Compensate activity), 550

TargetObject property (InvokeMethod activity), 223

TargetType property (InvokeMethod activity), 223

templates, 6

Terminate method (WorkflowApplication class), 132, 139

TerminateWorkflow activity, 102, 107

terminating activities, 693, 858

text, WriteLine activity for, 10

Text property

WriteLine activity, 11, 12

WorkflowDesigner class, 754, 755

TextWriter property

HostingDemoWorkflow sample and, 114

WriteLine activity and, 108

Then property (If activity), 104, 164

Throw activity, 32, 103, 109

Timeout property (TransactionScope activity), 540

timeout values, 119

TimeSpan value, 119, 131

TimeToPersist property (WorkflowIdleBehavior class), 444

TimeToUnload property (WorkflowIdleBehavior class), 444, 454

ToolboxCategory class, 755

ToolboxControl class, 755

ToolboxItemWrapper class, 755, 768

topmost (root) activity, 9

Track method (TrackingParticipant class), 578, 605, 609

Tracking namespace, 600

tracking participants, 566, 578, 604–618, 858

    custom, 604–618

    tracking profiles and, 574

tracking profiles, 566, 574–578, 591–604, 858

    loading from App.config file, 623–626

    targeting selected activities and, 596

tracking records, 566, 568–574, 858

    custom, 600–604

    serializing to XML, 605–608

    tracking participants and, 578

    tracking profiles for, 574, 591

    viewing tracking data and, 587, 623

tracking workflows, 50, 565–627, 858

    architecture of the workflow tracking mechanism, 566

    declarative workflow services and, 618–623

    migration and, 807

    reasons for using, 566

    SQL Server and, 68

    steps for implementing (list), 567

    viewing tracking data and, 579, 586, 623

TrackingParticipant class, 578, 605

TrackingProfile class, 574, 575

TrackingProvider class, 566

TrackingRecord class, 568

TransactedReceiveScope activity, 103, 107, 412, 541

transaction and compensation category (of standard activities), 108

transactions, 50, 540–549, 858

    host transactions and, 547

    workflows/workflow services and, 411

TransactionScope activity, 50, 103, 108, 411, 540–546

TransactionScope class, 540

transport protocol, identified by binding, 316

Trigger property (PickBranch activity), 105

Try property (TryCatch activity), 109, 530

try/catch blocks, 35, 531, 549

TryCatch activity, 103, 109, 410, 530–540

    multiple exceptions and, capturing, 537

    properties of, 530

TryCommand (InstanceStore class), 484, 488

U

Uniform Resource Identifier (URI), endpoint addresses and, 316

unit testing, 39–43

Unload method (WorkflowApplication class), 132

Unloaded delegate, WorkflowApplication class and, 128, 137

URI (Uniform Resource Identifier), endpoint addresses and, 316

using statement (C#), 10

■V

Validate method
(ActivityValidationServices class),
661, 663, 680

validation, 47, 661–683, 858

constraints for, 662, 669–679

executing manually, 679–683

mechanisms for (list), 662

validation attributes for, 662, 663–666

validation code for, 662, 667–669

validation errors, displaying, 777

ValidationContext property, 672

ValidationSettings class, 663, 680

value expressions, 632

Values property

ForEach activity, 105, 195

ParallelForEach activity, 196

Variable class, 56, 75, 90

Variable Editor, 27

variables, 75, 858

activity data flow and, 99

defining, 26, 235

scope and, 26, 100, 859

shipping charges calculator sample
application and, 85

shopping cart sample workflow and,
431, 445

Variables button (workflow designer), 10,
26

Variables Editor, 26

VB (Visual Basic), for expressions, 57–62,
859

versioning, 803

View property (WorkflowDesigner class),
754, 755

viewing modes, expanded/collapsed, 645–
649

visibility, 565

Visual Basic (VB), for expressions, 57–62,
859

Visual Studio

.NET Framework and, 804

privileges and, 329, 367

unit testing and, 39

WF 3.*x* and, 802

WF and, 4

workflow designer and. *See* workflow
designer

Visual Studio debugger, 48

Visual Studio Toolbox, 6, 301

VisualBasicReference class, 58

VisualBasicValue class, 58

■W

warnings, validation and, 669

WAS (Windows Process Activation
Service), 316

WCA.exe utility, 823, 826

WCF (Windows Communication
Foundation), 48, 314–317, 859

message exchange patterns and, 315,
317

WCF contracts and, 67

WF integration with, 3

workflow services and. *See* workflow services

WCF Service Configuration Editor (svcconfigeditor.exe), 342

WCF Test Client (WcfTestClient.exe), 342

web service activities, Interop activity and, 807

Web.config file

declarative workflow services and, 620

enhancing for workflow services publishing to IIS, 341

WF (Windows Workflow Foundation), 859

base classes and, 23

creating workflow in, 15

features missing from version 4.0 of, 66

features/capabilities of, 45–51

grand tour of, 45–69

migration strategies for, 51, 801–806

quick tour of, 1–44

reasons for using, 3

variable scope and, 27

version 4.0 of, 4, 859

WF 3.*x* and, 801–847, 859

WF 3.*x* vs. WF 4 (table), 861–868

While activity, 103, 104, 165–175

custom designers and, 650

WorkflowItemPresenter/WorkflowItems Presenter classes and, 632

while keyword, 48

Windows Communication Foundation. *See* WCF

Windows Event Viewer, 579, 586, 623

Windows Presentation Foundation (WPF) applications, 131, 160, 629

Windows Process Activation Service (WAS), 316

Windows Server AppFabric, 316

Windows Workflow Foundation. *See* WF

work categories, activities and, 72

workflow clients, implementing, 348–361

Workflow Console Application template, 6, 23, 235

workflow designer, 4, 8, 47

architecture/components of, 753–760

DesignerHost sample application illustrating, 760–799

hosting, 753–799

interface of, 10

rehosting, 51

Visual Studio and, 47

workflow extensions, 49, 276–286, 859

adding to workflows, 409

alternate extension and, 286–289

custom, 405–409, 426, 472–474

implementing, 406

workflow persistence and, 419

workflow projects

creating, 6

running, 15

workflow services, 48, 313–414, 860

behaviors and, 412

configuring, 316

controlling instances of, 327

correlation and, 324

credit approval sample workflow service and, 388–405

declarative, 618–623

declaring, 327–340

exceptions/faults and, 409

hosting, 316

message types and, 322

messaging activities for implementing, 317–322

order processing sample workflow service. *See* order processing (sample) workflow service

order shipment sample workflow service. *See* order shipment (sample) workflow service

OrderEntryService sample workflow service and, 445, 458, 464

publishing to IIS, 341

self-hosting, 361–368

transactions and, 411

WCF contracts and, 67

workflow instances, identifying, 325

workflow tracking. *See* tracking workflows

workflow workflow, 4

Workflow1.xaml file, 7, 15–17

WorkflowApplication class, 49, 57, 126–142, 860

creating instances of, 127

Delay activity and, 418

delegate members and, 127

GetExtension method and, 277

handling unhandled exceptions and, 507

ResumeBookmark method, 267

SqlWorkflowInstanceStore used with, 424–443

workflow extensions and, 277

workflow instance execution and, 130

workflow persistence and, 416, 419

vs. WorkflowInvoker class, 126, 273

WorkflowControlClient class, 480

WorkflowControlEndpoint, 479–483

tasks for implementing, 480

testing and, 482

WorkflowControlEndpoint class, 57, 443

WorkflowDesigner class, 754, 860

WorkflowExtensions property, 362, 405

WorkflowIdleBehavior class, 413, 443, 454

WorkflowInstanceQuery, 576

WorkflowInstanceRecord, 569, 576, 592

WorkflowInstanceStates class, 570

WorkflowInvoker class, 13, 49, 111–126, 267, 860

BeginInvoke method for, 113, 122, 124

EndInvoke method for, 113, 122, 124

executing activities via, 121

host transactions and, 547

instance methods for, 112, 122–126

Invoke method for, 111

InvokeAsync method for, 113, 122

static methods for, 111, 114–122

unhandled exceptions and, 507

workflow extensions and, 277

workflow persistence and, 416

vs. WorkflowApplication class, 126, 273

WorkflowItemPresenter class, 632, 651, 655, 660

WorkflowItemsPresenter class, 632, 655

WorkflowQueue (WF 3.x), migration and, 805

workflows, 1–44, 859

  aborting, 849

  activity data flow and, 99

  activity definition vs. activity instance, 55

  asynchronous execution and, 126

  bookmarks and, 131

  building blocks and, 97

  cancelling, 564, 851

  controlling workflow instances and, 132

  declarative activity model and, 45

  declarative workflow model and, 2

  declaring, 8–12, 17, 236

  dynamic updates, WF 3.x and, 68

  examples of. See samples

  executing, 13, 15, 111–161

  flowchart modeling for, 229–263

  hosting. See hosting workflows

  invoking from ASP.NET web applications, 145–149

  long-running, 265, 327, 479–483

  mental checklist for, 4

  multiple instances of, managing, 150–161

orphaned workflow instances and, 443

parallel execution, multiple activities and, 725–734

passing parameters to, 17–22

persistence and. See persistence

procedural modeling for, 163–194

reasons for using, 1

resumption of after becoming idle, 113

activities and. See activities; custom activities

stopping execution of, 132, 137

synchronous execution and, 148

timeout values for, 119

tracking. See tracking workflows

transactions and, 411

understanding as synonymous with activities, 46, 55

unit testing for, 39–43

updating, 508–564

workflow extensions and, 129, 409

Xaml workflow services and, 326

Xaml workflows and, 326

WorkflowServiceHost

  workflow persistence and, 443–467

  WorkflowControlEndpoint and, 480

WorkflowServiceHost class, 49, 361, 443, 860

  Delay activity and, 423

  ExternalDataExchangeService and, 823, 831

  multiple workflow instances and, 150

  workflow persistence and, 416, 422

WorkflowExtensions property, 362, 405

Xamlx workflow services and, 326

WorkflowUnhandledExceptionBehavior class, 57, 412

WorkflowViewElement class, 630

WPF (Windows Presentation Foundation) applications, 131, 160, 629

WriteLine activity, 10, 103, 108

    HostingDemoWorkflow sample and, 114

    inventory lookup sample and, 188

■**X**

x:Class attribute, 630, 636

Xaml, 15–17, 46, 860

    ActivityXamlServices class and, 142–144

    authoring activities and, 72

    breakpoints and, 38

Xaml workflows, 326

Xamlx workflow services, 326, 860

XML, serializing tracking records to, 605–608

xmln:s attribute, 637

xmlns:sapc attribute, 637

You Need the Companion eBook